THE NATIONAL UNDERWRITER COMPANY

2014 ERISA Facts

Frank J. Bitzer, Esq., FACEBC, and Nicholas W. Ferrigno, Jr., J.D., CLU®

It is readily acknowledged that the Employee Retirement Income Security Act (ERISA) is one of the most complicated of federal laws. Providing answers to more than 800 ERISA-related questions, *2014 ERISA Facts* unravels those mysteries and is a must-have easy-access resource for a wide range of employee benefits professionals, including:

- ERISA attorneys

- TPAs

- CPAs

- Employee benefits specialists

- Corporate counsel

- IFEBP members.

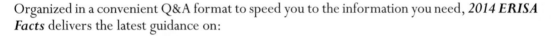

Organized in a convenient Q&A format to speed you to the information you need, *2014 ERISA Facts* delivers the latest guidance on:

- Fiduciary responsibility under ERISA

- Health insurance issues (HIPAA, COBRA, etc.)

- Plan administration issues

- Responsibilities related to plan investments and fiduciary liability

Highlights of the 2014 Edition:

- Updated questions and answers on Section 408(b)(2) Service Provider Disclosure Rules

- Updated information on Section 404(a)(5) Participant Fee Disclosure Rules

- Added information on new Department of Labor (DOL) guidance on ERISA Fee Recapture Accounts

- Updated DOL Model COBRA Election Notice

- Updated information on the PBGC Reporting Rules

- Discussion of Medicaid expansion provisions under the Affordable Care Act

- Additional information on how income is determined for purposes of Medicare Part B premiums

To place additional orders for *2014 ERISA Facts* or any of our products, or for additional information, contact Customer Service at **1-800-543-0874**.

2014
ERISA FACTS

Plan Administration • Fiduciary Duties and Liabilities
Prohibited Transactions and Exemptions
Investment Management • Health Benefits and Reform
Voluntary Compliance Programs • Enforcement Issues

Frank J. Bitzer, Esq., FACEBC
Nicholas W. Ferrigno, Jr., J.D., CLU®

2014 Edition

Circular 230 Notice – The content in this publication is not intended or written to be used, and it cannot be used, for the purposes of avoiding U.S. tax penalties.

ISBN: 978-1-939829-43-6

Copyright © 1998, 1999, 2000, 2001, 2002, 2003, 2004, 2005, 2006, 2007, 2008, 2009, 2010, 2011, 2012, 2013, 2014

The National Underwriter Company
Summit Business Media | www.SBMedia.com
5081 Olympic Boulevard, Erlanger, KY 41018

Printed in U.S.A.

ABOUT SUMMIT PROFESSIONAL NETWORKS

Summit Professional Networks supports the growth and vitality of the insurance, financial services and legal communities by providing professionals with the knowledge and education they need to succeed at every stage of their careers. We provide face-to-face and digital events, websites, mobile sites and apps, online information services, and magazines giving professionals multi-platform access to our critical resources, including Professional Development; Education & Certification; Prospecting & Data Tools; Industry News & Analysis; Reference Tools and Services; and Community Networking Opportunities.

Using all of our resources across each community we serve, we deliver measurable ROI for our sponsors through a range of turnkey services, including Research, Content Development, Integrated Media, Creative & Design, and Lead Generation.

For more information, go to http://www.SummitProfessionalNetworks.com.

ABOUT THE NATIONAL UNDERWRITER COMPANY

For over 110 years, The National Underwriter Company has been the first in line with the targeted tax, insurance, and financial planning information you need to make critical business decisions. Boasting nearly a century of expert experience, our reputable Editors are dedicated to putting accurate and relevant information right at your fingertips. With *Tax Facts, Tools & Techniques, National Underwriter Advanced Markets, Field Guide, FC&S®, FC&S Legal®* and other resources available in print, eBook, CD, and online, you can be assured that as the industry evolves National Underwriter will be at the forefront with the thorough and easy-to-use resources you rely on for success.

The National Underwriter Company
Update Service Notification

This National Underwriter Company publication is regularly updated to include coverage of developments and changes that affect the content. If you did not purchase this publication directly from The National Underwriter Company and you want to receive these important updates sent on a 30-day review basis and billed separately, please contact us at (800) 543-0874. Or you can mail your request with your name, company, address, and the title of the book to:

> The National Underwriter Company
> 5081 Olympic Boulevard
> Erlanger, KY 41018

If you purchased this publication from The National Underwriter Company directly, you have already been registered for the update service.

National Underwriter Company Contact Information

To order any National Underwriter Company title, please

- call 1-800-543-0874, 8-6 ET Monday – Thursday and 8 to 5 ET Friday

- online bookstore at www.nationalunderwriter.com, or

- mail to The National Underwriter Company, Orders Department, 5081 Olympic Blvd, Erlanger, KY 41018

DEDICATION

Frank dedicates this book to the joy in his life: his sons Griffin and Quinn. For Nick – thank you for being my friend, colleague, and co-author. It wouldn't have been possible without you.

Nick dedicated this book to the blessings in his life, Rhonda, Brittany, and Alexis and his mother, Kathé.

IN MEMORIAM

Nicholas W. Ferrigno, Jr. 1959 – 2009.

PREFACE

This edition goes to print at the end of a very interesting year. As I type, there is a national conversation focusing on the problematic roll-out of the Affordable Care Act and all of the problems that go along with it. I anticipate the coming year will see a great deal of pushing and pulling from the powers that be in our nation's capital to "fix" the problem in a manner that is most advantageous to each side of the political spectrum heading into the 2014 mid-term elections. "ObamaCare" will certainly be a hot topic between now and then. But, that is, perhaps, for the 2015 edition.

The 2014 edition elaborates on the following activities that have occurred since the last edition went to print:

- IRS updated Delinquent Filer Voluntary Compliance Program;

- Updated fiduciary guidance from the DOL on Target Date Funds;

- Further circuit court clarifications on the impact of the *Amara* decision;

- HHS issuance of final rules on HIPAA/HITECH;

- DOL issuance of an updated COBRA Model Election Notice;

- DOL expansion of the Abandoned Individual Account Plan rules;

- Advisory Opinion on ERISA Fee Recapture Accounts;

- DOL and SEC Agreement on the application of securities laws to participant level account disclosures;

- Updates and expansions on civil and criminal DOL field enforcement projects; and

- The usual litany of circuit and Supreme Court cases impacting the qualified benefit plans.

As you can see, the IRS, DOL, PBGC and the courts continue to be very active in their oversight responsibilities of the qualified plans universe. I've made a diligent effort to track these activities and updated the 2014 edition to bring you the most up-to-date and detailed analysis available in a desk reference text. As always, thank you kindly for your continued interest in, and support of, ERISA Facts. And again, I hope you continue to find this text as useful in your everyday efforts in the field of qualified benefits plans as I do.

Frank J. Bitzer

November 11, 2013

ABOUT THE AUTHORS

Frank J. Bitzer, Esq., FACEBC, is a practicing attorney in Cincinnati, Ohio. Mr. Bitzer is a graduate of the University of Cincinnati College of Education and received his Juris Doctorate from the University of San Diego School of Law in 1988. Mr. Bitzer has particular experience in both civil and criminal fiduciary matters pursuant to ERISA, having previously served as a Journeyman level Investigator with the United States Department of Labor – Employee Benefits Security Administration. Mr. Bitzer is the Past Chair of the Cincinnati Bar Association Employee Benefits Committee. He has been named a Cincy Leading Lawyer by *Cincy Magazine* in 2008, 2010, 2011, 2012, and 2013. He has also been recognized as a Super Lawyer for the State of Ohio by *Cincinnati* magazine and *Law & Politics* magazine in 2009, 2010, 2011, 2012, and 2013. In addition, he is a Fellow in the American College of Employee Benefits Counsel.

Mr. Bitzer is a featured speaker of The National Underwriter Company Speakers Bureau and has made presentations on ERISA fiduciary matters to organizations across the United States. He is a contributor of articles to the *Journal of Pension and Benefits*, *Spencer's Research Reports*, *The Pension Actuary*, *Pension Plan Administrator* and other publications. Mr. Bitzer also provides expert witness testimony in litigation matters focusing on ERISA. He is a member of the American Society of Pension Professionals & Actuaries and a former member of Government Affairs Committee, Sub-Committee on Department of Labor Enforcement. He is a member of the Internal Revenue Service Great Lakes Region Tax Exempt and Government Entities Joint Council, the International Foundation of Employee Benefit Plans, and the Cincinnati Bar Association-Employee Benefits Committee.

In addition to this text, Mr. Bitzer is a co-author of *Benefits Facts*, *The Insider's Guide to DOL Plan Audits*, *Quick Reference to ERISA Compliance – The Coverage and Nondiscrimination Answer Book*, and *The Pension Answer Book – Forms and Worksheets*, published by Wolters Kluwer.

The original edition of this book and the first ten annual updates were co-authored by Nicholas W. Ferrigno, Jr., Esq.

Nicholas W. Ferrigno, Jr., Esq., was a Member and Chairman of ERISA Controversy Team of the law firm of Greenebaum Doll & McDonald PLLC with offices in Covington, Frankfort, Lexington, and Louisville, Kentucky; and Cincinnati, Ohio. Mr. Ferrigno received his B.S. (Finance) from the University of Rhode Island and Juris Doctorate (cum laude) from the Salmon P. Chase College of Law, Northern Kentucky University. Mr. Ferrigno had particular experience in ERISA fiduciary and compliance matters, having previously served with the U.S. Department of Labor - Employee Benefits Security Administration.

Senior Developmental Editor

Rebecca von Gillern is a senior developmental editor with the Professional Publishing Division of the National Underwriter Company, Summit Professional Networks. She manages the editorial development of the Advisor's Guide and the Tools & Techniques series of investment and planning products. She also develops other financial services content for the company. Rebecca has been developing content for the higher education and business-to-business markets for the past sixteen years.

As the owner and principal editor for Bookworm Editorial Services, Rebecca was responsible for ensuring client satisfaction by collaborating with publishing company project teams and authors in the creation of publication strategies. Her work was focused on adding value through enhanced clarity, accuracy, and marketability of print and digital product.

She began her career with Thomson Learning, where she developed and revised federal and state taxation publications. At Thomson she also developed product in the disciplines of accounting, business communication, communication, introduction to business, management, marketing, and the sciences. She is a graduate of the University of Southern Mississippi.

Editorial Director

Diana B. Reitz, CPCU, AAI, is the editorial director of the Professional Publishing Division of The National Underwriter Company. As such she is responsible for the overall integrity of all division publications. She previously was the Director of the Property & Casualty Publishing Department of the Reference Division.

Ms. Reitz has been with The National Underwriter Company since 1998, when she was named editor of the Risk Financing and Self-Insurance manuals and associate editor of the *FC&S Bulletins*®. She also is co-author of the National Underwriter publication, *Workers Compensation Coverage Guide*, and has edited and contributed to numerous other books and publications, including *The Tools & Techniques of Risk Management and Insurance, Claims* magazine, ProducersWEB, and *National Underwriter Property & Casualty* newsweekly.

Prior to joining The National Underwriter she was with a regional insurance broker, concentrating on commercial insurance. She is a graduate of the University of Maryland and St. Francis College.

Editorial Services

Connie L. Jump, Supervisor, Electronic Publication Production
Patti O'Leary, Editorial Assistant

ABBREVIATIONS

ARRA 2009	American Recovery and Reinvestment Act of 2009
BNA	Bureau of National Affairs
CA or — Cir.	United States Court of Appeals
CB	Cumulative Bulletin of Internal Revenue Service
COBRA	Consolidated Omnibus Budget Reconciliation Act of 1985
DC	District Court
DOL	Department of Labor
DOL Adv. Op.	Department of Labor Advisory Opinion
EBSA	Employee Benefits Security Administration
EGTRRA 2001	Economic Growth and Tax Relief Reconciliation Act of 2001
ERISA	Employee Retirement Income Security Act of 1974
Fed. Reg.	Federal Register
FERSA	Federal Employees' Retirement System Act of 1986
F.2d	Federal Reporter, second series (later decisions of U.S. Court of Appeals to Mid-1993)
F.3rd	Federal Reporter, third series (decisions of U.S. Court of Appeals since Mid-1993)
F. Supp.	Federal Supplement (decisions of U.S. District Courts)
FERSA	Federal Employees Retirement System Act
FHLMC	Federal Home Loan Mortgage Corporation
FMLA	Family and Medical Leave Act of 1993
FNMA	Federal National Mortgage Association
GCM	General Counsel Memorandum (IRS)
GINA 2008	Genetic Information Nondiscrimination Act of 2008
GNMA	Government National Mortgage Association
HIPAA '96	Health Insurance Portability and Accountability Act
HITECH Act	Health Information Technology for Economic and Clinical Health Act of 2009
IB	Interpretive Bulletin
IRB	Internal Revenue Bulletin of Internal Revenue Service
IRC	Internal Revenue Code
IRS	Internal Revenue Service
Let. Rul.	Letter Ruling (issued by IRS)
MEWA	Multiple Employer Welfare Arrangements
MVRA	Mandatory Victim Restitution Act of 1996
NMHPA	Newborns' and Mothers' Health Protection Act of 1996
PBGC	Pension Benefit Guaranty Corporation
PBGC Adv. Op.	Pension Benefit Guaranty Corporation Advisory Opinion
PHS Act	Public Health Service Act
P.L.	Public Law
PPA 2006	Pension Protection Act of 2006
PPACA	Patient Protection and Affordable Care Act
PTE	Prohibited Transaction Exemption
Prop. Reg.	Proposed Regulation

QDRO	Qualified Domestic Relations Order
Reg.	Labor Regulation
Rev. Proc.	Revenue Procedure (issued by IRS)
SBJPA '96	Small Business Job Protection Act of 1996
TC	Tax Court (official reports)
TRA	Tax Reform Act of (year of enactment)
TRA '97	Taxpayer Relief Act of 1997
Treas. Reg.	Regulation (final)
US	United States Supreme Court decisions
USDL	United States Department of Labor News Release
USERRA	Uniformed Services Employment and Reemployment Rights Act of 1994
VHOBIA	Veteran's Housing Opportunity Benefits and Improvement Act of 2006
WPPDA	Welfare and Pension Plans Disclosure Act

SUMMARY TABLE OF CONTENTS

APPENDICES AND TABLES

LIST OF QUESTIONS
SECTION I

Establishment and Administration
Basic ERISA Requirements

1. What is the Employee Retirement Income Security Act of 1974 (ERISA)?

2. What employee benefit plans are subject to ERISA?

3. Must a plan be in writing in order to be subject to ERISA?

4. What are the additional requirements for establishing ERISA-covered plans?

5. What are the trust requirements in establishing an ERISA-covered plan?

6. What are the rules that govern trusts?

7. Are plans that are not established by an employer or employee organization subject to ERISA?

8. Which employee benefit plans does ERISA expressly exclude from coverage?

9. What welfare benefit plans are not subject to ERISA?

10. What type of group or group-type insurance programs are expressly excluded from ERISA coverage?

11. Which employee benefit pension plans are expressly excluded from ERISA coverage?

12. What is the safe harbor that permits an employer to establish an IRA payroll deduction program that is not subject to ERISA?

13. Does ERISA expressly exclude 403(b) tax sheltered annuities from ERISA coverage?

14. What ERISA-covered plans are exempt from ERISA's fiduciary provisions?

15. For purposes of ERISA, who is a participant and who is a beneficiary?

Vesting

16. What are the basic requirements for vesting under ERISA?

17. What kinds of service may a plan disregard for purposes of vesting?

18. What plans are subject to ERISA's vesting rules?

19. What plans are exempt from ERISA's vesting rules?

20. How are the vesting rules affected by the presence of a controlled group?

of employee benefit plan records?

60. What type of forms must a plan maintain regarding disability retirement benefits?

Reporting and Disclosure

61. What plans are subject to reporting rules?

62. What plans are exempt from the reporting rules?

63. What reports are required to be provided to the Internal Revenue Service?

64. What are the schedules that are filed with the Annual Report Form 5500?

65. What is the proper format and place for reporting delinquent participant contributions in the Annual Report Form 5500?

66. What are the required contents of the financial statements filed with Form 5500?

67. What is a reportable transaction for purposes of filing Form 5500?

68. What actuarial information is required to be provided in Schedule SB or Schedule MB of Form 5500?

69. What is the due date for filing Form 5500?

70. What is the Delinquent Filer Voluntary Compliance Program (DFVCP)?

71. Who is eligible to participate in the DFVCP?

72. What civil penalties may be assessed by the DOL against plan administrators who fail to file a timely annual report and do not participate in the DFVCP?

73. How does a plan administrator file a delinquent Form 5500 under the DFVCP?

74. Which version of the Form 5500 should be filed?

75. What is the applicable penalty amount under the DFVCP?

76. A plan administrator for a plan is delinquent on Form 5500 filings for multiple years. If during that period, the plan's classification has shifted between being a "large" and "small plan," which penalty cap applies to the plan's DFVC Program submission?

77. Is there a different "per plan" penalty cap that applies to administrators of small plans sponsored by IRC Section 501(c)(3) organizations (including IRC Section 403(b) small plans)?

78. Are extensions considered when calculating penalties under the DFVC Program?

79. Does a plan administrator waive any rights upon filing under the DFVCP?

80. If a filing has been made under the DFVCP, will the plan administrator be liable for any other Department of Labor annual reporting civil penalties?

81. Can plan assets be used to pay the civil penalties assessed under ERISA Section 502(c)(2)?

82. May an administrator of an apprenticeship and training plan, as described in 29 C.F.R. §2520.104-22, or an administrator of a "top hat" plan, as described in 29 C.F.R. §2520.104-23, participate in the DFVCP?

83. How does an administrator of an apprenticeship and training plan participate in the DFVCP?

84. How does an administrator of a "top hat" plan participate in the DFVCP?

85. Is the DFVCP applicable to filings made by direct filing entities (DFEs) (i.e., master trusts, pooled separate accounts, common/collective trusts, 103-12 Investment Entities (103-12 IEs), and group insurance arrangements)?

86. Is it possible to obtain a waiver from the applicable penalty amount under the DFVCP if the plan administrator can demonstrate that there is reasonable cause why the penalty should not be assessed?

87. Does participation in the DFVCP protect the plan administrator from other civil penalties that may be assessed by the Internal Revenue Service (IRS) or the Pension Benefit Guaranty Corporation (PBGC) for failing to timely file a Form 5500 Annual Return/Report?

88. What reports and disclosures are plans required to submit to the Department of Labor?

89. What are the summary plan description (SPD) filing requirements?

90. What are the filing requirements regarding the summary of material modifications (SMM)?

91. What are the filing requirements regarding terminal reports?

92. What are the filing requirements regarding a notice of plan amendments?

93. What reports and disclosures are required to be submitted to the Pension Benefit Guaranty Corporation?

94. What reports and disclosures are required to be furnished under the Multiemployer Pension Plan Amendments Act of 1980?

95. What are the disclosure requirements applicable to multiemployer plans under the Pension Protection Act of 2006?

96. What are the reports and disclosures that plans must provide to participants?

Qualified Domestic Relations Orders

SECTION II
Health Benefit Issues

158. How does HIPAA define a "preexisting condition"?

159. What are the general notice procedures for a preexisting-condition exclusion?

160. What preexisting conditions cannot be excluded from coverage under HIPAA?

161. May states modify HIPAA's portability requirements?

162. How do subsequent group health plans determine the length of a newly hired employee's preexisting-condition exclusion period?

163. Does HIPAA prohibit an employer from establishing a waiting period for enrollment in the plan?

164. What is creditable coverage?

165. How does crediting for prior coverage work under HIPAA?

166. Can an employee receive credit for previous COBRA continuation coverage?

167. Is there an alternative method to credit coverage under HIPAA?

168. What is involved in the certification of creditable coverage?

169. Who is responsible for providing information on a newly hired employee's prior health coverage?

170. When must group health plans and issuers provide certificates of creditable coverage?

171. What is the minimum period of time that should be covered by the certificate of creditable coverage?

172. What are the basic nondiscrimination requirements under HIPAA?

173. What are the special enrollment rules under HIPAA?

174. What are the special enrollment rules under the Children's Health Insurance Program (CHIP) Reauthorization Act of 2009?

175. Does HIPAA require employers to offer health coverage or require plans to provide specific benefits?

176. May an individual obtain guaranteed individual insurance coverage under HIPAA?

177. Does HIPAA extend COBRA continuation coverage?

178. What information must group health plans disclose to participants?

SECTION III
Fiduciaries

236. What is the settlor doctrine? May an employer rely on the settlor doctrine to avoid fiduciary status?

237. Is a trustee a fiduciary?

238. May an officer of the plan sponsor serve as a plan fiduciary?

239. When does a person render investment advice?

240. Is a person who renders investment advice a fiduciary?

241. What is a "fee or other compensation" for the rendering of investment advice?

242. Does the provision of research or recommendations by a broker-dealer constitute the rendering of "investment advice?"

243. Does the provision of investment-related information to participants and beneficiaries in participant-directed individual account plans constitute the rendering of "investment advice"?

244. Must a person who renders investment advice, but who does not exercise or have the right to exercise discretionary authority with respect to the assets of the plan, be bonded solely by reason of the provision of such investment advice?

245. Is a broker-dealer a fiduciary?

246. Who is an investment manager?

247. May an investment adviser who is neither a bank nor an insurance company, and who is not registered under the Investment Advisers Act of 1940, in reliance upon an exemption from registration provided in that Act, be appointed an investment manager under ERISA Section 402(c)(3)?

248. May an investment adviser who has a registration application pending under the Investment Advisers Act of 1940 function as an investment manager under the Act prior to the effective date of registration under the Investment Advisers Act?

249. What is the procedure for state-registered investment advisers to obtain investment manager status under ERISA?

250. What persons are barred from serving as fiduciaries?

251. May an employee pension or welfare benefit plan trustee be appointed for "life" subject to removal for "cause"?

SECTION IV

Fiduciary Duties

271. What guidance has the DOL provided for fiduciaries of terminated defined contribution plans with missing participants?

272. What are the mandatory search methods under FAB 2004-2?

273. What IRA distribution options are provided for under Field Assistance Bulletin 2004-02?

274. What alternative distribution options are provided under Field Assistance Bulletin 2004-02?

275. What is the DOL safe harbor for rollovers of mandatory cash-outs?

276. What are the safe harbor requirements for rollovers of mandatory distributions?

277. Are employers' communications to plan participants about business decisions that may affect pension benefits subject to the fiduciary standards?

278. What is the exclusive purpose rule?

279. What kinds of actions will result in a breach of the exclusive purpose rule?

280. Is a fiduciary prohibited from holding positions of dual loyalty?

281. Must a fiduciary with a conflict of interest resign?

282. Is the payment of expenses by a plan subject to the exclusive purpose rule?

283. Is the exclusive benefit rule violated if a plan pays expenses incurred in connection with business decisions, or "settlor" functions?

284. Is the exclusive benefit rule violated if a plan pays expenses incurred in implementing the plan's termination?

285. Is the exclusive benefit rule violated if an action intended to benefit the plan incidentally benefits the plan sponsor?

286. What is the prudence requirement of ERISA Section 404?

287. What is the standard for evaluating the prudence of a fiduciary's act?

288. What level of prudence applies to ERISA fiduciaries under the prudent man rule?

289. What is procedural prudence?

290. What is substantive prudence?

291. What substantive factors must be considered by a fiduciary with respect to plan investments?

292. What are the general guidelines with respect to a fiduciary's investment duties?

332. How does a named fiduciary monitor an investment manager's proxy voting?

333. Should a statement of proxy-voting policy be part of a comprehensive statement of investment policy?

334. What is the duty of diversification under ERISA?

335. What is the purpose of diversifying the assets of a plan?

336. Who has the burden of proof in an action based on a breach of the duty of diversification?

337. What is the proper degree of investment concentration necessary to satisfy the diversification requirement?

338. What are the factors for diversification under the "facts and circumstances" test?

339. Is there a prohibition against a fiduciary's investing a substantial portion of a plan's assets in a single security?

340. Is there a prohibition against a fiduciary's investing a substantial portion of a plan's assets in a single geographic area?

341. Is non-diversification a per se violation of ERISA?

342. Is diversification required if it is clearly prudent not to diversify?

343. Does the diversification requirement apply to the ultimate investment of plan assets?

344. Is the requirement to diversify applicable to investment managers?

345. How is the duty of diversification measured for an investment manager of a plan where the investments are distributed among several investment managers?

346. How is the diversification requirement applied to eligible individual account plans?

347. How is the diversification requirement applied to segregated asset accounts underlying annuities?

348. What is the rule regarding diversification of 401(k) plan investments in employer securities or employer real property?

349. May an investment manager rely on information furnished by a fiduciary?

350. What is a fiduciary's duty to act in accordance with the plan documents under ERISA?

351. Is a good-faith but erroneous exercise of the trustees' powers under the plan agreement a breach of ERISA Section 404(a)(1)(D)?

370. Who enforces the fiduciary standards?

371. What is an ERISA Section 404(c) participant-directed plan?

372. What are the default investment alternatives under participant-directed plans?

373. May defined benefit plan fiduciaries seek protection under the provisions of ERISA Section 404(c)?

374. Is compliance with ERISA Section 404(c) mandatory?

375. What are the "core investment alternatives"?

376. What is a "broad range of investment alternatives"?

377. What constitutes a "reasonable opportunity" to give investment instructions under an ERISA Section 404(c) plan?

378. What is "opportunity to exercise control" in an ERISA Section 404(c) plan?

379. To what extent may a fiduciary offer investment education and still maintain the protection from liability provided under ERISA Section 404(c)?

380. Are fiduciaries of ERISA Section 404(c) plans required to exercise prudence in the selection and monitoring of educators and advisers?

381. Which fiduciary responsibilities may not be relieved under ERISA Section 404(c)?

382. Does ERISA Section 404(c) apply to SIMPLE plans?

383. What are the disclosure requirements for plan sponsors attempting to comply with ERISA Section 404(c) regulations?

384. Under what circumstances may an ERISA Section 404(c) plan fiduciary refuse to follow affirmative investment instructions from a participant or beneficiary?

385. When may a participant or beneficiary invest in employer securities under an ERISA Section 404(c) plan?

386. How are ERISA Section 404(c) plans affected by the use of investment managers?

387. What are the fiduciary rules associated with investing automatic enrollment contributions of participants who do not provide investment direction in a participant-directed individual account plan?

388. May ERISA Section 404(c) plan trustees override the investment directions of missing participants?

SECTION V

Prohibited Transactions

Transaction Between a Plan and a Party in Interest

Transactions Between a Plan and a Fiduciary

Excise Taxes Under the Internal Revenue Code

Excise Taxes Under ERISA

SECTION VI

Statutory, Class, and Individual Exemptions

Class Exemptions

425. What are the class exemptions recognized by the Department of Labor and the Internal Revenue Service?

426. What is the broker-dealer exemption?

427. What is the foreign exchange class exemption?

428. What is the class exemption for securities transactions by plan fiduciaries?

429. What are the class exemptions for the purchase and sale of life insurance?

430. What is the class exemption regarding the sale of annuities, insurance, and annuity contracts by captive insurance companies?

431. What is the class exemption regarding the sale of insurance or annuity contracts by agents or brokers that sponsor the plan making the purchase?

432. What is the class exemption relating to insurance company pooled separate accounts?

433. Does the class exemption relating to insurance company pooled separate accounts apply to multiemployer plans?

434. What are the class exemptions regarding mutual fund "in-house" plans?

435. What is the class exemption regarding investment advisers who serve in a dual capacity to a plan?

436. What are the class exemptions that specifically apply to transactions with multiemployer plans?

437. What is the class exemption regarding multiemployer apprenticeship plans?

438. What is the class exemption regarding the plan's purchase of customer notes?

439. What is the class exemption regarding court-ordered transactions?

440. What is the class exemption regarding Department of Labor settlement agreements?

441. What is the class exemption for plans that enter into settlement agreements with private parties?

442. What is the abandoned plan qualified termination administrator exemption?

443. What is the class exemption regarding interest-free loans between a plan and parties in interest?

444. What is the class exemption regarding the purchase of securities by a plan in order to retire indebtedness to a party in interest?

Statutory Exemptions

SECTION VII

Fiduciary Liability Issues

506. May the ERISA Section 502(*l*) penalty be offset by other penalties?

507. Must the Department of Labor prove a breach of fiduciary duty to assess the ERISA Section 502(l) penalty?

508. Is a settlement agreement required for the assessment of an ERISA Section 502(*l*) penalty?

509. What is the scope of protection offered under the ERISA prohibition against interference with participant rights?

510. Does ERISA restrict an employer's right to discharge an employee for cause?

511. Who has the burden of proof with respect to establishing intentional interference with participant rights?

512. Are an employer's efforts to reduce costs by capping lifetime health benefits a violation of ERISA Section 510?

513. Do participants and beneficiaries have a right to seek civil enforcement of ERISA Section 510?

514. Do participants and beneficiaries have a right to seek criminal enforcement of ERISA?

Remedies

515. What remedies are available to participants, beneficiaries, and plans when a fiduciary duty is breached?

516. Can the DOL sue a fiduciary for money damages even though an identical claim brought by a class of participants against the same fiduciary has been the subject of a court-approved settlement?

517. Does a fiduciary breach that causes no damages mandate a remedy?

518. What are the rules regarding the favorable tax and qualification treatment of restorative payments from a fiduciary breach?

519. How are the losses determined if a breaching fiduciary is held personally liable?

520. Can a fiduciary be subject to punitive damages for a breach of fiduciary duty?

521. May a participant recover interest on improperly delayed benefits payments?

522. Are fiduciaries subject to civil liability for the interference with ERISA protected rights?

523. What are the rules regarding co-fiduciary liability?

524. Is there a right of co-fiduciary contribution?

SECTION VIII

Fidelity Bonding, Fiduciary Liability Insurance, and Exculpatory Provisions

Exemptions

Fiduciary Liability Insurance

SECTION IX

Investment Issues

579. Is a statement of investment policy consistent with the duty of loyalty and prudence?

580. Does the maintenance of a statement of investment policy by a named fiduciary relieve the named fiduciary of its fiduciary duties with respect to the appointment and monitoring of an investment manager or trustee?

581. May a fiduciary expressly require, as a condition of an investment management agreement, that an investment manager comply with the terms of a statement of investment policy?

582. Does ERISA Section 404(a)(1)(D) shield an investment manager from liability for imprudent actions taken in compliance with a statement of investment policy?

583. When will an employer be regulated as an investment adviser?

584. May a financial institution include the business of investment management of ERISA-covered plan assets under its control in the sales price of a fiduciary?

585. What are "plan assets"?

586. When do contributions to SIMPLE plans become plan assets?

587. What are the plan asset rules with respect to insurance company general accounts?

588. Must plan documents provide for a written funding policy?

589. Are there any restrictions on the types of investments that are permissible for a plan?

590. Are plan assets required to be held in a trust?

591. What are the exceptions to the requirement that plan assets be held in a trust?

592. May a plan participate in economically targeted investments? What are the asset management issues involved in economically targeted investments?

593. May an employer offer investment advice without incurring fiduciary liability?

594. What is the "plan information" safe harbor under Interpretive Bulletin 96-1?

595. What is the "general financial and investment information" safe harbor under Interpretive Bulletin 96-1?

596. What is the "asset allocation model" safe harbor under Interpretive Bulletin 96-1?

597. What is the "interactive investment materials" safe harbor under Interpretive Bulletin 96-1?

598. Are there any other types of information covered by Interpretive Bulletin 96-1?

599. When will the underlying assets of an insurance company issuing group annuity contracts be considered, or not considered, to be plan assets?

600. What are the asset management issues regarding investments in derivatives?

601. Is the cash asset value of a split dollar life insurance policy considered a plan asset?

602. May plans engage in securities lending arrangements utilizing plan assets?

603. May plans engage in repurchase agreements utilizing plan assets?

604. Under what circumstances may plans enter into "soft dollar" and directed-commission arrangements?

605. May plans enter into "soft dollar" and directed-commission arrangements where the plan sponsor has directed brokerage transactions?

606. What types of "soft dollar" and directed-commission arrangements fall outside Technical Release 86-1 and the limited safe harbor?

607. How does the limited safe harbor for "soft dollar" arrangements apply to recapture provisions?

608. Are there any proposed changes regarding the rules on "soft dollar" and commission recapture arrangements?

609. What are "qualifying employer securities"?

610. What is "qualifying employer real property"?

611. What rules apply to the acquisition and holding of employer securities and employer real property?

612. What is an employee stock ownership plan (ESOP)?

613. What is the difference between a stock bonus plan and a leveraged ESOP?

614. May an ESOP be maintained by an S corporation?

615. What are the requirements of an "exempt loan" used for the purchase of qualifying employer securities by an ESOP?

616. Does the use of an independent appraiser by an ESOP fiduciary ensure compliance with ERISA?

617. What are the "pass through" voting rights applicable to ESOPs?

618. What special diversification rules apply to ESOPs?

SECTION X

Taft-Hartley Plans
(Multiemployer Plans)

658. When and how are withdrawal liability payments to be made?

659. What happens in the event of a default on withdrawal liability payments?

660. Does interest accrue on delinquent withdrawal liability payments?

661. Are payments made by an employer for withdrawal liability deductible?

662. What happens when substantially all of the employers withdraw from a plan?

663. What is involved in filing the notice of termination for a multiemployer plan?

664. What is involved in filing the notice of benefit reductions?

665. What is involved in filing the notice of insolvency?

666. What is the penalty for failure to provide any of the required notices under the multiemployer plan provisions of ERISA?

667. Is the plan sponsor's determination of withdrawal liability presumed to be correct? How can a withdrawing employer challenge the plan sponsor's determination?

668. What are the rules regarding arbitration of multiemployer plan withdrawal liability disputes?

669. What are an arbitrator's powers and duties?

670. How are the awards and costs of arbitration handled?

671. May a party to an arbitration bring a post-award court action seeking enforcement, modification, or vacation of the award?

672. Is a withdrawing employer entitled to a refund for the overpayment of withdrawal liability payments?

673. Must a plan sponsor seek PBGC approval of a plan amendment to utilize a nonstatutory, alternative method for computing withdrawal liability? What information must a request for approval of such an amendment contain?

674. What is the 50% insolvency rule?

675. What rules apply to the sale of assets to an unrelated employer?

676. What are the rules applicable to the merger of multiemployer plans?

677. What occurs if there is a withdrawal following a merger?

678. How is "transfer of assets or liabilities" defined?

679. Is the transfer of assets or liabilities between plans a prohibited transaction?

680. What are the asset transfer rules for multiemployer plans?

681. What rules apply to the transfer of assets between multiemployer and single-employer plans?

682. What special asset transfer rules apply to multiemployer welfare benefit plans?

683. What rules apply to transfers where there has been a change in collective bargaining representatives?

684. What rules apply where an employer withdraws from a plan after a transfer due to a change in bargaining representatives?

685. Do the rules regarding the transfer of assets and liabilities as a result of a change in collective bargaining representatives apply to a transfer to a defined contribution plan?

686. When will the PBGC order the partitioning of a multiemployer plan?

687. Does ERISA require contributions to a multiemployer plan?

688. How are claims for contributions and withdrawal liability handled in bankruptcy?

689. What happens if an employer that has previously withdrawn from a multiemployer plan reenters the plan?

690. Who has standing to bring a civil action regarding a multiemployer plan?

691. What is the statute of limitations for civil actions regarding multiemployer plans?

SECTION XI

Multiple Employer Benefit Arrangements

692. What are the issues regarding multiple employer benefit arrangements?

693. What is a multiple employer welfare arrangement (MEWA)?

694. When does an arrangement offer or provide benefits to the employees of two or more employers?

695. Is a welfare benefit arrangement maintained by a group or association of unrelated employers considered to be provided by two or more employers?

SECTION XII

Civil Compliance and Enforcement Issues

Employee Benefits Security Administration

Investigations of Service Providers

Investigations of Financial Institutions

General Employee Benefits Security Administration Investigations

769. What are the initial DOL inquiries regarding non-income-producing assets that may be held by the plan?

770. What are the initial DOL inquiries regarding the accounting records of a subject plan?

771. What are the initial DOL inquiries regarding the bonding and insurance coverage of a subject plan?

Investigative Findings and Compliance

772. What can a plan sponsor expect after the DOL has completed its investigation?

773. What techniques does the Employee Benefits Security Administration use to correct ERISA violations?

774. Which types of cases involving ERISA violations are appropriate for voluntary compliance?

775. Which types of cases involving ERISA violations may not be suitable for voluntary compliance?

776. Are any cases involving ERISA violations not suitable for voluntary compliance?

777. How are plan fiduciaries or others notified of the opportunity for voluntary compliance?

778. What is a voluntary compliance notice letter?

779. How long will the Employee Benefits Security Administration conduct voluntary compliance negotiations?

780. What settlement terms are acceptable under voluntary correction?

781. What actions are taken by the Employee Benefits Security Administration when voluntary compliance attempts are unsuccessful?

782. What is a closing letter?

783. What action should be taken when fiduciaries agree with the DOL's official findings in an investigation?

784. What action should be taken when fiduciaries disagree with the DOL's official findings in an investigation?

785. What is the "interagency referral agreement"?

DOL Civil Actions

786. What types of civil actions may be brought by the DOL?

787. Can the DOL intervene in an existing ERISA-related civil action?

ERISA Preemption

788. What is the scope of ERISA preemption?

789. What are the exceptions to the broad reach of ERISA preemption?

790. What are EBSA Field Assistance Bulletins?

Pension Benefit Guaranty Corporation

791. What is Title IV of ERISA?

792. What are the investigative powers and authority of the PBGC and which plans do they cover?

793. What ERISA-covered plans are exempt from PBGC coverage?

794. What is the PBGC premium program?

795. What are the PBGC proposed regulations that implement PPA changes to variable-rate premiums for single-employer plans?

796. What are the reportable events that must be directed to the attention of the PBGC?

797. What are the details of the PBGC streamlined filing and notice requirements to facilitate use of electronic media?

798. What are the methods of filing provided under the PBGC's streamlined rules?

799. What are the methods of issuance under the PBGC's streamlined rules?

800. What are the dates of filing or issuance under the PBGC's streamlined rules?

801. What are the "computation of time" rules under the PBGC's streamlined requirements?

802. What are the electronic means of record retention under the PBGC's streamlined requirements?

803. What is the PBGC Participant Notice Voluntary Correction Program?

Plan Terminations

804. What is a "standard termination"?

805. Who must receive notice when a plan sponsor intends to terminate a defined benefit plan? And what information must such individuals receive?

806. What other notice requirements are required in a defined benefit plan termination?

807. What is a distress termination?

808. What are the PBGC proposed regulations on providing information to affected parties in distress or PBGC-initiated plan terminations?

809. What must a plan sponsor do if the plan does not satisfy the requirements of a distress termination?

810. What benefits are guaranteed by the PBGC?

811. Will the PBGC guarantee benefits in a plan that the IRS has disqualified?

812. How will a plan amendment affect the PBGC guarantee upon a plan's termination?

813. Who are "affected parties" in a defined benefit plan termination?

814. What is the importance of a defined benefit plan's termination date?

815. When will the PBGC initiate a plan termination?

816. What is involved in the final distribution of assets in a defined benefit plan standard termination?

817. Does the Pension Benefits Guaranty Corporation (PBGC) retain any responsibility for the provision of benefits after the purchase of annuities by a terminating pension plan?

818. How are the assets of missing participants handled when a defined benefit plan terminates?

819. What help is available from the PBGC for former participants attempting to locate vested benefits in plans of former employers?

820. Who has authority to enforce certain plan terminations in a civil action?

Civil Actions Under ERISA

821. What is the appropriate jurisdiction and venue to bring a civil action under ERISA Section 4070?

822. What is the statute of limitations for any civil action brought under ERISA Section 4070?

823. Who may bring a civil action against the PBGC?

824. What is the appropriate jurisdiction and venue in which to bring a civil action against the PBGC?

825. What is the statute of limitations on civil actions brought against the PBGC?

826. When may the PBGC bring a civil action?

SECTION XIII

Criminal Enforcement

ERISA Criminal Code Provisions

United States Criminal Code Provisions

868. Is any person subject to conviction under 18 U.S.C. Section 1027?

869. What does the term "knowingly" mean for purposes of 18 U.S.C. Section 1027?

870. What documents are covered under the provisions of 18 U.S.C. Section 1027?

871. What documents are "published" for purposes of 18 U.S.C. Section 1027?

872. What documents are "kept" for purposes of 18 U.S.C. Section 1027?

873. What documents are "certified by the plan administrator" for purposes of 18 U.S.C. Section 1027?

874. What is an offer, acceptance, or solicitation to influence operations of an employee benefit plan?

875. Who is a recipient for purposes of 18 U.S.C. Section 1954?

876. Who is a "giver" under 18 U.S.C. Section 1954?

877. Must the "receiver" directly receive a payment to be prosecuted under 18 U.S.C. Section 1954?

878. Must the defendant receive a kickback both "because of" and "with the intent to be influenced" to be convicted under 18 U.S.C. Section 1954?

879. Must the defendant have the actual ability to control the decisions of a benefit plan to be convicted under 18 U.S.C. Section 1954?

880. Must the person who paid the kickback know of the recipient's position with respect to a plan in order to be convicted under 18 U.S.C. Section 1954?

881. Is a benefit or lack of injury to the plan a valid defense to a prosecution under 18 U.S.C. Section 1954?

882. What is a "thing of value" for purposes of 18 U.S.C. Section 1954?

883. What payments are not prohibited under 18 U.S.C. Section 1954?

884. How is "bona fide" defined for purposes of 18 U.S.C. Section 1954?

885. Do the criminal provisions of ERISA supersede local criminal laws?

SECTION I

Establishment and Administration
Basic ERISA Requirements
1. What is the Employee Retirement Income Security Act of 1974 (ERISA)?

The Employee Retirement Income Security Act of 1974 (ERISA)[1] is a federal law that sets minimum standards for most voluntarily established and maintained pension and health plans in private industry, to provide protection for individuals in these plans. Such plans are voluntarily established and maintained by an employer, by an employee organization, or jointly by one or more such employers and an employee organization.

Pension plans are established and maintained to provide retirement income or to defer income until termination of covered employment or beyond. Other employee benefit plans, called welfare plans, are established and maintained to provide health benefits, disability benefits, death benefits, prepaid legal services, vacation benefits, day care centers, scholarship funds, apprenticeship and training benefits, or other similar benefits.

In general, ERISA does not cover plans established or maintained by government entities or churches for their employees, or plans that are maintained solely to comply with workers' compensation, unemployment, or disability laws. ERISA also does not cover plans maintained outside the United States primarily for the benefit of nonresident aliens, or unfunded excess benefit plans.

ERISA requires plans to provide participants with plan information, including important information about plan features and funding; sets minimum standards for participation, vesting, benefit accrual, and funding; provides fiduciary responsibilities for those who manage and control plan assets; requires plans to establish a grievance and appeals process for participants to get benefits from their plans; gives participants the right to sue for benefits and breaches of fiduciary duty; and, if a defined benefit plan is terminated, guarantees payment of certain benefits through a non-profit, federally chartered corporation, known as the Pension Benefit Guaranty Corporation (PBGC).

The administration of ERISA is divided among the U.S. Department of Labor (DOL), the Internal Revenue Service of the Department of the Treasury (IRS), and the PBGC. Title I, which contains rules for reporting and disclosure, vesting, participation, funding, fiduciary conduct, and civil enforcement, is administered by the DOL. Title II of ERISA, which amended the Internal Revenue Code to parallel many of the Title I rules, is administered by the IRS. Title III is concerned with jurisdictional matters and with coordination of enforcement and regulatory activities by the DOL and the IRS. Title IV covers the insurance of defined benefit pension plans and is administered by the PBGC.

---

1. 29 U.S.C. §§1001 et seq.; 29 C.F.R. §§2509 et seq.

Part 5 of Title I of ERISA gives the DOL authority to bring a civil action to correct violations of the law, provides investigative authority to determine whether any person has violated Title I, and imposes criminal penalties on any person who willfully violates any provision of Part 1 of Title I.

The DOL also has jurisdiction over the prohibited transaction provisions of Title II of ERISA. However, the IRS generally administers the rest of Title II, as well as the standards of Title I of ERISA that address vesting, participation, nondiscrimination, and funding. The IRS is responsible for ensuring compliance with the Internal Revenue Code, which establishes the rules for operating a tax-qualified pension plan, including pension plan funding and vesting requirements (a pension plan that is tax-qualified can offer special tax benefits both to the employer sponsoring the plan and to the participants who receive pension benefits).

There have been a number of amendments to ERISA, expanding the protections available to health benefit plan participants and beneficiaries. One important amendment, the Consolidated Omnibus Budget Reconciliation Act (COBRA), provides some workers and their families with the right to continue their health coverage for a limited time after certain events, such as the loss of a job. Another amendment to ERISA is the Health Insurance Portability and Accountability Act (HIPAA), which provides important protections for working Americans and their families who have preexisting medical conditions, or might otherwise suffer discrimination in health coverage based on factors that relate to an individual's health. Other important amendments include the Newborns' and Mothers' Health Protection Act, the Mental Health Parity Act, and the Women's Health and Cancer Rights Act.[1]

2. What employee benefit plans are subject to ERISA?

ERISA Sections 3(1), 3(2), and 3(3) provide that for purposes of ERISA coverage, an "employee benefit plan" means an employee welfare benefit plan or an employee pension plan that is established or maintained by an employer or an employee organization for the purpose of providing benefits to participants and their beneficiaries.

An "employee welfare benefit plan" is one that has been established for the provision of:

1. Medical, surgical, or hospital care or benefits;

2. Benefits in the event of sickness, accident, disability, death, or unemployment;

3. Vacation benefits, apprenticeship, or other training programs;

4. Day care centers, scholarship funds, or prepaid legal services; or

5. Any benefit described under Section 302(c) of the Labor Management Relations Act of 1947 (excluding pensions on retirement or death, and insurance to provide for such pensions).

---

1. http://www.dol.gov/ebsa/faqs/faq_compliance_pension.html; http://www.dol.gov/asp/programs/guide/erisa.htm; http://www.dol.gov/ebsa/ aboutebsa/history.html; and http://www.dol.gov/dol/topic/health-plans/erisa.htm.

An "employee pension benefit plan" is any plan, fund, or program established for the provision of retirement income to employees or that results in the deferral of income by employees for periods extending to the termination of covered employment and beyond, regardless of the method of calculating the contribution made to the plan, the method of calculating the benefits under the plan, or the method of distributing benefits from the plan. The U.S. Supreme Court has ruled that a working owner of a corporation is covered by ERISA if that corporation's benefit plan covers at least one employee.[1]

An "employer" is any person acting directly as an employer, or indirectly in the interest of an employer, in relation to an employee benefit plan, and includes a group or association of employers acting for an employer in such capacity.[2] An "employee organization" is any labor union or any organization of any kind, or any agency or employee representation committee, association, group, or plan, in which employees participate and that exists for the purpose, in whole or part, of dealing with employers concerning an employee benefit plan.[3]

All plans that satisfy the definition of an ERISA covered plan are subject to the fiduciary rules set forth in ERISA. ERISA Section 402(a)(1) requires that all plans subject to ERISA provide for one or more named fiduciaries who jointly and severally have authority to control and manage the administration and operation of the plan.

3. Must a plan be in writing in order to be subject to ERISA?

Yes and no. ERISA requires that every employee benefit plan be established and maintained pursuant to a written instrument that provides for the identification of named fiduciaries with authority to manage and control plan operations, and it must provide procedures for funding, amending, allocating responsibilities for administration, and establishing a basis on which payments will be made from the plan.[4] However, the courts have ruled that certain unwritten policies of employers that provide for pension benefits or welfare benefits have been established plans subject to ERISA.

Court decisions have held that an employee benefit plan will be subject to ERISA if, from the surrounding circumstances, it is reasonable for a person to ascertain the intended benefits, the procedures for obtaining those benefits, the source of funding, and the intended beneficiaries.[5] Although a failure to establish a plan in writing is a violation of ERISA, it will not prevent the plan from being subject to the provisions of ERISA.[6] The mere decision to offer an extension of benefits will subject a plan to ERISA.[7]

---

1. See *Yates v. Hendon*, 124 S. Ct. 1330, 32 EBC 1097 (2004).
2. ERISA Sec. 3(5).
3. ERISA Sec. 3(4).
4. ERISA Secs. 402(a), 402(b).
5. *Scott v. Gulf Oil Corp.*, 754 F.2d 1499 (9th Cir. 1985); *Donovan v. Dillingham*, 688 F.2d 1367 (11th Cir. 1982); *Elmore v. Cone Mills Corp.*, 23 F.3d 855 (4th Cir. 1994).
6. *Adams v. Avondale Indus., Inc.*, 905 F.2d 943 (6th Cir. 1990).
7. *Donovan v. Dillingham*, 688 F.2d 1367 (11th Cir. 1982); *James v. National Bus. Sys.*, 924 F.2d 718 (7th Cir. 1991).

4. What are the additional requirements for establishing ERISA-covered plans?

In addition to the requirement that the plan be in writing and provide for the identification of named fiduciaries, ERISA Section 402(b) requires every employee benefit plan to:

1. Provide a procedure for establishing and carrying out a funding policy and method consistent with the objectives of the plan and the requirements of ERISA;

2. Describe any procedure under the plan for the allocation of responsibilities for the operation and administration of the plan;

3. Provide for a procedure for amending such plan, and for identifying persons who have authority to amend the plan; and

4. Specify the basis on which payments are made to and from the plan.

ERISA Section 405(c)(1) also provides that the plan may expressly provide for procedures for allocating fiduciary responsibilities (other than trustee responsibilities) among named fiduciaries, and for named fiduciaries to designate persons other than named fiduciaries to carry out fiduciary responsibilities (other than trustee responsibilities) under the plan. "Trustee responsibility" means any responsibility provided in the plan's trust instrument (see Q 5) to manage or control the assets of the plan, other than a power under the trust instrument of a named fiduciary to appoint an investment manager in accordance with the provisions of ERISA Section 402(c)(3).[1] See Q 373 to Q 387 for details of investment manager issues.

The employee benefit plan may provide that any person or group of persons may serve in more than one fiduciary capacity. It may also provide that a named fiduciary may employ one or more persons to render advice with regard to any responsibility such fiduciary has under the plan; or that a person who is a named fiduciary may appoint an investment manager or more than one person to manage (including the power to acquire and dispose of) any assets of the plan.[2]

5. What are the trust requirements in establishing an ERISA-covered plan?

ERISA Section 403 provides that all assets of an employee benefit plan must be held in trust by one or more trustees. Such trustees must either be named in the trust instrument or in the plan's governing documents or appointed by a named fiduciary. Upon acceptance of being named or appointed, the trustee or trustees must have exclusive authority and discretion to manage and control the assets of the plan, except to the extent that:

1. The plan expressly provides that such trustees are subject to the direction of a named fiduciary who is not a trustee, in which case the trustees must be subject to proper directions of such fiduciary that are made in accordance with the terms of the plan and are in accordance with the provisions of ERISA; or

---

1. ERISA Sec. 405(c)(3).
2. ERISA Secs. 402(c)(1), 402(c)(2), 402(c)(3).

2. Authority to manage, acquire, or dispose of assets of the plan is delegated to one or more investment managers (in accordance with the provisions of ERISA Section 402(c)(3)).

The Conference Committee Reports to ERISA (Pub. L. No. 93-406) state that a plan may provide for an investment committee to manage the plan's investments, so long as all members of the investment committee are named fiduciaries. The Committee Reports also provide that a trustee is not liable for the acts of a properly appointed investment manager.[1] See Section IV for details of the fiduciary responsibility of investment managers.

ERISA Section 403(b) holds that the trust requirements do not apply:

1. To any assets of a plan that consist of insurance contracts or policies issued by an insurance company qualified to do business in a state;

2. To any assets of such an insurance company or any assets of a plan that are held by such an insurance company;

3. To a plan in which some or all of the participants are self-employed (within the definition of IRC Section 401(c)(1)), or which consists of one or more individual retirement accounts (as described under IRC Section 408), to the extent that such plan's assets are held in one or more custodial accounts that are qualified under the Code;

4. To a plan that the Secretary of Labor has exempted from the trust requirements and that is not subject to the participation, vesting, funding, and plan termination insurance provisions of ERISA; or

5. To a tax sheltered annuity contract established under the provisions of IRC Section 403(b) to the extent the assets are held in one or more custodial accounts.

6. What are the rules that govern trusts?

Generally, all assets of an employee benefit plan must be held in trust by one or more trustees pursuant to a written trust instrument.[2] Trustees must either be named in the trust instrument or in the plan documents, or appointed by a named fiduciary. Upon acceptance of being named or appointed, such trustees must have exclusive authority and discretion to manage and control the assets of the plan, except to the extent that:

1. The plan instrument or the trust instrument expressly provides that the trustees are subject to the direction of a named fiduciary who is not a trustee, in which case the trustees shall be subject to the proper instructions of the named fiduciary; or

2. Authority to manage, acquire, or dispose of plan assets is delegated to one or more investment managers.[3]

---

1. H.R. Conf. Rep. No. 93-1280, 93d Cong., 2d Sess. 323 (1974) (ERISA Conference Report).
2. Labor Reg. §2550.403a-1.
3. Labor Reg. §2550.403a-1(c).

The written trust requirement will not be violated merely because securities of a plan are held in the name of a nominee or in street name, provided such securities are held on behalf of the plan by:

1. A bank or trust company that is subject to the supervision of the United States or of any state, or nominee of such bank or trust company;

2. A broker-dealer registered under the Securities Exchange Act of 1934, or a nominee of such broker-dealer; or

3. A "clearing agency" as defined in Section 3(a)(23) of the Securities Exchange Act of 1934, or its nominee.[1]

The trust requirement will also be satisfied if a corporation described under IRC Section 501(c)(3) holds real property on behalf of the plan if all stock of the corporation is held in trust on behalf of the plan.[2]

Where plan assets are invested in an entity such as a corporation or a partnership, the trust requirement is satisfied if the indicia of ownership (certificate or contract) of the plan's interest in the entity are held in trust on behalf of the plan.[3]

7. Are plans that are not established by an employer or employee organization subject to ERISA?

No. ERISA Section 4(a) states that ERISA will not apply to any employee benefit plan that is not established or maintained by any employer engaged in commerce or any industry or activity affecting commerce, or by an employee organization or organizations representing employees engaged in commerce or any industry or activity affecting commerce, or both.

8. Which employee benefit plans does ERISA expressly exclude from coverage?

ERISA Section 4(b) establishes that the provisions of ERISA do not apply to any employee benefit plan if:

1. The plan is a governmental plan (as defined under ERISA Section 3(32));

2. It is a church plan (as defined in ERISA Section 3(33)) that has not made an IRC Section 410(d) election to have participation, funding, and vesting provisions apply;

3. It is maintained solely for the purpose of complying with applicable workers' compensation laws or unemployment compensation laws or disability insurance laws;

4. It is maintained outside the United States primarily for the benefit of persons substantially all of whom are nonresident aliens; or

---

1. Labor Reg. §2550.403a-1(b).
2. Labor Reg. §2550.403a-1(b)(2).
3. Labor Reg. §2550.403a-1(b)(3).

5.   The plan is an unfunded excess benefit plan (as described under ERISA Section 3(36), which provides benefits for certain employees in excess of the limitations on contributions and benefits imposed by IRC Section 415).

9. What welfare benefit plans are not subject to ERISA?

The following welfare benefit arrangements are not subject to the general fiduciary provisions of ERISA:

1.   Payroll practices that are established by an employer and that provide for payment by an employer to employees on account of overtime pay, shift premiums, holiday premiums or weekend premiums, sick pay, vacation pay, jury duty pay, and pay while on leave for military service;[1]

2.   The maintenance of on-premises facilities such as recreation, dining, or medical/first aid for the treatment of work-related injuries or illness occurring during normal work hours, or other facilities (excluding day care centers) for use by employees;[2]

3.   Programs for the provision of holiday gifts such as turkeys or hams;[3]

4.   Sales to employees of articles or commodities (whether or not they are offered at below-market prices) of the kind the employer offers for sale in the regular course of business;[4]

5.   Hiring halls maintained by one or more employers, employee organizations, or both;[5]

6.   Remembrance funds under which contributions are made to provide remembrances such as flowers, small gifts, or obituary notices on occasion of the illness, hospitalization, or death of an employee;[6]

7.   Strike funds maintained by an employee organization to provide payment to its members during strikes and for related purposes;[7]

8.   Industry advancement programs that have no employee participants and do not provide benefits, regardless of whether the program serves as a conduit through which funds or other assets are channeled to employee benefit plans subject to ERISA;[8] and

9.   Unfunded scholarship programs, including tuition and education reimbursement programs, under which payments are made solely from the general assets of an employer or employee organization.[9]

---

1. Labor Reg. §2510.3-1(b).
2. Labor Reg. §2510.3-1(c).
3. Labor Reg. §2510.3-1(d).
4. Labor Reg. §2510.3-1(e).
5. Labor Reg. §2510.3-1(f).
6. Labor Reg. §2510.3-1(g).
7. Labor Reg. §2510.3-1(h).
8. Labor Reg. §2510.3-1(i).
9. Labor Reg. §2510.3-1(k).

10. What type of group or group-type insurance programs are expressly excluded from ERISA coverage?

For purposes of ERISA coverage, the term "employee welfare benefit plan" does not include a group or group-type employee pay-all insurance program offered by an insurer to employees or members of an employee organization, under which:

1.   No contributions are made by the employer or employee organization;

2.   Participation in the program is completely voluntary for employees or members;

3.   The sole functions of the employer or employee organization with respect to the program are, without endorsing the program, to permit the insurer to publicize the program to employees or members, to collect premiums through payroll deductions or dues checkoffs, and to remit them to the insurer; and

4.   The employer or employee organization receives no consideration in the form of cash or otherwise in connection with the program, other than reasonable compensation, excluding any profit, for administrative services actually rendered in connection with payroll deductions or dues checkoffs.[1]

A U.S. District Court in Florida ruled that a disability plan originally maintained by an employer remains subject to the provisions of ERISA even after it becomes an employee pay-all welfare benefit arrangement.[2]

Such employers who pay all of an insurance program may, unintentionally, find themselves subject to ERISA where the employer or employee organization that has offered the program inadvertently endorses it (e.g., advising employees that the program offers a "valuable" extension of existing insurance coverage, or the marketing pamphlets for the program contain the employer or employee organization's logos).[3]

11. Which employee benefit pension plans are expressly excluded from ERISA coverage?

The regulations provide that the following employer-sponsored plans will not be deemed employee benefit pension plans for purposes of ERISA coverage:

1.   Severance pay plans that provide for the payment of severance benefits on account of termination of an employee's service so long as:

a.   such payments are not contingent, directly or indirectly, upon the employee's retiring,

---

1. Labor Reg. §2510.3-1(j).
2. See *Stern v. Provident Life & Accident Ins. Co.*, 2003 U.S. Dist. LEXIS 23183 (M.D. Fla. 2003).
3. *Hansen v. Continental Ins. Co.*, 940 F.2d 971 (5th Cir. 1991).

  b. the total amount of such payments does not exceed the equivalent of twice the employee's annual compensation during the year immediately preceding the termination of his service, and

  c. all such payments to any employee are completed;[1]

2. Bonus programs that provide payments made by an employer to some or all of its employees as bonuses for work performed (unless such payments are systematically deferred to the termination of covered employment or beyond, so as to provide retirement income to employees);[2]

3. Individual retirement accounts established under IRC Section 408(a) and individual retirement annuities established under IRC Section 408(b) provided that there are no employer contributions, employee participation is voluntary, and the sole involvement of the employer or employee organization is without endorsement to permit the sponsor to publicize the availability of the program and to collect contributions through payroll deduction or dues checkoffs, for which the employer or employee organization receives no consideration from the sponsor other than reimbursement for services rendered in connection with payroll deductions or dues checkoffs.[3]

12. What is the safe harbor that permits an employer to establish an IRA payroll deduction program that is not subject to ERISA?

The DOL has issued an Interpretive Bulletin that sets forth a safe harbor under which an employer may establish a payroll deduction program to fund employee IRAs without the program's being subject to the employee benefit provisions of ERISA. The safe harbor will exempt a payroll deduction IRA program from ERISA if the program satisfies the following requirements:

1. In all communications to employees regarding the program, the employer must be neutral. The employer must make clear that it is involved in the program only to the extent that it is collecting the payroll deductions and remitting them to the IRA sponsor.

2. The employer may limit the number of IRA options it makes available to employees (to as few as one), if it fully discloses any costs or limitations on the employees' ability to roll over the contributions to another IRA. The Interpretive Bulletin cautions that the employer will fall outside the safe harbor if it negotiates special fees, terms, or conditions with the IRA sponsor that are not available to other IRA participants.

3. The employer may pay fees connected with the establishment and maintenance of the payroll deduction procedure for the program. But the employer is not permitted to pay any administrative, investment management, or other fee

---

1. Labor Reg. §2510.3-2(b).
2. Labor Reg. §2510.3-2(c).
3. Labor Reg. §2510.3-2(d).

that the IRA sponsor would charge employees for establishing and maintaining the IRA.

4.   The employer may be paid "reasonable compensation for services rendered in connection with payroll deductions and dues checkoffs." Payments from the IRA sponsor may not include any profit to the employer such as a payment based on a percentage of assets contributed by the employees or an extension of credit to the employer in exchange for making the program available.[1]

13. Does ERISA expressly exclude 403(b) tax sheltered annuities from ERISA coverage?

For purposes of ERISA, a program for the purchase of an annuity contract or the establishment of a custodial account as described under IRC Section 403(b), pursuant to salary reduction agreements or agreements to forgo an increase in salary and which satisfies the requirements of treasury regulations under Section 403(b), will not be considered "established or maintained by an employer" as that term is used in the definition of the terms "employee pension benefit plan" and "pension plan" if:

1.   Participation is completely voluntary for employees;

2.   All rights under the annuity contract or custodial account are enforceable solely by the employee, by a beneficiary of such employee, or any authorized representative of such employee or beneficiary;

3.   The sole involvement of the employer is limited to any of the following:

    a.   permitting annuity contractors to publicize their products to employees,

    b.   requesting information concerning proposed funding media, products, or annuity contractors,

    c.   summarizing or otherwise compiling the information provided with respect to the proposed funding media or products that are made available, or the annuity contractors whose services are provided, in order to facilitate review and analysis by the employees,

    d.   collecting annuity or custodial account considerations as required by salary reduction agreements or by agreements to forgo salary increases, remitting such considerations to annuity contractors, and maintaining records of such considerations,

    e.   holding in the employer's name one or more group annuity contracts covering its employees, and

---

1. I.B. 99-1, 64 Fed. Reg. 32,999 (June 18, 1999).

    f.   limiting the funding media or products available to employees, or the annuity contractors who may approach employees, to a number and selection that is designed to afford employees a reasonable choice in light of all relevant circumstances; and

    4.   The employer receives no direct or indirect consideration or compensation in cash or otherwise other than reasonable compensation to cover expenses properly and actually incurred by the employer.[1]

14. What ERISA-covered plans are exempt from ERISA's fiduciary provisions?

The fiduciary responsibility provisions of ERISA Part IV do not apply to any employee benefit plan that is an unfunded plan maintained by an employer primarily for the purpose of providing deferred compensation for a select group of management or highly compensated employees (commonly referred to as "top hat" plans).[2]

The fiduciary provisions of ERISA will also not apply to any agreement described in IRC Section 736 that provides payments to a retired partner or deceased partner or a deceased partner's successor in interest.[3]

15. For purposes of ERISA, who is a participant and who is a beneficiary?

ERISA Section 3(7) defines a "participant" as an employee or former employee of an employer, or any member or former member of an employee organization, who is or may become eligible to receive a benefit of any type from an employee benefit plan that covers employees of such employer or members of such organization, or whose beneficiaries may be eligible to receive any such benefit.

The Supreme Court has applied the term "may become eligible" to include employees in, or reasonably expected to be in, covered employment, or former employees who have a reasonable expectation of returning to covered employment or those who have a colorable claim to vested benefits.[4] A claim that a participant may become eligible for benefits is established if the claimant can establish a "colorable claim" that they will prevail in a suit for benefits, or that they will fulfill eligibility requirements in the future.[5]

A "beneficiary" means a person designated by the participant, or by the terms of an employee benefit plan, who is or may become entitled to a benefit under the plan.[6] ERISA preempts state laws invalidating beneficiary designations pursuant to divorce.[7]

---

1. Labor Reg. §2510.3-2(f).
2. ERISA Sec. 401(a)(1).
3. ERISA Sec. 401(a)(2).
4. *Firestone Tire & Rubber Co. v. Bruch*, 489 U.S. 101 (1989).
5. *Firestone Tire & Rubber Co. v. Bruch*, above.
6. ERISA Sec. 3(8).
7. *Egelhoff v. Egelhoff*, 532 U.S. 141, 25 EBC 2089 (2001), rev'g 989 P.2d 80 (Wash. 1999).

Vesting

16. What are the basic requirements for vesting under ERISA?

ERISA Section 203 establishes the minimum vesting standards for an ERISA-covered pension plan. Under that section, each pension plan must provide that an employee's right to his normal retirement benefit is nonforfeitable upon the attainment of normal retirement age. ERISA Section 203(a)(1) states that an employee's accrued benefit derived from the employee's own contributions must, at all times, be nonforfeitable.

Section 904 of the Pension Protection Act of 2006,[1] has altered the mandatory vesting requirements for qualified benefit plans by eliminating ERISA Section 203(a)(4) and IRC Section 411(a)(12). The PPA also amended ERISA Section 203(a)(4) and IRC Section 411(a)(2) by providing that for plan years beginning after 2006, employer non-elective contributions must vest at least as rapidly as the mandated vesting schedules for employer matching contributions— that is, either a three-year cliff vesting schedule or a schedule of 20 percent after two years, 40 percent after three years, 60 percent after four years, 80 percent after five years, and 100 percent after six years.

IRS Notice 2007-7 has clarified that employer discretionary contributions remitted to a plan trust prior to 2007 may remain under the pre-PPA vesting provisions of either a five-year cliff vesting schedule or a 3/20 schedule graduating at 20 percent per year after three years and culminating in 100 percent vesting after seven years.[2]

Most qualified retirement plans provide for a graduated vesting schedule on a "2/20" basis. That is a vesting schedule that provides for 2 percent vesting after two years of credited service and then increases the vesting percentage by 20 percent for each additional year of credited service until the participant becomes 100 percent vested. However, employer-matching contributions (as defined under IRC Section 401(m)(4)(A)) must be vested on a three-year cliff or six-year graded vesting schedule.[3]

For defined contribution plans, the "accrued benefit" is the balance of assets allocated to the participant's individual account.[4] For purposes of a defined benefit plan, "accrued benefit" is defined as the employee's accrued benefit as determined under the plan and expressed in the form of an annual benefit commencing at normal retirement age.[5]

Both ERISA and the Internal Revenue Code generally prohibit any plan amendment that has the effect of decreasing accrued benefits under a plan.[6] This would include any amendment increasing the vesting schedule. The IRS takes this provision very seriously and has disqualified plans for violations of this prohibition. Such violations are often referred to as the "death penalty" for qualified plans. See Q 24.

---

1. PPA; Pub. L. No. 109-280.
2. I.R.S. Notice 2007-7, 2007-5 I.R.B. 395.
3. ERISA Secs. 203(a)(2)(A) and 203(a)(2)(B).
4. IRC Sec. 411(a)(7)(A)(ii).
5. IRC Sec. 411(a)(7)(A)(i).
6. ERISA Sec. 204(g)(1); IRC Sec. 411(d)(6).

17. What kinds of service may a plan disregard for purposes of vesting?

In computing the period of service under a qualified plan for purposes of determining the nonforfeitable percentage of an employee's accrued benefit, all of an employee's years of service with the employer maintaining the plan must be taken into account, except that the following may be disregarded:

1. All years of service prior to age eighteen;

2. All years of service during a period for which the employee declined to contribute to a plan requiring employee contributions;

3. All years of service with an employer during any period for which the employer did not maintain the plan or a predecessor plan;

4. All years of service before January 1, 1971, unless the participant has had at least three years of service after December 31, 1970;

5. In general, all years of service accrued prior to a five-year break in service (see Q 33 to Q 35 for details); and

6. In the case of a multiemployer plan, years of service—

   a. with an employer after a complete withdrawal of such employer from the plan or a partial withdrawal in connection with the decertification of the collective bargaining representative, and

   b. with any employer under the plan after the termination date of the plan.[1]

In a Third Circuit case, the permissibility of using an employment classification exclusion that prevents an employee from participating in a plan after satisfying the age and service requirements was upheld.[2] In that case, the plaintiff had worked on an hourly basis for more than 18 years. The plan covered only salaried employees. The plaintiff entered the plan and participated as a salaried employee for three and one-half years until retirement. Upon retirement he filed suit claiming that because he had otherwise satisfied the age and service requirements, he should be given credit for the 18 years of service as an hourly paid employee. The court disagreed, holding that the words "and is otherwise entitled to participate in the plan" in ERISA Section 202(a)(4) permit employment classification as an exclusion if clearly spelled out in the plan provisions.[3]

18. What plans are subject to ERISA's vesting rules?

A plan will not be a "qualified" plan under IRC Section 401 unless it satisfies the minimum vesting standards established under IRC Section 411 (which are mirrored under ERISA Section 203(a)—see Q 16).[4] Under ERISA, these vesting rules apply to all pension plans that are established or maintained by any employer engaged in commerce or in any industry or activity

---

1. ERISA Sec. 203(b)(1); IRC Sec. 411(a)(4).
2. *Bauer v. Summit Bancorp*, 325 F.3d 155 (3d Cir. 2003).
3. *Bauer v. Summit Bancorp*, above.
4. IRC Sec. 401(a)(7).

affecting commerce, or by any employee organization or organizations representing employees engaged in commerce or in any industry or activity affecting commerce, or both.[1] As such, both qualified and nonqualified plans that provide for retirement income or result in the deferral of income to termination or retirement are generally subject to the vesting requirements of ERISA. See Q 19 for plans that are exempt from the general vesting rules.

19. What plans are exempt from ERISA's vesting rules?

The following types of plans are exempt from the general vesting rules of ERISA:

1. A governmental plan established or maintained by the government of the United States, any state or political subdivision, or agency or instrumentality thereof (including any plan to which the Railroad Retirement Act of 1935 or 1937 applies);[2]

2. Church plans (those plans established and maintained for its employees by a church or a convention of churches that is tax exempt under IRC Section 501) that have not made an irrevocable election to be subject to the participation, vesting, and funding rules of ERISA;[3]

3. Plans that are adopted by fraternal beneficiary societies and voluntary employee beneficiary associations that are tax exempt under IRC Section 501(c)(8) or IRC Section 501(c)(9) if no contributions are made by employers;[4]

4. Workers' compensation plans and plans established to comply with unemployment compensation or disability insurance laws;[5]

5. Plans maintained outside the United States primarily for persons substantially all of whom are nonresident aliens;[6]

6. Welfare benefit plans;[7]

7. A plan that is unfunded and maintained by an employer primarily for the purpose of providing deferred compensation for a select group of management or highly compensated employees (i.e., "top hat" plans);[8]

8. Excess benefit plans that are maintained solely for the purpose of providing benefits for certain employees in excess of the accrual limits under IRC Section 415;[9]

9. Any agreement described under IRC Section 736 that provides payments to a retired partner or deceased partner or a deceased partner's successor in interest;[10]

---

1. ERISA Secs. 4(a), 203(a).
2. ERISA Sec. 3(32); IRC Sec. 411(e)(1)(A).
3. ERISA Sec. 4(b)(2); IRC Secs. 410(d), 411(e)(1)(B).
4. ERISA Sec. 201(3)(A); IRC Sec. 411(e)(1)(D).
5. ERISA Sec. 4(b)(3).
6. ERISA Sec. 4(b)(4).
7. ERISA Sec. 201(1).
8. ERISA Sec. 201(2).
9. ERISA Sec. 201(7).
10. ERISA Sec. 201(5).

10.   Individual retirement accounts and individual retirement annuities;[1] and

11.   A Keogh plan that covers only self-employed individuals and does not extend coverage to common-law employees.[2]

20. How are the vesting rules affected by the presence of a controlled group?

All employees of all corporations that are members of a controlled group of corporations, and all employees of trades or businesses (whether or not incorporated) that are under common control, must be treated as employed by a single employer.[3] For credited service under an applicable vesting schedule, participants will be credited for all years of service with members of the controlled group of corporations or employers under common control, as defined under the terms of the plan's governing documents.

A "controlled group of corporations" can be one of three types: parent-subsidiary, brother-sister, and combined. All three types are defined under IRC Section 1563(a) as follows:

(1)   PARENT-SUBSIDIARY CONTROLLED GROUP. One or more chains of corporations connected through stock ownership with a common parent corporation if—

(A)   stock possessing at least 80 percent of the total combined voting power of all classes of stock entitled to vote or at least 80 percent of the total value of shares of all classes of stock of each of the corporations, except the common parent corporation, is owned ... by one or more of the other corporations, and

(B)   the common parent corporation owns ... stock possessing at least 80 percent of the total combined voting power of all classes of stock entitled to vote or at least 80 percent of the total value of shares of all classes of stock of at least one of the other corporations, excluding, in computing such voting power or value, stock owned directly by such other corporations.

(2)   BROTHER-SISTER CONTROLLED GROUP. Two or more corporations if five or fewer persons who are individuals, estates, or trusts own stock ... possessing—

(A)   at least 80 percent of the total combined voting power of all classes of stock entitled to vote or at least 80 percent of the total value of shares of all classes of the stock of each corporation, and

(B)   more than 50 percent of the total combined voting power of all classes of stock entitled to vote or more than 50 percent of the total value of shares of all classes of stock of each corporation, taking into account the stock ownership

---

1. ERISA Sec. 201(6).
2. Labor Reg. §§2510.3-3(b), 2510.3-3(c).
3. ERISA Secs. 210(c), 210(d).

of each such person only to the extent such stock ownership is identical with respect to each such corporation.

(3)   COMBINED GROUP. Three or more corporations each of which is a member of a group of corporations described in paragraphs (1) or (2), and one of which—

(A) is a common parent corporation included in a group of corporations described in paragraph (1), and also,

(B) is included in a group of corporations described in paragraph (2).

A combined group of trades or businesses under common control "means any group of three or more organizations, if (1) each such organization is a member of either a parent-subsidiary group of trades or businesses under common control or a brother-sister group of trades or businesses under common control, and (2) at least one such organization is the common parent organization of a parent-subsidiary group of trades or businesses under common control and is also a member of a brother-sister group of trades or businesses under common control."[1]

21. How are the vesting rules affected by the presence of an affiliated service group?

As with a controlled group of corporations and trades or businesses under common control, all employees of employers who are members of an affiliated service group are treated as employed by a single employer.[2] This is for purposes of the vesting provisions of IRC Section 411 and ERISA Section 203(a).

An affiliated service group is defined as a group consisting of a service organization (i.e., the "first organization") and one or more of the following:

(A)   Any service organization which—

(i)   is a shareholder or partner in the first organization, and

(ii) regularly performs services for the first organization or is regularly associated with the first organization in performing services for third persons, and

(B)   Any other organization if—

(i)   a significant portion of the business of such organization is the performance of services (for the first organization, for organizations described in subparagraph (A), or for both) of a type historically performed in such service field by employees, and

(ii) 10 percent or more of the interests in such organization is held by persons who are highly compensated employees (within the meaning of [IRC] [S]ection

---

1. Treas. Reg. §1.414(c)-2(d).
2. IRC Sec. 414(m)(1).

414(q)) of the first organization or an organization described in subparagraph (A).[1]

A "service organization" is any organization the principal business of which is the performance of services.[2]

22. What are the vesting rules for multiemployer plans?

Multiemployer plans are generally subject to the same vesting schedules that are applied to single employer plans. See Q 16.[3]

The change in vesting schedules does not apply to employees who do not have more than one hour of credited service under the multiemployer plan on or after the first day of the first plan year to which the change in vesting schedules applies.[4]

23. May plan fiduciaries amend plan vesting schedules?

Plans are permitted to change their vesting schedules through appropriate plan amendment processes. However, a plan amendment that changes a vesting schedule will not be treated as satisfying the vesting requirements of ERISA and the Code if the nonforfeitable percentage of the accrued benefit derived from employer contributions (determined as of the later of the date such amendment is adopted or becomes effective) of any employee who is a participant in the plan is less than such nonforfeitable percentage computed under the plan without regard to such amendment.[5]

A plan amendment that changes a vesting schedule also will not be treated as satisfying the vesting requirements unless each participant having three or more years of service is permitted to elect, within a reasonable period after the adoption of such amendment, to have his nonforfeitable percentage computed under the plan without regard to such amendment.[6] An election is not required where the amended vesting schedule would not result in a lesser vesting percentage.[7]

The period during which a participant may make such an election must begin no later than the date the plan amendment is adopted and must end no later than the following:

1. Sixty days after the date the amendment is adopted;

2. Sixty days after the date the amendment becomes effective; or

3. Sixty days after the date the participant is given written notice of the amendment by the employer or the plan administrator.[8]

---

1. IRC Sec. 414(m)(2).
2. IRC Sec. 414(m)(3).
3. SBJPA '96 §1442(b), *repealing* ERISA Sec. 203(a)(2)(C); SBJPA '96 §§1442(a)(1), 1442(a)(2), *repealing* IRC Sec. 411(a)(2)(C).
4. SBJPA '96 §1442(c).
5. ERISA Sec. 203(c)(1)(A); IRC Sec. 411(a)(10)(A).
6. IRC Sec. 411(a)(10)(B).
7. Temp. Treas. Reg. §1.411(a)-8T(b)(1).
8. Temp. Treas. Reg. §1.411(a)-8T(b)(2).

24. Will a plan amendment that establishes surrender charges under an annuity contract violate ERISA's minimum vesting and benefit accrual standards?

A violation of ERISA's minimum vesting and benefit accrual standards was found to occur where a plan amendment established surrender charges that had the effect of reducing participants' accrued benefits.[1] Generally, any plan amendment that has the effect of reducing a participant's accrued benefit under the plan is prohibited.[2]

In *Arakelian v. National Western Life Insurance Co.*, National Western argued that the amendment at issue merely reallocated front-end administrative costs. This position was unpersuasive to the court.[3] The court explained that the plan documents may have allowed surrender charges to be considered in establishing the accrued benefits under the plan; however, the original plan document did not impose any surrender charges. Therefore, the amendment establishing surrender charges decreased the accrued benefits of the plan participants.

Benefit Accrual and Forfeiture

25. What are the general benefit accrual rules under ERISA?

In the case of a defined benefit plan, the term "accrued benefit" means the employee's accrued benefit as determined under the plan and expressed in the form of an annual benefit commencing at normal retirement age.[4] In the case of an individual account defined contribution plan, the term "accrued benefit" means the balance of the employee's account (whether vested or not).[5]

Generally, the accrued benefits of participants may not be decreased by a plan amendment (commonly referred to as the "anti-cutback" rule).[6] For purposes of this rule, a plan amendment that has the effect, with respect to benefits attributable to service before the amendment, of eliminating or reducing an early retirement benefit or a retirement-type subsidy, or eliminating an optional form of benefit, will be treated as reducing accrued benefits.[7] A pension plan's cost-of-living adjustment has been deemed an accrued benefit that cannot be decreased by a plan amendment.[8]

An optional form of benefit is defined as a distribution form with respect to an employee's benefit that is available under the plan and is identical with respect to all features relating to the distribution form, including the payment schedule, timing, commencement, medium of distribution, the portion of the benefit to which such distribution features apply, and the election rights with respect to such optional forms.[9]

---

1. *Arakelian v. National W. Life Ins. Co.*, 724 F. Supp. 1033 (D.D.C. 1989).
2. ERISA Sec. 204(g)(1); IRC Sec. 411(d)(6).
3. *Arakelian v. National W. Life Ins. Co.*, above.
4. IRC Sec. 411(a)(7)(A)(i).
5. IRC Sec. 411(a)(7)(A)(ii).
6. ERISA Sec. 204(g)(1); IRC Sec. 411(d)(6).
7. ERISA Sec. 204(g)(2); IRC Sec. 411(d)(6)(B).
8. *Hickey v. Chicago Truck Drivers, Helpers & Warehouse Workers*, 980 F.2d 465 (7th Cir. 1992).
9. Treas. Reg. §1.411(d)-4(b).

26. May a retirement plan reduce the rate of future benefit accruals?

Yes. However, a defined benefit or money purchase pension plan may not be amended to provide for a significant reduction in the rate of future benefit accruals, unless the plan administrator provides a written notice setting forth the plan amendment and its effective date to the following:

1. Each plan participant;

2. Each beneficiary who is an alternate payee under an applicable qualified domestic relations order; and

3. Each employee organization representing participants in the plan.

This notice must be provided after the adoption of the plan amendment and not less than fifteen days before the effective date of the plan amendment.[1] The Court of Appeals for the Third Circuit has ruled that failure to provide the required notice under ERISA Section 204(h) invalidated an amendment to convert a money purchase pension plan into a discretionary profit sharing plan.[2]

27. What service must be taken into account for purposes of benefit accrual?

Participants will be credited with service for purposes of benefit accruals from the earliest date on which they become a participant in the plan.[3] The following service need not be considered for purposes of benefit accrual:

1. Service prior to the participant's becoming a participant in the plan;

2. Service that is not required to be taken into account under ERISA Section 202(b) and IRC Section 410(a)(5) as a result of a one-year break in service;

3. Service that is not required to be taken into account under ERISA Section 204(b) (4)(C) and IRC Section 411(b)(4)(C) because it is less than 1,000 hours during a 12-consecutive-month period; and

4. Service before the conclusion of a series of consecutive one-year breaks in service that permit the plan to disregard service that need not be counted for vesting on account of the rule of parity provided for under ERISA Section 203(b)(3)(D) and IRC Section 411(a)(6)(D).[4]

28. Are age-related reductions in accruals permissible?

A defined contribution plan will be deemed to have satisfied the basic accrual requirements of ERISA and the Code if allocations to the participant's account under the plan do not cease

---

1. ERISA Sec. 204(h).
2. *Brothers v. Miller Oral Surgery, Inc. Ret. Plan*, 230 F.3d 1348, 25 EBC 1369 (3d Cir. 2000).
3. *See* ERISA Sec. 204(b)(4); IRC Sec. 411(b)(4).
4. *See* Labor Reg. §2530.204-1(b).

and the rate at which amounts are allocated to the participant's account is not reduced because of the attainment of any age.[1]

A defined benefit plan will be deemed to have failed to satisfy the basic accrual requirements of ERISA and the Code if an employee's benefit accrual under the plan does cease or the rate of an employee's benefit accrual is reduced because of the attainment of any age.[2]

However, certain reductions in accruals are permissible. Defined benefit plans will not violate the basic accrual requirements where the plan (without regard to the participant's age) imposes a limitation on the amount of benefits that the plan provides or a limitation on the number of years of service or years of participation that are taken into account for purposes of determining benefit accruals under the plan.[3] Where a participant in a defined benefit plan continues to be actively employed by the plan sponsor beyond his attainment of the plan's normal retirement age, and the participant has commenced distribution of benefits, the rate of accrual may be reduced by the value of the actuarial equivalent of an in-service distribution of benefits to that participant. Further, where an actively employed participant works beyond normal retirement age and has not commenced distribution of her benefits, the plan may make an adjustment in the benefit payable due to the delay in the distribution of benefits after the attainment of normal retirement age.[4]

29. What are the benefit accrual rules specific to defined contribution plans?

As noted in Q 25, under a defined contribution plan, the participant's accrued benefit is the balance of assets in his individual account under the plan.[5] As such, separate accounting is required for each participant's accrued benefit.[6]

In general, defined contribution assets accrue when they are actually allocated to the participants' accounts. However, the Internal Revenue Service has ruled that accrual occurs when a participant is entitled to an allocation of assets under the terms of the plan, even where there has not been an actual crediting of the benefits to the participant's account.[7] Thus, the plan sponsor's determination of a discretionary annual profit sharing contribution that was committed to, but that was not yet allocated to the participants' accounts, was part of the accrued benefit.

The position taken by the IRS is in contradiction to a prior Fifth Circuit Court ruling, which held that the employer's contribution of employer stock did not accrue under the plan until actually allocated.[8] In that case, the court permitted the plan sponsor to amend the plan's provisions and revalue the stock before the contribution had actually accrued to the participants, without violating ERISA's restrictions on reductions in accrued benefits.

---

1. ERISA Sec. 204(b)(2)(A); IRC Sec. 411(b)(2).
2. ERISA Sec. 204(b)(1)(H); IRC Sec. 411(b)(1)(H).
3. ERISA Sec. 204(b)(1)(H)(ii); IRC Sec. 411(b)(1)(H)(ii).
4. ERISA Sec. 204(b)(1)(H)(iii); IRC Sec. 411(b)(1)(H)(iii).
5. IRC Sec. 411(a)(7)(A)(ii).
6. ERISA Sec. 204(b)(3)(B); IRC Sec. 411(b)(3)(B).
7. Priv. Ltr. Rul. 9735001.
8. *Izzarelli v. Rexene Prods. Co.*, 24 F.3d 1506 (5th Cir. 1994).

Practitioner's Pointer: It is always best to make a thorough evaluation of any contemplated amendment to a plan that may have an effect on the accrual of benefits. Given the seriousness with which the IRS considers the "anti-cutback" rules, the best service a trustee or fiduciary can offer the plan is to seek the professional opinion of qualified legal counsel before carrying out the considered amendment.

Voluntary Employee Contributions

The accrued benefit derived from contributions made by an employee is the balance of the employee's separate account consisting of his contributions and income, expenses, gains, and losses attributable thereto. If a separate account is not maintained for an employee's contributions, the accrued benefit derived from such contributions is the amount that bears the same ratio to the participant's total accrued benefit as the total amount of the employee's contributions (less withdrawals) bears to the sum of such contributions and the contributions made on his behalf by the employer (less withdrawals).[1]

For vesting purposes, voluntary employee contributions are always 100 percent vested.[2]

30. What are the benefit accrual rules specific to defined benefit plans?

As stated in Q 25, accrued pension or retirement benefits under a defined benefit plan are determined under the plan and expressed in the form of an annual benefit commencing at normal retirement age.[3]

Normal retirement age is defined as the earlier of:

1.   The time a plan participant attains normal retirement age under the plan; or

2.   The later of (a) the time a plan participant attains age sixty-five or (b) the fifth anniversary of the time a plan participant commenced participation in the plan.[4]

Defined benefit plan participants are required to have their accrued benefit provided by an annual benefit in the form of a single life annuity. If an employee's accrued benefit is to be determined as an amount other than an annual benefit commencing at normal retirement age, or if the accrued benefit derived from contributions made by an employee is to be determined with respect to a benefit other than an annual benefit in the form of a single life annuity commencing at normal retirement age, the employee's accrued benefit, or the accrued benefits derived from contributions made by an employee, must be actuarially adjusted.[5]

ERISA and the Code provide for three optional methods in calculating accruals under a defined benefit plan. In general, the three methods apply as follows:

1.   The "3 percent method" entitles a participant to a benefit at normal retirement age of not less than 3 percent of the normal retirement benefit to which she would

---

1. ERISA Sec. 204(c)(2)(A); IRC Sec. 411(c)(2)(A).
2. ERISA Sec. 203(a)(1); IRC Sec. 411(a)(1).
3. IRC Sec. 411(a)(7); Treas. Reg. §1.411(a)-7(a)(1).
4. ERISA Sec. 3(24); IRC Sec. 411(a)(8).
5. ERISA Sec. 204(c)(3); IRC Sec. 411(c)(3).

be entitled if she began participation at the earliest possible entry age under the plan and served continuously until the earlier of age sixty-five or the plan's normal retirement age, multiplied by the number of years (not in excess of 33⅓ percent) of her participation in the plan;

2.   The "133⅓ percent rule" entitles a participant to a benefit at normal retirement age that is equal to the normal retirement benefit provided that (1) at Normal Retirement Age (NRA), a participant's Accrued Benefit = his or her Normal Retirement Benefit under the terms of the Plan and (2) the annual rate at which a participant can accrue benefits, under the plan formula, for a later year cannot exceed 133⅓ percent of the annual rate of benefit accrual for any prior year; or (3) The "fractional rule" provides that the accrued benefit to which a participant is entitled upon her separation from service is not less than a fraction of the annual benefit commencing at normal retirement age to which she would be entitled under the plan as in effect on the date of separation from service if she continued to earn annually until normal retirement age the same rate of compensation upon which her normal retirement benefit would be computed under the plan, determined as if she had attained normal retirement age on the date on which any such determination is made (but taking into account no more than ten years of service immediately preceding her separation from service). Such fraction must be a fraction, not exceeding one, the numerator of which is the total number of years of participation in the plan (as of the date of her separation from service) and the denominator of which is the total number of years she would have participated in the plan if she separated from service at the normal retirement age.[1]

These rules apply for an accrual of a defined benefit in an even manner that does not result in the acceleration of accruals for older participants or participants with extensive years of service over the rate of accrual for younger participants or participants who have attained fewer years of credited service.

Insurance Contract Plans

Defined benefit plans that are funded exclusively through the purchase of individual insurance contracts purchased on behalf of participants are not required to satisfy any of the three accrual methods detailed above.[2]

In order to satisfy this exemption from the defined benefit accrual rules, the insurance contracts must provide for level annual premium payments to be paid extending not later than the retirement age for each individual participating in the plan, and commencing with the date the individual became a participant in the plan (or in the case of an increase in benefits, commencing at the time such increase becomes effective). Also, the benefits provided by the plan must be equal to the benefits provided under each contract at normal retirement age under the plan and must be guaranteed by an insurance carrier to the extent the premiums have been paid.

---

1. ERISA Sec. 204(b)(1); IRC Sec. 411(b)(1).
2. ERISA Secs. 204(b)(1)(F), 301(a)(2); IRC Secs. 411(b)(1)(F), 412(h)(2).

Finally, all premiums must be paid for the plan year before the contract lapses (or there is reinstatement of the policy), no rights under the contracts may have been subject to a security interest at any time during the plan year, and no policy loans may be outstanding at any time during the plan year.[1] In order for the exemption from the defined benefit accrual standards to apply, the insurance contract plan must provide that the employee's accrued benefit as of any applicable date is not less than the cash surrender value the employee's insurance contracts would have on that date.[2]

31. For purposes of vesting and accrual, how is a participant's service computed?

An employee's statutory entitlement with regard to participation, vesting, and benefit accrual is generally determined by reference to years of service and years of participation completed by the employee and one-year breaks in service incurred by the employee. The units used for determining an employee's credit toward statutory participation, vesting, and benefit accrual entitlements are in turn defined in terms of the number of hours of service credited to the employee during a specified period — in general, a twelve-consecutive-month period referred to under ERISA as a "computation period."[3]

An employee who is credited with 1,000 hours of service during an eligibility computation period must generally be credited with a year of service for purposes of participation and vesting standards under ERISA and the Code.[4] A "year of service" is defined as a calendar year, plan year, or other twelve-consecutive-month period designated by the plan (and not prohibited under ERISA regulations) during which the participant has completed 1,000 hours of service.[5]

An "hour of service" must be counted for purposes of determining a year of service, a year of participation for benefit accrual, and breaks in service.[6] An "hour of service" is determined under ERISA regulations.[7] Three definitions are provided under ERISA regulations.

Under the first definition, an hour of service is each hour for which an employee is paid, or entitled to payment, for the performance of duties for the employer during the applicable computation period.[8]

The second definition of hour of service is each hour for which an employee is paid, or entitled to payment, by the employer on account of a period of time during which no duties are performed (irrespective of whether the employment relationship has terminated), due to vacation, holiday, illness, incapacity (including disability), layoff, jury duty, military duty, or leave of absence. However, no more than 501 hours of service are required to be credited to

---

1. ERISA Sec. 301(b); IRC Sec. 412(i).
2. ERISA Sec. 204(b)(1)(F); IRC Sec. 411(b)(1)(F); Treas. Reg. §1.411(b)-1(d)(2).
3. Labor Reg. §2530.200b-1(a).
4. Labor Reg. §2530.200b-1(a).
5. ERISA Sec. 203(b)(2)(A); IRC Sec. 411(a)(5).
6. Labor Reg. §2530.200b-2(a).
7. ERISA Sec. 202(a)(3)(C); IRC Sec. 410(a)(3)(C).
8. Labor Reg. §2530.200b-2(a)(1).

an employee on account of any single continuous period during which the employee performs no duties (whether or not such period occurs in a single computation period).[1]

Finally, an hour of service includes each hour for which back pay, irrespective of mitigation of damages, is either awarded or agreed to by the employer (however, there will be no credit for hours of service awarded under this provision if the same hours have already been granted to the participant by reason of the preceding two paragraphs).[2]

Hours of service need not be credited to a participant if payment is made or due under a plan maintained solely for the purpose of complying with applicable workers' compensation or disability insurance laws, nor for payments that solely reimburse an employee for medical and medically related expenses incurred by the employee.[3]

Alternative Methods for Crediting Hours of Service

Plans are permitted to adopt one of the following three alternative methods for crediting "hours of service":

1.   Counting hours of service: these are detailed above;[4]

2.   Use of equivalencies: a plan may adopt an equivalency of hours of service to be credited based upon:

   a.   periods of employment: days – ten hours; weeks – forty-five hours; semi-monthly – ninety-five hours; or monthly – 190 hours;[5]

   b.   earnings: for hourly rate employees, a plan must divide the employee's total earnings during a computation period by one of three hourly rates to establish the hours of service to be credited (actual hourly rates; employee's lowest hourly rate during the computation period; and lowest hourly rate paid to employees in the same or similar job classification) and 870 hours must be credited as equivalent to 1,000 hours and 435 hours must be credited as equivalent to 500 hours. For non-hourly employees, hours of service to be credited under this equivalency method are determined by dividing the employee's total earnings by the lowest hourly rate and 750 hours must be credited as equivalent to 1,000 hours and 375 hours must be credited as equivalent to 500 hours;[6] or

   c.   hours of working time: this is divided into two types — (i) in the case of those based on hours worked (i.e., those hours for which an employee is paid or is entitled to payment for the performance of duties, including back pay awards), 870 hours must be treated as equivalent to 1,000 hours and 375 hours must

---

1. Labor Reg. §2530.200b-2(a)(2).
2. Labor Reg. §2530.200b-2(a)(3).
3. Labor Reg. §§2530.200b-2(a)(2)(ii), 2530.200b-2(a)(2)(iii).
4. Labor Reg. §2530.200b-2(a).
5. Labor Reg. §2530.200-3(e).
6. Labor Reg. §2530.200-3(d).

be credited as equivalent to 500 hours; and (ii) in the case of those based on regular time (i.e., the same as the hours worked equivalency excluding overtime hours), 750 regular time hours must be treated as equivalent to 1,000 hours and 375 regular time hours must be treated as equivalent to 500 hours.[1]

Elapsed Time Calculation Method

In addition to the methods of crediting hours of service detailed above, a plan may determine hours of service to be credited for participation, vesting, and accrual purposes on an elapsed time method. Under this method, service is credited by reference to the total period of time that elapses while the employee is employed with the employer or the employer maintains the plan (regardless of the actual number of hours worked). Such service must be taken into account from the date the employee first performs an "hour of service" to the date of severance. The regulation states that the elapsed time method is designed to enable a plan to lessen the administrative burdens associated with maintenance of records by permitting each employee to be credited with his total period of service with the employer.[2]

Under the elapsed time method, the employer may not require as a condition of participation that an employee complete a period of service beyond the later of the employee's attaining:

1.   Age twenty-one; or

2.   The completion of a one-year period of service (based upon the one-year anniversary of employment commencement date).[3]

If the eligibility under the elapsed time method is satisfied, the participant must commence participation in the plan no later than the first day of the first plan year beginning after the date on which the employee satisfied the minimum requirements for eligibility to participate, or the date six months after the date on which the employee satisfied the minimum requirements.[4]

Excludable Service under the Elapsed Time Method

Plans that utilize the elapsed time method of calculating credited service may disregard the following forms of employee service:

1.   The period of service completed by the employee prior to the attainment of age eighteen;

2.   In the case of a plan that requires mandatory employee contributions, the period of service that falls within the period of time to which a particular employee contribution relates, if the employee had the opportunity to make a contribution for such period of time and failed to do so;

---

1. Labor Reg. §2530.200-3(f).
2. Treas. Reg. §1.410(a)-7(a).
3. Treas. Reg. §1.410(a)-7(c).
4. Treas. Reg. §1.410(a)-7(c)(3).

3.   The period of service during any period for which the employer did not maintain the plan or a predecessor plan;

4.   The period of service that is not required to be taken into account by reason of the break-in-service rules of IRC Section 410(d)(4);

5.   The period of service completed by an employee prior to January 1, 1971, unless the employee completes at least three years of service at any time after December 31, 1970; and

6.   The period of service completed before the first plan year for which IRC Section 410 applies to the plan, if such service would have been disregarded under the plan rules relating to breaks in service in effect at that time.[1]

Break in Service

A one-year break in service is a twelve-consecutive-month period beginning on the employee's severance from employment and ending on the first anniversary of that date, provided that the employee fails to perform an "hour of service" (as defined under ERISA regulations, see above) during that twelve-consecutive-month period for the employer maintaining the plan. Under the elapsed time method, the term "one-year break in service" will be substituted with the term "one-year period of severance."[2]

Service completed prior to a one-year break in service or a one-year period of severance is not required to be taken into account for the determination of eligibility and vesting until the employee has completed one year of service upon his return to active employment.[3]

32. What are the basic "break in service" rules?

A one-year break in service is defined as a calendar year, plan year, or other twelve-consecutive-month period designated by the plan during which the participant has not completed 500 or more hours of service.[4] The computation period to be used in applying the break-in-service rules is the computation period established under the plan for purposes of calculating eligibility, benefit accruals, and vesting.

One-Year Break in Service

In the case of an employee who has had any one-year break in service, years of service completed before such break are not required to be taken into account until the participant has completed a year of service after her return to employment.[5]

Where an employee has performed one year of service upon reemployment (after a one-year break in service), she must receive credit for all pre-break and post-break service (including the reemployment waiting year) for purposes of benefit accrual and vesting.

---

1. Treas. Reg. §1.410(a)-7(d)(2).
2. Treas. Reg. §1.410(a)-7(d)(4).
3. Treas. Reg. §1.410(a)-7(d)(5).
4. ERISA Sec. 203(b)(3)(A); IRC Sec. 411(a)(6)(A).
5. ERISA Sec. 203(b)(3)(B); IRC Sec. 411(a)(6)(B).

Five Consecutive One-Year Breaks in Service

In the case of a participant in an individual account plan or an insured defined benefit plan who has five consecutive one-year breaks in service, years of service after such five consecutive one-year breaks in service will not be required to be taken into account for purposes of determining the nonforfeitable percentage of her accrued benefit derived from employer contributions that accrued prior to the five-year period.[1]

Rule of Parity

In the case of an employee who has no vested benefits, years of service with the employer maintaining the plan before any period of consecutive one-year breaks in service need not be taken into account if the number of consecutive one-year breaks in service within such period equals or exceeds the greater of five, or the aggregate number of years of service before such period.[2] If the participant returns to work within five years, she must be given credit for her pre-break years of service for purposes of vesting.[3]

33. How is the five-year break-in-service rule applied to a reemployed participant who had previously terminated with a vested percentage under the plan?

In a defined contribution plan, where a participant has accumulated five or more consecutive one-year breaks in service, all service of the participant must be taken into account upon his reemployment (including all service credited prior to his reemployment) if the participant was partially vested in employer contributions at the time of his separation from service.[4]

34. How is a participant's credited service accrued prior to five consecutive one-year breaks in service treated where the number of years of service before the break exceeds the number of consecutive one-year breaks in service?

Upon reemployment, if a participant has five or more consecutive one-year breaks in service, she must be given full credit for all pre-termination breaks in service, for purposes of vesting and benefit accrual, if the number of years of service prior to termination exceeds the number of consecutive one-year breaks in service.[5]

For plans that utilize the elapsed time method in determining years of service, the plan is also required to provide full credit for all service completed for vesting purposes if the period of consecutive one-year periods of severance does not exceed the number of years of pre-termination service.

---

1. ERISA Sec. 203(b)(3)(C); IRC Sec. 411(a)(6)(C).
2. ERISA Sec. 203(b)(3)(D); IRC Sec. 411(a)(6)(D).
3. ERISA Sec. 203(b)(3)(D)(iii); IRC Sec. 411(a)(6)(D)(iii).
4. IRS Alert Guidelines No. 2, III.
5. IRS Alert Guidelines No. 2, III.

35. What are the rights of veterans upon reemployment after a severance from service for military service?

The Uniformed Services Employment and Reemployment Rights Act of 1994 (USERRA) establishes that upon reemployment after a period of military service, participants are entitled to all rights and benefits based upon seniority that they would have accrued with reasonable certainty had they maintained continuous employment without the separation from service for military service (including basic seniority).[1]

Depending on the length of the military service, a returning servicemember is entitled to take from one (for periods of service not exceeding thirty-one days) to ninety (for periods of service exceeding 180 days) days following the military service before reporting back to work.[2] The employer is generally required to rehire the employee within two weeks of application for reemployment "absent unusual circumstances."[3]

Regulations make it clear that this period must be treated as service with the employer for purposes of eligibility, vesting, and benefit accrual.[4]

With respect to qualified retirement plans, reemployed veterans are given an opportunity to make up elective deferrals that they would have made had it not been for the separation from service for military service. The compensation considered in making up salary deferrals will be the amount of compensation the reemployed veteran would have made from the employer had he not separated from service for military service. Where it would be difficult to establish the compensation the reemployed veteran would have been paid had he not incurred a separation from service, the plan must use the reemployed veteran's average compensation from the 12-month period preceding the break in service for military service. Any makeup of employee salary deferrals and matching contributions will not result in the plan's violating the limits on contributions or minimum participation rules.[5] The returning employee is not required to pay interest (lost opportunity costs) on made-up contributions.[6]

If the missed elective deferrals cannot be made up by the employee, the employee will not receive the employer match or the accrued benefits attributable to his or her contribution, because the employer is required to make contributions that are contingent on or attributable to the employee's contributions or elective deferrals only to the extent that the employee makes up payments to the plan.[7]

Employer contributions that are not contingent on employee contributions (or elective deferrals) must be made no later than 90 days after the date of reemployment, or when plan

---

1. IRC Sec. 414(u).
2. Labor Reg. §1002.115.
3. Prop. Labor Reg. §1002.181.
4. Labor Reg. §1002.259.
5. IRC Sec. 414(u)(2).
6. Labor Reg. §1002.263.
7. Labor Reg. §1002.262(b).

contributions are normally due for the year in which the uniformed service was performed, whichever is later.[1]

Additionally, reemployed veterans will not be treated as having incurred any breaks in service for the period of time spent on active military duty. That period of time is to be considered service with the employer even though the veteran was actually in active military status. This rule applies to the plan's rules regarding nonforfeitability of accrued benefits and for determining accruals under the plan.[2]

Finally, the plan is permitted to suspend any requirement of loan repayments by participants during the period the participants are in active military service.[3] If the returning employee withdrew part or all of his account balance prior to the military service, the employee must have buy-back rights, and must be allowed a certain amount of time to repay the amount withdrawn. In the case of a defined benefit plan, the employee must have the right to buy back the interest that would have otherwise accrued.[4]

Regarding multiemployer plans, the regulations specify that a returning servicemember does not have to be reemployed by the same employer for whom the employee worked prior to the period of service in order to be reinstated under the plan with all of his or her USERRA rights. An employer of a returning servicemember who is entitled to benefits under a plan is required to notify the plan administrator of the reemployment within thirty days.[5]

USERRA covers ERISA-qualified group health plans, including multiemployer plans.[6] If the employee has coverage under such a plan, the plan must permit employees to elect to continue coverage for themselves and their dependents for a period of time that is the lesser of the twenty-four-month period beginning on the date on which their leave of absence for military service begins, or the date on which their absence for military service begins and ending on the date when they fail to return from service or apply for reemployment.[7]

Regarding veterans' reemployment rights under a health plan, the regulations describe two situations in which health coverage may be canceled upon departure for uniformed service:

1.   The departing employee fails to give advance notice of service and fails to elect continuation coverage;[8] and

2.   An employee leaves for a period of service exceeding thirty days and gives advance notice of service but fails to elect continuation coverage.[9]

---

1. Labor Reg. §1002.262(a).
2. IRC Sec. 414(u)(8).
3. IRC Sec. 414(u)(4).
4. Labor Reg. §1002.264.
5. Labor Reg. §1002.266.
6. Labor Reg. §1002.163.
7. Labor Reg. §1002.164(a)(1) and (2).
8. Labor Reg. §1002.167(a).
9. Labor Reg. §1002.167(b).

If the employee is in active military service for less than thirty-one days, he or she cannot be required to pay more than the regular employee share, if any, for the health coverage.[1] Employees in military service thirty-one or more days may be required to pay no more than 102 percent of the full premium under the plan, which represents the employer's share, plus the employee's share, plus 2 percent for administrative costs.[2] Plans may also adopt reasonable rules allowing cancellation of continuation coverage if timely payment is not made.[3]

However, if a departing employee who fails to give advance notice and fails to elect continuation coverage was excused from giving advance notice of service under USERRA's provisions because of military necessity, impossibility, or unreasonableness, then coverage must be retroactively reinstated upon the employee's election to continue coverage and upon his or her payment of all amounts due (no administrative reinstatement costs can be charged).[4]

If the employee who has provided advance notice of leave exceeding thirty days but has failed to elect coverage subsequently elects to continue coverage, the scope of his reinstatement right depends upon whether the plan has developed reasonable rules regarding the period within which employees may elect continuing coverage. If reasonable rules have been established, then the plan must permit retroactive reinstatement of uninterrupted coverage upon the employee's election and payment of all unpaid amounts due within periods established under the plan rules. If the plan has not established reasonable rules regarding the election period, it must permit retroactive reinstatement of uninterrupted coverage upon the employee's election and payment of all unpaid amounts at any time during the maximum coverage period under USERRA.[5]

The Veterans' Housing Opportunity and Benefits Improvement Act of 2006 (VHOBIA) extended employer health plan continuation and reinstatement rights to reservists entitled to the federal government's health insurance program for all branches of the military. The program, known as TRICARE, provides health care coverage to civilian dependents of military servicemembers. VHOBIA extends TRICARE participation rights to active-duty reservists and their dependents upon being called to active duty. It also extends USERRA continuation coverage rights to reservists upon termination of active-duty status. The USERRA rights apply even if reservists' active-duty orders are cancelled and they do not actually leave employment to perform active military service.

Reservists who receive active-duty orders with delayed effective dates are treated as if called to active duty for more than thirty days, starting on the later of the date the order was issued or ninety days before the date for active service. When these reservists are considered on "active duty," they and their family members are eligible for military health and dental benefits under TRICARE.

---

1. Labor Reg. §1002.166(a).
2. Labor Reg. §1002.166(b).
3. Labor Reg. §1002.167(c).
4. Labor Reg. §1002.167(a).
5. Labor Reg. §1002.167(b)(1) and (2).

Practitioner's Pointer: An employer who fails to establish reasonable rules regarding the election period may find itself bound to longer maximum coverage periods than those otherwise mandated under USERRA.

The regulations indicate that where health plans are also covered by COBRA, it may be reasonable to adopt COBRA-compliant rules regarding election of and payment for continuing coverage, so long as those rules do not conflict with USERRA or the new cancellation rules. This has the effect of allowing plan sponsors to streamline their health plan administrative provisions by implementing applicable COBRA provisions already in place (except where they would violate USERRA).[1]

The definition of "employer" under the final regulations excludes entities to which employers or plan sponsors have delegated purely ministerial functions, such as third-party administrators. The preamble to the final regulations indicates that the definition of employer was intended to apply to insurance companies administering employers' health plans, "so that such entities cannot refuse to modify their policies in order for employers to comply with requirements under" USERRA, adding that employers with insured health plans are "obliged to negotiate coverage that is compliant with USERRA"[2]

On June 17, 2008, President Bush signed the Heroes Earnings Assistance and Relief Tax Act of 2008 into law.[3] The Heroes Act makes specific modifications to USERRA in an effort to assist veterans who die or become totally disabled while on active military duty and the beneficiaries of veterans who die on active military duty.

After December 31, 2006, the Heroes Act requires 401(k) and other qualified retirement plans to provide the survivors of a plan participant who dies while performing qualified military service with any additional benefits (such as accelerated vesting and ancillary life insurance benefits) that would have been provided if the participant had resumed employment and then died.[4]

Another provision of the Heroes Act permits (but does not require) 401(k) and other qualified retirement plans to be amended to treat individuals who die or become disabled while performing qualified military service as if they had resumed employment in accordance with their USERRA reemployment rights on the day before death or disability, and then terminated employment on the date of death or disability. This provision allows a plan to provide such "deemed rehired employees" (or their survivors) partial or full retroactive benefit accruals that the plan must provide to reemployed servicemembers under USERRA. These additional benefit accruals must be credited on a reasonably equivalent basis to all individuals who die or become disabled during their military service. Under this rule, when determining the amount of matching contributions, individuals are treated as having made deferrals based on their average deferrals for the 12 months immediately before qualified military service.[5] This provision applies to deaths or disabilities occurring after December 31, 2006.

---

1. Labor Reg. §1002.167(c).
2. Labor Reg. §1002.5(d)(1).
3. Pub. L. No. 110-245, 122 Stat. 1624 (hereinafter Heroes Act).
4. IRC Sec. 401(a)(37), *as amended by Heroes Act* §104(a).
5. IRC Sec. 414(u)(9), *as added by Heroes Act* §104(b).

36. How are the break-in-service rules affected by parental leaves?

For participation and vesting purposes, a participant will be deemed to have completed all hours of service for which the participant was absent (not to exceed 501 hours) if the leave of service was for the purpose of parental leave taken for the following purposes:

1. The participant's pregnancy;

2. The birth of the participant's child;

3. The placement of a child as a result of adoption by the participant; or

4. The care of a child during that period immediately following the birth or placement of the child through adoption.[1]

Hours of service are to be based upon the actual hours the participant would have completed, or eight hours for each day the participant was absent if the actual number of hours cannot be reasonably calculated.[2]

Hours credited under these circumstances are not required to be credited for purposes of benefit accruals under the plan; they are required to be credited only for participation and vesting.[3]

37. What are the general rules regarding plan forfeitures?

Any accrued benefit that has vested in the participant may not be forfeitable.[4] In general, an accrued benefit is considered to be nonforfeitable at any given time if it is an unconditional right. Where there is a conditional right to a benefit, such as a right to a benefit that is conditioned upon the occurrence of a subsequent event, performance, or forbearance, the plan may be amended to provide for the reduction or elimination of that benefit.[5]

Rights that are conditioned upon the sufficiency of plan assets in the event of plan termination or partial termination are considered to be forfeitable.[6]

If a participant retires and begins the receipt of retirement benefits under the plan, it is not considered a forfeiture of monthly benefits where such payments attributable to employer contributions are suspended upon the reemployment of the participant.[7] Benefit payments that are attributable to employee contributions may not be suspended once they have commenced.

Retirement plans generally may not be amended to retroactively reduce benefits that have already accrued to a participant.[8] However, a pension plan is permitted to reduce benefits accrued in the current plan year if an amendment specifying the reduction is adopted within 2½ months

---

1. ERISA Sec. 203(b)(3)(E); IRC Sec. 411(a)(6)(E).
2. ERISA Sec. 203(b)(3)(E)(ii); IRC Sec. 411(a)(6)(E)(ii).
3. ERISA Sec. 203(b)(3)(E)(i), flush language; IRC Sec. 411(a)(6)(E)(i), flush language.
4. ERISA Sec. 203(a); IRC Sec. 411(a).
5. See Treas. Reg. §1.411(a)-4.
6. Treas. Reg. §1.411(a)-4.
7. ERISA Sec. 203(a)(3)(B); IRC Sec. 411(a)(3)(B).
8. ERISA Sec. 204(g)(1); IRC Sec. 411(d)(6).

after the close of the affected plan year. The amendment may not retroactively reduce benefits accrued in prior plan years. Further, such amendment must be approved by the Department of Labor following a determination that such amendment is necessary due to a substantial business hardship incurred by the plan sponsor.[1]

Also, participants in contributory pension plans who withdraw mandatory employee contributions may have their vested portion of employer contributions forfeited if, at the time of the withdrawal of mandatory employee contributions, they were less than 50 percent vested in such employer contributions.[2] However, a pension plan that contains such a forfeiture provision must permit the participant an opportunity to "buy back" the forfeited employer contributions upon the repayment by the participant of the full amount of the withdrawal and, in the case of a defined benefit plan, interest.[3]

Once a forfeiture has occurred (where there is a terminated non-vested participant), such amounts in a pension plan must be applied to reduce future employer contributions. In a profit sharing or 401(k) plan, the plan document may provide that such forfeitures may be used to reduce future employer contributions or reallocated to the accounts of remaining participants.

Prenuptial Waiver of Benefits Not Valid under ERISA

The U.S. Magistrate Judge of the U.S. District Court for the Eastern District of Wisconsin ruled in a dispute over the benefits between a widow, Renee J. Propst, and her husband's estate that a prenuptial agreement did not satisfy the ERISA requirements for a valid spousal waiver of benefits.[4] The Magistrate held that the case turned on the fact that under ERISA only "spouses" can waive rights to their partners' retirement assets. Because the agreement was necessarily signed before the wedding, the benefit waiver it contained was not valid under ERISA.

After a marriage lasting only several months, the Propsts separated. Alan Propst initiated divorce proceedings in February 2006 but died in an August 2006 motorcycle accident before the divorce was finalized.

38. May a plan forfeit a participant's benefits in the event of the participant's death prior to retirement?

A plan generally may forfeit a participant's vested benefits that are attributable to employer contributions in the event of the participant's death prior to retirement.[5] However, in the event a vested participant dies before retirement and the participant has a surviving spouse, the plan must provide for the issuance of a qualified preretirement survivor annuity to the surviving spouse.[6]

---

1. ERISA Sec. 302(c)(8); IRC Sec. 412(c)(8).
2. ERISA Sec. 203(a)(3)(D); IRC Sec. 411(a)(3)(D).
3. ERISA Sec. 203(a)(3)(D)(ii); IRC Sec. 411(a)(3)(D)(ii).
4. *John Deere Deferred Sav. Plan for Wage Employees v. Estate of Propst*, No. 06-C-1235 (E.D. Wis. Dec. 28, 2007).
5. ERISA Sec. 203(a)(3)(A); IRC Sec. 411(a)(3)(A).
6. ERISA Sec. 205(a)(2); IRC Sec. 401(a)(11); Treas. Reg. §1.401(a)-11.

39. Are noncompetition and "bad boy" clauses that result in the forfeiture of benefits enforceable?

A noncompetition agreement that authorizes the plan to deny or defer benefits provided by the plan sponsor in the event that a participant terminated employment with the plan sponsor and began employment with one of the plan sponsor's competitors may, generally, be enforced. However, such a forfeiture may never be applied to employee contributions.[1]

"Bad boy" clauses traditionally are plan provisions that call for the forfeiture of plan benefits in the event, during the period of employment with the plan sponsor, of any act of dishonesty, fraud, or theft or a felony conviction by a participant.

ERISA Section 206(d)(4) provides that the anti-alienation provisions of ERISA will not apply to any offset of a participant's benefits provided under an employee pension plan against an amount that the participant is ordered or required to pay to the plan if the order or requirement to pay arises under a judgment of conviction for a crime involving such plan; under a civil judgment entered by a court in an action brought in connection with a violation of the fiduciary provisions of ERISA; or pursuant to a settlement agreement between the DOL and the participant or the PBGC and the participant in connection with a violation (or alleged violation) of the fiduciary provisions of ERISA by a fiduciary or any other person. Further, the judgment, decree, order, or settlement agreement must expressly provide for the offset.

Courts have denied forfeiture of benefits under "bad boy" clauses that are related to acts of fraud committed by the participant.[2] The courts reasoned that a fraud exception to the nonforfeitability provisions of ERISA Section 203(a) and IRC Section 411(a) would be improper. However, courts have upheld forfeiture provisions as a result of fraudulent acts as they applied to non-vested benefit accruals and benefits in excess of minimum vesting standards under the plan.[3]

A forfeiture of benefits under a "bad boy" clause in a plan provision that applied in the event of a participant's conviction of a criminal act in connection with his employment with the plan sponsor (outside any actions involving the plan) was enforceable in that it did not violate the participant's rights to equal protection under the U.S. Constitution.[4]

Garnishment of Benefits to Pay Criminal Fines

The IRS has determined that where a federal court is seeking to collect a fine in an individual's criminal case, the employer would not violate the IRC Section 401(a)(13) (ERISA Section 206(d)(4)) anti-alienation rule by garnishing his 401(k) plan account balance.[5]

Under a federal criminal procedure rule[6], a fine imposed as part of either (1) a criminal sentence, or (2) an order of restitution, is a lien in favor of the federal government on all property

---

1. *Brower v. Comark Merch., Inc.*, 949 F. Supp. 1183 (D.N.J. 1996).
2. *Crausman v. Curtiss-Wright Corp.*, 676 F. Supp. 1302 (D.N.J. 1988); *Vink v. SVH N. Am. Holding Corp.*, 549 F. Supp. 268 (S.D.N.Y. 1982).
3. *Clark v. Lauren Young Tire Ctr. Profit Sharing Trust*, 816 F.2d 480 (9th Cir. 1987); *Montgomery v. Lowe*, 507 F. Supp. 618 (S.D. Tex. 1981); *Noell v. American Design, Inc. Profit Sharing Plan*, 764 F.2d 827 (11th Cir. 1985).
4. *Parente v. Town of West Warwick*, 685 F. Supp. 873 (D.R.I. 1988), *aff'd*, 868 F.2d 522 (1st Cir. 1989).
5. Priv. Ltr. Rul. 200342007.
6. 18 U.S.C. §3613(c).

of the person fined, as if the liability of the person fined were a tax liability. Thus, IRS ruled, the federal government is authorized to collect a fine from an individual's interest in a qualified retirement plan. Here, the only other issue to be resolved was whether the collection would violate the IRC Section 401(a)(13) anti-alienation rule.

Three federal court cases have held that the federal government can collect criminal fines from a pension plan without disqualifying the plan. In *United States v. Tyson*,[1] a participant in a retirement plan was convicted in federal court and ordered to pay restitution. The federal government filed an application for a writ of continuing garnishment under the Fair Debt Collection Practices Act (FDCPA), and the court ruled that the government was entitled to garnish the participant's interest in the plan.

The collection of restitution fell within the exception provided by Proposed Treasury Regulation Section 1.401(a)-13(b)(2)(ii), under which the federal government can collect on a judgment resulting from an unpaid tax assessment.

Similarly, in *United States v. Clark*,[2] a participant was convicted of a crime and fined $240,000. Relying on *Tyson* above, the court allowed the garnishment to proceed, holding that a plan is subject to garnishment to satisfy a criminal fine under the FDCPA.

IRS concluded that a judgment rendered by a federal court imposing a fine payable to the federal government is to be treated as a tax liability. Thus, it is reasonable to interpret Proposed Treasury Regulation Section 1.401(a)-13(b)(2)(ii) as authorizing the enforcement of the judgment against a plan participant's interest in a qualified plan irrespective of the anti-alienation rule, IRS reasoned.

The Second Circuit Court of Appeals noted in *United States v. Irving*[3] that Congress created an exception from ERISA's anti-alienation provision when it enacted the Mandatory Victims Restitution Act of 1996 (MVRA). In this case, the defendant was found guilty of child pornography charges unrelated to his employment or to the underlying qualified plan. He was sentenced to time in prison and a fine of $200,000. The Second Circuit permitted the seizure of his vested plan assets because under MVRA, the federal government may enforce a judgment imposing a fine against all property, exempting only property that it could not reach for unpaid federal income taxes. Since ERISA-qualified assets held in trust can be reached for the payment of such fines and unpaid taxes, they can be garnished under MVRA for the payment of criminal fines.

The Ninth Circuit Court of Appeals has ruled that garnishment of vested benefits pursuant to MVRA is an exception to the anti-alienation restrictions of ERISA.[4] In issuing this finding, the Ninth Circuit relied on the provisions of MVRA directing that restitution orders are to be enforced by the government "using all of the remedies that are available for the collection of criminal fines."[5] Further, the Court noted that MVRA elevates liabilities created under the Act to

---

1. 265 F. Supp. 2d 788 (E.D. Mich. 2003).
2. 2003 WL 22889389 (E.D. Mich. 2003).
3. 2005 U.S. App. LEXIS 28493 (2d Cir. 2005).
4. *United States v. Novak*, 37 EBC 1172 (9th Cir. 2006).
5. 18 U.S.C. §3664(m)(1)(A)(i).

be the equivalent of a tax liability assessed under the Internal Revenue Code.[1] As such, criminal restitution orders are an exception to the anti-alienation restrictions of ERISA, as ERISA assets are not among the enumerated items being exempt from tax levy actions.[2]

The Sixth Circuit has ruled that Michigan's State Correctional Facilities Reimbursement Act (SCFRA) is void as a violation of ERISA's anti-alienation rule as an involuntary transfer of benefits. SCFRA required prison wardens to notify pension plans that future benefits checks should be mailed to the prisoner at the prison address. Once received at the prison, the payments were to be automatically deposited into the prisoner's institutional account. The orders also required the prison warden to distribute to the state 90 percent of each deposit to reimburse the costs of caring for the prisoner. The court noted that once a plan has sent benefit payments to a participant and relinquished control of those payments, ERISA does not prevent creditors from attaching the funds. However, under ERISA the distributions must be at the voluntary request of the prisoners; as such, the mandate of SCFRA that such payments be remitted to the State absent prisoner consent is void as violative of ERISA.[3]

Garnishment under Federal Mandatory Victims Restitution Act of 1996

The Ninth Circuit Court of Appeals has created an exception to the anti-assignment provisions of ERISA Section 206(d) for garnishment orders presented under MVRA. In following the 1990 Supreme Court holding in *Guidry v. Sheet Metal Workers National Pension Fund*,[4] which allows a garnishment or constructive levy on ERISA assets only if some exception to the general statutory ban is available, the Ninth Circuit determined that the MVRA requirement that a court order restitution for victims in cases involving property loss[5] is just such an exception. In *United States v. Novak*,[6] the defendant and his wife were convicted of stealing high-value telephone boards from his wife's employer, Nestle, and then transporting them in interstate commerce in violation of federal criminal law, as they sold them. In upholding the exception to the ERISA anti-alienation restriction, the court relied on a provision of MVRA that holds that restitution orders are to be enforced by the government using "all of the remedies that are available for the collection of criminal fines."[7]

40. May a participant's assets in an ERISA-covered plan be accessed by her creditors when the participant files bankruptcy?

No, a participant's plan assets generally may not be accessed by her creditors in bankruptcy proceedings filed by the participant.[8] This is one of two exceptions (referred to as "applicable nonbankruptcy law") to the United States Bankruptcy Code provision that generally holds that an

---

1. 18 U.S.C. §3613.
2. 18 U.S.C. §3613(a).
3. *DaimlerChrysler Corp. v. Cox*, 2006 U.S. App. LEXIS 12599 (6th Cir. 2006).
4. 493 U.S. 365 (1990).
5. 18 U.S.C. §3663A.
6. *39 EBC 2825 (9th Cir. Feb. 22, 2007)*.
7. 18 U.S.C. §3664(m)(1)(A)(i).
8. See 11 U.S.C. §541(c)(2).

individual's bankruptcy estate includes all property in which the debtor has a legal or equitable interest at the time of the bankruptcy proceedings.[1]

The U.S. Supreme Court settled the issue of whether the anti-alienation provisions of ERISA Section 206(d)(1) qualified as "applicable nonbankruptcy law" that would exclude the participant's plan assets from his individual bankruptcy estate.[2] ERISA Section 206(d)(1) states that "each pension plan shall provide that benefits provided under the plan may not be assigned or alienated." The Supreme Court ruled this plain language to be the "applicable nonbankruptcy law," which constitutes a restriction on the transfer of assets in bankruptcy proceedings. However, the Ninth Circuit Court of Appeals ruled under then-applicable law (see below for 2005 legislation) that ERISA's exclusion of qualified plan benefits from a debtor's bankruptcy estate did not extend to an individual who was the owner and sole participant in the plan, because such a plan was not covered by ERISA.[3]

A federal court in the Northern District of Indiana has ruled that participant assets held in the banking accounts of a third-party administrator that had filed bankruptcy were beyond the reach of the third-party administrator's non-ERISA creditors.[4]

Generally speaking, an ERISA-qualified plan's anti-alienation provision is not enforceable against the IRS, in part because ERISA does not supersede other federal law, including federal tax law.[5] The IRS has announced its acquiescence in the 2003 decision of *United States v. Snyder*, a Ninth Circuit case holding that the IRS's tax lien against a debtor's property did not give rise to a secured bankruptcy claim against the debtor's interest in an ERISA-qualified plan.[6]

The Ninth Circuit in *Snyder* rejected the IRS's secured claim in bankruptcy. According to the Ninth Circuit, the rights of secured creditors under Bankruptcy Code Section 506(a) are established only in property that is included in the bankruptcy estate. Thus, any bankruptcy exclusion under Bankruptcy Code Section 541(c)(2) is determined before the rights of secured creditors. According to the court, the denial of secured status in bankruptcy for the IRS claim prevents the IRS from using the debtor's bankruptcy to accelerate the payment of liens that would not have been paid until the plan interest was in pay status.

This is consistent with an announcement the IRS made in Chief Counsel Notice 2004-033, regarding claims against debtors in bankruptcy. The IRS stated that it will no longer argue that it may include in its secured claim against a debtor in bankruptcy the value of the debtor's interest in a pension plan that is otherwise excluded from the debtor's bankruptcy estate. However, the Chief Counsel Notice adds that the IRS will enforce its lien and levy against a debtor's plan interest outside the bankruptcy process (when the benefit would otherwise become distributable under the applicable provisions of the underlying plan). This is consistent with the advice of the Ninth Circuit in the *Snyder* opinion.

---

1. 11 U.S.C. §541(a).
2. *Patterson v. Shumate*, 504 U.S. 753 (1992).
3. *In re Lowenschuss*, 171 F.3d 673 (9th Cir. 1999).
4. *In re GS Consulting, Inc.*, 2009 WL 301917 (N.D. Ind. 2009).
5. ERISA Sec. 514(d).
6. See *United States v. Snyder*, 343 F.3d 1171 (9th Cir. 2003), acq. 2004-41 I.R.B. 4.

Participants in retirement plans that are not covered by the anti-alienation provisions of ERISA (e.g., IRAs, plans covered by the Railroad Retirement Act, church plans, etc.) may have their plan assets protected from alienation in bankruptcy proceedings by the second major exception to the general holding of the Bankruptcy Code, which is referred to as the "federal pension exemption." Under this exemption, an individual debtor may exempt from his bankruptcy estate his right to receive a payment under a stock bonus, pension, profit sharing, annuity, or similar plan or contract on account of illness, disability, death, age, or length of service, to the extent reasonably necessary for the support of the debtor and any dependent of the debtor.[1] In order for this exemption to apply, the plan must be qualified under IRC Section 401(a), 403(a), 403(b), or 408.[2]

The Ninth Circuit has ruled that liability for breach of fiduciary duty under ERISA is dischargeable in bankruptcy if it does not involve the misappropriation of funds or failure to provide a proper accounting of funds.[3]

Bankruptcies Filed on or after October 17, 2005

The Bankruptcy Abuse Prevention and Consumer Protection Act of 2005 changed the treatment of retirement plan assets for all debtors who file bankruptcy petitions on or after its effective date of October 17, 2005. The Act specifically *exempts* from the bankruptcy estate "retirement assets to the extent that those funds are in a fund or account that is exempt from taxation" under any qualified pension, profit sharing, and stock bonus plans, as well as any employee annuities, including tax sheltered annuities; traditional IRAs, including SEPs and SIMPLE IRAs; Roth IRAs; governmental, church, and multi-employer plans; and certain deferred compensation plans of state and local governments and tax-exempt organizations. The exemption for traditional and Roth IRAs is subject to an aggregate limit (i.e., per debtor) of $1 million; however, this limit does not apply to rollover amounts, nor to amounts held in simplified employee pensions or SIMPLE IRAs.

41. Are retirees' pension and health benefits protected when their former employer files bankruptcy?

Under the federal bankruptcy code, companies that have filed bankruptcy under Chapter 11 of the Bankruptcy Code are required to continue paying retiree benefits until a modification of those benefits is agreed to by the parties or is ordered by the court.[4] These benefits include medical, surgical, or hospital care benefits, or those benefits payable in the event of sickness, disability, or death under any plan established or maintained by the company prior to the bankruptcy filing.

These rules are not applicable to retirees with gross income in excess of $250,000 per year, unless comparable coverage cannot be obtained.

---

1. 11 U.S.C. §522(d)(10).
2. 11 U.S.C. §522(d)(10)(E).
3. *Corse v. Hemmeter*, 2001 U.S. App. LEXIS 4559 (9th Cir. 2001).
4. 11 U.S.C. §1114.

The court will allow these retiree benefits the status of an allowed administrative expense under the Bankruptcy Code. These benefits may be modified in the bankruptcy proceedings if it is necessary to permit the reorganization of the employer, it is clearly favored by a balance of the equities, and it is fair and equitable to all affected parties.

Retirees are protected where there are attempts to reverse claims for which they had received payments.

One court has held that early retirement benefits payable to an employee who was terminated following his employer's bankruptcy filing were not entitled to priority as allowed administrative expenses of the bankruptcy, since those benefits had accrued over the course of employment, and were not new benefits earned upon termination of employment.[1]

The Sixth Circuit Court of Appeals has ruled that a debtor-employer who might have qualified as an ERISA fiduciary was *not* a fiduciary within the meaning of the bankruptcy discharge rules.[2] Therefore, the $99,000 debt for unpaid employer contributions that the employer owed to ERISA plans was dischargeable in bankruptcy. The trial court in the matter did hold that the unpaid wage withholdings of participants were not dischargeable, as the plan sponsor was functioning in the role of a plan fiduciary and trustee regarding the management and handling of the withholdings as plan assets. Under 11 U.S.C. §523(a)(4), an individual debtor is not discharged from any debt for fraud or defalcation while acting in a fiduciary capacity. This holding was not challenged on appeal.

This holding concurs with the Eighth Circuit holding on the same issue.[3] It disagrees with the Ninth Circuit's position on the same matter.[4]

The Sixth Circuit concluded that the defendant had only a contractual obligation to pay the employer contributions. That was not enough to preclude the discharge of the obligation.[5]

Claims Procedures

42. What procedures must a plan have in place regarding participant claims?

Every employee benefit plan must provide adequate notice, in writing, to any participant or beneficiary whose claim for benefits under a plan has been denied. That notice must also set forth the specific reasons for the denial in a "manner calculated to be understood by the participant."[6]

Every employee benefit plan must also establish and maintain reasonable claims procedures. These procedures must be set forth in the plan's summary plan description (SPD), and they may

---

1. *In re Bethlehem Steel Corp.* 2007 WL 625202 (2d Cir. 2007).
2. *Board of Trs. of Ohio Carpenters Pension Fund v. Bucci*, 2007 WL 1891736 (6th Cir. 2007).
3. *Hunter v. Philpott*, 373 F.3d 873 (8th Cir. 2004).
4. *In re Hemmeter*, 242 F.3d 1186 (9th Cir. 2001).
5. *Board of Trs. of Ohio Carpenters Pension Fund v. Bucci*, 2007 WL 1891736 (6th Cir. 2007).
6. ERISA Sec. 503(1).

not contain any provisions or be administered in such a way as to unduly inhibit or hamper the processing of a participant claim.[1]

A claim is a request for a plan benefit that has been submitted by a participant or beneficiary. Where a plan has failed to establish a reasonable procedure for filing claims, a claim shall be deemed filed when a written or oral request is made by the claimant that is reasonably calculated to bring such claim to the attention of the persons or business unit that customarily handles employee benefits matters of the plan sponsor.[2] Under the "federal mailbox rule" as applied in benefits dispute cases, a participant can document the timing of his application for benefits through the mail by the date on the postmark or certified mail return receipt.[3]

If a participant's or beneficiary's claim for benefits is partially or wholly denied, notice of the decision must be furnished to the claimant within a reasonable period of time, not to exceed 90 days, after receipt of the claim by the plan.[4]

If an ERISA plan does not have claims procedures in place, or it fails to follow the new rules, participants and beneficiaries may have direct access to courts in seeking assistance because they will be "deemed" to have exhausted the plan's internal appeals procedures (short cutting the "exhaust all plan remedies" requirement for other claims).[5] Furthermore, the plan claims procedures must allow a claimant's authorized representative to pursue a claim or appeal.[6]

The written notice to be provided in the event of a denial of a claim for benefits must contain the following information:

1. The specific time limits for the plan to resolve a claim;

2. Specific reference to pertinent plan provisions on which the denial is based;

3. A description of any additional material or information necessary for the claimant to perfect the claim and an explanation of why such material or information is necessary; and

4. Appropriate information as to the steps to be taken if the participant or beneficiary wishes to submit his or her claim for review.[7]

If the notice is not provided in a reasonable period of time, the claim is deemed to have been denied and the participant may proceed to the claims review stage.[8] Numerous federal court cases have required claimants to "exhaust their remedies" before they may file an action in federal court under a claim of denial of benefits. This means that participants are required to follow through on a plan's claims procedures, including the review procedures. The U.S.

---

1. Labor Reg. §2560.503-1(b).
2. Labor Reg. §2560.503-1(d).
3. See *Schikore v. Bankamerica Supp. Ret. Plan*, 2001 U.S. App. LEXIS 22384 (9th Cir. 2001).
4. Labor Reg. §2560.503-1(e).
5. Labor Reg. §2560.503-1(l).
6. Labor Reg. §2560.503-1(b)(4).
7. Labor Reg. §2560.503-1(f).
8. Labor Reg. §2560.503-1(e)(2).

District Court for the Northern District of Georgia has awarded a participant $32,400 in statutory penalties because of a plan administrator's negligent failure to provide a SPD that adequately described the underlying plan's appeals process, thereby interfering with the participant's ability to properly exhaust her appeals rights.[1]

43. What regulations expedite and strengthen participant health benefit claims procedures?

Final regulations speed up the time health plans would have to respond to urgent health care claims. The final regulations provide that benefit claims involving urgent care must be resolved within seventy-two hours of submission, and participants must be notified of incomplete benefit claims within twenty-four hours of submission.[2]

Further, the regulations contain provisions that require pre-service claims to be decided within a maximum of fifteen days after the receipt of the claim by the plan. This period can be extended by an additional fifteen days if the plan administrator determines it is necessary due to matters beyond the control of the plan and the claimant is notified prior to the close of the initial fifteen days.[3] Adverse benefit determinations for post-service claims must be provided within thirty days of receipt of the claim by the plan. As with pre-service claims, the plan administrator may extend the deadline by an additional fifteen days if it is necessary due to matters beyond the control of the plan and the claimant is notified prior to the close of the initial thirty-day period.[4]

In notifying a participant of an adverse benefit determination, the plan is required to provide a written or electronic notification. Such notification must disclose to the participant the specific reason for the adverse determination as well as the specific provisions of the plan upon which such determination was made. Participants must also be advised of any material or information necessary to perfect the claim, along with an explanation as to why the material or information is necessary. The notice of adverse determination must disclose the plan's review procedures and the time limits for undertaking such procedures. Finally, the notice of adverse determination must notify the participant of his right to file a civil action under ERISA Section 502(a), should the participant believe there is a cause of action due to the adverse benefit determination.[5]

The Department of Labor has provided detailed guidance on the new claims procedure regulations in the form of frequently asked questions and answers.[6]

44. What are a participant's rights with respect to appealing a denial of a claim for benefits?

Every employee benefit plan must provide a reasonable opportunity to a participant who has had a claim for benefits denied to have a "full and fair review" of the denial.[7]

---

1. *Palmeri v. Coca-Cola Co.*, No. 1:01-CV-3498-TWT (N.D. Ga. Aug. 28, 2006).
2. Labor Reg. §§2560.503-1(o), 2560.503-1(f).
3. Labor Reg. §2560.503-1(f)(iii)(A).
4. Labor Reg. §2560.503-1(f)(iii)(B).
5. Labor Reg. §2560.503-1(g).
6. That information is available on the Internet at http://askpwba.dol.gov/faq-claims-proc-reg.html.
7. ERISA Sec. 503(2).

The review procedure must allow the participant a reasonable opportunity to appeal a denied claim to an appropriate named fiduciary (or a person designated by such fiduciary) under which a full and fair review of the claim and its denial may be obtained. That fiduciary cannot be the individual who made the initial benefit determination, nor may it be one of his or her subordinates.[1]

Under the review procedure, participants must

1. Request a review upon written application to the plan;

2. Be provided reasonable access to, and copies of all documents, records, and other information relevant to their claims without charge;

3. Submit written comments, documents, records, and other information relating to the benefits claim.[2]

Employee benefit plans may establish a limited period within which a participant must file a request for review of a denial. This period may not be less than sixty days from the date of the receipt of the written denial by the participant.[3] A decision on the review by an appropriate named fiduciary shall not ordinarily be made more than sixty days after the receipt of the request for a review by the plan. The sixty-day limit may be extended to no more than 120 days under special circumstances that require an extension of time for processing the claimant's appeal for review. Written notice of such an extension must be provided to the claimant.[4] If the plan provides for the review of appeals by an appointed board or committee that meets at least quarterly, the sixty-day limit will not apply. The board must review the matter at its first meeting after the request is filed (unless the request is filed within thirty days of a scheduled meeting, in which case it can be delayed until the next scheduled meeting).[5]

The decision on review must be furnished to the claimant in writing and must include specific reasons for the decision, as well as specific references to the pertinent plan provisions on which the decision is based.[6]

If an appeal is denied, the notice must include the following information provided in a manner calculated to be understood by the claimant:

1. The specific reason(s) for the adverse determination;

2. Reference to the specific plan provisions on which the determination was based;

3. A statement of the claimant's right to receive, at no cost, information and copies of documents relevant to the claim, even if such information was not relied upon in making the determination;

---

1. Labor Reg. §2560.503-1(h)(3)(ii).
2. Labor Reg. §2560.503-1(g).
3. Labor Reg. §2560.503-1(g)(3).
4. Labor Reg. §2560.503-1(h).
5. Labor Reg. §2560.503-1(h)(1)(ii).
6. Labor Reg. §2560.503-1(h)(3).

4.   A description of any voluntary appeals procedures of the plan and how to receive information about those procedures; and

5.   A statement of the claimant's right to sue under ERISA.[1]

A failure to have a formal, written claims procedure is a procedural violation of ERISA.[2] Where a plan provides for compulsory arbitration to settle an employee benefits dispute under its claims procedure, any requirement that the claimant bear an equal share of the expenses of arbitration (with the plan bearing an equal share) is a violation of ERISA.[3]

The Ninth Circuit has ruled for a new standard of review to be applied in reviewing a plan administrator's decision to deny ERISA benefits where the record shows that there is a conflict of interest for the administrator and the case shows serious disregard for ERISA's procedural requirements in handling benefits.[4] This standard of review allows the court flexibility to consider the level and depth of the conflict of interest, as well as accompanying evidence of failing to rely on credible evidence in favor of the participant. Repeated denials of claims for benefits, failure to properly investigate claims, and incorrectly interpreting the provisions of the plan.

The Tenth Circuit Court of Appeals has ruled that the appeals regulations[5] do not require "a plan administrator to provide a claimant with access to the medical opinion reports of appeal-level reviewers prior to a final decision on appeal." Rather, the court ruled, "[T]he regulations mandate provision of relevant documents, including medical opinion reports, at two discrete stages of the administrative process. First, relevant documents generated or relied upon during the initial claims determination must be disclosed prior to or at the outset of an administrative appeal.... Second, relevant documents generated during the administrative appeal — along with the claimant's file from the initial determination — must be disclosed after a final decision on appeal."[6]

In elaborating upon its position, the Tenth Circuit opined that "[p]ermitting a claimant to receive and rebut medical opinion reports generated in the course of an administrative appeal — even when those reports contain no new factual information and deny benefits on the same basis as the initial decision — would set up an unnecessary cycle of submission, review, re-submission, and re-review. This would undoubtedly prolong the appeal process, which, under the regulations, should normally be completed within forty-five days."

Therefore, the court determined that "so long as appeal-level reports analyze evidence already known to the claimant and contain no new factual information or novel diagnoses," providing documents at the two specific times detailed herein is all that is required.[6]

---

1. Labor Reg. §2560.503-1(h), (i), and (j).
2. See *Harris v. Pullman Standard, Inc.*, 809 F.2d 1495 (11th Cir. 1987).
3. DOL Adv. Op. 82-46A.
4. *Abatie v. Alta Health & Life Ins. Co.* 458 F.3d 955 (9th Cir. 2006).
5. Labor Reg. §§2560.501-1 et seq.
6. *Metzger v. UNUM Life Ins. Co.*, 2007 U.S. App. LEXIS 3755 (10th Cir. 2007).

In a similar ruling, the Eleventh Circuit held that a plaintiff does not have a right to documents in a denial of claim review that is still pending.[1] The court advised that the same regulations the Ninth Circuit relied upon (above) indicate that a document is relevant if it was "relied upon in making the benefit determination." If the claim review was still pending, then no determination had been made. The court went on to advise that it is the position of the DOL that the document production regulations are intended to assist claimants in assessing the need to further appeal an adverse determination. Therefore, producing the documents before a decision is rendered would not serve the intent of the regulations because the claimant would not yet know whether there was an adverse determination.

The Ninth Circuit has ruled that the insurer for an ERISA plan may be sued for benefits under ERISA Section 502(a)(1)(B) to recover benefits owed under the terms of the plan or to enforce or clarify rights under the plan.[2] The ruling provides that an insurer may be sued where the insurer effectively controls the decision whether to honor or deny a claim under the plan. In doing so, the court overruled four earlier Ninth Circuit decisions suggesting otherwise.

Funding Standards

45. What plans are covered by ERISA's funding standards?

ERISA Section 302 establishes minimum funding standards that are applicable to every employee pension benefit plan subject to the coverage provisions of ERISA (see Q 7, Q 8, Q 11, and Q 13). Thus, ERISA's minimum funding standards apply to defined benefit plans, money purchase plans, and target benefit arrangements, as well as certain nonqualified deferred compensation arrangements.

46. What plans are specifically exempted from ERISA's funding standards?

The following plans are expressly exempted from ERISA's funding requirements:

1. An employee welfare benefit plan;

2. A plan that is unfunded and is maintained for the provision of benefits to a select group of management or highly compensated employees;

3. An insurance contract plan funded exclusively by individual annuity contracts;

4. A plan that has not required employer contributions after January 1, 1975;

5. Individual retirement accounts or annuities;

6. Agreements providing payments to retired or deceased partners;

7. Excess benefit plans;

8. Individual account plans (other than money purchase and target benefit plans); or

---

1. *Glazer v. Reliance Standard Life Ins. Co.*, 2008 WL 1775437 (11th Cir. 2008).
2. *Cyr v. Reliance Standard Life Ins. Co.*, 642 F.3d 1202 (9th Cir. 2011) (en banc).

9.   Any plan in which an employer, all of whose stock is owned by employees, former employees, or beneficiaries, proposes through an unfunded arrangement to compensate retired employees for benefits that were forfeited under a plan maintained by a former employer prior to the date that such plan became subject to ERISA.[1]

Additionally, plans designed to comply with workers' compensation, unemployment compensation, or disability insurance laws and plans maintained outside the United States for the primary benefit of nonresident aliens are exempted.[2]

47. What are the minimum funding standards under ERISA?

A plan shall be treated as satisfying the minimum funding standard for a plan year if:[3]

1.   In the case of a defined benefit plan that is not a multiemployer plan, the employer makes contributions to or under the plan for the plan year that, in the aggregate, are not less than the minimum required contribution determined under IRC Section 430 for the plan for the plan year;

2.   In the case of a money purchase plan that is not a multiemployer plan, the employer makes contributions to or under the plan for the plan year that are required under the terms of the plan;

3.   In the case of a multiemployer plan, the employers make contributions to or under the plan for any plan year that, in the aggregate, are sufficient to ensure that the plan does not have an accumulated funding deficiency under IRC Section 431 as of the end of the plan year.

48. What funding requirements must be determined using actuarial assumptions?

Normal retirement benefit costs, accrued liability, past service liabilities, and experience gains and losses must be determined under the funding method used to determine costs under the plan.[4] The costs, liabilities, rates of interest, and other factors under the plan must be determined on the basis of actuarial assumptions and methods.[5]

The actuarial assumptions and methods utilized must be reasonable (taking into account the experience of the plan and reasonable expectations) or, when aggregated, must result in a total contribution equivalent to that which would be determined if each such assumption and method were reasonable.[6] In addition, when taken together, such actuarial assumptions and methods must offer the actuary's best estimate of anticipated experiences under the plan.[7]

---

1. ERISA Sec. 301(a).
2. ERISA Secs. 4(b)(3), 4(b)(4).
3. IRC Sec. 412(a).
4. ERISA Sec. 302(c)(1); IRC Sec. 412(c)(1).
5. ERISA Sec. 302(c)(3); IRC Sec. 412(c)(3).
6. ERISA Sec. 302(c)(3)(A); IRC Sec. 412(c)(3)(A).
7. ERISA Sec. 302(c)(3)(B); IRC Sec. 412(c)(3)(B).

49. What is the alternative minimum funding standard?

A plan that uses a funding method requiring contributions in all years not less than those required under the entry age normal funding method may maintain an alternative minimum funding standard account for any plan year.[1]

Such minimum funding standard accounts for a plan year must be charged with the sum of:

1. The lesser of normal cost under the funding method used under the plan or normal cost determined under the unit credit method;

2. The excess, if any, of the present value of accrued benefits under the plan over the fair market value of the assets; and

3. An amount equal to the excess, if any, of credits to the alternative minimum funding standard account for all prior plan years over charges to such account for all such years.[2]

Further, alternative minimum funding standard accounts must be credited with the amount considered contributed by the employer to or under the plan for the plan year.[3]

Alternative minimum funding standard accounts must be charged or credited with interest in the same manner as interest charged or credited to the funding standard account.[4]

50. What are the employer deduction limits for minimum required funding contributions?

Generally, contributions paid by an employer to a pension plan are deductible in the taxable year when paid.[5] The amount that is deductible is based on:

1. The amount necessary to provide the remaining unfunded cost of past and current service credits over the remaining future service of each such employee; or

2. The amount equal to the normal cost of the plan, plus the amount necessary to amortize the unfunded past service costs attributable to such credits in equal annual payments over ten years.[6]

Where the plan is subject to the full funding limitation in a given year, the maximum deduction may not exceed the full funding limit.[7] However, any amount paid in a taxable year in excess of the deductible amount for such year will be deductible in the succeeding taxable years (in order of time) to the extent of the difference between the amount paid and deductible in each such succeeding year and the maximum amount deductible for such year.[8]

---

1. ERISA Sec. 305(a)(1); IRC Sec. 412(g)(1).
2. ERISA Sec. 305(b)(1); IRC Sec. 412(g)(2)(A).
3. ERISA Sec. 305(b)(2); IRC Sec. 412(g)(2)(B).
4. ERISA Sec. 305(c); IRC Sec. 412(g)(3).
5. IRC Sec. 404(a).
6. IRC Sec. 404(a)(1)(A).
7. IRC Sec. 404(a)(1)(A)(i).
8. IRC Sec. 404(a)(1)(E).

For non-multiemployer defined benefit plans with more than one-hundred participants, the maximum amount deductible will not be less than the unfunded current liability as determined under IRC Section 412(*l*). For purposes of determining whether a plan has one-hundred participants, all defined benefit plans maintained by the same employer (or any member of the employer's controlled group) are treated as one plan, but only employees of such controlled group member or employer are taken into account.[1]

If a collectively bargained plan has satisfied the full funding limitation in a plan year and, as a result of an amendment applying to such year, the current liability of the plan exceeds the full funding limitation, the plan may elect the maximum amount of the deduction for such plan year to be equal to the lesser of:

1. The full funding limitation for such year, taking into account any decrease in the present value of unamortized liability as a result of the amendment; or

2. The normal cost under the plan reduced by the amount necessary to amortize in equal annual installments over ten years (until fully amortized) the amount of the decrease in the present value of unamortized liability as a result of the amendment.[2]

If the election is taken, the amount deductible with respect to any of the plan years following the plan year for which the election was made must be reduced by the amount required to amortize the benefit reduction.

51. How are the terms "full-funding limitation," "current liability" and "interest rate" defined?

"Full-funding limitation" as in effect prior to 2004, was defined as the excess (if any) of:

1. The lesser of 170 percent (in 2003, 165 percent in 2002) of current liability (including the expected increase in current liability due to benefits accruing during the plan year) or the accrued liability (including normal cost) under the plan; over

2. The lesser of the fair market value of the plan's assets or the value of such assets determined on the basis of any reasonable actuarial method of valuation that takes into account fair market value and is permitted under Treasury regulations.[3]

"Current liability" is defined as all liabilities to participants and beneficiaries under the plan.[4] Any calculation of current liability must utilize a rate of interest within the "permissible range" established under ERISA and the Code. For plan years beginning in 2004 and 2005, the rate of interest used to determine current liability is a blended corporate rate based on investment-grade long-term corporate bonds.[5]

---

1. IRC Sec. 404(a)(1)(D).
2. IRC Sec. 404(a)(1)(B).
3. ERISA Sec. 302(c)(7); IRC Sec. 412(c)(7).
4. ERISA Sec. 302(d)(7); IRC Sec. 412(l)(7).
5. See IRC Secs. 412(l)(7)(C)(i)(IV), 412(b)(5)(B)(i)(II); Notice 2004-34, 2004-18 I.R.B. 848.

The interest rate used under the plan must be determined without taking into account the experience of the plan and reasonable expectations, but consistent with the assumptions that reflect the purchase rates that would be used by insurance companies to satisfy the liabilities under the plan.[1]

52. May a pension plan subject to the minimum funding standards be converted to an insurance contract plan?

A defined benefit pension plan is permitted to convert to an insurance contract plan wherein premium payments would replace minimum funding requirements.[2] The conversion to an insurance contract plan will result in premium payments starting after the date that employees began participating in the plan, in apparent violation of IRC Section 412(i) (see Q 30). However, an existing defined benefit plan that is converted in accordance with the requirements listed below will not be considered to fail to meet the requirements of IRC Section 412(i) merely because of participation in the plan before level annual premiums commence.

Such conversion will be effective on the first day of the plan year in which the following conditions have been satisfied:

1. The plan is funded by level premium annuity contracts under which all benefits accruing for each participant on or after the date of conversion are funded by level annual premium contracts;

2. All benefits accrued for each participant prior to the date of the conversion are guaranteed through insurance or annuity contracts, the purchase price of which equals the minimum amount required by the life insurance company for a contract that guarantees the provision of accrued benefits to participants; and

3. There are "meaningful continuing benefit accruals" under the plan after the conversion (for at least three plan years after the conversion date).

The following actions must occur prior to, or on, the effective date of the conversion:

1. Insurance contracts that guarantee benefits that have accrued prior to the conversion date are purchased (this includes contracts purchased within one month after the first day of the plan year);

2. The remaining plan assets are applied to the payment of premiums for the level annual premium contracts; and

3. All necessary amendments to satisfy the requirements of IRC Section 403(a), IRC Section 404(a)(2), and IRC Section 412(i) have been adopted.

Where a plan has failed to satisfy the necessary requirements prior to the effective date of the conversion, the prior minimum funding requirements will continue to apply to the plan.

---

1. ERISA Sec. 302(b)(5)(B)(iii); IRC Sec. 412(b)(5)(B)(iii).
2. Rev. Rul. 94-75, 1994-2 C.B. 59.

Where a plan terminates prior to providing meaningful continuing benefit accruals for at least three plan years after the conversion date, the plan will be subject to the minimum funding requirements for the period of time after the effective date of the conversion.[1]

53. What is the employer's deduction limit for converted insurance contract plans?

For plan years beginning after the effective date of the conversion from a defined benefit plan to an insurance contract plan, the employer's deductible limit in the conversion year and subsequent plan years will equal the sum of:

1.   An amount equal to the *normal cost* of the insurance contract plan established on the conversion date for post-conversion benefit accruals for guidance on what constitutes "normal cost";[2]

2.   The limit adjustments for any ten-year amortization base created because the plan was treated as if terminated on the last day of the plan year immediately preceding the conversion year; and

3.   The limit adjustments for any ten-year amortization bases remaining unamortized as of the conversion date that are maintained for purposes of IRC Section 404(a)(1)(A)(iii).[3]

Normal cost is generally based upon the annual premiums for level annual premium contracts providing for the post-conversion benefit accruals (including increases in benefits) that are reasonable in view of the funding mechanism and reasonable expectations regarding the effects of mortality, interest, and other relevant factors.

54. What are the general rules regarding the amortization of pension costs?

The minimum funding standards of ERISA Section 302 mandate that the annual contributions to a defined benefit plan must be enough to satisfy the normal costs of retirement benefits accrued during that plan year and be sufficient to satisfy the amortization of unfunded past service liability and changes in past service liability due to plan amendments, assumption changes, and experience gains and losses. For a review of the specific rules regarding the amortization of normal costs, initial past service costs, and experience gains and losses, see Q 47 and Q 48.

The interest rate charged in calculating the amount of amortization is the same rate that is applied to initial past service liabilities for a new plan, as found under ERISA Section 302(b)(5)(B)—see Q 51 for details.

---

1. For special limitations applying to insurance contract plans, see Rev. Proc. 2005-25, 2005-17 I.R.B. 962; Rev. Rul. 2004-21, 2004-1 C.B. 544; Rev. Rul. 2004-20, 2004-1 C.B. 546; Treas. Reg. §1.402(a)-1.
2. See Rev. Rul. 2004-20, 2004-10 I.R.B. 546.
3. Rev. Rul. 94-75, 1994-2 C.B. 59.

Experience Gains and Losses

A change in benefits under the Social Security Act or in other retirement benefits created under federal or state law, a change in the definition of the term "wages" under IRC Section 3121, or a change in the amount of such wages taken into account under applicable Treasury regulations that results in an increase or decrease in the accrued liability of a plan will be treated as an experience gain or loss.[1] A determination of experience gains and losses and a valuation of the plan's liability are required to be completed at least once every plan year.[2] Such adjustments to experience gains or losses will result in an adjustment to the plan sponsor's deduction for plan contributions.[3]

Extensions in Amortization Periods

The period of years required to amortize any unfunded liability of a plan may be extended for a period of time not to exceed ten years if the Secretary of Labor determines that such an extension would provide adequate protection for participants and beneficiaries, and if the Secretary determines that the failure to permit such an extension would:

1. Result in a substantial risk to the voluntary continuation of the plan;

2. Result in a substantial curtailment of pension benefit levels or employee compensation; and

3. Be adverse to the interests of plan participants in the aggregate.[4]

When an application for an extension of the amortization period is going to be filed, the plan administrator is required to provide notice of such application to the participants, beneficiaries, alternate payees, and any employee organization representing employees, which details the extent to which the plan is funded for benefits guaranteed by the Pension Benefit Guaranty Corporation (PBGC) and for benefit liabilities.[5]

The following facts generally must be furnished when an application for the extension of an amortization period is requested:

1. The unfunded liability for which the extension is being requested (i.e., past service costs, etc.);

2. The reasons that detail the necessity for the extension;

3. The period of time for which the extension is being requested (not to exceed ten years); and

4. A numerical illustration that details how the annual plan costs will be affected by the extension.[6]

---

1. ERISA Sec. 302(c)(4); IRC Sec. 412(c)(4).
2. ERISA Sec. 302(c)(9); IRC Sec. 412(c)(9).
3. IRC Sec. 404(a)(1)(A).
4. ERISA Sec. 304(a); IRC Sec. 412(e).
5. IRC Sec. 412(f)(4)(A).
6. Rev. Proc. 2008-67, 2008-48 I.R.B. 1211(for post-2007 plan years); Rev. Rul. 79-408, 1979-2 C.B. 191.

Applications must also be accompanied by the annual financial statements of the plan sponsor for the previous five years, the most recent Annual Report Form 5500, and the most recent actuarial valuation report.[1]

The application for an extension of the amortization period should be sent to the following address:

Internal Revenue Service
Attention: CP:E:EP
P.O. Box 14073, Ben Franklin Station
Washington, DC 20044

A user fee will also be required.[2]

Where an application for an extension of the amortization period has been granted, a copy of the letter granting the approval must be attached to the plan's Annual Report Form 5500, Schedule B, for the applicable plan year.

55. What are the financial accounting standards applicable to pension plans?

The Financial Accounting Standards Board (FASB) is the body that is charged with the development of generally accepted accounting principles. Generally, employee benefit plans are required to file a financial statement based upon an examination of the books and records of the plan presented fairly in conformity with generally accepted accounting principles applied on a basis consistent with that report prepared and filed for the previous plan year.[3]

Regarding those principles to be applied in review of the accounting practices of pension plans, FASB has issued three pertinent statements to offer guidance to accountants who are charged with preparing annual financial statements for pension plans.

FASB Statement No. 35, titled "Accounting and Reporting by Defined Benefit Pension Plans," stipulates that defined benefit, multiemployer, governmental, and church pension plans' financial statements be prepared on an accrual basis. The financial statement is required to detail the actuarial value of accumulated benefits (at the start or end of the plan year) based upon earnings and services provided by participants prior to the measurement date. Significant changes that affect the accumulated benefits must also be disclosed. The financial statements are required to provide information on net assets available for benefits and any changes affecting those net assets available for the payment of benefits.

FASB Statement No. 87, titled "Employer's Accounting for Pensions," stipulates the reporting required for employers who offer pension plans. Under FASB Statement No. 87, employers are required to report pension liabilities on an accrual basis. The statement also requires employers

---

1. See Rev. Proc. 2008-67, above.
2. See Rev. Proc. 95-8, 1995-1 C.B. 485, 492.
3. ERISA Sec. 103(a)(3)(A).

to provide information on the delayed recognition of retroactive plan amendments and changes in pension liabilities, offsetting assets and liabilities, and the reporting of net periodic pension costs that are in accordance with the standards detailed under FASB Statement No. 87.

FASB Statement No. 88, titled "Employer's Accounting for Settlements and Curtailments of Defined Benefit Pension Plans and Termination Benefits," stipulates that employers detail the settlement of defined benefit pension obligations, curtailments of defined benefit plans, and any special termination benefits offered by plans in accordance with the separate accounting standards spelled out under FASB Statement No. 88.

56. What are the financial accounting standards applicable to post-employment and postretirement benefits other than pension plans?

The Financial Accounting Standards Board (FASB) has issued *FASB Statement No. 112*, titled "Employer's Accounting for Post-Employment Benefits." FASB Statement No. 112 requires employers to account for severance benefits, termination benefits, supplemental unemployment benefits, disability benefits, health care continuation benefits, survivor benefits, and all other post-employment benefits that are not pension retirement benefits on an accrual basis, in advance (just as they are required to do for pension benefits).

FASB Statement No. 112 requires employers to accrue liabilities for post-employment benefits other than pensions where:

1.   The obligation is attributable to services previously provided;

2.   Employee rights to the benefits accumulate or vest;

3.   Payment of the benefits is probable; and

4.   The amount of benefits can be reasonably estimated.

FASB Statement No. 106, titled "Employer's Accounting for Post-Retirement Benefits other than Pensions," stipulates that employers charge the cost of postretirement benefits other than pensions against income during the years an employee provides services to the employer.

The DOL has issued a Notice advising that Form 5500s filed by multiemployer welfare plans will be rejected if the accountant's opinion accompanying the Form is "qualified" or "adverse" due to a failure to comply with the financial statement disclosure provisions of AICPA Statement of Position 92-6, which is mirrored in FASB Statement No. 106. This notice is a rejection by the DOL of its previously proposed policy of non-enforcement, issued in 1997, wherein the DOL advised that it would not reject Form 5500 filings of multiemployer welfare plans for any funds that did not comply with the reporting standards.[1] The DOL advises that Form 5500s of multiemployer welfare benefit plans will be subject to rejection if there is any material qualification in the accountant's opinion due to failure to comply with FASB Statement No. 106.[2]

---

1. FASB Statement No. 106, 62 Fed. Reg. 11,929 (Mar. 13, 1997).
2. Notice of Annual Reporting Enforcement Policy, 63 Fed. Reg. 65,505 (Nov. 25, 1998).

57. What are the financial accounting standards applicable to employer disclosures about pensions and other postretirement benefits?

The Financial Accounting Standards Board (FASB) has issued *FASB Statement No. 132*, titled "Employer's Disclosures about Pensions and other Postretirement Benefits." That statement provides that FASB Statements No. 87 (Employer's Accounting for Pensions), No. 88 (Employer's Accounting for Settlements and Curtailments of Defined Benefit Pension Plans and Termination Benefits), and No. 106 (Employer's Accounting for Postretirement Benefits other than Pensions) have been amended to provide standardized disclosure requirements for pension and postretirement benefits. The statement also requires additional information on changes in the benefit obligations and the fair values of plan assets that will improve financial analysis and eliminate certain disclosure requirements.

The disclosure requirements eliminated under FASB Statement 132 include:

1.   The requirement to provide a description of the plan, including employee groups covered, types of assets held and benefit formulas, funding policy, significant non-benefit liabilities, and the effect of significant matters affecting comparability of information for all periods presented; and

2.   Alternative measures of the benefit obligation, including vested benefit obligations, accumulated benefit obligations for pension plans with assets in excess of the accumulated benefit obligation, and various portions of postretirement benefit obligations for retirees, other active participants, and other fully eligible participants.

Plan sponsors with two or more plans are permitted under FASB Statement 132 to aggregate required disclosures for their defined benefit pension plans and defined benefit postretirement benefit plans. FASB Statement 132 also eliminates the requirement to disaggregate disclosures for plans with accumulated pension benefit obligations that exceed plan assets. FASB Statement 132 permits the aggregation of these disclosures with other disclosures about plans with accumulated benefit obligations in excess of assets.

Defined contribution plan sponsors are required under FASB Statement 132 to disclose the amount of cost recognized for the plan or other postretirement benefit plan during the period separately from the amount of cost recognized for a defined benefit plan. Defined contribution plan sponsors are also required to include in disclosures a description of any significant changes that would affect comparability (i.e., changes in the rate of sponsor contributions).

FASB Statement 132 requires defined benefit pension plan sponsors and defined benefit postretirement plan sponsors to provide the following information:

1.   A reconciliation of the beginning and ending balances of the benefit obligation for the period;

2.   A reconciliation of the beginning and ending balances of the fair value of plan assets;

3.   The funding status of the plans;

4.   All amounts not recognized in the statement of financial position;

5.   All amounts recognized in the statement of financial position;

6.   The amount of net periodic benefit costs recognized in net income and the amount recognized in other comprehensive income;

7.   The following assumptions used in the accounting for the plans (on a weighted basis):

   a.   assumed discount rate,

   b.   rate of compensation increase (pay-related plans),

   c.   health care cost trend rate, and

   d.   the expected long-term rate of return on plan assets;

8.   The effect of a one percentage point increase and decrease in the weighted average of the assumed health care cost trend rates on:

   a.   the aggregate of the service and interest cost components of net periodic postretirement health care benefit costs, and

   b.   the accumulated postretirement benefit obligation for health care benefits, and

9.   An explanation of any significant change in the benefit obligations or plan assets not otherwise apparent in the other disclosure required by the statement.

FASB Statement 132 requires employers to disclose the amount of contributions to multiemployer plans.

Recordkeeping

58. What employee recordkeeping is required to be maintained under ERISA?

In administering a qualified plan, plan sponsors must maintain certain records in order to assure that they are maintaining and operating the plan in accordance with the participation, accrual, vesting, and distribution requirements of ERISA and the Code. ERISA Section 209 says that every employer must maintain records, with respect to each employee, which are sufficient to determine the benefits that are due or may become due to such employees. That section goes on to require that the employer furnish the plan administrator with the information necessary to prepare mandated reports for participants. These reports include statements of account balances and vested percentages, as well as summary annual reports. Records necessary for the preparation of required reports include those pertaining to employment history, birth, pay, and marital status.

Employment History Records

In addition to the necessity of maintaining employment history records for non-retirement benefit reasons, these records will be necessary for determining:

1. Eligibility to participate (in general, ERISA Section 202(a)(1) and IRC Section 410(a)(1)(A) mandate participation in a qualified plan upon the completion of one year of service and the attainment of age twenty-one);

2. Benefit accrual (ERISA Section 202(a)(3)(A) and IRC Section 410(a)(3)(A) define a "year of service" for purposes of qualifying for a benefit accrual, and ERISA Section 203(b)(2) and IRC Section 411(a)(5) define a year of service for vesting purposes as 1,000 hours of service — excluding seasonal or part-time employees, who have alternative rules);

3. Vesting (see the discussion of vesting requirements in Q 16); and

4. In certain cases, eligibility for early retirement benefit incentives.

Employment records must also be maintained for purposes of determining whether an employee has experienced a "break in service." "Break in service" rules state that any participant who has not completed 500 hours of service in a plan year has experienced a break in service. A break in service will have an impact upon a participant's accrual of vesting percentages and may require the participant, upon re-attainment of full-time status (1,000 hours of service), to satisfy the plan's active-service requirements before returning to active participation in the underlying plan.[1]

Birth Records

Employee birth records are required to be maintained for purposes of determining eligibility to participate in the plan (see ERISA Section 202(a)(1) and IRC Section 410(a)(1)(A) — referred to above); vesting (ERISA Section 203(b) and IRC Section 411(a)(4) mandate that all years of service with a plan sponsor after the attainment of age eighteen must be taken into consideration when calculating a participant's vesting percentage); and to receive distributions from the plan, either through early retirement benefits or upon the attainment of normal retirement age. A qualified plan must commence the payment of benefits — unless the participant elects otherwise — not later than the sixtieth day after the latest of the close of the plan year:

1. In which the participant attains the earlier of age sixty-five or the normal retirement age specified under the plan,

2. In which the tenth anniversary occurs of the year in which the participant began to participate in the plan, or

3. In which the participant terminates his service with the employer.[2]

Pay Records

IRC Section 415 details the limitations on benefits and contributions under qualified plans. These limitations are typically based upon the compensation paid to participants, and govern annual contributions under individual account plans (the lesser of $50,000 (in 2012) or 100

---

1. ERISA Sec. 202(b)(1); IRC Sec. 410(a)(5).
2. IRC Sec. 401(a)(14).

percent of compensation) and annual benefit limits for participants under defined benefit plans. Plan administrators must pay particular attention to these records and their accuracy because the IRS considers violations under IRC Section 415 limits to be very serious. Indeed, plans that violate the Section 415 limits face the very real possibility of disqualification.

Marital Status Records

Records of the marital status of plan participants are necessary in order to determine eligibility for mandated spousal benefits under ERISA and the Internal Revenue Code. Where a participant with vested benefits under a plan dies prior to attaining the earliest retirement age under the plan (i.e., generally the time when benefits under a plan are payable in the form of an annuity), the surviving spouse, if any, is entitled to a qualified preretirement survivor annuity (QPSA) (with certain exceptions).[1]

The surviving spouse of a participant who dies after reaching the earliest retirement age under the plan generally must be provided a qualified joint and survivor annuity (QJSA) (again, with certain exceptions). A QJSA is defined as an annuity for the life of the spouse that is not less than 50 percent of (and not greater than 100 percent of) the amount of the annuity that is payable during the joint lives of the participant and the spouse and that is the actuarial equivalent of a single annuity for the life of the participant.[2] Qualified plans subject to the spousal annuity rules must also provide written explanations to participants of their QPSA and QJSA rights.[3] Spouses must consent in writing to any waiver of their preretirement survivor annuity and joint and survivor annuity rights.[4]

Where a participant has experienced a divorce, the former spouse may be eligible to receive benefits under a qualified domestic relations order (QDRO). The plan administrator will need to maintain accurate participant benefit records in this situation in order to ascertain the exact amount of accrued benefits the participant must provide to the participant's ex-spouse under a court-ordered QDRO. A QDRO is defined as any judgment, decree, or order that relates to the provision of child support, alimony payments, or marital property rights (including accrued retirement benefits) to a spouse, former spouse, child, or other dependent of a participant, and that is made pursuant to a state domestic relations law (including community property law).[5]

Marital records are also necessary when a plan permits participants to access their accrued benefits through participant loans. If the plan is subject to the spousal annuity rules, the plan must obtain the written consent of the participant's spouse, within ninety days of issuance, for any participant loan under the plan in excess of $5,000.[6]

---

1. ERISA Sec. 205(e)(1); IRC Sec. 417(c).
2. ERISA Sec. 205(d)(1); IRC Sec. 417(b).
3. ERISA Sec. 205(c)(3); IRC Sec. 417(a)(3).
4. ERISA Sec. 205(c)(2); IRC Sec. 417(a)(2).
5. ERISA Sec. 206(d)(3)(B)(ii); IRC Sec. 414(p)(1)(B).
6. Treas. Reg. §1.401(a)-20, A-24.

59. What are the rules regarding the use of electronic media for the maintenance and retention of employee benefit plan records?

The DOL has issued final safe harbor rules for disclosure of employee benefit plan information to participants and beneficiaries.[1] The final rules also detail requirements for the maintenance and retention of employee benefit plan records in electronic form.

The IRS published proposed regulations expanding on a number of existing rules for using electronic media to meet various Code and regulatory requirements. These regulations require that certain retirement plan notices, elections, and consents be in writing and coordinate with the requirements of the E-SIGN statute.[2] In October 2006, the IRS published final regulations establishing uniform standards for electronic systems that make use of an electronic medium to provide notices to plan participants and beneficiaries, or to transmit elections or consents relating to employee benefit arrangements.[3] These regulations apply to all Tax Code requirements regarding electronic notice and consent issues, as well as the parallel provisions under ERISA.[4]

The final regulations continue to be a "safe harbor," meaning that plans are not required to comply, but compliance ensures that the DOL and courts will find a plan's electronic delivery method consistent with the general requirement that documents be furnished by a method "reasonably calculated to ensure actual receipt."

Expanded Application to All Benefit Plan Documents

The regulation expands the safe harbor to encompass all ERISA Title I disclosures.[5] The original temporary rules limited electronic disclosure to summary plan descriptions, summaries of material modifications, and summary annual reports. The expanded provisions include all information that must be provided to participants and beneficiaries after written request, individual benefit statements, and plan investment information.

Covered Participants

Electronic delivery may be used for employees both inside and outside the workplace, so long as the employee has ready access to the employer's computer system at a location where the employee is reasonably expected to perform his duties. Access for the employee to the employer's computer system must be an integral part of the employee's duties under the regulation (i.e., intranet or e-mail).[6] Therefore, a kiosk or computer set aside in a common area will not be acceptable.

Electronic delivery may be used for non-employees as well. The final regulations permit a plan to provide documents electronically to others required to receive ERISA disclosures (i.e., e-mail, Internet, CD, DVD, or computer disc not dependent on electronic

---

1. Labor Reg. §2520.104b-1, *as amended.*
2. Electronic Signatures in Global and National Commerce Act, Pub. L. No. 106-229.
3. Treas. Reg. §1.401(a)-21; T.D. 9294 (Oct. 20, 2006).
4. Treas. Reg. §1.401(a)-21(g).
5. Labor Reg. §2520.104b-1(c).
6. Labor Reg. §2520.104b-1(c)(2)(i)(A) and (B).

transmission). To do this, the other individuals must provide an address for delivery of the documents and must affirmatively consent to the electronic disclosure in a manner that reasonably demonstrates the individual's ability to access information in electronic form.[1] Alternatively, the new IRS regulations state that the consent can be made using a written paper document or through some other nonelectronic means, but only if the participant confirms the consent in a way that reasonably demonstrates that he can access the notice in the electronic form to be provided.[2]

Mandated Procedures

Electronic delivery must be reasonably calculated to ensure actual receipt. The plan administrator must take appropriate and necessary steps to ensure that the system for furnishing documents results in actual receipt of the transmitted information.[3]

Further, the documents must be presented in a format that is consistent with the style and content requirements applicable to the particular document.[4] When the applicable notice is provided, the electronic transmission must alert the recipient to the significance of the transmittal (including the identification of the subject matter of the notice), and provide any instructions needed to access the notice, in a manner that is readily understandable and accessible.[5]

The Ninth Circuit has ruled that a plan administrator may not rely on a summary plan description posted on the plan sponsor intranet without evidence of measures in place to ensure actual receipt by participants.[6] An employee sued to recover disability benefits under the employer's disability plan. The employer, in rejecting the claim for disability benefits, relied on an SPD that had been posted on its intranet site. The electronic version of the SPD differed from the version of the SPD in the administrative record of the employee's benefit claim. The court held that the employer could not rely on the intranet SPD because it had "submitted nothing on the record to suggest that the mere placement of an updated SPD on its intranet site could ensure that [the employee] would actually receive the transmitted information."

Individuals must have the right to request paper versions of the electronic forms.[7]

Individuals must receive notice of electronically delivered items at the time the item is delivered. That notice must tell individuals of their right to request and receive paper versions of any documents being sent electronically. In addition, the notice is required to apprise the individuals of the significance of the document being sent electronically when it is not otherwise evident as transmitted.[8]

---

1. Labor Reg. §2520.104b-1(c)(2)(ii)(A) and (B).
2. Treas. Reg. §1.401(a)-21.
3. Labor Reg. §2520.104b-1(c)(1)(i)(A).
4. Labor Reg. §2520.104b-1(c)(1)(ii)(B).
5. Treas. Reg. §1.401(a)-21(a)(5).
6. *Gertjejansen v. Kemper Ins. Cos.*, 2008 WL 1787484 (9th Cir. 2008).
7. Labor Reg. §2520.104b-1(c)(1)(iv)(B).
8. Labor Reg. §2520.104b-1(c)(1)(iii)(B).

Where an employer desires to make electronic disclosure available to participants, beneficiaries, and other payees outside the workplace, the plan administrator must, in advance, provide a clear and conspicuous statement that contains the following information:

- The types of documents to which the consent would apply;

- That consent can be withdrawn at any time without charge;

- The procedures for withdrawing consent and updating the participant's, beneficiary's, or other individual's address for receipt of electronically furnished documents or other information;

- The right to request and obtain a paper version of an electronically furnished document, including whether the paper version will be furnished free of charge; and

- Any hardware and software requirements for accessing and retaining the documents.[1]

If the hardware or software requirements change, new consent must be obtained from the participant.[2]

Participant Elections

The final Treasury regulations establish the requirements that apply if a consent or election is made by a person using an electronic system.[3] Specifically, the regulations require that:

1.   The electronic medium under an electronic system used to make a participant election must be a medium that the appropriate individual is effectively able to access;

2.   The electronic system must be reasonably designed to preclude any person other than the appropriate individual from making the participant election—reasonableness to be based on the facts and circumstances;

3.   The electronic system used in making the elections must provide the person making the participant election with a reasonable opportunity to review, confirm, modify, or rescind the terms of the election before it becomes effective;

4.   The person making the participant election must receive, within a reasonable time period, a confirmation of the election through either a written paper document or an electronic medium under a system that satisfies the applicable consumer consent or exemption requirements of Treasury Regulation Section 1.401(a)-21(b) or Treasury Regulation Section 1.401(a)-21(c), respectively; and

5.   In the case of a participant election that must be witnessed by a plan representative or a notary public (such as a spousal consent under the IRC Section 417 qualified joint

---

1. Labor Reg. §2520.104b-1(c)(2)(ii)(C); Treas. Reg. §1.401(a)-21(b).
2. Treas. Reg. §1.401(a)-21(b).
3. Treas. Reg. §1.401(a)-21(d).

and survivor annuity rules), the signature of the individual making the participant election must be witnessed in the physical presence of a plan representative or a notary public.

With respect to requirement five, above, the IRS recognizes that at some point in the future, technology could exist that would provide the same safeguards as the physical presence requirement. Accordingly, the Treasury regulations provide that the IRS may, by publishing guidance in the Internal Revenue Bulletin, provide that the use of procedures under an electronic system with respect to an electronic medium is deemed to satisfy the physical presence requirement. However, the IRS can do so only if those procedures with respect to the electronic system provide the same safeguards for participant elections as provided through the physical presence requirement.[1]

Confidentiality Requirements

There are confidentiality requirements where documents contain personal information relating to accounts, benefits, and investments. The plan administrator must take reasonable steps to safeguard the confidentiality of personal information relating to the individual's accounts and benefits.[2]

The DOL has not provided guidance under the regulations as to what constitutes "reasonable steps."

Imposition of Fees for Printing Copies of Electronic Documents

The final regulations provide that the plan administrator may charge a nominal fee for printing any documents that are *not* required disclosures under ERISA.[3] The regulations do not spell out what a "nominal fee" is, but DOL investigators are trained to question any copy charge in excess of twenty-five cents per page.

Recordkeeping Requirements

The record maintenance and retention requirements of ERISA Sections 107 and 209 are satisfied when using electronic media if:

- The electronic recordkeeping system has reasonable controls to ensure the integrity, accuracy, authenticity, and reliability of the records kept in electronic form;

- The electronic records are maintained in reasonable order and in a safe and accessible place, and in such a manner as they may be readily inspected or examined;

- The electronic records are readily convertible into legible and readable paper copy as may be needed to satisfy reporting and disclosure requirements or any other obligation under Title I of ERISA;

---

1. Preamble to T.D. 9294 (Oct. 20, 2006); Treas. Reg. §1.401(a)-21(d).
2. Labor Reg. §2520.104b-1(c)(1)(i)(B).
3. 67 Fed. Reg. 17,268 (Apr. 9, 2002).

- The electronic recordkeeping system is not subject, in whole or in part, to any agreement or restriction that would, directly or indirectly, compromise or limit a person's ability to comply with any reporting and disclosure obligation; and

- Adequate records management practices are established and implemented (secure storage, adequate backup, etc.).[1]

All electronic records must exhibit a high degree of legibility and readability when displayed on a video display terminal or other method of electronic transmission and when reproduced in paper form.[2]

Original paper records may be disposed of any time they are transferred to an electronic recordkeeping system that complies with the requirements of the final regulations. However, documents may not be discarded if the electronic record would not constitute a duplicate or substitute copy under the terms of the plan and applicable federal or state law.[3]

60. What type of forms must a plan maintain regarding disability retirement benefits?

Where a qualified plan permits the distribution of accrued benefits in the case of the disability of a participant, the plan will need to maintain a basic disability application to be completed by the participant, and a separate form for the certification of disability to be completed by the participant's physician.

The basic application for disability benefits will provide for the standard information all participants will be required to provide when they apply for benefits. In addition, this form will allow sufficient space for the participant to detail the disability and provide the identification of attending physicians who have diagnosed and treated the disability.

The certification form will be completed, and attested, by the attending physician, who satisfies the plan or plan sponsor's requirements for competency in determining the nature and extent of the participant's disability. Most plan sponsors have established written procedures to designate a physician of their choosing for the completion of this form. Multiemployer plans will often provide for a medical board to review these determinations and will often provide for a union-appointed physician to review the disability claims of a participant.

Reporting and Disclosure

61. What plans are subject to reporting rules?

The ERISA provisions governing reporting and disclosure are applicable to an employee benefit plan established or maintained by an employer engaged in commerce or in an industry affecting commerce. In addition, these provisions are applicable to employee organizations representing employees engaged in commerce or in an industry affecting commerce.[4]

---

1. Labor Reg. §2520.107-1(b)(1) to (5).
2. Labor Reg. §2520.107-1(c).
3. Labor Reg. §2520.107-1(d).
4. *Baucom v. Pilot Life Ins. Co.*, 674 F. Supp. 1175 (M.D.N.C. 1987).

62. What plans are exempt from the reporting rules?

The provisions of Title I of ERISA do not apply to an employee benefit plan if the plan is:

1.   A governmental plan (as defined in ERISA Section 3(32));

2.   A church plan (as defined in ERISA Section 3(33)) with respect to which no election has been made under IRC Section 410(d);

3.   Maintained solely for the purpose of complying with applicable workers' compensation, unemployment compensation, or disability insurance laws;

4.   Maintained outside the United States primarily for the benefit of persons substantially all of whom are nonresident aliens; or

5.   An excess benefit plan (as defined in ERISA Section 3(36)), and is unfunded.[1]

In addition, individual retirement accounts and individual retirement annuities (IRAs, as defined in IRC Section 408), Keogh plans that cover a single self-employed individual, and Health Savings Accounts are also exempt from ERISA's reporting rules.

63. What reports are required to be provided to the Internal Revenue Service?

ERISA-covered plans must comply with certain duties of disclosure and reporting, set forth in ERISA Section 101.

Annual Report, Schedules, and Supplemental Information

The reporting obligations include the furnishing of an annual report that satisfies the requirements of ERISA Section 103.[2] ERISA Section 103 details the information on the characteristics and financial operations of the plan for which the annual report has been filed.

The Annual Report Form 5500 (i.e., the 5500) must be filed with the Employee Benefits Security Administration by the last day of the seventh month after the close of the plan year. The DOL will process these reports after receipt and provide a copy of the 5500 to the IRS (thereby eliminating the need for the plan administrator to file two copies of the same report). As detailed in Section XII, the DOL utilizes the 5500s it receives in enforcement and other program activities.

Under the recently revised 5500 format the prior Form 5500-C/R filed by small plans (those with fewer than 100 participants) was eliminated, and the Form 5500-EZ was retained. Under the revised format, there are 13 schedules that accompany the new Form 5500. A plan will complete and file only those schedules that apply. The 13 schedules include the prior eight schedules (A, B, C, E, F, G, P, and SSA) and five additional schedules (D, H, I, R, and T). Schedules A, C, and G have undergone substantial revisions. See Q 64 for details on these new schedules.

---

1. ERISA Sec. 4(b).
2. ERISA Sec. 101(b)(4).

Plans with one-hundred or more participants are required to file a supplemental report prepared by an independent qualified public accountant that provides for the accountant's opinion (unqualified or qualified) on the financial statements and schedules contained in the 5500, the accounting principles and practices utilized in the preparation of the 5500, and any changes in the accounting principles that may have affected the information in the financial statements. This requirement is also subject to final rules issued by the DOL that require some plans with fewer than 100 participants to file supplemental reports prepared by independent qualified public accountants. See Q 110 for details of these small plan audit requirements.

DOL guidance provides that in order for electronic filing under EFAST2 to be timely, Form 5500 must be received by EFAST2 by midnight in the plan administrator's time zone, as determined by the plan administrator's address stated on Line 3a of Form 5500 Main Body. If a plan attempts to submit Form 5500 but it is not successfully received by EFAST2 before the deadline, the DOL advises that the plan should print the unsuccessful submission notice and include it with the resubmitted Form 5500 (tagging it as an "other attachment"). The DOL states that penalties may still be assessed in this situation based upon their review of the facts and circumstances surrounding the original unprocessable submission and subsequent resubmission. If imposed, penalties will be calculated starting from the original due date if EFAST2 receives the resubmitted Form 5500 after the deadline.[1]

The DOL has updated its "Troubleshooter's Guide to Filing the ERISA Annual Report (Form 5500 and Form 5500-SF)." The guide contains practical tips for complying with the Form 5500 reporting requirements and avoiding common reporting errors.[2]

Short Form 5500 for Certain Small Plans

Form 5500-SF is retained for certain small plans (generally, fewer than 100 participants) with secure and easy-to-value investment portfolios. Potentially eligible plans include certain small pension plans that qualify for the audit waiver and small welfare plans that do not otherwise qualify for a filing exemption.

The two-page Form 5500-SF is to be used to satisfy the voluntary alternative reporting option imposed by the PPA for certain pension plans with fewer than twenty-five participants.[3]

Notice of Plan Changes

A plan administrator who is required to file an annual registration statement (known as Schedule SSA, see Q 64) is also required to notify the IRS of:

1.   A change in the name of the plan;

2.   A change in the name or address of the plan administrator;

---

1. EBSA FAQs: EFAST2 All-Electronic Filing System (Mar. 2010), http://www.dol.gov/ebsa/faqs/faq-EFAST2.html.

2. Troubleshooter's Guide to Filing the ERISA Annual Report (Form 5500 and Form 5500-SF) (Oct. 2010), http://www.dol.gov/ebsa/pdf/troubleshootersguide.pdf. To research returns submitted under the EFAST2 program, go to http://www.efast.dol.gov/welcome.html.

3. Annual Reporting and Disclosure, Revision of Annual Information Return/Reports, Final Rule, 29 C.F.R. pt. 2520, 72 Fed. Reg. 64,709 (Nov. 16, 2007); Notice of Adoption of Revisions to Annual Return/Report Forms, 72 Fed. Reg. 64,731 (Nov. 16, 2007).

3.   The termination of the plan; or

4.   The merger or consolidation of the plan with any other plan, or its division into two or more plans (on Form 5310-A).[1]

Furthermore, plan administrators are required to notify the IRS in the event of a plan termination. This notification may be made by checking the "Final Return" box at the top of the Form 5500 filed by the plan. Plan administrators may file Form 5310 with the IRS to seek a favorable opinion on the plan's qualification; however, such a filing is not required. It is recommended that terminating plans seek a favorable IRS determination to ensure that funds distributed from the terminating plan and transferred to other qualified plans or individual retirement accounts will retain their tax-deferred status.

Electronic Filing of Form 5500/EFAST2 All-Electronic Filing System

Beginning with the 2009 reporting years, all plans must file the 5500 and related schedules electronically through the computerized system known as EFAST (ERISA Filing Acceptance System).[2] Under EFAST2, Forms 5500 are required to be filed in one of two computer scanable formats: "machine print" and "hand print." The EFAST2 system is designed to accept 5500 filings only on one of these two approved forms. All 5500 submissions were required to be in one of the two approved formats. The EFAST2 system may not properly process forms that do not meet the new specifications. This could result in non-standard form filings' being rejected as deficient. For information on both EFAST2-approved forms, as well as a list of approved EFAST2 software providers, see the official DOL EFAST2 Web site at http://www.efast.dol. gov. The DOL's EFAST2 Web site now contains forty-five frequently asked questions (FAQs) addressing EFAST2, the all-electronic filing system for Form 5500. These FAQs cover such topics as short plan years, third-party software, registering for credentials, and filing issues. This online assistance is available at http://www.dol.gov/ebsa/faqs/faq-EFAST2.html.

Anyone required to sign a Form 5500 must register online to obtain "Filing Signer" credentials, which will give them a personal identification number (PIN) that serves as an electronic signature for Form 5500 purposes. Question 33 of the FAQs discusses whether a plan administrator can give its PIN to a third-party administrator (TPA) or other Form 5500 preparer, who can then use it to sign the filing before submitting it. The DOL says no and explains that because the plan administrator is required to examine any Form 5500 before it is submitted, use of the PIN— the plan administrator's electronic signature—attests to the fact that the Form 5500 has been examined and "to the best of [the plan administrator's] knowledge and belief, it is true, correct, and complete." As a result, the PIN must be used only by the plan administrator. Registration for EFAST2 credentials is performed on the EFAST2 Web site at http://www.efast.dol.gov. The registration requires five brief steps, after which, within five minutes of submission and acceptance, the credentials are generated.[3]

---

1. IRC Sec. 6057(b).
2. Annual Reporting and Disclosure, Revision of Annual Information Return/Reports, Final Rule, 29 C.F.R. pt. 2520, 72 Fed. Reg. 64,709 (Nov. 16, 2007); Notice of Adoption of Revisions to Annual Return/Report Forms, 72 Fed. Reg. 64,731 (Nov. 16, 2007).
3. DOL FAQ on EFAST2 Credentials (Dec. 2010).

The DOL has announced a new e-signature option for filing Form 5500 under EFAST2. Under EFAST2, prior to addition of this new e-signature option, plan administrators were required to obtain their own PINs in order to electronically sign the Form 5500. Also, plan administrators could not share their PINs with third-party preparers. In response to concerns submitted to the DOL on the PIN-sharing prohibition, the new e-signature option is designed "to simplify the electronic filing process, especially for small businesses that use service providers to complete and file their annual reports." Third-party preparers may now obtain their own EFAST2 signing credentials and submit a Form 5500 on a plan administrator's behalf. The preparer must receive and retain the plan administrator's specific written authorization to submit the electronic filing. The plan administrator must manually sign a paper copy of the Form 5500, and the preparer is required to include a PDF copy of the first two pages of the manually signed form as an attachment to the electronic submission. Further, the preparer must advise the plan administrator that by using the e-signature option, the plan administrator's manual signature will be part of the Form 5500 that is posted by the DOL on the Internet for public disclosure. The preparer also must communicate to the plan administrator any inquiries and information received from EFAST2, the DOL, the IRS, or the PBGC regarding the Form 5500. NOTE: Q/A-33a reminds preparers that they may not affix a plan administrator's PIN to Form 5500 filings.[1]

The Electronic Filing Rule explains that electronic filing by the administrator of a pension or welfare benefit plan would constitute compliance with the applicable limited exemption, alternative method of compliance, and/or simplified reporting requirements, as applicable, prescribed in Labor Regulation Sections 2520.103-1 et seq. and promulgated in accordance with Sections 104(a) and 110 of Title I of ERISA. For purposes of the PBGC's annual filing and reporting requirements under Section 4065 of Title IV of ERISA, a plan administrator's electronic filing of a Form 5500 Annual Return/Report or the proposed Short Form 5500, in accordance with the instructions, will be treated as satisfying the administrator's annual reporting obligation under Section 4065 of Title IV of ERISA. The instructions for authorized service provider signatures have been updated to clarify how a service provider who manages the filing process for a plan can obtain EFAST2 signing credentials and submit the filings on behalf of the plan. The service provider must:

1.   Receive specific written authorization from the plan administrator to submit the plan's electronic filing;

2.   Manually sign a paper copy of the electronically completed Form 5500, and the service provider must include a PDF copy of the first two pages of the manually signed Form 5500 as an attachment to the electronic Form 5500 submitted to EFAST2;

3.   Communicate to the plan administrator any inquiries received from EFAST2, DOL, IRS, or PBGC regarding the filing;

---

1. EFAST2 FAQs: Signing A Return/Report (May 2010), http://www.dol.gov/ebsa/faqs/faq-EFAST2.html#SigningAReturn/Report; EFAST2 FAQs: FAQs on Electronic Filing for Small Businesses, http://www.dol.gov/ebsa/faqs/faq-EFAST2-smallbusiness.html.

4.   Communicate to the plan administrator that, by electing to use this option, the image of the plan administrator's manual signature will be included with the rest of the return/report posted by the Labor Department on the Internet for public disclosure; and

5.   Keep the manually signed copy of the Form 5500, with all required schedules and attachments, as part of the plan's records.[1]

Similarly, for purposes of the annual filing and reporting requirements of the Internal Revenue Code, the IRS has advised the DOL that, although there are no mandatory electronic filing requirements for a Form 5500 Annual Return/Report or the proposed Short Form 5500 under the Code or the Treasury regulations, the electronic filing of a Form 5500 Annual Return/Report or the proposed Short Form 5500 (described below), in accordance with the instructions and other guidance the IRS may provide, will be treated as satisfying the annual filing and reporting requirements under IRC Sections 6058(a) and 6059(a). The IRS intends that plan administrators, employers, and certain other entities that are subject to various other filing and reporting requirements under IRC Sections 6033(a), 6047(e), 6057, and 6058(a) must continue to satisfy these requirements in accordance with IRS revenue procedures, regulations, publications, forms, and instructions.

The Form 5500-EZ is used by certain plans that are not subject to the requirements of Section 104(a) of ERISA to satisfy the annual reporting and filing obligations imposed by the Code. To ease the burdens on these filers, the IRS has also advised the DOL that certain Form 5500-EZ filers will be permitted to satisfy the requirement to file the Form 5500-EZ with the IRS by filing the proposed Short Form 5500 electronically through the EFAST2 processing system.

Therefore, under the IRS's proposal, certain Form 5500-EZ filers will be provided both electronic and paper filing options. The electronic option will allow Form 5500-EZ filers to complete and electronically file selected information on the Short Form 5500. Form 5500-EZ filers will also have the option to file a paper Form 5500-EZ. Under the voluntary electronic filing option, 5500-EZ filers filing an amended return for a plan year must file the amended return electronically using the Form 5500-SF if they initially filed electronically for the plan year and must file with the IRS using the paper Form 5500-EZ if they filed for the plan year with the IRS on a paper Form 5500-EZ.

At the same time as the Electronic Filing Rule was developed, the DOL and IRS undertook a comprehensive review of the current forms and instructions in an effort to improve the data collected and to determine what, if any, design or data changes should be made in anticipation of the new processing system. The proposed revision of the forms and instructions, in conjunction with the Electronic Filing Rule, is intended to streamline the return/report, facilitate the electronic filing requirement, and reduce the burden on plans that file the Form 5500 Annual Return/Report.

The preamble to the final rule states the DOL, in deciding whether to assess annual reporting civil penalties, will take into account technical and logistical obstacles experienced by plan

---

1. Instructions to 2011 Form 5500, http://www.dol.gov/ebsa/pdf/2011-5500inst.pdf.

administrators who acted prudently and in good faith in attempting to timely file a complete annual report in the first year of the wholly electronic filing system. The revised and streamlined data requirements for the Form 5500 Annual Return/Report as proposed are intended to be applicable for the reporting year for which the new e-filing system is implemented.

The proposed revisions to the annual return/report forms involve the following major categories of changes, along with other technical revisions and updates, to the current structure and content of the Form 5500 Annual Return/Report:

1. Establishment of the Form 5500-SF Annual Return/Report (Short Form or Short Form 5500) as a new simplified report for certain small plans;

2. Removal of the IRS-only schedules from the Form 5500 Annual Return/Report as part of the move to a wholly electronic filing system;

3. Elimination of the special limited financial reporting rules for IRC Section 403(b) plans;

4. Revision of the Schedule C (Service Provider Information) to clarify the reporting requirements and improve the information plan officials receive regarding amounts being received by plan service providers; and

5. Addition of new questions to improve information on pension plan funding and compliance with minimum funding requirements.

Because of the electronic filing requirement for the revised Form 5500 Annual Return/ Report, including the proposed Short Form 5500, copies of facsimile forms and schedules will not be acceptable for filing under ERISA. Rather, the facsimile forms and schedules the Agencies anticipate publishing in conjunction with the final regulation will show the required format for satisfying disclosure obligations under ERISA, including the plan administrator's obligation to furnish copies of the annual report to participants and beneficiaries on request pursuant to Section 104(b) of ERISA; but paper versions will not be able to be used for filing.[1]

64. What are the schedules that are filed with the Annual Report Form 5500?

A filed Form 5500 must be accompanied by the appropriate schedules that are designed to provide detailed information supporting the basic facts and figures reported on Form 5500. The following is a brief review of the schedules, the information they must contain, and which plans are required to file each schedule. These schedules are available for electronic and paper filing.[2]

The DOL, IRS, and PBGC have jointly issued final Form 5500 regulations and have adopted final revisions to the Form 5500 that are applicable for 2009 and later plan year filings.[3]

---

1. 71 Fed. Reg. 41,615 (July 21, 2006).
2. They can be viewed and printed from the DOL's Web site at http://www.dol.gov/ebsa/5500main.html.
3. Annual Reporting and Disclosure, Revision of Annual Information Return/Reports, Final Rule, 29 C.F.R. pt. 2520, 72 Fed. Reg. 64,709 (Nov. 16, 2007); Notice of Adoption of Revisions to Annual Return/Report Forms, 72 Fed. Reg. 64,731 (Nov. 16, 2007).

Schedule A

Schedule A is filed by those plans that provide benefits through an insurance company. It provides a statement from the insurance company that details the premium rate for subscription charge, the total subscription charges paid to each insurance carrier, and the number of individuals covered by each class of benefits. Schedule A also reports the total amount of premiums received by the insurance carrier, the number of individuals covered in each class of benefits, and the total amount of claims paid. The information provided in Schedule A is required by ERISA Section 103(e). Schedule A is designed to collect information on the types of insurance products, the types of coverage, and insured benefits being reported. It is also designed to conform required reporting to various accounting industry changes (Generally Accepted Accounting Principles) on current value financial reporting of investment-type contracts with insurance companies.

Under the final regulations, the DOL has retained the broad definition of fees and commissions required to be reported on Schedule A (as set out in Advisory Opinion 2005-02A). However, the new Schedule A contains a special rule under which compensation paid by an insurer to third parties for recordkeeping, claims processing, and other similar types of administrative services will not be required to be reported as fees and commissions on Schedule A, provided that certain detailed conditions are satisfied. Also, the new Schedule A will exclude "occasional and insubstantial non-monetary compensation" paid by insurers to brokers and others (similar to the rule also added to Schedule C, discussed below).[1]

Schedule A is not required from plans that file a Form 5500-EZ.

Schedule B

Schedule B is filed by defined benefit plans to provide details on the actuarial information for those plans to which the minimum funding standards of IRC Section 412 apply. It is prepared and signed by an enrolled actuary. Schedule B contains a description of the funding method and actuarial assumptions used to determine the costs of the plan and a certification of the contribution necessary to reduce the accumulated funding deficiency (if any) to zero.

Schedule B — Schedule SB, Schedule MB

Under the final regulations, the new Schedule B has been updated for certain Pension Protection Act of 2006 (PPA) changes that became effective in 2007. Schedule B is phased out and has been replaced by Schedule SB for single-employer plans and by Schedule MB for multiemployer plans. In addition, defined benefit plans with 1,000 or more participants must file financial asset breakdown information on Schedule R, and multiemployer plans must provide supplemental information on Schedule R.

DOL EFAST2 guidance provides that if the filing requires the submission of the following attachments, the plan must upload these documents separately into the appropriate attachment "tag" or else EFAST 2 may generate an error message:

---

1. Annual Reporting and Disclosure, Revision of Annual Information Return/Reports, Final Rule, 29 C.F.R. pt. 2520, 72 Fed. Reg. 64,709 (Nov. 16, 2007); Notice of Adoption of Revisions to Annual Return/Report Forms, 72 Fed. Reg. 64,731 (Nov. 16, 2007).

- Schedule of Funding Standard Account Bases;

- Summary of Plan Provisions;

- Statement of Actuarial Assumptions/Methods;

- Balances Subject to Binding Agreement with the PBGC;

- Description of Weighted Average Retirement Age;

- Alternative Seventeen-Year Funding Schedule for Airlines;

- Information on Use of Substitute Mortality Tables;

- Change in Actuarial Assumptions;

- Schedule of Active Participant Data;

- Change in Method;

- Schedule of Amortization Bases;

- Additional Information for Plans in At-Risk Status;

- Illustration Supporting Actuarial Certification Status;

- Actuarial Certification Status;

- Summary of Funding Improvement Plan;

- Summary of Rehabilitation Plan;

- Reorganization Status Explanation;

- Reorganization Status Worksheet;

- Justification for Change in Actuarial Assumptions;

- Schedule MB/SB in PDF Format; and

- Schedule MB and Schedule SB Statement by Enrolled Actuary.

If the plan does not have the software capable of slitting the files apart or cannot separate the files from the plan's actuary, the plan may create separate documents with a brief statement that the required attachment is included in the Actuary Statement file, and upload the document where the plan would otherwise upload the required attachment using the correct tag for that attachment.[1]

---

1. EFAST2 FAQs: Completing an Annual Return/Report (Form 5500 or Form 5500-SF), Attachments, Q 24b (Aug. 2010).

The Schedule SB and the Schedule MB instructions have been updated to reflect provisions of the Preservation of Access to Care for Medicare Beneficiaries and Pension Relief Act of 2010 (PRA 2010).[1]

Schedule C

Schedule C details the service provider and trustee information. It is used to report those service providers receiving, directly or indirectly, $5,000 or more in compensation for services provided to the plan during the plan year being reported. Schedule C also details information regarding service providers who have terminated (or were terminated from) services to the plan during the reporting year. Schedule C reports only the forty top-paid service providers. Terminated service provider reporting applies only to terminating accountants and enrolled actuaries. The Schedule C instructions have been updated to advise that in the case of a multiemployer or multiple-employer plan, where the "plan sponsor" would be the joint board of trustees for the plan, payments by contributing employers, directly or through an employer association, or by participating employee organizations, should be treated the same as payments by a plan sponsor.

The final regulations have expanded the compensation reporting obligations under Schedule C. The final Schedule C requires direct compensation paid by the plan to be reported on a separate line item from indirect compensation of various types from various sources other than the plan or the plan sponsor. This includes an expansion of the codes required to identify the types of services provided. It also requires expanded codes for the reporting of fees received by service providers (i.e., "float" revenue, securities brokerage commissions, and revenue sharing among affiliates and other "bundled service providers").

Schedule C will not require inclusion of compensation consisting of "ordinary business gifts" (i.e., meals, entertainment, and other gratuities) that are occasional and insubstantial — less than $50 in the case of a single gift from one source.

The Notice advises that the DOL is working on a regulation setting forth the standards applicable for the prohibited transaction exemption that permits a plan to make reasonable contractual arrangements with a party in interest for services.

Instructions for Schedule C are modified to clarify that welfare plans with one-hundred or more covered participants at the beginning of the plan year, that are exempt from filing Schedule H and an accountant's opinion because they rely on the trust non-enforcement policy of Technical Release 92-01, are also exempt from filing Schedule C to report service provider compensation paid by or received from the plan.[2]

The DOL has issued 40 frequently asked questions (FAQs) on Schedule C disclosures to be required for 2009 and later plans years. The DOL further issued twenty-five additional questions supplementing the 40 questions. This guidance is available at http://www.dol.gov/ebsa/faqs/faq-sch-C-supplement.html. As background, both pension and welfare plans required to file Form 5500 must include revised Schedule C to report compensation received

---

1. Instructions to 2011 Form 5500, http://www.dol.gov/ebsa/pdf/2011-5500inst.pdf.
2. Annual Reporting and Disclosure, Revision of Annual Information Return/Reports, Final Rule, 29 C.F.R. pt. 2520, 72 Fed. Reg. 64,709 (Nov. 16, 2007); Notice of Adoption of Revisions to Annual Return/Report Forms, 72 Fed. Reg. 64,731 (Nov. 16, 2007).

by service providers in connection with services to the plan.[1] However, if Technical Release 92-01 is satisfied, insured welfare plans and those receiving participant contributions through a cafeteria plan will not be required to file Schedule C (even if service providers are paid from those contributions, which are plan assets by definition). The end result is that Schedule C will not be required for a welfare plan unless it has a trust (or should have a trust because Technical Release 92-01 does not apply). Here is a sampling of the guidance.

According to FAQ-6, commissions paid to an agent in connection with the sale of an investment, product, or service to a plan constitute reportable indirect compensation because that term includes payment of "finder's fees" or other payments by a service provider to an independent agent or employee for a transaction or service involving the plan.

Pursuant to FAQs-11 and -12, "float" income is indirect compensation whether it is received on the account of a single plan or on an omnibus account involving multiple plans. Disclosures satisfying DOL Field Assistance Bulletin 2002-03 (regarding float disclosures in the prohibited transactions context) will generally be sufficient to allow float income to be reported as eligible indirect compensation under the alternative reporting option.

Fees that must be broken out and reported separately are discussed under FAQ-14. They detail that any person in the bundle receiving separate fees charged against a plan's investment (e.g., investment management fees, float revenue, and other asset-based fees, such as shareholder servicing fees, 12b-1 fees, and wrap fees if charged in addition to the investment management fee) must be treated as receiving separately reportable compensation; and compensation must be separately reported if (i) the compensation is received by any person in the bundle who is one of the service providers enumerated on Line 3 of Schedule C, and (ii) the compensation received is "commissions and other transaction based fees, finders' fees, float revenue, soft dollars and other non-monetary compensation." Examples of separate fees charged against a plan's investment for purposes of this exception are revenue-sharing payments for shareholder services, recordkeeping services, or compliance services that are paid by an investment provider to a third-party administrator (TPA) if they are charged against the plan's investment as a separate amount or pursuant to a separate formula. Thus, if the investment provider pays the TPA out of an overall investment management or shareholder services charge assessed against the plan's investment, the payment to the TPA by the investment manager out of its fees would not be a separate fee for this purpose.

FAQ-23 states that the spread earned by a broker on principal transactions involving the plan is not "eligible indirect compensation." Securities commissions for Schedule C purposes would include a markup, markdown, commission equivalent, or other fee paid by a managed account to a dealer for executing a transaction where the fee and transaction price are fully and separately disclosed on the confirmation and the transaction is reported under conditions that provide independent and objective verification of the transaction price subject to self-regulatory organization oversight. Fees paid for eligible riskless principal transactions that are reported under NASD Rule 4632, 4642, or 6420 would fall within this interpretation.

---

1. http://www.dol.gov/ebsa/faqs/faq_scheduleC.html.

FAQs-32 through -35 discuss the reporting rules regarding the receipt of gifts, meals, entertainment, and attendance at conferences and seminars.

Whenever the plan sponsor seeks reimbursement for fees paid a service provider, FAQ-37 states that the Schedule C should reflect a direct payment from the plan to the provider and not a payment to the employer.

Service providers who fail to provide necessary Schedule C information must be identified on the new Schedule C. FAQ-40 excuses the identification requirement if the plan administrator receives a statement from the service provider that (1) it made a good-faith effort to make any necessary recordkeeping and information system changes in a timely fashion, and (2) despite such efforts, was unable to complete the changes for the 2009 plan year.

Two new questions have been added by the DOL to its FAQs about Schedule C disclosures. The questions focus on how pharmacy benefit managers (PBMs) that provide services to ERISA plans are to report direct and indirect compensation for purposes of Schedule C reporting obligations.

Under FAQ-26, for Schedule C reporting purposes, payments provided to a PBM by a plan (or payments made to a PBM by a plan sponsor that are reimbursed by the plan) are reportable as direct compensation. This includes fees that are paid to a PBM acting as TPA for an ERISA plan prescription drug program, whether the fees are paid as administrative fees or as dispensing fees that are charged for each prescription and paid for with plan assets. In addition, payments provided for the provision of ancillary administrative services such as recordkeeping, data management and information reporting, and formulary management are also reportable as direct compensation.

According to FAQ-27, discounts and rebates generally do not need to be reported as indirect compensation for Schedule C purposes, even though they may be attributable to a PBM's business with ERISA plans. However, if a plan and the PBM agree that rebates or discounts are to be used to compensate the PBM for services rendered to the plan, then that revenue would be reportable indirect compensation on Schedule C.[1]

Schedule D

Schedule D serves two purposes:

1. Part I provides a standardized reporting format for any Direct Filing Entity (DFE) (the primary plan reporting); and

2. Part II provides a standardized reporting form for plans participating in the primary plan reporting (including Master Trust Investment Accounts (MTIAs)).

Schedule F

Schedule F is required to be filed by cafeteria plans and educational assistance programs.

---

1. (DOL Supplemental FAQs About the 2009 Schedule C (Feb. 5, 2010), http://www.dol.gov/ebsa/faqs/faq-sch-C-supplement.html.)

Schedule G

Schedule G is required to be filed by all large plans (one-hundred or more participants) and DFEs and MTIAs. The financial schedules provided in Schedule G are designed to provide a uniform method for the reporting of investment and asset information, including loans and fixed-income obligations in default or determined to be uncollectible and non-exempt prohibited transactions (see Q 66 for details).

Schedule H

Schedule H contains required reporting of financial information for larger plans and DFEs. It reports financial details about the plan, including asset and liability information as well as income and expense information. The DOL has issued additional FAQs relevant to welfare and 401(k) plans that address permitted special characters and the handling of combined attachment files for Schedule H (large plan financial information). If an independent qualified public accountant (IQPA) report under Schedule H includes both the signed accountant's opinion and supporting financial statements in the same file, that file need not be separated into two documents. Instead, the entire IQPA report may be uploaded (using the "AO" attachment tag) as a single PDF file. If the combined file includes the Schedule of Assets or a Schedule of Reportable Transactions, they must be uploaded separately using the appropriate attachment tag. The DOL states that if the plan does not have separate files of these Schedules, this may be addressed either by resubmitting the combined file (which could create transmission problems due to the file size) or by filing brief statements referring the DOL back to the audit report attachment.[1]

Schedule I

Schedule I serves the same function as Schedule H; however, it is required filing for smaller plans. The new Schedule I closely resembles the simplified financial statements contained in the old Form 5500-R. The Schedule I instructions have been updated to advise that in the case of a plan with fewer than 100 participants at the beginning of the plan year, any amount deposited with such plan not later than the seventh business day following the day on which such amount is received by the employer (in the case of amounts that a participant or beneficiary pays to an employer), or the seventh business day following the day on which such amount would otherwise have been payable to the participant in cash (in the case of amounts withheld by an employer from a participant's wages), shall be deemed to be contributed or repaid to such plan on the earliest date on which such contributions or participant loan repayments can reasonably be segregated from the employer's general assets.[2]

Schedule P

Schedule P is the Annual Return of Fiduciary of Employee Benefit Trust. It is filed by a trustee or custodian with either Form 5500 or 5500-EZ.

Schedule P was removed from Form 5500 filings beginning with the 2006 plan year in anticipation of the move to electronic filing.[3]

---

1. EFAST2 FAQs: Completing an Annual Return/Report (Form 5500 or Form 5500-SF), Attachments (Aug. 2010)).
2. See 29 C.F.R. §2510.3-102(a)(2) for further guidance. (Instructions to 2011 Form 5500, http://www.dol.gov/ebsa/pdf/2011-5500inst.pdf.)
3. IRS Ann. 2007-63, 2007-30 I.R.B. 65.

Schedule R

Schedule R is required for both tax-qualified and nonqualified pension benefit plans (large and small) that are required to file Form 5500 (except for Section 403(b) plans). Schedule R reports certain information about the plan's participants, asset distribution, and funding. It also requires the reporting of any plan amendments that have the effect of increasing the value of benefits in a defined benefit plan.

Form 8955-SSA

The IRS has eliminated Schedule SSA as a schedule of the Form 5500 Annual Return/ Report. In its place, the IRS has introduced Form 8955-SSA. Plan administrators must file this new form with the IRS and *not through the EFAST2 filing system.* Form 8955-SSA is a stand-alone reporting form that must be filed with the IRS. Generally, Form 8955-SSA must be filed by the last day of the seventh month following the last day of the plan year to which the Form applies (the same deadline and extension rules that apply to Form 5500.)[1] Form 5558 — Application for Extension of Time to File Certain Employee Plan Returns — can be used to extend the filing date.[2]

After the Form 8955-SSA and related instructions are available for filing, plan administrators should expect to have a reasonable amount of time to complete and file the form by the special due date.

The IRS advises that the information to be reported on the new form will be similar to the information previously required for Schedule SSA.[3]

Schedule T

Schedule T (Qualified Pension Plan Coverage Information) was removed from Form 5500 filings beginning with the 2005 plan year. The IRS notes that this change was not intended to affect the applicable required or optional nondiscrimination testing (including the testing options described in Revenue Procedure 93-42[4]).

65. What is the proper format and place for reporting delinquent participant contributions in the Annual Report Form 5500?

The DOL has stated that amounts paid by a plan participant or beneficiary or withheld by an employer from a participant's wages for contribution to a plan are plan assets on the earliest date that they can reasonably be segregated from the employer's general assets, but in no event later than:

1.   For pension plans, the fiftieth business day of the month following the month in which the participant contributions are withheld or received by the employer; and

---

1. IRS Ann. 2011-21, 2011-12 I.R.B. 567.
2. IRS Ann. 2011-21, 2011-12 I.R.B. 567.
3. http://www.irs.gov/retirement/article/0,,id=117588,00.html.
4. 1993-2 C.B. 540.

2.   For welfare plans, ninety days from the date on which such amounts are withheld or received by the employer.[1] (See Q 587 for further details on participant contributions as plan assets.)

Plan administrators are required to report in their annual Form 5500 schedules delinquent participant contributions[2] on the financial schedules (Schedule H for large plans and Schedule I for small plans).

When an employer is delinquent in forwarding participant contributions and holds them commingled with its general assets, the DOL states that the employer will have engaged in a prohibited transaction under ERISA Section 406. Plans filing Schedule H that report nonexempt prohibited transactions on Line 4d also are required to file a Schedule G to report detailed information regarding the nonexempt prohibited transactions.

The Form 5500 instructions state that delinquent participant contributions reported on Line 4a should be treated as part of the supplemental schedules for purposes of reporting on the plan's financial statements by the independent qualified public accountant (IQPA). The instructions also advise that if the information contained on Line 4a is not presented in accordance with the DOL's regulatory requirements, the IQPA report must make the appropriate disclosures in accordance with generally accepted accounting standards (a summary paragraph detailing the matter and indicating whether it results in the IQPA's issuing a "qualified" report).[3]

For delinquent contributions that are corrected in a subsequent plan year, the information reported in the 5500 Schedule H or I for the year of the initial delinquency will be carried over into subsequent year reporting until corrected.

In Advisory Opinion 2002-02A, the Department stated that participant loan repayments paid to or withheld by an employer for purposes of transmittal to a plan are sufficiently similar to participant contributions to justify, in the absence of regulations providing otherwise, the application of principles similar to those underlying the participant contribution regulations. Delinquent forwarding of participant loan repayments is eligible for correction under the Voluntary Fiduciary Correction Program (VFC Program) and PTE 2002-51 (see Q 412 for details regarding the correction of delinquent contribution violations through the VFC Program). Accordingly, the DOL advises that it will not reject a Form 5500 report based solely on the fact that delinquent forwarding of participant loan repayments is included on Line 4a of the Schedule H or Schedule I.[4]

66. What are the required contents of the financial statements filed with Form 5500?

Schedule G to the Annual Report Form 5500 is used for the reporting of financial statements. Schedule G is used to report the following:

---

1. Labor Reg. §2510.3-102.
2. As defined in Labor Reg. §2510.3-102, above.
3. See *AICPA Audit and Accounting Guide for Audits of Employee Benefit Plans* paras. 13.09-13.19.
4. Source: http://www.dol.gov/ebsa/faqs/faq_compliance_5500.html.

1.   A statement of assets and liabilities;

2.   A statement of changes in the fund balance;

3.   A statement of changes in financial position; and

4.   A statement of changes in net assets available for plan benefits.

The financial statement with respect to an employee welfare benefit plan provides a statement of assets and liabilities, changes in the fund balance, and changes in the financial position of the plan. In the notes to the financial statements, disclosures concerning the following items must be considered by the accountant:

1.   A description of the plan, including any significant changes in the plan made during the period and the impact of such changes on benefits;

2.   A description of material lease commitments, other commitments, and contingent liabilities;

3.   A description of agreements and transactions with people known to be parties in interest;

4.   A general description of priorities upon termination of the plan;

5.   Information concerning whether or not a tax ruling or determination letter has been obtained; and

6.   Any other matters necessary to fully and fairly present the financial statements of the plan.[1]

The financial statement with respect to an employee retirement benefit plan will contain a statement of assets and liabilities and a statement of changes in net assets available for plan benefits that must include details of revenues and expenses and other charges aggregated by general source and application. In the notes to financial statements, disclosures concerning the following items must be considered by the accountant:

1.   A description of the plan, including any significant changes in the plan made during the period and the impact of those changes on benefits;

2.   The funding policy (including the policy with respect to prior service cost), and any changes with respect to those policies during the year;

3.   A description of any significant changes in plan benefits made during the period;

4.   A description of material lease commitments, other commitments, and contingent liabilities;

5.   A description of agreements and transactions with people known to be parties in interest;

---

1. ERISA Sec. 103(b)(1).

6.　　A general description of priorities upon termination of the plan;

7.　　Information concerning whether or not a tax ruling or determination letter has been obtained; and

8.　　Any other matters necessary to fully and fairly present the financial statements of the retirement benefits plan.[1]

All employee benefit plans must have attached the following information in separate schedules:

1.　　A statement of the assets and liabilities of the plan aggregated by categories and valued at their current value, and the same data displayed in comparative form for the end of the previous fiscal year of the plan;

2.　　A statement of receipts and disbursements during the preceding twelve-month period aggregated by general sources and applications;

3.　　A schedule of all assets held for investment purposes aggregated and identified by issuer, borrower, lessor, or similar party to the transaction (including a notation as to whether the party is known to be a party in interest), maturity date, rate of interest, collateral, par or maturity value, cost, and current value;

4.　　A schedule of each transaction involving a person known to be a party in interest and each nonexempt transaction in which the person is involved;

5.　　A list of all leases that were in default or were classified as uncollectible;

6.　　A list of all loans or fixed income obligations that were in default as of the close of the plan year;

7.　　If some or all of the assets of a plan or plans are held in a common or collective investment trust maintained by a bank or similar institution or in a separate account maintained by an insurance carrier or a separate trust maintained by a bank as trustee, the report must include the most recent annual statement of assets and liabilities of the common or collective trust; and

8.　　A schedule of each reportable transaction (see Q 67 for details on reportable events).[2]

67. What is a reportable transaction for purposes of filing Form 5500?

A reportable transaction required to be detailed in Form 5500 for a reporting year is a transaction, or series of transactions, with or in conjunction with the same person that, when aggregated, regardless of the category of the asset and the gain or loss on any transaction, involves an amount in excess of 5 percent of the current value of plan assets.[3]

The schedule of reportable transactions will apply to any series of transactions (other than transactions with respect to securities) within the plan year or with or in conjunction with the

---

1. ERISA Sec. 103(b)(2).
2. ERISA Sec. 103(b)(3).
3. Labor Reg. §2520.103-6(c).

same person that, when aggregated (regardless of the category of asset and the gain or loss on any transaction), involves an amount in excess of 5 percent of the current value of plan assets. It also includes any transaction within the plan year involving securities of the same issue if within the plan year any series of transactions with respect to the securities, when aggregated, involves an amount in excess of 5 percent of the current value of plan assets.[1]

Plans whose assets are held in whole or in part in a common or collective trust or a pooled separate account (as provided under Labor Regulation Section 2520.203-3 and Labor Regulation Section 2520.103-4 and that satisfy the requirements of those sections) are not required to prepare schedules of reportable transactions with respect to the individual transactions of the common or collective trust or pooled separate account.[2]

The schedule of reportable transactions requires the following information as to each transaction or series of transactions:

1. The name of each party, except that in the case of a transaction or series of transactions involving a purchase or sale of a security on the market, the schedule need not include the person from whom it was purchased or to whom it was sold (a purchase or sale on the market is a purchase or sale of a security through a registered broker-dealer acting as a broker under the Securities Exchange Act of 1934);

2. A brief description of each asset;

3. The purchase or selling price in the case of a purchase or sale, the rental cost in the case of a lease, and the amount of principal, interest rate, payment schedule (e.g., fully amortized, partly amortized with balloon), and maturity date in the case of a loan;

4. Expenses incurred, including, but not limited to, any fees or commissions;

5. The cost of any asset;

6. The current value of any asset acquired or disposed of at the time of acquisition or disposition; and

7. The net gain or loss.[3]

The term "current value" is defined as the fair market value where available, and otherwise the fair value as determined in good faith by a trustee or a named fiduciary pursuant to the terms of the plan and in accordance with the ERISA's regulations, assuming an orderly liquidation at the time of the determination.[4]

There is an exemption from the 5 percent reportable transaction requirements for any plan assets held in common or collective trusts maintained by a bank, trust company, or similar

---

1. Labor Reg. §2520.103-6(c).
2. Labor Reg. §2520.103-6(c)(3).
3. Labor Reg. §2520.103-6(d)(1).
4. ERISA Sec. 3(26).

institution, or assets held in an insurance company pooled separate account. The plan is not required to include in the annual report any information concerning the individual transaction of the common or collective trust or pooled separate account.[1]

68. What actuarial information is required to be provided in Schedule SB or Schedule MB of Form 5500?

Schedule SB (single-employer) or Schedule MB (multiemployer) of Form 5500 is required to be filed on an annual basis by a defined benefit plan that is subject to the minimum funding standards of ERISA. The completed Schedule B must be signed by an enrolled actuary and based upon an actuarial valuation of the plan. The information reported on Schedule B includes:

1. A description of the funding method and actuarial assumptions used to determine the plan costs;

2. A certification of the contribution necessary to fully fund the plan;

3. A statement that the report is complete and accurate and that the actuarial assumptions are reasonable and represent the actuary's best estimate of anticipated experience under the plan; and

4. Any other information necessary to fully and fairly disclose the actuarial position of the plan.

69. What is the due date for filing Form 5500?

Form 5500 is required to be filed (with its accompanying schedules) on or before the last day of the seventh month following the close of the plan year. For plans operating on a calendar year basis, that date is July 31. Form 5500 is filed with the DOL. A plan being absorbed in a merger has a short plan year ending on the date of the merger, for which the accountant's report is required to be filed with Annual Report Form 5500.[2]

Where the plan requires an extension of time beyond the filing date, the plan sponsor may receive an automatic extension if the plan year is the same as the plan sponsor's tax year, and the plan sponsor has been granted an extension to file its federal income tax return. In order to receive the automatic extension, a copy of the extension to file the federal income tax return must be attached to Form 5500 when it is filed.

An extension for filing may also be requested by filing Form 5558 prior to the initial due date for filing. This form requires a detailed statement that explains why the extension is necessary. If granted, the extension may be for up to two and one-half months beyond the original filing deadline. If refused, the plan will receive a ten-day grace period beyond the original filing deadline in order to timely file the annual report.

---

1. Labor Regs. §§2520.103-3, 2520.103-4.
2. *PWBA v. USAirways, Inc.*, 24 EBC 2604 (Office of Admin. Law Judges 2000).

Practitioner's Pointer: The extension of time for filing Form 5500 that has been granted through an automatic extension or through a Form 5558 filing does not provide the employer with an extension of time for the filing of PBGC Form 1. Forms 5558 that are filed by the initial due date are automatically approved.

---

70. What is the Delinquent Filer Voluntary Compliance Program (DFVCP or DFVC Program)?

The Delinquent Filer Voluntary Compliance Program (DFVCP, DFVC Program) was adopted by the Department of Labor's Employee Benefits Security Administration (formerly the Pension and Welfare Benefits Administration)[1] in an effort to encourage delinquent filers to voluntarily comply with the annual reporting requirements under Title I of ERISA. As adopted, the DFVCP permitted eligible plan administrators the opportunity to avoid the assessment of civil penalties otherwise applicable to administrators who failed to file timely annual reports (commonly referred to as the Form 5500) by voluntarily complying with the filing requirements under Title I of ERISA and paying reduced civil penalties specified in the DFVCP.

In early 2013, the DOL updated the DFVCP to reflect the mandatory electronic filing requirement for the Form 5500 under EFAST 2. The updated DFVCP replaces the program adopted on April 27, 1995, and updated on March 28, 2002, and became effective on January 29, 2013. The updated program maintains the penalty structure that was announced in the 2002 update.[2]

In an effort to further encourage and facilitate voluntary compliance by plan administrators with the annual reporting requirements of Title I of ERISA, the DOL updated the DFVCP by simplifying the procedures governing participation and lowering the civil penalty assessments thereunder.

According to DOL guidance, the penalty structure under the DFVCP is as follows:

- Reduced per-day penalty: The basic penalty under the program was reduced from $50 to $10 per day for delinquent filings.

- Reduced per-filing cap: The maximum penalty for a single late annual report was reduced from $2,000 to $750 for a small plan (generally a plan with fewer than 100 participants at the beginning of the plan year) and from $5,000 to $2,000 for a large plan.

- "Per plan" cap: The DFVCP's "per plan" cap is designed to encourage reporting compliance by plan administrators who have failed to file an annual report for a plan for multiple years. The "per plan" cap limits the penalty to $1,500 for a small plan

---

1. 60 Fed. Reg. 20,874.
2. Delinquent Filer Voluntary Compliance Program, 78 Fed Reg. 6135 (January 29, 2013): http://www.gpo.gov/fdsys/pkg/FR-2013-01-29/pdf/2013-01616.pdf.

and $4,000 for a large plan regardless of the number of late annual reports filed for the plan at the same time. There is no "per administrator" or "per sponsor" cap. If the same person is the administrator or sponsor of several plans required to file annual reports under Title I of ERISA, the maximum applicable penalty amounts would apply for each plan.

- Small plans sponsored by certain tax-exempt organizations: A special "per plan" cap of $750 applies to a small plan sponsored by an organization that is tax-exempt under Internal Revenue Code Section 501(c)(3). The $750 limitation applies regardless of the number of late annual reports filed for the plan at the same time. It is not available, however, if as of the date the plan files under the DFVCP, there is a delinquent annual report for a plan year during which the plan was a large plan.

- Top hat plans and apprenticeship and training plans: The penalty amount for "top hat" plans and apprenticeship and training plans was reduced to $750.

Questions about the DFVCP should be directed to EBSA by calling (202) 693.8360 or accessing its Web site at *http://www.dol.gov/ebsa*.

71. Who is eligible to participate in the DFVCP?

The DOL has stated that:

Plan administrators are eligible to pay reduced civil penalties under the program if the required filings under the DFVCP are made prior to the date on which the administrator is notified in writing by the department of a failure to file a timely annual report under Title I of the Employee Retirement Security Act of 1974 (ERISA). DFVCP is not available to plans that are not covered by Title I of ERISA. DFVCP relief is available only if the plan is required to file an annual report under Title I of ERISA. If a Form 5500-EZ is filed late, the plan administrator may request relief from the IRS for any applicable tax code penalties.

Participation under the DFVCP is not available to all Form 5500 series filers. The relief under the DFVCP is available only to the extent that a Form 5500 is required to be filed under Title I of ERISA. For example, Form 5500-EZ filers and Form 5500 filers for plans without employees[1] are not eligible to participate in the DFVCP because such plans are not subject to Title I of ERISA. Plan administrators may call (202) 693-8360 if they have questions about whether the program applies to their filings.[2]

NOTE: Form 8955-SSA. DFVCP does not apply to late filings of IRS Form 8955-SSA. Late filings should be sent to the IRS. A reasonable cause penalty waiver may be requested with that late filing.

---

1. As described in 29 CFR §2510.3-3(b) and (c)).
2. DOL Procedure: PWBA's Delinquent Filer Voluntary Compliance Program, Office of Chief Accountant Frequently Asked Questions, Delinquent Filer Voluntary Compliance Program, http://www.dol.gov/ebsa/faqs/faq_dfvc.html.

72. What civil penalties may be assessed by the DOL against plan administrators who fail to file a timely annual report and do not participate in the DFVCP?

The DOL has the authority, under ERISA Section 502(c)(2), to assess civil penalties of up to $1,100 a day against plan administrators who fail or refuse to file complete and timely annual reports (Form 5500 Series Annual Return/Reports) as required under ERISA Section 101(b)(4) and the DOL regulations.[1] Pursuant to the regulations, EBSA has maintained a program for the assessment of civil penalties for noncompliance with the annual reporting requirements.[2] Under this program, plan administrators filing annual reports after the date on which a report was required to be filed may be assessed $50 per day for each day an annual report is filed after the date on which the annual report or reports were required to be filed, without regard to any extensions for filing. Plan administrators who fail to file an annual report may be assessed a penalty of $300 per day, up to $30,000 per year, until a complete annual report is filed. Penalties are applicable to each annual report required to be filed under Title I of ERISA. The DOL may, in its discretion, waive all or part of a civil penalty assessed under ERISA Section 502(c)(2) upon a showing by the administrator that there was reasonable cause for the failure to file a complete and timely annual report.

The DOL states that "the following penalties may be assessed by the DOL against plan administrators:

- *Late filers.* Plan administrators filing a late annual report (i.e., after the date the report was required to be filed, including extensions) may be assessed $50 per day, with no limit, for the period they failed to file, determined without regard to any extensions for filing.

- *Non-filers.* Plan administrators who fail to file an annual report may be assessed a penalty of $300 per day, up to $30,000 per year, until a complete annual report is filed.

For example, assume an administrator for a plan with a calendar plan year files the annual report for the 2009 plan year on October 31, 2010, and does not participate in the DFVCP. The administrator would receive a written notice indicating the department's intent to assess a penalty of $4,600 ($50 × 92 days delinquent). If there are other annual reports that either have not been filed or have been filed late, the plan administrator may be subject to the assessment of additional penalties because the penalties are separately calculated for each filing.

Pursuant to the department's regulations, upon issuance by the department of a notice of intent to assess a penalty, the plan administrator may file a statement of reasonable cause why the penalty, as calculated, should not be assessed. A showing of reasonable cause must

---

1. See 29 C.F.R. pt. 2520; Labor Reg. §2570.502c-2, *redesignated* as Labor Reg. §2575.502-2; 64 Fed. Reg. 2246 (Aug. 3, 1999).
2. See Labor Reg. §§2560.502c-2, 2570.60 et seq.

be in the form of a written statement setting forth all the facts alleged as reasonable cause and must contain a declaration by the administrator that the statement is made under penalty of perjury."[1]

73. How does a plan administrator file a delinquent Form 5500 under the DFVCP?

Under the 2013 updates to the DFVC Program, all delinquent filings are made through EFAST2, even for pre-2009 plan years when a different filing system was in effect and electronic filing was not mandatory.[2]

For a delinquent return relating to a pre-2009 plan year, there are special procedures that apply for filing delinquent returns/reports relating to such years. The applicant must submit the filing using the current filing year Form 5500, schedules, and instructions. The electronic filing on the current filing year Form 5500, however, must indicate, in the appropriate space at the beginning of the Form 5500, the plan year for which the annual return/report is being filed.[3]

If any of the schedules listed below were required with a pre-2009 plan year being filed late, the correct-year schedule (that is, the schedule as it existed for the plan year for which the delinquent filing relates) must be completed in accordance with the related correct-year instructions:

- Schedule B, SB, or MB (Actuarial Information),

- Schedule E (ESOP Annual Information),

- Schedule P (Annual Return of Fiduciary of Employee Benefit Trust),

- Schedule R (Retirement Plan Information) and

- Schedule T (Qualified Pension Plan Coverage Information).[4]

The correct-year Schedule C may (but is not required to) be filed in lieu of the current filing year Schedule C. Any pre-2009 schedules used for the delinquent or amended filing must be completed in blue or black ink and attached as a PDF image and tagged as "other attachments." To obtain correct-year schedules and related instructions, go to http://www. dol.gov/ebsa/5500main.html and print the schedules and instructions of the form year that corresponds to the plan year being filed.[5]

---

1. DOL Procedure: PWBA's Delinquent Filer Voluntary Compliance Program, Office of Chief Accountant Frequently Asked Questions, Delinquent Filer Voluntary Compliance Program, http://www.dol.gov/ebsa/faqs/faq_dfvc.html.
2. Delinquent Filer Voluntary Compliance Program, 78 Fed Reg. 6135 (January 29, 2013): http://www.gpo.gov/fdsys/pkg/FR-2013-01-29/pdf/2013-01616.pdf.
3. Delinquent Filer Voluntary Compliance Program, section 3.02, 78 Fed Reg. 6135 (January 29, 2013): http://www.gpo.gov/fdsys/pkg/FR-2013-01-29/pdf/2013-01616.pdf.
4. Delinquent Filer Voluntary Compliance Program, 78 Fed Reg. 6135 (January 29, 2013): http://www.gpo.gov/fdsys/pkg/FR-2013-01-29/pdf/2013-01616.pdf.
5. Delinquent Filer Voluntary Compliance Program, 78 Fed Reg. 6135 (January 29, 2013): http://www.gpo.gov/fdsys/pkg/FR-2013-01-29/pdf/2013-01616.pdf.

For a 403(b) plan making a delinquent pre-2009 filing, use the current year Form 5500 but complete only Part I, and lines 1-4 and 8 of Part II.[1]

There are two steps to obtaining penalty relief under the DFVCP. One is to file the late returns through EFAST2, and the other is to pay the DFVC applicable penalty amount. Payment is made separately from the EFAST2 delinquent filing.

For electronic payments, the DOL provides an online calculator tool for determining the penalty under the DFVC Program.[2] Once the penalty is calculated with the online tool, there is a link to continue to an online payment center for electronic payment. If electronic payment is used, there are no additional filing requirements other than the delinquent filing through DFVC, as described above.[3]

Instead of making an electronic payment, the plan administrator may send the penalty payment by check to:

DFVC DOL
P.O. Box 71361
Philadelphia, PA 19176-1361.

If the check payment method is used, a paper copy of the Form 5500 or 5500-SF (without schedules or attachments), must be included with the check. NOTE: the EFAST2 delinquent filing described above is still required.[4]

It is recommended that all filings for a plan be submitted to the DFVCP in the same envelope or package in order to ensure that those filings count toward the "per plan" capped penalty amount." See Q 75, Q 76.[5]

If a joint employer-union board of trustees or committee is the administrator, at least one employer representative and one union representative must sign the form.

74. Which version of the Form 5500 should be filed?

According to guidance published by the DOL, the plan administrator must file either:

- The most current Form 5500 Annual Return/Report form issued (and, if necessary, indicate in the appropriate space on the first page of the Form 5500 the plan year for which the annual return/report is being filed), or

---

1. Delinquent Filer Voluntary Compliance Program, 78 Fed Reg. 6135 (January 29, 2013): http://www.gpo.gov/fdsys/pkg/FR-2013-01-29/pdf/2013-01616.pdf.
2. See http://www.dol.gov/ebsa/calculator/dfvcpmain.html.
3. Delinquent Filer Voluntary Compliance Program section 3.03(a); 78 Fed Reg. 6135 (January 29, 2013): http://www.gpo.gov/fdsys/pkg/FR-2013-01-29/pdf/2013-01616.pdf.
4. Delinquent Filer Voluntary Compliance Program section 3.03(a); 78 Fed Reg. 6135 (January 29, 2013): http://www.gpo.gov/fdsys/pkg/FR-2013-01-29/pdf/2013-01616.pdf."
5. DOL Procedure: PWBA's Delinquent Filer Voluntary Compliance Program, Office of Chief Accountant Frequently Asked Questions, Delinquent Filer Voluntary Compliance Program, http://www.dol.gov/ebsa/faqs/faq_dfvc.html.

- The Form 5500 Series Annual Return/Report form issued for the plan year for which the relief is sought.[1]

If an amended or delinquent filing is being made with respect to a pre-2009 plan year, either Form 5500 or Form 5500-EZ, whichever is applicable, must be used. Form 5500-SF, which first became available for the 2009 plan year, is not available for a pre-2009 delinquent filing under the DFVCP, even if the plan would have qualified for Form 5500-SF had that form been in effect for such year. If the current Form 5500 is being filed for a pre-2009 year, the procedures described above should be used. If Form 5500-EZ is being filed for a pre-2009 year, the correct prior year paper version must be used and filed with the IRS. Note that the DFVC procedures are not applicable to late Form 5500-EZ filers.[2]

For Plan Years beginning on or after January 1, 2009, the filing is made under EFAST2 either using the forms and schedules relating to the plan year being filed or the current year forms.[3] The form may be the Form 5500 or the Form 5500-SF, whichever would have applied to that delinquent year. The Form 5500 Version Selection Tool (http://www.dol.gov/ebsa/5500selectorinstructions.html) is used to determine which version of the Form 5500 and which schedules should be used for an amended or delinquent filing. If applicable, there are boxes to check if the filing is an amended return (a late return requires no box to be checked), or if the filing will be for a 403(b) plan or for a Direct Filing Entity (DFE).

For a delinquent filing for a post-2008 plan year that *is more than three years late*, use the latest available Form 5500 (or 5500-SF, if applicable), and the current year schedules that apply, except that the Schedule SB or MB, if applicable, from the delinquent plan year must be used, attached as a PDF image (Other Attachment) in lieu of the current year schedule.[4]

75. What is the applicable penalty amount under the DFVCP?

With the 2013 restructuring of the DFVC Program, the following penalty structure applies for a late filing made through DFVC. NOTE: The DOL online calculator[5] automatically computes the penalty based on this rate structure.

The basic late filing penalty under the DFVCP is $10 per day (reduced in 2002 from $50 per day under the original 1995 procedure). The "per day" penalty runs from the date the annual report was due, determined without regard to extensions. If a Form 5558 was filed to extend the return, but the filing is not completed by the extended deadline, the penalty is calculated from the original deadline. This basic penalty applies regardless of the size of the plan.[6]

1. DOL Procedure: PWBA's Delinquent Filer Voluntary Compliance Program, Office of Chief Accountant Frequently Asked Questions, Delinquent Filer Voluntary Compliance Program, http://www.dol.gov/ebsa/faqs/faq_dfvc.html.
2. Delinquent Filer Voluntary Compliance Program, 78 Fed Reg. 6135 (January 29, 2013): http://www.gpo.gov/fdsys/pkg/FR-2013-01-29/pdf/2013-01616.pdf.
3. Delinquent Filer Voluntary Compliance Program, Section 3.02(1); 78 Fed Reg. 6135 (January 29, 2013): http://www.gpo.gov/fdsys/pkg/FR-2013-01-29/pdf/2013-01616.pdf.
4. Delinquent Filer Voluntary Compliance Program, 78 Fed Reg. 6135 (January 29, 2013): http://www.gpo.gov/fdsys/pkg/FR-2013-01-29/pdf/2013-01616.pdf.
5. (See http://www.dol.gov/ebsa/calculator/dfvcpmain.html).
6. Delinquent Filer Voluntary Compliance Program, 78 Fed Reg. 6135 (January 29, 2013): http://www.gpo.gov/fdsys/pkg/FR-2013-01-29/pdf/2013-01616.pdf.

For small plan filers (a plan with fewer than 100 participants at the beginning of the plan year) or a plan that is treated as a small plan filer under the "80-to-120" participant rule in DOL Reg. Sec. 2520.103-1(d)), the maximum penalty for a delinquent filing is $750.[1]

For large plan filers (a plan with 100 or more participants at the beginning of the plan year) or a plan that is treated as a large plan filer under the "80-to-120" participant rule in DOL Reg. Sec. 2520.103-1(d)), the maximum penalty for a delinquent filing is $2,000. This is a substantial relief over the original penalties and reflects the DOL's attitude of encouraging compliance for late filers.[2]

For multiple plan year submissions there is a per-plan cap which provides a maximum penalty for plans that have failed to file for multiple years and seek DFVC relief with respect to those multiple years. The per-plan cap is $1,500 for small plan filers and $4,000 for large plan filers.[3] The only time a multiple-plan-year DFVC filing will have a lower fee is if only two plan years are involved and, for the more recent plan year, the maximum per-return cap has not been reached for that plan year.[4]

A plan also might be subject to penalties under the tax code for late Form 5500 filings. Under the 2002 updates, the IRS announced that it would waive the tax code penalties for a late filing if the plan administrator has obtained relief under the DFVC Program.[5] As of the date of publication of the 2014 edition of this text, it is anticipated that the IRS will announce the continuation of that penalty waiver for filings made under the 2013 update of the DFVC Program.[6]

76. A plan administrator for a plan is delinquent on Form 5500 filings for multiple years. If during that period, the plan's classification has shifted between being a "large" and "small plan," which penalty cap applies to the plan's DFVC Program submission?

DOL guidance explains that:

If, during the years of non-filing, there is at least one year where the plan is a large plan, for purposes of the DFVCP the plan must use the large plan penalty amounts of $10 per day up to a maximum of $2,000 per filing, not to exceed $4,000 per plan.[7]

---

1. Delinquent Filer Voluntary Compliance Program, 78 Fed Reg. 6135 (January 29, 2013): http://www.gpo.gov/fdsys/pkg/FR-2013-01-29/pdf/2013-01616.pdf.

2. Delinquent Filer Voluntary Compliance Program, 78 Fed Reg. 6135 (January 29, 2013): http://www.gpo.gov/fdsys/pkg/FR-2013-01-29/pdf/2013-01616.pdf.

3. Delinquent Filer Voluntary Compliance Program, 78 Fed Reg. 6135 (January 29, 2013): http://www.gpo.gov/fdsys/pkg/FR-2013-01-29/pdf/2013-01616.pdf.

4. Delinquent Filer Voluntary Compliance Program, 78 Fed Reg. 6135 (January 29, 2013): http://www.gpo.gov/fdsys/pkg/FR-2013-01-29/pdf/2013-01616.pdf.

5. (IRS Notice 2002-23).

6. Delinquent Filer Voluntary Compliance Program, section 5.02; 78 Fed Reg. 6135 (January 29, 2013): http://www.gpo.gov/fdsys/pkg/FR-2013-01-29/pdf/2013-01616.pdf.

7. DOL Procedure: PWBA's Delinquent Filer Voluntary Compliance Program, Office of Chief Accountant Frequently Asked Questions, Delinquent Filer Voluntary Compliance Program, http://www.dol.gov/ebsa/faqs/faq_dfvc.html.

77. Is there a different "per plan" penalty cap that applies to administrators of small plans sponsored by IRC Section 501(c)(3) organizations (including IRC Section 403(b) small plans)?

Guidance from the DOL states that:

Yes. In the case of a small plan sponsored by a Code section 501(c)(3) organization (including a Code section 403(b) small plan), the applicable penalty amount is $10 per day for each day the annual report is filed after the date on which the annual report was due (without regard to any extensions), not to exceed $750 regardless of the number of delinquent annual reports for the plan submitted as part of the same DFVCP submission.

This "per-plan" penalty cap, however, will not be available if, as of the date the plan files under the DFVCP, there is a delinquent or late annual report due for a plan year during which the plan was a large plan. (See Q 75, Q 76.)

Small plan filings that are eligible for this special "per-plan" penalty cap must bear the notation "501(c)(3) Plan" in the upper-right corner of the first page of the Form 5500 that is submitted to the DFVCP in Charlotte, North Carolina. This notation should not be included in the filing made with EBSA in Lawrence, Kansas.[1]

Under the 2013 updates to the DFVC Program, the per-plan cap for a small plan filer applies only if the plan is a small plan filer for all plan years involved in the DFVC submission.[2]

78. Are extensions considered when calculating penalties under the DFVC Program?

The DOL states:

No. All penalties under the DFVCP are calculated at $10 per day, beginning on the day after the date the filing was due, without regard to any extensions.[3]

79. Does a plan administrator waive any rights upon filing under the DFVCP?

The DOL has answered this question as follows:

Yes. Payment of the penalty amount under the terms of the DFVCP constitutes, with regard to the filings submitted under the Program, a waiver of the right both to receive notice

---

1. DOL Procedure: PWBA's Delinquent Filer Voluntary Compliance Program, Office of Chief Accountant Frequently Asked Questions, Delinquent Filer Voluntary Compliance Program, http://www.dol.gov/ebsa/faqs/faq_dfvc.html.
2. Delinquent Filer Voluntary Compliance Program, section 3.03(b)(3); 78 Fed Reg. 6135 (January 29, 2013): http://www.gpo.gov/fdsys/pkg/FR-2013-01-29/pdf/2013-01616.pdf.
3. DOL Procedure: PWBA's Delinquent Filer Voluntary Compliance Program, Office of Chief Accountant Frequently Asked Questions, Delinquent Filer Voluntary Compliance Program, http://www.dol.gov/ebsa/faqs/faq_dfvc.html.

of the assessment from the department and to contest the department's assessment of the DFVCP penalty amount.[1]

80. If a filing has been made under the DFVCP, will the plan administrator be liable for any other Department of Labor annual reporting civil penalties?

The DOL answers this question as follows:

Annual reports that are filed under the DFVCP are subject to the usual edit checks. Plan administrators will have an opportunity to correct deficiencies in accordance with the procedures described in 29 CFR §2560.502c-2. The failure to correct deficiencies in accordance with these procedures may result in the assessment of further deficient filer penalties.[2]

81. Can plan assets be used to pay the civil penalties assessed under ERISA Section 502(c)(2)?

Guidance on this question from the DOL says:

No. The plan administrator is personally liable for the payment of civil penalties assessed under ERISA Section 502(c)(2). Therefore, civil penalties, including penalties paid under the DFVC Program, may not be paid from the assets of an employee benefit plan.[3]

See Sections 3.04 and 4.04 of the DFVC Program for details. The DOL states that payment of the penalty with plan assets would constitute a prohibited transaction and also would violate the exclusive benefit rule.[4]

82. May an administrator of an apprenticeship and training plan, as described in 29 C.F.R. §2520.104-22, or an administrator of a "top hat" plan, as described in 29 C.F.R. §2520.104-23, participate in the DFVC Program?

Yes. Administrators of apprenticeship and training plans and administrators of pension plans for a select group of management or highly compensated employees ("top hat plans"), may file the applicable notice and statement described in regulation Sections 2520.104-22 and 2520.104-23, respectively, under the DFVCP in lieu of filing any past due annual reports. By properly filing these statements and meeting the other applicable DFVC Program requirements (see Q 83, Q 85), administrators will be considered as having elected compliance with the exemption and/or alternative method of compliance prescribed in Sections 2520.104-22 or 2520.104-23, as appropriate, for all subsequent plan years.[5]

1. DOL Procedure: PWBA's Delinquent Filer Voluntary Compliance Program, Office of Chief Accountant Frequently Asked Questions, Delinquent Filer Voluntary Compliance Program, http://www.dol.gov/ebsa/faqs/faq_dfvc.html.

2. DOL Procedure: PWBA's Delinquent Filer Voluntary Compliance Program, Office of Chief Accountant Frequently Asked Questions, Delinquent Filer Voluntary Compliance Program, http://www.dol.gov/ebsa/faqs/faq_dfvc.html.

3. DOL Procedure: PWBA's Delinquent Filer Voluntary Compliance Program, Office of Chief Accountant Frequently Asked Questions, Delinquent Filer Voluntary Compliance Program, http://www.dol.gov/ebsa/faqs/faq_dfvc.html.

4. Delinquent Filer Voluntary Compliance Program, 78 Fed Reg. 6135 (January 29, 2013): http://www.gpo.gov/fdsys/pkg/FR-2013-01-29/pdf/2013-01616.pdf.

5. *See* DOL Procedure: PWBA's Delinquent Filer Voluntary Compliance Program, Office of Chief Accountant Frequently Asked Questions, Delinquent Filer Voluntary Compliance Program, http://www.dol.gov/ebsa/faqs/faq_dfvc.html.

Under the 2013 updates, penalty relief is available for apprenticeship and training plans and for "top hat" plans. These plans are not subject to Form 5500 filing requirements if the employer timely files with the EBSA notice described in DOL Reg. Sec. 2520.104-22 (apprenticeship and training plans) or the statement described in DOL Reg. Sec. 2520.104-23 (top hat plans). Under the DFVC Program, the employer can file the applicable notice or statement in lieu of filing any past due annual reports. These procedures are set forth in section 4 of the DFVCP. The apprenticeship and training plan notice must be sent to the DOL in accordance with the instructions in DOL Reg. Sec. 2520.104-22 or in DOL Reg. Sec. 2520.104-22, as appropriate.[1]

83. How does an administrator of an apprenticeship and training plan participate in the DFVCP?

In this situation, guidance from the DOL states:

[T]he plan administrator must prepare the statement described in … 29 CFR Section 2520.104-22 and file it at the following address:

> U.S. Department of Labor
> Employee Benefits Security Administration
> Apprenticeship and Training Plan Exemption
> 200 Constitution Avenue, NW, Suite N-1513
> Washington, DC 20210

The plan administrator must also complete the most current Form 5500 Annual Return/ Report (without schedules or attachments), items 1a-1b, 2a-2c, 3a-3c, and use plan number 999 for all apprenticeship and training plans. The paper copy of the form must be signed and dated, and be accompanied by a check for $750 made payable to the U.S. Department of Labor.

Effective March 29, 2011, the address for the DFVC lockbox has changed to:

> **DFVC DOL**
> P.O. Box 71361
> Philadelphia, PA 19176-1361

Do not send express mail. There is no overnight delivery address.

The applicable $750 penalty amount is for each DFVCP submission, without regard to the number of plans maintained by the same plan sponsor for which the notices and statements are being filed or the number of participants covered by the plan or plans.[2]

---

1. Delinquent Filer Voluntary Compliance Program, 78 Fed Reg. 6135 (January 29, 2013): http://www.gpo.gov/fdsys/pkg/FR-2013-01-29/pdf/2013-01616.pdf.

2. DOL Procedure: PWBA's Delinquent Filer Voluntary Compliance Program, Office of Chief Accountant Frequently Asked Questions, Delinquent Filer Voluntary Compliance Program, http://www.dol.gov/ebsa/faqs/faq_dfvc.html.

84. How does an administrator of a "top hat" plan participate in the DFVCP?

The DOL has stated that the plan administrator must prepare the statement described in 29 C.F.R. §2520.104-23 and file it at the following address:

U.S. Department of Labor
Employee Benefits Security Administration
Top Hat Plan Exemption
200 Constitution Avenue, NW, Suite N-1513
Washington, DC 20210

Note: The plan sponsor need only prepare one statement to cover all of its top hat plans. DOL Reg. Sec. 2520.104-23(b) does not require a separate statement for each top hat plan. However, separate notices are required for each apprenticeship and training plan.[1]

The plan administrator must also complete the most current Form 5500 Annual Return/ Report (without schedules or attachments), items 1a-1b, 2a-2c, 3a-3c, and use plan number 888 for all "top-hat" plans. The paper copy of the form must be signed, dated, and accompanied by a check for $750 made payable to the U.S. Department of Labor.

Effective March 29, 2011, the address for the DFVC lockbox has changed to:

DFVC DOL
P.O. Box 71361
Philadelphia, PA 19176-1361

Do not send express mail. There is no overnight delivery address.

The applicable $750 penalty amount is for each DFVC submission, without regard to the number of plans maintained by the same plan sponsor for which the notices and statements are being filed or the number of participants covered by the plan or plans."[2]

According to the 2013 update to the DFVC Program, if a check is sent, then a paper copy of the most current Form 5500 with only items 1a-1b, 2a-2c, and 3a-3c completed must be sent with that check. If there is a least one apprenticeship and training plan and at least one top hat plan, a copy of a separate Form 5500 must be prepared (with only the enumerated items completed) for each type of plan, showing plan number 888 for a top hat plan and plan number 999 for an apprenticeship and training plan. If a Form 5500 is required because the check payment method is used, that form is not submitted through EFAST2, but rather submitted with the penalty payment. If the plan administrator makes the payment electronically, it will

---

1. Delinquent Filer Voluntary Compliance Program, 78 Fed Reg. 6135 (January 29, 2013): http://www.gpo.gov/fdsys/pkg/FR-2013-01-29/pdf/2013-01616.pdf.
2. DOL Procedure: PWBA's Delinquent Filer Voluntary Compliance Program, Office of Chief Accountant Frequently Asked Questions, Delinquent Filer Voluntary Compliance Program, http://www.dol.gov/ebsa/faqs/faq_dfvc.html.

provide relevant information as part of that process, and a paper copy of a partially-completed Form 5500 is not sent to the DOL.[1]

85. Is the DFVCP applicable to filings made by direct filing entities (DFEs) (i.e., master trusts, pooled separate accounts, common/collective trusts, 103-12 Investment Entities (103-12 IEs), and group insurance arrangements)?

The DOL answers this question as follows:

The DFVCP is not applicable to DFE filings made for master trusts, pooled separate accounts, common/collective trusts and 103-12 IEs. The Form 5500 filed by these DFEs is an integral part of the annual report of the participating employee benefit plans. If a Form 5500 was timely filed for the participating employee benefit plans, a failure to timely file a DFE Form 5500 for these entities may cause the plan's annual report to be incomplete or inaccurate, but it does not result in the plan being a late or non-filer. The plan's Form 5500, however, may be subject to rejection for being incomplete or inaccurate, and, if rejected, a plan administrator who failed to correct the problem would be subject to penalty assessments by the department.

A Form 5500 filed for a group insurance arrangement (GIA) under the department's regulations relieves the plan administrators of the individual plans participating in the GIA from the requirement to file a separate Form 5500 for each plan. The department will allow a GIA that failed to file a GIA Form 5500 on time to use the DFVCP to correct the late filing. GIAs participating in the DFVCP are subject to the conditions applicable to large plan filers. (See Q 75.)[2]

86. Is it possible to obtain a waiver from the applicable penalty amount under the DFVCP if the plan administrator can demonstrate that there is reasonable cause why the penalty should not be assessed?

According to the DOL:

No. Payment of a penalty under the terms of the DFVCP constitutes a waiver of an administrator's right both to receive a notice of assessment from the department and to contest the department's assessment of the penalty amount. If the plan administrator chooses not to waive these rights, the plan administrator must file with EFAST in Lawrence, Kansas in the regular manner and not pursuant to the DFVCP.

---

1. Delinquent Filer Voluntary Compliance Program, 78 Fed Reg. 6135 (January 29, 2013): http://www.gpo.gov/fdsys/pkg/FR-2013-01-29/pdf/2013-01616.pdf.
2. DOL Procedure: PWBA's Delinquent Filer Voluntary Compliance Program, Office of Chief Accountant Frequently Asked Questions, Delinquent Filer Voluntary Compliance Program, http://www.dol.gov/ebsa/faqs/faq_dfvc.html.

See Q 72 regarding possible civil penalties that may be assessed by the DOL under ERISA Section 502(c)(2), and the DOL's regulations that provide the plan administrator with the opportunity to file a statement of reasonable cause.[1]

87. Does participation in the DFVC Program protect the plan administrator from other civil penalties that may be assessed by the Internal Revenue Service (IRS) or the Pension Benefit Guaranty Corporation (PBGC) for failing to timely file a Form 5500 Annual Return/Report?

The DOL answers this question as follows:

Both the IRS and PBGC have agreed to provide certain penalty relief under the Code and Title IV of ERISA for delinquent Form 5500s filed for Title I plans where the conditions of the DFVCP have been satisfied.[2]

Although the PBGC has authority under ERISA Section 4071 to impose penalties for a late Form 5500 filing, the PBGC has agreed not to assess a penalty under ERISA Section 4071 if DFVC relief has been obtained. See section 5.03 of the DFVC Program for further details.[3]

88. What reports and disclosures are plans required to submit to the Department of Labor?

Employee benefit plan administrators are required to file the following documents with the Department of Labor:

1.   Summary Plan Description (only upon request of the DOL) (see Q 89);

2.   Annual Reports (actual filing is made to the IRS) (see Q 63 through Q 69);

3.   Notice of Material Modifications (only upon request of DOL) (see Q 90);

4.   Terminal Reports (see Q 91); and

5.   Notice of Plan Amendments (see Q 92).

The DOL may request copies of SPDs and other relevant plan documents from third-party administrators only on behalf of requesting participants, fiduciaries, alternate payees under a QDRO (or prospective alternate payees under a QDRO), qualified COBRA beneficiaries, alternative recipients under a qualified medical child support order (or prospective alternate payees under a qualified child medical support order), or a duly authorized representative of any of the foregoing. Failure to comply with a DOL request may result in the imposition of penalties for each such failure up to $110 per day from the date of such failure (not to exceed $1,100).

---

1. DOL Procedure: PWBA's Delinquent Filer Voluntary Compliance Program, Office of Chief Accountant Frequently Asked Questions, Delinquent Filer Voluntary Compliance Program, http://www.dol.gov/ebsa/faqs/faq_dfvc.html.

2. *See* Sections 5.02 and 5.03 of the DFVC Program Federal Register Notice and IRS Notice 2002-23. *See also* DOL Procedure: PWBA's Delinquent Filer Voluntary Compliance Program, Office of Chief Accountant Frequently Asked Questions, Delinquent Filer Voluntary Compliance Program, http://www.dol.gov/ebsa/faqs/faq_dfvc.html.

3. Delinquent Filer Voluntary Compliance Program, 78 Fed Reg. 6135 (January 29, 2013): http://www.gpo.gov/fdsys/pkg/FR-2013-01-29/pdf/2013-01616.pdf.

The DOL can waive all or a part of the penalty if the third-party administrator can show that the failure or refusal to comply was due to matters reasonably beyond the control of the third-party administrator. The third-party administrator has thirty days from receipt of a notice of intent to assess the penalty to provide an explanation as to why it should not be assessed.[1]

89. What are the summary plan description (SPD) filing requirements?

ERISA Section 104(a)(6) provides that a plan administrator must file a copy of the plan's SPD with the Department of Labor (DOL) only if it is requested by the DOL.

For a detailed review of the format and content requirements of an SPD, as well as the obligations to provide the SPD to participants and beneficiaries, see Q 98.

90. What are the filing requirements regarding the summary of material modifications (SMM)?

A plan administrator is required to provide an SMM to the DOL only upon the request of the DOL.[2] The DOL may impose a civil penalty of up to $110 per day (up to a maximum of $1,100) against a plan administrator for failure to respond within thirty days to a DOL request for an SMM.[3]

91. What are the filing requirements regarding terminal reports?

Each administrator of a defined benefit plan that is winding up its affairs and terminating must file "such terminal reports as the Secretary [of Labor] may consider necessary." A copy of the terminal report is also required to be filed with the Pension Benefit Guaranty Corporation.[4] The terminal report is required to be filed regardless of the number of people actively participating in the plan.

The Department of Labor may also require a terminal report to be filed on behalf of a welfare benefit plan that is terminating.

92. What are the filing requirements regarding a notice of plan amendments?

Any amendment applying to a plan year that reduces the accrued benefits of a participant may not take effect unless the plan administrator files a notice with the Department of Labor.[5]

93. What reports and disclosures are required to be submitted to the Pension Benefit Guaranty Corporation?

The Pension Benefit Guaranty Corporation (PBGC) is a corporation wholly owned by the federal government. It is charged with the administration of the defined benefit plan termination rules detailed in Title IV of ERISA. The PBGC is also charged with establishing and maintaining

---

1. RIN 1210-AA67 and RIN 1210-AA68, 64 Fed. Reg. 42,797 (Aug. 5, 1999); ERISA Secs. 104(a)(6), 502(c)(6); Labor Reg. §2560.502c-
2. ERISA Sec. 104(a)(6).
3. ERISA Sec. 502(c)(6).
4. ERISA Sec. 101(c).
5. ERISA Sec. 302(c)(8)(C).

the defined benefit plan benefit insurance program. See Section XII for a detailed review of the PBGC and its operations regarding defined benefit plans.

Defined benefit plans subject to PBGC jurisdiction are required to file the following forms with the PBGC:

1. PBGC Form 1, Annual Premium Payment;

2. PBGC Form 1-ES (Annual Premium Payment Form for plans with 500 or more participants that must pay an estimated premium by the last day of the second full calendar month after the close of the prior plan year);

3. Notice of Reportable Events (see Q 798 for a detailed review of the contents of a Notice of Reportable Events);

4. Notice of Intent to Terminate (see Q 807 for a detailed review of the contents of a Notice of Intent to Terminate);

5. Notice of the Withdrawal of a Substantial Employer;

6. Annual Reports (Form 5500); and

7. Terminal Reports.

94. What reports and disclosures are required to be furnished under the Multiemployer Pension Plan Amendments Act of 1980?

The Multiemployer Pension Plan Amendments Act of 1980 provides that a multiemployer plan in reorganization may be amended to reduce or eliminate accrued benefits in accordance with ERISA Section 4244A where the contributions are not eligible for the Pension Benefit Guaranty Corporation's (PBGC's) guarantee. Accrued benefits may not be reduced unless a notice has been given to the following at least six months before the first day of the plan year in which the amendment reducing benefits is adopted:

1. Plan participants and beneficiaries;

2. Each employer who has an obligation to contribute under the plan; and

3. Each employee organization that, for purposes of collective bargaining, represents plan participants employed by the employer.[1]

The notice must advise recipients that the plan is in reorganization and that if contributions under the plan are not increased, accrued benefits under the plan will be reduced or an excise tax will be imposed on the employers.

The plan sponsors should include in any notice issued to plan participants and beneficiaries information as to the rights and remedies of plan participants and beneficiaries, as well as how to contact the Department of Labor for further information and assistance where appropriate.

---

1. ERISA Sec. 4244A(b)(1)(A).

If the plan sponsor of a plan in reorganization determines that the plan may become insolvent, the plan sponsor must notify the following that if the insolvency occurs, certain benefit payments will be suspended but basic benefits will continue to be paid:

1.   The Secretary of the Treasury;

2.   The PBGC;

3.   Each employer who has an obligation to contribute under the plan;

4.   Each employee organization that represents plan participants employed by that employer; and

5.   The plan participants and beneficiaries.[1]

95. What are the disclosure requirements applicable to multiemployer plans under the Pension Protection Act of 2006?

Section 502(a)(1) of the Pension Protection Act of 2006 added Section 101(k) to ERISA. That provision mandates that the plan administrator of a multiemployer plan must, upon written request, furnish within thirty days a copy of certain actuarial, financial, and funding-related documents to any plan participant, beneficiary, employee representative, or any employer that has an obligation to contribute to the plan.

Pursuant to ERISA Section 101(k), a plan administrator must furnish the following documents:

1.   A copy of any periodic actuarial report (including sensitivity testing) received by the plan for any plan year that has been in the plan's possession for at least thirty days;

2.   A copy of any quarterly, semi-annual, or annual financial report prepared for the plan by any plan investment manager or adviser or other fiduciary that has been in the plan's possession for at least thirty days; and

3.   A copy of any application filed with the Secretary of the Treasury requesting an amortization extension under Section 304 of ERISA and the determination of the Secretary pursuant to such application.

Under the Proposed Regulations, in general, the administrator of a multiemployer pension plan must furnish copies of actuarial, financial, and funding-related documents detailed below to

1.   Any participant within the meaning of Section 3(7) of the Act (see Q 15 for details);

2.   Any beneficiary receiving benefits under the plan;

3.   Any labor organization representing participants under the plan; and

---

1. ERISA Sec. 4245(e)(1).

4.   Any employer that is a party to the collective bargaining agreement(s) pursuant to which the plan is maintained or who otherwise may be subject to withdrawal liability.[1]

The administrator of a multiemployer pension plan must, not later than thirty days after receipt of a written request for a document or documents described below from an eligible party, furnish the requested document or documents to the requester. The documents must be furnished in a manner consistent with existing ERISA disclosure rules, including those applicable to electronic disclosures.[2]

Under the Proposed Regulations, the requesting party is entitled to receive a copy of any

a.   Periodic actuarial report (including any sensitivity testing) received by the plan for any plan year that has been in the plan's possession for at least thirty days prior to the date of the written request;

b.   Quarterly, semi-annual, or annual financial report prepared for the plan by any plan investment manager or adviser (without regard to whether such adviser is a fiduciary within the meaning of Section 3(21) of the Act) or other fiduciary that has been in the plan's possession for at least thirty days prior to the date of the written request; and

c.   Application filed with the Secretary of the Treasury requesting an extension under Section 304 of ERISA or IRC Section 431(d) and the determination of such Secretary pursuant to such application.[3]

The mandated disclosures do not include the provision of any information or data that served as the basis for any report or application required to be disclosed, although there is nothing restricting the right that a requesting person may have to review or obtain such information under other applicable provisions of ERISA. Nor shall such mandated disclosures include any information that the plan administrator reasonably determines to be either

1.   Individually identifiable information regarding any plan participant, beneficiary, employee, fiduciary, or contributing employer, or

2.   Proprietary information regarding the plan, any contributing employer, or entity providing services to the plan.[4]

A plan administrator must inform the requester if it withholds any such information included within a request under the proposed regulations.

Individuals may make such disclosure requests only once in any twelve-month period. The plan administrator is entitled to charge a reasonable fee to cover the costs of furnishing

---

1. Labor Reg. §§2520.101-6(a), 2520.101-6(d).
2. Labor Reg. §§2520.101-6(b)(1), 2520.101-6(2).
3. Labor Reg. §2520.101-6(c)(1).
4. Labor Reg. §§2520.101-6(c)(2)(A), 2520.101-6(b).

the requested documents. Such fee may not exceed the lesser of the actual cost to the plan for the least expensive means of acceptable reproduction of the document(s) or twenty-five cents per page, plus the cost of mailing or delivery of the document.[1] These charges include costs for furnishing statements or documents, including the latest updated summary plan description; the latest annual report; and any terminal report, the bargaining agreement, trust agreement, contract, or other instruments under which the plan is established or operated.[2]

96. What are the reports and disclosures that plans must provide to participants?

In the ongoing operation of an ERISA-covered employee benefit plan, the plan administrator is required to provide participants certain reports and disclosures. At various points in time and upon the occurrence of specific events, the plan administrator is required to provide participants the following documents:

1.   Summary Plan Description (see Q 98);

2.   Notice of Material Plan Changes (see Q 103);

3.   Summary of Annual Reports (see Q 104);

4.   Written Explanation of Joint and Survivor Annuity Option (see Q 105) and the Preretirement Survivor Annuity Option (see Q 106);

5.   Rollover Distribution Notice (see Q 107);

6.   Statement of Participant's Rights (see Q 109);

7.   Annual Funding Notice (see Q 114);

8.   Statement of Participant's Accrued and Vested Benefits (see Q 111);

9.   Notice to Participants in Underfunded Plans (see Q 114);

10.   Notice of Failure to Fund (see Q 115);

11.   Notice to Missing Participants (see Q 116); and

12.   COBRA Notices (see Q 189).

ERISA Section 104(b) requires the plan to produce only the "latest" annual report and summary plan description. It does not require plans to produce documents that simply do not exist.[3]

Practitioner's Pointer: The ruling in *Staib v. Vaughn Industries* is important in that it minimizes the ability of attorneys and participants to conduct legal "fishing expeditions" in which they request "any and all documents" in an effort to discover any potential issue for litigation.

---

1. Labor Reg. §§2520.101-6(b)(3), 2520.101-6(b)(4).
2. Labor Reg. §2520.101-6, 2520.104b-30; 75 Fed. Reg. 9334, (March. 2, 2010).
3. *Staib v. Vaughn Indus.*, 2001 U.S. Dist. LEXIS 17838 (N.D. Ohio 2001).

Federal courts have been increasingly active in ruling when plan fiduciaries must disclose plan amendments and other actions that may affect benefit levels within a plan (under the concept of "serious consideration"). In one such ruling, the Second Circuit ruled that the fiduciary duty to deal fairly and honestly with beneficiaries prohibits fiduciaries from making false or misrepresentative statements regarding future benefit enhancements wherein an inquiry seeking relevant, accurate information has been presented.[1]

The Ninth Circuit opined that there is no affirmative duty to provide considered changes in benefits after an amendment is under serious consideration, *but* where the employer has agreed to follow up with an inquiring employee, it must provide affirmative disclosure when the consideration later comes under serious consideration.[2]

Effective for violations occurring after March 24, 2003, the penalty under ERISA Section 502(*l*)(6) for a failure to furnish documents upon request as required under ERISA Section 104(a)(6) (SPD, governing documents, etc.) is increased. The penalty changes from $100 per day (but not greater than $1,000 per request) to $110 per day (but not greater than $1,100 per request).[3] A penalty of $35,000 under Section 502(*l*) was upheld for an employer's failure to respond timely to a document request made by a surviving spouse.[4]

The Sixth Circuit has ruled that a former participant was awarded $10,500 in civil penalties for a plan sponsor's failure to provide her with the plan documents she had requested in writing. The fine was calculated from the date on which the former employee filed suit, rather than thirty days after the documents were requested, because the plan administrator had in good faith believed that the request had been withdrawn.[5]

Conversely, the same Circuit has ruled that a failure to furnish enrollment forms and other specifically requested related documents does not trigger the $110 daily fine for failure to timely provide mandated information. In arriving at this decision, the Sixth Circuit advised that the requested enrollment form, a returned envelope showing that plan-related information had been sent to an obsolete address, and an e-mail from a representative of the employer were not instruments under which the plan was established or operated and, therefore, not subject to the statutory penalty.[6]

The United States District Court for the Western District of Wisconsin imposed penalties against a plan sponsor for the failure to provide requested plan documents that were in the exclusive possession and control of the plan's third-party administrator. The trial court reiterated ERISA's position that only the employer, as plan administrator, could be held liable under ERISA for delays in providing requested plan documents. The court concluded that the employer breached its fiduciary duty to the participant by not taking additional steps to assist her in obtaining the requested documents.[7]

In distinguishing a "lawyer-to-lawyer device" from the exercise of a participant's ERISA rights, the Fifth Circuit has held that a plan sponsor's failure to comply with a litigation discovery request did not trigger statutory penalties for violation of its ERISA obligation to provide plan documents on request.[8]

---

1. *Caputo v. Pfizer, Inc.*, 2001 U.S. App. LEXIS 21707 (2d Cir. 2001).
2. *Bins v. Exxon Co.* USA, 24 EBC 2377 (9th Cir. 2000).
3. See Labor Reg. §2575.502c-6; 68 Fed. Reg. 2875 (Jan. 22, 2003).
4. *Lowe v. McGraw-Hill Cos.*, 361 F.3d 335 (7th Cir. 2004).
5. *Zirnhelt v. Michigan Consol. Gas Co.* 526 F.3d 282 (6th Cir. 2008).
6. *Jordan v. Tyson Foods, Inc.*, 2008 WL 3876422 (6th Cir. 2008).
7. *Mondry v. American Family Mut. Ins. Co.*, 2010 WL 3730910 (W.D. Wis. 2010).
8. *Kujanek v. Houston Poly Bag I, Ltd.*, 2011 WL 4445993 (5th Cir. 2011).

97. What are the fiduciary requirements for disclosure in participant-directed individual account plans?

The DOL advises that the investment of plan assets is a fiduciary act governed by the fiduciary standards of ERISA Section 404(a)(1)(A) and (B). Pursuant to new regulations issued on October 20, 2010, when the governing documents of an individual account plan provide for the allocation of investment responsibilities to participants or beneficiaries, the plan administrator must take steps to ensure that such participants and beneficiaries, on a regular and periodic basis, are made aware of their rights and responsibilities with respect to the investment of assets held in, or contributed to, their accounts and are provided sufficient information regarding the plan, including fees and expenses, and regarding designated investment alternatives, so that they can make informed decisions with regard to the management of their individual accounts.[1] On June 1, 2011, the DOL issued a notice proposing amendments to the fiduciary-level and participant-level fee disclosure regulations to more closely align the initial compliance dates for the two rules. The DOL has now issued a final rule that extends and aligns the initial compliance date to January 2, 2012, and to amend the transitional rule (detailed below) to extend it from sixty days to 120 days.[2] See also Q 402.

In general, the plan administrator of a covered individual account plan must comply with the disclosure requirements set forth below for each participant or beneficiary that, pursuant to the terms of the plan, has the right to direct the investment of assets held in, or contributed to, their individual account. Compliance with these requirements will satisfy the duty to make the regular and periodic disclosures, provided that the information contained in such disclosures is complete and accurate. A plan administrator will not be liable for the completeness and accuracy of information used to satisfy these disclosure requirements when the plan administrator reasonably and in good faith relies on information received from or provided by a plan service provider or the issuer of a designated investment alternative.[3]

For purposes of these disclosure rules, a "covered individual account plan" is any participant-directed individual account plan as defined in Section 3(34) of ERISA, except that such term shall not include plans involving IRA, SEP, or SIMPLE arrangements.[4]

Nothing within these rules is intended to relieve a fiduciary from its duty to prudently select and monitor providers of services to the plan or designated investment alternatives offered under the plan.[5]

Disclosure of Plan-Related Information

A plan administrator (or person designated by the plan administrator) shall provide to each participant or beneficiary the plan-related information described below based on the latest information available to the plan:

---

1. Labor Reg. §2550.404a-5(a); 75 Fed. Reg. 64,910 (Oct. 20, 2010).
2. Requirements for Fee Disclosure to Plan Fiduciaries and Participants—Applicability Dates, 29 C.F.R. pt. 2550, 76 Fed. Reg. 42539 (July 19, 2011).
3. Labor Reg. §2550.404a-5(b)(1).
4. Labor Reg. §2550.404a-5(b)(2).
5. Labor Reg. §2550.404a-5(f).

1. On or before the date on which a participant or beneficiary can first direct their investments and at least annually thereafter:

    a. An explanation of the circumstances under which participants and beneficiaries may give investment instructions;

    b. An explanation of any specified limitations on such instructions under the terms of the plan, including any restrictions on transfer to or from a designated investment alternative;

    c. A description of or reference to plan provisions relating to the exercise of voting, tender, and similar rights appurtenant to an investment in a designated investment alternative as well as any restrictions on such rights;

    d. An identification of any designated investment alternatives offered under the plan;

    e. An identification of any designated investment managers; and

    f. A description of any "brokerage windows," "self-directed brokerage accounts," or similar plan arrangements that enable participants and beneficiaries to select investments beyond those designated by the plan.[1]

2. If there is a change to this information each participant and beneficiary must be furnished a description of such change at least thirty days, but not more than ninety days, in advance of the effective date of such change, unless the inability to provide such advance notice is due to events that were unforeseeable or circumstances beyond the control of the plan administrator, in which case notice of such change must be furnished as soon as reasonably practicable.[2]

Administrative Expenses

On or before the date on which a participant or beneficiary can first direct their investments and at least annually thereafter, they must be provided an explanation of any fees and expenses for general plan administrative services (e.g., legal, accounting, recordkeeping), which may be charged against the individual accounts of participants and beneficiaries and are not reflected in the total annual operating expenses of any designated investment alternative, as well as the basis on which such charges will be allocated (e.g., pro rata, per capita) to, or affect the balance of, each individual account.[3] If there is a change to this information, each participant and beneficiary must be furnished a description of such change at least thirty days, but not more than ninety days, in advance of the effective date of such change, unless the inability to provide such advance notice is due to events that were unforeseeable or circumstances beyond

---

1. Labor Reg. §2550.404a-5(c)(1)(i)(A) to (F).
2. Labor Reg. §2550.404a-5(c)(1)(ii).
3. Labor Reg. §2550.404a-5(c)(2)(i)(A).

the control of the plan administrator, in which case notice of such change must be furnished as soon as reasonably practicable.[1]

At least quarterly, participants and beneficiaries must be provided a statement that includes:

1.   The dollar amount of the fees and expenses that are actually charged (whether by liquidating shares or deducting dollars) during the preceding quarter to the participant's or beneficiary's account for such services;

2.   A description of the services to which the charges relate (e.g., plan administration, including recordkeeping, legal, accounting services); and

3.   If applicable, an explanation that, in addition to the fees and expenses, some of the plan's administrative expenses for the preceding quarter were paid from the total annual operating expenses of one or more of the plan's designated investment alternatives (e.g., through revenue sharing arrangements, Rule 12b-1 fees, sub-transfer agent fees).[2]

Individual Expenses

On or before the date on which participants or beneficiaries can first direct their investments and at least annually thereafter, they must be provided an explanation of any fees and expenses that may be charged against the individual account of a participant or beneficiary on an individual, rather than on a plan wide, basis (e.g., fees attendant to processing plan loans or qualified domestic relations orders, fees for investment advice, fees for brokerage windows, commissions, front- or back-end loads or sales charges, redemption fees, transfer fees and similar expenses, and optional rider charges in annuity contracts) and which are not reflected in the total annual operating expenses of any designated investment alternative.[3] If there is a change to this information, each participant and beneficiary must be furnished a description of such change at least thirty days, but not more than ninety days, in advance of the effective date of such change, unless the inability to provide such advance notice is due to events that were unforeseeable or circumstances beyond the control of the plan administrator, in which case notice of such change must be furnished as soon as reasonably practicable.[4]

At least quarterly, participants and beneficiaries must be provided a statement that includes:

1.   The dollar amount of the fees and expenses that are actually individually charged (whether by liquidating shares or deducting dollars) during the preceding quarter to the participant's or beneficiary's account for individual services; and

2.   A description of the services to which the charges relate (e.g., loan processing fee).[5]

---

1. Labor Reg. §2550.404a-5(c)(2)(i)(B).
2. Labor Reg. §2550.404a-5(c)(2)(ii)(A) to (C).
3. Labor Reg. §2550.404a-5(c)(3)(i)(A).
4. Labor Reg. §2550.404a-5(c)(3)(i)(B).
5. Labor Reg. §2550.404a-5(c)(3)(ii)(B).

Disclosures on or Before First Investment

Requirements to furnish information on or before the date on which participants or beneficiaries can first direct their investments may be satisfied by furnishing to them the most recent annual disclosure furnished to participants and beneficiaries detailed above and any updates to that information.[1]

Disclosure of Investment-Related Information
to Be Provided Automatically

The plan administrator, based on the latest information available to the plan, must provide each participant or beneficiary on or before the date on which they first direct their investments and at least annually thereafter, the following information with respect to each designated investment alternative offered under the plan:

1.   The name of each designated investment alternative; and the type or category of the investment (e.g., money market fund, balanced fund (stocks and bonds), large-cap stock fund, employer stock fund, employer securities);

2.   For designated investment alternatives with respect to which the return is not fixed, the average annual total return of the investment for one-, five-, and ten-calendar year periods (or for the life of the alternative, if shorter) ending on the date of the most recently completed calendar year; as well as a statement indicating that an investment's past performance is not necessarily an indication of how the investment will perform in the future; and

3.   For designated investment alternatives with respect to which the return is fixed or stated for the term of the investment, both the fixed or stated annual rate of return and the term of the investment. If, with respect to such a designated investment alternative, the issuer reserves the right to adjust the fixed or stated rate of return prospectively during the term of the contract or agreement, the current rate of return, the minimum rate guaranteed under the contract, if any, and a statement advising participants and beneficiaries that the issuer may adjust the rate of return prospectively and how to obtain (e.g., telephone or Web site) the most recent rate of return required under this section.[2]

For designated investment alternatives with respect to which the return is not fixed, participants and beneficiaries are to receive the name and returns of an appropriate broad-based securities market index over the one-, five-, and ten-calendar year periods (or for the life of the alternative, if shorter) comparable to the performance data periods and that is not administered by an affiliate of the investment issuer, its investment adviser, or a principal underwriter, unless the index is widely recognized and used.[3]

---

1. Labor Reg. §2550.404a-5(c)(4).
2. Labor Reg. §2550.404a-5(d)(1)(i) and (ii).
3. Labor Reg. §2550.404a-5(d)(1)(iii).

The final rule on fee disclosures, released on February 3, 2012,[1] (see Q 402 for a detailed analysis of these rules) adds to the disclosure requirements for descriptions of annual operating expenses (e.g., expense ratio) of a designated investment alternative under these individual account plan disclosure rules. The final rule now requires the disclosure of total annual operating expenses for designated investment alternatives, expressed as a percentage, made to participants. The percentage is to be calculated in accordance with the new Labor Regulation Section 2550.404a-5(h)(5). In addition, the final rule requires disclosure of any other information relating to designated investment alternatives that is within the control of, or reasonably available to, the covered service provider under the fee disclosure rules, if the information is considered investment-related information that must be provided automatically under these participant-directed disclosure rules.[2] See also Q 402.

Practitioner's Pointer: Plan administrators are reminded that the final rule's July 1, 2012, effective date will also affect when disclosures must first be made under the participant-level disclosure regulations. The initial annual disclosure of "plan level" and "investment level" information (including associated fees and expenses) were required to be furnished no later than August 30, 2012, (sixty days after the final rule's effective date). The first quarterly statement must then be furnished no later than November 14, 2012, (forty-five days after the end of the third quarter during which the initial disclosures were first required). This quarterly statement need only reflect the fees and expenses actually deducted from the participant's or beneficiary's account during the third calendar quarter to which the statement relates.

Furthermore, for designated investment alternatives with respect to which the return is not fixed participants and beneficiaries are also required to be provided the following fee and expense information:

1. The amount and a description of each shareholder-type fee (fees charged directly against a participant's or beneficiary's investment, such as commissions, sales loads, sales charges, deferred sales charges, redemption fees, surrender charges, exchange fees, account fees, and purchase fees, which are not included in the total annual operating expenses of any designated investment alternative) and a description of any restriction or limitation that may be applicable to a purchase, transfer, or withdrawal of the investment in whole or in part (such as round trip, equity wash, or other restrictions);

2. The total annual operating expenses of the investment expressed as a percentage (i.e., expense ratio);

3. The total annual operating expenses of the investment for a one-year period expressed as a dollar amount for a $1,000 investment (assuming no returns);

4. A statement indicating that fees and expenses are only one of several factors that participants and beneficiaries should consider when making investment decisions; and

---

1. 77 Fed. Reg. 5632 (Feb. 3, 2012).
2. Labor Reg. §2550.408b-2(c)(1)(iv)(E).

5.   A statement that the cumulative effect of fees and expenses can substantially reduce the growth of a participant's or beneficiary's retirement account and that participants and beneficiaries can visit the EBSA's Web site for an example demonstrating the long-term effect of fees and expenses.[1]

For designated investment alternatives with respect to which the return is fixed for the term of the investment, the amount and a description of any shareholder-type fees and a description of any restriction or limitation that may be applicable to a purchase, transfer, or withdrawal of the investment in whole or in part are also required to be provided to participants and beneficiaries.[2]

Participants and beneficiaries must be given an Internet Web site address and a glossary that is sufficiently specific to provide them access to the following information regarding the designated investment alternative:

1.   The name of the alternative's issuer;

2.   The alternative's objectives or goals in a manner consistent with Securities and Exchange Commission Form N-1A or N-3, as appropriate;

3.   The alternative's principal strategies (including a general description of the types of assets held by the investment) and principal risks in a manner consistent with Securities and Exchange Commission Form N-1A or N-3, as appropriate;

4.   The alternative's portfolio turnover rate in a manner consistent with Securities and Exchange Commission Form N-1A or N-3, as appropriate;

5.   The alternative's performance data updated on at least a quarterly basis, or more frequently if required by other applicable law; and

6.   The alternative's fee and expense information.[3]

If a designated investment alternative is part of a contract, fund, or product that permits participants or beneficiaries to allocate contributions toward the future purchase of a stream of retirement income payments guaranteed by an insurance company (an annuity product), participants and beneficiaries are to receive the annuity-specific information detailed below, to the extent such information is not otherwise included in the general investment-related fees and expenses described above.[4]

The disclosures that must be issued on or before the date on which the participant or beneficiary can first direct his investments may be satisfied by furnishing to the participant or beneficiary the most recent annual disclosure furnished to participants and beneficiaries.[5]

---

1. Labor Reg. §2550.404a-5(d)(1)(ii)(1) to (5).
2. Labor Reg. §2550.404a-5(d)(1)(iv)(B).
3. Labor Reg. §§2550.404a-5(d)(1)(v)(A) to (F), 2550.404a-4(d)(1)(vi).
4. Labor Reg. §2550.404a-5(d)(1)(vii).
5. Labor Reg. §2550.404a-5(d)(1)(viii).

Comparative Format — Charts

Participants and beneficiaries are to be provided the above information, and, if applicable, the employer stock and annuity-specific information detailed below in a chart or similar format that is designed to facilitate a comparison of such information for each designated investment alternative available under the plan and prominently displays the date, and that includes:

1. A statement indicating the name, address, and telephone number of the plan administrator (or a person or persons designated by the plan administrator to act on its behalf) to contact for the provision of the required information required;

2. A statement that additional investment-related information (including more current performance information) is available at the listed Internet Web site addresses; and

3. A statement explaining how to request and obtain, free of charge, paper copies of the information required to be made available on a Web site relating to annuity options, or fixed-return investments, of this section.[1]

Nothing in the regulation precludes plan administrators from including additional information that they determine to be appropriate for such comparisons, provided such information is not inaccurate or misleading.[2]

Information to Be Provided Subsequent to Investment

The plan administrator must furnish to each investing participant or beneficiary, subsequent to an investment in a designated investment alternative, any materials provided to the plan relating to the exercise of voting, tender, and similar rights appurtenant to the investment, to the extent that such rights are passed through to such participant or beneficiary under the terms of the plan.[3]

Information to Be Provided upon Request

Upon request, the plan administrator must furnish to each participant or beneficiary, either at the mandated times specified above, or upon request, the following information relating to designated investment alternatives:

1. Copies of prospectuses (or, alternatively, any short-form or summary prospectus, the form of which has been approved by the Securities and Exchange Commission) for the disclosure of information to investors by entities registered under either the Securities Act of 1933 or the Investment Company Act of 1940, or similar documents relating to designated investment alternatives that are provided by entities that are not registered under either of these Acts;

2. Copies of any financial statements or reports, such as statements of additional information and shareholder reports, and of any other similar materials relating

---

1. Labor Reg. §2550.404a-5(d)(2)(i)(A) to (C).
2. Labor Reg. §2550.404a-5(d)(2)(ii).
3. Labor Reg. §2550.404a-5(d)(3).

to the plan's designated investment alternatives, to the extent such materials are provided to the plan;

3.   A statement of the value of a share or unit of each designated investment alternative as well as the date of the valuation; and

4.   A list of the assets comprising the portfolio of each designated investment alternative which constitute plan assets within the meaning of 29 CFR 2510.3-101 and the value of each such asset (or the proportion of the investment which it comprises).[1]

Form of Disclosure

The information required to be disclosed may be provided as part of the plan's summary plan description or as part of a pension benefit statement (for defined benefit plans), if such summary plan description or pension benefit statement is furnished at a frequency that comports with this regulation.[2]

A plan administrator that uses and accurately completes the model disclosure provided in the Appendix to the disclosure regulations, taking into account each designated investment alternative offered under the plan, will be deemed to have satisfied the requirements of the regulation.[3]

Fees and expenses may be expressed in terms of a monetary amount, formula, percentage of assets, or per capita charge, unless this regulation specifies a different format.[4]

As with all disclosures given to participants and beneficiaries as required under ERISA, the information prepared by the plan administrator for disclosure under these rules (as required) must be written in a manner that can be understood by the average plan participant.[5]

The DOL has revised and reissued its interim policy on electronic distribution of participant-level fee disclosures with two clarifications.[6] The interim policy states that the DOL will not take enforcement action based solely on a plan administrator's use of electronic media to make the required disclosures under the participant fee disclosure regulation if the administrator complies with the conditions in the technical release. The DOL clarified that release through the issuance of Technical Release 2011-03R (Dec. 8, 2011) to provide that the revised technical release is identical to Technical Release 2011-03 except as necessary to clarify that (1) continuous access Web sites are permissible if the administrator complies with the conditions in the technical release; and (2) investment-related information under paragraph (d) of the participant-level fee disclosure regulation may be furnished as part of, or along with, a pension benefit statement, either electronically under the conditions in the technical release or in paper form.[7] See also Q 402.

---

1. Labor Reg. §2550.404a-5(d)(4)(i) to (iv).
2. Labor Reg. §2550.404a-5(e)(1) and (2).
3. Labor Reg. §2550.404a-5(e)(3).
4. Labor Reg. §2550.404a-5(e)(4).
5. Labor Reg. §2550.404a-5(e)(5).
6. DOL Technical Release 2011-03 (Sept. 13, 2011).
7. DOL Technical Release 2011-03R (Dec. 8, 2011).

Target Date or Similar Funds

On November 30, 2010, the DOL issued a proposed regulation updating the disclosure rules specific to disclosures on target date or life cycle funds offered as designated investment alternatives.[1] Regarding these investment alternatives, the plan administrator must provide as an appendix or appendices to the chart or similar document, in addition to the general information detailed above, the following:

1.　An explanation of the asset allocation, how that allocation will change over time, and the point in time when the alternative will reach its most conservative asset allocation (including a chart, table, or other illustration of change in allocations over time that does not obscure or impede a participant's or beneficiary's understanding of the disclosures);

2.　If the alternative is described with reference to a target date, an explanation of the age group for whom it is designed, the relevance of that date, and any assumptions about a participant's or beneficiary's contribution and withdrawal intentions on or after such date; and

3.　A statement that the participant or beneficiary may lose money by investing in the alternative, including losses near and following retirement, and that there is no guarantee that the alternative will provide adequate retirement income.[2]

The DOL has issued informal guidance on fiduciary responsibility with respect to Target Date Funds (TDFs). The guidance provides tips to plan fiduciaries with respect to their fiduciary duty in selecting and monitoring Target Date Funds.[3] The guidance notes that with the growth in participant directed investment accounts, TDFs have become an increasingly attractive investment option for employees who do not want to actively manage their retirement savings. TDFs automatically rebalance to become more conservative as an employee gets closer to retirement. Because of these features, many plans have adopted a TDF as the qualified default investment alternative. Among investment options qualifying as TDFs, however, there can be wide disparities as to investment strategies, glide paths (i.e., the shift in asset allocation over time as the TDF becomes more conservatively invested as the individual ages), as well as in the associated fees. It is therefore, imperative, the guidance notes, that fiduciaries understand these differences when selecting a TDF as an investment option under a plan."

Brokerage Windows

The DOL has issued subsequent guidance on the fee disclosure regulations through a series of questions and answers in Field Advisory Bulletin 2012-02R. One of the key points issued in this bulletin is the position of the DOL that adding a brokerage window to an individual account plan is a fiduciary duty wherein the plan fiduciary will be responsible for the prudent selection and monitoring of the designated investment manager, which is a provider of brokerage window

---

1. 75 Fed. Reg. 73,987 (Nov. 30, 2010).
2. Prop. Labor Reg. §2550.404a-5(i)(4)(i) to (iii).
3. Target Date Retirement Funds—Tips for ERISA Plan Fiduciaries; http://www.dol.gov/ebsa/newsroom/fsTDF.html.

services to the plan.[1] Further, the DOL provides "The regulation covers "brokerage windows," "self-directed brokerage accounts," and other similar plan arrangements that enable participants and beneficiaries to select investments beyond those designated by the plan."[2]

Coverage of brokerage windows under the regulation, however, is limited to the disclosure requirements relating to plan-related information. The disclosure requirements regarding investment-related information do not apply to brokerage windows, self-directed brokerage accounts, and similar arrangements, because such windows, accounts, and arrangements are not designated investment alternatives. Nor, do the disclosure requirements apply to any investment selected by a participant or beneficiary that is not designated by the plan (*i.e.*, any investments made through the window, account, or arrangement).[3]

Specific disclosures for brokerage windows under the final regulations include the following. First, a plan administrator must provide a general description of any such window, account, or arrangement.[4] The regulation does not state how specific and detailed a description must be to satisfy this requirement. Whether a particular description is satisfactory will depend on the facts and circumstances of the specific plan and the specific window, account, or arrangement. At a minimum, however, this description must provide sufficient information to enable participants and beneficiaries to understand how the window, account, or arrangement works (*e.g.*, how and to whom to give investment instructions; account balance requirements, if any; restrictions or limitations on trading, if any; how the window, account, or arrangement differs from the plan's designated investment alternatives) and whom to contact with questions.[5]

Second, a plan administrator also must provide an explanation of any fees and expenses that may be charged against the individual account of a participant or beneficiary on an individual, rather than on a plan-wide, basis in connection with any such window, account, or arrangement.[6] This would include:

1. Any fee or expense necessary for the participant or beneficiary to start, open, or initially access such a window, account, or arrangement (such as enrollment, initiation, or start up fees), or to stop, close or terminate access;

2. Any ongoing fee or expense (annual, monthly, or any other similarly charged fee or expense) necessary for the participant to maintain access to the window, account, or arrangement, including inactivity fees and minimum balance fees; and

3. Any commissions or fees (*e.g.*, per trade fee) charged in connection with the purchase or sale of a security, including front or back end sales loads if known; but would not include any fees or expenses of the investment selected by the participant

---

1. FAB 2012–02R (July 30, 2012).
2. FAB 2012–02R, Q&A 29 (July 30, 2012).
3. FAB 2012–02R, Q&A 29 (July 30, 2012).
4. 29 CFR § 2550.404a-5(c)(1)(i)(F) FAB 2012–02R, Q&A 13, (July 30, 2012).
5. FAB 2012–02R, Q&A 13, (July 30, 2012).
6. 29 CFR § 2550.404a-5(c)(3)(i)(A); FAB 2012–02R, Q&A 13, (July 30, 2012).

or beneficiary (*e.g.*, Rule 12b-1 or similar fees reflected in the investment's total annual operating expenses).[1]

The DOL understands that in some circumstances the specific amount of certain fees associated with the purchase or sale of a security through a window, account, or arrangement, such as front end sales loads for open-end management investment companies registered under the Investment Company Act of 1940, may vary across investments available through the window or may not be known by the plan administrator or provider of the window, account, or arrangement in advance of the purchase or sale of the security by a participant or beneficiary. In recognition of the foregoing, a general statement that such fees exist and that they may be charged against the individual account of a purchasing or selling participant or beneficiary, and directions as to how the participant can obtain information about such fees in connection with any particular investment, ordinarily will satisfy the requirements of 29 CFR § 2550.404a-5(c)(3)(i)(A). Otherwise, plan administrators might inundate participants and beneficiaries with information about the cost of buying or selling all the various securities available through a window, account, or arrangement, despite the fact that participants and beneficiaries may not have the interest or expertise to purchase or sell each or any such security. Further, the statement should advise participants and beneficiaries to ask the provider of the window, account, or arrangement about any fees, including any undisclosed fees, associated with the purchase or sale of a particular security through a window, account, or arrangement, before purchasing or selling such security.[2]

Third, a plan administrator also must provide participants and beneficiaries with a statement of the dollar amount of fees and expenses that actually were charged during the preceding quarter against their individual accounts in connection with any such window, account, or arrangement.[3] A statement of these fees must include a description of the services to which the charge relates.[4] The description of the services must clearly explain the charges (*e.g.*, $19.99 brokerage trades, $25.00 brokerage account minimum balance fee, $13.00 brokerage account wire transfer fee, $44.00 front end sales load).[5]

Where a covered plan offers an investment platform that includes a brokerage window, self-directed brokerage account, or similar plan arrangement, and the plan fiduciary does not designate any of the funds on the platform or available through the brokerage window, self-directed brokerage account, or similar plan arrangement as "designated investment alternatives" under the plan, the platform or the brokerage window, self-directed brokerage account, or similar plan arrangement is not a designated investment alternative for purposes of the fee disclosure regulations.[6] The DOL elaborates: "Whether an investment alternative is a "designated investment alternative" (DIA) for purposes of the regulation depends on whether it is specifically identified as available under the plan. The regulation does not require that a plan have a particular number of DIAs, and nothing in this Bulletin prohibits the use of a platform or a

---

1. FAB 2012-02R, Q&A 13, (July 30, 2012).
2. FAB 2012-02R, Q&A 13, (July 30, 2012).
3. 29 CFR § 2550.404a-5(c)(3)(ii)(A); FAB 2012-02R, Q&A 13, (July 30, 2012).
4. 29 CFR 2550.404a-5(c)(3)(ii)(B); FAB 2012-02R, Q&A 13, (July 30, 2012).
5. FAB 2012-02R, Q&A 13, (July 30, 2012).
6. FAB 2012-02R (July 30, 2012).

brokerage window, self-directed brokerage account, or similar plan arrangement in an individual account plan. The Bulletin also does not change the 404(c) regulation or the requirements for relief from fiduciary liability under section 404(c) of ERISA. Nonetheless, in the case of a 401(k) or other individual account plan covered under the regulation, a plan fiduciary's failure to designate investment alternatives, for example, to avoid investment disclosures under the regulation, raises questions under ERISA section 404(a)'s general statutory fiduciary duties of prudence and loyalty. Also, fiduciaries of such plans with platforms or brokerage windows, self-directed brokerage accounts, or similar plan arrangements that enable participants and beneficiaries to select investments beyond those designated by the plan are still bound by ERISA section 404(a)'s statutory duties of prudence and loyalty to participants and beneficiaries who use the platform or the brokerage window, self-directed brokerage account, or similar plan arrangement, including taking into account the nature and quality of services provided in connection with the platform or the brokerage window, self-directed brokerage account, or similar plan arrangement."[1]

Qualifying Employer Securities

In the case of designated investment alternatives designed to invest in, or primarily in, qualifying employer securities, within the meaning of Section 407 of ERISA, in lieu of the general disclosure requirements detailed above, the following disclosures apply:

1. For principal strategies and principal risks, plan administrators must provide an explanation of the importance of a well-balanced and diversified investment portfolio;

2. The rules regarding portfolio turnover rate do not apply to such designated investment alternative;

3. The rules relating to fee and expense information also do not apply to such designated investment alternatives, unless the designated investment alternative is a fund with respect to which participants or beneficiaries acquire units of participation, rather than actual shares, in exchange for their investment;

4. Disclosures of total annual operating expenses expressed as a percentage do not apply to such designated investment alternatives, unless the designated investment alternative is a fund with respect to which participants or beneficiaries acquire units of participation, rather than actual shares, in exchange for their investment;

5. Disclosures of total annual operating expenses expressed as a dollar amount per $1,000 invested do not apply to such designated investment alternatives, unless the designated investment alternative is a fund with respect to which participants or beneficiaries acquire units of participation, rather than actual shares, in exchange for their investment; and

6. For information relating to performance data for one, five, and 10-year periods, the definition of "average annual total return" shall apply to such designated investment

---

1. FAB 2012-02R (July 30, 2012).

alternatives in lieu of the specific calculation of the average annual return called for under 2550.404a-5(h)(3) of these regulations if the qualifying employer securities are publicly traded on a national exchange or generally recognized market and the designated investment alternative is not a fund with respect to which participants or beneficiaries acquire units of participation, rather than actual shares, in exchange for their investment.[1]

The term "average annual total return" means the change in value of an investment in one share of stock on an annualized basis over a specified period, calculated by taking the sum of the dividends paid during the measurement period, assuming reinvestment, plus the difference between the stock price (consistent with ERISA Section 3(18)) at the end and at the beginning of the measurement period, and dividing by the stock price at the beginning of the measurement period; reinvestment of dividends is assumed to be in stock at market prices at approximately the same time actual dividends are paid.[2] This definition of "average annual total return" shall apply to such designated investment alternatives consisting of employer securities that are not publicly traded on a national exchange or generally recognized market, unless the designated investment alternative is a fund with respect to which participants or beneficiaries acquire units of participation, rather than actual shares, in exchange for their investment.[3]

Annuity Options

In the case of a designated investment alternative that is an annuity product, the plan administrator shall, in lieu of the general disclosure information required above, provide each participant or beneficiary the following information with respect to each such option:

1.   The name of the contract, fund, or product;

2.   The option's objectives or goals (e.g., to provide a stream of fixed retirement income payments for life);

3.   The benefits and factors that determine the price (e.g., age, interest rates, form of distribution) of the guaranteed income payments;

4.   Any limitations on the ability of a participant or beneficiary to withdraw or transfer amounts allocated to the option (e.g., lock-ups) and any fees or charges applicable to such withdrawals or transfers;

5.   Any fees that will reduce the value of amounts allocated by participants or beneficiaries to the option, such as surrender charges, market value adjustments, and administrative fees;

6.   A statement that guarantees of an insurance company are subject to its long-term financial strength and claims-paying ability; and

---

1. Labor Reg. §2550.404a-5(i)(1)(i) to (vi).
2. Labor Reg. §2550.404a-5(i)(1)(vi)(B).
3. Labor Reg. §2550.404a-5(i)(1)(vi)(B).

7. An Internet Web site address that is sufficiently specific to provide participants and beneficiaries access to the following information—

    a. The name of the option's issuer and of the contract, fund, or product;

    b. Description of the option's objectives or goals;

    c. Description of the option's distribution alternatives/guaranteed income payments (e.g., payments for life, payments for a specified term, joint and survivor payments, optional rider payments), including any limitations on the right of a participant or beneficiary to receive such payments;

    d. Description of costs and/or factors taken into account in determining the price of benefits under an option's distribution alternatives/guaranteed income payments (e.g., age, interest rates, other annuitization assumptions);

    e. Description of any limitations on the right of a participant or beneficiary to withdraw or transfer amounts allocated to the option and any fees or charges applicable to a withdrawal or transfer; and

    f. Description of any fees that will reduce the value of amounts allocated by participants or beneficiaries to the option (e.g., surrender charges, market value adjustments, administrative fees).[1]

The DOL is currently working on proposed regulations pertaining to periodic employee benefit statements required under ERISA Sec. 105. As part of that proposal, the DOL intends to require that statements issued by defined contribution plans express a participant's or beneficiary's account balance as an annuity (lifetime income stream) in addition to the dollar amount of the account balance. On May 8, 2013, the DOL issued an advance notice of proposed regulations that would require employee benefit statements for Defined Contribution plans to include equivalent annuity information with respect to current and projected account balances Advance Notice of Proposed Rulemaking (ANPRM).[2]

The purpose of the ANPRM is to disclose to the public its current draft of the portion of the regulations that will impose this requirement. The DOL advises that the ANRPM is issued under the authority of ERISA Sec. 105(a)(2)(A)(i)(I), which requires a benefit statement to indicate a participant's or beneficiary's "total benefits accrued," and ERISA Sec. 505, which gives the DOL the ability to prescribe such regulations as it finds "necessary or appropriate" to carry out the provisions of Title I of ERISA. The DOL believes that by having information about the annuity equivalent of the account balance, the benefit statement will provide a more accurate picture of the participant's or beneficiary's total benefits accrued. In mandating annuity equivalents for both the current account balance and a projected account balance, the DOL believes that participants will be encouraged to increase contribution levels with a view toward reaching a more adequate retirement income level.

---

1. Labor Reg. §2550.404a-5(i)(2)(i) to (vii).
2. Prop. DOL Reg. §2520.105-1, 78 F.R. 26727-26739 (May 8, 2013).

There are four core requirements that would be included in the DOL's proposed regulation. The proposed regulations provide that the "individual" receiving the benefit statement to indicate that either a participant or a beneficiary might be receiving the statement.

(1)   The statement would have to express the individual's current account balance as a lifetime income stream,[1] based on the fair market value of the account balance as of the last day of the period covered by the statement.[2] The lifetime income stream would have to be expressed as a monthly benefit payable for the life of the individual beginning on the assumed commencement date (see (b) below), as determined using reasonable actuarial assumptions (see (a) below).[3]

(a) To compute the lifetime income stream, general principles (see (i) below), allow the plan to select assumptions that satisfy those principles, and a safe harbor (see (ii) below). However, see (iii) below for alternative assumptions that might have to be used for plans that offer annuity distribution options.

(i) **General principles**. The interest and mortality assumptions used to determine the lifetime income stream must each be reasonable taking into account generally accepted actuarial principles.[4]

(ii) **Safe harbor option**. As an alternative, safe harbor assumptions may be used that are deemed to be reasonable.[5] The safe harbor interest assumption would be the ten-year constant maturity Treasury securities rate for the first business day of the last month of the period to which the statement relates (e.g., the first business day of December for a statement period ending December 31).[6] The safe harbor mortality assumption would be the applicable mortality table under IRC Sec. 417(e)(3)(B) in effect for the month that contains the last day of the period to which the statement relates (e.g., December for a statement period ending December 31).[7]

(iii) **Substitution of plan terms**. If the plan offers an annuity form of distribution pursuant to a contract with an issuer licensed under applicable state law, the plan would be required to substitute actual plan terms for the assumptions in (i) and (ii) above.[8]

(b) The lifetime income stream would be based on an assumed commencement date that is the first day following the period to which the statement relates. For example, if the statement is for the period October 1 through

1. ANPRM Sec. 2520.105-1(c)(2)(vii).
2. ANPRM Sec. 2520.105-1(c)(2)(v)).
3. ANPRM Sec. 2520.105-1(e)(1)(i) and (iii).
4. ANPRM Sec. 2520.105-1(e)(2)(i).
5. ANPRM Sec. 2520.105-1(e)(2)(ii).
6. ANPRM Sec. 2520.105-1(e)(2)(ii)(A).
7. ANPRM Sec. 2520.105-1(e)(2)(ii)(B).
8. ANPRM Sec. 2520.105-1(e)(3).

December 31. The assumed commencement date would be the next January 1. For an individual who has not reached normal retirement age, the annuity would be calculated under the assumption that the individual has reached the plan's normal retirement age. For an individual who has passed the normal retirement age, then the actual age is used.[1]

(2)   If the participant has not reached the plan's normal retirement age, the statement also would have to include a projected account balance, expressed in current dollars, as well as the lifetime income stream generated by that projected balance. The assumptions for converting the projected account balance to a lifetime income stream would be the same as used for the current account balance ((1)(a) and (1) (b) above).[2]

(a) The proposal would prescribe general principles for projecting the account balance ((i) below), but offer a safe harbor option ((ii) below);

(i) The projection would have to be based on reasonable assumptions taking into account generally accepted investment theories. A projection would not be reasonable unless it is expressed in current dollars (i.e., an inflation factor must be considered) and takes into account future contributions and investment returns.[3]

(ii)The projection would be deemed to be reasonable (safe harbor) if it is based on the following assumptions: (1) that contributions continue to normal retirement age at the current annual dollar amount, increased at a rate of 3 percent per year, (2) investment returns are 7 percent per year (nominal), and (3) a discount rate of 3 percent per year (to establish the value in current dollars).[4]

(3)   If the individual has a spouse, the lifetime income stream illustration would also have to include a level monthly payment, payable for the life of the individual at the assumed commencement date (see (1)(b) above), with a survivor's benefit which is equal to 50 percent of the monthly payment payable to the individual, and which is payable for the life of the surviving spouse.[5]

(4)   The benefit statement would have to contain: (a) an understandable explanation of the assumptions behind the lifetime income stream illustrations, including both the assumptions used to calculate the present value of the projected account balance and the assumptions used to establish the lifetime income stream, and (b) a statement that the lifetime income stream illustrations are illustrations only, and that actual monthly payments may be received at normal retirement age will

---

1. ANPRM Sec. 2520.105-1(e)(4).
2. ANPRM Sec. 2520.105-1(c)(vi) and (viii).
3. ANPRM Sec. 2520.105-1(d)(1).
4. ANPRM Sec. 2520.105-1(d)(2).
5. ANPRM Sec. 2520.105-1(e)(1)(ii).

depend on numerous factors and may vary from the illustrations in the benefit statement.[1]

Fixed-Return Investments

In the case of a designated investment alternative with respect to which the return is fixed for the term of the investment, the plan administrator shall, in lieu of complying with the general disclosure requirements detailed above, provide participants and beneficiaries an Internet Web site address that is sufficiently specific to provide the following information:

1. The name of the alternative's issuer;

2. The alternative's objectives or goals (e.g., to provide stability of principal and guarantee a minimum rate of return);

3. The alternative's performance data (described in paragraph (d)(1)(ii)(B) of § 2550.404a-5 Fiduciary requirements for disclosure in participant-directed individual account plans) updated on at least a quarterly basis, or more frequently if required by other applicable law;

4. The alternative's fee and expense information described in the general disclosure requirements detailed above.

DOL-SEC Agreement on Application of Securities Laws to Participant-Level Disclosure Regulations

In response to a request from DOL, the Securities and Exchange Commission (SEC) has issued a no-action letter in which SEC has agreed to treat investment-related information provided by a plan administrator to plan participants to comply with EBSA's disclosure regulations as though the information were a communication that satisfies the requirements of Rule 482 of the Securities Act of 1933.[2] The DOL requested this guidance in order to address concerns raised by plan representatives and their financial service providers regarding their obligations under ERISA and Rule 482 — which establishes requirements that open-ended investment companies must follow when placing performance information in their advertising. Specifically, the DOL sought a no-action letter from SEC indicating that a plan's compliance with the DOL disclosure requirements would not result in action by SEC related to Rule 482.

The SEC has also elaborated beyond the DOL request by indicating that the investment-related information provided to plan participants and beneficiaries need not be filed under Rule 497 of the Securities Act and Section 24(b) of the Investment Company Act with SEC or certain national securities associations, such as the Financial Industry Regulatory Authority (FINRA). The SEC noted that it has been informed by FINRA's staff that FINRA intends to interpret its own rules that apply to the information provided by a plan administrator to plan participants that is required by, and complies with, the disclosure requirements under the DOL disclosure regulations. See also Q 402.

---

1. ANPRM Sec. 2520.105-1(c)(6).
2. SEC No-Action: Dep't of Labor (Oct. 26, 2011).

Effective Date and Applicability Date

These rules for fiduciary requirements for disclosure in participant-directed individual account plans went into effect on December 20, 2010.[1] These rules apply to covered individual account plans for plan years beginning on or after January 2, 2012.[2]

Transitional Rules

The initial disclosures required on or before the date on which a participant or beneficiary can first direct his investments must be furnished no later than 120 days after such applicability date to participants or beneficiaries who had the right to direct the investment of assets held in, or contributed to, their individual account on the applicability date.[3]

For plan years beginning before October 1, 2021, if a plan administrator reasonably and in good faith determines that it does not have the information on expenses attributable to the plan that is necessary to calculate, in accordance with the regulatory definition contained within these rules, the five-year and ten-year average annual total returns for a designated investment alternative that is not registered under the Investment Company Act of 1940, the plan administrator may use a reasonable estimate of such expenses or the plan administrator may use the most recently reported total annual operating expenses of the designated investment alternative as a substitute for such expenses. When a plan administrator uses a reasonable estimate or the most recently reported total annual operating expenses as a substitute for actual expenses pursuant to this paragraph, the administrator shall inform participants of the basis on which the returns were determined. Disclosure of returns for periods before the inception of a designated investment alternative are not required.[4]

The DOL has issued a Field Assistance Bulletin announcing a temporary non-enforcement policy under which plans may reset the deadline for annual distribution of the comparative charts used to disclose investment-related information. As background, DOL regulations require plan administrators of 401(k) plans (and other participant-directed individual account plans) to make annual and quarterly disclosures under ERISA Section 404(a)(5).

DOL Field Assistance Bulletin 2013-2 gives employers an extension to provide the 2013 disclosures. Instead of being due twelve months after the 2012 disclosures, they are now due eighteen months afterwards. This provides a one-time "reset" of the disclosure deadline, which would facilitate employers providing the information. The extension is available if the plan administrator reasonably determines that using the extension will benefit participants and beneficiaries.

This relief is limited to the information in the annual disclosures. It does not affect the requirements to:

---

1. Labor Reg. §2550.404a-5(j)(1).
2. Labor Reg. §2550.404a-5(j)(2).
3. Labor Reg. §2550.404a-5(j)(3)(i); Requirements for Fee Disclosure to Plan Fiduciaries and Participants—Applicability Dates, 29 C.F.R. pt. 2550, 76 Fed. Reg. 42539 (July 19, 2011).
4. Labor Reg. §2550.404a-5(j)(3)(ii); 75 Fed. Reg. 64,910 (Oct. 20, 2010).

- Provide quarterly expense disclosures

- Notify participants of changes

- Update investment information on the internet/intranet web sites

The DOL also announced that it is considering amending the regulation to allow a thirty-forty-five day "window" to provide annual disclosures.[1]

98. What information must be contained in the Summary Plan Description (SPD)?

The requirement that a plan administrator file a copy of the SPD with the Department of Labor (DOL) has been eliminated, unless the plan administrator is specifically requested by the DOL to do so.[2] The SPD must accurately reflect the contents of the plan as of a date not earlier than 120 days prior to the date that the SPD is disclosed.[3]

The following information must be included in the SPD of both employee welfare benefit plans and employee pension benefit plans:

1. The name of the plan, and, if different, the name by which the plan is commonly known by its participants and beneficiaries;

2. The name and address of:

    a. in the case of a single employer plan, the employer whose employees are covered by the plan;

    b. in the case of a plan maintained by an employee organization, the employee organization that maintains the plan;

    c. in the case of a collectively bargained plan established or maintained by one or more employee organizations, the representative organization of the parties that established or maintain the plan, as well as: (i) a statement that a complete list of the employer and employee organizations sponsoring the plan may be obtained by participants and beneficiaries upon written request, and the list is available for examination by participants and beneficiaries in accordance with the appropriate regulations, or (ii) a statement that participants and beneficiaries may receive from the plan administrator, upon written request, information as to whether a particular employer or employee organization is a sponsor of the plan, and, if the employer or employee organization is a plan sponsor, the sponsor's address;

---

1. DOL Field Assistance Bulletin 2013-02 (July 22, 2013).
2. ERISA Sec. 104(a)(6).
3. Labor Reg. §2520.102-3.

    d.   in the case of a plan established or maintained by two or more employers, the representative organization of the parties who established or maintain the plan, as well as: (i) a statement that a complete list of the employers sponsoring the plan may be obtained by participants and beneficiaries upon written request to the plan administrator, and the list is available for examination by participants and beneficiaries, as required by applicable regulations, or (ii) a statement that participants and beneficiaries may receive from the plan administrator, upon written request, information as to whether a particular employer is a sponsor of the plan, and if the employer is a plan sponsor, the sponsor's address;

3.   The employer identification number assigned by the Internal Revenue Service to the plan sponsor and the plan number assigned by the plan sponsor;

4.   The type of pension or welfare plan (e.g., for pension plans — defined benefit, money purchase, profit sharing, ERISA Section 404(c), etc., and for welfare plans — hospitalization, disability, prepaid legal service, etc.);

5.   The type of administration of the plan (e.g., contract administration, insurer administration, etc.);

6.   The name, business address, and business telephone number of the plan administrator (as defined in ERISA Section 3(16));

7.   The name of the person designated as agent for service of legal process, the address at which process may be served on that person, and a statement that service of legal process may be made upon a plan trustee or the plan administrator;

8.   The name, title, and address of the principal place of business of each trustee of the plan;

9.   If a plan is maintained pursuant to one or more collective bargaining agreements, a statement that the plan is so maintained and that a copy of the collective bargaining agreement may be obtained by participants and beneficiaries upon written request to the plan administrator, and that it is available for examination by participants and beneficiaries, as required by applicable regulations;

10.   The plan's requirements respecting eligibility for participation and for benefits; the SPD must describe the plan's provisions relating to eligibility to participate in the plan, such as the age or years of service requirements, and the following items (as appropriate):

    a.   for employee pension benefit plans, it must also include a statement describing the plan's normal retirement age (as defined in ERISA Section 3(24)), and a statement describing any other conditions that must be met before a participant will be eligible to receive benefits; the benefits must be described or summarized; and

       b. for employee welfare benefit plans, it must also include a statement of the conditions pertaining to eligibility to receive benefits and a description or summary of the benefits;

11.   In the case of an employee pension benefit plan, a statement describing any joint and survivor benefits provided under the plan, including any requirement that an election be made as a condition to select or reject the joint and survivor annuity;

12.   For both pension and welfare benefit plans, a statement clearly identifying circumstances that may result in disqualification, ineligibility, denial, loss, forfeiture, or suspension of any benefits that a participant or beneficiary might otherwise reasonably expect the plan to provide on the basis of the benefits required by (10) and (11), above;

13.   For an employee pension benefit plan the following information:

       a. if the benefits of the plan are not insured by the Pension Benefit Guaranty Corporation (PBGC), a statement of this fact, and the reason for the lack of insurance; and

       b. if the benefits of the plan are insured by the PBGC, a statement of this fact, a summary of the Pension Benefit Guaranty Corporation provisions of Title IV of ERISA, and a statement indicating that further information on the provisions of Title IV can be obtained from the plan administrator or the PBGC; the address of the PBGC must be provided;

14.   In the case of an employee pension benefit plan, a description and explanation of the plan provisions for determining years of service for eligibility to participate, vesting, breaks in service, and years of participation for benefit accrual; the description must state the service required to accrue full benefits and the manner in which accrual of benefits is prorated for employees failing to complete full service for a year;

15.   In the case of an employee pension benefit plan that will use the "cutback" rule of Revenue Ruling 76-378,[1] to make retroactive changes in the vesting or accrual provisions described in the SPD, a statement that certain provisions of the plan are subject to amendment that directly or indirectly modifies certain plan rights and benefits, the nature of those modifications, and the identification by reference of the portions of the SPD where those provisions are described; the statement may be either printed within the text of the SPD or printed in a separate sheet and disclosed together with the SPD;

16.   The sources of contributions to the plan — for example, employer, employee organization, employees — and the method by which the amount of contributions is calculated; defined benefit pension plans may state without further explanation that the contribution is actuarially determined;

---

1. 1976-2 C.B. 112.

17. The identity of any funding medium used for the accumulation of assets through which benefits are provided; the SPD must identify the insurance company, trust fund, or any other institution, organization, or entity that maintains a fund on behalf of the plan or through which the plan is funded or benefits are provided;

18. The date of the end of the year for purposes of maintaining the plan's fiscal records; and

19. The procedures to be followed in presenting claims for benefits under the plan and the remedies available under the plan for the redress of claims that are denied in whole or in part.[1]

Final rules also require the SPD for welfare benefit plans to include a description or summary of the benefits and service providers available under the plan. If the schedule of benefits and/or service providers is extensive, the plan sponsor may provide the lists under separate documents if such documents are referenced in the SPD and participants are advised in the SPD that such lists are available without cost to any participant or beneficiary who requests one.[2] Such welfare benefit plans are also required to disclose to participants and beneficiaries such cost-sharing measures as the plan may have in place with insurance providers (premiums, deductibles, coinsurance, etc.), as well as any annual or lifetime caps, which preventative services are offered, whether, and under what circumstances existing and new drugs are covered, and any other conditions or limits on the type and availability of coverage offered.[3] These final rules became effective as of the first day of the second plan year beginning on or after January 22, 2001.

Other provisions of the final rules include a requirement that plans include a description of the procedures governing QDROs, or a statement that participants and beneficiaries can obtain, without charge, a copy of such procedures.[4] A description of the procedures governing qualified medical child support orders is also required to be disclosed in the SPD of welfare benefit plans.[5] In addition, welfare plans are required to disclose COBRA rights and any model language required as a result of the Newborns' and Mothers' Health Protection Act.[6]

SPDs must be written in a manner calculated to be understood by the average plan participant, and they must be sufficiently accurate and comprehensive to reasonably apprise participants and beneficiaries of their rights and obligations under the plan.[7]

A non-English language notice of assistance must be displayed prominently in the summary plan description (SPD) of any plan that:

---

1. Labor Reg. §2520.102-3.
2. Labor Reg. §2520.102-3(j)(2) and (3).
3. Labor Reg. §2520.102-3(j)(3).
4. Labor Reg. §2520.102-3(j)(1).
5. Labor Reg. §2520.102-3(j)(2).
6. Labor Reg. §2520.102-3(t)(2) and (u)(1).
7. ERISA Sec. 102(a).

1. Covers fewer than one-hundred participants at the beginning of the plan year, and under which at least 25 percent of all plan participants are literate only in the same non-English language; or

2. Covers one-hundred or more participants at the beginning of the plan year, and under which the lesser of:

    a. 500 or more participants, or

    b. at least 10 percent of the plan participants are literate only in the same non-English language.[1]

The Supreme Court in *CIGNA Corp. v. Amara* has ruled that ERISA Section 502(a)(1)(B) does not permit a court to *reform* a plan document to comport with an erroneous SPD because the SPD is a communication "about the plan" and does not "constitute the *terms* of the plan." In this holding, the Supreme Court rejected the DOL's position as stated in its Amicus Brief because the Supreme Court was unable to reconcile the DOL's position with ERISA Section 102(a), which provides that an SPD is an informal explanation of plan benefits and cannot be considered a part of a plan's governing documents. See Q 355 and Q 518 for a detailed elaboration on the impact of this decision on the issues of fiduciaries' being required to follow the written terms of a governing plan document and the application of this ruling to remedies and equitable estoppel/equitable relief.[2]

The Sixth Circuit has held that a plan's beneficiary designation procedures, as detailed in the SPD are enforceable by plan and not in conflict with the Amara opinion.[3] The Sixth Circuit upheld a decision by the trial court that the subject plan Administrative Committee's decision was not arbitrary and capricious. The plan specifically authorizes the Administrative Committee to prescribe the form and procedures for filing a beneficiary designation. The Committee did so in the SPD. The court ruled that relying on the SPD to determine the procedures for making a beneficiary designation does not contradict the holding in *CIGNA Corp. v. Amara*,[4] because there is no conflict between the SPD and the plan. Here, the plan authorizes the Committee to prescribe beneficiary designation procedures, and it did that in the SPD. An SPD can be a document or instrument governing the plan without constituting the terms of the plan.

99. What are the summary plan description (SPD) requirements in a successor plan situation?

The ERISA regulations establish an alternative method of SPD compliance for certain successor pension plans.[5] Where a portion of plan participants and beneficiaries have rights established under a successor plan, while continuing to be eligible for benefits under the former plan that

---

1. Labor Reg. §2520.102-2(c)(1).
2. *CIGNA Corp. v. Amara*, No. 08-804, 50 EBC 2569 (U.S. May 16, 2011).
3. *Liss v. Fidelity Employer Services Company, LLC*, 2013 WL 677280 (6th Cir. February 26, 2013) (not selected for publication in the Federal Register).
4. 131 S.Ct. 1866 (2011),
5. Labor Reg. §2520.104-4.

has been merged into the successor plan, the plan administrator is not required to describe the relevant provisions of the old plan in the SPD of the successor plan.

The provisions of this alternative compliance method are applicable only to plan mergers that occur after the issuance by the successor plan of the initial SPD under ERISA.

The alternative method of compliance is available only if the plan administrator of the successor plan furnishes to the participants covered under the merged plan and beneficiaries receiving pension benefits under the merged plan, within ninety days after the effective date of the merger, the following:

1. A copy of the most recent SPD of the successor plan;

2. A copy of any summaries of material modifications to the successor plan not incorporated in the most recent SPD; and

3. A separate statement containing a brief description of the merger; a description of the provisions of, and benefits provided by, the merged and successor plans that are applicable to the participants and beneficiaries of the merged plan; and a notice that copies of the merged and successor plan documents, as well as the plan merger documents (including the portions of any corporate merger documents that describe or control the plan merger), are available for inspection and that copies may be obtained upon written request for a duplication charge (in accordance with the provisions of Labor Regulation Section 2520.104b-2(a)).

After the merger, the plan administrator in all subsequent SPDs must clearly and conspicuously identify the class of participants and beneficiaries affected by the provisions of the merged plans, and state that the documents above are available for inspection and those copies may be obtained upon written request for a duplication charge.

100. What are the distribution requirements for the summary plan description (SPD)?

A plan administrator is required to furnish to each plan participant and beneficiary receiving benefits under the plan a copy of the SPD as well as a statement of ERISA rights. These documents must be provided within ninety days after a person becomes a participant, or (in the case of a beneficiary) within ninety days after he first receives benefits or, if later, within 120 days after the plan becomes subject to the reporting and disclosure provisions of ERISA.[1]

Where a plan is made prospectively effective to take effect after a certain date or after a condition is satisfied, the date upon which the plan becomes subject to the reporting and disclosure provisions of ERISA is the day after the date the condition is satisfied. Where a plan is adopted with a retroactive effective date, the 120-day period begins on the day after the plan is adopted. Where a plan is made retroactively effective dependent on a condition, the day on which the plan becomes subject to the reporting and disclosure provisions of ERISA is the day

---

1. ERISA Sec. 104(b)(1); Labor Reg. §2520.104b-2(a).

after the day on which the condition is satisfied. Where a plan is made retroactively effective subject to a contingency that may or may not occur in the future, the day on which the plan becomes subject to the reporting and disclosure provisions of ERISA is the day after the day on which the contingency occurs.[1]

ERISA also requires a plan administrator to provide a copy of the latest SPD upon the *written request* of a participant or beneficiary.[2] The penalty for failure to comply with such a written request is $110 per day.[3] The Ninth Circuit Court of Appeals has held that a participant's request for an SPD under this provision[4] did not have to be in writing for this penalty to apply, because the SPD was something the participant is entitled to receive automatically, without any request.[5]

According to a district court ruling, a plan sponsor's established administrative practices may serve as evidence that an SPD was timely furnished.[6] In that case, a participant applied for disability retirement benefits five years after termination. However, the claim was denied because the plan document and SPD clearly spelled out that such claims must be filed within two years. The plaintiff claimed that she never received the SPD. Two employees of the plan sponsor's human resources department testified that it was standard practice to personally provide the SPD to new hires and employees who change employment status. The plaintiff had such a change in employment status, and the records clearly indicated that she received other documents regarding her benefits. In light of this, and the evidence of the plan sponsor's administrative practice, the court held that it was "more likely true than not" that the plaintiff had actually received the SPD.

The Court of Appeals for the Fourth Circuit has ruled that the failure of an employer to deliver the SPD to an employee is not a breach of fiduciary duty where the employer was able to demonstrate that it had "by sufficiently reliable means" submitted materials adequate to inform the participant of the plan's conditions for enrollment.[7]

The Court of Appeals for the Fifth Circuit has issued an opinion stating that information in a plan's "Enrollment Guide" that conflicted with the plan's SPD was not controlling because the SPD is the primary disclosure document.[8]

The U.S. District Court for the Eastern District of Virginia has held that no penalties shall apply for the failure to provide a terminated participant with a copy of the SPD to the participant's health plan absent a specific written request of the participant.[9] The court ruled that although there is a requirement to automatically provide an SPD within ninety days after a person becomes a participant, there are no statutory penalties under ERISA for failure to do so,

1. Labor Reg. §2520.104b-2(a)(3).
2. ERISA Sec. 104(b)(4) (*emphasis added*).
3. ERISA Sec. 502(c)(1); Labor Reg. §2570.502c-1.
4. ERISA Sec. 104(b)(4).
5. *Crotty v. Cook*, 121 F.3d 541 (9th Cir. 1997).
6. See *Hunter v. Lockheed Martin Corp.*, 202 U.S. Dist. LEXIS 13797 (N.D. Cal. 2002).
7. *Brenner v. Johns Hopkins Univ.*, 2004 U.S. App. LEXIS 2339 (4th Cir. 2004).
8. *Bailey v. CIGNA Ins.*, 32 EBC 1720 (5th Cir. 2004).
9. *Middlebrooks v. St. Coletta of Greater Wash., Inc.*, 2010 WL 3521760 (E.D. Va. 2010), and 2010 WL 3522084 (E.D. Va. 2010).

absent a written request. The court also found no requirement to provide an SPD upon termination of coverage, absent a written request.

The Federal Court for the eastern District of Virginia imposed the maximum penalty of $110 per day against the employer of a group health plan participant in its role as plan administrator for failing to timely provide the most current SPD upon a written request. The employer provided an older, inaccurate version of the SPD when there was a more current, and accurate, version containing material changes to the definition of long-term disability that impacted the participant's claim for benefits.[1]

101. What information regarding plan termination must be contained in the summary plan description (SPD)?

An SPD is required to include information regarding the provisions of the plan that relate to the termination of the plan. It is the position of the Department of Labor that since a plan termination may result in the denial or loss of benefits to participants and beneficiaries, the SPD must include the following:

1. A summary of any plan provisions on the rights of the plan sponsor, or other entity, to terminate the plan, and the circumstances, if any, under which the plan may be terminated;

2. A summary of plan provisions that govern the benefits, rights, and obligations of participants and beneficiaries, including provisions on the accrual and vesting of benefits under the plan upon termination; and

3. A summary of those provisions of the plan that deal with the allocation and disposition of plan assets upon termination.[2]

102. What are the plan's obligations regarding the updating of the summary plan description (SPD)?

The administrator must furnish to each participant, and to each beneficiary receiving benefits under the plan, an updated SPD that integrates all plan amendments made within a five-year period. The updated SPD must be distributed every fifth year after the plan becomes subject to the reporting and disclosure provisions of ERISA. If no amendments have been made during the five-year period, this requirement does not apply. The administrator must furnish to each participant, and to each beneficiary receiving benefits under the plan, the SPD every tenth year after the plan becomes subject to the reporting and disclosure provisions of ERISA.[3]

Updated SPDs must be provided to each participant and beneficiary receiving benefits under the plan no later than 210 days following the end of the plan year in which a five-year or ten-year period (described above) ends.[4]

---

1. *Latimer v. Wash. Gas Light Co.*, 2012 WL 2119254 (E.D. Va. 2012).
2. DOL Technical Release 84-1, 5A Pens. Plan Guide (CCH) ¶22,475.
3. ERISA Sec. 104(b)(1).
4. Labor Reg. §2520.104b-2(b).

103. What information regarding material plan changes must be provided to participants?

A summary of material modifications (SMM) in plan provisions is required to be provided to participants and beneficiaries. The SMM must be provided within 210 days after the close of the plan year in which the modification was adopted (even for the adoption of amendments that take effect on a date in the future), and must be written in a manner calculated to be understood by the average participant.[1]

The disclosure date is not affected by retroactive applications to a prior plan year of an amendment that makes a material modification to the plan; a modification does not occur before it is adopted.[2]

The SMM is not required where it has been rescinded or otherwise does not take effect.[3] Also, an SMM is not required if the changes or modifications are described in a timely SPD.[4]

Where an SPD has been provided to participants in accordance with ERISA, it must be accompanied by all SMMs or changes in information required to be included in the SPD that have not been incorporated into that SPD.

Any change in the name of a plan trustee is a modification or change that must be disclosed to participants and beneficiaries through an SMM.[5]

For plan changes in a group health plan that is subject to the provisions of HIPAA '96, changes must be disclosed to participants and beneficiaries no later than sixty days after the first day of the first plan year.[6]

Plan changes to maternity and newborn infant hospital coverage in a group health plan that is subject to the provisions of the Newborns' and Mothers' Health Protection Act of 1996 (NMHPA) must be disclosed to participants and beneficiaries no later than sixty days after the first day of the first plan year.[7]

104. What are the Summary Annual Report (SAR) requirements?

The plan administrator is required to furnish annually to each participant and beneficiary receiving benefits an SAR.[8] Regulations dictate the content, style, and format requirements for SARs and even provide prototype formats to be reproduced for pension and welfare benefit plans. Plan administrators may not vary the format of the SAR; however, information that is not applicable to the plan may be omitted. Also, plan administrators may elaborate upon information

---

1. ERISA Secs. 102(a)(1), 104(b)(1); Labor Reg. §2520.104b-3(a).
2. Labor Reg. §2520.104b-3(a).
3. Labor Reg. §2520.104b-3(a).
4. Labor Reg. §2520.104b-3(b).
5. DOL Adv. Op. 80-32A.
6. Labor Reg. §2520.102-3(v)(1).
7. ERISA Sec. 711(d); Labor Reg. §2520.1023(v)(2).
8. ERISA Sec. 104(b)(3); Labor Reg. §2520.104b-10.

contained within the SAR. The information used to complete the forms must be based upon information contained in the most recent annual report of the plan.[1]

The SAR is required to be provided to participants and beneficiaries receiving benefits under the plan no later than nine months after the close of the plan year. In the case of welfare benefit plans that use group health insurance arrangements, the SAR is required to be provided within nine months of the close of the fiscal year of the trust or other entity that files the report.[2]

A plan that covers fewer than one-hundred participants at the beginning of a plan year in which 25 percent or more of the plan participants are literate only in the same non-English language, or a plan that covers one-hundred or more participants in which 500 or more participants or 10 percent or more of all plan participants, whichever is less, are literate only in the same non-English language, must provide to these non-English language participants an English-language SAR that prominently displays a notice, in the non-English language common to these participants, offering them assistance. The actual assistance provided need not be in writing. The notice must clearly set forth any procedures participants must follow to obtain the assistance. Further, plans that provide an explanatory notice accompanying Form 5500-R or the notice of the availability of Form 5500-R must also provide a notice, in the non-English language common to these participants, offering assistance.[3]

The following plans are exempted from the SAR provisions of ERISA:

1. Totally unfunded welfare benefit plans;

2. Small unfunded or insured welfare benefit plans (that satisfy these definitions in Labor Regulation Section 2520.104b-20(b));

3. An apprenticeship or other training plan;

4. A pension or welfare plan for selected employees;

5. A day care center; and

6. A dues-financed pension or welfare plan.[4]

It is the opinion of the Department of Labor that ERISA and its attendant regulations require SARs to be distributed to affected participants and beneficiaries for the plan year in which the plan terminates. This information is necessary to assist participants and beneficiaries in evaluating the financial information relating to the distribution of residual assets of the plan.[5]

For defined benefit plans, if the current value of the assets of the plan is less than 70 percent of the current liability under the plan, this must be disclosed in a statement in the annual report

---

1. Labor Reg. §§2520.104b-10(d)(3), 2520.104b-10(d)(4).
2. Labor Reg. §2520.104b-10(c).
3. Labor Reg. §2520.104b-10(e).
4. Labor Reg. §2520.104b-10(g).
5. DOL Adv. Op. 79-64A.

that indicates the level to which the plan is underfunded (see Q 116 for further details).[1] A similar notice of underfunding is required to be placed in the SAR.[2]

105. What are the plan disclosure obligations regarding the joint and survivor annuity option?

A plan that provides a qualified joint and survivor annuity must provide to each participant, within a reasonable period of time before the annuity starting date, a written explanation of:

1. The terms and conditions of the qualified joint and survivor annuity;

2. The participant's right to make, and the effect of, an election to waive the joint and survivor annuity form of benefits;

3. The rights of the participant's spouse; and

4. The right to make, and the effect of, a revocation of an election.[3]

The provision of a written notice is not required if the plan fully subsidized the cost of the benefit and the plan does not permit a participant to waive the benefit or designate another beneficiary.[4] The Pension Protection Act of 2006 (PPA) amended ERISA Section 205(c)(7)(A) to require that distribution notices must be furnished to participants no less than 30 days and no more than 180 days before the date of distribution.

The PPA also amended ERISA Sections 205(c) and (d), providing that, beginning January 1, 2008, if a plan's mandatory joint and survivor annuity is less than 75 percent, the plan must offer as an option a survivor annuity that equals 75 percent of the annuity payable during the joint lives of participants and their spouses. If the plan's joint and survivor annuity is equal to or exceeds 75 percent, the plan must offer a 50 percent survivor annuity.

106. What is the plan disclosure obligation regarding the qualified pre-retirement survivor annuity?

A plan must provide a written explanation of the qualified pre-retirement survivor annuity to each participant that details:

1. The terms and conditions of the qualified pre-retirement survivor annuity;

2. The participant's right to make, and the effect of, an election to waive the qualified pre-retirement survivor annuity;

3. The rights of the participant's spouse; and

4. The right to make, and the effect of making, a revocation of an election.[5]

---

1. ERISA Sec. 103(d)(11).
2. ERISA Sec. 104(b)(3).
3. ERISA Sec. 205(c)(3); IRC Sec. 417(a)(3)(A).
4. ERISA Sec. 205(c)(5)(A); IRC Sec. 417(a)(5)(A).
5. ERISA Sec. 205(c)(3)(B); IRC Sec. 417(a)(3)(B)(i).

This information must be provided no later than whichever of the following periods ends last:

1.   The period beginning with the first day of the plan year in which the participant attains age thirty-two and ending with the close of the plan year preceding the plan year in which the participant attains age thirty-five;

2.   A reasonable period after the individual becomes a participant;

3.   A reasonable period of time after the end of the subsidization by the plan of a survivor benefit with respect to a participant;

4.   A reasonable period of time after the survivor benefit provisions of ERISA Section 205 become applicable to a participant; or

5.   A reasonable period of time after separation from service in the case of a participant who separates from service before the age of thirty-five.[1]

The provision of a written notice is not required if the plan fully subsidized the cost of the benefit and the plan does not permit a participant to waive the benefit or designate another beneficiary.[2]

The Pension Protection Act of 2006 amended ERISA Section 205(c) and (d), providing that if a plan's mandatory joint and survivor annuity is less than 75 percent, the plan must offer as an option a survivor annuity that equals 75 percent of the annuity payable during the joint lives of participants and their spouses. If the plan's joint and survivor annuity is equal to, or exceeds 75 percent, the plan must offer a 50 percent survivor annuity.

107. What is the plan obligation regarding the rollover distribution notice?

The plan administrator of a plan must, within a reasonable period of time before making an eligible rollover distribution from an eligible retirement plan, provide a written explanation to the recipient of:

1.   The provisions under which the recipient may have the distribution directly transferred to another eligible retirement plan, and that the automatic distribution by direct transfer applies to certain distributions;

2.   The provisions that require the withholding of tax on the distribution if it is not directly transferred to another eligible retirement plan;

3.   The provisions under which the distribution will not be subject to tax if transferred to an eligible retirement plan within sixty days after the date on which the recipient received the distribution; and

4.   If applicable, the tax on lump-sum distributions (of IRC Section 402(d)) or related taxability rules (of IRC Section 402(e)).[3]

---

1. ERISA Sec. 205(c)(3)(B); IRC Sec. 417(a)(3)(B)(ii).
2. ERISA Sec. 205(c)(5)(A); IRC Sec. 417(a)(5)(A).
3. IRC Sec. 402(f).

108. What guidance has the DOL provided concerning rollovers of mandatory cash-outs?

The DOL has issued final regulations providing a safe harbor for plan fiduciaries handling automatic rollovers to IRAs of mandatory cash-outs from qualified plans. The regulations finalized proposed regulations issued in 2004 and expanded the availability of the safe harbor to also cover mandatory distributions of $1,000 or less. For details on this safe harbor, see Q 277 and Q 278.[1]

In conjunction with the final regulations, the DOL also finalized a prohibited transaction class exemption (PTE 2004-16) that allows financial institutions (or their affiliates) who are plan administrators to designate themselves (or their affiliates) as the IRA provider to receive the automatic rollover of the cash-outs. For more information on this PTE, see Q 460.

109. What information is required to be contained in the statement of ERISA rights?

A plan administrator is required to furnish, in the summary plan description (SPD), to each participant and beneficiary receiving benefits under the plan, a statement of ERISA rights of participants and beneficiaries. The statement of rights must appear as one consolidated statement.[2] A model statement of ERISA rights is contained in the regulations.[3] An SPD will be deemed to comply with the statement of rights requirements if it includes the model statement (excluding inapplicable material). The statement of rights must disclose that participants and beneficiaries are entitled to certain rights, including the rights to:

1. Examine, without charge, all plan documents, supporting documents, and documents filed with the Department of Labor (DOL);

2. Obtain copies of the plan documents upon written request to the plan administrator (who may make a reasonable charge for these copies);

3. Receive the plan's Summary Annual Report;

4. Obtain a statement of any right to receive a pension upon the attainment of normal retirement age, and what that pension would be at normal retirement age should the employee terminate employment now;

5. Obtain a statement, upon written request, of how many more years an employee must work to obtain a pension benefit upon the attainment of normal retirement age;

6. Receive an explanation of the fiduciary duties imposed upon plan fiduciaries (including the prohibition against discriminating against participants and beneficiaries for seeking to enforce their rights under ERISA);

7. Obtain a written explanation of any reason for the denial of a claim for benefits under the plan;

---

1. See also Labor Reg. §2550.404a-2.
2. ERISA Sec. 104(c).
3. See Labor Reg. §2520.102-3(t)(2).

8.   Appeal the denial of a claim for benefits; and

9.   Enforce their rights by taking certain specified steps (i.e., civil action or seeking DOL assistance).[1]

The style and format of the statement must not have the effect of misleading, misinforming, or failing to inform participants and beneficiaries. All information contained in the statement of rights must be written in a manner calculated to be understood by the average plan participant, taking into account factors such as the level of comprehension and education of typical participants in the plan and the complexity of the items required in the statement of rights. Inaccurate, incomprehensible, or misleading explanatory material will fail to meet the requirements of the statement of rights. If the plan administrator finds it desirable to make additional mention of certain rights elsewhere in the SPD, it may do so. The SPD may state that the statement of ERISA rights is required by federal law and regulations.[2]

For group health plans, the model statement of ERISA rights may be modified under the regulations to require group health plans to instruct participants and beneficiaries to contact the nearest DOL field office, or the DOL Division of Technical Assistance and Inquiries, with questions regarding their rights.[3]

110. Does ERISA provide additional protection to small business retirement plans?

ERISA Section 103(a)(3)(A) requires qualified plans to engage an independent qualified public accountant and to file the opinion of the accountant with the plan's Annual Report Form 5500. Regulations provide a waiver of the annual examination and report of an independent qualified public accountant for plans with fewer than one-hundred participants as of the beginning of the plan year.[4] The Department of Labor (DOL) has issued final regulations that are designed to increase the security of assets in small business retirement plans. The regulations apply to retirement plans covering fewer than one-hundred participants and impose additional requirements in order to remain exempt from having an annual audit of the plan.

The regulations provide that the administrator of a qualified plan with fewer than 100 participants is not required to comply with the annual audit requirement if, with respect to each plan year, the following conditions are satisfied:

1.   At least 95 percent of the assets of the plan constitute "qualifying plan assets," as defined below; or

2.   Any person who handles assets of the plan that do not constitute qualifying plan assets is bonded under ERISA Section 412 with the amount of the bond being not less than the value of the non-qualifying assets.[5]

---

1. Labor Reg. §2520.102-3(t)(2).
2. Labor Reg. §2520.102-3(t)(1).
3. Labor Reg. §2520.102-3(t)(2).
4. Labor Reg. §2520.104-46.
5. Labor Reg. §2520.104-46(b)(1)(i)(A)(1) and (2).

"Qualifying plan assets" are defined under the final regulations as:

1. Qualifying employer securities as defined in ERISA Section 407(d)(1);

2. Participant loans meeting the requirements of ERISA Section 408(b)(1);

3. Shares issued by a registered investment company (mutual fund);

4. Investment and annuity contracts issued by an insurance company; and

5. Any assets held by the following institutions: (a) a bank or similar financial institution as defined in Labor Regulation Section 2550.408b-4(c); (b) an insurance company; (c) a broker-dealer registered under the Securities and Exchange Act of 1934; or (d) any other organization authorized to act as a trustee for individual retirement accounts under IRC Section 408.[1]

The summary annual report for the plan must also include the following enhanced disclosures:

1. The name of each institution holding qualifying plan assets and the amount of such assets held by each institution as of the end of the plan year (excluding employer securities, participant loans that satisfy ERISA Section 408(b)(1), and participant-directed individual accounts);

2. The name of the surety company issuing any bond required under the regulation;

3. A notice indicating that participants and beneficiaries may, upon request and without charge, examine or receive copies of evidence of any bond required under the regulation and copies of the statements received from each institution holding qualified assets that describe the assets held by the institution as of the end of the plan year; and

4. A notice stating that participants and beneficiaries should contact the Pension and Welfare Benefits Administration of the DOL if they are unable to examine or obtain copies of the statements or evidence of the bond.[2]

Further, the plan administrator must, upon the request of a participant or beneficiary, make available for inspection, or provide copies of (at no charge), the evidence of any bond required by the regulation and the statement of assets from the financial institutions holding qualifying assets.[3]

111. What is the Statement of Participant's Accrued and Vested Benefits?

Each plan administrator of an employee pension benefit plan must furnish to any plan participant or beneficiary who so requests in writing, a statement indicating, on the basis of the

---

1. Labor Reg. §2520.104-46(b)(1)(ii)(C)(4).
2. Labor Reg. §2520.104-46(b)(1)(i)(B).
3. Labor Reg. §2520.104-46(b)(1)(i)(C).

latest available information, the total benefits accrued, and the nonforfeitable pension benefits, if any, that have accrued, or the earliest date on which benefits will become nonforfeitable.[1]

Plan sponsors must maintain records with respect to each of their employees sufficient to determine the benefits due or that may become due to those employees. The plan administrator must make a report, in such a form as required by regulations, to each employee who is a participant under the plan and who:

1.   Requests the report, in the manner and at the time as is provided in the regulations;

2.   Terminates his service with the employer; or

3.   Has a one-year break in service.[2]

The Pension Protection Act of 2006 amends ERISA Section 105(a) to require defined contribution plans (other than one-participant plans) and tax-deferred annuities to provide:

1.   Quarterly benefit statements to participants with a right to direct their own investments within individual accounts;

2.   Annual statements to participants who do not have the right to direct investments within their individual accounts; and

3.   Benefit statements upon written request (not to exceed more than one per year).

In addition, defined benefit plans would be required to furnish benefit statements every three years (or alternatively, annually furnish a notice of availability of statements) to vested participants, or provide benefit statements upon written request (not to exceed one per year).

These updated benefit statement requirements stipulate that they must include, among other things, information regarding accrued or vested benefits to date, the value of the participant's investments as of the most recent valuation date, an explanation of the importance of diversification, and a direction to the DOL's Web site for investment and diversification information. These statements may be delivered in either written or electronic format.[3]

Failure to furnish benefit statements may result in penalties up to $100 per day per participant.[4]

112. What guidance has the DOL provided participants who wish to learn more about the fees and expenses of their 401(k) plan?

In 1998, the DOL released the results of its study on 401(k) plan fees and expenses. The study was undertaken on behalf of the DOL by an independent firm, in an effort to develop information allowing participants to understand the ways service providers charge for different

1. ERISA Sec. 105(a).
2. ERISA Sec. 209(a).
3. See Field Assistance Bull. 2006-3.
4. ERISA Sec. 502(a)(1).

services. The study also pointed out that many plan sponsors are not fully aware of how fees are calculated and where they may be charged against participant accounts.

Although the report makes no recommendations, it does provide a checklist for plan sponsors and participants to use in reviewing their 401(k) plan fees and expenses. This checklist helps the user to see how fees and expenses affect investment returns and impact retirement income. The checklist provides the following 10 questions for readers to ask in evaluating the fees and expenses of their 401(k) plan:

1. What investment options are offered under your company's 401(k) plan?

2. Do you have all available documentation about the investment choices under your plan and the fees charged to your plan?

3. What types of investment education are available to you under your plan?

4. What arrangement is used to provide services under your plan?

5. Do you and other participants use most or all of the optional services offered under your 401(k) plan, such as participant loan programs and insurance coverages?

6. If administrative services are paid separately from investment management fees, are they paid for by the plan, paid for by your employer, or shared?

7. Are the investment options tracking an established market index or is there a higher level of investment management services being provided?

8. Do any of the investment options under your plan include sales charges (such as loads or commissions)?

9. Do any of the investment options under your plan include any fees related to specific investments, such as 12b-1 fees, insurance charges, or surrender fees, and what do they cover?

10. Does your plan offer any special funds or special classes of stock (which are generally sold to larger group investors)?

The full text of the DOL's release, titled "Study of 401(k) Plan Fees and Expenses," as well as its participant handbook entitled *A Look at 401(k) Plan Fees* are available on the DOL's Web site at http://www.dol.gov/dol/pwba.

113. How can a plan sponsor understand and evaluate the fees and expenses related to its 401(k) plan?

Plan sponsors, or their assigned representatives, when establishing a 401(k) plan, are responsible for the selection of investment options from which participants will choose. They are also responsible for the selection of service providers to the plan, as well as the monitoring of the services provided and of the performance of the investment options. It is the stated view of the DOL that all of these duties require a fiduciary of the plan sponsor to consider the costs to the plan while complying with the fiduciary standards under ERISA.

In addition, the DOL advises in its pamphlet *A Look at 401(k) Plan Fees for Employers* that "understanding fees and expenses is important in providing for the services necessary for" a plan's operation. The DOL also says that "after careful evaluation during the initial selection, the plan's fees and expenses should be monitored to determine whether they continue to be reasonable."

As part of the evaluation process, the DOL offers 10 questions to assist in the evaluation and consideration of fees and expenses:

1. Have you given each of your prospective service providers complete and identical information with regard to your plan?

2. Do you know what features you want to provide (e.g., loans, number of investment options, types of investments, Internet trading)?

3. Have you decided which fees and expenses you, as plan sponsor, will pay, which your employees will pay, and/or which you will share?

4. Do you know which fees and expenses are charged directly to the plan and which are deducted from investment returns?

5. Do you know what services are covered under the base fee and what services incur an extra charge? Do you know what the fees are for extra or customized services?

6. Do you understand that some investment options have higher fees than others because of the nature of the investment?

7. Does the prospective service arrangement have any restrictions, such as charges for early termination of your relationship with the provider?

8. Does the prospective arrangement assist your employees in making informed investment decisions for their individual accounts (e.g., providing investment education, information on fees, and the like) and how are you charged for this service?

9. Have you considered asking potential providers to present uniform fee information that includes all fees charged?

10. What information will you receive on a regular basis from the prospective provider so that you can monitor the provision of services and the investments that you select and make changes, if necessary?

The DOL recommends, in its 401(k) pamphlet described above, that the plan sponsor provide all prospective service providers "with complete and identical information about the plan" and to consider the specific services desired for the plan. The DOL cites as examples "the types and frequency of reports to the employer, communications to participants, educational materials and meetings for participants and the availability and frequency of participant investment transfers, the level of responsibility you (the plan sponsor) want the prospective service provider to assume, what services must be included and what are possible extras or customized services, and optional features such as loans, Internet trading and telephone transfers."

To assist in gathering this information and in making equivalent comparisons, the DOL has developed a 401(k) Plan Fee Disclosure Form to help plan sponsors make informed cost-benefit decisions with a plan and compare investment product fees and plan administration expenses charged by competing service providers, regardless of how each service provider structures its fees.[1]

114. What are the Annual Funding Notice and Notice to Participants in Underfunded Plans?

Defined Benefit Plan Annual Funding Notice

ERISA Section 101(f), as expanded by Section 501(a) of the Pension Protection Act of 2006, requires administrators of all defined benefit plans to provide an annual funding notice to the PBGC, to each plan participant and beneficiary, and in the case of multiemployer plans, to each employer that has an obligation to contribute to the plan.[2] The annual funding notice must contain, among other things, the plan's funding percentage (not only to the plan year to which the notice applies, but also to the two plan years preceding that year), a statement of the value of the plan's assets and liabilities and a description of how the plan's assets are invested as of specific dates, and a description of the benefits that are eligible to be guaranteed by the PBGC.[3] The notice may be provided in written, electronic, or other appropriate form to the extent the form is reasonably accessible to persons to whom the notice is required to be provided.[4]

The DOL has provided two model annual funding notices (for single-employer plans and for multiemployer plans) under Field Assistance Bulletin (FAB) 2009-01, along with a series of FAQs to elaborate on DOL guidance. Use of the model notices will be deemed to satisfy the content requirements of ERISA Section 101(f).

Notice to Participants in Underfunded Plans

The plan administrator of a plan that is less than 90 percent funded must provide, in a form and manner and at such time as prescribed in Pension Benefits Guaranty Corporation (PBGC) regulations, notice to plan participants and beneficiaries of the plan's funding status and the limits on the PBGC's guarantee should the plan terminate while underfunded. This notice must be written in a manner calculated to be understood by the average plan participant.[5]

The notice for a plan year must be issued no later than two months after the deadline for filing the plan's Form 5500.[6] The notice must explain the employer's obligation to fund the plan and indicate the percentage at which the plan is actually funded. The notice is also required to disclose the dollar amount the employer must pay in satisfaction of the minimum funding standards.[7]

---

1. A copy of the DOL pamphlet on 401(k) plan fee disclosure is available on the Internet at http://www.dol.gov/ebsa/.
2. ERISA Sec. 101(f).
3. ERISA Sec. 101(f)(2)(B)(i) and (ii).
4. ERISA Sec. 101(f)(4)(C); DOL FAB 2009-01.
5. ERISA Sec. 4011.
6. PBGC Reg. §4011.8.
7. PBGC Reg. §4011.10.

The PBGC has established a model notice that plan administrators may use in providing notice to participants in underfunded plans.[1]

115. What is the Notice of Failure to Fund?

If an employer maintaining a plan (other than a multiemployer plan) fails to make a required payment, it must notify each participant and beneficiary (including alternate payees) of the failure to make a required installment or other payment required to meet the minimum funding standard to a plan. The notice must be made before the sixtieth day following the due date for the installment or other payment.[2]

In FAB 2007-03, the DOL modified prior guidance that provided a forty-five-day deadline for the annual benefit statement for defined contribution plans. FAB 2007-03 extends the deadline to the date the plan files its Form 5500 for the plan year to which the statement relates (but in no event later than the date, including extensions, on which the plan is required to file its Form 5500).

In issuing this extension, the DOL acknowledged the feedback from the benefits industry. The plan sponsors of many profit sharing plans do not determine or contribute profit sharing contributions until after the sponsor has completed its corporate (or partnership) tax return for the year. As such, the forty-five-day deadline was practically difficult to attain and was potentially a heavy expense for many of these plans to meet. Because the majority of the information required to be disclosed in the benefit statements is compiled as a part of the Annual Report Form 5500 compilation, plan sponsors indicated to the DOL that it would be helpful to have the annual benefit statement and Form 5500 deadlines correspond.[3]

A plan administrator who fails to meet this notice requirement may be held liable to participants and beneficiaries in the amount of up to $110 a day from the date of the failure to provide notice.[4]

116. How can a plan distribute notices to missing participants?

The Department of Labor has advised that plan administrators must attempt to locate missing participants to satisfy their fiduciary obligations.[5] Where a plan administrator, after a diligent good-faith effort, is having difficulty locating missing plan participants, she may seek the assistance of the Internal Revenue Service (IRS). For recent DOL guidance on rollovers of mandatory cash-outs for missing participants, see Q 273 to Q 278.

The IRS discontinued the use of their letter-forwarding program in 2012.

Under IRS Project 753, the plan administrator is required to submit a flat fee of $1,750 per request, along with $.50 for each letter to be forwarded and $.01 per address search.[6]

---

1. PBGC Reg. §4011 app. A. See Appendix A.
2. ERISA Sec. 101(d).
3. DOL Field Assistance Bull. 2007-03 (Oct. 12, 2007), http://www.dol.gov/ebsa/regs/fab2007-3.html.
4. ERISA Sec. 502(c)(1).
5. DOL Adv. Op. 11-86.
6. Rev. Proc. 94-22, 1994-1 C.B. 608.

For defined benefit plans subject to Pension Benefit Guaranty Corporation (PBGC) coverage that are terminating, the PBGC advises that the plan must purchase an irrevocable commitment from an insurance company for the provision of benefits to any missing participant who is entitled to $5,000 or more in benefits. Missing participants who were married as of their separation from service must have a joint and survivor annuity purchased on their behalf.[1]

For further details on the PBGC's role in locating missing participants, see Q 820.

The PBGC has asked for public comments to help it implement a missing participants program for terminating individual account plans, including 401(k) plans. PBGC is soliciting information from the public on issues related to missing participants in terminating individual account plans. PBGC seeks comments on any and all relevant issues, including the following:

- Among individual account plans that service providers are familiar with, what proportion has participants they cannot find? Among such plans, what is the average number of participants the plan cannot find? What is the average account balance, and what is the range of account balances, for participants that cannot be found?

- What if any services for missing participants in individual account plans are unavailable in the competitive private marketplace (for example, handling very small benefits or QJSA benefits)? Why are they unavailable (for example, because it is not cost-effective to provide them)?

- If PBGC provided services for missing participants' accounts in terminating individual account plans that were comparable to the services provided by the private sector and charged comparable fees, would you be likely to choose the PBGC program or the private sector program and why? Would it make a difference if PBGC provided a narrower range of services than typical private-sector providers?

- How would individual account plans' choice to use a PBGC missing participants program for such plans— rather than a private-sector service—be affected by (1) The level of fees PBGC might charge, (2) the minimum benefit size PBGC might accept, (3) optional or mandatory electronic filing, and (4) other possible program features?

- How would you view the value (such as convenience and reliability) of a single database of missing participants' benefits in terminated individual account plans, maintained by PBGC, compared to the burden on plans to provide the data and the burden on PBGC to maintain the database? How would the comparison change if plan reporting of data were voluntary rather than mandatory, making the database less comprehensive? What information should be in the database?

---

1. PBGC Adv. Op. 91-8.

It is anticipated that the PBGC will evaluate the responses received and attempt to formulate a program to assist the individual account plan market place in locating missing participants.[1]

Qualified Domestic Relations Orders

117. What is a qualified domestic relations order?

ERISA and the Internal Revenue Code do not permit a participant to assign or alienate his interest in a qualified plan to another person. These "anti-assignment and alienation" rules are intended to ensure that a participant's retirement benefits are actually available to provide financial support during the participant's retirement years. A limited exception to the anti-assignment and alienation rules permits the assignment of pension benefits through a qualified domestic relations order (QDRO).[2]

Under the QDRO exception, a domestic relations order may assign some or all of a participant's pension benefits to a spouse, former spouse, child, or other dependent to satisfy family support or marital property obligations, but only if the order is a "qualified domestic relations order." ERISA and the Code require that qualified plans pay benefits in accordance with the applicable requirements of any "qualified domestic relations order" that has been submitted to the plan administrator. The plan administrator's determination of whether a domestic relations order is a QDRO, therefore, has significant implications both for the parties to a domestic relations proceeding and for the plan.

A *qualified* domestic relations order is defined as a domestic relations order (see Q 118):

1.   That creates or recognizes the existence of an "alternate payee's" right to receive, or assigns to an alternate payee the right to receive (see Q 119) benefits under the plan;

2.   Under which all or a portion of the benefits are payable with respect to a participant under a pension plan; and

3.   That includes certain information (see Q 120) and meets certain other requirements. (For details, see Q 121 to Q 135.)[3]

118. What is a domestic relations order?

To be recognized as a QDRO, an order must first be a "domestic relations order." A domestic relations order is defined as a judgment, decree, or order (including the approval of a property settlement):

1.   That is made pursuant to state domestic relations law (including community property law); and

---

1. Missing Participants in Individual Account Plans, Request for Information, 78 Fed. Reg. 37598 (June 21, 2013).
2. ERISA Sec. 206(d)(3)(A); IRC Sec. 414(p).
3. ERISA Sec. 206(d)(3)(B); IRC Sec. 414(p)(1)(A).

2.   That relates to the provision of child support, alimony payments, or marital property rights for the benefit of a spouse, former spouse, child, or other dependent of a participant.[1]

The DOL has stated that "[a] state authority, generally a court, must actually issue a judgment, order, or decree or otherwise formally approve a property settlement agreement before it can be considered a 'domestic relations order' under ERISA and the Code."[2] "The mere fact that a property settlement has been agreed to and signed by the parties will not, in and of itself, cause the agreement to be a domestic relations order."

"There is no requirement that both parties to a marital proceeding sign or otherwise endorse or approve an order. It is also not necessary that the pension plan be brought into state court or made a party to a domestic relations proceeding for an order issued in that proceeding to be considered a 'domestic relations order' or a 'qualified domestic relations order.' Indeed, because state law is generally preempted to the extent that it relates to pension plans, the Department takes the position that pension plans cannot be joined as a party in a domestic relations proceeding pursuant to state law. Moreover, pension plans are neither permitted nor required to follow the terms of domestic relations orders purporting to assign pension benefits unless they are QDROs."[3]

119. Who can be an "alternate payee" under a QDRO?

According to the DOL, "a domestic relations order can be a QDRO only if it creates or recognizes the existence of an alternate payee's right to receive, or assigns to an alternate payee the right to receive, all or part of a participant's benefits. For purposes of the QDRO provisions, an alternate payee cannot be anyone other than a spouse, former spouse, child, or other dependent of a participant."[4]

The Court of Appeals for the Ninth Circuit held that an alternate payee could perfect a domestic relations order into a QDRO after the participant's death where the plan was on notice of the domestic relations order before the death of the participant.[5]

In finding the non-married partner of a plan participant to be a "dependant" of the participant, the U.S. District Court for the Western District of Washington has upheld a QDRO issued in state court ordering the partner's pension plan to award 50 percent of each monthly pension payment to the non-married partner.[6] The participant was retired and was receiving monthly benefits from a multiemployer pension plan. He and his partner, while never legally married, had lived together in a "quasi-marital relationship" for more than thirty years. The participant was the sole-employed member of the household and his partner stayed home to care for the couple's two children.

---

1. ERISA Sec. 206(d)(3)(B)(ii); IRC Sec. 414(p)(1)(B).
2. ERISA Sec. 206(d)(3)(B)(ii); IRC Sec. 414(p)(1)(B).
3. IRC Sec. 2530.206.
4. Pension & Welfare Benefits Admin., Dep't of Labor, QDROs: The Division of Pensions Through Qualified Domestic Relations Orders, Question 1-4 (1997). See ERISA Sec. 206(d)(3)(K); IRC Sec. 414(p)(8).
5. *Trustees of the Dirs. Guild of Am.–Producer Pension Benefit Plans v. Tise*, 2000 U.S. App. LEXIS 31161 (9th Cir. 2000).
6. *Owens v. Automotive Machinists Pension Trust*, No. C06-943Z (W.D. Wash. Jan. 19, 2007).

Upon separation the partner sought an equitable distribution of their assets in state court. The court entered a QDRO granting the distribution. The plan administrator determined that, because the couple had never married, the Order did not relate to "the provision of child support, alimony payments, or marital property rights," so the Order was not qualified as mandated by ERISA. The partner sued in the U.S. District Court.

The District Court held that the Order was a QDRO. In reviewing the claim that the Order did not relate to "marital property rights," the court noted that this issue was determined by Washington State's domestic relations law, which grants state courts authority to divide property following the breakup of "quasi-marital relationships" to the same extent that it empowers them to divide community property following the breakup of legal marriages. Therefore, the "quasi-marital property rights" addressed in the Order qualified as "marital property rights." In response to the claim that the partner was not an "alternate payee" because she was not a spouse, the court concluded that she qualified as an "alternate payee" because she was his dependent.[4] ERISA Section 206(d)(3)(K) defines an "alternate payee" to include any "other dependent" of the participant.[1]

120. What information must a domestic relations order contain in order to be considered a QDRO?

The DOL has stated that QDROs must contain the following information:

1. The name and last known mailing address of the participant and each alternate payee;

2. The name of each plan to which the order applies;

3. The dollar amount or percentage (or the method of determining either) of the benefit to be paid to the alternate payee; and

4. The number of payments or the time period to which the order applies.[2]

The Pension Protection Act of 2006, Section 1001, mandated that the DOL issue, by August 17, 2007, regulations clarifying the status of certain domestic relations orders, including that a domestic relations order will not fail to be qualified solely because it is issued after, or modifies, a previous domestic relations order or QDRO, or because of the time at which it is issued.[3] These regulations were finalized effective August 9, 2010, and are elaborated on in the following questions.[4]

121. What is a QDRO prohibited from containing?

DOL guidance states that there are certain provisions that a QDRO must not contain. The order *must not*:

---

1. *Owens v. Automotive Machinists Pension Trust*, above.
2. Pension & Welfare Benefits Admin., Dep't of Labor, QDROs: The Division of Pensions Through Qualified Domestic Relations Orders, Question 1-5 (1997). See ERISA Sec. 206(d)(3)(C); IRC Sec. 414(p)(2).
3. See Labor Reg. §2530.206.
4. 75 Fed. Reg. 32,846 (Aug. 18, 2010).

1. Require a plan to provide an alternate payee or participant with any type or form of benefit, or any option, not otherwise provided under the plan;

2. Require a plan to provide for increased benefits (determined on the basis of actuarial value);

3. Require a plan to pay benefits to an alternate payee that are required to be paid to another alternate payee under another order previously determined to be a QDRO; and

4. Require a plan to pay benefits to an alternate payee in the form of a qualified joint and survivor annuity for the lives of the alternate payee and his or her subsequent spouse.[1]

122. May a QDRO provide for payment to the guardian of an alternate payee?

Yes. "If an alternate payee is a minor or is legally incompetent, the order can require payment to someone with legal responsibility for the alternate payee (such as a guardian or a party acting *in loco parentis* in the case of a child, or a trustee acting as an agent for the alternate payee)."[2]

123. Can a QDRO cover more than one plan?

Yes. According to the Department of Labor, "[a] QDRO can assign rights to pension benefits under more than one pension plan of the same or different employers as long as each plan and the assignment of benefit rights under each plan are clearly specified."[3]

124. Who determines whether a domestic relations order is "qualified"?

The DOL has addressed this question as follows:

Under Federal law, the administrator of the pension plan that provides the benefits affected by an order is the individual (or entity) initially responsible for determining whether a domestic relations order is a QDRO. Plan administrators have specific responsibilities and duties with respect to determining whether a domestic relations order is a QDRO. Plan administrators, as plan fiduciaries, are required to discharge their duties prudently and solely in the interest of plan participants and beneficiaries. Among other things, plans must establish reasonable procedures to determine the qualified status of domestic relations orders and to administer distributions pursuant to qualified orders. Administrators are required to follow the plan's procedures for making QDRO determinations. Administrators also are required to furnish notice to participants and alternate payees of the receipt of a

1. Pension & Welfare Benefits Admin., Dep't of Labor, QDROs: The Division of Pensions Through Qualified Domestic Relations Orders, Question 1-6 (1997). See ERISA Secs. 206(d)(3)(D), 206(d)(3)(E)(i)(III); IRC Secs. 414(p)(3), 414(p)(4)(A)(iii).
2. Pension & Welfare Benefits Admin., Dep't of Labor, QDROs: The Division of Pensions Through Qualified Domestic Relations Orders, Question 1-9 (1997). See also General Explanation of the Tax Reform Act of 1984, 100th Cong., 1st Sess. 222.
3. Pension & Welfare Benefits Admin., Dep't of Labor, QDROs: The Division of Pensions Through Qualified Domestic Relations Orders, Question 1-10 (1997). See ERISA Sec. 206(d)(3)(C)(iv); IRC Sec. 414(p)(2)(D).

domestic relations order and to furnish a copy of the plan's procedures for determining the qualified status of such orders.

It is the view of the DOL that a state court (or other state agency or instrumentality with the authority to issue domestic relations orders) does not have jurisdiction to determine whether an issued domestic relations order constitutes a "qualified domestic relations order." In the view of the Department, jurisdiction to challenge a plan administrator's decision about the qualified status of an order lies exclusively in Federal court.[1]

In a 1999 Advisory Opinion, the DOL stated that when a plan administrator is made aware of evidence indicating that a domestic relations order was fraudulently obtained, he must take reasonable steps to determine the credibility of the evidence.

If the administrator determines that the evidence is credible, the administrator must decide how best to resolve the question of the validity of the order without inappropriately spending plan assets or inappropriately involving the plan in the State domestic relations proceeding. The appropriate course of action will depend on the facts and circumstances of the particular case and may vary depending on the fiduciary's exercise of discretion. However, in these circumstances, we note that appropriate action could include relaying the evidence of invalidity to the State court or agency that issued the order and informing the court or agency that its resolution of the matter may affect the administrator's determination of whether the order is a QDRO under ERISA.... If, however, the administrator is unable to obtain a response from the court or agency within a reasonable time, the administrator may not independently determine that the order is not valid under State law and therefore is not a "domestic relations order" [under ERISA], but should rather proceed with the determination of whether the order is a QDRO.[2]

The California Supreme Court, in contrast, has rejected the argument that the federal courts have exclusive jurisdiction over the question whether a state domestic relations order is qualified under ERISA.[3] Instead, the court concluded that state courts have subject matter jurisdiction, concurrent with that of the federal courts, over whether a domestic relations order is a QDRO. According to the court, the determining factor in deciding whether there is state court jurisdiction to decide whether a superior court's order was a QDRO under ERISA is whether the action is one by a beneficiary to recover, enforce rights to, or clarify future benefits under the terms of a plan, within the meaning of 29 U.S.C. §1132(a)(1)(B).

The DOL has ruled that a plan administrator may determine that a second order modifying an original order may qualify as a QDRO. Payments made under the prior order discharge liability to the participant and alternate payee for the period it was in effect, and the second order is applicable only on a prospective basis.[4]

---

1. Pension & Welfare Benefits Admin., Dep't of Labor, QDROs: The Division of Pensions Through Qualified Domestic Relations Orders, Question 1-12 (1997). See ERISA Sec. 206(d)(3)(G)(i)(II); IRC Sec. 414(p)(6)(A)(ii).
2. DOL Adv. Op. 99-13A.
3. *In re Marriage of Odino*, 939 P.2d 1266 (Cal. 1997), cert. denied, 118 S. Ct. 1302 (1998).
4. See DOL Adv. Op. 2004-02A (Feb. 17, 2004).

Since "Congress extended concurrent state jurisdiction to any action by a participant or beneficiary to obtain or clarify benefits under the terms of a plan," the court agreed that "an action to qualify a domestic relations order and obtain benefits pursuant to it is an action to obtain or clarify benefits claimed under the terms of a plan. While Congress clearly intended that actions to enforce rights created by ERISA's Title I would be limited to federal courts, rights to benefits awarded in a QDRO are not derived from ERISA, but from state law and plan terms." Thus, a former spouse, who seeks enforcement of a state court order giving the former spouse a right to a portion of the participant's plan benefits, is not seeking to enforce ERISA but rather to obtain benefits the former spouse claims are due the former spouse under the terms of the plan and the state court order. Accordingly, a state has concurrent subject matter jurisdiction if a former spouse is seeking payment of benefits the alternate payee claims are due him or her under the plan and under a superior court's division of marital property.[1]

125. What are the requirements of a plan's QDRO procedures?

According to the DOL, a qualified plan's "QDRO procedures must:

- Be in writing;

- Be reasonable;

- Provide that each person specified in a domestic relations order as entitled to payment of benefits under the plan will be notified (at the address specified in the domestic relations order) of the plan's procedures for making QDRO determinations upon receipt of a domestic relations order; and

- Permit an alternate payee to designate a representative for receipt of copies of notices and plan information that are sent to the alternate payee with respect to domestic relations orders.

It is the view of the Department that a plan's QDRO procedures would not be considered 'reasonable' if they unduly inhibited or hampered the obtaining of a QDRO determination or the making of distributions under a QDRO."[2]

126. Is a plan administrator required to reject a domestic relations order as defective if the order fails to specify factual identifying information that is easily obtainable by the plan administrator?

No. According to the DOL, a domestic relations order that is submitted to a plan that clearly describes the identity and rights of the parties, but is "incomplete only with respect to factual identifying information within the plan administrator's knowledge or easily obtained

---

1. *In re Marriage of Odino*, above.
2. Pension & Welfare Benefits Admin., Dep't of Labor, QDROs: The Division of Pensions Through Qualified Domestic Relations Orders, Question 2-4 (1997). See ERISA Sec. 206(d)(3)(G)(ii); IRC Sec. 414(p)(6); DOL Adv. Op. 94-32A.

through a simple communication with the alternate payee or the participant" should not be rejected on that basis. "For example, an order may misstate the plan's name or the names of participants or alternate payees, and the plan administrator can clearly determine the correct names, or an order may omit the addresses of participants or alternate payees, and the plan administrator's records include this information. In such a case, the plan administrator should supplement the order with the appropriate identifying information, rather than rejecting the order as not qualified."[1]

127. What is the time limit within which an administrator must determine the qualification of a domestic relations order?

The DOL has stated that "[p]lan administrators must determine whether a domestic relations order is a QDRO within a reasonable period of time after receiving the order. What is a reasonable period of time will depend on the specific circumstances.... Plans are required to adopt reasonable procedures for determining the qualified status of domestic relations orders. Compliance with such procedures should ensure that determinations of the qualified status of an order take place within a reasonable period of time. Procedures that unduly inhibit or hamper the QDRO determination process will not be considered reasonable procedures."[2]

128. How can a plan protect against wrongly paying benefits to the participant (instead of the alternate payee) during the determination process?

The DOL addresses this issue as follows:

During any period in which the qualification of a domestic relations order is being determined (by a plan administrator, by a court of competent jurisdiction, or otherwise), ERISA requires that the plan administrator separately account for the amounts that would be payable to an alternate payee under the terms of the order during such period if the order had been determined to be qualified. These amounts are referred to as "segregated amounts." During the period in which the status of a domestic relations order is being determined, the plan administrator must take steps to ensure that amounts that would have been payable to the alternate payee, if the order were a QDRO, are not distributed to the participant or any other person.

The plan administrator's duty to separately account for and to preserve the segregated amounts is limited in time. ERISA provides that the plan administrator must preserve the segregated amounts for not longer than the end of an "18-month period." This "18-month period" does not begin until the first date (after the plan receives the order) that the order would require payment to the alternate payee...

---

1. Pension & Welfare Benefits Admin., Dep't of Labor, QDROs: The Division of Pensions Through Qualified Domestic Relations Orders, Question 2-9 (1997). See ERISA Secs. 206(d)(3)(C), 206(d)(3)(I); IRC Sec. 414(p)(2); *see also* S. Rep. No. 98-575, 98th Cong., 2d Sess. 20 (1984).
2. Pension & Welfare Benefits Admin., Dep't of Labor, QDROs: The Division of Pensions Through Qualified Domestic Relations Orders, Question 2-10 (1997). See ERISA Sec. 206(d)(3)(G)(i)(II); IRC Sec. 414(p)(6)(A)(ii).

… [D]uring the determination period, the administrator, as a plan fiduciary, may not permit distributions to the participant or any other person of any amounts that would be payable to the alternate payee if the domestic relations order were determined to be a QDRO. If the domestic relations order is determined to be a QDRO before the first date on which benefits are payable to the alternate payee, the plan administrator has a continuing duty to account for and to protect the alternate payee's interest in the plan to the same extent that the plan administrator is obliged to account for and to protect the interests of the plan's participants. The plan administrator also has a fiduciary duty to pay out benefits in accordance with the terms of the QDRO.[1]

The Fifth Circuit Court of Appeals has held that a QDRO may not be issued after the death of a participant in order to establish a former spouse's interest in a qualified joint and survivor annuity under applicable state community property law when the survivor annuity is payable to the participant's current spouse.[2]

The Fifth Circuit has also ruled that a pension plan administrator could not recover benefits distributed to alternate payees under QDROs, despite evidence that the underlying divorces were orchestrated by participants and their spouses solely to enable them to receive lump-sum, in-service distributions not otherwise permitted under the plan.[3]

129. What type of notice is required to be provided by a plan administrator following a qualification determination?

According to the Department of Labor:

The plan administrator is required to notify the participant and each alternate payee of the administrator's determination as to whether the order constitutes a QDRO. This notice should be in writing and furnished promptly following a determination.

In the case of a determination that an order is not qualified, the notice should include the reasons for the rejection.… [I]n most instances where there has been a reasonable good faith effort to prepare a qualified domestic relations order, the parties will attempt to correct any deficiencies in the order and resubmit a corrected order for the plan administrator to review. The Department believes that where a reasonable good faith effort has been made to draft a QDRO, prudent plan administration requires the plan administrator to furnish to the parties the information, advice, and guidance that is reasonably required to understand the reasons for a rejection, either as part of the notification process or otherwise, if such information, advice, and guidance could serve to reduce multiple submissions of deficient orders and, therefore, the burdens and costs to plans attendant on review of such orders.[4]

---

1. Pension & Welfare Benefits Admin., Dep't of Labor, QDROs: The Division of Pensions Through Qualified Domestic Relations Orders, Questions 2-11, 2-12 (1997). See ERISA Sec. 206(d)(3)(H); IRC Sec. 414(p)(7).

2. *Rivers v. Central & S. W. Corp.*, 186 F.3d 681 (5th Cir. 1999).

3. *Brown v. Continental Airlines, Inc.*, 2011 WL 2780505 (5th Cir. 2011).

4. Pension & Welfare Benefits Admin., Dep't of Labor, QDROs: The Division of Pensions Through Qualified Domestic Relations Orders, Question 2-14 (1997). See ERISA Sec. 206(d)(3)(G); IRC Sec. 414(p)(6).

Where a plan administrator, comprising a committee of plan trustees and officers of the plan sponsor, failed to inform the former spouse of a plan participant and committee member of its decision that a domestic relations order the former spouse presented to the plan was not qualified, the Ninth Circuit ruled that the committee violated its fiduciary duties.[1] Specifically, the participant spouse on the committee violated his duty to carry out the plan's written QDRO procedures, and the other committee members violated their duties as co-fiduciaries in failing to exercise their affirmative duty to prevent the spouse committee member from breaching his fiduciary duties. The failure to inform the former spouse of the plan's QDRO procedures and of the decision that the domestic relations order she presented was not qualified denied her the opportunity to obtain a valid QDRO. The fiduciary violations gave the former spouse standing to sue the committee members in order to protect her rights and interests as an alternate payee.

130. What must be disclosed to an alternate payee under a QDRO?

Guidance issued by the Department of Labor states:

[A] person who is an alternate payee under a QDRO generally shall be considered a beneficiary under the plan for purposes of ERISA. Accordingly, the alternate payee must be furnished, upon written request, copies of a variety of documents, including the latest summary plan description, the latest annual report, any final annual report, and the bargaining agreement, trust agreement, contract, or other instrument under which the plan is established or operated. The administrator may impose a reasonable charge to cover the cost of furnishing such copies. It is the view of the Department that, at such time as benefit payments to the alternate payee commence under the QDRO, the alternate payee must be treated as a "beneficiary receiving benefits under the plan" and automatically furnished with the summary plan description, summaries of material plan changes, and the plan's summary annual report.[2]

131. What happens to rights created under a QDRO if the underlying plan is amended, merged, or maintained by a successor employer?

According to the DOL, "[t]he rights of an alternate payee under a QDRO are protected in the event of plan amendments, a plan merger, or a change in the sponsor of the plan to the same extent that rights of participants or beneficiaries are protected with respect to benefits accrued as of the date of the event."[3]

132. What happens to the rights created by a QDRO if a plan is terminated?

The DOL has stated that "[i]n the view of the Department, the rights granted by a QDRO must be taken into account in the termination of a plan as if the terms of the QDRO were part of the plan. To the extent that the QDRO grants the alternate payee part of the participant's

---

1. *Stewart v. Thorpe Holding Co. Profit Sharing Plan*, 207 F.3d 1143 (9th Cir. 2000).

2. Pension & Welfare Benefits Admin., Dep't of Labor, QDROs: The Division of Pensions Through Qualified Domestic Relations Orders, Question 2-16 (1997). *See* ERISA Secs. 203(d)(3)(J), 104(b); Labor Reg. §§2520.104b-1 et seq.

3. Pension & Welfare Benefits Admin., Dep't of Labor, QDROs: The Division of Pensions Through Qualified Domestic Relations Orders, Question 2-17 (1997). *See* ERISA Secs. 204(g), 206(d)(3)(A), 403(c)(1); IRC Secs. 401(a)(13)(B), 411(d)(6); *see also* General Explanation of the Tax Reform Act of 1984, 100th Cong., 1st Sess. 224.

benefits, the plan administrator, in terminating the plan, must provide the alternate payee with the notification, consent, payment, or other rights that it would have provided to the participant with respect to that portion of the participant's benefits."[1]

133. What happens to the rights created by a QDRO if a defined benefit plan is terminated and the PBGC becomes trustee of the plan?

Guidance issued by the Department of Labor states:

When [a Pension Benefit Guaranty Corporation ("PBGC") insured defined benefit] ... plan terminates without enough money to pay all guaranteed benefits, PBGC becomes trustee of the terminating plan and pays the plan benefits, subject to certain limits on amount and form. For instance, PBGC does not pay certain death and supplemental benefits. In addition, benefit amounts paid by PBGC are limited by ERISA, and the forms of benefit PBGC pays are also limited.

PBGC has special rules that apply to the payment of benefits under QDROs. For example, if a QDRO is issued prior to plan termination, PBGC will not modify the form of benefit payable to an alternate payee specified in the QDRO. If, in contrast, a QDRO is issued after plan termination, PBGC will generally limit the form of benefit that PBGC will pay under the QDRO to the form permitted by PBGC in other circumstances (generally a single life annuity). There are other special rules that apply to the administration by PBGC of QDROs. These rules are explained in PBGC's booklet, *Divorce Orders & PBGC*.[2]

134. How much can be provided to an alternate payee through a QDRO?

In guidance addressing this issue, the DOL has stated:

A QDRO can give an alternate payee any part or all of the pension benefits payable with respect to a participant under a pension plan. However, the QDRO cannot require the plan to provide increased benefits (determined on the basis of actuarial value); nor can a QDRO require a plan to provide a type or form of benefit, or any option, not otherwise provided under the plan (with one exception ... for an alternate payee's right to receive payment at the participant's "earliest retirement age"). The QDRO also cannot require the payment of benefits to an alternate payee that are required to be paid to another alternate payee under another QDRO already recognized by the plan.[3]

Although ERISA provides that a QDRO cannot require a plan to pay a type or form of benefit not otherwise available under the plan, the DOL has issued an Advisory Opinion that holds that any interest a participant has in a plan (for example, incidental death benefits) is

1. Pension & Welfare Benefits Admin., Dep't of Labor, QDROs: The Division of Pensions Through Qualified Domestic Relations Orders, Question 2-18 (1997). *See* ERISA Secs. 206(d)(3)(A), 403(d).
2. Pension & Welfare Benefits Admin., Dep't of Labor, QDROs: The Division of Pensions Through Qualified Domestic Relations Orders, Question 2-19 (1997).
3. Pension & Welfare Benefits Admin., Dep't of Labor, QDROs: The Division of Pensions Through Qualified Domestic Relations Orders, Question 3-2 (1997). See ERISA Secs. 206(d)(3)(D), 206(d)(3)(E); IRC Secs. 414(p)(3); 414(p)(4). See Q 135.

subject to being paid to an alternate payee under a QDRO.[1] In the fact pattern subject to the Advisory Opinion, a former spouse sought a ruling that the QDRO received in the divorce from the plan participant covered the incidental company-paid survivor benefits provided under the plan, even though the plan provisions specifically limited potential recipients of these incidental benefits to surviving current spouses, minor children, or surviving parents of the participant.

135. What is the significance of "earliest retirement age" in regard to a QDRO?

According to the DOL:

For QDROs, Federal law provides a very specific definition of "earliest retirement age," which is the earliest date as of which a QDRO can order payment to an alternate payee (unless the plan permits payments at an earlier date). The "earliest retirement age" applicable to a QDRO depends on the terms of the pension plan and the participant's age. "Earliest retirement age" is the *earlier* of two dates:

- The date on which the participant is entitled to receive a distribution under the plan; or

- The *later* of either:

    o   the date the participant reaches age fifty, or

    o   the earliest date on which the participant could begin receiving benefits under the plan if the participant separated from service with the employer.[2]

136. Does a domestic relations order fail to be a qualified domestic relations order solely because the order is issued after, or revises, another domestic relations order or qualified domestic relations order?

No. In accordance with Section 1001 of the Pension Protection Act of 2006 (PPA),[3] the Department of Labor (DOL) released Labor Regulation Section 2530.206, which clarifies certain issues relating to the timing and order of domestic relations orders under Section 206(d)(3) of ERISA and Section 414(p) of the Code.[4] As explained below, the interim regulations clarify that a domestic relations order otherwise meeting the requirements to be a QDRO, including the requirements of ERISA Section 206(d)(3)(D) and IRC Section 414(p)(3), shall not fail to be treated as a QDRO solely because (1) the order is issued after, or revises, another domestic relations order or QDRO; or (2) of the time at which it is issued. Section 1001 of the PPA also requires that the regulations clarify that such orders are subject to all of the same requirements

1. DOL Adv. Op. 2000-09A.
2. Pension & Welfare Benefits Admin., Dep't of Labor, QDROs: The Division of Pensions Through Qualified Domestic Relations Orders, Question 3-10 (1997). See ERISA Sec. 206(d)(3)(E)(ii); IRC Sec. 414(p)(4)(B).
3. Pub. L. No. 109-280.
4. 75 Fed. Reg. 32,846 (June 10, 2010).

and protections that apply to QDROs, including the provisions of ERISA Section 206(d)(3)(H) and IRC Section 414(p)(7).

Subsequent Domestic Relations Orders

Paragraph (b)(1) of the Labor Regulation Section 2530.206 provides that a domestic relations order otherwise meeting ERISA's requirements to be a QDRO shall not fail to be treated as a QDRO solely because the order is issued after, or revises, another domestic relations order or QDRO. The rule described in paragraph (b)(2) of the regulation is illustrated by the following examples:

> *Example (1). Subsequent domestic relations order between the same parties.* Participant and Spouse divorce, and the administrator of Participant's 401(k) plan receives a domestic relations order. The administrator determines that the order is a QDRO. The QDRO allocates a portion of Participant's benefits to Spouse as the alternate payee. Subsequently, before benefit payments have commenced, Participant and Spouse seek and receive a second domestic relations order. The second order reduces the portion of Participant's benefits that Spouse was to receive under the QDRO. The second order does not fail to be treated as a QDRO solely because the second order is issued after, and reduces the prior assignment contained in, the first order.

> *Example (2). Subsequent domestic relations order between different parties.* Participant and Spouse divorce, and the administrator of Participant's 401(k) plan receives a domestic relations order. The administrator determines that the order is a QDRO. The QDRO allocates a portion of Participant's benefits to Spouse 1 as the alternate payee. Participant marries Spouse 2, and then they divorce. Participant's 401(k) plan administrator subsequently receives a domestic relations order pertaining to Spouse 2. The order assigns to Spouse 2 a portion of Participant's 401(k) benefits not already allocated to Spouse 1. The second order does not fail to be a QDRO solely because the second order is issued after the plan administrator has determined that an earlier order pertaining to Spouse 1 is a QDRO.

Timing of Domestic Relations Order

Paragraph (c)(1) of Labor Regulation Section 2530.206 provides that a domestic relations order otherwise meeting ERISA's requirements to be a QDRO shall not fail to be treated as a QDRO solely because of the time at which it is issued. The rule described in paragraph (c)(2) of the regulation is illustrated by the following examples:

> *Example (1). Orders issued after death.* Participant and Spouse divorce, and the administrator of Participant's plan receives a domestic relations order, but the administrator finds the order deficient and determines that it is not a QDRO. Shortly thereafter, Participant dies while actively employed. A second domestic relations order correcting the defects in the first order is subsequently submitted to the plan. The second order does not fail to be treated as a QDRO solely because it is issued after the death of the Participant. The result would be the same if the order were instead to increase the prior assignment contained in the first order.

> *Example (2). Orders issued after divorce.* Participant and Spouse divorce. As a result, Spouse no longer meets the definition of "surviving spouse" under the terms of the plan. Subsequently, the plan administrator receives a domestic relations order requiring that Spouse be treated as the Participant's surviving spouse for purposes of receiving a death benefit payable under the terms of the plan only to a participant's surviving spouse. The order does not fail to be treated as a QDRO solely because, at the time it is issued, Spouse no longer meets the definition of a "surviving spouse" under the terms of the plan.

> *Example (3). Orders issued after annuity starting date.* Participant retires and commences benefit payments in the form of a straight life annuity equal to $1,000 per month, with respect to which Spouse waives the surviving spousal rights provided under the plan and section 205 of ERISA. Subsequent to the commencement of benefits, Participant and Spouse divorce after Participant's annuity starting date and present the plan with a

domestic relations order requiring 50 percent ($500) of Participant's future monthly annuity payments under the plan to be paid instead to Spouse, as an alternate payee (so that monthly payments of $500 are to be made to Spouse during the Participant's lifetime). Pursuant to paragraph (c)(1) of regulation section 2530.206, the order does not fail to be a QDRO solely because it is issued after the annuity starting date. If the order instead had required payments to Spouse for the lifetime of Spouse, this would constitute a re-annuitization with a new annuity starting date, rather than merely allocating to Spouse a part of the determined annuity payments due to Participant, so that the order, while not failing to be a QDRO because of the timing of the order, would fail to meet the requirements of section 206(d)(3)(D)(i) of ERISA (unless the plan otherwise permits such a change after the participant's annuity starting date). See *Example (4)* below.

Requirements and Protections

Paragraph (d)(1) of Labor Regulation Section 2530.206 provides that any domestic relations order described in paragraph (b) or (c) of the regulation shall be subject to the same requirements and protections that apply to all QDROs under Section 206(d)(3) of ERISA. The rule described in paragraph (d)(2) of the regulation is illustrated by the following examples:

Example (1). Type or form of benefit. Participant and Spouse divorce, and their divorce decree provides that the parties will prepare a domestic relations order assigning 50 percent of Participant's benefits under a 401(k) plan to Spouse to be paid in monthly installments over a ten-year period. Shortly thereafter, Participant dies while actively employed. A domestic relations order consistent with the decree is subsequently submitted to the 401(k) plan; however, the plan does not provide for ten-year installment payments of the type described in the order. Pursuant to paragraph (c)(1) of regulation section 2530.206, the order does not fail to be treated as a QDRO solely because it is issued after the death of Participant, but the order would fail to be a QDRO under ERISA section 206(d)(3)(D)(i) and paragraph (d)(1) of regulation section 2530.206 because the order requires the plan to provide a type or form of benefit, or any option, not otherwise provided under the plan.

Example (2). Segregation of payable benefits. Participant and Spouse divorce, and the administrator of Participant's plan receives a domestic relations order under which Spouse would begin to receive benefits immediately if the order is determined to be a QDRO. The plan administrator separately accounts for the amounts covered by the domestic relations order as is required under section 206(d)(3)(H)(v) of ERISA. The plan administrator finds the order deficient and determines that it is not a QDRO. Subsequently, after the expiration of the segregation period pertaining to that order, the plan administrator receives a second domestic relations order relating to the same parties under which Spouse would begin to receive benefits immediately if the second order is determined to be a QDRO. Notwithstanding the expiration of the first segregation period, the amounts covered by the second order must be separately accounted for by the plan administrator for an eighteen-month period, in accordance with section 206(d)(3)(H) of ERISA and paragraph (d)(1) of regulation section 2530.206.

Example (3). Previously assigned benefits. Participant and Spouse divorce and the administrator of Participant's 401(k) plan receives a domestic relations order. The administrator determines that the order is a QDRO. The QDRO assigns a portion of Participant's benefits to Spouse 1 as the alternate payee. Participant marries Spouse 2, and then they divorce. Participant's 401(k) plan administrator subsequently receives a domestic relations order pertaining to Spouse 2. The order assigns to Spouse 2 a portion of Participant's 401(k) benefits already assigned to Spouse 1. The second order does not fail to be treated as a QDRO solely because the second order is issued after the plan administrator has determined that an earlier order pertaining to Spouse 1 is a QDRO. The second order, however, would fail to be a QDRO under ERISA section 206(d)(3)(D) (iii) and paragraph (d)(1) of regulation section 2530.206 because it assigns all or a portion of Participant's benefits that are already assigned to Spouse 1 by the prior QDRO.

Example (4). Type or form of benefit. Participant retires and commences benefit payments in the form of a straight life annuity based on the life of the Participant, with respect to which Spouse consents to the waiver of the surviving spousal rights provided under the plan and section 205 of ERISA. Participant and Spouse divorce after the annuity starting date and present the plan with a domestic relations order that eliminates the straight life annuity based on Participant's life and provides for Spouse, as alternate payee, to receive all future benefits in the form of a straight life annuity based on the life of Spouse. The plan does not allow for re-annuitization with a new annuity starting date, as defined in section 205(h)(2) of ERISA (and as further explained in 26 CFR 1.401(a)-20, Q&A-10(b)). Pursuant to paragraph (c)(1) of Reg Sec. 2530.206, the order does not fail to be a QDRO solely because it is issued after the annuity starting date, but the order would fail to be a QDRO under section 206(d)(3)(D)(i) and paragraph (d)(1) of Reg. Sec. 2530.206 because the order requires the plan to provide a type or form of benefit, or any option, not otherwise provided under the plan. However, the order would not fail to be a QDRO under section 206(d)(3)(D)(i) and Reg. Sec. 2530.206 if instead it were to require all of Participant's future payments under the plan to be paid instead to Spouse, as an alternate payee (so that payments that would otherwise be paid to Participant during the Participant's lifetime are instead to be made to the Spouse during the participant's lifetime).

According to the DOL, the examples above, which are set forth in paragraphs (b)(2), (c)(2), and (d)(2) of Labor Regulation Section 2530.206, illustrate how the rules in paragraphs (b)(1), (c)(1), and (d)(1), respectively, apply to specific facts. They do not represent the only circumstances for which these rules would provide clarification.

SECTION II

Health Benefit Issues

137. What services are provided to employers by the DOL regarding interactive help with health benefit laws?

The DOL announced in late 2006 the introduction of an interactive Web site, called the Health Benefits Advisor (the Advisor). The Advisor is designed to help employers and other plan officials understand their responsibilities in operating their group health plans. It details explanations of legislation, statutes, and regulations. Further, it provides summary guidance (not intended to rise to the level of legal guidance). The laws discussed in the Advisor are included in Parts 6 and 7 of Title I of ERISA (COBRA and HIPAA).[1]

To coincide with the fourth anniversary of the HIPAA Privacy Rule, the Office of Civil Rights (OCR) of the Department of Health and Human Services (HHS) has launched an enhanced Web site on HIPAA privacy compliance and enforcement. The Web site is divided into three sections: (1) Enforcement Process; (2) Enforcement Highlights; and (3) Case Examples.[2] The first section gives an overview of the OCR complaint process, which currently is the principal method OCR uses to enforce the HIPAA Privacy Rule. The Web site lists the various items the Centers for Medicare & Medicaid Services (CMS) considers when deciding whether to take action on a complaint. The second part of the Web site, Enforcement Highlights, contains statistics on the OCR's enforcement activity to date. The final section of the Web site provides examples of the types of complaints that OCR has investigated and resolved.

On August 11 and 15, 2011, HHS submitted to Congress (and posted on its Web site) the first set of annual reports on breach notifications and HIPAA privacy and security compliance required by the Health Information Technology for Economic and Clinical Health (HITECH) Act, enacted as part of the American Recovery and Reinvestment Act of 2009.[3]

HIPAA Requirements

138. What is the Health Insurance Portability and Accountability Act of 1996?

The Health Insurance Portability and Accountability Act of 1996 (HIPAA) includes protections for employees and their families who have preexisting medical conditions or might suffer discrimination in health coverage based on a factor that relates to an individual's health. HIPAA's provisions amend Title I of ERISA (Protection of Employee Benefit Rights) as well as the Internal Revenue Code and the Public Health Service Act. Additionally, HIPAA places

---

1. EBSA News Release (Oct. 6, 2006).

2. HHS-OCR Web site: HIPAA Privacy Compliance & Enforcement, available at http://www.hhs.gov/ocr/privacy/enforcement/.

3. Annual Report to Congress on Breaches of Unsecured Protected Health Information (Aug. 15, 2011); Annual Report to Congress on HIPAA Privacy Rule and Security Rule Compliance (Aug. 11, 2011).

requirements on employer-sponsored group health plans, insurance companies, and health maintenance organizations (HMOs). HIPAA includes changes that:

1.   Limit exclusions for preexisting conditions;

2.   Prohibit discrimination against employees and dependents based upon their health status;

3.   Guarantee renewability and availability of health coverage to certain employers and individuals; and

4.   Protect many workers who lose health coverage by providing better access to individual health insurance coverage.

The DOL, the IRS, and the HHS jointly issued final regulations, which were designed to provide guidance on the nondiscrimination provisions of HIPAA.[1] The final version of the regulations differs very little from the interim final regulations. Overall, they fine-tune the interim regulations to improve portability and lessen the compliance burden of group health plans and group health insurers.

The final rule includes the following provisions:

1.   Plans may not prohibit eligibility or enrollment in health plans for individuals who engage in inherently dangerous activities, such as bungee jumping and skiing. However, plans may deny coverage for injuries sustained while undertaking such inherently dangerous leisure time activities;[2]

2.   Plans may not deny benefits for injuries resulting from acts of domestic violence or a physical or mental condition. The rules provide the example of injuries sustained in a failed suicide attempt where the actions were the result of the mental condition of depression;[3]

3.   Plans may not implement non-confinement clauses that deny eligibility to individuals confined to a hospital or who are unable to engage in normal life activities;[4]

4.   Plans may not implement an "actively at work" clause that restricts eligibility to people who are on the job when a new benefit program takes effect, unless the plan defines "on the job" to include employees who are absent from work due to health factors;[5]

5.   Plans may provide differing levels of benefits and services, as long as they are applied uniformly to people covered by the plan (even though differing levels may affect individuals with health problems more severely than others). This does not mean,

---

1. 69 Fed. Reg. 78,720 (Dec. 30, 2004).
2. Labor Reg. §§2590.702(b)(2)(iii)(A), 2590.702(b)(2)(iii)(B) Ex. 2.
3. Labor Reg. §§2590.702(b)(2)(iii)(A), 2590.702(b)(2)(iii)(B) Ex. 1.
4. Labor Reg. §2590.702(e)(1).
5. Labor Reg. §2590.702(e)(2).

however, that individuals with health problems may be subject to less favorable eligibility or enrollment standards;[1] and

6.   Plans may not be amended to reduce benefits for a specific treatment or service as a result of a specific individual's claim for those benefits. There is a presumption, however, that a plan amendment reducing or eliminating such benefits as of the first day of the next plan year is not directed at a specific individual.[2]

In addition to the final HIPAA nondiscrimination regulations, the Department of the Treasury, the DOL, and HHS has issued final HIPAA wellness program regulations.[3] The final nondiscrimination regulations do not replace the interim and final 2001 rules. Rather, they clarify the source of injury rules and how they apply to the timing of a diagnosis of a medical condition. Regarding wellness programs, the final regulations provide clarification on previously ambiguous text and other modest changes to organization and text.

The final regulations clarify the rule regarding source-of-injury exclusions and further clarify that the rule applies even if the medical condition in question is not diagnosed prior to the injury. If a group health plan or group health insurance coverage generally provides benefits for a type of injury, the plan or issuer may not deny benefits otherwise provided for treatment of the injury if the injury results from an act of domestic violence or a medical condition (including both physical and mental health conditions).[4]

Under the final regulations, wellness programs must meet a five-part test. The benefit of satisfying the criteria of wellness program is that the plan may offer a reward to participants who satisfy objective criteria based on health-related factors. A wellness program that requires satisfaction of a standard that is based on a health-related factor will satisfy the final regulations if:

1.   The reward does not exceed 20 percent of the cost of coverage;

2.   The program is reasonably designed to promote health or prevent disease;

3.   The program gives eligible individuals the opportunity to qualify for the reward at least once a year;

4.   The reward is available to all similarly situated individuals (including making available a reasonable alternative standard to qualify for the reward if it is unreasonably difficult for an individual to satisfy the otherwise applicable standard because of a medical condition or if it is medically inadvisable for an individual to attempt to satisfy the standard); and

5.   The plan discloses the availability of a reasonable alternative standard in all plan materials that describe the terms of the program.[5]

---

1. Labor Reg. §§2590.702(b)(2)(i)(A), 2590.702(b)(2)(i)(B).
2. Labor Reg. §§2590.702(b)(2)(i)(B), 2590.702(b)(2)(i)(C).
3. 26 C.F.R. pt. 54; 29 C.F.R. pt. 2590; 45 C.F.R. pt. 146; 71 Fed. Reg. 75,014 (Dec. 13, 2006). For a copy of the final regulations, go to http://edocket.access.gpo.gov/2006/pdf/06-9557.pdf.
4. Labor Reg. §2590.702(b)(2)(iii)(A).
5. Labor Reg. §§2590.702-1(f)(2)(i) to 2590.702-1(f)(2)(iv), 2590.702(f)(2)(A)(1), and 2590.702(f)(2)(A)(2).

The final regulations permit a plan to seek verification, such as a statement from an individual's physician, that because of a health factor it is unreasonably difficult or medically inadvisable for the individual to satisfy or attempt to satisfy the otherwise applicable standard.[1]

The final regulations state that certain wellness programs do not have to satisfy any additional conditions. If none of the requirements for obtaining a wellness program reward is based on satisfaction of a standard related to a health factor, and if participation in the program is available to all similarly situated individuals, nothing more is required. Wellness programs in this category could include programs that reimburse the cost of membership in a fitness center, diagnostic testing programs that base the reward on participation rather than on the test results; programs that reimburse employees for the costs of smoking-cessation programs without regard to whether employees quit smoking; and a program that provides a reward for attending a monthly health education seminar.[2]

139. What is the DOL enforcement safe harbor for supplemental plans under HIPAA portability, MHPA, WHCRA, and NMHPA rules?

In general, the health reform provisions of HIPAA, the Mental Health Parity Act, Women's Health and Cancer Rights Act, and the Newborns' and Mothers' Health Protection Act apply to group health plans (generally plans established or maintained by employers or employee organizations, or both) and health insurance issuers in the group or individual market. But these provisions do not apply to certain excepted benefits provided for under ERISA Sections 732(c)(3) and 733(c)(4) (certain "supplemental" coverage provided under a separate policy, certificate, or contract of insurance). Under the language of the exception, supplemental coverage includes:

1.   Medicare supplemental health insurance (commonly referred to as "Medigap" insurance);

2.   Insured Tricare supplements; and

3.   "Similar supplemental coverage provided to coverage under a group health plan."

In December 2007, the DOL issued DOL Field Assistance Bulletin 2007-04,[3] which establishes an enforcement safe harbor for supplemental types of health coverage that are excepted from the provisions of Part 7 of ERISA.

In issuing FAB 2007-04, the DOL says that it, along with the IRS and HHS, have concerns that certain insurance products in the industry have been marketed as supplemental coverage in an effort to circumvent compliance with ERISA's health reform provisions. This is done by issuing multiple insurance contracts in connection with a plan. In general, if all benefits under a plan or coverage are excepted benefits, then the plan and any health insurance coverage under the plan do not have to comply with the health reform requirements and the coverage may not qualify as creditable coverage.

---

1. Labor Reg. §2590.702(f)(2)(B).
2. Labor Reg. §§2590.702(f)(1)(i), 2590.702(f)(1)(ii), 2590.702(f)(1)(iv), and 2590.702(f)(1)(v).
3. http://www.dol.gov/ebsa/regs/fab2007-4.html (Dec. 7, 2007).

"To fall within the safe harbor for determining excepted benefits, a policy, certificate, or contract of insurance must be issued by an entity that does not provide the primary coverage under the plan and must be specifically designed to fill gaps in primary coverage." The safe harbor brings guidance to properly determining what constitutes "similar supplemental coverage" for purposes of being excepted from Part 7 of ERISA.

Specifically, under the FAB's safe harbor the DOL will treat coverage as "similar supplemental coverage" if it is a separate policy, certificate, or contract of insurance that meets these criteria:

1. It must be specifically designed to supplement gaps in the primary coverage, such as the payment of co-insurance or deductibles (a plan that merely becomes secondary or supplemental to the primary plan under its coordination of benefits provisions is not considered to be specifically designed to fill in gaps in the primary coverage).

2. The cost of the supplemental coverage must not exceed 15 percent of the cost of primary coverage (for this determination, the DOL will calculate the cost in the same manner as the cost of COBRA continuation coverage is calculated, even if the coverage is not subject to COBRA, except that the cost will be 100 percent of the applicable premium, not 102 percent generally permitted to be charged as the COBRA premium).

3. It does not differentiate among individuals in eligibility, benefits, or premiums based on any health factor of an individual (a Medigap requirement extended under this interpretation).

140. Who is a "dependent" under HIPAA?

The final regulations on HIPAA provide a new definition for purposes of administration and coverage. Pursuant to Labor Regulation Section 2590.701-2, "dependent" means any individual who is or may become eligible for coverage under the terms of a group health plan because of a relationship to a participant.[1]

141. Does the DOL offer guidance in understanding COBRA, HIPAA, and NMHPA?

The Department of Labor has made available at its Internet Web site (http://www.dol.gov/dol/ebsa) three brochures designed to familiarize participants in employer-sponsored health plans with the provisions of COBRA (see Q 189 to Q 203), HIPAA (see Q 138 to Q 180), and NMHPA, as well as how these protections and rights apply to life changes and health benefits.

The brochure "Top 10 Ways to Make Your Health Benefits Work for You" sets forth guidance for participants who are selecting a health plan or are changing their benefits under existing health coverage. The brochure advises individuals of the right to change benefits under HIPAA and the right to continuation of health coverage under COBRA when changing jobs.

---

1. 69 Fed. Reg. 78,720 (Dec. 30, 2004).

"Life Changes Require Health Choices" provides readers with guidance on what an employee may do when the employee experiences a life-changing event, such as the birth of a child. It also explains how COBRA, HIPAA, and NMHPA provide health care rights under certain life-changing events.

The final brochure "Work Changes Require Health Choices" details the effect of retirement, lay-off, termination, or job changes on the provision of health benefits. It provides details on employee rights under COBRA and HIPAA where certain health benefits are protected when a work change occurs.

142. What is the Privacy Rule under HIPAA?

On August 14, 2002, the Department of Health and Human Services published the final HIPAA Privacy Rule.[1] The Privacy Rule prohibits a health plan from using or disclosing an individual's Protected Health Information (PHI) unless specifically authorized by the individual or otherwise allowed under the Privacy Rule.[2]

The Privacy Rule allows a plan to use or disclose an individual's PHI, without the individual's authorization, as necessary for "treatment, payment or health care operations."[3] Generally, once a plan determines that it may use or disclose PHI, it must take reasonable measures to limit the use or disclosure to the minimum amount necessary to accomplish the intended purpose of the use or disclosure (see Q 143 through Q 156).[4]

In January, 2013, HHS issued the Omnibus Final Regulations to HIPAA/HITECH.[5] Effective March 26, 2013, the final rule adopts the majority of the previously issued proposed rules from 2009 with some clarifications and changes (noted in detail under Q 143 through Q 156 and Q 211).

Enforcement and Penalties

The American Recovery and Reinvestment Act of 2009 (ARRA 2009)[6] authorizes the Secretary of Health and Human Services to conduct periodic audits of covered entities and Business Associates to ensure compliance with HIPAA and ARRA 2009 requirements.[7] These new provisions fundamentally change the enforcement of HIPAA violations and extend these penalties and liabilities to Business Associates.

The Secretary is required to impose civil penalties if a violation is due to willful neglect and to formally investigate any complaint if a preliminary investigation indicates the potential of violation due to willful neglect.[8]

---

1. 67 Fed. Reg. 53,181 (Aug. 14, 2002).
2. 45 C.F.R. §§164.508(a), 164.502(a)(1).
3. 45 C.F.R. §164.506.
4. 45 C.F.R. §164.502(b)(1).
5. 78 Fed. Reg. 5566, (Jan. 25, 2013).
6. Pub.L.No.111-5.
7. ARRA 2009 §13411.
8. ARRA 2009 §13410(a)(1).

"Willful neglect" is defined as "conscious, intentional failure, or reckless indifference to the obligation to comply with the HITECH Act requirements.[1]

Since the willful neglect provisions became effective on February 16, 2011, the Secretary was required to impose the monetary penalties discussed below for those violations.[2]

For cases involving violations for which the individual can establish the affirmative defense that he did not know of the violation or would not have known of the violation by exercising reasonable diligence, and the violation is corrected during the 30-day period beginning on the first date the covered entity knew, or by exercising reasonable diligence would have known, that the violation occurred (or such longer period as the Secretary may deem appropriate), corrective action rather than penalty may still be used.[3] "Reasonable diligence" is defined as the business care and prudence expected from a person seeking to satisfy a legal requirement under similar circumstances.[4]

In the case of a violation in which it is established that the person did not know (and by exercising reasonable diligence would not have known) that such person violated such provision, there may be a penalty of $100 to $50,000 for each such violation, except that the total amount imposed on the person for all such violations of an identical requirement or prohibition during a calendar year may not exceed $1,500,000.[5]

In the case of a violation in which it is established that the violation was due to reasonable cause and not to willful neglect, there may be a penalty for each such violation in the amount of $1,000 to $50,000 for each such violation, except that the total amount imposed on the person for all such violations of an identical requirement or prohibition during a calendar year may not exceed $1,500,000.[6] "Reasonable cause" is defined as circumstances that would make it unreasonable for the covered entity, despite the exercise of ordinary business care and prudence, to comply with the violated provisions of the HITECH Act.[7]

In the case of a violation in which it is established that the violation was due to willful neglect, and where the violation has been corrected during the 30-day period beginning on the first date the covered entity liable for the penalty knew, or by exercising reasonable diligence, should have known that the violation occurred, there may be a penalty of $10,000 to $50,000 for each such violation, except that the total amount imposed on the person for all such violations of an identical requirement or prohibition during a calendar year may not exceed $1,500,000.[8] For each violation that is due to willful neglect that is not corrected during the thirty-day period beginning on the first date the covered entity liable for the penalty knew, or by exercising reasonable diligence, should have known that the violation occurred, the amount of the penalty is $50,000 for each such violation, except that the total amount imposed on the

1. 45 C.F.R. §160.401; 74 Fed. Reg. 56,123 (Oct. 30, 2009).
2. ARRA 2009 §13410(b); 45 C.F.R. §160.404(b)(1)(i); 74 Fed. Reg. 56,123 (Oct. 30, 2009).
3. ARRA 2009 §13410(f); 45 C.F.R. §160.410(b)(1), (2); 74 Fed. Reg. 56,123 (Oct. 30, 2009).
4. 45 C.F.R. 160.401; 74 Fed. Reg. 56,123 (Oct. 30, 2009).
5. ARRA 2009 §13410(d)(1), (2); 45 C.F.R. §404(b)(2)(i)(A), (B); 74 Fed. Reg. 56,123 (Oct. 30, 2009).
6. ARRA 2009 §13410(d)(1), (2); 45 C.F.R. §404(b)(2)(ii)(A), (B); 74 Fed. Reg. 56,123 (Oct. 30, 2009).
7. 45 C.F.R. §160.401; 74 Fed. Reg. 56,123 (Oct. 30, 2009).
8. 45 C.F.R. §404(b)(2)(iii)(A), (B); 74 Fed. Reg. 56,123 (Oct. 30, 2009).

person for all such violations of an identical requirement or prohibition during a calendar year may not exceed $1,500,000.[1]

In determining the amount of a penalty under this section for a violation, the Secretary of HHS shall base such determinations on the nature and extent of the violation and the nature and extent of the harm resulting from such violation.[2] The Government Accountability Office is charged with recommending to the Secretary a methodology under which harmed individuals under HIPAA would receive a percentage of any monetary penalty or monetary settlement collected with respect to HIPAA violations. The Secretary was required to establish regulations for implementing this methodology by February 16, 2012.[3]

On January 25, 2013 HHS issued the Omnibus Final Rules on HIPAA and HITECH. Under these final regulations, covered entities and business associates will be liable for the acts of their business associate agents in accordance with the Federal common law of agency, regardless of whether the covered entity has a compliant business associate agreement in place.[4]

Under the Final Rule, in determining the amount of any civil money penalty, HHS may consider the following factors, which may be mitigating or aggravating as appropriate:

    (a)   The nature and extent of the violation, consideration of which may include but is not limited to:

        (1) The number of individuals affected; and

        (2) The time period during which the violation occurred;

    (b)   The nature and extent of the harm resulting from the violation, consideration of which may include but is not limited to:

        (1) Whether the violation caused physical harm;

        (2) Whether the violation resulted in financial harm;

        (3) Whether the violation resulted in harm to an individual's reputation; and

        (4) Whether the violation hindered an individual's ability to obtain health care;

    (c)   The history of prior compliance with the administrative simplification provisions, including violations, by the covered entity or business associate, consideration of which may include but is not limited to:

        (1) Whether the current violation is the same or similar to previous indications of noncompliance;

        (2) Whether and to what extent the covered entity or business associate has attempted to correct previous indications of noncompliance;

---

1. ARRA 2009 §13410(d)(1), (2); 45 C.F.R. §404(b)(2)(iv); 74 Fed. Reg. 56,123 (Oct 30, 2009).
2. Social Security Act §1176(a)(1), as amended by ARRA 2009 §13410(d)(1).
3. ARRA 2009 §13410(c)(3).
4. 45 CFR 160.402(c); 78 Fed. Reg. 5566, (Jan. 25, 2013).

(3) How the covered entity or business associate has responded to technical assistance from HHS provided in the context of a compliance effort; and

(4) How the covered entity or business associate has responded to prior complaints;

(d)   The financial condition of the covered entity or business associate, consideration of which may include but is not limited to:

(1) Whether the covered entity or business associate had financial difficulties that affected its ability to comply;

(2) Whether the imposition of a civil money penalty would jeopardize the ability of the covered entity or business associate to continue to provide, or to pay for, health care; and

(3) The size of the covered entity or business associate; and

(e)   Such other matters as justice may require.[1]

The Fifth Circuit Court has ruled that HIPAA does not expressly create a private right of action. In issuing the decision, the court noted that enforcement of HIPAA is delegated to HHS for civil penalties and the U.S. Department of Justice for criminal penalties.[2]

HHS has announced a resolution agreement between its Office for Civil Rights (OCR) and a WellPoint, Inc., a health plan network (WellPoint) to settle alleged violations of HIPAA's privacy and security rules. OCR opened its investigation after WellPoint notified HHS of a breach of electronic PHI following a software upgrade to its web based application data base. WellPoint agreed to pay HHS $1.7 million to settle potential violations of the HIPAA Privacy and Security Rules. The report indicated that security weaknesses in an online application database left the electronic protected health information (ePHI) of 612,402 individuals accessible to unauthorized individuals over the Internet. OCR's investigation indicated that WellPoint did not implement appropriate administrative and technical safeguards as required under the HIPAA Security Rule.[3]

HHS has also announced a Resolution Agreement with Affinity Health Plan (Affinity) a health plan to settle potential HIPAA privacy and security violations relating to ePHI found on the hard drives of leased photocopiers after the health plan returned them to the leasing company. The agreement requires Affinity, a HIPAA covered entity, to pay over $1.2 million and comply with a Corrective Action Plan (CAP).

According to the HHS news release, Affinity learned of the problem from a television network that purchased one of the photocopiers as part of an investigative report. Affinity submitted a breach notification to HHS, which prompted an investigation by HHS's Office for Civil Rights (OCR). OCR's investigation revealed that Affinity had failed to properly erase

---

1. 45 CFR 160.408(a)-(e); 78 Fed. Reg. 5566, (Jan. 25, 2013).
2. *Acara v. Banks*, 2006 U.S. App. LEXIS 28120 (5th Cir. Nov. 13, 2006).
3. HHS Resolution Agreement; HHS News Release (July 11, 2013).

multiple photocopier hard drives prior to returning them to the leasing company—resulting in the impermissible disclosure of ePHI of up to 344,579 individuals. According to the Resolution Agreement, Affinity also failed to consider the photocopiers in its HIPAA security risk assessment and failed to implement appropriate policies for the disposal of ePHI. A copy of the resolution agreement may be viewed here: http://www.hhs.gov/ocr/privacy/hipaa/enforcement/examples/affinity_agreement.pdf."

Practitioner's Pointer: The HITECH Act requires HHS to conduct periodic audits to ensure that covered entities and business associates are complying with HIPAA's privacy and security rules and breach notification requirements. To implement this mandate, HHS's Office for Civil Rights (OCR) has launched a three-stage pilot audit program, which is now detailed on their Web site. To implement this mandate, the OCR is piloting a program to perform up to 150 audits of covered entities to assess privacy and security compliance. Audits conducted during the pilot phase began November 2011 and conclude by December 2012. The objectives of this enforcement program are described as thus: "The audit program serves as a new part of OCR's health information privacy and security compliance program. OCR will use the audit program to assess HIPAA compliance efforts by a range of covered entities. Audits present a new opportunity to examine mechanisms for compliance, identify best practices and discover risks and vulnerabilities that may not have come to light through OCR's ongoing complaint investigations and compliance reviews. OCR will broadly share best practices gleaned through the audit process and guidance targeted to observed compliance challenges via this web site and other outreach portals."[1]

The OCR has announced an agreement with The General Hospital Corporation and Massachusetts General Physicians Organization, Inc., to settle potential violations of the HIPAA privacy rule. The agreement requires the hospital, a covered entity, to pay $1 million and comply with a detailed CAP that requires it to develop and implement a comprehensive set of policies and procedures to safeguard the privacy of its patients.[2]

The OCR has also announced an agreement with the UCLA Health System to settle potential HIPAA privacy and security violations. The agreement, which requires the health system to pay $865,500 and to implement a three-year CAP, settles potential violations discovered during the OCR's investigation of violations of the privacy rights of two celebrities when employees of UCLA Health System accessed their protected health information absent a permissible reason. The CAP is designed to address gaps discovered with UCLA Health System's compliance with HIPAA privacy and security rules.[3]

---

143. What is "protected health information" under the Privacy Rule?

In general, an individual's "protected health information" (PHI) covers virtually all "individually identifiable health information" that is transmitted or maintained by a health plan, regardless of its form. "Individually identifiable health information" is defined broadly to include health information that is created or received by a plan or health care provider that relates to an individual's physical or mental health or condition, including information related to an individual's care or the payment for such care. Further, the health information must identify

---

1. HHS Web site: OCR HIPAA Audit Program (Nov. 8, 2011). For full details on this enforcement program, see http://www.hhs.gov/ocr/privacy/hipaa/enforcement/audit/index.html.
2. HHS Resolution Agreement (Feb. 14, 2011); HHS News Release (Feb. 24, 2011), http://www.hhs.gov/ocr/privacy/hipaa/news/mghnews.html.
3. HHS Resolution Agreement (July 6, 2011); HHS News Release (July 7, 2011), http://www.hhs.gov/ocr/privacy/hipaa/news/uclahs.html.

the individual, or there must be a reasonable basis to believe that the information could be used to identify the individual.[1]

144. What information is not considered "protected health information"?

Any information that falls outside the definition of protected health information[2] may be freely disclosed because it is not subject to the privacy regulations.

De-Identified Information

Protected health information that has been edited to eliminate the identifiers detailed below (referred to as "de-identified information" in the Privacy Rule) does not constitute PHI and may also be used and disclosed freely.[3]

A covered entity may determine that health information is not individually identifiable if the following identifiers of the individual, relatives of the individual, employers, or household members, are removed:

1.   Names;

2.   Full-face photographic images;

3.   Biometric identifiers (finger and voice prints);

4.   Geographic subdivisions smaller than state (street address, city, county, zip code);

5.   Dates related to the individual (except year);

6.   Telephone and fax numbers;

7.   E-mail addresses, Web Universal Resource Locators (URLs), and Internet Protocol (IP) addresses;

8.   Social Security numbers;

9.   Medical record numbers;

10. Plan beneficiary numbers;

11. Account numbers;

12. Certificate/license numbers;

13. Vehicle identifiers and serial numbers (including license plates); and

14. Any other unique identifying number or characteristic.[4]

---

1. 45 C.F.R. §160.103.
2. As defined under 45 C.F.R. §160.103.
3. 45 C.F.R. §§164.502(d)(1), 164.502(d)(2), and 164.514(a).
4. 45 C.F.R. §§164.514(b)(2)(i)(A) to 164.514(b)(2)(i)(I).

The Omnibus Final Rule expands the definition of protected health information to exclude:

1. Individually identifiable health information;

2. Education records covered by The Family Educational Rights and Privacy Act;

3. Employment records held by a covered entity in its role as an employer; and

4. Any information regarding an individual who has been deceased for at least fifty years.[1]

145. What are the covered entities to which the Privacy Rule applies?

The Privacy Rule applies only to "covered entities," which include health plans, health care providers, and health care clearinghouses.[2]

The term "health plan" is defined broadly to include practically every authorized program that provides health-related services, including:

1. A group health plan (any employee welfare benefit plan as described under ERISA Section 3(1);

2. A health insurance issuer;

3. An HMO;

4. An employee welfare benefit plan;

5. CHAMPUS;

6. Medicare Parts A, B, C, and D, including Medicare Advantage;

7. Medicaid;

8. Veterans' health care programs;

9. Active military health care programs; and

10. Practically any other mechanism designed to provide or pay for the cost of medical coverage, unless specifically excluded under the regulations.[3]

The Department of Health and Human Services has final regulations regarding the ability of nonfederal governmental entities to opt out of HIPAA coverage if specific requirements are satisfied, including timely notice to participants and a timely filed election (prior to the first day of the affected plan year) to opt out submitted to the Centers for Medicare and Medicaid Services, Private Health Insurance Group.[4]

But the definition of health plans does not include plans with fewer than fifty participants that are self-administered by the plan sponsor. In addition, the Privacy Rule does not apply to

---

1. 45 CFR 160.103(2)(i)-(iv); 78 Fed. Reg. 5566, (Jan. 25, 2013).
2. 45 C.F.R. §§160.102(a) and 164.104.
3. 45 C.F.R. §160.103.
4. 45 C.F.R. §146.180, 69 Fed. Reg. 43,926 (July 23, 2004).

certain plans that are exempt from HIPAA's portability, special enrollment, and nondiscrimination requirements (i.e., plans that provide accident coverage, disability income coverage, and workers' compensation benefits).[1]

Plan sponsors and third-party administrators (TPAs) are not "covered entities" under the Privacy Rule.[2] But the rules do extend some coverage to plan sponsors and TPAs through plan document and contractual requirements (detailed below).

A "health care provider" is defined as a provider of medical or health services and any other person or organization who furnishes, bills, or is paid for health care in the normal course of business.[3]

A covered entity must use the standard unique employer identifier (EIN) of the appropriate employer in standard transactions that require an employer identifier to identify a person or entity as an employer, including where situationally required.[4]

A "health care clearinghouse" is defined as a public or private entity, including a billing service, re-pricing company, community health management information system, or "value added" network or switch, that does either of the following:

1.   Processes or facilitates the processing of health information received from another entity in a nonstandard format or containing nonstandard data content into standard data elements, or a standard transaction; or

2.   Receives a standard transaction from another entity and processes or facilitates the processing of health information into nonstandard format or nonstandard data content for the receiving entity.[5]

HHS has issued proposed regulations that would require health plans to obtain a unique health plan identifier (HPID). Section 1104(c)(1) of the Affordable Care Act, enacted on March 23, 2010, directs HHS to promulgate a final rule establishing a unique health plan identifier on an interim final basis effective not later than October 1, 2012. The Affordable Care Act specifically calls for the establishment of a unique identifier for health plans.[6] There are however, other entities that are not health plans but that perform certain health plan functions and are currently identified in the standard transactions in the same fields using the same types of identifiers as health plans. For example, health care clearinghouses, TPAs, and re-pricers often contract with insurance companies, self-funded employer health care plans, and provider- or hospital-run health plans to perform claims administration, premium collection, enrollment, and other administrative functions. In some cases, TPAs or other entities are identified in the same fields as health plans in the transactions, depending on the contractual relationships. The

---

1. 45 C.F.R. §160.103.
2. 45 C.F.R. §160.103.
3. 45 C.F.R. §160.103.
4. 45 C.F.R. §162.610, 69 Fed. Reg. 3434 (Jan. 23, 2004).
5. 45 C.F.R. §160.103.
6. 45 CFR 162.506; 77 Fed. Reg. 74 (Apr. 17, 2012).

proposed regulation adopts a data element — an "other entity identifier" (OEID) — to serve as an identifier for these other entities.[1]

The proposed regulation mandates HPID usage requirements for all HIPAA wherever a covered entity identifies a health plan in a covered transaction.[2] Covered entities would obtain the HPIDs of health plans from the health plans themselves or from the Enumeration System, provided for under the proposed regulation.[3] If a covered entity uses a business associate to conduct standard transactions on its behalf, the covered entity must require that its business associate use an HPID in each field where the business associate identifies a health plan in all covered transactions.[4]

The HPID may also be used for any other lawful purpose that requires the identification of health plans. Some examples of permitted uses include the following:

- Health plans may use HPIDs in their internal files to facilitate processing of health care transactions.

- A health plan may use an HPID on a health insurance card.

- The HPID may be used as a cross-reference in health care fraud and abuse files and other program integrity files.

- Health care clearinghouses may use HPIDs in their internal files to create and process standard and non-standard transactions, and in communications with health plans and health care providers.

- HPIDs may be used in patient medical records to help specify patients' health care benefit package(s).

- HPIDs may be used to identify health plans in electronic health records (EHRs).

- HPIDs may be used to identify health plans in Health Information Exchanges (HIEs).

- HPIDs may be used to identify health plans in Federal and State health insurance exchanges.

- HPIDs may be used to identify health plans for public health data reporting purposes.[5]

---

1. 45 CFR 162.514; 77 Fed. Reg. 74 (Apr. 17, 2012).
2. 45 CFR 162.510; 77 Fed Reg 74 (Apr. 17, 2012).
3. 45 CFR 162.508; 77 Fed. Reg. 74 (Apr. 17, 2012).
4. 45 CFR 162.510(b); 77 Fed. Reg. 74 (Apr. 17, 2012).
5. Preamble to 45 CFR 162, sub-part E, 77 Fed. Reg. 74 (Apr. 17, 2012).

146. What disclosures are not permitted without the valid authorization of the affected individual?

A covered entity may not use or disclose PHI without valid authorization for any of the following purposes:

1.   Psychotherapy notes (except those necessary for treatment, payment, or health care operations; use by the originator of the notes for treatment; for structured internal training purposes; and for defense in a legal action brought by the individual); and

2.   Marketing purposes (except if it is in the form of face-to-face communication from a covered entity to the individual).[1]

For other restricted health information, a covered entity may use or disclose PHI provided that the individual is orally informed in advance of the use or disclosure and has an opportunity to orally agree, prohibit, or restrict such use or disclosure.[2] Such use and disclosure includes:

1.   Use and disclosure for a directory of individuals within the covered entity's facility;

2.   Disclosure to a family member, other relative or a close personal friend, or any other person identified by the individual, of the PHI directly relevant to such person's involvement with the individual's care or payment related to the individual's care;

3.   Notification of a family member, personal representative, or another person responsible for the care of the individual of the individual's location, general condition, or death.[3]

The Omnibus Final Rule provides that an authorization for use or disclosure of protected health information may not be combined with any other document to create a compound authorization, except as follows:

1.   An authorization for the use or disclosure of protected health information for a research study may be combined with any other type of written permission for the same or another research study. This exception includes combining an authorization for the use or disclosure of protected health information for a research study with another authorization for the same research study, with an authorization for the creation or maintenance of a research database or repository, or with consent to participate in research. Where a covered health care provider has conditioned the provision of research-related treatment on the provision of one of the authorizations, as permitted above, any compound authorization must clearly differentiate between the conditioned and unconditioned components and provide the individual with an opportunity to opt in to the research activities described in the unconditioned authorization.

---

1. 45 C.F.R. §§164.508(a)(1), 164.508(a)(2), and 164.508(a)(3).
2. 45 C.F.R. §164.510.
3. 45 C.F.R. §§164.510(b)(1)(i) and 164.510(b)(1)(ii).

2.   An authorization for a use or disclosure of psychotherapy notes may only be combined with another authorization for a use or disclosure of psychotherapy notes.

3.   An authorization, other than an authorization for a use or disclosure of psychotherapy notes, may be combined with any other such authorization except when a covered entity has conditioned the provision of treatment, payment, enrollment in the health plan, or eligibility for benefits under the above rules on the provision of one of the authorizations.[1]

147. What are the contents of a valid authorization?

A valid authorization must contain at least the following information:

1.   A description of the information to be used and disclosed that identifies the information in a specific and meaningful fashion;

2.   The name and other specific identification of the person(s) or class of persons authorized to make the requested use or disclosure;

3.   The name or other specific identification of the person(s) or class of persons to whom the covered entity may make the requested use or disclosure;

4.   A description of each purpose of the requested use or disclosure;

5.   An expiration date or expiration event that relates to the individual or the purpose of the use or disclosure; and

6.   The signature of the individual and the date. If the authorization is signed by a representative of the individual, a description of such representative's authority to act must also be provided.[2]

Prohibition on Sales of Electronic Health Records or PHI

ARRA 2009 toughened the prohibition on selling PHI by specifically prohibiting a covered entity or business associate from receiving remuneration in exchange for PHI without the individual's authorization,[3] unless the exchange is made for certain purposes, such as the following:

1.   Public health activities;[4]

2.   Research, if the price charged reflects the cost of preparation and transmittal of data;[5]

3.   Treatment of the individual;[6]

4.   The sale, transfer, merger, or consolidation of all or a part of a covered entity with another covered entity, and due diligence related to that activity;[7]

---

1. 45 CFR 164.508(b)(3)(i)-(iii); 78 Fed. Reg. 5566, (Jan. 25, 2013).
2. 45 C.F.R. §§164.508(b)(1), 164.508(c)(1), and 164.508(c)(2).
3. ARRA 2009 §13405(d)(1).
4. ARRA 2009 §13405(d)(2)(A).
5. ARRA 2009 §13405(d)(2)(B).
6. ARRA 2009 §13405(d)(2)(C).
7. ARRA 2009 §13405(d)(2)(D).

5.   Paying a business associate under a business associate agreement for services rendered;[1]

6.   Providing an individual with access to his or her PHI;[2] or

7.   An exchange made pursuant to an arrangement determined by the Secretary of Health and Human Services to be similarly necessary and appropriate as compared to the enumerated exceptions.[3]

> *Note:* Business associates should immediately review their business associate agreements to ensure that, if payments are made between a covered entity and the business associate, those payment terms are contained in the business associate agreement and no other remuneration is received by the business associate in exchange for the PHI unless one of the exceptions noted above is delineated.

148. What are the uses of PHI for which authorization is not required?

A covered entity may use or disclose protected health information without the consent of the individual in the following circumstances:

1.   Uses and disclosures required by law;

2.   Release of PHI for public health activities to:

     a.   a public health authority for the prevention or control of disease,

     b.   a public health authority for reports of child abuse or neglect,

     c.   a person subject to FDA jurisdiction with respect to an FDA-regulated product or activity,

     d.   persons exposed to a communicable disease or otherwise at risk of contracting or spreading a disease, or

     e.   an employer concerning an employee, to conduct an evaluation relating to medical surveillance of the workplace or to evaluate whether the employee has a workplace-related illness or injury (provided written notice of the release is given the employee);

3.   Release of PHI where the covered entity reasonably believes the individual to be a victim of abuse, neglect, or domestic violence, and where such information is released to a government authority as required by law;

4.   Disclosures for health oversight activities authorized by law, such as audits; civil, administrative, or criminal investigations; inspections; and licensure proceedings;

---

1. ARRA 2009 §13405(d)(2)(E).
2. ARRA 2009 §13405(d)(2)(F).
3. ARRA 2009 §13405(d)(2)(G).

5. Disclosures for judicial and administrative proceedings in response to a court order, subpoena, or discovery request;

6. Disclosures for law enforcement-related purposes;

7. Limited release of information for identification and location purposes in response to a law enforcement official's request;

8. Disclosure of information upon request of a law enforcement official regarding an individual suspected to be a victim of a crime (including report of the death of an individual and the commission and nature of a crime);

9. Disclosure of information to coroners and funeral directors;

10. Release of information to an organ donation entity for the facilitation of donations;

11. Disclosure for research (under stringent approval and usage guidelines detailed in the regulations);

12. Good-faith disclosures to avert serious threat to the health or safety of a person or the public (including information necessary for law enforcement to identify and apprehend an individual);

13. Uses and disclosures for specialized government functions (armed forces personnel, veterans, and foreign military personnel, protective services for the President, correctional institutions, governmental entities providing public benefits, and national security and intelligence activities); and

14. Disclosures to maintain compliance with applicable workers' compensation statutes.[1]

The Omnibus Final Rule expands the uses for which authorization is not required to include situations where the covered entity is a covered health care provider who provides health care to the individual at the request of the employer.[2]

The Final Rule also expands the uses for which authorization is not required to include a school, for information about an individual who is a student or prospective student of the school, if:

1. The protected health information that is disclosed is limited to proof of immunization;

2. The school is required by State or other law to have such proof of immunization prior to admitting the individual; and

3. The covered entity obtains and documents the agreement to the disclosure from either:

    a. A parent, guardian, or other person acting in loco parentis of the individual, if the individual is an unemancipated minor; or

    b. The individual, if the individual is an adult or emancipated minor.[3]

---

1. 45 C.F.R. §164.512(a) to (l).
2. 45 CFR 164.512(b)(v)(A); 78 Fed. Reg. 5566, (Jan. 25, 2013).
3. 45 CFR 164.512(b)(vi)(A)-(C)(i)(ii); 78 Fed. Reg. 5566, (Jan. 25, 2013).

Clarification of the "Minimum Necessary" standard

A covered entity will be considered to be in compliance with the minimum necessary standard (see Q 142) if, to the extent possible, the covered entity limits the disclosure to a limited data set or to the minimum data necessary to accomplish the intended purpose of the disclosure or use of the information.[1]

The covered entity or business associate disclosing such information must determine what constitutes the minimum necessary to accomplish the intended purpose of such disclosure.[2]

> *Note:* Business associates should review the types of disclosures they make on a routine basis and confirm that the information disclosed constitutes a limited data set or that the disclosures are limited to the minimum necessary amount of PHI to accomplish the intended purpose of the disclosure.

The Omnibus Final Rule clarifies that when using or disclosing PHI or when requesting PHI from another covered entity or business associate, a covered entity or business associate must make reasonable efforts to limit protected health information to the minimum necessary to accomplish the intended purpose of the use, disclosure, or request.[3]

149. What guidelines are applicable to the disclosure of PHI to business associates?

Health plans have a legitimate need to disclose PHI to certain noncovered entities that perform functions on behalf of the health plan. The privacy rules have been drafted to provide guidance where such information is shared with service providers, such as TPAs, claims administrators, and attorneys. These outside entities are referred to in the Privacy Rule as "business associates" and are defined to include any person who, on behalf of a covered entity or health care arrangement in which the covered entity participates (aside from members of the workforce), performs or assists in the performance of a function or activity involving the use or disclosure of individually identifiable health information, including claims processing or administration, data analysis, utilization review, quality assurance, billing, benefit management, practice management, or re-pricing. Business associates also include providers of legal, actuarial, accounting, consulting, management, administrative accreditation, or financial services to, or for, such covered entity.[4] The Omnibus Final Rule expands the definition of business associate to include a Health Information Organization, E-prescribing Gateway, or other person that provides data transmission services with respect to protected health information to a covered entity and that requires access on a routine basis to such protected health information. It also expands the definition to include a person who offers a personal health record to one or more individuals on behalf of a covered entity.[5]

---

1. ARRA 2009 §13405(b)(1)(A); 45 C.F.R. §164.502(b).
2. ARRA 2009 §13405(b)(2).
3. 45 CFR 164.502(b)(1); 78 Fed. Reg. 5566, (Jan. 25, 2013).
4. 45 C.F.R. §160.103.
5. 45 CFR 160.103; 78 Fed. Reg. 5566, (Jan. 25, 2013).

A covered entity may disclose PHI to a business associate if the plan obtains "satisfactory assurances" that the business associate will properly safeguard the information. Satisfactory assurances must be in the form of a written agreement.[1] The covered entity must document the satisfactory assurances through a written contract or other written agreement or arrangement with the business associate.[2] The Omnibus Final Rule clarifies that a covered entity is not required to obtain such satisfactory assurances from a business associate that is a subcontractor.[3]

Any contract between a covered entity and a business associate must:

1. Establish the permitted and required uses and disclosures of such information by the business associate (except that the contract may not permit the use of PHI in a manner inconsistent with the Privacy Rule);[4] and

2. Provide that the business associate will:

    a. not use or further disclose the information other than as permitted by the contract or law,

    b. use appropriate safeguards to prevent use or disclosure of PHI other than as provided for by the contract,

    c. report to the covered entity any use or disclosure of the information not provided for by the contract of which it becomes aware,

    d. ensure that any agents and subcontractors to whom it provides PHI received from, or created or received by the business associate on behalf of the covered entity, agree to the same restrictions and conditions that apply to the business associate with respect to such information,

    e. make available PHI in accordance with an individual's right to access it,

    f. make available PHI for amendment in accordance with an individual's right,

    g. make available information regarding accurate accounting of disclosures in accordance with an individual's right,

    h. make its internal practices, books, and records relating to the use and disclosure of PHI received from, or created or received by, the business associate on behalf of the covered entity available to HHS for inspection, and

    i. at termination of the contract, if feasible, return or destroy all PHI received from, or created or received by, the business associate on behalf of the covered entity that the business associate still maintains in any form and retain no such

---

1. 45 C.F.R. §164.502(e)(1).
2. 45 C.F.R. §164.502(e)(2).
3. 45 CFR 164.502(e)(1)(i); 78 Fed. Reg. 5566, (Jan. 25, 2013).
4. 45 C.F.R. §164.502(e)(2)(i).

copies. If destruction or return is infeasible, extend the protections of the contract to the information and limit further uses and disclosures.[1]

Furthermore, any contract between a covered entity and a business associate must provide that the covered entity may terminate the contract upon determination that the business associate has violated a material term of the contract.[2]

The Omnibus Final Rule expands the guidelines regarding subcontractors to business associates. Under the Final Rule, a business associate may disclose PHI to a business associate that is a subcontractor and may allow the subcontractor to create, receive, maintain, or transmit PHI on its behalf, if the business associate obtains satisfactory assurances, (as provided in the preceding information), that the subcontractor will appropriately safeguard the information. The satisfactory assurances must be documented through a written contract or other written agreement or arrangement with the business associate that meets the applicable requirements noted herein.[3]

Finally, the Omnibus Final Rule clarifies that a covered entity must comply with the requirements disclosures to business associates with respect to the PHI of a deceased individual for a period of fifty years following the death of the individual.[4]

Business Associates Required to Comply with HIPAA Privacy and Security Rules

Title 13 of ARRA 2009[5] made a number of modifications to HIPAA regarding privacy and security rules. This title is often referred to as the "Health Information Technology for Economic and Clinical Health Act" or the "HITECH Act." There are significant changes for all covered entities (defined under HIPAA as health care providers that conduct certain electronic transactions, health care clearinghouses, and health plans),[6] but are most challenging for business associates—individuals or corporations that perform *any* function or activity involving the use of PHI, who now face a host of new requirements.

Prior to the enactment of ARRA 2009, HIPAA only required a contract between the business associate and the HIPAA-covered entity, and the only sanction that business associates faced for failure to protect health information was a breach of contract claim. However, ARRA 2009 makes significant changes to the way business associates are treated under HIPAA. This includes the extension to them of security provisions and civil and criminal penalties previously applicable only to covered entities.[7] Specifically, ARRA 2009 requires that the administrative, physical, and technical safeguards and the policy, procedure, and documentation requirements of HIPAA ARRA 2009's security rule apply to business associates of a covered entity in the same manner as they apply to the covered entity.

1. 45 C.F.R. §§164.504(e)(2)(ii)(A) to 164.504(e)(2)(ii)(I).
2. 45 C.F.R. §164.504(e)(2)(iii).
3. 45 CFR 164.502(e)(1)(ii); 78 Fed. Reg. 5566, (Jan. 25, 2013).
4. 45 CFR 164.502(e)(2); 78 Fed. Reg. 5566, (Jan. 25, 2013).
5. Pub. L. No. 111-5 (2009), signed into law by the President on February 17, 2009.
6. 45 C.F.R. §160.103.
7. ARRA 2009 §§13401(a) and 13401(b).

ARRA 2009 has expanded the types of entities required to enter into business associate agreements with covered entities. It specifies that *any* entity that engages in health information exchanges or provides data transmission of PHI, and that requires access on a routine basis to such protected health information (such as a Health Information Exchange Organization, Regional Health Information Organization, E-prescribing Gateway, or each vendor that contracts with a covered entity to allow that covered entity to offer a personal health record to patients as part of its electronic health record) is considered a business associate. As such, these entities must enter into a business associate contract with the covered entity and will be subject to ARRA 2009's civil and criminal penalty provisions.[1] These provisions were effective as of February 17, 2010.[2] The Omnibus Final Rule applies these administrative, physical, and technical safeguards, as well as the Security Rule's policies, procedures, and documentation requirements to business associates. They also finalize the extension of the civil and criminal liability provisions to business associates.[3]

The additional requirements must be incorporated into business associate contracts and agreements and must include notification provisions for a breach and the application of ARRA 2009's criminal and civil penalties.[4]

> *Note:* A business associate is now subject to sanctions if it has knowledge of a pattern or practice that would constitute a material breach or violation of its business association agreement with a covered entity, and subsequently fails to take action to cure the breach or terminate the agreement.

With regard to HIPAA's privacy rules, business associates are prohibited from using or disclosing any PHI in a manner that is not in compliance with the business associate contract or agreement-required terms under HIPAA.[5] These additional requirements were effective February 17, 2010 (one year after the enactment of ARRA 2009).[6]

> *Note:* These changes will require business associates and vendors to business associates to update their current HIPAA policies and procedures as well as requiring the redrafting of their existing HIPAA agreements in order to bring them into compliance with these new legal requirements.

> *Note:* Under the HITECH Act a breach of the new business associate agreement requirements now constitutes a violation of law as well as a breach of contract.

Additional Restrictions on Business Associates' Marketing Communications

ARRA 2009 addresses marketing communications made by business associates. It clarifies that a marketing communication made by a business associate about a product or service that

---

1. ARRA 2009 §13408.
2. ARRA 2009 §13423.
3. 45 CFR 164.308; 164.310; 164.312; and 164.316; 78 Fed. Reg. 5566, (Jan. 25, 2013).
4. ARRA 2009 §§13404(b) and 13404(c).
5. ARRA 2009 §13404(a).
6. ARRA 2009 §13423.

encourages the recipient to purchase or use the product or service may not be considered an otherwise permissible "health care operation" unless the communication relates to a health care–related product or services offered by a covered entity, or the communication otherwise relates to the treatment of the individual.[1] These provisions were effective February 17, 2010.[2]

> *Note:* Business associates should review whether their communications to patients constitute marketing and, if so, should limit those communications so they relate to a covered-entity-offered health care product or service or relate to the individual's treatment.

The Final Rule modifies the marketing restrictions by requiring authorization for all treatment and health care operations communications where the covered entity receives financial renumeration for making the communications from a third party whose product is being marketed. This final rule also extends to business associates and subcontractors.[3]

150. What are the individual privacy rights with respect to PHI?

The Privacy Rule establishes substantial rights for individuals with respect to their PHI. These rights include the right of an individual to:

- Request privacy protection for PHI,[4]

- Access their PHI maintained by the plan,[5]

- Request amendments to their PHI, and[6]

- Request an accounting of the disclosures of their PHI by the plan.[7]

Expansion of Accounting and Disclosures

ARRA 2009 changed the existing limitations on accounting for disclosures of health information to individuals who request the disclosure. If a covered entity uses or maintains an electronic health record (EHR), then individuals will be allowed to receive, upon request, an accounting of the disclosures of PHI for treatment, payment, and health care operations made from the EHR.[8] The period of mandated disclosure is limited to the three-year period prior to the individual's request.[9] A reasonable fee may be charged to the requesting individual, provided the fee is not greater than the labor costs involved in complying with the request.[10]

---

1. ARRA 2009 §13406(a).
2. ARRA 2009 §13406(c).
3. 45 CFR 164.502(5)(ii)(A); (B)(1) and (2); 78 Fed. Reg. 5566, (Jan. 25, 2013).
4. 45 C.F.R. §164.522(a)(1).
5. 45 C.F.R. §164.524(a)(1).
6. 45 C.F.R. §164.526(a)(1).
7. 45 C.F.R. §164.528(a)(1).
8. ARRA 2009 §13405(c)(1)(B).
9. ARRA 2009 §13405(c)(1)(B).
10. ARRA 2009 §13405(e)(2).

In response to a request from an individual for an accounting, a covered entity must elect to provide either:

- An accounting for disclosures of PHI that are made by such covered entity and by a business associate acting on behalf of the covered entity; or

- An accounting for disclosures that are made by such covered entity and provide a list of all business associates acting on behalf of the covered entity, including contact information for such associates (such as mailing address, phone, and e-mail address).[1]

A business associate included on a list in the preceding paragraph must provide an accounting of disclosures made by the business associate upon a request made by an individual directly to the business associate for such an accounting.[2]

Covered entities that began using EHR prior to January 1, 2009, will be required to provide the accounting upon request effective January 1, 2014.[3]

Covered entities that begin using EHR after January 1, 2009, are required to provide the accounting upon request effective January 1, 2011, or the date that it acquires the EHR.[4]

> *Note:* Business associates will be required not only to maintain a record of the required disclosures but also to implement a new procedure for responding to patient requests.

> *Note:* This business associate requirement will apply when a covered entity uses an EHR and chooses to list the business associate in responding to the patient request. This requirement will apply to the business associate even if the business associate does not use or maintain an EHR itself.

Mandatory Restrictions on Disclosure of PHI When Requested by Individuals

Prior to ARRA 2009, a covered entity had the right to reject a request from an individual seeking restrictions on disclosures of their PHI. Under ARRA 2009, individuals are now given the right to restrict the disclosure of PHI related to treatment, payment, and health care operations provided:

- The restriction relates to disclosure for purposes of payment or health care operations;[5]

- The restriction does not relate to disclosure for purposes of treatment;[6] and

---

1. ARRA 2009 §13405(c)(3).
2. ARRA 2009 §13405(c)(3).
3. ARRA 2009 §13405(c)(4)(A).
4. ARRA 2009 §13405(c)(4)(B)(i) and (ii).
5. ARRA 2009 §13405(a)(1).
6. ARRA 2009 §13405(a)(1).

- The PHI relates only to an item or service for which the provider has already received payment in full out-of-pocket from the individual.[1]

   Note: This new rule will likely require most covered entities to link their accounts receivable and patient treatment recordkeeping functions in order to determine how best to honor such nondisclosure requests as part of their newly expanded procedures for responding to patient requests.

Right of Individuals to Receive Electronic Records

If a covered entity maintains EHRs that contain PHI, ARRA 2009 provides individuals with the right to obtain a copy of their records in an electronic format or to request that the record be transmitted to a third party. The covered entity may not charge the individual requesting the copies more than the total cost of labor incurred by the entity in transmitting the copies.[2]

151. What requirements are imposed on plan sponsors under the Privacy Rule?

The Department of Health and Human Services (HHS) indirectly regulates plan sponsors by placing restrictions and requirements on the exchange of health information between covered entities (group health plans) and noncovered entities (plan sponsors). These requirements depend upon whether the plan sponsor intends to obtain PHI from its health plan.

In many health care arrangements (particularly self-funded plans), the employer is both the plan sponsor and the plan administrator. In this situation, the employer requires access to PHI in order to fulfill its ERISA fiduciary duties to the health plan (e.g., serving as the claims fiduciary for appeals of claims). Disclosure of PHI by a health plan to a plan sponsor under the Privacy Rule in order to facilitate compliance with fiduciary obligations is permissible if the following requirements are satisfied:

1. The plan document is amended to include the following items relating to the receipt and use of PHI:

   a.   the permitted uses and disclosures of PHI to the plan sponsor (consistent with the Privacy Rule);

   b.   a provision that the plan will disclose PHI to the plan sponsor only upon certification that the plan documents have been amended to incorporate the following provisions and that the plan sponsor agrees to:

   i.   not use or further disclose the information other than as permitted by plan documents or the law,

   ii. ensure that any agents and subcontractors to whom it provides PHI agree to the same restrictions and conditions applicable to the plan sponsor,

---

1. ARRA 2009 §13405(a)(2).
2. ARRA 2009 §13405(e)(1).

iii. not use or disclose the PHI for employment-related actions and decisions,

iv. report to the plan any use or disclosure of the information that is inconsistent with the Privacy Rule (see below for further information on security incident–reporting obligations),

v. make available PHI to individuals in accordance with their rights to access such information,

vi. make available PHI to individuals within their rights to amend it,

vii. make available PHI to individuals within their rights to seek an accounting of disclosures,

viii. make its internal practices, books, and records relating to the use and disclosure of protected information available to HHS for purposes of determining compliance with the Privacy Rule,

ix. if feasible, return or destroy all PHI received from the plan that the sponsor still maintains in any form and retain no copies of such information when no longer needed for the purpose for which the disclosure was made, and

x. ensure that the adequate separation described below is established.[1]

2. The plan sponsor must amend the plan document for the health plan to establish adequate separation between the group health plan and the plan sponsor regarding employees that have access to PHI and the uses of the PHI by the plan sponsor, including "an effective mechanism for resolving any issues of noncompliance" (i.e., use of information for non-health-plan-related purposes).[2]

HHS has updated its content on HIPAA administrative simplification to provide detailed information and guidance on security incident–reporting obligations for business associates and plan sponsors. These may be accessed at http://www.cms.gov/Regulations-and-Guidance/HIPAA-Administrative-Simplification/HIPAAGenInfo/index.html.[3]

A covered entity "may consider some of the following questions: what specific actions would be considered security incidents; how will incidents be documented and reported; what information should be contained in the documentation; how often and to whom should incidents be reported; what are the appropriate responses to certain incidents; and whether identifying patterns of attempted security incidents is reasonable and appropriate... While internal reporting of security incidents is an inherent part of security incident policies and procedures, the Security Rule generally does not require a covered entity to report incidents to outside entities. However, 45 C.F.R. §§ 164.314(a)(2)(i)(C) and 164.314(b)(2)(iv) require contracts between a covered entity and a business associate, and plan documents of group health

---

1. 45 C.F.R. §164.504(f)(2)(ii)(A) to (J).
2. 45 C.F.R. §§164.504(f)(2)(iii)(A), 164.504(f)(2)(iii)(B), and 164.504(f)(2)(iii)(C).
3. Updated October 11, 2013.

plans, respectively, to include provisions that require business associates and plan sponsors to report to the covered entity any security incidents of which they become aware."

Regarding business associates and plan sponsors, although they may not be covered entities under HIPAA, they would "nevertheless be contractually obligated, through its business associate contract, to report such security incidents to the covered entity." HHS further states that contracts between a covered entity and its business associate or a plan sponsor could serve as the vehicle to establish the covered entity's specific reporting requirements and should be developed to meet the entity's specific needs. The covered entity and business associate or plan sponsor must document the specifics of the reporting requirements, including the frequency, level of detail, format, and other relevant considerations (e.g., in aggregate or per incident, weekly or monthly).

In addressing this required implementation specification, a covered entity and its business associate or plan sponsor may consider some of the following questions:

1. What specific actions would be considered security incidents?

2. How will incidents be documented and reported?

3. What information should be contained in the documentation?

4. How often and to whom within the covered entity should incidents be reported?

5. What are the appropriate responses to certain incidents?

6. Whether identifying patterns of attempted security incidents are reasonable and appropriate?

Disclosure of Only Summary Health Information to the Plan Sponsor

Plan sponsors can avoid the above requirements (i.e., plan document amendments and the certification) imposed on them by only receiving summary health information and enrollment/disenrollment information relating to the health plan.

The summary health information may only be disclosed to the plan sponsor for the limited purposes of obtaining premium bids for health insurance coverage under the health plan and for amending or terminating the plan.[1]

Summary health information is defined as information that summarizes the claims history, claims expenses, or types of claims for individuals enrolled in the group health plan after certain individual identifiers have been removed.[2] As a result, employers that sponsor fully insured plans and that do not act as the plan administrator would be able to avoid having to amend their plan document and complete the certification to the plan if they limited the information they received from the insurer to only summary health information.

---

1. 45 C.F.R. §164.504(f)(1)(ii).
2. 45 C.F.R. §164.504(a).

152. What are the required elements of the privacy notice?

The Privacy Rule requires plans to provide notice to each individual who's PHI will be used or maintained by the plan.[1]

The notice must describe elements required under the Privacy Rule, in plain English, including:

1. The uses and disclosures that the plan may make of each individual's PHI;[2]

2. The individual's rights and the plan's obligations with respect to the PHI;[3]

3. The covered entity's duties;[4]

4. The right to file complaints with the Secretary of HHS;[5] and

5. The name, or title and telephone number, of the person or office to contact for further information.[6]

No less than once every three years, the health plan must notify individuals covered under the plan of the availability of the notice and how to obtain it.[7]

Health care providers who maintain a "physical service delivery site" must have the notice available for inspection and copying for individuals who request it, and the notice must be posted in a clear and prominent location "where it is reasonable to expect individuals seeking service … to be able to read" the notice.[8]

The Omnibus Final Rule issued on January 25, 2013, mandates that covered entities must modify their privacy notices to include additional items including the uses and disclosures of PHI that require authorization under the applicable regulations (detailed in the preceding information); a statement that individuals can restrict disclosure of protected health information to a health plan if the disclosure is for payment or health care operations and pertains to a health care item or service for which the individual has paid out of pocket in full; and that affected individuals have the right to be notified following a breach.[9]

153. What rules apply to electronic delivery of the notice?

A covered entity that maintains a Web site that provides information about its services or benefits must prominently post its notice on the Web site and make the notice available electronically through its Web site.[10]

---

1. 45 C.F.R. §164.520(a)(1).
2. 45 C.F.R. §164.520(b)(1)(ii).
3. 45 C.F.R. §164.520(b)(1)(iv).
4. 45 C.F.R. §164.520(b)(1)(v).
5. 45 C.F.R. §164.520(b)(1)(vi).
6. 45 C.F.R. §164.520(b)(1)(vii).
7. 45 C.F.R. §164.520(c)(1)(ii).
8. 45 C.F.R. §§164.520(c)(2)(ii)(A) and 164.520(c)(2)(ii)(B).
9. 45 CFR 164.520(b); 78 Fed. Reg. 5566, (Jan. 25, 2013).
10. 45 C.F.R. §164.520(c)(3)(i).

A covered entity may provide the notice to an individual by e-mail, if the individual agrees to electronic notice and such agreement has not been withdrawn. Where the covered entity has reason to believe the electronic delivery of the notice has failed, a paper copy of the notice must be provided.[1]

Recipients of electronic delivery always retain the right to request and receive a paper copy of the notice.[2]

154. What is the HIPAA Security Rule regarding electronic transactions, and how is it applied?

The HIPAA Security Rule regarding electronic transactions requires administrative, physical, and technical safeguards detailed under eighteen standards to ensure the confidentiality, integrity, and availability of electronic protected health information (PHI) that is maintained, used, or transmitted by a health plan or provider. Designed to be technology neutral, the Security Rule allows covered entities to devise policies, procedures, training, and implementation approaches that will work with their existing system capabilities.

The Security Rule standards are broken down into two types: required and addressable. Required standards are those that must be addressed by all covered entities in order to attain and maintain compliance with the Security Rule. Standards that are "addressable" provide some flexibility to covered entities in that if the covered entity decides that the addressable implementation specification is not reasonable and appropriate, it must document that determination and implement an equivalent alternative measure, presuming that the alternative is reasonable and appropriate. Or if the standard can otherwise be met, the covered entity may choose to not implement the implementation specification or any equivalent alternative measure.

The Security Rule does not expressly prohibit the use of e-mail for sending electronic PHI. But the standards for access control,[3] integrity,[4] and transmission security[5] require covered entities to implement policies and procedures to restrict access to, protect the integrity of, and guard against the unauthorized access to electronic PHI. The standard for transmission security[6] also includes addressable specifications for integrity controls and encryption. The Security Rule allows for electronic PHI to be sent over an electronic open network as long as it is adequately protected.

The Security Rule makes the use of encryption an addressable implementation specification.[7] In other words, there is no mandatory format for achieving a secure encryption. Covered entities are free to address this particular issue in any manner that best suits their particular requirements.

---

1. 45 C.F.R. §164.520(c)(3)(ii).
2. 45 C.F.R. §164.520(c)(3)(iv).
3. 45 C.F.R. §164.312(a).
4. 45 C.F.R. §164.312(c)(1).
5. 45 C.F.R. §164.312(e)(1).
6. 45 C.F.R. §164.312(e).
7. 45 C.F.R. §§164.312(a)(2)(iv) and 164.312(e)(2)(ii).

Physical safeguards under the Security Rule are physical measures, policies, and procedures to protect a covered entity's electronic information systems and related buildings and equipment from natural and environmental hazards and unauthorized intrusion. The standards under physical safeguards include facility access controls, workstation use, workstation security, and device and media controls.

The Security Rule does not apply to written or oral communications (they are covered under the broader PHI rule). This includes paper-to-paper faxes, video teleconferencing, and messages left on voice mail (because the information exchanged did not exist in an electronic format prior to transmission). The electronic Security Rule does apply to PHI transmitted via telephone voice response and faxback systems because they are used as input and output devices for computers.

If an individual (i.e., a subscriber or a patient) uses his or her credit or debit card to pay for health care, related costs are exempt from the Security Rule unless the individual making the payment is acting in some capacity on behalf of a covered entity.

Covered entities that allow employees to telecommute or work out of home-based offices and allow them to have access to electronic PHI must implement appropriate safeguards to protect the organization's data. The automatic logoff implementation specification is addressable. But the information access management and access control standards require the covered entity to implement policies and procedures for authorizing access to electronic PHI and technical policies and procedures to allow access only to those persons or software programs that have been appropriately granted access rights.[1]

The Department of Health and Human Services (HHS) has issued Security Guidance on the protection of electronic PHI when accessed or stored offsite and outside of the covered entity's control.[2] HHS notes that recent advances in the technology involving the transmission of data throughout the health care industry have created complications and increased the risk of theft loss and unauthorized use and disclosure of PHI. As such, the guidance issued provides a review of some strategies that HHS deems reasonable for covered entities to follow under the Security Rule.

Of particular concern to HHS are laptops, home-based computers, personal digital assistants (PDAs), CDs, DVDs, smart phones, USB flash drives, e-mail, public workstations, memory cards, and public wireless access points. HHS urges covered entities to be "extremely cautious about allowing the offsite use of, or access to" electronic PHI. Covered entities should allow offsite use or access only when necessary and only "where great rigor has been taken to ensure that policies, procedures and workforce training have been effectively deployed and access is consistent with" the Security Rule.

The guidance notes that with respect to remote access to or use of electronic PHI, the covered entity "should place significant emphasis and attention" on their:

1.   Risk analysis and risk management strategies;

2.   Policies and procedures for safeguarding electronic PHI; and

---

1. Centers for Medicare & Medicaid Servs., HIPAA Q&A, http://questions.cms.hhs.gov/.
2. HIPAA Security Guidance for Remote Use of and Access to Electronic Protected Health Information (Jan. 2007).

3.   Security awareness and training on the policies and procedures for safeguarding electronic PHI.

In addressing security incidents and noncompliance with remote access and portable devices, HHS notes that the covered entity's security incident procedures must specify the actions workforce members must take to manage the harmful effects of the loss. Further, a sanction policy must be in place and effectively communicated so that workforce members understand the consequences of failing to maintain compliance with the security policies and procedures. Regarding off-site storage and use of electronic PHI, the six-page guidance provides practical advice on possible risk management strategies regarding the access and storage of electronic PHI. The guidance is available for access on the Internet at http://www.cms.hhs.gov/SecurityStandard/Downloads/SecurityGuidanceforRemoteUseFinal122806.pdf. HHS has issued interim final rules regarding the adoption of operating rules for eligibility for a health plan, and for health care claim status transactions. The operating rules attempt to define the rights and responsibilities of all parties, security requirements, transmission formats, response times, liabilities, exception processing, error resolution, and more, in order to facilitate successful interoperability between data systems of different entities.[1]

Methods of Securing PHI

The Secretary of Health and Human Services has issued guidance regarding the acceptable methods of securing PHI—including standards for encryption and the disposal of PHI.[2] Covered entities and business associates that comply with these safeguards are "safe harbored" from the new notification requirements, which apply to breaches of *unsecured* PHI (see Q 155). If PHI is rendered unusable, unreadable, or indecipherable to unauthorized individuals by an HHS-approved method, the data will not be considered "unsecured."[3] There are two ways to secure PHI: (1) encryption or (2) destruction.

Electronic PHI encryption is achieved by "the use of an algorithmic process to transform data into a form in which there is a low probability of assigning meaning without use of a confidential process or key," and such confidential process or key that might enable decryption had not been breached. The guidance identifies acceptable encryption processes that have been tested by the National Institute of Standards and technology and judged to meet this standard.[4]

The media on which the PHI is stored or recorded is considered destroyed if managed in one of the following ways:

1.   Paper, film, or other hard copy media have been shredded or destroyed such that the PHI cannot be read or reconstructed; or

2.   Electronic media have been cleared, purged, or destroyed consistent with NIST standards such that the PHI cannot be retrieved.[5]

---

1. Administrative Simplification: Adoption of Operating Rules for Eligibility for a Health Plan and Health Care Claim Status Transactions, 45 C.F.R. pts. 160 and 162, 76 Fed. Reg. 40,458 (July 8, 2011).
2. 74 Fed. Reg. 19,006 (Apr. 27, 2009). Under ARRA 2009 §13402, the Secretary was required to issue guidelines that specify the technologies and methodologies that render PHI unusable, unreadable, or indecipherable to unauthorized individuals (i.e., encryption).
3. 45 C.F.R. §164.402(2)(iii); 74 Fed. Reg. 42,740 (Aug. 24, 2009).
4. 74 Fed. Reg. 19,006 (Apr. 27, 2009).
5. 74 Fed. Reg. 19,006 (Apr. 27, 2009).

155. What are the administrative requirements imposed under the Privacy Rule?

The Privacy Rule also imposes additional administrative requirements on covered entities.

The covered entity must designate, and document, a privacy official who is responsible for the development and implementation of the policies and procedures of the entity. Furthermore, a covered entity must designate a contact person or office responsible for receiving complaints and providing further information about matters covered by the notice requirement set forth below.[1]

A covered entity is also required to train all members of its workforce, no later than the compliance dates, on the policies and procedures with respect to PHI "as necessary and appropriate for the members ... to carry out their function." Such training must be documented. Further training must be provided to each new member of the covered entity and includes training on all material changes to policies and procedures.[2]

Additional administrative requirements include the following:

1. Covered entities must take appropriate administrative, technical, and physical safeguards to protect the privacy of PHI;[3]

2. Covered entities must provide a process for individuals to make complaints concerning the covered entity's policies and procedures (including documentation of complaints and their disposition);[4]

3. Covered entities must provide standard sanctions against members of their workforces who fail to comply with policies and procedures;[5]

4. Covered entities must mitigate, to the extent practicable, any harmful effect that is known to the covered entity of a use or disclosure of PHI in violation of policies and procedures;[6] and

5. Covered entities may not intimidate, threaten, coerce, discriminate, or take retaliatory action against any individual who seeks to exercise any rights under the privacy provisions of HIPAA.[7]

Notice to Individuals of Privacy and Security Breaches

ARRA 2009 also imposes certain notification requirements on covered entities and business associates in the event of a breach of "unsecured protected health information." A breach is defined as "the unauthorized acquisition, access, use, or disclosure of protected health information which compromises the security or privacy of such information, except where an authorized

---

1. 45 C.F.R. §§164.530(a)(1)(i), 164.530(a)(1)(ii), and 164.530(a)(2).
2. 45 C.F.R. §§164.530(b)(1) and 164.530(b)(2).
3. 45 C.F.R. §164.530(c)(1)
4. 45 C.F.R. §164.530(d)(1).
5. 45 C.F.R. §154.530(e)(1).
6. 45 C.F.R. §154.530(f).
7. 45 C.F.R. §154.530(g).

person to whom such information is disclosed would not reasonably have been able to retain such information."[1]

"Unsecured protected health information" is defined as protected health information that the covered entity or business associate has not secured via standards approved by the Secretary of Health and Human Services (Secretary of HHS).[2]

The Omnibus Final Rule, issued in 2013, provides that the final rule of Breach Notification for Unsecured Protected Health Information under HITECH replaces the breach notification "harm" threshold with a more objective standard for determining when a breach notification must issue. That new objective standard provides that an acquisition, access, use, or disclosure of protected health information in a manner not permitted is presumed to be a breach unless the covered entity or business associate, as applicable, demonstrates that there is a low probability that the protected health information has been compromised based on a risk assessment of at least the following factors:

1.   The nature and extent of the protected health information involved, including the types of identifiers and the likelihood of re-identification;

2.   The unauthorized person who used the protected health information or to whom the disclosure was made;

3.   Whether the protected health information was actually acquired or viewed; and

4.   The extent to which the risk to the protected health information has been mitigated.[3]

A covered entity that accesses, maintains, retains, modifies, records, stores, destroys, or otherwise holds, uses, or discloses unsecured protected health information must, in the case of a breach of such information that is discovered by the covered entity, notify each individual whose unsecured protected health information has been, or is reasonably believed to have been, accessed, acquired, or disclosed as a result of such breach.[4] The notice must be in plain language[5] and contain the following information:

1.   A brief description of what happened, including the date of the breach and the date of the discovery of the breach, if known;

2.   A description of the types of unsecured protected health information that were involved in the breach (personal identifiers, diagnosis, disability code, etc.);

3.   Any steps individuals should take to protect themselves from potential harm resulting from the breach;

4.   A brief description of what the covered entity involved is doing to investigate the breach, to mitigate harm to individuals, and to protect against any further breaches; and

---

1. ARRA 2009 §§13400(i)(A) and 13400(i)(B).
2. ARRA 2009 §13402(h)(1).
3. 45 CFR 164.402(2)(i)-(iv); 78 Fed. Reg. 5566, (Jan. 25, 2013).
4. ARRA 2009 §13402(a).
5. 45 C.F.R. §164.404(c)(2); 74 Fed. Reg. 42,740 (Aug. 24, 2009).

5.   Contact procedures for individuals to ask questions or learn additional information, which must include a toll-free number, an e-mail address, Web site, or postal address.[1]

For breaches involving minors, incapacitated, or deceased individuals, notice must be made to the personal representative or next of kin of the individual.[2]

If unauthorized access, use, or disclosure is not a violation of the existing privacy rules, no notice is required. Such examples would include the unintentional access or use of PHI by a workforce member of a covered entity or business associate if it occurred in good faith and within the scope of authority and does not result in further use or disclosure. It also includes any inadvertent disclosure by an authorized person at a covered entity or business associate to another person authorized to access protected health information at the same covered entity or business associate or organized health care arrangement in which the covered entity participates, and the information received is not further used or disclosed in a manner not permitted under the Privacy Rule.[3]

Business associates of a covered entity that access, maintain, retain, modify, record, store, destroy, or otherwise hold, use, or disclose unsecured protected health information must, following the discovery of a breach of such information, notify the covered entity of such breach.[4] A breach is treated as discovered by a business associate as of the first day on which such breach is known to the business associate or, by exercising reasonable diligence, would have been known to any person, other than the individual committing the breach, who is an employee, officer, or agent of the business associate.[5] Such notice must include the identification of each individual whose unsecured protected health information has been, or is reasonably believed to have been, accessed, acquired, or disclosed during such breach.[6]

Generally, the notification of a breach must be provided "without unreasonable delay," but in no case later than sixty days after the discovery of the breach or when the breach should reasonably have been discovered.[7] Since the sixty days is the outer limit for notification, if the full sixty-day window is used, the covered entity or business associates involved in the breach must be prepared to justify their reasons for not providing notification of the breach sooner. However, notice of a breach may be delayed provided that notification would hinder a criminal investigation and/or injure national security (as determined by a law enforcement official).[8]

Note: The sixty-day deadline under this provision does not give the business associate a license to wait. Department of Labor audits will focus on the "without unreasonable delay" standard under a facts-and-circumstances test to determine if the business associate has complied with this deadline.

---

1. 45 C.F.R. §164.404(c)(1)(A) to (E); 74 Fed. Reg. 42,740 (Aug. 24, 2009).
2. 45 C.F.R. §164.404(d)(1)(ii); 74 Fed. Reg. 42,740 (Aug. 24, 2009).
3. 45 C.F.R. §164.402(2)(i), (ii); 74 Fed. Reg. 42,740 (Aug. 24, 2009).
4. 45 C.F.R. §164.410(a)(1); 74 Fed. Reg. 42,740 (Aug. 24, 2009).
5. 45 C.F.R. §164.410(a)(2); 74 Fed. Reg. 42,740 (Aug. 24, 2009).
6. ARRA 2009 §13402(b); 45 C.F.R. §164.410(c)(1); 74 Fed. Reg. 42,740 (Aug. 24, 2009).
7. ARRA 2009 §13402(d)(1); 45 C.F.R. §164.404(b); 74 Fed. Reg. 42,740 (Aug. 24, 2009).
8. 45 C.F.R. §164.412(a), (b); 74 Fed. Reg. 42,740 (Aug. 24, 2009).

In general, notification to affected individuals must be sent via first-class mail.[1] For breaches involving fewer than ten people, the notice may be provided by an alternative form of written notice, telephone, or "other means."[2] However, where a breach involves ten or more individuals whose contact information is out-of-date or deficient, notification must be conspicuously posted for a period of ninety days to the covered entity's Web site or conspicuously published in major print or broadcast media in geographic areas where persons affected by the breach likely reside.[3] Such alternative notice must also include a toll-free number that remains active for ninety days where an individual may be able to learn whether their unsecured PHI was involved in the breach.[4] For a breach that involves 500 or more individuals, the covered entity involved in the breach must also give notice to prominent media outlets in the applicable jurisdiction or state "without unreasonable delay and in no case later than sixty days after the discovery of the breach."[5] Most media notifications should be press releases to local newspapers or general-interest papers with circulation throughout the region of the affected individuals.

> *Note:* Where there exists the possibility of imminent misuse of PHI obtained through a privacy and security breach, notice by telephone may be issued if it is followed up with a written notice that complies with these updated provisions.[6]

Notice of all breaches must be provided to the Secretary of HHS.[7] If the breach affects 500 or more individuals, the covered entity involved in the breach must immediately notify the Secretary.[8] For breaches that affect fewer than 500 individuals, the covered entity involved in the breach may notify the Secretary of any breaches on an annual basis not later than sixty days after the close of the calendar year.[9]

The covered entity or business associate implicated in a breach has the burden of proof in demonstrating that all notifications were made as required by the interim final rule, or that the use and disclosure did not constitute a breach.[10]

156. Do the HIPAA privacy rules preempt applicable state privacy laws?

In general, HIPAA preempts all such state laws that establish standards that are contrary to the Privacy Rule.[11] (This includes the traditional preemption analysis under ERISA regarding any state law that "relates to an employee benefit plan" being preempted by ERISA.) But state laws that are deemed to be "more stringent" than the Privacy Rule are not preempted under the privacy regulations.[12]

---

1. ARRA 2009 §13402(e)(1)(A); 45 C.F.R. §164.404(d)(1); 74 Fed. Reg. 42,740 (Aug. 24, 2009).
2. 45 C.F.R. §164.404(d)(2)(i); 74 Fed. Reg. 42,740 (Aug. 24, 2009).
3. ARRA 2009 §13402(e)(1)(B); 45 C.F.R. §164.404(d)(2)(ii)(A); 74 Fed. Reg. 42,740 (Aug. 24, 2009).
4. 45 C.F.R. §164.404(d)(2)(ii)(B); 74 Fed. Reg. 42,740 (Aug. 24, 2009).
5. 45 C.F.R. §164.406(a), (b); 74 Fed. Reg. 42,740 (Aug. 24, 2009).
6. 45 C.F.R. §164.404(d)(3); 74 Fed. Reg. 42,740 (Aug. 24, 2009).
7. ARRA 2009 §13402(e)(3); 45 C.F.R. §164.408(a); 74 Fed. Reg. 42,740 (Aug. 24, 2009).
8. ARRA 2009 §13402(e)(3); 45 C.F.R. §164.408(b); 74 Fed. Reg. 42,740 (Aug. 24, 2009).
9. ARRA 2009 §13402(e)(3); 45 C.F.R. §164.408(c); 74 Fed. Reg. 42,740 (Aug. 24, 2009).
10. 45 C.F.R. §164.414(b); 74 Fed. Reg. 42,740 (Aug. 24, 2009).
11. 45 C.F.R. §160.203.
12. 45 C.F.R. §160.203(b).

What this does, in effect, is establish under federal law a baseline approach that permits many state privacy laws to continue to apply. (New York's and California's stringent privacy statutes come to mind.)

The Eleventh Circuit has ruled that HIPAA preempts a Florida law that required disclosure of decedents' medical records. In that case, several nursing facilities (covered entities under HIPAA) challenged a pre-HIPAA Florida law that required state-licensed nursing homes to furnish a current or former resident's medical records to certain individuals who request them (i.e., the resident's spouse, guardian, surrogate, proxy, or attorney in fact).[1]

157. What are the preexisting-condition exclusions under HIPAA?

Under HIPAA, a group health plan or a health insurance issuer offering group health insurance coverage may impose preexisting-condition exclusion with respect to a participant or beneficiary only if the following requirements are satisfied:

1. The preexisting-condition exclusion must relate to a condition for which medical advice, diagnosis, care, or treatment was recommended or received during the six-month period prior to an individual's enrollment date.[2] The final regulations advise that a plan or issuer may use a shorter look-back period for purposes of applying the six-month look-back rule.[3]

2. The preexisting-condition exclusion may not last for more than twelve months (eighteen months for late enrollees) after an individual's enrollment date.[4]

3. This twelve-month (or eighteen-month) period must be reduced by the number of days of the individual's prior creditable coverage, excluding coverage before any break in coverage of sixty-three days or more.[5]

The final regulations have modified the preexisting-condition exclusion to provide that a plan exclusion is subject to HIPAA if it restricts benefits for a condition that exists before the effective date of coverage under a group health plan, whether or not any medical advice, diagnosis, care, or treatment was recommended before that day.[6]

If an individual is diagnosed with a preexisting condition that relates to a genetic condition, the plan may impose preexisting-condition exclusion with respect to the condition if the above elements are also satisfied.[7]

For individuals reinstated into a health plan following active military duty, the final regulations provide that USERRA may affect the application of preexisting-condition exclusion.[8] Therefore, it is important for an employer to be aware of the reason that a former participant is reentering the plan.

1. *OPIS Mgmt. Resources LLC v. Secretary, Fla. Agency for Health Care Admin.*, 2013 WL 1405035 (11th Cir. 2013).
2. IRC Sec. 9801(a); Labor Reg. §2590.701-3(a)(1); Temp. Treas. Reg. §54.9801-3T(a)(1).
3. Labor Reg. §2590.703-(a)(2)(i).
4. IRC Sec. 9801(a); Labor Reg. §2590.701-3(a)(2); Temp. Treas. Reg. §54.9801-3T(a)(1).
5. IRC Sec. 9801(a); Labor Reg. §2590.701-4; Temp. Treas. Reg. §54.9801-4T.
6. Labor Reg. §2590.701-3(a)(1)(i).
7. Labor Reg. §2590.701-3(a)(6)(i).
8. Labor Reg. §2590.701-3(a)(2)(iv).

158. How does HIPAA define a "preexisting condition"?

HIPAA states that a "preexisting condition" is a condition present before an individual's enrollment date in any new health plan. Under HIPAA, the only preexisting conditions that may be excluded under preexisting-condition exclusion are those for which medical advice, diagnosis, care, or treatment were recommended or received within the six-month period ending on the individual's enrollment date.[1]

If an employee has had a medical condition in the past, but has not received any medical advice, diagnosis, care, or treatment within the six-month period prior to his or her enrollment date in the plan, the employee's prior condition is not a "preexisting condition" for which an exclusion can be applied.[2]

159. What are the general notice procedures for preexisting-condition exclusion?

Pursuant to the final regulations, a group health plan, or a group health insurance issuer, imposing preexisting-condition exclusion must provide written general notice of the preexisting-condition exclusion before it can become effective. The requirements of a general notice are as follows:

1. It must be provided as part of any written application materials distributed for purposes of enrollment.

2. If these materials are not distributed, the plan or issuer must furnish the notice by the earliest date after a request for enrollment that the plan or issuer, acting in a reasonable and prompt fashion, can provide the notice.[3]

The general notice must notify participants of the following:

1. The existence and terms of any preexisting-condition exclusion under the plan (including the length of the look-back period);

2. The maximum exclusion period under the plan;

3. How the plan will reduce the maximum excluding period by creditable coverage;

4. A description of the rights of individuals to demonstrate creditable coverage and any applicable waiting periods (which must include a description of the right of the individual to request a certificate from a prior plan provider); and

5. A person to contact (address and telephone number) for obtaining additional information or assistance.[4]

---

1. IRC Sec. 9801(a)(1).
2. Labor Reg. §§2590.701-2, 2590.701-3; Temp. Treas. Reg. §54.9801-3T.
3. Labor Reg. §2590.701-3(c)(1).
4. Labor Reg. §2590.701-3(c)(2).

160. What preexisting conditions cannot be excluded from coverage under HIPAA?

Preexisting-condition exclusions cannot be applied to pregnancy, regardless of whether the woman had previous coverage.[1] In addition, a preexisting-condition exclusion cannot be applied to a newborn, adopted child under age eighteen, or a child under eighteen placed for adoption, as long as the child became covered under the health plan within thirty days of birth, adoption, or placement for adoption, and provided that the child does not incur a subsequent sixty-three-day (or longer) break in coverage.[2]

161. May states modify HIPAA's portability requirements?

Yes, in certain circumstances. States may impose stricter obligations on health insurance issuers in the seven areas listed below. If certain requirements are met, states may:

1.   Shorten the 6-month "look-back" period prior to the enrollment date to determine what is a preexisting condition;

2.   Shorten the twelve-month and eighteen-month maximum preexisting-condition exclusion periods;

3.   Increase the sixty-three-day significant break in coverage period;

4.   Increase the thirty-day period for newborns, adopted children, and children placed for adoption to enroll in the plan so that no preexisting-condition exclusion period may be applied thereafter;

5.   Expand the prohibitions on conditions and people to whom a preexisting-condition exclusion period may be applied beyond the "exceptions" described in federal law (see Q 160);

6.   Require additional special enrollment periods; and

7.   Reduce the maximum HMO affiliation period to less than two months (three months for late enrollees).[3]

Therefore, if employee health coverage is offered through an HMO or an insurance policy issued by an insurance company, the employee should check with the state insurance commissioner's office regarding the rules in his state.

162. How do subsequent group health plans determine the length of a newly hired employee's preexisting-condition exclusion period?

A plan can exclude coverage for a preexisting condition only if it relates to a condition (whether physical or mental, and regardless of the cause of the condition) for which medical advice, diagnosis, care, or treatment was recommended or received within the six-month "look-back" period ending on an individual's "enrollment date." The enrollment date is the first day

---

1. IRC Sec. 9801(d)(3).
2. IRC Sec. 9801(d); Labor Reg. §2590.701-3(b); Temp. Treas. Reg. §54.9801-3T(b).
3. Labor Reg. §§2590.701-1(b), 2590.701-4(b)(2); Temp. Treas. Reg. §§54.9801-1T(b), 54.9801-4T(b)(2).

of coverage, or, if there is a waiting period, the first day of the waiting period (typically, the date of hire).[1]

The maximum length of a preexisting-condition exclusion period is twelve months after the enrollment date, or eighteen months in the case of a "late enrollee." A "late enrollee" is an individual who enrolls in a plan on a date other than (1) the earliest date on which coverage can become effective under the terms of the plan, or (2) a special enrollment date.[2]

A plan must reduce an individual's preexisting-condition exclusion period by the number of days of an individual's "creditable coverage" (see Q 164). But a plan is not required to take into account any days of creditable coverage that precede a break in coverage of sixty-three days or more, known as a "significant break in coverage."[3] A plan generally receives information about an individual's creditable coverage from a certificate furnished by a prior plan or issuer (e.g., an insurance company or HMO).

163. Does HIPAA prohibit an employer from establishing a waiting period for enrollment in the plan?

HIPAA does not prohibit a plan or issuer from establishing a waiting period. But if a plan has a waiting period and a preexisting-condition exclusion period, the preexisting-condition exclusion period must begin when the waiting period begins.[4]

For group health plans, a "waiting period" is the period that must pass before an employee or a dependent is eligible to enroll under the terms of a group health plan. But if the employee or dependent is a late enrollee or a special enrollee, any period before such late or special enrollment is not a waiting period.[5]

If an individual seeks and obtains coverage by purchasing an individual insurance policy, the period between the date when the individual files a substantially complete application for coverage and the first day of coverage is a waiting period.[6]

164. What is creditable coverage?

Most health coverage is creditable coverage. It is defined as coverage of an individual under many types of health plans, including a group health plan, health insurance coverage, HMO, individual health insurance policy, Part A or Part B of Title XVIII of the Social Security Act (Medicare), a state health benefits risk pool, and a public health plan.[7]

Creditable coverage does not include coverage consisting solely of "excepted benefits," such as coverage solely for dental or vision benefits. Days in a waiting period during which an individual has no other coverage are not creditable coverage under the plan, nor are these days

---

1. Labor Reg. §§2590.701-2, 2590.701-3; Temp. Treas. Reg. §54.9801-3T(a)(2).
2. Labor Reg. §2590.701-3(a)(2); Temp. Treas. Reg. §54.9801-3T(a)(2).
3. IRC Sec. 9801(c)(2)(A); Labor Reg. §2590.701-4; Temp. Treas. Reg. §54.9801-4T.
4. Labor Reg. §2590.701-2; Temp. Treas. Reg. §54.9801-2T.
5. Labor Reg. §2590.701-3(a)(2); Temp. Treas. Reg. §54.9801-3T(a)(2).
6. Labor Reg. §2590.701-2.
7. IRC Sec. 9801(c)(1).

taken into account when determining a significant break in coverage (i.e., a break of sixty-three days or more).[1]

A preexisting-condition exclusion period is not permitted to extend for more than twelve months (or eighteen months for late enrollees) after an individual's enrollment date in the plan. The period of any preexisting-condition exclusion that would apply under a group health plan is generally reduced by the number of days of creditable coverage.

A plan or issuer may modify an initial determination of an individual's creditable coverage if a notice of the new determination meeting the requirements of a second individual notice (as described under Labor Regulation Section 2590.701-3(f)) is provided. Until the new notice is issued, the plan and issuer must act consistently with the initial determination for purposes of approving access to medical services.[2]

165. How does crediting for prior coverage work under HIPAA?

Most plans use the "standard method" of crediting coverage. Under the standard method, an employee receives credit for her previous coverage that occurred without a break in coverage of sixty-three days or more. Any coverage occurring prior to a break in coverage of sixty-three days or more is not credited against a preexisting-condition exclusion period.[3]

In accordance with the final regulations, a plan or issuer may not impose any limit on the amount of time that an individual has to present a certificate or other evidence of creditable coverage.[4]

It is also important to remember that, during any preexisting-condition exclusion period under a new plan, an employee may be entitled to COBRA continuation coverage under her former plan. "COBRA" is the name for a federal law that provides workers and their families with the opportunity to purchase group health coverage through their employer's health plan for a limited period of time (generally eighteen, twenty-nine, or thirty-six months) if they lose coverage due to specified events, including termination of employment, divorce, or death. Workers in companies with twenty or more employees generally qualify for COBRA. Some states have laws similar to COBRA that may apply to smaller companies. See Q 189 to Q 203.

166. Can an employee receive credit for previous COBRA continuation coverage?

Yes. Under HIPAA, any period of time during which an employee was receiving COBRA continuation coverage is counted as previous health coverage, as long as the coverage occurred without a break in coverage of sixty-three days or more.[5]

For example, if an employee was covered continuously for five months by a previous health plan, and then received seven months of COBRA continuation coverage, the employee would be entitled to receive credit for twelve months of coverage under the new group health plan.

---

1. Labor Reg. §2590.701-4(a); Temp. Treas. Reg. §54.9801-4T(a).
2. Labor Reg. §2590.701-3(f).
3. Labor Reg. §2590.701-4(b)(2)(iv); Temp. Treas. Reg. §54.9801-4T(b)(2)(iv).
4. Labor Reg. §2590.701-3(d)(2).
5. Labor Reg. §2590.701-6; Temp. Treas. Reg. §54.9801-6T.

Under the Trade Act of 2002, individuals who qualify for Trade Act assistance who did not initially elect COBRA coverage during the initial election period are entitled to a second election period. For an individual who elects COBRA continuation coverage during the second election period, the days between the date an individual loses group health coverage and the first day of the second COBRA election period are disregarded in determining whether a significant break in coverage has occurred.[1]

167. Is there an alternative method to credit coverage under HIPAA?

Yes, a plan or issuer may elect the "alternative method" for crediting coverage for all employees. Under the alternative method of counting creditable coverage, the plan or issuer determines the amount of an individual's creditable coverage for any of the five specified categories of benefits. These categories are (1) mental health; (2) substance abuse treatment; (3) prescription drugs; (4) dental care; and (5) vision care.[2] The standard method (see Q 165) is used to determine an individual's creditable coverage for benefits that are not within any of the five categories that a plan or issuer may use. (The plan or issuer may use some or all of these categories.)

When using the alternative method, the plan or issuer looks to see if an individual has coverage within a category of benefits, regardless of the specific level of benefits provided within that category.

If an employer's plan requests information from a new employee's former plan regarding any of the five categories of benefits under the alternative method, the former plan must provide the information regarding coverage under the categories of benefits.[3]

168. What is involved in the certification of creditable coverage?

Group health plans and health insurance issuers are required to furnish a certificate of coverage to an individual to provide documentation of the individual's prior creditable coverage. A certificate of creditable coverage:

1. Must be provided automatically by the plan or issuer when an individual either loses coverage under the plan or becomes entitled to elect COBRA continuation coverage, and when an individual's COBRA continuation coverage ceases;

2. Must be provided, if requested, before the individual loses coverage or within twenty-four months of losing coverage;

3. May be provided through the use of the Model Certificate;[4]

4. Must include an educational statement explaining:

    a. the restrictions on the availability of a plan or issuer to impose a pre-existing condition exclusion,

    b. special enrollment rights,

1. Labor Reg. §2590.701-4(b)(2)(iv).
2. Labor Reg. §2590.701-4(c); Temp. Treas. Reg. §54.9801-4T(c).
3. Labor Reg. §2590.701-5; Temp. Treas. Reg. §54.9801-5T(b).
4. Labor Reg. §2590.701-5; Temp. Treas. Reg. §54.9801-5T.

    c. prohibitions against discrimination based on any health factor,

    d. the right to individual health coverage,

    e. that state law may require issuers to provide additional protections, and

    f. where to obtain additional information.[1]

A single certificate of creditable coverage is permissible for both a participant and the participant's dependents if the information is the same for each individual. But dependents are entitled to receive individualized certificates under the same circumstances as other individuals. Disparate information may also be set out in a single form if it provides all required information for each individual and separately states the information that is not identical.[2]

In general, the certificate of coverage is required to be furnished in writing. But the final rules indicate that presentation in any other medium approved by the Secretary of HHS, IRS, or DOL is permissible.[3]

169. Who is responsible for providing information on a newly hired employee's prior health coverage?

Under HIPAA, providing information about an employee's prior health coverage is the responsibility of an employee's former group health plan and/or the insurance company providing such coverage.[4] HIPAA sets specific disclosure and certification requirements for group health plans, insurance companies, and HMOs.

A certificate stating when an employee was covered under the plan must be provided automatically to the employee when he loses coverage under the plan, or otherwise becomes entitled to elect COBRA continuation coverage, as well as when COBRA continuation coverage ceases.[5]

Employees may also request a certificate, free of charge, until twenty-four months after the time when their coverage ended. An employee may request a certificate even before his coverage ends.[6]

170. When must group health plans and issuers provide certificates of creditable coverage?

Plans and issuers must furnish a certificate of creditable coverage automatically to:

    1.   An individual who is entitled to elect COBRA continuation coverage at a time no later than when a notice is required to be provided for a qualifying event under COBRA;

---

1. Labor Reg. §2590.701-5(a)(3).
2. Labor Reg. §§2590.703-5(a)(2)(i) and 2590.703-5(a)(3)(iv).
3. Labor Reg. §2590.701-5(a)(3)(i)(A).
4. Labor Reg. §2590.701-5(a); Temp. Treas. Reg. §54.9801-5T(a).
5. Labor Reg. §2590.701-5(a)(2)(ii).
6. Labor Reg. §2590.701-5(a)(2)(iii).

2.   An individual who loses coverage under a group health plan and who is not entitled to elect COBRA continuation coverage, within a reasonable time after coverage ceases; and

3.   An individual who has elected COBRA continuation coverage, either within a reasonable time after the plan learns that COBRA continuation coverage ceased, or, if applicable, within a reasonable time after the individual's grace period for the payment of COBRA premiums ends.

Plans and issuers must also generally provide a certificate to an employee if she requests one, or if someone requests one on her behalf (with the employee's permission), at the earliest time that a plan or issuer, acting in a reasonable and prompt fashion, can provide the certificate.[1]

171. What is the minimum period of time that should be covered by the certificate of creditable coverage?

The minimum period of time that should be covered by the certificate depends on whether the certificate is issued automatically or upon request. A certificate that is issued automatically should reflect the most recent period of continuous coverage ending on the date when the coverage ceased. A certificate that is issued upon request should reflect each period of continuous coverage ending within the twenty-four-month period ending (or continuing) on the date of the request. Separate certificates may be provided for each such period of continuous coverage.[2]

At no time must the certificate reflect more than eighteen months of creditable coverage that is not interrupted by a break in coverage of sixty-three days or more.

172. What are the basic nondiscrimination requirements under HIPAA?

Individuals may not be excluded from coverage under the terms of the plan, or charged more for benefits offered by a plan or issuer, based upon specified factors related to health status.[3]

Group health plans and issuers may not establish rules for eligibility (including continued eligibility) of any individual to enroll under the terms of the plan based on "health status-related factors."[4] These factors are:

1.   Health status;

2.   Medical condition (physical or mental);

3.   Claims experience;

4.   Receipt of health care;

5.   Medical history;

---

1. Labor Reg. §2590.701-5(a)(2); Temp. Treas. Reg. §54.9801-5T(a)(2).
2. Labor Reg. §2590.701-5(a)(3)(iii); Temp. Treas. Reg. §54.9801-5T(a)(3)(iii).
3. IRC Secs. 9802(a)(1), 9802(b)(1).
4. IRC Sec. 9802(a)(1).

6.   Genetic information;

7.   Evidence of insurability; and

8.   Disability.

An employee cannot be excluded or dropped from coverage under his health plan just because he has a particular illness.[1]

Plans may establish limits or restrictions on benefits or coverage for similarly situated individuals.[2] In addition, a plan may change covered services or benefits if it gives participants notice of such "material reductions" within sixty days after the change is adopted.

Also, plans may not require an individual to pay a premium or contribution greater than that for a similarly situated individual based on a health status-related factor.[3]

173. What are the special enrollment rules under HIPAA?

Group health plans and health insurance issuers are required to permit special enrollment rights for certain employees and their dependents. These rights are provided to:

1.   Employees who were eligible but declined enrollment in the plan when first offered because they were covered under another plan; and

2.   Individuals upon marriage, birth, adoption, or placement for adoption of a new dependent.

These special enrollment rights permit these individuals to enroll without having to wait until the plan's next regular enrollment period.[4]

A special enrollment occurs if an individual with other health insurance coverage loses that coverage, or if a person becomes a dependent through marriage, birth, adoption, or placement for adoption. A special enrollee is not treated as a late enrollee. Therefore, the maximum preexisting-condition exclusion period that may be applied to a special enrollee is twelve months, and that twelve-month period is reduced by the special enrollee's creditable coverage. A newborn, adopted child, or child placed for adoption cannot be subject to a preexisting-condition exclusion period if the child is enrolled within thirty days of birth, adoption, or placement for adoption.[5]

A plan must provide a description of the plan's special enrollment rights to an employee on or before the time when he is offered the opportunity to enroll in group health coverage.[6]

---

1. Labor Reg. §2590.702; Treas. Reg. §54.9802-1.
2. Treas. Reg. §54.9802-1.
3. IRC Sec. 9802(b)(1); Labor Reg. §2590.702(b); Treas. Reg. §54.9802-1(c).
4. Labor Reg. §§2590.701-6(a), 2590.701-6(b).
5. IRC Sec. 9801(d); Labor Reg. §§2590.701-6(a), 2590.701-6(b).
6. Labor Reg. §2590.701-6(c).

The final regulations provide that a loss of eligibility for coverage is still considered to exist even if there is a subsequent coverage opportunity. Under these rules, an individual need not elect COBRA continuation coverage in order to preserve her right to special enrollment.[1]

Special enrollees must be treated the same as those individuals who enroll for group health coverage under the plan at the first opportunity.[2]

174. What are the special enrollment rules under the Children's Health Insurance Program (CHIP) Reauthorization Act of 2009?

Group health plans must permit special enrollment opportunities for employees regarding the eligibility of the employee or a dependent under either the Medicaid program pursuant to Title XIX of the Social Security Act or the Children's Health Insurance Program (CHIP) under Title XXI of the Social Security Act. Under these rules, a group health plan must permit an employee or the employee's dependent who is eligible for coverage under the employee's employer's group health plan, but not enrolled, to enroll for coverage under the employer's plan if either:

1.   The employee or dependent is covered under a Medicaid plan or a state CHIP, and

   a.   coverage of the employee or dependent is terminated as a result of loss of eligibility, and

   b.   the employee requests coverage under the group health plan no later than sixty days after the coverage terminates.[3]

2.   The employee or dependent becomes eligible for assistance under a Medicaid plan or state CHIP, and the employee requests coverage under the group health plan no later than sixty days after the date the employee or dependent is determined to be eligible for assistance.[4]

The Children's Health Insurance Program Reauthorization Act of 2009 (CHIPRA 2009)[5] extends and expands state CHIP. The Act permits states to subsidize premiums for employer-provided group health coverage for eligible children and families. In addition to special enrollment rights, it requires new notice and disclosure obligations for employers that maintain group health plans. Beginning April 1, 2009, covered plans must accommodate requests for the new special enrollment rights.

Notice to Employees

Employers that maintain group health plans in states that provide Medicaid or CHIP assistance in the form of premium assistance subsidies are required to provide written notices to their employees, informing them of the potential opportunities for premium assistance in

---

1. Labor Reg. §2590.701-6(a)(3).
2. Labor Reg. §2590.701-6(d)(2).
3. ERISA Sec. 701(f)(3)(A)(i), as added by CHIPRA 2009, Pub. L. No. 111-3, §311(a).
4. ERISA Sec. 701(f)(3)(A)(ii), as added by CHIPRA 2009, Pub. L. No. 111-3, §311(a).
5. CHIPRA 2009, Pub. L. No. 111-3, §311.

the states in which they reside to help pay for health coverage for employees or dependents.[1] The national and state-specific model notices were issued by the HHS on February 4, 2010.[2] Employers may provide these notices along with other plan materials notifying the employees of health plan eligibility with open enrollment materials, or when furnishing the SPD.[3] The notice requirement is effective for plan years beginning after the date on which model notices are first issued.[4]

Disclosure to States

The new law also requires group health plan administrators to disclose information about plan benefits to states upon request when a plan participant or beneficiary is covered under Medicaid or CHIP in order to allow states to determine the cost effectiveness of providing premium assistance for the purchase of coverage under the plan and to provide supplemental benefits.[5]

The new law provides for civil penalties of up to $100 a day for failure to comply with the new notice and disclosure requirements to an employee. Each violation to any single employee will be treated as a separate violation.[6] There are mirror penalty provisions for any failure to comply with the notice and disclosure requirements to any state.[7]

175. Does HIPAA require employers to offer health coverage or require plans to provide specific benefits?

No. The provision of health coverage by an employer is voluntary. HIPAA does not require specific benefits, nor does it prohibit a plan from restricting the amount or nature of benefits for similarly situated individuals.[8]

There is no requirement for any employer to offer health insurance coverage. If a subsequent employer does not offer health insurance, the individual may be able to continue coverage under his previous employer's plan through COBRA continuation coverage. See Q 189 et seq.

176. May an individual obtain guaranteed individual insurance coverage under HIPAA?

Yes. Individuals may be able to obtain coverage under an individual insurance policy issued by an insurance company.[9] HIPAA guarantees access to individual insurance for "eligible individuals." Eligible individuals are individuals who:

1.   Have had coverage for at least eighteen months, and the most recent period of coverage was under a group health plan;

---

1. IRC Sec. 9801(f)(3)(B)(i)(I).
2. EBSA Notice, 75 Fed. Reg. 5808 (Feb. 4, 2010).
3. ERISA Sec. 102(b), as amended by CHIPRA 2009, Pub. L. No. 111-3, §311(b)(1)(B).
4. CHIPRA 2009, Pub. L. No. 111-3, §3(a).
5. ERISA Sec 701(f)(3), *as amended by* CHIPRA 2009, Pub. L. No. 111-3, §311(b)(1)(A).
6. ERISA Sec. 502(c)(9)(A), *as amended by* CHIPRA 2009, Pub. L. No. 111-3, §311(b)(1)(E)(ii).
7. ERISA Sec. 502(c)(9)(B).
8. Treas. Reg. §54.9802-1(b)(2).
9. Health & Human Servs. Regs., 45 C.F.R. §§148.102, 148.103.

2.   Did not have their group coverage terminated because of fraud or nonpayment of premiums;

3.   Are ineligible for COBRA continuation coverage or have exhausted their COBRA benefits (or continuation coverage under a similar state provision); and

4.   Are not eligible for coverage under another group health plan, Medicare, Medicaid, or any other health insurance coverage.

The opportunity to buy an individual insurance policy is the same whether the individual is laid off or is voluntarily or involuntarily terminated.

HIPAA does not set premium rates, but it does prohibit plans and issuers from charging an individual more than similarly situated individuals in the same plan because of health status. Plans may offer premium discounts or rebates for participation in wellness programs.[1]

In addition, many states limit insurance premiums. HIPAA does not preempt such current or future state laws regulating the cost of insurance.

177. Does HIPAA extend COBRA continuation coverage?

Generally, no. HIPAA makes two changes to the length of the COBRA continuation coverage period. Qualified beneficiaries who are determined to be disabled under the Social Security Act within the first sixty days of COBRA continuation coverage will be able to purchase an additional eleven months of coverage beyond the usual eighteen-month coverage period.[2] This is a change from the old law, which required that a qualified beneficiary be determined to be disabled at the time of the qualifying event in order to receive twenty-nine months of COBRA continuation coverage.

This extension of coverage is also available to nondisabled family members who are entitled to COBRA continuation coverage.[3] See Q 199.

COBRA rules are also modified and clarified to ensure that children who are born or adopted during the continuation coverage period are treated as "qualified beneficiaries."[4] A model notice discussing these changes appears in Appendix A. See Q 191.

178. What information must group health plans disclose to participants?

HIPAA and other legislation made important changes in ERISA's disclosure requirements for group health plans. Group health plans must ensure that their summary plan descriptions (SPDs) and summaries of material modifications (SMMs):

1.   Notify participants and beneficiaries of "material reductions in covered services or benefits" (for example, reductions in benefits and increases in deductibles and co-payments), generally within sixty days of adoption of the change (see Q 179);

---

1. Treas. Reg. §54.9802-1(c).
2. IRC Sec. 4980B(f)(2)(B)(i); DOL Technical Release 96-1.
3. Treas. Reg. §54.4980B-7, A-5.
4. Treas. Reg. §54.4980B-3, A-1.

2.   Disclose to participants and beneficiaries information about the role of issuers (e.g., insurance companies and HMOs) with respect to their group health plan—in particular, the name and address of the issuer, whether and to what extent benefits under the plan are guaranteed under a contract or policy of insurance issued by the issuer, and the nature of any administrative services (e.g., payment of claims) provided by the issuer;

3.   Tell participants and beneficiaries which DOL office they should contact for assistance or information on their rights under ERISA and HIPAA; and

4.   Tell participants and beneficiaries that federal law generally prohibits the plan and health insurance issuers from limiting hospital stays for childbirth to under forty-eight hours for normal deliveries and ninety-six hours for delivery by caesarean section.[1]

In addition, the SPD must describe:

1.   Any cost-sharing provisions (including premiums, deductibles, coinsurance, and co-payment amounts), any annual or lifetime caps or other limits on benefits, the extent to which preventive services are covered under the plan, which existing and new drugs are covered under the plan (this may be done by reference to a schedule), and the coverage provided for medical tests, devices, and procedures;

2.   Any provisions governing the use of network providers, the composition of the provider network (this may be provided in a separate document, if referenced in the SPD and provided without charge), and whether coverage is provided for out-of-network services (and, if so, under what circumstances); and

3.   Any conditions or limits on the selection of primary care providers or specialists, any conditions or limits applicable to emergency medical care; and any provisions requiring pre-authorizations or utilization review as a condition to obtaining a benefit or service under the plan.[2]

Group health plans subject to the COBRA continuation coverage rules (see Q 189) must include information concerning the rights and obligations of participants and beneficiaries under COBRA. The regulations also provide that the initial COBRA notice obligation (see Q 193) will be satisfied by furnishing the covered employee and spouse with an SPD that includes the COBRA continuation coverage notice information at the time when their plan coverage commences.[3]

The SPD of a group health plan must set forth the claims procedure (see Q 201), including any plan procedures for pre-authorization, approval, or utilization review. A plan may furnish the claims procedures as a separate document, so long as: (1) that separate document satisfies the style and format requirements of Labor Regulation §2520.102-2; (2) such claims procedures set forth in a separate document are provided (a) automatically with the SPD and (b) without

---

1. Labor Reg. §§2520.102-3, 2520.104b-3.
2. Labor Reg. §2520.102-3(j)(3).
3. Labor Reg. §2520.102-3(o).

charge; and (3) the SPD contains a statement indicating that the claims procedures are furnished automatically, without charge, as a separate document.[1]

Funded health plans with 100 or more participants are subject to disclosure rules under revised standards issued by the American Institute of Certified Public Accountants (AICPA). Plans providing benefits entirely through insurance contracts and plans with fewer than 100 participants are exempt from these standards.[2]

179. What is a material reduction in covered services or benefits subject to the sixty-day notice requirement?

A "material reduction in covered services or benefits" means any modification to a group health plan or change in the information required to be included in the summary plan description that, independently or in conjunction with other contemporaneous modifications or changes, would be considered by the average plan participant to be an important reduction in covered services or benefits under the group health plan.[3]

The regulations cite examples of "reductions in covered services or benefits" as generally including any plan modification or change that:

1. Eliminates benefits payable under the plan;

2. Reduces benefits payable under the plan, including a reduction that occurs as a result of a change in the formulas, methodologies, or schedules that serve as the basis for benefit determinations;

3. Increases deductibles, co-payments, or other amounts to be paid by a participant or beneficiary;

4. Reduces the service area covered by a health maintenance organization; or

5. Establishes new conditions or requirements (e.g., pre-authorization requirements) to obtain services or benefits under the plan.[4]

If COBRA continuation coverage is eliminated in *anticipation* of a qualifying event, such as in anticipation of a divorce or legal separation, the actual elimination is disregarded in determining whether the qualifying event causes a loss of coverage. In order for a qualifying beneficiary who has lost his health coverage as a result of an anticipated divorce or legal separation to perfect his right to COBRA coverage, the plan administrator must be given notice within sixty days of the actual divorce or separation.[5] Consequently, the IRS has ruled that when an employee eliminates his spouse's group health plan coverage in anticipation of the couple's divorce, a plan that is required to make COBRA continuation coverage available to the spouse must begin to make that coverage available as of the date of the divorce, and not the date of the actual elimination.[6]

---

1. Labor Reg. §2520.102-3(s).
2. AICPA SOP 01-2 (Accounting and Reporting by Health and Welfare Plans).
3. Labor Reg. §2520.104b-3(d)(3).
4. Labor Reg. §2520.104b-3(d)(3)(ii).
5. Treas. Reg. §54.4980B-6, Q&A 2.
6. Rev. Rul. 2002-88, 2002-2 C.B. 995.

180. Who has the authority to enforce HIPAA?

The Secretary of Labor enforces the health care portability provisions of HIPAA under ERISA, including self-insured health care arrangements. In addition, participants and beneficiaries can file suit to enforce their rights under ERISA, as amended by HIPAA.

The Secretary of the Treasury enforces the health care portability provisions of HIPAA under the Internal Revenue Code, including self-insured health care arrangements. A taxpayer that fails to comply with these provisions may be subject to an excise tax.

States also have enforcement responsibility for group and individual requirements imposed on health insurance issuers, including available sanctions under state law. If a state does not act in the areas of its responsibility, the Secretary of Health and Human Services may make a determination that the state has failed "to substantially enforce" the law, assert federal authority to enforce the law, and impose sanctions on health insurance issuers as specified in the statute, including civil money penalties.

The Department of the Treasury, the Department of Labor, and the Department of Health and Human Services entered into a Memorandum of Understanding, which formally established an interagency agreement among the Secretary of the Treasury, the Secretary of Labor, and the Secretary of Health and Human Services. This agreement is intended to ensure the coordination of the regulations, rulings, and interpretations relating to changes made by HIPAA, and to coordinate policies relating to HIPAA enforcement in order to avoid duplication of enforcement efforts and to assign priorities in enforcement.[1]

HHS has delegated to the Office for Civil Rights (OCR) authority under HIPAA to administer and enforce the security standards for the protection of electronic protected health information. Among other things, the delegation gives OCR the authority to impose civil penalties, issue subpoenas, administer regulations, and interpret and enforce the security standards. OCR already had enforcement authority over the Privacy Rule and, according to an HHS news release, combining the enforcement authority in one agency will eliminate duplication and increase the efficiency of investigations and resolutions of failures to comply with both the Privacy Rule and the Security Rule.[2]

The U.S. District Court for the District of Columbia has ruled in the case *Runkle v. Gonzales*[3] that an employee has no private right of action under the HIPAA Privacy Rule for the inappropriate disclosure of medical information to others in the workplace.

Practitioner's Pointer: The HITECH Act required HHS to conduct periodic audits to ensure that covered entities and business associates are complying with HIPAA's privacy and security rules and breach notification standards. Previously, HHS's Office for Civil Rights (OCR) posted information on its website about its pilot program to perform 115 audits of covered entities to assess privacy and security compliance. Audits conducted during the pilot phase began November 2011 and concluded in December 2012. The actual audit protocols are detailed on the HHS website at: http://www.hhs.gov/ocr/privacy/hipaa/enforcement/audit/auditpilotprogram.html An analysis of these protocols shows them to be a convenient compliance tool for self-audits and program analysis for all covered entities.

---

1. 64 Fed. Reg. 70,163. See also http://www.dol.gov/ebsa/regs/fedreg/notices/99032500.htm.
2. Office for Civil Rights; Delegation of Authority, 74 Fed. Reg. 38,630 (Aug. 4, 2009).
3. 2005 U.S. Dist. LEXIS 22219 (D.D.C. 2005).

The court in *Runkle* did not address the potential right of action the employee may have if the information disclosed was issued in relation to an ERISA-qualified welfare benefit plan or if it were employer information (as opposed to protected health information, which falls under the purview of HIPAA).

For purposes of criminal enforcement provisions, the American Recovery and Reinvestment Act of 2009 (ARRA 2009) provides that "a person (including an employee or other individual)" is considered to have obtained or disclosed individually identifiable health information in violation of HIPAA if such information is maintained by a covered entity and the individual obtained or disclosed such information without authorization.[1] This includes people and organizations other than covered entities.

> *Note:* This provision permits the Office for Civil Rights to pursue an investigation and the imposition of civil monetary penalties against *any individual* (not just the covered entity of the business associate) for an alleged criminal violation of the HIPAA rules, if the Justice Department has not prosecuted the individual. Regulations were required to be issued by August 16, 2009, which would apply to penalties imposed on or after February 16, 2011.[2]

A state's Attorney General may bring a civil action under ARRA 2009 on behalf of state residents who have been or are threatened to be harmed by a violation to obtain injunctive relief or damages, as well as attorneys' fees. Notice must be given to the Secretary of Health and Human Services, and the Secretary is permitted to intervene. The state's Attorney General may not bring an action if a federal action by the Secretary is already pending. These provisions only apply to violations that occur after February 17, 2009 (the date of enactment).[3]

> *Note:* This will most likely result in an increase in regulatory oversight and enforcement activities.

ARRA 2009 requires Health and Human Services to conduct periodic audits of business associates to ensure their compliance with these newly amended HIPAA rules. This requirement went into effect on February 17, 2010.

The Eighth Circuit has approved a private suit for HIPAA nondiscrimination violations under ERISA Section 502.[4] In *Werdehausen v. Benicorp Insurance Co.*, the participant sued the insurer under his employer's health plan after it retroactively canceled his coverage due to an alleged material misrepresentation in his enrollment application (failure to disclose that neck surgery had been recommended by his physician). Under the insurance policy, the insurer had two possible responses to the misrepresentation. The insurer either could retroactively rescind the participant's coverage or retroactively increase plan premiums—paid 75 percent by the plan sponsor, 25 percent by the participants—to cover the extra cost of the surgery. After

---

1. ARRA 2009 §13409.

2. ARRA 2009 §§13410(b)(1) and 13410(b)(2).

3. Social Security Act §1176, as amended by ARRA 2009 §13410(e), by adding §§1176(d)(1) to 1176(d)(8).

4. *Werdehausen v. Benicorp Ins. Co.*, 2007 U.S. App. LEXIS 12348 (8th Cir. 2007). For a copy of the opinion, visit http://www.ca8.uscourts.gov/opndir/07/05/062818P.pdf.

the participant had the recommended neck surgery, the insurer retroactively rescinded the participant's coverage to the first day of enrollment and denied all the claims for the surgery expenses.

The participant alleged that the insurer violated HIPAA by discriminating against him in eligibility based on a health status factor, effectively making him ineligible to participate in the plan because he had a neck condition. The trial court dismissed these claims, stating that HIPAA does not provide a private right of action. The Eighth Circuit Court of Appeals reversed, ruling that HIPAA's nondiscrimination rules may be enforced under ERISA Section 502, which allows, among other things, a participant to sue to enjoin specified statutory violations.

A jury for the U.S. District Court for the Southern District of Florida found the owner of a company guilty of wrongfully obtaining individually identifiable health information with the intent to sell, transfer, or use it for personal gain.[1] The defendant, Fernando Ferrer, Jr., had paid an employee of the Cleveland Clinic in Weston, Florida, to provide him with individually identifiable health information for the purpose of committing Medicare fraud. (The clinic employee, Isis Machado, who was the defendant's cousin, pled guilty early in 2007 and testified against the defendant at trial.) Using that information, Ferrer submitted more than $7 million in fraudulent Medicare claims, with approximately $2.5 million paid to providers and suppliers. Ferrer was also convicted of conspiring to defraud the United States, computer fraud, and multiple counts of aggravated identity theft.

181. What are the provisions of the Patient Protection and Affordable Care Act mandating health care coverage for adult children to age twenty-six?

On May 13, 2010, the DOL, IRS, and HHS issued interim final regulations requiring health care coverage for young adults until age twenty-six.[2] The Patient Protection and Affordable Care Act[3] (Affordable Care Act) amends the Public Health Services Act (PHS Act) by adding Section 2714 mandating that a health insurance issuer or a health plan that makes available dependent coverage of children must make such coverage available for children until attainment of age twenty-six.[4]

The Affordable Care Act also added Section 715 to ERISA and Section 9815 to the Internal Revenue Code to make part A of the PHS Act (including the extension of coverage to dependent children until age twenty-six) applicable under ERISA and the Code to qualified health plans. In addition to the interim final regulations, the DOL issued a fact sheet and a series of twenty-one Frequently Asked Questions and Answers.[5] The IRS has also issued Notice 2010-38, which provides details on the exemption from taxable income for the value of employer-provided coverage for adult children covered until age twenty-six. PHS Act Section 2714 was effective September 23, 2010.[6]

---

1. *United States v. Ferrer*, No. 06-CR-60261-JIC (S.D. Fla. Jan. 24, 2007).
2. Treas. Reg. §54.9815-2714T; 75 Fed. Reg. 27,122 (May 13, 2010).
3. Pub. L. No. 111-148.
4. Treas. Reg. §54.9815-2714T(a)(1); Labor Reg. §2590.715-2714(a)(1).
5. http://www.dol.gov/ebsa/faqs/faq-dependentcoverage.html.
6. PHS Act §1004; Treas. Reg. §54.9815-2714T(f)(3); Labor Reg. §2590.715-2714(f)(3).

A health plan or health insurance issuer may not define dependent for purposes of eligibility for dependent coverage of children other than in terms of a relationship between a child and the participant. Both married and unmarried children qualify for this extended coverage.[1] By way of example, plans and issuers may not deny coverage to a child who has not attained age twenty-six by reason of the child's marital status, student status, or financial dependency on the parents. Grandchildren, however, are not covered under this mandate of extended coverage.[2]

Special Open Enrollment and Notice Requirements

Qualified individuals who lost coverage because of a loss of dependent status in place prior to the effective date of these extended coverage rules must be offered all of the benefit packages available to children who did not lose coverage because of loss of dependent status.[3] Insurers and employers that sponsor health plans will be required to inform young adults of continued eligibility for coverage until the age of twenty-six. Insurers and employers will provide notice for a special open enrollment period, which must be at least thirty days beginning on September 23, 2010.[4]

Any child enrolling in a covered health plan under these rules must be treated as a special enrollee as that term is defined under HIPAA.[5] In other words, the child must be offered all the benefit packages available to a similarly situated individual who did not lose coverage by reason of cessation of dependent status.[6]

The written notice must include a statement that children whose coverage ended, or who were denied coverage because their eligibility ended prior to attainment of age twenty-six, are eligible to enroll in the plan. The notice may be provided to an employee on behalf of the employee's child. Also, the notice may be included in open enrollment materials, provided that it is prominent.[7]

Grandfathered Plans

The Affordable Care Act, Section 1251, defines a grandfathered plan as a group or individual health coverage plan that was in existence on March 23, 2010. A grandfathered plan can remain grandfathered indefinitely. For plan years beginning before January 1, 2014, a grandfathered plan that makes available dependent coverage of children may exclude an adult child who has not reached age twenty-six from dependent coverage if the child is eligible to enroll in an employer-sponsored health plan other than a group health plan of a parent.[8] Grandfathered health plans must comply with these extended coverage requirements for plan years beginning on or after January 1, 2014.[9]

---

1. Treas. Reg. §54.9815-2714T(b); Labor Reg. §2590.715-2714(b).
2. Treas. Reg. §54.9815-2714T(c); Labor Reg. §2590.715-2714(c).
3. Treas. Reg. §54.9815-2714T(f)(1)(i), (ii), and (f)(4); Labor Reg. §2590.715-2714(f)(1)(i), (ii), and (f)(4).
4. Treas. Reg. §54.9815-2714T(f)(2); Labor Reg. §2590.715-2714(f)(2).
5. Labor Reg. §2590.701-6(d); see Q 173 for further details. See also Treas. Reg. §54.9815-2714T(f)(4); Labor Reg. §2590.715-2714(f)(4).
6. Treas. Reg. §54.9815-2714T(f)(4); Labor Reg. §2590.715-2714(f)(4).
7. Treas. Reg. §54.9815-2714T(f)(2)(ii); Labor Reg. §2590.715-2714(f)(2)(ii).
8. Treas. Reg. §54.9815-2714T(g)(1); Labor Reg. §2590.715-2714(g)(1).
9. Treas. Reg. §54.9815-2714T(g)(2); Labor Reg. §2590.715-2714(g)(2).

As of September 23, 2010, newly adopted plans and plans that lose grandfathered status must immediately comply with these requirements or face a penalty that is equal to $100 per day for each highly compensated employee to whom the failure relates (capped at an annual maximum of $500,000 or 10 percent of the employer's annual health expenses of the previous year—whichever is lesser).[1]

Value of Coverage for Covered Adult Children Exempt from Taxation

Effective March 30, 2010, the value of any employer-provided health coverage for an employee's child is excluded from the employee's income through the end of the taxable year in which the child turns twenty-six. This tax benefit applies regardless of whether the plan or the insurer is required by law to extend health care coverage to the adult child or the plan or insurer voluntarily extends the coverage.[2]

Women's Health and Cancer Rights

182. What is the Women's Health and Cancer Rights Act of 1998?

The Women's Health and Cancer Rights Act (Women's Health Act), added Section 713 to ERISA and Sections 2706 and 2752 to the Public Health Service Act (PHS Act). Under the Women's Health Act, insured and self-insured group health plans of private and governmental employers, collectively bargained health plans, insurance companies, and health maintenance organizations (HMOs) that provide coverage for medical and surgical benefits with respect to a mastectomy must also provide coverage for reconstructive surgery, in a manner determined in consultation between the attending physician and the patient. Coverage includes reconstruction of the breast on which the mastectomy was performed, surgery and reconstruction of the other breast to produce a symmetrical appearance, and prostheses and treatment of physical complications at all stages of the mastectomy, including lymphedemas. The requirements for individual health insurance policies were placed in the PHS Act within the jurisdiction of the Department of Health and Human Services (HHS).

The Women's Health Act permits the imposition of deductibles or coinsurance requirements for reconstructive surgery in connection with a mastectomy, but only if the deductibles and coinsurance are consistent with those established for other benefits under the plan or coverage. But the Women's Health Act prohibits a patient from being denied eligibility, or continued eligibility, to enroll or to renew coverage under the terms of the plan, in order to avoid the requirements of the Women's Health Act. In addition, a plan may not penalize or otherwise reduce or limit the reimbursement of an attending provider, or provide incentives (monetary or otherwise) to an attending provider, to induce the provider to provide care to an individual participant or beneficiary in a manner inconsistent with the Women's Health Act. But the Women's Health Act does not prevent a group health plan or a health insurance issuer offering group health insurance coverage from negotiating the level and type of reimbursement with a provider for the coverage prescribed by the Women's Health Act.[3]

---

1. PHS Act §2714.
2. IRS Notice 2010-38.
3. Women's Health and Cancer Rights Act of 1998, Pub. L. No. 105-277. See http://www.dol.gov/ebsa/publications/whcra.html for Questions & Answers from the DOL about the Women's Health Act.

The U.S. District Court for the Southern District of Iowa has ruled that surgical benefits were not required under the Women's Health Act where the underlying welfare benefit plan did not provide benefits for breast reduction, augmentation, and reconstruction, nor for any complications related to such treatments.[1]

In the case *Krauss v. Oxford Health Plans, Inc.*,[2] the court ruled that the Women's Health Act does not require the payment of more than the previously disclosed plan maximum for breast reconstruction. The facts under *Krauss* showed that the insurer's maximum coverage for breast reconstruction was based on its determination of the usual, customary, and reasonable (UCR) rate for the procedure in the same geographic area and on a policy limiting payment for bilateral surgeries to 150 percent of the UCR rate for a single surgery. The court determined that the UCR fell within that portion of the Women's Health Act that permits reconstruction coverage to "be subject to annual deductibles and coinsurance provisions as may be deemed appropriate and as are consistent with those established for other benefits."

183. What are the notice requirements of the Women's Health Act?

The Women's Health Act requires that group health plans, insurance companies, and HMOs that offer coverage for medical and surgical benefits with respect to a mastectomy provide two separate notices regarding the coverage required under the Women's Health Act. The first notice is a one-time requirement, under which group health plans, and their insurance companies or HMOs, must furnish a written description of the benefits that the Women's Health Act requires. The second notice must also describe the required benefits, but it must be provided upon enrollment in the plan and it must be furnished annually thereafter. In addition, the Women's Health Act requires that the notices be in writing and prominently positioned in any literature or correspondence made available or distributed by the plan or issuer.[3]

The DOL has issued a Model Annual Notice designed to provide additional compliance assistance.[4]

An employee in the Federal Court for the Northern District of New York sued the claims administrator under her employer's self-insured health plan after it refused to pay the full cost of her breast reconstruction surgery. The employee was diagnosed with breast cancer and underwent a double mastectomy and bilateral breast reconstruction. Prior to undergoing the reconstructive procedure, she received a letter advising that the procedure had been "approved for payment."

After the health plan failed to pay the full cost of the breast reconstruction surgery, the employee filed a civil case, challenging the adequacy of the administrator's claims procedures and arguing that it provided a late and inadequate notice of adverse benefit determination. The employee also alleged that the claims administrator failed to provide the written notice required

---

1. Davidson v. Wal-Mart Assocs. Health & Welfare Plan, 2004 U.S. Dist. LEXIS 2598 (S.D. Iowa 2004).
2. 2005 U.S. Dist. LEXIS 34379 (S.D.N.Y. 2005).
3. Women's Health and Cancer Rights Act of 1998, Pub. L. No. 105-277. See http://www.dol.gov/ebsa/publications/whcra.html for Questions & Answers from the DOL.
4. See http://www.dol.gov/ebsa/publications/healthlawsnotice.html.

under WHCRA. The court concluded that the employee had shown that communication of the benefit denial was very inadequate in satisfying ERISA's requirements in that it did not explain the reason for the denial, reference any plan provisions or describe the appeals process. The actual notice of the benefits denial was a short notation on a check stub. Based upon this, the court concluded that the employee had adequately alleged that the claims administrator did not provide notice of the denial until four months after the claim, even though the SPD required notice within thirty days. However, the court dismissed the employee's claim that she had not received a WHCRA notice. Finding that the plan's SPD contained an entire subsection on WHCRA and clear notice of covered treatments, the court concluded that the SPD had provided adequate notice of the coverage required by WHCRA.[1]

184. What information must be included in the Women's Health Act notices?

The notices must describe the benefits required under the Women's Health Act. According to the DOL, the notice must indicate that coverage will be provided in a manner determined in consultation between the attending physician and the patient, for:

1.   Reconstruction of the breast on which the mastectomy was performed;

2.   Surgery and reconstruction of the other breast to produce a symmetrical appearance; and

3.   Prostheses and treatment of physical complications at all stages of the mastectomy, including lymphedemas.

The notice must also describe any deductibles and coinsurance limitations applicable to such coverage.[2]

185. How must the notices required by the Women's Health Act be delivered to participants and beneficiaries?

These notices must be delivered in accordance with the regulations applicable to summary plan descriptions (SPDs). See Q 100 et seq.[3] The notices may be provided, for example, by first-class mail or by any other means of delivery prescribed in the regulations. In addition, a separate notice must be furnished to a group health plan beneficiary, where the last known address of the beneficiary is different from the last known address of the covered participant.

186. Must group health plans that have already provided the coverage required by the Women's Health Act provide the initial one-time notice?

A group health plan that, prior to the date of enactment of the Women's Health Act (October 21, 1998), had already provided the coverage required under the Act (and continues to provide such coverage) will have satisfied the initial one-time notice requirement if the

---

1. *Haag v. MVP Healthcare*, 2013 WL 2018205 (N.D.N.Y 2013).
2. Women's Health and Cancer Rights Act of 1998, Pub. L. No. 105-277. See http://www.dol.gov/ebsa/publications/whcra.html for Questions & Answers from the DOL.
3. *See also* Labor Reg. §2520.104b-1.

information that must be provided in the initial notice was previously furnished to participants and beneficiaries in accordance with the regulations on disclosure of information to participants and beneficiaries. See Q 100 et seq.[1]

187. Must a group health plan, and its insurance companies or HMOs, furnish separate notices under the Women's Health Act?

No. In order to avoid duplication of notices, the DOL allows a group health plan or its insurance companies or HMOs to satisfy the notice requirements of the Women's Health Act by contracting with another party to provide the required notice. For example, in the case of a group health plan funded through an insurance policy, the group health plan satisfies the notice requirements with respect to a participant or beneficiary if the insurance company or HMO actually provides the notice that includes the information required by the Women's Health Act.[2]

188. Does the Women's Health Act preempt state laws requiring similar coverage for breast reconstruction?

It depends. The federal Women's Health Act permits state law protections to apply to certain health coverage. State law protections apply if the state law was in effect on October 21, 1998 (the date of enactment of the Women's Health Act), and the state law requires at least the level of coverage for reconstructive breast surgery required under the federal Women's Health Act.

According to the DOL, if a state law meets these requirements, then the state law applies to coverage provided by an insurance company or HMO ("insured" coverage). But if coverage is not provided by an insurance company or HMO (e.g., coverage is provided under a self-funded health plan), then state law does not apply.[3]

COBRA Requirements

189. What is COBRA?

Health insurance programs allow workers and their families to take care of essential medical needs. These programs can be one of the most important benefits provided by an employer. Prior to the enactment of the Consolidated Omnibus Budget Reconciliation Act of 1985 (COBRA), there was a time when group health coverage may have been terminated when a worker lost his job or changed employment. That changed in 1986 with the passage of the health benefit provisions in COBRA, which amended ERISA, the Internal Revenue Code, and the Public Health Service Act to provide continuation of group health coverage that otherwise would be terminated. Under COBRA, employees and beneficiaries who lose coverage because of certain "qualifying events" may be able to buy group coverage for limited periods of time.[4]

---

1. Women's Health and Cancer Act of 1998, Pub. L. No. 105-277. See http://www.dol.gov/ebsa/publications/whcra.html for Questions & Answers from the DOL.
2. Women's Health and Cancer Act of 1998, Pub. L. No. 105-277. See http://www.dol.gov/ebsa/publications/whcra.html for Questions & Answers from the DOL.
3. Women's Health and Cancer Act of 1998, Pub. L. No. 105-277. See http://www.dol.gov/ebsa/publications/whcra.html for Questions & Answers from the DOL.
4. ERISA Secs. 601, 607(1); IRC Secs. 4980B(f), 4980B(g)(2); Treas. Reg. §54.4980B-5, A-1.

The DOL issued final regulations in May 2004 relating to various notice requirements for group health plan sponsors, administrators, and covered employees and qualified beneficiaries.[1] The final regulations outline the timing and content requirements for COBRA notices. See Q 193 to Q 196 for details of these regulations.

If a participant or beneficiary is entitled to COBRA benefits, the health plan must provide such individual with a notice stating his right to choose to continue benefits provided by the plan (see Q 193). Participants and beneficiaries have sixty days to elect COBRA coverage or lose all rights to benefits. Once COBRA coverage is chosen, terminated participants may be required to pay for the coverage.

COBRA provides certain former employees, retirees, spouses, and dependent children with the right to temporary continuation of health coverage at group rates. This coverage is only available if such an individual has lost coverage as a result of a "qualifying event" (see Q 191). Group health coverage for COBRA participants is usually more expensive than health coverage for active employees because the employer usually pays a part of the premium for active employees, while COBRA participants generally pay the entire premium themselves. COBRA coverage is ordinarily less expensive than individual health coverage.

COBRA applies to plans in the private sector and those sponsored by state and local governments that are administered by the Department of Health and Human Services. But the law does not apply to plans sponsored by the federal government, certain church-related organizations, or small employer plans. A small employer plan is defined as a group health plan maintained by an employer that normally employed fewer than twenty employees during the preceding calendar year—except in the case of a multiemployer plan (see Section X).[2]

Under COBRA, a group health plan ordinarily is defined as a plan that provides health care for the individuals who have an employment-related connection to the employer or employee organization or to their families through insurance or another mechanism, such as a trust, health maintenance organization, self-funded pay-as-you-go basis, reimbursement, or combination of these.[3] (See Q 197.) Medical benefits provided under the terms of the plan and available to COBRA beneficiaries may include:

1.   Inpatient and outpatient hospital care;

2.   Physician care;

3.   Surgery and other major medical benefits;

4.   Prescription drugs; and

5.   Any other medical benefits, such as dental and vision care.

But life insurance is not covered under COBRA.

---

1. See Labor Reg. §§2590.606-1 to 2590.606-4; 69 Fed. Reg. 30,084 (May 26, 2004).
2. Treas. Reg. §54.4980B-2, A-4 and A-5.
3. ERISA Sec. 607(1); IRC Sec. 4980B(g)(2); Treas. Reg. §54.4980B-2, A-1.

Practitioner's Pointer: What is the definition of "involuntary termination" in relation to the COBRA subsidy? Does a person qualify if let go for "just cause"—such as being late to work or calling in everyday or failing drug tests? The IRS has partially addressed this issue. "Involuntary termination" includes involuntary termination "for cause." However, for purposes of COBRA, if the termination of employment is due to "gross misconduct of the employee," the termination is *not* a qualifying event and the employee and other family members losing health coverage by reason of the employee's termination of employment are not eligible for COBRA.[1] Unfortunately, COBRA contains no definition of "gross misconduct." Based solely on the legislative history, it is clear that termination for gross misconduct is not the same as termination simply "for cause." The courts have not agreed on a common standard to apply in gross misconduct cases. Certain federal courts have looked to the unemployment insurance laws of the state in which the court sits because these laws often deny unemployment benefits to employees terminated for "gross misconduct," "misconduct," or "willful misconduct." This approach, however, has not led to a uniform definition of gross misconduct because state unemployment law concepts vary according to the state in which the federal court deciding a COBRA case sits. Other federal courts have rejected the state-by-state approach in favor of a uniform federal standard of gross misconduct. One court fashioned the following definition: "Gross misconduct may be intentional, wanton, willful, deliberate, reckless or in deliberate indifference to the employer's interest. It is misconduct beyond mere minor breaches of employee standards, but conduct which would be considered gross in nature." Other courts similarly have defined gross misconduct without reference to state law, and one court referred both to state law and to federal case law in fashioning a definition of gross misconduct.

The Federal Employee Health Benefits Amendments Act of 1988 (the COBRA analog for federal employees) also contains a gross-misconduct exception. Regulations issued under that Act define gross misconduct as "a flagrant and extreme transgression of law or established rule of action."[2]

One approach to the statute's failure to define gross misconduct may be for the employer to notify all employees, in advance, of the types of behavior that will be considered gross misconduct for COBRA purposes. This may enhance the likelihood that a court will uphold the denial of a COBRA election.

Being chronically late or consistently calling in to "take a day off" likely does not rise to the level of gross misconduct for purposes of denying COBRA coverage to an employee terminated for such conduct. On the other hand, failing a drug test, which is likely proof positive of illegal activity by the employee, would probably rise to the level of gross misconduct for purposes of denying COBRA coverage. The best way to make such a denial for coverage immune to attack would be to have a solid written COBRA policy and procedure that clearly spells out that termination for gross misconduct will result in COBRA's being unavailable, and that any act of gross misconduct will result in immediate termination. Employers should develop a workable definition of what constitutes gross misconduct of a sort that will be reasonable in application and easily understood by the average adult (the best approach may be to adopt a definition that parallels what the federal government has adopted for its own employees).

A Federal court in the Eastern District of Pennsylvania has ruled that an employer who had been sued for withdrawing a COBRA offer after determining that two employees had been terminated for "gross misconduct" must reinstate, retroactively, the COBRA coverage offer because the DOL had investigated the matter and ruled that the employees behavior had not constituted "gross misconduct" for purposes of denying COBRA coverage.[3]

---

1. IRS Notice 2009-27, Q-6.
2. 5 USC 8901.
3. *Danois v. i3 Archive Inc.*, 2013 WL 3556083 (E.D. Pa. 2013).

190. Who has the obligation to make COBRA coverage available to qualified beneficiaries where there has been a business reorganization or employer withdrawal from a multiemployer plan?

Since the introduction of COBRA coverage, the IRS has been concerned with cases of coverage being dropped or denied in the context of certain corporate transactions. In many cases, as it turns out, both the buyer and the seller have told qualified beneficiaries that the other party is responsible for the provision of COBRA coverage.

The regulations make clear that the parties to a transaction are free to allocate the responsibility for the provision of COBRA coverage by contract, even if the contract imposes responsibility on a different party than would the regulations. As long as the party who has assumed this responsibility under the contract performs its obligations, the other party will have no responsibility for providing COBRA coverage. But if the party assuming the contractual obligation to provide COBRA coverage defaults on its obligation, and if, under the regulations, the other party would have the obligation to provide COBRA coverage in the absence of the contractual agreement, then that other party would retain that obligation. The party with the underlying obligation under the regulations may insist on appropriate security and may pursue contractual remedies against the defaulting party.[1]

For sales of stock and sales of substantial assets, the seller retains the obligation to keep COBRA coverage available to existing qualified beneficiaries. In addition, where the seller ceases to provide any group health plan to any employees in connection with the sale and, therefore, is not responsible for providing COBRA continuation coverage (which will be determined on the facts and circumstances of each case), the buyer is responsible for providing COBRA continuation coverage to existing qualified beneficiaries. This secondary liability for buyers applies in all stock sales, and in all sales of substantial assets in which the buyer continues the business operations associated with the assets without interruption or substantial change.[2]

Where an employer ceases contributions to a multiemployer group health plan, the multiemployer plan generally continues to have the obligation to make COBRA coverage available to all qualified beneficiaries associated with that employer.[3] But there is no obligation on the part of the multiemployer plan to make COBRA coverage available to continuing employees of the withdrawing employer, as cessation of contributions is not a qualifying event.[4] Once the withdrawing employer makes group health coverage available to a class of its employees who were formerly covered under the multiemployer group health plan, or starts contributing to another multiemployer group health plan on their behalf, the employer's plan (or the new multiemployer group health plan) would then assume the obligation to make COBRA coverage available to the existing qualified beneficiaries.[5]

---

1. Treas. Reg. §54.4980B-9, A-7.
2. Treas. Reg. §54.4980B-9, A-8.
3. Treas. Reg. §54.4980B-9, A-10.
4. Treas. Reg. §54.4980B-9, A-9.
5. Treas. Reg. §54.4980B-9, A-10.

191. Who is entitled to COBRA benefits?

There are three elements to qualifying for COBRA benefits. COBRA establishes specific criteria for plans, beneficiaries, and events that initiate the coverage.

All group health plans are subject to COBRA, except small employer plans (see Q 189), church plans (within the meaning of IRC Section 414(e)), and governmental plans (within the meaning of IRC Section 414(d)).[1] The term "employees" includes all full-time and part-time employees, as well as self-employed individuals.[2] For this purpose, the term "employees" also includes agents, independent contractors, and directors, but only if they are eligible to participate in a group health plan.[3]

A "merger and acquisition qualified beneficiary" is defined as an individual who is a qualified beneficiary whose qualifying event occurred before, or in conjunction with, the acquisition and who is, or whose qualifying event occurred in connection with, a covered employee whose last employment before the qualifying event was associated with the assets being sold or the acquired organization in a stock sale.[4]

A qualified beneficiary who does not elect COBRA continuation coverage in connection with a qualifying event ceases to be a qualified beneficiary at the end of the election period.[5]

Leased employees, for the purposes of COBRA coverage requirements, are to be treated as employees of the recipient of the employee's services.[6]

A nonresident alien with no U.S. source of income from the employer during his period as a covered employee is not a qualified beneficiary. Under this rule, the nonresident alien's spouse or dependent children would also not be considered "qualified beneficiaries."[7]

The Defense of Marriage Act[8] provides that under applicable federal statutes, a domestic partner will not qualify as either a spouse or dependent child. Therefore, a covered employee's domestic partner, even if covered under the employer's group health plan, will not be considered a qualified beneficiary and will have no independent COBRA election rights.

"Qualifying events" are certain types of events that, but for COBRA continuation coverage, would cause an individual to lose health coverage. The type of qualifying event will determine who the qualified beneficiaries are and the required amount of time that a plan must offer COBRA coverage to them. A plan, at its discretion, may provide longer periods of continuation coverage. The types of qualifying events for employees are:

1. Voluntary or involuntary termination of employment, for reasons other than "gross misconduct";

2. Reduction in the number of hours of employment; and

---

1. Treas. Reg. §54.4980B-4, A-1.
2. ERISA Sec. 607(2); IRC Sec. 4980B(f)(7).
3. IRC Sec. 4980B(f)(7).
4. Treas. Reg. §54.4980B-9, A-4.
5. Treas. Reg. §54.4980B-3, A-1(f).
6. IRC Secs. 414(n)(1), 414(n)(3)(C).
7. IRC Sec. 4980B(g)(1)(C); Treas. Reg. §54.4980B-3, A-1(e).
8. Pub. L. No. 104-199, 110 Stat. 2419 (Sept. 21, 1996).

3.   A proceeding in bankruptcy under Title 11 of the U.S. Code with respect to an employer from whose employment a covered employee retired at any time.

The types of qualifying events for spouses are:

1.   The death of the covered employee;

2.   Divorce or legal separation from the covered employee;

3.   The covered employee's becoming entitled to Medicare;

4.   Reduction in the hours worked by the covered employee; and

5.   Termination of the covered employee's employment, for any reason other than "gross misconduct."[1]

COBRA coverage is not required to be provided in the event of a sham termination of employment between an employee and an employer.[2]

The U.S. District Court in Minnesota has ruled that going on strike is a COBRA qualifying event. After union employees went on strike, the employer in this case demanded that the strikers pay the full premium within a week or have their coverage terminated retroactively to a date shortly after the strike began. The employer did not issue COBRA notices to the workers or their covered dependents. The court, in ruling on the employees' request for a temporary restraining order, found that the company's threatened discontinuance of employer contributions constituted a COBRA loss of coverage. Although the court did not take note of it, IRS COBRA regulations hold that "a strike or a lockout is a termination or reduction of hours that constitutes a qualifying event if the strike or lockout results in a loss of coverage."[3]

The types of qualifying events for dependent children are the same as for the spouse with one addition: the loss of "dependent child" status under the rules of the plan.

Final COBRA regulations introduce the term "similarly situated non-COBRA beneficiaries," which is defined as the group of covered employees, their spouses, or dependent children receiving coverage under a group health plan maintained by the employer or employee organization who are receiving that coverage for a reason other than the rights provided under COBRA, and who are most similarly situated to the situation of the qualified beneficiary just before the qualifying event, based on all the facts and circumstances.[4]

192. For purposes of COBRA, how is the number of group health plans that an employer or employee organization maintains determined?

Proposed regulations permit employers and employee organizations broad discretion in determining the number of group health plans that they maintain. This reduces burdens on employers and employee organizations by permitting them to structure their group health

---

1. ERISA Sec. 603; IRC Sec. 4980B(f)(3); Treas. Reg. §54.4980B-4, A-1.
2. *Powell v. Strategic Outsourcing Inc.*, 2009 WL 746253 (S.D. Tex. 2009).
3. *Teamsters Local No. 120 v. Marathon Petroleum Co. LLC*, 2006 U.S. Dist. LEXIS 61933 (D. Minn. 2006).
4. Treas. Reg. §54.4980B-3, A-3.

plans in an efficient and cost-effective manner, and to satisfy their COBRA obligations based upon that structure. The number of group health plans pursuant to which those benefits are provided is determined by the instruments governing the arrangement or arrangements. But a multiemployer plan and a non-multiemployer plan are always separate arrangements.[1] Where it is not clear from the governing instruments how many group health plans provide benefits, or if there are no governing instruments, then all health care benefits will be deemed to be provided under a single plan.[2]

But if the principal purpose of establishing separate plans is to evade any requirement of law, then separate plans will be considered to be a single plan to the extent necessary to prevent this evasion.[3]

193. What are the notice and election procedures under COBRA?

An initial general notice must be furnished to employees covered under the group health plan, their covered spouses, and newly hired employees informing them of their rights under COBRA and describing provisions of the law.[4] Group health plans must provide a written notice of COBRA rights to covered employees and their spouses when their coverage begins. Plan administrators often include this general COBRA notice in their plans' SPDs.

The DOL has posted on its website Spanish language versions of the Model General Notice and the Model Election Notice.[5]

Regulations generally require plan administrators to furnish this notice within ninety days after coverage begins.[6] A plan could address a single notice to the covered employee and the employee's spouse if they live together and their coverage begins at the same time (or if the covered employee's coverage does not begin more than ninety days before the spouse's coverage).[7] In other circumstances, plans will have to furnish separate notices to both the covered employee and the spouse. The regulations permit the delivery of a single notice addressed to a covered employee and the employee's spouse at a joint residence, if the latest information on file with the plan indicates they reside at the same address. The single notice is not permitted where the spousal coverage begins at a later date than the employee coverage (but it is permitted where the spousal coverage begins before the date on which the notice must be provided the employee).[8]

Under the regulations, the ninety-day period for issuing the general notice begins on the date in which the covered employee or spouse first becomes covered under the plan.[9]

---

1. Treas. Reg. §54.4980B-2, A-6(b).
2. Treas. Reg. §54.4980B-2, A-6(a).
3. Treas. Reg. §54.4980B-2, A-6(c).
4. ERISA Sec. 606(a)(1); IRC Sec. 4980B(f)(6)(A).
5. For a copy of the Model General Notice, see http://www.dol.gov/ebsa/ModelGeneralNoticeSP.doc. For a copy of the Model Election Notice, see http://www.dol.gov/ebsa/ModelElectionNoticeSP.doc.
6. See Labor Reg. §2590.606-1(b); 69 Fed. Reg. 30,084 (May 26, 2004).
7. Labor Reg. §2590.606-1(f).
8. Labor Reg. §2590.606-1(d).
9. Labor Reg. §2590.606-4(b).

The regulations are subdivided into four parts: (1) general notice of continuation coverage; (2) notice requirement for employers; (3) notice requirements for covered employees and qualified beneficiaries; and (4) notice requirements for plan administrators.[1] The regulations clarify interpretations on good-faith efforts at compliance.

In addition, specific notice requirements are triggered for employers, qualified beneficiaries, and plan administrators when a qualifying event occurs.

Notice Requirements for Employers

Employers must notify plan administrators within thirty days after an employee's death, termination, reduction in hours of employment, or entitlement to Medicare. Multiemployer plans may provide for a longer period of time.[2]

Under the regulations, the employer notice has to "include sufficient information to enable the administrator to determine the plan, the covered employee, the qualifying event, and the date of the qualifying event."[3]

In the case *Ayres v. Balousek*,[4] the Court ruled that the employer and the plan administrator were not required to provide a COBRA election notice after the underlying health plan had terminated.

The First Circuit Court of Appeals has ruled that where a participant is terminated for gross misconduct, no COBRA notice is required.[5] The district court ruled that because COBRA does not contain a definition of "gross misconduct" in order for the employer to establish termination due to gross misconduct, it would have to prove that the employee engaged in job-related misconduct and was fired for that misconduct. This decision was affirmed by the First Circuit Court of Appeals.

Notice Requirements for Covered Employees and Qualified Beneficiaries

The covered employee or qualified beneficiary must notify the plan administrator within sixty days if the qualifying event is the covered employee's divorce or legal separation, or if a dependent child ceases to be eligible for coverage as a dependent under the plan's terms.[6] If covered employees or qualified beneficiaries fail to timely notify the plan administrator of these qualifying events, they forfeit their rights to COBRA benefits.

The covered employee or qualified beneficiary also is responsible for notifying the plan administrator within sixty days of experiencing a second qualifying event after COBRA coverage begins. Furthermore, it is the covered employee's or qualified beneficiary's responsibility to notify the plan administrator if the Social Security Administration determines he or she is disabled, and thus eligible for the eleven-month COBRA disability extension, or determines he or she is no longer disabled.[7]

---

1. Labor Reg. §§2590.606-1 to 2590.606-4.
2. ERISA Sec. 606(a)(2); IRC Sec. 4980B(f)(6)(B).
3. Labor Reg. §2590.606-2(c).
4. 2005 U.S. Dist. LEXIS 17471 (E.D. Mich. 2005).
5. *Pomales v. Celulares Telefonica, Inc.*, Civ. No. 02-1256 (D.P.R. 2005), aff'd, 2006 U.S. App. LEXIS 11585 (1st Cir. 2006).
6. ERISA Sec. 606(a)(3).
7. Labor Reg. §§2590.606-3(a)(4) and 2590.606-3(a)(5).

The regulations would require plans to establish "reasonable procedures" for covered employees or qualified beneficiaries to furnish these notices. The plan's procedures would be deemed reasonable if they: (1) are described in the plan's SPD; (2) specify the individual or entity designated to receive such notices; (3) describe the information about the qualifying event or disability determination the plan administrator needs to provide the covered employee or qualified beneficiary with the appropriate COBRA rights; and (4) satisfy certain other requirements.[1] The regulations detail that if a plan does not have reasonable procedures for notice to qualified beneficiaries, notice will be considered as having been provided if certain information adequately identifying a specific qualifying event is communicated in writing or orally to any of the parties that would customarily be considered in charge of the plan. Plans are free to mandate that notices be submitted in a specific form if the form is easily available to qualified beneficiaries without cost.[2]

Plans would be required to accept the notice from the covered employee or qualified beneficiary, or from a representative acting on behalf of the covered employee or qualified beneficiary. A notice provided to the plan by any one of these individuals would be treated as satisfying the notice requirement for all related qualified beneficiaries with respect to the qualifying event.[3]

A qualified beneficiary must notify the plan administrator within sixty days after events such as divorce, legal separation, or a child's ceasing to be covered as a dependent under plan rules.[4]

A court-ordered separation during divorce proceedings was ruled to not be a "legal separation" for purposes of issuing a COBRA notice of eligibility for benefits. The court ruled that the subsequent divorce was the qualifying event and sanctioned the plan administrator for issuing the notice upon the separation and failing to do so upon the granting of the divorce and awarded damages to the plaintiff for out-of-pocket expenses relating to the failure to issue the notice at the proper time.[5]

Disabled beneficiaries must notify plan administrators of Social Security disability determinations. A notice must be provided within sixty days of a disability determination and prior to the expiration of the eighteen-month period of COBRA coverage. These beneficiaries must also notify the plan administrator within thirty days of a final determination that they are no longer disabled.[6]

Notice Requirements for Plan Administrators

Plan administrators, upon notification of a qualifying event, must automatically provide employees and family members with a notice of their right to elect COBRA coverage. The notice must be provided in person or by first-class mail within fourteen days of receiving information

---

1. Labor Reg. §§2590.606-3(b)(1) and 2590.606-3(b)(2)(i) to 2590.606-3(b)(2)(v).
2. Labor Reg. §§2590.606-3(b)(3) and 2590.606-3(b)(4).
3. Labor Reg. §2590.606-3(e).
4. ERISA Sec. 606(a)(3); IRC Sec. 4980B(f)(6)(C).
5. *Simpson v. T.D. Williamson, Inc.*, 2003 U.S. Dist. LEXIS 25498 (N.D. Okla. 2003), judgment entered in 2004 U.S. Dist. LEXIS 11531 (N.D. Okla. 2004).
6. ERISA Sec. 606(a)(3); IRC Sec. 4980B(f)(6)(C).

that a qualifying event has occurred, and must be provided to each qualified beneficiary.[1] The DOL has advised that this requirement may, in some cases, be met by mailing one election notice where more than one qualified beneficiary resides at the same address. Where, at the time of the notification, the last known addresses of the covered employee, the covered employee's spouse, and dependent children (if any) are the same, the DOL will consider a single first-class mailing addressed to the covered employee, the covered employee's spouse, and dependent children (if any) to be good-faith compliance with the election notice requirements of ERISA Section 606(a)(4).[2] The Federal Court for the Western District of Oklahoma has upheld this long-standing DOL position by concluding that there is no legal requirement that the plan administrator prove the qualified beneficiary actually received the COBRA notices; instead, the only requirement is to prove that the notices were sent to the last known address. A former employee sued her employer for (among other things) failing to timely provide a COBRA election notice under its group health plan. She claimed that she did not receive an election notice until she complained to the HR director three months after her termination. The plan administrator refuted this allegation with proof that it had timely mailed the Notice to the former employee's last known mailing address it had on file.[3]

Significantly, the regulations clarify that in cases where the employer is responsible for notifying the plan administrator of a qualifying event, and the employer is the plan administrator, the employer generally has forty-four days from the date of the qualifying event to provide the COBRA election notice.[4]

Among other things, the regulations require the COBRA election notice to include the following:

1.   An explanation of the consequences of failing to elect or waiving COBRA coverage, including the possible effects on the individual's HIPAA portability and special enrollment rights;

2.   A description of the COBRA coverage that will be made available under the plan;

3.   An explanation of how long COBRA coverage will last, including an explanation of any events that may cause coverage to be discontinued earlier; and

4.   A description of how much the COBRA coverage will cost the individual, and the requirements and procedures for paying COBRA premiums.[5]

The regulations include a model notice plan administrators could use to satisfy these content requirements.

Finally, the regulations establish two additional notice requirements for plan administrators. The first applies only in circumstances where the covered employee or qualified beneficiary is required to notify the plan administrator of a qualifying event. In this case, if the plan administrator

---

1. ERISA Sec. 606(a)(4).
2. DOL Adv. Op. 99-14A.
3. *Somers v. Cudd Energy Services, Inc.*, 2012 WL 1836269 (W.D. Okla. 2012).
4. Labor Reg. §2590.606-4(b)(2).
5. Labor Reg. §§2590.606-4(b)(4)(i) to 2590.606-4(b)(4)(xiv).

receives such a notice and determines the individual is not entitled to COBRA coverage, the plan administrator has to notify the individual of that determination within fourteen days and include an explanation of why the individual cannot elect COBRA coverage.[1]

The second would apply when a plan administrator prematurely terminates a qualified beneficiary's COBRA coverage. (This usually happens when the qualified beneficiary fails to timely pay COBRA premiums.) In this case, the regulations require the plan administrator to notify the qualified beneficiary "as soon as practicable" after deciding to terminate coverage. The notice would have to explain why the plan administrator is terminating coverage, and any other rights to coverage the qualified beneficiary may have under the plan or applicable law, including conversion rights.[2]

The mere posting of the election notice at the place of employment is not considered adequate.[3]

There are two special exceptions to the notice requirements for multiemployer plans. First, the time frame for providing notices may be extended beyond the fourteen-day and thirty-day requirements if allowed by plan rules.[4] Second, employers are relieved of the obligation to notify plan administrators when employees terminate or reduce their work hours.[5] Plan administrators are responsible for determining whether these qualifying events have occurred.[6]

The election period is the period of time during which each qualified beneficiary may choose whether to continue health care coverage under an employer's group health plan. Qualified beneficiaries have a sixty-day period to elect whether to continue coverage. This period is measured from the later of the coverage loss date or the date when the notice to elect COBRA coverage is sent. COBRA coverage is retroactive to the loss of coverage if the qualified beneficiary elects and pays for the coverage retroactively.[7] An election is considered to be made on the date it is sent to the plan administrator. The election period must begin no later than the date when the qualified beneficiary would lose coverage on account of the qualifying event.[8]

A covered employee or the covered employee's spouse may elect COBRA coverage on behalf of any other qualified beneficiary. But each qualified beneficiary may independently elect COBRA coverage. A parent or legal guardian may make the election on behalf of a minor child.[9]

If COBRA continuation coverage is eliminated in *anticipation* of a qualifying event, such as in anticipation of a divorce or legal separation, the actual elimination is disregarded in determining whether the qualifying event causes a loss of coverage. In order for a qualifying beneficiary who

---

1. Labor Reg. §2590.606-4(b)(1).
2. Labor Reg. §§2590.606-4(d)(1) to 2590.606-4(d)(3).
3. COBRA Conf. Rep. No. 453, 99th Cong., 1st Sess. 563 (1985).
4. IRC Sec. 4980B(f)(6)(D).
5. IRC Sec. 4980B(f)(6)(B).
6. IRC Sec. 4980B(f)(6)(D).
7. ERISA Sec. 605(1); IRC Sec. 4980B(f)(5)(A).
8. Treas. Reg. §54.4980B-6, A-1.
9. Treas. Reg. §54.4980B-6, A-6.

has lost his health coverage as a result of an anticipated divorce or legal separation to perfect his right to COBRA coverage, the plan administrator must be given notice within sixty days of the actual divorce or separation.[1] Consequently, the IRS has ruled that when an employee eliminates his spouse's group health plan coverage in anticipation of the couple's divorce, a plan that is required to make COBRA continuation coverage available to the spouse must begin to make that coverage available as of the date of the divorce, and not the date of the actual elimination of coverage.[2]

A waiver of coverage may be revoked by or on behalf of a qualified beneficiary before the end of the election period. The waiver, or revocation of waiver, is considered to have been made on the date that it has been sent to the plan or plan administrator. A beneficiary may then reinstate coverage, in which case the plan need only provide continuation coverage beginning on the date when the waiver is revoked.[3] Coerced waivers that are obtained through the withholding of benefits are invalid.[4]

The United States District Court for the Eastern District of Louisiana has ruled that an employer has no duty to provide a COBRA election notice for the termination of long-term disability coverage because COBRA does not require such notification.[5]

The Fourth Circuit Court of Appeals has ruled that a human resources manager had no obligation to provide details on COBRA continuation rights to the inquiring mother of a hospitalized beneficiary.[6]

Due to COBRA's and ERISA's being vague on the issue of a statute of limitations for the filing of claims, one trial court looked to the most analogous state statute for determining whether a COBRA claim filed four years after termination was time barred (it was not barred; instead, a six-year limitation was applied).[7]

The U.S. District Court for the Southern District of Illinois has ruled that an employer is liable for a participant's medical bills where the participant takes a leave of absence due to illness and the plan administrator fails to provide the participant with a timely COBRA notice and fails to provide the plan with notice of a qualifying event. The failure to give the plan notice of the qualifying event relieved the plan of any obligation to cover the deceased employee's medical expenses.[8]

The First Circuit Court of Appeals has ruled that there can be no good-faith compliance with COBRA if the election notice was knowingly sent by the employer to an invalid address.[9]

1. Treas. Reg. §54.4980B-6, Q&A 2.
2. Rev. Rul. 2002-88, 2002-2 C.B. 995.
3. Treas. Reg. §54.4980B-6, A-4.
4. *Meadows v. Cagle's, Inc.*, 954 F.2d 686 (11th Cir. 1992).
5. *Goldman v. Hartford Life & Accident Ins. Co.*, 2004 U.S. Dist. LEXIS 18266 (E.D. La. 2004).
6. *Estate of Weeks v. Advance Stores Co.*, 2004 U.S. App. LEXIS 10637 (4th Cir. 2004).
7. *Mattson v. Farrell Distrib. Corp.*, 2001 U.S. Dist. LEXIS 16159 (D. Vt. 2001).
8. *Uthell v. Mid-Illinois Concrete, Inc.*, 2006 U.S. Dist. LEXIS 89314 (S.D. Ill. 2006).
9. *Torres-Negron v. Merck & Co.*, 2007 U.S. App. LEXIS 12034 (1st Cir. 2007).

The Eighth Circuit Court of Appeals has ruled that where an employee was terminated from his position after failing to return to work after the expiration of leave taken under the FMLA, the plan administrator's COBRA election notice was sufficient for compliance based upon date-stamped evidence of mailing by the U.S. Postal Service as a method "reasonably calculated to reach" the plaintiff even though the plaintiff claims to have never received the notice.[1]

The DOL has updated its model COBRA election notice in order to make it available in modifiable, electronic form. The revised notice appears on the DOL website (http://www.dol.gov/ebsa/cobra.html), along with a redline version highlighting the changes.[2] A copy of the updated model notice also appears in the Appendices of this text.

194. What is the special second COBRA election period?

The Trade Act of 2002, which expanded trade adjustment assistance (TAA) benefits available to workers dislocated by import competition or shifts of production to other countries, also amended the Internal Revenue Code by adding a new second COBRA election period for qualifying individuals. An individual qualifies for the second election period if she:

- Receives TAA benefits (or would be eligible to receive TAA benefits but for the requirement that the individual first exhaust unemployment benefits);

- Lost health coverage due to a termination of employment that resulted in the individual's becoming eligible for TAA benefits; and

- Did not elect COBRA coverage during the regular COBRA election period.

Qualifying individuals may then elect COBRA coverage during the second election period, which is the sixty-day period that begins on the first day of the month in which the individual becomes a qualifying individual, but only if the election is made not later than six months after the initial loss of coverage (e.g., the loss of coverage at termination of employment). Once elected, the COBRA coverage commences on the first day of the second election period (coverage is *not* retroactive to the date of the initial loss of coverage).

The maximum coverage period for COBRA elected in the second election period is still to be measured from the initial loss of coverage. Because qualification for TAA benefits is not immediate, affected individuals would not be eligible for the maximum COBRA coverage period. However, there are some indications that additional guidance from the IRS may hold that the date from which the maximum coverage period is calculated would be the first day of the second election period (thereby allowing a full maximum coverage period).

The IRS has ruled that a covered employee's becoming entitled to Medicare after a qualifying event, but while the employee's spouse or dependent child has COBRA continuation coverage, is *not* a second qualifying event entitling the spouse or dependent child to extend continuation

---

1. *Hearst v. Progressive Foam Techs., Inc.*, 2011 WL 2201064 (8th Cir. 2011).
2. DOL Technical Release No. 2013-02 (May 8, 2013), http://www.dol.gov/ebsa/cobra.html; Model COBRA Continuation Coverage Election Notice and Redline Version Showing May 2013 Changes.

coverage to a total of thirty-six months, *unless* the Medicare entitlement would have resulted in a loss of coverage under the employer's group health plan for the spouse or dependent child under the plan before the employee was terminated.[1]

> *NOTE:* The proposed regulations relate specifically to the COBRA notice requirements codified in ERISA. However, the proposals also would apply to the COBRA notice provisions codified at IRC Section 4980B in most circumstances. As a result, non-ERISA group health plans subject to IRC Section 4980B should be interested in the DOL's proposals.

195. What are the content requirements for the general COBRA notice?

Final regulations spell out the content requirements for the general COBRA notice. The primary items the notice must set forth include:

1. The plan's name and the name and contact information for the party responsible for administering COBRA benefits;

2. A general description of the plan's COBRA provisions, including information about COBRA qualifying events, when COBRA benefits can be extended, and the plan's requirements relating to paying COBRA premiums;

3. An explanation of when a COBRA qualified beneficiary is responsible for notifying the plan administrator about a qualifying event and the plan's procedures for providing such notice; and

4. A statement that more complete information about COBRA is available from the plan administrator and in the plan's SPD.[2]

As noted, the regulations include a model notice plan administrators can use to satisfy these content requirements (see Appendix A for a copy of this sample notice).

196. What are the SPD content disclosures for welfare benefit plans regarding COBRA?

Under the final regulations, the DOL takes the position that group health plan summary plan descriptions (SPDs) should include information about the new health insurance tax credit for trade-displaced workers as part of the discussion about participants' COBRA rights and responsibilities. The final regulations confirm that plans can continue to satisfy this general COBRA notice requirement by including all the required information in the plan's SPD. But in order for this to be effective compliance, the plan administrator must furnish the SPD to covered employees and their spouses within the ninety-day time period required by the proposed regulations.[3]

Practitioner's Pointer: Because of this rule by the DOL, many plan administrators probably will need to issue a summary of material modifications (SMM) to their SPDs to comply with the Department's position.

---

1. Rev. Rul. 2004-22, 2004-10 I.R.B. 553.
2. Labor Reg. §§2590.606-1(c)(1) to 2590.606-1(c)(6); 69 Fed. Reg. 3083 (May 26, 2004).
3. Labor Reg. §2590.606-1(e); 69 Fed. Reg. 30,083 (May 26, 2004).

197. What benefits and plans are covered by COBRA?

Each qualified beneficiary must be offered coverage identical to that available to similarly situated beneficiaries who are not receiving COBRA coverage under the plan. Generally, this is the same coverage that the qualified beneficiary had immediately before qualifying for continuation coverage.

A change in the benefits under the plan for the active employees will also apply to the qualified beneficiary(ies).[1] Qualified beneficiaries must be allowed to make the same choices given to non-COBRA beneficiaries under the plan, such as during periods of open enrollment by the plan. If the plan allows similarly situated active employees, with respect to whom a qualifying event has not occurred, to choose among several options during an open enrollment period, then each qualified beneficiary must also be offered to the ability choose, during an open enrollment period, among the options made available to similarly situated active employees.[2] The coverage may not be conditioned upon, or discriminate on the basis of, the insurability of a designated beneficiary.[3]

In general, COBRA includes the medical, dental, and vision plans offered by the qualified beneficiary's former employer under the continuation of benefits guidelines. The qualified beneficiary may continue only those plans in which they were enrolled on the date of loss of eligibility.

> *Example,* A qualified beneficiary was enrolled in a PPO medical and vision plan while an active employee. The beneficiary may continue either or both of these two plans. However, the qualified beneficiary would not be ineligible to elect participation in a dental plan, and would be ineligible to change to an HMO medical plan, until the next annual Open Enrollment period.

198. How do the COBRA continuation coverage requirements apply to cafeteria plans and other flexible benefit arrangements?

In the case of a cafeteria plan or other flexible benefit arrangement, the COBRA coverage requirements apply only to the health care benefits thereunder that an employee has actually chosen to receive (and is actually receiving on the day before the qualifying event).[4]

199. What is the duration of COBRA coverage?

COBRA establishes required periods of coverage for continuation health benefits. A plan, may, however, provide longer periods of coverage than those required by COBRA. COBRA beneficiaries generally are eligible to purchase group coverage for a maximum of eighteen months in the case of qualifying events due to employment termination or reduction in work hours. Certain qualifying events, or a second qualifying event during the initial period of coverage, may permit a beneficiary to purchase a maximum of thirty-six months of coverage.[5]

---

1. ERISA Sec. 602(1); IRC Sec. 4980B(f)(2)(A).
2. Treas. Reg. §54.4980B-6, A-6.
3. ERISA Sec. 602(4); IRC Sec. 4980B(f)(2).
4. Treas. Reg. §54.4980B-2, A-8.
5. ERISA Secs. 602(2)(A)(i), 602(2)(A)(ii); IRC Secs. 4980B(f)(2)(B)(i), 4980B(f)(2)(B)(ii); Treas. Reg. §54.5980B-7, A-6.

Special rules for disabled individuals may extend the maximum periods of coverage. If a qualified beneficiary is determined, under Title II or XVI of the Social Security Act, to have been disabled at any time during the first sixty days of continuation coverage, and the beneficiary properly notifies the plan administrator of the disability determination before the expiration of the eighteen-month period, then the eighteen-month period is expanded to twenty-nine months (see Q 177).[1]

Regulations clarify that this extension of coverage to twenty-nine months due to disability is available if three conditions are satisfied: (1) a termination or reduction of hours of a covered employee's employment occurs; (2) an individual (whether or not the covered employee) who is a qualified beneficiary in connection with the qualifying event described in (1) is determined to have been disabled at any time during the first sixty days of COBRA coverage; and (3) any of the qualified beneficiaries affected by the qualifying event described in (1) provides notice to the plan administrator of the disability determination on a date that is both within sixty days after the date the determination is issued and before the end of the original eighteen-month period. This extension due to disability applies independently to each qualified beneficiary, whether or not the beneficiary is disabled.[2]

Coverage begins on the date when coverage would otherwise end because of a qualifying event, and can end when:

1.   The last day of the maximum coverage period is reached;

2.   Premiums are not paid on a timely basis;

3.   The employer ceases to maintain any group health plan;

4.   The individual "becomes covered" under another employer group health plan that does not contain any exclusion or limitation with respect to any preexisting condition of such beneficiary, and

5.   A beneficiary is entitled to Medicare benefits.[3]

If a determination is made that a qualified beneficiary is no longer disabled, then a plan may terminate the COBRA coverage prior to the end of the disability extension (however, not before the end of the maximum coverage period that would apply without regard to the disability extension).[4]

A group health plan can terminate for cause the coverage of a qualified beneficiary receiving COBRA coverage on the same basis that the plan terminates for cause the coverage of similarly situated non-COBRA beneficiaries (i.e., the submission of a fraudulent claim).[5] But the coverage of a qualified beneficiary can be terminated for failure to make timely payment to the plan only if the payment is not "timely" under the regulations (see Q 200).[6]

---

1. ERISA Sec. 602(2)(A)(iv); IRC Sec. 4980B(f)(2)(B)(i).
2. Treas. Reg. §54.4980B-7, A-5.
3. ERISA Sec. 602(2); IRC Sec. 4980B(f)(2).
4. Treas. Reg. §54.4980B-7, A-4(c).
5. Treas. Reg. §54.4980B-7, A-1(b).
6. Treas. Reg. §54.4980B-8, A-5.

When a qualified beneficiary first becomes covered under another group health plan after the date on which COBRA continuation coverage is elected for the qualified beneficiary, the plan may terminate the qualified beneficiary's COBRA coverage as of the date on which the qualified beneficiary first becomes covered under the other group health plan.[1] By contrast, if a qualified beneficiary first becomes covered under another group health plan on or before the date on which COBRA coverage is elected, then that other coverage cannot be a basis for terminating the qualified beneficiary's COBRA coverage.[2]

Although COBRA specifies certain maximum required periods of time that continued health coverage must be offered to qualified beneficiaries, COBRA does not prohibit plans from offering continuation health coverage beyond the COBRA periods.[3]

Some plans allow beneficiaries to convert group health coverage to an individual policy. If this conversion option is available under the plan, it must be offered to qualified beneficiaries. In this case, the beneficiary must have the option to enroll in a conversion health plan within 180 days before COBRA coverage ends. The premium is generally not at a group rate. The conversion option, however, need not be available if the beneficiary ends COBRA coverage before reaching the maximum period of entitlement.[4]

200. What rules govern the payment for COBRA coverage?

Beneficiaries may be required to pay the entire premium for coverage. The premium cannot exceed 102 percent of the cost to the plan for similarly situated individuals who have not incurred a qualifying event.[5] Premiums reflect the total cost of group health coverage, including both the portion paid by active employees and any portion paid by the employer before the qualifying event, plus 2 percent for administrative costs.[6]

In the case of disabled beneficiaries receiving an additional eleven months of coverage after the initial 18 months, the premium for those additional months may be increased to 150 percent of the plan's total cost of coverage.[7] If a qualified beneficiary entitled to a disability extension experiences a second qualifying event within the original eighteen-month maximum coverage period, then the plan is not permitted to require the payment of an amount that exceeds 102 percent of the applicable premium for any period of COBRA coverage. By contrast, if a qualified beneficiary entitled to a disability extension experiences a second qualifying event after the end of the original eighteen-month maximum coverage period, the plan may require the payment of an amount up to 150 percent of the applicable premium for the remainder of the period of COBRA continuation coverage, as long as the disabled qualified beneficiary is included in that coverage.[8]

---

1. Treas. Reg. §54.4980B-7, A-2.
2. *Geissal v. Moore Med. Corp.*, 524 U.S. 74 (1998); Treas. Reg. §54.4980B-7, A-2(a).
3. Treas. Reg. §54.4980B-7, A-6.
4. Treas. Reg. §54.4980B-7, A-8.
5. ERISA Sec. 602(3); IRC Sec. 4980B(f)(2)(C).
6. ERISA Sec. 602(3); IRC Sec. 4980B(f)(2)(C).
7. ERISA Sec. 602(3); IRC Sec. 4980B(f)(2)(C).
8. Treas. Reg. §54.4980B-8, A-1(b).

Premiums may be increased if the costs to the plan increase, but generally must be fixed in advance of each twelve-month premium cycle.[1] The plan must allow terminated participants to pay premiums on a monthly basis if they ask to do so.[2]

The initial premium payment must be made within forty-five days after the date of the qualified beneficiary's COBRA election.[3] Payment generally must cover the period of coverage from the date of COBRA election retroactive to the date of the loss of coverage due to the qualifying event. Premiums for successive periods of coverage are due on the date stated in the plan, with a minimum thirty-day grace period.[4] The due date may not be prior to the first day of the period of coverage. A group health plan must allow payment for COBRA coverage to be made in monthly installments. The plan may also allow alternative payment intervals such as weekly, quarterly, or semiannually.[5]

An employer cannot require a beneficiary to pay premiums for a period of continuation coverage exceeding the length of coverage requested by the beneficiary.[6]

Premiums for the rest of the COBRA period must be made within thirty days after the due date for each such premium or longer period as provided by the plan. But the plan is not obligated to send monthly premium notices.

A plan must treat a timely payment that is not significantly less than the amount required as full payment, unless the plan notifies the qualified beneficiary of the amount of the deficiency and grants a reasonable period for payment. A reasonable period of time for this purpose is thirty days after the date when notice is provided. An amount will be considered as "not significantly less" if the shortfall is no greater than the lesser of $50 or 10 percent of the amount the plan requires to be paid.[7]

COBRA beneficiaries remain subject to the rules of the plan, and therefore must satisfy all costs related to deductibles, catastrophic events, and other benefit limits.

The Federal Court for the Southern District of Indiana has held that a former employee has no COBRA rights when their COBRA coverage has been terminated for nonpayment of premiums. The employee in this case sued his employer for failing to provide a COBRA election notice when his employment terminated due to his failure to return from a leave of absence. During the leave, the employee had initially maintained his health coverage by paying his portion of the premiums directly to the plan administrator, but he subsequently ceased making payments. His coverage was canceled as a result. In issuing a Summary judgment in favor the defendant, the Court ruled that the former employee's group coverage did not cease because of his termination, instead it ended because he failed to pay his premiums. Therefore, the former employee's termination does not constitute a qualifying event for the purposes of COBRA.[8]

---

1. IRC Sec. 4980B(f)(4)(C).
2. ERISA Sec. 602(3); IRC Sec. 4980B(f)(2)(C).
3. ERISA Sec. 602(3); IRC Sec. 4980B(f)(2)(C).
4. ERISA Sec. 602(2)(C); IRC Sec. 4980B(f)(2)(B)(iii).
5. Treas. Reg. §54.4980B-8, A-3.
6. *Popovits v. Circuit City Stores Inc.*, 185 F.3d 726 (7th Cir. 1999).
7. Treas. Reg. §54.4980B-8, A-5(b).
8. *Shedlock v. Visteon Corp.*, 2012 WL 2912722 (S.D. Ind. 2012).

201. What are the claims procedures for COBRA?

Health plan rules must explain how to obtain benefits and must include written procedures for processing claims. Claims procedures are to be included in the SPD booklet. See Q 98.

Terminated participants should submit a written claim for benefits to whoever is designated to operate the health plan (e.g., employer, plan administrator). If the claim is denied, notice of denial must be in writing and furnished generally within ninety days after the claim is filed. The notice should state the reasons for the denial, as well as any additional information needed to support the claim and procedures for appealing the denial.

Participants have sixty days after a claim is denied in which to appeal the denial.[1] Such participants must receive a decision on the appeal within sixty days after appealing unless the plan:

1.   Provides for a special hearing or

2.   Requires that the decision be made by a group that meets only on a periodic basis.

202. How does COBRA coverage coordinate with other benefits?

The Family and Medical Leave Act of 1993 (FMLA) requires an employer to maintain coverage under any "group health plan" for an employee on FMLA leave, under the same conditions that coverage would have been provided if the employee had continued working. Coverage provided under the FMLA is not COBRA coverage, and FMLA leave is not a qualifying event under COBRA.[2] A COBRA qualifying event may occur, however, when an employer's obligation to maintain health benefits under FMLA ceases, such as when an employee notifies an employer of his intent not to return to work following FMLA leave. The qualifying event occurs on the last day of FMLA leave. The employer must notify the plan administrator within thirty days of the last day of FMLA leave.[3]

The Uniformed Services Employment and Reemployment Rights Act of 1994 (USERRA) gives certain members of the military reserves the right to purchase up to eighteen months of COBRA coverage when they are called to active duty. The final regulations clarify that USERRA coverage is alternative coverage, and, therefore, the USERRA and COBRA periods of continuation coverage run concurrently.[4]

The Sixth Circuit Court of Appeals has ruled that no COBRA Notice of Rights was required at the end of combined FMLA and non-FMLA leave where the employee did not pay health coverage premiums while on leave.[5] In the case, the employer permitted an employee to take FMLA leave and allowed the leave to continue an additional six months beyond the mandated length of FMLA leave. During this leave the participant failed to pay his mandated portion of health premiums for employer-provided coverage.

---

1. 28 USC § 2107.
2. Treas. Reg. §54.4980B-10, A-1.
3. Notice 94-103, 1994-2 C.B. 569; Treas. Reg. §54.4980B-10, A-2.
4. Treas. Reg. §54.4980B-7, A-7.
5. *Jordan v. Tyson Foods, Inc.*, 2007 WL 4455435 (6th Cir. 2007).

As a result, following a corporate merger that occurred during the leave, the employee was not allowed to enroll in the successor employer's health plan. When the employee failed to return to work at the end of his leave, the successor employer terminated his employment. The employee then sued both employers for failure to provide COBRA. The Sixth Circuit cited the IRS regulations, under which the end of an FMLA leave results in a COBRA qualifying event if an employee:

1.   Was covered under an employer's health plan the day before taking FMLA leave,

2.   Does not return to employment at the end of FMLA leave, and

3.   Would lose coverage in the absence of COBRA.

The court ruled that the third condition had not been met. Noting that without COBRA, the employee could have remained covered under the health plan for the remainder of his approved leave so long as he had paid his premiums, the court held that the FMLA leave did not result in a qualifying event.[1]

A federal court in Utah has ruled that a health plan insurer could not terminate COBRA coverage for the minor who was a qualified beneficiary and who was also enrolled in a state Medicaid program.[2] The court opined that COBRA coverage cannot be terminated by reason of an individual's eligibility for Medicaid, noting that federal and state laws evidenced a clear policy of prohibiting insurers from shifting their obligation for medical expenses to the taxpayer-funded Medicaid program. Relying upon ERISA Section 609(b)(2), which prohibits group health plans from taking into account an individual's eligibility for or participation in a state Medicaid program, the court ruled that the son of the parent who had acquired the COBRA coverage had coverage under the plan.

203. What are the applicable sanctions and penalties under COBRA?

Any administrator who fails to meet the notice requirements of COBRA may be subject to (1) a civil penalty, and/or (2) personal liability. Further, plan administrators who fail to provide timely notice may be subject to a fine of up to $110 per day, "and the court may in its discretion order such other relief as it deems proper."[3] In *Phillips v. Riverside*,[4] the court deemed proper and awarded relief in the amount that would place the beneficiary in the same position he would have been in had full continuation coverage under COBRA been provided. ERISA statutory penalties awarded for COBRA notice violation extend only to the participant.[5]

In the case of *Rodriguez v. International College of Business & Technology, Inc.*,[6] the court ruled that the daily penalties for a failure to provide a COBRA election notice do not stop until the maximum 18-month coverage period has expired. This was in response to a motion of the plan administrator to request that the Court apply the daily penalty to a shorter period that

1. *Jordan v. Tyson Foods, Inc.*, 2007 WL 4455435 (6th Cir. 2007).
2. *Mellor v. Wasatch Crest Mut. Ins. Co.*, 2009 WL 172773 (D. Utah 2009).
3. ERISA Sec. 502(c)(1); Labor Reg. §2575.502c-1.
4. *Phillips v. Riverside*, 796 F. Supp. 403 (E.D. Ark. 1992).
5. *Wright v. Hanna Steel Corp.*, 2001 U.S. App. LEXIS 22878 (11th Cir. 2001).
6. 2005 U.S. Dist. LEXIS 2351 (D.P.R. 2005).

ended when the participant filed the lawsuit, or at the latest, when the administrator filed its response to the suit. Issuance of a COBRA notice beyond the mandatory issuance deadline stops the accrual of penalties even if a corrected notice is subsequently issued to correct an error in the initial notice.[1]

No statutory penalty of $110 per day is permitted under COBRA where an employer allows a participant to elect COBRA coverage retroactive to the date of termination.[2]

ERISA Section 502(a)(1) authorizes participants or beneficiaries to bring a civil action to enforce their rights under COBRA, clarify their rights to future benefits, or recover benefits due to them under the terms of the plan. Because ERISA does not prescribe a specific statute of limitations under which a claim under COBRA may be litigated, courts must rely on the most analogous state law statute of limitations for guidance. Under the case *Treanor v. Metropolitan Transportation Authority*,[3] the Court ruled that a claim not filed within the applicable three-year limitations period under New York's Unfair Insurance Practices statute of limitations is barred.

The court, in its discretion, may allow reasonable attorneys' fees and costs of action incurred under a civil suit to enforce COBRA rights, and such other legal or equitable relief as the court deems appropriate.[4] Various court cases have established the following factors for the courts to consider in determining an award of attorneys' fees:

1. The degree of the opposing party's culpability or bad faith;

2. The ability of the opposing party to personally satisfy an award of fees;

3. Whether the award would deter other parties from acting in a similar way under similar circumstances;

4. Whether the party requesting the fees sought to benefit all plan participants and beneficiaries or to resolve a significant legal question; and

5. The relative merits of the opposing party's position.[5]

Internal Revenue Code Section 4980B(a) provides for the imposition of an excise tax against any group health plan that fails to meet the requirements of COBRA continuation coverage. The excise tax is $100 for each day that a group health plan fails to meet the continuation coverage requirements, which is doubled to $200 per day where there is more than one beneficiary with respect to the same qualifying event.[6] The employer or the plan itself (in the case of a multiemployer plan) will be held liable for the excise tax (unless the plan is exempt from the COBRA rules).[7]

---

1. *Fiveash v. Commerce Lexington Inc.*, 2009 WL 331387 (E.D. Ky. 2009).
2. *Gigliotti v. Sprint Spectrum, L.P.*, 2001 U.S. Dist. LEXIS 20221 (N.D.N.Y. 2001).
3. 2005 U.S. Dist. LEXIS 35861 (S.D.N.Y. 2005).
4. ERISA Sec. 502(g)(1).
5. *Eaves v. Penn*, 587 F.2d 453 (10th Cir. 1978); *Gordon v. United States Steel Corp.*, 724 F.2d 106 (10th Cir. 1983); *Krogh v. Chamberlain*, 708 F. Supp. 1235 (D. Utah 1989).
6. IRC Secs. 4980B(b), 4980B(c)(3)(B).
7. IRC Sec. 4980B(e)(1)(A); Treas. Reg. § 54.4980B-2, A-10.

There is a thirty-day grace period to correct a failure due to reasonable cause and not willful neglect. If the failure is corrected within the grace period, the excise tax will not be imposed.[1]

Where there has been an inadvertent compliance failure during any period in which the persons who would be liable for the tax did not know, or could not know through the exercise of reasonable diligence, of the failure, the excise tax will not be imposed.[2]

The annual limit on the liability for the excise tax that must be paid during an employer's tax year is the lesser of 10 percent of the total amount paid or incurred by the employer or predecessor employer (or trust, in the case of a multiemployer plan) during the preceding tax year for the employer's group health plans, or $500,000.[3]

The Third Circuit Court of Appeals has upheld the statutory penalties under COBRA where the employer, in the absence of bad faith, failed to timely issue the COBRA continuation notice to the plaintiff.[4]

The Seventh Circuit has ruled that no penalties will apply to an employer for COBRA notice failures to two employees where the errors were discovered and corrected through the employer's program of compliance audits.[5] The employer admitted that the plaintiffs were not provided with timely COBRA election notices. But an annual internal audit, performed for the employer by an outside auditor, revealed that between May 2004 and January 2006, an estimated 266 of the 1,570 participants who experienced qualifying events apparently did not timely receive their COBRA notices. The company promptly contacted those individuals, provided the overdue notices, allowed retroactive election of benefits, and offered to negotiate payment plans for those who could not afford to immediately pay the accrued premium obligations. The court declined to impose the penalties, noting that neither plaintiff was significantly prejudiced by the delay in notification, that there was no indication of bad faith or gross negligence, and that the company offered to provide retroactive coverage through a payment plan.[6]

The federal court for the Southern District of Indiana has issued a $1.8 million COBRA Notice penalty against a large employer, in its role as plan administrator of the company's group health plan. The Court ruled that the employer/plan administrator had neglected its duty as plan administrator to ensure that COBRA election notices were sent on a timely basis. According to a federal district court, the employer/plan administrator had a poorly designed notice system and failed to regularly audit its COBRA program. The court added that the employer's use of a third-party administrator did not relief it of legal liability as the official "plan administrator."[7]

---

1. IRC Sec. 4980B(c)(2).
2. IRC Sec. 4980B(c)(1).
3. IRC Sec. 4980B(c)(4)(A)(i).
4. *Veneziano v. Long Island Pipe Fabrication & Supply,* 79 Fed. Appx. 506, 2003 U.S. App. LEXIS 21735 (3d Cir. 2003).
5. *Gomez v. St. Vincent's Health,* 2011 WL 3559924 (7th Cir. 2011).
6. *Gomez v. St. Vincent's Health,* 2011 WL 3559924 (7th Cir. 2011).
7. *Pierce v. Visteon Corp.,* 2013 WL 3225832 (S.D. Ind. 2013).

Practitioner's Pointer: The IRS has issued their audit techniques and summary of tax law for the examination of COBRA cases under the Internal Revenue Code. These examination procedures make a model self-audit protocol for monitoring ongoing COBRA compliance by employers and plan administrators. These guidelines are available on-line at: http://www.irs.gov/Businesses/Small-Businesses-&-Self-Employed/Audit-Techniques-and-Tax-Law-to-Examine-COBRA-Cases-%28Continuation-of-Employee-Health-Care-Coverage%29.

Qualified Medical Child Support Orders

204. What are the DOL rules regarding qualified medical child support order notices?

ERISA requires employer-sponsored group health plans to extend health care coverage to the children of a parent/employee who is divorced, separated, or never married when ordered to do so by state authorities. A state court or agency may require an ERISA-covered health plan to provide benefits coverage to children by issuing a qualified medical child support order (QMSCO). A state child support enforcement agency may also obtain group health coverage for a child by issuing a qualified National Medical Support Notice (NMSN).

The DOL provides a compliance assistance guide to help employers, plan sponsors, service providers, and state officials understand the federal health benefits law regarding QMCSOs. The new compliance guide for QMCSOs is located on Employment Standards Administration's Web site (http://www.dol.gov/esa) under "Publications."

ERISA Section 609(a) provides that each group health plan must provide benefits in accordance with applicable requirements of any QMCSO. ERISA Section 609(a)(2) defines a QMCSO as a medical child support order issued under any state law that creates or recognizes the existence of an "alternate recipient's" right to receive benefits for which a participant or beneficiary is eligible under a group health plan. Upon receipt of a medical child support order, the plan administrator of a group health plan is required to determine, within a reasonable period of time, whether a medical child support order received by the plan is qualified.[1]

Congress enacted Section 401 of the Child Support Performance and Incentive Act of 1998 to amend both ERISA and the Social Security Act to require state agencies to enforce the medical child support obligations of noncustodial parents by issuing to their employers an NMSN. ERISA requires plan administrators, upon receipt of the notice from the employer, to accept an appropriately completed notice that also complies with the requirements of ERISA Section 609(a) as a QMCSO. The DOL and the Department of Health and Human Services have issued final rules that grant states the authority to serve NMSNs upon employers of noncustodial parents.[2] Accompanying these final rules was the release of a model "National Medical Support Notice," which included model Part A "Notice to Withhold for Health Care Coverage" and model Part B "Medical Support Notice to Plan Administrator." These model forms are included in Appendix A.

---

1. ERISA Sec. 609(a)(5).
2. 29 C.F.R. pt. 2590; 65 Fed. Reg. 82,128 (Dec. 27, 2000).

Under the final rules, the two-part NMSN would be issued to an employer of a noncustodial parent. Part A, the employer withholding notice, advises employers of an identified employee's obligation to provide medical coverage for a child (or children) to whom the QMCSO applies. Within 20 business days, the employer is then required to forward Part B of the NMSN, the "Medical Support Notice to Plan Administrator," to its group health plan administrator. Under Part A, the employer is also required to withhold from the earnings of the employee any participant contributions required under the plan for coverage of the identified child and to transmit those amounts to the plan.

The plan administrator, after receipt of Part B, would determine whether group health coverage of the child is available under plan provisions, whether the child has been enrolled in the plan, and, if not, what steps must be taken to provide coverage under the plan. The plan administrator is required to provide a report back to the state issuing the NMSM within forty days of receipt of the Notice.[1]

Under the final rules, an employer must provide covered benefits to a child under its group health plan even if:

1.   The child is born out of wedlock;

2.   The child does not reside within the plan's service area;

3.   The employee does not claim the child as a dependent; or

4.   The child would have to be added outside the plan's open enrollment period.

Part A of the NMSN contained in the rules includes a draft "employer response" form, which an employer would complete and file with a state if health coverage does not exist or if state or federal withholding limitations preclude the employer from withholding. The employer response also contains general instructions that identify the various types of health coverage that may be required by the QMCSO, and a warning that penalties may apply if the employer fails to withhold pursuant to the NMSN.

Health Savings Accounts

205. Are employer-provided HSAs ERISA-covered Plans?

According to DOL Field Assistance Bulletin 2004-1, ERISA will not apply to an employee's health savings account (HSA) even though the employer contributes to the account, as long as the employee's HSA was established voluntarily and the employer's involvement is minimal.[2]

Normally, a welfare benefit plan described in ERISA Section 3(1) that is established, maintained, or contributed to by an employer is covered by ERISA. But Labor Regulation Section 2510.3-1(j) provides a safe harbor under which an employee benefit arrangement *will not* be subject to ERISA if:

1.   There are no employer contributions;

2.   Employee participation is voluntary;

---

1. 29 C.F.R. pt. 2590; 65 Fed. Reg. 82,128 (Dec. 27, 2000).
2. DOL Field Assistance Bull. 2004-1 (Apr. 7, 2004).

3.   The employer does not endorse the program; and

4.   The employer receives no consideration in connection with the program, other than reasonable compensation for administrative services actually rendered in connection with payroll deductions.

The DOL states that HSAs are personal health care savings vehicles under the control of the account beneficiary, and HSA funds cannot be used to pay group health insurance premiums. Therefore, although employer contributions to a group health plan are generally considered to be persuasive that the arrangement is one covered by ERISA, employer contributions to HSAs are not significant in applying a similar analysis to HSAs. In reviewing the recently enacted HSA guidance, the DOL says that HSAs meeting the safe harbor criteria of Labor Regulation Section 2510.3-1(j) would not be considered "welfare benefit plans" subject to ERISA.

In fleshing this position out, FAB 2004-1 holds that it will not find that employer contributions to HSAs give rise to an ERISA plan where establishment of the HSAs is completely voluntary on the part of the employees, as long as the employer does *not*:

1.   Limit the ability of eligible individuals to move their funds to another HSA beyond restrictions imposed by IRC Section 223;

2.   Impose conditions on use of HSA funds beyond those permitted under IRC Section 223;

3.   Make or influence the investment decisions with respect to funds contributed to an HSA;

4.   Represent that the HSAs are an employee welfare benefit plan established or maintained by the employer; or

5.   Receive any payment or compensation in connection with an HSA.

Safe harbor treatment would still apply in the event the employer: (1) imposes terms and conditions on contributions that would be required to satisfy requirements of IRC Section 223; or (2) limits the forwarding of contributions through its payroll system to a single HSA provider (or permits only a limited number of HSA providers to advertise or market their HSA products in the workplace) unless the employer or the HSA provider restricts the employee's ability to move funds to another HSA beyond the restrictions imposed by IRC Section 223.

Of course, FAB 2004-1 cautions that the guidance offered therein does not exempt from ERISA coverage the high-deductible health care plans with which HSAs are affiliated. That must be determined as a separate issue.

Genetic Information Nondiscrimination Act

206. What is the Genetic Information Nondiscrimination Act of 2008, and what restrictions under ERISA does it place on group health plans?

On May 21, 2008, the Genetic Information Nondiscrimination Act of 2008[1] was signed into law by President George W. Bush. Sections 101 through 104 of GINA amended ERISA, the

---

1. GINA 2008, Pub. L. No. 110-233).

Internal Revenue Code, the Social Security Act, and the Public Health Service Act to prohibit discrimination against an individual on the basis of the individual's genetic information in regard to hiring, discharge, compensation, terms, conditions, or privileges of employment.[1] Covered entities, under GINA, are prohibited from discriminating against any individual in retaliation against the individual for opposition to any act or practice made unlawful by GINA, or against such individual who has made a charge, testified, assisted, or participated in any manner in any investigation, proceeding, or hearing under GINA.[2] Title II of GINA restricts the requesting, requiring, or purchasing of genetic information by covered entities, prohibits use of genetic information in employment decision making, requires that genetic information be kept confidential, and places strict limits on disclosure of genetic information.[3] "Manifestation" or "manifested" means, that an individual has been or could reasonably be diagnosed with a disease, disorder, or pathological condition by a health care professional with appropriate training and expertise in the field of medicine. A disease, disorder, or pathological condition is not manifested if the diagnosis is based principally on genetic information.[4]

Specifically, it prohibits group health plans and group health insurance issuers from using genetic information to adjust premium or contribution amounts for the group covered under the plan.[5] However, group health plans and group health issuers may increase the premium rate for an employer based on the manifestation of a disease or disorder of an individual enrolled in the plan. The manifestation of a disease or disorder in one individual cannot be used as genetic information about other group members to increase premiums.[6] The IRS, DOL and HHS have jointly released interim final rules prohibiting discrimination based on genetic information in health insurance coverage and group health plans. The rules implement GINA's group and individual market requirements, which generally parallel one another. For purposes of these rules, the term "genetic information" includes family medical history.[7]

A "covered entity" for purposes of GINA means an employer, employing office, employment agency, labor organization, or joint labor-management committee.[8] "Employee" for purposes of GINA means "an individual employed by a covered entity, as well as an applicant for employment and a former employee."[9] "Employer" under GINA means "any person that employs an employee defined above, and any agent of such person, except that, as limited by section 701(b)(1) and (2) of the Civil Rights Act of 1964, 42 U.S.C. 2000e(b) (1) and (2), an employer does not include an Indian tribe, or a bona fide private club (other than a labor organization) that is exempt from taxation under section 501(c) of the Internal Revenue Code of 1986."[10]

---

1. 29 C.F.R. §1635.4(a).
2. 29 C.F.R. §1635.7.
3. 75 Fed. Reg. 68,912 (Nov. 9, 2010).
4. 29 C.F.R. §1635.3(g).
5. ERISA Sec. 702(b)(3)(A), *as added by* Section 101(a)(2) of GINA.
6. ERISA Sec. 702(b)(3)(B), *as added by* Section 101(a)(2) of GINA.
7. 29 C.F.R. §2590.701-2 et seq.; 74 Fed. Reg. 51,664 (Oct. 7, 2009).
8. 29 C.F.R. §1635.2(b).
9. 29 C.F.R. §1635.2(c).
10. 29 C.F.R. §1635.2(d).

GINA also creates ERISA Section 702(c), which prohibits group health plans and group health issuers from requesting or requiring an individual or family member of an individual to undergo a genetic test.[1] Group health plans and group health issuers are not precluded from obtaining or using the results of a genetic test to make a determination regarding payment. However, they are limited to using only the minimum amount of information necessary.[2]

Activities conducted in determining and making a plan "payment" include: (a) the activities undertaken by a health plan to obtain premiums or determine or fulfill its responsibility for coverage and provision of benefits under the health plan; (b) the activities undertaken by a health care provider or a health plan to obtain or provide reimbursement for the provision of health care; and (c) the above activities in relation to an individual to whom health care is provided, including:

   i.   such matters as determinations of eligibility and coverage (including coordination of benefits or the determination of cost-sharing amounts); and

   ii.   adjudication or subrogation of health benefits claims, as well as risk-adjusting amounts due based on enrollee health status and demographic characteristics, billing claims management, pre-certification, etc.[3]

The restriction on a group health plan or group health insurer requesting an individual or an individual's family member from undergoing a genetic test does not limit the authority of a health care professional who is providing health care services to an individual to request that such individual undergo a genetic test.[4]

GINA also places the following prohibitions on group health plans and group health insurers regarding the collection of genetic information:

   1.   The request, requirement, or purchase of genetic information for underwriting purposes (as defined under ERISA Section 733, below); and

   2.   The request, requirement, or purchase of genetic information with respect to any individual prior to such individual's enrollment under the plan or coverage in connection with such enrollment.[5]

If a group health plan or group health insurer obtains genetic information incidental to request-ing, requiring, or purchasing other information concerning any individual, such requirement, request, or purchase will not be considered a violation of the restriction regarding individual genetic information gathering in connection with enrollment if such request, requirement, or purchase has not been done for purposes of underwriting.[6] Furthermore, a covered entity may not request, require, or purchase genetic information of an individual or family member of the

---

1. ERISA Sec. 702(c)(1), *as added by* Section 101(b) of GINA.
2. ERISA Secs. 702(c)(3)(A) and 702(c)(3)(B), as added by Section 101(b) of GINA.
3. 45 C.F.R. §164.501.
4. ERISA Sec. 702(c)(2), *as added by* Section 101(b) of GINA.
5. ERISA Secs. 702(d)(1) and 702(d)(2), as added by Section 101(b) of GINA. Interim Final Rule, 29 C.F.R. §2590.702-1(c)(4)(D)(2); 74 Fed. Reg. 51,664 (Oct. 7, 2009).
6. ERISA Sec. 702(d)(3), *as added by* Section 101(b) of GINA.

individual, except as specifically provided below. "Request" includes conducting an Internet search on an individual in a way that is likely to result in a covered entity obtaining genetic information; actively listening to third-party conversations or searching an individual's personal effects for the purpose of obtaining genetic information; and making requests for information about an individual's current health status in a way that is likely to result in a covered entity's obtaining genetic information.[1] The prohibition against requesting, requiring, or purchasing genetic information does not apply where a covered entity inadvertently requests or requires genetic information of the individual or family member of the individual.[2]

If a covered entity acquires genetic information in response to a lawful request for medical information, the acquisition of genetic information will not generally be considered inadvertent unless the covered entity directs the individual and/or health care provider from whom it requested medical information (in writing, or verbally, where the covered entity does not typically make requests for medical information in writing) not to provide genetic information.[3] If a covered entity uses a notice containing language such as the following, any receipt of genetic information in response to the request for medical information will be deemed inadvertent: "The Genetic Information Nondiscrimination Act of 2008 (GINA) prohibits employers and other entities covered by GINA Title II from requesting or requiring genetic information of an individual or family member of the individual, except as specifically allowed by this law. To comply with this law, we are asking that you not provide any genetic information when responding to this request for medical information. 'Genetic information' as defined by GINA, includes an individual's family medical history, the results of an individual's or family member's genetic tests, the fact that an individual or an individual's family member sought or received genetic services, and genetic information of a fetus carried by an individual or an individual's family member or an embryo lawfully held by an individual or family member receiving assistive reproductive services."[4] A covered entity's failure to give such a notice or to use this or similar language will not prevent it from establishing that a particular receipt of genetic information was inadvertent if its request for medical information was not "likely to result in a covered entity obtaining genetic information" (for example, where an overly broad response is received in response to a tailored request for medical information).[5] The term "genetic information" for purposes of GINA does not include information about the sex or age of any individual, the sex or age of family members, or information about the race or ethnicity of the individual or family members that is not derived from a genetic test.[6]

The provisions of GINA Title II are not intended to apply to uses and disclosures of health information governed by the HIPAA Privacy Rule.[7] Therefore, nothing in the proposed regulations under GINA should be construed as applying to the use or disclosure of genetic information that is protected health information subject to the HIPAA Privacy Rule.[8]

---

1. 29 C.F.R. §1635.8(a).
2. 29 C.F.R. §1635.8(b)(1).
3. 29 C.F.R. §1635.8(b)(1)(i)(A).
4. 29 C.F.R. §1635.8(b)(1)(i)(B).
5. 29 C.F.R. §1635.8(b)(1)(i)(C).
6. ERISA Sec. 733(d)(6)(C), *as added by* Section 101(d) of GINA; 29 C.F.R. §1635.3(c)(2).
7. GINA Sec. 206(c).
8. 29 C.F.R. §1635.9(c).

The DOL has published a series of fourteen FAQs focusing on the requirements of Title I of GINA under ERISA, prohibiting discrimination in group health plan coverage based on genetic information. These FAQs are available at http://www.dol.gov/ebsa/faqs/faq-GINA.html.

207. When may a group health plan or group health insurance issuer request a participant or beneficiary to undergo a genetic test?

A group health plan or group health insurer may request, but not require, a participant or beneficiary to undergo a genetic test if each of the following conditions is met:

1. The request is made, in writing, pursuant to HIPAA rules for the protection of the subjects of human medical testing, or equivalent federal regulations, and any applicable state or local laws or regulations for the protection of human subjects in research;

2. The plan clearly indicates to each participant or beneficiary, or in the case of a minor child, to the legal guardian of such beneficiary, to whom the request is made that:

    i. compliance with the request is voluntary, and

    ii. noncompliance will have no effect on enrollment status or premium or contribution amounts;

3. No genetic information collected or acquired under ERISA Section 702(c)(4) shall be used for underwriting purposes;

4. The plan or issuer notifies the DOL in writing that the plan or issuer is conducting activities pursuant to the exceptions provided under ERISA Section 702(c)(4), including a description of the activities conducted; and

5. The plan or issuer complies with such other conditions as the DOL may, by regulation, require for activities conducted under ERISA Section 702(c)(4).[1]

208. How are "family member" and "family medical history" defined for purposes of GINA?

"Family member" for purposes of GINA, means with respect to any individual:

(A) A person who is a dependent of that individual as the result of marriage, birth, adoption, or placement for adoption; or

(B) A first-degree, second-degree, third-degree, or fourth-degree relative of the individual, or of a dependent of the individual under one, above.[2]

First-degree relatives include an individual's parents, siblings, and children. Second-degree relatives include an individual's grandparents, grandchildren, uncles, aunts, nephews,

---

1. ERISA Secs. 702(c)(4)(A) to 702(c)(4) (E), *as added by* Section 101(b) of GINA.
2. 29 C.F.R. §1635.3(a)(1).

nieces, and half-siblings. Third-degree relatives include an individual's great-grandparents, great grandchildren, great uncles/aunts, and first cousins. Fourth-degree relatives include an individual's great-great-grandparents, great-great-grandchildren, and first cousins once-removed (i.e., the children of the individual's first cousins).[1]

"Family medical history" for purposes of GINA means information about the manifestation of disease or disorder in family members of the individual.[2]

209. What are the provisions of GINA that apply to pregnant individuals and beneficiaries and their fetuses?

Any reference in ERISA Section 702 to genetic information concerning an individual or a family member of an individual: (1) must include with respect to such individual or family member of an individual who is pregnant, genetic information of any fetus carried by such pregnant woman; (2) and with respect to an individual or family member utilizing assisting reproductive technology, must include genetic information of any embryo legally held by the individual or family member.[3]

Under the proposed regulations, the genetic information of a fetus carried by a covered individual or by a pregnant woman who is a family member of the covered individual includes the genetic information of any embryo legally held by the covered individual or a family member using assisted reproductive technology.[4]

210. How is "genetic test" defined for purposes of GINA?

"Genetic test," for purposes of GINA, means an analysis of human DNA, RNA, chromosomes, proteins, or metabolites that detects genotypes, mutations, or chromosomal changes.[5] "Genetic test" does not include: an analysis of proteins or metabolites that does not detect genotypes, mutations, or chromosomal changes; or an analysis of proteins or metabolites that is directly related to a manifested disease, disorder, or pathological condition that could reasonably be detected by a health care professional with appropriate training and expertise in the field of medicine involved.[6]

Genetic tests include, but are not limited to:

1. A test to determine whether someone has the BRCA1 or BRCA2 variant evidencing a predisposition to breast cancer, a test to determine whether someone has a genetic variant associated with hereditary nonpolyposis colon cancer, and a test for a genetic variant for Huntington's Disease;

2. Carrier screening for adults using genetic analysis to determine the risk of conditions such as cystic fibrosis, sickle cell anemia, spinal muscular atrophy, or fragile X syndrome in future offspring;

---

1. 29 C.F.R. §1635.3(a)(2)(i)-(iv).
2. 29 C.F.R. §1635.3(b).
3. ERISA Secs. 702(f)(1) and 702(f)(2), as added by Section 101(c) of GINA.
4. 29 C.F.R. §1635.3(c)(1)(v), 74 Fed. Reg. 9056 (Mar. 2, 2009).
5. ERISA Sec. 733(d)(7)(A), as added by Section 101(d) of GINA.
6. ERISA Secs. 733(d)(7)(B)(i) and 733(d)(7)B)(ii), *as added by* Section 101(d) of GINA.

3. Amniocentesis and other evaluations used to determine the presence of genetic abnormalities in a fetus during pregnancy;

4. Newborn screening analysis that uses DNA, RNA, protein, or metabolite analysis to detect or indicate genotypes, mutations, or chromosomal changes, such as a test for PKU performed so that treatment can begin before a disease manifests;

5. Preimplantation genetic diagnosis performed on embryos created using in vitro fertilization;

6. Pharmacogenetic tests that detect genotypes, mutations, or chromosomal changes that indicate how an individual will react to a drug or a particular dosage of a drug;

7. DNA testing to detect genetic markers that are associated with information about ancestry; and

8. DNA testing that reveals family relationships, such as paternity.[1]

The following are examples of tests or procedures that are not genetic tests:

1. An analysis of proteins or metabolites that does not detect genotypes, mutations, or chromosomal changes;

2. A medical examination that tests for the presence of a virus that is not composed of human DNA, RNA, chromosomes, proteins, or metabolites;

3. A test for infectious and communicable diseases that may be transmitted through food handling;

4. Complete blood counts, cholesterol tests, and liver-function tests; and

5. A test for the presence of alcohol or illegal drugs.[2]

A test to determine whether an individual has a genetic predisposition for alcoholism or drug use is a genetic test.[3]

211. How is "underwriting purposes" defined for group health insurance issuers under GINA?

The term "underwriting purposes" for purposes of GINA means, with respect to any group health plan or group health insurance coverage offered in connection with a group health plan:

1. Rules for, or determination of, eligibility (including enrollment and continued eligibility) for benefits under the plan or coverage;

2. The computation of premium or contribution amounts under the plan or coverage;

---

1. 29 C.F.R. §1635.3(f)(2)(i)-(viii).
2. 29 C.F.R. §§1635.3(f)(3)(i)-(v), 1635.3(f)(4)(i).
3. 29 C.F.R. §1635.3(f)(4)(ii).

3.   The application of any preexisting-condition exclusion under the plan or coverage; and

4.   Other activities related to the creation, renewal, or replacement of a contract of
health insurance or health benefits.[1]

On January 25, 2013, HHS issued the omnibus final rule on HIPAA and HITECH.[2] The final
rule adopts the 2009 interim final rule "Prohibiting Discrimination based on Genetic Information
in Health Insurance Coverage and Group Health Plans that provided that the prohibition against
collection of genetic information for underwriting purposes is construed broadly to include rules
for eligibility for benefits and the computation of premium or contribution amounts.[3] Section
105 of GINA requires HHS to modify the Privacy Rule to prohibit ''a covered entity that is a
group health plan, health insurance issuer that issues health insurance coverage, or issuer of a
Medicare supplemental policy'' from using or disclosing genetic information for underwriting
purposes. In the NPRM, the Department, using both its authority under GINA as well as
its broad authority under HIPAA, proposed to apply the prohibition on using and disclosing
protected health information that is genetic information for underwriting to all health plans
that are subject to the Privacy Rule, rather than solely to the plans GINA explicitly requires be
subject to the prohibition. The final rule adopts the approach of the proposed rule to apply the
prohibition on using or disclosing protected health information that is genetic information for
underwriting purposes to all health plans that are covered entities under the HIPAA Privacy
Rule, including those to which GINA does not expressly apply, except with regard to issuers
of long term care policies.

The final rule modifies HHS regulations under the Privacy Rule to: (1) Revise the definition
of "health information" to make clear that the term includes "genetic information;" (2) add
definitions for the GINA-related terms of "family member," "genetic information," "genetic
services," "genetic test," and "manifestation or manifested;" and (3) make technical corrections
to the definition of "health plan."[4]

For purposes of determining whether a benefit is medically appropriate, plans and insurers
may use genetic information (limited to the minimum necessary amount) without violating the
prohibition on using genetic information for underwriting purposes.[5]

212. What are the exceptions under GINA for wellness programs?

Where a covered entity offers health or genetic services, including such services offered as
part of a voluntary wellness program, the exceptions to the prohibitions on the acquisition of
genetic information apply where:

1.   The provision of genetic information by the individual is voluntary (the covered
entity neither requires the individual to provide genetic information nor penalizes
those who choose not to provide it);

---

1. ERISA Sec. 733(d)(9), as added by Section 101(d) of GINA.
2. 78 Fed. Reg. 5566, (Jan. 25, 2013).
3. Interim Final Rule, 29 CFR 2590.702-1(c)(4)(D)(1)(i) and 2590.702-1(c)(4)(D)(1)(ii), 74 Fed. Reg. 51664 (Oct. 7, 2009).
4. 45 CFR 160.103; 45 CFR 164.502(a)(5); 78 Fed. Reg. 5566, (Jan. 25, 2013).
5. Interim Final Rule, 29 C.F.R. §2590.702-1(c)(4)(D)(1)(iii); 74 Fed. Reg. 51,664 (Oct. 7, 2009).

2.   The individual provides prior knowing, voluntary, and written authorization (written in a manner reasonably likely to be understood), which may include authorization in electronic format (which also describes the type of genetic information that will be obtained and the general purposes for which it will be used; and describes the restrictions on disclosure of genetic information);

3.   Individually identifiable genetic information is provided only to the individual (or family member if the family member is receiving genetic services) and the licensed health care professionals or board-certified genetic counselors involved in providing such services, and is not accessible to managers, supervisors, or others who make employment decisions, or to anyone else in the workplace; and

4.   Any individually identifiable genetic information provided is only available for purposes of such services and is not disclosed to the covered entity except in aggregate terms that do not disclose the identity of specific individuals (a covered entity will not violate the requirement that it receives information only in aggregate terms if it receives information that, for reasons outside the control of the provider or the covered entity (such as the small number of participants), makes the genetic information of a particular individual readily identifiable with no effort on the covered entity's part).[1]

A covered entity may not offer a financial inducement for individuals to provide genetic information but may offer financial inducements for completion of health risk assessments that include questions about family medical history or other genetic information, provided the covered entity makes clear, in language reasonably likely to be understood by those completing the health risk assessment, that the inducement will be made available whether or not the participant answers questions regarding genetic information.[2]

A covered entity may offer financial inducements to encourage individuals who have voluntarily provided genetic information (e.g., family medical history) that indicates that they are at increased risk of acquiring a health condition in the future to participate in disease management programs or other programs that promote healthy lifestyles, and/or to meet particular health goals as part of a health or genetic service. However, to comply with Title II of GINA, these programs must also be offered to individuals with current health conditions and/or to individuals whose lifestyle choices put them at increased risk of developing a condition.[3]

213. What are the statutory penalties for violations of GINA?

GINA amends ERISA Section 502 to allow the DOL to impose a penalty of $100 per day/per individual affected against any plan sponsor of a group health plan, or any health insurance issuer offering health insurance coverage in connection with the plan. And, for any failure to satisfy the requirements regarding the provisions of ERISA added and amended by GINA.

---

1. 29 C.F.R. §1635.8(b)(2)(i)(A), (B)(1)-(3), (C), and (D).
2. 29 C.F.R. §1635.8(b)(2)(ii).
3. 29 C.F.R. §1635.8(b)(2)(iii).

Specifically, the penalty applies to noncompliance regarding genetic information with respect to each participant or beneficiary to whom such failure relates.[1]

For purposes of imposition of the $100 daily penalty, the term "noncompliance period" means, with respect to any failure, the period beginning on the date such failure first occurs and ending on the date the failure is corrected.[2]

In the case of one or more failures with respect to a participant or beneficiary that are not corrected before the date on which the plan receives notice from the DOL of such violation, and that occurred or continued during the period involved, the amount of the penalty imposed by reason of such failure with respect to such participant or beneficiary shall not be less than $2,500. To the extent violations are more than *de minimis*, the amount of the penalty with respect to such participant or beneficiary shall not be less than $15,000.[3]

However, no penalties will apply on any failure during any period for which it is established to the satisfaction of the DOL that the person otherwise liable for such penalty did not know, and exercising reasonable diligence would not have known, that such failure to comply with GINA existed.[4]

Furthermore, no penalty will apply on any failure to comply with GINA if such failure was due to reasonable cause and not willful neglect, and is corrected during the thirty-day period beginning on the first date the person otherwise liable for such penalty knew, or exercising reasonable diligence would have known, that such failure existed.[5]

In the case of failures that are due to reasonable cause and not to willful neglect, the penalty shall not exceed the amount equal to the lesser of: (a) 10 percent of the aggregate amount paid or incurred by the plan sponsor (or predecessor plan sponsor) during the taxable year for group health plans, or (b) $500,000.[6]

In the case of a failure that is due to reasonable cause and not to willful neglect, the DOL may waive all or part of the penalty to the extent that the payment of such penalty would be excessive relative to the failure involved.[7]

Every covered entity is required to post and keep posted in conspicuous places upon its premises where notices to employees, applicants for employment, and members are customarily posted a notice to be prepared or approved by the EEOC setting forth excerpts from or, summaries of, the pertinent provisions of this regulation and information pertinent to the filing of a complaint. A willful violation of this requirement is punishable by a fine of not more than $100 for each separate offense.[8]

---

1. ERISA Secs. 502(a)(9)(A) and 502(a)(9)(B)(i), *as amended by* Section 101(e) of GINA.
2. ERISA Secs. 502(a)(9)(B)(ii)(I) and 502(a)(9)(B)(ii)(II), *as amended by* Section 101(e) of GINA.
3. ERISA Secs. 502(a)(9)(C)(i) and 502(a)(9)(C)(ii), *as amended by* Section 101(e) of GINA.
4. ERISA Sec. 502(a)(9)(D)(i), *as amended by* Section 101(e) of GINA.
5. ERISA Sec. 502(a)(9)(D)(ii), *as amended by* Section 101(e) of GINA.
6. ERISA Secs. 501(a)(9)(D)(iii)(I) and 501(a)(9)(D)(iii)(II), *as amended by* Section 101(e) of GINA.
7. ERISA Sec. 502(a)(9)(E), *as amended by* Section 101(e) of GINA.
8. 29 C.F.R. §1635.10(c).

Michelle's Law

214. What is "Michelle's Law," and how does it apply to students with medical coverage under their parents' health care plan?

"Michelle's Law" is legislation that was signed into law in November 2008.[1] It ensures the continuity of health plan coverage for students covered under their parents' health care plan who, because of injury or illness, are unable to maintain full-time student status. The law is named in memory of Michelle Morse, a full-time college student who was forced to maintain a full-time college course load while undergoing extensive chemotherapy for colon cancer in order to maintain health insurance coverage. Her parents' health care plan only extended coverage to adult children while they were full-time college students.

Prior to Michelle's law, ERISA and the Internal Revenue Code did not prohibit the ability of a health plan to terminate coverage of a covered dependent who was a full-time student in a post-secondary program if the student had to leave full-time status for medical reasons. The new law prohibits group health plans from terminating such coverage. Specifically, Michelle's Law prevents a group health plan from terminating coverage of a dependent child due to a medically necessary leave of absence, before the earlier of:

1. The date that is one year after the first day of the medically necessary leave of absence; or

2. The date on which the coverage would otherwise terminate under the plan's terms.[2]

"Medically necessary leave of absence" is defined for purposes of this statute as:

1. The child's leave of absence from a post-secondary educational institution; or

2. "Any other change in enrollment" of the child at the institution, that:

   i. begins while the child is suffering from serious illness or injury;

   ii. is certified as medically necessary by an attending physician; and

   iii. causes the child to lose student status for purposes of coverage, under the terms of the plan or coverage.[3]

Under Michelle's Law, a "dependent child" is defined as a group health plan beneficiary who:

1. Is a dependent child of a plan participant or beneficiary under the plan's terms; and

2. Was enrolled in the plan, based on being a student at a post-secondary educational institution immediately before the first day of the medically necessary leave of absence.[4]

---

1. Pub. L. No. 110-381 (Oct. 9, 2008); H.R. 2851, signed into law by President Bush on November 8, 2008.
2. ERISA Secs. 714(b)(1)(A) and 714(b)(1)(B); IRC Secs. 9813(b)(1)(A) and 9813(b)(1)(B).
3. ERISA Secs. 714(a)(1), 714(a)(2), and 714(a)(3); IRC Secs. 9813(a)(1), 9813(a)(2), and 9813(a)(3).
4. ERISA Secs. 714(b)(2)(A) and 714(b)(2)(B); IRC Secs. 9813(b)(2)(A) and 9813(b)(2)(B).

In order to maintain the coverage, the plan or the health insurer issuing coverage under the plan must receive a written certification from the treating physician attesting that the covered dependent is suffering from a serious illness or injury and that the leave of absence or change of enrollment is medically necessary.[1]

A plan must include a description of the rules for certification of student status for coverage under a group health plan requiring continued coverage during medically necessary leaves of absence in a language that is understandable to the typical plan participant.[2]

During the medically necessary leave of absence, the dependent child must be entitled to the same benefits as if the child had continued to be a student at the post-secondary educational institution and was not on a medically necessary leave of absence.[3]

If the dependent child's coverage changes during the medically necessary leave of absence, the child is entitled to continued coverage for the remainder of the period of the medically necessary leave of absence, in the same manner as the coverage would have applied if the changed coverage had been the previous coverage, as long as:

1. The dependent child of a participant or beneficiary is in a period of coverage under the group health plan, pursuant to the child's medically necessary leave of absence;

2. The manner in which the participant or beneficiary is covered under the plan changes, whether through a change in health insurance coverage or health insurance issuer, a change between health insurance coverage and self-insured coverage, or otherwise; and

3. The coverage, as so changed, continues to provide coverage of beneficiaries as dependent children.[4]

---

1. ERISA Sec 714(b)(3); IRC Sec. 9813(b)(3).
2. ERISA Sec. 714(c); IRC Sec. 9813(c).
3. ERISA Sec. 714(d); IRC Sec. 9813(d).
4. ERISA Secs. 714(e)(1), 714(e)(2), and 714(e)(3); IRC Secs. 9813(e)(1), 9813(e)(2), and 9813(e)(3).

SECTION III

Fiduciaries

215. Who is an ERISA fiduciary?

The term "fiduciary" is broadly defined to include any *person* (see Q 216) who: (1) exercises any discretionary authority or discretionary control respecting management of the plan; (2) exercises any authority or control respecting management or disposition of its assets; (3) renders investment advice for a fee or other compensation, direct or indirect, with respect to any moneys or other property of the plan, or has any authority or responsibility to do so; or (4) has any discretionary authority or discretionary responsibility in the administration of the plan.[1]

It is important to determine who the fiduciaries are of any employee benefit plan covered by ERISA because parties who are considered fiduciaries with respect to the plan have specified duties and responsibilities, must conduct plan business under established standards of care, and are prohibited from engaging or causing the plan to engage in certain transactions under ERISA. Fiduciaries that breach these requirements are often held liable for actions taken with respect to the plan.

In late 2010, the DOL released proposed regulations that have a significant impact on determining fiduciary status regarding advice and management decisions focusing on plan assets.[2] You will find a detailed analysis of these proposed regulations and the impact they have on plan assets and individuals involved in the decisions and management of them under Q 240. The DOL has announced that it will re-propose regulations on the definition of an ERISA fiduciary in the context of persons giving investment advice to an employee benefit plan or plan participants. The previously proposed regulations would have updated a 1975 regulation defining when a person providing investment advice becomes a fiduciary under ERISA, in order to adapt the rule to the current retirement marketplace. The proposal's goal is to ensure that potential conflicts of interest among advisers are not allowed to compromise the quality of investment advice that millions of American workers rely on, so they can retire with the dignity that they have worked hard to achieve. While the DOL anticipated this rule's being released in early 2012, as of October 30, 2013, the DOL had not released the final rule.[3]

216. What types of "persons" can be fiduciaries?

The term "person" means any individual, partnership, joint venture, corporation, mutual company, joint-stock company, trust, estate, unincorporated organization, association, or employee organization.[4]

217. How is fiduciary status determined under ERISA?

A person can be deemed a fiduciary by performing certain specified acts (see Q 215) with or without authority to do so, by holding certain positions with duties and responsibilities that

---

1. ERISA Secs. 3(21)(A) and 3(9).
2. Prop. Labor Reg. §2510.3-21; 75 Fed. Reg. 65,263 (Oct. 22, 2010).
3. DOL News Release No. 11-1382-NAT (Sept. 19, 2011).
4. ERISA Sec. 3(9).

require by their very nature, performance of those acts, or by being expressly designated or named as a fiduciary in the plan document.[1]

In the case of *Leimkuehler v. American United Life Insurance Co.*, the Seventh Circuit Court of Appeals has held that neither actions taken by plan recordkeeper nor authority reserved by that recordkeeper to substitute or delete available investment funds as plan options made it a functional fiduciary. The Court reasoned that actual actions or exercise of authority must involve the basis of the claims that allege the fiduciary breach. The claims presented by the plaintiff focused on actions taken by AUL that would allegedly violate ERISA's fiduciary standards if AUL is acting in the capacity of a fiduciary of the plan. In order for the case to proceed to the merits of whether AUL violated fiduciary duties by receiving revenue sharing compensation, the plaintiffs required the court to find that AUL was a fiduciary of the plan. Since AUL was not a named fiduciary in the plan, its fiduciary responsibility must stem from its status as a functional fiduciary. AUL's contractual reservation of the right to substitute or delete funds made available to the plan participants was not, in itself, an exercise of authority or control, especially since AUL never affirmatively exercised its contractual right in a way that gives rise to a claim of fiduciary breach the Seventh Circuit ruled. Since the court did not find AUL to be a fiduciary, it did not rule on whether the revenue-sharing arrangement resulted in a breach of fiduciary duty.[2]

218. How is a person deemed a fiduciary?

Any person who performs one or more of the fiduciary functions described in ERISA Section 3(21)(A) (see Q 215) performs activities that confer fiduciary status. "The term fiduciary is to be broadly construed and a person's title does not necessarily determine if one is a fiduciary."[3] "ERISA defines 'fiduciary' not in terms of formal trusteeship, but in functional terms of control and authority over the plan, thus expanding the universe of persons subject to fiduciary duties."[4]

Status as a fiduciary is determined by a person's functions with respect to the plan, rather than by the person's title, office, or formal designation. Under this functional test, fiduciary status is determined with reference to an individual's activities with respect to a plan and does not depend upon a formal undertaking or agreement.[5] Additionally, it is the nature and extent of a person's duties and responsibilities with respect to the plan that determines a person's status as a fiduciary.[6] A person becomes a fiduciary under ERISA Section 3(21)(A) "only when fulfilling certain defined functions, including the exercise of discretionary authority or control over plan management or administration."[7] A party is considered a fiduciary to the extent it actually exercises control over the disposition of plan assets, even if it did not possess any discretionary authority.[8] The absence of any grant of authority does not automatically preclude a finding of

---

1. ERISA Sec. 3(21)(A).

2. *Leimkuehler v. American United Life Insurance Co.*, 713 F.3d 905 (7th Cir. Ind. April 16, 2013)."

3. *Consolidated Beef Indus., Inc. v. New York Life Ins. Co.*, 949 F.2d 960 (8th Cir. 1991), cert. denied, 503 U.S. 985 (1992).

4. *Mertens v. Hewitt Assocs.*, 508 U.S. 248 (1993).

5. H.R. Conf. Rep. No. 93-1280, 93d Cong., 2d Sess. 323 (1974) (ERISA Conference Report).

6. *Swint v. Protective Life Ins. Co.*, 779 F. Supp. 532 (S.D. Ala. 1991).

7. *Lockheed Corp. v. Spink*, 116 S. Ct. 1783 (1996) (quoting *Siskind v. Sperry Ret. Program*, 47 F.3d 498 (2d Cir. 1995)).

8. *Slyman v. Equitable Life Assurance Soc'y*, 1987 U.S. Dist. LEXIS 8652 (N.D.N.Y. 1987).

fiduciary status.[1] "[T]he linchpin of fiduciary status under ERISA is discretion."[2] Thus, whether an individual is a fiduciary within the meaning of ERISA Section 3(21)(A) is inherently factual and will depend on the particular discretionary actions or functions that a person performs on behalf of a plan.[3]

219. What is an automatic fiduciary?

According to the Department of Labor, some offices or positions of an employee benefit plan by their very nature require persons who hold them to perform one or more of the functions described in Section 3(21)(A)(iii) of ERISA.[4] Thus, with certain exceptions, fiduciary status will automatically be conferred upon the persons who hold these positions. For instance, a plan administrator or a trustee of a plan is, per se, a fiduciary because he must have "discretionary authority or discretionary responsibility in the administration" of the plan within the meaning of ERISA Section 3(21)(A)(iii).[5] "As the administrator of the employee benefit plan, [the entity] is a fiduciary for ERISA purposes."[6] "[T]he statute, regulations and case law lead to the conclusion that trustees are fiduciaries by virtue of their position."[7]

On the other hand, a plan administrator who does not possess discretionary authority with respect to a plan is not a fiduciary for purposes of ERISA.[8] Similarly, trustees may not be considered fiduciaries where the plan instrument "does not accord the trustees any discretionary authority over investment decisions" of the plan and the plan does not name the trustees as fiduciaries.[9] Thus, whether automatic fiduciary status exists with respect to a particular office or position is dependent upon the facts and circumstances and whether the office or position performs any of the functions described in ERISA Section 3(21)(A).[10]

The United States District Court for the Northern District of Oklahoma has ruled that a chief executive officer of a plan sponsor employer who never exercised his signature power over a plan claims account was not a fiduciary where bank trustee policies prevented the CEO from accessing the claims account of the plan for purposes of making deposits, thereby eliminating the ability of the CEO to exercise any control over the funds. The court dismissed the charges against the CEO and allowed the remaining claims of breach of fiduciary duty and negligence to proceed against the plan sponsor.[11]

Conversely, the Sixth Circuit Court of Appeals has ruled that where a TPA exercised power to write checks on a plan account, it was a fiduciary.[12] In this case, the TPA alleged that it was not a fiduciary because it had contracted to provide merely ministerial services. But the Sixth Circuit

---

1. *Olson v. E.F. Hutton & Co.*, 957 F.2d 622 (8th Cir. 1992).
2. *Curcio v. John Hancock Mut. Life Ins. Co.*, 33 F.3d 226 (3d Cir. 1994).
3. Labor Reg. §§2509.75-5, 2509.75-8.
4. Labor Reg. §2509.75-8, D-3.
5. *U.S. Steel Mining Co. v. District 17, United Mine Workers of Am.*, 897 F.2d 149 (4th Cir. 1990).
6. *Reilly v. Blue Cross & Blue Shield United of Wis.*, 846 F.2d 416 (7th Cir.), cert. denied, 488 U.S. 856 (1988).
7. *Reich v. Hosking*, No. 94-CV-10363-BC, 20 EBC 1090 (E.D. Mich. 1996).
8. *Pohl v. National Benefits Consultants, Inc.*, 956 F.2d 126 (7th Cir. 1992).
9. *Arakelian v. National W. Life Ins. Co.*, 748 F. Supp. 17 (D.D.C. 1990).
10. *See* Labor Reg. §2509.75-8, D-3.
11. *Gross v. Hale-Halsell Co.*, 2006 U.S. Dist. LEXIS 66304 (N.D. Okla. 2006).
12. *Briscoe v. Fine*, 2006 U.S. App. LEXIS 9208 (6th Cir. 2006).

ruled that when the TPA paid itself an administrative fee out of the plan trust, wrote checks to pay claims, deposited COBRA premiums, and later—after terminating services—issued two checks to the employer for COBRA premiums received and for remittance of the balance of the trust, it had exercised control over the assets in such a manner as to render it a fiduciary. The case was remanded to the District Court for a determination of whether the TPA, as a fiduciary, was liable for more than $300,000 in unpaid claims under the plan.

220. What is a named fiduciary?

Every employee benefit plan must provide for one or more named fiduciaries.[1] A "named fiduciary" is a fiduciary who is named in the plan document or who is identified as a fiduciary, pursuant to a procedure specified in the plan, (1) by a person who is an employer or employee organization with respect to the plan, or (2) by such an employer and such an employee organization acting jointly.[2] The named fiduciaries have joint or several authority to control and manage the operation and administration of the plan. Since the "named fiduciary" is a fiduciary who is named in the plan document or who is identified as a fiduciary, it is the only person who is a fiduciary by title.

221. What is the purpose of having a named fiduciary?

The purpose of naming a fiduciary in the plan document is to enable employees and other interested persons to ascertain who is responsible for operating the plan. A plan must designate a named fiduciary "so that responsibility for managing and operating the plan and liability for mismanagement are focused with a degree of certainty."[3]

222. Who may be a named fiduciary?

A named fiduciary may be any "person" meeting the definition of fiduciary set forth in ERISA Section 3(21)(A). A named fiduciary may be a person whose name actually appears in the document, or may be a person who holds an office specified in the document, such as the company president. A named fiduciary also may be a person who is identified by the employer or union, under a procedure set forth in the document. For example, the plan may provide that the employer's board of directors will choose the person who manages or controls the plan. In addition, a named fiduciary may be a person identified by the employers and union acting jointly. Further, the members of a joint board of trustees of a Taft-Hartley plan would usually be named fiduciaries (see Q 640).[4]

223. How should named fiduciaries be designated in the plan document?

According to DOL guidance, the preferred practice is to explicitly designate the plan's named fiduciaries in the plan document.[5] However, the "named fiduciary" requirement of ERISA Section 402(a) is fulfilled by clearly identifying one or more persons, by name or title,

---

1. ERISA Sec. 402(a)(1).
2. ERISA Sec. 402(a)(2).
3. *Birmingham v. Sogen-Swiss Int'l Corp. Ret. Plan*, 718 F.2d 515 (2d Cir. 1983) (citing H.R. Conf. Rep. No. 93-1280, 93d Cong., 2d Sess. (1974) (ERISA Conference Report)).
4. H.R. Conf. Rep. No. 93-1280, 93d Cong., 2d Sess. 297 (1974) (ERISA Conference Report).
5. Labor Reg. §2509.75-5, FR-1.

combined with a statement that such person or persons have authority to control and manage the operation and administration of the plan. For example, a plan document that provides that "the plan committee shall control and manage the operation and administration of the plan," and specifies, by name or position, who will constitute the committee, fulfills this latter requirement. Likewise, a plan document of a union-negotiated employee benefit plan, which provides that a clearly identified joint board on which employees and employers are equally represented will control and manage the operation and administration of the plan, adequately satisfies the "named fiduciary" requirement in ERISA Section 402(a). In the latter case, the persons designated to be members of the joint board would be named fiduciaries under ERISA Section 402(a).[1]

224. May an employee benefit plan covering employees of a corporation designate the corporation as the "named fiduciary"?

Yes. The DOL has stated that under ERISA Section 402(a)(2), "a 'named fiduciary' is a fiduciary either named in the plan instrument or designated according to a procedure set forth in the plan instrument. A fiduciary is a 'person' falling within the definition of fiduciary set forth in ERISA Section 3(21)(A). A 'person' may be a corporation under the definition of person contained in ERISA Section 3(9). While such a designation satisfies the requirement of enabling employees and other interested persons to ascertain the person or persons responsible for operating the plan, a plan instrument which designates a corporation or other entity as 'named fiduciary' should provide for designation by the corporation of specified individuals or other persons to carry out specified fiduciary responsibilities under the plan...."[2]

225. Are persons who perform administrative functions fiduciaries?

A person who performs purely ministerial functions for an employee benefit plan within a framework of policies, interpretations, rules, practices, and procedures made by other persons is not a fiduciary because such a person does not perform the discretionary functions within ERISA Section 3(21)(A), nor have the power to make such decisions. These persons are not fiduciaries because they do not exercise any discretionary authority or discretionary control respecting management of the plan or the disposition of its assets.

The DOL has provided guidance concerning what types of functions will make a person a fiduciary with respect to a plan. Specifically, the following types of administrative activities are *not* considered to be fiduciary functions:[3]

1.   Application of rules determining eligibility for participation or benefits;

2.   Calculation of services and compensation credits for benefits;

3.   Preparation of employee communications material;

4.   Maintenance of participants' service and employment records;

---

1. *See* Labor Reg. §2509.75-5, FR-1.
2. Labor Reg. §2509.75-5, FR-3 (ERISA Interpretive Bull. 75-5).
3. Labor Reg. §2509.75-8, D-2.

5.   Preparation of reports required by government agencies;

6.   Calculation of benefits;

7.   Orientation of new participants and advising participants of their rights and options under the plan;

8.   Collection of contributions and application of contributions as provided in the plan;

9.   Preparation of reports concerning participant's benefits;

10.   Processing claims; and

11.   Making recommendations to others for decisions with respect to plan administration.

Pursuant to these provisions, the determination of whether a person is a fiduciary with respect to a plan, or is one who merely performs ministerial duties, requires an analysis of the types of functions performed and actions taken by the person on behalf of the plan to determine whether particular functions or actions are fiduciary in nature and, therefore, subject to ERISA's fiduciary responsibility provisions. The Fourth Circuit has ruled that plan administrators are not liable as fiduciaries for the miscalculation of benefits because the calculation of benefits is not a fiduciary function.[1]

For example, a plan might designate as a "benefit supervisor" a plan employee whose sole function is to calculate the amount of benefits to which each plan participant is entitled in accordance with a mathematical formula contained in the written instrument pursuant to which the plan is maintained. The benefit supervisor, after calculating the benefits, would then inform the plan administrator of the results of her calculations, and the plan administrator would authorize the payment of benefits to a particular plan participant. The benefit supervisor does not perform any of the functions described in ERISA Section 3(21)(A) and, therefore, is not a plan fiduciary.[2]

On the other hand, the plan might designate as a "benefit supervisor" a plan employee who has the final authority to authorize or disallow benefit payments in cases where a dispute exists as to the interpretation of plan provisions relating to eligibility for benefits. Under these circumstances, the benefit supervisor would be a fiduciary within the meaning of ERISA Section 3(21)(A).[3]

Whether a person is a fiduciary with respect to a plan or one who merely performs ministerial duties is often determined in the courts. For example, a party who performs only clerical or ministerial tasks is not a fiduciary.[4] "It is well established that one who performs only ministerial tasks is not cloaked with fiduciary status."[5] Similarly, performing administrative actions within a framework of policies established by others is not considered the exercise of fiduciary responsibility.[6] A claims processor is not a fiduciary if he has not been granted the

---

1. *Cunningham Pension Plan v. Mathieu*, 153 F.3d 720 (4th Cir. 1998).
2. See Labor Reg. §2509.75-8, D-3.
3. See Labor Reg. §2509.75-8, D-3.
4. *Pohl v. National Benefits Consultants, Inc.*, 956 F.2d 126 (7th Cir. 1992).
5. *Olson v. E.F. Hutton & Co.*, 957 F.2d 622 (8th Cir. 1992) (citing *Anoka Orthopaedic Assocs., P.A. v. Lechner*, 910 F.2d 514 (8th Cir. 1990)).
6. *Gelardi v. Pertec Computer Corp.*, 761 F.2d 1323 (9th Cir. 1985) (per curiam).

authority to review benefits denials and make the ultimate decisions regarding eligibility.[1] Nor is a plan supervisor who merely calculates claims according to the plan document a fiduciary.[2] However, a claims processor who acts beyond a purely ministerial capacity risks being deemed a fiduciary.[3]

A third-party service provider who was not identified as a plan fiduciary under plan documents and service agreements was held to be a "functional fiduciary" because the service provider undertook the discretionary authority to grant or deny claims and to write checks against plan assets to make payment on claims.[4]

Although a person who performs only functions listed above may not be a plan fiduciary, she may be subject to the bonding requirements contained in ERISA Section 412 if she handles funds or other property of the plan.[5]

226. Are professional service providers such as an attorney, accountant, consultant, or actuary fiduciaries?

Many courts have held that professional service providers such as attorneys, accountants, actuaries, or consultants who render legal, accounting, actuarial, or consulting services to employee benefit plans (other than an investment adviser to the plan) are not fiduciaries to a plan solely by virtue of the rendering of such services.[6] The courts support this position by reading the terms "discretionary authority," "discretionary control," and "discretionary responsibility" in ERISA Section 3(21)(A) as speaking to actual decision-making power, rather than to the influence that a professional may have over the decisions made by the plan trustees "that the professional advises."[7]

According to the courts, the power to act for the plan is essential to status as a fiduciary under ERISA. Thus, without the ability to exercise any decision-making authority over the plan or plan assets, lawyers, accountants, actuaries, and consultants may render services to employers, plan trustees, and plan beneficiaries without becoming a fiduciary of the plan. The mere provision of professional services to employers, plan trustees, and plan beneficiaries "does not give lawyers, accountants, and actuaries decision-making authority over the plan or plan assets, since the power to act for the plan is essential to status as ERISA fiduciary."[8] Further, attorneys do not become fiduciaries even when legal advice is commingled with incidental business observation and investment-related observations, especially in the case of giving advice to sophisticated businesspersons.[9]

---

1. *Howard v. Parisian, Inc.*, 807 F.2d 1560 (11th Cir. 1987).
2. *Confer v. Custom Eng'g Co.*, 952 F.2d 34 (3d Cir. 1991). See also *Baxter v. C.A. Muer Corp.*, 941 F.2d 451 (6th Cir. 1991) (affirming that a plan administrator was not an ERISA plan fiduciary but rather simply a claims processor).
3. *IT Corp. v. General Am. Life Ins. Co.*, 107 F.3d 1415 (9th Cir. 1997).
4. *Guardsmark, Inc. v. Blue Cross & Blue Shield of Tenn.*, 313 F. Supp. 2d 739 (W.D. Tenn. 2004).
5. Labor Reg. §2509.75-8, D-2.
6. See *Anoka Orthopaedic Assocs., P.A. v. Lechner*, 910 F.2d 514 (8th Cir. 1990) (lawyers and financial consultants); *Painters of Phila. Dist. Council v. Price Waterhouse*, 879 F.2d 1146 (3d Cir. 1989) (accountants); *Yeseta v. Baima*, 837 F.2d 380 (9th Cir. 1988) (neither attorney who reviewed plan's compliance with law nor accountant who prepared tax returns and financial statements was fiduciaries); and *Chapman v. Klemick*, 3 F.3d 1508 (11th Cir. 1993), cert. denied, 510 U.S. 1165 (1994) (attorney for plan beneficiary). See also *Nieto v. Ecker*, 845 F.2d 868 (9th Cir. 1988) (attorney who gave professional advice to a plan not a fiduciary).
7. *Pappas v. Buck Consultants, Inc.*, 923 F.2d 531 (7th Cir. 1991) (actuaries performing ordinary professional functions).
8. *Associates in Adolescent Psychiatry v. Home Life Ins. Co.*, 941 F.2d 561 (7th Cir. 1991), cert. denied, 502 U.S. 1099 (1992).
9. *Useden v. Acker*, 947 F.2d 1563 (11th Cir. 1991), cert. denied, 508 U.S. 959 (1993).

While attorneys, accountants, actuaries, and consultants performing their usual professional functions will ordinarily not be considered fiduciaries, if the factual situation in a particular case indicates that such a person exercises discretionary authority or discretionary control over the management or administration of the plan, or exercises authority or control respecting management or disposition of the plan's assets, such professionals would be regarded as fiduciaries.[1] Fiduciary status could also encompass consultants and advisers whose special expertise leads them to formulate and act on discretionary judgments while performing administrative functions not otherwise contemplated as those of a fiduciary.[2] In addition, fiduciary status was imposed on accountants when they provided far more than ministerial professional accounting services and, instead, "recommended transactions, structured deals, and provided investment advice to such an extent that they exercised effective control over the ESOP's assets, since none of the other corporate insiders had the expertise in accounting and employee benefits law needed to spin the tangled web of transactions at issue."[3]

The Seventh Circuit Court of Appeals has ruled that a pharmacy benefits manager (PBM) is not an ERISA fiduciary where the PBM lacked the "ultimate discretionary authority" over the content of the formulary and any drug-switching decisions of the underlying plan, which was contractually reserved by the plan.[4]

The health plan sued its PBM, alleging that it had breached ERISA fiduciary duties by:

1.   Not passing along to the plan 100 percent of price discounts negotiated with pharmacies and drug manufacturers; and

2.   Manipulating the drugs used under the plan to cause more manufacturer rebates to be paid to the PBM and not sharing rebates and other financial incentives with the plan.

The plan argued that the PBM was an ERISA fiduciary because: (1) it had discretion to negotiate drug prices and to administer the plan's formulary (that listed preferred brand-name drugs) and drug-switching program (that encouraged use of lower-priced drugs); and (2) the PBM controlled rebates received from drug manufacturers, which may constitute plan assets if payable to the plan. The PBM countered that it was not a fiduciary because the arm's-length contract with the plan did not require it to share discounts or rebates, but set out specific drug prices to be paid by the plan and fixed rebates to be paid by the PBM.

On appeal, the Seventh Circuit upheld the trial court, agreeing that the contract did not require the PBM to share with the plan all of the discounts and rebates it negotiated, and holding that the contract's fixed prices and rebates had resulted from arm's-length negotiations with the PBM, which did not make the PBM a fiduciary. Finally, the court rejected the plan asset argument, holding that the PBM did not collect rebates on behalf of the plan but rather controlled its own assets in making any contractually required rebate payments to the plan.

1. Labor Reg. §2509.75-5, D-1.
2. *Eaton v. D'Amato*, 581 F. Supp. 743 (D.D.C. 1980) (citing H.R. Conf. Rep. No. 93-1280, 93d Cong., 2d Sess. 323 (1974) (ERISA Conference Report)).
3. *Martin v. Feilen*, 965 F.2d 660 (8th Cir. 1992), cert. denied sub nom. *Henss v. Martin*, 506 U.S. 1054 (1993); *Coldesina v. Estate of Simper*, 407 F.3d 1126 (10th Cir. 2005).
4. *Chicago Dist. Council of Carpenters Welfare Fund v. Caremark, Inc.*, 2007 U.S. App. LEXIS 1128 (7th Cir. 2007).

227. Are officers, members of the board of directors, or employees of a plan sponsor fiduciaries?

According to the DOL, members of the board of directors, officers, and employees of an employer or employee organization that maintains an employee benefit plan are not fiduciaries solely by reason of holding such office or employment.[1] In comparison, the court in *Kayes v. Pacific Lumber Co.*[2] rejected the Third Circuit's interpretation in *Confer* that an officer who acts on behalf of a named fiduciary corporation cannot be a fiduciary if he acts within his official capacity, and if no fiduciary duties are delegated to him individually. See also *Thomas v. Peacock*,[3] in which the court determined that a corporate officer was a fiduciary.

Members of the board of directors, officers, and employees will be fiduciaries to the extent that they have responsibility for the functions described in ERISA Section 3(21)(A). If an employer has no power with respect to a plan other than to appoint the plan administrator and the trustees, then its fiduciary duty extends only to those functions.[4] Additionally, "plan officers, directors and members of the investment or administrative committees are fiduciaries, in that they exercise discretionary authority or control over plan management and asset disposition. Similarly, an officer and director of a plan sponsor are fiduciaries if they exercise control through the selection of the investment committee, administrative committee or plan officers or directors."[5] Additionally, "officers and directors of an employer who sponsors a pension plan may be fiduciaries to the extent they maintain authority for the selection, oversight, or retention of plan administrators."[6]

If the members of the board of directors are responsible for the selection and retention of plan fiduciaries and exercise "discretionary authority or discretionary control respecting management of such plan," they are fiduciaries with respect to the plan. However, their responsibility, and, consequently, their liability, is limited to the selection and retention of fiduciaries (apart from co-fiduciary liability arising under circumstances described in ERISA Section 405(a)). In addition, if the directors are made named fiduciaries of the plan, their liability may be limited pursuant to a procedure provided for in the plan instrument for the allocation of fiduciary responsibilities among named fiduciaries or for the designation of persons other than named fiduciaries to carry out fiduciary responsibilities, as provided in ERISA Section 405(c)(2).[7]

228. Are insurance companies and insurance agents fiduciaries?

An insurance company may be a fiduciary of a plan, depending upon the degree to which it exercises discretionary control over the assets or administration of the plan. An insurance

---

1. Labor Reg. §2509.75-8, D-4, D-5. See also *Confer v. Custom Eng'g Co.*, 952 F.2d 34 (3d Cir. 1991) (holding that individual officers of an ERISA plan are not fiduciaries by virtue of their offices).
2. 51 F.3d 1449 (9th Cir. 1995).
3. 39 F.3d 493 (4th Cir. 1994).
4. *Gelardi v. Pertec Computer Corp.*, 761 F.2d 1323 (9th Cir. 1985).
5. *Eaves v. Penn*, 587 F.2d 453 (10th Cir. 1978) (citing S. Rep. No. 93-383, 93d Cong., 1st Sess. 3).
6. *Martin v. Schwab*, 15 EBC 2135 (W.D. Mo. 1992); see also *Leigh v. Engle*, 727 F.2d 113 (7th Cir. 1984), remanded, 669 F. Supp. 1390 (N.D. Ill. 1985), aff'd, 858 F.2d 361 (7th Cir. 1988), cert. denied, 489 U.S. 1078 (1989); *Newton v. Van Otterloo*, 756 F. Supp. 1121 (N.D. Ind. 1991); *Sandoval v. Simmons*, 622 F. Supp. 1174 (C.D. Ill. 1985); *Shaw v. International Ass'n of Machinists & Aerospace Workers Pension Plan*, 563 F. Supp. 653 (C.D. Cal. 1983), aff'd, 750 F.2d 1458 (9th Cir.), cert. denied, 471 U.S. 1137 (1985).
7. Labor Reg. §2509.75-8, D-4, D-5.

company does *not* become an ERISA "fiduciary" simply by performing administrative functions and claims processing within a framework of rules established by an employer.[1] Where an insurance company provides only administrative claims-processing services to a plan within a framework established by the employer, and is not granted authority to review benefit denials nor to make ultimate decisions regarding eligibility, it is not a fiduciary.[2] Payment of claims pursuant to provisions of a benefits plan does not clothe the administrator with discretionary authority to such an extent as to make the administrator's role that of a fiduciary.

However, fiduciary status may be invoked if an insurance company has the ability to make policy decisions outside a preexisting or separate framework of policies, practices, and procedures.[3] Similarly, an insurance company may be a fiduciary if it has the discretionary authority to grant or deny claims in the administration of the plan.[4] In addition, an insurance company can become a fiduciary where it makes payments of claims using the money of the plan and it makes final dispositions of denied claims.[5] An insurance company that processes claims may be a fiduciary if it exceeds its purely ministerial capacity by exercising discretionary authority in deciding doubtful or disputed claims for referral back to the plan sponsor and it controls the plan's bank account for the payment of claims.[6]

In addition, an insurance company was held to be a plan fiduciary where it retained the power to amend certain terms of an annuity without the consent of the plan's trustees.[7] An insurance company also was held to be a fiduciary where it had the power to unilaterally amend an annuity contract covering employee benefit plan assets in a guaranteed rate account to the extent of its obligations connected with the amendment. The policy itself, as an asset of the plan, and the insurance company's ability to amend it and thereby alter its value, were not qualitatively different from the insurance company's ability to choose investments for the plan in its exercise of control over the assets of the plan.[8] The Supreme Court has held that an insurance company has a fiduciary responsibility for management of "free funds" or the non-guaranteed portion of group annuity contracts issued to a pension plan, to the extent that the insurance company engages in the discretionary management of assets attributable to that phase of the contract that provides no guarantee of benefit payments and no fixed rates of return, and where the investment risk was borne primarily by the contract holder.[9]

However, simply urging "the purchase of its products does not make an insurance company an ERISA fiduciary with respect to those products."[10] In addition, simply issuing insurance policies

1. *Gelardi v. Pertec Computer Corp.*, 761 F.2d 1323 (9th Cir. 1985).
2. *Baker v. Big Star Div. of Grand Union Co.*, 893 F.2d 288 (11th Cir. 1989). See also *DeGeare v. Alpha Portland Indus., Inc.*, 652 F. Supp. 946 (E.D. Mo. 1986).
3. *Munoz v. Prudential Ins. Co. of Am.*, 633 F. Supp. 564 (D. Colo. 1986).
4. *Confer v. Custom Eng'g Co.*, 952 F.2d 41 (3d Cir. 1991) (citing *McLaughlin v. Connecticut Gen. Life Ins. Co.*, 565 F. Supp. 434 (N.D. Cal. 1983)).
5. *See Sixty-Five Sec. Plan v. Blue Cross & Blue Shield*, 583 F. Supp. 380 (S.D.N.Y. 1984); *Blue Cross v. Peacock's Apothecary, Inc.*, 567 F. Supp. 1258 (N.D. Ala. 1983); *McLaughlin v. Connecticut Gen. Life Ins. Co.*, 565 F. Supp. 434 (N.D. Cal. 1983).
6. *IT Corp. v. General Am. Life Ins. Co.*, 107 F.3d 1415 (9th Cir. 1997).
7. *Associates in Adolescent Psychiatry v. Home Life Ins. Co.*, 941 F.2d 561 (7th Cir. 1991), cert. denied, 502 U.S. 1099 (1992).
8. *Chicago Bd. of Options v. Connecticut Gen. Life Ins. Co.*, 713 F.2d 256 (7th Cir. 1983).
9. *Harris Trust & Sav. Bank v. John Hancock Mut. Life Ins. Co.*, 510 U.S. 86 (1993).
10. *American Fed'n of Unions, Local 102 v. Equitable Life Assurance Soc'y*, 841 F.2d 658 (5th Cir. 1988).

to a covered plan does not render an insurance company a fiduciary.[1] An insurance company is not a fiduciary if it develops a retirement plan in conjunction with the plan fiduciaries, does not control the plan assets, and does not recommend specific investments beyond selling its own annuities to the plan.[2] An insurance company's suggestion that a health and welfare plan self-insure did not make it a fiduciary because its suggestion did not fit within the definition of investment advice under ERISA where the advice was not given on a regular basis, pursuant to a mutual agreement for a fee.[3]

An insurance agent who markets and sells his insurance company's Section 401(k) plan and financial products, who does not provide investment advice to the plan, and who acts merely as a salesperson earning commissions is not a plan fiduciary.[4] However, an agent who works on amendments to a plan, informs employees about the plan, meets with the company's independent accountant to discuss key issues affecting the plan, consults on plan investments, and has the authority to make press releases concerning the plan, may be exercising discretionary authority with respect to the administration or management of a plan and may be considered a fiduciary.

An insurance agent who sold life and health policies to a health and welfare fund, then later became a fund administrator, was held to be a fiduciary.[5] Even though his compensation arrangement was agreed on prior to his becoming an administrator, the court noted that his compensation was directly linked to his discretionary activities in determining which claims would be paid. As a result, he was a fiduciary with respect to the commissions and administrative expenses paid to him, and to the extent those amounts were paid to ineligible persons, he was liable to the fund.[6]

229. Can a person be a fiduciary for a limited purpose?

Yes, a person can be a fiduciary only *to the extent* that she has responsibility for the functions described in ERISA Section 3(21)(A).[7] The phrase "to the extent" indicates that a person is a fiduciary only with respect to those aspects of the plan over which she exercises authority or control.[8] "It is a well established principle that under ERISA, fiduciary status is not an all or nothing proposition."[9] "ERISA recognizes that a person may be a fiduciary for some purposes and not others."[10]

---

1. *Austin v. General Am. Life Ins. Co.*, 498 F. Supp. 844 (N.D. Ala. 1980); *Cate v. Blue Cross & Blue Shield of Ala.*, 434 F. Supp. 1187 (E.D. Tenn. 1977). See also *Lederman v. Pacific Mut. Life Ins. Co.*, 494 F. Supp. 1020 (C.D. Cal. 1980) (dicta).
2. *Consolidated Beef Indus., Inc. v. New York Life Ins. Co.*, 949 F.2d 960 (8th Cir. 1991).
3. *American Fed'n of Unions, Local 102 v. Equitable Life Assurance Soc'y*, 841 F.2d 658 (5th Cir. 1988).
4. *Consolidated Beef Indus., Inc. v. New York Life Ins. Co.*, 949 F.2d 960 (8th Cir. 1991).
5. *Monson v. Century Mfg. Co.*, 739 F.2d 1293 (8th Cir. 1984).
6. *American Fed'n of Unions, Local 102 v. Equitable Life Assurance Soc'y*, 841 F.2d 658 (5th Cir. 1988).
7. Labor Reg. §2509.75-8, D-4.
8. *Sommers Drug Stores Co. Profit Sharing Trust v. Corrigan Enters., Inc.*, 793 F.2d 1456 (5th Cir. 1986), cert. denied, 479 U.S. 1034 (1987) (citing *Brandt v. Grounds*, 687 F.2d 895 (7th Cir. 1982)). See also *Arakelian v. National W. Life Ins. Co.*, 748 F. Supp. 17 (D.D.C. 1990) (trustees were not liable for certain fiduciary breaches involving surrender charges and investment decisions because of a lack of discretionary authority over the investment of plan assets).
9. *Demaio v. Cigna Corp.*, 16 EBC 1627 (E.D. Pa. 1993).
10. *Leigh v. Engle*, 727 F.2d 113 (7th Cir. 1984).

230. How many fiduciaries must an employee benefit plan have?

Although a plan is not required to have a specified number of fiduciaries, each plan must have at least one named fiduciary who serves as plan administrator.[1] Additionally, if the plan assets are held in trust, the plan must have at least one trustee. There is no limit on the number of fiduciaries a plan may have. A plan may have as few or as many fiduciaries as are necessary for its operation and administration. Furthermore, if the plan so provides, any person or group of persons may serve in more than one fiduciary capacity, including serving both as trustee and as administrator.[2]

231. Is person's state of mind or title a prerequisite to fiduciary status?

No. A person's belief or formal title is irrelevant in determining his fiduciary status under ERISA.[3] Congress intended the term to be broadly construed. "The definition includes persons who have authority and responsibility with respect to the matter in question, regardless of their formal title."[4] Thus, whether or not an individual or entity is an ERISA fiduciary rests on an objective evaluation of functions performed, and not on an individual's state of mind, or the title held.

232. Who is a plan administrator?

The term "administrator" means: (1) the person specifically so designated by the terms of the instrument under which the plan is operated; (2) if an administrator is not so designated, the plan sponsor; or (3) in the case of a plan for which an administrator is not designated and a plan sponsor cannot be identified, such other person as the Department of Labor may by regulation prescribe.[5] Plan documents generally designate the person or entity who is assigned the role of the plan administrator. If the document is silent as to this position, the plan sponsor is designated in accordance with the statute.

233. Is a plan administrator a fiduciary?

Although nothing in ERISA specifically states that a plan administrator is a fiduciary, both the courts and the Department of Labor are in accord that the holder of this position automatically has fiduciary status solely on the basis of her role as plan administrator because, by the very nature of the position, plan administrators have "discretionary authority or discretionary responsibility in the administration" of the plan. Thus, a plan administrator who has discretionary authority or discretionary responsibility in the administration of the plan is a fiduciary within the terms of ERISA Section 3(21)(A)(iii) and has a duty to act in accordance with the rules of fiduciary conduct under ERISA.[6] A plan administrator who does not possess discretionary authority over the plan or its assets but merely performs "ministerial" functions is not a fiduciary. For an explanation of what actions constitute "ministerial" functions, see Q 225.

---

1. Labor Reg. §2509.75-8, FR-12.
2. ERISA Sec. 402(c)(1).
3. *See, e.g., Freund v. Marshall & Ilsley Bank*, 485 F. Supp. 629 (W.D. Wis. 1979); *Donovan v. Mercer*, 747 F.2d 304 (5th Cir. 1984); *McNeese v. Health Plan Mktg., Inc.*, 647 F. Supp. 981 (N.D. Ala. 1986).
4. H.R. Rep. No. 93-1280, 93d Cong., 2d Sess. (1974) (ERISA Conference Report*); Blatt v. Marshall & Lassman*, 812 F.2d 810 (2d Cir. 1987).
5. ERISA Sec. 3(16)(A).
6. Labor Reg. §2509.75-8, D-3; see *Hozier v. Midwest Fasteners, Inc.*, 908 F.2d 1155 (3d Cir. 1990); *U.S. Steel Mining Co. v. District 17, United Mine Workers of Am.*, 897 F.2d 149 (4th Cir. 1990).

The DOL has stated that the determination of whether a third-party administrator (TPA) is a fiduciary is a *functional test*.[1] Furthermore, if a TPA exercises discretionary control she is probably a fiduciary. Kaplan added that courts have been expanding the definition of fiduciary, and that contracts disclaiming fiduciary responsibility do not provide the protection they once did.

The Ninth Circuit has ruled that a TPA was not a fiduciary under ERISA and did not have a duty to disclose to participants its suspicion of asset embezzlement by the plan sponsor CEO/co-trustee because the TPA's primary duty was the preparation of financial reports on behalf of the plan. The court ruled that since the TPA lacked discretionary control over the plan, and control remained with the CEO/co-trustee, the TPA could not be deemed a fiduciary under ERISA.[2]

The Eleventh Circuit expressly held that a TPA could not be a *de facto* plan administrator for purposes of ERISA because, pursuant to the terms of the plan document, the plan sponsor retained ultimate decision-making authority over the plan and benefits determinations.[3] The court recognized that employers can be *de facto* plan administrators in certain situations, but it refused to extend the theory to TPAs. The court held that if it were to extend the theory of *de facto* plan administrator liability to TPAs, it would undercut the ability of employers to obtain the administrative services necessary to operate their ERISA plans.

In determining that the employer was the plan administrator, the Eleventh Circuit analyzed the benefit denial under the "arbitrary and capricious" standard of review (rejecting the trial court's de novo standard of review). In order for a TPA to be a Plan Administrator for purposes of ERISA Section 3(16)(A), the governing documents must specifically identify the TPA as plan administrator and grant to it the discretion and authority over the plan and benefits determinations.

234. Who is a plan sponsor?

A plan sponsor is: (1) the employer, in the case of an employee benefit plan established or maintained by a single employer; (2) the employee organization, in the case of a plan established or maintained by an employee organization; or (3) in the case of a plan established or maintained by two or more employers or jointly by one or more employers and one or more employee organizations, the association, committee, joint board of trustees, or other similar group of representatives of the parties who establish or maintain the plan.[4]

235. When does a plan sponsor act as a fiduciary?

"ERISA allows employers to wear 'two hats,' and they act as a fiduciary 'only when and to the extent' that they function in their capacity as plan administrators, not when they conduct business that is not regulated by ERISA."[5] Since the roles of plan administrator and plan sponsor are distinct, a plan sponsor who does not serve in the capacity of a trustee, named fiduciary, or

---

1. Sherwin Kaplan, Deputy Solicitor Gen., Plan Benefit Sec. Div., Dep't of Labor, Speaking at the Meeting of Workers in Employee Benefits (Feb. 18, 1998).

2. *CSA 401(k) Plan v. Pension Prof'ls, Inc.*, 195 F.3d 1135 (9th Cir. 1999).

3. *Oliver v. Coca Cola Co.*, 2007 WL 2429394 (11th Cir. 2007).

4. ERISA Sec. 3(16)(B).

5. *Amato v. Western Union Int'l, Inc.*, 773 F.2d 1402 (2d Cir. 1985), cert. denied, 474 U.S. 1113 (1986).

plan administrator is not deemed to be a fiduciary. Thus, a plan sponsor steps into the role of a fiduciary under ERISA Section 3(21)(A) only when exercising discretionary authority or control over the plan management or administration.[1] For example, if an employer has no power with respect to a plan other than to appoint the plan administrator and the trustees, then its fiduciary duty extends only to those functions.[2] However, a plan sponsor may be found to be a fiduciary if it controls the trustee's investment decisions (either through the use of its position or otherwise) by causing the trustees to relinquish their independent discretion in making investment decisions for the plan and to follow an investment course prescribed by the plan sponsor.[3]

Fiduciary status may also attach in the situation where a plan sponsor serves in the dual capacity as both a plan sponsor and a plan administrator. Although not all of a plan sponsor's business activities involve plan management or administration, a plan sponsor may act in the capacity of a plan fiduciary and not as an employer in communicating to plan participants about "business decisions" that may affect plan benefits. In communicating to employees, a plan sponsor may wear its "fiduciary" as well as its "employer" hat. In communicating business decisions with respect to a plan and their effect on the plan benefits, reasonable employees may not be able to distinguish consciously between the plan sponsor's roles as employer and as plan administrator. Thus, an employer may be exercising "discretionary authority" respecting the plan's "management" or "administration" in communicating the business decision, combined with a plan-related nature of the decision, if a reasonable employee would believe that the plan sponsor is communicating to him in the capacity of plan administrator.[4] See Q 236.

Taking the holding in the *Varity* case one step further, the court in the case of *Hensley v. P.H. Glatfelter Co.*[5] ruled that the omission of material information, which constitutes material misstatements or the provision of incomplete, inconsistent, or contradictory disclosures, that misinforms beneficiaries may be a breach of fiduciary duty if such actions serve to provide assurances to participants and beneficiaries about a specified course of action regarding the plan, while simultaneously withholding information that constitutes a substantial risk to benefits under the scenario.

A plan sponsor acts as a fiduciary of a plan with respect to retaining the authority in the selection and retention of plan fiduciaries. For example, plan sponsors often have the responsibility for the appointment of and removal of the plan's trustees, administrators, or members of an administrative committee that administers the plan. By virtue of this responsibility, and by virtue of the plan sponsor's exercise of the appointment power, the plan sponsor is a fiduciary of the plan within the meaning of ERISA.[6]

---

1. *Siskind v. Sperry Ret. Program*, 47 F.3d 498 (2d Cir. 1995).

2. See *Gelardi v. Pertec Computer Corp.*, 761 F.2d 1323 (9th Cir. 1985); *Leigh v. Engle*, 727 F.2d 113 (7th Cir. 1984); Labor Reg. §2509.75-8, D-4.

3. *Sommers Drug Stores Co. Profit Sharing Trust v. Corrigan Enters., Inc.*, 793 F.2d 1456 (5th Cir. 1986), cert. denied, 479 U.S. 1034 (1987).

4. *Varity Corp. v. Howe*, 514 U.S. 1082 (1996).

5. 2005 U.S. Dist. LEXIS 31136 (W.D.N.C. 2005).

6. ERISA Sec. 3(21)(A); see *Eaves v. Penn*, 587 F.2d 453 (10th Cir. 1978); *Batchelor v. Oak Hill Med. Grp.*, 870 F.2d 1446 (9th Cir. 1989) (consortium of physicians operating medical clinics held liable for breach of fiduciary duty in selection of a third party as fund administrator); *Hickman v. Tosco Corp.*, 840 F.2d 564 (8th Cir. 1988) (company was a fiduciary within the meaning of ERISA because it appointed and removed the members of the administrative committee that administered the pension plan); *Whitfield v. Tomasso*, 682 F. Supp. 1287 (E.D.N.Y. 1988) (union that had authority to appoint and remove trustees had exercised discretionary control over the management of the welfare fund and was, therefore, a fiduciary to the fund); *McKinnon v. Cairns*, 698 F. Supp. 852 (W.D. Okla. 1988); *Moehle v. NL Indus., Inc.*, 646 F. Supp. 769 (E.D. Mo. 1986) (employer that appointed and removed plan committee members was a fiduciary).

236. What is the settlor doctrine? May an employer rely on the settlor doctrine to avoid fiduciary status?

Relying on the distinction between an employer's role as a plan fiduciary and an employer's role in conducting business, the settlor doctrine sets forth the theory that certain actions of an employer in the course of the design, establishment, and termination of a plan are settlor functions (see Q 256), which are not governed by the fiduciary standards of ERISA. However, as explained below, an employer cannot necessarily rely on this doctrine under all circumstances.

It is well established that decisions involving the design, establishment, and termination of a plan are employer tasks, and not within the purview of the fiduciary provisions of ERISA. These settlor functions are discretionary activities that relate to the formation, rather than the management, of a plan and, thus, are allowed to be made without considering the interests of plan participants and beneficiaries. Moreover, Congress made it clear that "ERISA does not require that day-to-day corporate business transactions, which may have a collateral effect on prospective, contingent employee benefits, be performed solely in the interest of plan participants."[1]

In effect, "ERISA permits employers to wear 'two hats,' and they assume fiduciary status 'only when and to the extent' that they function in their capacity as plan administrators, not when they conduct business that is not regulated by ERISA." Thus, under the settlor doctrine, ordinary business decisions that directly affect the plan and plan participants, such as the decision to modify or terminate welfare benefits, are not governed by ERISA's fiduciary obligations because they do not involve discretionary administration of the plan.[2]

The ability of an employer to rely on this settlor doctrine, however, is limited. The Supreme Court has held that an employer serving in the dual capacity as both a plan sponsor and plan administrator may invoke fiduciary status upon itself in communicating to plan participants about "business decisions" that may affect plan benefits, thus subjecting it to the fiduciary standards of ERISA.[3]

The employer in *Varity* intentionally misled employees about the financial health of a subsidiary it had created, leading them to forfeit benefits in a financially sound plan in exchange for benefits backed by a subsidiary that the employer knew was insolvent. In the lawsuit that later ensued, the employer argued that its deceptive statements about the subsidiary's financial health were made in its capacity as an employer, not as a plan fiduciary.

The Court rejected the employer's argument, stating that "reasonable employees … could have thought that Varity was communicating with them *both* in its capacity as employer *and* in its capacity as plan administrator. Reasonable employees might not have distinguished consciously between the two roles. But they would have known that the employer was their plan's administrator and had expert knowledge about how their plan worked." The Court noted

---

1. *Adams v. Avondale Indus., Inc.*, 905 F.2d 943 (6th Cir.), cert. denied, 498 U.S. 984 (1990).

2. See *Curtiss-Wright Corp. v. Schoonejongen*, 514 U.S. 73 (1995).

3. *Varity Corp. v. Howe*, 514 U.S. 1082 (1996).

further that the employees' conclusion that their benefits with the subsidiary would be secure "could well have drawn strength from their awareness of that expertise," and, in fact, that such a perception was the employer's intention.

The Court concluded that while the employer in *Varity* had made an employer business decision with respect to the plan (i.e., splitting off unprofitable divisions into a subsidiary, as well as transferring a number of employees and debts—including the liability for their benefits—to that subsidiary), it acted in a fiduciary capacity when it discussed the decision and its impact on the plan benefits to employees. Indeed, its intentional misleading of employees as to the future of plan benefits in that context was an act of plan administration, and the employer was found liable for its actions.

Thus, under *Varity*, although a business decision relating to the plan should not, in itself, trigger the fiduciary standards, an employer's communications to employees about the effect of the business decision on the plan's benefits may likely be considered a fiduciary act, thereby subjecting it to scrutiny under the fiduciary provisions of ERISA.

237. Is a trustee a fiduciary?

Yes, under most circumstances. With certain exceptions, ERISA generally mandates that all assets of an employee benefit plan must be held in trust by one or more trustees.[1] The trustees must either be named in the plan document, be named in the trust agreement, or appointed by a named fiduciary. The trustees have exclusive authority and discretion to acquire, manage, control, and dispose of the assets of the plan, except to the extent trustees are subject to the direction of a named fiduciary (non-trustee), or where these functions are delegated to an investment manager. Thus, trustees who have the authority and discretion to acquire, manage, control, and dispose of the assets of the plan, by definition, are fiduciaries.[2]

238. May an officer of the plan sponsor serve as a plan fiduciary?

Yes. ERISA specifically allows an officer, employee, agent, or other representative of a union or plan sponsor to also serve as a fiduciary of the plan sponsor's employee benefit plan. ERISA Section 408(c) states that "nothing in ... this title shall be construed to prohibit any fiduciary from ... serving as a fiduciary in addition to being an officer, employee, agent, or other representative of a party in interest."

In addition, the courts have held that there is no inherent conflict of interest where an officer of a corporation is also a fiduciary of the corporation's benefit plan. In fact, ERISA contemplates such a situation where an officer of a corporation wears two hats; when acting in the capacity of an employee of the corporation, the officer owes a duty to act on behalf of the corporation.[3] For example, a trustee of an employee benefit plan does not violate ERISA merely by also serving in a position with an employee organization or employer that requires him to represent the entity in the collective bargaining negotiations that determine the funding

---

1. ERISA Sec. 403(a).
2. ERISA Sec. 3(21)(A)(i).
3. See *Amato v. Western Union Int'l, Inc.*, 773 F.2d 1402 (2d Cir. 1985), cert. denied, 474 U.S. 1113 (1986).

of the plan. In those negotiations, the bargaining representative represents either the employer or the employees.[1]

On the other hand, an officer of the plan sponsor also owes a duty to the plan as plan fiduciary to avoid placing herself in a position where her role as an officer of the plan sponsor prevents her from functioning with complete loyalty to the participants of the plan.[2] Thus, when an officer of a plan sponsor acts in the capacity of a plan fiduciary, the officer owes a duty to act in the best interest of the plan's participants and beneficiaries.

An officer of a plan sponsor was held to be a fiduciary with respect to his obligation to timely deposit withheld employee contributions, in spite of the fact that he was not the plan administrator nor otherwise designated as a fiduciary.[3]

239. When does a person render investment advice?

A person renders "investment advice" (within the meaning of ERISA Section 3(21)(A)) only if:

1. The person renders advice to the plan as to the value of securities or other property, or makes recommendations as to the advisability of investing in, purchasing, or selling securities or other property; and

2. The person either directly or indirectly (e.g., through or together with any affiliate): (a) has discretionary authority or control, whether or not pursuant to agreement, arrangement or understanding, with respect to purchasing or selling securities or other property for the plan; or (b) renders any advice described in paragraph (1), above, on a regular basis to the plan pursuant to a mutual agreement, arrangement or understanding, written or otherwise, between such person and the plan or a fiduciary with respect to the plan, that the services will serve as a primary basis for investment decisions with respect to plan assets, and that such person will render individualized investment advice to the plan based on the particular needs of the plan regarding such matters as, among other things, investment policies or strategy, overall portfolio composition, or diversification of plan investments.[4]

240. Is a person who renders investment advice a fiduciary?

A person is considered a fiduciary with respect to an employee benefit plan to the extent that he "renders investment advice for a fee or other compensation, direct or indirect, with respect to any moneys or other property of such plan, or has any authority to do so." Accordingly, the definition of fiduciary is a two-part test requiring both the provision of "investment advice" and the receipt of a "fee or other compensation" for such advice.[5]

On October 22, 2010, the DOL issued proposed regulations that will, if adopted in final format, dramatically change this two-part test by replacing it with rules that would subject more

1. *Evans v. Bexley*, 750 F.2d 1498 (11th Cir. 1985).
2. *Donovan v. Bierwirth*, 680 F.2d 263 (2d Cir.), cert. denied, 459 U.S. 1069 (1982).
3. See *LoPresti v. Terwilliger*, 126 F.3d 34 (2d Cir. 1997).
4. Labor Reg. §2510.3-21(c).
5. ERISA Sec. 3(21)(A)(ii).

people to ERISA's fiduciary rules by providing that a person is a fiduciary under ERISA if that person provides, for a fee or other compensation, direct or indirect, to a plan, a plan fiduciary, plan participant, or beneficiary:

1. Advice, or an appraisal or fairness opinion about the value of securities or other property;

2. Recommendations as to the advisability of investing, buying, or selling securities or other property; or

3. Advice or recommendations as to the management of securities and other property.[1]

And, such person also, either directly or indirectly (e.g., through, or together with, any affiliate):

1. Represents or acknowledges that it is acting as an ERISA fiduciary with respect to providing the above advice or recommendations;

2. Is a fiduciary with respect to the plan within the meaning of the ERISA Section 3(21)(a)(i) or (iii) basic definition of a fiduciary;

3. Is an investment adviser within the definition contained in the Investment Advisers Act of 1940; or

4. Provides advice or makes recommendations as described above pursuant to an agreement, arrangement, or understanding, written or otherwise, between such person and the plan, a plan fiduciary, or a plan participant or beneficiary that such advice may be considered in connection with making investment or management decisions with respect to plan assets, and will be individualized to the needs of the plan, a plan fiduciary, or a participant or beneficiary.[2]

The DOL has announced that it will re-propose regulations on the definition of an ERISA fiduciary in the context of persons giving investment advice to an employee benefit plan or plan participants. The previously proposed regulations would have updated a 1975 regulation defining when a person providing investment advice becomes a fiduciary under ERISA, in order to adapt the rule to the current retirement marketplace. The proposal's goal is to ensure that potential conflicts of interest among advisers are not allowed to compromise the quality of investment advice that millions of American workers rely on, so they can retire with the dignity that they have worked hard to achieve. As of October 16, 2013, the DOL has yet to release the final rule.[3]

It is important to note that the proposed regulation eliminates the requirement that the advice be rendered on a "regular basis" or as the "primary basis" elements of the current regulation while simultaneously expanding fiduciary status for the provision of advice or recommendations to participants and beneficiaries. This is quite an expansion of the circumstances under which a person may find herself a fiduciary. The DOL noted that its adoption of these

---

1. Prop. Labor Reg. §2510.3-21(c)(1)(i)(A)(1) to (3).
2. Prop. Labor Reg. §2510.3-21(c)(1)(i)(B)(ii)(A) to (D).
3. DOL News Release No. 11-1382-NAT (Sept. 19, 2011).

proposed regulations "would protect beneficiaries of pension plans and individual retirement accounts by more broadly defining the circumstances under which a person is considered to be a 'fiduciary' by reason of giving investment advice to an employee benefit plan or a plan's Participants." In adopting the proposed regulations, the DOL provides that they are intended to take account of significant changes in the financial industry, to meet the expectations of plan officials and participants who receive investment advice, and to protect participants from conflicts of interest and self-dealing.[1]

Exceptions

The proposed regulation does contain limits on this dramatic expansion of fiduciary status determination. Specifically, as it pertains to financial sales activities, a person will not be considered a fiduciary with respect to the provision of advice or recommendations if, with respect to a person other than one who acknowledges acting as a fiduciary with respect to providing investment advice or recommendations (e.g., investment manager), such person can demonstrate that the recipient of the advice knows or, under the circumstances, reasonably should know, that the person is providing the advice or making the recommendation in its capacity as a purchaser or seller of a security or other property, or as an agent of, or appraiser for, such a purchaser or seller, whose interests are adverse to the interests of the plan or its participants or beneficiaries, and that the person is not undertaking to provide impartial investment advice.[2] These limitations also except from fiduciary status:

1. Anyone providing investment education pursuant to the provisions of Interpretive Bulletin 96-1 (see Q 595 for details of this Interpretive Bulletin);

2. The marketing or making available through a platform or similar mechanism, investment options a plan sponsor may select for plan participants *only if* the investment options are made available without regard to the individualized needs of the plan or its participants and the service provider makes a written disclosure to the plan that it is *not* providing impartial investment advice;

3. The provision of general financial information or data in connection with a plan fiduciary's selection and monitoring of investments *only if* the provider makes a written disclosure to the plan that it is *not* providing impartial investment advice; and

4. The provision of appraisals and valuations that do not include a report or statement that indicates that the value of the investment is being provided for purposes of compliance with the reporting and disclosure provisions of ERISA and the Internal Revenue Code, *unless* the appraisal or valuation covers an asset for which there is no generally recognized market, and serves as the basis on which a plan may make distributions to participants and beneficiaries.[3]

Effective Date

Comments are still being taken on this proposal thus no effective date has been implemented.

---

1. Preamble to Prop. Labor Reg. §2520.3-21(c); 75 Fed. Reg. 65,263 (Oct. 22, 2010).

2. Prop. Labor Reg. §2510.3-21(c)(2)(i).

3. Prop. Labor Reg. §§2510.3-21(c)(2)(ii)(A) to (C) & 2520.3-21(c)(2)(iii).

241. What is a "fee or other compensation" for the rendering of investment advice?

According to the Department of Labor, "a fee or other compensation," direct or indirect, for the rendering of investment advice to a plan by a fiduciary, is deemed to include all fees or other compensation incident to the transaction in which the investment advice to the plan has been rendered or will be rendered. This may include, for example, brokerage commissions, mutual fund sales commissions, and insurance sales commissions.[1]

242. Does the provision of research or recommendations by a broker-dealer constitute the rendering of "investment advice?"

Generally, no. But according to the Department of Labor, the provision by broker-dealers of research, information, and advice concerning securities to a plan in the ordinary course of their business as broker-dealers would not, in and of itself, constitute the rendering of "investment advice" unless the services are rendered pursuant to a mutual agreement (written or otherwise) to provide individualized advice to a plan on a regular basis, which will serve as the primary basis for plan investment decisions. Thus, for example, the provision of general research materials to a broker-dealer's customers, including employee benefit plans, would not fall into that category. In other instances, a determination of whether the provision of research or recommendations by a broker-dealer constitutes the rendering of "investment advice" within the meaning of ERISA Section 3(21)(A)(ii) will depend on the particular facts and circumstances.[2]

243. Does the provision of investment-related information to participants and beneficiaries in participant-directed individual account plans constitute the rendering of "investment advice"?

Not necessarily. The Department of Labor has issued guidance identifying categories of investment-related information and related materials that an employer may make available to participants without the provision of such items constituting "investment advice" for purposes of the definition of "fiduciary" under ERISA.[3] For an explanation of the regulations under ERISA Section 3(21)(A)(ii), with respect to what constitutes the rendering of "investment advice," see Q 381.

The "safe harbor" treatment of these items applies regardless of who provides the information, how often it is shared, the form in which it is provided (e.g., in writing, via video or software, on an individual or group basis), or whether an identified category of information and materials is furnished alone or in combination with other identified categories of information and materials. The materials identified by the DOL include:

1. Information and materials that inform participants about the benefits of plan participation, the benefits of increasing plan contributions, the impact of

---

1. DOL Adv. Op. 83-60A; DOL Adv. Op. 84-36A.
2. DOL Adv. Op. 83-60A.
3. See Labor Reg. §2509.96-1 (I.B. 96-1), 61 Fed. Reg. 29,586 (June 11, 1996).

pre-retirement withdrawals, the operation and terms of the plan, and investment alternatives available under the plan (including their investment objectives and philosophies, risk and return characteristics, and historical return information), see Q 596;

2.   General financial and investment concepts, such as risk and return, diversification, dollar cost averaging, compounded return, and tax-deferred investing, historical differences in rates of return between different asset classes based on standard market indices, effects of inflation, estimating future retirement needs, determining investment time horizons, and assessing risk tolerance, provided that the information has no direct relationship to investment alternatives available under the plan, see Q 597;

3.   Asset allocation information (e.g., pie charts, case studies, or graphs) made available to all participants and beneficiaries, that provide participants with models of asset allocation portfolios of hypothetical individuals with different time horizons and risk profiles (however, the models must be based on accepted investment theories and all material facts and assumptions on which the models are based must be specified, and the models must include certain other disclosures), see Q 598; and

4.   Interactive investment materials, such as questionnaires, worksheets, software, and similar materials that provide participants a means of estimating future retirement income needs, provided that requirements similar to those for asset allocation information in (3), above, are met; see Q 599.[1]

244. Must a person who renders investment advice, but who does not exercise or have the right to exercise discretionary authority with respect to the assets of the plan, be bonded solely by reason of the provision of such investment advice?

No. A person who renders investment advice, but who does not exercise or have the right to exercise discretionary authority with respect to plan assets, is not required to be bonded solely by reason of the provision of such investment advice. Such a person is not considered to be "handling" funds within the meaning of the temporary bonding regulations.[2] See Section VIII for a discussion of the bonding requirements.

245. Is a broker-dealer a fiduciary?

Generally, no. A broker or dealer registered under the Securities Exchange Act of 1934, a reporting dealer in United States government or agency securities, or a supervised bank (federal or state) will not be considered a fiduciary merely because the person executes transactions for the purchase or sale of securities on behalf of an employee benefit plan if the following requirements are met:

1.   The transactions are executed (a) in the ordinary course of the business of the broker, dealer, or bank; and (b) pursuant to the instructions of a plan fiduciary;

---

1. Labor Reg. §2509.96-1(d).
2. Labor Reg. §2509.75-5, FR-7.

2.   The fiduciary or its affiliates are not affiliated with the broker, dealer, or bank; and

3.   The fiduciary's instructions specify (a) the security to be purchased or sold, (b) a price range within which such security is to be purchased or sold, (c) a time span during which the security may be purchased or sold (not to exceed five business days), and (d) the minimum or maximum quantity of the security that may be purchased or sold within the price range.[1]

However, subject to the provisions governing co-fiduciary liability and the rules governing prohibited transactions as a party-in-interest,[2] a broker-dealer, reporting dealer, or bank is not considered a fiduciary regarding any plan assets with respect to which it:

1.   Does not have any discretionary authority, discretionary control, or discretionary responsibility;

2.   Does not exercise any authority or control;

3.   Does not render investment advice for a fee or other compensation; *and*

4.   Does not have any authority or responsibility to render such investment advice.[3]

The foregoing regulations have been interpreted as requiring all of the following five elements in order to support a finding of fiduciary status of a broker-dealer: (1) individualized investment advice was provided; (2) the advice was given pursuant to a mutual understanding; (3) the advice was provided on a regular basis; (4) the advice pertained to the value of the property or consisted of recommendations as to the advisability of investing in certain property; and (5) the advice was rendered for a fee.[4]

A broker-dealer who recommended securities for a plan to purchase was held to be merely a broker and not a fiduciary because the broker-dealer had no discretionary authority over the plan, he had no discretion to dispose of any of the plan's assets, and there was no mutual understanding that the broker-dealer would provide to the plan individualized investment advice that would be the primary basis for the plan's investment decisions. Thus, the broker-dealer did not rise to the status of a fiduciary by merely selling suggested securities to the plan in a sales pitch, which the court described as "the very cornerstone of a typical broker-client relationship."[5] In addition, a finding that the investment adviser rendered advice on a "regular basis" is essential to a determination that a fiduciary relationship existed.[6]

246. Who is an investment manager?

An "investment manager" is a fiduciary (other than a trustee or named fiduciary) who has the power to manage, acquire, or dispose of any asset of a plan. This power is delegated by a named fiduciary for the purpose of managing the assets of a plan. The investment manager

---

1. Labor Reg. §2510.3-21(d)(1).
2. See ERISA Secs. 405(a), 3(14)(B).
3. Labor Reg. §2510.3-21(d)(2).
4. See *Thomas, Head & Greisen Emps. Trust v. Buster*, 24 F.3d 1114 (9th Cir. 1994).
5. *Farm King Supply, Inc. v. Edward D. Jones & Co.*, 884 F.2d 288 (7th Cir. 1989).
6. *American Fed'n of Unions, Local 102 v. Equitable Life Assurance Soc'y*, 841 F.2d 658 (5th Cir. 1988).

must be either registered as an investment adviser under the Investment Advisers Act of 1940, a bank (as defined in that Act), or an insurance company with the power to manage, acquire, or dispose of any asset of a plan under the laws of more than one state. In addition, an investment manager is required to acknowledge in writing that it is a fiduciary with respect to the plan.[1]

247. May an investment adviser who is neither a bank nor an insurance company, and who is not registered under the Investment Advisers Act of 1940, in reliance upon an exemption from registration provided in that Act, be appointed an investment manager under ERISA Section 402(c)(3)?

No. The only persons who may be appointed as an investment manager under ERISA Section 402(c)(3) are persons who meet the requirements of ERISA Section 3(38)—namely, banks,[2] insurance companies qualified under the laws of more than one state to manage, acquire, and dispose of plan assets, or persons registered as investment advisers under the Investment Advisers Act of 1940.[3]

248. May an investment adviser who has a registration application pending under the Investment Advisers Act of 1940 function as an investment manager under the Act prior to the effective date of registration under the Investment Advisers Act?

No, for the same reasons as stated in Q 247[4]

249. What is the procedure for state-registered investment advisers to obtain investment manager status under ERISA?

Under temporary procedures instituted by the Department of Labor, state-registered investment advisers seeking investment manager status under ERISA must file with the Department of Labor a copy of their most recently filed state registration form and any subsequent filings. Generally, this filing requirement applies to investment advisers who manage less than $25 million and who are required to register under state law. Advisers who are required to register in multiple states need only provide the DOL a copy of the registration form filed in the state where they maintain their principal office and place of business.

Copies of these filings should be mailed to the DOL at the following address:

Investment Adviser Filings, Room N-5638
U.S. Department of Labor, PWBA
Office of Program Services
200 Constitution Avenue, NW
Washington, DC 20210

---

1. ERISA Secs. 3(38), 402(c)(3).
2. As defined in the Investment Advisers Act of 1940.
3. Labor Reg. §2509.75-5, FR-6.
4. Labor Reg. §2509.75-5, FR-7.

As a temporary filing requirement, the procedures are scheduled to remain in effect only until a centralized database containing the registration forms (or substantially similar information) is available through the Securities and Exchange Commission (SEC) or other organization. At that time the DOL intends to provide notice that filing with the DOL is no longer necessary.[1]

250. What persons are barred from serving as fiduciaries?

Any person who has been convicted of any of a broad range of crimes is barred from serving as a fiduciary or service provider of an employee benefit plan.[2] The statute automatically disqualifies individuals by its terms and subjects these persons to prosecution for violating its provisions. Anyone who has been convicted of, or imprisoned as a result of, the following offenses is prohibited from serving as a fiduciary:

1. Robbery, bribery, extortion, embezzlement, fraud, grand larceny, burglary, arson, murder;

2. Rape, kidnapping, perjury, assault with intent to kill;

3. A felony violation of federal or state law involving "controlled substances" defined in Section 802(6) of Title 21 of the U.S. Code (Comprehensive Drug Abuse Prevention and Control Act of 1970);

4. Any crime described in Section 80a-9(a)(1) of Title 15, U.S. Code (Investment Company Act of 1940);

5. Any crime in ERISA (Sections 411, 501, and 511);

6. A violation of Section 186 of Title 29, U.S. Code (prohibited payments to labor unions, labor union officials, and employee representatives);

7. A violation of Chapter 63 of Title 18, U.S. Code (e.g., mail fraud, wire fraud, etc.);

8. A violation of Section 874, 1027, 1503, 1505, 1506, 1510, 1951, or 1954 of Title 18, U.S. Code;

9. A violation of the Labor-Management Reporting and Disclosure Act of 1959, Section 401 of Title 29, U.S. Code;

10. Any felony involving abuse or misuse of such person's position or employment in a labor organization or employee benefit plan to seek or obtain an illegal gain at the expense of the members of the labor organization or the beneficiaries of the employee benefit plan;

11. A conspiracy or attempt to commit any of the foregoing crimes; and

12. Any crime in which any of crimes described in ERISA Section 411 is an element.

See Section XIII, Criminal Enforcement, for further discussion.

---

1. ERISA Sec. 3(38)(B), *as amended by* Pub. L. No. 105-72.
2. ERISA Sec. 411.

251. May an employee pension or welfare benefit plan trustee be appointed for "life" subject to removal for "cause"?

In Advisory Opinion 85-41A (Dec. 5, 1985), the DOL expressed the view that a lifetime term of appointment for a pension plan trustee would generally be inconsistent with ERISA's fiduciary responsibility provisions. In addition, applicable regulations state, in part, that a contract or arrangement to provide trustee or other services to the plan is reasonable only if it permits termination of the contract or arrangement by the plan on reasonably short notice without penalty to the plan.[1]

The principles articulated in Advisory Opinion 85-41A apply equally to the terms of the appointment of trustees of funded welfare plans according to the DOL in Advisory Opinion 99-17A. Accordingly, an arrangement whereby trustees are to serve for unlimited terms subject to removal only upon proof of malfeasance, misconduct, or incapacity, or upon their own voluntary resignation or death, would not be reasonable within the meaning of the regulation.

---

1. Labor Reg. §2550.408b-2c.

SECTION IV
Fiduciary Duties

252. What standards of conduct does ERISA impose on fiduciaries?

Borrowing from trust law, ERISA imposes high standards of fiduciary duty upon those responsible for administering an ERISA plan and investing and disposing of its assets. The general standards governing fiduciary conduct require, among other things, that fiduciaries discharge their duties solely in the interest of plan participants and beneficiaries, for the exclusive purpose of providing them benefits "with the care, skill, prudence, and diligence" of a "prudent man acting in a like capacity and familiar with such matters," and in accordance with the documents and instruments governing the plan.[1] This section explains these duties and the standards of care governing the conduct of employee benefit plan fiduciaries.

253. What are the fiduciary duties prescribed by ERISA?

In addition to making certain actions by fiduciaries illegal per se, ERISA also codified the common law duties of loyalty and prudence for ERISA trustees. The central and fundamental obligations imposed on fiduciaries by ERISA are contained in Title I of ERISA (at Subtitle B, Part 4), titled *Fiduciary Responsibility*. This section sets forth the standards of conduct applicable to fiduciaries of employee benefit plans. In relevant part, the fiduciary provisions of ERISA Section 404(a) require that a plan fiduciary discharge his duties with respect to an employee benefit plan solely in the interest of the participants and beneficiaries, and

1. For the exclusive purpose of (a) providing benefits to participants and their beneficiaries and (b) defraying reasonable expenses of administering the plan;

2. With the care, skill, prudence, and diligence under the circumstances then prevailing that a prudent man acting in a like capacity and familiar with such matters would use in the conduct of an enterprise of a like character and with like aims;

3. By diversifying the investments of the plan so as to minimize the risk of large losses, unless under the circumstances it is clearly prudent not to do so; and

4. In accordance with the documents and instruments governing the plan insofar as such documents and instruments are consistent with the provisions of ERISA.

The fiduciary provisions of ERISA Section 404 embody the "central and fundamental obligation imposed on fiduciaries by ERISA," containing a carefully tailored law of trusts, including the requirements of undivided loyalty to beneficiaries, the prudent man rule, the rule requiring diversification of investments, and the requirement that fiduciaries comply with the provisions of plan documents to the extent that they are not inconsistent with ERISA.[2] These rules are supplemented by ERISA Section 403(c)(1), which provides that "the assets of a plan

---

1. ERISA Sec. 404.
2. *Eaves v. Penn*, 587 F.2d 453 (10th Cir. 1978).

shall never inure to the benefit of any employer and shall be held for the exclusive purposes of providing benefits to participants in the plan and their beneficiaries and defraying reasonable expenses of administering the plan."

In addition to these fiduciary standards, other sections of ERISA supplement these duties by expressly prohibiting numerous specific transactions between the plans and their affiliated "parties in interest" and by placing limits on the acquisition and holding of employer securities and real property by plans.[1] Counterbalancing these duties and prohibitions are certain statutory and administrative exemptions.[2]

ERISA Section 404(a) establishes uniform fiduciary standards to prevent transactions that dissipate or endanger plan assets. Much of the content of these provisions was drawn from the common law of trusts, which was the law governing most benefit plans before ERISA's enactment. In constructing the provisions of ERISA, Congress invoked the common law of trusts to define the general scope of fiduciaries' authority and responsibility, rather than explicitly enumerating all of the powers and duties of trustees and other fiduciaries.[3] Still, while ERISA imposes trust-like fiduciary standards, Congress expected that the courts would interpret these various fiduciary standards, bearing in mind the special nature and purpose of modern employee benefit plans.[4]

254. What plans are covered by the fiduciary rules?

The fiduciary rules of ERISA generally apply to employee welfare and pension benefit plans maintained by employers and employee organizations, or both, that are engaged in commerce, industry, or activity that affects commerce.[5]

255. What plans are exempted from the fiduciary rules?

Not all employee benefit plans are subject to the fiduciary duty requirements of ERISA Section 404(a). The fiduciary rules do not apply to the following types of employee benefit plans:[6]

1.   Governmental plans;[7]

2.   Church plans (as defined in ERISA Section 3(33)) for which no election under IRC Sec. 410(d) has been made to relate the participation, vesting, and funding provisions;[8]

3.   Plans that are maintained solely for the purpose of complying with applicable workers' compensation laws or unemployment compensation or disability insurance laws;

---

1. See ERISA Secs. 406, 407.
2. See ERISA Sec. 408.
3. See *Varity Corp. v. Howe,* 514 U.S. 1082 (1996).
4. See *Varity Corp. v. Howe,* 514 U.S. 1082 (1996).
5. ERISA Secs. 401(a), 3(3), 4, 5.
6. See ERISA Secs. 4(b), 401(a).
7. As defined in ERISA Section 3(32).
8. IRC Sec. 410(d).

4. Plans that are maintained outside the United States primarily for the benefit of persons substantially all of whom are nonresident aliens;

5. Plans that are unfunded excess benefit plans;[1]

6. Plans that are unfunded and are maintained by an employer primarily for the purpose of providing deferred compensation for a select group of management or highly compensated employees; and

7. Any agreement described in IRC Section 736 that provides payments to a retired partner or deceased partner or a deceased partner's successor in interest.

In order to fit within exemption (6) above, a plan must satisfy two prerequisites: it must be unfunded, and it must be maintained by an employer primarily for the purpose of providing deferred income for select employees. An unfunded plan is one in which only the employer provides the necessary funding for the benefits under the plan.[2] If the employer itself is the source of all the benefits and payments under the plan, and no contributions are made by the employee or any other third party, the plan is unfunded for purposes of exemption (6) above. Thus, the plan is exempt from the fiduciary duty requirements of ERISA.[3]

256. What is a "settlor" function?

A "settlor" function is a discretionary activity undertaken by a plan sponsor that relates to the formation, rather than the administration or management, of a plan. These so-called "settlor" functions include decisions made by the plan sponsor (or the employers and labor representatives in the case of a collectively bargained plan) relating to the establishment, termination, and design of plans.

Both the Department of Labor and a number of courts have agreed that these "settlor" functions, or business activities, as distinguished from administrative functions, are not fiduciary activities, and therefore not subject to ERISA's fiduciary duty requirements in light of the voluntary nature of the private pension system and ERISA's overall statutory scheme. Therefore, in undertaking "settlor" functions, an employer does not act in the capacity of a fiduciary because she is not exercising any discretionary authority or discretionary control respecting management of a plan under the definition of a fiduciary in ERISA Section 3(21)(A). Instead, these activities are analogous to those of the settlor of a trust, and when an employer acts in its capacity as a settlor, it is not regulated by the fiduciary duties set forth in ERISA Section 404(a). Thus, employers or other plan sponsors generally have the complete discretion to adopt, modify, or terminate employee benefit plans without acting in the capacity of a fiduciary.[4]

Fiduciaries are permitted to implement settlor functions in a non-fiduciary capacity, as an agent of the plan sponsor, on behalf of an employee benefit plan.[5] In general, settlor functions are not subject to the fiduciary provisions of ERISA where the fiduciaries who carry them out

---

1. As defined in ERISA Section 3(36).
2. See *Bruch v. Firestone Tire & Rubber Co.*, 828 F.2d 134 (3d Cir. 1987) (an unfunded plan is one where "every dollar provided in benefits is a dollar spent by ... the employer"), *aff'd* in part, *rev'd* in part, 489 U.S. 101 (1989); *Miller v. Eichleay Eng'rs, Inc.*, 886 F.2d 30 (3d Cir. 1989) (same).
3. *Crumley v. Stonhard, Inc.*, 920 F. Supp. 589 (D.N.J.), *aff'd*, 106 F.3d 384 (3d Cir. 1996) ("phantom stock" plan).
4. See DOL Op. Ltr. to John N. Erlenborn, 13 Pens. Rep. (BNA) 472 (Mar. 13, 1986). See, e.g., *Lockheed Corp. v. Spink*, 517 U.S. 882 (1996); *Adams v. Avondale Indus., Inc.*, 905 F.2d 943 (6th Cir.), cert. denied, 498 U.S. 984 (1990).
5. *NLRB v. Amax Coal Co.*, 453 U.S. 322 (1981); *Siskind v. Sperry Ret. Program*, 47 F.3d 498 (3d Cir. 1995).

do so without the exercise of any discretion.[1] Even where the fiduciary has exercised some discretion in the carrying out of settlor functions, fiduciary obligations will not normally be attached if the settlor functions have been properly documented and exercised as they relate to the general business activities of the employer.

The ability of an employer to avoid the fiduciary standards of ERISA by relying on the argument that it was performing purely settlor functions may be limited when, in fact, reasonable persons would conclude that it was acting in a dual capacity as both employer and plan fiduciary. See Q 236.

257. What guidance has the DOL provided with respect to fiduciary obligations for dealing with missing participants in a terminating defined contribution plan?

The DOL has issued Field Assistance Bulletin 2004-02 (FAB 2004-02), September 30, 2004, providing guidance to its field investigators as to the obligations of a fiduciary of a defined contribution plan to missing participants when the plan terminates. Specifically, FAB 2004-02 addresses the issue of what a fiduciary needs to do to fulfill its fiduciary obligations under ERISA with respect to (1) locating a missing participant of a terminated defined contribution plan and (2) distributing an account balance when efforts to communicate with a missing participant fail to secure a distribution election.

The DOL states that although the decision to terminate a plan is a settlor decision, the steps taken to actually implement that decision, including steps to locate missing participants, are fiduciary obligations pursuant to ERISA. Further, because distribution of a participant's vested account balance will terminate his or her status as a participant, the choice of a distribution option is also a fiduciary decision.

In attempting to locate a missing participant, FAB 2004-02 provides a series of particular search methods that should be taken to locate a participant before declaring the participant missing. But the DOL notes "in determining any additional steps that may be appropriate with regard to a particular participant, a plan fiduciary must consider the size of the participant's account balance and the expenses involved in attempting to locate the missing participant. Accordingly, the specific steps that a plan fiduciary takes to locate a missing participant may vary depending on the facts and circumstances."

FAB 2004-02 states that the search methods listed below involve nominal expense and such potential for effectiveness that a fiduciary must always use them, regardless of the size of the participant's account. The search methods that should be used, according to the Field Assistance Bulletin, are

1.   Sending correspondence to the participant via certified mail;

2.   Checking related plan records, including such things as the employer's own records or records of the group health plan maintained by the employer (if there are privacy

---

1. *Akers v. Palmer*, 71 F.3d 226 (6th Cir. 1995), cert. denied, _488 U.S.817 (1996); *Trenton v. Scott Paper Co.*, 832 F.2d 806 (3d Cir. 1987), cert. denied, 485 U.S. 1022 (1988).

concerns, the plan can instead ask the holder of the records to contact the participant directly and ask that the participant contact the plan fiduciary);

3.   Checking with any designated plan beneficiary on file;

4.   Miscellaneous other methods such as Internet search tools, commercial locator services, and credit reporting agencies. (If the cost of using these services will be charged to the missing participant's account, plan fiduciaries will need to consider the size of the participant's account balance in relation to the cost of the services when deciding whether the use of such services is appropriate.)

Where the above search methods are fruitless, FAB 2004-02 details the following distribution options that the DOL deems as satisfying the fiduciary's obligations in order to terminate the plan:

1.   The FAB says that a rollover to an IRA is the preferred distribution option because it is more likely to preserve assets for retirement purposes than any of the other identified options.

2.   If the fiduciary is unable to locate an IRA provider that will accept the rollover, it is suggested that the fiduciary consider either establishing an interest-bearing federally insured bank account in the name of the missing participant or escheating the account balances of missing participants to state unclaimed property funds in the state of the participant's last known residence or work location.

In FAB 2004-02, the DOL states that the decision to roll assets over to an IRA raises additional fiduciary issues as to the particular choice of an individual retirement plan trustee, custodian, or issuer, as well as the selection of an initial individual retirement plan investment to receive the distribution. It refers fiduciaries to Labor Regulation Section 2550.404a-2, which provides a safe harbor for plan fiduciaries to satisfy their fiduciary responsibility under ERISA Section 404(a) when selecting individual retirement plan providers and initial investments in connection with the rollovers of certain mandatory distributions to individual retirement plans.

The DOL has previously held that if a state unclaimed property statute were applied to require an ongoing plan to pay to the state amounts held by the plan on behalf of terminated employees, the application of that statute would be preempted by ERISA. But under FAB 2004-02, the DOL offers that "we do not believe that the principles set forth in Advisory Opinion 94-41A, which dealt with a plan fiduciary's duty to preserve plan assets held in trust for an ongoing plan, prevent a plan fiduciary from voluntarily deciding to escheat missing participants' account balances under a state's unclaimed property statute in order to complete the plan termination process."

A plan fiduciary's transfer of a missing participant's account balance from a terminated defined contribution plan to a state's unclaimed property fund would constitute a plan distribution, which ends both the property owner's status as a plan participant and the property's status as a plan asset under ERISA. Any transfer to state unclaimed property funds must comply with state law requirements.

In deciding between distribution into a state unclaimed property fund and distribution into a federally insured bank account, a plan fiduciary should evaluate any interest accrual and fees associated with a bank account against the availability of the state unclaimed property fund's searchable database that may facilitate the potential for recovery.

Should fiduciaries consider issuing a distribution with 100 percent withholding forwarded to the IRS? FAB 2004-02 says that after reviewing this option with the IRS, the DOL has concluded that the use of this option would not be in the interest of participants and beneficiaries and, therefore, would violate ERISA's fiduciary requirements. This is because under the IRS's current data processing, the 100 percent withholding distribution option would not necessarily result in the withheld amounts being matched or applied to the missing participants'/taxpayers' income tax liabilities, resulting in a refund of the amount in excess of such tax liabilities. This option, therefore, should not be used by plan fiduciaries as a means to distribute benefits to plan participants and beneficiaries.

Footnote five of FAB 2004-02 spells out that the above rules will not apply to any plan that has an annuity option. For these plans, the qualified joint and survivor annuity (QJSA) requirements will apply. Further, these rules will not apply if the employer maintains another defined contribution plan. In that case, the missing participant's assets must be transferred to the ongoing plan and all optional forms of benefits available from the transferring plan must be protected.

258. What guidance has the DOL provided regarding abandoned individual account plans?

The DOL has issued three rules to assist in the orderly and proper termination of individual account plans, and the distribution of benefits where the plans have been abandoned by their sponsoring employers. The DOL has also issued notice of a class prohibited transaction exemption that would permit a Qualified Termination Administrator (QTA) of an abandoned individual account plan to select and pay fees to itself or to an affiliate for performing termination-related services to the plan.[1] In December 2012, the DOL issued updated proposed regulations expanding the abandoned individual account plan rules to include plans sponsored by employers undergoing Chapter 7 bankruptcy proceedings. See the next question for detailed guidance on this.[2]

The rule establishes a framework through which financial institutions and other entities holding plan assets can terminate the abandoned plan and distribute the assets while incurring minimal liability. The initial determination of plan abandonment and the initial steps necessary to properly terminate the plan will need to be made by a QTA. A person or entity may qualify as a QTA only if it is qualified to serve as a trustee or as an issuer of IRAs, and it actually holds the assets of the plan for which it proposes to be the QTA.

A QTA may find that an individual account plan has been abandoned if there have been no contributions for more than twelve continuous months or where the facts and circumstances

---

1. Prop. Labor Reg. §§2578.1, 2520.103-13, 2550.404a-3; PTE Application No. D-11201 (70 Fed. Reg. 12,046 (Mar. 10, 2005)); as updated 77 Fed. Reg. 74063 (December 12, 2012).
2. Prop. DOL Reg. §§2520.103-13, 2550.404a-3, 2578.1, 77 Fed. Reg. 74063 (December 12, 2012).

known to the QTA indicate that the plan is, or may become, abandoned. Such circumstances could include the bankruptcy and cessation of operations by the plan sponsor, or communications between the plan, plan sponsor, and/or participants and beneficiaries that indicate abandonment or intent to abandon the subject plan. The latter would obviate the need to establish that twelve consecutive months have passed without a distribution and allow for more immediate steps to terminate the plan.

A second step for the QTA in determining abandonment requires the QTA to follow reasonable efforts to locate or communicate with the known plan sponsor, and determine that the plan sponsor no longer exists, cannot be located, or is unable to maintain the plan (due to physical, mental, financial, legal, or other impediments that, in the judgment of the QTA, prevent the sponsor from maintaining the plan in compliance with the governing documents and all applicable rules and regulations). "Reasonable notice" would include the provision of a notice from the QTA of its intent to terminate the plan and distribute the assets. The proposed regulation contains a model notice for this purpose.

Upon a finding of abandonment by the QTA, the regulation holds that the plan will be deemed terminated on the ninetieth day following the day on which the QTA issues notice to the DOL of its determination of plan abandonment and its election to serve as the QTA. This is intended to allow the DOL ample opportunity to review the circumstances and determine if it has any objections to the proposed activities of the QTA. The DOL also retains the right to waive or reduce the 90-day time period if, in its view, the QTA is accurate and the reduction of the time period would not put the assets at risk. The notice filed by the QTA with the DOL must include:

1.   Name of QTA;

2.   Employer identification number of QTA;

3.   Address and telephone number of QTA;

4.   Summary of steps taken to communicate with the plan and plan sponsor;

5.   Statement of election to terminate and wind up the plan;

6.   Itemized estimate of expenses the QTA expects to pay in terminating the plan;

7.   Details on any investigations, examination, or enforcement action by specified federal authorities;

8.   Plan name;

9.   Number of participants;

10.   Estimated assets of the plan;

11.   Known names and addresses of service providers to the plan; and

12.   Last known address of the plan sponsor.

In carrying out the termination, the QTA must take reasonable and diligent efforts to locate and update plan records necessary to determine benefits payable under the plan.

Under the regulation, the QTA will not be deemed to have failed to act reasonably and diligently merely because it determines in good faith that updating the records is either impossible or involves significant cost to the plan in relation to the total assets of the plan. In such circumstances, the QTA may determine benefits on less than complete or accurate records. But the QTA must take reasonable care in calculating the benefits payable based upon the available records.

The QTA must also provide a notice to participants and beneficiaries at their last known address. The notice must provide:

1.   A statement that the plan has been terminated;

2.   The participant's or beneficiary's account balance;

3.   Distribution options available under the plan;

4.   A request for the participant or beneficiary to make a distribution election;

5.   A statement that should a distribution election fail to be made, the assets will be rolled over into an IRA and invested in an investment product that is designed to preserve principal and provide a reasonable rate of return and liquidity; and

6.   The name, address, and telephone number of an appropriate contact person for questions that may arise.

If the notice is returned as undeliverable, the QTA must undertake those steps detailed in FAB 2004-02 (see Q 257 for details) for locating missing participants in a terminated defined contribution plan.

The QTA is permitted to engage those service providers it deems necessary to wind up the affairs of the plan and distribute the assets. The reasonable expenses of both the QTA and any service providers engaged may be paid from the assets of the plan. An expense will be deemed reasonable if

1.   It is necessary to wind up the affairs of the plan and distribute the benefits;

2.   It is consistent with industry rates for those services provided;

3.   It is not in excess of rates normally charged by the QTA to other customers for similar services; and

4.   Such services do not constitute a prohibited transaction or they are otherwise exempt from ERISA's prohibited transaction provisions.

The DOL has published, in conjunction with the regulations, a prohibited transaction exemption D-11201, which clarifies that QTAs (or their affiliates) can be reimbursed or compensated for services performed pursuant to the dictates of these proposed regulations.[1]

---

1. 70 Fed. Reg. 12,074 (Mar. 10, 2005).

The final step for the QTA in winding up the affairs of an abandoned individual account plan requires the filing of a notice to the DOL that all benefits have been distributed in accordance with the proposed regulation. This notice must include:

1. A statement that the plan has been terminated;

2. A statement that all assets have been distributed to participants and beneficiaries on the basis of the best available information;

3. A statement that the terminal report has accompanied the filing of the notice;

4. A statement that any plan expenses paid out of the trust were paid in compliance with applicable federal law; and

5. In cases where the expenses paid to the QTA exceed the estimate by 20 percent or more, a statement acknowledging and detailing the overrun.

The regulation contains a model final notice for this filing purpose.

Where the terms of the abandoned plan's governing documents contain provisions that would restrict the otherwise orderly termination of the plan and distribution of the assets pursuant to the terms of the regulation, Labor Regulation Section 2578.1(d)(3) allows for a determination by the QTA that the necessary plan amendments to permit the termination have been deemed to have occurred.

Finally, the rules hold that if the QTA carries out its responsibilities with regard to winding up the affairs of the abandoned plan in accordance with the above detailed provisions of the regulations, the QTA is deemed to have satisfied any responsibilities it may have under ERISA Section 404(a), except for the selection and monitoring of service providers. If, in selecting and monitoring the service providers, the QTA acted in accordance with the provisions of Part 4 of ERISA, it will not be liable for the service providers' acts and omissions of which the QTA has no knowledge.

259. What are the Proposed Regulations that would expand the Orphan Plan Termination Program to allow bankruptcy trustees to terminate plans maintained by plan sponsors who are liquidating under Chapter 7 of the Bankruptcy Code?

Under proposed regulations issued by the DOL, a bankruptcy trustee could terminate and liquidate a plan maintained by a plan sponsor that is liquidating under Chapter 7 of the Bankruptcy Code ("Chapter 7 plans"). In issuing the proposed regulations, the DOL cites "on-going challenges associated with terminating and winding up Chapter 7 plans as the reason for the proposal.[1]

Under the special rules proffered under the proposed regulations, a Chapter 7 plan may be terminated and liquidated upon the entry of an order for relief under Chapter 7 of the

---

1. Prop. DOL Reg. sections 2520.103-13, 2550.404a-3, 2578.1, 77 F.R. 74063 (December 12, 2012).

Bankruptcy Code.[1] No other finding needs to be made as would normally be required under DOL Reg. Sec. 2578.1(b).

A Chapter 7 plan would be deemed terminated as of the 90th day following the date of the letter from the DOL acknowledging receipt of the Notice of Plan Abandonment (described below). If, at any time before the plan is deemed terminated, the plan sponsor's Chapter 7 liquidation proceeding is dismissed or converted to a reorganization proceeding under Chapter 11 of the Bankruptcy Code, the plan will cease to be considered abandoned.[2]

Normally, the Qualified Termination Administrator (QTA) is restricted to a person (usually a financial institution) that is eligible to service as a trustee or issuer of an IRA and that holds assets of the abandoned plan. For a Chapter 7 plan, the QTA may be the bankruptcy trustee or an "eligible designee," which is defined as a person who is designated by the bankruptcy trustee and who would be eligible to be a QTA under the normal definition of a QTA.[3] NOTE: under the proposed regulations, the bankruptcy trustee would be responsible for the selection and monitoring of any eligible designee in accordance with the fiduciary standards under ERISA section 404(a)(1).

To commence the termination proceedings under the abandoned plan regulations, the QTA for the Chapter 7 plan would have to furnish a Notice of Plan Abandonment to the DOL that is signed and dated by the QTA and contains the following information.[4]

The Notice of Plan Abandonment must contain the following information:

1.   The name, address (including email address), and telephone number of the bankruptcy trustee and, if applicable, the name, EIN, address (including email address), and telephone number of any eligible designee acting as the QTA;

2.   The name, address, telephone number, account number, EIN, and plan number of the plan with respect to which the person is serving as the QTA, the name and last known address and telephone number of the plan sponsor, and the estimated number of participants and beneficiaries with accounts in the plan;

3.   A statement that the plan is considered to be abandoned due to an entry of an order for relief under Chapter 7 of the U.S. Bankruptcy Code, and a copy of the notice or order entered in the case reflecting the bankruptcy trustee's appointment to administer the plan sponsor's case;

4.   The estimated value of the plan's assets as of the date of the entry of an order for relief, the name, EIN, address (including email address) and telephone number of the entity that is holding these assets, and the length of time plan assets have been held by such entity, if the period of time is less than twelve months, an identification of any assets with respect to which there is no readily ascertainable fair market

---

1. Prop. DOL Reg. Sec. 2578.1(j)(1)(i).
2. Prop. DOL Reg. Sec. 2578.1(j)(1)(i).
3. Prop. DOL Reg. Sec. 2578.1(j)(1)(ii).
4. Prop. DOL Reg. Sec. 2578.1(j)(2).

value, as well as information, if any, concerning the value of such assets, and an identification of known delinquent contributions;

5.   The name, address, and telephone number of known service providers (e.g., recordkeeper, accountant, lawyer, other asset custodian(s)) to the plan, and an identification of any services considered necessary to carry out the QTA's authority and responsibility under this section, the name of the service provider(s) that is expected to provide such services, and an itemized estimate of expenses attendant thereto expected to be paid out of plan assets by the QTA; and

6.   A statement that the information being provided in the notice is true and complete based on the knowledge of the person electing to be the QTA, and that the information is being provided by the QTA under penalty of perjury.[1]

The procedures prescribed in existing DOL Regulation section 2578.1(d) (see prior question for details) would apply to the winding up of a Chapter 7 plan, subject to the modifications described subsequently.[2]

The QTA, consistent with the duties under ERISA section 404(a)(1), would have to take reasonable and good faith steps to collect known delinquent contributions on behalf of the plan, taking into account the value of the plan assets involved, the likelihood of a successful recovery, and the expenses expected to be incurred in connection with collection.

If the bankruptcy trustee designates an eligible designee, the bankruptcy trustee at the time of such designation would have to notify the eligible designee of any known delinquent contributions.[3] The DOL advises that an eligible designee's duty to collect delinquent contributions is limited expressly to those delinquent contributions it knows about based on the information provided by the bankruptcy trustee at the time of the designation. Thus, an eligible designee would have no duty to collect delinquent contributions if the bankruptcy trustee failed to disclose them to the eligible designee.

The QTA would have to report contributions (employer and employee) owed to the plan, and any activity that the QTA believes may be evidence of other fiduciary breaches that involve plan assets by a prior plan fiduciary. This information must be reported to the DOL in conjunction with the filing of the Notice of Abandonment described above, or in the Final Notice described in DOL Reg. Sec. 2578.1(d)(2)(ix) (see prior question for details). If a bankruptcy trustee designates an eligible designee, the bankruptcy trustee would have to provide the eligible designee with records under the control of the bankruptcy trustee to enable the eligible designee to carry out its responsibilities to make this report. If, after the eligible designee completes the winding up of the plan, the bankruptcy trustee, in administering the debtor's estate, discovers additional information not already reported in the Notice of Abandonment that it believes may be evidence of fiduciary breaches that involve plan assets by a prior plan fiduciary, the bankruptcy trustee would have to report such activity to the DOL in a time and manner specified in instructions

---

1. Prop. DOL Reg. sec. 2578.1(j)(2).
2. Prop. DOL Reg. sec. 2578.1(j)(3).
3. Prop. DOL Reg. sec. 2578.1(j)(3)(i).

developed by the Office of Enforcement, Employee Benefits Security Administration, U.S. Department of Labor.[1]

In the notice to participants required under DOL Reg. Sec. 2578.1(d)(2)(vi)(A), in lieu of the statement to participants that the plan has been abandoned by the employer, the notice would have to include a statement that the plan sponsor is in liquidation under chapter 7 of title 11 of the United States Code and, therefore, the plan has been terminated by the bankruptcy trustee (or its eligible designee).[2]

In the Final Notice described in DOL Reg. sec. 2578.1(d)(2)(ix), in lieu of the identifying information described in section 2578.1(d)(2)(ix)(A), the Final Notice would have to include the name, address (including email address), and telephone number of the bankruptcy trustee and, if applicable, the name, EIN, address (including email address), and telephone number of the eligible designee.[3]

The provision in DOL Reg. Sec. 2578.1(d)(2)(vii)(C) which allows a QTA to designate itself as the transferee of distribution proceeds in accordance with DOL Reg. Sec. 2550.404a-3 would not apply in the case of a QTA that is the plan sponsor's bankruptcy trustee.[4]

Under DOL Reg. Section 2578.1(d)(2)(v)(B), expenses paid of plan assets for plan administration are considered reasonable if specific conditions have been satisfied. One of those conditions is that the expenses are consistent with industry rates for such similar services, based on the experience of the QTA, and are not in excess of rates ordinarily charged by the QTA for same or similar services provided to customers that are not terminated abandoned plans, if the QTA provides same or similar services to such other customers.[5] This condition is modified if the QTA is the bankruptcy trustee. Instead, it would have to be shown that the expenses are consistent with industry rates for such or similar services ordinarily charged by a QTA.[6]

An eligible designee would be permitted to pay the bankruptcy trustee, from plan assets, for reasonable expenses incurred in the selection and monitoring of the eligible designee.[7] The DOL notes in the preamble that the rates charged to the plan by the bankruptcy trustee for selecting and monitoring the eligible designee are to be judged in relation to the rates charged by a plan fiduciary for similar services, rather than the generally higher fees charged by bankruptcy trustees for legal services provided to the bankruptcy estate. The eligible designee is required to apply the rules in DOL Reg. sec. 2578.1(d)(2)(v) in determining whether the payment to the bankruptcy trustee for monitoring services is reasonable.

The bankruptcy trustee or eligible designee would not be permitted to, through waiver or otherwise, seek a release from liability under ERISA, or assert a defense of derived judicial

---

1. Prop. DOL Reg. sec. 2578.1(j)(3)(ii).
2. Prop. DOL Reg. §2578.1(j)(3)(iii).
3. Prop. DOL Reg. §2578.1(j)(3)(iv).
4. Prop. DOL Reg. sec. 2578.1(j)(3)(v).
5. DOL Reg. Sec. 2578.1(d)(2)(v)(B)(2).
6. Prop. DOL Reg. Sec. 2578.1(j)(3)(vi)(A).
7. Prop. DOL Reg. Sec. 2578.1(j)(3)(vi)(C).

immunity (or similar defense) in any action brought against the bankruptcy trustee or eligible designee arising out of its conduct under this regulation.[1]

In distributing benefits, the procedures under DOL Reg. Sec. 2550.404a-3 is available to bankruptcy trustees who serve as QTAs. However, in the case of *de minimis* account ($1,000 or less), the bankruptcy trustee would be able to transfer the account to an interest-bearing bank account or to the unclaimed property fund of the State in which the participant's or beneficiary's last known address is located only if, after reasonable good faith efforts, is unable to locate an IRA provider who will accept the distribution.[2]

260. What are the final rules for determining a plan has been abandoned for purposes of termination?

The DOL final rules for terminating abandoned plans and distributing their benefits were effective May 22, 2006.[3] The purpose of these rules is to establish standards for the termination and winding up of an individual account plan (as defined in ERISA Section 3(34) with respect to which a Qualified Termination Administrator (QTA—see Q 261, following) has determined there is no responsible plan sponsor or plan administrator within the meaning of ERISA Section 3(16)(B) and (A) to perform such acts.

A QTA may find an individual account plan to be abandoned when either

1. No contributions to, or distributions from, the plan have been made for a period of at least twelve consecutive months immediately preceding the date on which the determination is being made; *or*

2. Other facts and circumstances (such as a filing by or against the plan sponsor for liquidation under title 11 of the United States Code or communications from participants and beneficiaries regarding distributions) known to the qualified termination administrator suggest that the plan is or may become abandoned by the plan sponsor; *and*

3. Following reasonable efforts to locate or communicate with the plan sponsor, the qualified termination administrator determines that the plan sponsor

   a. no longer exists,

   b. cannot be located, or

   c. is unable to maintain the plan.[4]

A QTA may not find a plan to be abandoned if, at any time before the plan is deemed terminated, the QTA receives an objection from the plan sponsor regarding the finding of abandonment and proposed termination.[5]

---

1. Prop. DOL Reg. sec. 2578.1(j)(4).
2. Prop. DOL Reg. sec. 2550.404a-3(d)(iv).
3. Labor Reg. §2578.1; 71 Fed. Reg. 20,820 (Apr. 21, 2006).
4. Labor Reg. §§2578.1(b)(1)(i)(A), 2578.1(b)(1)(i)(B), 2578.1(b)(1)(ii).
5. Labor Reg. §2578.1(b)(2).

Labor Regulation Section 2578.1(b)(3) and (4) provide that a QTA shall be deemed to have made a reasonable effort to locate or communicate with the plan sponsor if the QTA sends to the last known address of the plan sponsor, and, in the case of a plan sponsor that is a corporation, to the address of the person designated as the corporation's agent for service of legal process, by a method of delivery requiring acknowledgment of receipt, the notice described in Labor Regulation Section 2578.1(b)(5). If receipt of the notice is not acknowledged, the QTA shall be deemed to have made a reasonable effort to locate or communicate with the plan sponsor if the QTA contacts known service providers (other than itself) of the plan and requests the current address of the plan sponsor from such service providers and, if such information is provided, the QTA sends to each such address, by a method of delivery requiring acknowledgment of receipt, the notice.

The required notice shall contain the following information:

1. Name and address of the QTA;

2. Name of the plan;

3. Account number or other identifying information relating to the plan;

4. A statement that the plan may be terminated and benefits distributed pursuant to these regulations if the plan sponsor fails to contact the QTA within thirty days;

5. Name, address, and telephone number of the person, office, or department that the plan sponsor must contact regarding the plan;

6. A statement that if the plan is terminated pursuant to these regulations, notice of such termination will be furnished to the U.S. Department of Labor's Employee Benefits Security Administration;

7. The following statement: "The U.S. Department of Labor requires that you be informed that, as a fiduciary or plan administrator or both, you may be personally liable for costs, civil penalties, excise taxes, etc., as a result of your acts or omissions with respect to this plan. The termination of this plan will not relieve you of your liability for any such costs, penalties, taxes, etc."; and

8. A statement that the plan sponsor may contact the DOL for more information about the federal law governing the termination and winding-up process for abandoned plans and the telephone number of the appropriate EBSA contact person.[1]

If a QTA finds that an individual account plan has been abandoned, the plan shall be deemed to be terminated on the ninetieth day following the date of the letter from EBSA's Office of Enforcement acknowledging receipt of the notice of plan abandonment.[2] If, prior to the end of the ninety-day period the DOL notifies the QTA that it objects to the termination of the plan, the plan shall not be deemed terminated until the QTA is notified that the DOL has withdrawn

---

1. Labor Reg. §2578.1(b)(5)(i)-(viii).
2. Labor Reg. §2578.1(c)(1).

its objection. If the DOL notifies the QTA that it waives the ninety-day period, the plan shall be deemed terminated upon the QTA's receipt of such notification.[1]

261. What is a Qualified Termination Administrator (QTA) for purposes of an abandoned individual account plan?

Labor Regulation Section 2578.1(g)(1) and (2) provide that a Qualified Termination Administrator (QTA), for purposes of the abandoned plans termination regulations, is qualified if:

1. It is eligible to serve as a trustee or issuer of an individual retirement plan, within the meaning of IRC Section 7701(a)(37), and

2. It holds assets of the plan that is considered abandoned pursuant to Labor Regulation Section 2578.1(b) (see Q 260 for details).

To the extent that the activities enumerated under wind-up rules for terminating an abandoned plan (see Q 263) involve the exercise of discretionary authority or control that would make the QTA a fiduciary within the meaning of ERISA Section 3(21), the QTA shall be deemed to satisfy its responsibilities under ERISA Section 404(a) with respect to such activities, provided that the QTA complies with the wind-up rules.[2]

A QTA is responsible for the selection and monitoring of any service provider (with the exception of when a QTA determines that the survivor annuity requirements in IRC Sections 401(a)(11) and 417 (or ERISA Section 205) prevent a distribution under these abandoned plan termination regulations (see Q 263 below)) determined by the QTA to be necessary to the winding up of the affairs of the plan, as well as ensuring the reasonableness of the compensation paid for such services. If a QTA selects and monitors a service provider in accordance with the requirements of ERISA Section 404(a)(1), the QTA shall not be liable for the acts or omissions of the service provider with respect to which the QTA does not have knowledge.[3]

For purposes of a distribution where a QTA determines that the survivor annuity requirements in IRC Sections 401(a)(11) and 417 (or ERISA Section 205) prevent a distribution under these abandoned plan termination regulations, a QTA shall be responsible for the selection of an annuity provider in accordance with ERISA Section 404.[4]

Nothing under the abandoned plan termination regulations can be construed to impose an obligation on the QTA to conduct an inquiry or review to determine whether or what breaches of fiduciary responsibility may have occurred with respect to a plan prior to becoming the QTA for such plan.[5] If assets of an abandoned plan are held by a person other than the QTA, such person shall not be treated as in violation of ERISA Section 404(a) solely on the basis that the person cooperated with and followed the directions of the QTA in carrying out its responsibilities

---

1. Labor Reg. §§2578.1(c)(2)(i), 2578.1(c)(2)(ii).
2. Labor Reg. §2578.1(e)(i).
3. Labor Reg. §2578.1(e)(ii).
4. Labor Reg. §2578.1(e)(iii)(1).
5. Labor Reg. §2578.1(e)(iii)(2).

with respect to such plan, provided that, in advance of any transfer or disposition of any assets at the direction of the QTA, such person confirms with the DOL that the person representing herself to be the QTA with respect to the plan is the QTA recognized by the DOL.[1]

Nothing under the abandoned plans termination regulations shall serve to relieve or limit the liability of any person other than the QTA due to a violation of ERISA.[2]

262. What notice must a QTA provide the DOL upon a finding of plan abandonment?

Labor Regulation Section 2578.1(c)(3) holds that following a QTA's finding that an individual account plan has been abandoned, the QTA shall furnish to the DOL a notice of plan abandonment that is signed and dated by the QTA and that includes the following information:

QTA information:

1. Name, EIN, address, and telephone number of the person electing to be the QTA, including the address, e-mail address, and telephone number of the person signing the notice (or other contact person, if different from the person signing the notice).

2. A statement that the person electing to be the QTA is a QTA within the meaning of abandoned plan termination regulations and elects to terminate and wind up the plan in accordance with the regulations.

3. Identification whether the person electing to be the QTA or its affiliate is, or within the past twenty-four months has been, the subject of an investigation, examination, or enforcement action by the DOL, IRS, or SEC concerning such entity's conduct as a fiduciary or party in interest with respect to any plan covered by ERISA.[3]

Plan information:

1. Name, address, telephone number, account number, EIN, and plan number of the plan with respect to which the person is electing to serve as the QTA.

2. Name and last known address and telephone number of the plan sponsor.

3. Estimated number of participants in the plan.[4]

The QTA must also include a statement that the QTA finds that the plan is abandoned. This statement shall include an explanation of the basis for such a finding, specifically referring to the provisions of Labor Regulation Section 2578.1(b)(1) (above), a description of the specific steps taken to locate or communicate with the known plan sponsor, and a statement that no

---

1. Labor Reg. §§2578.1(e)(iii)(2), 2578.1(e)(iii)(3).
2. Labor Reg. §2578.1(f).
3. Labor Reg. §2578.1(c)(3)(i)(A), (B), and (C).
4. Labor Reg. §2578.1(c)(3)(ii)(A), (B), and (C).

objection has been received from the plan sponsor.[1] The following plan asset information must also be detailed in this statement:

1. Estimated value of the plan's assets held by the QTA;

2. Length of time the plan assets have been held by the QTA, if such period of time is less than twelve months;

3. Identification of any assets with respect to which there is no readily ascertainable fair market value, as well as information, if any, concerning the value of such assets; and

4. Identification of known delinquent contributions to the plan.[2]

Finally, the following service provider information must also be detailed:

1. Name, address, and telephone number of known service providers (e.g., record keeper, accountant, lawyer, other asset custodian(s)) to the plan; and

2. Identification of any services considered necessary to wind up the plan in accordance with this section, the name of the service provider(s) that is expected to provide such services, and an itemized estimate of expenses attendant thereto expected to be paid out of plan assets by the QTA.[3]

In closing, the required statement must contain a perjury statement that the information being provided in the notice is true and complete based on the knowledge of the person electing to be the QTA, and that the information is being provided by the QTA.[4]

263. How does the QTA wind up the affairs of an abandoned plan?

In any case where an individual account plan is deemed to be terminated, the QTA must take steps as may be necessary or appropriate to wind up the affairs of the plan and distribute benefits to the plan's participants and beneficiaries. The QTA shall undertake reasonable and diligent efforts to locate and update plan records necessary to determine the benefits payable under the terms of the plan to each participant and beneficiary.[5]

A QTA must not have failed to make reasonable and diligent efforts to update plan records merely because the administrator determines in good faith that updating the records is either impossible or involves significant cost to the plan in relation to the total assets of the plan. The QTA must also use reasonable care in calculating the benefits payable to each participant or beneficiary based on plan records. A QTA shall not have failed to use reasonable care in calculating benefits payable solely because the QTA

1. Treats as forfeited an account balance that, taking into account estimated forfeitures and other assets allocable to the account, is less than the estimated share of plan

---

1. Labor Reg. §2578.1(c)(3)(iii).
2. Labor Reg. §2578.1(c)(3)(iv)(A)-(D).
3. Labor Reg. §2578.1(c)(3)(v).
4. Labor Reg. §2578.1(c)(3)(vi).
5. Labor Reg. §§2578.1(d)(1), 2578.1(d)(2).

expenses allocable to that account, and reallocates that account balance to defray plan expenses or to other plan accounts;

2. Allocates expenses and unallocated assets in accordance with the plan documents, or, if the plan document is not available, if the plan document is ambiguous, or if compliance with the plan is unfeasible,

  a. allocates unallocated assets (including forfeitures and assets in a suspense account) to participant accounts on a per capita basis (allocated equally to all accounts); and

  b. allocates expenses on a pro rata basis (proportionately in the ratio that each individual account balance bears to the total of all individual account balances) or on a per capita basis (allocated equally to all accounts).[1]

Labor Regulation Section 2578.1(d)(2)(iii)(A) requires the QTA to notify the DOL of any known contributions (either employer or employee) owed to the plan in conjunction with the filing of the notification. No provision of the abandoned plan termination regulations, nor any other provision of ERISA, shall be construed to impose an obligation on the QTA to collect delinquent contributions on behalf of the plan, provided that the QTA satisfies the requirements detailed in this question.

Engage Service Providers and Pay Expenses

The QTA must engage, on behalf of the plan, such service providers as are necessary for the QTA to wind up the affairs of the plan and distribute benefits to the plan's participants and beneficiaries. In so doing, the QTA may pay reasonable expenses from plan assets in carrying out the termination of the plan.[2]

Expenses of plan administration shall be considered reasonable if

1. Such expenses are for services necessary to wind up the affairs of the plan and distribute benefits to the plan's participants and beneficiaries;

2. Such expenses

  a. are consistent with industry rates for such or similar services, based on the experience of the QTA; and

  b. are not in excess of rates ordinarily charged by the QTA (or affiliate) for the same or similar services provided to customers that are not plans terminated under these abandoned plans regulations, if the QTA (or affiliate) provides the same or similar services to such other customers; and

---

1. Labor Reg. §§2578.1(d)(2)(i)(A) and (B), 2578.1(d)(2)(ii)(A) and (B).
2. Labor Reg. §§2578.1(d)(2)(iv), 2578.1(d)(2)(v)(A).

3.   The payment of such expenses would not constitute a prohibited transaction under ERISA or is exempted from such prohibited transaction provisions pursuant to Section 408(a).[1]

Notify Participant

Labor Regulation Section 2578.1(d)(2)(vi)(A) requires the QTA to furnish to each participant or beneficiary of the plan a notice written in a manner calculated to be understood by the average plan participant and containing the following:

1.   Name of the plan;

2.   A statement that the plan has been determined to be abandoned by the plan sponsor and, therefore, has been terminated pursuant to regulations issued by the U.S. Department of Labor;

3.   A statement of the account balance and the date on which it was calculated by the QTA, and the following statement: "The actual amount of your distribution may be more or less than the amount stated in this letter depending on investment gains or losses and the administrative cost of terminating your plan and distributing your benefits";

4.   Description of the distribution options available under the plan and a request that the participant or beneficiary elect a form of distribution and inform the QTA (or designee) of that election;

5.   A statement explaining that, if a participant or beneficiary fails to make an election within thirty days from receipt of the notice, the QTA (or designee) will distribute the account balance of the participant or beneficiary directly:

   a.   to an individual retirement plan (i.e., individual retirement account or annuity),

   b.   to an individual account described in Labor Regulation Section 2550.404a-3(d)(1)(ii) in the case of a distribution on behalf of a distributee other than a participant or spouse,

   c.   in any case where the amount to be distributed meets the conditions in Labor Regulation Section 2550.404a-3(d)(1)(iii), to an interest-bearing federally insured bank account, the unclaimed property fund of the state of the last known address of the participant or beneficiary, or an individual retirement plan in the case of a distribution on behalf of a distributee other than a participant or spouse, or

   d.   to an annuity provider in any case where the QTA determines that the survivor annuity requirements in IRC Sections 401(a)(11) and 417 (or ERISA Section 205) prevent a distribution under the abandoned plan termination regulations;

---

1. Labor Reg. §2578.1(d)(2)(v)(B)(1), (2), and (3).

6. In the case of a distribution to an individual retirement plan, a statement explaining that the account balance will be invested in an investment product designed to preserve principal and provide a reasonable rate of return and liquidity;

7. A statement of the fees, if any, that will be paid from the participant or beneficiary's individual retirement plan or other account, if such information is known at the time of the furnishing of this notice;

8. Name, address, and telephone number of the provider of the individual retirement plan, qualified survivor annuity, or other account, if such information is known at the time of the furnishing of this notice; and

9. Name, address, and telephone number of the QTA and, if different, the name, address, and phone number of a contact person (or entity) for additional information concerning the termination and distribution of benefits.[1]

The notice shall be furnished to each participant or beneficiary to the last known address of the participant or beneficiary. In the case of a notice that is returned to the plan as undeliverable, the QTA shall, consistent with the duties of a fiduciary under ERISA Section 404(a)(1), take steps to locate and provide notice to the participant or beneficiary prior to making a distribution. If, after such steps, the QTA is unsuccessful in locating and furnishing notice to a participant or beneficiary, the participant or beneficiary shall be deemed to have been furnished the notice and to have failed to make an election within the thirty-day period required.[2]

Distribute Benefits

The QTA must distribute benefits in accordance with the form of distribution elected by each participant or beneficiary with spousal consent, if required. If the participant or beneficiary fails to make an election within thirty days from the date the notice is furnished, the QTA must distribute benefits

1. In accordance with Labor Regulation Section 2550.404a-3 of the abandoned plan termination regulations; or

2. In any manner reasonably determined to achieve compliance with those requirements if the QTA determines that the survivor annuity requirements in IRC Sections 401(a)(11) and 417 (or ERISA Section 205) prevent a distribution under these abandoned plan termination regulations.[3]

The QTA may designate itself (or an affiliate) as the transferee of such proceeds, and invest such proceeds in a product in which it (or an affiliate) has an interest, only if such designation and investment is exempted from the prohibited transaction provisions pursuant to ERISA Section 408(a).[4]

---

1. Labor Reg. §2578.1(d)(2)(vi)(A)(1)-(9).
2. Labor Reg. §§2578.1(d)(2)(vi)(B)(1), 2578.1(d)(2)(vi)(B)(2).
3. Labor Reg. §§2578.1(d)(2)(vii)(A), 2578.1(d)(2)(vii)(B)(1), 2578.1(d)(2)(vii)(B)(2).
4. Labor Reg. §2578.1(d)(2)(vii)(C).

The QTA must then file the Special Terminal Report for Abandoned Plans. See Q 258 for details.[1]

Final Notice

Labor Regulation Section 2578.1(d)(2)(ix) provides that no later than two months after the end of the month in which the QTA satisfies the requirements of the abandoned plan termination regulations, the QTA must furnish to the Office of Enforcement, Employee Benefits Security Administration, U.S. Department of Labor, 200 Constitution Avenue, NW, Washington, DC 20210, a notice, signed and dated by the QTA, containing the following information:

1.   Name, EIN, address, e-mail address, and telephone number of the QTA, including the address and telephone number of the person signing the notice (or other contact person, if different from the person signing the notice);

2.   Name, account number, EIN, and plan number of the plan with respect to which the person served as the QTA;

3.   A statement that the plan has been terminated and all the plan's assets have been distributed to the plan's participants and beneficiaries on the basis of the best available information;

4.   A statement that plan expenses were paid out of plan assets by the QTA in accordance with these regulations;

5.   If fees and expenses paid to the QTA (or its affiliate) exceed by 20 percent or more the estimate required, a statement that actual fees and expenses exceeded estimated fees and expenses and the reasons for such additional costs;

6.   Identification of known delinquent contributions (if not already reported); and

7.   A statement that the information being provided in the notice is true and complete based on the knowledge of the QTA, and that the information is being provided by the QTA under penalty of perjury.[2]

All Required Amendments "Deemed"

Under the abandoned plan termination regulations, the terms of the plan shall, for purposes of Title I of ERISA, be deemed amended to the extent necessary to allow the QTA to wind up the plan.[3]

264. How can a QTA file a simplified final annual report Form 5500 for an abandoned plan?

Labor Regulation Section 2520.103-13 provides a simplified method for the QTA to file a final Form 5500 for abandoned plans. In anticipation of the implementation of a mandatory

---

1. Labor Reg. §2578.1(d)(2)(viii).
2. Labor Reg. §2578.1(d)(2)(ix)(A)-(G).
3. Labor Reg. §2578.1(d)(3).

electronic filing system for Form 5500, the final Form 5500 is no longer required to be an attachment to the final EBSA notice under the abandonment procedure (although the DOL anticipates that, for now, final Form 5500s will be filed as attachments to final EBSA notices.) The QTA is not required to file any previously unfiled Form 5500s, but the plan sponsor or other plan fiduciaries would remain liable for all unfiled Form 5500s.[1]

The terminal report required to be filed by the QTA shall consist of the following items:

1. Identification information concerning the QTA and the plan being terminated;

2. Total assets of the plan as of the date the plan was deemed terminated, prior to any reduction for termination expenses and distributions to participants and beneficiaries;

3. Total termination expenses paid by the plan and a separate schedule identifying each service provider and amount received, itemized by expense;

4. Total distributions made and a statement regarding whether any such distributions were transfers; and

5. Identification, fair market value, and method of valuation of any assets with respect to which there is no readily ascertainable fair market value.[2]

The terminal report shall be filed on the most recent Form 5500 available as of the date the QTA satisfies the requirements of the abandoned plan termination regulations and in accordance with the Form's instructions pertaining to terminal reports of QTAs.[3] The QTA must file the terminal report within two months after the end of the month in which the QTA satisfies the requirements of the abandoned plan termination regulations.[4]

Along with the simplified final 5500 regulations, the DOL released prohibited transaction exemption 2006-06 permitting a QTA to select and pay itself to provide services and investment products in connection with the termination of an abandoned plan. See Q 444 for details.

265. What is the fiduciary safe harbor provided for automatic rollovers from terminated defined contribution plans?

Labor Regulation Section 2550.404a-3 provides a fiduciary safe harbor for QTAs to make distributions to IRAs on behalf of participants who fail to make distribution elections under the abandonment procedure.[5] The final safe harbor regulation codifies those parts of Field Assistance Bulletin 2004-02 (Sept. 30, 2004) relating to the distribution of assets to an individual retirement plan from terminating individual account plans in those instances in which a participant or beneficiary fails to make a distribution election. FAB 2004-02 did not address abandoned plans. These safe harbor rules are not limited to abandoned defined contribution

---

1. 71 Fed. Reg. 20,820 (Apr. 21, 2006).
2. Labor Reg. §2520.103-13(b)(1) to (5).
3. Labor Reg. §§2520.103-13(c)(1), 2520.103-13(c)(2).
4. Labor Reg. §2520.103-13(d).
5. 71 Fed. Reg. 20,820 (Apr. 21, 2006).

plans. They also apply to terminated plans where the participants and beneficiaries fail to make an affirmative election with respect to a distribution. These latter plans must be in compliance with IRC Section 401(a), 403(a), or 403(b) at the time of the distribution.[1]

The final regulation holds that if the conditions of the safe harbor are met, a fiduciary (including a QTA for an abandoned plan) is deemed to have satisfied the requirements of ERISA Section 404(a) with respect to the distribution of benefits, selection of an individual retirement plan provider or other account provider, and the investment of funds in connection with the distribution.[2]

In order for the safe harbor to apply, the fiduciary must demonstrate that the participant or beneficiary on whose behalf the distribution will be made was furnished the required notice and that the participant or beneficiary failed to elect a form of distribution within thirty days of the furnishing of the notice. Such distribution must be made

1.   To an individual retirement plan;

2.   In the case of a distribution on behalf of a distributee other than a participant or spouse, within the meaning of IRC Section 402(c), to an account (other than an individual retirement plan) with an institution eligible to establish and maintain individual retirement plans; or

3.   In the case of a distribution by a QTA with respect to which the amount to be distributed is $1,000 or less and that amount is less than the minimum amount required to be invested in an individual retirement plan product offered by the QTA to the public at the time of the distribution, to

   a.   an interest-bearing federally insured bank or savings association account in the name of the participant or beneficiary,

   b.   the unclaimed property fund of the state in which the participant's or beneficiary's last known address is located, or

   c.   an individual retirement plan offered by a financial institution other than the qualified termination administrator to the public at the time of the distribution.[3]

Except with respect to distributions to state unclaimed property funds, the fiduciary must enter into a written agreement with the transferee entity that provides that the distributed funds shall be invested in an investment product designed to preserve principal and provide a reasonable rate of return, whether or not such return is guaranteed, consistent with liquidity (except that distributions to a bank or savings account are not required to be invested in such a product).[4]

---

1. Labor Reg. §2550.404a-3(a)(2)(ii).
2. Labor Reg. §2550.404a-3(c).
3. Labor Reg. §2550.404a-3(d)(i), (ii), and (iii).
4. Labor Reg. §§2550.404a-3(d)(2)(i), 2550.404a-3(d)(2)(ii).

The investment product shall seek to maintain, over the term of the investment, the dollar value that is equal to the amount invested in the product by the individual retirement plan or other account, and be offered by a state or federally regulated financial institution, which shall be: a bank or savings association, the deposits of which are insured by the Federal Deposit Insurance Corporation; a credit union, the member accounts of which are insured within the meaning of Section 101(7) of the Federal Credit Union Act; an insurance company, the products of which are protected by state guaranty associations; or an investment company registered under the Investment Company Act of 1940.[1]

Labor Regulation Section 2550.404a-3(d)(2)(iii) and (iv) state that all fees and expenses attendant to the transferee plan or account, including investments of such plan or account (e.g., establishment charges, maintenance fees, investment expenses, termination costs, and surrender charges) shall not exceed the fees and expenses charged by the provider of the plan or account for comparable plans or accounts established for reasons other than the receipt of a distribution under this section; and the participant or beneficiary on whose behalf the fiduciary makes a distribution shall have the right to enforce the terms of the contractual agreement establishing the plan or account, with regard to his transferred account balance, against the plan or account provider.

Each participant or beneficiary of the plan shall be furnished a notice written in a manner calculated to be understood by the average plan participant and containing the following:

1. Name of the plan;

2. A statement of the account balance, the date on which the amount was calculated, and, if relevant, an indication that the amount to be distributed may be more or less than the amount stated in the notice, depending on investment gains or losses and the administrative cost of terminating the plan and distributing benefits;

3. A description of the distribution options available under the plan and a request that the participant or beneficiary elect a form of distribution and inform the plan administrator (or other fiduciary) of that election;

4. A statement explaining that, if a participant or beneficiary fails to make an election within 30 days from receipt of the notice, the plan will distribute the account balance of the participant or beneficiary to an individual retirement plan or other account and the account balance will be invested in an investment product designed to preserve principal and provide a reasonable rate of return and liquidity;

5. A statement explaining what fees, if any, will be paid from the participant or beneficiary's individual retirement plan or other account, if such information is known at the time of the furnishing of this notice;

---

1. Labor Reg. §§2550.404a-3(d)(2)(ii)(A), 2550.404a-3(d)(2)(ii)(B).

6. Name, address, and telephone number of the individual retirement plan or other account provider, if such information is known at the time of the furnishing of this notice; and

7. Name, address, and telephone number of the plan administrator (or other fiduciary) from whom a participant or beneficiary may obtain additional information concerning the termination.[1]

The notice shall be furnished to each participant or beneficiary at the last known address of the participant or beneficiary; and in the case of a notice that is returned to the plan as undeliverable, the plan fiduciary shall, consistent with its duties under ERISA Section 404(a)(1), take steps to locate the participant or beneficiary and provide notice prior to making the distribution. If, after such steps, the fiduciary is unsuccessful in locating and furnishing notice to a participant or beneficiary, the participant or beneficiary shall be deemed to have been furnished the notice and to have failed to make an election within thirty days for purposes of the safe harbor.[2]

Labor Regulation Section 2550.404a-3(f) provides that the Model Notice (see Appendix A) may be used to discharge the notification requirements of the safe harbor. Use of the model notice is not mandatory, but use of an appropriately completed model notice will be deemed to satisfy the notice requirements of the regulation.

266. Are expenses incurred in the execution of settlor functions payable out of plan assets?

In a Department of Labor (DOL) Information Letter to Kirk Maldonado (dated March 2, 1987), the DOL advised that "the use of plan assets to pay fees and expenses incurred in connection with the provision of services would not be a reasonable expense of administering a plan if the payments are made for the employer's benefit or involve services for which an employer could reasonably be expected to bear the cost in the normal course of such business or operations. In this regard, certain services provided in conjunction with the establishment, termination and design of plans, so called 'settlor' functions, relate to the business activities of an employer and, therefore, generally would not be the proper subject of payment by an employee benefit plan."

The letter goes on to provide that the prohibited transaction provisions of ERISA come into play in connection with payments for administrative services. ERISA Section 408(b)(2) exempts from the prohibited transaction provisions of ERISA Section 406(a) any contract or reasonable arrangement with a party in interest for office space, or legal or accounting or other services necessary for the establishment or operation of a plan. Such expenditures are to be reviewed on a case-by-case basis by taking into consideration all relevant facts and circumstances. "Thus, the fiduciaries of a plan should review all services provided to determine whether such services are 'necessary services' for which payment would be lawful."

---

1. Labor Reg. §2550.404a-3(e)(1)(i) to (vii).
2. Labor Reg. §2550.404a-3(e)(2).

The DOL later reiterated the position set forth in the Maldonado letter. In discussing its long-standing position forbidding plans from reimbursing settlor expenses to the plan sponsor, the DOL advises that "[e]xpenses incurred in the connection with the performance of settlor functions would not be reasonable expenses of a plan as they would be incurred for the benefit of the employer and would involve services for which an employer could reasonably be expected to bear the cost in the normal course of its business operations."[1] Although start-up expenses may not be paid out of plan expenses, a nonrefundable tax credit of 50 percent of certain administrative and retirement-education expenses is available to small employers (100 employees or less) adopting a new qualified plan, SIMPLE IRA plan, SEP, or payroll deduction IRA program. The credit applies to the first $1,000 of such expenses for the plan for each of the first three plan years.[2] For a discussion of the reimbursement to the plan sponsor of expenses incurred in the ongoing maintenance of the tax-qualified status of a plan, see Q 267.

267. What plan expenses may be paid out of plan assets?

Plan documents must expressly provide for the payment of plan expenses out of plan assets in order for the plan to be allowed to pay them. ERISA Section 402(b)(4) requires plans to specify the basis upon which payments will be made from the plan. ERISA Section 403(c)(1) provides that the assets of a plan shall never inure to the benefit of any employer and shall be held for the exclusive purposes of providing benefits to participants in the plan and their beneficiaries and defraying reasonable expenses of administering the plan. This is mirrored in ERISA Section 404(a)(1)(A), which requires fiduciaries to discharge their duties for the exclusive purpose of providing benefits to participants and beneficiaries and defraying reasonable expenses of administering the plan.

Reimbursable expenses include those that are reasonable and are for services rendered to the plan by a fiduciary.[3] Whether or not compensation paid to a party in interest by the plan is reasonable under ERISA Section 408(b)(2) and ERISA Section 408(c)(2) depends on the particular facts and circumstances of each case.[4] Reasonable compensation does not include any compensation to a fiduciary who is already receiving full-time pay from an employer or association of employers or from an employee organization, except for the reimbursement of direct expenses properly and actually incurred and not otherwise reimbursed.[5]

An expense is not a direct expense to the extent that it would have been sustained had the service not been provided or if it represents an allocable portion of overhead costs.[6]

The reimbursement of reasonable compensation to service provider arrangements where plan sponsor employees act in a fiduciary capacity may be a properly reimbursable direct expense if

1. The expense would not have been sustained had the service not been provided;

2. The expense can be properly allocated to the services provided;

---

1. DOL Adv. Op. 2001-01A.
2. IRC Sec. 45E.
3. ERISA Sec. 408(c).
4. Labor Reg. §2550.408c-2.
5. Labor Reg. §2550.408c-2(b)(2).
6. Labor Reg. §2550.408c-2(b)(3).

3.   The expense does not represent an allocable portion of overhead costs; and

4.   The service is a necessary service.[1]

The general fiduciary requirements of prudence will apply to these arrangements. Therefore, a proper evaluation of the arrangement that includes employees of the plan sponsor will be necessary, as well as the obligation to properly monitor the ongoing activities of such employees under the arrangement.

The DOL has issued guidance to assist plan sponsors in determining the extent to which an employee benefit plan may pay the costs attendant to maintaining tax-qualified status, without regard to the fact that tax qualification confers a benefit on the plan sponsor. Implementation of a tax-qualified plan is, the DOL advises, a settlor function for which a plan may not pay (see Q 266). But the ongoing maintenance of a plan's tax-qualified status may require fiduciaries to undertake certain activities for which a plan may pay reasonable expenses. The Advisory Opinion offers six hypothetical situations to provide clarification and facilitate compliance on this issue.[2]

268. How do ERISA Fee Recapture Accounts impact the rules on plan expenses being paid out of plan assets?

In Advisory Opinion 2013-03A (AO 2013-03A) the DOL addresses the different types of ERISA recapture accounts and discusses the ERISA plan asset and prohibited transaction rules that apply to them. In AO 2013-03A, the DOL describes two types of ERISA recapture accounts – the *bookkeeping account* and the *plan account*. Each requires a different approach in identifying how ERISA applies.

Under the *bookkeeping account approach*, the financial institution receives the revenue sharing payments and under an agreement with the plan establishes this account on the financial institution's records. The bookkeeping account reflects credits that under a written plan agreement or under the direction of a plan fiduciary, will apply these credits to pay plan service providers. In this approach, amounts in the bookkeeping account are *not* ERISA plan assets. Therefore, plan fees of any type may be paid under this approach.

However, the DOL advises that if there is an agreement in place for plan fees to be paid from this account and the financial institution fails to make such specified payments, the plan would have a claim against the financial institution and that claim *is* a plan asset.

Under the *plan account approach*, the financial institution receives the revenue sharing payments directly and under written agreement with the plan transfers some or all of the revenue sharing payments to the plan. The plan administrator then uses the plan account to pay service providers. IF, at the close of the plan year, amounts remain in the plan account, the plan administrator will then allocate them to participants as additional plan earnings.

---

1. DOL Adv. Op. 93-06A.
2. DOL Adv. Op. 2001-01A (clarifying DOL Adv. Op. 97-03A).

With the *plan account approach*, the amounts received in the account *are* plan assets. If the plan has a contract with the financial institution to transfer the funds to the plan, and the financial institution fails to make those payments, the plan would have a claim against the financial institution and that claim would be a plan asset. Therefore, under *plan account approach*, the guidelines spelled out above (under Advisory Opinion 93-06A) would govern the payment and reimbursement of plan expenses.

Regardless of the approach selected, the responsible plan fiduciary has the standard ERISA Section 404 fiduciary duties to act prudently and in the best interests of plan fiduciaries in deciding to enter into such an ERISA fee recapture/revenue sharing arrangement as well as the same duties in the ongoing monitoring of the arrangement.

AO 2013-03A does not mandate any plan language/provision updates in order to avail the plan to ERISA fee recapture arrangements.

269. May plan expenses be allocated among plan participants in a defined contribution plan?

Field Assistance Bulletin (FAB) 2003-03 sets forth guidelines on the allocation of administrative expenses among plan participants in a defined contribution plan. The FAB was issued in response to a number of questions being raised by the national and regional offices of the DOL in the course of investigations and otherwise concerning the propriety of certain expense allocation practices in defined contribution plans.

By way of background, the DOL noted in the FAB that ERISA contains no provisions specifically addressing how plan expenses may be allocated among participants and beneficiaries. But ERISA and implementing regulations do address certain instances in which a plan may impose charges on particular participants and beneficiaries. For example, ERISA Section 104(b)(4) provides that the plan administrator may impose a reasonable charge to cover the cost of furnishing copies of plan documents and instruments upon request of a participant or beneficiary.[1]

Also, ERISA Section 602 permits group health plans, subject to certain conditions, to require the payment of 102 percent of the applicable premium for any period of continuation coverage elected by an eligible participant or beneficiary. Further, the Labor regulations under ERISA Sections 404(c) and 408(b)(1) provide that reasonable expenses associated with a participant's exercise of an option under the plan to direct investments or to take a participant loan may be separately charged to the account of the individual participant.[2] By contrast, regulations may limit the ability of a plan to charge a particular participant or beneficiary by requiring that information be furnished free of charge upon request of a participant or beneficiary.[3]

According to the DOL, assuming that the expenses at issue are both proper expenses of the defined contribution plan and reasonable expenses with respect to the services to which they relate, FAB 2003-3 states that, for purposes of Title I of ERISA, certain administrative expenses

---

1. See Labor Reg. §§2520.104b-30, 2520.104-4(b)(2)(ii).
2. See Labor Reg. §2550.404c-1(b)(2)(ii)(A) and 54 Fed. Reg. 30,520, at 30,522 (July 20, 1989) (the preamble to Labor Reg. §2550.408b-1).
3. See Labor Reg. §§2520.104-46(b)(1)(i)(C), 2520.104b-1(c)(1)(iii) and (iv), 2520.104b-30.

may be allocated on a pro rata basis and certain administrative expenses may properly be charged to an individual participant rather than allocated among all plan participants.

But not every method of allocating plan expenses is reasonable, and a method that is not reasonable could result in a significant detriment. For example, allocating the expenses of active employees pro rata to all accounts, including the accounts of both active and former employees, while allocating the expenses of former employees only to their accounts would not be reasonable since former employees would be bearing more than an equitable portion of the plan's expenses.

Accordingly, such an allocation of expenses could be a significant detriment. Unfortunately, FAB 2003-03 relates solely to the application of Title I of ERISA, and is silent as to whether any particular allocation of expenses might violate the Internal Revenue Code or any other federal statute.

Allocating Expenses as a General Plan Expense

In the view of the DOL, when the plan documents are silent or ambiguous on this issue, fiduciaries must select the method or methods for allocating plan expenses. In doing so, a plan fiduciary must be prudent in the selection of the method of allocation. Prudence in such instances would, at a minimum, require a process by which the fiduciary weighs the competing interests of various classes of the plan's participants and the effects of various allocation methods on those interests. In addition to a deliberative process, a fiduciary's decision must satisfy the "solely in the interest of participants" standard set forth in ERISA §404. In this regard, a method of allocating expenses would not fail to be "solely in the interest of participants" merely because the selected method disfavors one class of participants, provided that a rational basis exists for the selected method, in the view of the DOL. (FAB 2003-3 cites the judicial standard as whether the fiduciary acted in an arbitrary or capricious manner in reviewing the propriety of such fiduciary actions. In meeting this standard, the fiduciary has a duty of impartiality to all the plan's participants and may appropriately balance the interests of different classes of participants in evaluating a proposed method of expense allocation.)[1]

But if a method of allocation has no reasonable relationship to the services furnished or available to an individual account, the DOL believes that a case might be made that the fiduciary breached his fiduciary duties to act prudently and "solely in the interest of participants" in selecting the allocation method. Further, in the case where the fiduciary is also a plan participant, the selection of the method of allocation may raise issues under the prohibited transaction provisions of ERISA Section 406 where the benefit to the fiduciary is more than merely incidental.[2] For example, if in anticipation of the plan fiduciary's own divorce, the fiduciary who is also a plan participant decides to change the allocation of expenses related to a determination of whether a domestic relations order constitutes a "qualified" order from the account incurring the expense to the plan as a whole, such a change by the fiduciary could constitute an act of self-dealing under ERISA Section 406, according to the DOL.

---

1. See *Varity Corp. v. Howe*, 516 U.S. 489, 514 (1996); Restatement (Second) of Trusts §183.
2. See DOL Advisory Op. 2000-10A.

While a pro rata method of allocating expenses among individual accounts (i.e., allocations made on the basis of assets in the individual account) would appear in most cases to be an equitable method of allocation of expenses among participants, it is not the only permissible method, in the view of the DOL. A per capita method of allocating expenses among individual accounts (i.e., expenses charged equally to each account, without regard to assets in the individual account) may also provide a reasonable method of allocating certain fixed administrative expenses of the plan, such as recordkeeping, legal, auditing, annual reporting, claims processing, and similar administrative expenses.

On the other hand, where fees or charges to the plan are determined on the basis of account balances, such as investment management fees, a per capita method of allocating such expenses among all participants would appear arbitrary to the DOL. With regard to services that provide investment advice to individual participants, a fiduciary may be able to justify the allocation of such expenses on either a pro rata or per capita basis and without regard to actual utilization of the services by particular individual accounts. Investment advice services might also be charged on a utilization basis, as discussed below, whereby the expense will be allocated to an individual account solely on the basis of a participant's utilization of the service.

Allocating Expenses to an Individual

In contrast to the methods of allocating plan expenses among all participants, in some circumstances, according to the DOL, an expense may be allocated (or charged) solely to a particular participant's individual account, rather than allocated among the accounts of all participants (e.g., on a pro rata or per capita basis). Some guidance on this issue was previous issued by the DOL in Advisory Opinion No. 94-32A. In analyzing the extent to which a plan may charge a participant (or alternate payee) for a determination as to whether a domestic relations order constitutes a "qualified" order, the DOL concluded in Advisory Opinion 94-32A that imposing the costs of a QDRO determination solely on the participant (or alternate payee) seeking the QDRO, rather than the plan as a whole, would violate ERISA.

Subsequent to the issuance of Advisory Opinion 94-32A, the DOL reviewed the basis for its position and concluded that neither the analyses nor conclusions set forth in Advisory Opinion No. 94-32A were legally compelled by the language of ERISA. In this regard, the DOL reversed its position in Advisory Opinion 94-32A and concluded that the same principles applicable to determining the method of allocating expenses among all participants, as discussed above, apply to determining the permissibility of allocating specific expenses to the account of an individual participant, rather than the plan as a whole (i.e., among all participants).

The DOL guidance in FAB 2003-3 provides the following examples of plan expenses that may be allocated to the account of a participant or beneficiary:

- *Hardship withdrawals.* A defined contribution plan may allocate reasonable expenses attendant to hardship withdrawals to the account of the participant or beneficiary seeking the withdrawal.

- *Calculation of benefits payable under different plan distribution options.* A defined contribution plan may allocate reasonable expenses attendant to the calculation of benefits payable under different distribution options available under the plan to the account of the participant or beneficiary seeking the information.

- *Benefit distributions.* A defined contribution plan may allocate reasonable expenses attendant to the distribution of benefits to the account of the participant or beneficiary seeking the distribution.

- *Accounts of separated vested participants.* In general, a defined contribution plan may charge the reasonable expenses of administering a plan to the individual accounts of the plan's participants and beneficiaries.

In the view of the DOL, nothing in Title I of ERISA limits the ability of a plan sponsor to pay only certain plan expenses or only expenses on behalf of certain plan participants. In the latter case, such payments by a plan sponsor on behalf of certain plan participants are equivalent to the plan sponsor's providing an increased benefit to those employees on whose behalf the expenses are paid. Therefore, plans may charge vested separated participant accounts the account's share (e.g., pro rata or per capita) of reasonable plan expenses, without regard to whether the accounts of active participants are charged such expenses and without regard to whether the vested separated participant was afforded the option of withdrawing the funds from her account or the option to roll the funds over to another plan or individual retirement account.

Qualified domestic relations orders (QDROs) and qualified medical child support order (QMCSO) determinations. A defined contribution plan may allocate reasonable expenses attendant to QDRO or QMCSO determinations to the account of the participant or beneficiary seeking the determination.

Practitioner's Pointer: As pointed out in the FAB, it should be noted that, pursuant to Labor Regulation Section 2520.102-3(*l*), plans are required to include in the summary plan description a summary of any provisions that may result in the imposition of a fee or charge on a participant or beneficiary, or the individual account thereof, the payment of which is a condition to the receipt of benefits under the plan. In addition, Labor Regulation Section 2520.102-3(*l*) provides that summary plan descriptions must include a statement identifying the circumstances that may result in the "offset, [or] reduction … of any benefits that a participant or beneficiary might otherwise reasonably expect the plan to provide on the basis of the description of benefits." Accordingly, a plan sponsor should review the summary plan description to see that it conforms to the above content requirements, especially if the plan sponsor changes the method of allocating plan expenses in reaction to the guidance in FAB 2003-3.

For the view of the Internal Revenue Service on this issue, see Revenue Ruling 2004-10,[1] in which the IRS held that an allocation of administrative expenses of a defined contribution plan to the individual account of a participant who does not consent to a distribution is not a significant detriment within the meaning of Treasury Regulation Section 1.411(a)-11(c)(2)(i) if that allocation is reasonable and otherwise satisfies the requirements of Title I of ERISA, such as a pro rata allocation.

---

1. 2004-7 I.R.B. 484.

270. Are business decisions of an employer fiduciary acts?

No. Under ERISA, purely business decisions by an employer are not governed by the fiduciary standards set forth in ERISA Section 404. "ERISA … envisions that employers will act in a dual capacity as both fiduciary to the plan and as employer. ERISA does not prohibit an employer from acting in accordance with its interests as employer when not administering the plan or investing its assets."[1]

But the DOL has determined that the selection of health care services for an employer-sponsored health care plan is a fiduciary function as an exercise of authority and control, due to the disposition of plan assets in paying for such services. The DOL has advised that since this selection is a fiduciary function, employers have a fiduciary duty to consider the quality of service to be rendered under the plan when making the selection, and failure to do so will constitute a breach thereof.[2]

"ERISA does not require that day-to-day corporate business transactions, which may have a collateral effect on prospective, contingent employee benefits, be performed solely in the interest of plan participants."[3] Thus, ordinary business decisions, such as whether to pay a dividend or whether to incur debt, may be made without fear of liability for a breach of fiduciary duty under ERISA, even though they may turn out to have negative consequences for plan participants. Even business decisions that directly affect the plan and plan participants, such as the decision to modify or terminate welfare benefits, are not governed by ERISA's fiduciary obligations because they do not involve discretionary administration of the plan.[4] For example, under the exclusion from fiduciary standards for business decisions, corporate actions by plan administrators seeking to reduce the amount of unaccrued plan benefits, terminating a pension plan, and deciding whether or not to establish a plan, have all been found nonfiduciary in nature.[5]

The Tenth Circuit Court of Appeals ruled that where a corporate CEO made corporate asset allocation decisions completely isolated to his position as CEO that negatively impacted the corporate health plan, resulting in approximately $1 million in unpaid medical claims, he was not functioning in his role as welfare plan fiduciary and, therefore, could not be held liable for alleged fiduciary breaches stemming from his decisions.[6]

After their financially troubled employer filed for bankruptcy and terminated the plan, participants filed a class-action lawsuit. The complaint alleged that while the plan was underfunded, the company's CEO, who was also a plan fiduciary, authorized a variety of payments from the company's assets, including substantial distributions to the company's

---

1. *Hickman v. Tosco Corp.*, 840 F.2d 564 (8th Cir. 1988) (quoting *Phillips v. Amoco Oil Co.*, 799 F.2d 1464 (11th Cir. 1986)). See also *Trenton v. Scott Paper Co.*, 832 F.2d 806 (3d Cir. 1987), cert. denied, 485 U.S. 1022 (1988).
2. DOL Information Letter to Service Employees' International Union (Feb. 19, 1998).
3. *Hickman v. Tosco Corp.*, above; see also *Adams v. Avondale Indus., Inc.*, 905 F.2d 943 (6th Cir.), cert. denied, 498 U.S. 984 (1990).
4. See *Curtiss-Wright Corp. v. Schoonejongen*, 514 U.S. 73 (1995). (The Supreme Court in *Curtiss-Wright* also quoted *Adams v. Avondale Indus., Inc.*, above, for the proposition that "a company does not act in a fiduciary capacity when deciding to amend or terminate a welfare benefits plan.")
5. *West v. Greyhound Corp.*, 813 F.2d 951 (9th Cir. 1987); *Cunha v. Ward Foods, Inc.*, 804 F.2d 1418 (9th Cir. 1986); *Moore v. Reynolds Metals Co.*, 740 F.2d 454 (6th Cir. 1984), cert. denied, 469 U.S. 1109 (1985).
6. *Holdeman v. Devine*, 2007 U.S. App. LEXIS 928 (10th Cir. 2007).

owners. The district court concluded that the CEO did not breach his ERISA fiduciary duties to the plan or its participants. The employees appealed, claiming that the CEO breached his ERISA fiduciary duties by, among other things, (1) failing to ensure that the plan was fully funded and (2) not challenging (in his capacity as plan fiduciary) his own decision authorizing distributions of company assets to the company's owners (made in his capacity as CEO).

On appeal, the Tenth Circuit advised that while an ERISA fiduciary may wear two hats, the CEO lacked authority, in his role as plan fiduciary, to decide whether to allocate company assets to the plan or elsewhere. Those decisions could only be made in the CEO's role as CEO. Because he was wearing his "CEO hat" at all times when he decided how to allocate company assets, he was not acting in his fiduciary capacity. Consequently, those decisions could not result in a breach of fiduciary duties. The court returned the case to the trial court for additional consideration of several claims the trial court failed to address earlier.[1]

271. Do employers owe a fiduciary duty to participants?

Generally, employers owe no fiduciary duty toward plan beneficiaries under ERISA. But when employers choose to "wear two hats" (i.e., act as both employer and plan administrator), they become subject to ERISA fiduciary duties regarding plan administration.[2] See also Q 236. Employers who act as plan administrators "assume fiduciary status only when and to the extent that they function in their capacity as plan administrators, not when they conduct business that is not regulated by ERISA."[3]

The Eighth Circuit ruled that an employer did not breach any fiduciary duty to participants by not following through on a "promise" to provide, once financial stability was recovered, missed contributions to two pension plans that were amended to provide that contributions were being suspended during a financial crisis.[4]

The Seventh Circuit affirmed a lower court's decision that plan fiduciaries were not obligated to tell thrift plan participants that they had decided to sell their own holdings in company stock, both within the plan and otherwise.[5]

In its opinion, the appellate court pointed out the fiduciaries had disclosed the sale of their stock held through the thrift plan—and also stock they were able to acquire by exercising vested options they had received in their roles as managers or directors of Indianapolis Power & Light—in filings with the Securities and Exchange Commission (SEC) and the markets. The court noted that rank-and-file workers do not read such filings, but investment analysts do, and the fiduciaries had hired Merrill Lynch to provide advice to each participant personally.

According to the ruling, ERISA "does not hold a fiduciary responsible for the decline in an investment's value, when an informed and independent investment adviser has been furnished

---

1. *Holdeman v. Devine*, 2007 U.S. App. LEXIS 928 (10th Cir. 2007). See also Q 282 and Q 283 for further details on this matter.
2. See *Payonk v. HMW Indus., Inc.*, 883 F.2d 221 (3d Cir. 1989).
3. *Payonk v. HMW Indus., Inc.*, above (quoting *Amato v. Western Union Int'l, Inc.*, 773 F.2d 1402 (2d Cir. 1985), cert. dismissed, 474 U.S. 1113 (1986)).
4. *Kalda v. Sioux Valley Physician Partners Inc.*, 481 F.3d 639 (8th Cir. 2007).
5. *Nelson v. Hodowal*, 512 F.3d 347 (7th Cir. 2008).

without charge to all beneficiaries, who exercise full control over which investments their accounts will hold."[1]

The Third Circuit Court of Appeals has ruled that a plan sponsor's alleged misrepresentations that caused a nonemployee spouse of a plan participant to retire were not a fiduciary breach.[2] In that case, the participant and his spouse claimed that there should be fiduciary liability based upon their detrimental reliance on a series of letters and worksheets regarding the participant's pension benefits. The letters to the participant, a longtime employee of the employer and its predecessor companies, addressed how his length of service would be calculated under the plan. The participant claimed that he calculated his expected pension benefits based on one of the letters that indicated he would be able to retire with a full pension. As a result, the spouse retired from her job at a different company. In later correspondence, however, the employer informed the participant that his benefit would be significantly less than previously stated due to his credited service calculation being complicated by a change in ownership. In denying the detrimental reliance allegation, the Third Circuit stated that although the couple may have taken action based on the employer's letters in deciding that the spouse should retire, this decision did not implicate either the participant's or the spouse's benefits under the employer's pension plan. Thus, this kind of reliance was "too attenuated" to hold the employer liable as a fiduciary.[3]

272. Are the notice obligations imposed on a plan administrator under the provisions of COBRA fiduciary duties?

In the case of *Onyebuchi v. Volt Management Corp.*,[4] the district court ruled, in dismissing the claim for damages under the theory of breach of fiduciary duty, that the failure to properly issue the notice mandated under COBRA does not rise to the level of a fiduciary breach for interference with rights under ERISA. The court ruled that the proper remedy in this matter was set forth in the statutory penalties already delineated under COBRA.

Practitioner's Pointer: The better course of action for the plaintiff under the *Onyebuchi* case would have been to investigate the ability of pursuing the claim for COBRA benefits under ERISA Section 502(a)(1)(B), which would have permitted him to recover benefits under the terms of the plan document.

---

273. What guidance has the DOL provided for fiduciaries of terminated defined contribution plans with missing participants?

Field Assistance Bulletin (FAB) 2004-02 provides guidance on the responsibilities of employee benefit plan fiduciaries in connection with missing participants in terminated defined contribution plans governed by ERISA. The guidance provides the steps fiduciaries must take

---

1. *Nelson v. Hodowal*, 512 F.3d at 351.
2. *Shook v. Avaya, Inc.*, 2010 WL 4292065 (3d Cir. 2010).
3. *Shook v. Avaya, Inc.*, 2010 WL 4292065 (3d Cir. 2010).
4. 2005 U.S. Dist. LEXIS 5175 (N.D. Tex. 2005).

to locate missing participants and beneficiaries in order to satisfy ongoing obligations under ERISA Section 404(c).[1]

The steps fiduciaries must take include checking related plan records and using the IRS's or Social Security Administration's letter-forwarding services. In addition, plan fiduciaries can follow the safe harbor regulations governing automatic rollovers for guidance on distributing benefits.

Under the Internal Revenue Code, a terminated plan is required to distribute all plan assets as soon as administratively feasible after the plan's termination date. In this FAB, the DOL explains the responsibilities of plan fiduciaries in connection with missing participants in terminated defined contribution plans governed by ERISA (see Q 274 to Q 278).

The application of the guidance is limited to terminated defined contribution plans that do not provide an annuity option, and to employers sponsoring those plans, so long as the employers do not maintain any other defined contribution plans to which the account balances of the terminated plan could be transferred. Fiduciaries of ongoing plans with missing participants may find the discussion of the search methods useful, but neither this guidance nor the DOL's automatic rollover safe harbor regulations address fiduciary issues or distribution options for missing participants in ongoing plans.

274. What are the mandatory search methods under FAB 2004-2?

Field Assistance Bulletin (FAB) 2004-02 (see Q 273) provides that standard methods for delivering plan termination and distribution notices to participants (i.e., first-class mail or electronic notification) are adequate in most instances. If these methods fail to generate the needed information or if the fiduciary has reason to believe the participant's address on file is incorrect, fiduciaries must take additional search measures (regardless of the size of the account). The four mandatory steps are:

1.   Certified mailing to last known address;

2.   Checking related plan records, such as the employer's group health plan, for a more current address (ask the employer and the plan administrator of other plans);

3.   Checking with the participant's designated plan beneficiaries (request they forward a letter if they raise privacy concerns); and

In accordance with the provisions of FAB 2003-03, reasonable expenses attendant to locating a missing participant may be charged to a participant's account, provided that the amount of the expenses is reasonable and the method of allocation is consistent with the terms of the plan and the plan fiduciary's duties under ERISA.[2]

The DOL advises in the FAB that fiduciaries should consider other search options, such as Internet searches, commercial locator services, and credit reporting agencies. If the cost of

---

1. EBSA FAB 2004-02 (Sept. 30, 2004), available at http://www.dol.gov/ebsa/pdf/fab-2004-2.pdf.
2. EBSA FAB 2004-02 (Sept. 30, 2004).

these additional search options will be charged to participants' accounts, plan fiduciaries must consider the size of a participant's account in relation to the cost of the search when deciding whether the search option is appropriate.

275. What IRA distribution options are provided for under Field Assistance Bulletin 2004-02?

If the four mandatory efforts described in Q 274 fail and the participants cannot be found, the FAB provides that the preferred distribution option is to set up an IRA for the missing participant, because an IRA rollover allows for preservation of capital by avoiding both the 20 percent withholding requirement and any applicable 10 percent early distribution penalty that may otherwise apply.

The DOL has issued guidance providing a safe harbor for mandatory IRA rollovers ($5,000 or less where the participant has failed to make a distribution election) and the selection of the trustee and custodian.[1] The FAB says that fiduciaries that establish IRAs using the DOL's automatic rollover safe harbor regulations for missing participants (without regard to the amount involved in the rollover) should, as an enforcement matter, be treated as satisfying their fiduciary duties.[2]

Practitioner's Pointer: Although the FAB allows the establishment of a rollover IRA for missing participants, the selection of the underlying investment vehicles within the IRA is still considered a fiduciary duty under ERISA. The DOL has provided no guidance as to what constitutes the appropriate exercise of such discretion in this matter.

---

276. What alternative distribution options are provided under Field Assistance Bulletin 2004-02?

If a plan fiduciary cannot locate a financial institution willing to establish a rollover IRA for a missing participant (many financial institutions will not open an IRA absent a participant's signature), the fiduciary may consider establishing separate interest-bearing, federally insured bank accounts in each missing participant's name. Such an account must provide the participant with an unconditional right to the assets upon a request for distribution.

Alternatively, the fiduciary may consider transferring missing participants' account balances to state unclaimed property funds. The assets should be submitted to the state where the participant had his last known address on file with the plan.

The DOL advises that under the situations addressed within the FAB, listing the state unclaimed property fund as an allowable transfer option for missing participants' account balances is not considered an alienation of benefits preempted under ERISA Section 514(a). This holding differs from the DOL position stated in ERISA Opinion Letter 94-41A, which concluded that if a state unclaimed property statute were to require an ongoing plan to pay to the state

---

1. See Labor Regulation Section 2550.404a-2 and Q 278).
2. EBSA FAB 2004-02 (Sept. 30, 2004).

amounts held on behalf of terminated employees, the statute would be preempted by ERISA Section 514(a). According to the FAB, a transfer of a missing participant's account balance from a terminated defined contribution plan to a state's unclaimed property fund would constitute a plan distribution, which would end the account holder's status as a plan participant, and the account's status as a plan asset under ERISA.

Under either option, the FAB notes that either transfer (i.e., to an interest-bearing bank account or to a state unclaimed property fund) will subject the funds to income taxation and possibly to the 10 percent early distribution penalty.

The FAB states that undertaking a 100 percent income tax withholding on a missing participant's account is not a valid distribution option.[1]

277. What is the DOL safe harbor for rollovers of mandatory cash-outs?

The Internal Revenue Code requires that, for a plan with a mandatory cash-out provision to remain tax-qualified, the plan must require that the plan administrator transfer the cash-out distribution to an IRA of a designated trustee or IRA issuer if:

- A distribution of a nonforfeitable accrued benefit of more than $1,000, but no more than $5,000 is made; and

- The plan participant (or beneficiary) receiving the distribution does not elect to have the distribution paid directly to another qualified plan or IRA (a direct rollover), and does not elect to receive the distribution herself.[2]

These provisions were not scheduled to take effect until after the DOL issued final regulations providing a safe harbor for plan fiduciaries who handle automatic rollovers to IRAs of mandatory cash-outs from qualified plans. Such regulations were issued in 2004, and took effect March 28, 2005.

The final regulations establish a safe harbor pursuant to which a fiduciary of a pension plan subject to Title I of ERISA will be deemed to have satisfied her fiduciary responsibilities in connection with automatic rollovers of certain mandatory distributions to individual retirement plans. The regulations also extend the safe harbor to cover mandatory distributions of $1,000 or less.[3]

In conjunction with the final regulations, the DOL has issued Prohibited Transaction Exemption (PTE) 2004-16, which allows financial institutions (or their affiliates) who are plan administrators to designate themselves (or their affiliates) as the IRA provider to receive the automatic rollover of the cash-outs. See Q 278.[4]

---

1. EBSA FAB 2004-02 (Sept. 30, 2004).
2. See IRC Sec. 401(a)(31)(B).
3. See Labor Reg. 2550.404a-2(d).
4. See Labor Reg. 2550.404a-2.

278. What are the safe harbor requirements for rollovers of mandatory distributions?

Final regulations provide that safe harbor relief depends on a fiduciary's satisfying the conditions explained below. If these conditions of the safe harbor are met, fiduciaries will be deemed to have satisfied their fiduciary duties under ERISA Section 404(a) with respect to both the selection of an individual retirement plan provider and the investment of funds in connection with an automatic rollover of a mandatory distribution described in IRC Section 401(a)(31)(B) to an individual retirement plan, within the meaning of IRC Section 7701(a)(37).[1]

With respect to an automatic rollover of a mandatory distribution, a fiduciary will qualify for the safe harbor if all the following occur:

1. The present value of the nonforfeitable accrued benefit does not exceed $5,000.[2]

2. The mandatory distribution is to an individual retirement plan as defined under IRC Section 408.[3]

3. In connection with the distribution of rolled-over funds to an individual retirement plan, the fiduciary enters into a written agreement with an individual retirement plan provider that provides that

    a. the rolled-over funds will be invested in an investment product designed to preserve principal and provide a reasonable rate of return, whether or not such return is guaranteed, consistent with liquidity;

    b. the investment product selected for the rolled-over funds shall seek to maintain, over the term of the investment, the dollar value that is equal to the amount invested in the product by the individual retirement plan;

    c. the investment product selected for the rolled-over funds shall be offered by a state or federally regulated financial institution, which shall be: a bank or savings association, the deposits of which are insured by the FDIC; a credit union, the member accounts of which are insured within the Federal Credit Union Act; an insurance company, the products of which are protected by state guaranty associations; or an investment company registered under the Investment Company Act of 1940;

    d. all fees and expenses attendant to an individual retirement plan, including investments of such plan (e.g., establishment charges, maintenance fees, investment expenses, termination costs, and surrender charges) shall not exceed the fees and expenses charged by the individual retirement plan provider for comparable individual retirement plans established for reasons other than the receipt of an automatic rollover distribution; and

---

1. See Labor Reg. §2550.404a-2(b).
2. Labor Reg. §2550.404a-2(c)(1).
3. Labor Reg. §2550.404a-2(c)(2).

e. the participant on whose behalf the fiduciary makes an automatic rollover shall have the right to enforce the terms of the contractual agreement establishing the individual retirement plan, with regard to his rolled-over funds, against the individual retirement plan provider.[1]

Further, the regulations require that participants be furnished a summary plan description, or a summary of material modifications, that describes the plan's automatic rollover provisions, including an explanation that the mandatory distribution will be invested in an investment product designed to preserve principal and provide a reasonable rate of return and liquidity, a statement indicating how fees and expenses attendant to the individual retirement plan will be allocated (i.e., the extent to which expenses will be borne by the account holder alone or shared with the distributing plan or plan sponsor), and the name, address, and phone number of a plan contact (to the extent not otherwise provided in the summary plan description or summary of material modifications) for further information concerning the plan's automatic rollover provisions, the individual retirement plan provider, and the fees and expenses attendant to the individual retirement plan.[2]

Finally, neither the fiduciary's selection of an individual retirement plan nor the investment of funds may result in a prohibited transaction, unless such actions are exempted by a prohibited transaction exemption under ERISA Section 408(a).[3]

The safe harbor regulations apply to any mandatory rollover distribution made after March 27, 2005.[4]

279. Are employers' communications to plan participants about business decisions that may affect pension benefits subject to the fiduciary standards?

They can be. The Supreme Court articulated a standard for determining the existence of fiduciary status when it held that conveying information about the likely future of plan benefits, in the context of communicating about a business decision, is a fiduciary act, and an employer breached its fiduciary duties by lying to the plan participants.[5]

In *Varity* (see Q 236), the employer made intentional misrepresentations for the purpose of inducing employees to make a choice about continued participation in an employee benefit plan. The Supreme Court emphasized the importance of that factual context in its conclusions that the employer's acts were acts of "plan administration" and, therefore, were subject to fiduciary review. Abandoning the statutory definition of what constitutes fiduciary conduct, and replacing it with a rule that turns on the subjective perceptions of plan participants, the Court held that an employer who sponsors an ERISA-covered plan, and who communicates to participants about a business decision, may rise to the status of a fiduciary if the communications pertain to or bear on the "likely future of plan benefits."

---

1. Labor Reg. §2550.404a-2(c)(3)(i) to (v).
2. Labor Reg. §2550.404a-2(c)(4).
3. Labor Reg. §2550.404a-2(c)(5).
4. Labor Reg. §2550.404a-2(e).
5. *Varity Corp. v. Howe*, 514 U.S. 1082 (1996).

The Sixth Circuit has ruled that an employer has a fiduciary duty to avoid making material misrepresentations concerning benefit entitlements as soon as any plan enhancements are subject to "serious consideration" by the plan sponsor.[1] The case arose because the plan sponsor offered certain employees an early retirement incentive plan while, unbeknownst to the employees offered early retirement, developing an enhanced retirement plan that became effective soon after the employees retired. The retired employees sued, claiming that the plan sponsor used material misrepresentations and deliberate nondisclosure to fraudulently induce them to opt for early retirement rather than using a leave of absence option that would have made them eligible for the enhanced benefit plan. In the ruling, the court relied on a Third Circuit ruling[2] applying a three-part "serious consideration" test. Under the test, "serious consideration" occurs "when (1) a specified proposal (2) is being discussed for purposes of implementation (3) by senior management with the authority to implement the change."[3]

The Ninth Circuit has expanded the Sixth Circuit's "serious consideration" rule in holding that "actively misled" employees were entitled to involuntary termination benefits despite retiring before the benefits were under "serious consideration."[4] In a suit filed by retired Chevron workers, the Ninth Circuit determined that those employees who had retired before an involuntary termination benefit program was under "serious consideration" by Chevron were nonetheless entitled to the benefits since they had been "actively misled" by Chevron regarding the program's future availability.

Even though the serious consideration test was not met until after the plaintiffs had retired (a matter of weeks), the district court, following the Ninth Circuit's decision in *Wayne v. Pacific Bell*,[5] determined that several pre–May 1999 statements by management were material and so amounted to fiduciary breaches. Although Chevron argued that these statements had to have been knowingly false (rather than merely misleading) for liability to attach, the Ninth Circuit disagreed, stating that under the common law of trusts, liability attaches for information that the trustee should have known was misleading. Chevron disseminated the information in its capacity as fiduciary because the information related to future plan benefits and not just employment matters.

But, in another case, the Seventh Circuit ruled that there is no fiduciary duty to disclose separation benefits offered under a new plan (distinguishing this case from the *Chevron* case above) that was established after the former participant's retirement.[6]

280. What is the exclusive purpose rule?

The "exclusive purpose" rule of ERISA Section 404(a)(1)(A) requires a fiduciary to discharge his duties with respect to a plan solely in the interests of the plan participants and beneficiaries and for the exclusive purpose of providing benefits to participants and beneficiaries and defraying

---

1. *McAuley v. IBM Corp.*, 165 F.3d 1038 (6th Cir. 1999).
2. *Fischer v. Philadelphia Elec. Co.*, 96 F.3d 1533 (3d Cir. 1996).
3. *McAuley v. IBM Corp.*, 165 F.3d 1038 (6th Cir. 1999).
4. *Mathews v. Chevron Corp.*, 362 F.3d 1172 (9th Cir. 2004).
5. 238 F.3d 1048 (9th Cir. 2001).
6. *Beach v. Commonwealth Edison Co.*, 2004 U.S. App. LEXIS 17956 (7th Cir. 2004).

reasonable expenses of administering the plan. Federal courts have described this responsibility as the "duty to act with complete and undivided loyalty to the beneficiaries,"[1] and with an "eye single to the interests of the participants and beneficiaries."[2]

Under this duty of loyalty, a trustee bears an unwavering duty of complete loyalty to the beneficiary of the trust, to the exclusion of the interests of all other parties.[3] This includes the trustee's own interests, as well as the interests of the trust's creditors.[4] A fiduciary must not subordinate the interests of participants and beneficiaries to unrelated objectives. Thus, in deciding whether and to what extent to enter into a course of action with respect to a plan, a fiduciary must ordinarily consider only factors relating to the interests of plan participants and beneficiaries; he may not be influenced by factors unrelated to these interests. Although nothing in ERISA Section 404(a)(1) expressly prohibits or limits the exercise of any particular method of decision making by plan fiduciaries, any decision by a fiduciary that subordinates the interests of the plan's participants and beneficiaries may contravene the exclusive purpose rule.

281. What kinds of actions will result in a breach of the exclusive purpose rule?

The exclusive purpose requirement is violated if plan assets have been removed or diverted for the benefit of anyone other than plan participants. This was illustrated when plan fiduciaries caused or permitted virtually all of a plan's assets to be loaned back to the sponsoring companies in exchange for unsecured promissory notes. The complete lack of security on the notes presented significant risks for the plan, and the interest rates paid on the notes did not adequately compensate for the risks involved. The court compared the exclusive benefit rule to the duty of loyalty under the common law of trusts, stating that the trustees had the duty to act with "complete and undivided loyalty to the beneficiaries of the trust" and with an "eye single to the interests of the participants and beneficiaries."[5]

The DOL ruled that transferring the accumulated surplus from a union-sponsored vacation and holiday fund to the local union would violate the exclusive purpose rule, in that it would not be for the exclusive purpose of providing benefits to participants and their beneficiaries and defraying reasonable expenses of administering the fund.[6]

An employer acting as a trustee of a parent plan and a spin-off plan (thus owing obligations of loyalty to the members of both plans) violated the exclusive purpose rule to participants in the spun-off plan in its allocation of investment gains realized on the parent plan assets to the spun-off plan. The employer failed to allocate the investment gains realized on the parent plan assets to the spun-off plan during the interim period after the closing date of the spin-off but before the transfers of the plan assets, despite the fact that 90 percent of those parent plan assets were attributable to members of the spun-off plan. The court noted that the employer's duty

---

1. See *Freund v. Marshall & Ilsley Bank*, 485 F. Supp. 629 (W.D. Wis. 1979).
2. See *Donovan v. Bierwirth*, 680 F.2d 263 (2d Cir.), cert. denied, 459 U.S. 1069 (1982).
3. *NLRB v. Amax Coal Co.*, 453 U.S. 322 (1981) (citing Restatement (Second) of Trusts §170(1); Scott on Trusts §170).
4. See *General Am. Life Ins. Co. v. Castonguay*, 984 F.2d 1518 (9th Cir. 1993).
5. *Freund v. Marshall & Ilsley Bank*, 485 F. Supp. 629 (W.D. Wis. 1979).
6. DOL Adv. Op. 77-56A.

of loyalty to its parent plan members did not extend to giving them a windfall at the expense of the spun-off plan participants. Because its conduct was inconsistent with the strict duty owed to the spun-off plan participants, it violated its fiduciary duties.[1]

Similarly, the trustees of a union-sponsored pension plan violated their duty of loyalty when they acted in the interest of the plan sponsor rather than "with an eye single to the interests of the participants and beneficiaries of the plan" and thereby violated the exclusive purpose and prudence requirements by authorizing loan transactions with an association that was closely related to the union. The evidence indicated that the trustees were on both sides of negotiations that resulted in the association's purchase of a loan note from the plan for well below the note's accounting value.[2]

The use of assets of an employee benefit plan to pay benefits to individuals who were not participants in that plan, or beneficiaries of such individuals, also contravened the exclusive purpose requirement. According to the Department of Labor, the payment of a gratuitous death benefit by plan trustees to the widow of a plan fiduciary would constitute a violation of the exclusive purpose standards of ERISA Section 403(c)(1) and ERISA Section 404(a)(1)(A), since the payment could not be characterized as either compensation for services performed or as a reasonable expense of administration of the plan. Furthermore, the payment proposed to be made to the widow would not have been made to her as a participant or as a beneficiary of the plan; thus, such a payment would violate the requirements of ERISA Section 403(c)(1) and ERISA Section 404(a)(1)(A) unless it constituted a reasonable expense of administering the plans.[3] Likewise, trustees of collectively bargained pension and welfare benefit plans violated the exclusive purpose rule by improperly causing the plans to extend coverage and pay benefits to themselves and the plans' attorney as participants in the plans.[4]

The use of plan assets by corporate management either as an offensive or defensive tool in battles for corporate control also violates the exclusive purpose rule, and such attempts are particularly monitored by the Department of Labor. This was illustrated when plan fiduciaries invested a plan's assets in companies involved in corporate control contests. The fiduciaries themselves were actively engaged in the control contests, they had substantial interests in them, and their investment decisions never deviated from their own best interests. In addition, where it might be possible to question the fiduciaries' loyalty, they are obliged at a minimum to engage in an intensive and scrupulous independent investigation of their options, in order to ensure that they are acting in the best interests of the plan beneficiaries.[5] Since ERISA requires plan fiduciaries to make investment decisions, including tender offer decisions, based on the facts and circumstances applicable to the investment and the plan, fiduciaries must take the course of action that is in the best economic interests of the pension plan, recognizing the pension trust as a separate legal entity designed to provide retirement income.[6]

---

1. *John Blair Commc'ns, Inc. Profit Sharing Plan v. Telemundo Grp., Inc.*, 26 F.3d 360 (2d Cir. 1994).
2. *Reich v. Compton*, 57 F.3d 270 (3d Cir. 1995).
3. DOL Adv. Op. 81-52A.
4. *Donovan v. Daugherty*, 550 F. Supp. 390 (S.D. Ala. 1982).
5. *Leigh v. Engle*, 727 F.2d 113 (7th Cir. 1984); see also *Donovan v. Bierwirth*, 680 F.2d 263 (2d Cir.), cert. denied, 459 U.S. 1069 (1982).
6. DOL News Release No. 89-52 (Jan. 31, 1989).

The exclusive purpose rule also was held to prohibit a fiduciary from granting preferences, as between a plan's participants or its beneficiaries, with respect to the administration of the plan.[1] In carrying out this obligation, the trustees of a plan must exercise their discretion to serve the interests of all the participants of the plan.[2] For example, the trustees of an employer-sponsored pension plan failed to administer the plan for the exclusive purpose of providing retirement income benefits to all of the plan participants and beneficiaries when they extended credit to a limited number of plan participants at unreasonably low interest rates. The low rates of interest charged on the loans to the selected participants resulted in correspondingly low rates of return on the investment of the plan assets for all of the plan participants. By extending credit to a limited number of plan participants at unreasonably low rates, the plan trustees failed to administer the plan for the exclusive purpose of providing retirement income benefits to all plan participants and beneficiaries.[3]

The Fourth Circuit has upheld a district court's removal of plan fiduciaries because they abdicated their fiduciary responsibilities.[4] The court also affirmed an award of $720,000 against the fiduciaries for unpaid contributions and would not allow the fiduciaries to offset their liabilities against excess contributions that may have been made in previous years. From 1982 through 1994, the plan fiduciaries provided annual contributions to the trust. They stopped doing so in 1995. In 2003, the DOL filed suit alleging the fiduciaries breached their duties by failing to make the required contributions from 1995 through 2003. The court held that the actions of the fiduciaries in failing to remit required contributions and attempting to take inappropriate refunds (in excess of $700,000) from the trust were not in the best interests of the participants and beneficiaries.

282. Is a fiduciary prohibited from holding positions of dual loyalty?

ERISA does not explicitly prohibit a fiduciary from holding positions of dual loyalty with conflicting interests; for example, an employer is permitted to act both as plan sponsor and plan administrator.[5] Employers who choose to administer their own plans assume responsibilities to both the company and the plan and, accordingly, owe duties of loyalty and care to both entities. In permitting such arrangements, which ordinary trust law generally forbids due to the inherent potential for a conflict of interest, Congress understood that the interests of the plan might be sacrificed if an employer were forced to choose between the company and the plan. Hence, Congress imposed on plan administrators a duty of care that requires them to discharge their duties with respect to a plan solely in the interests of the participants and beneficiaries.

Congress never intended ERISA Section 404(a)(1) to establish a *per se* rule of fiduciary conduct.[6] Consequently, a court will not create a prohibited transaction and conflict of interest

---

1. *Winpisinger v. Aurora Corp.*, 456 F. Supp. 559 (N.D. Ohio 1978).
2. *Talarico v. United Furniture Workers Pension Fund A*, 479 F. Supp. 1072 (D. Neb. 1979).
3. *McLaughlin v. Rowley*, 698 F. Supp. 1333 (N.D. Tex. 1988).
4. *Chao v. Malkani*, 452 F.3d 290 (4th Cir. 2006).
5. See ERISA Sec. 408(c)(3).
6. *Fentron Indus., Inc. v. National Shopmen Pension Fund*, 674 F.2d 1300 (9th Cir. 1982).

where Congress and precedent have not indicated one.[1] Thus, for example, a bank does not commit a violation of ERISA Section 404(a)(1) by the mere act of becoming a trustee with conflicting interests, and a trustee does not necessarily violate ERISA Section 404(a)(1) by accepting a trusteeship with dual loyalties.[2]

283. Must a fiduciary with a conflict of interest resign?

Not necessarily. But fiduciaries must be mindful that "outside pressure leading fiduciaries to consider anyone's interest other than that of the beneficiaries seriously undermines ERISA's core principles."[3] If a potential conflict of interest exists, a fiduciary must uphold its duty to act solely in the interests of the beneficiaries and for the exclusive purpose of providing them with benefits. Where the potential for conflicts is substantial, it may be difficult for a fiduciary to discharge his duties with an "eye single" to the interests of the beneficiaries, and the fiduciary may need to step aside, at least temporarily, from the management of assets where he faces potentially conflicting interests.[4]

Nevertheless, when a fiduciary has dual loyalties, the prudent person standard requires that he make a careful and impartial investigation of all investment decisions.[5] Where it might be possible to question the fiduciaries' loyalty, fiduciaries are obliged at a minimum to engage in an intensive and scrupulous independent investigation of their options to ensure that they act in the best interests of the plan participants and beneficiaries.[6] In addition, courts may look closely at whether the fiduciaries investigated alternative actions and relied on outside advisers before implementing a challenged transaction.[7]

In further clarifying the role of a fiduciary dealing with a conflict of interest, the DOL noted in an information letter to a Taft-Hartley trustee that "a fiduciary's duty to act prudently and solely in the interests of the plan and its participants and beneficiaries does not end with respect to a particular plan decision because a fiduciary may have recused himself from that decision and avoided prohibited transactions. In this regard, if a fiduciary has material information, including information regarding potential service providers, that would be necessary in order for other plan fiduciaries to make an appropriate and prudent decision, we believe the fiduciary's duties under [ERISA Section 404] would require informing the deciding fiduciaries of that information."[8]

In other words, a fiduciary with a conflict of interest who has recused himself from a decision-making process has a further obligation to share material information that may have impacted the decision to recuse himself with other fiduciaries charged in the decision-making process.

---

1. *Ershick v. United Mo. Bank of Kan. City*, 948 F.2d 660 (10th Cir. 1991). See also *Brock v. Citizens Bank of Clovis*, 841 F.2d 344 (10th Cir.), cert. denied, 488 U.S. 829 (1988), which pointed out that courts have been unwilling to create "a per se violation [of ERISA Section 406(b)] when Congress has not done so."
2. *Friend v. Sanwa Bank Cal.*, 35 F.3d 466 (9th Cir. 1994).
3. *General Am. Life Ins. Co. v. Castonguay*, 984 F.2d 1518 (9th Cir. 1993).
4. *Leigh v. Engle*, 727 F.2d 113 (7th Cir. 1984).
5. *Schaefer v. Arkansas Med. Soc'y*, 853 F.2d 1487 (8th Cir. 1988) (citing *Donovan v. Bierwirth*, 680 F.2d 263 (2d Cir.), cert. denied, 459 U.S. 1069 (1982)).
6. *Leigh v. Engle*, 727 F.2d 113 (7th Cir. 1984) (citing *Donovan v. Bierwirth*, 680 F.2d 263 (2d Cir.), cert. denied, 459 U.S. 1069 (1982)).
7. *Martin v. Feilen*, 965 F.2d 660 (8th Cir. 1992). See *Donovan v. Cunningham*, 716 F.2d 1467 (5th Cir. 1983); *Newton v. Van Otterloo*, 756 F. Supp. 1121 (N.D. Ind. 1991).
8. DOL Information Letter (Feb. 23, 2005), http://www.dol.gov/ebsa/regs/ILs/il022305.html.

284. Is the payment of expenses by a plan subject to the exclusive purpose rule?

A payment that is not a distribution of benefits to participants or beneficiaries of a plan is not consistent with the requirements of ERISA unless it is used to defray a reasonable expense of administering the plan.[1] As a general rule, reasonable expenses of administering a plan include direct expenses properly and actually incurred in the performance of a fiduciary's duties to the plan. The determination of whether a particular expense is a reasonable administrative expense under ERISA Section 404(a)(1)(A) is the responsibility of the appropriate plan fiduciaries.

In making such a determination, a fiduciary must act prudently and solely in the interest of the plan participants and beneficiaries, and in accordance with the documents and instruments governing the plan insofar as they are consistent with the provisions of ERISA. In this regard, the fiduciary must assure that payment of the expenses by the plan is authorized by the plan and is in the interest of the plan participants and beneficiaries, as well as that the amount of the expense is reasonable. For example, the use of plan assets to pay fees and expenses incurred in connection with the provision of services would not be a reasonable expense of administering a plan if the payments are made for the employer's benefit or involve services for which an employer could reasonably be expected to bear the cost in the normal course of the employer's business or operations.[2]

285. Is the exclusive benefit rule violated if a plan pays expenses incurred in connection with business decisions, or "settlor" functions?

Yes. A plan may pay only those expenses incurred in connection with plan administration and fiduciary decision making, but may not pay expenses incurred in connection with business decisions, or "settlor" functions. These so-called "settlor" functions, which relate to the formation, rather than the management, of plans, include decisions relating to the establishment, design, and termination of plans and generally are not fiduciary activities subject to Title I of ERISA. See Q 256.[3] Expenses incurred in connection with the performance of settlor functions are not reasonable plan expenses because they are incurred for the benefit of the employer and involve services for which an employer could reasonably be expected to bear the cost in the normal course of its business or operations.[4]

The Court of Appeals for the Fourth Circuit has ruled that the collecting and forwarding of employee contributions to a third-party administrator is a fiduciary function under ERISA. As such, it is not to be considered a settlor function. The court noted that an employer entrusted with employee contributions for remittance to a claims administrator is acting in a fiduciary capacity under ERISA, especially in light of the DOL regulation expressly providing that employee contributions are plan assets. Further, the court also found that the employer's

---

1. ERISA Secs. 403(c)(1), 404(a)(1)(A).
2. DOL Op. Letter to Kirk F. Maldonado (Mar. 2, 1987).
3. See also DOL Op. Letter to John N. Erlenborn (Mar. 13, 1986).
4. See DOL Op. Letter to Kirk F. Maldonado (Mar. 2, 1987).

officers were fiduciaries when they directed that the employee contributions be diverted to pay other corporate expenses.[1]

286. Is the exclusive benefit rule violated if a plan pays expenses incurred in implementing the plan's termination?

Although the decision to terminate a plan is a settlor or business function, activities undertaken to implement the plan termination decision are generally fiduciary in nature.[2] Accordingly, reasonable expenses incurred in implementing a plan termination would generally be payable by the plan. These termination expenses include expenses incurred in auditing the plan, preparing and filing annual reports, preparing benefit statements and calculating accrued benefits, notifying participants and beneficiaries of their benefits under the plan, and, in certain circumstances, amending the plan to effectuate an orderly termination that benefits the participants and beneficiaries.

287. Is the exclusive benefit rule violated if an action intended to benefit the plan incidentally benefits the plan sponsor?

Not necessarily. Although a fiduciary has a duty under ERISA to act for the exclusive benefit of trust beneficiaries, "Congress did not intend ... [ERISA] to penalize employers for exercising their discretion to make rational economic decisions which are both in the best interests of the preservation of the fund and which are also not adverse to the employer's interests."[3] Thus, the fact that a fiduciary's action incidentally benefits an employer does not necessarily mean that the fiduciary has breached her duty.

A transaction that incidentally benefits the plan sponsor or the fiduciaries does not violate the exclusive purpose requirements if: (a) after careful and impartial investigation, the fiduciaries reasonably conclude that the transaction is best to promote the interests of participants and beneficiaries; and (b) their decisions are made with an "eye single to the interests of the participants and beneficiaries."[4]

For example, a plan sponsor did not violate the exclusive purpose requirement to participants in a merged pension plan by instituting a program designed to encourage early retirement through the payment of supplemental early retirement benefits from the plan, since any incidental economic benefit that the employer derived from the reductions in employees did not violate ERISA's exclusive benefit rule prohibiting plan assets from inuring to the employer's benefit. Thus, the exclusive benefit rule prohibits the use of plan assets for the primary benefit of an employer, but does not prohibit incidental benefits to an employer when the primary benefits go to participants.[5]

1. *Phelps v. C.T. Enters., Inc.*, 2005 U.S. App. LEXIS 497 (4th Cir. 2005).
2. See DOL Adv. Op. 97-03A.
3. *Holliday v. Xerox Corp.*, 732 F.2d 548 (6th Cir.), cert. denied, 469 U.S. 917 (1984).
4. *Donovan v. Bierwirth*, 680 F.2d 263 (2d Cir.), cert. denied, 459 U.S. 1069 (1982).
5. In re Gulf Pension Litig., 764 F. Supp. 1149 (S.D. Tex. 1991). See also *United Steelworkers of Am., Local 2116 v. Cyclops Corp.*, 860 F.2d 189 (6th Cir. 1988); *McDonald v. Pan Am. World Air., Inc.*, 859 F.2d 742 (9th Cir. 1988); *Morse v. Stanley*, 732 F.2d 1139 (2d Cir. 1984).

288. What is the prudence requirement of ERISA Section 404?

ERISA requires that a fiduciary discharge his duties "with the care, skill, prudence, and diligence under the circumstances then prevailing that a prudent man acting in a like capacity and familiar with such matters would use in the conduct of an enterprise of like character and with like aims."[1] Known as the "prudent man" rule, this section defines the obligation of a trustee in investing the plan's assets. The prudent man standard, combined with the duty of loyalty, imposes an unwavering duty on an ERISA trustee to make decisions with single-minded devotion to a plan's participants and beneficiaries and, in so doing, to act as a prudent person would act in a similar situation. These familiar principles evolved from the common law of trusts that Congress codified and made applicable to ERISA trustees.[2]

The case law gives meaning to the "prudence" standard and is replete with examples of imprudent behavior by plan fiduciaries.[3] Courts have focused the inquiry under the "prudent man" rule on a review of the fiduciary's independent investigation of the merits of a particular investment.

For example, the Fifth Circuit Court of Appeals has ruled that the fiduciaries' decision to purchase stock for their plan in reliance upon a consultant's totally inaccurate appraisal of the stock's fair market value violated ERISA Section 404(a)(1)(B). The evidence showed that during the two years between the time of the appraisal and consummation of the transaction, the trustees failed to consider whether the facts and assumptions underlying the consultant's appraisal remained valid.[4]

Breaches of fiduciary duty constituting imprudent behavior are also recounted in *Katsaros v. Cody*.[5] The trustees in *Katsaros* breached their fiduciary duty of prudence when they approved a $2 million loan to a bank that they knew was destined to fail based on its financial condition, performance, and creditworthiness at the time of the transaction, as well as when they failed to collect the unreimbursed expenses incurred by the fund in connection with a second aborted loan. The trustees' handling of the $2 million loan was particularly imprudent, since they approved it without obtaining independent professional analysis of the bank's financial statements.

The records that should have been examined in *Katsaros* would have shown (1) that the bank had never earned enough money to service the debt and probably would not be able to do so in the future, (2) that the bank was undercapitalized, and (3) that the bank was deeply in debt. Moreover, several local banks, including the subject bank's principal creditor, had refused to extend credit to it, and some of the collateral that was to secure the loan had been seized for back taxes, while the remainder was worth one-third less than the stated value. The court found that the trustees who were involved in this transaction violated ERISA Section 404(a)(1)(B).

---

1. ERISA Sec. 404(a)(1)(B).
2. *Morse v. Stanley*, 732 F.2d 1139 (2d Cir. 1984).
3. See, e.g., *Donovan v. Bierwirth*, 680 F.2d 263 (2d Cir.), cert. denied, 459 U.S. 1069 (1982); *Marshall v. Glass/Metal Ass'n*, 507 F. Supp. 378 (D. Haw. 1980); *Freund v. Marshall & Ilsley Bank*, 485 F. Supp. 629 (W.D. Wis. 1979).
4. See *Donovan v. Cunningham*, 716 F.2d 1455 (5th Cir. 1983).
5. 744 F.2d 270 (2d Cir. 1984).

Patently imprudent behavior was also committed by plan trustees in *Donovan v. Mazzola*.[1] The focus in *Mazzola*, as in *Katsaros*, was the prudence of a $1.5 million loan of pension fund assets to another fund secured by real estate. Of primary concern to the court was the trustees' retention and reliance upon the advice of a consultant whom they knew or should have known lacked the expertise to analyze the value of the collateral. The evidence showed that the consultant had never made a feasibility study of, or advised others about, property of the sort in question. He also failed to discuss the significance of his report with the trustees and did not submit an update when one was appropriate. An expert called by the DOL testified that the trustees' conduct prior to making the loan fell far short of industry standards because (1) they failed to ascertain the value of the property deeded by the debtor as security for the loan; (2) they did not determine the extent to which the pension fund's interest in the collateral would be subordinate to other security interests; (3) they neglected to discover that the debtor had previously been unable to make regular payments on previous loans from the fund; and (4) they granted the loan at a rate below the prevailing interest rates for comparable mortgages at the time.[2]

In contrast, there was no imprudent behavior present where plan trustees charged participants who obtained mortgages from the plan more than two percentage points below the prevailing market rate.[3] In developing the loan program, the trustees consulted with lawyers, accountants, actuaries, and mortgage bankers over a six-month period in 1979. The trustees examined loan rates charged by major commercial financial institutions in the area and determined that if they applied those rates, they would have virtually no loan activity. The trustees also considered the rates of nontraditional mortgage loans in the area, such as owner-financed loans. Each borrower's employment background was examined, and in addition to pledging their accrued pension benefits, borrowers whose equity was less than 20 percent were required to obtain mortgage insurance. The interest rates established were at a higher rate of return than any of the other assets in the fund's portfolio and were in excess of the fund's actuarial and funding requirements. The loans accounted for about 10 percent of the portfolio. The court held that the term "reasonable rate of interest" is not synonymous with the term "prevailing or market rate of interest" and that a reasonable rate of interest may be below the prevailing market rate.

289. What is the standard for evaluating the prudence of a fiduciary's act?

Prudence is measured according to the objective "prudent person" standard developed in the common law of trusts.[4] The fiduciary responsibility section of ERISA, in essence, codifies and makes applicable to fiduciaries certain principles developed in the evolution of the law of trusts. "Consistent with these common law principles, the courts measure 'prudence' according to an objective standard, focusing on a fiduciary's conduct in arriving at an investment decision, not on its results, and asking whether a fiduciary employed the appropriate methods to investigate and determine the merits of a particular investment at the time they engaged in the challenged transactions."[5] In addition, the prudence requirement is flexible, such that the adequacy of a

1. 716 F.2d 1226 (9th Cir. 1983).
2. See also *Katsaros v. Cody*, 568 F. Supp. 360 (E.D.N.Y. 1983).
3. See *Brock v. Walton*, 609 F. Supp. 1221 (S.D. Fla. 1985), aff'd, 794 F.2d 586 (11th Cir. 1986).
4. See *Donovan v. Mazzola*, 716 F.2d 1226 (9th Cir. 1983), *cert. denied*, 464 U.S. 1040 (1984); S. Rep. No. 93-127, 93d Cong., 2d Sess.
5. *Donovan v. Mazzola*, 716 F.2d 1226 (9th Cir. 1983), *cert. denied*, 464 U.S. 1040 (1984).

fiduciary's independent investigation and ultimate investment selection is evaluated in light of the "character and aims" of the particular type of plan he serves.[1] Moreover, the fiduciary's subjective good-faith belief in an investment does not insulate him from the charges that he acted imprudently.[2]

Similarly, the Department of Labor regulations concerning the investment duties of ERISA fiduciaries provide that the requirements of ERISA Section 404(a)(1)(B) are satisfied if fiduciaries give "appropriate consideration to those facts and circumstances that, given the scope of such fiduciary's investment duties, the fiduciary knows or should know are relevant to the particular investment or investment course of action involved, including the role the investment plays in that portion of the plan's investment portfolio with respect to which the fiduciary has investment duties; and has acted accordingly."[3]

In reviewing a challenged transaction, the courts consider the prudence of a fiduciary's conduct at the time he engaged in the challenged transaction, rather than from the vantage point of hindsight.[4]

290. What level of prudence applies to ERISA fiduciaries under the prudent man rule?

The standard of prudence that applies to plan fiduciaries "is not that of a prudent lay person but rather that of a prudent fiduciary with experience dealing with a similar enterprise."[5] Under the objective standard of the prudent person rule, fiduciaries are judged "according to the standards of others 'acting in a like capacity and familiar with such matters.'"[6] These principles hold fiduciaries to a more exacting standard than the common law of trusts standards.[7] The duties of an ERISA trustee are "the highest known to the law."[8]

In the context of investing plan assets, the prudent person standard "requires that the fiduciary's behavior be measured as against the standards in the investment industry."[9] In contrast, the Fifth Circuit took exception to the premise that the reference in ERISA Section 404 to a prudent man "familiar with such matters" creates a "prudent expert" standard under ERISA.[10] It was that court's view that the emphasis of ERISA Section 404 is on flexibility and that the level of knowledge required of a fiduciary will vary with the nature of the plan. The court agreed that the prudence requirement is flexible, such that the adequacy of a fiduciary's independent investigation and ultimate investment selection is evaluated in light of the "character and aims" of the particular type of plan he serves.[11]

---

1. *Donovan v. Cunningham*, 716 F.2d 1455 (5th Cir. 1983), *cert. denied*, 467 U.S. 1251 (1984).
2. *Donovan v. Bierwirth*, 538 F. Supp. 463 (E.D.N.Y. 1981), *aff'd*, 680 F.2d 263 (2d Cir.), *cert. denied*, 459 U.S. 1069 (1982).
3. Labor Reg. §2550.404a-1(b)(1).
4. *American Comm'ns Ass'n, Local 10 v. Retirement Plan for Emps. of RCA Corp.*, 488 F. Supp. 479 (S.D.N.Y.), *aff'd*, 646 F.2d 559 (2d Cir. 1980).
5. *Marshall v. Snyder*, 430 F. Supp. 1224 (E.D.N.Y. 1977); *Donovan v. Mazzola*, 716 F.2d 1226 (9th Cir. 1983), cert. denied, 464 U.S. 1040 (1984).
6. *Marshall v. Glass/Metal Ass'n*, 507 F. Supp. 378 (D. Haw. 1980).
7. *Donovan v. Mazzola*, 716 F.2d 1226 (9th Cir. 1983).
8. *Donovan v. Bierwirth*, 680 F.2d 263 (2d Cir.), cert. denied, 459 U.S. 1069 (1982).
9. *Lanka v. O'Higgins*, 810 F. Supp. 379 (N.D.N.Y. 1992) (citing *Jones v. O'Higgins*, 736 F. Supp. 1243 (N.D.N.Y. 1989)).
10. *Donovan v. Cunningham*, 716 F.2d 1455 (5th Cir. 1983).
11. See *Donovan v. Cunningham*, 716 F.2d 1455 (5th Cir. 1983*); In re Unisys Sav. Plan Litig.*, 74 F.3d 420 (3d Cir. 1996), reh'g denied, 173 F.3d 145 (3d Cir. 1999).

291. What is procedural prudence?

Procedural prudence—as distinguished from substantive prudence (see Q 292)—is the conduct or process by which a fiduciary makes her decision. The focus of the inquiry is on how the fiduciary acted in her selection of the investment; it considers the trustee's conduct and not the success or failure of the investment.[1] In the context of investing the assets of a plan, procedural prudence requires that a fiduciary (1) employ proper methods to investigate, evaluate, and structure the investment; (2) act in a manner as would others who have a capacity and familiarity with such matters; and (3) exercise independent judgment when making investment decisions.[2]

292. What is substantive prudence?

In contrast to procedural prudence, which focuses on a fiduciary's conduct in arriving at an investment decision (see Q 291), substantive prudence concerns whether a fiduciary properly evaluated the merits of a particular investment.[3]

293. What substantive factors must be considered by a fiduciary with respect to plan investments?

NOTE: In late 2010, and again in 2011, the DOL released proposed regulations that have a significant impact on determining fiduciary status regarding advice and management decisions focusing on plan assets.[4] You will find a detailed analysis of these proposed regulations and the impact they have on plan assets and individuals involved in the decisions and management of them under Q 240.

According to the Department of Labor, the prudence requirement is satisfied with respect to the investment duties of a fiduciary provided that the fiduciary "has given appropriate consideration to those facts and circumstances that, given the scope of such fiduciary's investment duties, the fiduciary knows or should know are relevant to the particular investment or investment course of action involved" and has acted accordingly. The substantive factors to which such consideration must be given include (but are not necessarily limited to)

1.   A determination by the fiduciary that the particular investment or investment course of action is reasonably designed, as part of the portfolio, to further the purposes of the plan, taking into consideration the risk of loss and the opportunity for gain associated with the investment or investment course of action; and

2.   Consideration of the composition of the portfolio with regard to (a) diversification; (b) the liquidity and current return of the portfolio relative to the anticipated cash flow requirements of the plan; and (c) the projected return of the portfolio relative to the funding objectives of the plan (see Q 292 for further discussion).[5]

---

1. *Donovan v. Cunningham*, 716 F.2d 1455 (5th Cir. 1983).
2. *Katsaros v. Cody*, 744 F.2d 270 (2d Cir.), cert. denied, 469 U.S. 1072 (1984).
3. *Donovan v. Cunningham*, 716 F.2d 1455 (5th Cir. 1983); *Katsaros v. Cody*, 744 F.2d 270 (2d Cir.), cert. denied, 469 U.S. 1072 (1984).
4. Prop. Labor Reg. §2510.3-21; 75 Fed. Reg. 65,263 (Oct. 22, 2010).
5. Labor Reg. §2550.404a-1(b).

In addition, the Department of Labor has advised that a prudent plan fiduciary "must consider, among other factors, the availability, riskiness, and potential return of alternative investments for his or her plan." Furthermore, it has indicated that investments will not be considered prudent if they provide a plan with less return, in comparison to risk, than comparable investments available to the plan, or if they involve a greater risk to the security of plan assets than other investments offering a similar return.[1]

294. What are the general guidelines with respect to a fiduciary's investment duties?

Regulations under ERISA prescribe general guidelines with respect to an investment or investment course of action (i.e., any series or program of investments or actions related to a fiduciary's performance of her investment duties) taken by a fiduciary pursuant to her investment duties to a plan. In accordance with these regulations, the prudence requirements are satisfied if the fiduciary

1. Has given appropriate consideration to those facts and circumstances that, given the scope of the fiduciary's investment duties, the fiduciary knows or should know are relevant to the particular investment or investment course of action involved, including the role the investment or investment course of action plays in that portion of the plan's investment portfolio with respect to which the fiduciary has investment duties; and

2. Has acted accordingly.[2]

The regulation incorporates the views of the Department of Labor that generally, the relative riskiness of a specific investment or investment course of action does not render an investment or investment course of action either prudent or imprudent *per se*, and that the prudence of an investment decision should not be judged without regard to the role that the proposed investment or investment course of action plays within the overall plan portfolio. In addition, a fiduciary should not have to expend unreasonable efforts in discharging her duties, or to consider matters outside the scope of those duties. Thus, in accordance with the regulation, the scope of the fiduciary's inquiry is limited to those facts and circumstances that a prudent person having similar duties and familiar with such matters would consider relevant.[3]

The DOL, in Advisory Opinion 2006-08A, has stated that a fiduciary's proposed investment strategy for a defined benefit plan, designed in part to reduce funding volatility for the plan sponsor, would not violate ERISA's fiduciary obligations and would, in fact, be prudent and consistent with the fiduciary duties detailed under ERISA Section 404. The DOL stated that it "does not believe that there is anything in the statute or the regulations that would limit a plan fiduciary's ability to take into account the risks associated with benefit liabilities or how those

---

1. DOL Adv. Op. 88-16A.
2. Labor Reg. §2550.404a-1.
3. *See* Labor Reg. §2550.404a-1.

risks relate to the portfolio management in designing an investment strategy. See Q 577 for further details on what constitutes a "prudent investment program."

295. What is "appropriate consideration"?

For purposes of the regulations under ERISA Section 404(a), "appropriate consideration" includes, but is not necessarily limited to, a determination by the fiduciary that the particular investment or investment course of action is reasonably designed, as part of the portfolio (or, where applicable, that portion of the plan portfolio with respect to which the fiduciary has investment duties), to further the purposes of the plan, taking into consideration the risk of loss and the opportunity for gain (or other return) associated with the investment or investment course of action, and consideration of the following factors as they relate to such portion of the portfolio:

1.   Composition of the portfolio with regard to diversification ("diversification" is given its customary meaning as a mechanism for reducing the risk of large losses);

2.   Liquidity and current return of the portfolio relative to the anticipated cash flow requirements of the plan (its principal subject matter is all anticipated cash requirements of the plan, and not solely those arising by reason of payment of benefits); and

3.   Projected return of the portfolio relative to the funding objectives of the plan.[1]

This includes giving appropriate consideration to the role that the investment or investment course of action plays (in terms of such factors as diversification, liquidity, and risk/return characteristics) with respect to that portion of the plan's investment portfolio within the scope of the fiduciary's responsibility.[2]

296. What is the meaning of the term "investment duties"?

The term "investment duties" refers to any duties imposed upon, or assumed or undertaken by, a person in connection with the investment of plan assets that make or will make the person a fiduciary, or that are performed by a fiduciary.[3]

297. Is there a "safe harbor" method of satisfying the prudence requirement?

Yes. In the view of the Department of Labor, Labor Regulation Section 2550.404a-1 acts as a "safe harbor" provision, and fiduciaries who comply with its provisions (see Q 294) satisfy the requirements of the prudence rule. Although the "safe harbor" is a manner of satisfying the requirements of the prudence rule, it does not necessarily constitute the exclusive method for satisfying the requirements of the prudence rule, and does not impose any additional requirements or constraints upon plan fiduciaries.

---

1. Labor Reg. §2550.404a-1.
2. Labor Reg. §2550.404a-1.
3. As defined in ERISA Section 3(21)(A)(i) or ERISA Section 3(21)(A)(ii).

298. What factors are included in an evaluation of an investment or investment course of action under the "safe harbor" provisions?

If a fiduciary desires to rely on the provisions of the "safe harbor," the fiduciary must consider the following factors, to the extent applicable, in its evaluation of an investment or investment course of action:

1.   Composition of the portfolio with regard to diversification (as a mechanism for reducing the risk of large losses);

2.   Liquidity and current return of the portfolio relative to the anticipated cash flow requirements of the plan (i.e., all anticipated cash requirements of the plan, and not solely those required for payment of benefits); and

3.   Projected return of the portfolio relative to the funding objectives of the plan.[1]

299. What investments are approved by the Department of Labor?

None. The Department of Labor does not consider it appropriate to develop any list of investments, classes of investment, or investment techniques that might be permissible under the "prudence" rule. In the Department's view, no such list could be complete; moreover, the Department does not intend to create or suggest a "legal list" of investments for plan fiduciaries.

300. Are high-risk investments inherently imprudent?

Not necessarily. The risk level of an investment does not alone make the investment prudent or imprudent per se. Thus, an investment is not deemed imprudent merely because the investment, in isolation, is characterized by a relatively high degree of risk. But a fiduciary must consider the risk characteristics of an investment in determining its suitability for the plan.[2]

301. Are fiduciaries required to invest in expensive systems or analysis to make investment decisions?

Not necessarily. The prudence standard establishes a standard of conduct measured by how a prudent fiduciary with experience dealing in a similar capacity and familiar with administration of employee benefit plans would act. Under the "prudence" rule, the standard to which a fiduciary is held is defined, in part, by what a prudent person acting in a like capacity and familiar with such matters would do. Thus, for example, it would not seem necessary for a fiduciary of a plan with assets of $50,000 to employ, in all respects, the same investment management techniques as would a fiduciary of a plan with assets of $50,000,000.[3]

302. Is a fiduciary "immunized" from liability once it has considered relevant facts and circumstances in the selection of an investment?

No. According to the Department of Labor, a trustee's ERISA responsibilities do not terminate solely because the fiduciary has given consideration to relevant facts and circumstances

---

1. Labor Reg. §2550.404a-1.
2. Labor Reg. §2550.404a-1.
3. Labor Reg. §2550.404a-1.

with regard to the initial decision to invest plan assets.[1] Likewise, courts have agreed that upon the conclusion of a preliminary investigation and purchase of an investment, a fiduciary has a duty to monitor the performance of an investment with reasonable diligence and to withdraw an investment if it becomes clear that the investment is unsuitable for the plan.[2] "ERISA fiduciaries must monitor investments with reasonable diligence and dispose of investments which are improper to keep."[3] Thus, in accordance with the "prudent man" rule, a fiduciary has a duty to continually monitor the performance of an investment and dispose of any investment in the event it becomes undesirable for the plan.

Employer Stock

The Fifth Circuit has adopted a "prudence" presumption in a case involving a stock drop in value allegedly causing a fiduciary breach for a failure to divest the employer stock.[4] 401(k) participants sued when the plan sponsor disclosed that it had engaged in sham transactions causing the price of its stock to drop about 40 percent in one week. The Fifth Circuit, in relying on precedent established in the Third Circuit,[5] held that even if the plan sponsor and committee were fiduciaries with respect to the investments in employer stock, they were entitled to a presumption that they acted prudently with respect to the employer stock investments. The court advised that mere fluctuations in value, including a significant downward trend, are not sufficient to overcome the presumption of prudence. In affirming the trial court's granting of summary judgment for the defendants, the court noted that the facts presented in this case were "much less grave" than the circumstances presented in other cases that failed to find a breach of fiduciary duty.

In a matter in which the plan documents mandated that a portion of plan assets be invested in employer stock, participants brought suit alleging breach of fiduciary duty by the plan sponsor because of a drop in stock price stemming from the disclosure of an inventory write-down for obsolete and unmarketable inventory.[6] The suit alleged that the plan sponsor failed to act prudently and in the best interests of participants by failing to divest the plan of employer stock that they knew to be artificially inflated because of the pending inventory write-down. The court disagreed with the plaintiff's position. Relying on the same Third Circuit holding as the case above, the court ruled that there is a presumption that an ESOP fiduciary's investment in employer securities is consistent with ERISA. Plaintiffs may attempt to rebut this position by demonstrating circumstances that would make an investment in employer stock contrary to plan purposes. Here, the court again noted that mere fluctuations in the value of employer stock, even severe downward trends, are insufficient to establish imprudence. The court noted that price fluctuations do not rise to the level of a dire situation that would require fiduciaries to violate the plan document provisions by not investing the assets in employer stock. In the matter at hand,

---

1. Labor Reg. §2550.404a-1.
2. See *Whitfield v. Cohen*, 682 F. Supp. 188 (S.D.N.Y. 1988) (citing *Public Serv. Co. of Colo. v. Chase Manhattan Bank*, 577 F. Supp. 92 (S.D.N.Y. 1983)).
3. *Hunt v. Magnell*, 758 F. Supp. 1292 (D. Minn. 1991).
4. *Kirschbaum v. Reliant Energy, Inc.*, 2008 WL 1838324 (5th Cir. 2008).
5. *Moench v Robertson*, 62 F.3d 553 (3d Cir. 1995).
6. *In re RadioShack ERISA Litig.*, 2008 WL 1808329 (N.D. Tex. 2008).

the court noted that the price of the stock rebounded in less than a year from the disclosure of the inventory write-down.[1]

303. Is a fiduciary liable for losses to a plan for failing to investigate and evaluate a proposed investment?

Not necessarily. A fiduciary's failure to investigate and evaluate an investment decision alone is not sufficient to make him liable for losses to a plan. Instead, efforts to hold the fiduciary liable for a loss attributable to an inadequate investment decision must demonstrate a causal link between the failure to investigate and evaluate and the harm suffered by the plan.[2]

The cases that hold a trustee liable for losses for failing to investigate and evaluate the merits of an investment have based the trustee's liability on findings of fact that clearly established the unsoundness of the investment decision at the time it was made. If a court determines that a trustee failed to investigate a particular investment adequately, it will examine whether, considering the facts that an adequate and thorough investigation would have revealed, the investment was objectively imprudent.[3]

"[T]he determination of an objectively prudent investment is made on the basis of what the trustee knew or should have known; and the latter necessarily involves consideration of what facts would have come to his attention if he had fully complied with his duty to investigate and evaluate." It is the imprudent investment, rather than the failure to investigate and evaluate, that is the basis of liability. A failure to investigate and evaluate the potential investment is merely evidence demonstrating that the trustee should have known more than he knew in selecting the imprudent investment.[4] Thus, a fiduciary may be held liable for losses to the plan for failure to perform his fiduciary obligations to investigate and evaluate a proposed investment of plan assets if the investment decision was objectively imprudent.

304. Is the prudent person rule subject to the business judgment rules?

No. It is not a business judgment rule that applies to the question of prudence in the management of an ERISA plan, but rather a prudent person standard.[5]

305. Is a fiduciary an insurer of plan investments?

No. "[T]he prudence rule does not make the fiduciary an insurer of the plan's assets or of the success of its investments. ERISA does not require that a pension fund take no risk with its investments. Virtually every investment entails some degree of risk, and even the most carefully evaluated investments can fail while unpromising investments may succeed."[6] "The application of ERISA's prudence standard does not depend upon the ultimate outcome of an investment, but upon the prudence of the fiduciaries under the circumstances prevailing when they make their

---

1. *In re RadioShack ERISA Litig.*, 2008 WL 1808329 (N.D. Tex. 2008).
2. *Kuper v. Iovenko*, 66 F.3d 1447 (6th Cir. 1995).
3. *Fink v. National Sav. & Trust Co.*, 772 F.2d 951 (D.D.C. 1985) (Scalia, J., concurring in part and dissenting in part).
4. *Fink v. National Sav. & Trust Co.*, above.
5. *Lanka v. O'Higgins*, 810 F. Supp. 379 (N.D.N.Y. 1992) (citing *Donovan v. Mazzola*, 716 F.2d 1226 (9th Cir. 1983) (which expressly rejected the business judgment rule)).
6. *Donovan v. Mazzola*, 716 F.2d 1226 (9th Cir. 1983), *cert. denied*, 464 U.S. 1040 (1984).

decision and in light of the alternatives available to them."[1] The fiduciary duty of care requires prudence, not prescience.[2]

In addition, the mere fact that a plan's investment portfolio declines in value or suffers a diminution of income does not by itself establish imprudence. Market values are untrustworthy indicia of value especially in times of economic decline.[3] In that respect, whether a trustee is liable for losses to the plan depends upon the circumstances at the time when the investment is selected and not upon subsequent events. Thus, if at the time an investment is made, it is an investment a prudent person would make, there is no liability if the investment later depreciates in value absent a failure to monitor its performance.

306. Can a successor fiduciary be liable for the investment acts of its predecessor?

Yes. If the selection of plan investments by a predecessor fiduciary constitutes a breach of duty or a prohibited transaction, a successor fiduciary has a duty to dispose of these investments upon assuming her responsibilities as fiduciary.[4] A fiduciary has a continuing duty to advise the plan to divest of unlawful or imprudent investments, and its failure to do so gives rise to a new cause of action each time the fund was injured.[5]

307. Is a fiduciary's subjective good faith a defense to a breach of fiduciary duty?

No. The fact that a fiduciary may have acted in good faith is not a defense to a breach of fiduciary duties, because the sincerity of a fiduciary's belief that his actions are in the best interests of the plan is essentially irrelevant to a determination of the prudence of the fiduciary's conduct.[6] Thus, good faith alone is not recognized as a defense to a breach of fiduciary duties.[7]

308. Does the prudence requirement obligate a fiduciary to seek the assistance of an expert?

It depends. Although ERISA does not require a fiduciary to seek professional assistance in making plan investments, where a trustee does not possess the education, experience, and skill required to make a decision concerning the investment of a plan's assets, he has an affirmative duty to seek independent counsel in making the decision. The failure to do so is imprudent and constitutes a violation of ERISA Section 404(a)(1)(B).[8]

---

1. *Marshall v. Glass/Metal Ass'n*, 507 F. Supp. 378 (D. Haw. 1980).
2. *Debruyne v. Equitable Life Assurance Soc'y*, 720 F. Supp. 1342 (N.D. Ill. 1989).
3. *American Commc'ns Ass'n, Local 10 v. Retirement Plan for Emps.* of RCA Corp., 488 F. Supp. 479 (S.D.N.Y.), *aff'd*, 646 F.2d 559 (2d Cir. 1980).
4. See *Morrissey v. Curran*, 567 F.2d 546 (2d Cir. 1977). See also *McDougall v. Donovan*, 552 F. Supp. 1206 (N.D. Ill. 1983) (successor trustee has duty to dispose of prior improper investment upon becoming trustee); *Buccino v. Continental Assur.* Co., 578 F. Supp. 1518 (S.D.N.Y. 1983).
5. *PBGC v. Greene*, 570 F. Supp. 1483 (W.D. Pa. 1982), aff'd, 727 F.2d 1100 (3d Cir. 1984).
6. *Donovan v. Daugherty*, 550 F. Supp. 390 (S.D. Ala. 1982); *Marshall v. Glass/Metal Ass'n*, 507 F. Supp. 378 (D. Haw. 1980).
7. *Reich v. King*, 867 F. Supp. 341 (D. Md. 1994) ("a fiduciary's subjective good faith belief of his prudence will not insulate him from liability"); see also *Lanka v. O'Higgins*, 810 F. Supp. 379 (N.D.N.Y. 1992); *Donovan v. Bierwirth*, 538 F. Supp. 463 (E.D.N.Y. 1981), *aff'd* as modified, 680 F.2d 263 (2d Cir.), *cert. denied*, 459 U.S. 1069 (1982).
8. *Donovan v. Bierwirth*, 538 F. Supp. 463 (E.D.N.Y. 1981), *aff'd* as modified, 680 F.2d 263 (2d Cir.), *cert. denied*, 459 U.S. 1069 (1982).

The reasoning behind this requirement is that the investment selection process is an indication of the care and diligence of the trustee in arriving at an investment decision. Thus, while there is flexibility in the prudence standard, it is not a refuge for fiduciaries who are not equipped to evaluate a complex investment. If fiduciaries commit a pension plan's assets to investments that they do not fully understand, they will nonetheless be judged, as provided in the statute, according to the standards of others "acting in a like capacity and familiar with such matters." Consequently, a trustee's lack of familiarity with investments is no excuse when evaluating his prudence.[1]

309. Can a fiduciary avoid liability by relying on the professional advice of others?

While a trustee has a duty to seek independent advice where he lacks the requisite education, experience, and skill, the trustee, nevertheless, must make his own decision based on that advice.[2] The conduct of a trustee in making an independent investigation is an indication of the care and diligence of the trustee in arriving at an investment decision. A trustee unfamiliar with an unusual or difficult investment decision is charged with making an "independent inquiry into the merits of particular investments rather than [relying] wholly upon the advice of others."[3]

Although fiduciaries are not expected by the courts to duplicate their advisers' investigative efforts, fiduciaries are required to "review the data a consultant gathers, to assess its significance and to supplement it where necessary."[4] In addition, "[a]n independent appraisal is not a magic wand that fiduciaries may simply wave over a transaction to ensure that their responsibilities are fulfilled. It is a tool and like all tools, is useful only if used properly." But as the source of the information upon which the experts' opinions are based, the fiduciaries are responsible for ensuring that the information is complete and up-to-date.[5] Moreover, the thoroughness of a fiduciary's investigation is measured not only by the actions it took in performing it, but by the facts that an adequate evaluation would have uncovered.[6]

310. Do plan losses create a presumption of a breach of duty?

No. The test of prudence under the prudent man rule is one of conduct, and not a test of the result of performance of the investment. The focus of the inquiry is how the fiduciary acted in his selection of the investment, not whether his investments succeeded or failed.[7]

---

1. *Marshall v. Glass/Metal Ass'n*, 507 F. Supp. 378 (D. Haw. 1980).

2. *Donovan v. Bierwirth*, 680 F.2d 263 (2d Cir.), *cert. denied*, 459 U.S. 1069 (1982); *Donovan v. Mazzola*, 716 F.2d 1226 (9th Cir. 1983).

3. *Withers v. Teachers' Ret. Sys.*, 447 F. Supp. 1248 (S.D.N.Y. 1978), *aff'd mem.*, 595 F.2d 1210 (2d Cir. 1979).

4. *In re Unisys Sav. Plan Litig.*, 74 F.3d 420 (3d Cir. 1996), aff'd, 173 F.3d 145 (3d Cir. 1999).

5. *Donovan v. Cunningham*, 716 F.2d 1455 (5th Cir. 1983).

6. *In re Unisys Sav. Plan Litig.*, 74 F.3d 420 (3d Cir. 1996), *reh'g denied*, 173 F.3d 145 (3d Cir. 1999) (citing *Fink v. National Sav. & Trust Co.*, 772 F.2d 951 (D.C. Cir. 1985) (Scalia, J., concurring in part and dissenting in part)).

7. *Donovan v. Cunningham*, 716 F.2d 1455 (5th Cir. 1983).

311. What factors should be considered in the prudent selection of a person or entity to invest plan assets?

According to one court, there are "certain elements necessary to a prudent selection of a person or entity to invest ERISA plan assets."[1] Such considerations would require a prudent trustee to

1.   Evaluate the person's qualifications, including (a) his experience in the particular area of investments under consideration and with other ERISA plans; (b) his educational credentials; (c) whether he is registered with the Securities and Exchange Commission under the Investment Advisers Act of 1940; (d) an independent assessment of his qualifications by means of (i) a widely enjoyed reputation in the business of investments, (ii) client references, and/or (iii) the advice of a professional third-party consultant; *and* (e) his record of past performance with investments of the type contemplated;

2.   Ascertain the reasonableness of fees;

3.   Review documents reflecting the relationship to be entered into; *and*

4.   Ensure adequate, periodic accountings in the future.[2]

312. What is the position of the DOL with respect to fiduciary responsibility when mutual fund market-timing or late-trading abuses occur?

Employee Benefits Security Administration Assistant Secretary Ann L. Combs issued a statement addressing this issue on February 17, 2004. In the statement, she noted that in light of late-trading and market-timing problems identified by federal and state regulators, as fiduciaries conduct their review they must discharge their fiduciary duties prudently. "The exercise of prudence in this context requires a deliberative process. In this regard, fiduciaries, deciding whether to make any changes in mutual fund investments or investment options, must make decisions that are as well informed as possible under the circumstances."

The Assistant Secretary opined that "in cases where specific funds have been identified as under investigation by government agencies, fiduciaries should consider the nature of the alleged abuses, the potential economic impact of those abuses on the plan's investments, the steps taken by the fund to limit the potential for such abuses in the future, and any remedial action taken or contemplated to make investors whole. To the extent that such information has not been provided or is not otherwise available, a plan fiduciary should consider contacting the fund directly in an effort to obtain specific information. Fiduciaries of plans invested in such funds may ultimately have to decide whether to participate in settlements or lawsuits. In doing so, they will need to weigh the costs to the plan against the likelihood and amount of potential recoveries."

In determining an appropriate course of action, the statement notes that fiduciaries should "follow prudent plan procedures relating to investment decisions and document their decisions."

---

1. *Whitfield v. Cohen*, 682 F. Supp. 188 (S.D.N.Y. 1988).
2. *Whitfield v. Cohen*, above.

In considering appropriate courses of action, questions have been raised "as to whether a plan's offering of mutual fund or similar investments that impose reasonable redemption fees on sales of their shares would, in and of itself, affect the availability of relief under [ERISA Section 404(c)]. Similarly, questions have been raised as to whether reasonable plan or investment fund limits on the number of times a participant can move in and out of a particular investment within a particular period would, in and of itself, affect the availability of relief under [ERISA Section 404(c)]."

"Without expressing a view as to any particular plan or particular investment options," the DOL is of the belief that these two examples represent approaches to limiting market-timing that do not run afoul of the "volatility" and other requirements set forth in the DOL's regulation under ERISA Section 404(c), "provided that any such restrictions are allowed under the terms of the plan and clearly disclosed to the plan's participants and beneficiaries. The imposition of trading restrictions that are not contemplated under the terms of the plan raises issues concerning the application of ERISA Section 404(c), as well as issues as to whether such restrictions constitute the imposition of a 'blackout period' requiring advance notice to affected participants and beneficiaries."

The SEC, pursuant to Orders entered under several enforcement matters alleging late-trading and market-timing activities, has established settlement funds that will be available for distribution to mutual fund investors, including certain 401(k) and other ERISA plans that suffered losses. For each relevant mutual fund or series of funds, the SEC has appointed independent distribution consultants (IDCs) who will establish procedures to distribute settlement monies to the appropriate mutual fund shareholders. The DOL expects that there will be ERISA plans that will receive settlement monies directly from the settlement funds. There will also be other ERISA plans, as clients, entitled to a share of settlement monies received by an "omnibus account" operated by an intermediary, such as a broker, underwriter, or record keeper.

The DOL, in Field Assistance Bulletin 2006-01,[1] has provided guidance regarding the duties and responsibilities under ERISA of IDCs, plan service providers, and fiduciaries with respect to the allocation and distribution of mutual fund settlement proceeds to plans and participants.

In FAB 2006-01, the DOL offers the following guidance:

1.   The IDCs, in developing and implementing a distribution plan for plan allocations, are not ERISA fiduciaries.

2.   Settlement proceeds do not constitute "plan assets" under ERISA until distributed from the SEC settlement funds.

3.   Upon receipt by a plan or an intermediary, the settlement monies are plan assets that must be held in trust and managed in accordance with ERISA's fiduciary provisions.

4.   Intermediaries will be fiduciaries of their omnibus account clients that are ERISA plans and must act prudently and solely in the interests of plan participants.

---

1. Field Assistance Bull. 2006-01 (Apr. 19, 2006).

5. Plan fiduciaries (including intermediaries) have flexibility in designing and implementing a methodology for allocating settlement proceeds to participant accounts, but must ensure that the methodology does not violate the prudence and "solely in the interest" requirements of ERISA.

Fiduciaries will be deemed to satisfy the prudence requirement if they use an allocation methodology that is provided or required by an IDC, so long as they implement the methodology prudently.

Upon receipt of settlement proceeds, intermediaries that otherwise might not be ERISA fiduciaries will become subject to ERISA, including prohibited transaction rules that affect how the intermediaries can be compensated for their work in handling and allocating distributions received by omnibus accounts.

313. May a fiduciary consider the collateral effects of an investment opportunity?

According to the Department of Labor, the requirements of ERISA Sections 403 and 404 do not exclude the consideration of collateral benefits in a fiduciary's evaluation of a particular investment opportunity. The DOL has stated that arrangements designed to bring areas of investment opportunity that provide collateral benefits to the attention of plan fiduciaries will not, in and of themselves, violate ERISA Section 403 or ERISA Section 404, provided that the arrangements do not restrict the exercise of the fiduciary's investment discretion.[1]

For example, in Advisory Opinion 88-16A, the DOL considered an arrangement whereby a company and union proposed to make recommendations, for up to 5 percent of the annual contributions, of investments with the potential for providing collateral benefits to union members. The DOL concluded that the arrangement would not be inconsistent with the requirements of ERISA Section 403(c) and ERISA Section 404(a)(1), where the investment managers having responsibility with respect to these recommendations retained exclusive investment discretion and were required to secure, over the long term, the maximum attainable total return on investments in a manner consistent with the principles of sound pension fund management. Moreover, the DOL stated that in considering such investments, plan fiduciaries could be influenced by factors that were not related to the plan's expected investment return, only if such investments were equal or superior to alternative available investments.[2]

Similarly, in a case involving construction project financing, the DOL also concluded that participation in an organization that presents investment opportunities but does not limit the investment alternatives available to the plans, and does not obligate the plans to invest in any project presented for consideration, did not, in itself, violate any of ERISA's fiduciary standards. Moreover, the DOL concluded that in enforcing the plan's rights after making an investment, the fiduciary could consider factors unrelated to the plan's investment return only if, in the

---

1. Labor Reg. §2509.94-1 (IB 94-1), 59 Fed. Reg. 32,606 (June 23, 1994).
2. DOL Adv. Op. 88-16A.

fiduciary's judgment, the course of action taken would be at least as economically advantageous to the plan as any alternative course of action.[1]

In other letters, the DOL has stated that the existence of such collateral benefits may be decisive in evaluating an investment only if the fiduciary determines that the investment containing the collateral benefits is expected to provide an investment return to the plan commensurate with alternative investments having similar risks.[2] Thus, while every investment may cause a plan to forgo other investment opportunities, an investment is not imprudent merely because it provides a plan with a lower expected rate of return than available alternative investments with commensurate degrees of risk, nor because it is riskier than alternative available investments with commensurate rates of return.[3]

Although the DOL has stated that a plan fiduciary may consider collateral benefits in choosing between investments that have comparable risks and rates of return, it has also consistently stated that fiduciaries who are willing to accept expected reduced returns or greater risks to secure collateral benefits are in violation of ERISA.

314. What are the fiduciary issues regarding economically targeted investments?

Interpretive Bulletin 2008-1[4] sets forth the views of the Department of Labor concerning the legal standards imposed on fiduciaries of employee benefit plans by ERISA Section 403 and ERISA Section 404 when considering investments in "economically targeted investments," that is, investments selected for the economic benefits they create apart from their investment return to the employee benefit plan.

Interpretive Bulletin 2008-1 reiterates that ERISA requires that a fiduciary act solely in the interest of the plan's participants and beneficiaries and for the exclusive purpose of providing benefits to their participants and beneficiaries. ERISA specifically states, in relevant part, that:

> "[A]ssets of a plan shall never inure to the benefit of any employer and shall be held for the exclusive purposes of providing benefits to participants in the plan and their beneficiaries."[5]

> "[A] fiduciary shall discharge his duties with respect to a plan solely in the interest of the participants and beneficiaries and for the exclusive purpose of providing benefits to participants and their beneficiaries."[6]

It is the view of the DOL that ERISA's plain text does not permit fiduciaries to make investment decisions on the basis of any factor other than the economic interest of the plan.

1. DOL Op. Letter to George Cox (Jan. 16, 1981).
2. DOL Op. Letters to Theodore Groom (Jan. 16, 1981), Daniel O'Sullivan (Aug. 2, 1982), James Ray (July 8, 1988), and Stuart Cohen (May 14, 1993).
3. See DOL Op. Letters to the Trustees of the Twin City Carpenters and Joiners Pension Plan (May 19, 1981), William Ecklund (Dec. 18, 1985, and Jan. 16, 1986), Reed Larson (July 14, 1986), and Jack Kemp (Nov. 23, 1990).
4. Labor Reg. §2509.08-1.
5. ERISA Sec. 403(c)(1).
6. ERISA Sec. 404(a)(1)(A)(i).

Situations may arise, however, in which two or more investment alternatives are of equal economic value to a plan. The DOL has recognized in past guidance that, under these limited circumstances, fiduciaries can choose between the investment alternatives on the basis of a factor other than the economic interest of the plan. The DOL has interpreted the statute to permit this selection because: (1) ERISA requires fiduciaries to invest plan assets and to make choices between investment alternatives; (2) ERISA does not itself specifically provide a basis for making the investment choice in this circumstance; and (3) the economic interests of the plan are fully protected by the fact that the available investment alternatives are, from the plan's perspective, economically indistinguishable.

Given the significance of ERISA's requirement that fiduciaries act "solely in the interest of participants and beneficiaries," the DOL believes that, before selecting an economically targeted investment, fiduciaries must first conclude that the alternative options are truly equal, taking into account a quantitative and qualitative analysis of the economic impact on the plan. ERISA's fiduciary standards expressed in ERISA Section 403 and ERISA Section 404 do not permit fiduciaries to select investments based on factors outside the economic interests of the plan until they have concluded, based on economic factors, that alternative investments are equal. A less rigid rule would allow fiduciaries to act on the basis of factors outside the economic interest of the plan in situations where reliance on those factors might compromise or subordinate the interests of plan participants and their beneficiaries. The DOL rejects a construction of ERISA that would render ERISA's tight limits on the use of plan assets illusory, and that would permit plan fiduciaries to expend ERISA trust assets to promote myriad public policy preferences.[1]

The DOL also states that a plan fiduciary's analysis is required to comply with, but is not necessarily limited to, the requirements set forth in Labor Regulation Section 2550.404a-1(b). In evaluating the plan portfolio, as well as portions of the portfolio, the fiduciary is required to examine the level of diversification, the degree of liquidity, and the potential risk/return in comparison with available alternative investments. The same type of analysis must also be applied when choosing between investment alternatives. Potential investments should be compared to other investments that would fill a similar role in the portfolio with regard to diversification, liquidity, and risk/return.

In light of the rigorous requirements established by ERISA, the DOL believes that fiduciaries who rely on factors outside the economic interests of the plan in making investment choices and subsequently find their decision challenged will rarely be able to demonstrate compliance with ERISA absent a written record demonstrating that a contemporaneous economic analysis showed that the investment alternatives were of equal value.

The following examples are provided in Interpretive Bulletin 2008-1:

1.   A plan owns an interest in a limited partnership that is considering investing in a company that competes with the plan sponsor. The fiduciaries may not replace the limited partnership investment with another investment based on this fact unless

---

1. See Letters from DOL to Jonathan Hiatt (May 3, 2005), to Thomas Donahue (Dec. 21, 2007) (A.O. 2007-07A), and to David Chavern (June 27, 2008) (A.O. 2008-05A).

they prudently determine that a replacement investment is economically equal or superior to the limited partnership investment and would not adversely affect the plan's investment portfolio, taking into account factors including diversification, liquidity, risk, and expected return. The competition of the limited partnership with the plan sponsor is a factor outside the economic interests of the plan, and thus cannot be considered unless an alternative investment is equal or superior to the limited partnership.

2.   A multiemployer plan covering employees in a metropolitan area's construction industry wants to invest in a large loan for a construction project located in the same area because it will create local jobs. The plan has taken steps to ensure that the loan poses no prohibited transaction issues. The loan carries a return fully commensurate with the risk of nonpayment. Moreover, the loan's expected return is equal to or greater than construction loans of similar quality that are available to the plan. The plan has already made several other loans for construction projects in the same metropolitan area, however, and this loan could create a risk of large losses to the plan's portfolio due to lack of diversification. The fiduciaries may not choose this investment on the basis of the local job creation factor because, due to lack of diversification, the investment is not of equal economic value to the plan.

3.   A plan is considering an investment in a bond to finance affordable housing for people in the local community. The bond provides a return at least as favorable to the plan as other bonds with the same risk rating. However, the bond's size and lengthy duration raise a potential risk regarding the plan's ability to meet its predicted liquidity needs. Other available bonds under consideration by the plan do not pose this same risk. The return on the bond, although equal to or greater than the alternatives, would not be sufficient to offset the additional risk for the plan created by the role that this bond would play in the plan's portfolio. The plan's fiduciaries may not make this investment based on factors outside the economic interest of the plan because it is not of equal or greater economic value as compared to other investment alternatives.

4.   A plan sponsor adopts an investment policy that favors plan investment in companies meeting certain environmental criteria (so-called "green" companies). In carrying out the policy, the plan's fiduciaries may not simply consider investments only in green companies. They must consider all investments that meet the plan's prudent financial criteria. The fiduciaries may apply the investment policy to eliminate a company from consideration only if they appropriately determine that other available investments provide equal or better returns at the same or lower risks, and would play the same role in the plan's portfolio.

5.   A collective investment fund, which holds assets of several plans, is designed to invest in commercial real estate constructed or renovated with union labor. Fiduciaries of plans that invest in the fund must determine that the fund's overall risk and return characteristics are as favorable, or more favorable, to the plans as other available

investment alternatives that would play a similar role in their plans' portfolios. The fund's managers may select investments constructed or improved with union labor, after an economic analysis indicates that these investment options are equal or superior to their alternatives. The managers will best be able to justify their investment choice by recording their analysis in writing. If real estate investments that satisfy both ERISA's fiduciary requirements and the union labor criterion are unavailable, however, the fund managers may have to select investments without regard to the union labor criterion.

The guidance set forth in Interpretive Bulletin 2008-1 modifies and supersedes the DOL's prior guidance that was set forth in Interpretive Bulletin 94-1[1] that addressed the limited circumstances under which fiduciaries, consistent with the requirements of ERISA Section 403 and ERISA Section 404, could, in connection with investment decisions, take into account factors other than the economic interests of the plan.

315. May a fiduciary engage in shareholder activism with the intent to monitor or influence the management of corporations in which the plan owns stock?

According to the Department of Labor, an investment policy that contemplates activities intended to monitor or influence the management of corporations in which the plan owns stock is consistent with a fiduciary's obligations under ERISA where the responsible fiduciary concludes that there is a reasonable expectation that such monitoring or communication with management, by the plan alone or together with other shareholders, will enhance the economic value of the plan's investment in the corporation, after taking into account the costs involved. In the view of the DOL, such a reasonable expectation may exist in various circumstances; for example, where plan investments in corporate stock are held as long-term investments or where a plan may not be able to easily dispose of such an investment.

The DOL's views with respect to shareholder activism were set forth initially in Interpretive Bulletin 94-2[2] issued by the DOL in 1994. The DOL updated its views on October 17, 2008, with the issuance of Interpretive Bulletin 2008-2,[3] relating, in part, to shareholder activism. The Interpretive Bulletin updates the views of the DOL concerning the legal standards imposed by ERISA Section 402, ERISA Section 403, and ERISA Section 404 with respect to the written statements of investment policy, including interpretive positions issued by the DOL since 1994 on shareholder activism, as well as interpretive positions issued by the DOL since 1994 on shareholder activism and socially directed proxy voting initiatives. The guidance modifies and supersedes the guidance set forth in Interpretive Bulletin 94-2.[4]

---

1. Labor Reg. §2509.94-1.
2. Labor Reg. §2509.94-2.
3. Labor Reg. §2509.94-2.
4. Labor Reg. §2509.94-2.

316. What types of issues are involved in "shareholder activism"?

According to the Department of Labor, shareholder activism would generally concern such issues as the independence and expertise of candidates for the corporation's board of directors and assuring that the board has sufficient information to carry out its responsibility to monitor management. Other issues may include such matters as consideration of the appropriateness of executive compensation, the corporation's policy regarding mergers and acquisitions, the extent of debt financing and capitalization, the nature of long-term business plans, the corporation's investment in training to develop its work force, and other workplace practices and financial and non-financial measures of corporate performance that are reasonably likely to affect the economic value of the plan. Active monitoring and communication may be carried out through a variety of methods, including by means of correspondence and meetings with corporate management, as well as by exercising the legal rights of a shareholder. In creating an investment policy, a fiduciary shall consider only factors that relate to the economic interest of participants and their beneficiaries in plan assets, and shall not use an investment policy to promote myriad public policy preferences.[1]

The DOL's views with respect to shareholder activism was set forth initially in Interpretive Bulletin 94-2[2] issued by the DOL in 1994. The DOL updated its views on October 17, 2008, with the issuance of Interpretive Bulletin 2008-2,[3] relating, in part, to shareholder activism. The Interpretive Bulletin updates the views of the DOL concerning the legal standards imposed by ERISA Section 402, ERISA Section 403, and ERISA Section 404 with respect to the written statements of investment policy, including interpretive positions issued by the DOL since 1994 on shareholder activism, as well as interpretive positions issued by the DOL since 1994 on shareholder activism and socially directed proxy voting initiatives. The guidance modifies and supersedes the guidance set forth in Interpretive Bulletin 94-2.

317. May trustees be relieved from liability for the acts or omissions of an investment manager?

If an investment manager has been appointed, no trustee will be liable for the acts or omissions of such investment manager, nor will any trustee be under an obligation to invest or otherwise manage any asset of the plan that is subject to the management of the investment manager.[4]

But this relief does not totally excuse from liability the named fiduciary who appointed the investment manager. If the named fiduciary violated ERISA Section 404(a)(1) (see Q 253) with respect to the allocation or designation of fiduciary duties, in the establishment or implementation of procedures for allocating fiduciary duties, or in continuing the allocation or designation, then the named fiduciary will be liable for an act or omission of an appointed person.[5]

---

1. See DOL Adv. Op. 2008-05A (June 27, 2008); Letter from DOL to Jonathan P. Hiatt (May 3, 2005).
2. Labor Reg. §2509.94-2.
3. Labor Reg. §2509.08-2.
4. ERISA Sec. 405(d).
5. ERISA Sec. 405(c)(2)(A).

The limited relief from liability for the named fiduciary who has appointed the investment manager is also expressed in the legislative history of ERISA Section 405 as follows: "in choosing an investment manager, the named fiduciary must act prudently and in the interest of participants and beneficiaries, and also must act in this manner in continuing the use of the investment manager ... as long as the named fiduciary had chosen and retained the investment manager prudently, the named fiduciary would not be liable for the acts or omissions of the investment manager."[1]

Named fiduciaries and plan trustees may not avoid fiduciary liability by appointing an investment manager and delegating investment authority to him. Instead, plan fiduciaries and trustees retain oversight responsibility and have a duty to keep themselves apprised of plan investments to ensure that the investments are prudent and legal.[2]

318. What are the duties and responsibilities of an investment manager?

NOTE: In late 2010, and again in 2011, the DOL released proposed regulations that have a significant impact on determining fiduciary status regarding advice and management decisions focusing on plan assets.[3] You will find a detailed analysis of these proposed regulations and the impact they have on plan assets and individuals involved in the decisions about and management of them under Q 240.

The term "investment manager" means any fiduciary (other than a trustee or named fiduciary) who

1.   Has the power to manage, acquire, or dispose of any asset of a plan, and has acknowledged in writing that he is a fiduciary to the subject plan;

2.   Is either (a) registered as an investment adviser under the Investment Advisers Act of 1940 (the 1940 Act), (b) a bank (as defined under the 1940 Act), or (c) an insurance company qualified to perform investment management services under the laws of more than one state; and

3.   Has acknowledged in writing that he is a fiduciary with respect to the plan.[4]

The investment manager's duties and responsibilities, in addition to those just listed (and in Q 578), are the same as those general provisions applicable to all fiduciaries under ERISA Section 404 and ERISA Section 406. These obligations include the duty to diversify and follow the language of the plan.

In two arrangements reviewed by the DOL in issuing advisory opinions, performance-based compensation was permissible where

1.   The arrangements complied with SEC Rule 205-3 governing performance compensation arrangements;

---

1. H.R. Conf. Rep. No. 93-1280, 93d Cong., 2d Sess. 301-302 (1974) (ERISA Conference Report).
2. *Reich v. Hosking*, No. 94-CV-10363-BC, 20 EBC 1090 (E.D. Mich. 1996).
3. Prop. Labor Reg. §2510.3-21; 75 Fed. Reg. 65,263 (Oct. 22, 2010).
4. ERISA Sec. 3(38).

2. Performance was measured by a formula taking into account both realized and unrealized gains and losses during a pre-established valuation period;

3. A large majority of the investments would be made in securities with readily available market quotations, and those that were not would be independently valued by persons appointed by the plan and independent of the manager; and

4. Execution of the arrangement was allowed only with plans having aggregate assets of at least $50 million.

But DOL cautioned that a violation of ERISA could occur in the course of an investment manager's service. It noted that ERISA requires that a fiduciary act prudently in deciding to retain an investment manager under a performance-based compensation arrangement and in negotiating the specific formula under which compensation will be paid.[1]

Specifically, the DOL opines that a plan's payment of performance-based compensation to an investment manager may be allowed under ERISA's prohibited transaction rules if:

1. The payment satisfies the ERISA Section 408(b)(2) requirements (for the prohibited transaction exemption for the provision of necessary services by a party in interest— the investment manager); and

2. The investment manager, as plan fiduciary, has not engaged in self-dealing (in violation of ERISA Section 406(b)). Where the investment manager does not exercise any fiduciary authority, control, or responsibility to obtain from the plan additional fees for a service that he—or an entity in which he has an interest—provides, he will not violate ERISA Section 406(b)(1).

Under arrangements involving a percentage of net appreciation or pre-determined index, both realized and unrealized gains and losses during a pre-established valuation period would be taken into account. Investments would be made in securities for which market quotations were readily available or, if not readily available, would be made by persons independent of the manager. Selection criteria for securities composing the index and the way in which these securities would be weighted would be set forth in the investment manager agreement and would not be adjusted except after consultation with the client plan. In such an instance, the investment manager would not be exercising any of its fiduciary authority or control to cause a plan to pay an additional fee.

The Court of Appeals for the Eleventh Circuit ruled that an investment manager had breached his fiduciary duties to a plan where he failed to investigate the cash flow needs of the plan and to adequately diversify the fund, which resulted in losses to the plan.[2] The Court of Appeals for the Second Circuit held that an investment firm was liable, and its owner was personally liable, for a breach of fiduciary duty due to the failure of the investment manager to follow the written agreement governing the investment management arrangement between the plan

---

1. ERISA Op. Letter 86-20A (1986); ERISA Op. Letter 86-21A (1986).
2. See *GIW Indus., Inc. v. Trevor, Stewart, Burton & Jacobsen, Inc.*, 895 F.2d 729 (11th Cir. 1990).

and the investment manager.[1] The fact that the plan trustees in *Dardaganis* were aware of the investment manager's failure to follow the governing documents for more than 14 months, yet took no steps to correct the failure, did not relieve the investment manager from liability for the losses incurred as a result of his failure to follow the investment management agreement. In another case, the same court of appeals held that an investment manager was liable for losses incurred as a result of entering into a prohibited transaction with a plan, even though the plan trustees directed the investment manager to make the investments at issue.[2]

Investment managers, as fiduciaries, may receive reasonable compensation and reimbursement of expenses for services rendered to the plan.[3]

Practitioner's Pointer: Most investment managers are compensated with a specified percentage of the assets they have under management, in accordance with an agreed-upon fee schedule. But there has been a growing trend toward "performance-based fees." Plan fiduciaries need to be cautious when entering into such performance-based fee schedules because the Department of Labor has stated that where the fiduciary may use his authority, control, or responsibility to cause the plan to pay additional fees, such a performance-based fee agreement is a prohibited transaction.[4] Payment of performance-based fees will not be a prohibited transaction where the fees depend solely upon the fluctuation of value of the plan's securities.

ERISA Fee Recapture Accounts

Investment managers actively engage in the establishment and management of fee recapture accounts with plan assets under management. The DOL has addressed the duties and responsibilities of investment managers in accessing the monies in these fees recapture accounts to pay for their, and other service providers, plan related expenses. In Advisory Opinion 2013-03A (AO 2013-03A) the DOL addresses the different types of ERISA recapture accounts and discusses the ERISA plan asset and prohibited transaction rules that apply to them. In AO 2013-03A, the DOL describes two types of ERISA recapture accounts – *the bookkeeping account* and the *plan account*. Each requires a different approach in identifying how ERISA applies.

Under the *bookkeeping account approach*, the investment manager receives the revenue sharing payments and under an agreement with the plan establishes this account on the investment manager's records. The bookkeeping account reflects credits that under a written plan agreement or under the direction of a plan fiduciary, will apply these credits to pay plan service providers. In this approach, amounts in the bookkeeping account are *not* ERISA plan assets.

However, the DOL advises that if there is an agreement in place for plan fees to be paid from this account and the investment manager fails to make such specified payments, the plan would have a claim against the investment manager and that claim *is* a plan asset.

---

1. See *Dardaganis v. Grace Capital, Inc.*, 889 F.2d 1237 (2d Cir. 1989).
2. See *Lowen v. Tower Asset Mgmt., Inc.*, 829 F.2d 1209 (2d Cir. 1987).
3. ERISA Sec. 408(c)(2).
4. See DOL Adv. Op. 89-31A.

Under the *plan account approach*, the investment manager receives the revenue sharing payments directly and under written agreement with the plan transfers some or all of the revenue sharing payments to the plan. The plan administrator then uses the plan account to pay service providers. If, at the close of the plan year, amounts remain in the plan account, the plan administrator will then allocate them to participants as additional plan earnings.

With the *plan account approach*, the amounts received in the account *are* plan assets. If the plan has a contract with the investment manager to transfer the funds to the plan, and the investment manager fails to make those payments, the plan would have a claim against the investment manager and that claim would be a plan asset.

319. Are investment managers of pooled accounts required to comply with multiple investment policies?

It depends on the situation. An investment manager of a pooled investment vehicle that holds assets of more than one employee benefit plan may be subject to a proxy-voting policy of one plan that conflicts with the proxy-voting policy of another plan. If the investment manager determines that compliance with one of the conflicting voting policies would violate ERISA Section 404(a)(1), for example, by being imprudent or not solely in the economic interest of plan participants, the investment manager would be required to ignore the policy and vote in accordance with ERISA's obligations, according to the Department of Labor. If, however, the investment manager reasonably concludes that application of each plan's voting policy is consistent with ERISA's obligations, such as when the policies reflect different but reasonable judgments or when the plans have different economic interests, ERISA Section 404(a)(1)(D) would generally require the manager, to the extent permitted by applicable law, to vote the proxies in proportion to each plan's interest in the pooled investment vehicle.

It is also the view of the DOL that an investment manager may also require participating investors to accept the investment manager's own investment policy statement, including any statement of proxy-voting policy, before they are allowed to invest, which may help to avoid such potential conflicts. As with investment policies originating from named fiduciaries, a policy initiated by an investment manager and adopted by the participating plans would be regarded as an instrument governing the participating plans, and the investment manager's compliance with such a policy would be governed by ERISA Section 404(a)(1)(D).

On July 29, 1994, the DOL issued guidance with respect to the duties of employee benefit plan fiduciaries under ERISA Section 402, ERISA Section 403, and ERISA Section 404 to vote proxies appurtenant to shares of corporate stock held by their plans.[1] The guidance set forth in Interpretive Bulletin 2008-2 includes clarifications of the earlier guidance, as well as interpretive positions issued by the DOL since 1994 on shareholder activism and socially directed proxy-voting initiatives.[2]

---

1. Labor Reg. §2509.94-2.
2. See Labor Reg. §2509.08-2; I.B. 2008-2 (Oct. 17, 2008).

320. Does a named fiduciary responsible for appointment of investment managers have the authority to condition the appointment on acceptance of a statement of investment policy?

It is the view of the Department of Labor that in plans where investment management responsibility is delegated to one or more investment managers appointed by the named fiduciary pursuant to ERISA Section 402(c)(3), the named fiduciary responsible for appointment of investment managers has the authority, which is inherent in the authority to appoint an investment manager, to condition the appointment on acceptance of a statement of investment policy. Thus, such a named fiduciary may expressly require, as a condition of the investment management agreement, that an investment manager comply with the terms of a statement of investment policy that sets forth guidelines concerning investments and investment courses of action that the investment manager is authorized or is not authorized to make. Such investment policy may include a policy or guidelines on the voting of proxies on shares of stock for which the investment manager is responsible. Such guidelines must be consistent with the fiduciary obligations set forth in ERISA Section 404(a)(1)(A), ERISA Section 404(a)(1)(B), and Interpretive Bulletin 2008-2, and may not subordinate the economic interests of the plan participants to unrelated objectives.

In the absence of such an express requirement to comply with an investment policy, the authority to manage the plan assets placed under the control of the investment manager would lie exclusively with the investment manager. Although a trustee may be subject to the direction of a named fiduciary pursuant to ERISA Section 403(a)(1), an investment manager who has authority to make investment decisions, including proxy-voting decisions, would never be relieved of its fiduciary responsibility if it followed the direction as to specific investment decisions from the named fiduciary or any other person.

Statements of investment policy issued by a named fiduciary authorized to appoint investment managers would be part of the "documents and instruments governing the plan" within the meaning of ERISA Section 404(a)(1)(D). An investment manager to whom such investment policy applies would be required to comply with such policy, pursuant to ERISA Section 404(a)(1)(D) insofar as the policy directives or guidelines are consistent with Titles I and IV of ERISA. Therefore, if, for example, compliance with the guidelines in a given instance would be imprudent, then the investment manager's failure to follow the guidelines would not violate ERISA Section 404(a)(1)(D). Moreover, ERISA Section 404(a)(1)(D) does not shield the investment manager from liability for imprudent actions taken in compliance with a statement of investment policy.

The plan document or trust agreement may expressly provide a statement of investment policy to guide the trustee or may authorize a named fiduciary to issue a statement of investment policy applicable to a trustee. Where a plan trustee is subject to an investment policy, the trustee's duty to comply with such investment policy would also be analyzed under ERISA Section 404(a)(1)(D). Thus, the trustee would be required to comply with the statement of investment policy unless, for example, it would be imprudent to do so in a given instance.

Interpretive Bulletin 2008-2 sets forth the DOL's interpretation of ERISA Section 402, ERISA Section 403, and ERISA Section 404 as those sections apply to voting of proxies on securities held in employee benefit plan investment portfolios and the maintenance of and compliance with statements of investment policy, including proxy-voting policy. In addition Interpretive Bulletin 2008-2 provides guidance on the appropriateness under ERISA of active monitoring of corporate management by plan fiduciaries. The guidance set forth in Interpretive Bulletin 2008-2 modifies and supersedes the guidance set forth in Interpretive Bulletin 94-2.[1]

321. Does the maintenance of a statement of investment policy by a named fiduciary relieve the named fiduciary of its fiduciary obligations with respect to the appointment and monitoring of an investment manager or trustee?

No, according to the Department of Labor in Interpretive Bulletin 2008-2. In its view, maintaining a statement of investment policy by a named fiduciary does not relieve the named fiduciary of its obligations under ERISA Section 404(a) with respect to the appointment and monitoring of an investment manager or trustee. In this regard, the named fiduciary appointing an investment manager must periodically monitor the investment manager's activities with respect to management of the plan assets. Moreover, compliance with ERISA Section 404(a)(1)(B) would require maintenance of proper documentation of the activities of the investment manager and of the named fiduciary of the plan in monitoring the activities of the investment manager. In addition, in the view of the DOL, a named fiduciary's determination of the terms of a statement of investment policy is an exercise of fiduciary responsibility and, as such, statements may need to take into account factors such as the plan's funding policy and its liquidity needs, as well as issues of prudence, diversification, and other fiduciary requirements of ERISA.

Interpretive Bulletin 2008-2 sets forth the DOL's interpretation of ERISA Section 402, ERISA Section 403, and ERISA Section 404 as those sections apply to voting of proxies on securities held in employee benefit plan investment portfolios and the maintenance of and compliance with statements of investment policy, including proxy-voting policy. In addition Interpretive Bulletin 2008-2 provides guidance on the appropriateness under ERISA of active monitoring of corporate management by plan fiduciaries. The guidance set forth in Interpretive Bulletin 2008-2 modifies and supersedes the guidance set forth in Interpretive Bulletin 94-2.[2]

322. Does the prudence requirement extend to the resignation of a trustee?

Yes. The courts have held that a trustee's duty of prudence extends to his resignation, and that his resignation is valid only when he has made adequate provision for the continued prudent management of plan affairs.[3] This resignation requirement is a component of the prudence standard imposed by ERISA Section 404(a)(1)(B).[4]

---

1. Labor Reg. §2509.94-2.
2. Labor Reg. §2509.94-2.
3. *Freund v. Marshall & Ilsley Bank*, 485 F. Supp. 629 (W.D. Wis. 1979).
4. *PBGC v. Greene*, 570 F. Supp. 1483 (W.D. Pa. 1983), *aff'd*, 727 F.2d 1100 (3d Cir.), *cert. denied*, 469 U.S. 820 (1984); *Chambers v. Kaleidoscope, Inc.*, Profit Sharing Plan & Trust, 650 F. Supp. 359 (N.D. Ga. 1986); *Glaziers & Glassworkers Union Local 252 Annuity Fund v. Newbridge Sec., Inc.*, 93 F.3d 1171 (3d Cir. 1996). See also *Ream v. Frey*, 107 F.3d 147 (3d Cir. 1997) (bank that resigned as trustee of plan failed to provide a suitable and trustworthy successor, or advise the participants in advance of its termination and of the reasons for its termination).

323. May ERISA-covered plans invest in derivatives?

Yes, but fiduciaries should exercise extreme caution and due diligence in considering derivatives as investment options for plan assets. A derivative investment is a security that derives its value at any given time, in whole or in part, from the value of one or more underlying assets at the same point in time. Examples of derivatives include futures, options, collateralized mortgage obligations, and forward contracts. See Q 602 for an explanation of asset management issues regarding derivative investments.

The Department of Labor advised fiduciaries of its concern with plan assets being invested in derivatives, due to the extreme price volatility, high degree of leverage, and limited testing by markets associated with derivatives. In other words, the DOL expressed concern that the market value of derivatives is hard to establish due to the illiquid market conditions in which they exist. In considering the appropriateness of investments in derivatives, the DOL advised that fiduciaries must consider how they fit within a plan's investment policy, the plan's exposure to loss, and the role such derivatives would play in the plan's investment portfolio.[1]

Fiduciaries should carefully evaluate all information available on a potential derivative investment prior to making the investment. Review should be made of the credit risk and market risk, projected performance, and the legal risk involved with the derivative being considered. Once an investment has been made in a derivative security, fiduciaries are required to exercise prudence in the monitoring of it to make certain that it is performing its expected function in regard to the plan's portfolio.

324. May fiduciaries purchase annuities for the purpose of distributing pension plan benefits?

Yes, according to DOL News Release 95-72, 3/1/95; DOL Interpretive Bulletin 95-1, 3/6/95, and the Federal Register p. 12328 It is appropriate for fiduciaries to purchase annuities for the purpose of transferring the plan's benefit liabilities to an annuity provider (i.e., the insurance company). These annuities are referred to as benefit distribution annuities. Benefit distribution annuity contracts are purchased for participants and beneficiaries under a variety of circumstances, such as in connection with the termination of a plan or, in the case of an ongoing plan, for participants who are retiring or separating from service with accrued vested benefits.

325. Is the purchase of distribution annuities subject to the fiduciary standards of ERISA?

Yes. DOL Interpretive Bulletin 95-1 provides that the selection of an annuity provider for purposes of a pension benefit distribution, whether upon separation from service, retirement of a participant, or termination of a plan, is a fiduciary decision governed by ERISA. Thus, in choosing an annuity provider for the purpose of making a benefit distribution, fiduciaries must act solely in the interest of participants and beneficiaries and for the exclusive purpose of providing benefits to the participants and beneficiaries, as well as defraying reasonable expenses

---

1. DOL Information Letter to the Comptroller of the Currency (Mar. 21, 1996).

of administering the plan. In addition, the fiduciary obligation of prudence requires that a fiduciary conduct an objective, thorough, and analytical search in identifying and selecting the annuity providers, and must evaluate a potential annuity provider's claims-paying ability and creditworthiness (see Q 326).[1]

326. What factors should be considered in the selection of an annuity provider?

According to DOL Interpretive Bulletin 95-1, the types of factors a fiduciary should consider include, among other things:

1. Quality and diversification of the annuity provider's investment portfolio;

2. Size of the insurer relative to the proposed contract;

3. Level of the insurer's capital and surplus;

4. Lines of business of the annuity provider and other indications of an insurer's exposure to liability;

5. Structure of the annuity contract and guarantees supporting the annuities, such as the use of separate accounts; and

6. Availability of additional protection through state guaranty associations and the extent of their guarantees.

Fiduciaries who do not possess the expertise necessary to evaluate the preceding factors should obtain the advice of a qualified, independent expert. In addition, a fiduciary must not rely solely on ratings provided by insurance rating services to identify the safest annuity. A fiduciary may conclude, after conducting an appropriate search, that more than one annuity provider is able to offer the safest annuity available.[2]

327. Must the safest annuity be purchased?

Yes, in the view of the DOL. As set forth in DOL Interpretive Bulletin 95-1, the DOL believes that a fiduciary must obtain the safest annuity available unless, under the circumstances, it would be in the interests of participants and beneficiaries to do otherwise. Such a result may occur if the safest available annuity is only marginally safer, but disproportionately more expensive than competing annuities, and the participants and beneficiaries are likely to bear a significant portion of that increased cost. Other examples include the following:

1. It may be in the interest of the participants to choose a competing annuity where the participants in a terminating pension plan are likely to receive, in the form of increased benefits, a substantial share of the cost savings that would result from choosing the competing annuity.

---

1. Labor Reg. §2509.95-1(c).
2. Labor Reg. §2509.95-1(c).

2.   It may also be in the interest of the participants and beneficiaries to choose a competing annuity if the safest available annuity provider is unable to demonstrate the ability to administer the payment of benefits to the participants and beneficiaries.

Interpretive Bulletin 95-1 also provides that fiduciaries must conduct an objective, thorough, and analytical search for purposes of identifying providers from which to purchase annuities and sets forth the six factors described in Q 326 that should be considered by fiduciaries in evaluating a provider's claims-paying ability and creditworthiness.

The DOL issued Advisory Opinion 2002-14A[1] regarding the application of Interpretive Bulletin 95-1[2] to the purchase of annuities by defined contribution plans. Of specific import is the opinion of the DOL regarding cost as an appropriate consideration for a fiduciary of a defined contribution plan. The DOL stated that "it is appropriate for the fiduciary of a defined contribution plan in selecting an annuity provider to take into account the costs and benefits to the participant or beneficiary of competing annuity products." But the DOL added that "a lower cost cannot justify the purchase of an unsafe annuity even when the annuity would pay a higher benefit amount to the participant or beneficiary."[3]

But the DOL believes that the increased cost or other considerations may not justify risking the benefits of annuitized participants and beneficiaries by purchasing an unsafe annuity.[4] In contrast, the Court of Appeals for the Fourth Circuit has rejected the proposition that fiduciaries must purchase the safest annuity available.[5] Similarly, the Fifth Circuit has stated that the DOL Interpretive Bulletin mandating purchase of the "safest annuity available" exceeds the statutory mandate; but it is a useful guide regarding the fiduciary process.[6]

The DOL also expressed the view in Advisory Opinion 2002-14A that the general fiduciary principles set forth in Interpretive Bulletin 95-1 with regard to the selection of annuity providers apply equally to defined benefit and defined contribution plans. But Section 625 of the Pension Protection Act of 2006 (PPA 2006) directed the DOL to issue final regulations clarifying that the selection of an annuity contract as an optional form of distribution from an individual account plan is not subject to the safest available annuity standard under Interpretive Bulletin 95-1 and is subject to all otherwise applicable fiduciary standards.

Consistent with PPA 2006 Section 625, the DOL amended Interpretive Bulletin 95-1 in August 2007 to provide that Interpretive Bulletin 95-1 is applicable only to the selection of annuity providers for the purpose of benefit distributions from a defined benefit pension plan.

The DOL has issued an amendment to Interpretive Bulletin 95-1 finalizing the applicability of PPA 2006 Section 625 to defined benefit plans only.[7]

---

1. DOL Adv. Op. 2002-14A (Dec. 18, 2002).
2. Labor Reg. §2509.95-1.
3. DOL Adv. Op. 2002-14A (Dec. 18, 2002).
4. Labor Reg. §2509.95-1.
5. *Riley v. Murdock*, 83 F.3d 415 (4th Cir. 1996).
6. *Bussian v. RJR Nabisco*, 25 EBC 1120 (5th Cir. 2000).
7. 73 Fed. Reg. 58,447 (Oct. 7, 2008).

Selection of Annuity Providers for Individual Account Plans

Given that the fiduciary standards in Interpretive Bulletin 95-1 no longer apply to the selection of an annuity contract as an optional form of distribution from an individual account plan, in September 2007, the DOL issued Proposed Labor Regulation Section 2550.404a-4, titled "Selection of Annuity Providers for Individual Account Plans," which, in the form of a safe harbor, provides guidance concerning the fiduciary standards under ERISA Section 404 applicable to the selection of an annuity provider for the purpose of benefit distributions from an individual account plan or benefit distribution options made available to participants and beneficiaries under such a plan. The proposed regulation was finalized on October 7, 2008. The final regulation has restructured and clarified the safe harbor and is reflected in the following text.[1]

In general. The regulation provides that when an individual account plan purchases an annuity from an insurer as a distribution of benefits to a participant or beneficiary, the plan's liability for the payment of those benefits is transferred to the annuity provider. The selection of an annuity provider in connection with a benefit distribution, or a benefit distribution option made available to participants and beneficiaries under the plan, is governed by the fiduciary standards of ERISA Section 404(a)(1)(B). ERISA Section 404(a)(1)(B) requires a fiduciary to act with the care, skill, prudence, and diligence under the prevailing circumstances that a prudent person acting in a like capacity and familiar with such matters would use.[2] The final regulation clarifies that the safe harbor is an optional means for satisfying the fiduciary responsibilities under ERISA Section 404(a)(1)(B) with respect to the selection of an annuity provider or contract for benefit distributions. It does not establish the sole means for such selection of an annuity provider, nor does it establish minimum requirements for the selection of an annuity provider.[3]

Selection of an annuity provider and contract. With regard to a fiduciary's selection of an annuity provider and contract for purposes of benefit distributions from an individual account plan or benefit distribution options made available to participants and beneficiaries under such a plan, the requirements of ERISA Section 404(a)(1)(B) are satisfied if the fiduciary:

1. Engages in an objective, thorough, and analytical search for the purpose of identifying and selecting providers from which to purchase annuities;

2. Gives appropriate consideration to information sufficient to assess the ability of the annuity provider to make all future payments under the annuity contract;

3. Appropriately considers the cost of the annuity contract in relation to the benefits and administrative services to be provided under such contract;

4. Appropriately concludes that, at the time of the selection, the annuity provider is financially able to make all future payments under the annuity contract and the

---

1. 73 Fed. Reg. 58,447 (Oct. 7, 2008).
2. Labor Reg. §2550.404a-4(a)(1).
3. Labor Reg. §2550.404a-4(a)(2).

cost of the annuity contract is reasonable in relation to the benefits and services to be provided under the contract; and

5.   Appropriately determines either that the fiduciary had, at the time of the selection, the appropriate expertise to evaluate the selection or that the advice of a qualified, independent expert was necessary.[1]

For purposes of the preceding requirements, the "time of selection" may be either:

1.   Time that the annuity provider and contract are selected for distribution of benefits to a specific participant or beneficiary; or

2.   Time that the annuity provider is selected to provide annuity contracts at future dates to participants or beneficiaries, provided that the selecting fiduciary periodically reviews the continuing appropriateness of the conclusion noted in item 4, above, taking into account the factors described above in items 2, 3 and 5.[2]

A fiduciary is not required to review the appropriateness of this conclusion with respect to any annuity contract purchased for any specific participant or beneficiary.[3]

328. May a fiduciary consider the reversion of excess assets to the plan sponsor in selecting an annuity provider?

No. In the view of the DOL, a fiduciary may not purchase more risky, lower-priced annuities in order to ensure or maximize a reversion of excess assets that will be paid solely to the employer-sponsor in connection with the termination of an overfunded pension plan. Such a decision will violate the fiduciary's duties to act solely in the interest of the plan participants and beneficiaries, and will interfere with the fiduciary's ability to obtain the safest annuity available with no countervailing interests. Thus, a fiduciary in such circumstances must make diligent efforts to ensure that the safest available annuity is purchased.[4]

329. May fiduciaries be relieved of liability by purchasing annuities for the distribution of plan assets to terminated participants or in connection with the termination of a plan?

In certain instances. The general rule is that liability for benefits promised under a plan is transferred from the plan where the provision of benefits has been arranged for through the purchase of an annuity contract. Once the contract is issued, the participants covered under it cease to be plan participants, and the liability for the provision of benefits is transferred to the insurance company issuing the annuity contracts if

1.   Contract has received transfer of the entire rights and benefits of the participant or beneficiary,

---

1. Labor Reg. §2550-414a-4(b)(1) to (5).
2. Labor Reg. §§2550.404a-4(c)(1), 2550.404a-4(c)(2).
3. Labor Reg. §2550.404a-4(c)(2).
4. Labor Reg. §2509.95-1.

2.   Benefits are guaranteed by the insurance company, and

3.   Rights of the participants and beneficiaries are enforceable at law by the sole choice of the participant or beneficiary.[1]

But in the event that the purchase of an insurance contract or insurance annuity in connection with termination of an individual's status as a participant constitutes a violation of ERISA fiduciary obligations or the terms of the plan, the terminated participant or beneficiary has standing to seek relief.[2] As such, these former participants and beneficiaries may sue the plan fiduciaries for any breaches that they may have committed in the termination of a pension plan or in the purchase of annuity contracts.

330. Who is responsible for the voting of proxies?

According to the Department of Labor, the fiduciary act of managing plan assets that are shares of corporate stock includes the management of voting rights appurtenant to those shares of stock.[3] As a result, the responsibility for voting or deciding not to vote proxies lies exclusively with the plan trustee except to the extent that either (1) the trustee is subject to the direction of a named fiduciary pursuant to ERISA Section 403(a)(1); or (2) the power to manage, acquire, or dispose of the relevant assets has been delegated by a named fiduciary to one or more investment managers pursuant to ERISA Section 403(a)(2).

If the authority to manage plan assets has been delegated to an investment manager pursuant to ERISA Section 403(a)(2), no person other than the investment manager has authority to make voting decisions for proxies appurtenant to such plan assets except to the extent that the named fiduciary has reserved to itself (or to another named fiduciary so authorized by the plan document) the right to direct a plan trustee regarding the voting of proxies.

On July 29, 1994, the DOL issued guidance with respect to the duties of employee benefit plan fiduciaries under ERISA Section 402, ERISA Section 403, and ERISA Section 404 to vote proxies appurtenant to shares of corporate stock held by their plans.[4] The guidance set forth in Interpretive Bulletin 2008-2 includes clarifications of the earlier guidance.[5]

331. May a named fiduciary reserve the right to direct the voting of proxies?

Yes, in the view of the Department of Labor. A named fiduciary that delegates investment management authority to an investment manager could reserve to itself the right to direct a trustee with respect to the voting of all proxies or reserve to itself the right to direct a trustee as to the voting of only those proxies relating to specified assets or issues.

Additionally, if the plan document or investment management agreement provides that the investment manager is not required to vote proxies, but does not expressly preclude the investment manager from voting proxies, the investment manager would have exclusive

---

1. Labor Reg. §2510.33(d)(2)(ii); PBGC Adv. Op. 91-1; PBGC Adv. Op. 85-9.
2. ERISA Sec. 502(a)(9).
3. See Letter from the DOL to Helmut Fandl (Feb. 23, 1988).
4. Labor Reg. §2509.94-2.
5. See Labor Reg. §2509.08-2; I.B. 2008-2 (Oct. 17, 2008).

responsibility for proxy-voting decisions, according to the DOL. Moreover, an investment manager would not be relieved of its own fiduciary responsibilities by following directions of some other person regarding the voting of proxies, or by delegating such responsibility to another person. If, however, the plan document or the investment management contract expressly precludes the investment manager from voting proxies, the responsibility for voting proxies would lie exclusively with the trustee. The trustee, however, consistent with the requirements of ERISA Section 403(a)(1), may be subject to the directions of a named fiduciary if the plan so provides, in the view of the DOL.

On July 29, 1994, the DOL issued guidance with respect to the duties of employee benefit plan fiduciaries under ERISA Section 402, ERISA Section 403, and ERISA Section 404 to vote proxies appurtenant to shares of corporate stock held by their plans.[1] The guidance set forth in Interpretive Bulletin 2008-2 includes clarifications of the earlier guidance.[2]

332. Do the fiduciary standards apply to the voting of proxies?

Yes, according to the Department of Labor. The fiduciary duties, described at ERISA Section 404(a)(1)(A) and ERISA Section 404(a)(1)(B), require that, in voting proxies, regardless of whether the vote is made pursuant to a statement of investment policy, the responsible fiduciary shall consider only those factors that relate to the economic value of the plan's investment and shall not subordinate the interests of the participants and beneficiaries in their retirement income to unrelated objectives. Votes shall only be cast in accordance with a plan's economic interests. If the responsible fiduciary reasonably determines that the cost of voting (including the cost of research, if necessary, to determine how to vote) is likely to exceed the expected economic benefits of voting, or if the exercise of voting results in the imposition of unwarranted trading or other restrictions, the fiduciary has an obligation to refrain from voting.[3] In making this determination, objectives, considerations, and economic effects unrelated to the plan's economic interests cannot be considered.

The fiduciary obligations of prudence and loyalty to plan participants and beneficiaries require the responsible fiduciary to vote proxies on issues that may affect the economic value of the plan's investment; however, fiduciaries also need to take into account costs when deciding whether and how to exercise their shareholder rights, including the voting of shares. Such costs include, but are not limited to, expenditures related to developing proxy resolutions, proxy-voting services, and the analysis of the likely net effect of a particular issue on the economic value of the plan's investment. Fiduciaries must take all of these factors into account in determining whether the exercise of such rights (e.g., the voting of a proxy), independently or in conjunction with other shareholders, is expected to have an effect on the economic value of the plan's investment that will outweigh the cost of exercising such rights. With respect to proxies appurtenant to shares of foreign corporations, a fiduciary, in deciding whether to purchase shares of a foreign corporation, should consider whether any additional difficulty and expense in voting such shares is reflected in their market price.

---

1. Labor Reg. §2509.94-2.
2. See Labor Reg. §2509.08-2; I.B. 2008-2 (Oct. 17, 2008).
3. See DOL Adv. Op. 2007-07A (Dec. 21, 2007).

The fiduciary's duties under ERISA Section 404(a)(1)(A) and ERISA Section 404(a)(1)(B) also require that the named fiduciary appointing an investment manager periodically monitor the activities of the investment manager with respect to the management of plan assets, including decisions made and actions taken by the investment manager with regard to proxy-voting decisions. The named fiduciary must carry out this responsibility solely in the participants' and beneficiaries' interest in the economic value of the plan assets and without regard to the fiduciary's relationship to the plan sponsor.

On July 29, 1994, the DOL issued guidance with respect to the duties of employee benefit plan fiduciaries under ERISA Section 402, ERISA Section 403, and ERISA Section 404 to vote proxies appurtenant to shares of corporate stock held by their plans.[1] The guidance set forth in Interpretive Bulletin 2008-2 includes clarifications of the earlier guidance.[2]

333. May plan fiduciaries use their fiduciary authority to attempt to further legislative, regulatory, or public policy issues or to monitor or influence the management of a corporation through the proxy-voting process?

It is the view of the DOL, set forth in Interpretive Bulletin 2008-2, that plan fiduciaries risk violating the exclusive purpose rule when they exercise their fiduciary authority in an attempt to further legislative, regulatory, or public policy issues through the proxy-voting process. In such cases, the DOL would expect fiduciaries to be able to demonstrate in enforcement actions their compliance with the requirements of ERISA Section 404(a)(1)(A) and ERISA Section 404(a)(1)(B). The mere fact that plans are shareholders in the corporations in which they invest does not itself provide a rationale for a fiduciary to spend plan assets to pursue, support, or oppose such proxy proposals. Because of the heightened potential for abuse in such cases, the fiduciaries must be prepared to articulate a clear basis for concluding that the proxy vote, the investment policy, or the activity intended to monitor or influence the management of the corporation is more likely than not to enhance the economic value of the plan's investment before expending plan assets.

The use of pension plan assets by plan fiduciaries to further policy or political issues through proxy resolutions that have no connection to enhancing the economic value of the plan's investment in a corporation would, in the view of the DOL, violate the prudence and exclusive purpose requirements of ERISA Section 404(a)(1)(A) and ERISA Section 404(a)(1)(B). For example, the likelihood that the adoption of a proxy resolution or proposal requiring corporate directors and officers to disclose their personal political contributions would enhance the economic value of a plan's investment in the corporation appears sufficiently remote that the expenditure of plan assets to further such a resolution or proposal clearly raises compliance issues under ERISA Section 404(a)(1)(A) and ERISA Section 404(a)(1)(B).[3]

Interpretive Bulletin 2008-2 sets forth the DOL's interpretation of ERISA Section 402, ERISA Section 403, and ERISA Section 404 as those sections apply to voting of proxies on

---

1. Labor Reg. §2509.94-2.
2. See Labor Reg. §2509.08-2; I.B. 2008-2 (Oct. 17, 2008).
3. See DOL Adv. Op. 2007-07A (Dec. 21, 2007).

securities held in employee benefit plan investment portfolios and the maintenance of and compliance with statements of investment policy, including proxy-voting policy. In addition, Interpretive Bulletin 2008-2 provides guidance on the appropriateness under ERISA of active monitoring of corporate management by plan fiduciaries. The guidance set forth in Interpretive Bulletin 2008-2 modifies and supersedes the guidance set forth in Interpretive Bulletin 94-2.[1]

334. How does a named fiduciary monitor an investment manager's proxy voting?

According to the Department of Labor, compliance with the duty to monitor necessitates proper documentation of the activities that are subject to monitoring. Thus, the investment manager or other responsible fiduciary would be required to maintain accurate records as to proxy-voting decisions, including, where appropriate, cost-benefit analyses.[2] Moreover, if the named fiduciary is to be able to carry out its responsibilities under ERISA Section 404(a) in determining whether the investment manager is fulfilling its fiduciary obligations in investing plans assets in a manner that justifies the continuation of the management appointment, the proxy-voting records must enable the named fiduciary not only to review the investment manager's voting procedure with respect to plan-owned stock, but also to review the actions taken in individual proxy-voting situations.

On July 29, 1994, the DOL issued guidance with respect to the duties of employee benefit plan fiduciaries under ERISA Section 402, ERISA Section 403, and ERISA Section 404 to vote proxies appurtenant to shares of corporate stock held by their plans.[3] The guidance set forth in Interpretive Bulletin 2008-2 includes clarifications of the earlier guidance.[4]

335. Should a statement of proxy-voting policy be part of a comprehensive statement of investment policy?

Yes, according to the Department of Labor. It is the view of the DOL that the maintenance by an employee benefit plan of a statement of investment policy designed to further the purposes of the plan and its funding policy is consistent with the fiduciary obligations set forth in ERISA Section 404(a)(1)(A) and ERISA Section 404(a)(1)(B). Because the fiduciary act of managing plan assets that are shares of corporate stock includes the voting, where appropriate, of proxies appurtenant to those shares of stock, a statement of proxy-voting policy would be an important part of any comprehensive statement of investment policy. For purposes of this document, the term "statement of investment policy" means a written statement that provides the fiduciaries who are responsible for plan investments with guidelines or general instructions concerning various types or categories of investment management decisions, which may include proxy-voting decisions. A statement of investment policy is distinguished from directions as to the purchase or sale of a specific investment at a specific time or as to voting specific plan proxies.

---

1. Labor Reg. §2509.94-2. See also Labor Reg. §2509.08-2; I.B. 2008-2 (Oct. 17, 2008).
2. See Letter from the DOL to Robert Monks (Jan. 23, 1990).
3. Labor Reg. §2509.94-2.
4. See Labor Reg. §2509.08-2; I.B. 2008-2 (Oct. 17, 2008).

On July 29, 1994, the DOL issued guidance with respect to the duties of employee benefit plan fiduciaries under ERISA Section 402, ERISA Section 403, and ERISA Section 404 to vote proxies appurtenant to shares of corporate stock held by their plans.[1] The guidance set forth in Interpretive Bulletin 2008-2 includes clarifications of the earlier guidance.

336. What is the duty of diversification under ERISA?

A fiduciary has a duty to discharge her responsibilities with respect to an employee benefit plan by diversifying the investments of the plan, so as to minimize the risk of large losses, unless under the circumstances it is clearly prudent not to do so.[2] The diversification requirement imposes a duty on plan fiduciaries to spread the risk of loss to the plan. Just as ERISA Section 404(a)(1)(B) requires that a fiduciary be prudent in each investment decision, ERISA Section 404(a)(1)(C) requires that a fiduciary be prudent in deciding not to diversify a plan's investments.[3] In general, a determination of whether the plan assets are sufficiently diversified is made by examining the ultimate investment of the plan assets.[4]

Breaches of a fiduciary's duty to diversify plan assets have been found, for example, where the trustees invested 70 percent of the plan's assets in thirty-year U.S. Treasury bonds without considering the plan's cash-flow requirements.[5] Similarly, the duty to diversify was breached where the plan had up to 85 percent of its assets invested in commercial real estate first mortgages in a single geographic area.[6]

A proposed loan constituting 23 percent of the plan's assets to finance a single, speculative, real estate venture amounted to a failure to diversify, considering the special risks of the venture (including the previous failure of the project, one participant's being in bankruptcy, and the trustees' inexperience).[7]

337. What is the purpose of diversifying the assets of a plan?

The purpose of diversifying the assets of a plan is to "distribute the risks of loss in order to maintain the trust principal, usually by limiting the proportion of total trust assets invested in any one stock or class of securities."[8] By spreading asset purchases throughout a number of varying types of securities or investments, a fiduciary may protect the trust, to a certain extent, against adverse economic and market conditions or against the fortunes of a particular field of business or industry, and thereby minimize the risk of large losses.[9]

By allocating funds to different types of investments, the potential losses that might occur in one area due to a particular economic event may be offset by gains in another area. Even

1. Labor Reg. §2509.94-2.
2. ERISA Sec. 404(a)(1)(C).
3. See *Reich v. King*, 867 F. Supp. 341 (D. Md. 1994).
4. H.R. Conf. Rep. No. 93-1280, 93d Cong., 2d Sess. 304 (1974) (ERISA Conference Report).
5. See *GIW Indus., Inc. v. Trevor, Stewart, Burton & Jacobsen, Inc.*, 895 F.2d 729 (11th Cir. 1990).
6. See *Brock v. Citizens Bank of Clovis*, 841 F.2d 344 (10th Cir.), *cert. denied*, 488 U.S. 829 (1988).
7. *Marshall v. Glass/Metal Ass'n*, 507 F. Supp. 378 (D. Haw. 1980); see also *Donovan v. Guaranty Nat'l Bank of Huntington*, 4 EBC 1686 (S.D. W. Va. 1983) (plan that invested entirely in residential real estate mortgages in one geographic area was not diversified because of risk associated with interest rates).
8. G. Bogert, The Law of Trusts & Trustees §612, at 18 (2d ed. 1980). See also *Marshall v. Glass/Metal Ass'n*, 507 F. Supp. 378 (D. Haw. 1980).
9. *GIW Indus., Inc. v. Trevor, Stewart, Burton & Jacobsen, Inc.*, 10 EBC 2290 (S.D. Ga. 1989).

if such a loss is not offset, its impact may be at least limited to a relatively small portion of the fund. In addition, by prudently diversifying investments and allowing for some degree of liquidity in a plan, trustees can prevent the risk of large losses and, at the same time, have funds available that can be shifted relatively quickly in order to profit from changes in economic conditions.[1]

Conversely, a plan fiduciary who pursues a strategy of non-diversification runs a risk of incurring substantial losses if a particular investment vehicle, or one of a few large investments chosen, performs poorly. Under such circumstances, one particular negative economic event can devastate the entire plan, or a great portion of it. Thus, while diversification of plan assets is important as a prophylactic measure to guard against losses occasioned by unforeseeable events, it may also result in relatively stable earnings generated by those investments, as well as in the preservation of trust principal, by neutralizing the risk of a particular investment when that investment is combined with others.[2]

When proper diversification is achieved, the risk inherent in the entire portfolio is less than that of any particular investment within that portfolio, with a result that the only risk remaining is primarily market risk. Moreover, "the return from a portfolio over time should be more stable than that of isolated investments within that portfolio."[3]

338. Who has the burden of proof in an action based on a breach of the duty of diversification?

The duty of diversification requires fiduciaries to diversify plan assets to minimize the risk of large losses, unless under the circumstances it is clearly prudent not to diversify. But Congress did not intend that a more stringent standard of prudence be established with the use of the term "clearly prudent." Instead, by using this term it intended that in an action for plan losses based on a breach of the diversification requirement, the plaintiff's initial burden will be to demonstrate that there has been a failure to diversify.[4] To establish a violation, a plaintiff must demonstrate that the portfolio is not diversified "on its face."[5]

Once a plaintiff proves that non-diversification exists, the burden shifts to the fiduciary to demonstrate that the failure to diversify was prudent.[6] The basic policy under ERISA Section 404(a)(1)(C) is to require diversification, and if diversification on its face does not exist, then the burden of justifying a failure to follow this general policy is on the fiduciary who engages in such conduct. The burden is not merely to prove that the investment was prudent, but that there was no risk of large loss resulting from the non-diversification.[7] But the "facts and circumstances" surrounding each plan and investment "ought to caution judicial review of investment decisions … and [i]t is clearly imprudent to evaluate diversification in hindsight."[8]

1. *Donovan v. Guaranty Nat'l Bank of Huntington*, 4 EBC 1686 (S.D. W. Va. 1983).
2. See Frank K. Reilly, Investment Analysis & Portfolio Management 5 (Dryden Press 1979).
3. *Leigh v. Engle*, 858 F.2d 361 (7th Cir. 1988).
4. H.R. Conf. Rep. No. 93-1280, 93d Cong., 2d Sess. 304 (1974) (ERISA Conference Report).
5. *Reich v. King*, 867 F. Supp. 341 (D. Md. 1994).
6. *In re Unisys Sav. Plan Litig.*, 74 F.3d 420 (3d Cir. 1996), *reh'g denied*, 173 F.3d 145 (3d Cir. 1999).
7. See ERISA Conference Report at 304; *Marshall v. Glass/Metal Ass'n*, 507 F. Supp. 378 (D. Haw. 1980).
8. *Metzler v. Graham*, 112 F.3d 207 (5th Cir. 1997).

339. What is the proper degree of investment concentration necessary to satisfy the diversification requirement?

ERISA and the regulations thereunder do not specify what constitutes "diversification" of the investments of a plan. But Congress recognized that the diversification requirement of ERISA imposes a separate duty on plan fiduciaries to spread the risk to the plan of loss from the investments. In fashioning the diversification provisions of ERISA, Congress did not choose to establish a specific percentage requirement for investment concentration or a fixed percentage limit on any one investment. Instead, it imposed a requirement of diversification that requires a prudent fiduciary to consider the facts and circumstances surrounding each plan and investment, thereby providing plan fiduciaries discretion and latitude in selecting an investment portfolio for a plan.[1]

340. What are the factors for diversification under the "facts and circumstances" test?

The extent to which a fiduciary has complied with the duty to diversify, as set forth in ERISA, is not measured by hard-and-fast rules or formulas. However, in prescribing that a prudent fiduciary consider the facts and circumstances surrounding each plan and investment, Congress established seven specific factors that should be considered by a plan fiduciary in determining the degree of concentration for prudent diversification:

1.   Purpose of the plan;

2.   Amount of the plan assets;

3.   Financial and industrial conditions;

4.   Type of investment, whether mortgages, bonds, stocks, or otherwise;

5.   Distribution as to geographic location;

6.   Distribution as to industries; and

7.   Dates of maturity.[2]

341. Is there a prohibition against a fiduciary's investing a substantial portion of a plan's assets in a single security?

As a general proposition, ERISA's duty to diversify prohibits a fiduciary from investing disproportionately in a particular investment or enterprise. The key principle behind the requirements of ERISA Section 404(a)(1)(C) is to prevent plan assets from being exposed to certain shared risks through a concentration of plan assets in a single investment or a single class of investments.[3]

---

1. H.R. Conf. Rep. No. 93-1280, 93d Cong., 2d Sess. 304 (1974) (ERISA Conference Report).
2. See H.R. Conf. Rep. No. 93-1280, 93d Cong., 2d Sess. 304 (1974) (ERISA Conference Report).
3. See H.R. Conf. Rep. No. 93-1280, 93d Cong., 2d Sess. 304 (1974) (ERISA Conference Report); *Marshall v. Teamsters Local 282 Pension Trust Fund*, 458 F. Supp. 986 (E.D.N.Y. 1978).

Although a fiduciary may be authorized to invest in a particular type of investment, "[o]rdinarily the fiduciary should not invest the whole or an unduly large proportion of the trust property in one type of security or in various types of securities dependent upon the success of one enterprise or upon conditions in one locality since the effect is to increase the risk of large losses."[1]

Disproportionate amounts of investment in a single security, industry, or class of property have been held to constitute a breach of the fiduciary's duty to diversify. For example, a fiduciary breached its duty to diversify where 23 percent of a pension plan's total assets were invested in a single loan. Committing a large percentage of plan assets to the loan violated the diversification requirement, since both on its face and according to standards of experienced lenders, it subjected a disproportionate amount of the plan's assets to the risk of a large loss.[2] Similarly, a court held that the trustee's concentration of between 25 percent and 89 percent of the ERISA plan's assets to one type of investment also violated the diversification requirement.[3] The trustees' investment of more than 65 percent of the plan's assets in commercial real estate first mortgages was found to violate the diversification requirements.[4] In that case, the trustees were held liable since they failed to establish that such investments were prudent notwithstanding the lack of diversification. Conversely, a district court found that a fiduciary had *not* violated ERISA's diversification requirements where 18.5 percent of the trust's total market value had been invested in one corporation, approximately 11 percent in another, and nearly 14 percent in a third corporation.[5]

342. Is there a prohibition against a fiduciary's investing a substantial portion of a plan's assets in a single geographic area?

Although concentrating a plan's investments in a particular geographic area is not prohibited by ERISA, such a strategy entails a great risk of loss to the plan by leaving the plan at the whimsy of the economic fate of the area.[6] Congress has stated that ordinarily the fiduciary should not invest the whole or an unduly large proportion of the trust property in one type of security, or in various types of securities that are dependent upon the success of one enterprise or conditions in one locality, since the effect is to increase the risk of large losses.[7] If a fiduciary invests in mortgages on real estate, he should not invest a disproportionate amount of the trust fund in mortgages in a particular district or upon a particular class of property so that a decline in property values in that district or of that class might cause a large loss.[8]

For example, in *Donovan*, (Footnote 6), the plan trustees violated the diversification requirement by investing virtually all of the plan assets in real estate mortgage loans concentrated in a single geographic area of Huntington, West Virginia. By concentrating

---

1. ERISA Conference Report, above.
2. *Marshall v. Glass/Metal Ass'n*, 507 F. Supp. 378 (D. Haw. 1980).
3. *Whitfield v. Tomasso*, 682 F. Supp. 1287 (E.D.N.Y. 1988).
4. *Brock v. Citizens Bank of Clovis*, 841 F.2d 344 (10th Cir.), *cert. denied*, 488 U.S. 829 (1988).
5. See *Sandoval v. Simmons*, 622 F. Supp. 1174 (C.D. Ill. 1985).
6. *Donovan v. Guaranty Nat'l Bank of Huntington*, 4 EBC 1686 (S.D. W. Va. 1983).
7. See H.R. Conf. Rep. No. 93-1280, 93d Cong., 2d Sess. (1974) (ERISA Conference Report).
8. See ERISA Conference Report, above.

the plan assets in real estate mortgages in the single geographic area, the trustees were not able to take advantage of changing market conditions. Although the trustees attempted to spread the risk of large losses by making a large number of individual investments within a particular class (real estate mortgage loans), the degree of protection afforded the plan was not sufficient diversification under ERISA.

Similarly, in another case involving real estate mortgages, the trustees of a plan violated ERISA by investing more than 65 percent of the plan's assets in commercial real estate mortgages in the area of Clovis, New Mexico.[1] The diversification requirement was not met because the trustees had chosen to invest in "one type of security," which did not protect against a multitude of risks, and the trustees failed to establish that the investments were prudent, notwithstanding the lack of diversification. In addition, the lack of diversification was not made moot by the trustees' reduction of the percentage of the plan's outstanding mortgages, because the trustees refused to assure the court that they would maintain a reduced level of real estate investments and insisted on maintaining independence in selecting plan investments.

343. Is non-diversification a per se violation of ERISA?

No. Non-diversification is not a per se violation of ERISA Section 404(a)(1)(C), and neither the case law nor the statutory language support the proposition that it is. "The degree of concentration in any asset or in any particular type of asset which would violate ERISA is determined on an ad hoc basis."[2] The language of ERISA Section 404(a)(1)(C), in effect, mandates a finding of fact that non-diversification is clearly imprudent before a finding of a fiduciary's liability.[3]

344. Is diversification required if it is clearly prudent not to diversify?

No. ERISA does not require the diversification of plan assets in circumstances when it is clearly prudent not to diversify. But in charting a course of non-diversification, fiduciaries should be aware that the "heavy burden" on the plan fiduciary in a non-diversification challenge "is not merely to prove that [an] investment is prudent, but that there is no risk of large loss resulting from the non-diversification."[4]

The diversification requirement and the clearly prudent exception are analyzed from the perspective of their purpose: to reduce the risk of large losses. Thus, if a course of non-diversification is clearly prudent, diversification is not required. For example, a pension plan administrator's purchase of a single tract of undeveloped land comprising 63 percent of the plan's assets was not in violation of his fiduciary duty to diversify, so as to minimize the risk of large losses.[5] The court held that the disproportionate amount of assets invested in undeveloped land was clearly prudent under all the circumstances. Even if the plan lacked diversification of its assets, the fiduciary did not imprudently introduce a risk of large loss to the plan by purchasing the property. The plan had adequate cash and short-term financial instruments to meet its projected long-term cash

---

1. See *Brock v. Citizens Bank of Clovis*, 841 F.2d 344 (10th Cir.), *cert. denied*, 488 U.S. 829 (1988).
2. *Brock v. Citizens Bank of Clovis*, 841 F.2d 344 (10th Cir.), *cert. denied*, 488 U.S. 829 (1988).
3. *Reich v. King*, 867 F. Supp. 341 (D. Md. 1994) (*citing Lanka v. O'Higgins*, 810 F. Supp. 379 (N.D.N.Y. 1992)).
4. *Marshall v. Glass/Metal Ass'n*, 507 F. Supp. 378 (D. Haw. 1980).
5. *Metzler v. Graham*, 112 F.3d 207 (5th Cir. 1997).

flows, the property was appropriate as a hedge against inflation, there was a significant cushion between the purchase price and the independent appraisal, and the fiduciary had expertise in the development of this type of property and the local real estate market.[1]

Similarly, although the plan's trustee breached the diversification requirement by investing about 70 percent of a plan's assets in real estate mortgages located in a single county in Maryland, the plan's trustee met the burden of showing that the plan did not face risk of large losses due to the non-diversification. Thus, the plan's investments, though not diversified, were otherwise clearly prudent because expert testimony demonstrated that the mortgage loan investments had low loan-to-value ratios, mortgages were five-year balloon mortgages (limiting the risk of inflation), and the trustee had knowledge of the local real estate market. In addition, the Department of Labor's expert had based his opinions on textbook-type theories that appeared far removed from actual realities of mortgages in the geographic area.[2]

Likewise, plan fiduciaries were clearly prudent in following a "contrarian" investment strategy even though the plan sustained heavy losses while 90 percent of the plan's assets were invested in stock of only three companies. Although the facts demonstrated a prima facie case of failure to diversify, the court held that the highly concentrated investments were prudent under the circumstances since the contrarian investment strategy was within industry standards.[3]

345. Does the diversification requirement apply to the ultimate investment of plan assets?

Yes. Congress intended that, in general, whether the plan assets are sufficiently diversified is to be determined by examining the ultimate investment of the plan assets. For example, Congress understands that for efficiency and economy, plans may invest all their assets in a single bank or other pooled investment fund, but that the pooled fund itself could have diversified investments. Known as the "look-through" rule, it is the intent of Congress that the diversification rule be applied to the plan by examining the diversification of the investments in the pooled fund. The same is true with respect to investments in a mutual fund. Also, a plan may be invested wholly in insurance or annuity contracts without violating the diversification rules, since generally an insurance company's assets are invested in a diversified manner.[4]

In addition, according to the Department of Labor, in the case of a plan that has invested in a single limited partnership, the underlying investments of the limited partnership are considered investments of the plan.[5] Similarly, in the case of a plan that invests in a real estate investment trust (REIT), it is the Department of Labor's view that the investments of the REIT are considered investments of the plan to the extent of the plan's interest in the REIT. The DOL noted that the fiduciaries of a plan are also under a duty to consider and examine a REIT in the light of the facts and circumstances relevant to the plan and the particular investment

---

1. *Metzler v. Graham*, above; see also *Etter v. J. Pease Constr. Co.*, 963 F.2d 1005 (7th Cir. 1992).
2. *Reich v. King*, 867 F. Supp. 341 (D. Md. 1994).
3. *Jones v. O'Higgins*, 736 F. Supp. 1243 (N.D.N.Y. 1989).
4. H.R. Conf. Rep. No. 93-1280, 93d Cong., 2d Sess. 304-305 (1974) (ERISA Conference Report).
5. DOL Adv. Op. 81-13A.

or investment course of action involved, and the role the investment or investment course of action plays in the plan's investment portfolio.[1]

This "look through" concept was not an adequate defense to a breach of fiduciary duty by a trustee who failed to investigate the objectives and needs of the plan, and imprudently invested too large a portion of the plan's assets in a guaranteed investment contract (GIC) issued by an insurer (Executive Life) that subsequently became insolvent. The court held that the investment in the Executive Life GIC did not meet the prudent person standard of diversification for the plan, considering the known risks of Executive Life and the objectives and needs of the plan.[2]

346. Is the requirement to diversify applicable to investment managers?

Yes. If the assets of a plan are managed by one or more investment managers, each investment manager must invest solely in accordance with the instructions of the named fiduciary and must diversify its portion of the plan investments in accordance with the diversification standard, the prudent man standard, and all other provisions applicable to the investment manager as a fiduciary.

For example, one investment manager, A, may be responsible for 10 percent of the assets of a plan and instructed by the named fiduciary or trustee to invest solely in bonds; another investment manager, B, may be responsible for a different 10 percent of the assets of the same plan and instructed to invest solely in equities. In these circumstances, A would invest solely in bonds in accordance with his instructions and would diversify the bond investments in accordance with the diversification standard, the prudent man standard, and all other provisions applicable to A as a fiduciary. Similarly, B would invest solely in equities in accordance with his instructions and these standards. Neither A nor B would incur any liability for diversifying assets subject to his management in accordance with his instructions.[3]

347. How is the duty of diversification measured for an investment manager of a plan where the investments are distributed among several investment managers?

The Court of Appeals for the Eleventh Circuit, in keeping with the intent of Congress, and persuaded by the approach of the Court of Appeals for the Third Circuit, concluded that if a plan's investments are distributed among several investment managers with each responsible for the investment of a particular segment of the plan's investments, then each investment manager's diversification is properly assessed by examining the plan segment for which that manager is responsible rather than the plan's universe of investment funds.[4] Since the risk of loss managed by an individual investment manager is not distributed among the total investments of the plan, but only spread among the individual investments within that segment, the satisfaction

---

1. DOL Adv. Op. 78-30A.
2. *Bruner v. Boatmen's Trust Co.*, 918 F. Supp. 1347 (E.D. Mo. 1996).
3. H.R. Conf. Rep. No. 93-1280, 93d Cong., 2d Sess. 304-05 (1974) (ERISA Conference Report).
4. See *GIW Indus., Inc. v. Trevor, Stewart, Burton & Jacobsen, Inc.*, 895 F.2d 729 (11th Cir. 1990).

of the duty to diversify is properly assessed by examining the particular segment managed by the investment manager.[1]

348. How is the diversification requirement applied to eligible individual account plans?

The diversification requirement of ERISA Section 404(a)(1)(C) is eased somewhat in the case of an eligible individual account plan, which is defined under ERISA as an individual account plan that is a profit sharing, stock bonus, thrift, or savings plan, an employee stock ownership plan (ESOP), or a pre-ERISA money purchase plan.[2] ERISA provides that in the case of an eligible individual account plan, the diversification requirement is not violated by the acquisition or holding of qualifying employer real property or qualifying employer securities.[3]

349. How is the diversification requirement applied to segregated asset accounts underlying annuities?

A Treasury regulation provides that investments of a segregated asset account that underlie a variable annuity, endowment, or life insurance contract are considered adequately diversified only if

1. No more than 55 percent of the value of the total assets of the account is represented by any one investment;

2. No more than 70 percent of the value of the total assets of the account is represented by any two investments;

3. No more than 80 percent of the value of the total assets of the account is represented by any three investments; and

4. No more than 90 percent of the value of the total assets of the account is represented by any four investments.[4]

The regulation also provides for an alternative diversification requirement for variable life insurance contracts.[5]

Segregated asset accounts are generally considered diversified during start-up and liquidation periods. For segregated accounts that are not invested in real property, the start-up period is the one-year period that begins on the date that any amount received under the life insurance or annuity contract is first allocated to the account. The liquidation period is the one-year period that begins on the date the plan of liquidation is adopted. For segregated asset accounts that invest in real property, the start-up period is the five-year period beginning on the date that any amount received under the contract is first allocated. The liquidation period for real

---

1. *In re Unisys Sav. Plan Litig.*, 74 F.3d 420 (3d Cir. 1996), *reh'g denied*, 173 F.3d 145 (3d Cir. 1999).
2. ERISA Sec. 407(d)(3).
3. See ERISA Sec. 404(a)(2).
4. Treas. Reg. §1.817-5(b)(1)(i).
5. Treas. Reg. §1.817-5(b)(3).

property accounts is two years. The start-up period rules do not apply if more than 30 percent of the amount allocated to a segregated asset account as of the last day of a calendar quarter is attributable to contracts entered into more than one year before such date.[1]

350. What is the rule regarding diversification of 401(k) plan investments in employer securities or employer real property?

ERISA places certain restrictions on IRC Section 401(k) plans that require 10 percent or more of employees' elective contributions to be invested in employer stock or employer real property.[2]

Such plans must treat the portion of a 401(k) plan that consists of elective deferrals that are required to be invested in qualifying employer securities or qualifying employer real property as a separate plan.

In application, this rule restricts 401(k) plans from *mandating* that employees place more than 10 percent of their plan funds in company stock or real property; however, employees are free to *elect* to place more than 10 percent of their plan assets in employer stock or employer real property.[3]

This restriction does not apply to ESOPs, nor to individual account plans where less than 1 percent of employee compensation is mandated to be invested in employer securities or employer real property.

ERISA Section 407(b) does not apply to any elective deferral that is invested in assets consisting of qualifying employer securities, qualifying employer real property, or both, if such assets were acquired before January 1, 1999.[4]

351. May an investment manager rely on information furnished by a fiduciary?

Yes. In the view of the DOL, an investment manager appointed to manage all or part of the assets of a plan, may, for purposes of compliance with her investment duties under ERISA Section 404(a)(1)(B), rely upon and act on the basis of information pertaining to the plan provided by or at the direction of the appointing fiduciary. But the information must be provided for the stated purpose of assisting the manager in the performance of her investment duties, and the investment manager must not know or have reason to know that the information is incorrect.[5]

In addition, a prudent investment manager has a duty not to act in accordance with a delegation of plan investment duties to the extent that she either knows or should know that the delegation involves a breach of fiduciary responsibility. Once the investment manager

---

1. Treas. Reg. §1.817-5(c).
2. See ERISA Sec. 407(b).
3. See ERISA Sec. 407(a)(2)(A)-(C).
4. See EGTRRA 2001 §665.
5. Labor Reg. §2550.404(a)-1(b)(3).

has considered factors otherwise necessary to assure herself that the delegation of investment authority and related specific instructions are appropriate, she may, in exercising such authority and carrying out such instructions, rely upon information provided to her by or at the direction of the appointing fiduciary.[1]

352. What is a fiduciary's duty to act in accordance with the plan documents under ERISA?

ERISA requires that fiduciaries discharge their duties in accordance with the documents and instruments governing the plan insofar as such documents or instruments are consistent with the provisions of Titles I and IV of ERISA.[2] But the duty to operate the plan "in accordance with the documents" is *subject to* the prudent person standard of ERISA Section 404(a)(1)(B).[3]

For example, a breach of the duty to operate the plan in accordance with the plan documents occurred in a case where the plan trustees allowed themselves and another defendant to participate in the plans and to cause the plans to make contributions on their behalf and on behalf of the defendant even though the plan documents made it clear that none of the trustees or the defendant was a proper participant.[4] Similarly, a plan fiduciary acted contrary to the terms of a plan document where the evidence demonstrated that he participated in a decision on a transaction, and where the plan document provided that an administrative committee member having an interest in a transaction was not to vote or participate with respect to the transaction.[5]

The Eighth Circuit Court of Appeals ruled that where a Summary Plan Description (SPD) is the only formal written document for an ERISA-qualified benefit plan, it is to be considered the governing document regardless of its label.[6] The case centered on the SPD language for a self-insured group health plan that had sought to recover more than $175,000 in expenses issued to cover a participant's health care stemming from a motor vehicle accident. The plan demanded reimbursement after the accident claims were settled. The employee refused and the plan sued the employee, relying on SPD language that gave the plan the right to be reimbursed for benefits from any judgment, settlement, or payment made because of an accident. The employee argued that the reimbursement provision in the SPD was unenforceable because it was not part of the formal plan document. On appeal, the Eighth Circuit ruled that the SPD was the only formal written document that the employer had for its health benefits and that the SPD informed participants that portions of it served as part of the official plan document. Therefore, the employer was entitled to rely upon it as a governing document. Adding that "the label of summary plan description ... is not dispositive," the court concluded that where no other source of benefits exists, the SPD is the formal plan document, regardless of its label.[7]

---

1. See Preamble to Labor Reg. §2550.404(a)-1(b)(3).
2. ERISA Sec. 404(a)(1)(D).
3. See *Morgan v. Independent Drivers Ass'n Pension Plan*, 975 F.2d 1467 (10th Cir. 1992).
4. See *Donovan v. Daugherty*, 550 F. Supp. 390 (S.D. Ala. 1982).
5. *Donovan v. Cunningham*, 716 F.2d 1455 (5th Cir. 1983).
6. *Administrative Comm. of the Wal-Mart Stores, Inc. Assocs.' Health & Welfare Plan v. Gamboa*, 2007 U.S. App. LEXIS 5240 (8th Cir. 2007).
7. *Administrative Comm. of the Wal-Mart Stores, Inc. Assocs.' Health & Welfare Plan v. Gamboa*, 2007 U.S. App. LEXIS 5240 (8th Cir. 2007).

Conversely, the majority of a Ninth Circuit panel deferred to a plan administrator's interpretation of plan terms to deny pension plan benefits to a surviving spouse, even though an ambiguous SPD could have been construed to entitle her to the benefits.[1]

In a similar ruling that determined that a short-term disability plan was not subject to ERISA, even though the SPD contained language indicating otherwise, the Sixth Circuit stated that "mere labeling by a plan sponsor or administrator is not determinative on whether a plan is governed by ERISA."[2] The Sixth Circuit affirmed a trial court determination that the disability plan was not an ERISA plan, but rather a payroll practice. "There is no evidence that DaimlerChrysler treated the DAP as an ERISA plan in its filings with the federal government, nor is there any evidence that the company partially funded benefits from a source other than general assets." Therefore, the court concluded the plan was not covered by ERISA.

The Fifth Circuit has ruled that a plan administrator's interpretation of a plan's default beneficiary provision that the term "children" did not include un-adopted step-children was a reasonable interpretation of the plan's governing provisions.[3] In this case, the deceased participant had named his wife as his beneficiary, but she predeceased him. Thus, he had no beneficiary designation at the time of his death. Under the plan's default beneficiary provision, a participant's "surviving children" are next in line after a surviving spouse. The participant had no biological or adopted children. On that basis, the plan administrator distributed the benefits to the participant's parents because third-in-line under the plan's default provision is a participant's surviving parents. The plaintiffs in this case were the participant's stepchildren. The participant had never adopted them. They argued that the plan's reference to "children" should be construed to include stepchildren. They cited their close relationship to the participant and the fact that he left his estate to them.

Since the plan document gives the plan administrator discretionary authority to determine the eligibility for benefits or to construe the terms of the plan, the court reviewed the plan administrator's interpretation of the plan for an abuse of discretion. Where an abuse-of-discretion standard of review applies, the court applies a two-step process, the first of which is whether the administrator's interpretation is legally correct. If it is, there is no further inquiry. If not, then further review is needed to determine if the administrator's decision was an abuse of discretion. Since the court concluded that the interpretation was legally correct it upheld the administrator's determination.

353. Is a good-faith but erroneous exercise of the trustees' powers under the plan agreement a breach of ERISA Section 404(a)(1)(D)?

Generally, no. The fiduciary provisions of ERISA Section 404(a)(1)(D) are not violated simply because a fiduciary does not follow the terms of the plan, so long as the action is undertaken pursuant to a good-faith (albeit erroneous) interpretation. Likewise, "trustees do not breach their fiduciary duties by interpreting the plan in good faith, even if their interpretation is later

---

1. *Weiss v. Northern Cal. Retail Clerks Unions & Food Emp'rs Joint Pension Plan*, 2007 WL 579776 (9th Cir. 2007).
2. *Langley v. DaimlerChrysler Corp.*, 2007 WL 2701091 (6th Cir. 2007).
3. *Herring and Herring v. Campbell*, 690 F.3d 413 (5th Cir. August 7, 2012).

determined to be incorrect."[1] To establish such a liability, willful or bad-faith conduct must be proven.[2] In addition, "the mere fact that [a fiduciary] has made a mistake of fact or of law in the exercise of his powers or performance of his duties does not render him liable for breach of trust. In such a case [the fiduciary] is liable for breach of trust if he is negligent, but not if he acts with proper care and caution." But a fiduciary could be liable under the law of trusts with respect to a mistake as to the extent of his duties and powers, even if made in good faith.[3] In support of the fiduciaries in the *Burke*, *Challenger*, and *Morgan* cases, it should be noted that the plan provisions were somewhat ambiguous and subject to different reasonable interpretations.

354. Must a fiduciary follow the terms of a plan document if the terms are inconsistent with ERISA?

No. Fiduciaries are required to interpret their plans "in accordance with the documents governing the plan insofar as such documents and instructions are consistent with [ERISA Section 404(a)(1)]."[4] The duty to conform to the provisions of a plan is not intended to override the fiduciary's foremost duty to serve the interests of plan participants and beneficiaries.[5] Thus, ERISA Section 404(a)(1)(D) does not excuse fiduciaries who act in a manner inconsistent with ERISA merely because they act according to a provision of a plan document.[6]

For example, a provision for pass-through voting under the terms of a plan's trust agreement was held not in the best economic interest of the plan participants and their beneficiaries (and inconsistent with the requirements of ERISA).[7] Deviating from the terms of the trust provided the participants with the ability to sell the shares at $12 per share, in contrast to $5 per share, which they would have received if the pass-through voting provision had been followed. The court noted that in accordance with the *Restatement (Second) of Trusts* §167 (1959), a court may "direct or permit the trustee to deviate from a term of the trust if owing to circumstances not known to the settlor and not anticipated by him compliance would defeat or substantially impair the accomplishment of the purposes of the trust; and in such case, if necessary to carry out the purposes of the trust, the court may direct or permit the trustee to do acts which are not authorized or are forbidden by the terms of the trust."[8]

On a related issue, the Supreme Court has ruled that a court may not reform a plan's document to comply with erroneous information provided in the plan's SPD because the SPD is a communication "about the plan" and does not "constitute the *terms* of the plan." The court relied, in part, upon ERISA Section 102(a), which provides that an SPD is an informal explanation of plan benefits and cannot be considered a part of a plan's governing documents.[9] See Q 98 and Q 517 for a further explanation of the impact of this ruling on SPD disclosure requirements and equitable remedies and equitable estoppel.

---

1. *Challenger v. Local Union No. 1*, 619 F.2d 645 (7th Cir. 1980).
2. *Burke v. Latrobe Steel Co.*, 775 F.2d 88 (3d Cir. 1985).
3. *Morgan v. Independent Drivers Ass'n Pension Plan*, 975 F.2d 1467 (10th Cir. 1992).
4. *Pratt v. Petroleum Prod. Mgmt. Emp. Sav. Plan*, 920 F.2d 651 (10th Cir. 1990).
5. *Moench v. Robertson*, 62 F.3d 553 (3d Cir. 1995) (citing *Kuper v. Quantum Chem. Corp.*, 852 F. Supp. 1389 (S.D. Ohio 1994)).
6. *Central States, Se. & Sw. Areas Pension Fund v. Central Transp., Inc.*, 472 U.S. 559 (1985).
7. See *Central Trust Co. v. American Avents Corp.*, 771 F. Supp. 871 (S.D. Ohio 1989).
8. *Central Trust. Co. v. American Avents Corp.*, above.
9. *CIGNA Corp. v. Amara*, No. 08-804, 50 EBC 2569 (U.S. May 16, 2011).

The Fifth Circuit Court of Appeals has ruled that a plan's SPD affects Plan interpretation, notwithstanding the Supreme Court decision in the *Amara* case. The Plaintiff-Appellant appealed the district court's summary judgment dismissing her suit to recover health insurance benefits under an ERISA governed employee benefits plan. Defendant-Appellee Aetna Health Inc., a Texas health maintenance organization ("HMO"), provided and administered the plan's health insurance benefits under an agreement giving Aetna discretion to interpret the plan's terms. Aetna refused to reimburse the Plaintiff for care she received from a specialist outside of the Aetna HMO to whom she had been referred by a physician in the HMO. Aetna denied her claim because the referral was not pre-authorized by Aetna. The district court found as a matter of law that Aetna did not abuse its discretion in denying coverage. The Fifth Circuit held that the plan was ambiguous and the need for pre-authorization was not clearly stated in Aetna's SPD of the plan. Therefore, under the circumstances it cannot be said as a matter of law that Aetna did not abuse its discretion in denying coverage. The district court ruling was over-turned and the case was remanded for further proceedings.[1]

The Federal District Court for the Middle District of Georgia has ruled that a health plan's SPD was considered to be a part of the plan's SPD as "a valid part of the plan instrument" (governing documents) for the purpose of identifying the plan administrator as required under ERISA where the insurance contract under the plan failed to identify the plan administrator. As such, the Court held that the employer was the plan administrator for purposes of liability for the statutory penalties for failing to timely furnish requested plan documents within the time frames required under ERISA.[2]

355. Are statements of investment policy part of the documents governing a plan?

In the view of the Department of Labor, statements of investment policy issued by a named fiduciary are part of the "documents and instruments governing the plan" within the meaning of ERISA Section 404(a)(1)(D). In that respect, a fiduciary must discharge his duties with respect to the plan in accordance with the documents and instruments, including statements of investment policy governing the plan, insofar as such documents and instruments are consistent with the provisions of ERISA. Thus, an investment manager to whom an investment policy applies would be required to comply with such policy to the extent permitted by ERISA Section 404(a)(1)(D).[3]

356. May a plan maintain the indicia of ownership of plan assets outside the jurisdiction of United States district courts?

No, with certain exceptions (see Q 357). In order to prevent "runaway assets," ERISA Section 404(b) prohibits an employee benefit plan from transferring or maintaining the indicia of ownership of plan assets outside the jurisdiction of United States district courts. The basic

---

1. *Koehler v. Aetna Health Inc.*, 2012 WL 1949166 (5th Cir. 2012).

2. *Cone v. Walmart Stores, Inc. Associates' Health and Welfare Plan*, 2012 WL 1946503 (M.D. Ga. 2012).

3. See *Dardaganis v. Grace Capital, Inc.*, 664 F. Supp. 105 (S.D.N.Y. 1987) (noncompliance with investment guidelines by an investment manager was held to violate ERISA Section 404(a)(1)(D)); *Marshall v. Teamsters Local 282 Pension Trust Fund*, 458 F. Supp. 986 (E.D.N.Y. 1978) (investment made in excess of trust percentage restrictions was held to violate ERISA Section 404(a)(1)(D)). See Labor Reg. §2509.94-2(2).

objective of this prohibition is to preclude frustration of adequate fiduciary supervision and remedies for breach of trust.[1] This prohibition is limited to the "indicia of ownership" (i.e., evidence of ownership of plan assets such as bonds or stock certificates), which may not be maintained outside the United States. Thus, the investment of employee benefit plan assets outside the United States is not prohibited if the investments are in the best interests of plan participants and made under appropriate circumstances and with proper safeguards.[2]

357. What are the "indicia of ownership" rules regarding the maintenance of plan assets outside the jurisdiction of United States district courts?

Regulations under ERISA detail exceptions under which the indicia of ownership of plan assets may be held abroad, provided that the conditions described below are satisfied with respect to the nature of the assets *and* the maintenance of them.[3]

Nature of Assets

The following assets may have indicia of ownership maintained outside the United States:

1. Securities that are issued by a person (other than an individual) that is not organized under the laws of the United States or a state and does not have its principal place of business within the United States;

2. Securities issued by a foreign government, state, or any political subdivision, agency, or instrumentality of a foreign government;

3. Securities issued by a person (other than an individual) where the principal trading market for the securities is outside the jurisdiction of the district courts of the United States; *or*

4. Currency issued by a foreign government if the currency is maintained outside the jurisdiction of the district courts of the United States solely as an incident to the purchase, sale, or maintenance of securities issued by a person that is organized under the laws of a foreign government and does not have its principal place of business within the United States.[4]

Maintenance of Assets

Furthermore, the requirements of either (1) or (2), as follow, must be met with respect to the maintenance and the indicia of ownership of the assets:

1. The assets must be either under the management and control of a fiduciary that is a corporation or partnership organized under the laws of the United States or a state, and that has its principal place of business within the United States; but the fiduciary must be either

---

1. H.R. Conf. Rep. No. 93-1280, 93d Cong., 2d Sess. 306 (1974) (ERISA Conference Report).
2. DOL Adv. Op. 75-80.
3. Labor Reg. §2550.404b-1(b).
4. Labor Reg. §2550.404b-1(a)(1).

a.   a bank as defined in Section 202(a)(2) of the Investment Advisers Act of 1940 that has, as of the last day of its most recent fiscal year, equity capital in excess of $1,000,000;

b.   an insurance company that is qualified under the laws of more than one state to manage, acquire, or dispose of any asset of a plan; that has, as of the last day of its most recent fiscal year, net worth in excess of $1,000,000; and that is subject to supervision and examination by the state authority having supervision over insurance companies; or

c.   an investment adviser registered under the Investment Advisers Act of 1940 that has, as of the last day of its most recent fiscal year, total client assets under its management and control in excess of $50,000,000 and either: (1) shareholders' or partners' equity in excess of $750,000; or (2) all of its obligations and liabilities assumed or guaranteed by a bank, insurance company, investment adviser, or broker-dealer described in this regulation.

2.   The indicia of ownership must be either

a.   in the physical possession of, or, as a result of normal business operations, in transit to the physical possession of, a person that is organized under the laws of the United States or a state. In addition, the person must have its principal place of business in the United States and must be

(i)   a bank as defined in Section 202(a)(2) of the Investment Advisers Act of 1940 that has, as of the last day of its most recent fiscal year, equity capital in excess of $1,000,000,

(ii)   a broker or dealer registered under the Securities Exchange Act of 1934 that has, as of the last day of its most recent fiscal year, net worth in excess of $750,000, or

(iii) a broker or dealer registered under the Securities Exchange Act of 1934 that has all of its obligations and liabilities assumed or guaranteed by a bank, insurance company, investment adviser, or broker-dealer described in the regulation, *or*

b.   maintained by a broker or dealer in the custody of an entity designated by the Securities and Exchange Commission as a "satisfactory control location" with respect to such broker or dealer pursuant to Rule 15c3-3 under the Securities Exchange Act of 1934, provided that

(i)   such entity holds the indicia of ownership as agent for the broker or dealer, and

(ii)   such broker or dealer is liable to the plan to the same extent it would be if it retained the physical possession of the indicia of ownership pursuant to paragraph (2)(a), above, *or*

c.   maintained by a bank described in (2)(a)(i), above, in the custody of an entity that is a foreign securities depository, foreign clearing agency which acts as a securities depository, or foreign bank, which entity is supervised or regulated by a government agency or regulatory authority in the foreign jurisdiction having authority over such depositories, clearing agencies, or banks, provided that

(i)   the foreign entity holds the indicia of ownership as agent for the bank,

(ii) the bank is liable to the plan to the same extent it would be if it retained the physical possession of the indicia of ownership within the United States,

(iii) the indicia of ownership are not subject to any right, charge, security interest, lien, or claim of any kind in favor of the foreign entity except for their safe custody or administration,

(iv) beneficial ownership of the assets represented by the indicia of ownership is freely transferable without the payment of money or value other than for safe custody or administration, *and*

(v)   upon request by the plan fiduciary who is responsible for the selection and retention of the bank, the bank identifies to the fiduciary the name, address, and principal place of business of the foreign entity that acts as custodian for the plan, and the name and address of the governmental agency or other regulatory authority that supervises or regulates that foreign entity.[1]

The regulation also permits the maintenance in Canada of the indicia of ownership of certain plan assets; see Q 358.

358. What is the alternative "indicia of ownership" rule for Canada-based assets?

A fiduciary may maintain in Canada the indicia of ownership of plan assets that are attributable to a contribution made on behalf of a plan participant who is a citizen or resident of Canada, if such indicia of ownership must remain in Canada in order for the plan to qualify for and to maintain tax-exempt status under the laws of Canada or to comply with other applicable laws of Canada or any Province of Canada.[2]

359. May fiduciary responsibility be allocated among fiduciaries?

Yes, ERISA expressly permits certain fiduciary responsibilities not involving the management and control of plan assets to be allocated among named fiduciaries. Named fiduciaries may also designate persons other than named fiduciaries to carry out the fiduciary responsibilities, provided that the plan instrument expressly provides procedures for the allocation or designation of the fiduciary responsibilities.[3]

---

1. Labor Reg. §2550.404b-1(a)(2).
2. Labor Reg. §2550.404b-1(b).
3. ERISA Sec. 405(c)(1); Labor Reg. §2509.75-8, FR-12.

360. Is a named fiduciary relieved of liability for acts and omissions allocated to other named fiduciaries?

Yes, under certain conditions and to a limited extent. Named fiduciaries are not liable for the acts and omissions of other named fiduciaries in carrying out the fiduciary responsibilities that have been allocated to other named fiduciaries, provided that the allocation is made prudently and in accordance with procedures contained in the plan document. But named fiduciaries are still liable for the acts and omissions of other named fiduciaries under ERISA Section 405(a) (relating to the general rules of co-fiduciary responsibility). In addition, if the plan document does not provide for a procedure for allocating fiduciary responsibilities among named fiduciaries, any allocation that the named fiduciaries made among themselves is ineffective to relieve a named fiduciary from responsibility or liability for the acts and omissions of the other named fiduciaries.[1]

361. May fiduciary responsibility be allocated to a person who is not a named fiduciary?

Yes, provided that the plan document provides for a procedure for designating the responsibilities of named fiduciaries to persons who are not named fiduciaries. In addition, the named fiduciaries of the plan will not be liable for the acts and omissions of the designated person except as provided in ERISA Section 405(a) (general rules of co-fiduciary liability), and ERISA Section 405(c)(2)(A) (designation of persons to carry out fiduciary responsibilities). However, the *selection* of a service provider to a qualified plan has been deemed by the DOL to be a fiduciary act for which named fiduciaries may be held liable.[2] And if the plan document does not provide for a procedure for designating persons who are not named fiduciaries to carry out fiduciary responsibilities, then the designation will not relieve the named fiduciaries from responsibility or liability for the acts and omissions of the designated persons.[3]

362. May a named fiduciary delegate the control and management of the plan assets?

Yes, subject to restrictions. A named fiduciary has the exclusive authority to control and manage the operation and administration of the plan. In accordance with that responsibility, the named fiduciary must appoint the trustees of a plan to manage and control the assets of the plan unless the plan document or trust agreement provides for that designation. In addition, only a named fiduciary may delegate the authority and discretion to manage and control the assets of a plan to others, provided that the plan document allows for the delegation. But the authority and discretion to manage and control the assets of a plan may be delegated only to other named fiduciaries, trustees, investment managers, and plan participants under limited circumstances.[4]

---

1. ERISA Sec. 405(c)(1); Labor Reg. §2509.75-8, FR-13.
2. PWBA Information Letter to Theodore Konshak (Dec. 1, 1997).
3. Labor Reg. §2509.75-8, FR-14.
4. See ERISA Secs. 402(a)(1), 402(c)(3), 403(a).

363. May a named fiduciary delegate responsibility for management and control of plan assets to anyone other than a person who is an investment manager?

No. ERISA does not allow named fiduciaries to delegate to others authority or discretion to manage or control plan assets.[1] But under the terms of ERISA Section 403(a)(2) and ERISA Section 402(c)(3), the authority and discretion may be delegated to persons who are investment managers as defined in ERISA Section 3(38). Further, under ERISA Section 402(c)(2), if the plan so provides, a named fiduciary may employ other persons to render advice to the named fiduciary to assist it in carrying out the named fiduciary's investment responsibilities under the plan.[2]

364. Can a fiduciary who is not a named fiduciary with respect to an employee benefit plan be personally liable for all phases of the management and administration of the plan?

A fiduciary with respect to the plan who is not a *named* fiduciary is a fiduciary only to the extent that she performs one or more of the fiduciary functions described in ERISA Section 3(21)(A). In addition, any fiduciary may become liable for breaches of fiduciary responsibility committed by another fiduciary of the same plan under circumstances giving rise to co-fiduciary liability, as provided in ERISA Section 405(a).[3]

365. What are the ongoing responsibilities of a fiduciary who has appointed trustees or other fiduciaries with respect to these appointments?

At reasonable intervals, the performance of trustees and other fiduciaries must be reviewed by the appointing fiduciary in a manner that is reasonably expected to ensure that their performance has been in compliance with the terms of the plan, has met the statutory standards, and satisfies the needs of the plan. No single procedure will be appropriate in all cases; the procedure adopted may vary in accordance with the nature of the plan and other facts and circumstances relevant to the choice of the procedure.[4]

The DOL and the Securities and Exchange Commission (SEC) have jointly published guidance to assist fiduciaries in the evaluation of potential conflicts of interest in the selection and monitoring of pension consultants.[5]

A 2005 report by the SEC raises serious questions concerning whether some pension consultants are fully disclosing potential conflicts of interest that may affect the objectivity of the advice they are providing to their pension plan clients.[6] "The SEC examination staff concluded in its report that the business alliances among pension consultants and money managers (in offering

---

1. ERISA Sec. 405(c)(1).
2. Labor Reg. §2509.75-8, FR-15.
3. Labor Reg. §2509.75-8, FR-16.
4. Labor Reg. §2509.75-8, FR-17.
5. DOL Fact Sheet "Selecting and Monitoring Pension Consultants: Tips for Plan Fiduciaries" (May 2005), http://www.dol.gov/ebsa/newsroom/fs053105.html.
6. See http://www.sec.gov/news/studies/pensionexamstudy.pdf.

bundled services such as brokerage, fund selection, and money management services) can give rise to serious potential conflicts of interest under the Advisers Act that need to be monitored and disclosed to plan fiduciaries."

To assist fiduciaries in this area, the DOL and SEC present ten questions to ask consultants that are designed to foster better disclosure of information that indicates potential conflicts of interest:

1. Are you registered with the SEC or a state securities regulator as an investment adviser? If so, have you provided us with all the disclosures required under those laws (including Part II of Form ADV)?

2. Do you or a related company have relationships with money managers that you recommend, consider for recommendation, or otherwise mention to the plan? If so, describe those relationships.

3. Do you or a related company receive any payments from money managers you recommend, consider for recommendation, or otherwise mention to the plan for our consideration? If so, what is the extent of these payments in relation to your other income (revenue)?

4. Do you have any policies or procedures to address conflicts of interest or to prevent these payments or relationships from being a factor when you provide advice to your clients?

5. If you allow plans to pay your consulting fees using the plan's brokerage commissions, do you monitor the amount of commissions paid and alert plans when consulting fees have been paid in full? If not, how can a plan make sure it does not over-pay its consulting fees?

6. If you allow plans to pay your consulting fees using the plan's brokerage commissions, what steps do you take to ensure that the plan receives best execution for its securities trades?

7. Do you have any arrangements with broker-dealers under which you or a related company will benefit if money managers place trades for their clients with such broker-dealers?

8. If you are hired, will you acknowledge in writing that you have a fiduciary obligation as an investment adviser to the plan while providing the consulting services we are seeking?

9. Do you consider yourself a fiduciary under ERISA with respect to the recommendations you provide the plan?

10. What percentage of your plan clients utilizes money managers, investment funds, brokerage services, or other service providers from whom you receive fees?

366. What guidance has the DOL issued regarding the fiduciary responsibilities of a directed trustee?

Many employee pension plans use directed trustees to carry out transactions according to instructions from a named fiduciary of the plan. In this regard, ERISA Section 403(a) specifically recognizes that a trustee or trustees will have limited authority or discretion when the plan expressly provides that the trustee or trustees are subject to the direction of a named fiduciary who is not a trustee, in which case the trustees shall be subject to proper directions of such fiduciary that are made in accordance with the terms of the plan and that are not contrary to the provisions of ERISA.

While ERISA Section 403(a)(1) does not remove a directed trustee from the purview of ERISA Section 3(21), it significantly limits such a trustee's responsibilities as a plan fiduciary. As the district court in *In re Enron Corp. Securities, Derivative & ERISA Litigation*[1] recognized:

> At least some fiduciary status and duties of a directed trustee are preserved, even though the scope of its exclusive authority and discretion to manage and control the assets of the plans has been substantially constricted by the directing named fiduciary's correspondingly broadened role.

The court in *In re WorldCom, Inc. ERISA Litigation*[2] also noted that, while the directed trustee provision serves as a limiting principle, ERISA Section 403(a) does not "eliminate the fiduciary status or duties that normally adhere to a trustee with responsibility over ERISA assets."[3] In further litigation stemming from the WorldCom matter, the court clarified that under the DOL's Field Assistance Bulletin 2004-03, "When a directed trustee receives a direction to invest plan assets in the securities of a company, or when plan assets are already invested in such securities, a directed trustee has a fiduciary duty of inquiry under ERISA when it knows or should know of reliable public information that calls into serious question the company's short-term viability as a going concern."[4] In reviewing the facts available at the time of the direction to make the investment in WorldCom stock, the directed trustee would have been under no obligation to investigate the prudence of investing in, and continuing to hold, the WorldCom shares.

The duties of a directed trustee under ERISA Section 403(a)(1) are significantly narrower than the duties generally ascribed to a discretionary trustee under common law trust principles.

The *Enron* and *WorldCom* cases have raised the DOL's awareness of the difficulties in defining the scope of a directed trustee's fiduciary duties, and in determining whether the directions they were following were "proper" and consistent with the terms of the plan document and ERISA. As noted above, DOL FAB 2004-03, which is consistent with the DOL's brief in the *Enron* case, clarifies that a directed trustee is a fiduciary under ERISA, responsible for carrying out its duties prudently and solely in the interest of the participants and beneficiaries of employee benefit plans.

---

1. 284 F. Supp. 2d 511, 601 (S.D. Tex. 2003).
2. 263 F. Supp. 2d 745 (S.D.N.Y. 2003).
3. 263 F. Supp. 2d at 762. See also *FirsTier Bank, N.A. v. Zeller*, 16 F.3d 907, 911 (8th Cir.), cert. denied sub nom. *Vercoe v. FirsTier Bank, N.A.*, 513 U.S. 871 (1994); *Herman v. NationsBank Trust Co.*, 126 F.3d 1354, 1361-62, 1370 (11th Cir. 1997).
4. *In re WorldCom, Inc. ERISA Litig.*, 2005 U.S. Dist. LEXIS 1218 (S.D.N.Y. 2005).

FAB 2004-03 also makes it clear that the named fiduciary, not the directed trustee, is primarily responsible for ensuring the prudence of plan investment decisions. A directed trustee must follow processes that are designed to avoid prohibited transactions. A directed trustee could satisfy its obligation by obtaining appropriate written representations from the directing fiduciary that the plan maintains and follows procedures for identifying prohibited transactions and, if prohibited, identifying the individual or class exemption applicable to the transaction. A directed trustee may rely on the representations of the directing fiduciary unless the directed trustee knows that the representations are false.

Under ERISA Section 403(a)(1), a directed trustee may not follow a direction that the trustee knows or should know is inconsistent with the terms of the plan. In order to make such determinations, directed trustees necessarily have a duty to request and review all the documents and instruments governing the plan that are relevant to its duties as a directed trustee. Accordingly, if a directed trustee either fails to request such documents or fails to review the documents furnished in response to its request and, as a result of such failure, follows a direction contrary to the terms of the plan, the directed trustee may be liable for following the direction because the directed trustee had a duty to request and review pertinent plan documents and, therefore, should have known that the direction was not in accordance with the terms of the plan. If, in the course of reviewing the propriety of a particular direction, a directed trustee determines that the terms of the relevant documents are ambiguous with respect to the permissibility of the direction, the directed trustee should obtain a clarification of the plan terms from the fiduciary responsible for interpreting such terms in order to ensure that the direction is proper. In this regard, the directed trustee may rely on the interpretation of such fiduciary.

The DOL notes in FAB 2004-03 that when a directed trustee has non-public information regarding a security that is necessary for a prudent decision by the directing plan fiduciary, the directed trustee has a duty to inquire about the named fiduciary's knowledge and consideration of the information. The primary circumstance in which such an obligation could arise is when the directed trustee possesses material non-public information regarding a security. "If a directed trustee has material non-public information that is necessary for a prudent decision, the directed trustee, prior to following a direction that would be affected by such information, has a duty to inquire about the named fiduciary's knowledge and consideration of the information with respect to the direction. For example, if a directed trustee has non-public information indicating that a company's public financial statements contain material misrepresentations that significantly inflate the company's earnings, the trustee could not simply follow a direction to purchase that company's stock at an artificially inflated price."

"Generally, the possession of non-public information by one part of an organization will not be imputed to the organization as a whole (including personnel providing directed trustee services) where the organization maintains procedures designed to prevent the illegal disclosure of such information under securities, banking or other laws. If, despite such procedures, the individuals responsible for the directed trustee services have actual knowledge of material non-public information, the directed trustee, prior to following a direction that would be affected by such information, has a duty, as indicated above, to inquire about the named fiduciary's knowledge and consideration of the information with respect to the direction. Similarly, if the directed trustee performs an internal analysis in which it concludes that the company's current financial statements are materially inaccurate, the directed trustee would have an obligation to disclose this analysis to the named fiduciary before making a determination whether to follow a direction to purchase the company's security. The directed trustee would not have an obligation to disclose reports and analyses that are available to the public."

In the case of public information, a directed trustee would be required to question the instructions of the directing fiduciary only in extraordinary circumstances "where there are clear and compelling public indicators, as evidenced by an 8-K filing with the Securities and Exchange Commission (SEC), a bankruptcy filing or similar public indicator, that call into serious question a company's viability as a going concern. In these situations, the directed trustee may have a duty not to follow the named fiduciary's instruction without further inquiry. For example, if a company filed for bankruptcy under circumstances which make it unlikely that there would be any distribution to equity-holders, or otherwise publicly stated that it was unlikely to survive the bankruptcy proceedings in a manner that would leave current equity-holders with any value, the directed trustee would have an obligation to question whether the named fiduciary has considered the prudence of the direction."

It also is the view of the DOL that, "in situations where a fiduciary who is a corporate employee gives an instruction to buy or hold stock of his company subsequent to the company, its officers or directors, being formally charged by state or federal regulators with financial irregularities, the directed trustee, taking such facts into account, may need to decline to follow the direction or may need to conduct an independent assessment of the transaction in order to assure itself that the instruction is consistent with ERISA. But if an independent fiduciary was appointed to manage the plan's investment in company stock, a directed trustee could follow the proper directions of the independent fiduciary without having to conduct its own independent assessment of the transaction."

It is the view of the DOL that the nature and scope of a directed trustee's fiduciary responsibility does not change "merely because the directed trustee, in carrying out its duties, raises questions concerning whether a direction is 'proper' or declines to follow a direction that the directed trustee does not believe is a proper direction within the meaning of Section 403(a)(1). For example, information provided to a named fiduciary concerning the prudence of a direction is not investment advice for purposes of ERISA Section 3(21)(A)(ii). Similarly, if a named fiduciary changes a direction in response to a directed trustee's inquiries or information, the directed trustee's fiduciary responsibility with respect to the changed direction remains governed by Section 403(a)(1). The directed trustee does not become primarily responsible for the prudence of the direction."

If a directed trustee has knowledge of a fiduciary breach, the directed trustee may be liable as a co-fiduciary under ERISA Section 405(a) unless the directed trustee takes reasonable steps to remedy the breach. "Thus, if the directed trustee knew that the named fiduciary was failing to discharge its obligations in accordance with ERISA's requirements, it could not simply follow directions from the breaching fiduciary." The DOL states that efforts to remedy the breach, or prevent its occurrence, may require the directed trustee to report the breach to other fiduciaries or to the DOL.

367. Does the inclusion of indemnification and limitation of liability language in a service provider contract violate ERISA's fiduciary provisions?

No. In regards to the general fiduciary obligations under ERISA Section 404(a)(1), and the prohibited transaction provisions of ERISA Section 406(a)(1)(C) and ERISA Section 406(a)(1)(D), the DOL states that the selection of service providers under ERISA is a fiduciary duty requiring the responsible fiduciary to "engage in an objective process designed to elicit information necessary to assess the qualifications of the provider." When soliciting bids among service providers, inquiring as to the presence of contractual provisions that limit liability or indemnify the service provider for acts of negligence allows the fiduciary to "obtain the necessary information relevant to the decision making process."

As such, the DOL opines that "in and of themselves, most limitation of liability and indemnification provisions in service provider contracts" are not imprudent under ERISA Section 404(a)(1), nor are they unreasonable arrangements with a party in interest under ERISA Section 408(b)(2). Further, the DOL says that "[o]ther limitations of liability and indemnification provisions, applying to negligence and unintentional malpractice may be consistent with ... ERISA when considered in connection with the reasonableness of the arrangement as a whole and the potential risks to participants and beneficiaries." The Advisory Opinion cautions that compliance with ERISA would require the fiduciary to assess the ability of the plan to obtain comparable services at comparable costs from other service providers that are willing to forgo such hold-harmless provisions in their contracts. Fiduciaries are also advised to assess the plan's exposure to risk of loss and costs that might result from the service provider's negligent act or omission under the contractual limitations.[1]

The advisory opinion expresses the DOL's belief that contractual limitations to acts of fraud and willful misconduct by a service provider are void against public policy and would be an act of imprudence for a fiduciary to agree to such provisions.

A district court has ruled that a plan provision relieving a plan trustee of the duty to monitor and collect employer contributions is void as against public policy.[2] In the case, the court held that ordinary notions of property rights include the right to collect unpaid contributions. The court then examined ERISA's trust requirement, concluding that ERISA Section 403 imposes a duty on trustees to monitor and collect unpaid contributions and that the plan provision eliminating that duty violated the trust requirement. The court concluded that the plan provision was void as against public policy under ERISA Section 410, so the court ordered the master plan sponsor to amend the plan documents to eliminate the provision.

368. Must a plan administrator solicit fee quotations in selecting a service provider to provide services to a plan?

Maybe. The selection of an actuary to provide the required services under ERISA Section 103(a)(4)(A) is an exercise of discretionary authority or control with respect to the management

1. DOL Adv. Op. 2002-08A.
2. *Solis v. Plan Benefit Servs. Inc.*, 2009 WL 799092 (D. Mass. 2009).

and administration of the plan, within the meaning of ERISA Section 3(21), and therefore constitutes a fiduciary act subject to the general fiduciary responsibility standards and prohibited transaction provisions of ERISA Section 404(a)(1), ERISA Section 406(a)(1)(C), and ERISA Section 406(a)(1)(D), respectively.[1] Although this guidance addresses the issue within the context of selecting the services of an actuary, the information letter's rationale generally would seem to warrant its extension to the selection of any provider of services to a plan.

According to the DOL, in selecting a service provider such as an enrolled actuary, the responsible plan fiduciary must engage in an objective process designed to elicit information necessary to assess the qualifications of the service provider, the quality of the work product, and the reasonableness of the fees charged in light of the services provided. In addition, such a process should be designed to avoid self-dealing, conflicts of interest, or other improper influence. What constitutes an appropriate method of selecting a service provider, however, will depend upon the particular facts and circumstances. In the view of the DOL, soliciting bids among service providers at the outset is a means by which the fiduciary can obtain the necessary information relevant to the decision-making process. Whether such a process is appropriate in subsequent years may depend, among other things, upon the fiduciary's knowledge of a service provider's work product, the cost and quality of services previously provided by the service provider, the fiduciary's knowledge of prevailing rates for the services, as well as the cost to the plan of conducting a particular selection process. But, regardless of the method used, the DOL cautions that the fiduciary must be able to demonstrate compliance with ERISA's fiduciary standards.[2]

Practitioner's Pointer: A fiduciary's ERISA Section 404 obligations are independent of the disclosure requirements related to the prohibited transaction exemption.[3] Thus, plan fiduciaries are required to obtain and carefully consider information necessary to assess the services to be provided to the plan, the reasonableness of the fees and expenses being paid for these services, and potential conflicts of interest that might affect the quality of the provided services. Ultimately, the responsible plan fiduciary will have to decide whether it has enough information about the services to be provided under a contract or arrangement to determine whether the cost of the services is reasonable. If a particular description of services provided by a covered service provider lacks sufficient detail to enable the fiduciary to make this determination, the fiduciary would have to request additional information concerning those services.[4] For additional information on the required disclosures for reasonable contracts and arrangements under the statutory exemption of ERISA Section 408(b)(2) for the provision of services or office space between a plan and a party-in-interest, see Q 402 and Q 464.

---

369. Must a plan administrator select the lowest quoted fee in selecting a service provider to provide services to a plan?

Not necessarily. Because a number of factors will necessarily be considered by a fiduciary when selecting a service provider, the DOL maintains that a fiduciary need not necessarily select the lowest bidder when soliciting bids, although the compensation paid to the service provider

---

1. Information Letter to Theodore Konshak from Bette J. Briggs (Dec. 1, 1997).
2. Information Letter to Theodore Konshak from Bette J. Briggs (Dec. 1, 1997).
3. Labor Reg. §2550.408b-2(c)(1)(i).
4. Labor Reg. §2550.408b-2(c).

by the plan must be reasonable in light of the services provided. But the fiduciary should not consider one factor, such as the lowest fee bid for services, to the exclusion of any other factor, such as the quality of the work product. Rather, the decision regarding which service provider to select should be based on an assessment of all the relevant factors, including both the quality and cost of the services.[1]

370. Is it appropriate for a trustee of an ERISA-covered health and welfare fund to consider quality in the selection of health care services?

Maybe. When the selection of a health care provider involves the disposition of employee benefit plan assets, such selection is an exercise of authority or control with respect to the management and disposition of the plan's assets within the meaning of ERISA Section 3(21)(A), and thus constitutes a fiduciary act subject to the general fiduciary responsibility standards and prohibited transaction provisions of ERISA Section 404(a)(1), ERISA Section 406(a)(1)(C), and ERISA Section 406(a)(1)(D), respectively.[2] Although this guidance addresses the issue within the context of selecting health care services, the same rationale would appear to apply to the selection of any provider of services to a plan.

According to the DOL, in selecting a health care provider in this context, as with the selection of any service provider under ERISA, the responsible plan fiduciary must engage in an objective process designed to elicit information necessary to assess the qualifications of the provider, the quality of services offered, and the reasonableness of the fees charged in light of the services provided. In addition, such a process should be designed to avoid self-dealing, conflicts of interest, or other improper influence. But what constitutes an appropriate method of selecting a health care provider will depend upon the particular facts and circumstances. Soliciting bids among service providers at the outset is a means by which the fiduciary can obtain the necessary information relevant to the decision-making process. Whether such a process is appropriate in subsequent years may depend, among other things, upon the fiduciary's knowledge of the service provider's work, the cost and quality of the services previously provided by the service provider, the fiduciary's knowledge of prevailing rates for similar services, as well as the cost to the plan of conducting a particular selection process. But, regardless of the method used, the DOL advises that the fiduciary must be able to demonstrate compliance with ERISA's fiduciary standards.

Because numerous factors necessarily will be considered by a fiduciary when selecting health care service providers, the DOL also notes that a fiduciary need not select the lowest bidder when soliciting bids, although the fiduciary must ensure that the compensation paid to a service provider is reasonable in light of the services provided to the plan. In addition, because "quality of services" is a factor relevant to selection of a service provider, it is the view of the DOL that a plan fiduciary's failure to take quality of services into account in the selection process would constitute a breach of the fiduciary's duty under ERISA when, in the case of a plan, the selection involves the disposition of plan assets.

---

1. Information Letter to Theodore Konshak from Bette J. Briggs (Dec. 1, 1997).
2. Information Letter to Diana Orantes Ceresi from Bette J. Briggs (Feb. 19, 1998).

In assessing "quality of services," the DOL believes that a plan fiduciary may, among other things, consider the scope of choices and qualifications of medical providers and specialists available to participants, ease of access to medical providers, ease of access to information concerning the operations of the health care provider, the extent to which internal procedures provide for timely consideration and resolution of patient questions and complaints, the extent to which internal procedures provide for the confidentiality of patient records, enrollee satisfaction statistics, and rating or accreditation of health care service providers by independent services or state agencies.[1]

371. May a fiduciary be relieved of liability for investment losses resulting from participant-directed investments?

Yes, to a limited degree. Generally, ERISA provides that if a plan that provides for individual accounts permits a participant or beneficiary to exercise control over assets in his account, and that participant or beneficiary in fact exercises control over assets in his account, then the participant or beneficiary is not deemed to be a fiduciary by reason of his exercise of control, and no person who is otherwise a fiduciary will be liable for any loss, or by reason of any breach, that results from such exercise of control.[2] Details as to safe harbor means by which a fiduciary may avail itself of ERISA Section 404(c) relief are explained in Q 373.

The Seventh Circuit Court of Appeals has issued a ruling that the plan administrator and the trustee of a company's profit sharing and pension plan that experienced investment losses did not breach their fiduciary duty with respect to that part of the plan under which participants were permitted to make limited investment decisions.[3]

Under the plan, participants were permitted to make investment directions into four mutual funds. The investment options were not changed after 1991. From 1991 to 2002, participants could change their investment directions only once per year. Beginning in 2002, participants could change investment directions every six months. The trustee did not review participants' investment decisions. When the plan experienced poor investment performance in 2002 and 2003, the participant brought suit against the owner, as trustee, and the plan sponsor, as administrator, alleging that they had breached their fiduciary duty by providing unduly restrictive means of directing their investments, failing to monitor the plan's investments, and failing to operate the plan according to ERISA, because control over plan assets was delegated to plan participants.

The Seventh Circuit found that although the plan gave the trustee power to invest, manage, and control the plan assets, the plan also permitted the participants to direct the trustee as to investment of the participants' accounts up to once per year. The court found that a plan that allows participant direction, but that does not meet the requirements of ERISA Section 404(c), does not violate ERISA if the trustee's actions in delegating decision-making authority otherwise satisfy the trustee's fiduciary duty.

---

1. Information Letter to Diana Orantes Ceresi from Bette J. Briggs (Feb. 19, 1998).
2. ERISA Sec. 404(c); Labor Reg. §2550.404c.
3. *Jenkins v. Yager*, 444 F.3d 916 (7th Cir. 2006).

372. Who enforces the fiduciary standards?

The Department of Labor has the sole authority for interpreting and enforcing the fiduciary provisions of ERISA, and it conducts investigations of violations thereof under its fiduciary investigations program.[1] A plan fiduciary who breaches any of the fiduciary obligations under ERISA Section 404 may be sued by the Secretary of Labor or other persons, and may be subjected to personal liability for losses to the plan and to all other appropriate equitable relief, including injunctive relief.[2]

373. What is an ERISA Section 404(c) participant-directed plan?

A participant-directed plan is one under which individual plan participants or beneficiaries may exercise control over assets in individual accounts maintained for them under the plan. Under ERISA, a person who exercises authority or control over the assets of a plan is a fiduciary and, therefore, has specific duties and responsibilities with respect to the plan and its participants and beneficiaries.

Regulations under ERISA Section 404(c) state that where a participant or beneficiary exercises control over the assets in her individual account in an individual account plan (e.g., a 401(k), money purchase, profit sharing, or 403(b) plan), then (1) the participant or beneficiary will not be deemed to be a fiduciary by reason of her exercise of control; and (2) no person who is otherwise a fiduciary will be liable under the fiduciary responsibility provisions of ERISA for any loss, or by reason of any breach, that results from such participant's or beneficiary's exercise of control, if certain requirements are met.[3]

The 404(c) regulations set forth specific rules that must be followed in order for plan fiduciaries to afford themselves the relief from liability allowed by ERISA Section 404(c). Additional guidance was issued in February 2004, addressing the obligation of fiduciaries to review their mutual fund and pooled investment funds for potential late-trading and market-timing abuses; see Appendix C.

In general, relief from liability is allowed under a 404(c) plan only if a participant or beneficiary actually exercises control over the assets in her account. A plan allows exercise of control if it provides the participant or beneficiary the opportunity under the plan to (1) choose from a broad range of investment alternatives, which consist of at least three diversified investment alternatives, each of which has materially different risk and return characteristics; (2) give investment instructions with a frequency that is appropriate in light of the market volatility of the investment alternatives, but not less frequently than once within any three-month period; (3) diversify investments within and among investment alternatives; and (4) obtain sufficient information to make informed investment decisions with respect to investment alternatives available under the plan.[4]

---

1. ERISA Secs. 502, 504, 505, 506; Reorganization Plan No. 4 of 1978, Sec. 102, 1979-1 C.B. 480; PWBA Enforcement Manual.
2. See ERISA Secs. 409, 502(a)(2), 502(a)(5).
3. Labor Reg. §2550.404c-1 (see Q 371).
4. See Labor Reg. §2550.404c-1.

374. What are the default investment alternatives under participant-directed plans?

Section 624(a) of the Pension Protection Act of 2006 (PPA 2006) provides that a participant of a participant-directed individual account pension plan will be deemed to have exercised control over assets in his account if, in the absence of investment directions from the participant, the plan invests in a Qualified Default Investment Alternative (QDIA). These new provisions went into effect January 1, 2007.[1] The DOL has issued final regulations to the QDIA.[2] The DOL has also issued technical clarifications to the final regulations.[3]

A fiduciary of a plan that complies with the regulation will not be liable for any loss, or by reason of any breach that occurs as a result of such investments. Plan fiduciaries remain responsible for the prudent selection and monitoring of the qualified default investment alternative.

As part of PPA 2006, ERISA Section 404(c) was amended to provide relief accorded by ERISA Section 404(c)(1) to fiduciaries that invest participant assets in certain types of default investment alternatives in the absence of participant investment direction.[4] Specifically, Section 624(a) of PPA 2006 added a new ERISA Section 404(c)(5). ERISA Section 404(c)(5)(A) provides that, for purposes of ERISA Section 404(c)(1), a participant in an individual account plan shall be treated as exercising control over the assets in the account with respect to the amount of contributions and earnings that, in the absence of an investment election by the participant, are invested by the plan in accordance with the regulations. It is not necessary for a plan to be an ERISA Section 404(c) plan in order for the fiduciary to obtain the relief accorded by this regulation.

Section 624(a) of PPA 2006 also added notice requirements in ERISA Section 404(c)(5)(B)(i) and ERISA Section 404(c)(5)(B)(ii). Section 404(c)(5)(B)(i) requires that each participant receive, within a reasonable period of time before each plan year, a notice explaining the employee's right under the plan to designate how contributions and earnings will be invested and explaining how, in the absence of any investment election by the participant, such contributions and earnings will be invested. The employee must have a reasonable period of time after receipt of such notice and before the beginning of the plan year to make such designation.

Section 404(c)(5)(B)(ii) requires each notice to be sufficiently accurate and comprehensive to appraise the employee of such rights and obligations, and to be written in a manner calculated to be understood by the average employee eligible to participate.

Like other investment alternatives made available under a plan, a plan fiduciary would be required to carefully consider investment fees and expenses in choosing a QDIA for purposes of the regulation. To the extent that a plan offers more than one investment alternative that could constitute a QDIA, the DOL anticipates that fees and expenses would be an important consideration in selecting among the alternatives.

---

1. Pub. L. No. 109-280.
2. 72 Fed. Reg. 60,451 (Oct. 24, 2007).
3. 73 Fed. Reg. 23,349 (Apr. 30, 2008).
4. Labor Reg. §2550.404c-5(a)(1).

The regulations have six conditions that must be satisfied in order for the fiduciary protections to apply.

The first condition requires that assets invested on behalf of participants or beneficiaries be placed in a "qualified default investment alternative."[1]

The second condition provides that the participant or beneficiary on whose behalf assets are being invested in a QDIA had the opportunity to direct the investment of assets in her account but did not direct the assets.[2] In other words, no relief is available when a participant or beneficiary has provided affirmative investment direction concerning the assets invested on the participant's or beneficiary's behalf.

The third condition requires that the participant or beneficiary on whose behalf an investment in a QDIA may be made is furnished notice at least thirty days in advance of the date of plan eligibility, or at least thirty days in advance of the date of any first investment in a QDIA. The notice may also be provided on or before the date of plan eligibility provided the participant has the opportunity to make a permissible withdrawal, and within a reasonable period of time of at least thirty days in advance of each subsequent plan year.[3] The specific content requirements for the notice are that it be written in a manner calculated to be understood by the average plan participant and contain the following:

1. A description of the circumstances under which assets in the individual account may be invested on behalf of the participant or beneficiary in a QDIA; and, if applicable, an explanation of the investment alternative; and if applicable, an explanation of the circumstances under which elective contributions will be made, the percentage of such contributions, and the right of the participant to elect not to have such contributions made on the participant's behalf (or to elect to have such contributions made at a different percentage);

2. An explanation of the right of participants and beneficiaries to direct the investment of assets in their individual accounts;

3. A description of the QDIA, including a description of the investment objectives, risk and return characteristics (if applicable), and fees and expenses attendant to the investment alternative;

4. A description of the right of the participants and beneficiaries on whose behalf assets are invested in a QDIA to direct the investment of those assets to any other investment alternative under the plan, including a description of any applicable restrictions, fees, or expenses in connection with such transfer; and

5. An explanation of where the participants and beneficiaries can obtain investment information concerning the other investment alternatives available under the plan.[4]

---

1. Labor Reg. §2550.404c-5(c)(1).
2. Labor Reg. §2550.404c-5(c)(2).
3. Labor Reg. §2550.404c-5(c)(3).
4. Labor Reg. §2550.404c-5(d).

The fourth condition of the regulation requires that any material provided to the plan relating to a participant's or beneficiary's investment in a QDIA (e.g., account statements, prospectuses, proxy voting material) will be provided to the participant or beneficiary.[1]

The fifth condition requires that any participant or beneficiary on whose behalf assets are invested in a QDIA may transfer, in whole or in part, such assets to any other investment alternative available under the plan with a frequency consistent with that afforded to a participant or beneficiary who elected to invest in the QDIA, but not less frequently than once within any three-month period. Furthermore, any transfer or permissible withdrawal of assets invested in a QDIA in whole or in part, resulting from the participant or beneficiary's election to make such a transfer or withdrawal during the ninety-day period beginning on the date of the participant's first elective contribution, or other first investment in a QDIA, shall not be subject to any restrictions, fees, expenses (including surrender charges, liquidation of exchange fees, redemption fees, and similar expenses charged in connection with the liquidation of, or transfer from, the investment). The preceding restriction on fees shall not apply to fees and expenses that are charged on an ongoing basis for the operation of the investment itself (such as investment management fees, 12b-1 fees, or legal, accounting, transfer agent, and similar administrative expenses), and are not imposed, or do not vary, based on a participant's or beneficiary's decision to withdraw, sell, or transfer assets out of the QDIA. Following the ninety-day period described above, any transfer or permissible withdrawal shall not be subject to any restrictions, fees, or expenses not otherwise applicable to a participant or beneficiary who elected to invest in that QDIA.[2]

The last condition requires that the plan offer participants and beneficiaries the opportunity to invest in a "broad range of investment alternatives" within the meaning of Labor Regulation Section 2550.404c-1(b)(3).[3] The DOL believes that the application of the "broad range of investment alternatives" standard of the Section 404(c) regulation provides participants and beneficiaries a sufficient range of investment alternatives to achieve a diversified portfolio with aggregate risk and return characteristics at any point within the range normally appropriate for the pension plan participant or beneficiary, without regard to whether such plans meet all the requirements for an ERISA Section 404(c) plan.[4]

The final regulations define a "qualified default investment alternative" as an investment that:

1. Does not hold or permit the acquisition of employer securities (with the exception of employer securities held or acquired by a mutual fund or a similar pooled investment vehicle made in accordance with stated investment objectives of the investment vehicle and independent of the plan sponsor or affiliate, or employer securities acquired as a matching contribution, or acquired prior to management by an investment management service that has discretion over the purchase and sale of such employer securities);

---

1. Labor Reg. §2550.404c-5(c)(4).
2. Labor Reg. §2550.404c-5(c)(5)(i), (ii), and (iii).
3. Labor Reg. §2550.404c-5(c)(6).
4. Preamble to Labor Reg. §2550.404c-5.

2. Satisfies the requirement that a participant or beneficiary have the ability to transfer, in whole or in part, her investment from the qualified default investment alternative to any other investment alternative available under the plan;

3. Is managed by an investment manager as defined within the meaning of ERISA Section 3(38); a trustee that meets the requirements of ERISA Section 3(38)(A), (B), and (C); the plan sponsor, or a committee comprised primarily of employees of the plan sponsor, which is a named fiduciary; an investment company registered under the Investment Company Act of 1940; or an investment product or fund described below; and

4. Constitutes one of the following:

    a. An investment fund product or model portfolio that applies generally accepted investment theories, is diversified so as to minimize the risk of large losses and is designed to provide varying degrees of long-term appreciation and capital preservation through a mix of equity and fixed-income exposures based on the participant's age, target retirement date (such as normal retirement age under the plan), or life expectancy (e.g., a life-cycle or targeted retirement date fund);

    b. An investment fund product or model portfolio that applies generally accepted investment theories, is diversified so as to minimize the risk of large losses, and is designed to provide long-term appreciation and capital preservation through a mix of equity and fixed-income exposures consistent with a target level of risk appropriate for participants of the plan as a whole (e.g., a balanced fund);

    c. An investment management service with respect to which a fiduciary (as noted in 3, above) applying generally accepted investment theories, allocates the assets of a participant's individual account to achieve varying degrees of long-term appreciation and capital preservation through a mix of equity and fixed-income exposures, offered through investment alternatives available under the plan, based on the participant's age, target retirement date, or life expectancy (e.g., a managed account);

    d. An investment product or fund designed to preserve principal and provide a reasonable rate of return, whether or not such return is guaranteed, consistent with liquidity, which seeks to maintain over the term of the investment, the dollar value that is equal to the amount invested in the product, and is offered by a state or federally regulated financial institution for no more than 120 days after the date following the participant's first elective contribution;

    e. An investment product or fund designed to guarantee principal and a rate of return generally consistent with that earned on intermediate investment grade bonds and provide liquidity for withdrawals by participants and beneficiaries, including transfers to other investment alternatives where there are no fees or surrender charges imposed in connection with withdrawals initiated by the participant or beneficiary and such investment product or fund invests primarily in investment products that are backed by state or federally regulated financial institutions (e.g., stable value funds); or

f.   An investment fund product or model portfolio that otherwise meets the requirements of a qualified default investment alternative that is offered through a variable annuity or similar contracts or through common or collective trust funds or pooled investment funds and without regard to whether such contracts or funds provide annuity purchase rights, investment guarantees, death benefit guarantees, or other features ancillary to the investment fund product or model portfolio.[1]

On November 30, 2010, the DOL issued a proposed regulation to update its guidance on QDIAs as they pertain to fiduciary relief for disclosure of certain investment-related information in general and specific to target date funds.[2]

The proposed regulations amend the October 20, 2010, final regulations on required disclosures under participant-directed individual account plans (see Q 97 for full details of those required disclosures) as they apply to QDIAs. Specifically, the proposed regulation provides that, in addition to the disclosure of investment-related information detailed at Q 97, a fiduciary must also provide the following information on QDIAs:

1.   A description of the QDIA including:

a.   name of the issuer;

b.   investment objectives;

c.   principal strategies and risks;

d.   historical investment performance;

e.   a statement that past performance is not an indication of how the investment will perform in the future; and,

f.   if applicable, a description of any fixed return, annuity, guarantee, death benefit, or other ancillary features;

2.   The QDIA's attendant fees and expenses, including:

a.   any fees charged directly against the amount invested in connection with the acquisition, sale, transfer, or withdrawal;

b.   any annual operating expenses; and

c.   any ongoing expenses in addition to annual operating expenses.[3]

---

1. Labor Reg. §2550.404c-5(e)(1) to (4)(i)-(vi), as corrected by regulatory amendment, 73 Fed. Reg. 23,349 (Apr. 30, 2008).
2. 75 Fed. Reg. 73,987 (Nov. 30, 2010).
3. Labor Reg. §§2550.404c-5(c)(4), 2550.404c-5(d)(3)(i) to (v)(A)-(C).

For QDIAs that are lifestyle funds, fiduciaries must also provide an explanation of the asset allocation, how the asset allocation will change over time, and the point in time when the QDIA will reach its most conservative asset allocation (including a chart, table, or graph that illustrates such change in asset allocation over time and in such a manner as to not obscure or impede a participant's or beneficiary's understanding).[1]

For QDIAs that are target date funds, fiduciaries must provide an explanation of the age group for whom it is designed, the relevance of the date and any assumptions about a participant's or beneficiary's contribution and withdrawal intentions on or after such date.[2]

Finally, the proposed regulations detail that participants and beneficiaries must receive a statement that (if applicable) they may lose money by investing in the QDIA, including losses near and following retirement, and that there is no guarantee that the QDIA will provide adequate retirement income; a description of their right to direct the investment of their assets out of the QDIA, along with a statement that certain fees and limitations may apply in connection with such a transfer; and an explanation of where they can obtain additional investment information regarding the QDIA and other investment options under the plan.[3]

In addition to the technical corrections noted above, the DOL has issued a Field Assistance Bulletin (FAB) that supplements the regulations.[4] The FAB addresses a number of issues. It affirms that fiduciary relief under the regulations can apply to assets invested in a QDIA before the regulations' effective date (December 24, 2007), if all conditions of the regulations are met. Fiduciary decisions made before that date are not eligible for relief. Fiduciary relief also can apply to assets that a participant elects to invest in a QDIA, so long as that election was made before the required notice was given. It is not necessary to distinguish between participants who invested in a QDIA intentionally and those who invested by default.

The FAB also advises that the information provided about QDIA fees and expenses, pending further guidance, generally should include: (1) the amount and description of any shareholder-type fees (e.g., current or deferred sales loads or charges, redemption fees, surrender charges, exchange fees, account fees, purchase fees, and mortality and expense fees); and (2) for investments with variable performance, the expense ratio. The fee and expense information can be provided in separate, simultaneously furnished documents (e.g., a prospectus or profile prospectus).

The QDIA notice can be furnished electronically, using either the IRS or DOL rules governing electronic media (see Q 59 for details). However, this freedom to use either set of rules does not extend to other information (e.g., investment materials).

The FAB states that the rule limiting fees and expenses during the ninety days that follow the initial QDIA investment does not apply to amounts invested before the regulations'

---

1. Labor Reg. §2550.404c-5(d)(3)(vi)(A).
2. Labor Reg. §2550.404c-5(d)(3)(vi)(B).
3. Labor Reg. §§2550.404c-5(d)(3)(vi)(C), 2550.404c-5(d)(4) and (5).
4. EBSA FAB 2008-03 (April 29, 2008), available at www.dol.gov/ebsa/regs/fab-2008-3.html.

December 24, 2007, effective date. Fees or expenses that might otherwise violate the rule will not be considered a violation if the plan sponsor or a plan service provider pays them.

Finally, the FAB details that grandfathering of stable value funds for amounts invested before the regulations' December 24, 2007, effective date was not contingent on issuing a notice thirty days before that date, but no fiduciary relief will apply until thirty days after the notice is furnished.

In a case involving a fiduciary's investment of participants' retirement plan accounts in a QDIA, the Sixth Circuit Court of Appeals upheld the trial court's decision in favor of the plan fiduciary holding that the DOL's fiduciary safe harbor for QDIA investments applied to the fiduciary's decision to transfer all participant assets in a stable value fund, as the then designated QDIA, into a lifestyle fund in order to bring their QDIA into alignment with recent DOL guidance regarding the inadequacy of stable value funds as QDIAs. The Court held this even though the plaintiff's had affirmatively elected to invest their plan assets into the stable value fund rather than having their assets placed into it by default. The action by the fiduciary in transferring 100 percent of plan assets in the stable value fund to the lifestyle fund caused the plaintiffs lost opportunity costs of approximately $85,000 and $16,900 dollars respectively.[1]

The Sixth Circuit has ruled that the QDIA safe harbor under ERISA section 404(c)(5) applies even though the funds transferred into the QDIA were originally invested by affirmative participant elections IF the safe harbor notice and other requisite conditions (detailed previously) have been satisfied.[2]

The plaintiffs in this case had affirmatively elected to invest their account balances into the Lincoln Stable Value Fund. At the time, the Stable Value Fund also was the default investment for participants who did not make affirmative elections. After the DOL released Reg. Sec. 2550.404c-5 on QDIAs, the plan sponsor decided to amend the plan's default investment to comply with those regulations. The new default investment was the Lincoln LifeSpan Fund, which satisfied the definition of a QDIA under the new regulations. The employer did not have records of which participants elected to invest in the Stable Value Fund though participants were invested in the fund by default. Accordingly, the employer sent notice of the change to all participants who were invested 100 percent in the Stable Value Fund, informing them that, if they did not provide instructions otherwise, their interest in the Stable Value Fund would be transferred to the LifeSpan Fund.

The plaintiffs claim they never received the notice and, as a result, their investments were transferred to the LifeSpan Fund without their knowledge. When they first learned of the transfer in the next quarterly account statement, they contacted the employer and had their investment switched back to the Stable Value Fund. Due to market fluctuations, they suffered losses during the time they were invested in the LifeSpan Fund.

The court ruled that the QDIA safe harbor under ERISA section 404(c)(5) is not confined to situations where a participant fails to make an investment election. It also may

---

1. *Bidwell v. Univ. Med. Ctr., Inc.*, 2012 WL 2477588 (6th Cir. 2012).
2. *Bidwell v. University Medical Center, Inc.*, 685 F.3d 613 (6th Cir. June 29, 2012).

apply with respect to transfers due to the replacement of the plan's default investment. As long as notice is furnished and participants have an opportunity to provide investment instructions, the QDIA safe harbor may apply to a situation where a participant was in an investment by election.

In so holding, the Sixth Circuit opined that the preamble to the regulations provides that the safe harbor applies to situations beyond automatic enrollment including circumstances such as "[t]he failure of a participant or beneficiary to provide investment direction following the elimination of an investment alternative or a change in service provider, the failure of a participant or beneficiary to provide investment instruction following a rollover from another plan, and any other failure of a participant or beneficiary to provide investment instruction."[1]

375. May defined benefit plan fiduciaries seek protection under the provisions of ERISA Section 404(c)?

No. The relief from fiduciary liability where participant direction of investments is allowed under ERISA Section 404(c) applies only to individual account plans. Individual account plans include (1) profit sharing plans, (2) Section 401(k) plans, (3) money purchase pension plans, and (4) Section 403(b) retirement savings plans.

Defined benefit plans provide for the payment of actuarially determined benefits to participants and beneficiaries. As such, benefits under defined benefit plans are paid from a single trust that is managed by plan fiduciaries under the general fiduciary provisions of ERISA.

376. Is compliance with ERISA Section 404(c) mandatory?

Compliance with the provisions of ERISA Section 404(c) and its attendant regulations is optional. The preamble to Labor Regulation Section 2550.404c-1 states that the transactional relief afforded under ERISA Section 404(c) is optional, and therefore, the regulations were not intended to establish standards for all ERISA-covered plans concerning the types of investments a fiduciary must make.

But the provisions of ERISA Section 404(c) do present an opportunity for plan fiduciaries to limit their exposure to liability under certain fiduciary responsibility provisions of ERISA regarding participant direction of investments in an individual account plan. It is the Department of Labor's view that the protection allowed under ERISA Section 404(c) is "similar to a statutory exception to the general fiduciary provisions of ERISA and, accordingly, the person asserting applicability of the exception will have the burden of proving that the conditions of ERISA Section 404(c) and any regulation thereunder have been met."[2] For guidance issued in 2004 on the obligations of fiduciaries to review their investments for potential mutual fund abuses, see Appendix C.

---

1. 72 Fed. Reg. 60453 (October 24, 2007).
2. See Preamble (Part I) to Labor Reg. §2550.404c-1.

377. What are the "core investment alternatives"?

Regulations state that a participant in an ERISA Section 404(c) plan must be able to select from among at least three investment alternatives

1.   Each of which is diversified;

2.   Each of which has materially different risk and return characteristics;

3.   That in the aggregate enable the participant or beneficiary, by choosing among them, to achieve a portfolio with risk and return characteristics at any point within the range normally appropriate for the participant or beneficiary; and

4.   Each of which, when combined with investment in the other alternatives, tends to minimize through diversification the overall risk of a participant's or beneficiary's portfolio.[1]

378. What is a "broad range of investment alternatives"?

An ERISA Section 404(c) plan satisfies the requisite provision of a broad range of investment alternatives if it provides the participant or beneficiary with a reasonable opportunity to

1.   Materially affect the potential degree of risk and the potential return on amounts held in his account;

2.   Choose from at least three diversified investment alternatives, each of which has materially different risk and return characteristics—core investment alternatives (see Q 377); and

3.   Diversify the investment of the portion of his individual account with respect to which he is permitted to exercise control, so as to minimize the risk of large losses, taking into account the nature of the plan and the size of participants' or beneficiaries' accounts.[2]

It is important to note that categories of investments must be diversified both between categories and within each category.[3]

For plans that have small participant account balances, the broad range of investment alternatives requirement can be met by offering "look through" investment vehicles.[4] The regulations define "look through" vehicles to include mutual funds, bank-maintained common or collective investment trust funds, bank deposits, guaranteed investment contracts, fixed-rate investment contracts, and pooled separate accounts.[5]

Only those alternatives for which sufficient information is available to participants can be taken into account in determining whether a plan provides a broad range of investment alternatives (for details as to the disclosure requirements, see Q 385).

---

1. Labor Reg. §2550.404c1(b)(3)(i)(B).
2. Labor Reg. §2550.404c-1(b)(3)(i).
3. See Labor Reg. §§2550.404c-1(b)(3)(i)(B)(1), 2550.404c-1(b)(3)(i)(C).
4. See Labor Reg. §2550.404c-1(b)(3)(ii).
5. Labor Reg. §2550.404c-1(e)(1).

The requirement of prudence will be applied to fiduciaries in the selection of "look through" investment vehicles and managers of "look through" vehicles. For guidance issued in 2004 on the obligations of fiduciaries to review their investments for potential mutual fund abuses, see Appendix C.

The Ninth Circuit has ruled that ERISA section 404(c) relief does not apply to the imprudent fiduciary decisions regarding the selection of investment options to be placed onto the plan's participant investment menu.[1]

This ruling brings the Ninth Circuit into agreement with the DOL's previously stated position on this issue (DOL Reg. Sec. 2550.404a-5(f)), as well as the Fourth[2], Sixth[3] and Seventh Circuits[4].

379. What constitutes a "reasonable opportunity" to give investment instructions under an ERISA Section 404(c) plan?

With regard to the three core investments that create the broad range of investment alternatives[5] (see Q 377), a 404(c) plan must give participants and beneficiaries a reasonable opportunity to give investment instructions no less frequently than once within any three-month period.[6]

The plan may impose reasonable restrictions on participants and beneficiaries as to the number of times they may give investment instructions. Such restrictions are reasonable only if they permit participants and beneficiaries to issue investment instructions with a frequency that is appropriate in light of the market volatility to which the investment alternative may reasonably be expected to be subject.[7]

In investment alternatives that are subject to a volatile market, the plan must permit the transfer of assets into one of the core investment alternatives with the same reasonable frequency as that which applies to the more volatile alternative (even if it is more frequent than once every three months). The preamble to the 404(c) regulations clearly states that the volatility rule allows more frequent transfers into the core alternatives and not in and out of the core alternatives.[8]

ERISA Section 404(c) plans may satisfy the volatility rule by permitting participants and beneficiaries to transfer their investments from volatile alternatives into "income producing, low risk, liquid funds" at least as often as they permit participants and beneficiaries to give investment instructions in the particular investment alternative. This allows for a safe place for participants and beneficiaries to place their assets (i.e., a "cash equivalency" vehicle), from

---

1. *Tibble v. Edison International*, 711 F. 3d 1061 (9th Cir. March 21, 2013).
2. *DiFelice v. U.S. Airways, Inc.*, 497 F.3d 410 (4th Cir. 2007).
3. *Pfeil v. State Street Bank & Trust Co.*, 671 F.3d 585 (6th Cir. 2012).
4. *Howell v. Motorola, Inc.*, 633 F.3d 552 (7th Cir. 2011)).
5. As mandated by Labor Reg. §2550.404c-1(b)(3)(i)(B).
6. See Labor Reg. §2550.404c-1(b)(2)(ii)(C)(1).
7. See Labor Reg. §2550.404c-1(b)(2)(ii)(C).
8. See Labor Reg. §2550.404c-1(b)(2)(ii)(C)(2)(i).

which they may then direct assets into another investment vehicle when the next scheduled opportunity presents itself.[1]

380. What is "opportunity to exercise control" in an ERISA Section 404(c) plan?

In an ERISA Section 404(c) plan, fiduciaries must provide specific instructions to participants and beneficiaries on how they may exercise control over the assets in their participant accounts. These instructions must be presented in writing.

Under the regulations, a participant or beneficiary is deemed to have exercised control over the assets in his account if the participant or beneficiary has

1.   A reasonable opportunity to give to an identified plan fiduciary investment instructions in writing (or by other means such as over the telephone) with an opportunity to receive a written confirmation that the instructions have been received and acted upon; and

2.   The opportunity to obtain sufficient information to make an informed investment decision.[2]

Instructions must be affirmatively given by participants and beneficiaries in order for the protections of ERISA Section 404(c) to cover plan fiduciaries. If a participant or beneficiary refuses to give investment instructions regarding his account under the plan, fiduciaries have an obligation to prudently invest those assets on behalf of the individual participant or beneficiary who refuses to exercise control.[3]

Plan fiduciaries may offer participants and beneficiaries an opportunity to exercise control over certain portions of their plan account assets and still maintain the protection available under ERISA Section 404(c). If fiduciaries limit such control for participants and beneficiaries, they will be afforded the protections of ERISA Section 404(c) only with regard to transactions over which they have provided participants and beneficiaries an opportunity to exercise control in conformity with the requirements of the regulations identified above.

Under the first prominent ERISA Section 404(c) case, the Court of Appeals for the Third Circuit ruled that any fiduciary who seeks protection under the ERISA provisions excusing a fiduciary from liability for any loss that results from a participant's exercise of control over an investment bears the burden of showing its application. Further, the court held that fiduciaries seeking protection must establish a causal nexus between the participant's exercise of control and the claimed loss.[4]

---

1. See Labor Reg. §2550.404c-1(b)(2)(ii)(C)(2)(ii).
2. Labor Reg. §§2550.404c-1(b)(2)(A), 2550.404c-1(b)(2)(B).
3. Preamble to Labor Reg. §2550.404c-1.
4. See *In re Unisys Sav. Plan Litig. v. Unisys Corp.*, 74 F.3d 420 (3d Cir. 1996), reh'g denied, 173 F.3d 145 (3d Cir. 1999).

Practitioner's Pointer: It is recommended, when setting up an ERISA Section 404(c) program for a plan, that "identified fiduciaries" to whom investment instructions are to be delivered be identified by their position title. This saves the time and effort necessary to amend the documents if the fiduciaries are identified by name and they subsequently vacate their positions as fiduciaries.

381. To what extent may a fiduciary offer investment education and still maintain the protection from liability provided under ERISA Section 404(c)?

Fiduciaries are not required to offer investment advice under an ERISA Section 404(c) plan.[1] But many plan sponsors recognize that some participants may not be able to make sound decisions regarding their plan accounts because they simply do not possess the investment expertise to do so. The DOL has provided guidance for plan sponsors who would like to provide some assistance for these participants and beneficiaries, while still maintaining their protection from liability.[2] For details of this guidance, see Q 243. For guidance issued in 2004 on the obligations of fiduciaries to review their investments for potential mutual fund abuses, see Appendix C.

Regulations under ERISA Section 3(21)(A)(ii) provide in pertinent part that a fiduciary "renders investment advice" if

1.   He renders advice as to the value of securities or other property, or makes recommendations as to the advisability of investing in, purchasing, or selling securities or other property; and

2.   He either directly or indirectly has discretionary authority or control with respect to purchasing or selling securities or other property for the participant or beneficiary, or renders any advice described in item one above, on a regular basis to the participant or beneficiary pursuant to an agreement, arrangement, or understanding, written or unwritten, between the person and the participant or beneficiary that such services will serve as the primary basis for the participant's or beneficiary's investment decisions with respect to plan assets, and that the person will render individualized investment advice to the participant or beneficiary based on the particular needs of the participant or beneficiary.

The decision whether the provision of investment education is the rendering of investment advice is made on a case-by-case basis, by considering the relevant facts and circumstances of the particular case. See Q 243 for a description of four "safe harbor" categories of information that may be provided that, in the opinion of the Department of Labor, will not constitute the rendering of investment advice under ERISA Section 3(21)(A)(ii) and Labor Regulation Section 2510.3-21(c).

The Securities and Exchange Commission has noted that plan sponsors (not third parties hired by the plan sponsor) who offer investment education under an ERISA Section 404(c)

---

1. Labor Reg. §2550.404c-1(c)(4).
2. See Labor Reg. §2509.96-1 (I.B. 96-1), 61 Fed. Reg. 29,586 (June 11, 1996).

plan will not be considered investment advisers for purposes of the Investment Advisers Act of 1940.[1]

382. Are fiduciaries of ERISA Section 404(c) plans required to exercise prudence in the selection and monitoring of educators and advisers?

Yes. In the context of an ERISA Section 404(c) plan, neither the designation of a person to provide education nor the designation of a beneficiary to provide investment advice to participants and beneficiaries will, in itself, give rise to fiduciary liability for loss with respect to any breach of the fiduciary responsibility provisions of ERISA (i.e., Part 4 of Title I) that is the direct and necessary result of a participant's or beneficiary's exercise of independent control over her account.[2]

Otherwise, the fiduciaries of an ERISA Section 404(c) plan are required to exercise the same prudence in the selection and monitoring of educators and advisers as is required with any designation of a service provider to a plan. Such a selection is an exercise of discretionary authority or control with respect to the management of the plan; consequently, persons making decisions regarding the appointment of persons to provide investment educational services or investment advice to plan participants and beneficiaries must act solely in the interests of those participants and beneficiaries (as required under ERISA Section 404(a)), as well as in continuing any such designations.[3]

However, the DOL also notes in Interpretive Bulletin 96-1 that a plan sponsor or fiduciary will have no fiduciary responsibility or liability with respect to the actions of a third party selected by a participant or beneficiary to provide education or investment advice where the plan sponsor or fiduciary neither selects nor endorses the educator or adviser, nor otherwise makes arrangements with the educator or adviser to provide such services.

The Sixth Circuit has ruled that a trustee's conduct was within the ERISA Section 404(c) safe harbor where the evidence was sufficient to demonstrate that the plaintiffs had exercised sufficient control over their individual accounts, including an agreement with the trustee that held that in order to purchase an asset, the plaintiffs would sign a directive telling the trustee what to do.[4] These forms expressly disclaimed the trustee's liability for the transaction. For directives to purchase loans, the forms instructed the trustee not to monitor the loans or investigate whether the transactions were somehow illegal. For directives purchasing assets that were not publicly traded, the forms directed the trustee to use the asset's cost basis rather than its market value (since there was none available) for accounting purposes.

The two plaintiffs had sued the plan's trustee after discovering that their accounts had suffered substantial losses through the actions of the investment adviser whom both participants had appointed to manage their individually directed accounts. The participants alleged that the trustee knew that their investment adviser was a criminal involved in theft and embezzlement

---

1. See I.B. 96-1, 61 Fed. Reg. 29,586 (June 11, 1996).
2. Labor Reg. §2509.96-1 (I.B. 96-1), 61 Fed. Reg. 29,586 (June 11, 1996).
3. Labor Reg. §2509.96-1(e) (I.B. 96-1(e)), above.
4. *Tullis v. UMB Bank N.A.*, 2011 WL 1885978 (6th Cir. 2011).

and had a duty to protect their account balances from the losses the plaintiffs experienced as a result of the theft of more than $1.5 million from their accounts by the investment adviser.[1]

383. Which fiduciary responsibilities may not be relieved under ERISA Section 404(c)?

Fiduciaries of ERISA Section 404(c) plans retain responsibility under ERISA for the general fiduciary provisions regarding the selection and monitoring of investment alternatives and investment managers (unless the plan participants have been granted authority to select investment managers under the plan and have exercised that authority). Fiduciaries are also obligated to observe the ERISA Section 406 restrictions on prohibited transactions. Furthermore, plan fiduciaries are responsible for providing notice under Labor Regulation Section 2550.404c-1 and for timely implementing the written investment instructions of ERISA Section 404(c) plan participants.

Fiduciaries of an ERISA Section 404(c) plan are also responsible for any situations of co-fiduciary liability that may arise under ERISA Section 405, with the exception of breaches that are the direct result of a participant's exercising direct control over the assets in his account. The regulations provide an example of this exception, where a participant independently exercises control over assets in his account by directing a fiduciary to invest 100 percent of his account balance in a single stock. In this situation, the participant will not be considered a fiduciary to the plan and the fiduciary will not be held liable for any losses that necessarily result from the participant's exercise of control.[2]

The Seventh Circuit has ruled that a plan sponsor's selection of investment options available to plan participants is not an action that falls under the protections of ERISA Section 404(c).[3] In this stock drop case, the Seventh Circuit considered, among other things, whether the safe-harbor protections for fiduciaries under ERISA Section 404(c) apply to the employer's investment fund selection for its participant-directed 401(k) plan. Though it ruled that the safe-harbor protections did not apply to the selection of the investment options, the court ruled that the 404(c) safe harbor protections did extend to the defendants regarding the failure to appoint competent fiduciaries to oversee the investment options.[4]

In a stock drop case, participants in two primary 401(k) retirement plans sponsored by General Motors claimed that the plan's fiduciary breached its duty by continuing to allow participants to invest their 401(k) plan accounts in employer stock even though public information indicated that the plan sponsor was headed for bankruptcy. The trial court dismissed the claim, holding, in part, that the participants could have transferred their individual account investments away from the stock fund at any time. On appeal, the Sixth Circuit ruled that the defendants claim that they were protected by the safe harbor provisions of ERISA section 404(c) was inappropriate for at the pleadings stage for purposes of granting a summary motion to dismiss. More importantly,

---

1. *Tullis v. UMB Bank N.A.*, 2011 WL 1885978 (6th Cir. 2011).
2. See Labor Reg. §2550.404c-1(f)(5).
3. *Howell v. Motorola Inc.*, 2011 WL 183966 (7th Cir. 2011).
4. *Howell v. Motorola Inc.*, above.

the Sixth Circuit also ruled against the defendants substantive 404(c) safe harbor protection claim by holding that "under the circumstances … it does not relieve fiduciaries of the responsibility to screen investments."[1]

384. Does ERISA Section 404(c) apply to SIMPLE plans?

Yes, ERISA Section 404(c) protections are extended to SIMPLE plan fiduciaries if a participant or beneficiary is treated as exercising control over the assets in his account as described below.

There are two different types of SIMPLE (Savings Incentive Match Plans for Employees) plans: SIMPLE IRA plans and SIMPLE 401(k) plans. Both are generally for employers who have 100 or fewer employees, and who do not sponsor any other qualified retirement plan (employers sponsoring a SIMPLE 401(k) plan may have another qualified plan provided it does not cover any of the same employees as covered by the SIMPLE 401(k) plan).

Under both types of SIMPLE plans, eligible employees may defer up to $11,500 (indexed in 2010) of earned income into their plan account on an annual basis. Generally, the employer must either provide a dollar-for-dollar matching contribution of up to 3 percent of compensation (a 1 percent match is available under limited circumstances in a SIMPLE IRA) or, alternately, a 2 percent of compensation nonelective contribution to all eligible participants, regardless of whether or not they are actively deferring earned income into the plan account. All contributions are immediately 100 percent vested in the plan participants.[2] Furthermore, certain catch-up contributions by participants age fifty or over may be permitted.[3]

SIMPLE plan fiduciaries are subject to the various fiduciary requirements of ERISA regarding the selection and monitoring of any financial institutions designated to receive plan contributions. A participant or beneficiary will be treated as exercising control over the assets in his account (and the protections of ERISA Section 404(c) will thus be extended to the SIMPLE plan fiduciaries) on the earliest of the following:

1. An affirmative election among investment options with respect to the initial investment of any contribution;

2. A rollover to any SIMPLE IRA or individual retirement plan; or

3. One year after the SIMPLE retirement account is established.

SIMPLE plans subject to ERISA Section 404(c) must also comply with all of the other requirements non-SIMPLE plans must satisfy in order to afford fiduciaries protection from liability.

385. What are the disclosure requirements for plan sponsors attempting to comply with ERISA Section 404(c) regulations?

If a participant, in fact, exercises control over the assets in his account, the regulations under ERISA Section 404(c) state that he is not treated as a fiduciary and fiduciaries of the plan will

1. *Pfeil v. State Street Bank & Trust Co.*, 2012 WL 555481 (6th Cir. 2012).
2. See IRC Secs. 408(p), 401(k)(11).
3. See IRC Sec. 414(v).

not be liable for any loss or for any breach of fiduciary duty that is the result of the participant's exercise of control over assets in his own account.[1]

In order to be afforded the protection of this limited liability, fiduciaries must comply with the requirement that they provide a broad range of investment alternatives (see Q 378), the requirement that they provide sufficient opportunities to give investment instructions regarding a participant's individual account (see Q 375), and the mandatory disclosure requirement of the items described below. For guidance issued in 2004 on the obligations of fiduciaries to review their investments for potential mutual fund abuses, see Appendix C.

Effective December 20, 2010, the DOL amended the ERISA Section 404(c) regulations to delete the former mandatory disclosure requirements (detailed below in items one through nine). In their place, the DOL has issued new individual account plan disclosure regulations, which are reviewed in detail under Q 97.[2] Under the former requirements, an identified plan fiduciary, or duly appointed representative, was required to provide each plan participant or beneficiary the following information:

1. A written explanation that the plan is intended to be an ERISA Section 404(c) plan and that plan fiduciaries may be relieved of liability for losses that are a result of participant investment instructions;

2. A description of the investment alternatives under the plan and a general description of the investment objectives and risk/return characteristics of each alternative, including information relating to the type and diversification of assets comprising that portfolio;

3. Identification of any designated investment managers the plan might provide for the participants;

4. An explanation of how to give investment instructions, any limits/restrictions on giving instructions (including information on withdrawal penalties and valuation adjustments) as well as any restrictions on the exercise of voting, tender, or similar rights;

5. A description of transaction fees or expenses that are charged to the participant's account (e.g., commissions);

6. If the plan provides for investment in employer securities, a description of those procedures established to provide for confidentiality to participants regarding their transactions in those securities—this requirement includes the name, address, and telephone number of any fiduciary in charge of maintaining such confidentiality and information on independent fiduciaries that are required in transactions that involve employer securities where there is a high potential for a conflict of interest;

---

1. Former Labor Reg. §2550.404c-1.
2. 75 Fed. Reg. 64,910 (Oct. 20, 2010).

7. Shareholder information, subsequent to a specific investment, including any material the plan receives regarding the exercise of voting and ownership rights to the extent such rights are passed through to the participant, along with references to any plan provisions regarding the exercise of these rights;

8. Copy of the most recent prospectus, which must be provided participants immediately after they have made an initial purchase of an investment that is subject to the Securities Act of 1933 (this may also be satisfied by providing the prospectus prior to the initial purchase); and

9. A description of those materials available only upon request (see below) and the identification of the person responsible for providing that information.[1]

NOTE: The DOL issued an advisory opinion stating that Section 404(c) plans may satisfy the disclosure requirement of the most recent prospectus (item eight, above) by providing participants with summaries of a prospectus, or "profiles," instead of providing a full prospectus that is less up-to-date. If requested by a participant, however, the plan was still required to provide a copy of the prospectus itself.[2]

In January 2009, the SEC published updated rules for an enhanced disclosure framework for mutual funds, including a new Summary Prospectus rule. The new Summary Prospectus rule provided for a Summary Prospectus as an optional means to comply with the Act's requirement to deliver a statutory prospectus to an investor upon the purchase of mutual fund shares. The Summary Prospectus was required to include information on how to obtain the full statutory prospectus. The DOL issued Field Assistance Bulletin 2009-03, which states that a mutual fund "Summary Prospectus" may be used to comply with the requirement in the ERISA 404(c) regulations that a plan fiduciary provide a prospectus to a participant or beneficiary.[3] The DOL advises that a Summary Prospectus would satisfy 404(c) regulations because the required contents of the Summary Prospectus provide the type of key information about a mutual fund that participants and beneficiaries need to make informed investment decisions. The DOL specifically notes that a fiduciary may satisfy the ERISA 404(c) requirement to furnish a prospectus immediately before or after a participant's initial investment in a mutual fund by delivering the most recent Summary Prospectus received by the plan. And if a participant requests a prospectus, and the most recent prospectus received by the plan is a Summary Prospectus, the fiduciary will comply with ERISA 404(c) if she provides such Summary Prospectus in response to the request.

Effective December 20, 2010, the DOL amended the ERISA Section 404(c) regulations to delete the former disclosure requirements that must issue upon request of the participant or beneficiary (detailed below in items one through five). In their place, the DOL has issued new individual account plan disclosure regulations, which are reviewed in detail under Q 97.[4]

---

1. See Labor Reg. §2550.404c-1(b)(2)(i)(B)(1).
2. DOL Adv. Op. 2003-11A.
3. DOL Field Assistance Bull. 2009-03 (Sept. 8, 2009).
4. 75 Fed. Reg. 64,910 (Oct. 20, 2010).

ERISA Section 404(c) plans must also provide the following information to participants and beneficiaries, but only if specifically requested:

1.   A description of the annual operating expenses borne by plan investment alternatives, such as investment management fees; also included would be any expense charges or recordkeeping fees, expressed as a percentage of the net assets of the investment, that may reduce the participant's return in the underlying investment;

2.   Copies of financial statements, annual reports, or other information relating to an investment alternative, to the extent it has been provided to the plan;

3.   List of assets in each designated investment alternative and the value of each asset, as well as the name of the contract issuer and the rate of return on fixed-rate investment contracts (such as GICs and BICs);

4.   Information concerning the share value or unit value of investment alternatives available to participants, as well as information concerning the past and current investment performance of the investment option; and

5.   Value of shares or units in investment alternatives held in the account of a participant.[1]

The Securities and Exchange Commission issued a final rule that permits mutual funds to offer investors an easier-to-read and less technical summary disclosure document referred to as a "profile" that is intended to make it easier for investors to understand a fund's risks, strategies, and performance. Mutual fund companies are permitted to tailor these profiles for 404(c) participants and to include enrollment forms for participating in the fund. The SEC appears to have considered the DOL's publicly stated concerns regarding the level of disclosure and understanding of information regarding risks and fees plan participants receive.[2]

386. Under what circumstances may an ERISA Section 404(c) plan fiduciary refuse to follow affirmative investment instructions from a participant or beneficiary?

Identified ERISA Section 404(c) plan fiduciaries are generally required to follow any affirmative investment instructions they receive from participants or beneficiaries. But identified plan fiduciaries are not required to follow affirmative investment instructions that, if carried out, would

1.   Result in the occurrence of a prohibited transaction (see Section IV);

2.   Result in the receipt of taxable income to the plan;

3.   Place the plan in jeopardy of losing its tax-qualified status under IRC Section 401;

4.   Violate the plan documents and the plan's governing instruments (insofar as they are consistent with the provisions of ERISA);

---

1. See Former Labor Reg. §2550.404c-1(b)(2)(i)(B)(2).
2. SEC Final Rule, 63 Fed. Reg. 13,968 (Mar. 23, 1998).

5.   Result in the maintenance of any indicia of ownership outside the United States or outside the jurisdiction of the United States district courts;

6.   Subject the participant's or beneficiary's account to a loss in excess of the actual account balance; or

7.   Result in the occurrence of prohibited self-dealing under ERISA (see Section IV), such as a sale, exchange, or leasing of property between a plan sponsor and the plan (except for ERISA Section 408 specified exemptions), a loan to a plan sponsor or affiliate, acquisition or sale of any employer real property, or the acquisition or sale of any employer securities (except for those specifically permitted under the regulations, see Q 387).[1]

387. When may a participant or beneficiary invest in employer securities under an ERISA Section 404(c) plan?

An ERISA Section 404(c) plan may permit the investment of participant or beneficiary assets in employer securities if the following requirements have been satisfied:

1.   The securities are "qualifying employer securities" (see Section VIII);

2.   The securities are (a) stock or (b) an equity interest in certain publicly traded partnerships;[2]

3.   The securities are publicly traded on a national exchange or other generally recognized market;

4.   The securities are traded with sufficient frequency and in sufficient volume to assure that participant or beneficiary directions to buy and sell the security may be acted upon promptly and efficiently;

5.   Information provided to shareholders of such securities is provided to participants and beneficiaries with accounts holding such securities;

6.   Voting, tender, and similar rights are passed through to participants and beneficiaries with accounts holding such securities;

7.   Information is maintained regarding the confidentiality procedures that relate to the purchase, holding, and sale of securities, and the exercise of voting, tender, and similar rights with respect to such securities by participants and beneficiaries, except to the extent necessary to comply with federal laws or state laws not preempted by ERISA;

8.   The plan designates a fiduciary who is responsible for ensuring that the confidentiality procedures designed to satisfy the safeguards mandated under the preceding paragraph (seven) are being followed; and

---

1. Labor Reg. §§2550.404c-1(b)(2)(ii)(B), 2550.404c-1(d)(2)(ii).
2. As defined in IRC Section 7704(b) and Labor Reg. §2550.404c-1(d)(2)(ii)(E)(4)(ii).

9.   An independent fiduciary is appointed to carry out activities where there is the potential for undue influence on participants and beneficiaries with regard to the direct or indirect exercise of shareholder rights.[1]

Where an ERISA Section 404(c) plan does permit employer securities as an investment alternative, participants or beneficiaries must be allowed to transfer the assets invested in the employer securities alternative into any of the three mandated core investments as frequently as the participant or beneficiary is allowed to give investment instructions to the employer securities alternative. Participants and beneficiaries must also be permitted to transfer their assets out of the employer securities alternative into the low income producing cash equivalency alternative as often as the participant or beneficiary is permitted to give investment instructions to the employer securities alternative.[2]

388. How are ERISA Section 404(c) plans affected by the use of investment managers?

Investment managers' decisions regarding the management of 404(c) plan participant assets "are not direct and necessary results" of their designation. In other words, the investment managers charged with the management and investment of ERISA Section 404(c) plan assets may not claim relief from their fiduciary obligations, and will retain responsibility for them, in spite of the fact that they have been appointed in accordance with the applicable regulations under ERISA Section 404(c).[3]

ERISA Section 404(c) plans may permit the selection of investment managers by individual participants, or the plan may provide for the designation of investment managers from whom the participants may make a selection. If this is the case, the employer will retain its fiduciary obligations to prudently select and monitor the investment managers. For guidance issued in 2004 on the obligations of fiduciaries to review their investments for potential mutual fund abuses, see Appendix C.

389. What are the fiduciary rules associated with investing automatic enrollment contributions of participants who do not provide investment direction in a participant-directed individual account plan?

The Pension Protection Act of 2006 (PPA 2006)[4] amended ERISA Section 404(c) to provide relief to fiduciaries that invest participant assets in certain types of default investment alternatives in the absence of participant investment direction.

Specifically, PPA 2006 Section 624(a) added new ERISA Section 404(c)(5)(A) and ERISA Section 404(c)(5)(B). ERISA Section 404(c)(5)(A) provides that, for purposes of ERISA Section 404(c)(1), a participant in an individual account plan will be treated as exercising control over the assets in the account for the amount of contributions and earnings that, in the absence of an

---

1. Labor Reg. §2550.404c-1(d)(2)(ii)(E)(4).
2. Labor Reg. §2550.404c-1(b)(2)(ii)(C)(3)(ii).
3. See Labor Reg. §2550.404c-1(d)(2)(iii).
4. Pub. L. No. 109-280.

investment election by the participant, are invested by the plan in accordance with regulations prescribed by the DOL, These regulations provide guidance on the appropriateness of designating default investments that include a mix of asset classes consistent with capital preservation or long-term capital appreciation, or a blend of both.

ERISA Section 404(c)(5)(B) provides that the notice requirements are satisfied if each participant

1.   Receives, within a reasonable period of time before each plan year, a notice explaining the employee's right under the plan to designate how contributions and earnings will be invested and explaining how, in the absence of any investment election by the participant, such contributions and earnings will be invested; and

2.   Has a reasonable period of time after receipt of such notice and before the beginning of the plan year to make such designation.

ERISA Section 404(c)(5) removes impediments to employers' adopting automatic enrollment arrangements, including employer fears about legal liability for market fluctuations and the applicability of state wage withholding laws.

In accordance with PPA 2006, the DOL issued Labor Regulation Section 2550.404c-5,[1] implementing the PPA 2006 provisions providing relief to plan fiduciaries who invest the assets of participants who do not provide investment direction in participant-directed plans (such as automatically enrolled workers) in "qualified default investment alternatives" or QDIAs.

A fiduciary of a plan that complies with Labor Regulation Section 2550.404c-5 will not be liable for any loss, or by reason of any breach, that occurs as a result of such investments. The regulation describes the types of investments that qualify as default investment alternatives under ERISA Section 404(c)(5), as described in detail below. But plan fiduciaries remain responsible for the prudent selection and monitoring of the QDIA. The regulation conditions relief upon advance notice to participants and beneficiaries describing the circumstances under which contributions or other assets will be invested on their behalf in a QDIA, the investment objectives of the QDIA, and the right of participants and beneficiaries to direct investments out of the QDIA.

The relief afforded by ERISA Section 404(c)(5) is not conditioned on a plan's being an ERISA 404(c) plan or otherwise meeting the requirements of Labor Regulation Section 2550.404c-5.[2] The amendments made by PPA 2006 Section 624 apply to plan years beginning after December 31, 2006, and Labor Regulation Section 2550.404c-5 is effective on December 24, 2007.

Scope of Relief under the Regulation

The scope of fiduciary relief provided by the regulation is the same as that extended to plan fiduciaries under ERISA Section 404(c)(1)(B) in connection with carrying out investment

---

1. 72 Fed. Reg. 60,452 (Oct. 24, 2007).
2. See Section A to the Preamble to Labor Regulation §2550.404c-1.

directions of plan participants and beneficiaries in an "ERISA Section 404(c) plan," as described in Labor Regulation Section 2550.404c-1(a). As with ERISA Section 404(c)(1) and Labor Regulation Section 2550.404c-1, the regulation does not provide relief from the general fiduciary rules applicable to the selection and monitoring of a particular qualified default investment alternative or from any liability that results from a failure to satisfy these duties, including liability for any resulting losses.

Under the regulation and the fiduciary relief afforded by ERISA Section 404(c)(5), a participant who does not give investment directions will be treated as exercising control over her account with respect to assets that the plan invests in a qualified default investment alternative, and a fiduciary of an individual account plan that permits participants and beneficiaries to direct the investment of assets in their accounts and that meets the conditions of the regulation is not liable for any loss under ERISA Section 404 or by reason of any breach that is the direct and necessary result of investing all or part of a participant's or beneficiary's account in any QDIA, or of investment decisions made by the entities described in the regulation in connection with the management of a QDIA. As long as a plan fiduciary selects any of the QDIAs, and otherwise complies with the conditions of the regulation, the plan fiduciary will obtain the fiduciary relief described in the regulation.

Conditions for Fiduciary Relief

Labor Regulation Section 2550.404c-5 contains six conditions for relief, set forth in paragraph (c) of the regulation, which provides that a fiduciary will qualify for the relief if all of the conditions below are satisfied:

1. Assets are invested in a qualified default investment alternative, as described in detail below.

2. The participant or beneficiary on whose behalf the investment is made had the opportunity to direct the investment of the assets in her account but did not direct the investment of the assets.

3. The participant or beneficiary on whose behalf an investment in a QDIA may be made is furnished a notice that meets the notice requirements described in detail below. The notice must be provided (a) at least thirty days in advance of the date of plan eligibility, or at least thirty days in advance of the date of any first investment in a QDIA on behalf of a participant or beneficiary described in condition two above; or (b) on or before the date of plan eligibility provided the participant has the opportunity to make a permissible withdrawal (as determined under IRC Section 414(w)); and within a reasonable period of time of at least thirty days in advance of each subsequent plan year.

Practitioner's Pointer: This condition requires both an initial notice and an annual notice. The initial notice generally must be furnished to participants and beneficiaries in advance of the first investment in the QDIA. The annual notice is provided yearly thereafter. The information that must be included in the notice is described in the regulation and below.

4. A fiduciary provides to a participant or beneficiary the material set forth in Labor Regulation Section 2550.404c-1(b)(2)(i)(B)(1)(viii), Labor Regulation Section 2550.404c-1(b)(2)(i)(B)(1)(ix), and Labor Regulation Section 2550.404c-1(b)(2)(i)(B)(2) relating to a participant's or beneficiary's investment in a QDIA (e.g., account statements, prospectuses, proxy voting material).

5. Any participant or beneficiary on whose behalf assets are invested in a QDIA may transfer, in whole or in part, such assets to any other investment alternative available under the plan with a frequency consistent with that afforded to a participant or beneficiary who elected to invest in the QDIA, but not less frequently than once within any three-month period.

Except as provided below, any such transfer, or any permissible withdrawal as determined under IRC Section 414(w)(2), by a participant or beneficiary of assets invested in a QDIA, in whole or in part, resulting from the participant's or beneficiary's election to make such a transfer or withdrawal during the 90-day period beginning on the date of the participant's first elective contribution as determined under IRC Section 414(w)(2)(B), or other first investment in a QDIA on behalf of a participant or beneficiary described above, may not be subject to any restrictions, fees, or expenses (including surrender charges, liquidation or exchange fees, redemption fees, and similar expenses charged in connection with the liquidation of, or transfer from, the investment). But such restrictions, fees, or expenses do not apply to fees and expenses that are charged on an ongoing basis for the operation of the investment itself—such as investment management fees, distribution and/or service fees, "12b-1" fees, or legal, accounting, transfer agent, and similar administrative expenses—and are not imposed, or do not vary, based on a participant's or beneficiary's decision to withdraw, sell, or transfer assets out of the qualified default investment alternative.

Additionally, following the end of the 90-day period described above, any transfer or permissible withdrawal is not subject to any restrictions, fees, or expenses not otherwise applicable to a participant or beneficiary who elected to invest in that QDIA.

Practitioner's Pointer: The fifth condition of the regulation requires that participants and beneficiaries must have the opportunity to direct investments out of a QDIA as frequently as from other plan investments, but at least quarterly, and includes three conditions applicable to a defaulted participant's or beneficiary's ability to move assets out of a QDIA. The regulation also limits the imposition of any restrictions, fees, or expenses (other than investment management and similar types of fees and expenses) during the first ninety days of a defaulted participant's or beneficiary's investment in the qualified default investment alternative. At the end of the ninety-day period, defaulted participants and beneficiaries may be subject to the restrictions, fees, or expenses that are otherwise applicable to participants and beneficiaries under the plan who elected to invest in that qualified default investment alternative.

---

6. The plan offers a "broad range of investment alternatives" within the meaning of Labor Regulation Section 2550.404c-1(b)(3) (and under ERISA Section 404(c)).

Qualified Default Investment Alternative

Labor Regulation Section 2550.404c-5(e) defines a qualified default investment alternative (QDIA) as an investment alternative available to participants and beneficiaries that

1.   Does not hold or permit the acquisition of employer securities, except (a) employer securities held or acquired by an investment company registered under the Investment Company Act of 1940 or a similar pooled investment vehicle regulated and subject to periodic examination by a state or federal agency and with respect to which investment in such securities is made in accordance with the stated investment objectives of the investment vehicle and independent of the plan sponsor or an affiliate thereof; or (b) with respect to a qualified default investment alternative that is an "investment management service" described in more detail below,[1] employer securities acquired as a matching contribution from the employer/plan sponsor, or employer securities acquired prior to management by the investment management service to the extent the investment management service has discretionary authority over the disposition of such employer securities;

2.   Satisfies the requirements of the regulation regarding the ability of a participant or beneficiary to transfer, in whole or in part, her investment from the qualified default investment alternative to any other investment alternative available under the plan;

3.   Is

     a.   managed by (i) an investment manager, within the meaning of ERISA Section 3(38); (ii) a trustee of the plan that meets the requirements of ERISA Section 3(38)(A), (B), and (C); or (iii) the plan sponsor who is a named fiduciary, within the meaning of ERISA Section 402(a)(2);

     b.   an investment company registered under the Investment Company Act of 1940; or

     c.   an investment product or fund described in Labor Regulation Section 2550.404c-5(e)(4)(iv) (discussed below); and

4.   Constitutes one of the following:

     a.   an investment fund product or model portfolio that applies generally accepted investment theories, is diversified so as to minimize the risk of large losses, and is designed to provide varying degrees of long-term appreciation and capital preservation through a mix of equity and fixed-income exposures based on the participant's age, target retirement date (such as normal retirement age under the plan), or life expectancy. Such products and portfolios change their asset allocations and associated risk levels over

---

1. See Labor Reg. §2550.404c-5(e)(4)(iii).

time with the objective of becoming more conservative (i.e., decreasing risk of losses) with increasing age. For this purpose, asset allocation decisions for such products and portfolios are not required to take into account risk tolerances, investments, or other preferences of an individual participant. An example of such a fund or portfolio may be a "life-cycle" or "targeted-retirement-date" fund or account.

b.   an investment fund product or model portfolio that applies generally accepted investment theories, is diversified so as to minimize the risk of large losses, and is designed to provide long-term appreciation and capital preservation through a mix of equity and fixed-income exposures consistent with a target level of risk appropriate for participants of the plan as a whole. For this purpose, asset allocation decisions for such products and portfolios are not required to take into account the age, risk tolerances, investments, or other preferences of an individual participant. An example of such a fund or portfolio may be a "balanced" fund.

Practitioner's Pointer: This alternative might be a "stand-alone" product or a "fund of funds" comprising various investment options otherwise available under the plan for participant investments. In the context of a "fund of funds" portfolio, it is likely that money market, stable value, and similarly performing capital preservation vehicles will play a role in the mix of equity and fixed-income exposures for this alternative.

c.   an investment management service with respect to which a fiduciary (i.e., an investment manager, within the meaning of ERISA Section 3(38); a trustee of the plan that meets the requirements of ERISA Section 3(38)(A), (B), and (C); or the plan sponsor who is a named fiduciary, within the meaning of ERISA Section 402(a)(2)), applying generally accepted investment theories, allocates the assets of a participant's individual account to achieve varying degrees of long-term appreciation and capital preservation through a mix of equity and fixed-income exposures, offered through investment alternatives available under the plan, based on the participant's age, target retirement date (such as normal retirement age under the plan), or life expectancy. Such portfolios are diversified so as to minimize the risk of large losses and change their asset allocations and associated risk levels for an individual account over time with the objective of becoming more conservative (i.e., decreasing risk of losses) with increasing age. For this purpose, asset allocation decisions are not required to take into account risk tolerances, investments, or other preferences of an individual participant. An example of such a service may be a "managed account."

d.   an investment product or fund designed to preserve principal and provide a reasonable rate of return, whether or not such return is guaranteed, consistent with liquidity. For this purpose, the investment product must (i) seek to maintain, over the term of the investment, the dollar value that is equal to the amount invested in the product; and (ii) be offered by a state- or federally regulated financial institution. But the investment product will only constitute a qualified default investment for no more than 120 days after the date of the participant's first elective contribution.[1]

Practitioner's Pointer: This limited capital preservation option allows plan sponsors to reduce investment risks following an employee's initial enrollment in the plan for purposes of contributions made on behalf of the participant for a 120-day period following the date of the participant's first elective contribution.

---

e. an investment product or fund designed to guarantee principal and a rate of return generally consistent with that earned on intermediate investment grade bonds, while providing liquidity for withdrawals by participants and beneficiaries, including transfers to other investment alternatives. Such investment product or fund will, for this purpose, meet the following requirements:

(i) there are no fees or surrender charges imposed in connection with withdrawals initiated by a participant or beneficiary; and

(ii) principal and rates of return are guaranteed by a state- or federally regulated financial institution.

This investment product or fund will constitute a qualified default investment alternative solely for purposes of assets invested in such product or fund before December 24, 2007.

Practitioner's Pointer: This option "grandfathers-in" stable value products and funds as qualified default investment alternatives if such investments were made prior to the effective date of the regulation. The transition rule does not provide relief for contributions to stable value products after the effective date of the regulation.

An investment fund product or model portfolio that otherwise meets the requirements of the regulation will not fail to constitute a product or portfolio for purposes of the types described in paragraphs (a) or (b) above solely because the product or portfolio is offered through a variable annuity or similar contracts or through common or collective trust funds or pooled investment funds and without regard to whether such contracts or funds provide annuity purchase rights, investment guarantees, death benefit guarantees, or other features ancillary to the investment fund product or model portfolio.

Notice Requirements

ERISA Section 404(c)(5)(A) provides that a participant in an individual account plan meeting the notice requirements of ERISA Section 404(c)(5)(B) will be treated as exercising control over the assets in the account with respect to the amount of contributions and earnings that, in

---

1. As determined under IRC Section 414(w)(2)(B).

the absence of an investment election by the participant, are invested by the plan in accordance with Labor Regulation Section 2550.404c-5. Specifically, the notice requirements of ERISA Section 404(c)(5)(B) are satisfied if each participant:

1. Receives, within a reasonable period of time before each plan year, a notice explaining the employee's right under the plan to designate how contributions and earnings will be invested and explaining how, in the absence of any investment election by the participant, such contributions and earnings will be invested; and

2. Has a reasonable period of time after receipt of such notice and before the beginning of the plan year to make such designation.

The form of the notice must comply with the requirements of IRC Section 401(k)(12)(D)(i) and IRC Section 401(k)(12)(D)(ii).

Labor Regulation Section 2550.404c-5(c)(3) conditions fiduciary relief on furnishing participants and beneficiaries advance notification concerning the default investment provisions of their plan that meets the requirements of Labor Regulation Section 2550.404c-5(d). Labor Regulation Section 2550.404c-5(d) provides that the notice required by Labor Regulation Section 2550.404c-5(d)(3) shall be written in a manner calculated to be understood by the average plan participant and shall contain the following:

1. A description of the circumstances under which assets in the individual account of a participant or beneficiary may be invested on behalf of the participant or beneficiary in a qualified default investment alternative; and, if applicable, an explanation of the circumstances under which elective contributions will be made on behalf of a participant, the percentage of such contributions, and the right of the participant to elect not to have such contributions made on the participant's behalf (or to elect to have such contributions made at a different percentage);

2. An explanation of the right of participants and beneficiaries to direct the investment of assets in their individual accounts;

3. A description of the QDIA, including a description of the investment objectives, risk and return characteristics (if applicable), and fees and expenses attendant to the investment alternative;

4. A description of the right of the participants and beneficiaries on whose behalf assets are invested in a QDIA to direct the investment of those assets to any other investment alternative under the plan, including a description of any applicable restrictions, fees, or expenses in connection with such transfer; and

5. An explanation of where the participants and beneficiaries can obtain investment information concerning the other investment alternatives available under the plan.

Civil Penalties under ERISA Section 502(c)(4)

Section 902(f)(2) of PPA 2006 amended ERISA Section 502(c)(4) to provide the Secretary of Labor with the authority to assess a civil penalty of not more than $1,000 a day for each violation of ERISA Section 514(e)(3), which requires the plan administrator to furnish a notice of rights and obligations under an automatic contribution arrangement.

Pursuant to the authority under ERISA Section 502(c)(4), on January 2, 2009, the DOL issued Labor Regulation Section 2560.502c-4, which establishes procedures relating to the assessment of civil penalties by the DOL under ERISA Section 502(c)(4). In general, the regulation sets forth how the maximum penalty amounts are computed, identifies the circumstances under which a penalty may be assessed, sets forth certain procedural rules for service and filing, and provides a plan administrator a means to contest an assessment by the DOL by requesting an administrative hearing.

Under the regulation, the administrator—within the meaning of ERISA Section 3(16)(A)—will be liable for civil penalties assessed by the DOL under ERISA Section 502(c)(4) for failure or refusal to furnish the notice of rights and obligations under an automatic contribution arrangement in accordance with ERISA Section 514(e)(3).

For purposes of this section, a failure or refusal to furnish the notice means a failure or refusal to furnish, in whole or in part, the notice at the relevant times and manners prescribed in ERISA Section 404(c)(5)(B).

The amount assessed under ERISA Section 502(c)(4) for each separate violation will be determined by the DOL, taking into consideration the degree or willfulness of the failure or refusal to furnish the notice. But the amount assessed for each violation under ERISA Section 502(c)(4) will not exceed $1,000 a day (or such other maximum amount as may be established by regulation pursuant to the Federal Civil Penalties Inflation Adjustment Act of 1990, as amended), computed from the date of the administrator's failure or refusal to furnish the notice.

Application of Final Rule to Circumstances Other Than Automatic Enrollment

It is the view of the DOL that nothing in Labor Regulation Section 2550.404c-5 limits the application of the fiduciary relief to investments made only on behalf of participants who are automatically enrolled in their plan. According to the DOL, the regulation applies to situations beyond automatic enrollment, such as, for example: the failure of a participant or beneficiary to provide investment direction following the elimination of an investment alternative or a change in service provider, the failure of a participant or beneficiary to provide investment instruction following a rollover from another plan, and any other failure of a participant to provide investment instruction. Thus, whenever a participant or beneficiary has the opportunity to direct the investment of assets in her account, but does not direct the investment of such assets, plan fiduciaries may avail themselves of the relief provided by the regulation, so long as all of its conditions have been satisfied.[1]

---

1. See Preamble to Labor Reg. §2550.404c-5, 72 Fed. Reg. 60,452 (Oct. 24, 2007).

Preemption of State Laws for Automatic Contribution Arrangement

PPA 2006 Section 902 added a new ERISA Section 514(e)(1), providing that, notwithstanding any other provision of Section 514, Title I of ERISA shall supersede any state law that would directly or indirectly prohibit or restrict the inclusion in any plan of an "automatic contribution arrangement."

PPA 2006 Section 902 also added ERISA Section 514(e)(2), defining the term "automatic contribution arrangement." For purposes of ERISA Section 514(e) and the preemption of state laws provisions in Labor Regulation Section 2550.404c-5(f), an automatic contribution arrangement is an arrangement (or the provisions of a plan) under which

1. A participant may elect to have the plan sponsor make payments as contributions under the plan on behalf of the participant or receive such payments directly in cash;

2. A participant is treated as having elected to have the plan sponsor make such contributions in an amount equal to a uniform percentage of compensation provided under the plan until the participant specifically elects not to have such contributions made (or specifically elects to have such contributions made at a different percentage); and

3. Contributions are invested in accordance with regulations prescribed by the DOL under ERISA Section 404(c)(5).

PPA 2006 Section 902 further added ERISA Section 514(e)(3), which requires a notice to be given to the participants of an automatic contribution requirement. Specifically, ERISA Section 514(e)(3)(A) provides that a plan administrator of an automatic contribution arrangement shall, within a reasonable period before such plan year, provide to each participant to whom the arrangement applies for such plan year notice of the participant's rights and obligations under the arrangement that

1. Is sufficiently accurate and comprehensive to apprise the participant of such rights and obligations, and

2. Is written in a manner calculated to be understood by the average participant to whom the arrangement applies.

ERISA Section 514(e)(3)(B) provides that a notice shall not be treated as meeting the requirements of ERISA Section 514(e) with respect to a participant unless

1. The notice includes an explanation of the participant's right under the arrangement not to have elective contributions made on the participant's behalf (or to elect to have such contributions made at a different percentage);

2. The participant has a reasonable period of time, after receipt of the notice and before the first elective contribution is made, to make such election; and

3. The notice explains how contributions made under the arrangement will be invested in the absence of any investment election by the participant.

In an effort to clarify the application of the preemption provisions of ERISA Section 514(e), and after reviewing the text and purpose of ERISA Section 514(e), the DOL added Labor Regulation §2550.404c-5(f)(2), which reflects its conclusion that ERISA Section 514(e) broadly preempts any state law that would restrict the use of an automatic contribution arrangement as to any pension plan, regardless of whether such plan includes an automatic contribution arrangement as defined in Labor Regulation Section 2550.404c-5(f).

In its view, Congress intended to occupy the field with respect to automatic contribution arrangements with the enactment of ERISA Section 514(e) and believes that its interpretation of ERISA Section 514(e) is consistent with the Technical Explanation of PPA 2206, and cites in the preamble to the final regulation a document prepared by the staff of the Joint Committee on Taxation. That document states, on page 230, "The State preemption rules under the bill are not limited to arrangements that meet the requirements of a qualified enrollment feature."

Thus, in the view of the DOL, ERISA Section 514(e) does not merely supersede state laws "insofar" as any particular plan complies with the final regulation, but rather generally supersedes any law "*which would directly or indirectly prohibit or restrict the inclusion in any plan of an automatic contribution arrangement.*" (Emphasis added.) Compare this language to the language of ERISA Section 514(a), which provides that "the provisions of this title and title IV shall supersede any and all State laws *insofar* as they may now or hereafter relate to any employee benefit plan." (Emphasis added.)

ERISA Section 514(e)(1) also provides the DOL with discretion to determine whether and to what extent preemption should be conditioned on plan compliance with minimum standards, stating that "[t]he Secretary may prescribe regulations which would establish minimum standards that such an arrangement would be required to satisfy in order for this subsection [on preemption] to apply in the case of such arrangement." According to the Preamble to Labor Regulation Section 2550.404c-5, the DOL has concluded pursuant to this grant of discretionary authority that it should not tie preemption to minimum standards for default investments under the regulation, and therefore, specifically provides in Labor Regulation Section 2550.404c-5(f)(4) that nothing in the regulation precludes a pension plan from including an automatic contribution arrangement that does not meet the conditions of ERISA Section 404(c)(5). Accordingly, state laws that hinder the use of any other default investments would, in the judgment of the DOL, be inconsistent with this conclusion, and with the discretionary authority Congress vested in the DOL over the scope of ERISA preemption.

Finally, the DOL intends that the furnishing of a notice in accordance with the timing and content requirements of the final regulation will satisfy not only the notice requirements of ERISA Section 404(c)(5)(B) but also the notice requirements under the preemption provisions of ERISA Section 514 applicable to an "automatic contribution arrangement," within the meaning of ERISA Section 514(e)(2). In that respect, Labor Regulation Section 2550.404c-5 specifically provides that the administrator of an automatic contribution arrangement (within the meaning of Labor Regulation Section 2550.404c-5(f)(1)) shall be considered to have satisfied the notice requirements of ERISA Section 514(e)(3) if notices are furnished in accordance with notice requirements described above.[1] Accordingly, satisfaction of the notice requirements under ERISA Section 404(c)(5) and Labor Regulation Section 2550.404c-5 also will serve to satisfy the separate notice requirements set forth in ERISA Section 514(e)(3) for automatic contribution arrangements. This eliminates the need for multiple notices by plan administrators of automatic contribution arrangements.[2]

Practitioner's Pointer: The rule provides that ERISA supersedes any state law that would prohibit or restrict automatic contribution arrangements, regardless of whether such automatic contribution arrangements qualify for the safe harbor.

---

390. May ERISA Section 404(c) plan trustees override the investment directions of missing participants?

Yes. The Department of Labor has stated that an individual account plan will maintain ERISA Section 404(c) status where the plan's trustees prudently invest the funds of missing participants who could not be found after a diligent search.[3]

The employer seeking the opinion of the DOL in Opinion Letter 96-02A presented a history of hiring documented immigrants, who were active participants in their 401(k) plan. Certain participants had unlawfully assumed the identities of properly documented workers. As a result of enforcement action by the Immigration and Naturalization Service, these employees were terminated and subsequently deported. The trustees made diligent efforts to locate the deported participants, but were unsuccessful.

The trustees were concerned that following the last investment instructions of missing participants would be imprudent due to a change in circumstances. The trustees proposed moving the missing participant account balances into a balanced mutual fund. The DOL advised that the plan would not lose its ERISA Section 404(c) status if the trustees prudently invested the assets of missing participants in a manner that contravened the last written investment instructions of missing participants.

But the DOL cautioned that ERISA Section 404(c) relief is provided only with respect to a transaction where a participant or beneficiary has exercised independent control "in fact" with respect to the investment of assets. Consequently, the DOL noted that any exercise of control by fiduciaries to override the last written investment instructions of a missing participant would not be afforded the transactional relief of ERISA Section 404(c).[4]

391. May ERISA Section 404(c) plan participants direct investments into collectibles?

No. The acquisition of any collectible by an individually directed account under a qualified plan (or by an IRA qualified under IRC Section 408) will be treated as a taxable distribution.[5]

---

1. Set forth in Labor Reg. §§2550.404c-5(c)(3), 2550.404c-5(d).
2. See Preamble to Labor Reg. §2550.404c-5 (72 Fed. Reg. 60,452).
3. See DOL Adv. Op. 96-02A.
4. See DOL Adv. Op. 96-02A.
5. IRC Sec. 408(m).

The term "collectible" generally means any work of art, rug or antique, metal or gem, stamp or coin, alcoholic beverage, or any other tangible property specified by the Secretary of the Treasury as a collectible for purposes of IRC Section 408(m). But certain bullion and certain gold, silver, or platinum coins are not considered collectibles for this purpose.[1]

392. What is the treatment of proceeds received by an employee welfare benefit plan in connection with a demutualization of an insurance company?

Generally, a mutual insurance company has no authorized, issued, or outstanding stock. Instead, the insurance and annuity policies issued by the mutual insurance company combine both insurance coverage and proprietary ownership rights in the company. The process of demutualization generally involves a reorganization that converts the company from a mutual insurance company to a stock insurance company. In such a case, the equity value of the company is distributed to eligible policyholders in the form of stock, cash, or policy credits in consideration of extinguishing the policyholders' membership interests in the company. Policyholder obligations generally remain unchanged and fully in force after the conversion. The amount of consideration each policyholder receives is generally dependent on various actuarial assumptions.

The U.S. Department of Labor (DOL) issued guidance on the treatment of demutualization proceeds received by an employee benefit plan in the form of an Information Letter dated February 18, 2002,[2] concurrently with two advisory opinion letters dealing with other issues involved in a demutualization.[3] The Information Letter addressed, in part, the applicability of ERISA's trust requirements to the treatment of proceeds received by an employee welfare benefit plan in connection with a demutualization of an insurance company and the alternatives available to a plan in such a case.

The DOL noted in the Information Letter that the application of the trust requirements of ERISA Section 403 depends on whether the demutualization proceeds received by a plan constitute plan assets. In the view of the DOL, generally, some or all of the proceeds paid to an ERISA-covered employee welfare benefit plan in consideration of a demutualization may constitute plan assets if the proceeds would be deemed to be owned by the plan under ordinary notions of property rights.[4] Additionally, if the plan participants pay a portion of the premiums to the plan, the portion of the demutualization proceeds attributable to participant contributions must be treated as plan assets. In determining what portion of the demutualization proceeds are attributable to participant contributions, the DOL noted that appropriate consideration should be made by the plan fiduciary to the facts and circumstances that the fiduciary knows or should know are relevant to the determination. Such a determination includes the documents and instruments governing the plan and the proportion of total participant contributions to the total premiums paid over an appropriate time period. Moreover, if the plan or trust is the

---

1. See IRC Secs. 401(m)(2), 401(m)(3).
2. DOL Information Letter, Groom Law Group (Feb. 18, 2001).
3. DOL Information Letter, Groom Law Group (Feb. 18, 2001).
4. See DOL Adv. Op. 92-02A (Jan. 17, 1992) (assets of a plan generally are to be identified on the basis of ordinary notions of property rights under non-ERISA law).

policyholder, or where the policy is paid for out of trust assets, the DOL believes that all of the proceeds received by the policyholder in connection with a demutualization would constitute plan assets.[1]

The Information Letter also provides DOL guidance on how to apply demutualization proceeds received by a plan. The DOL notes that, consistent with ERISA Section 403, the proceeds could be placed in trust until appropriately expended in accordance with the terms of the plan. Alternatively, prior to or simultaneous with the distribution of demutualization proceeds constituting plan assets, the DOL suggests that such assets could be applied to enhancing plan benefits under existing, supplemental, or new insurance policies or contracts; applied toward future participant premium payments; or otherwise held by the insurance company on behalf of the plan without violating the requirements of ERISA Section 403.[2]

Another issue involved in the treatment of proceeds received by an employee welfare benefit plan in connection with a demutualization of an insurance company is determining how to allocate the proceeds among the plan's participants. The DOL briefly addressed this issue in DOL Opinion Letter 2001-02A and noted that the general standards of fiduciary conduct under ERISA Section 404 apply. In particular, a fiduciary of a plan making such a determination must act with impartiality to the plan's participants, and not select an allocation method that benefits the fiduciary (as a plan participant) at the expense of other participants in the plan. Furthermore, if a single policy covers multiple plans, the use of proceeds generated by one plan to benefit the participants of another plan may constitute a breach of the duty of loyalty to the plan's participants.

Finally, although the application of the trust requirement of ERISA Section 403 may require that the proceeds of a demutualization be placed in trust for the benefit of plan participants and beneficiaries, the DOL addressed the issue of whether an employee welfare benefit plan funded solely by insurance contracts must establish a formal trust merely to receive and hold such proceeds for a limited period of time. In response to this issue, the DOL acknowledged that the costs and burdens involved in complying with ERISA's trust and reporting requirements for the one-time receipt of demutualization proceeds could be burdensome in some cases. In consideration of the nature of the affected plans and expected short-term exhaustion of demutualization proceeds, the DOL found it appropriate to provide relief, pending the release of further guidance on the matter, in the form of not asserting a violation in any enforcement proceeding solely because of a failure to hold demutualization proceeds in trust if the following conditions are satisfied:

1. The plan is not otherwise required to maintain a trust under ERISA Section 403.

2. The assets consist solely of proceeds received by the plan in connection with a demutualization.

---

1. DOL Information Letter, Groom Law Group (Feb. 18, 2001).
2. DOL Information Letter, Groom Law Group (Feb. 18, 2001).

3. The proceeds, and any earnings thereon, are placed in the name of the plan in an interest-bearing account, in the case of cash, or custodial account, in the case of stock, as soon as reasonably possible following receipt.

4. The assets are subject to the control of a designated plan fiduciary.

5. As soon as reasonably possible, but no later than twelve months following receipt, the proceeds are applied for

    a. the payment of participant premiums, or

    b. applied to plan benefit enhancements, or

    c. distributed to plan participants.

6. The designated fiduciary maintains such documents and records as are necessary under ERISA with respect to the foregoing.

For those plans satisfying the above conditions, the DOL also will not assert a violation in any enforcement proceeding or assess a civil penalty with respect to such plans because of a failure to meet the reporting requirements by reason of not coming within the limited exemptions set forth in Labor Regulation Section 2520.104-20 and Labor Regulation Section 2520.104-44 solely as a result of receiving demutualization proceeds constituting, in whole or in part, plan assets.[1]

The Sixth Circuit held that employees being paid benefits under a group annuity contract purchased by a terminated plan are entitled to the demutualization proceeds from the insurer.[2] The court based its ruling on the theory that the owner of the group annuity contract was the owner of the annuity contracts when the owner purchased them pursuant to the plan's termination. But in this case, once the annuities were purchased and distributed, the trustee allowed the remaining assets in the plan to revert to the employer, thus terminating the role of the trustee. The Sixth Circuit held that these acts caused the contracts to "lack an owner" for purposes of the demutualization proceeds. In relying on DOL Advisory Opinion 2003-05A, the court noted that terms of the annuity contracts and state law govern in resolving the issue of who is treated as owners of the policies. Following this, the court ruled that the employees were entitled to the demutualization proceeds as successors to the trustee as the contract holder.[3]

The U.S. District Court for the District of Columbia ruled that the demutualization proceeds from the life insurance company providing coverage to an ERISA welfare plan maintained by an employee organization are plan assets that are available to benefit all plan participants.

After the plan's life insurance company demutualized, a participant with life insurance coverage claimed that the $17 million payment made by the insurer to the plan's trust should be

---

1. DOL Information Letter, Groom Law Group (Feb. 18, 2001). See http://www.dol.gov/dol/pwba/public/programs/ori/advisory2001/opinion01. htm.
2. *Bank of New York v. Janowick*, 470 F.3d 264 (6th Cir. 2006).
3. *Bank of New York v. Janowick*, 470 F.3d 264 (6th Cir. 2006).

distributed to or used to benefit the life insurance participants only. The complaint stated that the plan administrator violated ERISA by using the proceeds for the benefit of all participants. The trial court found that plan language supported treatment of the demutualization proceeds as "plan assets." It further ruled that because the participant failed to show that the plan had been terminated, he had no conversion rights. Nor did the participant demonstrate a right to distribution of the proceeds.

In affirming, the D.C. Circuit Court of Appeals ruled that the plan language did not support the participant's argument that the demutualization was an "occurrence" similar to death, accident, sickness, or disability, leading to a "benefit" and that there were no other plan terms entitling him to the demutualization proceeds as a benefit. The court, in reviewing applicable DOL guidance, held that, where the premiums are fully paid by employees (with the trust as the policy holder), demutualization proceeds are surplus funds properly treated as plan assets and thus the plan administrator did not breach its fiduciary duty by using the proceeds to benefit all plan participants or by retroactively amending the plan to clarify how the proceeds would be used.[1]

393. What are the fiduciary responsibilities of a directed trustee in the context of publicly traded securities?

The DOL issued Field Assistance Bulletin 2004-03, which provides general guidance to EBSA regional offices regarding the DOL's views on the responsibilities of directed trustees under ERISA in response to questions that may arise regarding the scope of the directed trustee's fiduciary duties during investigations of transactions involving publicly traded securities by the DOL.

Fiduciary Status of Directed Trustee

In setting forth its position on the fiduciary status of directed trustees, the DOL notes that ERISA Section 403(a) provides that a plan trustee "shall have exclusive authority and discretion to manage and control the assets of the plan." ERISA Section 3(21)(A) provides that a person is a fiduciary with respect to a plan "to the extent … he … exercises any authority or control respecting management or disposition of its assets." A plan trustee, therefore, will, by definition, always be a "fiduciary" under ERISA as a result of its authority or control over plan assets, in the view of the DOL. But not all trustees have the same authority or discretion to manage or control the assets of a plan, observes the DOL. In this regard, ERISA Section 403(a) specifically recognizes that a trustee or trustees will have limited authority or discretion when

> the plan expressly provides that the trustee or trustees are subject to the direction of a named fiduciary who is not a trustee, in which case the trustees shall be subject to proper directions of such fiduciary which are made in accordance with the terms of the plan and which are not contrary to this Act.

---

1. *Stewart v. National Educ. Ass'n*, 2006 U.S. App. LEXIS 30830 (D.C. Cir. 2006).

Thus, the DOL notes that while ERISA Section 403(a)(1) does not remove a directed trustee from ERISA Section 3(21)'s purview, it significantly limits such a trustee's responsibilities as a plan fiduciary. The DOL adds that such a principle was supported by a district court,[1] which recognized that

> [a]t least some fiduciary status and duties of a directed trustee are preserved, even though the scope of its exclusive authority and discretion to manage and control the assets of the plan has been substantially constricted by the directing named fiduciary's correspondingly broadened role.

In further support, the DOL observes that the court in *In re WorldCom, Inc. ERISA Litigation*[2] also noted that, while the directed trustee provision serves as a limiting principle, ERISA Section 403(a) "does not ... eliminate the fiduciary status or duties that normally adhere to a trustee with responsibility over ERISA assets."[3]

Accordingly, in the view of the DOL, the duties of a directed trustee under ERISA Section 403(a)(1) are therefore significantly narrower than the duties generally ascribed to a discretionary trustee under common law trust principles. (The DOL assumes for purposes of FAB 2004-03 that discretionary authority or control over plan assets, beyond that discussed in FAB 2004-03 as applicable to a person serving as a directed trustee under ERISA Section 403(a)(1), has not been conferred upon a directed trustee under the terms of the plan, including trust and service provider agreements).

Determining Whether a Direction Is "Proper"

The DOL notes in FAB 2004-03 that, under ERISA Section 403(a)(1), a directed trustee is subject to proper directions of a named fiduciary, and for purposes of ERISA Section 403(a)(1), a direction is proper only if the direction is "made in accordance with the terms of the plan" and "not contrary to [ERISA]." Accordingly, it is the position of the DOL that when a directed trustee knows or should know that a direction from a named fiduciary is not made in accordance with the terms of the plan or is contrary to ERISA, the directed trustee may not follow the direction, consistent with its fiduciary responsibilities under ERISA.

In Accordance with Plan Terms

The DOL notes in FAB 2004-03 that, under ERISA Section 403(a)(1), a directed trustee may not follow a direction that the trustee knows or should know is inconsistent with the terms of the plan. In order to make such determinations, the DOL believes that directed trustees necessarily have a duty to request and review all the documents and instruments governing the plan that are relevant to its duties as directed trustee. Accordingly, the DOL maintains that if a directed trustee either fails to request such documents or fails to review the documents furnished in response to its request and, as a result of such failure, follows a

---

1. *In re Enron Corp. Sec., Derivative & ERISA Litig.*, 284 F. Supp. 2d 511, 601 (S.D. Tex. 2003).
2. 263 F. Supp. 2d 745, 762 (S.D.N.Y. 2003).
3. See also *FirsTier Bank, N.A. v. Zeller*, 16 F.3d 907, 911 (8th Cir.), *cert. denied* sub nom. *Vercoe v. FirsTier Bank, N.A.*, 513 U.S. 871 (1994); *Herman v. NationsBank Trust Co.*, 126 F.3d 1354, 1361-62, 1370 (11th Cir. 1997).

direction contrary to the terms of the plan, the directed trustee may be liable for following such direction because the directed trustee had a duty to request and review pertinent plan documents and, therefore, should have known that the direction was not in accordance with the terms of the plan. Additionally, if a directed trustee follows an improper direction, as would be the case where the purchase of a particular stock at the direction of the plan's named fiduciary is contrary to the plan's investment policy, the directed trustee may be liable for a breach of its fiduciary duty to follow only proper directions.

If the documents pursuant to which the plan is established and operated do not prohibit the direction, such a direction is consistent with the terms of a plan, in the view of the DOL. It is also the view of the DOL that if, in the course of reviewing the propriety of a particular direction, a directed trustee determines that the terms of the relevant documents are ambiguous with respect to the permissibility of the direction, the directed trustee should obtain a clarification of the plan terms from the fiduciary responsible for interpreting such terms in order to ensure that the direction is proper, and that the directed trustee may rely on the interpretation of such fiduciary.

Not Contrary to ERISA

The DOL also observes in FAB 2004-03 that even when a direction is consistent with the terms of the plan, the direction may nonetheless fail to be a proper direction because it is contrary to ERISA. The DOL notes that under ERISA Section 403(a)(1), a directed trustee may not follow a direction that the trustee knows or should know is contrary to ERISA. For example, the directed trustee cannot follow a direction that the directed trustee knows or should know would require the trustee to engage in a transaction prohibited under ERISA Section 406 or violate the prudence requirement of ERISA Section 404(a)(1). The DOL provides the following discussion in FAB 2004-03 to further clarify the duties of a directed trustee in this area.

Prohibited Transaction Determinations

In the view of the DOL, a directed trustee must follow processes that are designed to avoid prohibited transactions. It notes that a directed trustee could satisfy its obligation by obtaining appropriate written representations from the directing fiduciary that the plan maintains and follows procedures for identifying prohibited transactions and, if prohibited, identifying the individual or class exemption applicable to the transaction. A directed trustee may rely on the representations of the directing fiduciary unless the directed trustee knows that the representations are false.

Prudence Determinations

The DOL also provides in FAB 2004-03 that the named fiduciary has primary responsibility for determining the prudence of a particular transaction, whether the transaction involves buying, selling, or holding particular assets. Accordingly, the DOL observes that as the courts and it have long recognized, the scope of a directed trustee's responsibility is significantly limited. A directed trustee does not, in the view of the DOL, have an independent obligation to determine the prudence of every transaction. The directed trustee does not have an obligation to duplicate or second-guess the work of the plan fiduciaries that have discretionary authority over the management of plan assets and does not have a direct obligation to determine the prudence of a transaction. The DOL cites *In re WorldCom ERISA Litigation*[1] and *Herman v. NationsBank Trust Co.*[2] (directed trustee does not have a direct obligation of prudence under ERISA Section 404; its obligation is simply "to make sure" the "directions were proper, in accordance with the terms of the plan, and not contrary to ERISA") in support of its view.

Duty to Act on Non-public Information

The directed trustee's obligation to question market transactions involving publicly traded stock on prudence grounds is quite limited, notes the DOL in FAB 2004-03. The DOL observes that the primary circumstance in which such an obligation could arise is when the directed trustee possesses material non-public information regarding a security. In its view, if a directed trustee has material non-public information that is necessary for a prudent decision, the directed trustee, prior to following a direction that would be affected by such information, has a duty to inquire about the named fiduciary's knowledge and consideration of the information with respect to the direction. For example, if a directed trustee has non-public information indicating that a company's public financial statements contain material misrepresentations that significantly inflate the company's earnings, the trustee could not simply follow a direction to purchase that company's stock at an artificially inflated price, according to the DOL.

The DOL also remarks that, generally, the possession of non-public information by one part of an organization will not be imputed to the organization as a whole (including personnel providing directed trustee services) where the organization maintains procedures designed to prevent the illegal disclosure of such information under securities, banking, or other laws.[3] If, despite such procedures, the individuals responsible for the directed trustee services have actual knowledge of material non-public information, the DOL maintains that the directed trustee, prior to following a direction that would be affected by such information, has a duty, as indicated above, to inquire about the named fiduciary's knowledge and consideration of the information with respect to the direction. Similarly, if the directed trustee performs an internal analysis in which it concludes that the company's current financial statements are materially inaccurate, the DOL states the directed trustee would have an obligation to disclose this analysis to the named fiduciary before making a determination whether to follow a direction to purchase the company's security. But the directed trustee would not have an obligation to disclose reports and analyses that are available to the public.

Duty to Act on Public Information

It is also the view of the DOL, set forth in FAB 2004-03, that absent material non-public information, a directed trustee, given its limited fiduciary duties as determined by statute, will rarely have an obligation under ERISA to question the prudence of a direction to purchase publicly traded securities at the market price solely on the basis of publicly

---

1. 263 F. Supp. 2d at 761.
2. 126 F.3d at 1361-62, 1371.
3. In a footnote to FAB 2004-03, the DOL states that it expresses no view as to whether, or under what circumstances, other procedures established by an organization to limit the disclosure of information will serve to avoid the imputation of information to a directed trustee.

available information. The DOL offers three considerations as counsel in favor of this view: (1) markets generally are assumed to be efficient, so that stock prices reflect publicly available information and known risks; (2) in the case of employer securities, the securities laws impose substantial obligations on the company, its officers, and its accountants to state their financial records accurately; and (3) ERISA Section 404 requires the instructing fiduciary to adhere to a stringent standard of care.[1] Furthermore, the DOL adds that, because stock prices fluctuate as a matter of course, even a steep drop in a stock's price would not, in and of itself, indicate that a named fiduciary's direction to purchase or hold such stock is imprudent and, therefore, not a proper direction.

In limited, extraordinary circumstances, where there are clear and compelling public indicators, as evidenced by an 8-K filing with the Securities and Exchange Commission (SEC), a bankruptcy filing, or similar public indicator, that call into serious question a company's viability as a going concern,[2] the directed trustee may have a duty not to follow the named fiduciary's instruction without further inquiry.[3] The DOL provides, for example, if a company filed for bankruptcy under circumstances that make it unlikely that there would be any distribution to equity-holders, or otherwise publicly stated that it was unlikely to survive the bankruptcy proceedings in a manner that would leave current equity-holders with any value, the directed trustee would have an obligation to question whether the named fiduciary has considered the prudence of the direction.[4]

The DOL also expresses its view in FAB 2004-03 that, in situations where a fiduciary who is a corporate employee gives an instruction to buy or hold stock of his company after formal charges of financial irregularities have been brought against the company, its officers, or directors by state or federal regulators, the directed trustee, taking such facts into account, may need to decline to follow the direction or may need to conduct an independent assessment of the transaction in order to assure himself that the instruction is consistent with ERISA. (The DOL notes in a footnote that nothing in the text should be read to suggest that a directed trustee would have a heightened duty whenever a regulatory body opens an investigation of a company whose securities are the subject of a direction, merely based on the bare fact of the investigation.) But if an independent fiduciary was appointed to manage the plan's investment in company stock, a

---

1. The DOL in a footnote to FAB 2004-03 adds that it should be noted that, in the case of an individual account plan, the diversification requirements of ERISA Section 404(a)(1)(C) do not apply to the acquisition or holding of qualifying employer securities within the meaning of ERISA Section 407(d)(5).

2. The DOL notes in a footnote to FAB 2004-03 that Section 409 of the Sarbanes-Oxley Act of 2002, 15 U.S.C. §78(m)(1), requires public companies to disclose "on a rapid and current basis" material information regarding changes in the company's financial condition or operations as the SEC by rule determines to be necessary or useful for the protection of investors or in the public interest. The SEC has recently updated its disclosure requirements related to Form 8-K, expanding the number of reportable events and shortening the filing deadline for most items to four business days after the occurrence of the event triggering the disclosure requirements of the form. 69 Fed. Reg. 15,594 (Mar. 25, 2004). Not all 8-K filings regarding a company would trigger a duty on the part of a directed trustee to question a direction to purchase or hold securities of that company. Only those relatively few 8-Ks that call into serious question a company's ongoing viability may trigger a duty on the part of the directed trustee to take some action.

3. A directed trustee's actual knowledge of media or other public reports or analyses that merely speculate on the continued viability of a company does not, in and of itself, constitute knowledge of clear and compelling evidence concerning the company sufficient to give rise to a directed trustee's duty to act, according to the DOL in a footnote to FAB 2004-03.

4. In a footnote to FAB 2004-03, the DOL observes that even under such circumstances, it might not be imprudent to purchase or hold stock in a distressed company in bankruptcy. There may be situations in which the plan's fiduciaries could reasonably conclude that the stock investment makes sense, even for a long-term investor, in light of the proposed restructuring of the company's debts or other factors.

directed trustee could follow the proper directions of the independent fiduciary without having to conduct its own independent assessment of the transaction, according to the DOL.

Effect of Questioning Directions on Fiduciary Status

The DOL also states its view that the nature and scope of a directed trustee's fiduciary responsibility, as discussed in FAB 2004-03, does not change merely because the directed trustee, in carrying out its duties, raises questions concerning whether a direction is "proper" or declines to follow a direction that the directed trustee does not believe is a proper direction within the meaning of ERISA Section 403(a)(1). For example, information provided to a named fiduciary concerning the prudence of a direction is not investment advice for purposes of ERISA Section 3(21)(A)(ii). Similarly, if a named fiduciary changes a direction in response to a directed trustee's inquiries or information, the directed trustee's fiduciary responsibility with respect to the changed direction remains governed by ERISA Section 403(a)(1). The directed trustee does not become primarily responsible for the prudence of the direction.

Co-Fiduciary Duties

The DOL observes in FAB 2004-03 that, under ERISA Section 405(a)(1), a fiduciary is liable for the breach of another fiduciary if the fiduciary "participates knowingly" in the breach of the other fiduciary. Accordingly, if a directed trustee has knowledge of a fiduciary breach, the directed trustee may be liable as a co-fiduciary unless the directed trustee takes reasonable steps to remedy the breach. Thus, if the directed trustee knew that the named fiduciary was failing to discharge its obligations in accordance with ERISA's requirements, it could not simply follow directions from the breaching fiduciary. The DOL notes that efforts to remedy a breach (or to prevent an imminent breach) may include reporting the breach to other fiduciaries of the plan or the DOL.

394. What are the duties of fiduciaries in light of the events regarding Bernard L. Madoff Investment Securities, LLC?

According to the Department of Labor in guidance released on February 5, 2009, recent events regarding Bernard L. Madoff Investment Securities, LLC, have resulted in questions by fiduciaries, investment managers, and other investment service providers to the Department of Labor about steps they should be taking in connection with employee benefit plans they believe may have exposure to losses as a result of investment of plan assets invested with Madoff entities. Fiduciaries of employee benefit plans covered by ERISA should address these events in a manner consistent with their fiduciary duties of prudence and loyalty to the plan's participants and beneficiaries.

Where plan fiduciaries determine that plan assets were invested with Madoff entities and material losses are likely, appropriate steps should be taken to assess and protect the interests of the plan and its participants and beneficiaries. Such steps may include (1) requesting disclosures from investment managers, fund managers, and other investment intermediaries regarding the plan's potential exposure to Madoff-related losses; (2) seeking advice regarding the likelihood of losses due to investments that may be at risk; (3) making appropriate disclosures to other plan fiduciaries and plan participants and beneficiaries; and (4) considering whether the plan has claims that are reasonably likely to lead to recovery of Madoff-related losses that should be asserted against responsible fiduciaries or other intermediaries who placed plan assets with Madoff entities, as well as claims against the Madoff bankruptcy estate. Fiduciaries must ensure that claims are filed in accordance with applicable filing deadlines, such as those applicable to bankruptcy claims and for coverage by the Securities Investor Protection Corporation (SIPC).

The Web site of the court-appointed trustee for the liquidation of Bernard L. Madoff Investment Securities, LLC, is http://www.madofftrustee.com. This Web site contains the liquidation notice, claim forms, and related claims information, and deadlines for the filing of claims with the trustee.

SECTION V

Prohibited Transactions

395. In general, what are the prohibited transaction provisions of ERISA?

ERISA Section 406 supplements the general duties imposed on fiduciaries (discussed in detail in Section IV) by providing a list of specifically prohibited transactions between a plan and a "party in interest" (see Q 398). The questions in this section discuss the various types of prohibited transactions, who is subject to the prohibited transaction rules, the penalties for engaging in prohibited transactions, and how to correct prohibited transactions.

Both ERISA and the Internal Revenue Code statutorily exempt certain transactions from the prohibited transaction rules. In addition, the Department of Labor, and sometimes the Internal Revenue Service, may grant conditional and unconditional individual or class exemptions from all or part of the restrictions imposed by the prohibited transaction rules. Individual exemptions offer relief only to the person requesting the exemption, while class exemptions provide relief to parties who engage in transactions of the type specified by the class exemption. The exemptions and procedures to obtain exemptions are discussed in Section VI.

Rather than leaving all fiduciary transactions to be judged by the general standard of care found in ERISA Section 404, ERISA Section 406 was adopted by Congress to prevent plans from engaging in certain types of transactions that had been used previously to benefit other parties at the expense of the plans' participants and beneficiaries.[1] The prohibited transaction rules indicate a desire by Congress to prevent those transactions that offer a high potential for the loss of plan assets or for insider abuse, by prohibiting such transactions.[2]

The IRC maintains a nearly identical version of the prohibited transaction rules, which prohibit certain transactions between a plan and a "disqualified person."[3] Although the terms party in interest and disqualified person are similar, a party in interest under ERISA encompasses a broader range of persons.

In order for a transaction to be considered a prohibited transaction under ERISA, a "fiduciary" must cause the plan to engage in the transaction, and must (or should) know that such a transaction constitutes a prohibited transaction.[4] A fiduciary who violates the prohibitions set forth in ERISA is personally liable for any losses incurred by the plan and for any ill-gotten profits, and may be subject to other equitable and remedial relief that may be deemed appropriate by a court.[5] The Eleventh Circuit Court of Appeals has ruled that non-fiduciary parties in interest may be sued by the DOL for prohibited transaction violations due to ERISA Section 502(a)(5), which permits the DOL to seek equitable relief to redress such violations without restricting the types

---

1. *Reich v. Compton*, 57 F.3d 270 (3d Cir. 1995).
2. *Cutaiar v. Marshall*, 590 F.2d 523 (3d Cir. 1979); *Marshall v. Kelly*, 465 F. Supp. 341 (W.D. Okla. 1978).
3. See IRC Sec. 4975.
4. ERISA Sec. 406(a)(1).
5. ERISA Sec. 409.

of parties who may be sued.[1] In addition, a person who participates in a prohibited transaction may be subject to penalties and excise taxes under the IRC. These excise taxes are imposed automatically and significantly increase if the prohibited transaction is not timely corrected.[2] See Q 421.

396. What plans are subject to the prohibited transaction restrictions?

The prohibited transaction restrictions apply to all tax-qualified retirement plans, individual retirement accounts, individual retirement annuities, and medical savings accounts.

The prohibited transaction provisions do *not* apply to the following: (1) governmental plans; (2) church plans that have not elected to be subject to the participation, vesting, and funding standards under IRC Section 410; (3) plans maintained solely for the purpose of complying with applicable workers' compensation, unemployment compensation, or disability insurance laws; (4) plans maintained outside the United States primarily for the benefit of persons substantially all of whom are nonresident aliens; (5) unfunded excess benefit plans; (6) plans that are unfunded and maintained by an employer primarily for the purpose of providing deferred compensation for a select group of management or highly compensated employees; and (7) any agreement described in IRC Section 736, which provides payments to a retired partner or deceased partner or a deceased partner's successor in interest. In addition, under the Internal Revenue Code, the prohibited transaction restrictions do not apply to plans that are issued a guaranteed benefit policy, or to any assets of the insurance company, insurance service, or insurance organization merely because of its issuance of such policy.[3]

397. What is a prohibited transaction?

Under ERISA, the term "prohibited transaction" means a transaction in which a plan fiduciary causes the plan to engage, if he knows (or should know) that such transaction constitutes a direct or indirect: (1) sale or exchange, or leasing, of any property between the plan and a party in interest; (2) lending of money or other extension of credit between the plan and a party in interest; (3) furnishing of goods, services, or facilities between the plan and a party in interest; (4) transfer to, or use by or for the benefit of, a party in interest, of any plan assets; or (5) acquisition, on behalf of the plan, of any employer security or employer real property in violation of ERISA Section 407.[4]

Under the Internal Revenue Code, the term "prohibited transaction" means any direct or indirect: (1) sale or exchange, or leasing, of any property between a plan and a disqualified person; (2) lending of money or other extension of credit between a plan and a disqualified person; (3) furnishing of goods, services, or facilities between a plan and a disqualified person; (4) transfer to, or use by or for the benefit of, a disqualified person of plan income or assets; (5) act by a disqualified person who is a fiduciary whereby he deals with the income or assets of a plan in his own interest or for his own account; or (6) receipt of any consideration

---

1. *Herman v. South Carolina Nat'l Bank*, 140 F.3d 1413 (11th Cir. 1998), *cert. denied*, 119 S. Ct. 1030 (1999).
2. IRC Sec. 4975.
3. ERISA Secs. 4(b), 401(a); IRC Secs. 736, 4975.
4. ERISA Sec. 406(a)(1).

for a personal account by any disqualified person who is a fiduciary from any party dealing with the plan in connection with a transaction involving the income or assets of the plan.[1] In contrast to ERISA, the IRC does not contain restrictions relating to employer securities or real (like-kind) property.

The transactions described in ERISA are per se prohibited transactions, designed to prevent a trustee "from being put into a position where he has dual loyalties and therefore he cannot act exclusively for the benefit of a plan's participants and beneficiaries."[2] The per se nature of the prohibitions is emphasized by the fact that the existence of a violation does not depend on whether any harm results from the transaction.[3] Lack of harm to the plan or the good faith or lack of the same on the part of the borrower is not relevant, or controlling, under ERISA Section 406.[4] The transactions enumerated in ERISA Section 406(a)(1) are per se violations of ERISA regardless of the motivation that initiated the transaction, the prudence of the transaction, or the absence of any harm arising from the transaction.[5] However, acts that do not fall within the specific list of prohibitions proscribed by ERISA Section 406(a)(1) do not constitute per se violations of ERISA.[6]

398. Who is a party in interest or a disqualified person?

Party in Interest

The prohibited transaction rules under ERISA affect a party in interest. Under ERISA, a party in interest is defined as:

1. Any fiduciary (including, but not limited to, any administrator, officer, trustee, or custodian), counsel, or employee of such employee benefit plan;

2. A person providing services to such plan;

3. An employer any of whose employees are covered by such plan;

4. An employee organization any of whose members are covered by such plan;

5. A direct or indirect owner of 50 percent or more of:

    a. the combined voting power of all classes of stock entitled to vote or the total value of shares of all classes of stock of a corporation,

    b. the capital interest or the profits interest of a partnership, or

    c. the beneficial interest of a trust or unincorporated enterprise,

1. IRC Sec. 4975(c)(1).
2. *NLRB v. Amax Coal Co.*, 453 U.S. 950 (1981).
3. *Marshall v. Kelly*, 465 F. Supp. 341 (W.D. Okla. 1978).
4. *M & R Inv. Co. v. Fitzsimmons*, 484 F. Supp. 1041 (D. Nev. 1980).
5. *Beck v. Levering*, 947 F.2d 639 (2d Cir. 1991); *Donovan v. Cunningham*, 716 F.2d 1455 (5th Cir. 1983).
6. *Brock v. Citizens Bank of Clovis*, 841 F.2d 344 (10th Cir. 1988).

which is an employer or an employee organization described in (three) or (four) above (the Secretary of Labor, after consultation and coordination with the Secretary of the Treasury, may, by regulation, prescribe a percentage lower than 5 percent);

6.   A relative of any individual described in (one), (two), (three), or (five) above (ERISA Section 3(15) defines "relative" to mean a spouse, ancestor, lineal descendant, or spouse of a lineal descendant);

7.   A corporation, partnership, trust, or estate of which (or in which) 50 percent or more of:

   a.   the combined voting power of all classes of stock entitled to vote, or the total value of shares of all classes of stock of such corporation,

   b.   the capital interest or profits interest of such partnership, or

   c.   the beneficial interest of such trust or estate,

   is owned directly or indirectly, or held by persons described in (one), (two), (three), (four), or (five) above (the Secretary of Labor, after consultation and coordination with the Secretary of the Treasury, may, by regulation, prescribe a percentage lower than 50 percent);

8.   An employee, officer, director (or an individual having powers or responsibilities similar to those of officers or directors), or a 10 percent or more shareholder (directly or indirectly), of a person described in (two), (three), (four), (five), or (seven) above, or of the employee benefit plan (the Secretary of Labor, after consultation and coordination with the Secretary of the Treasury, may, by regulation, prescribe a percentage lower than 10 percent); or

9.   A 10 percent or more (directly or indirectly in capital or profits) partner or joint venturer of a person described in (two), (three), (four), (five), or (seven) above (the Secretary of Labor, after consultation and coordination with the Secretary of the Treasury, may, by regulation, prescribe a percentage lower than 10 percent).[1]

Disqualified Person

Under the Internal Revenue Code, the prohibited transaction rules apply to a "disqualified person" rather than a party in interest. The term "disqualified person" covers a range of people, including employers, unions, and their officials, fiduciaries, persons providing services to a plan, and persons whose relationship to the plan is not immediately apparent. More specifically, a disqualified person is defined as a person who is:

1.   A fiduciary;

2.   A person providing services to the plan;

---

1. ERISA Sec. 3(14).

3.   An employer, any of whose employees are covered by the plan;

4.   An employee organization, any of whose members are covered by the plan;

5.   A direct or indirect owner of 50 percent or more of:

    a.   the combined voting power of all classes of stock entitled to vote or the total value of shares of all classes of stock of a corporation,

    b.   the capital interest or the profits interest of a partnership, or

    c.   the beneficial interest of a trust or unincorporated enterprise,

    which is an employer or an employee organization described in (three) or (four) above (the Secretary of the Treasury, after consultation and coordination with the Secretary of Labor or his delegate, may, by regulation, prescribe a percentage lower than 50 percent);

6.   A member of the family of any individual described in (one), (two), (three), or (five) above (the family of an individual includes a spouse, ancestor, lineal descendant, and spouse of a lineal descendant);

7.   A corporation, partnership, trust, or estate of which (or in which) 50 percent or more of:

    a.   the combined voting power of all classes of stock entitled to vote or the total value of shares of all classes of stock of such corporation,

    b.   the capital interest or profits interest of such partnership, or

    c.   the beneficial interest of such trust or estate,

    is owned directly or indirectly, or held by persons described in (one), (two), (three), (four), or (five) above (the Secretary of the Treasury, after consultation and coordination with the Secretary of Labor or his delegate, may, by regulation, prescribe a percentage lower than 50 percent);

8.   An officer, director (or an individual having powers or responsibilities similar to those of officers or directors), a 10 percent or more shareholder, or a highly compensated employee (earning 10 percent or more of the yearly wages of an employer) of a person described in (three), (four), (five), or (seven) above (the Secretary of the Treasury, after consultation and coordination with the Secretary of Labor or his delegate, may, by regulation, prescribe a percentage lower than 10 percent); or

9.   A 10 percent or more (in capital or profits) partner or joint venturer of a person described in (three), (four), (five), or (seven) above (the Secretary of the Treasury,

after consultation and coordination with the Secretary of Labor or his delegate, may, by regulation, prescribe a percentage lower than 10 percent).[1]

A party in interest under ERISA and a "disqualified person" under the Internal Revenue Code include generally the same group of individuals and entities; however, employees who are highly compensated (earning 10 percent or more of the yearly wages of an employer) are disqualified persons only under the Internal Revenue Code.

A Tax Court case held that while an individual may not be a fiduciary as defined under ERISA, he may still be liable for excise taxes as a disqualified person under the IRC for participating in a prohibited transaction.[2] The court stated that although ERISA provides an exception for transactions conducted through individual account plans,[3] the IRC has no similar provisions preventing the attachment of liability. In so ruling, the court noted that, under ERISA, liability runs directly to the fiduciary for breaches of fiduciary duty. Under the IRC, however, liability runs to disqualified persons and applies whether or not a fiduciary has breached his duties under ERISA.[4]

Transaction Between a Plan and a Party in Interest

399. What are the rules regarding the sale, exchange, or leasing of property between a plan and a party in interest?

A plan fiduciary is prohibited from causing the plan to engage in a transaction if she knows (or should know) that the transaction constitutes a direct or indirect sale or exchange, or leasing, of any property between the plan and a party in interest.[5] ERISA protects a plan against influences exerted by a party in interest, as that term is defined in ERISA Section 3(14).[6] This prohibition is violated when, for example, one corporation's plan leases a building to a second corporation where both companies are 95 percent owned by the same individual.[7]

The acquisition of a jet by a plan from an aircraft firm, acting as a third-party dealer, where the aircraft company acquired the jet from the same union that represented the participants of the plan, was held to be an indirect sale prohibited by ERISA Section 406(a)(1)(A).[8] Knowing that the union was trading in the airplane, the plan trustees prepared a bid equivalent to the trade-in value of the airplane, and purchased the airplane on the same day that the union traded it in. The presence of the aircraft company as an intermediary did not add an "arm's length" element to remove the transaction from the prohibitions of ERISA. This case illustrates that the prohibitions of ERISA Section 406 cannot be easily circumvented or legitimized by the insertion of a third party—a party who, incidentally, could profit from its role.

1. IRC Sec. 4975(e)(2).
2. *Flahertys Arden Bowl, Inc. v. Commissioner*, 115 T.C. 269 (2000), *aff'd*, 88 A.F.T.R.2d 2001-5547 (8th Cir. 2001).
3. ERISA Sec. 404(c)(1).
4. *Flahertys Arden Bowl, Inc. v. Commissioner*, above.
5. ERISA Sec. 406(a)(1)(A).
6. *McDougall v. Donovan*, 552 F. Supp. 1206 (N.D. Ill. 1982).
7. DOL Adv. Op. 76-14.
8. *McDougall v. Donovan*, 552 F. Supp. 1206 (N.D. Ill. 1982).

According to a Department of Labor Opinion Letter, a transaction will not be prohibited if the transaction is an ordinary "blind" transaction purchase or sale of securities through an exchange where neither buyer nor seller (nor the agent of either) knows the identity of the other party involved.[1] That Opinion Letter addressed whether a bank would engage in a prohibited transaction if, in its capacity as directed trustee of an employee benefit plan, it purchased securities issued by its parent company on behalf of any such plan, at the proper direction of a named fiduciary having the authority to direct investments by the bank, or of an investment manager appointed by a named fiduciary.

According to the Opinion Letter, purchases and sales of a bank's stock in blind transactions executed by unaffiliated brokers at the proper direction of named fiduciaries of plans of the bank's customers will not constitute transactions described in ERISA Section 406(a)(1)(A). The Opinion Letter reasoned that there is no reason to impose a sanction on a fiduciary (or party in interest) merely because, by chance, the other party turns out to be a party in interest (or plan).[2]

In-kind contributions to a plan, which reduce the obligation of a plan sponsor or employer to make a contribution measured in terms of cash amounts, also constitute a prohibited transaction, unless a statutory or administrative exemption applies (see Section VI). For example, if a profit sharing plan required the employer to make annual contributions "in cash or in kind" equal to a given percentage of the employer's net profits for the year, an in-kind contribution used to reduce this obligation would constitute a prohibited transaction in the absence of an exemption, because the amount of the contribution obligation is measured in terms of cash amounts (a percentage of profits), even though the terms of the plan purport to permit in-kind contributions.[3]

In the Sixth Circuit, an employer, as plan fiduciary, did not engage in a prohibited transaction with a party in interest, when, in the course of a corporate spinoff, it caused its plan to sell or transfer assets to the other company's plan.[4] The successor company was not a party in interest, and the court said that to hold that the transfer was a prohibited transaction would be to construe the prohibited transaction rules to conflict with the permissive attitude of ERISA Section 208 toward plan mergers and transfers.

400. What are the rules regarding the lending of money or other extension of credit between the plan and a party in interest?

A plan fiduciary is prohibited from causing a plan to engage in a transaction, if he knows (or should know) that such transaction constitutes a direct or indirect lending of money (or other extension of credit) between the plan and a party in interest.[5] This prohibition often extends to a loan made by a plan to a plan sponsor, to a union that is a party in interest, or to a business owned by a party in interest. In addition, a prohibited transaction occurs when a

---

1. DOL Adv. Op. 92-23A.
2. DOL Adv. Op. 92-23A.
3. Labor Reg. §2509.94-3.
4. *United Steelworkers of Am., Local 2116 v. Cyclops Corp.*, 860 F.2d 189 (6th Cir. 1988).
5. ERISA Sec. 406(a)(1)(B).

plan loan is made to a third party, where the fiduciaries know and intend that the proceeds of the loan are to be transferred to a party in interest.[1]

For example, if a sole shareholder of the plan sponsor, acting as trustee of a plan, arranges loans from an employee benefit plan to a party in interest (in addition to making a loan to himself and causing the plan to renew outstanding loans to the plan sponsor), that transaction will violate the prohibition against lending of money or other extension of credit between a plan and a party in interest.[2]

The statute prohibits lending between the plan and a party in interest, and although the intention behind the statute is to keep parties in interest from borrowing from the plan, its plain reading prohibits loans in both directions.[3] This was illustrated in a case where the owners of the plan sponsor, acting as trustees of the plan, loaned money to the plan and executed guarantees on behalf of the plan. The court held that loans made by disqualified persons (the equivalent of parties in interest under the Internal Revenue Code) to plans are absolutely prohibited.[4]

There is, however, no per se prohibition against a fiduciary's lending money to an unrelated person who thereafter uses the loan proceeds to pay obligations to a party in interest. If a violation exists, it must arise by implication. This is the case if loans are made to third parties in order to avoid application of ERISA Section 406(a).[5]

A prohibited transaction under ERISA does not necessarily require that the assets of the plan be actually disbursed to a party in interest. In the case of a loan to a party in interest, even if the proceeds of the loan are never disbursed, there still may exist a lending of money where a contractually created right to the loan proceeds is not severable from the contract that created it.

In some cases, the culpability arises with the contract's creation, and not with the basically ministerial act of disbursing the funds.[6]

Lack of knowledge on the part of a fiduciary (the fact that he does not know or should not have known that a borrower is a party in interest) is not a defense under ERISA Section 406(a)(1)(B). Knowledge is imputed to a fiduciary by the requirement that a "'thorough investigation' is mandated in any 'significant transaction' to determine if the borrower is a party in interest," and knowledge, actual or constructive, on the part of fiduciary has no bearing on whether the transaction is prohibited.[7]

---

1. *Dole v. Lundberg*, 733 F. Supp. 895 (N.D. Texas 1989); *Donovan v. Bryans*, 566 F. Supp. 1258 (E.D. Pa. 1983).
2. *Marshall v. Kelly*, 465 F. Supp. 341 (W.D. Okla. 1978).
3. *Brock v. Citizens Bank of Clovis*, 841 F.2d 344 (10th Cir.), *cert. denied*, 488 U.S. 829 (1988); *Rutland v. Commissioner*, 89 T.C. 1137 (1987).
4. *Janpol v. Commissioner*, 101 T.C. 518 (1993).
5. *Brock v. Citizens Bank of Clovis*, 841 F.2d 344 (10th Cir. 1988).
6. *M & R Inv. Co. v. Fitzsimmons*, 685 F.2d 283 (9th Cir. 1982).
7. *M & R Inv. Co. v. Fitzsimmons*, 484 F. Supp. 1041 (D. Nev. 1980); see *Marshall v. Kelly*, 465 F. Supp. 341 (W.D. Okla. 1978).

401. What are the rules regarding furnishing goods, services, and facilities between the plan and a party in interest?

A plan fiduciary is prohibited from engaging in a transaction, if she knows (or should know) that such transaction constitutes a direct or indirect furnishing of goods, services, or facilities between the plan and a party in interest.[1] This prohibition is comprehensive and applies to the furnishing of living quarters, office space, equipment, and supplies, as well as accounting, legal, investment advisory, and computer services. This prohibition was illustrated where a corporation wholly owned by a union plan made excessive payments to the plan trustees for doing work for the local union as well as work for the corporation.[2]

On the other hand, a multiemployer plan was not seen as providing services to a participating employer merely because it undertook the task of directly reporting the third-party sick payments to recipient employees and to the IRS rather than providing the employers with the statements of those payments and obliging them to forward the information to the employees and to the IRS.[3]

In addition, the furnishing of goods and services by the subsidiary of the sponsoring employer (and, thus, a party in interest) to an unrelated tenant of real property owned by the plan, for the repair and maintenance of the property, was not a prohibited transaction. As the tenant was responsible for the maintenance of the property and only the tenant had enforceable rights under any service contracts it executed, the transaction was not between the plan and a party in interest, but was between a tenant and a provider of goods and services.[4]

Under certain circumstances, a party in interest may be exempted from the prohibition of furnishing goods and services to a plan. ERISA exempts from the prohibited transaction rules a plan's payment to a party in interest, including a fiduciary, for office space or any service (or a combination of services) if (1) the office space or service is necessary for the establishment or operation of the plan; (2) the office space or service is furnished under a contract or arrangement that is reasonable; and (3) no more than reasonable compensation is paid for such office space or service.[5]

402. What are the final rules governing the disclosure of service provider compensation and potential conflicts of interest under a reasonable contract or arrangement for services under ERISA Section 408(b)(2)?

As noted in Q 280 and pursuant to ERISA Section 404(a), when selecting or monitoring service providers for employee benefit plans, plan fiduciaries must act prudently and solely in the interest of the plan's participants and beneficiaries, and for the exclusive purposes of providing benefits and defraying reasonable expenses of plan administration. A fiduciary must have sufficient information to fulfill its obligations.

---

1. ERISA Sec. 406(a)(1)(C).
2. *Marshall v. Snyder*, 572 F.2d 894 (2d Cir. 1978).
3. DOL Adv. Op. 82-32A.
4. DOL Adv. Op. 83-45A.
5. ERISA Sec. 408(b)(2); see Section VI.

Covered Plans

When these requirements are applied to arrangements between plans and service providers that are exempt under ERISA Section 408(b)(2) (the contract or arrangement is reasonable; the services are necessary for the plan's establishment or operation; and no more than reasonable compensation is paid for the services), the DOL has issued final rules requiring that certain service providers to defined contribution and defined benefit pension plans[1] disclose information to assist fiduciaries "in assessing the reasonableness of contracts or arrangements, including the reasonableness of the service providers' compensation and potential conflicts of interest that may affect the service providers' performance."[2] These final regulations became effective on July 1, 2012, and they apply to contracts and arrangements between covered plans and covered service providers as of the effective date, regardless as to whether the arrangement had been entered into prior to the effective date. Further, the detailed disclosures below must be provided no later than the effective date.[3]

A "covered plan" does not include a "simplified employee pension," a "simple retirement account," an individual retirement account, or an individual retirement annuity.[4] In addition, 403(b) plan custodial accounts and annuity contracts subject to ERISA are also excluded if they were issued to affected employees before January 1, 2009, where the sponsoring employer ceased making contributions, where rights or benefits of individual owners are enforceable against the insurer or custodian without employer involvement, and where such individual owners are fully vested in the benefits provided under the contract or account.[5]

The final rule provides that a covered service provider must disclose the mandated information to the responsible plan fiduciary "reasonably in advance of the date the contract or arrangement is entered into, and extended or renewed."[6] The final rule does not provide any guidance as to what constitutes "reasonable time." Exceptions to this initial disclosure requirement apply when an investment arrangement is determined to not hold plan assets upon the plan's direct equity investment, but subsequently is determined to hold plan assets while the investment continues. In this case, the mandated disclosures must be provided as soon as practicable, but not later than thirty days from the date that it is discovered that the arrangement holds plan assets.[7] Another exception to the initial disclosure requirement applies where there is a subsequent designation of an investment alternative under the arrangement. Where that is the case, the mandated disclosures must be provided as soon as practicable, but not later than the date the investment alternative is designated by the covered plan.[8] A covered service provider must disclose a change to the required disclosure information as soon as practicable, but not later than 60 days from the date on which the covered service provider is informed of such change, unless the disclosure is precluded due to extraordinary circumstances beyond the control of the covered service

---

1. Labor Reg. §2550.408b-2(c)(1)(ii); 77 Fed. Reg. 5632 (Feb. 3, 2012).
2. 75 Fed. Reg. 41,600 (July 16, 2010).
3. Labor Reg. §2550.408b-2(c)(1)(xii).
4. Labor Reg. §2550.408b-2(c)(1)(ii).
5. Labor Reg. §2550.408b-2(c)(1)(ii).
6. Labor Reg. §2550.408b-2(c)(1)(v)(A).
7. Labor Reg. §2550.408b-2(c)(1)(v)(A)(1).
8. Labor Reg. §2550.408b-2(c)(1)(v)(A)(2).

provider, in which case the information must be disclosed as soon as practicable.[1] Finally, the covered service provider must disclose any changes to the investment disclosure requirements for fiduciary services (see subsequent information) and the investment disclosure requirements for recordkeeping and brokerage services (see subsequent information) at least annually.[2]

The final disclosure rule reserves a place for future development of provisions that would require a covered service provider to separately furnish a guide or similar tool designed to enable the responsible plan fiduciary to locate compensation information disclosed through multiple or complex documents. The preamble to the final rule states that the DOL intends to soon publish a Notice of Proposed Rulemaking on this matter. The DOL has provided a Sample Guide as an appendix to the final disclosure rule to encourage service providers to assist plan fiduciaries with their review of required disclosures.

Subsequent to the initial reporting requirements, covered service providers, upon receipt of a written request of the responsible plan fiduciary, must furnish, reasonably in advance of the date upon which such responsible plan fiduciary or covered plan administrator states that it must comply with the applicable reporting or disclosure requirement, any other information relating to compensation received in connection with the arrangement that is required for the covered plan to comply with its reporting and disclosure obligations under ERISA (unless disclosure is precluded by extraordinary circumstances beyond the service provider's control).[3]

Where it is discovered that a mandated disclosure, or a subsequent change to an initial disclosure, contains an error or omission, but that the service provider was acting in good faith and with reasonable diligence, the arrangement will still be considered reasonable if the service provider discloses the correct information as soon as practicable, but not more than thirty days after discovery of the error.[4]

The DOL has issued subsequent guidance on the fee disclosure regulations through a series of questions and answers in Field Advisory Bulletin 2012-02R. One of the key points issued in this bulletin is the position of the DOL that adding a brokerage window to an individual account plan is a fiduciary duty wherein the plan fiduciary will be responsible for the prudent selection and monitoring of the designated investment manager, which is a provider of brokerage window services to the plan.[5] Further, the DOL provides "The regulation covers "brokerage windows," "self-directed brokerage accounts," and other similar plan arrangements that enable participants and beneficiaries to select investments beyond those designated by the plan."[6]

Coverage of brokerage windows under the regulation, however, is limited to the disclosure requirements relating to plan-related information. The disclosure requirements regarding investment-related information do not apply to brokerage windows, self-directed brokerage accounts, and similar arrangements, because such windows, accounts, and arrangements are not

---

1. Labor Reg. §2550.408b-2(c)(1)(v)(B)(1).
2. Labor Reg. §2550.408b-2(c)(1)(v)(B)(2).
3. Labor Reg. §2550.408b-2(c)(1)(vi)(A) and (B).
4. Labor Reg. §2550.408b-2(c)(1)(vii).
5. FAB 2012-02R (July 30, 2012).
6. FAB 2012-02R, Q&A 29 (July 30, 2012).

designated investment alternatives. Nor, do the disclosure requirements apply to any investment selected by a participant or beneficiary that is not designated by the plan (*i.e.*, any investments made through the window, account, or arrangement).[1]

Specific disclosures for brokerage windows under the final regulations include the following. First, a plan administrator must provide a general description of any such window, account, or arrangement.[2] The regulation does not state how specific and detailed a description must be to satisfy this requirement. Whether a particular description is satisfactory will depend on the facts and circumstances of the specific plan and the specific window, account, or arrangement. At a minimum, however, this description must provide sufficient information to enable participants and beneficiaries to understand how the window, account, or arrangement works (*e.g.*, how and to whom to give investment instructions; account balance requirements, if any; restrictions or limitations on trading, if any; how the window, account, or arrangement differs from the plan's designated investment alternatives) and whom to contact with questions.[3]

Second, a plan administrator also must provide an explanation of any fees and expenses that may be charged against the individual account of a participant or beneficiary on an individual, rather than on a plan-wide, basis in connection with any such window, account, or arrangement.[4] This would include:

1. Any fee or expense necessary for the participant or beneficiary to start, open, or initially access such a window, account, or arrangement (such as enrollment, initiation, or start up fees), or to stop, close or terminate access;

2. Any ongoing fee or expense (annual, monthly, or any other similarly charged fee or expense) necessary for the participant to maintain access to the window, account, or arrangement, including inactivity fees and minimum balance fees; and

3. Any commissions or fees (*e.g.*, per trade fee) charged in connection with the purchase or sale of a security, including front or back end sales loads if known; but would not include any fees or expenses of the investment selected by the participant or beneficiary (*e.g.*, Rule 12b-1 or similar fees reflected in the investment's total annual operating expenses).[5]

The DOL understands that in some circumstances the specific amount of certain fees associated with the purchase or sale of a security through a window, account, or arrangement, such as front end sales loads for open-end management investment companies registered under the Investment Company Act of 1940, may vary across investments available through the window or may not be known by the plan administrator or provider of the window, account, or arrangement in advance of the purchase or sale of the security by a participant or beneficiary. In recognition of the foregoing, a general statement that such fees exist and that they may be charged against the individual account of a purchasing or selling participant or beneficiary, and

1. FAB 2012-02R, Q&A 29 (July 30, 2012).
2. 29 CFR § 2550.404a-5(c)(1)(i)(F) FAB 2012-02R, Q&A 13, (July 30, 2012).
3. FAB 2012-02R, Q&A 13, (July 30, 2012).
4. 29 CFR § 2550.404a-5(c)(3)(i)(A); FAB 2012-02R, Q&A 13, (July 30, 2012).
5. FAB 2012-02R, Q&A 13, (July 30, 2012).

directions as to how the participant can obtain information about such fees in connection with any particular investment, ordinarily will satisfy the requirements of 29 CFR § 2550.404a-5(c)(3)(i)(A). Otherwise, plan administrators might inundate participants and beneficiaries with information about the cost of buying or selling all the various securities available through a window, account, or arrangement, despite the fact that participants and beneficiaries may not have the interest or expertise to purchase or sell each or any such security. Further, the statement should advise participants and beneficiaries to ask the provider of the window, account, or arrangement about any fees, including any undisclosed fees, associated with the purchase or sale of a particular security through a window, account, or arrangement, before purchasing or selling such security.[1]

Third, a plan administrator also must provide participants and beneficiaries with a statement of the dollar amount of fees and expenses that actually were charged during the preceding quarter against their individual accounts in connection with any such window, account, or arrangement.[2] A statement of these fees must include a description of the services to which the charge relates.[3] The description of the services must clearly explain the charges (*e.g.*, $19.99 brokerage trades, $25.00 brokerage account minimum balance fee, $13.00 brokerage account wire transfer fee, $44.00 front end sales load).[4]

Where a covered plan offers an investment platform that includes a brokerage window, self-directed brokerage account, or similar plan arrangement, and the plan fiduciary does *not* designate any of the funds on the platform or available through the brokerage window, self-directed brokerage account, or similar plan arrangement as "designated investment alternatives" under the plan, the platform or the brokerage window, self-directed brokerage account, or similar plan arrangement is *not* a designated investment alternative for purposes of the fee disclosure regulations.[5] The DOL elaborates: "Whether an investment alternative is a Designated Investment Alternative (DIA) for purposes of the regulation depends on whether it is specifically identified as available under the plan. The regulation does not require that a plan have a particular number of DIAs, and nothing in this Bulletin prohibits the use of a platform or a brokerage window, self-directed brokerage account, or similar plan arrangement in an individual account plan. The Bulletin also does not change the 404(c) regulation or the requirements for relief from fiduciary liability under section 404(c) of ERISA. Nonetheless, in the case of a 401(k) or other individual account plan covered under the regulation, a plan fiduciary's failure to designate investment alternatives, for example, to avoid investment disclosures under the regulation, raises questions under ERISA section 404(a)'s general statutory fiduciary duties of prudence and loyalty. Also, fiduciaries of such plans with platforms or brokerage windows, self-directed brokerage accounts, or similar plan arrangements that enable participants and beneficiaries to select investments beyond those designated by the plan are still bound by ERISA section 404(a)'s statutory duties of prudence and loyalty to participants and beneficiaries who use the platform or the brokerage window, self-directed brokerage account, or similar plan arrangement, including taking into

---

1. FAB 2012-02R, Q&A 13, (July 30, 2012).
2. 29 CFR § 2550.404a-5(c)(3)(ii)(A); FAB 2012-02R, Q&A 13, (July 30, 2012).
3. 29 CFR § 2550.404a-5(c)(3)(ii)(B); FAB 2012-02R, Q&A 13, (July 30, 2012).
4. FAB 2012-02R, Q&A 13, (July 30, 2012).
5. FAB 2012-02R (July 30, 2012).

account the nature and quality of services provided in connection with the platform or the brokerage window, self-directed brokerage account, or similar plan arrangement."[1]

Reasonable Contract or Arrangement Applicability

Under the final regulations, in order for contracts and arrangements for services to be reasonable, the service provider must disclose the information specified below to a responsible plan fiduciary (one with authority to enter into or cause the plan to enter into, or extend or renew, the contract or arrangement). The following information is mandated under the interim final regulation to be disclosed in writing:

1.   A description of the services to be provided under the arrangement;

2.   If applicable, a statement that the service provider, an affiliate, or subcontractor will provide, or reasonably expects to provide, services pursuant to the arrangement directly to the plan (or to an investment contract, product, or entity that holds plan assets and in which the plan has a direct equity investment) as fiduciary (i.e., "platform provider"); and

3.   If applicable, a statement that the service provider, an affiliate, or subcontractor reasonably expects to provide services under the arrangement directly to the plan as an investment adviser registered under the Investment Advisers Act of 1940 or any state law.[2]

Covered Service Providers

A "covered service provider" is a service provider who enters into a contract or arrangement with the covered plan and reasonably expects to receive $1,000 or more in compensation directly or indirectly for providing the following services (regardless of whether such services will be performed, or compensation received, by the service provider, an affiliate, or a subcontractor):

1.   *Service as a fiduciary (within the meaning of ERISA Section 3(21)) or registered investment adviser* — acting as a fiduciary to an investment contract, product, or entity that holds plan assets and in which the plan has a direct equity investment, or services provided directly to the plan as an investment adviser registered under the Investment Advisers Act of 1940 or any state law;

2.   *Certain recordkeeping or brokerage services* — provided to individual account plans wherein participants and beneficiaries may direct the investment of their accounts, if one or more designated investment alternatives will be made available in connection with such recordkeeping or brokerage services; and

3.   *Other services for indirect compensation* — accounting, auditing, actuarial, appraisal, banking, consulting, custodial, insurance, investment advisory (for plan or

---

1. FAB 2012-02R (July 30, 2012).
2. Labor Reg. §2550.408b-2(c)(1)(iv)(A) and (B).

participants), legal, recordkeeping, securities or other investment brokerage, third-party administration, or valuation services.[1]

However, no person or entity will be a "covered service provider" solely by providing services:

1. As an affiliate or a subcontractor that is performing one or more of the services described in items one, two, and three, above, under the contract or arrangement with the covered plan. Thus, only the party directly responsible to the plan for the provision of services is the "covered service provider"—even if an affiliate or a subcontractor performs some of the services that determine a "covered service provider"; or

2. To an investment contract, product, or entity (i.e., an investment vehicle) in which the covered plan invests, regardless of whether (or not) the investment vehicle holds assets of the covered plan—where the services are provided *other than* as a fiduciary (as described in item two, in the preceding list). Thus, furnishing non-fiduciary services to investment vehicles for plan assets will *not* cause a person to be a covered service provider.[2]

Compensation or Fees Defined

"Compensation" is defined under the final regulation as "anything of monetary value (for example, money, gifts, awards, and trips), but does not include non-monetary compensation valued at $250 or less, in the aggregate, during the term of the contract or arrangement." "Direct compensation" is any compensation received directly from the plan. "Indirect compensation" is compensation received from any source other than the plan, the plan sponsor, the service provider, an affiliate, or subcontractor (if the subcontractor receives such compensation in connection with the services performed under the arrangement).[3]

A description of all direct and indirect compensation must be provided to the plan, either in the aggregate or by service that the service provider, an affiliate, or a subcontractor reasonably expects to receive for the covered services.[4] A description of the compensation or cost may be expressed as a monetary amount, formula, percentage of the covered plan's assets, or a per-capita charge for each participant or beneficiary or, if the compensation or cost cannot be reasonably expressed in such terms, by any other reasonable method. The description may include a reasonable and good-faith estimate if the covered service provider cannot otherwise readily describe compensation or cost and the covered service provider explains the methodology and assumptions used to prepare such estimate. Any estimate of recordkeeping cost must contain sufficient information to permit evaluation of the reasonableness of the compensation or cost.[5]

---

1. Labor Reg. §§2550.408b-2(c)(1)(iii)(A)(1)-(3), 2550.408b-2(c)(1)(iii)(B) and (C).
2. Labor Reg. §§2550.408b-2(c)(1)(iii)(D), 2550.408b-2(c).
3. Labor Reg. §2550.408b-2(c)(1)(viii)(A) and (B)(1) and (2).
4. Labor Reg. §2550.408b-2(c)(1)(iv)(C)(1) and (2).
5. Labor Reg. §2550.408b-2(c)(1)(viii)(D)(3).

Where compensation is to be paid among related parties, the plan fiduciary is to receive a description of any compensation that will be paid among the service provider, an affiliate, or subcontractor in connection with the covered services if it is set on a transaction basis (e.g., commissions, soft-dollars, finder's fees, or other incentive compensation based on business placed or retained) or is charged directly against the plan's investment (e.g., 12b-1 fees). This includes identification of the services for which the compensation will be paid and the identification of the payers and the recipients (including their status, if applicable, as an affiliate or subcontractor). These forms of compensation must be disclosed regardless of whether any other compensation is also required to be disclosed by any other parts of the final regulation.[1]

Where recordkeeping services are to be provided to the plan, a description of all direct and indirect compensation that the service provider, an affiliate, or subcontractor reasonably expects to receive must be disclosed (even when no explicit charge for recordkeeping is identified as part of the service package or contract). If the service provider reasonably expects the services to be provided, in whole or in part, without explicit compensation, or will be offset or rebated based on other compensation received, the service provider must provide a reasonable and good-faith estimate of the cost to the plan of the recordkeeping services. This explanation must include an explanation of the methodology and assumptions used in preparing the estimate along with a detailed explanation of the recordkeeping services to be provided. The estimate is to take into account the rates that the service provider, an affiliate, or subcontractor would be paid by third parties or the prevailing market rates charged for similar recordkeeping services for a similar plan with a similar number of participants and beneficiaries.[2] The recordkeeper must also advise the plan of the manner in which it will receive the fees — through plan billing or deduction directly from plan accounts and investments.[3]

Recordkeepers are also required to disclose the following information with respect to each investment contract, product, or entity that holds plan assets and in which the covered plan has a direct equity investment, and for which fiduciary services will be provided (a bundled service arrangement):

1. A description of any compensation that will be charged directly against an investment, such as commissions, sales loads, sales charges, deferred sales charges, redemption fees, surrender charges, exchange fees, account fees, and purchase fees, and that is not included in the annual operating expenses of the investment;

2. A description of the annual operating expenses (e.g., "expense ratio") if the return is not fixed and any ongoing expenses in addition to annual operating expenses (e.g., wrap fees, mortality and expense fees), or, for an investment that is a designated investment alternative (see Q 97 for full details on designated investment alternatives and disclosures under individual account plans), the total annual operating expenses

---

1. Labor Reg. §2550.408b-2(c)(1)(iv)(C)(3).
2. Labor Reg. §2550.408b-2(c)(1)(iv)(D)(1) and (2).
3. Labor Reg. §2550.408b-2(c)(1)(iv)(E).

expressed as a percentage and calculated in accordance with Labor Regulation Section 2550.404a-5(h)(5); and

3.   For an investment that is a designated investment alternative (again, see Q 97 for further details), any other information or data about the designated investment alternative that is within the control of, or reasonably available to, the covered service provider and is required to be disclosed under the individual account plan disclosure regulations.[1]

For service providers offering services as a fiduciary or registered investment adviser (brokerage services), an additional disclosure must be made to the plan with respect to each investment contract, product, or entity that holds plan assets and in which the plan has a direct equity investment, and for which fiduciary services will be provided.

An investment-related disclosure is required by recordkeepers, with respect to each designated investment alternative for which recordkeeping brokerage services will be provided. A covered service provider may comply with this requirement by providing current disclosure materials of the issuer of the designated investment alternative, or information replicated from such materials, that include the information, provided that:

1.   The issuer is not an affiliate;

2.   The issuer is a registered investment company, an insurance company qualified to do business in any state, an issuer of a publicly traded security, or a financial institution supervised by a state or federal agency; and

3.   The covered service provider acts in good faith and does not know that the materials are incomplete or inaccurate, and furnishes the responsible plan fiduciary with a statement that the covered service provider is making no representations as to the completeness or accuracy of such materials.[2]

There is nothing in the regulation that limits the ability of covered service providers to furnish information required by the regulation to responsible plan fiduciaries via electronic media. However, unless the covered service provider's disclosure information on a Web site is readily accessible to responsible plan fiduciaries, and fiduciaries have clear notification on how to gain such access, the information on the Web site may not be regarded as having been "furnished" within the meaning of the final regulation.[3]

Termination of the Contract or Arrangement

The final regulation stipulates that no contract or arrangement is reasonable within the meaning of the statutory exemption and regulations if it does not permit termination by the plan without penalty to the plan on reasonably short notice under the circumstances to prevent the plan from becoming locked into an arrangement that has become disadvantageous. A long-term

---

1. Labor Reg. §2550.408b-2(c)(1)(iv)(E).
2. Labor Reg. §2550.408b-2(c)(1)(iv)(F).
3. Preamble to Final Regulation, 77 Fed. Reg. 5632 (Feb. 3, 2012).

lease that may be terminated prior to expiration (without penalty to the plan) on reasonably short notice under the circumstances is not generally an unreasonable arrangement merely because of its long term. A provision that reasonably compensates the service provider or lessor for loss upon early termination is not a penalty. Similarly, a provision for a termination fee that covers reasonably foreseeable expenses related to the vacancy and reletting of the office space upon early termination is not a penalty. However, such provisions do not reasonably compensate for losses if they require payment in excess of the actual losses incurred or fail to require mitigation of damages.[1]

The final regulations stipulate that all covered service providers must disclose a description of any compensation that they, an affiliate, or a subcontractor reasonably expects to receive in connection with the termination of the arrangement, and how any prepaid amounts will be calculated and refunded upon such termination.[2]

Result of Failure to Comply

The DOL updated the final class exemption relating to the final regulations (see Q 460 for full details) to require, among other things, that the responsible plan fiduciary notify the DOL of a failure to comply by a covered service provider under certain circumstances.[3]

Service providers who fail to comply with the final regulation will be subject to the prohibited transaction rules of ERISA Section 406 and Code Section 4975 penalties.

Practitioner's Pointer: The notice requirement in the final class exemption does not relieve a plan administrator of the obligation to report a prohibited transaction in accordance with the instructions to the Annual Report Form 5500 Series, without regard to whether the covered service provider furnishes information in response to the fiduciary's request.

Effective Date

The final regulation is effective for both existing and new contracts and arrangements as of July 1, 2012.

Practitioner's Pointer: Plan administrators are reminded that the final rule's July 1, 2012, effective date will also impact when disclosures must first be made under the participant-level disclosure regulations (see Q 97 for full details). The initial annual disclosure of "plan level" and "investment level" information (including associated fees and expenses) must be furnished no later than August 30, 2012, (sixty days after the final rule's effective date). The first quarterly statement must then be furnished no later than November 14, 2012, (forty-five days after the end of the third quarter during which the initial disclosures were first required). This quarterly statement need only reflect the fees and expenses actually deducted from the participant or beneficiary's account during the third calendar quarter to which the statement relates.

---

1. Labor Reg. §2550.408b-2(c)(1)(xii).
2. Labor Reg. §2550.408b-2(c)(1)(iv)(C)(4).
3. Labor Reg. §2550.408b-2(c)(1)(ix).

ERISA Fee Recapture Accounts and 408(b)(2)
Service Provider Fee Disclosures

In Advisory Opinion 2013-03A (AO 2013-03A) the DOL addresses the different types of ERISA recapture accounts and discusses the ERISA plan asset and prohibited transaction rules that apply to them. In AO 2013-03A, the DOL describes two types of ERISA recapture accounts – the *bookkeeping account* and the *plan account*. Each requires a different approach in identifying how ERISA applies.

Under the *bookkeeping account approach*, the financial institution receives the revenue sharing payments and under an agreement with the plan and establishes this account on the financial institution's records. The bookkeeping account reflects credits that under a written plan agreement or under the direction of a plan fiduciary, will apply these credits to pay plan service providers. In this approach, amounts in the bookkeeping account are *not ERISA* plan assets.

However, the DOL advises that if there is an agreement in place for plan fees to be paid from this account and the financial institution fails to make such specified payments, the plan would have a claim against the financial institution and that claim is a plan asset.

Under the *plan account approach*, the financial institution receives the revenue sharing payments directly and under written agreement with the plan transfers some or all of the revenue sharing payments to the plan. The plan administrator then uses the plan account to pay service providers. If, at the close of the plan year, amounts remain in the plan account, the plan administrator will then allocate them to participants as additional plan earnings.

With the *plan account approach*, the amounts received in the account are plan assets. If the plan has a contract with the financial institution to transfer the funds to the plan, and the financial institution fails to make those payments, the plan would have a claim against the financial institution and that claim would be a plan asset.

Under the service provider fee disclosure rules of ERISA Section 408(b)(2), if the service provider is a "covered service provider" (it is) the covered service provider's receipt of revenue sharing payments constitutes "direct or indirect compensation" paid in connection with services and must be disclosed by the financial institution to the responsible plan fiduciary BEFORE entering into such an arrangement. Failure to disclose the arrangement in advance makes it "unreasonable" and a de facto prohibited transaction. The payments received under the ERISA recapture account must be reasonable and necessary in light of the facts and circumstances or they will constitute a prohibited transaction.

The responsible plan fiduciary has the standard ERISA section 404 fiduciary duties to act prudently and in the best interests of plan fiduciaries in deciding to enter into such an ERISA fee recapture/revenue sharing arrangement as well as the same duties in the ongoing monitoring of the arrangement.

AO 2013-03A does not mandate any plan language/provision updates in order to avail the plan to ERISA fee recapture arrangements."

DOL, SEC Agreement on Application of Securities Laws to Participant-Level Disclosure Regulations

In response to a request from DOL, the Securities and Exchange Commission (SEC) has issued a no-action letter in which SEC has agreed to treat investment related information provided by a plan administrator to plan participants to comply with EBSA's disclosure regulations, as though the information were a communication that satisfies the requirements of Rule 482 of the Securities Act of 1933 (the 33 Act).[1] The DOL requested this guidance in order to address concerns raised by plan sponsors and their financial service providers regarding their obligations under ERISA and Rule 482 of the 33 Act—which establishes requirements that open-ended investment companies must follow when placing performance information in their advertising. Specifically, the DOL sought a no-action letter from SEC indicating that a plan's compliance with the DOL disclosure requirements under ERISA section 408(b)(2) would not result in action by SEC related to Rule 482.

The SEC has also elaborated beyond the DOL's request by indicating that the investment-related information provided to plan participants and beneficiaries need not be filed under Rule 497 of the Securities Act and Section 24(b) of the Investment Company Act with SEC or certain national securities associations, such as the Financial Industry Regulatory Authority (FINRA).

However, the SEC notes that it has been informed by FINRA's staff that FINRA intends to interpret its own rules that apply to the information provided by a plan administrator to plan participants that is required by, and complies with, the disclosure requirements under the DOL disclosure regulations.

403. What are the rules regarding transfers of assets of the plan?

The direct or indirect transfer to, or use by or for the benefit of, a party in interest of any plan assets is prohibited.[2] For example, the trustees of a union-sponsored pension plan engaged in prohibited transactions by loaning money to an association that was "closely-related" to the union. A prohibited transaction occurs when a fiduciary has subjective intent to benefit a party in interest, and the fiduciary knows (or reasonably should know) that the transaction represents a use of plan assets for the benefit of a party in interest. Where the trustees of a plan subjectively intended to benefit the union through the lending of plan assets to the association, and the union did, in fact, benefit from the loans, the transaction violated ERISA Section 406(a)(1)(D).[3]

A fiduciary does not necessarily need to have a culpable motive in order to have engaged in a prohibited transaction under ERISA Section 406(a)(1)(D). For example, a plan trustee transferred assets from the plan trust to his own bank account allegedly to protect the plan from a fraudulent scheme by plan participants. Because ERISA Section 406 on its face does not require culpable motive, the trustee's motive for the transfer of assets was not a defense to the prohibited transaction.[4]

---

1. Dept. of Labor, SEC No-Action Letter (Oct. 26, 2011).
2. ERISA Sec. 406(a)(1)(D).
3. *Reich v. Compton*, 57 F.3d 270 (3d Cir. 1995).
4. *PBGC v. Fletcher*, 750 F. Supp. 233 (W.D. Tex. 1990).

A prohibited transaction also occurs if there is an arrangement under which a plan invests in, or retains its investment in, an investment company, and, as part of the arrangement, it is expected that the investment company will purchase securities from a party in interest. Similarly, the plan's purchase of an insurance policy, pursuant to an arrangement under which it is expected that the insurance company will make a loan to a party in interest, is a prohibited transaction.[1]

A prohibited transaction also occurs if a fiduciary, acting as plan trustee: (1) renews outstanding loans with the sponsor of the plan (thus allowing continued use of plan assets by the plan sponsor); (2) causes the plan to make a loan to himself (thus transferring plan assets to himself for his own use and benefit); and (3) causes the plan to transfer its assets to the plan sponsor.[2]

The trustees of collectively bargained pension and welfare plans violated ERISA by authorizing monthly payments for each other from the plans' assets as compensation for their services as trustees and by authorizing the plans to make contributions on their behalf, so as to make each other eligible for the receipt of benefits from the plans. The trustees' receipt of the monthly payments from the plans, the contributions made on their behalf, and the receipt of benefits from the plans each constituted a separate prohibited transaction in violation of ERISA Section 406(a)(1)(D).[3]

In another case, plan trustees released parties in interest from guarantees of a plan loan. The court held that this constituted "a direct or indirect transfer" of "assets of the plan" to parties in interest, or the use of "assets of the plan" for the benefit of parties in interest, in violation of ERISA Section 406(a)(1)(D), because prior to their release, the guarantees were assets of the plan. In addition, the release benefited the guarantors at the expense of the plan, because the plan no longer had the same security to enable it to collect on the outstanding amount of its loan. Thus, assets of the plan were transferred for the benefit of parties in interest, and the release of defendants' guarantees constituted a prohibited transaction under ERISA Section 406(a)(1)(D).[4]

In contrast, unless a transaction falls within the specific list of dealings proscribed by ERISA, it does not constitute a per se violation of the prohibited transaction rules. For example, a violation did not exist where a plan loaned money to unrelated persons, who then used all or a portion of the funds received to pay off loans to the employer of the plan's participants. Although the plan trustees were also employees of the plan sponsor, there was no evidence to support the hypothesis that they acted for their own benefit by approving the third-party loans to protect their employment with the plan sponsor.[5]

Likewise, a party in interest does not violate ERISA Section 406(a)(1)(D) merely because the party derives some incidental benefit from the investment of plan assets in shared investments that are made simultaneously with investments by a fiduciary for its own account on identical

---

1. Labor Reg. §2509.75-2.
2. *Marshall v. Kelly*, 465 F. Supp. 341 (W.D. Okla. 1978).
3. *Donovan v. Daugherty*, 550 F. Supp. 390 (S.D. Ala. 1982).
4. *Reich v. Polera Bldg. Corp.*, 20 EBC 1100 (S.D.N.Y. 1996).
5. *Brock v. Citizens Bank of Clovis*, 841 F.2d 344 (10th Cir.), *cert. denied*, 488 U.S. 829 (1988).

terms and in the same relative proportions. Any benefit that the fiduciary might derive from these circumstances is incidental and would not violate ERISA Section 406(a)(1)(D).[1]

The United States Supreme Court held that the payment of benefits by an employer pursuant to an early retirement program conditioned on the participants' release of employment-related claims did not constitute a prohibited transaction under ERISA Section 406(a)(1)(D).[2] Although the amendments to the plan offered increased benefits in exchange for a release of employment claims, and the employer received an incidental benefit from the releases, the amendments did not constitute the use of plan assets to "purchase" a significant benefit for the employer. The Court held that the payment of benefits pursuant to an amended plan, regardless of what the plan requires of the employee in return for those benefits, does not constitute a prohibited transaction, because ERISA Section 406(a)(1)(D) does not, in direct terms, include the payment of benefits by a plan administrator. In addition, the surrounding provisions suggest that the payment of benefits is in fact not a "transaction" in the sense that Congress used that term in ERISA Section 406(a). The Court reasoned that the prohibited "transactions" identified in ERISA Section 406(a) have in common the use of plan assets in a manner that is potentially harmful to the plan. However, the "payment of benefits conditioned on performance by plan participants cannot reasonably be said to share that characteristic."[3]

404. What are the rules regarding the acquisition, on behalf of a plan, of employer securities or employer real property?

A fiduciary is prohibited from causing a plan to engage in a transaction, if she knows (or should know) that such transaction constitutes a direct or indirect acquisition, on behalf of the plan, of any employer security or employer real property in violation of ERISA Section 407.[4]

This prohibition seeks to protect the judgment of fiduciaries against influences exerted by employers in the context of security and real property purchases. The United States Supreme Court emphasized that the purpose of ERISA Section 406(a)(1)(E) and related provisions is to insulate the trust from the employer's interest, and to ensure that the exclusive authority and discretion to arrange and control the assets of the plan rest in the fiduciaries alone, and not in the employer or union who might be responsible for the fiduciaries' appointments.[5] The purchase or sale of securities by a plan in an effort to manipulate the price of such securities to the advantage of a party in interest is an example of what would violate ERISA Section 406(a)(1)(E).[6]

Transactions Between a Plan and a Fiduciary

405. What are the rules regarding self-dealing and conflicts of interest?

In addition to the five specific prohibited transactions involving parties in interest under ERISA Section 406(a), ERISA Section 406(b) prohibits fiduciaries from engaging in various acts

---

1. PTE 88-93.
2. *Lockheed Corp. v. Spink*, 517 U.S. 882 (1996).
3. *Lockheed Corp. v. Spink*, above.
4. ERISA Sec. 406(a)(1)(E).
5. *NLRB v. Amax Coal Co.*, 453 U.S. 950 (1981).
6. H.R. Conf. Rep. No. 93-1280, 93d Cong., 2d Sess. 310 (1974).

of self-dealing or conflicts of interest, and transactions involving the plan in which the fiduciary personally profits. These transactions compromise the fiduciary's duties of loyalty to the plan and acting exclusively for the benefit of the plan or participants and beneficiaries. The purpose of ERISA Section 406(b) is to prevent a fiduciary from being put in a position where he has dual loyalties, and, therefore, cannot act exclusively for the benefit of a plan's participants and beneficiaries.

Under these prohibitions, a plan fiduciary may not: (1) deal with the assets of the plan in his own interest or for his own account; (2) in his individual or in any other capacity, act in any transaction involving the plan on behalf of a party (or represent a party) whose interests are adverse to the interests of the plan or the interests of its participants or beneficiaries; or (3) receive any consideration for his own personal account from any party dealing with such plan in connection with a transaction involving the assets of the plan.[1]

Similar to ERISA, under the Internal Revenue Code, a disqualified person who is a fiduciary may not: (1) deal with the income or assets of a plan in his own interest or for his own account; or (2) receive any consideration for his own personal account from any party dealing with the plan in connection with a transaction involving the income or assets of the plan.[2]

The prohibitions of ERISA Section 406(b) supplement the other prohibitions of ERISA Section 406(a), by imposing on parties in interest who are fiduciaries a duty of undivided loyalty to the plans for which they act. These prohibitions are imposed upon fiduciaries to deter them from exercising the authority, control, or responsibility that makes them fiduciaries when they have interests that may conflict with the interests of the plans. In such cases, the fiduciaries have interests in the transactions that may affect the exercise of their best judgment as fiduciaries.[3]

Thus, a fiduciary may not use the authority, control, or responsibility that makes such person a fiduciary to cause a plan to pay an additional fee to such fiduciary (or to a person in which such fiduciary has an interest that may affect the exercise of such fiduciary's best judgment as a fiduciary) to provide a service. Nor may a fiduciary use such authority, control, or responsibility to cause a plan to enter into a transaction involving plan assets whereby such fiduciary (or a person in which such fiduciary has an interest that may affect the exercise of such fiduciary's best judgment as a fiduciary) will receive consideration from a third party in connection with such transaction. A person in which a fiduciary has an interest that may affect the exercise of such fiduciary's best judgment as a fiduciary includes a person who is a party in interest.[4]

Thus, ERISA Section 406(b) is specifically directed at the problem of fiduciary self-dealing, and absolutely prohibits a fiduciary from acting in a conflict of interest situation where his loyalties to the plan may be compromised or divided.[5] The legislative history of ERISA Section 406(b)

---

1. ERISA Sec. 406(b).
2. IRC Secs. 4975(c)(1)(E), 4975(c)(1)(F).
3. Labor Reg. §2550.408b-2(e)(1); *Gilliam v. Edwards*, 492 F. Supp. 1255 (D.N.J. 1980).
4. Labor Reg. §2550.408b-2(e)(1).
5. *Donovan v. Daugherty*, 550 F. Supp. 390 (S.D. Ala. 1982).

and relevant case law indicate that Congress sought to prevent "kickbacks," making "illegal per se the types of transactions that experience had shown to entail a high potential for abuse."[1]

Additionally, even in the absence of bad faith, or in the presence of a fair and reasonable transaction, ERISA Section 406(b) creates a per se violation and establishes a blanket prohibition against certain acts, easily applied, in order to facilitate Congress's remedial interest in protecting employee benefit plans.[2]

406. What are the rules regarding dealing with the assets of the plan in one's own interest or for one's own account?

A fiduciary is prohibited from dealing with the assets of the plan in her own interest or for her own account.[3] This prohibition is aimed at a fiduciary's use of a plan's assets as a vehicle for advancing her own interests. Fiduciaries that cause pension plans to invest in companies in which they have financial interests, and that accept consulting and other fees from such companies, are examples of violators of this provision.[4]

A fiduciary, acting as plan trustee, dealt with the plan assets in his own interest by actively negotiating and designing an employment contract under which a pension fund was to pay him for his services as its administrator. The prohibited transaction was supported when the trustee made no attempt to disqualify himself or extract himself from the plan trustees' considerations. He also actively participated in or initiated the discussions leading to his employment as administrator, and was a guiding force at the trustees' meetings, encouraging them to award him the contract. The final contract was decidedly one-sided in his favor, and he reserved the sole ability to terminate it. Because the trustee had actively pursued and discussed the design of his own employment contract without proper regard for the interests of the fund, he had abandoned his fiduciary obligation to the pension plan in order to secure the best contract, in violation of ERISA Section 406(b)(1).[5]

A plan fiduciary also cannot use any of his fiduciary authority to cause the plan to make a loan to an entity in which he has an interest. This occurred where a plan fiduciary caused a plan to renew the loans to a company that he owned, caused the plan to make a loan to himself, and caused the plan to make a payment of plan assets to the same company that he owned.[6]

A violation also occurred when plan trustees authorized monthly payments for themselves from a plan as compensation for services rendered to the plan (they received full-time pay from contributing employers and unions), and they authorized the plan to make contributions on their behalf, so as to make themselves eligible to receive benefits from the plan.[7]

---

1. *Donovan v. Cunningham*, 716 F.2d 1455 (5th Cir. 1983), *cert. denied*, 467 U.S. 1251 (1984).
2. *Gilliam v. Edwards*, 492 F. Supp. 1255 (D.N.J. 1980); see also *Brink v. DaLesio*, 496 F. Supp. 1350 (D. Md. 1980), *aff'd* in part and *rev'd* in part, 667 F.2d 420 (4th Cir. 1981).
3. ERISA Sec. 406(b)(1).
4. *Lowen v. Tower Asset Mgmt., Inc.*, 653 F. Supp 1542 (S.D.N.Y. 1987).
5. *Gilliam v. Edwards*, 492 F. Supp. 1255 (D.N.J. 1980).
6. *Marshall v. Kelly*, 465 F. Supp. 341 (W.D. Okla. 1978).
7. *Donovan v. Daugherty*, 550 F. Supp. 390 (S.D. Ala. 1982).

Although a fiduciary is prohibited from dealing with the assets of the plan in her own interests of a financial nature, the term "interests" is not limited to financial interests. The term "interest" is read broadly to prevent the use of plan assets for any interest, financial or nonfinancial, other than the interests of the plan and its beneficiaries. For example, in a contest for corporate control, actions of the plan trustees (who were also officers of either the "target" or the "raider") who bought shares in a target corporation, in order to assist either the target's management or the raider in the quest for either corporate control or a control premium, could be seen as having a significant "interest" of their own in the outcome of the contest. The officers of the "target" might well be immediately concerned about holding onto their jobs, and the officers of the "raider" might find it in their interest, in terms of maintaining good relations with their superiors, to assist their corporation in its acquisition efforts.[1]

Similarly, a fiduciary of a plan engages in a violation if he retains his child to provide, for a fee, various kinds of administrative services necessary for the operation of the plan. The fiduciary has engaged in an act described in ERISA Section 406(b)(1), because the fiduciary's child is a person in whom the fiduciary has an "interest" that may affect the exercise of the fiduciary's best judgment as a fiduciary.[2]

In contrast, a fiduciary does not engage in a violation of ERISA Section 406(b)(1) if the fiduciary does not use any of the authority, control, or responsibility (which makes such person a fiduciary) to cause a plan to pay additional fees for a service furnished by such fiduciary or to pay a fee for a service furnished by a person in which such fiduciary has an interest that may affect the exercise of such fiduciary's best judgment as a fiduciary. This may occur, for example, when one fiduciary is retained by a second fiduciary on behalf of a plan to provide a service for an additional fee.[3]

Another example is when a plan's investment adviser, who is a plan fiduciary, also performs, for additional fees, services that are in addition to the services currently provided if the provision of the services is arranged and approved by an independent plan fiduciary. The investment adviser has not engaged in a prohibited transaction described in ERISA Section 406(b)(1), because the adviser does not use any of the authority, control, or responsibility that makes it a fiduciary (the provision of investment advisory services) to cause the plan to pay it additional fees for the provision of the additional services.[4]

Additionally, a plan may retain a bank, whose president is a trustee of the plan, to provide administrative services to it, if the bank president physically absents himself from all consideration of the bank's proposal to provide the services to the plan and does not otherwise exercise any of the authority, control, or responsibility that makes him a fiduciary to cause the plan to retain the bank. Under these circumstances, the bank president has not engaged in an act described in ERISA Section 406(b)(1). Further, the other trustees have not engaged in an act described in ERISA Section 406(b)(1) merely because the bank president is on the board of trustees of the

---

1. *Leigh v. Engle*, 727 F.2d 113 (7th Cir. 1984).
2. Labor Reg. §2550.408b-2(f), Ex. 6.
3. Labor Reg. §2550.408b-2(e)(2).
4. Labor Reg. §2550.408b-2(f), Ex. 1.

plan. This fact alone would not make them have an interest in the transaction that might affect the exercise of their best judgment as fiduciaries.[1]

However, the authority, control, or responsibility that makes a person a fiduciary may be exercised "in effect" as well as in form. Therefore, mere approval of the transaction by a second fiduciary does not mean that the first fiduciary has not used any of the authority, control, or responsibility that makes such person a fiduciary to cause the plan to pay the first fiduciary an additional fee for a service. For example, when plan fiduciary A retains fiduciary B to provide administrative services to the plan, and thereafter, fiduciary B retains fiduciary A to provide services to the plan for a fee in addition to the services currently provided to the plan by A, both A and B have engaged in a prohibited transaction. Regardless of any intent that he may have had at the time he retained B, A has engaged in a violation because A has, in effect, exercised the authority, control, or responsibility that makes A a fiduciary to cause the plan to pay A additional fees for the services. B, whose continued employment by the plan depends on A, has also engaged in a violation, because B has an interest in the transaction that might affect the exercise of B's best judgment as a fiduciary. As a result, B has dealt with plan assets in his own interest under ERISA Section 406(b)(1).[2]

407. What are the rules regarding transactions involving the plan on behalf of a party whose interests are adverse to the interests of the plan or the interests of its participants or beneficiaries?

Although not a prohibited transaction under the Internal Revenue Code, ERISA prohibits a plan fiduciary from acting in his individual or in any other capacity in any transaction involving the plan on behalf of a party (or representing a party) whose interests are adverse to the interests of the plan or its participants or beneficiaries.[3]

This provision is a blanket prohibition against a fiduciary's engaging in potential conflicts of interest. Like the prohibited transaction provisions of ERISA Section 406(a)(1), ERISA Section 406(b)(2) applies regardless of whether the transaction is "fair" to the plan.

An insurance company, as named fiduciary of a plan, violated ERISA Section 406(b)(2) when it engaged in a transaction involving a plan in which its interests were adverse to the plan's interests. The prohibited transaction occurred when the insurance company invested all of the plan's assets in annuity contracts issued by the insurance company. The insurance company's interest in the transaction involved the plan's purchase of its own group annuity contracts as investment vehicles to the insurance company's master pension plan. The insurance company maximized its profits by paying the lowest permissible return on the plan's investment and by charging the maximum permissible surrender charge. The plan's interest in the transaction was to maximize the sum of their investment by receiving the highest permissible rate of return and by minimizing or eliminating any surrender charges.[4]

---

1. Labor Reg. §2550.408b-2(f), Ex. 7.
2. Labor Reg. §2550.408b-2(f), Ex. 5.
3. ERISA Sec. 406(b)(2).
4. *Arakelian v. National W. Life Ins. Co.*, 680 F. Supp. 400 (D.D.C. 1987).

The scope of the prohibition also encompasses the lending of money between a plan and another party. A fiduciary cannot act in a loan transaction on behalf of a party borrowing from the plan without violating ERISA Section 406(b)(2), because the interests of a lender and a borrower are, by definition, adverse. This was illustrated in a case where an identical group of trustees managed a union pension fund and a union welfare fund. Because of decreased employer contributions, the welfare fund began to run short of cash, and the trustees agreed to loan money from the pension fund to the welfare fund. Despite the fact that the transaction involved no allegations of misconduct or unfair terms, the court held that ERISA Section 406(b)(2) had been violated because when identical trustees of two employee benefit plans whose participants and beneficiaries are not identical effect a loan between the plans, a per se violation of ERISA exists. The violation existed because the borrower and lender in the same transaction had adverse interests and the fiduciaries acting on both sides of the loan transaction could not negotiate the best terms for either plan.[1]

A bank, in its capacity as plan fiduciary, violated ERISA Section 406(b)(2) when it arranged construction loans simultaneously with permanent loans using common trust funds that included employee plan assets. The bank received origination fees from the borrowers in exchange for the bank's assistance in obtaining the permanent loans funded by the employee benefit plan assets. In addition to having a conflict of interest in representing both parties to the permanent loan transactions, by arranging the permanent financing to retire the construction loans it had made, the bank assured itself that the construction loans would be virtually without risk, and was thus acting in its own economic interest.[2]

Just as a plan fiduciary cannot act in a loan transaction on behalf of the borrower who is obtaining a loan from the plan without violating ERISA Section 406(b)(2), likewise, a plan fiduciary cannot, without violating ERISA Section 406(b)(1), use any of his fiduciary authority to cause the plan to make a loan to an entity in which he has an interest. Such was the case when pension plan trustees approved the investment of virtually all of a pension plan's assets in loans to sponsoring companies of which they were officers. All of the plan trustees held an ownership or management interest in each of the borrowing companies, and the companies were so related and interdependent that each fiduciary had an interest in each borrower, and, in effect, represented both the borrowers and the lender in the transaction. Accordingly, the court concluded that in making and approving such loans, the trustees violated ERISA Section 406(b)(2).[3]

408. What are the rules regarding receiving any consideration from any party dealing with a plan in connection with a transaction involving plan assets?

Commonly referred to as the "anti-kickback" provision is the prohibition against a plan fiduciary's receiving any payments or other forms of consideration for her own personal account

---

1. *Cutaiar v. Marshall*, 590 F.2d 523 (3d Cir. 1979); see also *Donovan v. Mazzola*, 606 F. Supp. 119 (N.D. Cal. 1981), *aff'd*, 716 F.2d 1226 (9th Cir. 1983).
2. *Martin v. National Bank of Alaska*, 828 F. Supp. 1427 (D. Alaska 1992).
3. *Freund v. Marshall & Ilsley Bank*, 485 F. Supp. 629 (W.D. Wis. 1979).

from any party dealing with such plan in connection with a transaction involving the assets of the plan.[1]

This prohibition is illustrated in the case of a union official, acting as a trustee of union benefit funds, who accepted free tax preparation services from an accounting firm that served both the union and the benefit funds. Although the accounting services in controversy were valued at only $500, the court held that receipt of gratuities violated ERISA Section 406(b)(3), without regard to whether the costs attributable to those services were passed on to the union or the benefit funds, and without regard to whether there was any demonstrable effect on the trustee's discretion concerning the selection and retention of accountants to perform services for those entities. Even though it had not been proven that the transaction was a quid pro quo for the gratuities or that harm had resulted, the court also held that a fiduciary charged with violating ERISA Section 406(b)(3) must prove by clear or convincing evidence that the compensation he received was for services other than a transaction involving the assets of the plan.[2]

In another kickback case, health and welfare fund trustees violated ERISA's conflict of interest provisions when they received kickbacks, in the form of monthly payments and the free use of a boat, from an individual who provided the plans' insurance policies.[3] Similarly, pension fund trustees violated ERISA Section 403(b)(3) when they received gratuities from the plan administrator that were used to give the trustees free trips and hotel rooms. Although no evidence was presented showing that the gratuity was made in connection with a transaction involving plan assets, the court held that logic dictates that the burden of proof should be placed on the trustees to prove the gratuity was not in connection with a transaction involving plan assets.[4]

Receipt of 12b-1 Fees

12b-1 fees are those fees paid by mutual funds for administrative and other fees to service providers such as banks, consultants, recordkeepers, and directed plan trustees in connection with plan investments in mutual funds. Mutual funds are willing to pay these fees because such bundled service arrangements (the combination of trust, custodial, and administrative services along with mutual fund investment options) common within the industry reduce the mutual fund's own administrative costs of providing shareholder services.

Previously, the DOL had held that the receipt of 12b-1 fees by plan trustees as a result of plan investments made in the underlying mutual funds violated the anti-kickback provisions of ERISA. With the release of Advisory Opinions 97-15A (the "Frost Letter") and 97-16A (the "Aetna Letter"), the DOL has ruled that the receipt of 12b-1 fees by a directed trustee from mutual funds involved in such bundled service arrangements will not violate the anti-kickback provisions, so long as the trustee does not exercise any fiduciary authority or control to cause the plans to invest in the mutual funds. The Aetna Letter applies this relief to recordkeepers from unrelated mutual funds that participate in the bundled service arrangement. The Frost Letter

---

1. ERISA Sec. 406(b)(3).
2. *Brink v. DaLesio*, 496 F. Supp. 1350 (D. Md. 1980), *aff'd in part and rev'd in part*, 667 F.2d 420 (4th Cir. 1981).
3. *Donovan v. Tricario*, 5 EBC 2057 (S.D. Fla. 1984).
4. *Secretary of Labor v. Carell*, 17 EBC 1159 (M.D. Tenn. 1993).

applies to bundled service products offered by a bank serving as trustee to customer plans as long as the bank acts according to investment directions from plan fiduciaries and participants, and does not otherwise exercise any authority or control to cause the plan to invest in the mutual funds. Further, the DOL ruled that where the bank exercises control over plan investments, there would be no violation of the anti-kickback provisions for the receipt of 12b-1 fees where the bank passes through to the plans a corresponding reduction in administrative fees in the amount of 12b-1 fees received by the bank from mutual funds to which it has directed plan investments.

The DOL has also determined that transactions, and related fees, taking place over an automated securities trading system, which matches buyers and sellers of a particular stock without requiring that the parties to the transaction reveal their identities, does not violate ERISA's prohibited transaction rules, because the transactions constitute a "blind" negotiation for the purchase or sale of securities.[1] However, the DOL advised that ERISA's general standards of fiduciary conduct would apply to the determination to buy or sell a particular stock, and to the decision to use a particular trading system.

Adviser Fees

The Seventh Circuit Court of Appeals has ruled that mutual fund adviser fees are best established by market competition free from judicial process. The court stated "Federal securities laws, of which the Investment Company Act is one component, work largely by requiring disclosure and then allowing price to be set by competition in which investors make their own choices." In affirming the trial court ruling for the defendants, the court stated that the law does not subject the fiduciary to a cap on compensation. "The trustees (and in the end investors, who vote with their feet and dollars), rather than a judge or jury, determine how much advisory services are worth."[2]

Revenue Sharing

In a case of first impression, a district court has held that ERISA does not mandate disclosure of 401(k) revenue-sharing arrangements.[3] The participants claimed that the plan sponsor, the investment provider, and a sister fund management firm of the investment provider violated their fiduciary duties to plan participants by providing investment options with "excessive and unreasonable fees and costs," and by failing to adequately disclose information about revenue sharing and the "hidden fees" and costs to plan participants.

In dismissing the claims of the participants, the district court stated that neither ERISA nor its regulations could be "reasonably read to require" the disclosure of revenue-sharing arrangements.[4] According to the district court, the disclosure in the 401(k) plans' annual reports (Form 5500) and the fund prospectuses accurately reflected the expenses paid to fund manager for fund management. (Each of the funds for which the fund manager served as investment adviser charged fund investors an asset-based fee. The fees are expressed as a percentage of total

---

1. DOL Adv. Op. 2004-05A (citing H.R. Rep. 93-1280).
2. *Jones v. Harris Assocs.*, No 07-1624 (7th Cir. 2008), http://www.plansponsor.com/uploadfiles/JonesvHarrisAssociates.pdf.
3. *Hecker v. Deere & Co.*, 2007 WL 1874367 (W.D. Wis. 2007), aff'd, 2009 WL 331285 (7th Cir. 2009).
4. *Hecker v. Deere & Co.*, 2007 WL 1874367 (W.D. Wis. 2007), aff'd, 2009 WL 331285 (7th Cir. 2009).

dollars invested in a particular fund. These fees, expressed as a percentage of assets invested, were set out in the prospectus for each fund, and were further itemized between management fees, service fees, and other expenses.) The court further noted that there was "no evidence of intent" in ERISA or DOL regulations that a plan's financial reports had to provide this type of detailed disclosure.

The court also dismissed claims that the plan sponsor had violated ERISA by not providing 401(k) plan investment options with lower annual fees than those charged by the investment provider.

Practitioner's Pointer: This holding is good news — the authors have always advised that investment options must be prudent and that the lowest cost is not always the determining factor as to what constitutes a prudent option.

See Q 97 for a discussion of the DOL's proposed regulations on fiduciary disclosures of plan- and investment-related information for participant-directed individual account plans.

409. Who enforces the prohibited transaction rules?

The Department of Labor (DOL) and the Internal Revenue Service (IRS) coordinate the administration of the prohibited transaction rules. In order to avoid unnecessary expense and duplication of these functions, the IRS transferred to the DOL general authority to issue regulations, rulings, opinions, and exceptions with respect to the prohibited transaction rules while retaining the authority to enforce the excise tax provisions of IRC Section 4975(a) and IRC Section 4975(b).[1] The IRS and the DOL consult with each other with respect to the excise tax provisions of IRC Section 4975 and with respect to the provisions relating to prohibited transactions and exemptions therefrom.[2] If the DOL obtains information indicating that a party in interest or disqualified person is violating the prohibited transaction rules, that information is transmitted to the IRS.[3]

410. What is the Department of Labor's Voluntary Fiduciary Correction Program?

The purpose of the Voluntary Fiduciary Correction Program (VFC Program or Program) is to protect the financial security of workers by encouraging the identification and correction of transactions that violate Part 4 of Title I of ERISA. Part 4 of Title I of ERISA sets out the responsibilities of employee benefit plan fiduciaries. ERISA Section 409 provides that a fiduciary who breaches any of these responsibilities is personally liable to make good to the plan any losses to the plan resulting from each breach, and the fiduciary must restore to the plan any profits that were made through the use of the plan's assets. ERISA Section 405 provides that a fiduciary may be liable, under certain circumstances, for a co-fiduciary's breach of fiduciary responsibilities. In addition, under certain circumstances, there may be liability for knowing participation in a fiduciary breach.

---

1. ERISA Reorganization Plan No. 4 of 1978, 1979-1 C.B. 480.
2. ERISA Sec. 3003(b).
3. ERISA Sec. 3003(c).

The VFC Program is designed to encourage employers and plan fiduciaries to voluntarily comply with ERISA and allows those who are potentially liable for certain specified fiduciary violations to voluntarily apply for relief from enforcement actions and certain penalties, provided they meet the VFC Program's criteria and follow the procedures outlined in the VFC Program. The Department of Labor (DOL) believes that many workers have benefited from the VFC Program as a result of the restoration of plan assets and payment of promised benefits. The VFC Program describes how to apply for relief, the specific transactions covered, acceptable methods for correcting violations, and examples of potential violations and corrective actions. Eligible applicants that satisfy the terms and conditions of the VFC Program receive a "no-action letter" from EBSA and are not subject to civil monetary penalties.

The Voluntary Fiduciary Correction Program was adopted by the DOL on a permanent basis in March 2002 (the original VFC Program). Prior to adoption in March 2002, the VFC Program was made available on an interim basis during which the DOL invited and considered public comments on the Program.[1] In 2002, the original VFC Program was further expanded to include a class exemption[2] providing excise tax relief for four specific VFC Program transactions.[3]

On April 6, 2005, the DOL published a revised VFC Program, which simplified and expanded the original VFC Program. The DOL also proposed amendments to PTE 2002-51 to accommodate a new transaction contained in the revised VFC Program. The DOL finalized its revisions made to the DOL's VFC Program on April 19, 2006,[4] with some additional changes. The final version of the VFC program reflects changes made in response to comments the DOL received on the April 2005 revisions. The changes include the expansion of covered transactions and the coordination of participant loan violations with the IRS's revisions to Employee Plans Compliance Resolution System (EPCRS). Other changes include additional methods of correcting previously covered transactions, simplifying the calculation of the correction amount, and an on-line calculator to assist in making accurate corrections. A Model Application Form has been adopted (see Appendix B), and the amount of supporting documentation to accompany any filing has been reduced. Conforming amendments also have been made to PTE 2002-51, which now provides relief from the excise taxes imposed under the Code for certain transactions corrected in the VFC Program. The finalized VFC Program and the changes to PTE 2002-51 became effective May 19, 2006.[5]

The revised VFC Program describes how to apply the nineteen specific transactions covered, acceptable methods for correcting violations, and examples of potential violations and corrective actions. The VFC Program includes a Voluntary Fiduciary Correction Program Model Application Form (see Appendix B), which provides a recommended format for a VFC Program application, and a revised Voluntary Fiduciary Correction Program Checklist (see Appendix B) to ensure the submission of a complete VFC Program application.

---

1. See 65 Fed. Reg. 14,164 (Mar. 15, 2000).
2. PTE 2002-51.
3. PTE 2002-51, *published at* 67 Fed. Reg. 70,623 (Nov. 25, 2002).
4. 71 Fed. Reg. 20,262.
5. See 70 Fed. Reg. 17,476 (Apr. 6, 2005).

Corrections under the VFC Program may be made without the determination that there is an actual breach; there need only be a possible breach. Each prohibited transaction eligible for remediation under the VFC Program has one established correction method (detailed in following questions). Applications concerning correction of breaches not described in the Program will not be accepted. Also, the DOL reserves the right to reject an application when warranted by the facts and circumstances of a particular case.

The plan may not pay the cost of any corrections under the VFC Program. These costs must be borne by the affected fiduciary, plan sponsor, or other plan official.

411. What are the VFC Program eligibility and application procedures?
Who Is Eligible?

Anyone who may be liable for fiduciary violations under ERISA, including employee benefit plan sponsors, officials, and parties in interest, may voluntarily apply for relief from enforcement actions, provided they comply with the criteria and satisfy the procedures outlined in the VFC Program. Such persons may use the VFC Program if neither the plan nor the applicant is "under investigation" by the DOL and the application contains the evidence of criminal violations. A plan or an applicant is considered to be "under investigation" by the EBSA if the EBSA or any other federal agency is conducting an investigation, either ongoing or for which notice has been given, that specifically involves the plan or that specifically relates to the applicant or the plan sponsor in connection with an act or transaction directly related to the plan.[1] A plan is not considered to be "under investigation" by the EBSA merely because EBSA staff has contacted the plan, the applicant, or the plan sponsor in connection with a participant complaint, unless the participant complaint concerns the transaction described in the application. A plan also is not considered to be "under investigation" if the accountant of the plan is undergoing a work paper review by EBSA's Office of the Chief Accountant under the authority of ERISA Section 504(a).

> *Example 1.* On March 1, the plan sponsor of a profit sharing plan received written notification from an agent of the IRS that the plan has been scheduled for examination. As of March 1, the plan is ineligible for participation in the VFC Program because the plan sponsor has received a notice from the IRS concerning the IRS's intent to examine the plan.

> *Example 2.* Assume the same facts as in Example 1, except that the plan sponsor received written notification from a Federal agency of an investigation of the company regarding an alleged workplace safety violation. The plan's eligibility to participate in the VFC Program would not be affected because the investigation does not involve the plan or an act or transaction involving the plan.

The final rules include an optional disclosure provision under which eligibility is not barred if the investigation is a civil one by the PBGC, a state attorney general, or a state insurance commissioner and the applicant discloses the investigation in writing when submitting the correction application.[2]

---

1. Updated Voluntary Fiduciary Corrections Program, 71 Fed. Reg. 20,262 (Apr. 19, 2006).
2. Updated Voluntary Fiduciary Corrections Program, 71 Fed. Reg. 20,262 (Apr. 19, 2006).

VFC Program Criteria

Persons using the VFC Program must fully and accurately correct violations. Incomplete or unacceptable applications may be rejected. If rejected, applicants may be subject to enforcement action, including assessment of civil monetary penalties under ERISA Section 502(*l*) and ERISA Section 502(i) (for Health and Welfare Benefit Plans and non-qualified pension plans).

How to Apply

Applicants do not need to consult or negotiate with EBSA to use the VFC Program. They merely need to follow the procedures outlined in the notice published in the April 19, 2006, Federal Register.[1]

The application must be prepared by a plan official or his authorized representative. If a representative of the plan official is submitting the application, the application must include a statement signed by the plan official that the representative is authorized to represent the plan official. Any fees paid to such representative for services relating to the preparation and submission of the application may not be paid from plan assets.

Each application must include the name, address, and telephone number of a contact person. The contact person must be familiar with the contents of the application, and have authority to respond to inquiries from DOL. The applicant must provide to the DOL a detailed narrative describing the breach and the corrective action. The narrative must include:

1.   A list of all persons materially involved in the breach and its correction (e.g., fiduciaries, service providers, borrowers);

2.   The employer identification number (EIN), plan number, and address of the plan sponsor and administrator;

3.   The date the plan's most recent Form 5500 was filed;

4.   An explanation of the breach, including the date it occurred;

5.   An explanation of how the breach was corrected, by whom, and when;

6.   If the applicant performs a manual calculation in accordance with the VFC Program rules, specific calculations demonstrating how principal amount and lost earnings or, if applicable, restoration of profits was computed;

7.   If the applicant uses the Online Calculator, the data elements required to be input into the Online Calculator, as applicable (to satisfy this requirement, applicants may submit a copy of the page(s) that result from the "View Printable Results" function used after inputting data elements and completing use of the Online Calculator); and

8.   An explanation of why payment of lost earnings or restoration of profits was chosen to correct the breach.

---

1. See http://www.dol.gov/ebsa/regs/fedreg/notices/2006003674a.htm, for more information.

Acceptable Corrections

The VFC Program provides rules for making acceptable corrections involving the transactions listed above. Applicants generally must:

- Conduct valuations of plan assets using generally recognized markets for the assets or obtain written appraisal reports from qualified professionals that are based on generally accepted appraisal standards;

- Restore to the plan the principal amount involved, plus the greater of (1) lost earnings, starting on the date of the loss and extending to the recovery date, or (2) profits resulting from the use of the principal amount, starting on the date of the loss and extending to the date the profit is realized;

- Pay the expenses associated with correcting transactions, such as appraisal costs or fees associated with recalculating participant account balances; and

- Make supplemental distributions to former employees, beneficiaries, or alternate payees when appropriate, and provide proof of the payments.

VFC Program Documentation

Under the VFC Program, applicants must provide supporting documentation to the appropriate regional office of EBSA. Required documentation includes:

1. Copies of the relevant portions of the plan document and any other pertinent documents (such as the adoption agreement, trust agreement, or insurance contract);

2. Documentation that supports the narrative description of the transaction and its correction;

3. Documentation establishing the lost earnings amount;

4. Documentation establishing the amount of restoration of profits, if applicable;

5. All documents described in Section 7 of the VFC Program with respect to the transaction involved; and

6. Proof of payment of principal amount and lost earnings or restoration of profits.

Applicants using the Online Calculator may satisfy the lost earnings and restoration of profits documentation as to the amount of interest, if any, payable with respect to the profit amount, by submitting a copy of the page(s) that result from the "View Printable Results" function used after inputting data elements and completing use of the Online Calculator. Except for proof of payment, applicants correcting participant loan transactions in VFC Program Section 7.3 are not required to submit the other documentation described above.

Each application must also contain the following penalty of perjury statement signed and dated by a plan fiduciary with knowledge of the transaction that is the subject of the application and the authorized representative of the applicant, if any:

"Under penalties of perjury I certify that I am not Under Investigation (as defined in section 3(b)(3)) and that I have reviewed this application, including all supporting documentation, and to the best of my knowledge and belief the contents are true, correct, and complete."

In addition, each plan official applying under the VFC Program must sign and date the Penalty of Perjury statement. The statement must accompany the application and any subsequent additions to the application. Use of the Penalty of Perjury Statement included with the Model Application Form will satisfy this requirement.

A checklist[1] must be completed, signed, and submitted with the application. Use of the checklist included with the Model Application Form also will satisfy this requirement.

Restitution to Plans

Under the VFC Program, applicants must restore the plan, participants, and beneficiaries to the condition they would have been in had the breach not occurred. EBSA is also providing a new Internet tool on its Web site, the Online Calculator,[2] to assist applicants by automatically calculating correction amounts that must be paid to the plan. EBSA's Web site includes instructions for using the Online Calculator, examples, and manual calculations. Plans must then file, where necessary, amended returns to reflect corrected transactions or valuations. According to the DOL, use of the Online Calculator by applicants is recommended, but is not mandatory. Applicants may perform manual calculations in accordance with VFC Program Section 5(b), using the IRC underpayment rates and the IRS Factors.

The DOL states that the Online Calculator computes lost earnings and interest, if any. If the principal amount was used for a specific purpose such that a profit on the use of the principal amount is determinable, the Online Calculator also computes interest on the profit. The Online Calculator then compares lost earnings to restoration of profits and provides the applicant with the greater amount, which must be paid to the plan.

The Online Calculator uses IRC Section 6621(a)(2) and IRC Section 6621(c)(1) underpayment rates in effect during the time period and the corresponding factors from IRS Revenue Procedure 95-17 (IRS Factors), which reflect daily compounding. Under the VFC Program special rules for transactions involving large losses or large restorations, the Online Calculator automatically recomputes the amount of lost earnings and restoration of profits using the applicable IRC Section 6621(c)(1) rates.

Applicants also must provide proof of payment to participants and beneficiaries, or properly segregate the affected assets in cases where the plan is unable to identify the location

---

1. VFCP Rule — Updated Voluntary Fiduciary Corrections Program, 71 Fed. Reg. 20,262 app. B (Apr. 19, 2006).
2. http://www.askebsa.dol.gov/VFCPCalculator/WebCalculator.aspx.

of missing individuals. Payment of the correction amount may be made directly to the plan where distributions to separated participants would be less than $20 and the cost of correction exceeds the distributions owed.

Excise Tax Exemption

The DOL has added amendments to class exemption PTE 2002-51 to provide excise tax relief for prohibited transaction violations involved in "the holding of an illiquid asset previously purchased by a plan," one of the new transactions contained in the revised VFC Program. The first of these amendments were published in the April 6, 2002, Federal Register simultaneously with the revised VFC Program.

The second was published April 19, 2006. According to the DOL, the four transactions identified in PTE 2002-51 as originally granted will remain in effect there are now two additional transactions included in the amendments. The first of the transactions was introduced in the April 2005 VFC Program and the proposed Amendment to PTE 2002–51. That transaction has now become effective in the amended exemption. The transaction concerns the purchase of an asset (including real property) by a plan where the asset has later been determined to be illiquid as described in the final VFC Program, and/or the subsequent sale of the illiquid asset by the plan in a transaction that was prohibited pursuant to section 4975(c)(1) of the Code. The second transaction included in the amendment covers the use of plan assets to pay expenses to a service provider for services that are properly characterized as settlor expenses, provided such payments were not expressly prohibited in the plan documents.

A copy of PTE 2002-51, as well as a listing of Frequently Asked Questions on the exemption, is available at http://www.dol.gov/ebsa/compliance_assistance.html#section8, and the amendments to PTE 2002-51 may be obtained at http://www.dol.gov/ebsa/regs/fedreg/notices/2006003675.pdf.

Contacts for Additional Information

For additional information, the DOL instructs VFC Program applicants to contact the appropriate regional office at EBSA's toll-free Employee and Employer Hotline number: 1.866.444.EBSA (3272) and request the VFC Program coordinator.

Source: VFCP Fact Sheet — http://www.dol.gov/ebsa/newsroom/fsrevisedvfcp.html.

412. What are the covered transactions under the VFC Program?

The VFC Program[1] and its amendments[2] provide descriptions of nineteen transactions, in six categories, and their methods of correction. This program and its amendments update the original procedural regulations outlined in the Code for Federal Regulations.[3] Corrective remedies are prescribed for the following fiduciary violations involving employee benefit plans:

---

1. 67 Fed. Reg. 15062.
2. 70 Fed. Reg. 17476, and 71 Fed. Reg. 20262.
3. 29 CFR. 2570.

A.   Delinquent Remittance of Participant Contributions

   1.   Delinquent Participant Contributions and Participant Loan Repayments to Pension Plans

   2.   Delinquent Participant Contributions to Insured Welfare Plans

   3.   Delinquent Participant Contributions to Welfare Plan Trusts

B.   Loans

   1.   Loan at Fair Market Interest Rate to a Party in Interest With Respect to the Plan

   2.   Loan at Below-Market Interest Rate to a Party in Interest With Respect to the Plan

   3.   Loan at Below-Market Interest Rate to a Person Who Is Not a Party in Interest With Respect to the Plan

   4.   Loan at Below-Market Interest Rate Solely Due to a Delay in Perfecting the Plan's Security Interest

C.   Participant Loans

   1.   Loans Failing to Comply with Plan Provisions for Amount, Duration, or Level Amortization

   2.   Default Loans

D.   Purchases, Sales, and Exchanges

   1.   Purchase of an Asset (Including Real Property) by a Plan from a Party in Interest

   2.   Sale of an Asset (Including Real Property) by a Plan to a Party in Interest

   3.   Sale and Leaseback of Real Property to Employer

   4.   Purchase of an Asset (Including Real Property) by a Plan from a Person Who Is Not a Party in Interest With Respect to the Plan at a Price Other Than Fair Market Value

   5.   Sale of an Asset (Including Real Property) by a Plan to a Person Who Is Not a Party in Interest With Respect to the Plan at a Price Less Than Fair Market Value

   6.   Holding of an Illiquid Asset Previously Purchased by a Plan

E.   Benefits

1. Payment of Benefits without Properly Valuing Plan Assets on Which Payment Is Based

F.   Plan Expenses

1. Duplicative, Excessive, or Unnecessary Compensation Paid by a Plan

2. Expenses Improperly Paid by a Plan

3. Payment of Dual Compensation to a Plan Fiduciary

When filed with the DOL, each of the correction methods discussed below must be accompanied by specific supporting documentation as required under the Program.

Delinquent Remittance of Participant Funds

A breach occurs where an employer receives directly from participants, or withholds from employees' paychecks, certain amounts for either contribution to a pension plan or for repayment of participants' plan loans. Instead of forwarding participant contributions for investment in accordance with the provisions of the plan and by reference to the principles of Labor Regulation Section 2510.3-102, the employer retains such contributions for a longer period of time. Similarly, in the case of participant loan repayments, instead of applying such repayments to outstanding loan balances within a reasonable period of time determined by reference to the guiding principles of Labor Regulation Section 2510.3-102 and in accordance with the provisions of the plan, the employer retains such repayments for a longer period of time.

The breach for unpaid contributions or participant loan repayments is corrected by paying to the plan the principal amount plus the greater of (1) lost earnings on the principal amount or (2) restoration of profits resulting from the employer's use of the principal amount. The loss date for such contributions is the date on which each contribution reasonably could have been segregated from the employer's general assets. In no event shall the loss date for such contributions be later than the applicable maximum time period described in Labor Regulation Section 2510.3-102. The loss date for such repayments is the date on which each repayment reasonably could have been segregated from the employer's general assets consistent with the guiding principles of Labor Regulation Section 2510.3-102. Any penalties, late fees, or other charges shall be paid by the employer and not from participant loan repayments.

With respect to the breach for late contributions or participant loan repayments where participant contributions or loan repayments were remitted to the plan outside of the time periods described above, the only correction required is to pay to the plan the greater of (1) lost earnings or (2) restoration of profits resulting from the employer's use of the principal amount. Any penalties, late fees, or other charges shall be paid by the employer and not from participant loan repayments. The principal amount is the amount of delinquent participant contributions or loan repayments retained by the employer. In addition to the documentation required in see Q 411 the applicant must also submit the following documents:

1. A statement from a plan official identifying the earliest date on which the participant contributions and/or repayments reasonably could have been segregated from the employer's general assets, along with the supporting documentation on which the plan official relied in reaching this conclusion;

2. If restored participant contributions and/or repayments (exclusive of lost earnings) (a) total $50,000 or less, or (b) exceed $50,000 and were remitted to the plan within 180 calendar days from the date such amounts were received by the employer, or the date such amounts otherwise would have been payable to the participants in cash (regarding amounts withheld by an employer from employees' paychecks), submit:

   a. A narrative describing the applicant's contribution and/or repayment remittance practices before and after the period of unpaid or late contributions and/or repayments; and

   b. Summary documents demonstrating the amount of unpaid or late contributions and/or repayments; and

3. If restored participant contributions and/or repayments (exclusive of lost earnings) exceed $50,000 and were remitted more than 180 calendar days after the date such amounts were received by the employer, or the date such amounts otherwise would have been payable to the participants in cash (regarding amounts withheld by an employer from employees' paychecks), submit:

   a. A narrative describing the applicant's contribution and/or repayment remittance practices before and after the period of unpaid or late contributions and/or repayments;

   b. For participant contributions and/or repayments received from participants, a copy of the accounting records that identify the date and amount of each contribution received; and

   c. For participant contributions and/or repayments withheld from employees' paychecks, a copy of the payroll documents showing the date and amount of each withholding.

The items below outline the requirements for delinquent participant contributions.

1. Delinquent Participant Contributions to Insured Welfare Plans the employer fails to forward participant pay withholding amounts for benefits provided exclusively through an insurance contract issued by an insurance company or a similar organization for the provision of group health or other welfare benefits in accordance with the terms of the plan, or the requirements of Labor Regulation Section 2510.3-102. If there have been no denials of claims under the

plan or any lapse in coverage as a result of the failure to timely remit contributions, the plan may correct the transaction under VFC Program by doing the following:

    a.   Pay to the insurance provider or HMO the principal amount, as well as any penalties, late fees, or other charges necessary to prevent a lapse in coverage due to the failure.

    b.   In addition to the documentation required and detailed in Q 411, submit the following documents:

        i.   For participant contributions received directly from participants, a copy of the accounting records that identify the date and amount of each contribution received;

        ii.   For participant contributions withheld from employees' paychecks, a copy of the payroll documents showing the date and amount of each withholding;

        iii.   A statement from a plan official identifying the earliest date that participant contributions reasonably could have been segregated from the employer's general assets, along with the supporting documentation that the plan official relied on in reaching this conclusion;

        iv.   Copies of the insurance contract or contracts for the group health or other welfare benefits;

        v.   A statement from a plan official attesting that there are no instances in which claims have been denied under the plan for nonpayment, nor has there been any lapse in coverage; and

        vi.   A statement from a plan official attesting that any penalties, late fees, or other such charges have been paid by the employer and not from the participant contributions.

2.   Delinquent Participant Contributions to a Welfare Plan Trust

An employer receives directly from participants or withholds from employees' paychecks certain amounts that the employer forwards to a trust maintained to provide, through insurance or otherwise, group health or other welfare benefits. The employer fails to forward such amounts in accordance with the terms of the plan document or in violation of Labor Regulation Section 2510.3-102. If there have been no denials of claims under the plan or any lapse in coverage as a result of the failure to timely remit contributions, the plan may correct the transaction under the VFC Program by doing the following:

Pay to the trust the principal amount and, where applicable, any penalties, late fees, or other charges necessary to prevent a lapse in coverage due to the failure to make timely payments. Also pay to the trust the greater of (a) lost earnings on the principal amount or (b) restoration of profits resulting from the employer's use of the principal amount.

The "loss date" for such contributions is the date on which each contribution would become plan assets under Labor Regulation Section 2510.3-102.

Loans

There are four types of loans covered under the VFC procedure: loans at fair market rates made to a party in interest; loans at below-market rates made to a party in interest; loans at below-market interest rates made to a person who is not a party in interest; and loans made at below-market interest rates due to a delay in perfecting the plan's security interest.

1. Loan at Fair Market Interest Rate Made to a Party in Interest with Respect to the Plan

   Correction of these loans requires loan repayment in full, including any applicable prepayment penalties. An independent commercial lender is required to confirm, in writing, that the loan was made at a fair market interest rate for loans under similar terms to borrowers of similar creditworthiness.

   A narrative describing the process used to determine the fair market interest rate at the time of the loan, validated in writing by an independent commercial lender, must be filed with the application.

2. Loan at Below-Market Interest Rates Made to a Party in Interest with Respect to the Plan

   Correction of these loans requires the repayment in full of the amount of the loan to the plan plus the "principal amount" of the loan, and the greater of (a) lost earnings or (b) the restoration of profits on the principal amount, if any. For below-market rate loans, the principal amount is equal to the excess of the interest payments that would have been received had the loan been made at market rate, over interest payments actually received. The fair market interest rate must be determined by an independent financial institution. Finally, any supplemental distribution required as a result of the below-market loan must be made.

3. Loan at Below-Market Interest Rate to a Person Who Is Not a Party in Interest with Respect to the Plan

   Correction of these loans involves payment to the plan of the "principal amount" plus lost earnings through the recovery date on the principal amount. Each loan payment will have a principal amount equal to the excess of interest on the principal amount payments that would have been received had the loan been executed at a fair market interest rate, over the interest actually received. An independent commercial lender must determine the fair market rate.

4. Loan at Below-Market Rate Solely Due to Delay in Perfecting Plan's Security Interest

   The acceptable correction method for this loan violation is the payment of the "principal amount" plus lost earnings on the principal amount through the date on which the loan is fully secured. The principal amount is the difference between the interest payments actually received and the interest payments that would have been received if the loan had been issued at a fair market rate for an unsecured loan. The fair market rate must be determined by an independent lender. If the delay in perfecting the security caused a permanent change in the risk characteristics of the loan, an independent commercial lender must establish the fair market rate for the remaining term of the loan.

Participant Loans

1. Loans Failing to Comply with Plan Provisions for Amount, Duration, or Level Amortization

A breach occurs where a plan extended a loan to a plan participant who is a party in interest with respect to the plan based solely on the participant's status as an employee of any employer whose employees are covered by the plan, as defined in ERISA Section 3(14)(H). The loan was a prohibited transaction that failed to qualify for ERISA's statutory exemption for plan loan programs because the loan terms did not comply with applicable plan provisions, which incorporated the requirements of IRC Section 72(p) concerning:

    i.   The amount of the loan,

    ii. The duration of the loan, or

    iii. The level amortization of the loan repayment.

Correction of Transaction: Plan officials must make a voluntary correction of the loan with IRS approval under the Voluntary Correction Program of the IRS's Employee Plans Compliance Resolution System (EPCRS). The applicant is not required to submit any of the supporting documentation listed above, except that the applicant must provide proof of payment and a copy of the IRS compliance statement.

2. Default Loans

A breach occurs where a plan extends a loan to a plan participant who is a party in interest with respect to the plan based solely on the participant's status as an employee of any employer whose employees are covered by the plan, as defined in ERISA Section 3(14)(H). At origination, the loan qualified for ERISA's statutory exemption for plan loan programs because the loan complied with applicable plan provisions, which incorporated the requirements of IRC Section 72(p). During the loan repayment period, the plan official responsible for loan administration failed to properly withhold a number of loan repayments from the participant's wages and included the amount of such repayments in the participant's wages based on administrative or systems processing errors. The failure to withhold is a breach causing the loan to become non-compliant with applicable plan provisions, which incorporated the requirements of IRC Section 72(p).

Correction of Transaction: Plan officials must make a voluntary correction of the loan with IRS approval under the Voluntary Correction Program of the IRS's EPCRS. The applicant is not required to submit any of the supporting documentation listed above, except that the applicant must provide proof of payment and a copy of the IRS compliance statement.

Purchases, Sales, and Exchanges

1. Purchase of an Asset (Including Real Property) by a Plan from a Party in Interest

    A breach occurs where a plan purchases an asset with cash from a party in interest with respect to the plan, in a transaction to which no prohibited transaction exemption applies. The breach is corrected by having the plan sell the asset back to the party in interest who originally sold the asset to the plan or to a person who is not a party in interest. Whether the asset is sold to a person who is not a party in interest with respect to the plan or is sold back to the original seller, the plan must receive the higher of (a) the fair market value (FMV) of the asset at the time of resale, without a reduction for the costs of sale, plus restoration to the plan of the party in interest's investment return from the proceeds of the sale, to the extent they exceed the plan's net profits from owning the property; or (b) the principal amount, plus the greater of (i) lost earnings on the principal amount or (ii) the restoration of profits, if any.

    As an alternative to the correction described in the preceding paragraph, the plan may retain the asset and receive (a) the greater of (i) lost earnings or (ii) the restoration of profits, if any, on the principal amount, but only to the extent that such lost earnings or restoration of profits exceeds the difference between the FMV of the asset as of the recovery date and the original purchase price; and (b) the amount by which the principal amount exceeded the FMV of the asset (at the time of the original purchase), plus the greater of (i) lost earnings or (ii) restoration of profits, if any, on such excess; provided an independent fiduciary determines that the plan will realize a greater benefit from this correction than it would from the resale of the asset. For this transaction, the principal amount is the plan's original purchase price.

    In addition to the documentation required above, the applicant must submit the following documents:

    a. Documentation of the plan's purchase of the asset, including the date of the purchase, the plan's purchase price, and the identity of the seller;

    b. A narrative describing the relationship between the original seller of the asset and the plan;

    c. The qualified, independent appraiser's report addressing the FMV of the asset purchased by the plan, both at the time of the original purchase and at the recovery date; and

    d. If applicable, a report of the independent fiduciary's determination that the plan will realize a greater benefit by receiving the correction amount than by reselling the asset.

2. Sale of an Asset (Including Real Property) by a Plan to a Party in Interest

    Correction of the transaction requires the plan to receive the "principal amount" plus the greater of (a) lost earnings or (b) the restoration of profits, if any. The principal amount is the amount by which the fair market value of the asset at the time of the original sale exceeds the sale price. As an alternative, the plan may repurchase the asset from the party in interest at the lower of the price for which it sold the property or the fair market value as of the recovery date, plus restoration of the party in interest's net profits from owning the property, to the extent that they exceed the plan's investment return from the proceeds of the sale. The determination as to which correction method is best for the plan must be made by an independent fiduciary.

3. Sale and Leaseback of Real Property to the Employer

    The transaction is corrected by the sale of the property back to the plan sponsor or a non-party in interest. The plan must receive the higher of (a) fair market value at the time of the resale; or (b) the principal amount (original sale price), plus the greater of (i) lost earnings or (ii) the restoration of profits on the principal amount, if any.

    If the plan has not been receiving rent at fair market value (as determined by a qualified independent appraisal), the sale price should not be based on the below-market rent that was paid to the plan. If this is the case, the recovery amount must include the difference between the rent actually paid and the fair market rent that should have been paid. The additional rent payments, if any, must also include the greater of lost earnings or the restoration of profits.

4. Purchase of an Asset (Including Real Property) by a Plan from a Person Who Is Not a Party in Interest with Respect to the Plan at a Price Other Than Fair Market Value

    Correction of this transaction requires the plan to receive the principal amount (difference between the price paid and the fair market value at the time of the purchase), plus lost earnings.

5. Sale of an Asset (Including Real Property) by a Plan to a Person Who Is Not a Party in Interest with Respect to the Plan at a Price Less Than Fair Market Value

    Correction of the transaction requires the plan to receive the principal amount (the amount by which the fair market value, as of the recovery date, exceeds the price at which the plan sold the property), plus lost earnings.

6. Holding of an Illiquid Asset Previously Purchased by a Plan

    A breach occurs where a plan is holding an asset previously purchased from (a) a party in interest with respect to the plan in an acquisition for which relief was available under a statutory or administrative prohibited transaction exemption; (b) a party in interest with respect to the plan at no greater than FMV at that time in an acquisition to which no prohibited transaction exemption applied; (c) a person who was not a party in interest with respect to the plan in an acquisition in which a plan fiduciary failed to appropriately discharge her fiduciary duties; or (d) a person who was not a party in interest with respect to the plan in an acquisition in which a plan fiduciary appropriately discharged her fiduciary duties.

Currently, a plan fiduciary determines that such asset is an illiquid asset because: (a) the asset failed to appreciate, failed to provide a reasonable rate of return, or caused a loss to the plan; (b) the sale of the asset is in the best interest of the plan; and (c) following reasonable efforts to sell the asset to a person who is not a party in interest with respect to the plan, the asset cannot immediately be sold for its original purchase price, or its current FMV, if greater.

The transaction may be corrected by the sale of the asset to a party in interest, provided the plan receives the higher of (a) the FMV of the asset at the time of resale, without a reduction for the costs of sale; or (b) the principal amount, plus lost earnings. The plan official may cause the plan to sell the asset to a party in interest. This correction provides relief for both the original purchase of the asset, if required, and the sale of the illiquid asset by the plan to a party in interest; relief from the prohibited transaction excise tax also is provided if the plan official satisfies the applicable conditions of the VFC Program class exemption. For this transaction, the principal amount is the plan's original purchase price.

In addition to the documentation required in the preceding list, the applicant must submit the following documents:

a. Documentation of the plan's original purchase of the asset, including the date of the purchase, the plan's purchase price, the identity of the original seller, and a description of the relationship, if any, between the original seller and the plan;

b. The qualified, independent appraiser's report addressing the FMV of the asset purchased by the plan at the recovery date;

c. A narrative describing the plan's efforts to sell the asset to persons who are not parties in interest with respect to the plan and any documentation of such efforts to sell the asset;

d. A statement from a plan official attesting that:

   i. The asset failed to appreciate, failed to provide a reasonable rate of return, or caused a loss to the plan;

   ii. The sale of the asset is in the best interest of the plan;

   iii. The asset is an illiquid asset; and

   iv. The plan made reasonable efforts to sell the asset to persons who are not parties in interest with respect to the plan without success; and

e. In the case of an illiquid asset that is a parcel of real estate, a statement from a plan official attesting that no party in interest owns real estate that is contiguous to the plan's parcel of real estate on the recovery date.

Benefits

1. Payment of Benefits without Properly Valuing Plan Assets on Which Payment Is Based

Correction of this transaction requires a corrected valuation of the plan assets for each plan year, starting with the first plan year for which the assets were improperly valued. The next step is to restore, directly to the plan for distribution to the affected plan participants, or directly to those participants, the amount by which all participants were underpaid distributions to which they were entitled, plus the higher of lost earnings or the underpayment rate (defined under IRC Section 6621(a)(2)). The plan must also file an amended Form 5500 for each of the last three plan years, or for all plan years in which the assets were improperly valued (whichever period is less).

According to the DOL, a plan official, rather than an independent fiduciary or independent expert, must determine the fair market value of the improperly valued asset for each year in which the asset was valued improperly. Once the assets are properly valued, participant accounts must be adjusted accordingly.

Plan Expenses

1. Duplicative, Excessive, or Unnecessary Compensation Paid by a Plan

Correction of this transaction requires the restoration to the plan of the principal amount of the incorrect payment, plus the greater of (a) lost earnings or (b) restoration of profits resulting from the use of the incorrect payments. The procedure defines "principal amount" as the difference between the amount actually paid during the six years prior to the discontinuation of the unnecessary payments and the reasonable market value of the services actually rendered.

2. A breach occurs where a plan uses plan assets to pay expenses, including commissions or fees, that should have been paid by the plan sponsor, to a service provider (such as an attorney, accountant, recordkeeper, actuary, financial adviser, or insurance agent) for:

   a. Services provided in connection with the administration and maintenance of the plan ("plan expenses") in circumstances where a plan provision requires that such plan expenses be paid by the plan sponsor; or

   b. Services provided in connection with the establishment, design, or termination of the plan ("settlor expenses") that relate to the activities of the plan sponsor in its capacity as settlor.

Correction of transaction requires restoration to the plan principal amount, plus the greater of (a) lost earnings or (b) restoration of profits resulting from the use of the principal amount. The principal amount is the entire amount improperly paid by the plan to the service provider for expenses that should have been paid by the plan sponsor. In addition to the documentation required above, the applicant must submit copies of the plan's accounting records that show the date and amount of expenses paid by the plan to the service provider.

3. Payment of Dual Compensation to a Plan Fiduciary

Correction requires payment to the plan of the principal amount of the dual payment, plus the greater of (a) lost earnings or (b) restoration of profits resulting from the fiduciary's use of the principal amount. The principal amount is defined as the difference between the amount incorrectly paid during the six-year period prior to discontinuation of the payments and the amount that represents proper reimbursements of expenses actually incurred by the fiduciary.

413. What are the policies and procedures under the VFC Program for handling terminated participants, beneficiaries, and alternate payees who cannot be located to receive distributions?

Under the VFC Program, plans are required to make supplemental distributions to former employees, beneficiaries receiving benefits, or alternate payees if the original distributions were too low because of the breach.[1] The plan must demonstrate proof of payment to participants and beneficiaries whose current location is known to the plan and/or applicant.

Where plans are unable to locate participants, beneficiaries, or alternate payees, they must provide evidence that they have segregated adequate funds to pay the missing individuals and have commenced a process of locating the missing individuals either through the IRS and Social Security Administration locater services, or other comparable means. The costs of such efforts are part of the costs of correction and cannot be borne by the plan.

414. How are de minimis corrective distributions to be handled under the VFC Program?

For distributions required in amounts under $20 to individuals who neither have account balances with nor have a right to future benefits from the plan, where the applicant demonstrates in its submission that the cost of making the distribution to these individuals exceeds the amount of the payment to which the individuals are entitled, the applicant is not required to make distributions to these individuals.[2] However, the applicant must forfeit to the plan, as a whole, the total of the *de minimis* amounts not distributed to individuals.

415. What is the excise tax exemption with respect to certain transactions covered by the VFC Program?

In order to encourage use of the VFC Program, the Department of Labor granted a class exemption[3] providing limited relief from the excise taxes under the Internal Revenue Code imposed on certain transactions covered by the VFC Program. After amendment of

---

1. PTE 2002-51; 67 Fed. Reg. 70623.
2. 71 Fed. Reg. 20262 (April 19, 2006).
3. Prohibited Transaction Exemption 2002-51.

PTE 2002-51 to add items five and six below, six specific transactions are now exempt from excise tax, provided applicants comply with the conditions contained in the exemption:

1. Failure to transmit participant contributions to a pension plan within the time frames described in the regulations[1] and/or the failure to transmit participant loan repayments to a pension plan within a reasonable time after withholding or receipt by the employer;

2. Making of a loan by a plan at a fair market interest rate to a party in interest with respect to the plan;

3. Purchase or sale of an asset (including real property) between a plan and a party in interest at fair market value;

4. Sale of real property to a plan by the employer and the leaseback of such property to the employer, at fair market value and fair market rental value, respectively;

5. Holding of an illiquid asset previously purchased by a plan; and

6. Impermissible payment by a plan of certain expenses.

Under the exemption, applicants must repay delinquent contributions to plans no more than 180 days from the date the money was received by the employer or would be payable to participants in cash. The exemption also requires, except in the case of delinquent participant contributions, that no more than 10 percent of the fair market value of total plan assets be involved. In addition, the exemption requires that notice of the transaction and the correction be provided to interested persons. Finally, covered transactions under the exemption cannot be part of an arrangement or understanding that benefits a related party and the exemption does not apply to any transactions for which an application for a similar transaction was submitted under the VFC Program within the past three years.

According to the DOL:

It is not necessary to apply to the DOL for relief under the class exemption. However, parties must meet all of the applicable conditions in the exemption in order to obtain excise tax relief. In part, those conditions require participation in the VFC Program. Parties must meet all of the VFC Program's applicable requirements, and must receive a no action letter from EBSA with respect to the prohibited transaction described in the VFC application. Additionally, under the class exemption, parties must provide notice to interested persons regarding the transaction and its correction, and provide a copy of the notice to the appropriate Regional Office of the DOL, within 60 days after submission of an application under the VFC. (Parties should indicate on the checklist submitted with their VFC application that they will provide notice to interested persons and the Department's Regional Office.) [2]

---

1. Labor Reg. §2510.3-102.
2. 67 Fed. Reg. 70,623 (Nov. 25, 2002); http://www.dol.gov/ebsa/newsroom/0302afact_sheet.html, http://www.dol.gov/ebsa/faqs/faq_vfcp.html#section2.

Questions concerning the class exemption can be referred to the Department of Labor's Office of Exemption Determinations at (202) 693-8540.

As noted above, the DOL amended PTE 2002-51 to permit certain transactions identified in the VFC Program.[1] The amendment to PTE 2002-51 added the two additional transactions noted in items 5 and 6 above where the correction under VFC would otherwise be a prohibited transaction. The amendments to the exemption grant prohibited transaction relief under IRC Section 4975 for correction of these additional transactions through the VFC program. The prohibited transaction relief extends to the original acquisition by the plan of an illiquid asset if such acquisition would have otherwise been a prohibited transaction, but only so far as where the original acquisition price was no more than the fair market value of the property at that time.

The IRS submitted a requested modification to the current requirement in PTE 2002-51, which provides that an applicant must notify interested persons in writing of the transactions for which relief is being sought pursuant to the VFC Program and PTE 2002-51. The IRS requested that the notice requirement not apply in those situations where: (1) the excise tax due under IRC Section 4975 for a failure to timely transmit participant contributions and loan repayments is less than or equal to $100.00; (2) the excise tax that otherwise would be owed and payable to the United States Treasury is contributed to the plan; and (3) the contribution is allocated to the accounts of the plan's participants and beneficiaries in a manner consistent with the plan's provisions concerning the allocation of plan earnings.

The IRS noted that, under the circumstances outlined above, employers that meet the applicable conditions of the class exemption would not be required to file a Return of Excise Taxes Related to Employee Benefit Plans (IRS Form 5330) with the IRS. After considering the issue, the DOL determined to modify the final exemption as requested by the IRS. For the purpose of determining whether the excise tax due under IRC Section 4975 for failing to timely transmit participant contributions and loan repayments is less than or equal to $100, and determining the amount to be contributed to the plan, an applicant may calculate the excise tax that would otherwise be imposed by IRC Section 4975 based upon the lost earnings amount computed using the Online Calculator.

Excise Taxes under the Internal Revenue Code

416. What is the excise tax on prohibited transactions?

To induce the correction of a prohibited transaction, the Internal Revenue Code generally imposes a two-tier nondeductible excise tax on each prohibited transaction entered into by a disqualified person.[2] The DOL has a Prohibited Transaction Class Exemption that would relieve certain transactions from these excise taxes under specified conditions. After amendment of PTE 2002-51 these eligible transactions are: (1) failure to timely remit participant contributions to the trust; (2) loans to a party in interest at fair market rates; (3) purchase or sale of an asset

---

1. 71 Fed. Reg. 20,135 (Apr. 19, 2006).
2. IRC Sec. 4975.

(including real property) between a plan and a party in interest; (4) sale and leaseback of real property (at fair market value and fair rental value, respectively); (5) holding of an illiquid asset previously purchased by a plan; and (6) impermissible payment by a plan of certain expenses.[1] See Q 412.

First-Tier Tax

An initial tax is automatically imposed on a disqualified person (other than a fiduciary acting only as such) for each prohibited transaction. The tax imposed on the disqualified person is 15 percent of the "amount involved" in the transaction for each year or partial year (of the disqualified person) in the taxable period. Where a fiduciary participates in a prohibited transaction in a capacity other than as a fiduciary, he is treated as a disqualified person subject to the tax.[2]

Second-Tier Tax

If the prohibited transaction is not corrected within the taxable period, a tax of 100 percent of the "amount involved" is imposed on the disqualified person.[3] If the prohibited transaction is corrected during the correction period, the second-tier tax imposed with respect to the prohibited transaction will not be assessed. If the tax has been assessed, it will be abated. If the tax has been collected, it will be credited or refunded as an overpayment. The tax imposed includes interest, additions to the tax, and additional amounts.[4] The correction period ends ninety days after a notice of deficiency is mailed under IRC Section 6212 with respect to the second-tier tax and is extended by any periods during which the tax cannot be assessed due to a tax court proceeding and any period approved by the Secretary of the Treasury.[5]

Amount and Collection

The excise taxes under IRC Section 4975 are assessed annually and accumulate until the prohibited transaction is corrected. Pending the issuance of final regulations under IRC Section 4975, the excise tax is calculated in a similar manner as excise tax calculations with respect to private foundations under IRC Section 4941. In particular, the definitions of "amount involved" and "correction" are the same.[6]

The excise taxes imposed under IRC Section 4975 are collected by the IRS. Unless the IRS finds that the collection of a tax is in jeopardy, it will notify the DOL before sending a notice of deficiency with respect to the excise tax. This is intended to provide the DOL with a reasonable opportunity to comment on the imposition or waiver of the excise tax or to obtain a correction of the prohibited transaction. In the event that the imposition of the excise tax imposed under IRC Section 4975 is based on a recommendation by the DOL, the IRS will not conduct a separate

---

1. 67 Fed. Reg. 15,083.
2. IRC Sec. 4975(a).
3. IRC Sec. 4975(b).
4. IRC Sec. 4961(a).
5. IRC Sec. 4963(e).
6. Treas. Reg. §141.4975-13.

examination regarding the prohibited transaction. Upon receiving a written request to impose an excise tax from the DOL or from the Pension Benefit Guaranty Corporation (PBGC), the IRS will investigate whether the tax imposed by IRC Section 4975 should be applied to any person referred to in the request.[1]

Taxable Period

Generally, the term "taxable period" means the period beginning with the date on which the prohibited transaction occurs and ending on the earliest of: (1) the date of mailing of a notice of deficiency with respect to the tax imposed under IRC Section 4975(a); (2) the date on which correction of the prohibited transaction is completed; or (3) the date on which the tax imposed under IRC Section 4975(a) is assessed.[2]

A prohibited transaction occurs on the date when the terms and conditions of the transaction and the liabilities of the parties have been fixed. When a notice of deficiency is not mailed because there is a waiver of the restriction on assessment and collection of a deficiency, or because the deficiency is paid, the date of filing of the waiver or the date of payment of the deficiency is treated as the end of the taxable period.[3]

Amount Involved—First-Tier Tax

The "amount involved" in a prohibited transaction is the greater of (1) the amount of money and the fair market value of other property given; or (2) the amount of money and the fair market value of other property received in the transaction. The fair market value for first-tier tax purposes is measured as of the date of the prohibited transaction.[4]

> *Example.* A corporation that maintains a plan purchases equipment from the plan for $12,000. The fair market value of the equipment is $15,000. The amount involved on first-tier tax is $15,000. If the corporation pays $20,000 for the equipment, the amount involved is $20,000.

Exception—Excess Compensation

Services that are exempt from prohibited transaction treatment because they fall within the purview of the statutory exemptions relating to (1) arrangements for office space or certain other services necessary for the establishment or operation of the plan; or (2) reasonable compensation paid to a disqualified person for services rendered, are not subject to the excise tax penalty unless the compensation is deemed to be excessive. In such a case, the excessive compensation is the "amount involved" that is subject to the first-tier tax.[5]

> *Example.* An investment adviser to a plan is paid $100 per day for each day worked. It is determined that $60 per day is a reasonable amount for the services rendered. The "amount involved" is $40 per day.

---

1. ERISA Sec. 3003(a); IRC Sec. 4975(h).
2. IRC Sec. 4975(f)(2).
3. Treas. Reg. §53.4941(e)-1(a).
4. IRC Sec. 4975(f)(4).
5. IRC Sec. 4975(f)(4).

Exception—Use of Money or Property

Where the use of money or other property is involved, the "amount involved" is the greater of the amount paid for such use or the fair market value of such use for the period during which the money or other property is used.[1]

> *Example 1*. If a plan borrows $100,000 from an employer at 8 percent interest and the prevailing rate in the financial community for loans of a similar nature at the time of the loan is 15 percent, the "amount involved" is $15,000 ($100,000 loan × 15% interest rate). The amount of first-tier excise tax is $2,250 (15% × $15,000).

> *Example 2*. If the plan leases its building to a disqualified person for $10,000 a year and the fair rental value is $11,000, the "amount involved" is $11,000. However, if the fair rental value is $9,000, then the "amount involved" is $10,000.

Exception—Less Than Fair Market Value Received

In the case of a prohibited transaction that would otherwise be protected from the imposition of the excise tax by virtue of a statutory or administrative exemption or a transitional rule, but fails to meet the conditions of such exemption or transitional rule solely because the plan paid more, or received less, than fair market value for the property transferred or a reasonable interest rate in the case of loans, the "amount involved" is the difference between the fair market value over the amount that the plan paid or received, provided that the parties made a good-faith effort to determine fair market value. A good-faith effort is ordinarily made when: (1) the person making the valuation is (a) not a disqualified person, (b) competent to make such valuations, and (c) not in a position to derive an economic benefit from the value used; and (2) the valuation method is a generally accepted one for valuing comparable property for purposes of arm's-length business transactions.[2]

> *Example.* Assume that a good-faith effort is made to determine the fair market value of property involved in a transaction, and it is valued at $5,000. The amount paid in the transaction is $5,000, but later the true fair market value is determined to be $5,500. The "amount involved" is $500. If a good-faith effort had not been made, the amount involved would have been $5,500.

Amount Involved—Second-Tier Tax

For determining the "amount involved" for second-tier tax purposes, the first-tier tax guidelines are applied, except that the "amount involved" is the highest fair market value during the taxable period.[3] This provision is to ensure that the person subject to the tax will not postpone correction of the prohibited transaction in order to earn income on such amounts.

Correction Period

The correction period begins with the date on which the prohibited transaction occurs and ends ninety days after the date of mailing of a notice of deficiency with respect to the tax imposed by IRC Section 4975(b). The correction period is extended by any period in which a

---

1. IRC Sec. 4975(f)(4).
2. Treas. Reg. §53.4941(e)-1(b)(2)(iii).
3. IRC Sec. 4975(f)(4)(B).

deficiency cannot be assessed under IRC Section 6213(a) (relating to notices of deficiency and tax court petitions) and may be extended by the Secretary of Treasury for any other period that is reasonable and necessary to bring about correction of the prohibited transaction (including for taxes imposed under IRC Section 4975 and equitable relief sought by the Secretary of Labor). The correction period ordinarily will not be extended unless (1) the involved parties are actively seeking, in good faith, to correct the prohibited transaction; (2) adequate corrective action cannot reasonably be expected to result during the unextended correction period; and (3) the Secretary of Labor requests an extension because adequate corrective action cannot reasonably be expected to result during the unextended correction period.[1]

If the first-tier tax is paid within the unextended or normal correction period, the normal correction period is automatically extended to end on the later of: (1) ninety days after payment of the tax; or (2) the last day of the correction period, determined without regard to this extension.[2]

If a claim for refund is filed with respect to a tax imposed under IRC Section 4975(a) within the correction period, including extensions, the correction period is extended while the claim is pending, plus an additional ninety days. If a suit or proceeding referred to in IRC Section 7422(g) (regarding suits for the refund of certain excise taxes) is filed, the correction period will be extended while the suit or proceeding is pending.[3]

Settlement Agreement with DOL May Not Preclude Excise Tax

The Ninth Circuit held that where a fiduciary enters into a consent agreement with the DOL after undertaking a transaction to reverse an existing prohibited transaction, the IRS may impose excise taxes under IRC Section 4975.[4] In that case, the court held that although the settlement agreement stated that it was the "final adjudication of all claims" made by the DOL, the IRS was free to impose the excise tax under its enforcement authority. Ironically, PTE 94-71 exempts a disqualified person/party in interest from excise taxes on a transaction authorized by the DOL that occurs *after* the agreement is reached with the DOL. If *Baizer* had undertaken the corrective transaction after reaching a settlement agreement with the DOL, he would have been relieved of the excise taxes imposed by the IRS.

417. How is a prohibited transaction corrected?

In order to avoid the imposition of the second-level 100 percent excise tax, a prohibited transaction must be corrected within the taxable period. Correcting a prohibited transaction means undoing the transaction to the extent possible. In any case, the resulting financial position of the plan may be no worse than that in which it would have been had the disqualified person acted under the highest fiduciary standards.[5]

---

1. IRC Sec. 4963(e); Treas. Reg. §53.4963-1(e)(3).
2. Treas. Reg. §53.4963-1(e)(4).
3. Treas. Reg. §53.4963-1(e)(5).
4. *Baizer v. Commissioner*, 204 F.3d 1231 (9th Cir. 2000).
5. IRC Sec. 4975(f)(5).

The main significance of correcting a prohibited transaction is to avoid the second-level 100 percent tax set forth by IRC Section 4975(b). Correcting the prohibited transaction does not constitute another prohibited transaction, and in correcting the prohibited transaction, the higher of the fair market value of the property given or received, either at the occurrence of each prohibited transaction or at the time of correction, must be utilized.[1]

Revenue Ruling 2002-45[2] discusses the treatment of payments to a qualified plan as restoration, or replacement payments in connection with fiduciary breaches under ERISA. Payments rendered pursuant to a DOL order or court-approved settlement (including payments made under the VFC Program (see Q 410) attributable to fiduciary breach, and lost earnings calculated under the Employee Plans Compliance Resolution System) to a defined contribution plan are considered to be made on account of a reasonable risk of liability and, therefore, would qualify as restorative payments. Payments made under the VFC provisions regarding delinquent elective deferrals, or any other payments to a plan required under the IRC, are not considered restorative.

Correction Involving Use of Money or Property by a Disqualified Person

If a disqualified person uses the property or money of a plan, correction includes, but is not limited to, the termination of such use. In addition, the disqualified person must pay to the plan the excess, if any, of the fair market value (the greater of the value at the time of the prohibited transaction or at the time of correction) for the use of the money or property over the amount paid for the use until termination, plus the excess, if any, of the amount that would have been paid by the disqualified person for the period such disqualified person would have used the property if such termination had not occurred, over the fair market value (at the time of correction) for the use for such period.[3]

Correction Involving Use of Property by a Plan

If a plan uses the property of a disqualified person, correction includes, but is not limited to, termination of such use. In addition, the disqualified person must pay to the plan the excess, if any, of the amount received from the plan over the fair market value (the lesser of the value at the time of the prohibited transaction or at the time of correction) for the use of the property until the time of termination, plus the excess, if any, of the fair market value at the time of correction for the use of the property (for the period that the plan would have used the property if termination had not occurred), over the amount that would have been paid by the plan after termination for use in such period.[4]

Correction of Sales of Property by a Plan to a Disqualified Person

In the case of a sale of property by a plan to a disqualified person for cash, correcting the transaction includes, but is not limited to, rescinding the sale, if possible. The amount returned

1. Treas. Reg. §53.4941(e)-1(c).
2. 2002-2 C.B. 116.
3. Treas. Reg. §53.4941(e)-1(c)(4).
4. Treas. Reg. §53.4941(e)-1(c)(5).

to the disqualified person must not exceed the lesser of the cash received by the plan or the fair market value of the property received by the disqualified person. The fair market value to be returned is the lesser of the fair market value on the date that the prohibited transaction occurred or at the time of the rescission of the sale. The disqualified person must also return to the plan any net income derived from the use of the property, to the extent that it exceeds any income derived by the plan during the correction period from its use of the cash received from the original sale, exchange, or transfer.[1]

Resale by a Disqualified Person Prior to the End of the Correction Period

If, prior to the end of the correction period, the disqualified person resells the property discussed immediately above in an arm's-length transaction to a bona fide purchaser other than the plan or another disqualified person, rescission of the original sale is not required. The disqualified person must pay over to the plan the excess, if any, of (1) the greater of (a) the fair market value of the property on the date of correction (the date on which the money is paid over to the plan) or (b) the amount realized by the disqualified person from the arm's-length sale over (2) the amount that would have been returned to the disqualified person if rescission had been required. In addition, the disqualified person must pay over to the plan any net profits realized through the use of the property during the correction period.[2]

Correction of Sales of Property by a Disqualified Person to a Plan

In the case of a sale of property to a plan by a disqualified person for cash, correcting the transaction includes, but is not limited to, rescission of the sale where possible. In order to avoid placing the plan in a position worse than if such rescission were not required, the amount received from the disqualified person pursuant to the rescission must be the greatest of: (1) the cash paid to the disqualified person; (2) the fair market value of the property at the time of the original sale; or (3) the fair market value of the property at the time of rescission. In addition to rescission, the disqualified person is required to pay over to the plan any net profits realized after the original sale with respect to the consideration received from the sale, to the extent that such income during the correction period exceeds the income derived by the plan during the correction period from the property that the disqualified person originally transferred to the plan.[3]

Resale by the Plan Prior to the End of the Correction Period

If the plan resells the property before the end of the correction period in an arm's-length transaction to a bona fide purchaser, other than a disqualified person, no rescission is necessary. The disqualified person must pay over to the plan the excess, if any, of the amount that would have been paid to the plan in the case of a rescission over the amount that the plan realized on the resale of the property. Also, the disqualified person is required to pay to the plan any net profits realized after the original sale with respect to the consideration received from the sale,

---

1. Treas. Reg. §53.4941(e)-1(c)(2)(i).
2. Treas. Reg. §53.4941(e)-1(c)(2)(ii).
3. Treas. Reg. §53.4941(e)-1(c)(3)(i).

to the extent that such income during the correction period exceeds the income derived by the plan during the correction period from the property that the disqualified person originally transferred to the plan.[1]

Payment of Compensation to a Disqualified Person

If a plan pays compensation to a disqualified person for the performance of personal services that are reasonable and necessary to carry out the provisions of the plan, correction requires repaying to the plan any amount considered excessive. Termination of employment is not required.[2]

Less Than Fair Market Value Received

In the case of a transaction with respect to the exception for less than fair market value received (described in Q 416), correction will occur if the plan is paid an amount equal to the "amount involved," plus any additional amounts necessary to compensate it for the loss of the use of the money or other property during the period from the date of the prohibited transaction to the date of correction.[3]

418. Who is liable for the excise tax?

Any disqualified person who participates in a prohibited transaction is liable for the excise taxes imposed under IRC Section 4975. However, a person who participates in a prohibited transaction only as a fiduciary is not liable for the excise tax.[4] If more than one disqualified person is liable for the prohibited transaction excise taxes, all such persons are jointly and severally liable with respect to the transaction.[5]

419. What is the statute of limitations for assessing the excise tax under IRC Section 4975?

With respect to the excise taxes imposed under IRC Section 4975, the filing of Form 5500 starts the running of the statute of limitations for a prohibited transaction if the prohibited transaction is reported on the form. Form 5500 is the return for the plan only. Schedule P to Form 5500 is considered the annual return of the plan's trust. Filing Schedule P starts the running of the statute of limitations under IRC Section 6501(a) for any trust described in IRC Section 401(a).

The statute of limitations is three years if the prohibited transaction is disclosed on Form 5500; thus, the amount of any excise tax imposed by IRC Section 4975 must be assessed within three years after Form 5500 is filed.[6] If the Form 5500 fails to disclose the prohibited transaction, a six-year statute of limitations applies.[7]

---

1. Treas. Reg. §53.4941(e)-1(c)(3)(ii).
2. Treas. Reg. §53.4941(e)-1(c)(6).
3. Treas. Reg. §53.4941(e)-1(c)(7).
4. IRC Secs. 4975(a), 4975(b).
5. IRC Sec. 4975(f)(1).
6. IRC Sec. 6501(a).
7. IRC Sec. 6501(e)(3).

The determination of the statute of limitations is different for a "continuing" transaction (e.g., a loan or lease) versus a "discrete" transaction (e.g., a sale). In the case of a continuing transaction, the prohibited transaction is deemed to recur on the first day of each subsequent taxable year. The filing of Form 5500 starts the statute of limitations running for transactions occurring in that year only; a separate determination as to the expiration of the statute of limitations must be made for each taxable year thereafter if the prohibited transaction has not been corrected. In the case of a discrete transaction, a determination need only be made for the taxable year in which the transaction occurred.[1]

The period of limitations on collection may be suspended, and assessment or collection of the first- or second-tier tax may be prohibited, during the pendency of administrative and judicial proceedings conducted to determine a taxpayer's liability for the second-tier tax under IRC Section 4975(b).[2] Treasury Regulation Section 53.4961-2 provides rules relating to the suspension of the limitations period and the prohibitions on assessment and collection. It also describes the administrative and judicial proceedings to which these rules apply.

420. How are prohibited transactions and the excise taxes reported?

Any disqualified person who is liable for the excise tax under IRC Section 4975 due to participating in a prohibited transaction (other than a fiduciary acting only as such) for which there is no exception must file Form 5330 (Return of Excise Taxes Related to Employee Benefit Plans) by the last day of the seventh month after the end of her tax year. Form 5330 and tax payments are required for the year in which a disqualified person participates in a prohibited transaction and for each year (or part of a year) in the taxable period applicable to the prohibited transaction. A separate Form 5330 must be filed to report taxes with different filing due dates. In addition, failure to file or to pay the excise tax by the due dates (including extensions) subjects the individual to additional penalties on the unpaid tax unless the failure to file or pay on time was due to reasonable cause.[3]

Excise Taxes under ERISA

421. What are the prohibited transaction excise taxes under ERISA?

In addition to the excise taxes imposed under IRC Section 4975, ERISA authorizes the Secretary of Labor to assess a civil penalty against a party in interest who engages in a transaction prohibited under ERISA Section 406 with regard to either an employee welfare benefit plan or a nonqualified plan. The initial penalty is 5 percent of the total "amount involved" in the prohibited transaction (unless a lesser amount is otherwise agreed to by the parties). However, if the prohibited transaction is not corrected during the "correction period," the civil penalty is 100 percent of the "amount involved" (unless a lesser amount is otherwise agreed to by the parties).[4]

The civil penalty under ERISA Section 502(i) complements the excise tax imposed on tax-qualified pension plans by IRC Section 4975 and is designed to achieve correction of the prohibited

---

1. See Gen. Couns. Mem. 38,846 (Feb. 26, 1982), *as modified by* Gen. Couns. Mem. 39,475 (Feb. 10, 1986).
2. IRC Secs. 4961(b), 4961(c); Treas. Reg. §53.4961-2(a).
3. Treas. Reg. §54.6011-1(b); Instructions to Form 5330.
4. ERISA Sec. 502(i); Labor Reg. §2560.502i-1(a).

transaction. In contrast to the excise tax of the Internal Revenue Code, the assessment of the civil penalty under ERISA is not automatic but rather is at the discretion of the Department of Labor (DOL).

The Employee Benefits Security Administration (EBSA) of the DOL must notify a party in interest of its intention to assess the ERISA Section 502(i) penalty. The ability to assess an ERISA Section 502(i) penalty may be preserved by the DOL by the issuance of a voluntary compliance notice letter to a party in interest.[1]

First-Tier Penalty

The first-tier penalty under ERISA Section 502(i) is 5 percent of the amount involved. The ERISA regulations refer to the Treasury regulations to define "amount involved." In general, the amount involved means the greater of (1) the amount of money and the fair market value of the property given; or (2) the amount of money and the fair market value of the property received as of the date of the occurrence of the prohibited transaction.[2]

Amount Involved

When determining the amount involved, the DOL may distinguish between situations that involve the prohibited transfer of ownership (a sale or transfer of property) and the prohibited use of property (a lease or loan of property). Where the prohibited transaction involves the transfer of ownership, the penalty is based on the greater of the fair market value of the property or the actual amount of money that changed hands. In the situation where the prohibited transaction involves the use of money or property, the amount involved is the greater of the amount paid for the use or the fair market value of the use of the money or property. For example, in the event of a prohibited transaction that involves a prohibited loan, the amount involved is the greater of the interest actually paid or the fair market rate of interest for the loan. In the situation of a prohibited transaction involving a lease, the amount involved is the greater of the rent actually paid or the fair market rental value.

If a prohibited transaction involves the payment of compensation to a party in interest for services provided to the plan, the amount involved is limited to any excess compensation paid for those services.[3]

Discrete Transaction

The Department of Labor also may make a distinction between a discrete and continuing prohibited transaction in calculating the ERISA Section 502(i) civil penalty. In the case of discrete prohibited transactions (such as a sale of property), the first tier of the civil penalty is assessed simply as 5 percent of the amount involved for each taxable year (of the party in interest) or portion thereof until the prohibited transaction is corrected or the penalty is assessed. The penalty on discrete prohibited transactions is calculated on an annual basis and is not prorated

---

1. See PTE 94-71.
2. Labor Reg. §2560.502i-1(b); Treas. Reg. §53.4941(e)-1(b).
3. Treas. Reg. §53.4941(e)-1(b).

for a portion of the year. Therefore, the amount of the penalty is not proportionately reduced for transactions that occur in the middle of a year.

Continuing Transaction

Where the prohibited transaction is continuing (such as a lease or loan), a new prohibited transaction is deemed to occur on the first day of each year or portion thereof during which the transaction remains uncorrected. This results in an assessment of an additional ERISA Section 502(i) penalty for each year during which the prohibited transaction remains outstanding. In contrast to discrete transactions, the penalty on a continuing transaction is calculated on an annual basis, but is prorated for a portion of any year involved.[1]

Second-Tier Penalty

The second tier of the ERISA Section 502(i) civil penalty (100 percent of the amount involved) may be assessed in addition to the first-tier penalty if the prohibited transaction is not corrected within ninety days after a final agency order is issued with respect to such transaction.[2] "Final order" means the final decision or action of the DOL concerning the assessment of a civil sanction against a particular party under ERISA Section 502(i). Such final order may result from a decision of an administrative law judge or the Secretary of Labor, or from the failure of a party to invoke the procedures for hearings or appeals.[3]

The "amount involved" in the transaction, for purposes of the second tier of the ERISA Section 502(i) penalty, is the highest fair market value during the correction period.[4] In general, the correction period begins on the date when the prohibited transaction occurs and ends ninety days after a final agency order.[5]

ERISA Section 502(i) Appeals

Upon receipt of a notice of assessment, a party in interest who elects to contest the EBSA's findings and assessment may request a hearing before an administrative law judge (ALJ). In general, the party in interest may file an answer and request for a hearing with the ALJ within thirty days of service of process. The failure to file a timely answer will be deemed to be a waiver of the right to appear as well as an admission of the facts alleged.[6]

Unless otherwise waived, the party in interest may file an appeal to the Secretary of Labor within twenty days of the issuance of the ALJ's final decision. Upon such appeal, the Secretary of Labor may affirm, modify, or set aside, in whole or in part, the decision on appeal. The Secretary of Labor's review is not a *de novo* proceeding but rather a review of the record established before the ALJ.[7]

---

1. Labor Reg. §2560.502i-1(e); *EBSA Enforcement Manual* ch. 35.
2. Labor Reg. §2560.502i-1(d).
3. Labor Reg. §2570.2(g).
4. Treas. Reg. §53.4941(e)-1(b)(3).
5. Labor Reg. §2560.502i-1(d).
6. Labor Reg. §2570.5.
7. Labor Reg. §§2570.10, 2570.11, 2570.12.

422. What is the amount involved?

The term "amount involved" is defined as that term is defined under IRC Section 4975(f) (4).[1] Temporary excise tax regulations state that Treasury Regulation Section 53.4941(e)-1(b) is controlling with respect to the interpretation of the term "amount involved" under IRC Section 4975.[2] Accordingly, the Department of Labor applies the principles set out in the Treasury regulations to determine the "amount involved" in a transaction subject to the civil penalty provided under ERISA Section 502(i).[3] See Q 416.

423. What is the correction period?

In general, the "correction period" begins on the date when the prohibited transaction occurs and ends ninety days after a final agency order with respect to the transaction. When a party in interest seeks judicial review within ninety days of a final agency order in an ERISA Section 502(i) proceeding, the correction period will end ninety days after the entry of a final order in the judicial action.[4] The regulation provides the following examples to illustrate the operation of these rules:

A party in interest receives notice of the DOL's intent to impose the ERISA Section 502(i) penalty and does not invoke the ERISA Section 502(i) prohibited transaction penalty proceedings described in Labor Regulation Section 2570.1 within thirty days of such notice. As provided in Labor Regulation Section 2570.5, the notice of the intent to impose a penalty becomes a final order after thirty days. Thus, the "correction period" ends ninety days after the expiration of the thirty-day period.[5]

A party in interest contests a proposed ERISA Section 502(i) penalty, but does not appeal an adverse decision of the administrative law judge in the proceeding. As provided in Labor Regulation Section 2570.10(a), the decision of the administrative law judge becomes a final order of the DOL unless the decision is appealed within twenty days after the date of such order. Thus, the correction period ends ninety days after the expiration of such twenty-day period.[6]

The Secretary of Labor issues a decision to a party in interest upholding an administrative law judge's adverse decision. As provided in Labor Regulation Section 2570.12(b), the decision of the Secretary of Labor becomes a final order of the DOL immediately. Thus, the correction period will end ninety days after the issuance of the Secretary's order, unless the party in interest judicially contests the order within that ninety-day period. If the party in interest so contests the order, the correction period will end ninety days after the entry of a final order in the judicial action.[7]

---

1. ERISA Sec. 502(i).
2. Treas. Reg. §141.4975-13.
3. Labor Reg. §2560.502i-1(b).
4. Labor Reg. §2560.502i-1(d).
5. Labor Reg. §2560.502i-1(d)(3)(i).
6. Labor Reg. §2560.502i-1(d)(3)(ii).
7. Labor Reg. §2560.502i-1(d)(3)(iii).

424. How is the ERISA Section 502(i) penalty computed?

In general, the civil penalty under ERISA Section 502(i) is determined by applying the applicable percentage (5 percent or 100 percent) to the aggregate amount involved in the transaction. However, a continuing prohibited transaction, such as a lease or a loan, is treated as giving rise to a separate event subject to the sanction for each year (as measured from the anniversary date of the transaction) in which the transaction occurs.[1]

Labor regulations provide the following examples to illustrate the computation of the ERISA Section 502(i) penalty:

An employee benefit plan purchases property from a party in interest at a price of $10,000. The fair market value of the property is $5,000. The "amount involved" in that transaction, as determined under Treasury Regulation Section 53.4941(e)-1(b), is $10,000 (the greater of the amount paid by the plan or the fair market value of the property). The initial 5 percent penalty under ERISA Section 502(i) is $500 (5% of $10,000).[2]

An employee benefit plan executes a four-year lease with a party in interest at an annual rental of $10,000 (which is the fair rental value of the property). The amount involved in each year of that transaction, as determined under Treasury Regulation Section 53.4941(e)-1(b), is $10,000. The amount of the initial sanction under ERISA Section 502(i) would be a total of $5,000: $2,000 ($10,000 × 5% × 4 with respect to the rentals paid in the first year of the lease); $1,500 ($10,000 × 5% × 3 with respect to the second year); $1,000 ($10,000 × 5% × 2 with respect to the third year); $500 ($10,000 × 5% × 1 with respect to the fourth year).[3]

425. Can a prohibited transaction be authorized by the Department of Labor (DOL)?

Yes. In accordance with Prohibited Transaction Exemption 94-71 (PTE 94-71), a transaction will not be treated as a prohibited transaction under ERISA Section 406 and subject to the taxes imposed under IRC Section 4975 if the transaction is authorized by a settlement agreement with the DOL that results from an investigation of a plan by the DOL under ERISA Section 504, provided that: (1) the transaction is described in the settlement agreement; (2) the DOL is a party to the settlement agreement; (3) written notice is provided to the affected participants at least thirty days before the settlement agreement; (4) the notice and method of distribution are approved in advance by the DOL office that negotiated the settlement; and (5) the notice includes (a) a description of the corrective action, (b) the date when the action will occur, (c) the address of the DOL office that negotiated the settlement, and (d) a statement informing the participants of their right to forward comments to the DOL office. The relief offered under PTE 94-71 does not cover transactions prohibited under ERISA Section 406(b)(3) and IRC Section 4975(c)(1)(F) (i.e., receipt of kickbacks). However, action taken before an agreement is reached with the DOL may result in excise tax liability under IRC Section 4975 (see Q 416).

---

1. Labor Reg. §2560.502i-1(e)(1).
2. Labor Reg. §2560.502i-1(e)(2)(i).
3. Labor Reg. §2560.502i-1(e)(2)(ii).

SECTION VI

Statutory, Class, and Individual Exemptions

426. What exemptions from prohibited transactions are provided under ERISA and its regulations?

The exemption provisions from the classes of prohibited transactions between ERISA-covered employee benefit plans and certain parties, identified as "parties in interest," are detailed in ERISA Section 408 and its attendant regulations. There are three different types of exemptions provided for under ERISA:

1. Statutory exemptions under ERISA Section 408;

2. Class exemptions, which are blanket exemptions issued by the Department of Labor (DOL) to grant relief to parties for common transactions, provided that they meet stated terms and conditions; and

3. Individual exemptions, which must be applied for on a case-by-case basis, in which the applicant seeks an exemption from the prohibited transaction provisions for a particular transaction he is contemplating.

The majority of transactions that are prohibited under ERISA are also prohibited under the Internal Revenue Code, although the latter refers to parties in interest as "disqualified persons."[1] In 1978, the responsibility for granting exemptions to employee benefit plans was largely transferred to the DOL.[2] Therefore, the overwhelming majority of exemptions reviewed and granted in the past 20 years have come from the DOL.

In general, exemptions will be granted only if they are (1) administratively feasible; (2) in the interest of the plan, its participants, and beneficiaries; and (3) protective of the rights of the participants and beneficiaries of the plan.[3]

This section explains in detail all three types of prohibited transaction exemptions (PTEs), as well as how to seek an exemption and what rights are available when the DOL denies an application for a PTE.

Class Exemptions

427. What are the class exemptions recognized by the Department of Labor and the Internal Revenue Service?

Class exemptions provide relief from the prohibited transaction provisions of ERISA for common transactions between parties in interest—as defined under ERISA Section 3(14) (see Q 398)—and ERISA-covered employee benefit plans. In order for a class exemption to apply to a particular transaction, all of the requisite elements of the class exemption must be satisfied.

---

1. IRC Sec. 4975(e)(2).
2. Reorganization Plan No. 4 of 1978, 1979-1 C.B. 480.
3. ERISA Sec. 408(a).

The DOL and IRS have recognized the following class exemptions:

- Broker-dealers and banks (PTE 75-1 and PTE 2003-39; see Q 428);

- Foreign exchange transactions (PTE 94-20; see Q 429);

- Securities transactions by plan fiduciaries (PTE 86-128, replacing PTE 79-1 and PTE 84-46; see Q 430);

- Purchase and sale of life insurance between a plan and its participants (PTE 92-5, PTE 92-6, and PTE 77-7; see Q 431);

- Insurance agents and brokers as parties in interest (PTE 77-9, PTE 79-41, PTE 79-60, and PTE 90-1; see Q 432, Q 433, and Q 435);

- Insurance company pooled separate accounts (PTE 90-1; see Q 434 and Q 435);

- Mutual fund "in-house" plans (PTE 77-3; see Q 436);

- Closed-end investment companies (PTE 79-13; see Q 436);

- Investment advisory firms (PTE 77-4; see Q 437);

- Multiemployer plans (PTE 77-10; see Q 438);

- Multiemployer apprenticeship plans (PTE 78-6; see Q 439);

- Customer note sales (PTE 85-68; see Q 440);

- Court-ordered transactions (PTE 79-15; see Q 441);

- Transactions authorized under DOL settlement agreements (PTE 94-71; see Q 442);

- Interest-free loans between plans and parties in interest (PTE 80-26; see Q 445);

- Plan purchase of securities to retire debt owed to a party in interest (PTE 80-83; see Q 446);

- Short-term plan investments (PTE 81-8; see Q 447);

- Bank collective investment funds (PTE 91-38 and PTE 96-15A; see Q 448);

- Transactions with mortgage pool investment trusts (PTE 81-7 and PTE 88-59; see Q 450);

- Residential mortgage financing arrangements (PTE 88-59; see Q 451);

- Qualified professional asset managers (PTE 84-14; see Q 452);

- In-house asset managers (PTE 96-23; see Q 453);

- Individual retirement accounts (PTE 97-11; see Q 457);

- Accelerated exemption procedures (PTE 96-62; see Q 458);

- Insurance company general accounts (PTE 95-60; see Q 459);

- Compensation of fiduciaries for securities lending services (PTE 82-63; see Q 454);

- Transactions authorized under settlement agreements between private parties (PTE 2003-39; see Q 443); and

- Abandoned individual account plan termination administrators (PTE 2006-06; see Q 461).

This list, of course, is not intended to be an exhaustive review of all of the class exemptions granted by the DOL. It is merely a detailed overview of the more common situations among ERISA-covered employee benefit plans that have been granted a class exemption from the prohibited transaction provisions of ERISA.

428. What is the broker-dealer exemption?

Prohibited Transaction Exemption 75-1 provides a class exemption for transactions between plans and broker-dealers, reporting dealers, and banks that involve (1) the extension of credit, (2) principal transactions, (3) agency transactions and services, (4) underwriting, and (5) market making, if certain specified conditions are met.

Much of the relief granted under PTE 75-1 was subsequently incorporated in regulations detailing the rules under which parties in interest may provide services to a plan.[1] See Q 464.

Relief may also be available to a party in interest furnishing a plan with "any advice, either directly or through publications or writings, as to the value of securities or other property, the advisability of investing in, purchasing or selling securities or other property, or the availability of securities or other property or of purchasers or sellers of securities or other property, or of any analysis or reports concerning issuers, industries, securities or other property, economic factors or trends, or portfolio strategy, or the performance of accounts, under circumstances which do not make the party in interest a fiduciary with respect to the plan."[2]

---

1. Labor Reg. §2550.408b-2.
2. PTE 75-1.

An adviser will become a fiduciary only if she renders the advice detailed above to the plan on a regular basis "pursuant to a mutual agreement … written or otherwise … that such service will serve as a primary basis for investment decisions with respect to plan assets."[1]

In order for the exemption to apply, such advice, analysis, and reports must be "furnished to the plan, on terms at least as favorable to the plan as an arm's length transaction with an unrelated party."[2]

The DOL has amended PTE 75-1 to narrow the scope of fiduciary relationship necessary to preclude reliance on the exemption.

Specifically, for transactions other than the purchase or sale of shares in an open-end mutual fund, the broker-dealer, reporting dealer or bank involved in the transaction, and any affiliate thereof, may not have or exercise any discretionary authority or control (except as directed trustee) with respect to the investment *of the plan assets involved in the transaction* and may not render investment advice with respect to those assets. This narrows the prohibited fiduciary relationship so that the broker-dealer, reporting dealer or bank, or its affiliate, might serve in other fiduciary capacities not related to the assets at issue.

Also, the exemption is amended with respect to an extension of credit by a broker-dealer to a plan. A broker-dealer who extends credit to the plan may not have or exercise any discretionary control (except as directed trustee) with respect to the investment *of the plan assets involved in the transaction* and may not render investment advice with respect to those assets. This narrows the prohibited fiduciary role in a manner similar to the above amendment.[3]

Based upon feedback from practitioners and independent fiduciaries working to settle litigation in accordance with this exemption, the DOL has provided a proposed expansion of the type of consideration that can be accepted by an employee benefit plan in settlement of litigation. While the DOL encourages cash settlements, it recognizes that there are situations in which it may be in the interest of participants and beneficiaries to accept consideration other than cash in exchange for releasing the claims of the plan and/ or the plan fiduciary.

In addition, because ERISA does not permit plans to hold employer-issued stock rights, warrants, or most bonds, without an individual exemption, the transactions covered by PTE 2003-39 have been expanded to include acquisition, holding, and disposition of employer securities received in settlement of litigation, including bankruptcy litigation. Where non-cash assets or benefits enhancements are being considered, the authorizing fiduciary must first determine that a cash settlement is either not feasible or is less beneficial than the alternative. Both non-cash assets and benefits enhancements must be described in the written settlement agreement.[4]

---

1. Labor Reg. §2510.3-21(c).
2. PTE 75-1.
3. Amendment to PTE 75-1, 71 Fed. Reg. 5883 (Feb. 3, 2006).
4. 72 Fed. Reg. 65597 (Nov. 21, 2007).

429. What is the foreign exchange class exemption?

If certain conditions are met, class exemption relief may be available to banks, broker-dealers, and their affiliates who purchase and sell foreign currencies on behalf of the plans to which they serve as parties in interest. Specifically, relief is provided if the transaction is directed for the benefit of a plan by a fiduciary that is independent of the bank, the broker-dealer, or any affiliate of the bank or broker-dealer.[1]

At the time when the parties enter into the transaction, the general conditions of the exemption require that the terms of the transaction be "not less favorable to the plan than the terms generally available in comparable arm's length foreign exchange transactions between unrelated parties." The exemption also requires that "neither the bank, the broker-dealer, nor any affiliate thereof has any discretionary authority or control with respect to the investment of the plan assets involved in the transaction or renders investment advice with respect to the investment of those assets."[2]

In addition to satisfying the general conditions detailed above, the following specific conditions must be satisfied in order for the exemption to apply:

1.   At the time of the transaction, the terms must not be less favorable to the plan than the terms afforded by the bank, broker-dealer, or any of their affiliates in a comparable arm's-length transaction involving unrelated parties.

2.   The bank or broker-dealer must maintain, at all times, written policies and procedures detailing its handling of foreign exchange transactions with plans with respect to which the bank or broker-dealer is a trustee, custodian, fiduciary, or other party in interest "which assure that the person acting for the bank or broker-dealer knows that he or she is dealing with a plan."

3.   Within five business days, the independent fiduciary who directs the covered foreign exchange transaction must be issued a written confirmation statement for the covered transaction that contains the account name, transaction date, exchange rates, settlement date, amount of currency sold, and the amount of currency purchased.

4.   The bank or broker-dealer must maintain, within the United States or its territories, specific records of the transaction that would enable the DOL, the IRS, fiduciaries, plan sponsors, or contributing employers to "determine whether the applicable conditions of this exemption have been met." These records must be maintained for a period of six years from the date of the transaction.[3]

The DOL has expanded PTE 94-20 to permit the foreign exchange transactions, discussed above, between plans and certain banks and broker-dealers that are parties in interest, provided

---

1. PTE 94-20.
2. PTE 94-20.
3. PTE 94-20.

that such transactions are executed under standing instructions. If specific conditions are satisfied, this rule may be applied retroactively to June 18, 1991.[1]

430. What is the class exemption for securities transactions by plan fiduciaries?

Exemptive relief may be available to persons who serve as fiduciaries and trustees of plans executing securities transactions. Such relief is provided by PTE 86-128, which replaces PTE 79-1 and PTE 84-46. PTE 86-128 was amended effective October 17, 2002, to expand the definition of trustees eligible to effect securities transactions on behalf of qualified plans to include discretionary trustees.[2] Prior to the amendment, PTE 86-128 applied only to non-discretionary trustees.

Note that this exemption does not apply to plan trustees or to plan sponsors, unless they are executing covered transactions in which the plan is permitted to recapture (either through a direct return, or a credit to the plan) all profits earned in connection with the transaction.

Only agency transactions (e.g., a fiduciary selling on behalf of a third party) and cross transactions (e.g., both the buyer and seller utilizing the same broker) are authorized under PTE 86-128. In order for exemptive relief to apply to any cross transactions, the following conditions must be met: (1) the cross transaction must be for the purchase or sale for no consideration other than cash payment made against the prompt delivery of a security for which there is a readily available market quotation; (2) the cross transaction must be executed at a price between the current bid and current sale quotations; (3) the broker-dealer must not have any discretionary authority on either side of the transaction; (4) the fiduciary agent must disclose potentially conflicting loyalties regarding all parties involved in the transaction; and (5) the agent fiduciary must provide a summary of all cross transactions, commissions, and remuneration paid during the period being summarized.[3]

But there are no special requirements under the exemption for cross transactions in which the agent fiduciary conducting the transaction (1) does not render any investment advice to the subject plan for a fee; (2) has no investment discretion with respect to any of the plan's assets involved in the transaction; and (3) has no authority to engage, retain, or discharge any fiduciary regarding any plan assets.[4]

The exemption does not apply to principal transactions in which the fiduciary markets securities on his own; thus, that is still a prohibited transaction. See Q 428. The authorization requirement provides that the executing fiduciary must receive advance written authorization to complete the transaction on behalf of the plan.

For single customer accounts, the authorization must come from each plan that has assets involved in the transaction. The advance written authorization must be provided by a fiduciary that is independent of the fiduciary executing the trade. Further, at any time within a three-month period prior to the granting of initial authorization, the independent fiduciary must have been

---

1. PTE 98-5.
2. 67 Fed. Reg. 64,137 (Oct. 17, 2002).
3. PTE 86-128, §III(g).
4. PTE 86-128, §IV.

furnished with reasonably available information that the agent believes to be necessary in order for the independent fiduciary to decide whether such authorization should be granted. Such information must include: (1) a copy of PTE 86-128; (2) a form for Termination of Authorization (which must be provided annually); (3) a description of the agent fiduciary's brokerage placement practices; and (4) any additional information that the agent fiduciary believes to be relevant to the decision to be made by the independent fiduciary.[1]

In order for the authorization to be effective, the independent fiduciary must be able to terminate the authorization at will, in writing, and without penalty to the plan.

In addition, the exemption permits sponsors of pooled separate accounts and other pooled investment funds of more than one ERISA plan to execute transactions on behalf of a plan only if an independent fiduciary has provided advance authorization under the following circumstances:

1. At least thirty days prior to a grant of authorization, the independent fiduciary has been provided any information (including a description of any proposed material change to the arrangement) reasonably necessary to make a determination as to whether such authorization should be granted or continued.

2. The information provided contains a description of the fiduciary agent's brokerage placement practices.

3. The independent fiduciary is able to terminate the investment in the agent fiduciary's collective fund, without penalty to the plan, by the submission of a written notice to the fiduciary agent that there is an objection to the implementation of a material change in or a continuation of the arrangement.[2]

Where an independent fiduciary has terminated a plan's investment in the fiduciary agent's fund, it must be carried out within a time frame that allows for the withdrawal from the fund in such an orderly manner as to be equitable to all withdrawing and non-withdrawing plans. Such a withdrawal must be completed prior to the implementation of any material change in the brokerage arrangement.

The fiduciary agent must provide one of the following to each independent fiduciary:

1. A confirmation slip for each transaction covered under the brokerage arrangement (within ten business days) that complies with Rule 10b-10(a) of the Securities Exchange Act of 1934, or

2. A quarterly report, furnished within forty-five days of the end of the reporting period, that provides

   a. a compilation of the information contained in the brokerage slips,

   b. a total of all transaction-related charges incurred within the reporting period,

---

1. PTE 86-128, §III(d).
2. PTE 86-128, §IV(d).

    c.   the amount of transaction-related charges retained by the agent, and

    d.   the amount of such charges paid to third parties for appropriate services provided (such as executions of transactions).[1]

The agent fiduciary must also provide an annual report to each independent fiduciary with a summary of the information contained in the confirmation slips. This annual report must be provided within forty-five days of the close of the reporting year and must contain the portfolio turnover ratio and the annual totals of the information required under the optional quarterly report.

The exemption permits the payment of additional fees to fiduciary agents, so long as the amount of transactions is not excessive as to size or frequency. The limits on the size and frequency of such transactions have been designed to prevent agent fiduciaries from generating excessive compensation through the churning of plan portfolios.[2]

431. What are the class exemptions for the purchase and sale of life insurance?

There are two class exemptions that permit the purchase and sale of life insurance policies between a plan and its participants.

A plan may acquire an individual life insurance contract or annuity contract from (1) a participant for whom the contract was issued; or (2) an employer, any of whose employees are covered by the plan, if certain requirements are met. The exemptive relief will apply if

1.   The plan pays, transfers, or otherwise exchanges no more than the lesser of

    a.   the cash surrender value of the contract,

    b.   the value of the participant's accrued benefit at the time of the transaction (if the plan is a defined benefit plan), or

    c.   the value of the participant's account balance (if the plan is a defined contribution plan);

2.   The sale, transfer, or exchange does not involve a contract that is subject to a lien or mortgage that the plan would assume;

3.   The sale, transfer, or exchange does not violate any provision of the plan or trust documents; and

4.   If the plan is a welfare benefit plan, the plan does not discriminate, in form or in operation, in favor of participants who are officers, shareholders, or highly compensated employees with respect to the sale, transfer, or exchange.[3]

---

1. PTE 86-128.
2. PTE 86-128.
3. PTE 92-5.

If certain conditions are met, a plan may sell an individual life insurance or annuity contract for its cash surrender value to any of the following:

1. A participant covered by the policy;

2. A relative of the participant who is the beneficiary under the contract;

3. The plan sponsor; or

4. Another plan.

In order for the exemption described above to apply to the sale of a contract, the following conditions must be met:

1. The participant is insured under the contract;

2. The "relative" is a spouse, ancestor, lineal descendant, or spouse of a lineal descendant (as defined under ERISA Section 3(15)), or is a brother or sister of the insured (or spouse of such brother or sister), *and is the beneficiary under the contract*;

3. The insurance contract would be surrendered by the plan if it is not sold;

4. The participant is first informed of the proposed sale and is given the first opportunity to purchase the contract from the plan, or he delivers to the plan a written statement that he elects not to purchase the contract and consents to the plan's sale of the contract to the plan sponsor, relative, or another plan;

5. The amount received by the plan from the sale of the contract is at least equal to the amount necessary to put the plan in the same cash position as it would have been in had it kept the contract, surrendered it, and made any distribution owing to the participant of his vested interest under the plan; *and*

6. If the selling plan is a welfare benefit plan, it must not discriminate, in form or operation, in favor of participants who are officers, shareholders, or highly compensated employees with respect to the sale of the contract.[1]

The DOL has clarified PTE 92-6, so that if all of its other conditions are met, then

1. Two or more relatives who are the sole beneficiaries under the contract may be considered a single "relative."

2. The term "individual life insurance contract" may be read to include a contract covering the life of the participant and his spouse, to the extent that

   a. applicable state insurance law permits an individual life insurance policy to cover the lives of an individual and his spouse, and

   b. "applicable law and pertinent plan provisions" permit the plan to acquire and hold such a policy.

---

1. PTE 92-6.

3. The sale of a partial interest in a life insurance contract will constitute the sale of an "individual life insurance contract," provided that the portion of the interest in the contract sold and the portion of the interest in the contract retained would each:

    a. have all of the characteristics of life insurance contracts,

    b. be independently viable as life insurance contracts,

    c. be available for purchase in the marketplace as life insurance contracts, and

    d. qualify as life insurance contracts under applicable state law.[1]

In reviewing the applicability of PTE 92-6 to the sale of a second-to-die policy jointly to a husband and wife, both of whom were plan participants, the DOL has said that the policy is an individual life policy and, therefore, eligible for exemptive relief under PTE 92-6. It should be noted that the policy was paid for entirely with funds from the husband's rollover account in the plan and the plan granted discretion to participants in managing the assets in their accounts.[2]

432. What is the class exemption regarding the sale of annuities, insurance, and annuity contracts by captive insurance companies?

Insurance companies that are related to a plan sponsor through substantial stock or partnership interests may be permitted to sell life insurance, health insurance, or annuity contracts designed to fund employee benefit plans sponsored by such related employer.

The exemptive relief will apply if

1. The insurance company making the sale

    a. is a party in interest with respect to the plan by reason of a stock or partnership affiliation with the employer sponsoring the plan (including a joint venture),

    b. is licensed to sell insurance products in at least one of the United States or the District of Columbia, and

    c. has obtained a certificate of compliance from the insurance commissioner of its home state within eighteen months of the sale (or, in the alternative, when the home state last issued such certificates);

2. An independent certified public accountant has conducted a financial examination of the insurance company for its last completed taxable year, or its home state insurance commissioner has done so within the five years preceding the sale;

3. The plan pays no more than "adequate consideration" for the insurance contracts or annuities;

4. No commissions are paid with respect to the sale of such insurance contracts; and

1. DOL Adv. Op. 98-07A.
2. DOL Adv. Op. 2006-03A (Feb. 28, 2006).

5.   The total of all premiums and annuity considerations received by the insurance company for the sale of life and health insurance and annuity contracts to all employee benefit plans in which the insurance company is a party in interest does not exceed 50 percent of the premiums and annuity considerations it has received from all lines of insurance in that taxable year.[1]

Note that this exemption does not provide relief from ERISA Section 406(b)(3), which prohibits a plan fiduciary from receiving "any consideration for his own personal account from any party dealing with a transaction involving the assets of the plan."

433. What is the class exemption regarding the sale of insurance or annuity contracts by agents or brokers that sponsor the plan making the purchase?

Exemptive relief is provided with respect to the sale of insurance or annuity contracts to employee benefit plans, and the receipt of commissions with respect to the sales by agents or brokers who are (or are related to) the employer sponsoring and maintaining the plan. In order for the exemptive relief to be granted, the following requirements must be met:

1.   The insurance agent or broker conducting the sale and receiving the commissions must be

     a.   an employer whose employees are covered by the plan;

     b.   a 10 percent or more partner in the capital or profits of an employer whose employees are covered by the plan;

     c.   an employee, officer, director, or 10 percent or more shareholder of an employer whose employees are covered by the plan; or

     d.   a party in interest with respect to the plan by reason of an affiliation with the employer who is the plan sponsor (including sole proprietor plan sponsors);

2.   The plan must pay no more than adequate consideration for the insurance contracts or annuities; and

3.   The total commissions received by the agent or broker for the taxable year in which the sales to the plan took place must not exceed 5 percent of the total insurance premiums she has earned in that year.[2]

434. What is the class exemption relating to insurance company pooled separate accounts?

Exemptive relief allowing an insurance company pooled separate account to engage in transactions with persons who are parties in interest with respect to an employee benefit plan

---

1. PTE 79-41.
2. PTE 79-60.

investing in the pooled separate account may be available under PTE 90-1. This includes pooled separate accounts that acquire or hold employer securities or employer real property.

The exemptive relief will apply only if, at the time of such transaction:

1.   The assets of the plan in the pooled separate account do not exceed 10 percent of the total of all assets in the pooled separate account (if the transaction has occurred on or after July 1, 1988, different limitations apply in earlier years); or

2.   The pooled separate account is a specialized account that has a policy of investing, and invests substantially all of its assets in short-term obligations, including, but not limited to: (a) corporate or governmental obligations or related repurchase agreements, (b) certificates of deposit, (c) bankers acceptances, or (d) variable amount notes of borrowers of prime credit; and

3.   The party in interest is not (a) the insurance company that holds the plan assets in its pooled separate account, (b) any other account of the insurance company, or (c) any affiliate of the insurance company.

The exemption does not prohibit insurance company pooled separate accounts from engaging in transactions that exceed the previously described limits, if such transactions are with parties in interest with respect to an employee benefit plan that invests in the pooled separate account for the lease of real property and/or the incidental furnishing of goods.[1]

435. Does the class exemption relating to insurance company pooled separate accounts apply to multiemployer plans?

In general, parties in interest may engage in transactions with the same insurance company pooled separate accounts in which a plan has invested.[2] See Q 434.

This exemption also applies to any transaction between an employer (or its affiliates) of employees covered by a multiemployer plan and an insurance company pooled separate account in which the plan has an interest, or any acquisition or holding by the pooled separate account of employer securities or employer real property. In order for the exemption to apply, the following requirements must be satisfied at the time of the transaction:

1.   The multiemployer plan assets invested in the pooled separate account do not exceed 10 percent of the pooled separate account's total assets; and

2.   The employer is not a "substantial employer" with respect to the plan;[3] or

3.   The multiemployer plan assets invested in the pooled separate account exceed 10 percent of the pooled separate account's total assets, and the employer is not

1. PTE 90-1.
2. PTE 90-1.
3. As defined under ERISA Section 4001(a)(2).

a "substantial employer" with respect to the plan, and would not be a substantial employer if its contributions to the plan for each year constituting either

a.   the two immediately preceding plan years, or

b.   the first two of the three immediately preceding plan years,

totaled an amount greater than or equal to 5 percent of contributions required to be paid to the plan for that year.

This exemption does not prohibit insurance company pooled separate accounts from engaging in transactions that exceed the previously described limits with parties in interest that invest in pooled separate accounts for the lease of real property and/or the incidental furnishing of goods.[1]

436. What are the class exemptions regarding mutual fund "in-house" plans?

Exemptive relief is provided for certain situations in which an "in-house" employee benefit plan (i.e., a plan covering only employees of the mutual fund, its investment adviser or principal underwriters, or any affiliate of the investment adviser or principal underwriter) invests the assets of the plan into its own open-end mutual funds.

In order for the exemptive relief to apply, such plans are prohibited from paying

1.   Any investment management or investment advisory fees to the investment adviser, principal underwriter, or their affiliates;

2.   A sales commission for the acquisition or sale of shares; or

3.   A redemption fee for the sale of shares by the plan to the mutual fund, unless the fee is paid only to the investment company and the fee is disclosed in the mutual fund's prospectus, both at the time of the acquisition of the shares and at the time of the sale.[2]

The DOL has extended relief under PTE 77-3 to include investment by a bank's in-house plan, through an in-kind exchange of assets for mutual fund shares, in a mutual fund advised by the bank.[3]

The DOL, in Advisory Opinion 2006-06A, has offered further clarification as to the definition of "sales commissions" as they apply pursuant to PTE 77-3. In that Opinion, the DOL opines that the sale of proprietary mutual funds to a plan covering employees of the fund's adviser would be a covered transaction under PTE 77-3 even though distribution-related expenses such as 12b-1 fees were paid by the fund distributor and underwriter sponsoring the underlying plan to an unrelated broker.

---

1. PTE 90-1.
2. PTE 77-3.
3. DOL Adv. Op. 98-06A.

Another exemption[1] permits the acquisition and sale of shares of a closed-end mutual fund by employee benefit plans covering the employees of such closed-end mutual fund, its investment adviser, or an affiliate[2] of either. In order for this exemptive relief to apply, the plan *must not pay*

1. Any investment management or investment advisory fee to the investment adviser or an affiliate; or

2. A sales commission in regard to the purchase or sale of shares to the closed-end fund, investment adviser, or affiliated person.

All other dealings between the plan and (1) the open-end and/or closed-end mutual fund, (2) its investment adviser or principal underwriter, or (3) any affiliated person of the mutual fund or underwriter, must be on a basis no less favorable to the plan than that found in such dealings with the mutual fund's other shareholders.[3]

Section 15 of the Investment Advisers Act of 1940 permits both open-end and closed-end mutual funds to pay the investment advisory fees under the terms of the investment advisory agreement themselves (in place of the plan).

437. What is the class exemption regarding investment advisers who serve in a dual capacity to a plan?

Exemptive relief is provided for a plan's purchase and sale of shares of a registered open-end mutual fund when a plan fiduciary (e.g., the investment manager) is also the investment adviser for the mutual fund. In order for the exemptive relief to be applicable, the investment adviser must not be "an employer of employees covered by the plan."

In addition, the exemption will apply only if

1. The plan does not pay any sales commissions regarding the purchase or sale of shares of the mutual fund;

2. The plan does not pay a redemption fee for the sale of shares from the plan to the mutual fund, unless (a) the redemption fee is paid only to the mutual fund and (b) the redemption fee is disclosed in the mutual fund prospectus at the time of the purchase and at the time of the plan's sale of those shares back to the mutual fund; and

3. The plan does not pay any investment management, investment advisory, or similar fees regarding the plan assets invested in the mutual fund "for the entire period of the investment"; however, the mutual fund may pay investment advisory fees, including fees for the entire portfolio of plan assets "from which a credit has been subtracted representing the plan's pro rata share of investment advisory fees paid by" the mutual fund.

---

1. PTE 79-13.
2. As defined by Section 2(a)(3) of the Investment Company Act of 1940.
3. PTE 79-13.

Further, a second plan fiduciary, "who is independent of and unrelated to the fiduciary/ investment advisor," must receive a current plan prospectus for the mutual fund, along with a full and detailed written disclosure of all applicable fees, for the purpose of reviewing the investment adviser's decision to invest plan assets in the mutual fund and for the approval of the fee structure to which the plan will be subject.

The second independent fiduciary must also be notified of any change in any of the fees to which the plan is subject from the mutual fund. The second independent fiduciary must approve, in writing, any continued holding, purchase, or sale of shares of the mutual fund.[1]

The DOL has expressed the opinion that PTE 77-4 does not provide exemptive relief for the purchase of shares in mutual funds that have not been paid for in cash.[2] This would exclude from the exemption asset exchanges between mutual funds.

But the DOL does extend the exemptive relief of PTE 77-4 to employee benefit plan investments in a master-feeder arrangement, even if the master fund has no prospectus available. Because a master fund is exempt from the prospectus requirements, the DOL has stated that Form N-1A must be provided to an independent plan fiduciary along with a detailed description of all relevant information necessary to determine the approval or disapproval of the plan's investment in the master-feeder arrangement.[3] A master fund is one in which only other mutual funds (feeder funds) may invest. The master fund must be a registered investment company under the Investment Company Act of 1940 (the '40 Act), but not the Securities Act of 1933 (the '33 Act). The feeder funds must be registered under both the '40 Act and the '33 Act, and must be offered to the general public.[4]

438. What are the class exemptions that specifically apply to transactions with multiemployer plans?

If certain conditions are met, PTE 76-1 exempts multiemployer plans from the prohibited transaction rules with respect to the following:

1.   The extension of the period of time for submitting delinquent contributions;

2.   The acceptance of less than the full amount that the employer is obligated to contribute; and

3.   The termination of efforts to collect contributions deemed uncollectible, whether in whole or in part.

The exemption includes construction loans and the provision of office space, administrative services, and goods.

In order to qualify for this exemption, the decision to issue a construction loan from a multiemployer plan to a participating employer must be made by a bank, an insurance company,

---

1. PTE 77-4.
2. DOL Adv. Op. 94-35A.
3. DOL Adv. Op. 94-35A.
4. DOL Adv. Op. 94-35A.

or a savings and loan association. In addition, immediately after a construction loan is made: (1) the aggregate amount of plan assets invested in the loan to the participating employer must not exceed 10 percent of the fair market value of the plan's assets; and (2) the aggregate amount of plan assets invested in all loans to all participating employers of the multiemployer plan must not exceed 35 percent of the fair market value of the plan's assets.[1]

Certain provisions of PTE 76-1 were extended, in PTE 77-10, to include circumstances in which a multiemployer plan shares office space and/or receives administrative services and goods. In order for the exemptive relief to apply, all of the following conditions must be satisfied:

1. The costs of sharing office space, services, and/or goods must be assessed and paid on a pro rata basis with respect to each party's use of the space, services, and goods.

2. The plan must receive "reasonable compensation" for the leasing of office space or for the provision of administrative services or for the sale or lease of any goods (but the plan need not earn the profit that might otherwise have been realized in an arm's-length transaction).

3. Any plan participating in such an arrangement must be able to terminate the transaction on reasonably short notice.

4. Any plan involved in such an arrangement must maintain records, for a period of six years from the date of the termination of the arrangement that would enable the DOL, plan participants and beneficiaries, participating employers, and employee organizations, or any duly authorized representative, to determine whether the conditions of the exemption have been met.[2]

439. What is the class exemption regarding multiemployer apprenticeship plans?

The DOL has determined that multiemployer apprenticeship plans would not be able to operate in the manner for which they were designed without relief from the prohibited transaction rules. Thus, certain transactions between multiemployer apprenticeship plans and employers or employee organizations (unions) contributing to such plans are granted exemptive relief, provided that certain requirements are met.

The following classes of transactions between apprenticeship and training plans and employers and unions may be entitled to exemptive relief:

1. The plan's purchase of personal property from a contributing employer or union;

2. The plan's lease of personal property from a contributing employer or union;

---

1. PTE 76-1.
2. PTE 77-10.

3.   The plan's lease of real property from a contributing employer or union; and

4.   The plan's lease of personal property (incidental to the leasing of real property) from a contributing employer or union.

The classes of transactions described above are exempt only if

1.   The terms of the transaction are at least as favorable to the plan as those found in an arm's-length transaction;

2.   The transaction is appropriate and helpful to the plan in carrying out its purposes; and

3.   The plan maintains the appropriate records, for a period of six years from the termination of any exempted transaction, that would enable the DOL, any contributing employer (and its employees), any sponsoring union, or any person receiving benefits under the plan to determine if the requirements of the exemption have been satisfied.[1]

440. What is the class exemption regarding the plan's purchase of customer notes?

A plan may acquire, hold, sell, and accept in-kind contributions of the plan sponsor's customer notes without violating the prohibited transaction provisions of ERISA, provided that all of the following conditions are satisfied:

1.   The terms of the transaction must be at least as favorable to the plan as those found under an arm's-length transaction with an unrelated third party.

2.   Immediately following the acquisition, no more than 50 percent of the current value of the plan's assets may be invested in customer notes, nor may more than 10 percent of the current value of the plan's assets be invested in the notes of any one customer.

3.   An independent fiduciary must give written approval of the acquisition of the notes in advance of the purchase.

4.   An independent fiduciary must monitor the investments in the notes to ensure that

a.   payments are timely received,

b.   delinquencies are pursued, and

c.   the employer's guarantee to repurchase delinquent notes (with accrued interest) is enforced.

The employer must offer a written guarantee to repurchase delinquent notes from the plan in the event that the note is more than sixty days delinquent, or if the independent fiduciary has determined that other events have impaired the safety of the note as a plan investment. Upon

---

1. PTE 78-6.

a written request by the plan sponsor, the independent fiduciary may, in its discretion, extend the sixty-day period by an additional thirty days.

"Other events" that may impair the safety of the note include (1) faulty language in the note, (2) the obligor's insolvency, (3) the obligor's bankruptcy filing and/or its actions to reorganize, (4) appointment of a receiver of any property belonging to the obligor, and (5) the obligor's failure to maintain the property financed by the note.

A customer note is defined as "a two-party instrument, executed along with a security agreement for tangible personal property, which is accepted in connection with, and in the normal course of, an employer's primary business activity as a seller of such property." A two-party instrument is defined as "a promissory instrument used in connection with the extension of credit in which one party (the maker) promises to pay a second party (the payee) a sum of money."

The notes must be (1) secured by the property being financed; and (2) limited to a maximum term of five years.[1]

441. What is the class exemption regarding court-ordered transactions?

An exemption may be available for a transaction or activity ordered by a United States District Court.

The exemption provides that ERISA Section 406, ERISA Section 407(a), and IRC Section 4975(a) "shall not apply with respect to any transaction or activity which is authorized or required, prior to the occurrence of such transaction or activity, by an order of a United States District Court or by a settlement of litigation approved by such a court, provided that the nature of such transaction or activity is specifically described in such order or settlement, and provided further that the Secretary of Labor or the Internal Revenue Service is a party to the litigation at the time of such order or settlement."[2]

442. What is the class exemption regarding Department of Labor settlement agreements?

The DOL determined that a class exemption was needed in order to eliminate the necessity of providing individual exemptions each time a transaction ordered under a settlement agreement would have otherwise violated the fiduciary or prohibited transaction provisions of ERISA. Accordingly, a class exemption is available to certain parties in interest whom the DOL has authorized to make transactions with a plan as part of a DOL settlement agreement.

The exemption requires that the activity required under the DOL settlement agreement be authorized in advance. Further, in order for the exemptive relief to apply, each of the following conditions must be satisfied:

---

1. PTE 85-68.
2. PTE 79-15.

1.   The nature of such transaction or activity is specifically described, in writing, by the terms of such settlement agreement.

2.   The DOL is a party to the settlement agreement.

3.   The party engaging in the transaction provides written notice to affected participants and beneficiaries at least thirty days prior to entering into the settlement agreement.

4.   The DOL field office that negotiated the settlement approves the notice and the method of its distribution in advance.

5.   The notice contains

a.   the date of the transaction,

b.   a description of the transaction,

c.   the address of the DOL field office that negotiated the settlement agreement, and

d.   a statement advising participants and beneficiaries that they have a right to provide their comments on the settlement agreement to the DOL field office.

Relief is not provided under this exemption for any transactions or activities in violation of fiduciary duties that gave rise to the DOL investigation, and which were cited as such in a Voluntary Compliance Letter (see Section XII for a discussion of DOL enforcement activities and Voluntary Compliance Letters).[1]

443. What is the class exemption for plans that enter into settlement agreements with private parties?

The DOL issued a prohibited transaction exemption addressing this issue late in 2003.[2] The DOL amended this exemption in 2010. The exemption applies to the release of claims and extensions of credit in connection with litigation. It provides both prospective and retroactive relief for plans that settle pending or threatened litigation.

In litigation settlements involving payment from a party in interest to a plan, in exchange for the plan's release of the right to sue the party in interest, the payment could be construed as a prohibited sale or exchange of property between the plan and the party in interest or a prohibited transfer of plan assets to or for the benefit of a party in interest. The exemption also permits the plan's acquisition, holding, and disposition of employer securities received in settlement of litigation, including bankruptcy. Disposition of employer securities that are stock rights or warrants includes sale of these securities, as well as the exercise of the rights or

---

1. PTE 94-71.
2. See PTE 2003-39, 68 Fed. Reg. 75,632 (Dec. 31, 2003).

warrants.[1] In addition, if the party in interest pays the settlement amount in installments, the payments could be construed as impermissible loans from the plan to the party in interest. The DOL has not determined that settlements with parties in interest are prohibited transactions but rather has issued the exemption to address the "considerable uncertainty surrounding this issue."

As amended, the exemption is available for settlement agreements relating to an employer's failure to timely remit participant contributions to a plan, including certain transactions involving collectively bargained multiemployer or multiple-employer plans (but only to the extent of the settlement agreement between the trustee and the plan sponsor).

The exemption covers settlement of any type of suit that the plan has brought, but it does not cover

1.   Settlement of claims brought by a party in interest against the plan,

2.   Benefit claims disputes, or

3.   Claims of fiduciary self-dealing or conflicts.

The exemption provides relief for a partial or complete settlement of a plan's or plan fiduciary's claim in which the plan or independent plan fiduciary releases the plan's legal or equitable claim against a party in interest in exchange for consideration from the party in interest (or from a third party acting on behalf of the party in interest), including payment of the settlement amount in installments.

For settlements after the effective date (retroactive to January 1, 1975), a settlement will not be treated as a prohibited sale or exchange of property, loan, or transfer of plan assets with or to the party in interest if all of the following conditions are met:

1.   A genuine controversy involving the plan exists (a certified class action is deemed to meet this requirement).

2.   The settlement is authorized by an independent fiduciary having no prejudicial interest in the matter (other than an interest in the plan).

3.   The settlement is reasonable in light of the value of the plan's likely recovery, litigation risks, and costs.

4.   The settlement terms and conditions are as favorable to the plan as they would be in an arm's-length transaction.

5.   The settlement is not designed to benefit a party in interest.

6.   The terms of any installment payments are reasonable.

7.   PTE 76-1 (pertaining to delinquent employer contributions to certain collectively bargained plans) does not apply.

---

1. 75 Fed. Reg. 33,830 (June 15, 2010).

The following additional conditions apply for settlements entered into after January 30, 2004:

1.   Unless a class action is certified, an independent attorney must determine that a genuine plan-related controversy exists.

2.   All terms of the settlement agreement or consent decree must be written.

3.   The plan may receive non-cash assets from a party in interest only if necessary to rescind a transaction at issue in the litigation or if such assets are marketable securities (including employer securities) valued at fair market value as of a date set forth in the agreement.

4.   The settlement agreement must describe the non-cash assets and their value received by the plan.

5.   The plan's independent fiduciary must acknowledge its status in writing and maintain records for six years demonstrating that the terms of the exemption were met (with certain protections against liability for parties in interest that are not culpable or responsible for lost records).

6.   Non-proprietary and non-confidential plan records must be available for inspection by the DOL, the IRS, participants, beneficiaries, plan fiduciaries, contributing employers, and unions whose members are covered by the plan (including their respective representatives).

The restrictions on the plan's receipt of non-cash payments do not preclude application of the exemption to a settlement that requires making future contributions, adopting plan amendments, or providing additional employee benefits.

In non–class action litigation after January 30, 2004, a plan will be eligible for relief only if the plan incurs what is likely to be the considerable cost of hiring an independent fiduciary to authorize the transaction and an independent attorney to obtain a legal opinion.

For settlements occurring on or after June 15, 2010, the exemption applies where:

1.   The litigation has not been certified as a class action by the court, no federal or state agency is a plaintiff to the litigation, and an attorney or attorneys retained to advise the plan on the claim, and having no relationship to any of the parties involved in the claims (other than the plan), determines that there is a genuine controversy involving the plan;

2.   The settlement must be authorized by a fiduciary who has no interest to, or interest in, any of the parties involved in the claims (other than the plan) that might affect the exercise of such person's best judgment as a fiduciary, and who has acknowledged in writing that she is a fiduciary with respect to the settlement of the litigation on behalf of the plan;

3. The settlement terms, including the scope of the release of claims, the amount of cash, and the value of any non-cash assets received by the plan; and the amount of any attorney's fee award or any other sums to be paid from the recovery, are reasonable in light of the plan's likelihood of full recovery, the risks and costs of litigation, and the value of claims foregone;

4. The terms and conditions of the transaction are no less favorable to the plan than comparable arms-length terms and conditions that would have been agreed to by unrelated parties in similar circumstances;

5. The transaction is not a part of an agreement, arrangement, or understanding designed to benefit a party in interest;

6. Any extension of credit by the plan to a party in interest in connection with the settlement of a legal or equitable claim against the party in interest is on terms that are reasonable, taking into consideration the creditworthiness of the party in interest and the time value of money;

7. The transaction is not relating to delinquent employer contributions to multiemployer and multiple-employer collectively bargained plans; and

8. All terms of the settlement are specifically described in a written settlement agreement or consent decree.[1]

Non-cash assets (which may include employer securities, and written promises of future employer contributions) and/or a written agreement to adopt future plan amendments or provide additional employee benefits or corporate reforms may be provided to the plan by a party in interest in exchange for a release by the plan or a plan fiduciary only if:

1. The authorizing fiduciary determines that an all-cash settlement is either not feasible, or is less beneficial to the participants and beneficiaries than accepting all or a part of the settlement in non-cash assets and/or enhancements;

2. The non-cash assets are specifically described in writing as part of the settlement, and valued at their fair market value as of the date or dates specified in the settlement agreement utilizing objective third-party sources such as price quotations from persons independent of the issuer or the independent third-party pricing services for the non-cash assets (in instances where there is a generally recognized market for the assets) or utilizing an objective and generally recognized methodology for valuing the non-cash assets that is approved as reasonable by the authorizing fiduciary and fully described in the settlement agreement;

3. The enhancements are specifically described in writing as part of the settlement; and

4. The plan does not pay any commissions in connection with the acquisition of the assets.[2]

---

1. 75 Fed. Reg. 33,830 (June 15, 2010).
2. 75 Fed. Reg. 33,830 (June 15, 2010).

Enhancements may be included as part of the settlement without an independent appraisal.

In deciding whether to approve the release of a claim in exchange for enhancements, the authorizing fiduciary shall take into account all aspects of the settlement, including the cash or other assets to be received by the plan, the solvency of the party in interest, and the best interests of the class of participants harmed by the acts that are subject of the plan's claims.

The authorizing, or an independent, fiduciary must act on behalf of the plan for all purposes related to any property, including employer securities, received by the plan as part of the settlement. They must continue to act on behalf of the plan for the entire period that the plan holds the property (including employer securities) as part of the settlement. As such, the authorizing, or independent, fiduciary will have sole responsibility relating to the acquisition, holding, disposition, ongoing management, and where appropriate, exercise of all ownership rights, including the right to vote securities, unless the plan is a participant-directed individual account plan and the authorizing fiduciary allows participants and beneficiaries to exercise control over the securities allocated to their accounts.

The authorizing, or independent, fiduciary must maintain, or caused to be maintained, for six years the records necessary to determine that the conditions of the exemption have been met, including documents evidencing the steps taken to satisfy the settlement terms as required above (such as correspondence with attorneys or experts consulted in order to evaluate the plan's claims). The exemption has a retroactive effective date of January 1, 1975.

444. What is the abandoned plan qualified termination administrator exemption?

PTE 2006-06 permits a "qualified termination administrator" (QTA) of an individual account plan that has been abandoned by its sponsoring employer to select itself or an affiliate to

1.   Provide services to the plan in connection with the termination of the plan,

2.   Pay itself or an affiliate fees for those services, and

3.   Pay itself for services provided prior to the plan's deemed termination.[1]

The DOL advised, when issuing the exemption, that the purpose of the accompanying regulations are to "facilitate the orderly, efficient termination of abandoned individual account plans in order to give participants and beneficiaries of those plans access to the amounts held in their individual accounts, which are frequently unavailable to them because of the abandonment."

The exemption issued along, and in connection, with the DOL's final regulations relating to the Termination of Abandoned Individual Account Plans,[2] the Safe Harbor for Distributions from Terminated Individual Account Plans,[3] and the Terminal Report for Abandoned Individual Account Plans, published simultaneously[4] in the Federal Register.

---

1. 71 Fed. Reg. 20,856 (Apr. 21, 2006).
2. Labor Reg. §2578.1.
3. Labor Reg. §2550.404a-3.
4. Labor Reg. §2520.103-13.

The exemption also provides relief from the prohibited transaction provisions of ERISA where a QTA designates itself or an affiliate to receive the account balance of a participant that does not provide direction as to the disposition of such assets. The other accounts authorized by the exemption (other than an individual retirement account), may be accounts

1. Described in the Safe Harbor Regulation, for a distribution made to a distributee other than a participant or spouse, or

2. Interest-bearing, federally insured bank or savings association accounts for distributions of less than $1,000, as described in the Safe Harbor Regulation.

The qualified termination administrator is an entity that is eligible to serve as a trustee or issuer of an individual retirement plan within the meaning of IRC Section 7701(a)(37) and that holds the assets of the abandoned plan.

The exemption further permits the QTA to

1. Make the initial investment of the distributed proceeds in a proprietary investment product,

2. Receive fees in connection with the establishment or maintenance of the individual retirement plan or other account, and

3. Receive investment fees as a result of the investment of the individual retirement plan or other account's assets in a proprietary investment product in which the QTA or an affiliate has an interest.

The QTA must comply with the requirements of the QTA Regulation. Additionally, the QTA is required to provide, in a timely manner, any other reasonably available information requested by the DOL regarding the proposed termination.

The class exemption was effective May 22, 2006.

The DOL has amended PTE 2006-06 to specifically require, as a condition of relief for a QTA, that the benefit of a deceased participant must be directly rolled over into an IRC Section 402(c)(11) inherited IRA established to receive the distribution on behalf of any missing, nonspouse "designated beneficiary."[1]

Fees

Pursuant to the exemption, fees and expenses must be reasonable.[2]

Fees and expenses paid to the QTA and its affiliate for services must be consistent with industry rates for such or similar services, based on the experience of the QTA, and must not be in excess of rates charged by the QTA (or its affiliate) for the same or similar services provided to customers that are not individual account plans terminated pursuant to the QTA Regulation,

---

1. 73 Fed. Reg. 58,629 (Oct. 7, 2008).
2. As defined under IRC Section 4975(d)(2).

if the QTA (or its affiliate) provides the same or similar services to such other customers. Accordingly, a QTA who possesses knowledge about the services needed for a plan termination and industry rates for such or similar services may retain itself, an affiliate, and other service providers without going through a timely and costly bidding process.

Fees and expenses of the individual retirement plan or other account, including the investment of the assets of such plan or account (e.g., establishment charges, maintenance fees, investment expenses, termination costs, and surrender charges) must not exceed the fees and expenses charged by the QTA for comparable individual retirement plans or other accounts established for reasons other than the receipt of a distribution made pursuant to the QTA Regulation. Further, fees and expenses of the individual retirement plan or other account, other than establishment charges, may be charged only against the income earned by the individual retirement plan or other account.

But the individual retirement plan or other account may not pay a sales commission in connection with the acquisition of an eligible investment product.

Prior Service Provider Serving as QTA upon Plan Abandonment

The exemption covers payment for services performed by a service provider pursuant to the QTA Regulation prior to the deemed termination of the plan and the service provider's becoming a QTA. Such services will generally have been performed by the service provider in determining that a plan has been abandoned and in preparing the notice of plan abandonment as required by the QTA Regulation. Permissible payment for services provided in good faith pursuant to the terms of a written agreement prior to the service provider's becoming a QTA includes payment for services provided under a valid contract, as well as the continuation of such services after the contract had expired. The QTA must demonstrate to the DOL, in its initial notification of plan abandonment, that such services were actually performed. The QTA also must provide a copy of the executed contract between the QTA and the plan fiduciary or plan sponsor that authorized such services.

Participant Notice

The QTA must inform the participant or beneficiary in the required notice that

1.   Absent an election by the participant or beneficiary within the thirty-day period from receipt of the notice, the QTA will directly distribute the account balance of the participant or beneficiary to an individual retirement plan or other account offered by the QTA or its affiliate.

2.   The account balance may be invested in the QTA's own proprietary investment product, which is designed to preserve principal and provide a reasonable rate of return and liquidity.

3.   The account must be established and maintained for the exclusive benefit of the individual retirement plan or other account holder, or spouse or beneficiaries of such.

4.   The terms of the individual retirement plan or other account, including the fees and expenses for establishing and maintaining the individual retirement plan or other account, must be no less favorable than those available to comparable individual retirement plans or other accounts established for reasons other than the receipt of a distribution described in the QTA Regulation.

Eligible Investment Product Offered by a Regulated Financial Institution

Other than in the case of a bank or savings account for distributions of less than $1,000, the distribution must be invested in an eligible investment product offered through a regulated financial institution. The rate of return or the investment performance received by the individual retirement plan or other account from an investment product must be no less than that received by comparable individual retirement plans or other accounts that are not established pursuant to the QTA Regulation but are invested in the same product. An "eligible investment product" is an investment product designed to preserve principal and provide a reasonable rate of return, whether or not such return is guaranteed, consistent with liquidity.

The regulated financial institution must seek to maintain, over the term of the investment, a dollar value that is equal to the amount invested in the product by the individual retirement plan or other account. The term "eligible investment product" includes money market funds maintained by registered investment companies and interest-bearing savings accounts and certificates of deposit of a bank or similar financial institution. In addition, the term includes stable-value products issued by a financial institution that are fully "benefit responsive" to the individual retirement plan or other account holder. "Regulated financial institution" is defined to mean an entity that is subject to state or federal regulation, and is

1.   A bank or savings association, the deposits of which are insured by the Federal Deposit Insurance Corporation;

2.   A credit union, the member accounts of which are insured within the meaning of Section 101(7) of the Federal Credit Union Act;

3.   An insurance company, the products of which are protected by state guaranty associations; or

4.   An investment company registered under the Investment Company Act of 1940.

"Benefit responsive" means a stable-value product that provides a liquidity guarantee by a financially responsible third party of principal and previously accrued interest for liquidations or transfers initiated by the individual retirement plan or other account holder exercising a right to withdraw or transfer funds under the terms of an arrangement that does not include substantial restrictions to the account holder's access to the individual retirement plan or other account assets.

The individual retirement plan or other account holder must be able to transfer the individual retirement plan or other account balance to a different investment offered by the QTA or its affiliate, or to a different financial institution not related to the QTA or its affiliate. Such requests must be granted within a reasonable period of time after the request and without penalty to the principal amount of the investment.

See Q 265 for further details of the Safe Harbor for Individual Account Plans.

Recordkeeping

The QTA must maintain records to enable certain persons to determine whether the applicable conditions of the exemption have been met. The records must be made available for examination by the IRS, the DOL, and any account holder or duly authorized representative of such account holder of an individual retirement plan or other account, for at least six years from the date the QTA provides notice to the DOL of its determination of plan abandonment and its election to serve as the QTA.

445. What is the class exemption regarding interest-free loans between a plan and parties in interest?

A party in interest may make an interest-free loan or extension of credit to a plan if

1. "No interest or other fee is charged to the plan, and no discount for payment in cash is relinquished by the plan" in connection with the loan;

2. The proceeds of the loan are restricted, to be used only for the payment of ordinary operating expenses of the plan, including benefits that are paid in accordance with the terms of the plan and insurance premiums under an insurance or annuity contract, *or*

3. The loan is unsecured; and

4. The loan is not directly or indirectly made by an employee benefit plan.[1]

The DOL amended PTE 80-26 to eliminate the three-day rule with respect to interest-free loans made on or after December 15, 2004. The amendment requires interest-free loans issued under the exemption to be reduced to writing if the loan will have a term of sixty days or longer. The agreement must contain all material terms of the loan. If such loan is issued for the purpose of the payment of ordinary operating expenses of the plan, the written agreement rule was effective as of April 7, 2006. If the loan is for incidental expenses, the amendment applies the written documentation requirement to any outstanding loans made on or after December 15, 2005.[2]

All of the remaining rules continue to apply to such a loan or extension of credit made to a party in interest.[3]

The DOL issued an amendment to PTE 80-26 regarding certain no-interest loans and extensions of credit from related parties to plans affected by terrorist attacks.[4]

---

1. PTE 80-26.
2. Amendment to PTE 80-26, 71 Fed. Reg. 17,917 (Apr. 7, 2006).
3. ERISA Secs. 404, 406.
4. 71 Fed. Reg. 17917 (April 7, 2006).

The exemption allowed plans to receive temporary loans and extensions of credit from related parties (e.g., employers), if certain conditions were met. The conditions of the exemption allowed loans and extensions of credit for no more than 120 days, beginning on September 11, 2001. All loans were required to be repaid by January 9, 2002. Among the conditions of the temporary exemption were requirements that

- No interest or other fee was charged to the plan and no discount for payment in cash was relinquished by the plan;

- The loans and extensions of credit were unsecured;

- Proceeds of the loans and extensions of credit were used only for purposes incidental to ordinary plan operations that were affected by the September 11 terrorist attacks; and

- The loans or extension of credit were not directly or indirectly made by a plan.[1]

An interest-free loan to a plan from a plan trustee was permitted in order for the plan to satisfy a payment obligation under a Qualified Domestic Relations Order (QDRO), which was issued pursuant to the trustee's divorce. The DOL stated that an alternate payee under a QDRO is a plan beneficiary and the plan must provide for the payment of benefits to participants and beneficiaries in accordance with the provisions of the plan document (requiring the plan to pay under the provisions of a QDRO). As such, the loan could be issued for the payment of benefits under a QDRO.[2]

The DOL has proposed an amendment to PTE 80-26 to provide temporary relief for certain "related account" indemnifications typically found in brokerage or other investment agreements. The proposed amendment, if adopted, would give retroactive and temporary exemptive relief for certain guarantees of the payment of debits to plan investment accounts (including IRAs) by parties in interest to such plans as well as certain loans and loan repayments made pursuant to such guarantees.[3]

This proposed amendment, if adopted, would provide retroactive and temporary relief for a "Covered Extension of Credit." The exemption defines this term as an indemnification agreement, cross-collateralization agreement, or other grant of a security interest in favor of a financial institution, as set forth in an Account Opening Agreement between a plan and the financial institution, by which (1) assets in a Plan Account guarantee the payment of amounts debited to a Related Account, or (2) assets in a Related Account guarantee the payment of amounts debited to a Plan Account.

The term Covered Extension of Credit does not include a loan or payment under such agreement or security interest. A Plan Account is an account established with a financial

---

1. 66 Fed. Reg. 49,703 (Sept. 28, 2001).
2. DOL Adv. Op. 94-28A.
3. Notice of Proposed Amendment to Prohibited Transaction Exemption 80-26 for Certain Interest Free Loans to Employee Benefit Plans, 78 Fed. Reg. 31584 (May 24, 2013).

institution by an employee benefit plan as defined in section 3(3) of ERISA. A Related Account is an account established pursuant to an Account Opening Agreement with the financial institution that also covers a Plan Account and/or guarantees the payment of debits to the Plan Account.

Retroactive and temporary relief is additionally proposed for the lending of money (a Covered Loan) by a Related Account to a Plan Account, pursuant to a Covered Extension of Credit, if the Related Account is not itself a Plan Account. Finally, the retroactive and temporary relief extends to the repayment by a Plan Account to a Related Account of a Covered Loan (Covered Repayment).

The DOL is proposing the relief described above solely to enable financial institutions to remove Covered Extensions of Credit from Account Opening Agreements and conclude any outstanding Covered Loans that may exist.[1]

446. What is the class exemption regarding the purchase of securities by a plan in order to retire indebtedness to a party in interest?

An exemption may be available for a plan's purchase of securities, the proceeds of which may be used by the issuer to repay or reduce indebtedness to a party in interest.[2]

In order for the exemption to apply, the following general conditions must be met:

1. The securities must be sold as part of a public offering and the price paid for the securities must not exceed the original offering price.

2. The fiduciary must maintain records relating to such transaction, sufficiently detailed to enable any authorized person reviewing them to determine whether the requisite elements of the exemption have been satisfied, for a period of six years from the date of the transaction.

3. The records referenced above must be "unconditionally available at their customary location" for examination by

    a. employees of the DOL or the IRS,

    b. any fiduciary who has authority to manage or control plan assets,

    c. any contributing employer,

    d. any participant or beneficiary to the plan, and

    e. the duly authorized representative of the persons listed in (a) through (d).

---

1. Notice of Proposed Amendment to Prohibited Transaction Exemption 80-26 for Certain Interest Free Loans to Employee Benefit Plans, 78 Fed. Reg. 31584 (May 24, 2013).
2. PTE 80-83.

This exemption is only available to a party in interest who is a *fiduciary* if that fiduciary is a bank or bank affiliate. If such fiduciary has "knowledge" that the proceeds of the purchase will be used to reduce or retire a debt owed to the fiduciary, the exemption will apply to all otherwise prohibited transactions, with the exception of the restriction on the plan's holding employer securities and the restriction on the receipt of kickbacks, provided the following requirements are met:

1.   The securities must generally be purchased prior to the end of the first full business day after the public offering, except that

   a.   if the securities are offered for subscription upon exercise of rights, then they may be purchased on or before the fourth day preceding the day on which the rights offering terminates, or

   b.   if the securities are debt securities, they may be purchased on a day subsequent to the end of such first full business day after the public offering, if the effective interest rates on comparable debt securities offered to the public subsequent to such first full business day and prior to the purchase are less than the effective interest rate of the debt securities being purchased.

2.   The securities must be offered by the issuer pursuant to an underwriting agreement under which all of the members of the underwriting syndicate have committed to purchase all of the securities being offered, except where securities are purchased by others pursuant to a rights offering, or are offered pursuant to an over-allotment plan.

3.   The issuer must be in continuous operation for at least three years (including the operations of any predecessors); unless such securities are nonconvertible debt securities rated in one of the four highest rating categories by at least one nationally recognized statistical rating organization.

4.   The amount of securities acquired by the plan must not exceed 3 percent of the total amount of securities being offered.

5.   The consideration for the securities must not exceed 3 percent of the fair market value (as of the most recent valuation date prior to the purchase) of the plan assets that are subject to the control of the fiduciary.

6.   The total amount of securities purchased in a single offering by the fiduciary on behalf of the plan (and on behalf of any other plan for which it serves as a fiduciary) may not exceed 10 percent of the total value of the offering.

A fiduciary will be deemed to have knowledge that the proceeds will be used to reduce or retire indebtedness to the fiduciary if

1.   Such knowledge is actually communicated to the fiduciary; or

2.   The officers or employees of the fiduciary, who are both authorized with respect to and actually involved in carrying out the fiduciary's investment responsibilities,

obligations, and duties regarding such purchase, possess information sufficient to cause them to believe that the proceeds will be so used.

This exemption does *not* provide relief for the following prohibited transactions in which the fiduciary does not know the proceeds will be used to reduce or retire indebtedness to the fiduciary, or in which such fiduciary is not involved in the decision to purchase the securities:

1. Acquiring on behalf of the plan any employer security in violation of ERISA Section 407(a);[1]

2. For a fiduciary with authority to control plan assets, permitting the plan to hold any employer security if the fiduciary knows, or should know, that such holding violates ERISA Section 407(a);[2]

3. Dealing with plan assets in the fiduciary's own interest;[3]

4. Acting on behalf of any party whose interests are adverse to the interests of the plan, its participants, or its beneficiaries;[4] and

5. Receiving any consideration for his own personal account (i.e., kickbacks) from any party dealing with the plan in connection with a transaction involving plan assets.[5]

447. What is the class exemption relating to short-term investments?

Employee benefit plans may engage in transactions involving certain short-term investments, notwithstanding the prohibited transaction provisions of ERISA. Specifically, plans may invest in banker's acceptances, commercial paper, repurchase agreements, certificates of deposit, and securities of banks that are parties in interest with respect to the plan, if the following requirements are satisfied:

1. Banker's acceptances: a plan may invest in these if

    a. they are issued by a federal or state-supervised bank,

    b. they have a stated maturity rate of one year or less, and

    c. neither the issuing bank, nor any of its affiliates, have any discretionary authority regarding the plan's assets;

2. Commercial paper: a plan may invest in commercial paper if

    a. it is not issued by the plan sponsor or any of its affiliates,

    b. it has a stated maturity date of nine months or less,

---

1. ERISA Sec. 406(a)(1)(E).
2. ERISA Sec. 406(a)(2).
3. ERISA Sec. 406(b)(1).
4. ERISA Sec. 406(b)(2).
5. ERISA Sec. 406(b)(3).

    c.   it has a rating that is one of the three highest rating categories by a nationally recognized statistical rating organization, and

    d.   neither the issuer nor any guarantor has any discretionary authority over the plan's assets;

   3.   Repurchase agreements: a plan may invest in repurchase agreements if

    a.   they have a duration of one year or less,

    b.   the plan receives written terms and an interest rate at least as favorable as in an arm's-length transaction with an unrelated third party,

    c.   the seller furnishes the plan with detailed financial statements, and

    d.   neither the seller nor any of its affiliates have any discretionary authority over the plan's assets;

   4.   Certificates of deposit: a plan may invest in certificates of deposit if neither the issuing bank nor any of its affiliates have any discretion over the plan's assets; and

   5.   Bank securities: a plan may invest in a bank's securities if the bank is considered a party in interest to the plan because it furnishes the plan with a checking account or related services (clearing, recordkeeping, etc.), provided that

    a.   the transaction is at least as favorable to the plan as an arm's-length transaction with an unrelated third party would be, and

    b.   the investment is not involved in an arrangement wherein the bank would cause a transaction to be made by the plan for the benefit of a party in interest.[1]

This exemption does not extend relief with respect to prohibited transactions that result in the furnishing of goods, services, or facilities between the plan and a party in interest,[2] an acquisition on behalf of the plan of any employer security or real property that violates ERISA Section 407,[3] or the prohibitions against fiduciaries' dealing with the plan assets in their own interest, against their dealing with the plan assets in the interest of any individual whose interests are adverse to the plan, or against their receipt of any kickbacks.[4]

448. What is the class exemption for transactions between bank collective investment funds and parties in interest?

A bank collective investment fund in which plan assets are held may be permitted to engage in certain transactions with parties in interest, so long as the plan's assets in the collective investment fund do not exceed a specified percentage of the fund's total assets.

---

1. PTE 81-8.
2. ERISA Sec. 406(a)(1)(C).
3. ERISA Sec. 406(a)(1)(E).
4. ERISA Secs. 406(b)(1), 406(b)(2), 406(b)(3).

The DOL has issued an advisory opinion wherein the provisions of PTE 91-38 can be extended to a United States–based branch of a non–United States bank for transactions involving collective funds of employee benefit plans. The DOL opined that "a U.S. branch of a non-U.S. bank that has been licensed to engage in banking and trust business by a State regulator, and that is subject to the same level of oversight and regulation as any other comparable banking entity established in that State, would qualify as a 'bank or trust company' for purposes of" ERISA Section 408(b)(8) and PTE 91-38.[1]

General Transaction Requirements

The exemption contains four sections, which detail general and specific rules. All transactions for which exemptive relief is sought must satisfy the following requirements:

1. The terms of the transaction must not be less favorable to the collective investment fund than the terms of an arm's-length transaction between unrelated parties.

2. For a period of six years from the date of the transaction, the bank must maintain the records necessary to enable the DOL, the IRS, plan fiduciaries, contributing employers, participants, and beneficiaries to ascertain whether the conditions of the exemption have been satisfied.[2]

In general, exemptive relief is provided with respect to any transaction between a party in interest and a collective investment fund in which the plan has an interest, provided that

1. The party in interest is not the bank maintaining the collective investment fund, or an affiliate of such bank; and

2. The plan's interest in the collective investment fund, when combined with the interests of any other employee benefit plans maintained by the same employer or employee organization, does not exceed 10 percent of all interests held in the collective investment fund (5 percent if the transaction occurs between September 23, 1980, and June 30, 1990); or

3. The collective investment fund is a specialized fund investing in short-term obligations, including, but not limited to, (a) corporate or governmental obligations or related repurchase agreements, (b) certificates of deposit, (c) bankers' acceptances, or (d) variable-amount notes of borrowers of prime credit.[3]

Specific Transaction Requirements

Transactions between (1) an employer of employees covered under a multiple employer plan and (2) a collective investment fund holding plan assets may receive exemptive relief provided that

---

1. Connecticut branch of the Bank of Ireland. DOL Adv. Op. 2007-03A (June 8, 2007).
2. PTE 91-38, §III.
3. PTE 91-38, §I(a)(1)(A).

1.   The combined assets in the collective investment fund *do not* exceed the 10 percent investment limitation, *and* the employer is not a "substantial employer" with respect to the plan (within the definition of ERISA Section 4001(a)(2)); or

2.   The combined assets in the collective investment fund *do* exceed the 10 percent investment limitation, *and* the employer is not a "substantial employer" and would not be a "substantial employer" if 10 percent were substituted for 5 percent in that definition.[1]

Exemptive relief is provided for the purchase, sale, or holding of employer securities and employer real property that exceeds the investment limitations by a collective investment fund in which the plan has an interest, provided that no commission is paid to the bank, the employer, or any affiliates of either with regard to the transaction.[2]

Employer real property transactions must be for parcels of employer real property "and the improvements thereon" that are suitable for use by different tenants. If leased or held for lease to third parties, the property must be geographically dispersed.[3]

In the case of employer securities, the bank in whose collective investment fund the security is held cannot be an affiliate of the issuer. Further, if the security is an obligation of the issuer and the collective investment fund owns the obligation when the plan acquires an interest in the fund, the interests in the fund must be offered and redeemed in accordance with appropriate valuation procedures of the fund, which are applied on a reasonable and consistent basis. Alternatively, the exemption requirement is satisfied if, immediately after the acquisition of the obligation, the plan holds not more than 15 percent of the aggregate amount of the obligations issued and outstanding at the time of the acquisition. If the obligation is one that is a restricted security under Rule 144 of the Securities Act of 1933, at least 50 percent of the aggregate amount of obligations issued and outstanding at the time of the acquisition must be held by persons independent of the issuer. "The bank, its affiliates and any collective investment fund maintained by the bank shall be considered to be persons independent of the issuer if the bank is not an affiliate of the issuer."[4]

For plans that are not eligible individual account plans (i.e., defined benefit plans), exemptive relief will be provided only if, immediately after the acquisition of securities or employer real property, the aggregate fair market value of the securities or employer real property over which the bank exercises investment discretion does not exceed 10 percent of the fair market value of all of the assets of the plan over which the bank has investment discretion.[5]

Any transaction between a collective investment fund and parties in interest will be exempt if the service provider is not an affiliate of the bank maintaining the collective investment fund.

---

1. PTE 91-38, §I(a)(2).
2. PTE 91-38, §I(a)(3)(A).
3. PTE 91-38, §I(a)(3)(A)(i).
4. PTE 91-38, §I(a)(3)(A)(ii).
5. PTE 91-38, §I(a)(3)(B).

For this purpose, the term "parties in interest" refers to those considered to be parties in interest simply because they provide services to the plan that has an interest in the collective investment fund or because they are related to a service provider to the plan and they do not have or exercise discretionary authority or control over the investment of plan assets in the collective investment fund. Such parties in interest will be provided exemptive relief if the service provider is not an affiliate of the bank maintaining the collective investment fund.[1]

Exemptive relief will also be provided for the furnishing of goods or the leasing of employer real property if

1. The goods to be furnished are owned by the collective investment fund;

2. The party in interest is not the bank that maintains the collective investment fund, any of its affiliates, or any other collective investment fund maintained by the same bank; and

3. Any amount involved in the furnishing of goods or the leasing of real property does not exceed, in any calendar year, the greater of $25,000 or 0.5 percent of the fair market value of the assets of the collective investment fund.[2]

Qualifying employer securities and qualifying employer real property held by a collective investment fund holding plan assets will not be taken into consideration when applying the prohibitions and restrictions on the holding of any employer real property or employer securities.[3] This exemptive relief will only apply where the general 10 percent investment limitation has been satisfied (excepting the short-term securities collective investment fund that has no 10 percent limit).[4]

The exemptive relief will not apply to prohibited transactions involving fiduciaries who deal with the plan assets in their interest or account, or who receive a kickback from any party dealing with the plan in connection with any transaction.[5]

449. What is the class exemption that permits the conversion of collective investment funds transferred in-kind for shares of a registered investment company?

Plans may be permitted to purchase shares of a registered investment company (mutual funds), the investment adviser for which is a bank or plan adviser that also serves as a fiduciary of the plan, in exchange for plan assets transferred in-kind from a collective investment fund maintained by the bank or plan adviser.[6] This exemption applies both retroactively and prospectively, if certain conditions are satisfied.

---

1. PTE 91-38, §I(b)(1)(A).
2. PTE 91-38, §I(b)(1)(B).
3. ERISA Secs. 406(a)(1)(E), 406(a)(2), 407(a).
4. PTE 91-38, §II.
5. ERISA Secs. 406(b)(1), 406(b)(3).
6. PTE 97-41.

The exemption allows a bank or plan adviser that serves as a fiduciary to a plan, in addition to serving as an adviser to a mutual fund, to convert the plan's assets that are currently managed through a collective investment fund (CIF) into a mutual fund by the transfer of assets out of the CIF and into the mutual fund. The investment adviser must be registered under the Investment Advisers Act of 1940 in order for exemptive relief to be granted.

The exemption consists of four sections. Section I provides retroactive relief for transactions occurring from October 1, 1988, until August 8, 1997. Section II provides prospective relief for transactions that must meet certain additional conditions. Section III provides that a transaction meeting the applicable conditions of the exemption will be deemed a purchase by the plan of shares of an open-end investment company (mutual fund) registered under the Investment Advisers Act of 1940 for purposes of PTE 77-4 (see Q 437). Thus, a bank or adviser that complies with the terms of PTE 97-41 and PTE 77-4 is able to receive investment management and investment advisory fees from the mutual fund and the plan with respect to the plan's assets invested in shares of the mutual fund, to the extent permitted under PTE 77-4. Section III also provides that compliance with PTE 97-41 will constitute compliance with certain requirements of PTE 77-4. Section IV contains definitions for certain terms used in the exemption.

The operative language of the exemption emphasizes that it does not provide relief for any prohibited transactions that may arise in connection with terminating a CIF, permitting certain plans to withdraw from a CIF that is not terminating, liquidating, or transferring any plan assets held by the CIF. Therefore, the exemption only provides relief from ERISA Section 406(a), ERISA Section 406(b)(1), and ERISA Section 406(b)(2) for the purchase of mutual fund shares by a plan in exchange for assets that are transferred in-kind from a CIF.

Retroactive Exemptive Relief

Retroactive relief will be provided under Section I of the exemption if

1.   No sales commissions or other fees have been paid by the plan in connection with the purchase of mutual fund shares;

2.   All transferred assets were cash or securities for which market quotations are readily available;

3.   The transferred assets constituted the plan's pro rata portion of all assets that were held by the CIF immediately prior to the transfer;

4.   The plan received mutual fund shares that had a total net asset value equal to the value of the plan's transferred assets on the date of the transfer (valued in accordance with SEC Rule 17a-7);

5.   An independent fiduciary of the plan received advance written notice of an in-kind transfer and purchase of assets and full written disclosure of information concerning the mutual fund, which included the following:

     a.   a current prospectus for each mutual fund to which the CIF assets may be transferred,

    b.   a statement describing the fees charged to, or paid by, the plan and the mutual funds to the bank or plan adviser, including the nature and extent of any differential between the rates of fees,

    c.   a statement of the reasons why the bank or plan adviser considered the transfer and purchase to be appropriate for the plan, and

    d.   a statement of whether there were any limitations on the bank or plan adviser with respect to which plan assets may be invested in shares of the mutual funds, and, if so, the nature of such limitations;

6.   On the basis of the foregoing information, the independent fiduciary gave prior approval, in writing, for each purchase of mutual fund shares in exchange for the plan's assets transferred from the CIF, consistent with the responsibilities, obligations, and duties imposed on fiduciaries under Part 4 of Title I of ERISA;

7.   The bank or plan adviser sent a written confirmation of the transaction to the independent fiduciary by regular mail or personal delivery, no later than 105 days after the purchase, containing

    a.   the number of CIF units held by the client plan immediately before the in-kind transfer, the related per-unit value, and the total dollar amount of such CIF units, and

    b.   the number of shares in the mutual funds that were held by the plan immediately following the purchase, the related per-share net asset value, and the total dollar amount of such shares;

8.   As to each plan, the combined total of all fees received by the bank or plan adviser for the provision of services to the plan, and in connection with the provision of services to the mutual fund in which a plan holds shares purchased in connection with the in-kind transfer, was not in excess of "reasonable compensation," within the meaning of ERISA Section 408(b)(2); and

9.   All dealings in connection with the in-kind transfer and purchase between the plan and a mutual fund were on a basis no less favorable to the plan than dealings between the mutual fund and other shareholders.[1]

Prospective Exemptive Relief

All of the preceding conditions also apply to prospective relief, under Section II of the exemption. In addition, *prospective* relief will be granted only if

1.   The plan's independent fiduciary is provided with the following information in writing, in advance:

---

1. PTE 97-41, §I.

a. the identity of all securities that will be valued in accordance with Rule 17a-7(b)(4) and allocated on the basis of the plan's pro rata portion of all assets that were held in the CIF immediately prior to the transfer, and

b. the identity of any fixed-income securities that will be allocated on the basis of each plan's pro rata share of the aggregate value of such securities that were held in the CIF immediately prior to transfer;

2. The bank or plan adviser sends a written confirmation (by regular mail or personal delivery or, if prior approval has been granted by the independent fiduciary, by facsimile or electronic mail) to the independent fiduciary of each plan that purchases mutual fund shares in connection with the in-kind transfer, no later than thirty days after completion of the purchase, which contains

a. the identity of each transferred security that was valued for purposes of the purchase of mutual fund shares in accordance with SEC Rule 17a-7(b)(4),

b. the current market price, as of the date of the in-kind transfer, of each such security involved in the purchase of mutual fund shares, and

c. the identity of each pricing service or market-maker consulted in determining the current market price of such securities;

3. The bank or plan adviser provides the independent fiduciary of the plan with a current prospectus of each mutual fund in which the plan continues to hold shares acquired through the in-kind transfer, at least annually; and

4. Upon request, the independent fiduciary is provided with a report or statement (which may take the form of the most recent financial report, the current Statement of Additional Information, or some other written statement) containing a description of all fees paid by the mutual fund to the bank or plan adviser.[1]

450. What are the class exemptions regarding mortgage pool investment trusts?

Exemptive relief may be provided, under certain conditions, for transactions involving the origination, maintenance, and termination of mortgage pool investment trusts and the acquisition and holding of certain mortgage-backed pass-through certificates of mortgage pools by plans.[2] This exemption was updated and extended to transactions between plans and pools containing loans secured by mortgages or deeds of trust other than first lien loans, and

---

1. PTE 97-41, §II.
2. PTE 81-7.

contracts for the purchase or sale of one or more certificates that are to be determined at an agreed future settlement date (i.e., forward delivery commitments).[1]

In these arrangements, sponsors establish investment pools, which invest in first and second mortgage notes originated by the sponsor of the pool or purchased from the mortgage loan originator. These loans are transferred to a trustee, who issues certificates of beneficial interest in the mortgages back to the investment pool. These certificates are issued to investors in the mortgage pool, including plans that invest their assets in the mortgage pool. In exchange for their investment, investors receive fixed monthly payments, which are funded (passed through) by the principal and interest payments of the mortgagors.

In order for PTE 81-7 to apply, these general conditions must be met:

1. The sponsor and trustees of each mortgage pool must maintain a system for insuring and protecting the pooled mortgage loans and the underlying real property securing the loans, and for indemnifying certificate holders against reductions in pass-through payments due to defaults in loan payments or property damage.

2. Except in the case of a governmental or quasi-governmental entity, such as the Federal National Mortgage Association, the trustee for each pool must not be an affiliate of the pool sponsor.

3. The sum of all payments made to and retained by the mortgage pool sponsor, as well as all funds inuring to the benefit of the pool sponsor as a result of their administration of the mortgage pool, must not represent more than adequate consideration for selling the mortgage loans, plus reasonable compensation for services provided by the pool sponsor to the pool.[2]

Both exemptions permit the sale, exchange, or transfer of the certificates of beneficial ownership between the plan and plan fiduciaries who are also either the pool sponsor, a plan trustee, or an insurer, provided that

1. The transaction is expressly approved by an independent fiduciary who has authority to manage and control those plan assets being invested in the certificates of the trust;

2. The plan receives a price for the certificates that is at least as favorable to the plan as an arm's-length transaction with an unrelated third party;

3. There are no investment management, advisory, or underwriting fees or sales commissions paid to the pool sponsor;

4. The plan has not purchased certificates with an aggregate value in excess of 25 percent of the total amount of the certificates issued; and

---

1. PTE 83-1.
2. PTE 81-7.

5. At least 50 percent of the total value of the issue of certificates is purchased by persons independent of the pool sponsor, trustee, or insurer.[1]

Any transaction involving mortgage pool certificates between the plan and a sponsor of a mortgage pool, a trustee, or an insurer (where the pool sponsor, trustee, or insurer are parties in interest with respect to the plan, but are not fiduciaries) is permitted under PTE 81-7 and PTE 83-1 if the plan pays no more than fair market value for the pass-through certificates and the interests represented by the certificates purchased by the plan are not subordinated to the rights and interests of other certificates issued by the same pool.

The exemptive relief provided to fiduciaries under these exemptions does not extend to the prohibition on the receipt of kickbacks from any party dealing with the plan in connection with any transaction.[2]

451. What is the class exemption regarding residential mortgage financing arrangements?

PTE 82-87 provides exemptive relief for the investment of qualified plan assets in certain residential mortgage financing arrangements. In 1988, the DOL amended PTE 82-87 and re-issued it as PTE 88-59. The amended class exemption expanded the types of mortgage transactions exempted from the prohibited transaction rules.

In order for the class exemption to apply, the following general conditions must be satisfied:

1. Any mortgage purchased by the plan must qualify as a "recognized mortgage loan," which is a loan with respect to a residential unit that, at origination, was eligible for purchase by the Federal National Mortgage Association (FNMA), Government National Mortgage Association (GNMA), Federal Home Loan Mortgage Corporation (FHLMC), or any FHA-insured GNMA project mortgage loan, or qualify as a participation interest in such a loan.

2. All mortgages must be originated by an "established mortgage lender," with respect to which neither the plan nor the plan sponsor has controlling power over management or policies.

3. The price paid for the mortgage by the plan must be at least as favorable as a similar transaction involving unrelated parties.

4. No developer, builder, or lender involved in the construction of the subject dwelling units has exercised any discretionary authority or control, or has rendered any investment advice, that would cause such person to be considered to be a fiduciary with respect to the plan's decision to purchase a mortgage loan or a participation interest therein or with respect to setting the terms of the loan.

---

1. PTE 81-7; PTE 83-1.
2. ERISA Sec. 406(b)(3).

The exemption defines "established mortgage lender" as an organized business enterprise, which has as one of its principal purposes, in the normal course of its business, the origination of loans secured by real estate mortgages or deeds of trust. In addition, to qualify as an established mortgage lender, a lender must have satisfied one of the following qualification requirement categories:

1. Approval by the Secretary of the Department of Housing and Urban Development (HUD) for participation in any mortgage insurance program under the National Housing Act;

2. Approval by FNMA or the FHLMC as a qualified seller/servicer; or

3. Approval by a state agency or independent state authority empowered by state law to raise capital to provide financing for residential dwelling units.

If the general conditions referenced above are satisfied, PTE 88-59 exempts the following transactions:

1. Issuance of a commitment by one or more plans to provide mortgage financing to buyers of residential units, either by making or participating in loans directly to the buyers or by buying mortgages or participation interests in mortgages that have been originated by a third party;

2. The plan's receipt of a fee in exchange for the issuance of a commitment;

3. The making or purchase of a mortgage loan or participation interest pursuant to such commitment;

4. The direct making or purchase by a plan of a mortgage loan or a participation interest other than where a commitment has been issued; and

5. The sale, exchange, or transfer of a mortgage loan or participation interest by a plan prior to the maturity date of the instrument, whether or not it was acquired pursuant to PTE 88-59, provided that the ownership interest sold, exchanged, or transferred represents the plan's entire interest in such investment.

When a plan enters into a commitment to purchase either a mortgage loan or a participation interest, the following specific conditions must be satisfied in order for exemptive relief to apply:

1. The commitment must be (a) in writing, and (b) consistent with the customary practices in the residential finance industry.

2. The commitment must be at least as favorable to the plan as an arm's-length transaction between unrelated parties.

3. The commitment must provide for the use of underwriting guidelines and mortgage instruments, which will ensure that any mortgage loan originated under the commitment will be considered a "recognized mortgage loan."

When a plan commits to enter into a participation interest in mortgage loans, the following specific conditions must be satisfied in order for exemptive relief to apply:

1.   The participation agreement must provide that the rights and interests of the plan are not subordinated to the rights and interests of other holders in the participation agreement.

2.   The majority interest in the participation agreement must be owned by a person or entity independent of the person or entity selling the participation interest and/ or servicing the underlying mortgages.

3.   In the event of an inability to collect on the payments on the underlying mortgages, the decision to foreclose must be directed by persons other than the seller/servicer.

4.   The participation agreement must be

      a.   in writing,

      b.   at least as favorable to the plan as a participation agreement involving unrelated parties, and

      c.   consistent with the customary practices and procedures in the residential financing industry.

Any retirement plan entering into a mortgage loan or a participation interest transaction must maintain records, for the duration of the obligation that would enable any trustee, investment manager, participant, beneficiary, or any representative of the DOL or the IRS to determine whether the requirements of the exemption have been satisfied. No violation will be cited if the records were lost or destroyed due to circumstances beyond the control of the fiduciaries to the plan.

No exemptive relief will be provided, either retroactively or prospectively, if the transaction violates the self-dealing and anti-kickback provisions of ERISA Section 406(b).[1]

452. What is the class exemption regarding qualified professional asset managers?

Relief may be provided to parties in interest, permitting them to engage in transactions involving plan assets, provided that those assets are managed by Qualified Professional Asset Managers (QPAMs) who meet specified financial standards and are independent of the parties in interest.[2]

The exemption extends relief to employers for the furnishing of a limited amount of goods and services in the ordinary course of business to an investment fund in which the employer's plan has an interest, and which is managed by a QPAM.

---

1. PTE 82-87; PTE 88-59.
2. PTE 84-14.

Further, the exemption provides additional relief for the lease of office or commercial space between managed investment funds, QPAMs, and contributing employers.

QPAMs may be insurance companies, banks, or savings and loan associations. Additionally, a QPAM may be an investment advisor that (1) is registered under the Investment Advisers Act of 1940; (2) has under his management, as of the last day of his most recent fiscal year, investor assets in excess of $85 million; and (3) could demonstrate either $1 million in shareholder or partner equity, or a guarantee of payment of all liabilities by an affiliate that would satisfy the $1 million equity requirement, including any liability for a breach of ERISA fiduciary duties. The QPAM must also acknowledge, in a written agreement, that he is a fiduciary with respect to each plan that has retained him.

It is the intent of the exemption to broadly expand the investment alternatives available to plans, while maintaining the protection of participants and beneficiaries.

Under the general provisions of the exemption, a party in interest and an investment fund in which the plan has an interest and that is managed by a QPAM may engage in transactions involving plan assets held in the investment fund, provided that:

1. At the time of the transaction, the party in interest, or its affiliate, does not have, and has not had, for the one-year period immediately preceding the transaction, the authority to:

    a. appoint or terminate the QPAM as a manager of any plan assets, or

    b. negotiate, on behalf of the plan, the terms of the management agreement with the QPAM;

2. The terms of the transaction are negotiated on behalf of the investment fund by the QPAM, and either the QPAM or a property manager acting under written guidelines of the QPAM makes the decision on behalf of the fund to enter into the transaction (so long as the transaction is not designed to benefit a party in interest);

3. The party in interest is neither the QPAM, nor a "related person" (a person who owns a 5 percent or more interest in the QPAM or in whom the QPAM owns a 5 percent or more interest);

4. The assets utilized in the transaction, when combined with all employer-established plan assets managed by the QPAM, do not exceed 20 percent of the assets managed by the QPAM at the time of the transaction;

5. The terms of the transaction are at least as favorable to the plan as an arm's-length transaction between unrelated parties; and

6. Neither the QPAM, nor any of its affiliates, nor any person who owns 5 percent or more of the QPAM, has, within the ten-year period preceding the transaction, been convicted or released from prison as a result of any felony involving abuse

of a position with a plan, labor organization, bank, broker-dealer, insurance company, or fiduciary (including tax evasion, larceny, theft, embezzlement, fraudulent conversion, misappropriation of funds, or conspiracy relating to any of the above).[1]

Further, the exemption does not apply to transactions that have already received their own class exemptions, such as: (1) securities lending arrangements[2] (see Q 454); (2) acquisitions by plans of interests in mortgage pools[3] (see Q 450); and (3) mortgage financing arrangements.[4]

Exemptive relief is available for the sale, leasing, or servicing of goods and the furnishing of services to a QPAM-managed investment fund by a party in interest if:

1. The party in interest is the plan sponsor or its affiliate;

2. The transaction is necessary for the administration or management of the fund;

3. The transaction takes place in the ordinary course of a business engaged in by the parties in interest with the general public; and

4. In the taxable year of the transaction, the amount earned through party-in-interest transactions engaged in with the investment fund does not exceed 1 percent of the gross receipts from all sources for the party in interest's prior taxable year.[5]

Exemptive relief for the leasing of office space or commercial space by a QPAM-managed fund to a party in interest will be granted if:

1. The party in interest is the plan sponsor or its affiliate;

2. No commission or other fee is paid by the fund to the QPAM, plan sponsor, or any affiliate;

3. The space leased to the party in interest by the fund is suitable for use by different tenants;

4. The space covered by the lease does not exceed 15 percent of the rentable space in the subject building, office park, or commercial center; and

5. In the case of defined benefit plans, immediately after the transaction is entered into, the fair market value of employer real property and employer securities held by funds of the QPAM in which the plan has an interest does not exceed 10 percent of the fair market value of the plan assets held in those funds.[6]

---

1. PTE 84-14.
2. PTE 81-6.
3. PTE 83-1.
4. PTE 82-87.
5. PTE 84-14.
6. PTE 84-14.

The specific exemptions for both the provision of goods and services and the leasing of office space must also comply with the general exemption requirements detailed in the preceding paragraphs.

QPAMs will receive specific exemptive relief for the leasing of office or commercial space by a QPAM-managed fund to the QPAM or its affiliates, if:

1. The amount of space covered by the lease does not exceed the greater of 7,500 square feet or 1 percent of the rentable space of the office building, office park, or commercial center in which the investment fund has an investment;

2. The space leased is suitable for use by different tenants;

3. The terms of the lease are not more favorable to the lessee than an arm's-length transaction between unrelated parties; and

4. No commission or other fee is paid to the QPAM by the investment fund.[1]

Exemptive relief is extended for the transactions involving places of public accommodation (e.g., hotels) that are owned by a QPAM-managed fund for the furnishing of services and facilities to parties related to plans that participate in a QPAM-managed fund, if the services and facilities are made available to the general public on a comparable basis.[2]

DOL Clarifies Meaning of "Ownership Interests"

In a 2003 advisory opinion, the DOL's Employee Benefit Security Administration (EBSA) clarified the application of the 5 percent ownership interest rule in PTE 84-14. That ownership provision states that a party in interest is related to a QPAM if:

1. The party in interest (or a person controlling or controlled by the party in interest) owns a 5 percent or more interest in the QPAM, or

2. The QPAM (or a person controlling or controlled by the QPAM) owns a 5 percent or more interest in the party in interest.

In the 2003 advisory opinion, EBSA was asked whether the 5 percent or more ownership interest in the QPAM provision included only "interests owned by the QPAM and entities in its vertical chain of ownership," or whether all entities under common control of the QPAM were included.

Citing the preamble to PTE 84-14, EBSA stated that it was not necessary to include entities under common control with the QPAM for purposes of the 5 percent or more ownership rule. Thus, said EBSA, the 5 percent ownership rule is limited to only the party in interest itself, or to the QPAM itself, and not their affiliates. Therefore, if a party in interest is wholly owned by another company, and, in turn, a QPAM has a 5 percent or more interest in that company, the party in interest and the QPAM are not "related" for purposes of prohibited transaction exemptions of PTE 84-14.[3]

---

1. PTE 84-14.
2. PTE 84-14.
3. DOL Adv. Op. 2003-07A.

The DOL finalized the amended PTE 84-14a to provide additional exemptive relief for employers to furnish limited amounts of goods and services to a managed fund in the ordinary course of business. Limited relief is also provided for leases of office or commercial space between managed funds and QPAMs or contributing employers. Finally, relief is provided for transactions involving places of public accommodation owned by a managed fund. The amendment affects participants and beneficiaries of employee benefit plans, the sponsoring employers of such plans, and other persons engaging in the described transactions. The amendment was effective August 23, 2005.[1]

The prohibited transaction provisions of ERISA shall not apply to a transaction between a party in interest with respect to an employee benefit plan and an investment fund in which the plan has an interest, and which is managed by a QPAM, if the following conditions are satisfied:

1. At the time of the transaction the party in interest, or its affiliate, does not have the authority to—

    a. appoint or terminate the QPAM as a manager of the plan assets involved in the transaction, or

    b. negotiate on behalf of the plan the terms of the management agreement with the QPAM (including renewals or modifications thereof) with respect to the plan assets involved in the transaction;

    Notwithstanding the foregoing, in the case of an investment fund in which two or more unrelated plans have an interest, a transaction with a party in interest with respect to an employee benefit plan will be deemed to satisfy the requirements of Section I(a) if the assets of the plan managed by the QPAM in the investment fund, when combined with the assets of other plans established or maintained by the same employer or by the same employee organization, and managed in the same investment fund, represent less than 10 percent of the assets of the investment fund;

2. The transaction is not described in—

    a. PTE 81-6[2] (relating to securities lending arrangements),

    b. PTE 83-1[3] (relating to acquisitions by plans of interests in mortgage pools), or

    c. PTE 82-87[4] (relating to certain mortgage financing arrangements);

3. The terms of the transaction are negotiated on behalf of the investment fund by, or under the authority and general direction of, the QPAM, and either the QPAM, or (so long as the QPAM retains full fiduciary responsibility with respect to the

1. 70 Fed. Reg. 162 (Aug. 23, 2005).
2. 46 Fed. Reg. 7527 (Jan. 23, 1981).
3. 48 Fed. Reg. 895 (Jan. 7, 1983).
4. 47 Fed. Reg. 21,331 (May 18, 1982).

transaction) a property manager acting in accordance with written guidelines established and administered by the QPAM, makes the decision on behalf of the investment fund to enter into the transaction, provided that the transaction is not part of an agreement, arrangement, or understanding designed to benefit a party in interest;

4. The party in interest dealing with the investment fund is neither the QPAM nor a person related to the QPAM;

5. The transaction is not entered into with a party in interest with respect to any plan whose assets managed by the QPAM, when combined with the assets of other plans established or maintained by the same employer (or affiliate) or by the same employee organization, and managed by the QPAM, represent more than 20 percent of the total client assets managed by the QPAM at the time of the transaction;

6. At the time the transaction is entered into, and at the time of any subsequent renewal or modification thereof that requires the consent of the QPAM, the terms of the transaction are at least as favorable to the investment fund as the terms generally available in arm's-length transactions between unrelated parties;

7. Neither the QPAM nor any affiliate thereof, nor any owner, direct or indirect, of a 5 percent or more interest in the QPAM is a person who within the ten years immediately preceding the transaction has been either convicted or released from imprisonment, whichever is later, as a result of: any felony involving abuse or misuse of such person's employee benefit plan position or employment, or position or employment with a labor organization; any felony arising out of the conduct of the business of a broker, dealer, investment adviser, bank, insurance company, or fiduciary; income tax evasion; any felony involving the larceny, theft, robbery, extortion, forgery, counterfeiting, fraudulent concealment, embezzlement, fraudulent conversion, or misappropriation of funds or securities; conspiracy or attempt to commit any such crimes or a crime in which any of the foregoing crimes is an element; or any other crime described in ERISA Section 411. For purposes of this condition, a person shall be deemed to have been "convicted" from the date of the judgment of the trial court, regardless of whether that judgment remains under appeal.

Specific Exemption for Employers

The prohibited transaction provisions of ERISA shall not apply to the following:

1. The sale, leasing, or servicing of goods, or to the furnishing of services, to an investment fund managed by a QPAM by a party in interest with respect to a plan having an interest in the fund if

    a. the party in interest is an employer any of whose employees are covered by the plan or is a person who is a party in interest by virtue of a relationship to such an employer.

b.   the transaction is necessary for the administration or management of the investment fund.

c.   the transaction takes place in the ordinary course of a business engaged in by the party in interest with the general public.

d.   effective for taxable years of the party in interest furnishing goods and services after August 23, 2005, the amount attributable in any taxable year of the party in interest to transactions engaged in with an investment fund pursuant to this exemption does not exceed 1 percent of the gross receipts derived from all sources for the prior taxable year of the party in interest.

e.   the requirements of Sections I(c) through (g) are satisfied with respect to the transaction.

2.   The leasing of office or commercial space by an investment fund maintained by a QPAM to a party in interest with respect to a plan having an interest in the investment fund if

a.   the party in interest is an employer any of whose employees are covered by the plan or is a person who is a party in interest by virtue of a relationship to such an employer.

b.   no commission or other fee is paid by the investment fund to the QPAM or to the employer, or to an affiliate of the QPAM or employer, in connection with the transaction.

c.   Any unit of space leased to the party in interest by the investment fund is suitable (or adaptable without excessive cost) for use by different tenants.

d.   The amount of space covered by the lease does not exceed 15 percent of the rentable space of the office building, integrated office park, or commercial center (if the lease does not pertain to office space).

e.   In the case of a plan that is not an eligible individual account plan,[1] immediately after the transaction is entered into, the aggregate fair market value of employer real property and employer securities held by investment funds of the QPAM in which the plan has an interest does not exceed 10 percent of the fair market value of the assets of the plan held in those investment funds. In determining the aggregate fair market value of employer real property and employer securities as described herein, a plan shall be considered to own the same proportionate undivided interest in each asset of the investment fund or funds as its proportionate interest in the total assets of the investment fund(s).

---

1. As defined in ERISA Section 407(d)(3).

For purposes of this requirement, the term "employer real property" means real property leased to, and the term "employer securities" means securities issued by, an employer any of whose employees are covered by the plan or a party in interest of the plan by reason of a relationship to the employer described in ERISA Section 3(14)(E) or ERISA Section 3(14)(G).

f.   The requirements of Sections I(c) through (g) are satisfied with respect to the transaction.

Specific Lease Exemption for QPAMs

The prohibited transaction provisions of ERISA shall not apply to the leasing of office or commercial space by an investment fund managed by a QPAM to the QPAM, a person who is a party in interest of a plan by virtue of a relationship to such QPAM described in subparagraphs (G), (H), or (I) of ERISA Section 3(14) or a person not eligible for the General Exemption of Part I by reason of Section I(a), if

1.   The amount of space covered by the lease does not exceed the greater of 7,500 square feet or 1 percent of the rentable space of the office building, integrated office park, or commercial center in which the investment fund has the investment.

2.   The unit of space subject to the lease is suitable (or adaptable without excessive cost) for use by different tenants.

3.   At the time the transaction is entered into, and at the time of any subsequent renewal or modification thereof that requires the consent of the QPAM, the terms of the transaction are not more favorable to the lessee than the terms generally available in arm's-length transactions between unrelated parties.

4.   No commission or other fee is paid by the investment fund to the QPAM, any person possessing the disqualifying powers described in Section I(a), or any affiliate of such persons, in connection with the transaction.

Transactions Involving Places of Public Accommodation

The prohibited transaction provisions of ERISA shall not apply to the furnishing of services and facilities (and goods incidental thereto) by a place of public accommodation owned by an investment fund managed by a QPAM to a party in interest with respect to a plan having an interest in the investment fund, if the services and facilities (and incidental goods) are furnished on a comparable basis to the general public.

Investment Advice Provided by Broker-Dealer's Subsidiary

In an advisory opinion, the DOL has stated that transactions between a broker-dealer and a separate 401(k) plan account managed by a QPAM would come under PTE 84-14, despite the plan participants' receiving investment advice from a subsidiary of the broker-dealer for a fee. Because neither the broker-dealer nor its subsidiary would have the authority to appoint or terminate the QPAM, the subsidiary's provision of investment advice to participants, for a fee, would not violate Section I(a) of class PTE 84-14, EBSA said.[1]

As noted previously, under Section I(a) of class PTE 84-14, an exemption would not be available if a QPAM caused the investment fund to enter into a transaction with a party in interest dealing with the fund, if the party in interest or its "affiliate" (1) was authorized to appoint or terminate the QPAM as a manager of any of the plan's assets, (2) was authorized to negotiate the terms of the management agreement with the QPAM (including renewals or modifications thereof) on behalf of the plan, or (3) had exercised such powers in the immediately preceding year.

In requesting the Opinion Letter, the broker-dealer sought DOL guidance regarding a scenario under which a participant-directed 401(k) plan offers a separate account that is managed by a QPAM as one of its investment options. The QPAM is not related to either the broker-dealer, or its subsidiary, a fee-based investment adviser. The subsidiary's services would be limited to advising participants as to the allocation of their investments in the plan. The investment adviser would not have authority or control over participants' accounts and would not participate in the plan sponsor's selection or oversight of the plan's investment options. The plan sponsor (or a named fiduciary unrelated to the broker-dealer and the investment adviser) would have, and would exercise, the authority to appoint and terminate the QPAM, and neither the broker-dealer nor the investment adviser would participate in negotiating the terms of the QPAM's management agreement.

The DOL determined that transactions between the separate account and the broker-dealer would not be affected by the investment adviser's provision of fee-based investment advice because

1. The plan sponsor (or named fiduciary), and not the broker-dealer or investment adviser, would select the investment vehicles to be managed by a QPAM, and

2. The plan participants, and not the broker-dealer or the investment adviser, would have the power to select the options under the plan in which to invest.

Thus, a transaction between the separate account and the broker-dealer would not fail to meet the requirements of Section I(a) of class PTE 84-14 despite the provision of advice to participants by the investment adviser.

In making its determination, the DOL notes that Part I of class PTE 84-14 provides no relief for transactions described in ERISA Section 406(b). Thus, if the investment adviser were a fiduciary (by providing investment advice within the meaning of Labor Regulation Section 2510.3-21(c)), then providing investment advice would involve self-dealing, and would subject the fiduciary adviser to liability under ERISA Section 406(b).

---

1. ERISA Op Letter 2007-01A.

453. What is the class exemption relating to in-house asset managers?

The prohibited transaction class exemption relating to qualified professional asset managers (QPAMs–see Q 452) does not extend exemptive relief to transactions involving the assets of plans managed by in-house asset managers (INHAMs).[1]

Previously, when an INHAM wished to conduct a transaction similar to that authorized for QPAMs, he was required to seek an individual exemption from the DOL, or hire a QPAM to execute the transaction.

The DOL recognized the need for a class exemption to provide relief to INHAMs in a manner similar to the relief afforded QPAMs, and issued PTE 96-23. This exemption provides relief with respect to otherwise prohibited transactions with party-in-interest service providers (except the INHAM, or parties related to the INHAM) regarding the portion of plan assets managed by the INHAM, as follows:

- The sale, exchange, or leasing of property between a plan and a party in interest;[2]

- The lending of money or the extension of credit to a party in interest;[3]

- The furnishing of goods, services, or facilities between a plan and a party in interest; and[4]

- The transfer to, or use by, a party in interest, of any assets of a plan.[5]

The exemption also permits a plan to lease office and commercial space to the plan sponsor. It extends exemptive relief to the furnishing of goods and services to a party in interest by places of public accommodation (e.g., hotels, motels) that are owned by the plan and managed by the INHAM.

The exemption defines an INHAM as an organization that is

1. Either a direct or indirect wholly owned subsidiary of (a) an employer, or (b) a parent corporation of such employer; *or*

2. A member of a nonprofit corporation, a majority of whose members are officers or directors of the parent corporation or employer; *and*

3. A registered investment adviser that, as of the last day of its most recent fiscal year, had INHAM affiliate plan assets of at least $50 million under its management.

In addition, the aggregate amount of all employee benefit plan assets under management by the INHAM or its affiliates must be at least $250 million as of the last day of the INHAM's most recent fiscal year.[6]

---

1. PTE 84-18.
2. ERISA Sec. 406(a)(1)(A).
3. ERISA Sec. 406(a)(1)(B).
4. ERISA Sec. 406(a)(1)(C).
5. ERISA Sec. 406(a)(1)(D).
6. PTE 96-23.

The exemption requires that the INHAM have discretionary authority or control with respect to the plan assets involved in the transaction. If this is the case, exemptive relief will be extended to transactions between a party in interest and the INHAM if

1. The terms of the transaction are negotiated on behalf of the plan by the INHAM, and either the INHAM or a property manager acting under written guidelines established by the INHAM, makes the determination to enter into the transaction (provided the INHAM retains fiduciary responsibility where the property manager makes the decision). But if the transaction involves plan assets of $5,000,000 or more, the plan sponsor must retain veto rights over the INHAM's approval of the transaction.

2. The transaction is not part of an agreement that has been established to benefit a party in interest.

3. The terms of the transaction are at least as favorable to the plan as an arm's-length transaction between unrelated parties.

4. The party in interest (a) is a party in interest solely by reason of being a plan service provider, or an affiliate of such service provider, and (b) does not have discretionary authority or control over the plan assets and does not render investment advice regarding plan assets involved in the transaction.

5. The party in interest is neither the INHAM nor a person related to the INHAM.

6. The INHAM has implemented written policies and procedures that govern the compliance with the conditions of the exemption.

7. An exemption audit is conducted, on an annual basis, by an independent auditor who (a) documents sufficient technical training and experience with the fiduciary responsibility provisions of ERISA, and (b) issues a written report to the plan detailing its findings regarding compliance with the written policies and procedures.[1]

Note that, if the independent audit referenced in item seven, above, reveals a failure to satisfy the conditions of the exemption on a specific transaction, exemptive relief will not be extended to that transaction. Further, the INHAM's failure to comply with the general exemption requirements (detailed above) will result in no exemptive relief for such transaction.

In addition, the exemptive relief will not be extended to the following transactions, because they have already been granted specific class exemptions: (1) securities lending arrangements[2] (see Q 454); (2) acquisitions by plans of interests in mortgage pools[3] (see Q 450); and (3) mortgage financing arrangements[4] (see Q 451).

---

1. PTE 96-23.
2. PTE 81-6.
3. PTE 83-1.
4. PTE 88-59.

The exemption also specifically applies to the leasing of office or commercial space, owned by a plan managed by an INHAM, to a plan sponsor or sponsor affiliate, if

1. The plan acquires the office or commercial space as a result of foreclosure on a mortgage or deed of trust;

2. The INHAM makes the decision, on behalf of the plan, to foreclose on the mortgage or deed of trust in the exercise of its discretionary authority; and

3. The amount of space covered by the lease does not exceed 15 percent of the rentable space of the office building or commercial center.

Exemptive relief is also extended for the leasing of residential space by a INHAM-managed plan to a party in interest, if

1. The party in interest is an employee of the plan sponsor or its affiliate;

2. The leasing employee has no discretionary authority or control with respect to the investment of the assets involved in the lease transaction and does not render investment advice with respect to those assets;

3. The leasing employee is not an officer, director, or 10 percent or more shareholder of the plan sponsor or its affiliate;

4. The terms of the transaction are not less favorable to the plan than an arm's-length transaction between unrelated parties; and

5. The amount of space covered by the lease does not exceed 5 percent of the rentable space in the apartment building or multi-unit residential subdivision, and the aggregate amount of space leased to all employees of the plan sponsor, or sponsor affiliate, does not exceed 10 percent of the rentable space.[1]

Both the lease of office/commercial space and the lease of residential space must also comply with the general exemptive provisions.

Finally, a place of public accommodation (e.g., hotel, motel) that is owned by a plan and managed by an INHAM may furnish services and facilities to parties in interest, if the services and facilities are furnished on a comparable basis to the general public.[2]

454. What is the class exemption regarding the lending of securities by employee benefit plans?

In the financial services industry, the lending of securities to broker-dealers and banks is commonplace. Absent an exemption, such practices, when entered into by plans and parties in interest, would violate the prohibited transaction provisions of ERISA. For this reason, requests for individual and class exemptions permitting plans to lend securities to broker-dealers and banks who were parties in interest had been filed by such prominent organizations as Morgan

---

1. PTE 96-23.
2. PTE 96-23.

Guaranty and Trust, Salomon Brothers, The American Bankers Association, and the Grumman Corporation.

PTE 81-6, as amended, whose holdings are incorporated in PTE 2006-16 (discussed subsequently), provides relief with regard to the lending of securities that are plan assets to a broker-dealer registered under the Securities Exchange Act of 1934 (the 1934 Act) or a broker-dealer exempted from registration under Section 15(a) of the 1934 Act as a dealer in exempted government securities, or to a bank, if the following conditions are satisfied:

1.   The entity borrowing the securities, or any of its affiliates, has no discretionary authority or control over the investment of plan assets involved in the transaction, and does not render investment advice regarding those assets.

2.   Either by physical delivery or by book entry in an appropriate securities depository, the subject plan receives collateral from the borrower consisting of (a) cash, (b) securities issued or guaranteed by the U.S. Government, or (c) irrevocable bank letters of credit issued by an entity other than the borrower or its affiliates, and having a market value equal to not less than 100 percent of the market value of the securities being loaned. (The collateral must be delivered by the close of the lending fiduciary's business on the day when the securities are borrowed. The market value of the collateral must be determined as of the close of the business day preceding the business day on which the securities are borrowed.)

3.   Prior to the borrowing of any securities, the borrower has provided to the lending fiduciary

   a.   the most recent available audited statement of the borrower's financial condition,

   b.   the most recent available unaudited statement of the borrower's financial condition (if more recent than the audited statement), and

   c.   a statement that there has been no material adverse change in its financial condition since the date of the most recent financial statement furnished to the plan that has not already been disclosed to the lending fiduciary.

4.   The loan is made in accordance with a written loan agreement (which may be a master agreement covering a series of securities lending transactions), the terms of which are as favorable to the plan as a comparable arm's-length transaction with an unrelated third party.

5.   The plan providing the securities to be borrowed receives

   a.   an opportunity to earn compensation through the investment of any cash collateral, or

   b.   a reasonable fee that is earmarked to the value of the securities borrowed and the duration of the loan, and

    c.   an amount equal to all distributions made to the holders of the borrowed securities during the term of the loan (such distributions include cash dividends, interest payments, shares of stock from stock splits, and any rights to purchase additional securities).

6.   If, as of the close of any business day within the term of the loan, the value of the collateral should ever fall below 100 percent of the market value of the borrowed securities, the borrower must deliver, by the close of the following business day, an additional amount of collateral that, when combined with the fair market value of the existing collateral, equals at least 100 percent of the market value of the borrowed securities.

7.   The loan must be terminable at any time by the plan, and the borrower must deliver certificates for securities, identical to the borrowed securities, to the plan within the customary delivery period for such securities, five business days, or within the time negotiated for delivery by the plan and the borrower.

8.   In the event of a failure to return the borrowed securities, if the loan is terminated within the time frames described in item seven above, the plan may use the collateral provided by the borrower to purchase securities identical to the borrowed securities, and may also use the collateral to pay any other obligations of the borrower and any expenses related to the purchase of replacement securities. The borrower is obligated to pay to the plan any remaining obligations and expenses not covered by the collateral, plus a reasonable rate of interest.[1]

In reviewing the terms of any potential letters of credit under the terms of a securities lending arrangement, plan fiduciaries are not relieved of their duties under ERISA Section 404(a) (see Q 253), which require them to ensure, among other things, that they have made prudent decisions. Also, fiduciaries retain their general responsibility to continually monitor the market value of the securities and the collateral to ensure that the plan is adequately protected during the entire term of the loan.

The exemption does not provide relief from the self-dealing and kickback prohibitions of ERISA Section 406(b).

PTE 82-63, whose holdings are also incorporated in PTE 2006-16 (discussed subsequently), exempts certain compensation arrangements for the provision of securities lending services by a plan fiduciary to an employee benefit plan, provided that

1.   The loan of securities is not prohibited by ERISA Section 406(a),

2.   The lending fiduciary is authorized to engage in lending transactions on behalf of the plan,

3.   The compensation is reasonable and is paid in accordance with terms of a written instrument,

---

1. PTE 81-6.

4.   The compensation arrangement is approved by an independent fiduciary, and

5.   The authorization is provided only after the independent fiduciary has received all information necessary to approve the arrangement with the lending fiduciary.

In late 2006, the DOL issued PTE 2006-16, replacing PTE 81-6 and PTE 82-63.[1] Under the newly crafted exemption, the holdings of the prior exemptions are incorporated. Also, the opportunities for securities lending among pension plans, banks, and broker-dealers are expanded. The new exemption became effective on January 2, 2007.

Relief under PTE 2006-16 is limited to transactions in which a plan loans securities to a U.S. broker-dealer or an eligible foreign broker-dealer located on specified countries that are a party in interest to the plan. PTE 2006-16 also provides exemption for securities lending to U.S. banks and eligible foreign banks located in specified countries that are a party in interest to a plan. The loan must be executed pursuant to a written loan agreement that grants the lender a continuing security interest in, title to, or rights of a secured creditor with respect to the collateral received for the loan. The borrower must also furnish the lender with its most recent available audited statement of the borrower's financial condition, as audited by a U.S.-based certified public accounting firm or a firm that is eligible or authorized to issue audited financial statements in conformity with accounting principles generally accepted in the primary foreign jurisdiction of the borrower. The loan must also require that the fees and other consideration received by the plan in exchange for the loan be reasonable.

An eligible foreign broker-dealer is one that is registered and regulated under the relevant securities laws of a governmental entity of a country other than the United States where such securities laws were applicable to a broker-dealer (including, specifically, any securities commission of a Province of Canada that is a member of the Canadian Securities Administration; and those registered under the Financial Services Authority of the United Kingdom) that

1.   Has, as of the last day of its most recent fiscal year, equity capital of no less than $200 million;

2.   Received an individual exemption from the DOL involving a loan of securities by a plan to a broker-dealer; or

3.   Received a final authorization by the DOL to engage in an otherwise prohibited transaction pursuant to PTE 96-62.

An eligible foreign bank is one that is subject to regulation by the relevant governmental banking agencies of a country other than the United States and the regulation by these banking agencies was applicable to a bank that

1.   Has substantially similar powers to a United States bank, as defined under Section 202(a)(2) of the Investment Advisers Act;

---

1. 71 Fed. Reg. 63,786 (Oct. 31, 2006).

2. Has, as of the last day of its most recent fiscal year, equity capital of no less than $200 million;

3. Received an individual exemption from the DOL involving a loan of securities by a plan to a bank; or

4. Received a final authorization by the DOL to engage in an otherwise prohibited transaction pursuant to PTE 96-62.

Collateral must be provided to the lender that is either

1. U.S. collateral having a market value, or in the case of bank letters of credit, a stated amount at least equal to 100 percent of the market value of the securities lent; or

2. Foreign collateral having a market value, or in the case of bank letters of credit, a stated amount at least equal to 102 percent of the market value of the securities lent as valued on a recognized securities exchange or an automated trading system on which the securities are primarily traded if the collateral posted is denominated in the same currency as the securities lent; or

3. 105 percent of the market value of the securities lent as valued on a recognized securities exchange or an automated trading system on which the securities are primarily traded if the collateral posted is denominated in a different currency than the securities.

U.S. collateral is defined under the exemption as:

1. U.S. currency;

2. Government securities, as defined under Section 3(a)(42)(C) of the Exchange Act (issued or guaranteed by FHLMC, FNMA, Student Loan Marketing Association (SLMA or Sallie Mae), and/or the Financing Corporation);

3. Mortgage-backed securities meeting the definition of a mortgage-related security under Section 3(a)(41) of the Exchange Act;

4. Negotiable certificates of deposit and banker's acceptances issued by a bank, as defined under Section 3(a)(6) of the Exchange Act, and that are payable in the United States and deemed to have a ready market; or[1]

5. Irrevocable letters of credit issued by a U.S. bank other than the borrower or an affiliate, or any combination thereof.

Foreign collateral is defined under the exemption as

1. Securities issued or guaranteed as to principal and interest by the following Multilateral Development Banks: International Bank for Reconstruction and Development, Inter-American Development Bank, Asian Development Bank,

---

1. As defined under 17 C.F.R. §240.15c3-1.

African Development Bank, European Bank for Reconstruction and Development, and The International Finance Corporation;

2.   Foreign sovereign debt securities provided that at least one nationally recognized statistical rating organization has rated in one of its two highest categories either the issue, the issuer, or the guarantor;

3.   The British pound, the Canadian dollar, the Swiss franc, the Japanese yen, or the Euro;

4.   Irrevocable letters of credit issued by a foreign bank, other than the borrower or affiliate, that has a counter-party rating of investment grade or better as determined by a nationally recognized statistical rating organization; or

5.   Any type of collateral described under Rule 15c3-3 of the Exchange Act, provided that the lending fiduciary is either a U.S. bank or a U.S. broker-dealer and such fiduciary indemnifies the plan with respect to the difference between the replacement cost of the borrowed securities and the market value of the collateral on the date of default plus interest and costs arising from the default.

The plan must receive collateral from the borrowers by physical delivery, wire transfer, or book entry in a securities depository located in the United States. For foreign banks and foreign broker-dealers, the plan must receive the collateral by physical delivery, wire entry, or book entry in a securities depository located in the United States or held at an Eligible Securities Depository.[1]

Where the lending fiduciary is a U.S.-based bank or broker-dealer, the exemption requires that the lending fiduciary indemnify the plan for the difference, if any, between the replacement cost of the borrowed securities and the market value of the collateral on the date of default plus interest and any transaction costs (including attorneys' fees). Acceptable foreign collateral in this situation must have, as of the close of business on the day preceding the lending date, a market value, or in the case of bank letters of credit, a stated amount, equal to not less than

1.   100 percent of the then market value of the securities lent as valued on a recognized securities exchange or an automated trading system on which the securities are primarily traded if the posted collateral is of the same currency;

2.   101 percent of the market value of the securities lent as valued on a recognized securities exchange or an automated trading system on which the securities are traded if the collateral is in a different currency denominated in Euros, British pounds, Japanese yen, Swiss francs, or Canadian dollars; or

3.   105 percent of the market value of the securities lent as valued on a recognized securities exchange or automated trading system if the collateral is in a different currency from the securities lent and is not one of the delineated currencies noted above.

---

1. As defined under Rule 17f-7 of the Investment Company Act of 1940.

Under the exemption, the plan may terminate the loan at any time. Failure by the borrower to maintain compliance of the loan with the requirements of the exemption will not expose the lender to liability for fiduciary breaches under ERISA's prohibited transaction provisions.

In the case of foreign lending of securities, the lending fiduciary must maintain the situs of the loan agreement in accordance with the *indicia of ownership* rules found under ERISA Section 404(b). The foreign borrower must agree to submit to the jurisdiction of U.S. federal district courts and agree that the plan may, in its sole discretion, enforce the agreement in a U.S. court. The sole exception to the requirement that a foreign borrower agree to submit to U.S. court jurisdiction is if the fiduciary lender is a U.S. bank or broker-dealer operating under the mandatory indemnification provisions detailed herein.

Finally, the requirements of PTE 2006-16 do not need to be applied to a securities lending arrangement entered into under an arrangement that meets with the requirements of ERISA Section 408(b)(17).[1]

PTE 81-6 will also be amended to permit additional types of collateral to be used for the loan. U.S. banks and U.S. broker-dealers would be permitted to give plans foreign collateral for securities loans. Foreign collateral would be defined as

1.   The currency of the UK or Euros;

2.   Securities issued or guaranteed by the government of the UK or one of its agencies or instrumentalities;

3.   Sovereign debt of the member countries of the European Monetary Union (EMU) denominated in Euros; or

4.   Irrevocable letters of credit issued by a foreign bank, other than the borrower, that has a counter-party rating of investment grade or better as determined by a nationally recognized statistical rating organization.

To better protect the plan's interest, the DOL increases the amount of collateral required when foreign collateral is offered to the plan. As an additional safeguard, the DOL would require that when a plan receives foreign collateral or U.S. collateral from a foreign bank or broker-dealer, the collateral itself must be maintained on behalf of the plan at an "eligible securities depository."[2] Rule 17f-7 governs the custody of assets of registered management investment companies with custodians outside the United States.

455. What is the class exemption that permits banks to offer IRA, SEP, and Keogh plans services at reduced fees or no cost?

If certain conditions are met, a self-employed individual for whose benefit a Keogh plan (see Q 19) is established or maintained (or members of her family) may receive services at reduced or no cost from a bank that bases the eligibility to receive such services upon the account balance of

---

1. As added by Section 611(d)(1) of the Pension Protection Act of 2006.
2. As defined in Rule 17f-7 of the Investment Company Act of 1940, 15 U.S.C. §80a.

the plan. This exemption may also apply to services received by an individual for whose benefit an individual retirement account (IRA) is established or maintained (or members of her family). In addition, this exemption applies to Simplified Employee Pension plans (SEPs), including those SEPs that provide participants with an unrestricted authority to transfer the assets in their accounts to IRAs sponsored by different financial institutions. The DOL has amended PTE 93-33 to expand coverage of the exemption to SIMPLE retirement accounts.[1] In the preamble to the proposal of this amendment to PTE 93-33, the DOL indicated that Advisory Opinion 98-03A (see Q 457) should be read to extend the coverage of PTE 93-33 to include Roth IRAs.[2]

These conditions must be met for the exemption to apply:

1.   The Keogh plan, SEP, or IRA is established and maintained for the exclusive benefit of the participant or IRA owner, her spouse, or beneficiaries.

2.   The service is of the type that the bank itself could offer consistent with applicable federal and state banking law.

3.   The services are provided by the bank (or an affiliate) in the ordinary course of business to customers who qualify for reduced- or no-cost services but do not maintain IRAs, SEPs, or Keogh plans with the bank.

4.   In the determination of eligibility, the Keogh plan, SEP, or IRA account balance required is equal to the lowest balance required by the bank for any other type of account that the bank includes to determine eligibility to receive reduced- or no-cost services.

5.   The rate of return on the Keogh plan, SEP, or IRA investment is no less favorable than the rate of return on an identical investment that could have been made at the same time at the same branch of the bank by a customer who is not eligible for (or who does not receive) reduced- or no-cost services.

The term "service" includes incidental products of a *de minimis* value provided by third persons pursuant to an arrangement with the bank, which are directly related to the provision of banking services covered by the exemption.

The exemption specifically excludes relief from the prohibited transaction provisions of ERISA to investments in securities offered by the bank exclusively to Keogh plans and IRAs.[3]

456. What is the class exemption regarding the payment of consideration to IRA and Keogh account holders?

Banks and financial institutions traditionally offer incentives to new customers, in order to encourage them to open new accounts. Incentives have included products (such as radios and toasters), services (such as free checking accounts and free check-cashing privileges), and cash incentives (such as the payment of a set fee for the deposit of certain dollar amounts). In

---

1. 64 Fed. Reg. 11,044 (Mar. 8, 1999).
2. 63 Fed. Reg. 56,233 (Oct. 21, 1998).
3. PTE 93-33.

addition, credit unions traditionally provide group life insurance policies for their members, free of charge, in an amount equal to the value of the assets that the member has on deposit, up to a predetermined amount (usually $5,000).

Exemptive relief is granted for the provision of these goods and services to IRA account holders and Keogh plan sponsors by banks and financial institutions, which would otherwise be prohibited transactions. In order for exemptive relief to apply, the following conditions must be satisfied:

1. The IRA or Keogh plan must be established solely for the purpose of providing benefits to the participant, his spouse, or beneficiaries.

2. The cash, property, or other consideration must be offered only in regard to the establishment of the IRA or Keogh plan, or additional contributions made to, or the transfer of assets from another plan to, the IRA or Keogh plan.

3. The total of the fair market value of the property or other consideration provided to the sponsor of the Keogh plan or to the IRA owner must not be more than $10 in any taxable year for deposits of less than $5,000, and not more than $20 in any taxable year for deposits of more than $5,000.

4. In the case where the consideration provided is group term life insurance, the limitations set forth in items two and three will not apply, if, during any taxable year, no more than $5,000 of the face value of the insurance is attributable, on a dollar for dollar basis, to the assets of the IRA or Keogh plan.[1]

457. What is the class exemption permitting broker-dealers to offer IRA, Roth IRA, SEP, SIMPLE, and Keogh plans' services to clients at reduced fees or no cost?

Broker-dealers registered under the Securities Exchange Act of 1934 are permitted to offer reduced- or no-cost services to their IRA, Simplified Employee Pension (SEP) plan, and Keogh plan clients.[2] Subsequently, the DOL amended PTE 97-11 to expand its relief to SIMPLE retirement accounts.[3] In the preamble to the proposal of this amendment to PTE 97-11, the DOL indicated that Advisory Opinion 98-03A should be read as extending the coverage of PTE 97-11 to include Roth IRAs.[4]

The exemption was issued in order to place broker-dealers on a level playing field with banks, which have been permitted to offer these services to their clients under PTE 93-33. See Q 455. The conditions established under PTE 97-11 are essentially the same as those required under PTE 93-33, except for the necessary changes to reflect the terminology and operations of broker-dealers.

---

1. PTE 93-1.
2. PTE 97-11.
3. 64 Fed. Reg. 11,042 (Mar. 8, 1999).
4. 63 Fed. Reg. 56,231 (Oct. 21, 1998).

Brokers may now take into consideration retirement plan assets when determining whether an individual is eligible for free or low-cost brokerage services, without running afoul of the prohibited transaction rules. The services permitted under the exemption include financial planning, direct deposit/debit and automatic fund privileges, enhanced account statements, toll-free access to client service centers, check-writing privileges, debit/credit cards, special newsletters, and reduced brokerage and asset management fees.

Under the exemption, the following conditions apply with respect to the balances under IRAs (including SIMPLE IRAs and Roth IRAs), SEPs, and Keogh plans:

1. The balance taken into account for purposes of determining eligibility to receive relationship brokerage arrangement services must be established and maintained for the exclusive benefit of the clients, their spouses, and beneficiaries.

2. The relationship brokerage services must be of the type that the broker-dealer could offer, consistent with all applicable federal and state laws regulating broker-dealers.

3. The relationship brokerage services must be provided by the broker-dealer (or an affiliate) in the ordinary course of business, to clients who otherwise qualify for reduced-or no-cost services but do not maintain these types of plans with the broker-dealer.

4. For purposes of determining eligibility to receive services, the relationship brokerage arrangement must have eligibility requirements that

    a. if based on the balance, must be as favorable as any such requirements based on the value of any other type of account that the broker-dealer includes to determine eligibility,

    b. if based on fees, must be as favorable as any requirements based on the amount of fees incurred by any other type of account that the broker-dealer includes to determine eligibility.

5. The combined total of all fees for the provision of services must not exceed "reasonable compensation."[1]

6. The investment performance must be no less favorable than the investment performance of an identical investment that could have been made at the same time by a client of the broker-dealer who is not eligible for (or does not receive) reduced- or no-cost services.

7. The services offered under the arrangement to a participant must be the same as are offered to non-plan clients with account values of the same amount or the same amount of fees generated.[2]

---

1. As defined under IRC Section 4975(d)(2).
2. PTE 97-11.

458. What is the class exemption relating to accelerated exemption procedures?

The DOL has issued an exemption that permits ERISA plans to seek approval, on an accelerated basis, of certain transactions that would otherwise be prohibited transactions under ERISA.[1]

The exemption also provides a general exemption for the accelerated approval of transactions prohibited under ERISA Section 406(a) and a specific exemption for the accelerated approval of transactions involving a fiduciary's self-dealing and the representation of a party whose interests are adverse to a plan, which would otherwise be prohibited under ERISA Section 406(b)(1) and ERISA Section 406(b)(2).

Under these general and specific exemption provisions, relief will be extended to cover transactions between a plan and a party in interest, which would otherwise violate the general exemption provision and the self-dealing or adverse interest restrictions of ERISA, if

1.   The proposed transaction is substantially similar to transactions described in at least two individual exemptions that were granted by the DOL, and which provided relief from the same restriction, within the five-year period ending on the date on which the written submission for an accelerated approval is filed;

2.   There is little risk of abuse or loss to the participants and beneficiaries as a result of the transaction; and

3.   Prior to executing the transactions, a written submission has been filed with the DOL regarding the proposed transactions, which contains the following information:

  a.   a separate written declaration, from the party who wishes to engage in the transaction, that the submission has been made in order to demonstrate compliance with the conditions of the exemption,

  b.   all required information for an individual exemption (see Q 885 and Q 886),

  c.   a specific statement demonstrating that the proposed transaction poses little, if any, risk of loss or abuse to plan participants or beneficiaries,

  d.   a comparison of the proposed transaction(s) to at least two other substantially similar transactions that have been granted individual exemptions by the DOL within the five-year period ending on the date of the submission, as well as an explanation that any differences should not be considered material for the purpose of granting the exemption, and

  e.   a complete draft of the required notice to be issued to interested persons (discussed subsequently), and a description of the method to be used in distributing the notice.

---

1. PTE 96-62.

For the specific transactions involving self-dealing or adverse interests, the written submission must contain the following information:

1.   Identification of the independent fiduciary;

2.   A description of that fiduciary's independence from the parties in interest involved in the transaction;

3.   A written statement by the independent fiduciary that details why the independent fiduciary believes the transaction is in the interest of and protective of the participants and beneficiaries;

4.   An agreement by the independent fiduciary to represent the interests of the plan in the transaction; and

5.   A description of how the independent fiduciary will be replaced, if necessary, during the term of the transaction.[1]

Following a tentative authorization of the transaction by the DOL, the party requesting an accelerated approval of a requested exemption must provide written notice of the proposed transaction in such a manner that it is likely that (1) interested persons will (a) receive the notice, and (b) be informed of the date of expiration for the comment period; and (2) all substantial adverse comments that interested persons have submitted within the comment period will be resolved to the satisfaction of the DOL.[2]

The notice to interested persons must include a description of the proposed transaction, including all material terms and conditions, the approximate date on which the transaction will occur, and a statement that the proposed transaction has satisfied the requirements for a tentative authorization by the DOL.

459. What is the class exemption regarding life insurance company general accounts?

The U.S. Supreme Court ruled that assets of a plan allocated to the general accounts of an insurance company are plan assets for purposes of ERISA, and thus are subject to ERISA's fiduciary provisions, including the prohibition against certain transactions involving plan assets. As such, insurance companies holding plan assets in their general accounts are considered fiduciaries under ERISA if they exercise discretionary authority or control over such plan assets.[3] This holding exposed life insurance companies to heretofore unheard-of levels of liability regarding their dealings with their qualified retirement plan clients.

In response, the American Council of Life Insurance requested that the DOL issue a prohibited transaction exemption to counteract the effects of the *Hancock* ruling. The DOL complied with this request and issued PTE 95-60, which permits (prospectively and retroactively to January 1, 1975) certain transactions engaged in by insurance company general accounts in which plan

---

1. PTE 96-62.
2. PTE 96-62.
3. *John Hancock Mut. Life Ins. Co. v. Harris Trust & Sav. Bank*, 510 U.S. 86 (1993).

assets are invested. The exemption also extends relief to plans that engage in transactions with people who provide services to insurance company general accounts. The exemption also provides relief for transactions relating to the origination and operation of certain asset pool investment trusts in which an insurance company general account has an interest as a result of the acquisition of certificates issued by the trust.

The basic exemption provides relief from the restrictions of ERISA that prohibit the sale, exchange, or leasing of plan property, the extension of credit between the plan and a party in interest, the furnishing of goods and services, or transfer to or use by a party in interest of plan assets, and that prohibit the plan from holding employer real property or employer securities.[1] The exemption applies to the following:

1. Any transaction between an insurance company general account (in which a plan has an interest) and a party in interest, or any acquisition or holding by the general account of employer securities or employer real property, if, at the time of the transaction, the amount of reserves and liabilities for the general account contracts held on behalf of the plan, together with the amount of reserves and liabilities for the general account contracts held on behalf of any other plans maintained by the same employer (or the same employee organization), in the general account do not exceed 10 percent of the total reserves and liabilities of the general account, plus surplus; and

2. Any acquisition or holding of qualifying employer real property or qualifying employer securities by a plan (other than through an insurance company general account) if: (a) the acquisition or holding violates the restrictions of ERISA Section 406(a)(1)(E), ERISA Section 406(a)(2), and ERISA Section 407(a), solely because they are aggregated with employer real property or employer securities held by an insurance company general account in which the plan has an interest, and (b) the percentage limitation of item 1 (above) is satisfied.

The exemption provides relief from ERISA Sections 406(a)(1)(A) to 406(a)(1)(D) for transactions with parties in interest if they are parties in interest solely because they provide certain services to an insurance company general account in which the plan has an interest, or are affiliates of such service providers.

The exemption also provides relief from ERISA restrictions upon the furnishing of services, facilities, and any goods incidental to services and facilities to a party in interest by a place of public accommodation owned by an insurance company general account.[2] Such services and facilities must be available to the general public on a comparable basis in order for the exemptive relief to apply.

For the preceding transactions to receive exemptive relief, the following conditions must be satisfied at the time when the parties entered into the transaction:

---

1. ERISA Secs. 406(a), 407(a).
2. ERISA Secs. 406(a), 406(b), 407(a).

1.   The terms of the transaction must be at least as favorable to the plan as an arm's-length transaction between unrelated parties.

2.   The transaction must not be designed, as part of an agreement or arrangement, to benefit a party in interest.

3.   The party in interest must not be the insurance company, a pooled separate account of the insurance company, or an affiliate of the insurance company.

The specific exemption for the operation of asset pool investment trusts provides relief from ERISA Section 406(a), ERISA Section 406(b), and ERISA Section 407(a) for transactions in connection with the servicing, management, and operation of a trust in which an insurance company general account has an interest, if

1.   The trust is described in PTE 83-1 or in one of the "Underwriter Exemptions" (referring to specific exemptions identified in PTE 95-60);

2.   The conditions of PTE 83-1 or the applicable underwriter exemption are met, except that

   a.   the rights and interests evidenced by the trust certificates that were acquired by the general account are not subordinated to the rights and interests of the other certificates of the same trust, and

   b.   the certificates of the trust acquired by the general account, at the time of the acquisition, have earned a rating that is one of the three highest generic rating categories from Standard & Poor's, Moody's, Duff & Phelps, or Fitch Investors Service.

Exemptive relief will be extended to those who are parties in interest as a result of being a service provider to the plan solely because of the plan's ownership of certificates issued by a trust.

This exemption does not relieve a fiduciary or party in interest from the other provisions of ERISA, including any prohibited transaction provisions to which the exemption does not apply, and the general fiduciary provisions of ERISA Section 404.[1]

460. What is the class exemption allowing a fiduciary financial institution to select itself as the provider of IRAs with rollovers of missing participant accounts?

PTE 2004-16 generally provides relief from ERISA's prohibited transaction provisions for a plan fiduciary's selection of itself as the provider of an individual retirement plan and/or issuer of an investment in connection with rollovers of missing participant accounts for amounts up to $5,000. Relief also is provided for a plan fiduciary to select a proprietary product as the initial investment for such individual retirement plan.

---

1. PTE 95-60.

For the class exemption to apply, the plan sponsor (or affiliate) must also meet the automatic rollover safe-harbor requirements detailed under Labor Regulation Section 2550.404-a2 (see Q 277 and Q 278 for details of the safe harbor).[1]

In addition to the above requirements, in order for the provisions of PTE 2004-16 to apply, the following conditions must be met:

1. In connection with the IRC Section 402(f) written explanation provided to the separating participant, or in the plan's SPD or SMM, the plan fiduciary notifies the participant that, absent his election, the Mandatory Distribution will be rolled over to an individual retirement plan offered by the plan fiduciary or an affiliate, and that the plan fiduciary may select its own proprietary investment for the initial investment of the Mandatory Distribution.

2. The individual retirement plan is established and maintained for the exclusive benefit of the individual retirement plan account holder, his spouse, or their beneficiaries.

3. The terms of the individual retirement plan, including the fees and expenses for establishing and maintaining the individual retirement plan, are no less favorable than those available to comparable individual retirement plans established for reasons other than the receipt of a Mandatory Distribution made pursuant to IRC Section 401(a)(31)(B).

4. The Mandatory Distribution is invested in an Eligible Investment Product(s) (see below).

5. The rate of return or the investment performance of the individual retirement plan investment(s) is no less favorable than the rate of return or investment performance of an identical investment(s) that could have been made at the same time by comparable individual retirement plans established for reasons other than the receipt of a Mandatory Distribution made pursuant to IRC Section 401(a)(31)(B).

6. The individual retirement plan does not pay a sales commission in connection with the acquisition of an Eligible Investment Product.

7. The individual retirement plan account holder may, within a reasonable period of time after his request and without penalty to the principal amount of the investment, transfer his individual retirement plan balance to a different investment offered by the Individual Retirement Plan Provider, or transfer his individual retirement plan balance to an individual retirement plan sponsored at a different financial institution.

8. The fees and expenses attendant to the individual retirement plan, including the investment of the assets of such plan (e.g., establishment charges, maintenance fees, investment expenses, termination costs, and surrender charges) shall not exceed the fees and expenses charged by the Individual Retirement Plan Provider

---

1. 69 Fed. Reg. 187 (Sept. 28, 2004).

for comparable individual retirement plans established for reasons other than the receipt of a Mandatory Distribution made pursuant to IRC Section 401(a)(31)(B).

9. Fees and expenses attendant to the individual retirement plan, with the exception of establishment charges, may be charged only against the income earned by the individual retirement plan.

10. Fees and expenses are not in excess of reasonable compensation within the meaning of IRC Section 4975(d)(2).

11. The present value of the nonforfeitable accrued benefit, as determined under IRC Section 411(a)(11), does not exceed the maximum amount required to be rolled over under IRC Section 401(a)(31)(B) ($5,000).

The term "eligible investment product" means an investment product designed to preserve principal and provide a reasonable rate of return, whether or not such return is guaranteed, consistent with liquidity. For this purpose, the product must be offered by a regulated financial institution and shall seek to maintain, over the term of the investment, the dollar value that is equal to the amount invested in the product by the individual retirement plan. Such term includes money market funds maintained by registered investment companies, and interest-bearing savings accounts and certificates of deposit of a bank or similar financial institution. In addition, the term includes "stable value products" issued by a financial institution that are fully benefit-responsive to the individual retirement plan account holder—in other words, they provide a liquidity guarantee by a financially responsible third party of principal and previously accrued interest for liquidations or transfers initiated by the individual retirement plan account holder exercising her right to withdraw or transfer funds under the terms of an arrangement that does not include substantial restrictions on the account holder's access to the individual retirement plan's assets.

The individual retirement plan provider must maintain records to enable certain persons to determine whether the applicable conditions of the exemption have been met. The records must be available for examination by the IRS, the DOL, and account holders and their beneficiaries for at least six years from the date of each automatic rollover.

The exemption is effective for mandatory distributions made on or after March 28, 2005.

461. What is the class exemption for responsible fiduciaries protecting them from failure to disclose by a covered service provider?

Effective July 1, 2012, as a class prohibited transaction exemption, the restrictions of ERISA Section 406(a)(1)(C) and ERISA Section 406(a)(1)(D) will *not* apply to a "responsible plan fiduciary" (i.e., the plan fiduciary that uses its authority to cause an employee benefit plan to enter into, or extend or renew, a written contract or arrangement for the provision of services), *notwithstanding* the covered service provider's failure to disclose specified information (either as an initial disclosure or in response to a request by the responsible plan fiduciary or covered plan administrator)—but only if:

1. The responsible plan fiduciary did not know that the covered service provider failed, or would fail, to make required disclosures, and reasonably believed that the covered service provider disclosed the required information.

2. The responsible plan fiduciary, upon discovering that the covered service provider failed to disclose the required information, requests in writing that the covered service provider furnish the information.

3. Where the covered service provider fails to comply with the written request within ninety days of the request, then the responsible plan fiduciary notifies DOL of the covered service provider's failure (as provided in item five).

    The notice is to be filed within thirty days of the expiration of the ninety-day response time, then at this time, the responsible plan fiduciary will be covered by the exemption, but the covered service provider will continue to be engaging in a non-exempt prohibited transaction until such time as the service arrangement is terminated, or the disclosure failure has been cured.

4. The notice contains the following information:

    a. name of the plan;

    b. plan number used for the plan's annual report;

    c. plan sponsor's name, address, and EIN;

    d. name, address, and telephone number of the responsible plan fiduciary;

    e. name, address, phone number, and, if known, the EIN, of the covered service provider;

    f. a description of the services provided to the covered plan;

    g. a description of the information that the service provider failed to disclose;

    h. date on which the information was requested in writing from the covered service provider; and

    i. a statement as to whether the service provider continues to provide services to the plan;

5. The notice is filed with DOL not later than thirty days following the earlier of:

    a. the date of covered service provider's refusal to furnish the information that was requested in writing; or

    b. ninety days after the written request was made;

6. Effective September 14, 2012, the DOL has amended the final fiduciary-level service provider fee disclosure regulations to revise the DOL electronic and mailing

addresses for fiduciaries needing to notify the DOL of a delinquent service provider. The notice is to be sent to the following address:

> U.S. Department of Labor
> Employee Benefits Security Administration, Office of Enforcement
> P.O. Box 75296
> Washington, DC 20013.

Further, effective September 14, 2012, the DOL has eliminated the previously available email address (OEDelinquentSPnotice@dol.gov). Instead, pursuant to instructions that will be separately provided by the DOL, responsible plan fiduciaries who wish to submit notices electronically will be able to do so through a dedicated link on the Department's Web site, at www.dol.gov/ ebsa/regs/feedisclosurefailurenotice.html. This web page will include clear instructions for how to submit the required notification and will provide immediate confirmation to responsible plan fiduciaries that the notice has been received by the DOL.[1]

7.   If the covered service provider fails to comply with the written request within the ninety-day time frame, the responsible plan fiduciary shall determine whether to terminate or continue the service contract or arrangement consistent with its duty of prudence under ERISA Section 404. If the requested information relates to future services and is not disclosed promptly at the end of the ninety-day period, then the responsible plan fiduciary shall terminate the contract or arrangement as expeditiously as possible, consistent with such duty of prudence.[2]

In late 2012, the DOL issued a proposed amendment to PTE 2006-06 that will modify the conditions of the exemption to recognize bankruptcy trustees that might serve in a QTA capacity (see question 258A for details on this expansion of the QTA program to include Chapter 7 Bankruptcy issues).[3]

The definition of a QTA under Section V(a) of PTE 2006-06 would be expanded to include the bankruptcy trustee of a Chapter 7 plan. Proposed Section V(a)(2). The provisions of PTE 2006-06 would be extended to cover the bankruptcy trustee acting as the QTA, with certain limitations. Also, an eligible designee of the bankruptcy trustee serving as the QTA would have full access to PTE 2006-06, since it would satisfy the same requirements as a regular QTA. Proposed Section V(h) would be added to include a definition of an eligible designee.

Section II(b) of PTE 2006-06 would be amended to eliminate the requirement that fees and expenses paid to the QTA and its affiliate be consistent with industry rates for such or similar services, based on the experience of the QTA, if the QTA is the bankruptcy trustee. Instead, the requirement would be deemed met to the extent that the fees and expenses paid

---

1. 29 CFR Part 2550, 77 Fed. Reg. 41678 (July 16, 2012).
2. Labor Reg. §2550.408b-2(c)(1)(ix); 77 Fed. Reg. 5632 (Feb 3, 2012).
3. 77 F.R. 74056 (December 12, 2012).

to such QTA are: (1) for services necessary to wind-up the affairs of the plan and distribute benefits to the plan's participants and beneficiaries, and (2) consistent with industry rates for such or similar services ordinarily charged by regular type of QTA. This would make the exemption consistent with the rules in amended DOL Reg. Sec. 2578.1. This modification would not apply to an eligible designee of the bankruptcy trustee, because that entity would be a type of institution that could satisfy the regular conditions under Section II(b) of the exemption.

Section I(b) of PTE 2006-06 provides an exemption from the prohibited transaction rules for a QTA that designates itself or an affiliate as the provider of an IRA (or inherited IRA, in the case of a nonspouse beneficiary), or the provider of an interest bearing bank account, where the conditions of DOL Reg. Sec. 2550.404a-3 are satisfied. This section of the exemption also covers the initial investment of such IRA or account in a proprietary investment product of the QTA or its affiliate, fees for the establishment or maintenance of such IRA or account, and fees associated with a proprietary investment product. If a bankruptcy trustee, rather than an eligible designee, is acting as a QTA, this part of the exemption would not apply to the QTA."

Statutory Exemptions

462. What are the statutory exemptions to the prohibited transaction provisions of ERISA?

ERISA Section 408 details several specific exemptions, which permit employee benefit plans to engage in transactions that would otherwise be prohibited under various provisions of ERISA, the Internal Revenue Code, and other sources of governing authority. ERISA Section 408 generally provides statutory exemptions for

1.   Loans to participants[1] (see Q 463);

2.   Provision of office space or services reasonably necessary for the operation of the plan[2] (see Q 464);

3.   Loans to employee stock ownership plans[3] (see Q 465);

4.   Deposits in bank investments where the bank is a plan fiduciary[4] (see Q 466);

5.   Purchase of insurance and annuity products from an insurance company that is the sponsor of the plan[5] (see Q 467);

6.   Provision of ancillary bank services to a plan by a bank that is a party in interest[6] (see Q 468);

1. ERISA Sec. 408(b)(1).
2. ERISA Sec. 408(b)(2).
3. ERISA Sec. 408(b)(3).
4. ERISA Sec. 408(b)(4).
5. ERISA Sec. 408(b)(5).
6. ERISA Sec. 408(b)(6).

7.   Certain transactions between the plan and owner-employees[1] (see Q 469);

8.   Conversion of securities[2] (see Q 470);

9.   Transactions between a plan and a pooled investment fund maintained by a bank that is a party in interest[3] (see Q 471);

10. Receipt of benefits by a disqualified person[4] (see Q 472);

11. Distribution of plan assets in accordance with the plan documents upon plan termination[5] (see Q 473); and

12. Merger and transfer of assets and liabilities between multiemployer plans[6] (see Q 474).

463. What is the statutory exemption regarding plan loans to parties in interest?

The lending of money or other extension of credit between a plan and a party in interest is prohibited under ERISA Section 406(a)(1)(B). But a statutory exemption permits loans from plans to parties in interest who are participants or beneficiaries if

1.   The loans are made available to all participants and beneficiaries on a reasonably equivalent basis;

2.   The loans are not made available to highly compensated employees (as defined under IRC Section 414(g)) in an amount greater than the amount made available to other employees;

3.   The loans are made in accordance with specific provisions regarding participant loans, which are set forth in the plan;

4.   The loans bear a reasonable rate of interest; and

5.   The loans are adequately secured.[7]

A "participant loan" is defined as a loan arranged and approved by the fiduciary administering the loan program, which has been prudently established and administered primarily in the interest of the participants and beneficiaries.[8] The existence of a written loan program and supporting loan documents will not qualify as a participant loan for which exemptive relief is available under ERISA Section 408(b)(1) if, upon consideration of all relevant facts and circumstances, the DOL determines that the parties to the loan agreement did not intend for the loan to be repaid.

---

1. ERISA Sec. 408(d).
2. ERISA Secs. 3(18), 408(b)(7).
3. ERISA Sec. 408(b)(8).
4. IRC Secs. 4975(d)(9), 4975(d)(10).
5. ERISA Sec. 408(b)(10).
6. ERISA Sec. 408(b)(11).
7. ERISA Sec. 408(b)(1).
8. Labor Reg. §2550.408b-1(a)(3).

Section 408(d)(2) of ERISA has been amended to provide for loans from qualified plans to certain S corporation shareholders, partners, and sole proprietors. This expanded availability of participant loans is effective for plan years beginning after December 31, 2001.[1]

In order for loans to be made available on a reasonably equivalent basis, they must be available to all participants and beneficiaries without regard to race, color, religion, sex, age, or national origin.[2] That same regulation also requires that consideration be given only to those factors that would be considered in a normal setting by an entity in the business of making similar types of loans. Such factors may include a review of the applicant's creditworthiness and financial need.

A participant loan program will not fail to qualify for exemptive relief under ERISA Section 408(b)(1) merely because it has established a minimum loan amount. Plans may not establish minimum loan amounts in excess of $1,000.[3]

Participant loan programs contained within the plan's governing documents must include (but need not be limited to) the following provisions:

1.   Identification of the person or positions authorized to administer the loan program;

2.   Procedure for applying for loans;

3.   Basis on which loans will be approved or denied;

4.   Limitations on the types and amount of loans offered;

5.   Procedure under the program for determining a reasonable rate of interest;

6.   Types of collateral that may be used to secure a participant loan; and

7.   Events that would constitute default and the steps that will be taken to preserve plan assets in the event of such default.[4]

A reasonable rate of interest is one that provides the plan with a return that is commensurate with the interest rates charged by persons in the business of lending money under similar circumstances.[5]

Adequate security is defined under the regulations as "something in addition to and supporting a promise to pay, which is so pledged to the plan that it may be sold, foreclosed upon, or otherwise disposed of upon default of repayment of the loan, the value and liquidity of which security is such that it may reasonably be anticipated that the loss of principal or interest will not result from the loan."[6]

---

1. Title VI, Subtitle E, Section 612(b) and (c) of EGTRRA.
2. Labor Reg. §2550.408b-1(a)(3).
3. Labor Reg. §2550.408b-1(b)(2).
4. Labor Reg. §2550.408b-1(d)(2).
5. Labor Reg. §2550.408b-1(e).
6. Labor Reg. §2550.408b-1(f).

See IRC Section 72(p) and its attendant regulations for further details regarding the official restrictions on the number and amount of loans that can be made available under a participant loan program.

464. What is the statutory exemption for the provision of services or office space?

ERISA Section 408(b)(2) permits a plan to contract for or make reasonable arrangements with a party in interest for the provision of office space, or legal, accounting, or other services necessary for the establishment or operation of the plan, if no more than reasonable compensation is paid for such services or office space.

A necessary service is a service that is appropriate and helpful to the plan in carrying out the purposes for which the plan is established or maintained. A person providing such services may furnish goods that are necessary for the establishment or operation of the plan in the course of, and incidental to, the furnishing of such services to the plan.[1]

A reasonable contract or arrangement is one that permits the termination of services by the plan, without penalty, on reasonably short notice under the circumstances, in order to prevent the plan from becoming locked into an arrangement that has become disadvantageous. But a contract provision that reasonably compensates the service provider or lessor for loss upon early termination of a contract, arrangement, or lease is not a penalty. A lease provision for termination fees covering reasonably foreseeable expenses related to the vacancy and re-letting of the office space upon early termination of the lease (not to exceed the actual loss) is also not a penalty; but provisions for lease termination fees must also provide for mitigation of damages in order to avoid a DOL ruling that it is a penalty.[2]

Reasonable compensation may be paid to a party in interest or a fiduciary for services rendered to the plan or for the provision of office space if the services or office space are reasonable and necessary for the establishment and ongoing operation of the plan.[3] Under the regulations, the DOL will determine the reasonableness of compensation under a review of the particular facts and circumstances of each case. The payment of fees to a fiduciary who is already a paid full-time employee of the plan sponsor is not considered reasonable unless it is paid as reimbursement of direct expenses properly and actually incurred.[4] A fiduciary may also be granted an advance to cover direct expenses that it reasonably expects to incur in the immediate future. The fiduciary must provide an accounting of such expenses at the end of the period covered by the advance.[5]

The statutory exemption does not permit fiduciaries to use their authority, control, or responsibility to cause the plan to pay additional fees to the fiduciary for the provision of services.[6] Such an act would be considered a prohibited transaction in violation of the self-dealing

---

1. Labor Reg. §2550.408b-2(b).
2. Labor Reg. §2550.408b-2(c).
3. Labor Reg. §2550.408c-2.
4. Labor Reg. §2550.408b-2(d); DOL Adv. Op. 83-07A.
5. DOL Adv. Op. 89-28A.
6. Labor Reg. §2550.408b-2(e)(1).

prohibitions of ERISA Section 406(b). But the regulations provide that it is not, in and of itself, a violation of the self-dealing prohibitions for a fiduciary to provide services to the plan without receiving compensation.[1]

A fiduciary is forbidden from using his authority, control, or responsibility to cause a plan to pay additional fees for a service provided by an entity in which the fiduciary has an interest.[2]

The statutory exemption found under ERISA Section 408(b)(2) for the payment in settlement of a claim arising from a service arrangement has been extended. This exemption applies if

1. The service arrangement initially qualified for, and continues to qualify for, the exemption found under ERISA Section 408(b)(2), after considering (a) the settlement agreement, (b) the alleged conduct of the service provider giving rise to the claims, and (c) where appropriate, the ability of the plan to obtain a guarantee from the service provider that the conduct resulting in the claim will not be repeated, and the fiduciaries' ability to protect the plan from abuse that may be inherent in the relationship between the parties to the settlement claim and the plan;

2. The party in interest relationship arises only from the provision of services under the exemption; and

3. The fiduciaries have prudently determined that settlement would be reasonable because the plan will receive payment at least equal to the amount of the plan's claims, taking into account the risks of litigation and creditworthiness of any party who has received an extension of credit.[3]

Disclosure Requirements for "Reasonable" Service Contracts Effective July 1, 2012

Effective July 1, 2012, to better ensure that plan fiduciaries have sufficient information to fulfill their ERISA Section 404 obligations when selecting and monitoring service providers, a service contract will not be "reasonable" unless the service provider furnishes to the "responsible plan fiduciary," in writing, information on compensation and on the services provided. Thus, these disclosure requirements will have to be met in order for a service contract to qualify for the prohibited transaction exemption that allows service providers to contract with employee benefit plans.[4] See Q 402 for full details on these final regulations issued February 2, 2012.

465. What is the statutory exemption regarding ESOP loans?

Plan fiduciaries are prohibited from receiving any consideration for their own account from any party dealing with the plan in connection with a transaction involving the income or assets of the plan.[5] But exemptive relief is provided for a loan from a fiduciary or other party

---

1. Labor Reg. §2550.408b-2(e)(3).
2. Labor Reg. §2550.408b-2(e)(2).
3. DOL Adv. Op. 95-26.
4. Labor Reg. §2550.408b-2(c); 77 Fed. Reg. 5632 (Feb. 3, 2012).
5. ERISA Sec. 406(b).

in interest to an employee stock ownership plan (ESOP)[1] where (1) the loan is primarily for the benefit of participants and beneficiaries of the plan and (2) the loan's interest rate is not in excess of a reasonable rate of interest.[2]

If the plan provides collateral for a loan, such collateral may only consist of qualifying employer securities.[3]

The terms of the loan must be at least as favorable to the plan as the terms of a comparable loan resulting from an arm's-length transaction between unrelated third parties.[4]

The proceeds of an exempt loan may only be issued by the plan in order to (1) acquire qualifying employer securities, (2) repay the loan, or (3) repay a prior exempt loan.[5] No securities purchased with such loan may be subject to a put, call, or other option, or a buy-sell or similar arrangement while held by, or when distributed from, the plan.

An ESOP loan must be made without recourse against the plan. No one who is entitled to payment under the loan should have any right to assets of the plan other than (1) collateral given for the loan, (2) contributions made to satisfy the ESOP's loan obligation, and (3) earnings attributable to the collateral and the investment of such contributions.[6]

Where there has been a default upon an exempt loan, the value of plan assets transferred in satisfaction of the loan must not exceed the value of the default amount.[7]

In considering what constitutes a reasonable rate of interest on an ESOP loan, all relevant factors will be considered, including the amount and duration of the loan, the security and guarantee involved, the creditworthiness of the plan and the guarantor, and the interest rate available on comparable loans.[8]

The regulations provide a complicated formula to calculate the number of securities released from encumbrance as collateral for the loan. Basically, for each plan year during the life of the loan, the number of securities released from encumbrance must equal the number of encumbered securities held immediately before release for the current plan year, when multiplied by a fraction. The numerator of that fraction is the amount of principal and interest paid for the year. The denominator is the sum of the numerator plus the principal and interest to be paid in all future years.[9]

Securities acquired with the proceeds of an ESOP loan may be subject to a right of first refusal. Securities subject to such a right of first refusal must be stock or an equity security, or a debt security convertible into stock or an equity security. In addition, securities subject to a

---

1. As defined in ERISA Section 407(d)(6).
2. ERISA Sec. 408(b)(3).
3. As defined in ERISA Section 407(d)(5).
4. Labor Reg. §2550.408b-3(c)(3).
5. Labor Reg. §2550.408b-3(d).
6. Labor Reg. §2550.408b-3(e).
7. Labor Reg. §2550.408b-3(f).
8. Labor Reg. §2550.408b-3(g).
9. Labor Reg. §2550.408b-3(h).

right of first refusal must not be publicly traded at the time when the right may be exercised. The right of first refusal must be in favor of the plan sponsor, the plan, or both.[1]

466. What is the statutory exemption regarding investments in deposits of banks?

The investment of all or part of a plan's assets in deposits that bear a reasonable interest rate in a bank or similar financial institution supervised by the United States or a State is exempted from the prohibited transaction restrictions of ERISA Section 406(a), ERISA Section 406(b)(1), and ERISA Section 406(b)(2), if that bank or institution is a plan fiduciary, and

1.   The plan covers only employees of the bank or institution; or

2.   The investment is expressly authorized by a provision of the plan or by a fiduciary (other than the bank, institution, or an affiliate thereof) who is expressly empowered by the plan to instruct the plan trustee regarding the investment.[2]

But ERISA Section 408(b)(4) does not provide an exemption from the prohibited transaction provision of ERISA Section 406(b)(3), which prohibits a fiduciary from receiving consideration for her own account from any party dealing with a plan in connection with a transaction involving plan assets. Further, the regulations provide that the fiduciary provisions of ERISA Section 404 continue to apply to the exempt transaction. In other words, the transaction must comply with the prudence and diversification requirements of ERISA.[3]

467. What is the statutory exemption regarding the purchase of insurance from an employer?

A plan is permitted to purchase any contract for life insurance, health insurance, or annuities with one or more insurers qualified to conduct business in a state, provided that

1.   The plan pays no more than adequate consideration; and

2.   Each insurer is

   a.   the plan sponsor, or

   b.   a party in interest wholly owned (either indirectly or directly) by the plan sponsor, or by any person who is a party in interest to the plan, but only if the total premiums and annuity considerations written by such insurer for all plans (and their employers) with respect to which the insurer is a party in interest do not exceed 5 percent of the total premiums and annuity considerations written for all lines of insurance in that year by the insurer.

The 5 percent limitation excludes all premiums and annuity considerations paid for a plan that the insurer maintains.[4]

---

1. Labor Reg. §2550.408b-3(i).
2. ERISA Sec. 408(b)(4).
3. Labor Reg. §2550.408b-4(a).
4. ERISA Sec. 408(b)(5).

468. What is the statutory exemption regarding the provision of ancillary bank services?

Exemptive relief is provided for any ancillary service provided to a qualified plan by a bank or similar financial institution that is supervised by the United States or a state, if the bank or institution is a plan fiduciary, and

1. The bank or financial institution has adequate internal safeguards that ensure that the ancillary service is consistent with sound banking and financial practice (as determined by a federal or state supervisory authority); and

2. Stated guidelines provided by the bank or financial institution hold that ancillary services may not be provided in an excessive or unreasonable manner, or in a fashion that is inconsistent with the best interests of participants and beneficiaries of the plans.

Under this statutory exemption, ancillary services may not be provided at more than reasonable compensation.[1]

This exemptive relief extends to services provided by the bank or financial institution that would not meet the requirements of the statutory exemption of ERISA Section 408(b)(2) (regarding the contracting by a plan for necessary services) because the provision of these ancillary services involves an act otherwise prohibited under either ERISA Section 406(b)(1) (the prohibition against fiduciaries' dealing with plan assets in their own interest), or ERISA Section 406(b)(2) (the prohibition against fiduciaries' acting in any transaction involving the plan on behalf of a party whose interests are adverse to the interests of the plan). ERISA Section 408(b)(6) provides exemptive relief from ERISA Section 406(b)(1) and ERISA Section 406(b)(2) because it contemplates the provision of such ancillary services without the approval of a second fiduciary.[2]

But ERISA Section 408(b)(6) does not provide exemptive relief from ERISA Section 406(b)(3), the prohibition against fiduciaries' receiving consideration for their own personal account from any party dealing with a plan in connection with a transaction involving assets of a qualified plan.

Practitioner's Pointer: The transfer of idle cash balances in plan accounts to short-term investment vehicles (commonly referred to as "sweep services" or "overnight sweeps") by the party in interest bank or financial institution will not be a prohibited transaction in violation of the self-dealing rules if the plan is not required to pay an additional fee for the service. If the plan is required to pay a fee for any sweep services, the DOL is likely to consider the payment of fees to be a prohibited transaction.[3]

---

1. ERISA Sec. 408(b)(6).
2. Labor Reg. §2550.408b-6(a).
3. DOL Adv. Op. 88-2A.

469. What is the statutory exemption regarding owner-employee transactions?

ERISA Section 408(d) provides that certain provisions of ERISA (enumerated below) do not apply to transactions in which a plan (either directly or indirectly) (1) lends any part of the corpus or income of the plan; (2) pays any compensation for personal services rendered to the plan; or (3) acquires for the plan any property from, or sells any property to, any person who is an owner-employee of the plan sponsor, a member of the family of any such owner-employee,[1] or a corporation controlled by an owner-employee through the direct or indirect ownership of 50 percent or more of the total combined voting power of all classes of stock entitled to vote, or 50 percent or more of the total value of shares of all classes of stock of the corporation.

The ERISA provisions that will not apply to the transactions described above are

1.   10 percent limit on the acquisition of employer securities and employer real property;[2]

2.   Statutory exemptions;[3]

3.   Statutory provision permitting parties in interest to receive benefits earned under a plan;[4] and

4.   Statutory exemption for the purchase, sale, or lease of qualifying employee securities or real property.[5]

These rules also apply to shareholder-employees of a Subchapter S corporation, an owner of an IRA, individual retirement annuity, or bond (or his beneficiary), and an employer or association of employers that establishes such an account or annuity under IRC Section 408(c).

ERISA Section 408(d), however, does not prohibit an owner-employee from receiving benefits under the plan as a participant or beneficiary. The premature distribution of assets to an owner-employee was permitted when the amount distributed was calculated according to the plan document, the same calculation method was applied to all of the other participants and beneficiaries, and the method used to calculate the benefit did not provide a greater benefit to the owner-employee than other methods of payment.[6]

The owner-employees and 50 percent shareholders who are restricted from receiving plan loans are permitted to qualify for the exemption regarding plan loans if a special exemption is approved by the DOL.[7] The DOL will consider individual exemption applications for such loans on a case-by-case basis.

---

1. Defined under ERISA Section 267(c)(4) as brothers, sisters, spouse, ancestors, and lineal descendants.
2. ERISA Sec. 407(d).
3. ERISA Sec. 408(b).
4. ERISA Sec. 408(c).
5. ERISA Sec. 408(e).
6. Priv. Ltr. Rul. 7933029.
7. Labor Reg. §2550.408b-1(a)(2).

470. What is the statutory exemption for the conversion of securities?

The exercise of a privilege to convert securities is permitted, but only if the plan receives no more than adequate consideration pursuant to such conversion.[1]

"Adequate consideration," for securities in which there is a generally recognized market, means "the price of the security prevailing on a national securities exchange." In the case of securities for which there is no recognized market, "adequate consideration" means "a price not less favorable to the plan than the offering price for the security as established by the current bid and asked prices" quoted by persons independent of the issuer and parties in interest.[2]

A plan may hold or acquire certain employer securities. Some of these securities may be convertible (for example, from bonds to stock). The statutory exemption permits these conversions if the plan receives at least fair market value under the conversion. The ERISA Conference Report provides that "it is expected that a conversion will be permitted if all the securities of the class held by the plan are subject to the same terms." These terms must be as favorable to the plan as an arm's-length transaction, so that conversions cannot be tailored to apply only to a particular plan.[3]

471. What is the statutory exemption regarding pooled investment funds?

Any transaction between a plan and either (1) a common or collective trust fund or pooled investment fund maintained by a party in interest that is a bank or trust company supervised by a state or federal agency or (2) the pooled investment fund of an insurance company qualified to do business in a state is exempt from the prohibited transaction provisions of ERISA if

1.   The transaction is a sale or purchase of an interest in the fund;

2.   The bank, trust company, or insurance company does not receive more than reasonable compensation; and

3.   Such transaction is expressly permitted by the instrument under which the plan is maintained, or by a fiduciary (other than the bank, trust company, or insurance company, or any of their affiliates) who has authority to manage and control assets of the plan.[4]

The DOL has ruled that the investment of plan assets by a trustee bank in common trust funds maintained by the bank would not violate the prohibited transaction provisions of ERISA, since the bank trustee would not be exercising any of the authority, control, or responsibility that makes it a fiduciary to cause a plan to pay an additional fee.[5]

Further, fiduciaries may not use any of the authority, control, or responsibility that makes such a person a fiduciary to cause a plan to pay additional fees to the fiduciary (or to an entity

---

1. ERISA Sec. 408(b)(7).
2. ERISA Sec. 3(18).
3. H.R. Conf. Rep. No. 93-1280, 93d Cong., 2d Sess. 323 (1974) (ERISA Conference Report).
4. ERISA Sec. 408(b)(8).
5. DOL Adv. Op. 88-11A.

in which such fiduciary has an interest that may affect the exercise of his best judgment as a fiduciary) for the provision of a service.[1]

472. What is the statutory exemption for the receipt of benefits?

Parties in interest may receive any benefit to which they may be entitled as a participant or beneficiary of the plan.[2] Further, parties in interest may receive compensation for services rendered to the plan and for the reimbursement of reasonable expenses incurred in providing services to the plan.[3]

The payment of benefits must be computed and paid on the same basis that benefits are computed and paid to the other participants and beneficiaries.

473. What is the statutory exemption regarding termination distributions?

The decision to terminate a qualified retirement plan is exempt from ERISA's fiduciary provisions.[4] As such, the prohibited transaction provisions do not apply to a fiduciary's distribution of assets during the termination of the plan, if they are distributed in accordance with the written provisions of the plan's governing documents.[5]

474. What is the statutory exemption for the merger of multiemployer plans?

A merger of multiemployer plans, or the transfer of assets or liabilities between multiemployer plans, will be exempt from the prohibited transaction provisions of ERISA if the same requirements that must be satisfied in order for the Pension Benefits Guaranty Corporation (PBGC) to approve a merger of multiemployer plans[6] are satisfied.[7]

This statutory exemption does not provide relief from ERISA Section 406(b)(1), which prohibits a fiduciary from dealing with the plan assets in her own interest, or from ERISA Section 406(b)(3), which prohibits a fiduciary from receiving any consideration for her own account from any party dealing with such plan in connection with a transaction involving plan assets.

475. What is the statutory exemption for the provision of an eligible investment advice arrangement?

The Pension Protection Act of 2006[8] provided guidance on the extent to which plan sponsors and fiduciaries can arrange for the provision of investment advice directly to participants without assuming fiduciary liability. Effective January 1, 2007, Section 601 of PPA 2006 adds new ERISA Section 408(b)(14), which holds that any transaction in connection with the provision of investment advice described under ERISA Section 3(21)(A) to a participant or beneficiary of an

---

1. Labor Reg. §2550.408b-2(e)(2).
2. IRC Secs. 4975(d)(9), 4975(d)(10).
3. DOL Adv. Op. 89-9A.
4. ERISA Sec. 408(b)(10).
5. *District 65, UAW v. Harper & Row, Inc.*, 576 F. Supp. 1468 (S.D.N.Y. 1983).
6. See ERISA Section 4231.
7. ERISA Sec. 408(b)(11).
8. PPA 2006; Pub. L. No. 109-280 (Aug. 17, 2006).

individual account plan that permits such participant or beneficiary to direct the investment of assets in his individual accounts is exempt from the prohibited transaction provisions of ERISA if the transaction is:

1.   The provision of investment advice to the participant or beneficiary of the plan with respect to a security or other property available as an investment under the plan;

2.   The acquisition, holding, or sale of a security or other property available as an investment under the plan pursuant to investment advice; or

3.   The direct or indirect receipt of fees or other compensation by the fiduciary adviser or an affiliate thereof in connection with the provision of the advice or in connection with the acquisition, holding, or sale of a security or other property available as an investment under the plan pursuant to investment advice; and if

4.   The requirements of ERISA Section 408(g) are all satisfied.

On January 21, 2009, the DOL issued final regulations (subsequently withdrawn) containing guidance under ERISA Section 408(g) for the provision of investment advice under 401(k) plans and IRAs.[1] The DOL then announced the withdrawal of the final regulations.[2] The DOL indicated that public comments had raised sufficient doubts as to whether the conditions of the PTE could adequately protect the interests of plan participants and beneficiaries from potential conflicts of interest that could arise for investment advisers. The DOL reissued the final rule on October 25, 2011, with changes designed to mitigate fiduciary advisers' conflicts. The new final regulations became applicable as of December 27, 2011.[3]

Under the exemption, such advice must be issued by a "fiduciary adviser" (see subsequent information) under an "eligible investment advice arrangement" (see subsequent information).[4]

A plan sponsor or other person who is a fiduciary (other than a "fiduciary adviser") is exempt from the prohibited transaction provisions of ERISA for the provision of covered investment advice if:[5]

1.   The advice is provided by a fiduciary adviser pursuant to an "eligible investment advice arrangement" between the plan sponsor or other fiduciary and the fiduciary adviser for the provision by the fiduciary adviser of investment advice;

2.   The terms of the eligible investment advice arrangement require compliance by the fiduciary adviser with the requirements of ERISA Section 408(g); and

3.   The terms of the eligible investment advice arrangement include a written acknowledgment by the fiduciary adviser that the fiduciary adviser is a fiduciary of the plan with respect to the rendering of investment advice.[6]

---

1. Labor Reg. §2550.408g-1, 74 Fed. Reg. 3822 (Jan. 21, 2009).
2. 74 Fed. Reg. 60,156 (Nov. 20, 2009); 74 Fed. Reg. 59,092 (Nov. 17, 2009).
3. 76 Fed. Reg. 66,136 (Oct. 25, 2011).
4. ERISA Sec. 408(g)(1).
5. ERISA Sec. 3(21)(a).
6. ERISA Sec. 408(g)(10)(A).

A plan sponsor is not subject to fiduciary liability solely because of investment advice provided by a fiduciary adviser as long as the fiduciary adviser satisfies the requirements for the exemption. However, the employer *is* responsible for the prudent selection and periodic review of a fiduciary adviser.[1]

A "fiduciary adviser" is defined as a person who, with respect to a plan, is a fiduciary by reason of the provision of investment advice[2] and who is one of the following:

1. Registered as an investment adviser under the Investment Advisers Act of 1940, or under the state laws of the state in which the fiduciary maintains its principal office and place of business;

2. A bank, or similar financial institution, but only if the advice is provided through a trust department of the bank or similar financial institution or savings association that is subject to periodic examination and review by federal or state banking authorities;

3. An insurance company qualified to do business under state law;

4. A person registered as a broker or dealer under the Securities Exchange Act of 1934;

5. An affiliate of (one) through (four); or

6. An employee, agent, or registered representative of any of the preceding who satisfies the requirements of applicable insurance, banking, and securities laws relating to the provision of advice.[3]

The fiduciary adviser must provide the authorizing fiduciary with written notification that the adviser intends to comply with the exemption and that the annual audit report (see subsequent details) will be provided to the authorizing fiduciary within sixty days of its completion.[4]

An "eligible investment advice arrangement" is an arrangement that either uses a fee-leveling arrangement that does not vary the fee to the fiduciary adviser regardless of the investments selected by the participants, or utilizes a computer model that does not inappropriately favor investment options offered by the fiduciary adviser or generate greater income for the fiduciary adviser.[5] These restrictions also apply to any person with a material affiliation or contractual relationship with the fiduciary adviser.[6] The fee-leveling arrangement rules and the computer model arrangement rules are designed to establish additional safeguards against conflicts of interest and undue influence with the fiduciary adviser.[7]

---

1. ERISA Sec. 408(g)(10)(B).
2. As defined under ERISA Sec. 3(21)(A).
3. ERISA Sec. 408(g)(11)(A).
4. Labor Reg. §2550.408g-1(b)(8).
5. Labor Reg. §§2550.408g-1(b)(3)(i)(A)-(C) and 2550.408g-1(b)(4)(i)(A)-(F)(1) and (2).
6. Labor Reg. §§2550.408g-1(b)(3)(i)(D) and 2550.408g-1(b)(4)(i)(F)(1) and (2).
7. Preamble to Eligible Investment Advice regulations, 76 Fed. Reg. 66,136 (Oct. 25, 2011).

An eligible investment advice arrangement must be expressly authorized by a plan fiduciary *other than*:

1. The person offering the investment advice program;

2. Any person providing investment options under the plan; or

3. Any affiliate of a person described above.[1]

The only advice that may be provided under the exemption where the computer model is utilized is the advice generated by the computer model.[2] The computer model requirements are mirrored below in the certification requirements. In order to satisfy the certification requirement for the use of a computer model, an eligible investment expert must certify in writing, prior to the utilization of the computer model, that the computer model meets each of the following requirements:

1. Applies generally accepted investment theories that take into account the historic returns of different asset classes over defined periods of time;

2. Takes into account investment management and other fees and expenses attendant to the recommended investments;

3. Uses relevant information about the participant, which may include age, life expectancy, retirement age, risk tolerance, other assets or sources of income, and preferences as to certain types of investments;

4. Uses prescribed objective criteria to provide asset allocation portfolios comprising investment options under the plan;

5. Operates in a manner that is not biased in favor of the investments offered by the fiduciary adviser or a person with a material affiliation or contractual relationship with the fiduciary adviser;

6. Does not inappropriately favor fee investment options that may generate greater income for the fiduciary adviser or a person with a material affiliation or material contractual relationship with the fiduciary adviser; and

7. Takes into account all the investment options under the plan in specifying how a participant's account should be invested without inappropriate weighting of any investment option.[3]

The level-fee limitation applies to both the entity retained to provide the investment advice and to its employees, agents, or representatives. This prohibits the affiliate of a fiduciary adviser from sending financial incentives back to the fiduciary adviser or to any employees of that adviser.[4]

---

1. ERISA Sec. 408(g)(4).
2. ERISA Sec. 408(g)(3)(D)(i).
3. ERISA Secs. 408(g)(3)(A), 408(g)(3)(B), 408(g)(3)(C); Labor Reg. §2550.408g-1(b)(3)(i)(A)-(D); Labor Reg. §2550.408g-1(b)(4)(i)(E) and (F)(1) and (2).
4. Field Assistance Bull. 2007-1.

A person who develops the computer model used in the provision of the advice, or who markets the investment advice program or computer model, is also treated as both a fiduciary of the plan by reason of the provision of investment advice and as a fiduciary adviser.[1] Where the computer model has been subject to material modifications, it must be recertified. The term "eligible investment expert" means a person who, through employees or otherwise, has the appropriate technical training or experience and proficiency to analyze, determine, and certify whether a computer model meets the requirements of the eligible investment advice arrangement regulations. The term does not include any person who has any material affiliation or contractual relationship with the fiduciary adviser or with a person who has such a relationship with the fiduciary adviser, is an employee, agent, or registered representative of the foregoing, or develops the computer model to be utilized by the fiduciary adviser.[2] The eligible investment expert may not have any material affiliation or contractual relationship with any investment adviser or a related person thereof.[3]

Audit Requirements

An independent auditor (who must state in writing that he has appropriate technical training or experience and proficiency) must:

1.   Conduct an annual audit of the investment advice arrangement for compliance with the applicable requirements; and

2.   Within sixty days following completion of the audit, issue a written report to the fiduciary adviser and to each fiduciary who authorized the use of the investment advice arrangement setting forth the specific findings of the auditor regarding compliance with the requirements of ERISA Section 408(g).

If the report of the auditor identifies noncompliance, the fiduciary adviser shall, within thirty days of receipt of the report from the auditor, send a copy of the report to the DOL Office of Investment Advice Exemption Notification—Statutory, Room N-1513, 200 Constitution Avenue, NW, Washington, DC 20210.

The "independence" of an auditor is established where he is not related to either: (1) the person offering the investment advice arrangement to the plan, or (2) any person providing investment options under the plan.[4]

The auditor must not have had any role in the development of the investment advice arrangement or certification of the computer model used by the fiduciary adviser.[5] The audit disclosure regulations also provide detailed guidance on what the annual audit report must contain.

---

1. ERISA Sec. 408(g)(11)(A); Labor Reg. §2550.408g-1(b)(4).
2. Labor Reg. §2550.408g-1(b)(4)(iii).
3. ERISA Secs. 408(g)(3)(C)(i), 408(g)(3)(C)(ii), 408(g)(3)(C)(iii).
4. ERISA Secs. 408(g)(5)(A), 408(g)(5)(B).
5. Labor Reg. §2550.408g-1(b)(6).

Disclosure Requirements

An eligible investment advice arrangement must satisfy the following disclosure requirements:

1. The fiduciary adviser must provide without charge to a participant or a beneficiary *before the initial* provision of the investment advice concerning any security or other property offered as an investment option, a written notification (which may be through electronic communication):

    a. of the role of any party that has a material affiliation or contractual relationship with the financial adviser in (i) the development of the investment advice program, and (ii) the selection of investment options available under the plan;

    b. of the past performance and historical rates of return of the investment options available under the plan;

    c. of all fees or other compensation relating to the advice that the fiduciary adviser (or any affiliate) is to receive (including compensation provided by any third party) in connection with either (i) the provision of the advice, or (ii) the sale, acquisition, or holding of the security or other property;

    d. of any material affiliation or contractual relationship of the fiduciary adviser (or affiliates) in the security or other property;

    e. of the manner, and under what circumstances, any participant or beneficiary information provided under the arrangement will be used or disclosed;

    f. of the types of services provided by the fiduciary adviser in connection with the provision of investment advice by the fiduciary adviser, including, with respect to the computer model arrangement, any limitations on the ability of the computer model to take into account an investment primarily in qualifying employer securities;

    g. That the adviser is acting as a plan fiduciary in connection with the provision of the advice; and

    h. That a recipient of the advice may separately arrange for the provision of advice by another adviser that could have no material affiliation with, and receive no fees or other compensation in connection with, the security or other property.[1]

---

1. Labor Reg. §2550.408g-1(a)(7).

2. At all times while providing advisory services to the participant or beneficiary, the fiduciary adviser must:

   a. maintain the information described in item a, above, in accurate form, and in accordance with the required standards for presenting information (described next);

   b. provide, without charge, accurate information to the recipient of the advice, no less frequently than annually;

   c. provide, without charge, accurate information to the recipient of the advice, upon request of the recipient; and

   d. provide, without charge, accurate information to the recipient of the advice concerning any material change to the information required to be provided to that recipient, at a time reasonably contemporaneous to the change in information.[1]

Written Notice Requirements

Written notification that must be provided to participants and beneficiaries under the disclosure requirements must be written in a manner that is:

1. Clear and conspicuous;

2. Calculated to be understood by the average plan participant; and

3. Sufficiently accurate and comprehensive to reasonably apprise participants and beneficiaries of the information required to be provided in the notification.[2]

The DOL will be issuing a model notice for the disclosure of fees and compensation.[3]

Miscellaneous Requirements

The following requirements must also be satisfied:

1. The fiduciary adviser must provide appropriate disclosure in connection with the sale, acquisition, or holding of the security or other property in accordance with all applicable securities laws;

2. The sale, acquisition, or holding must occur solely at the direction of the recipient of the advice;

---

1. ERISA Secs. 408(g)(6)(A), 408(g)(6)(B); Labor Reg. §2550.408g-1(b)(7)(i).
2. ERISA Sec. 408(g)(8)(A); Labor Reg. §2550.408g-1(b)(7)(ii)(A).
3. ERISA Sec. 408(g)(8)(B); Labor Reg. §2550.408g-1(b)(7)(ii)(B).

3.   The compensation received by the fiduciary adviser (and affiliates) in connection with the sale, acquisition, or holding of the security or other property must be reasonable; and

4.   The terms of the sale, acquisition, or holding of the security or other property must be at least as favorable to the plan as an arm's-length transaction would be.[1]

Required Six-Year Compliance Period

Any fiduciary adviser who has provided advice under an eligible investment advice arrangement with respect to eligible exempt transactions must maintain for a period of not less than six years after the provision of the advice *any records necessary* for determining whether all of the requirements for the investment advice prohibited transaction exemption have been met. A prohibited transaction will *not* be considered to have occurred solely because the records are lost or destroyed before the end of the six-year period due to circumstances beyond the fiduciary adviser's control.[2]

476. What is the statutory exemption for securities cross-trading?

The Pension Protection Act of 2006 (PPA 2006) added ERISA Section 408(b)(19), which is the statutory exemption providing for securities cross-trades involving the purchase and sale of a security between a plan and any other account managed by the same investment manager.[3]

In order for the exemption to apply relief to cross-trades between a plan and a party in interest, or between a plan and a fiduciary;

1.   The transaction must be a purchase or sale, for no consideration other than cash payment against prompt delivery of a security for which market quotations are readily available;

2.   The transaction is effected at independent current market price of a security;[4]

3.   No brokerage commission, fee (except for customary transfer fees, the fact of which is disclosed as required subsequently), or other remuneration is paid in connection with the transaction;

4.   A fiduciary (other than the investment manager engaging in the cross-trades of any affiliate) for each plan participating in the transaction authorizes in advance of any cross-trade (in a document that is separate from any other written agreement of the parties) that the investment manager may engage in cross-trades at the investment manager's discretion, after such fiduciary has received disclosure regarding the conditions under which cross-trades may take place (but only if such disclosure is

---

1. ERISA Secs. 408(g)(7)(A), 408(g)(7)(B), 408(g)(7)(C), 408(g)(7)(D).
2. ERISA Sec. 408(g)(9); Labor Reg. §2550.408g-1(d) and (e).
3. PPA 2006 Sec. 611.
4. Within the meaning of 17 C.F.R. §270.17a-7(b).

separate from any other agreement or disclosure involving the asset management relationship), including the written policies and procedures of the investment manager (see next);

5. Each plan participating in the transaction has assets of at least $100,000,000, except that if the assets of a plan are invested in a master trust containing the assets of plans maintained by employers in the same controlled group,[1] the master trust has assets of at least $100,000,000;

6. The investment manager provides for the plan fiduciary who authorized cross-trading under item four (preceding) a quarterly report detailing all cross-trades executed by the investment manager in which the investment manager participated during such quarter, including the following information, as applicable;

    a. identity of each security bought or sold;

    b. number of shares or units traded;

    c. parties involved in the cross-trades; and

    d. trade price and the method used to establish the trade price;

7. The investment manager does not base its fee schedule on the plan's consent to cross-trading, and no other service (other than investment opportunities and cost savings available through a cross-trade) is conditioned on the plan's consent to cross-trading;

8. The investment manager has adopted, and cross-trades are effected in accordance with, written cross-trading policies and procedures that are fair and equitable to all accounts participating in the cross-trading program, and that includes a description of the manager's pricing policies and procedures, and the manager's policies and procedures for allocating cross-trades in an objective manner among accounts participating in the cross-trading program; and

9. The investment manager has designated an individual responsible for periodically reviewing such purchases and sales to ensure compliance with the written policies and procedures described above in item eight, and following such review, the individual shall issue an annual written report no later than ninety days following the period in which it relates, signed under penalty of perjury, to the plan fiduciary who authorized cross-trading under item four above, describing the steps performed during the course of the review, the level of compliance, and any specific instances of noncompliance. This written report shall also notify the plan fiduciary of the plan's right to terminate participation in the investment manager's cross-trading program at any time.

---

1. As defined under ERISA Section 407(d)(7).

Content of Written Cross-Trading Policies and Procedures

The mandatory policies and procedures to be implemented in order to maintain compliance with the exemption will have to include the following items:

1. A statement of policy that describes the criteria that will be applied by the investment manager in determining that execution of a securities transaction as a cross-trade will be beneficial to both parties of the transaction;

2. A description of how the investment manager will determine that cross-trades are effected at the "current market price" of the security,[1] including the identity of sources used to establish such price;

3. A description of the procedures for ensuring compliance with the $100,000,000 minimum asset size requirement. A plan or master trust will satisfy the minimum asset size requirement as to a transaction if it satisfies the requirement upon its initial participation in the cross-trading program and later on an annual basis;

4. A statement that any investment manager participating in a cross-trading program will have conflicting loyalties and responsibilities to the parties involved in any cross-trade transaction, and a description of how the investment manager will mitigate such conflicts;

5. A requirement that the investment manager allocate cross-trades among accounts in an objective and equitable manner, and a description of the allocation methods available to, and utilized by, the investment manager for ensuring an objective allocation among accounts participating in the cross-trading program; and if more than one allocation methodology may be used by the investment manager, a description of what circumstances will dictate the use of a particular methodology;

6. Identification of the compliance officer responsible for periodically reviewing the investment manager's compliance with ERISA, and a statement of the compliance officer's qualifications for this position;

7. A statement that the cross-trading statutory exemption requires satisfaction of several objective conditions in addition to the requirements that the investment manager adopt and effect cross-trades in accordance with written cross-trading policies and procedures; and

8. A statement that specifically describes the scope of the annual review conducted by the compliance officer.[2]

---

1. Within the meaning of 17 C.F.R. §270.17a-17(b) and SEC no-action and interpretive letters thereunder.
2. Labor Reg. §2550.408b-19(b)(3)(i)(A) to (H).

Individual Exemptions

477. What is an "individual prohibited transaction exemption," and how is such an exemption granted?

An individual prohibited transaction exemption is an administrative exemption, granted under ERISA Section 408(a) and IRC Section 4975(c)(2). An individual prohibited transaction exemption applies only to specific parties in interest, named or otherwise defined in the exemption.[1]

Under ERISA Section 408, the Department of Labor (DOL) is authorized to issue exemptions to the prohibited transaction rules under both ERISA and the Internal Revenue Code. Since 1978, the DOL has been the sole entity granting exemptions.[2] Prior to 1978, the IRS would issue exemptions from the prohibited transaction provisions of the IRC, and the DOL would issue exemptions from the prohibited transaction provisions of ERISA. As it stands today, any exemption application received by the DOL expressly seeking an exemption under the IRC or ERISA will be treated as an application filed under both laws if it relates to any transaction prohibited under both the IRC and ERISA.[3]

The DOL will review each application on its own merits. Even if an application satisfies all of the requirements as to content (which are detailed under the applicable regulation), there is no guarantee that the DOL will grant the relief requested. All exemptions granted by the DOL must be: (1) administratively feasible; (2) in the best interests of the plan and its participants and beneficiaries; and (3) protective of the rights of participants and beneficiaries of the plan.[4]

Some examples of individual prohibited transaction exemptions that the DOL has granted include

- Extension of credit between the plan and parties in interest;

- Sale, transfer, and use of plan assets by parties in interest;

- Payment of commissions to parties in interest;

- Leases between a plan and parties in interest;

- Loans between a plan and parties in interest;

- Provision of services between a plan and parties in interest;

- Transactions involving collective investment funds;

- Transactions between investment managers and parties in interest;

---

1. Labor Reg. §2570.31(e).
2. Reorganization Plan No. 4 of 1978, 1979-1 C.B. 480.
3. Labor Reg. §2570.30(b).
4. ERISA Sec. 408(a).

- Sale of leases, letters of credit, loans, and memberships in clubs; and

- Transactions between Keogh plans and IRAs.

478. How does one apply for an individual prohibited transaction exemption?

The DOL has issued final regulations that describe the procedures for the filing and processing of applications for individual prohibited transaction exemptions under ERISA and the Internal Revenue Code. These regulations detail the procedural and content requirements for filing an application for an individual prohibited transaction exemption.[1]

The DOL may initiate exemption proceedings on its own, usually where there is a need for a class exemption that has been recognized by the DOL as applicable on an industry wide basis.[2]

The DOL will not issue exemptions that have been requested orally. Although an applicant for an individual exemption may request and receive oral advice from DOL representatives in preparing an exemption application, the DOL has indicated that such advice does not constitute a part of the administrative record of the application and is not binding upon the DOL in processing an individual exemption application procedure.

The following questions explain the procedures for seeking an individual exemption application, including

- Where to file an individual exemption application (see Q 484);

- Who may apply for an individual exemption (see Q 479);

- What information an exemption application must contain (see Q 481 and Q 482);

- Which individual exemption applications the DOL will not consider (see Q 480);

- What to do if the applicant wishes to withdraw an individual exemption application (see Q 492);

- What the applicant's rights are should the DOL notify the applicant that the DOL intends to reject the individual exemption application (see Q 486 and Q 487);

- What the limits and effect of an individual exemption are once the exemption has been granted (see Q 496); and

- Whether the DOL may revoke or modify an individual exemption once it has been granted (see Q 497).

1. See Labor Reg. §§2570.1 et seq.
2. Labor Reg. §2570.32(a).

479. Who may apply for an individual exemption?

Regulations detail persons who may apply for individual exemptions.[1] In addition to the DOL's initiating exemption procedures on its own, the DOL will initiate exemption proceedings upon the receipt of an application from the following entities:

1. Any party in interest who is or may be a party to the transaction upon which the individual exemption is sought;

2. Any plan that is a party to the transaction for which the individual exemption is being sought; and

3. Regarding an application for an exemption that will affect a class of parties in interest or a class of transactions (in addition to those persons described in items one and two above), an association or organization representing parties in interest who may be parties to the transaction for which the individual exemption is being sought.[2]

If an application is being submitted on behalf of any of the above parties by an authorized representative of the applicant, the representative must submit proof of her authority in an executed Power of Attorney or a written certification from the applicant.[3] If the authorized representative submits the individual exemption application with proof of her authority to represent the applicant before the DOL, the DOL will direct all correspondence and inquiries regarding the application to the authorized representative, unless requested to do otherwise by the applicant.[4]

480. What type of individual exemption applications will the Department of Labor ordinarily not consider?

The DOL will ordinarily not consider any individual prohibited transaction application that does not include all of the required information contained under the application procedures (see Q 481 and Q 482).[5] The DOL will also not consider any application that does not conform to the requirements of the individual exemption application procedures.

The DOL will not consider for approval any application for an individual exemption that involves transactions that the DOL is currently investigating for possible violations of ERISA. The DOL will also not consider any application that involves any party in interest who is the subject of a DOL investigation, or is a defendant in any court action, whether brought by the DOL or the IRS, to enforce Parts 1 or 4 of Subtitle B of ERISA, Sections 8477 and 8478 of the Federal Employees' Retirement System Act of 1986, or the Internal Revenue Code.[6]

If the administrative record supporting an application designates as confidential any information required by the regulations or requested by the DOL, the DOL will determine

---

1. Labor Reg. §2570.32.
2. Labor Reg. §2570.32(a).
3. Labor Reg. §2570.32(b).
4. Labor Reg. §2570.32(c).
5. Labor Reg. §2570.33.
6. Labor Reg. §2570.33(a).

whether the information is material to the exemption determination. If the DOL rules that the information is material, the DOL will not process the application unless the applicant withdraws the claim of confidentiality.[1]

If the DOL is considering a class exemption relating to the type of transaction in which the DOL has received an individual exemption application, the DOL will ordinarily not consider the individual application on a separate basis.[2]

If the DOL determines that it will not consider an individual exemption application, the DOL will inform the applicant of that decision in writing, including the reasons for which it has declined to consider the application.[3]

Applications for Exemptions

481. What information must be contained in every exemption application?

In the summary of the final regulations for prohibited transaction exemption procedures, the DOL notes that the efficiency of the exemption application program could be greatly improved "if the quality of exemption applications filed were improved." The DOL further states that, "[i]n the past, applications have been incomplete, have omitted or misstated facts or legal analysis needed to justify requests for exemptive relief, and, in some cases, have been so poorly drafted that the details of the transactions for which exemptive relief is sought are unclear."[4] In an effort to improve the quality of the applications received, the regulations require that an application for exemption contain more detailed information, and that certain documents be included when such application is filed with the DOL.

Regulations detail the information that must be included in every exemption (class and individual) application submitted to the DOL.[5] For a detailed review of the additional information that must accompany individual exemption applications, see Q 482. *Every* exemption application must contain the following information:

1. Names of all applicants;

2. A detailed description of the proposed transaction for which exemptive relief is sought and the parties in interest for whom the exemption is being requested, including a description of any larger integrated transactions, of which the transaction at issue may be a part;

3. Whether there will be a dual representation of the plan and any of the parties in interest by the same person in regard to the exemption application;

4. The plan's reasons for entering into the proposed exempted transaction;

---

1. Labor Reg. §2570.33(c).
2. Labor Reg. §2570.33(d).
3. Labor Reg. §2570.33(b).
4. Prohibited Transaction Exemption Procedures; Employee Benefit Plans, 55 Fed. Reg. 32,836 (Aug. 10, 1990).
5. Labor Reg. §2570.34.

5. The provisions of ERISA that would otherwise prohibit the proposed transaction and the reason why the proposed transaction would violate each such provision;

6. Whether the proposed transaction is a type that is customary for the industry or class involved;

7. Statement detailing whether the proposed transaction is or has been the subject of an investigation or enforcement action by the DOL or the IRS; and

8. The hardship or economic loss that a denial of the application would cause to (a) the person(s) filing the exemption application, (b) the plan(s), and (c) participants and beneficiaries.[1]

In addition, all exemption applications must contain

1. A statement explaining that the requested exemption would be

   a. administratively feasible,

   b. in the interests of the plan(s), participants, and beneficiaries, and

   c. protective of the rights of plan participants and beneficiaries; and

2. A required notification (see Q 490) that must contain:

   a. a detailed description of those interested individuals to whom the applicant will provide notice of the application,

   b. the manner in which the notice will be provided, and

   c. an estimate of the length of time that the applicant must provide the notice to all interested parties following publication of a notice of the proposed exemption in the Federal Register.[2]

If an advisory opinion has been requested regarding any issue related to the exemption application, the application must contain (1) a copy of the response from the DOL that states its action on the advisory opinion request; *or* (2) if the DOL has not concluded its action on the request, both (a) a copy of the request (or the date on which it was submitted, along with the DOL's correspondence control number assigned in its acknowledgment letter), *and* (b) an explanation of what effect the granting of a favorable advisory opinion would have upon the proposed exemption transaction.[3]

If the application is to be signed by anyone other than those parties in interest for whom the exemption is sought, a statement must be provided that identifies the individual who will be signing the application and that individual's relationship to the applicant(s). The statement

---

1. Labor Reg. §2570.34(a).
2. Labor Reg. §2570.34(b).
3. Labor Reg. §2570.34(b).

will also need to contain a brief explanation of the signing party's familiarity with the matters discussed in the application.[1]

An exemption application may, but is not required to, include a draft of the requested exemption defining the proposed transaction for which relief is sought and the parties in interest to the proposed transaction along with an explanation of those specific conditions under which the exemption would apply.[2]

Finally, all exemption applications must contain the following declaration, which must be made under penalty of perjury:

"I declare that I am familiar with the matters discussed in this application, and, to the best of my knowledge and belief, the representations made in this application are true and correct."

This declaration must be signed and dated by

1. The individual party in interest seeking the exemption;

2. A corporate officer (if the applicant is a corporation);

3. A partner (if the applicant is a partnership); or

4. A plan fiduciary who will have authority and control regarding the exempted transaction (if the applicant seeking exemptive relief is a plan).[3]

Specialized statements from third-party experts submitted in support of an exemption application must also contain a statement of consent from the expert, acknowledging that the statement is being submitted to the DOL as part of an exemption application. The specialized statements may include, but are not limited to, appraisals or analyses of market conditions that support the proposed transaction.[4]

Where an exemption application requires an independent fiduciary to represent the plan with respect to the proposed transaction, that independent fiduciary must file a declaration, made under penalty of perjury, that to the best of his knowledge and belief, the representations made in the statement are true and correct.[5]

482. What information is required to be included in an individual exemption application?

In addition to the material required for *all* exemption applications (see Q 481), individual exemption applications are required to include the following information:

---

1. Labor Reg. §2570.34(b)(4).
2. Labor Reg. §2570.34(c).
3. Labor Reg. §2570.34(b)(5).
4. Labor Reg. §2570.34(b)(5)(iii).
5. Labor Reg. §2570.34(b)(5)(iv).

1. Name, address, telephone number, and type(s) of plan to which the requested exemption will apply;

2. Plan number and the employer identification number (EIN) used by the plan(s) on all reporting and disclosure requirements filed with the DOL;

3. Whether any plan or trust involved in the requested exemption has ever been found by the DOL, the IRS, or a court to have violated the exclusive benefit rule (of IRC Section 401(a)), or to have engaged in a prohibited transaction (under ERISA Section 406, ERISA Section 407(a), or IRC Section 503(b));

4. Whether any statutory relief under ERISA Section 408 or IRC Section 4975(c)(2) has been provided to, or requested by, the applicant or any of the parties for whom the exemption is being sought, and, if so, the exemption application number or the prohibited transaction exemption number;

5. Whether the applicant or any party in interest involved in the proposed transaction has been (or is currently) a defendant in any lawsuit or criminal action regarding his conduct as a fiduciary or party in interest with respect to any plan within the last five years;

6. Whether the applicant or any party in interest with respect to the proposed transaction has been convicted of any crime prohibited under ERISA Section 411 (prohibition against certain persons' holding fiduciary positions) within the last thirteen years;

7. Whether, within the last five years, any of the affected plans or any party in interest has been under investigation or examination by, or has been involved in litigation or a continuing controversy with, the DOL, the IRS, the PBGC, or the Federal Retirement Thrift Investment Board involving compliance with any of the provisions of ERISA, the employee benefit provisions of the Internal Revenue Code, or the provisions of the Federal Employees' Retirement System Act of 1986 (FERSA) relating to the Federal Thrift Savings Fund (if so, the affected parties must submit copies of all correspondence with the DOL, the IRS, the PBGC, the Justice Department, or the Federal Retirement Thrift Investment Board relating to the substantive issues involved in the investigation, examination, litigation, or controversy);

8. Whether any of the plans affected by the exemption application have experienced a reportable event under ERISA Section 4043 (plan mergers, consolidation, partial termination, termination, failure to meet minimum funding standards, etc.);

9. Whether a Notice of Intent to Terminate has been filed under ERISA Section 4041 relating to any of the plans affected by the proposed exemption;

10. Name, address, and taxpayer identification number of each party in interest with respect to the proposed transaction;

11. An estimate of the number of participants and beneficiaries in each plan affected by the proposed transaction (as of the date of the application);

12. What percentage of the assets of each affected plan, by fair market value, will be involved in the proposed transaction;

13. Whether the proposed transaction has been consummated or will be consummated only if the exemption is granted;

14. If the transaction has already been consummated, the circumstances under which fiduciaries caused the transaction to be consummated prior to seeking an exemption from the DOL, whether the transaction has been terminated, whether the transaction has been corrected,[1] whether Form 5330, *Return of Excise Taxes Related to Employee Benefit Plans*, has been filed with the IRS, in relation to the transaction, and whether all excise taxes due with respect to the transaction have been paid to the IRS;[2]

15. Identity of every person with investment discretion over any of the assets involved in the proposed transaction and their relationship to the parties in interest and their affiliates with respect to the proposed transaction;

16. If the assets of the plan are invested in (a) loans to any party in interest with respect to the transaction, (b) property that is leased to a party in interest, or (c) any securities issued by a party in interest, a statement with respect to each of these three types of investments that details

   a. to which of the three investment types the investment pertains,

   b. the fair market value of all of the plan investments of this type (as of the most recent plan valuation),

   c. the overall percentage of plan assets represented by this type of investment (as of the most recent plan valuation), and

   d. any applicable statutory or administrative exemption that covers the investments;

17. Aggregate fair market value of the assets of all of the plans involved in the proposed transaction;

18. Individuals responsible for the costs of the exemption application and the notification of interested persons; and

19. Identity of the independent fiduciaries involved in the transaction, if any, and the identity of those individuals bearing the responsibility for any fee payable to the independent fiduciary.[3]

All applications for individual exemptions must also include true copies of all contracts, deeds, agreements, and instruments, as well as relevant portions of each plan's governing documents, trust agreements, and any other documents that relate to the proposed transaction.

---

1. IRC Sec. 4975(f)(5).
2. IRC Secs. 4975(a), 4975(b).
3. Labor Reg. §2570.35(a).

Along with the relevant documents, there must also be an explanation of the relevant facts in these documents that have a bearing on the transaction, as well as an analysis of their relevance to the transaction.[1]

All applications must also be accompanied by a copy of the most recent financial statements of all plans affected by the requested exemption.[2]

483. What are the special rules for applications for individual exemptions involving pooled funds?

Individual prohibited transaction exemption applications involving pooled funds have specific requirements as to the information that they must contain.[3] Much of the information required for other individual exemption applications must also be provided in applications submitted by pooled funds. In addition, individual exemption applications submitted by pooled funds must contain an estimate of the number of plans that are participating (or will participate) in the pooled fund and the minimum and maximum limits imposed on participating plans regarding the total assets of each plan that may be invested in the pooled fund.

As noted above, the following information must be furnished with reference to the pooled funds seeking the individual exemption:

1. Name, address, and telephone number of the pooled fund(s) to which the requested exemption applies;

2. Employer identification number (EIN) used by such pooled fund(s);

3. Whether the DOL, the IRS, or a court has ever found any pooled fund affected by the requested exemption to have violated the exclusive benefit rule of IRC Section 401, or to have engaged in a prohibited transaction in violation of ERISA Section 406, ERISA Section 407(a), or IRC Section 503(b);

4. Whether relief under ERISA Section 408(a) or IRC Section 4975(c)(2) has been requested by, or provided to, the applicant or any of the parties on behalf of whom the application is sought, and, if so, the prohibited transaction exemption number or the exemption application number;

5. Whether presently, or in the past five years from the date of the application, the applicant or a party in interest with respect to the proposed exemption has been a defendant in any lawsuit or criminal action concerning her conduct as a fiduciary or party in interest with respect to plan assets invested in the pooled fund;

6. Whether the applicant or a party in interest with respect to the transaction has been convicted, within the last thirteen years from the date of the application, of any crime described in ERISA Section 441 (prohibition against certain persons' holding fiduciary positions);

---

1. Labor Reg. §2570.35(b).
2. Labor Reg. §2570.35(b)(3).
3. Labor Reg. §2570.35(c).

7. Whether, in the last five years from the date of the application, any plan affected by the transaction or any party in interest involved in the transaction has been under investigation or engaged in litigation or a continuing controversy with the DOL, the IRS, the PBGC, the Department of Justice, or the Federal Retirement Thrift Investment Board involving issues that relate to compliance with the provisions of Part 1 or 4 of Subtitle B of Title I of ERISA, IRC Section 4975, or Federal Employees' Retirement System Act (FERSA) Section 8477 or 8478 (excluding routine audits under FERSA Section 8477(g));

8. Whether the transaction has been consummated or will be consummated only if the exemption is granted;

9. If the transaction has been consummated:

   a. the circumstances that resulted in the pooled fund's engaging in the transaction before an exemption has been granted,

   b. whether the transaction has been terminated,

   c. whether the transaction has been corrected in accordance with IRC Section 4975(f)(5),

   d. whether Form 5330, *Return of Excise Taxes Related to Employee Benefit Plans*, has been filed with the IRS with respect to plans involved in the transaction, and

   e. whether any excise taxes, due by reason of the transaction under IRC Section 4975(a) and IRC Section 4975(b), have been paid;

10. Name of every person who has investment discretion over any assets involved in the transaction and the relationship of each of these people to the parties in interest involved in the transaction and their affiliates;

11. Whether assets of the affected plan are invested in loans to any party in interest, in property leased to any such party in interest, or in securities issued by any such party in interest involved in the transaction, and, if such investments exist, a statement with respect to each of these three types of investments that details

    a. type of investment to which the statement pertains,

    b. aggregate fair market value of all investments of this type,

    c. approximate percentage of the fair market value of the funds' total assets represented by all investments of this type, and

    d. statutory or administrative exemption covering plan assets involved in these investments, if any;

12. Approximate fair market value of the total assets of each of the pooled funds affected by the transaction;

13. Person(s) responsible for the costs of the exemption application and for notifying interested persons; and

14. Whether an independent fiduciary is, or will be, involved in the exemption transaction and, if so, the names of the persons who will bear the cost of the fee payable to such fiduciary.[1]

Each applicant for an individual exemption involving a pooled asset fund must also include copies of all contracts, deeds, agreements, and instruments, as well as all relevant portions of qualified retirement plan-related documents, trust agreements, and other documents with respect to the transaction.[2]

Applicants must also provide a discussion of the relevant facts relating to the transaction that are reflected in these documents, an analysis of their bearing on the requested exemption, and a copy of the most recent financial statement of each plan affected by the requested exemption.[3]

More detailed informational requirements apply to an exemption application that involves one or more pooled asset funds in which the investment of any participating plan is more than 20 percent of the total assets of the pooled fund or that covers employees of the party, or its affiliates, sponsoring the pooled fund or any fiduciary with investment discretion over the pooled fund's assets. Under these circumstances, the exemption application must include, with respect to each plan involved in the transaction, (1) the names, addresses, and taxpayer identification numbers of all parties in interest with respect to the plan involved in the transaction; (2) the percentage of the fair market value of the total assets of each affected plan that is involved in the transaction; and (3) the information required to be disclosed by pooled asset funds detailed previously in items one, two, three, five, six, seven, eight, nine, ten, eleven, thirteen, and fourteen, but only to the extent that the requested information applies to the plans involved in the transaction.[4]

484. Where are individual exemption applications filed?

The Department of Labor's prohibited transaction exemption program is administered by the Employee Benefits Security Administration (EBSA).[5] As such, all individual exemption applications, filed in accordance with the application procedures detailed under Labor Regulation Sections 2570.32 through 2570.47, should be delivered to:

Exemption Application
EBSA, Office of Exemption Determinations
U.S. Department of Labor
200 Constitution Avenue, NW, Suite N-5649
Washington, DC 20210

---

1. Labor Reg. §2570.35(a).
2. Labor Reg. §2570.35(b)(1).
3. Labor Reg. §§2570.35(b)(2), 2570.35(b)(3).
4. Labor Reg. §2570.35(c).
5. Labor Reg. §2570.36.

485. When do applicants have a duty to amend and supplement an individual exemption application?

After the initial filing of an individual exemption application, the applicant must notify the DOL Division of Exemptions, in writing, if it discovers that any material fact or representation contained in the original application is inaccurate. The applicant must also promptly notify the Division of Exemptions if any of the facts or representations in the application have changed, or if anything has occurred, while the application is pending, that may have an effect on the accuracy of the facts or representations contained in the application.[1]

The DOL Division of Exemptions must be promptly notified if any of the parties in interest with respect to the proposed transaction have become the subject of an investigation regarding issues of compliance with ERISA, the employee benefit provisions of the Internal Revenue Code, or the portions of the Federal Employees' Retirement System Act (FERSA) relating to the Federal Thrift Savings Fund. The notification must be made when the investigation or enforcement action has been undertaken by the DOL, the IRS, the Department of Justice, the PBGC, or the Federal Retirement Thrift Savings Fund.[2]

The DOL may also require applicants to provide any additional documentation that it believes may be necessary in order to verify statements in the application or its supporting documents.[3]

486. What options are available to individual exemption applicants when they receive a tentative denial letter from the Department of Labor?

The DOL notifies individual exemption applicants in writing of a tentative denial of an exemption application. The DOL also provides a brief written statement that lists its reasons for the tentative denial.[4]

Applicants who receive a tentative denial letter may, within twenty days from the date of the letter, request a conference or notify the DOL of their intent to submit, in writing, additional information to be considered under the exemption application. See Q 487 and Q 488. If, within the twenty-day period, the DOL has not received a written request for a conference or a written notice of the applicant's intention to submit additional written information, the DOL will issue a final denial letter. See Q 489.[5]

The DOL is under no obligation to issue a tentative denial letter where it has conducted a hearing on the exemption application pursuant to either a hearing held by interested persons in objection to the proposed exempted transaction (see Q 494), or where the DOL has scheduled and conducted a hearing on the application on its own volition due to its determination that issues within the application must be more fully explored (see Q 495).[6]

---

1. Labor Reg. §2570.37(a).
2. Labor Reg. §2570.37(b).
3. Labor Reg. §2570.37(c).
4. Labor Reg. §2570.38(a).
5. Labor Reg. §2570.38(b).
6. Labor Reg. §2570.38(c).

487. When may an applicant take the opportunity to submit additional information in support of an exemption application?

An applicant may submit additional information to the DOL regarding his exemption application according to the specific procedures outlined in the regulations.[1] If an applicant intends to submit additional information in support of his exemption application, he must notify the DOL of this intent. This notice may be made over the telephone or in writing to the address provided within a tentative denial letter (see Q 486). The notice should detail the type of additional information being provided.[2]

After the applicant has provided notice to the DOL, the applicant has thirty days from the date of that notice to submit in writing all of the additional material that he intends to provide to the DOL in support of his individual exemption application. The applicant must also submit a written declaration, made under penalty of perjury that attests to the truth and correctness of the information provided, and that is signed and dated by either the applicant or a person qualified to sign such a declaration.[3]

The applicant may request an extension of the thirty-day period if, for reasons beyond his control, he is unable to submit, in writing, all additional information he intends to provide in support of his application. Requests for extensions beyond the thirty-day period must be made prior to the close of the thirty-day period, and will be granted only in unusual circumstances.[4]

If the applicant is unable to submit the additional written information that he had previously notified the DOL he intended to submit, the applicant may withdraw his exemption application before the expiration of the thirty-day period, plus any additional extension that may have been granted. By withdrawing the exemption application before the expiration of the applicable time period, the applicant may later reinstate the application when he has prepared the additional information to be submitted in support of his application.[5]

The DOL will issue a final denial letter of an exemption application where the DOL has not received the additional information that the applicant intended to submit within the thirty-day period (plus any additional extension that has been granted). The DOL will also issue a final denial letter if the applicant did not file a request for a conference after the receipt of a tentative denial letter (see Q 486), or where the applicant has not withdrawn his exemption application.[6]

488. What are the procedures for an exemption application conference with the Department of Labor?

All conferences between the applicant(s) and the DOL regarding a pending individual exemption application will be held at the Washington, D.C., offices of the DOL. The DOL will, however, conduct a conference over the telephone at the applicant's request.[7]

---

1. Labor Reg. §2570.39.
2. Labor Reg. §2570.39(a).
3. Labor Reg. §§2570.39(b), 2570.34(b)(5).
4. Labor Reg. §2570.39(c).
5. Labor Reg. §2570.39(d).
6. Labor Reg. §2570.39(e).
7. Labor Reg. §2570.40(a).

The DOL will schedule conferences, at a mutually convenient time, within forty-five days following the later of

1.   The date when the DOL receives the applicant's request for a conference; or

2.   The date when the DOL notifies the applicant that it is still not prepared to propose the requested exemption, after the review of additional material presented by the applicant, in accordance with the provisions of Labor Regulation Section 2570.39 (see Q 487).

If an applicant fails to appear at a scheduled conference, or if the applicant fails to attend a conference at any time within the forty-five-day period, the DOL will deem the applicant to have waived his right to a conference, unless the applicant is unable to appear due to circumstances beyond his control.[1]

If the DOL has held a hearing on an individual exemption application pursuant to a request filed in opposition to the exemption application from an interested person, or a hearing scheduled by the DOL, on its own initiative, in an effort to develop further information regarding a pending exemption application (see Q 494), an applicant will not be entitled to an exemption application conference with the DOL. Otherwise, an applicant is entitled to one conference with respect to any exemption application.[2]

The DOL will consolidate conferences, with all applicants being present, where there is more than one applicant under an individual exemption application or where more than one applicant has filed an application with respect to similar types of transactions that the DOL is considering together as a request for a class transaction. The DOL will also hold joint conferences where more than one applicant has requested a conference and where the DOL is contemplating the rejection of an application.[3]

Within twenty days after the date of a conference, an applicant may submit a written record to the DOL, containing any additional information, arguments, or precedents discussed during the conference, but which were not previously or adequately presented in writing.[4]

In instances where the applicant has requested a conference and has notified the DOL of its intent to furnish additional information in support of the application, and has failed to furnish such information within forty days from the date of the tentative denial letter, the DOL will schedule a conference for a date and time that occurs within sixty days after the date of the issuance of the tentative denial letter. If for reasons beyond the applicant's control, the applicant cannot attend the conference within the sixty-day limit, they may request an extension of time for the scheduling of a conference, if such request is made before the expiration of the sixty-day limit. Such extension may only be granted at the exclusive discretion of the DOL for unusual circumstances and only for a brief period of time.[5]

---

1. Labor Reg. §2570.40(d).
2. Labor Reg. §2570.40(b).
3. Labor Reg. §2570.40(c).
4. Labor Reg. §2570.40(e).
5. Labor Reg. §2570.40(f).

489. When will the Department of Labor issue a final denial letter?

The DOL will issue a final denial letter regarding an individual exemption application in situations where

1.   The applicant has either failed to request a conference with the DOL, or failed to notify the DOL of her intent to submit additional information within the twenty-day period following the date of a tentative denial letter;

2.   The applicant has failed to appear at a requested conference or to submit additional information;

3.   The applicant has not withdrawn her application as permitted by Labor Regulation Section 2570.39(d);

4.   After issuing a tentative denial letter and receiving additional information, and after considering the entire record of the application, the DOL decides not to propose an exemption or to withdraw an exemption already proposed; or

5.   After proposing and conducting a hearing on the exemption, and after considering the entire record of the application, the DOL decides to withdraw the proposed exemption.[1]

490. How will the Department of Labor publicize its intention to tentatively grant an individual exemption application?

If, after consideration of all information submitted by an applicant, the DOL has made a tentative decision to grant an individual exemption application, it will publish a notice of proposed exemption in the Federal Register.[2] This notice will explain the exemption transaction, along with a summary of the information submitted to the DOL in support of the exemption application.[3]

The notice published in the Federal Register will also specify all conditions under which the exemption is proposed, and serves to inform interested persons of their rights to submit written comments to the DOL regarding the proposed exempt transaction, as well as to establish a deadline for the receipt of such comments.[4]

If the proposed exemption provides relief from the prohibited transaction provisions of ERISA Section 406(b), or the prohibitions found under IRC Section 4975(c)(1)(E) or IRC Section 4975(c)(1)(F), the notice published in the Federal Register will serve to inform interested persons of their rights to request a hearing in opposition to the exemption and to establish a deadline for the receipt of such opposition hearing requests.[5]

---

1. Labor Reg. §2570.41.
2. Labor Reg. §2570.42.
3. Labor Reg. §2570.42(a).
4. Labor Regs. §§2570.42(b), 2570.42(c).
5. Labor Reg. §2570.42(d).

491. When will an applicant be required to provide notice to interested persons of a proposed prohibited transaction exemption?

If the DOL determines that the publication of a proposed prohibited transaction exemption in the Federal Register will not provide sufficient notice to interested persons, the DOL is required to notify the applicant and to secure the applicant's written agreement to provide adequate notice to interested persons under the circumstances.[1]

If a notice of the proposed exemption is published in the Federal Register as a result of the DOL's tentative decision to grant the exemption, the applicant must notify interested persons of the pending exemption in the manner and time specified in the exemption application, or in any superseding agreement with the DOL. The notification must include a copy of the Notice of Proposed Exemption and a supplemental statement that provides the following notice:

> "You are hereby notified that the United States Department of Labor is considering granting an exemption from the prohibited transaction provisions of the Employee Retirement Income Security Act of 1974, the Internal Revenue Code of 1986, or the Federal Employees' Retirement System Act of 1986. The exemption under consideration is explained in the enclosed Notice of Proposed Exemption. As a person who may be affected by the exemption, you have the right to comment on the proposed exemption by [date]. [If you may be adversely affected by the grant of the exemption, you also have the right to request a hearing on the exemption by [date]].

> "Comments or requests for a hearing should be addressed to: Office of Exemption Determinations, Employee Benefits Security Administration, Room _____, U.S. Department of Labor, 200 Constitution Avenue, NW, Washington, D.C. 20210, ATTENTION: Application No. _____.

> "The Department will make no final decision on the proposed exemption until it reviews all comments received in response to the enclosed notice. If the Department decides to hold a hearing on the exemption before making its final decision, you will be notified of the time and place of the hearing."[2]

The method elected for the notice to interested persons must be "reasonably calculated" to ensure that all interested persons will actually receive the notice. In all cases, personal delivery and delivery by first-class mail will be considered reasonable methods of furnishing the required notice.[3]

After furnishing the required notice, an applicant must provide a statement to the DOL confirming that the required notice was furnished to the persons in the manner and time designated in its exemption application, or in any superseding agreement with the DOL.

The statement must also contain a declaration stating that, under penalty of perjury, the applicant attests to the truth of the information provided in the statement. This declaration must be signed by the applicant or a person qualified to sign such a declaration.[4]

---

1. Labor Reg. §2570.43(a).
2. Labor Reg. §2570.43(b).
3. Labor Reg. §2570.43(c).
4. Labor Reg. §2570.34(b)(5).

The DOL will not grant an exemption until such statement and accompanying declaration have been furnished to the DOL.[1]

492. What is involved in the withdrawal of an exemption application?

Applicants may wish to withdraw an exemption application where they have been notified of a tentative denial of the application by the DOL, or where the applicant will require additional time beyond the thirty-day period to compile and submit additional information in support of his application to the DOL (see Q 487). Withdrawing an application prior to an official denial from the DOL will permit the applicant to re-submit the application at a later time for reconsideration. An official denial will preclude the applicant from seeking an exemption from the DOL at any time thereafter. An applicant may withdraw his individual exemption application at any time by informing the DOL, either orally or in writing, of his intent to withdraw the application.[2]

The DOL will confirm the applicant's request for withdrawal of the application for an exemption by letter and will terminate all proceedings regarding the withdrawn application. The DOL will also publish a notice of the withdrawn application in the Federal Register if a notice of the proposed exemption had been published therein.[3]

Where the applicant proposes to withdraw an application that has been considered with other applications under a request for a class exemption, or where the application itself is for a class exemption, the DOL will inform all other applicants with respect to the exemption of the individual withdrawal. The DOL will continue to process remaining applications seeking the same exemption. Where all applicants provide notice of an intent to withdraw an application, the DOL will either terminate all proceedings related to the exemption, or it will propose the exemption upon its own motion.[4]

At any time after the timely withdrawal of an application, the applicant may seek to reinstate the application by submitting a letter to the DOL requesting that the application be reinstated and by referring to the application number assigned to the original application. If there was any additional information outstanding at the time of the withdrawal of the application (see Q 487), that information must accompany the letter that requests reinstatement of the original application. The information submitted to the DOL at the time of the original application does not need to be re-submitted with the request for reinstatement unless the application had been withdrawn more than two years prior to the request for reinstatement.[5]

The DOL will reinstate any application upon a request made in accordance with these procedures, and the DOL will take whatever steps remained at the time the application was withdrawn to process the application.[6]

---

1. Labor Reg. §2570.43(d).
2. Labor Reg. §2570.44(a).
3. Labor Reg. §2570.44(b).
4. Labor Reg. §2570.44(c).
5. Labor Reg. §2570.44(d).
6. Labor Reg. §2570.44(e).

493. What is involved in a request for the reconsideration of an exemption application?

Once a final denial has been issued, the DOL will grant one request for reconsideration of the denied exemption application if the applicant presents significant new information or arguments in support of the application that could not have been submitted for consideration during the DOL's initial review of the application.[1]

Such a request for reconsideration must be filed with the DOL within 180 days of the issuance of the final denial letter and must be accompanied by a copy of the final denial letter, along with a statement setting forth the new facts and arguments that provide the basis for the request for reconsideration.[2] The request for reconsideration must also contain a statement declaring that, under the penalty of perjury, the new information provided is true. This statement must be signed by either the applicant or a person qualified to sign such a declaration.[3]

If, after reviewing the additional facts and arguments, the DOL decides that the facts do not warrant reversal of the original denial, it will submit a letter to the applicant reaffirming the original denial.[4]

If, after reviewing the additional facts and arguments, the DOL decides that the facts *do* warrant reconsideration, the DOL will notify the applicant of this decision in writing. The DOL will then initiate whatever steps remained in order to process the original exemption application at the time it issued its original denial letter.[5] If, at any time during the reconsideration of an exemption application, the DOL again determines that the facts and arguments do not warrant the granting of the exemption, the DOL will issue a letter to the applicant reaffirming the original decision to deny the application.[6]

494. May either interested persons who oppose an exemption application, or the Department of Labor, seek a hearing regarding an exemption application on its own initiative?

Any interested person that may be adversely affected by an exemption that the DOL proposes to grant from the prohibited transaction provisions of ERISA Section 406(b) (prohibitions against self-dealing), IRC Section 4975(c)(1)(E) and IRC Section 4975(c)(1)(F), or Federal Employees' Retirement System Act (FERSA) Section 8477(c)(2) may request a hearing before the DOL within the deadline specified in the notice of the proposed transaction published in the Federal Register.[7]

---

1. Labor Reg. §2570.45(a).
2. Labor Reg. §2570.44(b).
3. Labor Regs. §§2570.45(c), 2570.34(b)(5).
4. Labor Reg. §2570.45(d).
5. Labor Reg. §2570.45(e).
6. Labor Reg. §2570.45(f).
7. Labor Reg. §2570.46.

All requests for hearings in opposition to exemptions must provide (1) the name, address, and telephone number of the person making the request; (2) the person's interest in the exemption and how the person would be adversely affected by the exemption; and (3) a written presentation of the issues to be addressed and a description of the evidence to be presented at the hearing.[1]

The DOL may grant a request for a hearing where it determines it is necessary to fully explore material and factual issues raised by the person requesting the hearing. But the DOL may decline a request for an opposition hearing where (1) the request fails to satisfy the above requirements, (2) the only issues raised by the party seeking the opposition hearing are matters of law, or (3) the factual issues raised can be adequately explored through the submission of written evidence.[2]

The DOL, in its discretion, may schedule a hearing on its own where it believes that issues relevant to the proposed exemption would be most fully or expeditiously explored in such a hearing.[3]

If the DOL grants a hearing in opposition to an exemption application, or of its own volition, the applicant seeking the exemption must notify interested persons in the form, time, and manner prescribed by the DOL. Ordinarily, adequate notification can be provided by giving interested persons a copy of the notice of hearing published by the DOL in the Federal Register within ten days of its publication, or using any method reasonably calculated to ensure that interested persons actually receive the notice. In all cases, the DOL considers personal delivery and delivery by first-class mail to be reasonable methods of furnishing notice.[4]

After providing the required notice, the applicant must provide the DOL with a written statement confirming that the notice was issued in the form, manner, and time prescribed. The statement must be accompanied by a declaration stating that, under penalty of perjury, the information provided in the written statement is true. This declaration must be signed by either the applicant or a person qualified to sign such a declaration.[5]

495. What steps will the Department of Labor take if it decides to grant an exemption?

If the DOL decides to grant an exemption, after taking into consideration all of the facts and representations presented by the applicant(s) in support of an exemption application and all comments received in response to the notice of proposed exemption, it will publish a notice in the Federal Register granting an exemption.[6]

---

1. Labor Reg. §2570.46(a).
2. Labor Reg. §2570.46(b).
3. Labor Reg. §2570.47.
4. Labor Reg. §2570.46(c).
5. Labor Reg. §§2570.46(d), 2570.34(b)(5).
6. Labor Reg. §2570.48(a).

The Federal Register notice of the grant of the exemption will provide a summary of the transaction or transactions for which the exemptive relief has been granted. The notice will also specify the conditions under which the exemptive relief is available.[1]

496. What are the limits on the effect of exemptions once they have been granted?

An exemption does not take effect unless the material facts and representations contained in the application and in any materials and documents submitted in support of the application were true and complete.[2]

Once an exemption has been granted, it is effective only for the period of time specified in the exemption, and remains in effect only if the specific conditions contained within the exemption are satisfied. Generally, the exemption will only provide exemptive relief for those parties specifically identified within the exemption. If the notice of the granted exemption does not limit the exemptive relief to specific identified parties, all parties to the exemption transaction may rely on the exemption.[3]

Such an exemption will not take effect or provide exemptive relief to parties involved in the transaction(s) unless the material facts and representations contained in the original application and all subsequent materials and documents submitted in support of the application are true and complete.

For transactions that are continuing in nature, the exemption ceases to be effective if there are material changes to the original facts and representations underlying the exemption, or if one or more of the exemption's conditions cease to be met.[4]

The determination as to whether, under the totality of the facts and circumstances, a particular statement contained in, or omitted from, an application constitutes a material fact or representation is made by the DOL.[5]

497. What will cause the revocation or modification of an exemption?

After the DOL has granted an exemption, it may take steps to revoke or modify the exemption if certain changes in the law or official DOL policy occur after an exemption has taken effect, and such changes have a potential bearing upon the continuing validity of the DOL's original decisions regarding the granting of the exemption.[6]

When the DOL has decided to revoke or modify an exemption, it will give written notice to the original applicant at least thirty days in advance of the revocation or modification. This notice will detail the DOL's reasons for taking the proposed action and will provide the

---

1. Labor Reg. §2570.48(b).
2. Labor Reg. §2570.49(a).
3. Labor Reg. §2570.49.
4. Labor Reg. §2570.49(d).
5. Labor Reg. §2570.49(e).
6. Labor Reg. §2570.50(a).

applicant with an opportunity to comment on such revocation or modification. The DOL will also publish a notice of its intended actions in the Federal Register. This notice will provide interested persons with an opportunity to comment on the proposed revocation or modification.[1]

When the DOL goes forward with an exemption modification or revocation, it will have only prospective effect.[2]

---

1. Labor Reg. §2570.50(b).
2. Labor Reg. §2570.50(c).

SECTION VII

Fiduciary Liability Issues

498. When, for what, and to whom may a fiduciary be held personally liable for a fiduciary breach?

Fiduciaries may be held personally liable only for breaches that occurred during their tenure as a fiduciary. ERISA states that "[n]o fiduciary shall be liable with respect to a breach of fiduciary duty under this title if such breach was committed *before he became a fiduciary or after he ceased to be a fiduciary.*"[1]

Anytime a plan fiduciary is found to have violated his fiduciary duties to a plan under the provisions of ERISA (see Section IV for a discussion of fiduciary duties), the Department of Labor, participants, beneficiaries, and certain former participants (see discussion of the Pension Annuitants Protection Act of 1994, next) may seek to enforce personal liability against the offending fiduciary for damages caused as a result of the breach.

A person who is a fiduciary with respect to a plan who breaches any of the responsibilities, obligations, or duties imposed upon fiduciaries will be personally liable to make good to such plan any losses resulting from each breach. A breaching fiduciary also must "restore to such plan any profits" that have been earned through the use of plan assets.[2]

In addition, a fiduciary who breaches a fiduciary duty "shall be subject to such other equitable or remedial relief as the court may deem appropriate, including removal of such fiduciary."[3] The Secretary of Labor, participants, or beneficiaries may bring a civil action under ERISA Section 502(a)(2) "for appropriate relief" under ERISA Section 409.

Further, civil penalties may be imposed against a fiduciary who has breached his fiduciary duty whenever the plan he holds fiduciary status with recovers an amount through a settlement agreement or judicial proceeding as a result of the breach. (See Q 500 for more detail on the application of civil penalties.)[4] However, the Ninth Circuit Court of Appeals ruled that liability for breach of fiduciary duty under ERISA is dischargeable in bankruptcy if it does not involve the misappropriation of funds or failure to provide a proper accounting of funds.[5]

A federal court for the Northern District of Georgia has ruled that a DOL claim seeking to impose personal liability on a fiduciary pursuant to ERISA Sections 409 and 502(a)(2) granted that fiduciary a right to a jury trial.[6] The court held that ERISA Section 502(a)(2) does not limit available remedies under ERISA to equities, and it expressly authorizes remedies that are

---

1. ERISA Sec. 409(b) (emphasis added).
2. ERISA Sec. 409(a).
3. ERISA Sec. 409(a).
4. ERISA Sec. 502(l).
5. *Blyler v. Hemmeter*, 2001 U.S. App. LEXIS 4559 (9th Cir. 2001).
6. *Chao v Meixner*, 2007 WL 4225069 (N.D. Ga. 2007).

compensatory in nature, which arise at law. Legal remedies, as opposed to equitable remedies, grant a defendant the right to a jury trial.[1]

The Pension Annuitants Protection Act of 1994[2] allows former participants and beneficiaries to seek "appropriate relief" from the fiduciaries of their former plan who violated their fiduciary duty in regard to the purchase of annuities that terminated the participants' and beneficiaries' active status under the plan (i.e., the termination removed them from the protections afforded active participants and beneficiaries under ERISA). Although the term "appropriate relief" is not defined, the statute does state that appropriate relief includes "the posting of security if necessary, to assure receipt by the participant or beneficiary of the amounts provided by such ... annuity, plus reasonable prejudgment interest on such amounts."[3] This statute was a direct response to the failures of life insurance companies that sold lesser-rated annuities to large pension plans for the benefit of terminated and retired participants (thereby removing them from active status under their plan), and then went bankrupt, leaving the annuities worthless and the annuitants without recourse to plan fiduciaries under ERISA.[4]

The Supreme Court has held that ERISA Section 409(a) was designed to protect the entire plan.[5] Consequently, ERISA's authorization of other appropriate relief (equitable or remedial) does not provide relief other than for the plan itself. In other words, disgorgement of profits and recoveries are not forms of relief available to individual participants or beneficiaries.

In distinguishing the *Massachusetts Mutual Life Insurance Co. v Russell* case, the Supreme Court has held that, for defined contribution plans, fiduciary misconduct of the type envisioned by ERISA Section 409 "need not threaten" the entire plan's solvency in order for the case to be actionable under ERISA Section 502(a)(2). In other words, when a violation of ERISA Section 409 reduces an individual account in a defined contribution plan, an action to have such loss recovered against the offending fiduciary may proceed. In this case, a 401(k) participant sought recovery of $150,000 in assets to his account that he claimed were "depleted" by the plan administrator's failure to follow his investment instructions.[6] The Second Circuit has ruled that the Supreme Court holding in the *LaRue* case does not extend beyond individual account plans.[7]

In a different case, the Supreme Court held that participants and beneficiaries may seek individual equitable relief for a breach of fiduciary duty under ERISA Section 502(a)(3), which authorizes appropriate equitable relief to "redress such violations or ... to enforce any provisions of this title or the terms of the plan." [8] In its ruling, the Court rejected the claim that ERISA Section 409 provides the exclusive remedy for a breach of fiduciary duty. The Court determined ERISA Section 502(a)(3) to be a "catch-all" provision that was consistent with ERISA's purpose of

---

1. *Chao v Meixner*, 2007 WL 4225069 (N.D. Ga. 2007).
2. Pub. L. No. 103-401.
3. ERISA Sec. 502(a)(9).
4. See *Kayes v. Pacific Lumber Co.*, 51 F.3d 1449 (9th Cir. 1995).
5. *Massachusetts Mut. Life Ins. Co. v. Russell*, 473 U.S. 134 (1985).
6. *LaRue v DeWolff, Boberg & Assocs., Inc.* 2008 WL 440748 (U.S. 2008).
7. *Fisher v Penn Traffic Co.*, 2009 WL 910388 (2d Cir. 2009).
8. *Varity Corp. v. Howe*, 514 U.S. 1082 (1996).

protecting the best interests of participants and beneficiaries. The holding authorized relief under ERISA Section 502(a)(3) only where appropriate equitable relief was not otherwise available.

The federal court for the Eastern District of Virginia has held that plan forfeitures cannot be used to offset the personal liability of fiduciaries found liable for their fiduciary breach.[1]

The Fourth Circuit has ruled that a participant's ERISA section 502(a)(2) claim for fiduciary breach with respect to investments made under an overfunded defined benefit lacked constitutional standing under Article III of the U.S. Constitution. Referring to the Supreme Court's opinion in *Hughes Aircraft Co. v. Jacobson*,[2] the court held that a participant in a defined benefit plan has an interest in his fixed future payments only, not the assets in the pension fund. Since the plan is overfunded, there is no injury-in-fact due to the losses incurred as a result of the alleged breach. If the plan becomes overfunded, the employer will be required to make additional contributions, and if the employer is unable to do so because of insolvency, the PBGC will guarantee the benefits.[3]

499. What are successor fiduciary responsibilities in regard to an actual or potential breach of fiduciary duty committed by a former fiduciary?

A successor fiduciary is obligated to take "reasonable steps" to remedy an outstanding breach committed by a predecessor fiduciary if she discovers sufficient information to determine that the actions of the prior fiduciary resulted in the outstanding breach. A failure to take remedial action constitutes a separate, current breach of fiduciary duty by the successor fiduciary.[4]

A successor fiduciary also has a duty to notify plan trustees or the Department of Labor if she has developed enough information to believe that a breach of fiduciary duty by a former fiduciary may have taken place.[5]

500. What are ERISA Section 502(l) penalties, and how are they applied?

ERISA provides for a mandatory civil penalty against a fiduciary who breaches a fiduciary responsibility or commits a violation of ERISA. Civil penalties are also imposed upon other persons who knowingly participate in such a breach or violation. The civil penalty is equal to 20 percent of the "applicable recovery amount" paid pursuant to a settlement agreement with the Department of Labor (DOL) or a court-ordered payment to a plan, participant, or beneficiary in a judicial proceeding instituted by the DOL.[6]

The DOL Regional Directors have been delegated authority in their respective geographic jurisdictions for assessing these civil penalties. This includes the authority to waive or reduce the penalty based upon a determination that the subject would be unable to restore all losses to the plan, participant, or beneficiary of the plan without incurring "severe financial hardship." The

---

1. *Chao v. Anderson*, 2007 U.S. Dist. LEXIS 34384 (E.D. Va. 2007).
2. 525 U.S. 432 (1999).
3. *David v. Alphin*, 704 F.3d 327 (4th Cir. January 14, 2013).
4. DOL Adv. Op. 76-95.
5. DOL Adv. Op. 77-79.
6. ERISA Sec. 502(l).

DOL Director of the Office of Exemption Determinations is delegated the authority to waive or reduce the civil penalties based upon a determination that an individual acted reasonably and in good faith in engaging in the fiduciary breach.[1]

The amount of the civil penalty is reduced by the amount of any penalty or tax imposed on the fiduciary or other person with respect to the transaction under ERISA Section 406 and ERISA Section 502(i) (5 percent of any amount involved in an ERISA Section 406 prohibited transaction; see Q 421), or IRC Section 4975.[2]

Practitioner's Pointer: In order for the DOL to impose civil penalties, the penalties must be applied against any recovery amount paid pursuant to a settlement agreement or court order. The plan fiduciaries must be placed on "official notice" that a prohibited transaction is outstanding and that the DOL or court is ordering that the violation be reversed. If a violation is discovered prior to the plan's being placed on official notice of its existence, it is important that the prohibited transaction be reversed prior to the issuance of the official notice (usually in the form of a "Notice Letter" from the Regional Office of the DOL). If the violation is reversed prior to issuance of an official notice, the 20 percent penalty may not be imposed by the DOL or a court.

501. What is the applicable recovery amount under ERISA Section 502(l)?

The term "applicable recovery amount" is defined as any amount that is recovered by an employee benefit plan, a participant or beneficiary of a plan, or a legal representative of a plan, or from a fiduciary or other person who knowingly participated in a breach of fiduciary duty or violation of the rules regarding fiduciary responsibility. The amount may be recovered pursuant to a settlement agreement with the Department of Labor (DOL) or a court order resulting from a judicial proceeding instituted by the DOL.[3] The applicable recovery amount with regard to a continuing violation is the total amount recovered pursuant to a settlement agreement or court order, reduced by the amount attributable to any element of the violation that occurred prior to December 19, 1989.[4]

502. What is a settlement agreement and court order?

A "settlement agreement" is an agreement between the Department of Labor (DOL) and a person whom the DOL alleges has committed a breach of fiduciary duty or violation of the rules regarding fiduciary responsibility. The agreement is pursuant to a claim for the breach or violation that is released in return for tender of cash or other property to a plan, a participant, or a beneficiary of a plan, or the legal representative of a plan or participants and beneficiaries.[5]

A "court order" is a judicial decree that either awards monetary damages or provides equitable relief.[6]

1. *EBSA Enforcement Manual* ch. 35.
2. ERISA Sec. 502(l)(4).
3. ERISA Sec. 502(l)(2).
4. Prop. Labor Reg. §2560.502l-1(c).
5. Prop. Labor Reg. §2560.502l-1(e).
6. Prop. Labor Reg. §2560.502l-1(e).

According to the Employee Benefits Security Administration (EBSA), in the absence of a signed agreement, but where corrective actions are taken by the recipient of a Voluntary Correction (VC) notice letter, the circumstances dictate whether a settlement agreement has been effected. A settlement agreement is deemed to occur in situations where the recipient of a VC notice letter, in response to that letter, corrects the described violations.[1]

503. How is the ERISA Section 502(*l*) penalty assessed?

The ERISA Section 502(*l*) penalty is assessed subsequent to the payment of the applicable recovery amount in accordance with a settlement agreement or court order. The civil penalty may be assessed against only the person who is required by the terms of the judgment or the settlement agreement to pay the applicable recovery amount, and can be assessed only for breaches or violations of ERISA that occurred on or after December 19, 1989.[2] With regard to a continuing violation, the 20 percent penalty may be assessed upon only that portion of the recovery that is attributable to violations occurring on or after December 19, 1989. EBSA offers this example: if only one of a group of fiduciaries agrees to restore losses to a plan pursuant to a settlement agreement, the civil penalty may be assessed against only that fiduciary. In certain circumstances, the penalty may be assessed against fiduciaries or knowing participants where the restitution to the plan is made on their behalf by a third party. Specifically, the penalty may be assessed when the third party has no independent obligation under ERISA to correct the violations.[3]

The regional office of EBSA serves on the person liable for making the payment a notice of assessment of a civil penalty equal to 20 percent of the applicable recovery amount.[4] The notice sent by the regional office is a document that contains a specified assessment, in monetary terms, of the civil penalty. The notice contains a brief factual description of the violation for which the assessment is being made, the identity of the person being assessed, the amount of the assessment, and the basis for assessing that particular person that particular penalty amount.[5]

Service of the notice is made by delivering a copy to the person being assessed, by leaving a copy at the principal office, place of business, or residence of such person, or by mailing a copy to the last known address of the person. Service by certified mail is completed upon mailing the notice; service by regular mail is completed upon receipt by the addressee.[6]

504. How is the ERISA Section 502(*l*) penalty calculated?

The penalty under ERISA Section 502(*l*) is equal to 20 percent of the "applicable recovery amount" paid pursuant to a settlement agreement with the Department of Labor (DOL) or a court order in a judicial proceeding instituted by the DOL under ERISA Section 502(a)(2) or ERISA Section 502(a)(5). The penalty is calculated as a percentage of the amount paid to a plan, participant, or beneficiary that represents losses incurred by the plan, disgorged profits, and

---

1. *EBSA Enforcement Manual* ch. 34, at 5.
2. ERISA Sec. 502(l)(2); Labor Reg. §2570.83.
3. *EBSA Enforcement Manual* ch. 35, at 5.
4. Labor Reg. §2570.83(a).
5. *EBSA Enforcement Manual* ch. 35, at 4.
6. Labor Reg. §2570.83(b); *EBSA Enforcement Manual* ch. 35, at 4-5.

amounts necessary to achieve correction of the ERISA violation. If correction is achieved without actual payment to a plan, participant, or beneficiary, no penalty may be assessed. An example of such an action is a fiduciary's taking administrative action to prevent future violations.[1]

505. What is the time period to pay the ERISA Section 502(l) penalty?

A person liable for the ERISA Section 502(l) penalty has sixty days from the service of the notice of assessment to pay the assessed amount. Subject to any tolling of the sixty-day payment period during the consideration of a waiver or reduction petition (see Q 506), the notice of assessment becomes a final agency action (meaning it is reviewable by a court)[2] on the first day following the sixty-day period. At any time prior to the expiration of that sixty-day period, a person may request one conference, per assessment, with the Department of Labor (DOL) to discuss the calculation of the assessment. If a conference is requested, the DOL will schedule one as soon as administratively feasible. The sixty-day payment period will not, however, be tolled upon such request.[3]

506. May the ERISA Section 502(l) penalty be reduced or waived?

At any time prior to the expiration of the sixty-day payment period, a person may petition the Department of Labor (DOL) to waive or reduce the assessed penalty on one of two grounds: (1) that the person acted reasonably and in good faith in engaging in the breach or violation; or (2) the person will not be able to restore all losses to the plan, participants, or beneficiaries of the plan without severe financial hardship unless the waiver or reduction is granted.[4] The petition for waiver or reduction of the penalty is submitted to the regional director who issued the notice of assessment of the penalty.[5]

As to whether a person acted reasonably and in good faith, the DOL examines the decision-making process with respect to the transaction in question to determine whether it was designed to adequately safeguard the interests of the participants and beneficiaries of the plan.

A person may request a financial hardship waiver not only with regard to actual losses to the plan, but also with regard to any disgorgement of profits gained through the relevant breach or violation, or amounts necessary for transfer to the plan in order to correct the relevant breach or violation.[6]

If the petition is based wholly on financial hardship, a written determination of whether to reduce or waive the penalty is made by the regional director within sixty days of receipt of the petition. If the petition is based in part on financial hardship and in part on good faith, the regional director makes a written determination of whether to reduce or waive the penalty only on the basis of financial hardship within sixty days of receipt. If the petitioner remains liable for any portion of the penalty after the regional director's written determination, the regional

---

1. *EBSA Enforcement Manual* ch. 35, at 5.
2. See 5 U.S.C. §704.
3. Labor Reg. §2570.84; *EBSA Enforcement Manual* ch. 35, at 5-6.
4. Labor Reg. §2570.85(a).
5. *EBSA Enforcement Manual* ch. 35, at 6.
6. Preamble to Labor Reg. §2570.80, nn. 4 & 5, 55 Fed. Reg. 25,284.

director forwards the petition to the Employee Benefits Security Administration's Office of Exemption Determinations for a determination of whether to reduce or waive the remaining portion of the penalty based on good faith. If the petition is based in whole on good faith, the regional director forwards the petition to EBSA's Office of Exemption Determinations for a determination of whether to reduce or waive the penalty.[1]

If the petition for waiver or reduction of penalty is submitted during the sixty-day payment period, the payment period for the penalty in question will be tolled pending the DOL's consideration of the petition. During the consideration, the petitioner is also entitled to one conference with the DOL. The DOL may, however, in its sole discretion, schedule or hold additional conferences with the petitioner concerning the actual allegations contained in the petition.[2]

Once the DOL has made a decision with regard to the petition, the petitioner will be served a written determination briefly informing him of the DOL's decision and the grounds for that decision. The determination is solely within the DOL's discretion and is a final, non-reviewable order. In the event that the DOL concludes that no waiver or reduction is granted, the payment period for the penalty in question, if previously tolled, will resume as of the date of service of the written determination on the petitioner.[3]

507. What are the required contents of a petition for a waiver of the ERISA Section 502(l) penalty?

A petition to waive or reduce the ERISA Section 502(*l*) civil penalty must be in writing and contain the following information: (1) the name of the petitioner; (2) a detailed description of the fiduciary duty, breach, or violation that is the subject of the penalty; (3) a detailed recitation of the facts that support the bases for waiver or reduction (see Q 506), accompanied by underlying documentation supporting such factual allegations; and (4) a declaration, signed and dated by the petitioner, which states, under penalty of perjury, that the petitioner is making true and correct representations to the best of her knowledge and belief.[4]

508. May the ERISA Section 502(l) penalty be offset by other penalties?

Yes. The ERISA Section 502(*l*) civil penalty assessed on a fiduciary or other person with respect to a transaction is reduced by the amount of a penalty or tax imposed on the fiduciary or other person with respect to ERISA Section 502(i) or Internal Revenue Code Section 4975.[5] ERISA Section 502(i) provides for a civil penalty against a party in interest who engages in a prohibited transaction with respect to an employee benefit plan. See Q 421. IRC Section 4975 provides for an excise tax against a disqualified person who engages in a prohibited transaction with a plan. See Q 414.

---

1. *EBSA Enforcement Manual* ch. 35, at 6.
2. Labor Reg. §2570.85(c).
3. Labor Reg. §2570.85(d).
4. Labor Reg. §2570.85(b).
5. Labor Reg. §2570.86.

In order to reduce the ERISA Section 502(*l*) penalty, a person must provide proof to the Department of Labor that an offsetting penalty was paid. The entire IRC Section 4975 excise tax or ERISA Section 502(i) penalty may offset an ERISA Section 502(*l*) civil penalty imposed due to the same transaction. The offset is limited to the identical parties on whom the excise tax or penalty is imposed. Any interest accrued on an ERISA Section 502(i) penalty or IRC Section 4975 excise tax assessment is not allowed as an offset to the ERISA Section 502(*l*) penalty.[1]

509. Must the Department of Labor prove a breach of fiduciary duty to assess the ERISA Section 502(l) penalty?

Yes. Absent a court order, in order to assess the penalty the Department of Labor (DOL) must prove a breach of fiduciary duty rather than unilaterally determine that a breach occurred because the statute does not contemplate punishment where no violation has occurred. ERISA Section 502(*l*) provides, in pertinent part, that in the case of any breach of fiduciary responsibility by a fiduciary, the DOL must assess a civil penalty against the fiduciary in an amount equal to 20 percent of the "applicable recovery amount" (any amount recovered from a fiduciary in accordance with a settlement agreement or court order).[2]

The DOL has contended that it is not required to prove a breach to assess the penalty when it has secured a settlement agreement, even if, in that settlement agreement, the party does not admit it breached a fiduciary duty. The DOL has argued that the words "in the case of any breach" are merely an instruction as to when to assess the penalty, and not an element of the penalty itself. The courts have rejected this argument because it would provide the DOL the unilateral determination of when a fiduciary breach has occurred and the "unchecked authority to impose a penalty" so long as there was a recovery through a settlement agreement. One court noted that a fiduciary may agree to a settlement to avoid an expensive legal battle even in the absence of a fiduciary breach.[3] In such a case, under the DOL's proposed reading of the statute, a fiduciary would subject itself to the 20 percent penalty because of the enforceable settlement agreement. In rejecting the DOL's contention, the court noted that in seeking the imposition of the ERISA Section 502(*l*) penalty, a trial may not be necessary to prove a breach of fiduciary duty if the facts (already developed in the course of the settlement negotiations) could establish a breach of fiduciary duty as a matter of law, or alternatively, if the DOL settled the case and required a sentence in the consent decree admitting that a violation occurred.[4]

510. Is a settlement agreement required for the assessment of an ERISA Section 502(l) penalty?

Yes. According to the court in *Rodgrigues v. Herman*, absent a court order the Department of Labor (DOL) may not impose an ERISA Section 502(*l*) penalty on fiduciaries who voluntarily correct a breach without entering into a settlement agreement.[5] The DOL may only assess a

---

1. ERISA Sec. 502(l); Labor Reg. §2570.86; *EBSA Enforcement Manual* ch. 35, at 6-7.
2. *Rodrigues v. Herman*, 121 F.3d 1352 (9th Cir. 1997); *Citywide Bank of Denver v. Herman*, F. Supp. 966 (D. Colo. 1997); *Huffer v. Herman*, 168 F. Supp. 2d 815 (S.D. Ohio 2001).
3. *Rodrigues v. Herman*, 121 F.3d 1352 (9th Cir. 1997).
4. *Rodrigues v. Herman*, 121 F.3d at 1355.
5. *Rodrigues v. Herman*, 121 F.3d at 1355.

civil penalty against the fiduciary in an amount equal to 20 percent of the "applicable recovery amount" (any amount that is recovered from a fiduciary in accordance with a settlement agreement or court order).[1] According to the court, the applicable recovery amount does not include amounts that are recovered by a voluntary correction that are not recovered pursuant to a settlement agreement.[2]

The essential elements of a settlement agreement are "a definitive offer and acceptance, consideration, and parties who have the capacity and authority to agree." As a contract, a settlement agreement is construed using ordinary principles of contract interpretation. In one case, a contract was not formed simply by an exchange of letters between the fiduciary and the DOL, including a voluntary correction letter issued by the DOL.[3] Also, the fiduciary repeatedly used precatory language in the letters, demonstrating that there was no definite offer upon which the parties could have a meeting of the minds, nor was there the presence of the essential elements of a contract. Because no contract or settlement agreement had been formed between the fiduciary and the DOL, the district court held that there was no statutory basis on which to impose the ERISA Section 502(*l*) penalty.[4] In *Huffer v. Herman*,[5] the U.S. District Court for the Southern District of Ohio noted that phrases such as "additional information may lead us to change our views" and "please advise … what action you propose to take" made the DOL Voluntary Compliance Letter something less than an offer to constitute a "settlement agreement" under ERISA Sec. 502(*l*).

511. What is the scope of protection offered under the ERISA prohibition against interference with participant rights?

ERISA Section 510 provides that "[i]t shall be unlawful for any person to discharge, fine, suspend, expel, discipline, or discriminate against a participant or beneficiary for exercising any right to which he is entitled" under the provisions of an employee benefit plan or ERISA.

The Supreme Court has held that ERISA Section 510 does not distinguish between rights that vest under ERISA and those that do not.[6] Therefore, ERISA Section 510 prohibits the interference with the attainment of any right to which a participant may become entitled. Further, the Court held that a plan sponsor's power to amend or eliminate a welfare benefit plan does not include the power to discharge, fine, suspend, expel, discipline, or discriminate against the plan's participants and beneficiaries for the purpose of interfering with the attainment of rights under the plan.[7]

This would appear to be an extension of an earlier Supreme Court ruling that a plan sponsor's right to amend its plans exists in balance with participant rights under ERISA Section 510 and may only be exercised in accordance with the plan's formal amendment procedures.[8]

---

1. ERISA Sec. 502(l).
2. *Rodrigues v. Herman*, 121 F.3d at 1355.
3. *Citywide Bank of Denver v. Herman*, 978 F. Supp. 966 (D. Colo. 1997).
4. *Citywide Bank of Denver v. Herman*, above.
5. 2001 WL 345455 (S.D. Ohio 2001).
6. *Inter-Modal Rail Emps. Ass'n v. Atchison, Topeka & Santa Fe Ry.*, 520 U.S. 510 (1997).
7. *Inter-Modal Rail Emps. Ass'n v. Atchison, Topeka & Santa Fe Ry.*, above.
8. See *Ingersoll-Rand Co. v. McClendon*, 498 U.S. 133 (1990).

ERISA Section 510 protects existing employees and does not extend to any issues involving a claim of a discriminatory refusal to hire an individual. Further, ERISA provides plan sponsors considerable discretion in the design and administration of qualified plans that they sponsor. Part of this discretion is a right to offer varying degrees of benefits to participants under the plans they sponsor. Previously laid-off employees, who were not rehired in spite of an upsurge in business because of the negative financial impact rehiring them would have on their former employer's retirement plans, were held to have no standing under ERISA Section 510 as it does not apply to former employees.[1]

In further clarification of the employer's expansive right to design and subsequently amend a plan, the Sixth Circuit ruled in *Coomer v. Bethesda Hospital, Inc.*[2] that ERISA Section 510 does not limit an employer's ability to amend a plan for the benefit of one participant while refusing to amend the plan in the same manner to benefit other individuals. In distinguishing this right, the court pointed out that deciding what the terms of a plan will be is a settlor function. Administering the provisions of the plan, as written or amended, is a fiduciary function. Specifically, the court states, "[T]o prevail under Section 510, a plaintiff must show that the alleged discrimination was designed either to retaliate for the exercise of a right or to interfere with the attainment of an entitled right." The court also cited two cases in support of this conclusion: *McGath v. Auto-Body North Shore,*[3] and *Haberern v. Kaupp Vascular Surgeons Ltd. Defined Benefit Pension Plan.*[4]

Earlier, the Sixth Circuit had expanded the coverage of ERISA Section 510 beyond the traditional plan sponsor or employer-employee relationship.[5] The court held that ERISA Section 510 was primarily, but not exclusively, aimed at employment situations. The holding by the court is that a Section 510 claim may be brought against any person who discharges, fines, expels, disciplines, or discriminates against a participant or beneficiary for exercising any right to which the participant or beneficiary is entitled under an employee benefit plan or ERISA. The case involved the widow of a participant, who had signed a prenuptial agreement that provided that if she survived her husband, she would be entitled to remain in the marital residence and receive a weekly allowance of $300 from the decedent's estate. In return, she surrendered all other claims against his estate. The widow learned of the decedent's benefits under a plan to which she, as the surviving spouse, was entitled. The plan administrator paid the widow those benefits in a lump sum. The decedent's estate determined that the widow's receipt of the lump-sum benefit from the plan was in violation of the prenuptial agreement and ceased the $300 weekly living stipend. The court held that, under ERISA Section 510, where a case does not involve an employment relationship, the list of proscribed actions should be read to mean adverse actions that affect the claimant's rights under the plan. The court held that the widow's case had met this threshold in that the estate had the power to interfere with the widow's enjoyment of the survivor benefits under the plan by offsetting them against the weekly payments made available

---

1. *Williams v. Mack Trucks*, 2000 U.S. Dist. LEXIS 18758 (E.D. Pa. 2000).
2. 32 EBC 2578 (6th Cir. 2004).
3. 7 F.3d 665 (7th Cir. 1993).
4. 24 F.3d 1491 (3d Cir. 1994).
5. *Mattei v. Mattei*, 126 F.3d 794 (6th Cir. 1997).

under the prenuptial agreement. Such alleged retaliation had a logical linkage to the widow's status as an ERISA beneficiary.[1]

The Ninth Circuit expanded the coverage of ERISA Section 510 to include a whistleblower claim brought by a former participant because the claimant was an active participant at the time of the alleged violation of ERISA Section 510.[2] The claimant was terminated from his employment with the plan sponsor three weeks after he, as a member of the ESOP committee, strongly urged that the DOL investigate the plan sponsor's proposed termination of the ESOP. The opinion of the court states that "[t]o hold otherwise would allow an employer simply by wrongfully firing a whistleblowing employee and then terminating the plan, wrongfully or otherwise, to deprive that employee of the right to sue the employer for retaliation prohibited by ERISA."[3]

In another case from the Sixth Circuit, a group of former employees claimed that their employer violated ERISA Section 510 when it closed the plant where they worked and discharged them to prevent their retirement eligibility.[4] When the plant closed, some of the employees were within only a year or two of qualifying for retirement benefits under the employer's defined benefit pension plan. The employer claimed that the plant was closed due to overcapacity (only 10 percent of the plant's available space was being used). The trial court dismissed the employees' claims, and the employees appealed. The Sixth Circuit affirmed the lower court's holding. The court concluded that the employees simply did not have sufficient evidence of improper motive to take the claim to a jury. (The employees' claim was undercut by the fact that two employees were subsequently recalled to work at another plant and actually completed the service necessary to become retirement eligible.[5])

The United States District Court for the Eastern District of Michigan has ruled that an employee's internal complaint of plan violations may be protected under ERISA Section 510.[6] After a participant complained to the plan sponsor about the plan sponsor's failure to timely deposit payroll contributions into the company-sponsored plan, the plan sponsor deposited the contributions, along with matching contributions and lost earnings. Three months later, the participant was terminated. In response, the participant filed suit alleging the termination was retaliatory and a violation of ERISA Section 510. The plan sponsor moved for a dismissal, claiming the complaint was not protected under ERISA Section 510 and that the intervening three months showed no causal link between the complaint and the termination. The court denied the motion, stating that the phrase "inquiry or proceeding" in ERISA Section 510 is broad enough to include an internal complaint. Further, the court noted that the plan sponsor may have needed the three-month interval to train a replacement for the terminated participant. Finally, although the employer offered evidence of unrelated legitimate reasons for the termination, the court ruled that there was sufficient evidence to believe these reasons were pretextual in nature (citing prior positive performance ratings and a lack of opportunity

1. *Mattei v. Mattei*, above.
2. *McBride v. PLM Int'l Inc.*, 179 F.3d 737 (9th Cir. 1999).
3. *McBride v. PLM Int'l Inc.*, 179 F.3d 746 (9th Cir. 1999).
4. *Crawford v. TRW Auto.* U.S. LLC, 2009 WL 818952 (6th Cir. 2009).
5. *Crawford v. TRW Auto.* U.S. LLC, 2009 WL 818952 (6th Cir. 2009).
6. *Dunn v. Elco Enters., Inc.*, 2006 U.S. Dist. LEXIS 26169 (E.D. Mich. 2006).

for corrective counseling/guidance on the issue for which the participant was terminated—in violation of company policy).

The Seventh Circuit has ruled that ERISA Section 510 extends to a participant's unsolicited comments made to their employer. *George v. Junior Achievement of Central Indiana, Inc.*,[1] With this ruling the Seventh Circuit has joined the Fifth Circuit (*Anderson v. Elec. Data Sys. Corp.*,[2]) and the Ninth Circuit (*Hashimoto v. Bank of Hawaii*,[3]) holdings that alleged retaliation for unsolicited comments is within the scope of ERISA section

However, the Second Circuit (*Nicolaou v. Horizon Media, Inc.*,[4]), Third Circuit (*Edwards v. A.H. Cornell & Sons, Inc.*,[5]), and Fourth Circuit (*King v. Marriott Int'l Inc.*,[6]) have held that ERISA section 510 does not reach alleged retaliation for unsolicited comments. These cases take the position that the reference to "inquiry or proceeding" suggests only a *formal* process, and that unsolicited comments made by an employee do not rise to that level."

Section 623 of the Pension Protection Act of 2006[7] amends ERISA Section 511 to provide that the penalty for any attempt to interfere with, or prevent the exercise of, participant rights under an employee benefit plan that involves "the use of fraud, force, violence, or the threat of the use of fraud, force, or violence" is a criminal act for which the perpetrator may be fined up to $100,000 (up from the previous maximum of $10,000), imprisoned up to ten years (up from the previous maximum of one year), or both.

512. Does ERISA restrict an employer's right to discharge an employee for cause?

No. Courts have held that an employee's discharge for cause is not interference with participant rights under ERISA Section 510. This includes discharge for breach of company policy, misconduct, and criminal activities.[8]

513. Who has the burden of proof with respect to establishing intentional interference with participant rights?

In order for a participant to establish a prima facie case of a violation of ERISA Section 510, the participant must show that the plan sponsor: (1) undertook prohibited action; (2) which was undertaken in an effort to interfere; (3) with the attainment of any right to which the participant may become entitled.[9]

---

1. 694 F.3d 812 (7th Cir. September 4, 2012).
2. 11 F.3d 1311 (5th Cir.1994.
3. 999 F.2d 408 (9th Cir.1993.
4. 402 F.3d 325 (2nd Cir. 2005.
5. 610 F.3d 217 (3rd Cir. 2010.
6. 337 F.3d 421 (4th Cir. 2003.
7. Pub. L. No. 109-280.
8. See *Furcini v. Equibank NA*, 660 F. Supp. 1436 (W.D. Pa. 1987).
9. *Rush v. United Techs. Otis Elevator Div.*, 930 F.2d 453 (6th Cir. 1991); *Hendricks v. Edgewater Steel Co.*, 898 F.2d 385 (3d Cir. 1990); *Baker v. O'Reilly Auto., Inc* 2001 U.S. Dist. LEXIS 15085 (N.D. Tex. 2001).

The burden of proof requires the complainant to demonstrate specific intent on the part of the plan sponsor to interfere with the attainment of rights under the plan. If this is established, the plan sponsor must articulate a legitimate, nondiscriminatory reason for the adverse actions it took. If the plan sponsor can do this, the participant must be able to demonstrate that the stated reason of the plan sponsor are pretextual.

The Tenth Circuit has ruled that employees terminated after their child had incurred large medical expenses could proceed with litigation filed under the Americans with Disabilities Act (ADA), which prohibits discrimination based upon association with a disabled person and prohibits intentional interference with ERISA rights, where the evidence supported a reasonable inference that the employees' involuntary termination was motivated by the high costs to their employer of their son's treatment.[1]

The court pointed out concerns expressed by the employer about the son's health care costs stemming from the treatment for a recurrence of brain cancer and the close "temporal proximity" of such treatment to the employees' termination (less than three weeks for the father and six weeks for the mother). The court also relied on evidence that the employer was aware of the costs for the treatment of the child and had included health care costs for each employee in its budget line item for labor costs. The court also noted the employer's failure to progressively discipline (rather than terminate) the employees for the alleged reasons resulting in termination. This created factual issues as to whether the employer's reason for terminating the employees was pretextual.

514. Are an employer's efforts to reduce costs by capping lifetime health benefits a violation of ERISA Section 510?

The Fifth Circuit Court of Appeals has held that retroactive modifications to the lifetime benefits available under an employer's health plan do not violate the anti-discrimination provisions of ERISA Section 510.[2] The plan sponsor placed a cap on the lifetime benefits under its health plan in an effort to reduce health care costs associated with AIDS treatment. The court decided that the plan sponsor's action in capping benefits was not discriminatory in that it affected all participants in the plan and not just those participants who were under treatment for AIDS.[3]

515. Do participants and beneficiaries have a right to seek civil enforcement of ERISA Section 510?

Yes. A participant, beneficiary, or fiduciary may bring a civil action to enjoin any act or practice that violates any provision of ERISA or the terms of the plan's governing documents, or to obtain other equitable relief to redress such violations and enforce any provision of ERISA (including ERISA Section 510).[4] Actions that may be brought by participants and beneficiaries include efforts to recover benefits due under the plan, enforce rights under the plan, or clarify

---

1. *Trujillo v. Pacificorp*, 2008 WL 1960765 (10th Cir. 2008).
2. *McGann v. H & H Music Co.*, 946 F.2d 401 (5th Cir. 1991).
3. *McGann v. H & H Music Co.*, above.
4. ERISA Sec. 502(a)(3).

rights to future benefits under the plan. Participants and beneficiaries may also bring suit against plan administrators for failure to comply with the notice requirements of ERISA.

Alleged violations of the fiduciary provisions of ERISA may be the subject of civil actions to enforce those provisions. Civil actions under these circumstances may be brought by the Department of Labor, participants, beneficiaries, and other plan fiduciaries.

In any civil action regarding causes of action under ERISA: (1) the party filing the action must have standing to sue; (2) the court in which the suit has been filed must have jurisdiction over the claim; and (3) the action must be brought in the proper venue.

The Third Circuit Court of Appeals has ruled that a former employee claiming that a fiduciary breach diminished his account value is a "participant" for purposes of determining his standing to sue.[1] In overturning a trial court ruling that the plaintiff, as a former plan participant who had cashed out of the plan, had no standing to sue under ERISA, the Third Circuit advised that ERISA defines a participant as "any employee or former employee ... who is or may become eligible to receive a benefit of any type from an employee benefit plan." The court went on to cite the Supreme Court's ruling in *Firestone Tire & Rubber Co. v. Bruch*, which held that the term "participant" covers a former employee with a colorable claim for "vested benefits." In granting the plaintiff standing to sue, the Third Circuit concluded that ERISA imposes fiduciary duties on plan administrators so that part of a participant's entitlement is the value of his account unencumbered by any fiduciary impropriety. "In other words," the court stated, "ERISA entitles individual account plan participants not only to what is in their accounts, but also to what should be there given the terms of the plan and ERISA's fiduciary obligations."[2]

The Seventh Circuit has ruled that former employees had standing to sue in an ERISA fiduciary breach action, even though before their amended complaint was filed they had received full payout of their defined contribution pension plan accounts.[3]

The U.S. District Court for the Western District of Michigan has ruled that a profit sharing plan trustee was entitled to a jury trial on his ERISA claim that the plan's former stock brokerage firm breached its fiduciary duties by failing to discover that the plan's former trustee had taken illegal plan loans.[4]

516. Do participants and beneficiaries have a right to seek criminal enforcement of ERISA?

No. The criminal provisions of ERISA Section 511 (prohibiting the interference with participant rights through the use or threat of force or intimidation) may be brought before the courts only by the Department of Justice.[5]

---

1. *Graden v. Conexant Sys. Inc.*, 2007 WL 2177170 (3d Cir. 2007).
2. *Graden v. Conexant Sys. Inc.*, above.
3. *Harzewski v. Guidant Corp.*, 2007 WL 1598097 (7th Cir. 2007).
4. *Ellis v. Rycenga Homes, Inc.*, 2007 WL 1032367 (W.D. Mich. 2007).
5. *West v. Butler*, 621 F.2d 240 (6th Cir. 1980).

This does not mean, however, that participants and beneficiaries who reasonably believe they have experienced an intentional interference with their rights under ERISA as a result of the use or threat of force or intimidation are without recourse. The aggrieved participants or beneficiaries have the right to present the evidence they have gathered, which led them to believe that a criminal violation of ERISA Section 511 occurred, to the Employee Benefits Security Administration (EBSA) field office that has jurisdiction for review and investigation. If the EBSA field office investigates the claims of criminal interference and establishes probable cause to believe that a participant or beneficiary has been the victim of criminal intimidation, the field office will present its findings to the appropriate U.S. Attorney's Office for consideration of prosecution. The U.S. Attorney's Office will review the results of the investigation, and if it agrees with EBSA's field office's findings, present the case to a grand jury to seek an indictment of the alleged perpetrators.

Remedies

517. What remedies are available to participants, beneficiaries, and plans when a fiduciary duty is breached?

Federal courts have broad discretion to fashion appropriate relief on behalf of plans, participants, beneficiaries, other fiduciaries, and the Department of Labor to remedy a breach of fiduciary duty, including the return of any profits earned through the use of plan assets. ERISA also provides for the legal remedy of monetary damages for the restoration of plan losses. Courts may fashion whatever equitable or remedial relief they deem appropriate, including the removal of an individual from his position as a fiduciary.[1]

ERISA Section 206(d)(4) permits the offset and alienation of benefits of fiduciaries who have been convicted or held liable for a criminal or civil judgment against the plan to which they serve as fiduciaries if the requirement to pay arises from:

1.   A judgment of conviction for a crime involving the plan;

2.   A civil judgment (or consent order or decree) that is entered by a court in an action brought in connection with a breach (or alleged breach) of fiduciary duty under ERISA; or

3.   A settlement agreement entered into by the participant and either the Secretary of Labor or the Employee Benefits Security Administration (EBSA) in connection with a breach of fiduciary duty.

The court order, judgment, decree, or settlement agreement must specifically require that all or a part of the amount to be paid to the plan be offset against the participant's plan benefits. According to the Conference Committee Report, such an offset is includable against the breaching fiduciary's income as of the date of the offset.[2]

---

1. ERISA Sec. 409(a).
2. H.R. Conf. Rep. No. 220, 105th Cong., 1st Sess. 756-57 (1997).

The Third Circuit Court of Appeals has held that an ERISA health plan's rights under its subrogation/reimbursement provision may be limited by the equitable principle of unjust enrichment, even if plan language indicates otherwise.[1] In the case, the employer sought subrogation of the full amount of medical care its plan paid for even though the subsequent recovery of the employee in litigation against the driver that struck him was, after attorney fees, lower than the amount the employer was seeking subrogation for. In reaching its conclusion the court held that "appropriate equitable relief" does not always equate with full reimbursement.[2]

The Eighth Circuit Court of Appeals has ruled that a 401(k) plan participant is not entitled to monetary damages from the plan sponsor for a three-and-one-half-year delay he experienced in obtaining his 401(k) distribution.[3]

The Tenth Circuit Court of Appeals has ruled that a plaintiff's failure to exhaust remedies regarding a claim for disability benefits results in judgment in favor of the defendant plan.[4]

The U.S. District Court for the Northern District of Texas has held that the monetary relief sought by the plan sponsor to recover an excess distribution of $220,106.94 from the former plan participant was outside the scope of equitable relief provided for under ERISA Section 502(a)(3).[5] While acknowledging that there is an exception for restitution in equity (in the form of a constructive trust or equitable lien), the court determined that because the former participant had spent the excess distribution, it would not apply in this case because the equitable distribution could no longer be traced to particular funds or property. The plan sponsor in this matter was, however, free to pursue a case of personal liability as a general creditor against the former participant. But such action would fall outside ERISA.

The Tenth Circuit Court of Appeals has ruled that an employer's error causing a delay in enrolling a participant in the employer's health plan—which caused the employee to not have coverage for several months, which in turn caused him to be subject to a preexisting-condition exclusion resulting in significant unpaid medical bills—meant that no remedy was available to the participant under ERISA.[6] The court ruled that the employer was a fiduciary and that its actions in failing to timely enroll the participant were a fiduciary breach. However, the monetary damages sought to pay the unpaid medical bills were not "equitable relief" and could not be granted. The court also held that an order of restitution was inapplicable because the employee had not asked for restitution of funds already paid. Finally, the court stated that an order correcting the employee's date of entry into the plan was not proper because the underlying insurer was not a party to the litigation and there was no basis for the court to order the insurer to treat the employee as having been enrolled prior to the time of actual enrollment.

The Eighth Circuit Court of Appeals has ruled that a participant must fully reimburse a plan from her special needs trust because the plan document required full reimbursement,

---

1. *US Airways, Inc. v. McCutchen*, 2011 WL 5557411 (3d Cir. 2011).
2. *US Airways, Inc. v. McCutchen*, above.
3. *Kerr v. Charles F. Vatterott & Co.*, 184 F.3d 938 (8th Cir. 1999).
4. *Getting v. Fortis Benefits*, 2001 U.S. App. LEXIS 3070 (10th Cir. 2001).
5. *Verizon Employee Benefits Comm. v. Adams*, 36 EBC 2878 (N.D. Tex. 2006).
6. *Negley v. Breads of the World Med. Plan*, 2007 U.S. App. LEXIS 5099 (10th Cir. 2007).

and such reimbursement was "appropriate equitable relief" under ERISA.[1] The plaintiff, a self-insured health plan, paid more than $469,000 in medical bills for the defendant participant who was injured in a car accident. The participant sued the parties who injured her and received a $700,000 settlement. After attorneys' fees and costs were paid, the balance ($417,477) was placed in the participant's special needs trust. The court refused to apply the make-whole and pro rata doctrines applicable under insurance law because these doctrines are inapplicable to self-insured health plans subject to ERISA. Further, the court held that their application would have altered the express terms of the plan.[2]

The Sixth Circuit Court of Appeals has held that an employee's state-law claims alleging entitlement to "reliance damages" for misrepresentations his employer made to him about the amount of pension benefits he would receive if he came to work for the employer were not preempted by ERISA.[3]

The Supreme Court declined to review a Fourth Circuit decision that the insurer of an ERISA accidental death and dismemberment plan did not have to pay benefits for a participant who died in a car crash that he caused while driving while legally intoxicated.[4]

Document Reformation and Equitable Estoppel

The U.S. Supreme Court has issued an opinion that ERISA Section 502(a)(1)(B) does not permit a court to *reform* a plan document to comport with an erroneous SPD because the SPD is a communication "about the plan" and does not "constitute the *terms* of the plan."[5] In this holding, the Supreme Court rejected the DOL's position as stated in its Amicus Brief because the Supreme Court was unable to reconcile the DOL's position with ERISA Section 102(a), which provides that an SPD is an informal explanation of plan benefits and cannot be considered a part of a plan's governing documents.

In its second part of that same ruling, the majority opinion discussed relief under ERISA Section 502(a)(3), asking if that provision would authorize relief to the plaintiffs in the form of document *reformation* as "other appropriate equitable relief" in order to prevent fraud or mistake on the theory that such relief has long been an established remedy in courts of equity. It is important to note that neither the parties, nor the DOL in its Amicus Brief, raised this issue, assuming it was not applicable under prior holdings (e.g., *Mertens*, *Knudson*). The six justices wrote that equity courts could reform contracts to reflect mutual understandings when fraudulent suppressions, omissions, or assertions materially affect the substance of the underlying contract. This is so even if the complaining party was also negligent in not realizing its mistake so long as the party's negligence does not fall below a standard of reasonable prudence or violate a legal duty.

1. *Administrative Comm. of the Wal-Mart Stores, Inc. Assocs.' Health & Welfare Plan v. Shank*, 2007 WL 2457664 (8th Cir. 2007).
2. *Administrative Comm. of the Wal-Mart Stores, Inc. Assocs.' Health & Welfare Plan v. Shank*, 2007 WL 2457664 (8th Cir. 2007).
3. *Thurman v. Pfizer, Inc.*, 484 F.3d 855 (6th Cir. 2007).
4. *Eckelberry v. ReliaStar Life Ins. Co.*, 469 F.3d 340 (4th Cir. 2006), cert. denied, 127 S. Ct. 2101 (2007).
5. *CIGNA Corp. v. Amara*, No. 08-804, 50 EBC 2569 (U.S. May 16, 2011).

In this second part of the majority opinion, the Court opined that equitable estoppel may constitute equitable relief available under ERISA Section 502(a)(3). More importantly, from an industry perspective, the six justices concluded that "surcharge" (i.e., monetary compensation) may constitute "equitable relief" for a breach of trust or fiduciary duty. In so holding, the six justices stated, "Equity courts possess the power to provide relief in the form of monetary compensation for a loss resulting from a breach of trust or to prevent unjust enrichment." Make-whole relief in the form of monetary compensation is available where the culpable defendant "is analogous to a trustee" (i.e., a benefits plan fiduciary). The Court distinguished its long-standing *Mertens* holding from the immediate case by explaining that in the prior decision, the Court had disallowed monetary relief because the defendant was a nonfiduciary provider of services to the plan.

The six justices went on to explain that ERISA sets no standard for showing "harm" (which would require proof of actual harm by a preponderance of evidence under the law of equity—and now under ERISA Section 502(a)(3)). In other words, each case must be substantively analyzed on the facts to determine if harm was more likely than not proven by the evidence of the case. The Court also commented that detrimental reliance was not required for reformation of plan documents under the law of equity, and now it should be the same with respect to reformation under ERISA Section 502(a)(3).

However, the six justices did say that equitable estoppel would require proof of detrimental reliance under the law of equity and also should require it under ERISA Section 502(a)(3) in order to provide relief under this doctrine. The Court remanded the case to the district court to determine what equitable relief, if any, would remedy the plaintiff's injury.[1]

Practitioner's Pointer: The majority opinion was not entirely without benefit to plan sponsors. The opinion indicates that if the Supreme Court has an opportunity to rule on the matter, an SPD cannot automatically be enforced as governing language when its language is more favorable to participants (this will overturn the precedent currently standing within the Second, Fourth, Fifth, Sixth, Seventh, and Ninth Circuits).

The opinion holds out the possibility that the participant-friendly rule of deferring to a favorable SPD error rule will soon be supplanted by the Court's new "reformation" doctrine. Plaintiffs would have to prove all of the elements of "reformation" before a governing plan document can be reformed in accordance with an SPD. Again, under *Amara*, ERISA Section 502(a)(1)(B) itself does not authorize reformation. But reformation may be available now as equitable relief under ERISA Section 502(a)(3).

In effect, this "reformation" doctrine may help plan sponsors in litigation, as all Circuits will now have to sort through all claims in their myriad contexts to resolve them. This will allow plan sponsors more opportunity to argue that SPD language errors should not be applicable to a case against them.

The Fifth Circuit Court of Appeals has ruled that a plan's SPD affects Plan interpretation, notwithstanding the Supreme Court decision in the *Amara* case. The Plaintiff-Appellant appealed the district court's summary judgment dismissing her suit to recover health insurance benefits under an ERISA governed employee benefits plan. Defendant-Appellee Aetna Health Inc., a Texas health maintenance organization ("HMO"), provided and administered the plan's health

---

1. *CIGNA Corp. v. Amara*, No. 08-804, 50 EBC 2569 (U.S. May 16, 2011).

insurance benefits under an agreement giving Aetna discretion to interpret the plan's terms. Aetna refused to reimburse the Plaintiff for care she received from a specialist outside of the Aetna HMO to whom she had been referred by a physician in the HMO. Aetna denied her claim because the referral was not pre-authorized by Aetna. The district court found as a matter of law that Aetna did not abuse its discretion in denying coverage. The Fifth Circuit held that the plan was ambiguous and the need for pre-authorization was not clearly stated in Aetna's SPD of the plan. Therefore, under the circumstances it cannot be said as a matter of law that Aetna did not abuse its discretion in denying coverage. The district court ruling was over-turned and the case was remanded for further proceedings.[1]

The Fifth Circuit has ruled, pursuant to the Amara ruling (preceding) that the issue of "surcharge" is a valid potential remedy under ERISA section 502(a)(3) in that a make-whole of the plaintiff for benefits lost may be pled as a plausible claim for relief.[2] This ruling specifically cites a similar holding by the Fourth Circuit wherein the Plaintiff was entitled to receive the financial value of improperly denied health care benefits instead of the amount of premiums paid for the denied coverage.[3]

In considering the limits of ERISA section 502(a)(3) for "appropriate equitable relief", the U.S. Supreme Court has resolved a split among Circuit Courts for ERISA health plans regarding equitable defenses such as unjust enrichment to defeat the express terms of the plan's governing documents. The Supreme Court has ruled that such equitable defenses do not take precedence over the express written terms of the plan. However, the Court did advise that when the plan's governing documents are silent on the issue before the court, the court may then consider equitable principles in seeking to fill in the terms of the plan, or constructing plan language.[4]

Cashed-Out Participants

A federal court for the Southern District of Iowa dismissed a claim brought by former participants in a 401(k) plan seeking compensatory damages because the participants lost money in investments made after cashing out their 401(k) accounts, stating such investments were not a part of the original 401(k) plan.[5] The court advised that the participants would be entitled to transfer their assets back into the 401(k) plan if they could demonstrate that they were deceived into transferring their money as a result of a fiduciary breach.

Conversely, the Fourth Circuit has ruled that 401(k) plan participants who have cashed out still have standing to bring suit under ERISA Section 502(a)(2), because cashed-out former employees remain "participants" in defined contribution retirement plans when seeking to recover amounts that should have been in their accounts but for the alleged fiduciary impropriety.[6]

On a similar note, the Eleventh Circuit Court of Appeals determined that former plan participants could bring an action for breach of fiduciary duty concerning a defined contribution plan's loss in value, since the action stated a claim for benefits under ERISA and was not a suit

---

1. *Koehler v. Aetna Health Inc.*, 2012 WL 1949166 (5th Cir. 2012).

2. *Gearlds v. Entergy Services, Inc.*, 2013 WL 610543 (5th Cir. 2013).

3. *McCravy v. Metro. Life Ins. Co.*, 690 F.3d 176, 180 (4th Cir. 2012).

4. *US Airways, Inc. v. McCutchen*, 2013 WL 1567371 (U.S. 2013).

5. *Young v. Principal Fin. Grp., Inc.*, 2008 WL 1776590 (S.D. Iowa 2008).

6. *In re Mutual Funds Inv. Litig.*, 529 F.3d 207 (4th Cir. 2008).

for damages.[1] The plaintiffs, all former employees of the plan sponsor, brought suit against plan fiduciaries, alleging that the fiduciaries violated their fiduciary duty by allowing the plan to invest in sponsor stock even though the fiduciaries were backdating stock options and creating fraudulent transactions that artificially inflated the price of the sponsor stock held in the plan. The plaintiffs sought restoration of all losses to their accounts caused by the alleged fiduciary breaches, restoration of lost opportunity costs from the losses created, and a purging from the fiduciaries of profits made as a result of the breaches. The lower court dismissed the case on the grounds that the former participants were not participants under ERISA Section 502(a)(2) and, therefore, lacked standing to sue for a breach of fiduciary duty under ERISA Section 409. On appeal, the Eleventh Circuit agreed with the plaintiff's position that they qualified as participants because their complaint asserted a claim for benefits instead of damages. In citing precedent, the court noted that under ERISA, a "participant" entitled to bring a civil action for breach of fiduciary duty includes any employee or former employee of an employer who is, or who may become, eligible to receive a benefit of any type from an employee benefit plan.[2] ERISA permits actions to recover benefits, but it does not permit actions seeking extra-contractual damages. As such, the court advised that whether the former employees had a colorable claim to vested benefits depended on the distinction between benefits and damages.[3]

Relying on prior decisions from the Third Circuit,[4] Sixth Circuit,[5] and the Seventh Circuit,[6] the Eleventh Circuit determined that a complaint involving the decreased value of a defined contribution account due to a fiduciary breach was not a claim for damages because the recovery sought was limited to the difference between the benefits actually received and the benefits that would have been received had the plan fiduciaries fulfilled their obligations.[7]

The Ninth Circuit has joined six other circuits (including those noted above in addition to the First Circuit) in holding that former employees who have cashed out their individual accounts in a former employer's defined contribution plan are still "participants" who can sue to recover losses arising from a breach of fiduciary duty that allegedly reduced the amount of their benefits. Ninth Circuit Court of Appeals held that because the cashed-out former employees had made a claim for benefits under the plans, they had the right to sue as participants for losses to their accounts alleged to have occurred while they were still in the plan.[8]

Scrivener's Error

Where there is "objective, convincing evidence" in considering an error in drafting a plan document that the error did not reflect the participant's reasonable benefit expectations, an equitable reformation of the scrivener's error to correct the plan document may be authorized. The plan document's description of the plan's complex pension formula included a multiplier mistakenly written to apply twice when the intent was to apply it only once. All

---

1. *Lanfear v. Home Depot, Inc.*, 2008 WL 2916390 (11th Cir. 2008).
2. *Firestone Tire & Rubber Co. v. Bruch*, 489 U.S. 101 (1989).
3. *Lanfear v. Home Depot, Inc.*, 2008 WL 2916390 (11th Cir. 2008).
4. *Graden v. Conexant Sys. Inc.*, 496 F.3d 291 (3d Cir. 2007).
5. *Bridges v. Am. Elec. Power Co.*, 498 F.3d 442 (6th Cir. 2007).
6. *Harzewski v. Guidant Corp.*, 489 F.3d 799 (7th Cir. 2007).
7. *Lanfear v. Home Depot, Inc.*, 2008 WL 2916390 (11th Cir. 2008).
8. *Vaughn v. Bay Envtl. Mgmt., Inc.*, 2008 WL 4276603 (9th Cir. 2008).

plan communications, benefit statements, and subsequent versions of the plan did not illustrate, nor contain, a double multiplier. A retired participant in payout status sued the plan, claiming that her pension, and that of approximately 14,000 other participants, should be doubled based upon the unambiguous plan language (drafted in error). The plaintiff also admitted that she never relied on the double-multiplier entered into the plan document in error. The Seventh Circuit Court of Appeals, in explaining that the high standard of "clear, precise, convincing" proof required to establish a scrivener's error should deter plan sponsors from pursuing reformation simply because a plan provision has proven to be unfavorable, ruled that the plan administrator had presented enough objective, convincing evidence that this was a scrivener's error.[1]

518. Can the DOL sue a fiduciary for money damages even though an identical claim brought by a class of participants against the same fiduciary has been the subject of a court-approved settlement?

Yes. Under the 1998 Eleventh Circuit holding in *Herman v. South Carolina National Bank*,[2] the Department of Labor (DOL) may sue a plan fiduciary for monetary damages even though an identical claim brought by a class of participants against the same fiduciary has been the subject of a court-approved settlement. The court ruled that the DOL may bring its identical suit even though it had prior notice of the participant's suit and the pending settlement.

In considering the fiduciary's argument that the DOL's actions were barred under the doctrine of res judicata, the court stated that it did not apply because the Secretary of Labor was not a party to the settlement and has "national public interests" that are "wholly distinct and separate from those of private litigants."

Practitioner's Pointer: When negotiating any settlement with a class of participants who have brought suit against a plan, attorneys are strongly urged to have the DOL join the action through ERISA Section 502(h). Unless and until ERISA is amended to eliminate this "double jeopardy," fiduciaries will be discouraged from settling participant suits, or will settle them for less (in anticipation of the later action by the DOL on the same issue).

---

519. Does a fiduciary breach that causes no damages mandate a remedy?

No, in limited circumstances. The Seventh Circuit Court of Appeals issued a very narrow ruling, holding the fact that a transaction is prohibited by ERISA, or violates some other provision of the Act, does not necessarily mandate a remedy.[3]

In that case, a participant sued the plan and the trustees, alleging that the trustees violated ERISA by engaging in two prohibited transactions and by failing to diversify plan investments. The alleged prohibited transactions included a loan from the plan to a party in interest (see Q 398), and a large investment in a real estate venture in which the plan trustees had a 63 percent financial stake.

---

1. *Young v. Verizon's Bell Atl. Cash Balance Plan*, 2010 WL 3122795 (7th Cir. 2010).
2. *cert. denied*, 119 S. Ct. 1030 (1999).
3. *Etter v. J. Pease Constr. Co.*, 963 F.2d 1005 (7th Cir. 1992).

The district court denied relief concerning the prohibited loan because it was well secured, carried an above market rate of interest, and was timely repaid. The district court further found that the real estate venture, which represented 88 percent of the plan's assets, did not constitute a prohibited transaction and that there was no duty to diversify because under the circumstances, it was prudent not to do so. The court based this decision on the experience and attention of the trustees and the significant profit of a 97 percent return the plan earned on its investment.

The Seventh Circuit affirmed the district court's decision, stating, "[T]he fact that a transaction is prohibited under ERISA does not necessarily mandate a remedy." Citing its decision in *Leigh v. Engle*,[1] the court further stated that the remedy of damages is not appropriate where there is no injury to the plan. In addition, the remedy of divestment is not possible where the plan cashed out of an investment, nor is the remedy of disgorgement of profits appropriate in the absence of evidence that the trustees engaged in self-dealing or transferred assets for their own personal interest.

Practitioner's Pointer: This holding should be strictly construed and narrowly applied. The Department of Labor (DOL) will aggressively enforce the prohibited transaction provisions[2] and the diversification provisions[3] of the Act. In the *Etter* case, the DOL was not involved in the detection of the investments in question nor in the enforcement efforts under ERISA to correct them. Had the DOL discovered such violations in the course of a routine investigation of the subject plan, the trustees probably would have been subject to an official enforcement order to correct the outstanding violations, and would have been subject to the possibility of ERISA Section 502(*l*) penalties (see Q 500) once they were placed on notice to reverse the prohibited transaction. The Seventh Circuit issued a caution in the *Etter* case that lends support to the DOL's enforcement position by saying that while prohibited transactions that do not result in losses may not be appropriate for a remedy, "it is a very dangerous area for trustees to explore, let alone attempt to exploit."

In addition, the Fifth Circuit Court of Appeals has held that although a fiduciary breach that did not result in a loss to a plan is not subject to monetary damages, there is available equitable relief such as the suspension or removal of a violating fiduciary.[4]

Plan Remedies for Recoupment of Overpayments/Subrogation

The Seventh Circuit has ruled that ERISA Section 502 is not the only mechanism through which ERISA-covered entities may obtain reimbursement from plan participants for overpayment.[5] Although plan fiduciaries are limited to obtaining equitable relief under ERISA Section 502(a)(3), the court noted that the statutory language does not address the possibility of a recoupment device to recapture overpayments by the plan. Therefore, the plan sponsor was not precluded by ERISA from invoking contractual remedies for reimbursement to suspend the payment of benefits as reimbursement for past disability and pension plan overpayments. The restriction in *Great-West Life & Annuity Insurance Co. v. Knudson*[6] did not apply here because the contractual

---

1. 727 F.2d 113 (7th Cir. 1984).
2. ERISA Sec. 406.
3. ERISA Sec. 404(a)(1)(C).
4. *Donovan v. Cunningham*, 716 F.2d 1455 (5th Cir. 1983), *cert. denied*, 467 U.S. 1257 (1984).
5. *Northcutt v. General Motors Hourly-Rate Emps. Pension Plan*, 467 F.3d 1031 (7th Cir. 2006).
6. *534 U.S. 204 (2002).*

remedy sought by the plan sponsor was not the seeking of judicial relief beyond the scope of ERISA.[1]

The Supreme Court has ruled that a plan's reimbursement claim is an acceptable form of equitable relief when identifiable funds are in the beneficiary's possession.[2] In *Sereboff*, the participant and her spouse received health plan coverage for injuries sustained in a motor vehicle accident in the amount of approximately $75,000. Under the terms of the plan, they were required to reimburse the plan if their injuries were the result of an act or omission of another person and they received recovery from a third party. The participant and her spouse settled a civil action stemming from their accident for $750,000. They refused a request to reimburse the plan for the $75,000 coverage provided, but in anticipation of the litigation, agreed to place the $75,000 into an investment account pending resolution of the litigation.

The participant argued that the Supreme Court's decision in *Great-West Life & Annuity Insurance Co. v. Knudson*[3] barred the plan's reimbursement claim because it was not "appropriate equitable relief" under ERISA. The Court rejected this argument, stating that the plan sought to recover identifiable funds within the participant's possession. This, the Court noted, differed from the *Great-West* case because Great West did not seek to recover a particular fund from the defendant. The plan language regarding subrogation was sufficient to create an equitable lien by agreement, which is considered equitable relief under ERISA.

The Ninth Circuit Court of Appeals has held that ERISA plans cannot exempt themselves from paying attorneys' fees and costs relating to a participants' personal-injury action when seeking reimbursement for medical expenses the plan paid to a participant. In this matter, the plan language expressly provided the plan with: (i) the right to reimbursement for medical expenses if the participant recovers funds from a third-party tortfeasor; (ii) an exemption from any responsibility for attorneys' fees paid in connection with any tort recovery by the participant; and (iii) the right to full reimbursement irrespective of whether the participant was made whole. The Court held that, even though the plan document clearly provided that the plan would not be responsible for the participant's attorneys' fees, the plan's equitable lien placed on the fees being held in trust by the attorney was unenforceable because the participant's attorney was a "nonsignatory" to the plan. The Court also remanded for further consideration of whether the plan could enforce plan provisions authorizing full reimbursement when the participant had not been made whole by her tort recovery.[4]

520. What are the rules regarding the favorable tax and qualification treatment of restorative payments from a fiduciary breach?

The IRS issued Revenue Ruling 2002-45 regarding the favorable tax and qualification treatment of payments issued to a qualified plan as restoration, or replacement payments, in connection with fiduciary breaches under ERISA.[5]

---

1. *Northcutt v. General Motors Hourly-Rate Emps. Pension Plan*, 467 F.3d 1031 (7th Cir. 2006).
2. *Sereboff v. Mid Atl. Med. Servs., Inc.* 126 S. Ct. 1869 (2006).
3. *534 U.S. 204 (2002).*
4. *CGI Technologies and Solutions Inc. v. Rose*, 2012 WL 2334230 (9th Cir. 2012).
5. Rev. Rul. 2002-45, 2002-2 C.B. 116 (July 22, 2002).

The IRS advises under the ruling that a payment based on a "reasonable determination that there is a reasonable risk of liability for a breach of fiduciary duty and to restore losses" is a *restorative payment* and, "as such, is not a contribution to a qualified plan." The determination as to whether or not a payment made to a plan qualifies as a restorative payment is based on the individual facts and circumstances. In general, payments made in order to restore some or all of a plan's losses due to the imprudent actions (or failure to act) of a fiduciary "that creates a reasonable risk of liability for breach of fiduciary duty" would be deemed to satisfy the facts-and-circumstances requirement of this ruling.[1]

Such restorative payments must be issued in a manner that treats plan participants who are similarly situated similarly with respect to the payment. However, the failure to allocate a share of a restorative payment to the account of fiduciary responsible for the losses will not result in a determination that there is different treatment for similarly situated participants.

Payments rendered pursuant to a Department of Labor (DOL) order or court-approved settlement (including payments made under the Voluntary Fiduciary Correction Program (VFC Program) attributable to fiduciary breach, and lost earnings calculated under the Employee Plans Compliance Resolution System (EPCRS) to a defined contribution plan are considered to be made on account of a reasonable risk of liability and, therefore, qualify as restorative payments. Payments made under the VFC Program provisions regarding delinquent elective deferrals, or any other payments to a plan required under the Internal Revenue Code, are not considered restorative.

Restorative payments made in accordance with Revenue Ruling 2002-45 are not subject to the annual additions limit of IRC Section 415(c) or the nondiscrimination requirements of IRC Section 401(a)(4) and, if applicable, IRC Section 401(k)(3) or 401(m). Finally, restorative payments are not subject to the IRC Section 404 limit on deductions, nor to the IRC Section 4972 excise tax on nondeductible contributions.

521. How are the losses determined if a breaching fiduciary is held personally liable?

The measure of damages to be applied to a breaching fiduciary is determined by establishing what the plan would have earned in an investment in the absence of the fiduciary's breach. This concept is referred to as "making the plan whole." Where there are several alternative returns that could have been earned in the absence of the fiduciary breach, the court applies the one that is most favorable to the plan and its participants and beneficiaries. This has been established and upheld repeatedly by the courts.[2]

A breaching fiduciary is not held liable for all profits earned while acting in the capacity of a fiduciary.[3] A breaching fiduciary is liable for only those profits earned through the use of

1. Rev. Rul. 2002-45, 2002-2 C.B. 116, 117 (July 22, 2002).
2. See *Leigh v. Engle*, 858 F.2d 361 (7th Cir. 1988); *Donovan v. Bierworth*, 754 F.2d 1049 (2d Cir. 1985); *Dardaganis v. Grace Capital, Inc.*, 755 F. Supp. 85 (S.D.N.Y. 1985).
3. *American Fed'n of Unions, Local 102 v. Equitable Life Assurance Soc'y*, 841 F.2d 658 (5th Cir. 1988).

plan assets in a breach of fiduciary duty, regardless of whether or not the plan suffered a loss as a result of the breach.[1]

Further, plan losses incurred through a fiduciary breach may not be offset by gains earned by the fiduciary in a separate and distinct transaction.[2]

522. Can a fiduciary be subject to punitive damages for a breach of fiduciary duty?

ERISA does not expressly permit the imposition of punitive damages. Some courts addressing the issue held that the imposition of punitive damages to be paid to a plan was within a court's discretion.[3]

The United States Supreme Court had originally left this question open.[4] However, the Court later held that participants and beneficiaries may not recover punitive damages from a fiduciary for a breach of fiduciary duty. The only available remedies are the restoration of losses and disgorgement of profits, both of which must be paid to the plan.[5]

523. May a participant recover interest on improperly delayed benefits payments?

Yes, the ability of participants to recover prejudgment interest for periods of delay in the awarding of benefits has recently received favorable rulings in three cases of note.

In the case of *Jackson v. Fortis Benefits Insurance Co.*,[6] the Eighth Circuit Court of Appeals held that prejudgment interest may be awarded even when a plaintiff has recovered the delayed benefits without resorting to litigation. According to the court, prejudgment interest is available under ERISA so long as the plaintiff demonstrates that the plan administrator breached either his statutory obligations under ERISA or the terms of the governing plan.

Under *Dunigan v. Metropolitan Life Insurance Co.*,[7] the Second Circuit Court of Appeals ruled that a participant may sue to recover interest on benefits that were awarded late. In this case, the defense argued that an award of interest was compensatory and not equitable, and, therefore, was not recoverable under ERISA Section 502(a)(3). In rejecting that argument, the court stated that an award of interest served to make the plaintiff whole in light of the defendant's unjustified delay in awarding the benefits. As such, the interest award qualified as equitable relief because it prevented the defendant from becoming unjustly enriched by retaining earnings on the monies involved during the period of unjustified delay.

Most recently, the United States District Court for the District of Minnesota ruled that "the plaintiff's suit for restitution (of interest on improperly delayed benefits payments) is equitable,

---

1. ERISA Sec. 409(a); *Donovan v. Mazzola*, 716 F.2d 1226 (9th Cir. 1983), *cert. denied*, 464 U.S. 1040 (1984).
2. *Leigh v. Engle*, 858 F.2d 361 (7th Cir. 1988).
3. See, e.g., *Monson v. Century Mfg. Co.*, 739 F.2d 1293 (8th Cir. 1984).
4. See *Massachusetts Mut. Life Ins. Co. v. Russell*, 473 U.S. 134 (1985).
5. *Mertens v. Hewitt Assocs.*, 508 U.S. 248 (1993).
6. 245 F.3d 748 (8th Cir. 2001).
7. 2002 U.S. App. LEXIS 337 (2d Cir. 2002).

not legal." In following the line of logic presented in the *Dunigan* case (above), the court opined that "[b]y not awarding her benefits during the periods which she claims were rightfully owed to her, defendant made a profit on that money in the form of interest earned. Plaintiff merely seeks to have defendant disgorge the interest it earned on the money due to her."[1]

Practitioner's Pointer: In the cases above, a review of the plan documents showed that the determination of whether to award benefits under applicable plan provisions was left to the discretion of the plan administrator. Specifically in the *Jackson* case, the court held that it was the abuse of this discretion that resulted in a violation of the plan document and the general fiduciary provisions of ERISA. In exercising such discretion under plan documents, plan administrators are urged to carefully document the reasons for any delays with all supporting information and materials that support their position. This may serve to blunt any claim that the delay was an abuse of discretion.

---

524. Are fiduciaries subject to civil liability for the interference with ERISA protected rights?

ERISA Section 510 states that "[i]t shall be unlawful for any person to discharge, fine, suspend, expel, discipline, or discriminate against a participant or beneficiary for exercising any right to which he is entitled under the provisions of an employee benefit plan" or ERISA or to interfere with the attainment of such rights. The provisions of ERISA Section 502 (Civil Enforcement) govern the enforcement of ERISA Section 510.

Courts have held that where such interference with ERISA-protected rights has been committed by a fiduciary that is also the employer, participants and beneficiaries may recover damages.[2]

525. What are the rules regarding co-fiduciary liability?

In addition to liability for their own conduct, plan fiduciaries may also be liable for a breach of fiduciary duty committed by co-fiduciaries. A fiduciary with respect to a plan may be liable for a breach of a fiduciary duty by another fiduciary with respect to the same plan in the following circumstances: (1) if he participates knowingly in, or knowingly undertakes to conceal, an act or omission of another fiduciary, knowing that the act or omission is a breach; (2) if, by a failure to comply with ERISA Section 404(a)(1) (requiring fiduciaries to discharge their duties solely in the interest of participants and their beneficiaries) in the administration of his responsibilities that give rise to his status as a fiduciary, *he enables another fiduciary to commit a breach*; or (3) if he has knowledge of a breach by another fiduciary, unless he makes reasonable efforts under the circumstances to remedy the breach.[3]

The ERISA Conference Report, as well as the Seventh Circuit, established the "knowing participation" rule, which holds that in order for a co-fiduciary to be held liable, he must know that: (1) the other person is a fiduciary with respect to the plan; (2) the other person participated in the act that constituted the breach; and (3) the act itself constituted a breach.[4]

---

1. *Parke v. First Reliance Standard Life Ins. Co.*, 2002 U.S. Dist. LEXIS 18762 (D. Minn. 2002).
2. See *Ingersoll-Rand Co. v. McClendon*, 498 U.S. 133 (1990); *Byrd v. MacPapers, Inc.*, 961 F.2d 157 (11th Cir. 1992).
3. ERISA Sec. 405(a).
4. H.R. Conf. Rep. No. 93-1280, 93d Cong., 2d Sess. 323 (1974) (ERISA Conference Report); *Thornton v. Evans*, 692 F.2d 1064 (7th Cir. 1982).

The ERISA Conference Report also states that a co-fiduciary is liable "if he knowingly undertakes to conceal a breach committed by the other [fiduciary]." In order for liability to be imposed for the concealment of a breach, the "knowing participation" rule is applied, as the Conference Report provides: "For the first fiduciary to be liable, he must know that the other is a fiduciary with regard to the plan, must know of the act, and must know it is a breach."

The First Circuit has held that, where an investment manager is involved, ERISA Section 405(d) specifically limits co-fiduciary liability to actions that involve a "knowing participation or concealment of" an act or omission of another fiduciary.[1] Thus, where a nondiscretionary trustee bank expressed concern over the real estate valuations of plan assets by the investment manager (which later proved to be inappropriately inflated), the bank did not assume the liability to ensure that the assets were properly valued. The court held that ERISA does not impose a "Good Samaritan" liability that would cause an institution to volunteer itself as a fiduciary regarding matters to which it would otherwise have no fiduciary liability simply because it undertakes reporting responsibilities that exceed its official mandate.[2]

A bank acting as a co-fiduciary was held liable under ERISA Section 405(a)(2) when it resigned as plan fiduciary and assigned the plan's assets to the administrator without taking the necessary steps to protect the assets of participants and beneficiaries, enabling the administrator to embezzle the plan's assets. The resigning fiduciary had reason to be concerned about the administrator (the plan sponsor's president) in that the administrator was repeatedly late in making remittances of the participant's 401(k) salary deferrals to the plan trust.[3]

In applying the "reasonable efforts" to remedy the breach requirement of ERISA Section 405(a)(3), regulations state that where a majority of plan fiduciaries plan on taking action that would clearly violate the prudence requirement of ERISA Section 404(a)(1)(B), the minority fiduciaries must take "all reasonable and legal steps" to prevent the majority fiduciaries from taking the planned action. If the minority fiduciaries can demonstrate that they unsuccessfully took all reasonable and legal steps to prevent the imprudent actions of the majority fiduciaries, they will not be held liable for the breach committed by the majority fiduciaries.[4]

A successor fiduciary is required to take whatever action is "reasonable" under the circumstances to remedy a breach by a former fiduciary if he knows of the existence of a breach by the prior fiduciary. The failure to take whatever steps are reasonable to remedy the breach will result in the successor fiduciary's being held liable for a separate breach of fiduciary responsibility.[5]

526. Is there a right of co-fiduciary contribution?

A civil action may be brought by a plan fiduciary, on behalf of the plan, against another plan fiduciary in an effort to "enjoin any act or practice that violates" ERISA or the terms of the plan to which they serve as fiduciaries. She may also bring a civil action on behalf of the plan

---

1. *Beddall v. State St. Bank & Trust Co.*, 137 F.3d 12 (1st Cir. 1998).
2. *Beddall v. State St. Bank & Trust Co.*, above.
3. *Ream v. Frey*, 107 F.3d 147 (3d Cir. 1997).
4. Labor Reg. §2509.75-5, FR-10.
5. DOL Adv. Op. 76-95.

to seek appropriate equitable relief and to enforce any provisions of ERISA that a co-fiduciary may be violating.[1]

ERISA, however, does not provide for, or preclude a right of contribution between co-fiduciaries. Consequently, the issue has been settled on both sides by different courts and is, for all intents and purposes, unresolved.

One court held that a federal right of contribution may only arise where Congress has expressly provided for it, has clearly implied a right of contribution, or has granted the courts power to fashion a right of contribution under federal common law. Since, under ERISA, there has been no such right of contribution expressed, there can be no right of contribution by a co-fiduciary.[2] In a similar holding, another court held that a plan administrator who has been found liable for a breach of fiduciary duty by engaging in prohibited transactions does not have a right of contribution against the plan's trustees.[3] The Supreme Court has held that ERISA Section 409 only establishes a right of remedy on behalf of the plan.[4] The Ninth Circuit Court of Appeals applied this holding when it held that a plan fiduciary is liable to the plan for any losses the plan suffers as a result of a breach, and because ERISA Section 409 only provides a remedy for the benefit of the plan, the breaching fiduciary has no right to the equitable remedy of contribution from co-fiduciaries.[5]

In holding that ERISA does not preclude a right of contribution from co-fiduciaries, a federal district court held that traditional trust law does provide for contribution under ERISA's federal common law.[6] The Seventh Circuit Court of Appeals has held in two separate cases that there is a right of contribution against more culpable trustees and that a district court has equitable power to require a more culpable fiduciary to indemnify passive co-fiduciaries for losses incurred by the plan.[7] Also, a federal court may not refuse to approve a settlement agreement between the Department of Labor and certain fiduciaries where certain third-party defendants who file an objection to the settlement agreement are not adversely affected by it.[8]

527. May nonfiduciaries who participate in a breach of fiduciary duty be held liable for monetary damages?

No. The Supreme Court has held that participants are not permitted to recover monetary damages from nonfiduciaries who knowingly participate in a fiduciary's breach of duty. The available relief to be applied against nonfiduciaries who knowingly participate in a fiduciary breach is found in equity.[9] Restitution has been deemed to be an appropriate equitable remedy that will require nonfiduciaries who are found liable for their active participation in a fiduciary breach to return to the plan all money earned through their active participation in the breach.[10]

1. ERISA Sec. 502(a)(3).
2. *Mutual Life Ins. Co. v. Yampol*, 706 F. Supp. 596 (N.D. Ill. 1988).
3. *Daniels v. National Emp. Benefit Servs., Inc.*, 877 F. Supp. 1067 (N.D. Ohio 1995).
4. *Massachusetts Mut. Life Ins. Co. v. Russell*, 473 U.S. 134 (1985).
5. *Kim v. Fujikawa*, 871 F.2d 1427 (9th Cir. 1989).
6. *Cohen v. Baker*, 845 F. Supp. 289 (E.D. Pa. 1994).
7. *Donovan v. Robbins*, 752 F.2d 1170 (7th Cir. 1985); *Free v. Briody*, 732 F.2d 1331 (7th Cir. 1984).
8. *Donovan v. Robbins*, above; *Free v. Briody*, above.
9. *Mertens v. Hewitt Assocs.*, 508 U.S. 248 (1993).
10. ERISA Sec. 502(a)(3); *Landwehr v. DuPree*, 72 F.3d 726 (9th Cir. 1995).

Likewise, nonfiduciaries are not subject to a right of contribution for their active participation in a breach.[1]

The First Circuit Court of Appeals has held that nonfiduciaries who do not benefit from their actions may not be subject to nonmonetary equitable remedies for their active participation in a fiduciary breach.[2] Under this holding the Department of Labor could not seek an injunction to bar a nonfiduciary consultant from providing his services to plans even though the consultant had previously advised plan fiduciaries to violate ERISA.

The Supreme Court has reconciled contradicting circuit court opinions on this issue, unanimously ruling that a fiduciary (even those culpable in the prohibited transaction at issue), participant, or beneficiary can sue a nonfiduciary party in interest for equitable relief for engaging in a prohibited transaction. Where the nonfiduciary party in interest engages in an ERISA Section 406 violation with a fiduciary, both may be held liable under ERISA Section 502(a)(3). The Supreme Court took a plan-based approach to this issue when reviewing ERISA Section 502(a)(3) by holding that it imposes a duty on nonfiduciary parties in interest that is separate and distinct from individual duties specifically imposed on fiduciaries under ERISA Sections 404 and 406.[3] This ruling may have a dramatic impact on future litigation stemming from prohibited transactions because it creates a potential second class of defendants in service providers (many of whom have much deeper pockets than individual fiduciaries) who knowingly participate in a fiduciary breach. The Supreme Court indicated in the *Harris Trust* ruling that an action for restitution under ERISA Section 502(a)(3) could be considered one for "equitable relief" as required in the *Mertens* case discussed above.

528. May a fiduciary enter into an agreement that relieves him from liability?

Generally speaking, no. Except as allowed by ERISA Section 405(b)(1) (a trust agreement that allocates specific duties) and ERISA Section 405(d) (delegation of authority to an investment manager), any provision in an agreement or instrument that purports to relieve a fiduciary from responsibility or liability for any responsibility, obligation, or duty under ERISA is void as against public policy.[4] However, plans and fiduciaries are allowed to purchase fiduciary insurance that provides coverage for potential liability for a fiduciary breach occurring in regard to an employee benefit plan.[5]

Plan fiduciaries are permitted to indemnify their employees who actually perform fiduciary services for the plan because this does not relieve the fiduciaries of their responsibilities under ERISA. An indemnification agreement that maintains a fiduciary's liability, but permits another party to satisfy any liability incurred by the fiduciary in a manner such as insurance coverage would provide, is permissible.[6]

---

1. *Glaziers & Glassblowers Union Local 252 Annuity Fund v. Newbridge Sec., Inc.*, 823 F. Supp. 1191 (E.D. Pa. 1993).
2. *Reich v. Rowe*, 20 F.3d 25 (1st Cir. 1994).
3. *Harris Trust & Sav. Bank v. Salomon Smith Barney Inc.*, 530 U.S. 238 (2000).
4. ERISA Sec. 410(a).
5. ERISA Sec. 410(b).
6. Labor Reg. §2509.75-4.

Further, the Seventh Circuit Court of Appeals has held that ERISA permits a plan trustee to be indemnified by a more culpable trustee for plan losses incurred due to a breach of fiduciary duty.[1]

Releases have been allowed from participants that relieve a fiduciary from past liability for a fiduciary breach where the releases were used to settle a bona fide dispute and had been given in exchange for consideration.[2] A release that conditions the distribution of a vested interest from a plan on the execution of the release must be provided for in the plan document in order for it to be valid under ERISA.[3]

529. Under what circumstances may liquidated damages be awarded in a civil action for a breach of fiduciary duty?

There is case precedent that in civil actions under ERISA's civil enforcement provisions, reasonable liquidated damages may be awarded at the discretion of the court.[4]

Federal common law principles require the satisfaction of two conditions in order to award liquidated damages: (1) the damages caused by the breach must be difficult or impossible to estimate; and (2) the amount of the award must be a reasonable forecast of just compensation for the harm caused.[5]

Statute of Limitations

530. What is the statute of limitations for bringing a civil action for a fiduciary breach?

ERISA Section 413(a) provides that "[n]o action may be commenced under this title with respect to a fiduciary's breach of any responsibility, duty, or obligation under this part, after the earlier of:

1.   Six years after (a) the date of the last action which constituted a part of the breach or violation, or (b) in the case of an omission, the latest date on which the fiduciary could have cured the breach or violation; or

2.   Three years after the earliest date on which the plaintiff had actual knowledge of the breach or violation; except that in the case of fraud or concealment, such action may be commenced not later than six years after the date of discovery of such breach or violation."

The Department of Labor (DOL) distinguishes fiduciary violations as either discrete or continuing violations. A discrete violation is one that occurs at a single moment in time. An example of a discrete violation would be the purchase of real property for more than fair market value. For a

1. *Free v. Briody*, 732 F.2d 1331 (7th Cir. 1984).
2. *Blessing & Grossman v. Struthers-Dunn, Inc.*, 1985 U.S. Dist. LEXIS 14159 (E.D. Pa. 1985).
3. *Haberern v. Kaupp Vascular Surgeons Ltd. Defined Benefit Plan & Trust Agreement*, 24 F.3d 1491 (3d Cir. 1994), *cert. denied*, 513 U.S. 1149 (1995).
4. See *Doolan v. Doolan Steel Corp.*, 591 F. Supp. 1506 (E.D. Pa. 1984).
5. *Idaho Plumbers Funds v. United Mech. Contractors, Inc.*, 875 F.2d 212 (9th Cir. 1989).

single discrete violation, the period for the statute of limitations is computed in a straightforward manner.

A continuing violation is one that continues past the initial moment when it occurs. An example of a continuing violation is an outstanding loan to a party in interest (which continues to be an ongoing violation so long as the loan is outstanding). With continuing violations, the DOL has argued the theory that the statute of limitations should have no direct effect other than making monetary relief unavailable with respect to pre–limitations period portions of a violation.

In response to this argument, the Ninth Circuit Court of Appeals has stated, "The application of the continuing violation theory founders on the plain language of [ERISA Section 413(a)(2)]. This section requires the plaintiff's knowledge to be measured from the 'earliest date' on which he or she knew of the breach.... Once a plaintiff knew of one breach, an awareness of later breaches would impart nothing materially new.... The earliest date on which a plaintiff became aware of any breach would thus start the limitation period of [ERISA Section 413(a)(2)] running."[1]

In an earlier similar ruling, the Ninth Circuit Court held that a continuous series of breaches may allow a plaintiff to argue for a new cause of action with each new breach. However, if the breaches are of the same nature and the plaintiff had actual knowledge of one of the breaches more than three years before bringing the civil action, ERISA Section 413(a)(2) bars the action.[2]

The Second Circuit Court of Appeals has accepted the "continuing violation" theory allowing for a claim beyond the original three- and six-year statute of limitations under a specific application of the "prudent investor rule"[3] (see Q 288). Under the prudent investor rule, fiduciaries have a continuing obligation to monitor plan investments and to review and advise the subject plan to divest itself of unlawful or imprudent investments. The court held that a fiduciary obligation to continually monitor plan investments effectively permits actions under ERISA Section 404(a)(1)(B) to be brought after the initial three- or six-year statute of limitations.[4]

The Eighth Circuit Court of Appeals has applied a ten-year statute of limitations to lawsuits for benefit claims under ERISA.[5] In that case, the plaintiff filed a claim for benefits under her employer's health benefits plan in late 1997 and in early 1998. In mid-2001, she filed suit against her employer, seeking to be compensated for the cost of medical procedures she claimed were wrongfully denied under the plan. The employer argued that the claim was barred due to the expiration of the statute of limitations under ERISA. The court noted that ERISA does not provide a statute of limitations for "abuse of discretion" and, therefore, the court looked to Iowa statutes for guidance. The court argued that the employer's improper denial for pre-authorization of a health benefits claim and abuse of discretion in denying the request for pre-authorization were

---

1. *Phillips v. Alaska Hotel & Rest. Emps. Pension Fund*, 944 F.2d 509 (9th Cir. 1991).
2. *Ziegler v. Connecticut Gen. Life Ins. Co.*, 916 F.2d 548 (9th Cir. 1990).
3. ERISA Sec. 404(a)(1)(B).
4. *Morrissey v. Curran*, 567 F.2d 546 (2d Cir. 1977).
5. *Shaw v. McFarland Clinic, P.C.*, 2004 U.S. App. LEXIS 6408 (8th Cir. 2004).

analogous to an insured's claim against her insurer and a breach of contract subject to Iowa state law. Under that law, a ten-year statute of limitations applied.

The Ninth Circuit has ruled that the ERISA section 413(1) six year statute of limitations on fiduciary breach claims involving investment menu selection generally runs from the time the menu option at issue is added.[1]

Practitioner's Pointer: The DOL is likely to continue in its efforts to establish cases that accept the "continuing violation" theory to extend the statute of limitations when there is a failure to correct outstanding breaches that are of the same kind and nature as those that have been outstanding beyond the ERISA Section 413(a)(2) limits. Because of this, should plan representatives become aware of any outstanding violations, or of a series of actions by plan fiduciaries that may be violations of the same kind and nature, they should take remedial action to reverse or correct the violations that would create isolated violations and clearly establish the time frame under which the statute of limitations would run.

531. Can a plan impose a statute of limitations on participants' right to file suit?

Under ERISA, a participant may file suit in federal court to recover benefits after her claim for benefits has been denied by an ERISA-qualified plan. The individual has a right to sue only after having exhausted a plan's claim procedures. Because of this, ERISA does not mandate a statute of limitations for a denial of benefits. This leaves states to rely on the most analogous state laws in managing such claims (usually contracts law).

In *Dye v. Associates First Capital Corp. Cafeteria Plan*,[2] the court upheld a provision in a plan that provided that "no legal action may be commenced against an ERISA covered plan more than 120 days after receipt of the decision on appeal." The court found that the plaintiff's claims were barred by this governing plan provision if not pursued within 120 days.

In determining whether this plan-imposed statute of limitations was enforceable, the court employed a three-factor test:

1. Is the plan-imposed statute of limitations a subterfuge to avoid lawsuits? (In this case, no; the plan was self-funded and did not exist to make a profit.)

2. Does the plan impose a similar time frame on the administrator to complete the review of the claim? (In this case, yes.)

3. Does the applicable statute of limitations begin to run prior to the exhaustion of internal appeals? (In this case, no.)

532. How is the statute of limitations affected by an act of fraud or concealment by a fiduciary?

If a breaching fiduciary has taken affirmative steps to hide his breach of fiduciary duty, the statute of limitations for bringing a civil action against him is six years from the discovery of

---

1. *Tibble v. Edison International*, 711 F.3d 1061 (9th Cir. March 21, 2013).
2. 2006 WL 2612743 (E.D. Tex. 2006).

the breach or violation. In determining whether the six-year statute of limitations applies, the issue is whether or not the fiduciary took affirmative steps to conceal his breach, not whether or not the civil complaint actually alleges fraud.[1]

The plan or participant bringing a civil action must prove that the fiduciary undertook a course of conduct designed to conceal evidence of the wrongdoing, and that the plan and the participants did not have actual or constructive knowledge of evidence of the violation, despite the exercise of reasonable diligence.[2]

533. When does an ERISA cause of action accrue for purposes of the statute of limitations?

ERISA is silent as to what event constitutes the fiduciary breach at issue or the knowledge of that breach. There are, however, two different theories that have developed. The "discovery rule" holds that the statute of limitations begins to run when the violation is discovered.[3] The "actual knowledge of breach or violation" rule states that the participant plaintiff must have knowledge of all of the relevant facts that are sufficient to provide the participant knowledge that a fiduciary duty has been breached or that a provision of ERISA has been violated.[4]

The Ninth Circuit Court of Appeals has ruled that a clear breach of ERISA Section 503 duties regarding notification and review after the denial of a participant's claims, while not dispositive, is a significant factor for determining if the statute of limitations has started to run against the participant.[5] The Ninth Circuit Court holds that an ERISA cause of action accrues under Section 503 either at the time the benefits are actually denied or when the insured has reason to know the claim has been denied. The court noted that the facts indicated that the participant had reason to know of the denial of benefits more than six years before he filed suit. Therefore, the court ruled that the claim was time barred due to expiration of the statute of limitations.

534. When does the statute of limitations begin to run for a denial of benefits claim?

The statute of limitations for a denial of benefits claim begins to run when the participant receives notice of the denial.[6] Where a participant has made no formal request for benefits, the statute of limitations begins to run at the time that the participant "should have known" she was entitled to benefits.[7]

A claim for denial of benefits is time barred where the plaintiff could have obtained knowledge, through due diligence, that the denial of benefits was a fiduciary violation.[8]

---

1. ERISA Sec. 413; *Kurz v. Philadelphia Elec. Co.*, 96 F.3d 1544 (3d Cir. 1996).
2. *J. Geils Band Emp. Benefit Plan v. Smith Barney Shearson, Inc.*, 76 F.3d 1245 (1st Cir. 1996).
3. *Connors v. Hallmark & Sons Coal Co.*, 935 F.2d 336 (D.C. Cir. 1991).
4. *Gluck v. Unisys Corp.*, 960 F.2d 1168 (3d Cir. 1992).
5. *Chuck v. Hewlett Packard Co.*, 2006 WL 2052288 (9th Cir. 2006).
6. *Price v. Provident Life & Accident Ins. Co.*, 2 F.3d 986 (9th Cir. 1993).
7. *Brown v. Cuttermill Bus Serv.*, 1991 U.S. Dist. LEXIS 9487 (E.D.N.Y. 1991).
8. *Vernau v. Vic's Mkt.*, 896 F.2d 43 (3d Cir. 1990).

535. Is knowledge of a breach by a former fiduciary imputed to a successor fiduciary for purposes of the statute of limitations?

The statute of limitations for a fiduciary breach begins to run when the plaintiff has actual knowledge of the breach. As such, knowledge of a former fiduciary's breach cannot be imputed to a successor fiduciary. A claim for a fiduciary breach filed by a successor trustee more than three years after the prior trustees had knowledge of the violation is not time barred.[1]

536. What is the statute of limitations in fiduciary cases where ERISA does not provide one?

ERISA specifically provides for a specific time limit under which suits to enforce certain fiduciary standards may be brought. Where ERISA does not expressly provide a statute of limitations for bringing a civil action relating to a plan, courts have applied state statutes of limitation that are most analogous to the claim.[2] In a civil action under ERISA Section 510 alleging discrimination or interference with a protected right, the analogous state statute of limitations is that governing employment discrimination, wrongful termination, or wrongful discharge.[3]

When a state statute of limitations expresses a hostile stance toward federal causes of action, it will not be applied to an action brought under ERISA. The Tenth Circuit has held that a very brief state statute of limitations that governed civil actions "seeking to impose liability based on a federal statute" would not be applied.[4]

537. How can the statute of limitations be tolled?

"Tolling" the statute of limitations (i.e., delaying it from running) can be accomplished by filing a civil action relating to the fiduciary issue in a state court. However, if the issue is one that should be filed in a federal court, the statute of limitations will not be tolled by the state action for purposes of filing a subsequent ERISA claim in federal court.[5]

Attorneys' Fees

538. When does a court have discretion to award attorneys' fees?

A court has discretion to award reasonable attorneys' fees to participants, beneficiaries, or fiduciaries.[6] This has been interpreted to include the costs of a civil action through appeal, paralegal fees, and the costs of collecting a post-judgment ERISA award.[7]

---

1. *District 65 Ret. Trust v. Prudential Sec.*, 925 F. Supp. 1551 (N.D. Ga. 1996).
2. See, e.g., *Kennedy v. Electricians Pension Plan IBEW #995*, 954 F.2d 1116 (5th Cir. 1992); *Meade v. Pension Appeals & Review Comm.*, 966 F.2d 190 (6th Cir. 1992); *Tolle v. Touche, Inc.*, 977 F.2d 1129 (7th Cir. 1992); *Lumpkin v. Envirodyne Indus., Inc.*, 933 F.2d 449 (7th Cir.), *cert. denied*, 502 U.S. 939 (1991); *Held v. Manufacturers Hanover Leasing Corp.*, 912 F.2d 1197 (10th Cir. 1990); *Giuffre v. Delta Airlines*, 746 F. Supp. 238 (D. Mass. 1990); *Bologna v. NMU Pension Trust*, 654 F. Supp. 637 (S.D.N.Y. 1987); *Nolan v. Aetna Life Ins. Co.*, 588 F. Supp. 1375 (E.D. Mich. 1984).
3. *Sandberg v. KPMG Peat Marwick, LLP*, 111 F.3d 331 (2d Cir. 1997); *Rich v. Zeneca, Inc.*, 845 F. Supp. 162 (D. Del. 1994).
4. *Trustees of the Wyo. Laborers Health & Welfare Plan v. Morgan & Oswood Constr. Co.*, 850 F.2d 613 (10th Cir. 1988).
5. *Shofer v. Stuart Hack Co.*, 970 F.2d 1316 (4th Cir. 1992).
6. ERISA Sec. 502(g)(1).
7. *Free v. Briody*, 793 F.2d 807 (7th Cir. 1986); *Mendez v. Teachers Ins. & Annuity Ass'n & College Ret. Equities Fund*, 789 F. Supp 139 (S.D.N.Y. 1993); *Parise v. Ricelli Haulers, Inc.*, 672 F. Supp. 72 (N.D.N.Y. 1987).

Courts have the discretion to deny attorneys' fees in cases that are not timely filed.[1]

In determining what are "reasonable" attorneys' fees under ERISA Section 502(g)(1), courts will utilize what is commonly referred to as the "lodestar method." Using the lodestar method, the court determines a reasonable number of hours spent on the case and then multiplies the hours by a reasonable hourly rate. The court may take into consideration such factors as the complexity of the case and the prevailing hourly rates of local attorneys.[2]

The Eleventh Circuit Court of Appeals has held that a district court abuses its discretion regarding the decision whether or not to award attorneys' fees when it denies a motion for fees without stating the reasons for doing so.[3]

The Fifth Circuit Court of Appeals has ruled that a dismissal of an action under ERISA for lack of subject matter jurisdiction precludes an award of attorneys' fees under ERISA Section 502(g)(1).[4]

539. Who may be awarded attorneys' fees in an ERISA civil action?

ERISA Section 502(g)(1) provides that "[i]n any action under [ERISA] by a participant, beneficiary, or fiduciary, the court in its discretion may allow a reasonable attorneys' fee and costs of action *to either party*" (emphasis added). Some courts have strictly interpreted this and have limited the recovery of attorneys' fees to only a participant, beneficiary or fiduciary.[5]

However, there have been cases where attorneys' fees were awarded to employers, pension plans, and insurance companies as prevailing parties.[6]

Further, out-of-court settlements of ERISA actions are not a bar to the awarding of attorneys' fees.[7]

The Eighth Circuit Court of Appeals awarded attorneys' fees to an employee benefit plan administrator (under the Equal Access to Justice Act) because the administrator was the victim of a "baseless claim" filed by the Department of Labor (DOL).[8] The DOL filed suit claiming that the administrator should have done more to ensure medical claim payments from the bankrupt plan sponsor of an ERISA-covered health plan. The court stated that the DOL failed to show that it was "justified in substance or in the main" in filing suit against the administrator because it knew that the administrator had made "reasonable, prudent, and largely successful efforts to obtain as much funding as possible" for the health plan.[9]

1. *Schake v. Colt Indus. Operating Corp. Severance Plan*, 960 F.2d 1188 (3rd Cir. 1992).
2. *D'Emanuaelle v. Montgomery Ward & Co.*, 904 F.2d 1379 (9th Cir. 1990). See *Bowen v. Southtrust Bank of Ala.*, 760 F. Supp. 889 (M.D. Ala. 1991); *Motion Picture Indus. Pension Plan v. Klages Group*, 757 F. Supp. 1082 (C.D. Cal. 1991).
3. *Evans v. Bexley*, 750 F.2d 1498 (11th Cir. 1985).
4. *Cliburn v. Police Jury Ass'n of La.*, 165 F.3d 315 (5th Cir. 1999).
5. See *Self Ins. Inst. of Am., Inc. v. Korioth*, 53 F.3d 694 (5th Cir. 1995); *Saladino v. I.L.G.W.U. Nat'l Ret. Fund*, 754 F.2d 473 (2d Cir. 1985); *M & R Inv. Co. v. Fitzsimmons*, 685 F.2d 283 (9th Cir. 1982).
6. See *Credit Managers Ass'n v. Kennesaw Life & Accident Ins. Co.*, 25 F.3d 743 (9th Cir. 1994); *Continental Can Co. v. Chicago Truck Drivers & Warehouse Workers Union Pension Fund*, 921 F.2d 126 (7th Cir. 1990).
7. *Cefali v. Buffalo Brass Co.*, 748 F. Supp. 1011 (W.D.N.Y. 1990).
8. *Herman v. Schwent*, 177 F.3d 1063 (8th Cir. 1999).
9. *Herman v. Schwent*, above.

540. What factors will a court consider in awarding attorneys' fees?

The majority of courts have applied a five-factor test for determining whether or not to award attorneys' fees in an ERISA civil action. The five factors are: (1) the degree of the offending party's culpability (bad faith); (2) the ability of the offending party to pay an award of attorneys' fees; (3) the deterrent factor of such an award; (4) whether or not the motion for an award of attorneys' fees is to benefit all participants and beneficiaries, or if the action was brought forth to resolve a significant legal question regarding ERISA; and (5) the relative merits of the parties' positions.[1]

All five factors need not be present in order for a court to award attorneys' fees. One court held that the element of bad faith did not need to be established in all instances in order for the court to exercise its discretion in awarding attorneys' fees.[2]

Another court held that attorneys' fees could be awarded on behalf of a plaintiff seeking payment of his vested interest in the plan after his termination where the plaintiff had limited financial resources and a favorable judgment would otherwise leave the plaintiff with an empty victory.[3]

The Supreme Court held that an award of attorneys' fees should not be reduced if a party has garnered substantial relief on the majority of the claims where the lawsuit consists of a number of related claims.[4]

Attorneys' fees may be awarded if the plaintiff succeeds on any significant issue that achieves part of the benefits sought in filing the initial action.[5]

An ERISA Section 502(g) award of attorneys' fees is inappropriate when such fees are specified as being contingent.[6]

In applying the five-factor test, the Ninth Circuit Court of Appeals ruled that a plan participant who filed suit seeking correction of a miscalculation of her benefits was entitled to a recovery of attorneys' fees in spite of the fact that her employer had filed for IRS approval of a correction of the miscalculation at issue under what was then called the IRS' Voluntary Compliance Resolution (VCR) program.[7] The court awarded attorneys' fees because it deemed the employer to have "relative culpability and bad faith" by refusing to advise the participant of the VCR submission, thereby making it necessary for her to file her civil action under an expiring statute of limitations in order to guarantee that her claim was protected.[8]

---

1. *Kimbro v. Atlantic Richfield Co.*, 889 F.2d 869 (9th Cir. 1989); *Gray v. New England Tel. & Tel. Co.*, 792 F.2d 251 (1st Cir. 1986); *Ironworkers Local No. 272 v. Bowen*, 695 F.2d 531 (11th Cir. 1983); *Eaves v. Penn*, 587 F.2d 453 (10th Cir. 1978).
2. *Gennamore v. Buffalo Sheet Metals, Inc. Pension Plan & Trust*, 568 F. Supp. 931 (W.D.N.Y. 1983).
3. *Morales v. Plaxall, Inc.*, 541 F. Supp. 1387 (E.D.N.Y. 1982).
4. *Hensley v. Eckerhart*, 461 U.S. 424 (1983).
5. *International Bhd. of Teamsters Local No. 710 Pension Fund v. Janowski*, 812 F.2d 295 (7th Cir. 1987).
6. *Martin v. Arkansas Blue Cross/Blue Shield*, 2001 U.S. App. LEXIS 22940 (8th Cir. 2001).
7. *McElwaine v. US W., Inc.*, 176 F.3d 1167 (9th Cir. 1999).
8. *McElwaine v. US West, Inc.*, 176 F.3d 1167 (9th Cir. 1999).

The Supreme Court provided a new standard for awarding attorneys' fees under ERISA, holding that benefits claimants and other litigants need not be "prevailing parties" to be eligible for an award of attorneys' fees if they demonstrate "some degree of success on the merits."[1] The Supreme Court noted that the words "prevailing party" do not appear in the ERISA provision on attorneys' fees. They advise, instead, that courts are permitted to award attorneys' fees to either party in their discretion. The requirement of demonstrating "some degree of success on the merits" is not met where a claimant achieves "trivial success on the merits" or a "purely procedural victory." A court must be able to view the litigation's outcome as some success on the merits without closely reviewing whether the success was substantial or involved a central issue.[2]

541. Does ERISA provide for the recovery of reasonable costs in addition to attorneys' fees?

ERISA provides for the recovery of "reasonable attorneys' fees and costs of action."[3] The Ninth Circuit Court of Appeals held that the term "reasonable" applies as a modifier to the term "legal fees" and not to the term "costs."[4] As such, the plaintiff was not permitted to recover "reasonable costs" for the full amount of fees charged by an expert witness. The court stated that the awarding of expert witness fees is governed by the Federal Rules of Civil Procedure (FRCP).[5]

Under the FRCP, an award of attorneys' fees may only be for the actual fees and costs that were incurred as a result of the conduct at issue.[6]

542. Can an award of attorneys' fees be discharged in bankruptcy, and can attorneys' charge fees in a bankruptcy case?

Under the following circumstances attorneys' fees may not be discharged. If a fiduciary has been held accountable for an award of attorneys' fees for conduct that goes beyond mere negligence, the attorneys' fees may not be discharged in a bankruptcy proceeding. Further, there must be a fiduciary relationship between the parties to the suit, and the offending action must have occurred as a result of a breach of, or a failure to satisfy, a fiduciary obligation.[7]

Regarding attorneys' fees related to bankruptcy cases, when plan sponsors of defined benefit plans file for bankruptcy protection, the Pension Benefits Guaranty Corporation (PBGC) becomes a creditor. In 1992, the PBGC established its Bankruptcy Fee Monitoring Section to monitor attorneys' fees that are charged in large bankruptcy proceedings in which the PBGC is a major creditor (i.e., obligated to pay any unfunded liability to the bankrupt corporation's defined benefit plan). Established within the PBGC's General Counsel's office, the program is designed to prevent excessive attorney and other professional fees from being charged in large bankruptcy cases.[8]

---

1. *Hardt v. Reliance Standard Life Ins. Co.*, 2010 WL 2025127 (U.S. 2010).
2. *Hardt v. Reliance Standard Life Ins. Co.*, above.
3. ERISA Sec. 502(g)(1).
4. *Agredano v. Mutual of Omaha Cos.*, 75 F.3d 541 (9th Cir. 1996).
5. *Agredano v. Mutual of Omaha Cos.*, above.
6. *Browning v. Kramer*, 931 F.2d 340 (5th Cir. 1991).
7. *In re Eisenberg*, 189 B.R. 725 (Bankr. E.D. Wis. 1995).
8. *Department of Labor News Release*, USDL 92-343 (June 5, 1992).

Multiemployer Plans

543. What special remedies exist for multiemployer plans?

Fiduciaries, participants, beneficiaries, employer organizations, and plan sponsors may bring civil actions to seek legal or equitable relief for damages caused by an act or omission of a party in relation to an ERISA-covered multiemployer plan. Such actions may not be brought against the Department of Labor or the Pension Benefits Guaranty Corporation.[1]

The majority of cases against multiemployer plans involve actions seeking the payment of unpaid or delinquent plan contributions into the plan trust. Participating employers are required to make contributions to a multiemployer plan trust in accordance with "the terms of the plan or under the terms of a collectively bargained agreement."[2] Such actions may only be brought by fiduciaries to the multiemployer plan, not participants or beneficiaries.[3] Multiemployer plans are permitted to utilize the defense that they have relied on the terms of the collective bargaining agreement as it has been written. Therefore, any provision within the collective bargaining agreement that may have been incorrectly written may, nonetheless, be relied upon by the parties to the action.[4]

The National Labor Relations Board (NLRB) has exclusive jurisdiction in determining liability for delinquent multiemployer plan contributions under an expired collective bargaining agreement. This is based on the theory of unfair labor practices. Unless, and until, the collective bargaining agreement has expired, federal district courts retain jurisdiction to hear cases against multiemployer plans for delinquent contributions.[5] If the NLRB determines that a collective bargaining agreement is invalid, the participating employers are not obligated to continue making contributions to the plan under the agreement. If the collective bargaining agreement has not been invalid from inception, participating employers must continue to make contributions to the plan unless, and until, the NLRB has ruled on the validity of it. Participating employers may not unilaterally cease making contributions to a multiemployer plan on the basis of a complaint filed with the NLRB regarding the validity of the collective bargaining agreement.[6]

In cases seeking the payment of delinquent contributions to a multiemployer plan brought by a fiduciary against a participating employer, the court *must* award attorneys' fees and costs of the action where a judgment was awarded in favor of the plan.[7]

Actions to enforce ERISA's multiemployer plan provisions must be brought (1) within six years after the date on which the cause of action arises, or (2) three years after the earliest date on which the plaintiff acquires actual knowledge of the existence of the cause of action, whichever is later. As in any ERISA case where there has been an act of fraud or concealment

---

1. ERISA Sec. 4301(a).
2. ERISA Sec. 515.
3. ERISA Sec. 502(g).
4. *Central Pa. Teamsters Pension Fund v. McCormack Dray Line, Inc.*, 85 F.3d 1098 (3d Cir. 1996).
5. *Smith v. Candler Coffee Shop*, 1996 U.S. Dist. LEXIS 10935 (S.D.N.Y. 1996).
6. *MacKillop v. Lowe's Mkt., Inc.*, 58 F.3d 1441 (9th Cir. 1995).
7. ERISA Sec. 502(g)(2); *O'Hare v. General Marine Transp. Corp.*, 740 F.2d 160 (2d Cir. 1984); *Greater Kan. City Laborers Pension Fund v. Thummel*, 738 F.2d 926 (8th Cir. 1984); *Operating Eng'rs Pension Trust v. Reed*, 726 F.2d 513 (9th Cir. 1984).

regarding the fiduciary violation, the three-year limitations period is extended to six years after the date of discovery of the act of fraud or concealment.[1]

Member employers in a multiemployer plan are required to make contributions to the plan under the terms of the collective bargaining agreement.[2] In a civil action to recover delinquent employer contributions wherein the plan emerges victorious on its claim, the court must award prejudgment interest on the delinquent contributions.[3] Further, the court must award the plan under such a judgment the greater of interest on the unpaid contributions or liquidated damages that have been provided for under the terms of the plan, plus reasonable attorneys' fees and costs of the action to enforce the contribution obligation. Liquidated damages are limited to 20 percent of the total amount of the outstanding delinquency.[4]

In a civil action to force a participating employer to make payments to a multiemployer plan under the terms of a collective bargaining agreement, a court must award, if it rules in favor of the plan, an amount equal to the greater of interest on the unpaid liability or liquidated damages (paid to the plan), reasonable attorneys' fees, and the costs of bringing the civil action.[5]

---

1. ERISA Sec. 4301(f).
2. ERISA Sec. 515.
3. ERISA Sec. 502(g)(2)(B); *Bricklayers Pension Trust Fund v. Taiariol*, 671 F.2d 988 (6th Cir. 1982).
4. ERISA Secs. 502(g)(2)(C), 502(g)(2)(D); *Teamsters Pension Trust Fund v. John Tinney Delivery Serv., Inc.*, 732 F.2d 319 (3d Cir. 1984).
5. ERISA Sec. 502(g).

SECTION VIII

Fidelity Bonding, Fiduciary Liability Insurance, and Exculpatory Provisions

544. Does ERISA require bonding or insurance for plans or plan fiduciaries, administrators, officers, or employees?

ERISA requires that every administrator, officer, and employee of any employee welfare benefit plan or employee pension benefit plan who handles funds or other property of the plan be bonded in order to protect benefit funds against loss by acts of fraud or dishonesty.[1] A bond that covers against loss resulting from dishonest or fraudulent acts of bonded employees is generally known as a fidelity bond.

ERISA refers to persons who handle funds or other property of an employee benefit plan as "plan officials." A plan official must be bonded for at least 10 percent of the amount of funds she handles, subject to a minimum bond amount of $1,000 per plan with respect to which the plan official has handling functions. In most instances, the maximum bond amount that can be required under ERISA with respect to any one plan official is $500,000 per plan. Effective for plan years beginning on or after January 1, 2007, however, the Pension Protection Act of 2006[2] amended the maximum required bond amount to $1,000,000 for plan officials of plans that hold employer securities.

ERISA permits a plan to purchase fiduciary insurance for its fiduciaries or for itself to cover liability or losses resulting from acts or omissions of the fiduciary. However, ERISA prohibits any agreement or instrument that purports to relieve a fiduciary from responsibility or liability for any obligation or duty under ERISA.

545. What are the bonding requirements of ERISA?

With exceptions, ERISA mandates that every fiduciary of an employee benefit plan and every person who "handles" (see Q 551) funds or other property of such a plan (a "plan official") be bonded, in order to protect the plan against loss by reason of acts of fraud or dishonesty on the part of the plan official, directly or through connivance with others.[3]

ERISA also provides that it is unlawful for any plan official to receive, handle, disburse, or otherwise exercise custody or control over any of the funds or other property of any employee benefit plan without being properly bonded. Additionally, it is unlawful under ERISA for any plan official, or any other person with authority, to permit a plan official who is not bonded to receive, handle, disburse, or otherwise exercise custody or control of any of the funds or other property of any employee benefit plan.[4] The required bond must be in an approved form or type, and is required to have as surety an acceptable corporate surety company.[5]

---

1. ERISA Sec. 412.
2. Pub. L. No. 109-280, 120 Stat. 780 (2006).
3. ERISA Sec. 412(a).
4. ERISA Sec. 412(b); *Brock v. Ardito*, 8 EBC 2303 (E.D.N.Y. 1987).
5. ERISA Sec. 412(a).

Pending the issuance of permanent regulations with respect to the bonding provisions of ERISA Section 412, the DOL has concluded that plan officials will be in compliance with ERISA's bonding requirements if they are in compliance with Section 13 of the Welfare and Pension Plans Disclosure Act (WPPDA), as amended, and its regulations, as well as the temporary bonding rules of ERISA. These temporary bonding rules apply to all employee benefit plans covered by ERISA. Any bond (or rider thereto) that contains a reference to the WPPDA is construed as referring to ERISA, provided that the surety company agrees. References to the WPPDA in the temporary bonding regulations are intended to refer to ERISA Section 412, and the language in ERISA supersedes similar language with a different meaning in the WPPDA and its regulations.[1]

546. What plans are exempt from the bonding requirements?

The bonding requirements of ERISA Section 412 do not apply to an administrator, officer, or employee of a plan if the benefits of the plan are paid from the general assets of an employer or a union. This exception from the bonding provisions applies only to completely unfunded plans in which the plan benefits derive solely from the general assets of a union or employer, and in which the plan assets are not segregated from the general assets of an employer or union, and remain solely within the general assets until the time of distribution of benefits.[2]

The plan itself is not exempt from the bonding requirements if the plan is one in which: (1) any benefits are provided or underwritten by an insurance carrier or service or other organization; (2) there is a trust or other separate entity to which contributions are made or out of which benefits are paid; (3) employees make contributions to the plan, either through withholding or otherwise, or from any source other than the employer or union involved; or (4) there are separately maintained bank accounts or separately maintained books and records for the plan, or other evidence of the existence of a segregated or separately maintained or administered fund out of which plan benefits are to be provided.[3]

As a general rule, the presence of special ledger accounts or accounting entries for plan funds as an integral part of the general books and records of an employer or union will not, in and of itself, be deemed sufficient evidence of segregation of plan funds to take a plan out of the exempt category, but will be considered along with the other factors and criteria discussed above in determining whether the exemption applies. The fact that a plan is not exempt from the bonding requirements does not necessarily mean that its administrators, officers, or employees are required to be bonded. This will depend in each case on whether or not they "handle" funds or other property of the plan within the meaning of ERISA Section 412, and under the standards set forth in the regulations (see Q 551).[4]

547. What are the exceptions to the bonding requirements for fiduciaries?

The bonding requirements do not apply to a fiduciary (or any director, officer, or employee of such fiduciary) if the fiduciary: (1) is a corporation organized and doing business under federal

---

1. Labor Reg. §2550.412-1.
2. ERISA Sec. 412(a)(1); Labor Reg. §2580.412-2.
3. Labor Reg. §2580.412-2.
4. Labor Regs. §§2580.412-2, 2580.412-6.

or state law; (2) is legally authorized to exercise trust powers or to conduct an insurance business; (3) is subject to supervision or examination by federal or state authorities; and (4) at all times has a combined capital and surplus of at least $1,000,000.[1]

A bank or other financial institution that is authorized to exercise trust powers and the deposits of which are not insured by the Federal Deposit Insurance Corporation (FDIC) may satisfy this exception if it meets bonding or similar requirements under state law that are at least equivalent to those imposed on banks by federal law.[2]

548. Who must be bonded?

Every administrator, officer, and employee of any benefit plan subject to ERISA who "handles" (see Q 551) funds or other property of such plan must be bonded.[3]

A plan "administrator" is either: (1) the person or persons designated under the terms of the plan or the collective bargaining agreement with responsibility for the ultimate control, disposition, or management of the money received or contributed; or (2) in the absence of such designation, the person or persons actually responsible for the control, disposition, or management of the money received or contributed, irrespective of whether such control, disposition, or management is exercised directly or through an agent or trustee designated by such person or persons.[4]

If the term *administrator* (as defined previously, or in regulations, interpretations, or opinions in regard to this definition) embodies natural persons such as members of the board of trustees of a trust, the bonding requirements will apply to such persons. However, if the term (as defined above, or in regulations, interpretations, or opinions in regard to this definition) is deemed to apply to an entity such as a partnership, corporation, mutual company, joint stock company, trust, unincorporated organization, union, or employees' beneficiary association, the term will apply, in meeting the bonding requirements, only to those natural persons: (1) who are vested under the authority of the entity-administrator with the responsibility for carrying out functions constituting control, disposition, or management of the money received or contributed within the definition of administrator, or who, acting on behalf of or under the actual or apparent authority of the entity-administrator, actually perform such functions; and (2) who *handle* (see Q 551 for the definition of "handle") funds or other property of the plan within the meaning of the regulations to ERISA Section 412.[5]

The term "officer," for purposes of the bonding provisions, includes any person designated under the terms of a plan or collective bargaining agreement as an officer, any person performing or authorized to perform executive functions of the plan, or any member of a board of trustees or similar governing body of a plan. The term includes such persons, regardless of whether they are representatives of or selected by an employer, employees, or an employee organization. In

---

1. ERISA Sec. 412(a)(2).
2. ERISA Sec. 412(a)(2).
3. ERISA Sec. 412(a).
4. Labor Reg. §2580.412-3(a)(1).
5. Labor Regs. §§2580.412-3(a)(2), 2580.412-3(a)(3).

its most frequent application, the term *officer* encompasses those natural persons appointed or elected as officers of the plan or as members of boards or committees performing executive or supervisory functions for the plan, but who do not fall within the definition of *administrator*.[1]

For purposes of the bonding provisions, the term "employee," to the extent a person performs functions not falling within the definition of *officer* or *administrator*, includes any employee who performs work for or directly related to a covered plan, regardless of whether, technically, he is employed, directly or indirectly, by or for a plan, a plan administrator, or a trust, or by an employee organization or employer.[2]

For purposes of the bonding requirements, the terms "administrator, officer, or employee" also include any persons performing functions for the plan normally performed by administrators, officers, or employees of a plan. As such, the terms include persons indirectly employed, or otherwise delegated, to perform this type of work for the plan, such as pension consultants and planners, and attorneys who perform handling functions, within the meaning of the regulations. In contrast, the terms do not include those brokers or independent contractors who have contracted for the performance of functions that are not ordinarily carried out by the administrators, officers, or employees of a plan, such as securities brokers who purchase and sell securities, or armored motor vehicle companies.[3]

In November 2000, the PWBA (now known as the Employee Benefits Security Administration) announced that it was undertaking a review of the temporary bonding regulations under ERISA Section 412 for the purpose of developing a regulation that would exempt certain investment advisers and broker-dealers from the definition of "plan officials" required to be bonded under ERISA Section 412(a).[4]

549. What are "funds or other property" of a plan?

The term "funds or other property" is intended to include all property that is used or may be used as a source for the payment of benefits to plan participants. It does not include permanent assets used in the operation of the plan (e.g., land and buildings, furniture and fixtures, or office and delivery equipment). It does include all items in the nature of quick (i.e., liquid) assets (e.g., cash, checks, and other negotiable instruments, government obligations, and marketable securities).

Funds or other property also includes all other property or items convertible into cash or having a cash value and held or acquired for the ultimate purpose of distribution to plan participants or beneficiaries. In the case of a plan that has investments, this would include all the investments of the plan, even though such investments are not in the nature of quick assets (e.g., land and buildings, mortgages, and securities in closely held corporations). However, in a given case, the question of whether a person was *handling* (see Q 551 for the definition of "handling") such *funds or other property* so as to require bonding depends upon whether his relationship to this

---

1. Labor Reg. §2580.412-3(b).
2. Labor Reg. §2580.412-3(c).
3. Labor Reg. §2580.412-3(d).
4. 65 Fed. Reg. 74,071 (Nov. 30, 2000).

property is such that there is a risk that he, alone or in connivance with others, could cause a loss of such *funds or other property* through fraud or dishonesty.[1]

550. When do items contributed to a plan become the "funds or other property" of the plan?

The point at which any item or amount contributed to a plan from any source (including employers, employees, or employee organizations) becomes *funds or other property* (see Q 549) of a plan for purposes of the bonding provisions is determined according to whether the plan administrator is the employer or employee organization that established the plan.

If the plan administrator is a board of trustees, person, or body *other than* the employer or employee organization establishing the plan, a contribution to the plan from any source becomes *funds or other property* of the plan at the time it is received by the plan administrator. Employee contributions collected by an employer and later turned over to the plan administrator would not become *funds or other property* of the plan until the funds are received by the plan administrator.

If the employer or employee organization establishing the plan is itself the plan administrator, the following rules apply:

1. Contributions from employees or other persons who are plan participants would normally become *funds or other property* of the plan when the contributions are received by the employer or employee organization; however, contributions made by withholding from employees' salaries are not considered *funds or other property* of the plan for purposes of the bonding provisions, so long as they are retained in and not segregated in any way from the general assets of the withholding employer or employee organization; and

2. Contributions made to a plan by an employer or employee organization and contributions made by withholding from employees' salaries would normally become *funds or other property* of the plan if and when they are: (a) taken out of the general assets of the employer or employee organization and placed in a special bank account or investment account; (b) identified on a separate set of books and records; (c) paid over to a corporate trustee or used to purchase benefits from an insurance carrier or service or other organization; or (d) otherwise segregated, paid out, or used for plan purposes, whichever occurs first. Thus, if a plan is operated by a corporate trustee and no segregation from general assets is made of monies to be turned over to the corporate trustee prior to the actual transmittal of such monies, the transmitted contribution becomes *funds or other property* of the plan at the time when the corporate trustee receives it. On the other hand, if a special fund is first established, from which monies are paid over to the corporate trustee, a contribution would become *funds or other property* of the plan when it is placed in the special fund. Similarly, if plan benefits are provided through an insurance carrier or service or other organization and no segregation from general assets of monies

---

1. Labor Reg. §2580.412-4.

used to purchase such benefits is made prior to turning such monies over to the organization contracting to provide benefits, status as *funds or other property* comes into being when the insurance carrier or service or other organization receives payment for such benefits. In these circumstances, the *funds or other property* of the plan would be represented by the insurance contract or other obligations to pay benefits, and would not be normally subject to *handling* (see Q 551). Bonding would not be required for any person with respect to the purchase of such benefits directly from general assets nor with respect to the bare existence of the contract obligation to pay benefits. However, if the particular arrangement were such that monies derived from, or by virtue of, the contract subsequently flowed back to the plan, bonding may be required if such monies returning to the plan are *handled* by plan *administrators, officers, or employees.*[1]

551. When are funds or other property "handled" so as to require bonding?

A plan administrator, officer, or employee will be considered to be "handling" funds or other property of a plan, and, thus, required to be bonded under ERISA, whenever the person's duties or activities with respect to the plan's *funds or other property* present a risk that the plan's funds or other property could be lost in the event of fraud or dishonesty on the part of the person, whether acting alone or in collusion with others. Generally, plan administrators, officers, and employees who *handle* funds within the meaning of ERISA will be persons with duties related to the receipt, safekeeping, and disbursement of funds; however, the scope of the term *handles* and the prohibitions of ERISA are deemed to include any relationship of an administrator, officer, or employee with respect to funds or other property, which can give rise to a risk of loss through fraud or dishonesty. This includes relationships such as those that involve access to funds or other property or decision-making powers with respect to funds or property that can give rise to such risk of loss.[2]

The determination of the existence of risk of loss is not based on the amount involved or the amount or value of funds or other property *handled*. A given duty or relationship to funds or other property is not considered *handling*, and bonding is not required, where it occurs under conditions and circumstances in which the risk of loss through fraud or dishonesty is negligible, regardless of the amount involved (e.g., where the risk of mishandling is precluded by the nature of the funds or other property, such as checks, securities, or title papers, which cannot be negotiated by the persons performing duties with respect to them and where significant risk of mishandling in the performance of duties of an essentially clerical character is precluded by fiscal controls).[3]

General Criteria

The regulations detail the general criteria (see next) for determining whether there is *handling* so as to require bonding, subject to the application of the basic standard of risk of loss to each situation.

---

1. Labor Reg. §2580.412-5.
2. Labor Reg. §2580.412-6(a)(1).
3. Labor Reg. §2580.412-6(a)(2).

Physical contact with cash, checks, or similar property generally constitutes handling. However, persons who, from time to time, perform counting, packaging, tabulating, messenger, or similar duties of an essentially clerical character involving physical contact with funds or other property would not be *handling* when they perform these duties under conditions and circumstances where risk of loss is negligible because of factors such as close supervision and control, or the nature of the property.[1]

The power to exercise physical contact or control is also determinative of *handling*. Whether or not physical contact actually takes place, the power to secure physical possession of cash, checks, or similar property through factors such as access to a safe deposit box or similar depository, access to cash or negotiable assets, powers of custody or safekeeping, or power to withdraw funds from a bank or other account generally constitutes *handling*, regardless of whether the person in question has specific duties in these matters and regardless of whether the power or access is authorized.[2]

The power to transfer to oneself or a third party or to negotiate for value is also an example of *handling*. With respect to property such as mortgages, title to land and buildings, or securities, while physical contact or the possibility of physical contact may not, of itself, give rise to risk of loss so as to constitute handling, a person shall be regarded as handling such items where she, through actual or apparent authority, could cause those items to be transferred to herself or to a third party or to be negotiated for value.[3]

The disbursement of funds or other property by persons such as officers or trustees who are authorized to sign checks or other negotiable instruments, or persons authorized to make cash disbursements, will be considered *handling*. Whether other persons who may influence, authorize, or direct disbursements or the signing or endorsing of checks or similar instruments will be considered to be *handling* funds or other property will be determined by reference to the particular duties or responsibilities of such persons as applied to the basic criteria of risk of loss.[4]

The signing or endorsing of checks or other negotiable instruments by persons with the power to do so, or to otherwise render them transferable, in connection with disbursements or otherwise, whether individually or as co-signers with one or more persons, is considered to be *handling* of such funds or other property.[5]

To the extent that the *supervisory or decision-making responsibility* of a person factors in to the relationship to funds discussed above, such persons will be considered to be *handling* in the same manner as any person to whom the criteria of those paragraphs apply. These persons are considered to be *handling* whenever the facts of the particular case raise the possibility that funds or other property of the plan is likely to be lost in the event of their fraud or dishonesty, and to the extent that only general responsibility for the conduct of the business affairs of the plan is involved, including such functions as approval of contracts, authorization of disbursements,

---

1. Labor Reg. §2580.412-6(b)(1).
2. Labor Reg. §2580.412-6(b)(2).
3. Labor Reg. §2580.412-6(b)(3).
4. Labor Reg. §2580.412-6(b)(4).
5. Labor Reg. §2580.412-6(b)(5).

auditing of accounts, investment decisions, determination of benefit claims, and similar responsibilities. The existence of general supervision would not necessarily, in and of itself, mean that such persons are *handling*. Factors to be considered are: the system of fiscal controls; the closeness and continuity of supervision; and who is in fact charged with, or actually exercising, final responsibility for determining whether specific disbursements, investments, contracts, or benefit claims are bona fide, regular, and made in accordance with the applicable trust instrument or other plan documents.

For example, certain persons with supervisory or decision-making responsibility would be considered to be *handling* to the extent they: (1) act in the capacity of plan *administrator* and have ultimate responsibility for the plan (within the meaning of "administrator" (see Q 548)), except to the extent that it can be shown that such persons could not, in fact, cause a loss to the plan through fraud or dishonesty; (2) exercise close supervision over corporate trustees or other parties charged with dealing with plan funds or other property, or exercise such close control over investment policy that they, in effect, determine all specific investments; (3) conduct, in effect, a continuing daily audit of the persons who *handle* funds; or (4) regularly review and have veto power over the actions of a disbursing officer, whose duties are essentially ministerial.

However, persons having supervisory or decision-making responsibility would not be *handling* to the extent that: (1) they merely conduct a periodic or sporadic audit of the persons who *handle* funds; (2) their duties with respect to investment policy are essentially advisory; (3) they make a broad general allocation of funds or general authorization of disbursements intended to permit expenditures by a disbursing officer who has final responsibility for determining the propriety of any specific expenditure and making the actual disbursement; (4) a bank or corporate trustee has all the day-to-day functions of administering the plan; or (5) they are in the nature of a board of directors of a corporation or similar authority acting for the corporation, rather than for the plan, and do not perform specific functions with respect to the operations of the plan.[1]

Finally, *insured plan arrangements* that would not normally be subject to bonding except to the extent that monies returned by way of benefit payments, cash surrender, dividends, credits, or otherwise, and which by the terms of the plan belonged to the plan (rather than to the employer, employee organization, insurance carrier, or service or other organization) were subject to *handling* by plan administrators, officers, or employees. In many cases, plan contributions made by employers or employee organizations or by withholding from employees' salaries are not segregated from the general assets of the employer or employee organization until payment for purchase of benefits from an insurance carrier or service or other organization. No bonding is required with respect to the payment of premiums or other payments made to purchase such benefits directly from general assets, nor with respect to the bare existence of the contract obligation to pay benefits.[2]

---

1. Labor Reg. §2580.412-6(b)(6).
2. Labor Reg. §2580.412-6(b)(7).

Scope and Form of the Bond

552. What is the meaning of "fraud or dishonesty" in terms of the scope of the protection provided by the bond?

The scope of coverage under ERISA Section 412 requires that the bond protect the plan against loss by reason of acts of fraud or dishonesty on the part of a plan administrator, officer, or employee, directly or through connivance with others. This coverage is limited to protection for those duties and activities from which loss can arise through *fraud or dishonesty*.

Coverage for "fraud or dishonesty" encompasses all those risks of loss that might arise through fraudulent or dishonest acts in *handling* plan funds (see Q 551 for the definition of "handling"). "As such, the bond must provide recovery for loss occasioned by such acts even though no personal gain accrues to the person committing the act and the act is not subject to punishment as a crime or misdemeanor, provided that within the law of the state in which the act is committed, a court would afford recovery under a bond providing protection against fraud or dishonesty."[1] The term *fraud or dishonesty*, as usually applied under state laws, encompasses such matters as larceny, theft, embezzlement, forgery, misappropriation, wrongful abstraction, wrongful conversion, willful misapplication, or any other fraudulent or dishonest acts. Other fraudulent or dishonest acts also include acts where losses result through any act or arrangement that violates the federal law prohibiting offers, acceptances, or solicitations to influence the operations of an employee benefit plan.[2]

553. What is an individual or schedule or blanket form of bonds?

ERISA provides that bonds are to be "in a form or of a type approved by the Secretary of Labor, including individual bonds or schedule or blanket forms of bonds which cover a group or class."[3] An individual, schedule, or blanket bond, or combination thereof, is acceptable under ERISA Section 412, provided that the form of the bond, in its particular clauses and application, is not inconsistent with meeting (1) the substantive requirements of ERISA for the persons and plan involved, and (2) the specific requirements of the regulations.

Basic types of bonds in general usage are: (1) individual bonds, covering a named individual in a stated penalty; (2) name schedule bonds, covering a number of named individuals in the respective amounts set opposite their names; (3) position schedule bonds, covering each of the occupants of positions listed in the schedule in the respective amounts set opposite such positions; and (4) blanket bonds, covering all of the insured's officers and employees with no schedule or list of those covered being necessary and with all new officers and employees becoming bonded automatically, in a blanket penalty that takes two forms, an aggregate penalty bond and a multiple penalty bond.

The aggregate penalty blanket bond, such as the commercial blanket bond, is a bond in which the amount of the bond is available for dishonesty losses caused by persons covered by

---

1. Labor Reg. §2580.412-9.
2. Labor Reg. §2580.412-9.
3. ERISA Sec. 412(a).

the bond, or losses in which such person is concerned or implicated. Payment of loss on account of any such person does not reduce the amount of coverage available for losses other than those caused by such person or in which he was concerned or implicated.

The multiple penalty bond, such as the blanket position bond, gives separate coverage on each person for a uniform amount, the net effect being the same as though a separate bond were issued on each person covered by the bond and all of such bonds being for a uniform amount.

For the purpose of ERISA Section 412, blanket bonds (which are either aggregate penalty or multiple penalty in form) are permissible only if they otherwise meet the requirements of ERISA and the regulations.

"Bonding, to the extent required, of persons indirectly employed, or otherwise delegated, to perform functions for the plan which are normally performed by 'administrators, officers, or employees' … may be accomplished either by including them under individual or schedule bonds or other forms of bonds meeting the requirements of [ERISA], or naming them in what is known under general trade usage as an 'Agents Rider' attached to a Blanket Bond."[1]

Amount of the Bond

554. What is the amount of the bond?

Each individual must be bonded for at least 10 percent of the amount of funds she *handles* (see Q 551 for a definition of "handles"). The amount of the bond is fixed at the beginning of each calendar, policy, or other fiscal year that constitutes the plan year. The amount of the bond is subject to a minimum of $1,000 and a maximum of $500,000. The Secretary of Labor may prescribe that a person be bonded for an amount in excess of $500,000, subject to the 10 percent limitation of the funds handled, upon due notice, opportunity for hearing to all interested parties, and after consideration of the record.[2]

Section 622(a) of the Pension Protection Act of 2006 (PPA)[3] amended ERISA Section 412 by increasing the maximum amount of the bond to $1,000,000 in circumstances when a plan holds employer securities within the meaning of ERISA Section 407(d)(1) for plan years beginning after December 31, 2007. However, every plan whose investments include employer securities is not subject to the increased maximum bond amount of $1,000,000. According to EBSA, the Staff Report of the Joint Committee on Taxation contains a technical explanation of the amended provision, which states that "[a] plan would not be considered to hold employer securities within the meaning of this section where the only securities held by the plan are part of a broadly diversified fund of assets, such as mutual or index funds."[4]Accordingly, it is EBSA's view that a plan is not considered to be holding employer securities, for purposes of the increased bonding requirement, merely because the plan invests in a broadly diversified

---

1. Labor Reg. §2580.412-10.
2. ERISA Sec. 412(a)(2)(D); Labor Reg. §2580.412-11.
3. Pub. L. No. 109-280, 120 Stat. 780.
4. See Field Assistance Bull. 2008-4, Q-38.

common or pooled investment vehicle that holds employer securities but that is independent of the employer and any of its affiliates.

555. How is the amount of the bond determined?

For purposes of fixing the amount of the bond for the current plan year, the amount of funds handled by the person, group, or class covered by the bond, and by their predecessor or predecessors, if any, during the preceding plan year must be determined; however, if the plan has no preceding plan year, the amount of the bond is determined by estimating the amount of funds to be handled during the current plan year by such person, group, or class.[1]

If the amount of funds handled increases during the plan year after the bond is purchased, the regulations do not require that the bond be updated during the plan year to reflect the increase because the regulations require that, with respect to each covered person, the bond amount be fixed annually. The bond must be fixed or estimated at the beginning of the plan's reporting year—that is, as soon after the date when such year begins as the necessary information from the preceding reporting year can practicably be ascertained. The amount of the bond must be based on the highest amount of funds handled by the person in the preceding plan year.[2]

556. What are the required recovery provisions of a bond?

The bond must meet certain requirements relating to reimbursement for loss. Reimbursement to a plan suffering a loss must be from the first dollar of loss up to the full amount for which the person causing the loss is bonded. The regulations do not permit the use of a deductible or any feature by which a portion of the risk with the amount of the bond is assumed by the insured. If a plan is already insured under a blanket bond covering all employees of the employer, but the bond has a deductible provision, the deductible provision must be either eliminated or modified so as not to apply to loss of plan funds caused by an administrator, officer, or employee of the plan; otherwise, a new bond must be secured covering the plan.[3]

557. What is the relationship between determining the amount of the bond and the "handling" of funds or other property?

The determination of whether an administrator, officer, or employee is required to be bonded depends on whether he *handles* funds or other property. (See Q 551 for a definition of "handle.") Determining the amount of the bond requires a determination of which funds or other property are being *handled* or which amounts of funds or other property are subject to risk of loss with respect to the duties or powers of an administrator, officer, or employee of a covered plan. Once this calculation is made, the required amount for which that person must be covered by a bond, either by himself or as a part of a group or class being bonded under a blanket or schedule bond, is not less than 10 percent of the amount *handled* or $1,000, whichever is the greater amount, except that a bond is not required in an amount greater than $500,000.[4]As noted in Q 554, the Secretary of Labor may prescribe an amount in excess of $500,000 subject

1. ERISA Sec. 412(a); Labor Reg. §2580.412-11.
2. See ERISA Sec. 412; 29 C.F.R. §§2580.412-11, 2580.412-14, 2580.412-19.
3. Labor Reg. §2580.412-11.
4. Labor Reg. §2580.412-12.

to the 10 percent limitation in certain circumstances. In addition, the maximum amount of the bond is increased to $1,000,000 if a plan holds employer securities within the meaning of ERISA Section 407(d)(1) for plan years beginning after December 31, 2007. See Q 554 for discussion of the amendment to ERISA Section 412 by Section 622(a) of the Pension Protection Act of 2006.[1]

558. What is the meaning of "funds" in determining the amount of the bond?

The amount of the bond depends on the amount of *funds handled* (see Q 551 for a definition of "handle"), and must be sufficient to provide bonding protection against risk of loss through fraud or dishonesty for all plan funds, including other property similar to funds or in the nature of funds. As such, the term "funds" is deemed to include and be equivalent to *funds and other property* of the plan. (See Q 549 for a definition of "funds or other property.") With respect to any item of *funds or other property* that does not have a cash value or readily ascertainable market value, the value of such property may be estimated on such basis as will reasonably reflect the potential loss to the plan if it were mishandled.[2]

559. How is the amount of funds "handled" during the preceding reporting year determined?

The amount of funds *handled* by an administrator, officer, or employee (or his predecessors) during the preceding reporting year is the total of funds subject to risk of loss, within the meaning of the definition of handling (see Q 551), through acts of fraud or dishonesty, directly or in connivance with others, by such person or his predecessors during the preceding reporting year.

The relationship between determining the amount of funds *handled* and determining who is *handling* those funds can best be illustrated by a situation that commonly arises with respect to executive personnel of a plan, where a bank or corporate trustee has the responsibility for the receipt, safekeeping, physical handling, and investment of a plan's assets, and the basic function of the executive personnel is to authorize payments to beneficiaries and payments for services to the corporate trustee, the actuary, and the employees of the plan itself. Normally, in any given year, only a small portion of the plan's total assets is disbursed, and the question arises as to whether an administrator or executive personnel is *handling* only the amounts actually disbursed each year or whether he is *handling* the total amounts of the assets. The answer to this question depends on the same basic criterion that governs all questions of *handling*, namely, the possibility of loss. If the authorized duties of the persons in question are strictly limited to disbursements of benefits and payments for services, and the fiscal controls and practical realities of the situation are such that these persons cannot gain access to funds that they are not legitimately allowed to disburse, the amount on which the bond is based may be limited to the amount actually disbursed in the reporting year. This would depend, in part, on the extent to which the bank or corporate trustee that has physical possession of the funds also has final responsibility for questioning and limiting disbursements from the plan, and on whether this responsibility is embodied in the original plan instruments.

---

1. Pub. L. No. 109-280, 120 Stat. 780.
2. Labor Reg. §2580.412-13.

On the other hand, where insufficient fiscal controls exist, so that the persons involved have free access to, or can obtain control of, the total amount of the fund, the bond must reflect this fact and the amount *handled* must be based on the total amount of the fund. This would generally occur with respect to persons such as the *administrator* (see Q 548 for a definition of "administrator"), regardless of which functions are performed by a bank or corporate trustee, since the *administrator*, by definition, retains ultimate power to revoke any arrangement with a bank or corporate trustee. In such a case, the *administrator* would have the power to commit the total amount of funds involved to his control, unless the plan itself or other specific agreement: (1) prevents the *administrator* from so doing; or (2) requires that an arrangement with a bank or corporate trustee cannot be revoked unless a new agreement providing for similar controls and limitations on the *handling* of funds is entered into simultaneously.

Where the circumstances of *handling* are such that the total amount of a given account or fund is subject to *handling*, the amount *handled* must include the total of all the funds on hand at the beginning of the reporting year, plus any items received during the year for any reason, such as contributions or income, or items received as a result of sales, investments, reinvestment, interest, or otherwise. It would not, however, be necessary to count the same item twice in arriving at the total funds *handled* by a given person during a reporting year.

For example, a given person may have various duties or powers involving receipt, safekeeping, or disbursement of funds, which would place him in contact with the same funds at several times during the same year. Different duties, however, would not make it necessary to count the same item twice in arriving at the total *handled* by such person. Similarly, where a person has several different positions with respect to a plan, it would not be necessary to count the same funds each time that they are *handled* by him in these different positions, so long as the amount of the bond is sufficient to meet the 10 percent requirement with respect to the total funds *handled* by him subject to risk of loss through his fraud or dishonesty, whether acting alone or in collusion with others. In general, once an item that is properly within the category of *funds* has been counted as *handled* by a given person, it need not be counted again even though it is subsequently *handled* by the same person acting in another capacity during the same year.[1]

560. What are the procedures to be used for estimating the amount of funds to be "handled" during the current reporting year in those cases where there is no preceding reporting year?

If, for any reason, a plan does not have a complete preceding reporting year, the amount *handled* (see Q 551 for a definition of "handle") by persons required to be covered by a bond is estimated at the beginning of the calendar, policy, or other fiscal year that would constitute either the operating year or the reporting year of the plan, whichever occurs first, according to the rules below.

In the case of a plan having a previous experience year, even though it has no preceding reporting year, the estimate of the amount to be handled for any person who must be covered is based on the

1. Labor Reg. §2580.412-14.

experience in the previous year, by applying the same standards and criteria as in a plan that has a preceding reporting year. Similarly, where a plan is recently established, but has had, at the time when a bond is obtained, sufficient experience to reasonably estimate a complete year's experience for persons who must be bonded, the amount of funds to be handled is projected for the complete year on the basis of the period in which the plan has had experience, unless, to the knowledge of the plan administrator, the given period of experience is so seasonal or unrepresentative of a complete year's experience as not to provide a reasonable basis for projecting the estimate for the complete year.

Where a plan does not have any prior experience sufficient to allow it to estimate the amount handled in the manner outlined above, the amount to be handled by the administrators, officers, and employees of the plan during the current reporting year is that amount initially required to fund or set up the plan, plus the amount of contributions required under the plan formula from any source during the current reporting year. In most cases, the amount of contributions will be calculated by multiplying the total yearly contribution per participant (required by the plan formula from either employers, employees, employer organizations, or any other source) by the number of participants in the plan at the beginning of such reporting year. In cases where the per capita contribution cannot readily be determined, such as in the case of certain insured plans covered by ERISA, the amount of contributions is estimated based on the amount of insurance premiums that are actuarially estimated as necessary to support the plan, or on such other actuarially estimated basis as may be applicable. In the case of a newly formed profit sharing plan covered by ERISA, if the employer establishing the plan has a previous year of experience, the amount of contributions required by the plan formula is estimated on the basis of the profits of the previous year. The amount of the bond is then fixed at 10 percent of this calculation, but not more than $500,000 (except in the case of exceptions outlined in Q 554). A bond for this amount is obtained in any form the plan desires on all of the persons who are administrators, officers, or employees of the plan and who handle funds or other property of the plan.[1]

561. What is the amount of bond required in blanket, schedule, or individual bonds or where more than one plan is insured in the same bond?

ERISA permits the use of blanket, schedule, and individual bonds, so long as the amount of the bond is sufficient to meet the requirements of ERISA for any person who is an administrator, officer, or employee of a plan handling funds or other property of the plan (see Q 553). Each person must be bonded for 10 percent of the amount he handles, and the amount of the bond must be sufficient to indemnify the plan for any losses in which the person is involved up to that amount.

When individual or schedule bonds are written, the amount of the bond for each person must represent not less than 10 percent of the funds *handled* (see Q 551 for a definition of "handle") by the named individual or by the person in the named position. When a blanket bond is written, the amount of the bond must be at least 10 percent of the highest amount handled by any administrator, officer, or employee to be covered under the bond. If an individual (or group

---

1. Labor Reg. §2580.412-15.

or class) covered under a blanket bond "handles" a large amount of funds or other property, while the remaining bondable persons "handle" only a smaller amount, it is permissible to obtain a blanket bond in an amount sufficient to meet the 10 percent requirements for all except the individual, group, or class handling the larger amounts. For those individuals handling larger amounts, an excess indemnity must be secured in an amount sufficient to meet the 10 percent requirement.

ERISA does not prohibit more than one plan from being named as insured under the same bond. However, the bond must allow for recovery by each plan in an amount at least equal to that which would be required if bonded separately. This requirement is applicable where a person (or persons) to be bonded has handling functions in more than one plan covered under the bond. In such a case, the amount of the bond must be sufficient to cover the persons having functions in more than one plan for at least 10 percent of the total amount handled by them in all of the plans covered under the bond.

For example, X is the administrator of two welfare plans sponsored by the same employer, and he handled $100,000 in the preceding reporting year for Plan A and $500,000 in the preceding reporting year for Plan B. If both plans are covered under the same bond, the amount of the bond with respect to X must be at least $60,000, or 10 percent of the total handled by X for both plans covered under the bond in which X has powers and duties of handling, since Plan B is required to carry a bond of at least $50,000 and Plan A is required to carry a bond of at least $10,000.

Additionally, in order to meet the requirement that each plan be protected, it is necessary that an arrangement be made either by the terms of the bond or rider to the bond or by separate agreement among the parties concerned that payment of a loss sustained by one of the insureds must not work to the detriment of any other plan covered under the bond with respect to the amount for which that plan is required to be covered.

For example, if Plan A (as described previously) suffered a loss of $30,000, and such loss was recompensed in its entirety by the surety company, it would receive $20,000 more than the $10,000 protection required under ERISA, and only $30,000 would be available for recovery with respect to further losses caused by X. In a subsequently discovered defalcation of $40,000 by X from Plan B, it would be necessary that the bond, rider, or separate agreement provide that such amount of recovery paid to Plan A in excess of the $10,000 for which it is required to be covered be made available by such insured to, or held for the use of, Plan B in such amount as Plan B would receive if bonded separately. Thus, in this example, Plan B would be able to recover the full $40,000 of its loss. Where the funds or other property of several plans are commingled (if permitted by law) with each other or with other funds, such an arrangement must allow recovery to be attributed proportionately to the amount for which each plan is required to be protected. Thus, in this example, if funds or other property were commingled, and X caused a loss of these funds through fraud or dishonesty, one-sixth of the loss would be attributable to Plan A and five-sixths of the loss attributable to Plan B.

The maximum amount of any bond with respect to any person in any one plan is $500,000, but bonds covering more than one plan may be in excess of $500,000 in order to meet the requirements of ERISA Section 412, since persons covered by such a bond may have handling functions in more than one plan. The $500,000 limitation for such persons applies only with respect to each separate plan in which they have such functions. The minimum bond coverage for any administrator, officer, or employee handling funds or other property of a plan is $1,000 with respect to each plan in which he has handling functions.[1]

General Bonding Rules

562. What are the general bonding rules?

Naming of Insureds

Where a single plan is the only insured under a bond, that plan is entitled to receive reimbursement for loss as the named insured. However, where a plan is insured jointly with other plans, or with an employer or an employee organization, the plan must be afforded the same protection that it would have under its own separate bond. A plan must receive preference (up to 10 percent of funds handled) when a loss is common to the plan and to the employer or employee organization. It is possible to achieve this result through a pay-over rider, an agreement among the parties that any reimbursement collected on a bond will be for the benefit and use of the plan suffering the loss (at least up to the statutory bonding minimum), or a combination of the two. Such rider or agreement must clearly be enforceable by all plans that do not have other direct recourse on the bond. Such a rider or agreement is always required: (1) where the employer or employee organization is first named joint insured with one or more plans; or (2) two or more plans are named joint insureds under a single bond with the first named acting for all insureds for the purpose of orderly servicing of the bond. Payment to one plan must not reduce the amount another plan is entitled to up to the bond amount required by ERISA for the other plan.[2]

Term of the Bond

The amount of any required bond must be based on the amount of funds "handled" (see Q 551), and must be fixed or estimated at the beginning of the plan's reporting year—that is, as soon after the date when this year begins as the necessary information from the preceding reporting year can practicably be ascertained. This does not mean, however, that a new bond must be obtained each year. ERISA does not prohibit a bond for a term longer than one year, with whatever advantages such a bond might offer by way of a lower premium. However, at the beginning of each reporting year, the bond must be in at least the requisite amount. If, for any reason, the bond is below the required level at that time, the existing bond must either be increased to the proper amount, or a supplemental bond must be obtained.[3]

Discovery Period

The bond must provide a discovery period of no less than one year after the termination or cancellation of the bond in which to discover the loss. A discovery period is the period after termination of the bond during which the insured is allowed to uncover a loss that occurred

---

1. Labor Reg. §2580.412-16.
2. Labor Reg. §2580.412-18.
3. Labor Reg. §2580.412-19.

while the bond was in force. Any standard form written on a "discovery" basis (i.e., providing that a loss must be discovered within the bond period as a prerequisite to recovery of such loss) will not be required to have a discovery period if it contains a provision giving the insured the right to purchase a discovery period of one year in the event of termination or cancellation and the insured has already given the surety notice that it desires such a discovery period.[1]

Additional Rules

A bond does not adequately meet the requirements of ERISA Section 412 if it contains a clause in contravention of the law of the state in which it is executed, or is otherwise in contravention of the law of such state.[2]

As long as a particular bond meets the requirements of ERISA Section 412 as to the persons who must be bonded, and provides coverage for these persons in at least the minimum required amount, additional coverage as to persons or amount may be taken in any form, either on the same or a separate bond.

If an existing bond is adequate to meet the bonding requirements or if it is modified to meet these requirements through a rider, modification, or separate agreement between the parties, no further bonding is required.

The choice of whether persons required to be bonded are bonded separately or under the same bond, whether given plans are bonded separately or under the same bond, whether existing bonds are used or separate bonds are obtained, or whether the bond is underwritten by a single surety company or more than one surety company, either separately or on a co-surety basis, is left to the judgment of the parties concerned, so long as the bonding program adopted meets the requirements of ERISA and the regulations thereunder.

More than one plan may be insured under the same bond, but the bond providing the coverage must allow for recovery by each plan in an amount at least equal to that which would be required if the plans were bonded separately. If a person handles the funds of more than one plan, she should be bonded in a manner that provides protection in the total of the amounts required by ERISA for each plan.[3]

The United States District Court for the District of Colorado has ruled that a welfare benefit plan may pursue a state law action against its insurance broker for failing to procure a fidelity bond for the plan that was in compliance with the requirements of ERISA.[4] In this case, the insurance broker provided a bond that failed to properly cover everyone who handled property and assets of the plan. The investment manager for the fund fraudulently caused the plan to lose more than $500,000, and when a claim for coverage on the bond was submitted, it was rejected because the bond did not cover the acts of the investment manager. In deciding the case, the court relied on prior cases holding that state law claims by ERISA plans against non-fiduciary third parties alleging professional malpractice are not preempted by ERISA.

---

1. Labor Reg. §2580.412-19.
2. Labor Reg. §2580.412-19(c).
3. Labor Reg. §2580.412-20.
4. *Colorado Operating Eng'rs Health & Welfare Trust Fund v. Clarke & Sampson, Inc.*, 2006 U.S. Dist. LEXIS 94085 (D. Colo. 2006).

563. What is an approved surety company?

ERISA Section 412(a) requires that bonds be written only by a corporate surety approved by the Treasury Department as an acceptable surety of federal bonds.[1] In order for a surety company to be eligible for a grant of authority, it must be incorporated under the laws of the United States or of any state, and the Secretary of the Treasury must be satisfied of certain facts relating to its authority and capitalization. Approved surety companies are evidenced by certificates of authority issued by the Secretary of the Treasury; these expire and are renewable annually. Companies holding certificates of authority as acceptable sureties on federal bonds are also acceptable as reinsuring companies.

A list of the companies holding such certificates of authority is published annually in the Federal Register, usually in May or June. This list is also published annually in the Department of the Treasury's Listing of Approved Sureties (Department Circular 570). Changes in the list, occurring between May 1 and April 30, either by addition to or removal from the list of companies, are also published in the Federal Register following each such change.[2]

If the bond is for a term of more than one year, the plan administrator must confirm that the surety is on the approved list at the beginning of each year. When a company is removed from the approved list, the plan administrator must secure a new bond from an approved company as soon as he learns of such removal.

564. What are the party-in-interest restrictions with respect to procuring the bond?

A bond for a plan may not be placed with any surety or other company or through any agent or broker in whose business operations such plan or any party in interest in the plan has any significant control or financial interest, direct or indirect.[3] The application of this prohibition requires a determination of whether the financial interest or control held is sufficiently significant to disqualify the agent, broker, or surety. Although no rule of guidance is established to govern each and every case in which this question arises, in general, the essential test is whether the existing financial interest or control held is incompatible with an unbiased exercise of judgment in regard to procuring the bond or bonding the plan's personnel. Lack of knowledge or consent on the part of persons responsible for procuring bonds with respect to the existence of a significant financial interest or control rendering the bonding arrangement unlawful is not deemed a mitigating factor where the persons have failed to make a reasonable examination into the pertinent circumstances affecting the procuring of the bond.[4]

The party-in-interest prohibition appears to indicate that the intent of Congress was to eliminate those instances where the existing financial interest or control held by the party in interest in the agent, broker, surety, or other company is incompatible with an unbiased exercise of judgment in regard to procuring the bond or bonding the plan's personnel. Accordingly,

---

1. *See Treasury Dep't Circular 570*, available at http://www.fms.treas.gov/c570/c570.html.
2. Labor Reg. §2580.412-21.
3. ERISA Sec. 412(c).
4. Labor Reg. §2580.412-35.

not all parties in interest are disqualified from procuring or providing bonds for the plan. Thus, where a party in interest or its affiliate provides multiple benefit plan services to plans, persons are not prohibited from availing themselves of the bonding services provided by the party in interest or its affiliate merely because the plan has already availed itself, or will avail itself, of other services provided by the party in interest. In this case, it is inherent in the nature of the party in interest or its affiliate as an individual or organization providing multiple benefit plan services, one of which is a bonding service, that the existing financial interest or control held is not, in and of itself, incompatible with an unbiased exercise of judgment in regard to procuring the bond or bonding the plan's personnel. In short, there is no distinction between this type of relationship and the ordinary arm's-length business relationship that may be established between a plan customer and an agent, broker, or surety company, a relationship that Congress could not have intended to disturb.

However, where a party in interest in the plan or an affiliate does not provide a bonding service as part of its general business operations, ERISA Section 412 would prohibit any person from procuring the bond through or with any agent, broker, surety, or other company, with respect to which the party in interest has any significant control or financial interest, direct or indirect. In this case, the failure of the party in interest or its affiliate to provide a bonding service as part of its general business operations raises the possibility of less than an arm's-length business relationship between the plan and the agent, broker, surety, or other company, since the objectivity of either the plan or the agent, broker, or surety may be influenced by the party in interest.[1]

The application of the principles discussed above is illustrated by the following examples:

> *Example 1*: B, a broker, renders actuarial and consultant service to plan P. B has also procured a group life insurance policy for plan P. B may also place a bond for P with surety company S, provided that neither B nor P has any significant control or financial interest, direct or indirect, in S, and provided that neither P nor any other party in interest in P (e.g., an officer of the plan) has any significant control or financial interest, direct or indirect, in B or S.

> *Example 2*: I, a life insurance company, has provided a group life insurance policy for plan P. I is affiliated with S, a surety company, and has a significant financial interest or control in S. P is not prohibited from obtaining a bond from S, since I's affiliation with S does not ordinarily, in and of itself, affect the objectivity of P in procuring the bond or the objectivity of S in bonding P's personnel. However, if any other party in interest (as defined in ERISA Section 3(14)), such as the employer whose employees are covered by P, should have a significant financial interest or control in S, S could not write the bond for P, since the employer's interest affects the objectivity of P and S.[2]

Exemptions

565. What is the exemption to the bonding requirements for bonds placed with certain reinsuring companies?

Although all bonds required under ERISA must be issued by a corporate surety company that is an acceptable surety on federal bonds, an exemption exists for companies authorized

---

1. Labor Reg. §2580.412-36.
2. Labor Reg. §2580.412-36.

by the Secretary of the Treasury as acceptable reinsurers on federal bonds. The exemption is conditioned on the fact that if, for any reason, the authority of any such company to act as an acceptable reinsuring company is terminated, the administrator of an insured plan will, upon knowledge of the fact, be responsible for securing a new bond with a company acceptable under ERISA. In obtaining or renewing a bond, or if the bond is for a term of more than one year, the plan administrator, at the beginning of each reporting year, must ascertain that the surety satisfies the requirements of ERISA.[1]

566. What is the exemption to the bonding requirements for bonds placed with underwriters at Lloyds, London?

Bonding arrangements (which otherwise comply with the requirements of ERISA Section 412 and its attendant regulations) placed with the underwriters at Lloyds, London will be deemed to satisfy the bonding requirements of ERISA if certain requirements are met. This exemption applies only to the requirements of ERISA Section 412(a), which requires that all bonds required thereunder have as surety thereon a corporate surety company that is an acceptable surety on federal bonds under authority granted to the Secretary of the Treasury.[2]

The exemption will be granted if the following conditions are met:

1. Underwriters at Lloyds, London must continue to be licensed in a state of the United States to enter into bonding arrangements of the type required by ERISA.

2. Underwriters at Lloyds, London must file two copies of each annual statement, required to be made to the Commissioner of Insurance of those states in which underwriters at Lloyds, London are licensed, with the Office of Pension and Welfare Benefit Programs. Copies of annual statements must be filed with the Office of Pension and Welfare Benefit Programs within the same period required by the respective states.

3. All bonding arrangements entered into by underwriters at Lloyds, London under ERISA Section 412 must contain a "Service of Suit Clause" in substantial conformity with that set forth in the petition for exemption.[3]

567. What are the exemptions to the bonding requirements for banking institutions and trust companies?

Banking institutions and trust companies subject to regulation and examination by (1) the Comptroller of the Currency, (2) the Board of Governors of the Federal Reserve System, or (3) the Federal Deposit Insurance Corporation (FDIC) are exempt from the bonding requirements with respect to welfare and pension benefit plans.[4]

---

1. Labor Regs. §§2580.412-23, 2580.412-24.
2. ERISA Sec. 412(a)(2)(D).
3. Labor Regs. §§2580.412-25, 2580.412-26.
4. Labor Regs. §§2580.412-27, 2580.412-28.

568. What are the exemptions to the bonding requirements for savings and loan associations subject to federal regulation?

Savings and loan associations (including building and loan associations, cooperative banks, and homestead associations) that are subject to regulation and examination by the Federal Home Loan Bank Board are exempt from the bonding requirements, if such associations are the administrators of welfare and pension benefit plans benefiting their own employees.[1]

569. What are the exemptions to the bonding requirements for insurance carriers, service, and other similar organizations?

Insurance carriers or service or other similar organizations that provide or underwrite welfare or pension plan benefits in accordance with state law are exempt from the bonding requirements with respect to welfare or pension plans established or maintained for the benefit of persons other than the employees of the insurance carrier or service or other similar organization.[2]

570. What are the exemptions to the bonding requirements for broker-dealers?

The DOL proposes to amend the temporary bonding regulations for broker-dealers and investment advisers subject to federal regulation. Under the proposed regulation, if a broker-dealer maintains a fidelity bond covering the broker-dealer and/or an affiliated investment adviser that complies with the bonding requirements of its governing self-regulatory organization, and the bond meets minimum limits of coverage, the following persons will be considered bonded under ERISA Section 412: (1) any broker-dealer registered under the Securities Exchange Act of 1934 (Exchange Act); and (2) any investment adviser registered under the Investment Advisers Act of 1940 who controls, is controlled by, or is under common control with a broker-dealer registered under the Exchange Act (investment adviser affiliate), and does not maintain actual custody or possession of assets of employee benefit plans, and is named as an additional insured on the registered broker-dealer's bond.

As indicated above, the bond must meet minimum limits of coverage, irrespective of the limits prescribed by the governing self-regulatory organization. These limits are:

Securities and money values in possession and control	Basic minimum coverage
$0 – 50 million	$1 million
$50 – 100 million	$3 million
$100 – 500 million	$5 million
$500 million – 1 billion	$10 million
$1 – 2 billion	$25 million
Above $2 billion	$50 million

---

1. Labor Regs. §§2580.412-29, 2580.412-30.
2. Labor Regs. §§2580.412-31, 2580.412-32.

For purposes of this proposed exception, the terms "broker-dealer" and "investment adviser" include any partner, director, officer, or employee of such broker-dealer or investment adviser. The term "control" means the power to exercise a controlling influence over the management or policies of a person other than an individual. The bond must have a corporate surety company that is an acceptable surety on federal bonds under authority granted by the Secretary of the Treasury.[1]

Section 611(b) of the Pension Protection Act of 2006 (PPA)[2] amended ERISA Section 412 to provide that no bond is required of any entity that is registered as a broker or a dealer under Section 15(b) of the Securities Exchange Act of 1934[3] if the broker or dealer is subject to the fidelity bond requirements of a self-regulatory organization (within the meaning of Section 3(a)(26) of such Act (15 U.S.C. §78c(a)(26)).

The amendment provides an exception to the ERISA bonding requirement for an entity registered as a broker or a dealer under the Securities Exchange Act of 1934 if the broker or dealer is subject to the fidelity bond requirements of a self-regulatory organization (within the meaning of the Securities Exchange Act of 1934). The provision is effective for plan years beginning after August 17, 2006.

571. What are the exemptions to the bonding requirements for other bonding arrangements or adequate financial conditions of the plan?

The Secretary of Labor may exempt a plan from the bonding requirements in circumstances where other bonding arrangements or the overall financial condition of the plan is adequate to protect the interests of the beneficiaries and participants. For example, if the Secretary of Labor determines that the plan administrator presents adequate evidence of the financial responsibility of the plan, or that other bonding arrangements would provide adequate protection of the beneficiaries and participants, the plan may be exempted from the bonding requirements.[4]

Although the Secretary of Labor is authorized to exempt plans from the bonding requirement in specified situations, depositing plan-owned assets with the Secretary of Labor in lieu of obtaining a fiduciary bond from a corporate surety company does not satisfy the bonding requirement of ERISA. This was illustrated in a case where the plan trustees proposed that a plan set aside certain amounts of its own assets to provide a source from which "reimbursements" could be made to the fund in the event that one of the fund fiduciaries breached a duty to the plan. The court held that such a scheme did not protect the assets of the fund in the event of a breach of fiduciary duty by one of the fund's trustees, because the plan's assets would be diminished by the amount of the damage caused by the breach.[5]

1. Prop. Labor Reg. §2580.412-33.
2. Pub. L. No. 109-280.
3. 15 U.S.C. §78o(b).
4. ERISA Sec. 412(e).
5. *Musso v. Baker*, 834 F.2d 78 (3d Cir. 1987), *cert. denied*, 487 U.S. 1205 (1988).

Fiduciary Liability Insurance

572. May a plan purchase insurance to cover liability or losses due to the acts or omissions of a fiduciary?

Yes. ERISA allows, but does not require, a plan to purchase fiduciary insurance for its fiduciaries (or for itself) to cover liability or losses resulting from acts or omissions of the fiduciary. However, the insurance policy must permit recourse by the insurer against the fiduciary for a breach of its fiduciary obligation.[1] Therefore, if, under an insurance agreement, a fiduciary remains liable to the extent that there is a breach of fiduciary responsibility, such agreement would not be exculpatory and would be permissible under ERISA Section 410(a). The decision to purchase fiduciary insurance, as well as the particular arrangement entered into, can be made only by the appropriate plan fiduciaries, consistent with their fiduciary responsibilities in accordance with ERISA Section 404(a)(1).[2]

573. May a fiduciary purchase insurance to cover his own liability or to cover liability or losses resulting from his own acts or omissions?

Yes. ERISA Section 410(b) also permits plan fiduciaries to purchase insurance to protect themselves from any liability or losses resulting from their own acts or omissions. However, it is not necessary for the insurance policy to provide the insurer with recourse against the fiduciaries.[3]

574. May an employer or an employee organization purchase insurance to cover potential liability of persons who serve in a fiduciary capacity?

Yes. An employer or an employee organization may purchase insurance to cover potential liability of persons serving in a fiduciary capacity with respect to an employee benefit plan. It is not necessary for the insurance policy to provide the insurer with recourse against the fiduciaries.[4]

Liability for an employer's decision to terminate a welfare plan was not covered under the employer's fiduciary liability insurance policy because the policy covered the corporate employers' fiduciary violations in the administration and management of the plan but did not cover the everyday business decisions of the employer. The decision of the employer to terminate the welfare plan was considered a "business decision," rather than a fiduciary decision, and, thus, was not covered as a breach of fiduciary duty under the policy.[5]

575. Does the FDIC provide coverage for ERISA plan assets held at banks and savings and loans?

Yes. An FDIC Financial Institution Letter[6] advises that through December 31, 2013, the FDIC will provide federal deposit insurance coverage up to $250,000 for the money a consumer has

---

1. ERISA Sec. 410(b).
2. DOL Adv. Op. 76-23.
3. ERISA Sec. 410(b)(2); Labor Reg. §2509.75-4.
4. ERISA Sec. 410(b)(3); Labor Reg. §2509.75-4.
5. *Gulf Res. & Chem. Corp. v. Gavine*, 763 F. Supp. 1073 (D. Idaho 1991).
6. Financial Institution Letter FIL-22-2009 (May 22, 2009) (citing Helping Families Save Their Homes Act of 2009, Pub. L. No. 111-22). The legislation provides that the $250,000 limit will return to $100,000 on January 1, 2014.

in retirement accounts held at banks or savings insitutions. Although the temporarily increased insurance limit is aimed at traditional and Roth IRAs, at one insured institution it also provides coverage for employer-sponsored defined contribution plan accounts that are self-directed by the participants. Also included in the temporarily increased insurance schedule are self-directed Keogh accounts, 457 plans for state government employees, and defined contribution plans. Further, the retirement accounts that will be protected under the temporary $250,000 increase are insured separately from other accounts at the same institution, which will continue to be insured up to at least $100,000.

SECTION IX

Investment Issues

576. Must fiduciaries adhere to the plan's governing documents in managing and investing plan assets?

Yes, fiduciaries must discharge their duties with respect to a plan in accordance with the documents and instruments governing the plan (insofar as they are consistent with the provisions of ERISA).[1] This duty is reviewed in the overall context of the "prudent man" standard of care established under ERISA Section 404(a)(1)(B).

577. What are the general guidelines for a prudent investment program?

The requirements of ERISA Section 404(a)(1)(B) (the prudent man standard) are satisfied with regard to an investment course of action taken by a fiduciary if the fiduciary has given appropriate consideration to those facts and circumstances that the fiduciary knows or should know are relevant to the particular investment, or to the role the investment course of action plays in that portion of the plan's investment portfolio with respect to which the fiduciary has investment duties, and she has acted accordingly.[2]

"Appropriate consideration" includes (but is not limited to) a determination by the fiduciary that the particular investment course of action is reasonably designed, as part of the portfolio, to further the purposes of the plan, taking into consideration the risk of loss and the opportunity for gain associated with the investment or investment course of action. "Adequate consideration" also means consideration of the following factors as they relate to such portion of the plan's investment portfolio:

1. Composition of the portfolio with regard to diversification;

2. Liquidity and current return of the portfolio relative to the anticipated cash flow requirements of the plan; and

3. Projected return of the portfolio relative to the funding objectives of the plan.[3]

In carrying out a plan's investment program, a fiduciary's failure to investigate the investments it administers violates the prudent man standard of care *only* if adequate investigation would have revealed to a prudent fiduciary that the investment at issue was inappropriate, or somehow not in the best interests of the participants and beneficiaries of the plan.[4] In other words, ERISA does not state that a fiduciary is prohibited from making a bad investment; rather, it states that a fiduciary may not make an imprudent investment.

The DOL, in Advisory Opinion 2006-08A, has stated that a fiduciary's proposed investment strategy for a defined benefit plan, designed in part to reduce funding volatility for the plan

---

1. ERISA Sec. 404(a)(1)(D).
2. Labor Reg. §2550.404a-1.
3. Labor Reg. §2550.404a-1(b)(2).
4. See *Katsaros v. Cody*, 744 F.2d 270 (2d Cir. 1984); *Roth v. Sawyer-Cleator Lumber Co.*, 16 F.3d 915 (8th Cir. 1994).

sponsor, would not violate ERISA's fiduciary obligations and would, in fact, be prudent and consistent with the fiduciary duties detailed under ERISA Section 404. The DOL stated that it "does not believe that there is anything in the statute or the regulations that would limit a plan fiduciary's ability to take into account the risks associated with benefit liabilities or how those risks relate to the portfolio management in designing an investment strategy."

578. May plan fiduciaries delegate investment management responsibilities to others?

The plan documents may provide that the named fiduciaries (see next) have the authority to delegate the management and investment of plan assets (including the power to acquire and dispose of plan assets) to an investment manager.[1] These individuals need not be specifically identified within the plan documents.

A *named fiduciary* is a fiduciary who is identified in the plan's governing documents, or who, pursuant to a procedure specified in the plan, is identified as a fiduciary by: (1) a person who is an employer or employee organization with respect to the plan, or (2) the employer and employee organization acting jointly.[2]

The ongoing responsibilities of named fiduciaries who have appointed trustees or other fiduciaries, such as investment managers, include a continuing obligation to monitor the performance of the appointed individuals at reasonable intervals. Their performance should be reviewed in such a manner as may be reasonably expected to ensure that such performance has been in compliance with the terms of the plan and statutory standards, and that it satisfies the needs of the plan. No single procedure will be appropriate in all cases. The procedures adopted for the monitoring of investment managers may vary in accordance with the nature of the plan and other facts and circumstances relevant to the choice of procedure.[3]

579. What is a "statement of investment policy"?

A "statement of investment policy" is defined as a written statement that provides the fiduciaries who are responsible for plan investments with guidelines or general instructions concerning various types or categories of investment management decisions, which may include proxy-voting decisions. A statement of investment policy provides general instructions or guidelines to be applied in all applicable situations, such as identification of acceptable classes or types of investments, limitations on investment categories as a percentage of the plan's portfolio, or generally applicable guidelines regarding voting positions in proxy contests (e.g., criteria regarding the support of or opposition to recurring issues, such as proposals to create classified boards of directors or to provide for cumulative voting for board members). A statement of investment policy does not provide specific instructions as to the purchase or sale of a specific investment at a specific time or specific instructions to vote specific plan proxies a certain way. Because the fiduciary act of managing plan assets that are shares of corporate stock includes the

---

1. ERISA Sec. 402(c)(3).
2. ERISA Sec. 402(a)(2).
3. See Labor Reg. §2509.75-8, Q&A FR-17.

voting of proxies appurtenant to those shares of stock, a statement of proxy-voting policy is an important part of any comprehensive statement of investment policy.[1]

580. Are statements of investment policy required by ERISA?

No. The maintenance of a statement of investment policy is not specifically required under ERISA. However, the Department of Labor believes that statements of investment policy serve a legitimate purpose in many plans by helping to ensure that investments are made in a rational manner and are designed to further the purposes of the plan and its funding policy. For example, a statement of investment policy that includes a statement on proxy voting may increase the likelihood that proxy-voting decisions are consistent with other aspects of the investment policy. Additionally, in plans with multiple investment managers, a written proxy-voting policy may also prevent (where such prevention is desirable) the managers from taking conflicting positions on a given voting decision.[2]

581. Is a statement of investment policy consistent with the duty of loyalty and prudence?

Yes. The Department of Labor issued Interpretive Bulletin 94-2 in part to clarify that the maintenance by an employee benefit plan of a statement of investment policy designed to further the purposes of the plan and its funding policy is consistent with the fiduciary obligations of loyalty and prudence. In the view of the DOL, a named fiduciary's determination of the terms of a statement of investment policy is an exercise of fiduciary responsibility and, as such, statements may need to take into account factors such as the plan's funding policy and its liquidity needs as well as issues of prudence, diversification, and any other fiduciary requirements of ERISA.[3]

582. Does the maintenance of a statement of investment policy by a named fiduciary relieve the named fiduciary of its fiduciary duties with respect to the appointment and monitoring of an investment manager or trustee?

No. In the view of the Department of Labor, maintenance of a statement of investment policy by a named fiduciary does not relieve the named fiduciary of its obligations under ERISA Section 404(a) with respect to the appointment and monitoring of an investment manager or trustee. In this respect, the named fiduciary appointing an investment manager must periodically monitor the investment manager's activities with respect to management of the plan assets. Moreover, complying with the duty of prudence requires maintenance of proper documentation of the activities of the investment manager and of the named fiduciary in monitoring the activities of the investment manager.[4]

---

1. Labor Reg. §2509.94-2(2); I.B. 94-2, 59 Fed. Reg. 38,860 (July 29, 1994).
2. See Labor Reg. §2509.08-2(2); I.B. 08-2 (Oct. 17, 2008).
3. See Labor Reg. §2509.08-2(2); I.B. 08-2 (Oct. 17, 2008).
4. See Labor Reg. §2509.08-2(2); I.B. 08-2 (Oct. 17, 2008).

583. May a fiduciary expressly require, as a condition of an investment management agreement, that an investment manager comply with the terms of a statement of investment policy?

Yes. According to the Department of Labor, the named fiduciary responsible for the appointment of investment managers in plans that delegate investment management responsibility to one or more investment managers has the authority to condition the appointment on acceptance of a statement of investment policy. Thus, the named fiduciary may expressly require, as a condition of the investment management agreement, that an investment manager comply with the terms of a statement of investment policy that sets forth guidelines concerning investments and investment courses of action that the investment manager is authorized to make or is precluded from making. However, in the absence of an express requirement of compliance with an investment policy, the authority to manage the plan assets placed under the control of an investment manager would lie exclusively with the investment manager.[1]

584. Does ERISA Section 404(a)(1)(D) shield an investment manager from liability for imprudent actions taken in compliance with a statement of investment policy?

No. According to the Department of Labor, acting in accordance with the plan documents does not shield an investment manager from liability for imprudent actions taken in compliance with a statement of investment policy. Even though an investment manager may be subject to the directions of a named fiduciary pursuant to ERISA Section 403(a)(1), an investment manager who has authority to make investment decisions is not relieved of its fiduciary responsibility if it followed directions as to specific investment decisions from the named fiduciary or any other person. An investment manager who operates under an investment policy is required to comply with the policy, pursuant to ERISA Section 404(a)(1)(D), insofar as the policy's directives or guidelines are consistent with ERISA. If compliance with the guidelines is imprudent, then the investment manager's refusal to follow the guidelines is not a violation of ERISA Section 404(a)(1)(D).[2]

585. When will an employer be regulated as an investment adviser?

If an employer is "in the business of providing investment advice," it is subject to the registration requirements and regulation under the Investment Advisers Act of 1940 if it:

1.   Holds itself out to the public as providing investment advice; or

2.   Receives separate or additional compensation from employees or third parties that represents a clearly definable charge for providing investment advice.[3]

---

1. See Labor Reg. §2509.08-2(2); I.B. 08-2 (Oct. 17, 2008).
2. See Labor Reg. §2509.08-2(2); I.B. 08-2 (Oct. 17, 2008).
3. Letter from Jack W. Murphy, Associate Director of the SEC, to Olena Berg, Assistant Secretary of the Pension and Welfare Benefits Administration (Dec. 5, 1995).

If an employer is merely offering various investment options under a defined contribution plan, it will not be considered an investment adviser, unless it is otherwise in the business of providing investment advice.

If any money or other property of an employee benefit plan is invested in securities issued by an investment company registered under the Investment Company Act of 1940, the investment will not by itself cause the investment company or its investment adviser or principal underwriter to be deemed to be a fiduciary or party in interest, except to the extent that the adviser or underwriter acts in connection with an employee benefit plan covering employees of the investment company, of the investment adviser, or of the principal underwriter.[1]

586. May a financial institution include the business of investment management of ERISA-covered plan assets under its control in the sales price of a fiduciary?

The Department of Labor (DOL) has strongly cautioned financial firms not to use employee benefit plan assets in negotiating corporate sales. In PWBA News Release 97-82, the DOL stated that it is an abuse of fiduciary duty for a financial institution to hire investment managers and service providers for plans by including the business of managing plans under their control in the sales price of a subsidiary or division.

The news release quotes Assistant Secretary Alan D. Lebowitz as saying, "The department is concerned that other financial institutions may be using their plans to barter for higher purchase prices. There is no gray area under the law. Employers cannot promise prospective buyers that they will get plan business, especially if they stand to profit by reaping a higher price on the sale of an affiliate."

The DOL cautions that financial institutions that include in the sales price of a related subsidiary the business of managing plans under their control could be placing their interest ahead of the interests of the plans and participants in violation of ERISA Section 404(a)(1) and ERISA Section 406(b)(1).

587. What are plan assets?

ERISA defines plan assets in two contexts: plan investments and employee contributions.

Plan Investments

When a plan invests in another entity, the *plan assets* generally include its own investments but do not, solely by reason of such investment, include any of the underlying assets of the entity. ERISA expressly provides that a plan's investment in the shares of a mutual fund does not by itself cause the fund or its investment adviser to be deemed a fiduciary.[2] ERISA also provides that a plan's assets do not, solely by reason of such an investment, include any assets of the fund.[3] The

---

1. ERISA Sec. 3(21)(B).
2. ERISA Sec. 3(21)(B).
3. ERISA Sec. 401(b)(1).

DOL has affirmed that the assets of "target date" and "lifecycle" mutual funds do not constitute plan assets of investing employee benefit plans, and the investment advisers to such mutual funds are not fiduciaries to investing plans merely because the funds invest in other, affiliated mutual funds.[1] However, there is a "look-through" rule, which provides that in the case of a plan's investment in an equity interest of an entity that is neither a publicly offered security nor a security issued by an investment company registered under the Investment Company Act of 1940 (i.e., generally mutual funds), that plan's assets will include both the equity interest and an undivided interest in each of the underlying assets of the entity, unless it is established that:

1.   The entity is an operating company; or

2.   Equity participation in the entity by benefit plan investors is not significant.[2]

If the look-through rule does apply, any person who exercises authority or control over the management and disposition of the underlying assets, or who provides investment advice with respect to such assets, is a fiduciary of the investing plan.

Generally, an investment by a plan in securities of a corporation or partnership will not, solely by reason of such investment, be considered an investment in the underlying assets of the corporation or partnership so as to make the assets of the entity "plan assets." Consequently, a subsequent transaction between the party in interest and the corporation or partnership generally would not constitute a prohibited transaction merely on account of such an investment.[3] In an appeal of seven- and ten-year prison sentences for the theft of unpaid plan contributions under ERISA's theft statute[4] (see Q 861); the two defendants argued that unpaid employer contributions did not constitute plan assets under the theft statute until they were paid into the plan. The Fourth Circuit Court of Appeals disagreed with this line of reasoning, ruling that the unpaid employer contributions became plan assets when they were "due and payable" to the plan.[5]

ERISA Fee Recapture Accounts

In Advisory Opinion 2013-03A (AO 2013-03A) the DOL addresses the different types of ERISA recapture accounts and discusses the ERISA plan asset and prohibited transaction rules that apply to them. In AO 2013-03A, the DOL describes two types of ERISA recapture accounts — the *bookkeeping account* and the *plan account*. Each requires a different approach in identifying how ERISA plan asset rules apply.

Under the *bookkeeping account approach*, the financial institution receives the revenue sharing payments and under an agreement with the plan establishes this account on the financial institution's records. The bookkeeping account reflects that it will, under a written plan agreement or under the direction of a plan fiduciary, apply these credits to pay plan service providers. In this approach, amounts in the bookkeeping account are *not* ERISA plan assets.

---

1. DOL Adv. Op. 2009-04A (Dec. 4, 2009).
2. See Labor Reg. §2510.3-101(a).
3. See Labor Reg. §2509.75-2(a).
4. 18 U.S.C. §664.
5. *United States v. Jackson*, 2008 WL 1903485 (4th Cir. 2008).

However, the DOL advises that if there is an agreement in place for plan fees to be paid from this account and the financial institution fails to make such specified payments, the plan would have a claim against the financial institution and that claim *is* a plan asset.

Under the *plan account approach*, the financial institution receives the revenue sharing payments directly and under written agreement with the plan transfers some or all of the revenue sharing payments to the plan. The plan administrator then uses the plan account to pay service providers. If, at the close of the plan year, amounts remain in the plan account, the plan administrator will then allocate them to participants as additional plan earnings.

With the *plan account approach*, the amounts received in the account *are* plan assets. If the plan has a contract with the financial institution to transfer the funds to the plan, and the financial institution fails to make those payments, the plan would have a claim against the financial institution and that claim would be a plan asset.

Employee Contributions

Under applicable regulations, plan assets include amounts (other than union dues) that a participant or beneficiary pays to an employer, or amounts that a participant has withheld from his wages by an employer, for contribution to the plan as of the earliest date on which such contributions can reasonably be segregated from the employer's general assets.[1] However, in no case may such employee contributions be paid to the plan later than the fifteenth business day of the month following the month in which the contributions were withheld or received by the employer.[2]

NOTE: The fifteenth-day business rule for participant contributions does not apply to welfare benefit plans. Therefore, participant contributions to a welfare benefit plan become plan assets as of the earliest date on which they can reasonably be segregated from the employer's general assets, but in no event later than ninety days from the date on which contributions are received or withheld by the employer.[3]

EBSA has amended the plan asset regulations to provide for a safe harbor under which participant contributions to a pension or welfare benefit plan with fewer than one-hundred participants at the beginning of the plan year will be treated as having been made to the plan in accordance with the general rule when contributions are deposited with the plan no later than: (1) the seventh business day following the day on which such amount is received by the employer; or (2) the seventh business day on which such amount would otherwise have been payable to the participant in cash.[4] The Department of Labor has stated that in all other issues regarding plan assets, it will apply the rules of property rights for the determination of what constitutes plan assets. Plan assets will generally include any property, tangible or intangible, in which the plan holds a beneficial ownership interest. Beneficial ownership exists where:

---

1. Labor Reg. §2510.3-102(a).
2. Labor Reg. §2510.3-102(b).
3. Labor Reg. §2510.3-102(c).
4. Labor Reg. §2510.3-102(a)(2); 75 Fed. Reg. 2068 (Jan. 14, 2010).

1. An employer has established a trust on behalf of the plan;

2. The employer has set up a separate account with a bank or third party in the name of the plan; *and*

3. The plan documents state that separately maintained funds belong to the plan.[1]

The DOL finalized the seven-business-day safe harbor for depositing participant contributions and loan repayments into small plans on January 14, 2010.[2] Under the final safe harbor, employers who sponsor plans with fewer than one-hundred participants are treated as having made a timely deposit under the plan asset rule if the contributions are deposited within seven business days after they (1) are received (if the contributions are paid to the employer), or (2) would have been paid in cash (if the contributions are withheld from wages). The safe harbor applies only to plans with fewer than one-hundred participants at the beginning of the plan year and became effective January 14, 2010.

The final rule extends the general deposit timing rule and safe harbor to participant loan repayments. The final rule includes a new subsection affirming that the seven-business-day rule is merely a safe harbor and not the exclusive means for determining whether the general deposit timing rule has been met.

In Field Assistance Bulletin 2008-01 (Feb. 1, 2008), the DOL advises that the responsibility for collecting employer and employee contributions is a trustee responsibility. The FAB elaborates that a named or functional fiduciary that has the authority to appoint a plan's trustees must make certain that the proper party has been assigned the obligation of collecting plan contributions.

The FAB does provide two exceptions to the general holding of trustee responsibility: (1) where the plan expressly provides that the trustee will be a directed trustee with respect to contributions; and (2) where the authority to collect contributions is delegated to an investment manager.[3]

In issuing the FAB, the DOL notes that it has encountered numerous trustee agreements with financial institutions relieving the institution serving as trustee of the responsibility to collect delinquent contributions without adequately assigning that duty to someone else. If no trustee or investment manager has the responsibility to make sure plan contributions are collected, the fiduciary with authority to hire trustees may be liable for plan losses based on to a failure to collect contributions due to the failure to properly assign the responsibility.

In late 2010, the DOL announced new civil and criminal enforcement actions to protect contributory retirement and health plan benefits (retirement and health plans for which employees have funds withheld from their paychecks to be deposited in their retirement plan's trust or to provide health benefits). In 2009, the DOL closed more than 1,000 401(k) plan

---

1. DOL Adv. Op. 92-24A.
2. Definition of "Plan Assets"—Participant Contributions, Labor Reg. §2510.3-102, 75 Fed. Reg. 2068 (Jan. 14, 2010).
3. ERISA Secs. 403(a)(1), 403(a)(2).

investigations, with 910 of those closed involving corrected violations. The DOL described over twenty-five new civil actions filed in 2011 and 2012, to recover misused retirement and welfare plan contributions.

The DOL announced its first criminal national enforcement initiative targeting persons who commit fraud and abuse against contributory 401(k) and health plans. The initiative targets employers sponsoring plans as well as "unscrupulous" service providers that have embezzled plan funds or stolen participants' identity information to access plan funds. The DOL coordinates these criminal investigations with U.S. attorneys as well as state and local law enforcement agencies nationwide to bring criminal prosecutions under ERISA. In 2009, the DOL closed sixty-four 401(k) criminal investigations, with thirty-three of those resulting in criminal indictments. The Retirement Security Initiatives fact sheet described ten criminal convictions obtained in recent years. Seven convictions resulted in prison sentences ranging from six months to 151 months. The remaining defendants received probation or house confinement and nearly all were ordered to pay restitution.[1]

As part of the announcement of the retirement security initiatives, the DOL posted "Ten Warning Signs That Your 401(k) Contributions Are Being Misused" on its Web site to help employees identify potential 401(k) plan abuse.[2]

The U.S. District Court for the Northern District of New York has ruled that plan fiduciaries can be personally liable for a failure to remit participant salary deferral contributions.[3] The court granted the DOL's motion for summary judgment and found the fiduciaries (father and son) jointly and severally liable to restore more than $43,000 in contributions to the plan, with interest. In addition, the court permanently barred them from serving as ERISA plan fiduciaries.

The Seventh Circuit Court of Appeals has upheld a criminal conviction for the owner of a plan sponsor who diverted funds withheld for salary deferral contributions and health benefits coverage.[4] The trial court found that the owner was guilty of using salary deferrals to pay his own management fees and expenses instead of remitting them to the trust. Further, he was found guilty of failing to use participant contributions for insurance coverage under the health benefits plan, causing large unpaid medical claims for participants. He was sentenced to ninety months in prison and ordered to pay more than $1 million in restitution. The Seventh Circuit affirmed, noting that the salary deferrals were the property of plan participants until deposited, and thus were tantamount to ERISA funds and not subject to conversion.

The Eleventh Circuit has ruled that Davis-Bacon Prevailing Wage contributions are *not* plan assets.[5] For a six-month period, the employer failed to make the prevailing wage

---

1. Employee Contributions Initiative, Retirement Security Initiatives, Contributory Plans Criminal Project (Nov. 2010), http://www.dol.gov/ebsa/newsroom/ECI/main.html.
2. Employee Contributions Initiative, Retirement Security Initiatives, Contributory Plans Criminal Project, Ten Warning Signs That Your 401(k) Contributions Are Being Misused (Nov. 2010), http://www.dol.gov/ebsa/newsroom/ECI/main.html.
3. *Chao v. James C. Docster, Inc.*, No. 3:01-CV-827 (N.D.N.Y. 2006).
4. *United States v. Whiting*, 2006 U.S. App. LEXIS 30833 (7th Cir. 2006).
5. *Pantoja v. Edward Engel & Son Express, Inc.*, 2012 W.L. 6117886 (11th Cir. December 11, 2012).

contributions, using the money instead to pay its payroll taxes. The court noted that DOL Reg. Sec. 2510.102-3 addresses only the issue of when participant contributions become plan assets. In the absence of Federal regulations regarding the issue of when employer contributions are plan assets, the Eleventh Circuit's position is that unpaid employer contributions are not plan assets unless specific and clear language in the plan documents or other evidence so indicates.

Participant Loans

The DOL has issued Advisory Opinion 2002-02A, which provides guidance on when participant loan repayments are considered plan assets. Under the advisory opinion, the DOL states that the employer's failure to transmit participant loan repayments to a plan "as soon as the repayments are considered assets of the plan" would constitute a prohibited transaction under ERISA Section 406.

The 2010 amendments to the plan asset regulations extend the application of the regulations to amounts paid by a participant or beneficiary or withheld by an employer from a participant's wages for purposes of repaying a participant's loan.[1] The amendments to the regulations also extend the seven-business-day safe harbor for plans with fewer than one-hundred participants to participant loan repayments.

Practitioner's Pointer: The *outside* window under the Labor Regulation principle applied is the fifteenth business day of the month following the month in which the repayment was withheld from the participant's wages. *However,* from a compliance and regulatory enforcement perspective, the DOL considers any repayment or salary withholding held beyond the normal time the employer processes payroll to be held for an "unreasonable" period of time (and, therefore, in violation of ERISA Section 406).

---

588. When do contributions to SIMPLE plans become plan assets?

The answer depends on whether the plan is a SIMPLE IRA or a SIMPLE 401(k) plan. In the case of SIMPLE IRAs, the Internal Revenue Code states that an employer must make salary reduction contributions to the financial institution maintaining the SIMPLE IRA plan no later than the close of the 30-day period following the last day of the month with respect to which the contributions are to be made.[2] Regulations under ERISA mirror this provision.[3]

The maximum period for holding SIMPLE 401(k) plan salary deferral contributions prior to their becoming plan assets is the same as under traditional 401(k) plans (see Q 587); thus, such amounts become plan assets no later than the fiftieth business day of the month following the month in which the contributions are received by the employer or would have otherwise been payable to the employee.[4]

---

1. Labor Reg. §2510.3-102(a)(1); 75 Fed. Reg. 2068 (Jan. 14, 2010).
2. IRC Sec. 408(p)(5)(A)(i).
3. See Labor Reg. §2510.3-102(b)(2).
4. See Labor Reg. §2510.3-102(b)(1).

589. What are the plan asset rules with respect to insurance company general accounts?

The U.S. Supreme Court has ruled that certain retirement plan assets held in the general accounts of insurance companies are plan assets under the rules of ERISA.[1] As such, these assets are subject to the fiduciary and prohibited transaction provisions of ERISA. This ruling contradicted two decades of insurance company practices that had been supported through Department of Labor guidance indicating that the consideration paid by an employee benefit plan for a contract or policy of insurance that is placed into the insurance company's general account was not to be considered plan assets.[2]

Insurance company general accounts are assets held by, and commingled with the assets of, an insurance company that are not legally segregated and allocated to separate accounts.

Final regulations further clarify the application of the provisions of ERISA to insurance company general accounts. These regulations offer guidelines for determining what percentage of insurance company general account assets may be considered ERISA "plan assets" where the insurer has provided a policy for the benefit of an ERISA-covered employee benefit plan that is supported by the insurer's underlying general account.[3]

The general rule is that when a plan acquires a policy issued by an insurer on or before December 31, 1998 (i.e., a "transition policy") that is supported by assets of the insurer's general account, the plan's assets include the policy, but do not include any of the underlying assets of the insurer's general account if the insurer satisfies the following general requirements:[4]

1.   An independent plan fiduciary with appropriate authority expressly authorizes the purchase of the transition policy;

2.   Certain disclosure requirements detailed under the regulations are satisfied both prior to the issuance of the transition policy and on an annual basis thereafter, including:

   a.   a description of the method by which any income, ongoing fees, and expenses of the insurer's general account are allocated to the policy during the term of the policy and upon policy termination;

   b.   a report of the actual return to the plan under the policy;

   c.   a description of the policyholder's rights to transfer or withdraw amounts credited to any "accumulation fund" established under the policy;

   d.   a statement of the method used to calculate any charges, fees, credits, or market value adjustments that may be imposed with connection to the transfer or withdrawal; and

---

1. See *John Hancock Mut. Life Ins. Co. v. Harris Trust & Sav. Bank*, 510 U.S. 86 (1993).
2. See I.B. 75-2; Labor Reg. §2509.75-2.
3. See Labor Reg. §2550.401c-1.
4. See Labor Reg. §§2550.401c-1(a)(2), 2550.401c-1(h)(6)(i).

3. Mandatory statement language required under the regulations is provided for with the disclosure material. Such statements must provide information regarding the difference in risks and legal rights between insurance company general accounts and insurance company separate accounts (which are segregated funds not commingled with the general account).

The DOL has issued an opinion letter covering the application of the "significant participation test" of ERISA's plan asset regulations to an investment in an entity by a wholly owned subsidiary of an insurer's general account that holds plan assets for purposes of determining whether that entity holds plan assets.[1] Pursuant to Labor Regulation Section 2510.3-101(f)'s "significant participation" test, equity participation in an entity by benefit plan investors is "significant" if on any date immediately after the most recent acquisition of any equity interest in the entity, 25 percent or more of the value of any class of equity interests in the entity is held by benefit plan investors. However, the regulation is silent as to its application to the general accounts of an insurance company. In response to this, the DOL ruled that, for purposes of the significant participation test the wholly owned subsidiary is disregarded and its equity interest in the entity is treated as held by the insurance company's general account, provided that the subsidiary is wholly owned at all times during the period of the entity's existence.

590. Must plan documents provide for a written funding policy?

Yes. Every employee benefit plan must provide a procedure for establishing and carrying out a funding policy and a method consistent with the objectives of the plan and the requirements of ERISA.[2] There has been a great deal of debate as to whether this policy must be in writing, but due to the emphasis that the Department of Labor places on plan funding and investment issues, it is strongly recommended that the funding policy be formalized in a written document.

The Conference Committee Report to ERISA states that the procedures relating to funding are to enable plan fiduciaries to determine the plan's long-term and short-term financial needs (growth vs. liquidity) and to use this information in establishing the funding and investment policy for the plan.[3] As noted in Q 577, the funding and investment policy should take into consideration the composition of the portfolio with regard to diversification and the projected return of the portfolio relative to the funding objectives of the plan (in addition to the liquidity and return characteristics).

The funding policy should also take into consideration:

1. General investment philosophy and objectives of the plan;

2. Standards for the identification and selection of appropriate investments;

3. Acceptable risk/return ratios;

4. Benchmarks for the measurement of investment performance;

---

1. ERISA Op. Letter 2005-19A (2005).
2. ERISA Sec. 402(b)(1).
3. See H.R. Conf. Rep. No. 93-1280, 93d Cong., 2d Sess. (1974) (ERISA Conference Report).

5.   Size of the plan; and

6.   Appropriate procedures for the monitoring and evaluation of investments.

Practitioner's Pointer: Plan fiduciaries should periodically review the plan's funding and investment policies to evaluate the necessity of any changes that may be required due to the changing circumstances of the plan as it grows. It is recommended that fiduciaries review the funding and investment policies at least once a year.

---

591. Are there any restrictions on the types of investments that are permissible for a plan?

ERISA does not mandate any specific investments or investment portfolio for employee benefit plans. The only restrictions on plan investments are the requirements that the investments be prudent, that they be for the exclusive benefit of participants and beneficiaries, and that they not violate the prohibited transaction provisions of ERISA (see Section IV and Section V for details on fiduciary issues and prohibited transactions, respectively). Otherwise, fiduciaries are free to select any investment they deem to be within the funding and investment policies of the plan.

592. Are plan assets required to be held in a trust?

Yes, except as explained in Q 593. ERISA states that all assets of an employee benefit plan shall be held in a trust by one or more trustees.[1] Such trustees must either be named in the trust instrument or plan document, or appointed by a person who is a named fiduciary. The trustee has the exclusive authority and discretion to manage and control the assets of the plan, except where:

1.   The plan expressly provides that the trustee is subject to the direction of a named fiduciary who is not a trustee (in which case the trustee will be subject to the proper directions of the named fiduciary); and

2.   Authority to manage, acquire, or dispose of assets has been delegated to one or more investment managers pursuant to ERISA Section 402(c)(3).

The Conference Committee Report to ERISA provides that a plan may allow for an investment committee to manage plan investments. Because investment decisions are basic to plan operations, the members of the investment committee must be named fiduciaries (see Q 578). They may be named by title (president, vice president, etc.), which would mean any person who holds that position becomes a named fiduciary with respect to the plan. Trustees are obligated to follow the investment committee's recommendations (if the plan permits the appointment of such committee), unless the recommendations are contrary to the terms of the plan document or the provisions of ERISA.[2]

---

1. ERISA Sec. 403(a).
2. See H.R. Conf. Rep. No. 93-1280, 93d Cong., 2d Sess. (1974) (ERISA Conference Report).

593. What are the exceptions to the requirement that plan assets be held in a trust?

The requirement that plan assets be held in a trust does not apply to:

1. Any assets that consist of insurance contracts or policies issued by an insurance company qualified to do business in a state;

2. Any assets of such an insurance company or any assets of a plan that are held by the insurer;

3. A plan in which some or all of the participants are self-employed or that consists of IRAs, to the extent that such plan's assets are held in one or more custodial accounts;

4. A plan that the Secretary of Labor exempts from the requirement that plan assets be held in a trust, and that is not subject to the participation, vesting, funding, and plan termination insurance provisions of ERISA; and

5. A tax sheltered annuity contract established and maintained under IRC Section 403(b) to the extent that such assets are held in one or more custodial accounts pursuant to IRC Section 403(b)(7).[1]

The ERISA Conference Committee Report states that although assets consisting of insurance contracts and policies are not required to be held in a trust, any individual who holds these contracts is a fiduciary and must act in accordance with the fiduciary provisions of ERISA.[2] As such, plan assets held by an insurance company are "plan assets" and the insurance company is to be treated as a fiduciary with respect to the plan whose assets it is holding.

The trust requirement will not be violated merely because securities of a plan are held in the name of a nominee or in a street name, provided such securities are held on behalf of the plan by a bank or trust company, a broker-dealer registered under the Securities Exchange Act of 1934, or a clearing agency.[3]

The trust requirement will also be satisfied for any real property held in an IRC Section 501(c)(2) tax-exempt corporation on behalf of a plan if the stock of the corporation is held in trust on behalf of the plan.[4]

Finally, if the assets of an entity in which a plan invests (e.g., a partnership) include plan assets by reason of the plan's investment in the entity, the trust requirement will be satisfied with respect to that entity if the indicia of ownership of the plan's interest in the entity are held in trust on behalf of the plan by one or more trustees.[5]

---

1. ERISA Sec. 403(b).
2. H.R. Conf. Rep. No. 93-1280, 93d Cong., 2d Sess. (1974) (*ERISA Conference Report*).
3. As defined in Section 3(a)(23) of the Securities Exchange Act of 1934. Labor Reg. §2550.403a-1(b)(1).
4. Labor Reg. §2550.403a-1(b)(2).
5. Labor Reg. §2550.403a-1(b)(3).

594. May a plan participate in economically targeted investments? What are the asset management issues involved in economically targeted investments?

Yes, under limited circumstances. An economically targeted investment (ETI) is an investment that is selected for the economic benefit it creates, in addition to the investment return to the employee benefit plan investor. Interpretive Bulletin 94-1[1] provides that "ETIs fall within a wide variety of asset categories, including real estate, venture capital and small business investments. Although some of these asset categories may require a longer time to generate significant investment returns, may be less liquid, and may not have as much readily available information on their risk and returns as other asset categories, nothing in ERISA precludes trustees and investment managers from considering ETIs in constructing plan portfolios." The Department of Labor believes that while some of these asset categories may require special expertise to evaluate, they may be attractive to sophisticated, long-term investors "including many pension plans." For an explanation of the *fiduciary* issues involved in economically targeted investments, see Q 314.

595. May an employer offer investment advice without incurring fiduciary liability?

[*NOTE:* In late 2010, and again in 2011, the DOL released proposed regulations that have a significant impact on determining fiduciary status regarding advice and management decisions focusing on plan assets.[2] You will find a detailed analysis of these proposed regulations and the impact they have on plan assets and individuals involved in the decisions and management of them in Q 240. It is important to note that in these proposed regulations, the DOL reaffirms its position that the following information regarding investment education rendered pursuant to Interpretive Bulletin 96-1 remains intact and is, in no way, altered by the proposed regulations on fiduciary status in rendering investment advice.]

Yes, within certain limitations. The Department of Labor has noted that with the growth of participant-directed individual account plans, more employees are directing the investment of their retirement plan assets and thereby assuming more responsibility for ensuring the adequacy of their retirement income. Simultaneously, the DOL has expressed increasing concern that many participants may not have sufficient understanding of investment principles and strategies to make their own informed investment decisions.

An Interpretive Bulletin[3] (see Q 243) provides final guidance on the provision of investment education for participants who are entitled to direct their own investments in an individual account plan. This guidance sets forth the views of the DOL regarding the circumstances under which the provision of investment-related information to participants will not constitute the "rendering of investment advice" under ERISA Section 3(21)(A)(ii).[4]

---

1. See Labor Reg. §2509.08-1; I.B. 08-1 (Oct. 17, 2008).
2. Prop. Labor Reg. §2510.3-21; 75 Fed. Reg. 65,263 (Oct. 22, 2010).
3. I.B. 96-1.
4. See Labor Reg. §2509.96-1 (I.B. 96-1).

The regulation establishes a series of graduated safe harbors for plan sponsors and service providers who provide participants and beneficiaries with the following specific categories of investment information and materials:

1. Investment education (see Q 596);

2. General financial and investment education (see Q 597);

3. Asset allocation models (see Q 598); and

4. Interactive investment materials (see Q 599).

For details as to what constitutes the "rendering of investment advice," see Q 380. See Q 600 regarding other types of information that may be covered under Interpretive Bulletin 96-1.

596. What is the "plan information" safe harbor under Interpretive Bulletin 96-1?

Interpretive Bulletin 96-1 provides a safe harbor for the provision of investment education to participants in an individual account plan by an employer or service provider without such information's constituting the "rendering of investment advice" (which results in certain persons' becoming, under ERISA Section 3(21)(A)(ii) and Labor Regulation Section 2510.3-21(c), a fiduciary with respect to the plan).

This first of the four safe harbors under Interpretive Bulletin 96-1 states that providing information and materials that inform a participant or beneficiary about the benefits of plan participation, the benefits of increasing plan contributions, the impact of pre-retirement withdrawals on retirement income, the terms of the plan, or the operation of the plan, that are made without reference to the appropriateness of any individual investment option for a participant or beneficiary will not be considered the rendering of investment advice. Furthermore, the regulation allows for the provision of information regarding investment alternatives, including descriptions of investment objectives, risk and return characteristics, historical performance information, prospectuses, and basic asset classes (such as bonds, equities, and cash equivalents) of such alternatives.[1]

597. What is the "general financial and investment information" safe harbor under Interpretive Bulletin 96-1?

Interpretive Bulletin 96-1 states that the provision of general financial and investment information by a plan sponsor or service provider will not constitute the rendering of investment advice if the materials inform participants and beneficiaries concerning:

1. General financial and investment concepts, such as risk and return, diversification, dollar cost averaging, compounded return, and tax-deferred investments;

2. Historic differences in rates of return between different asset classes (e.g., equities, bonds, and cash) based on standard market indices;

---

1. See Labor Reg. §2509.96-1(d)(1).

3.   The effects of inflation;

4.   Estimating future retirement income needs;

5.   Determining investment time horizons; and

6.   Assessing risk tolerance.

This information is considered, under the regulation, to be general financial and investment information that has no direct relationship to investment alternatives available to participants and beneficiaries under a plan. As such, the provision of it is not considered the rendering of investment advice or the making of recommendations to a participant or beneficiary.[1]

598. What is the "asset allocation model" safe harbor under Interpretive Bulletin 96-1?

Interpretive Bulletin 96-1 establishes a safe harbor under which the provision of asset allocation models will not be considered the rendering of investment advice or the making of recommendations for purposes of conferring fiduciary status upon the plan sponsor or service provider offering such information.[2]

Under the safe harbor, this applies to information and materials (e.g., pie charts, graphs, or case studies) that provide participants and beneficiaries with models of asset allocation portfolios of hypothetical individuals with different time horizons and risk profiles where:

1.   Such models are based on generally accepted investment theories that take into account the historic returns of different asset classes (e.g., equities, bonds, or cash) over defined periods of time;

2.   All material facts and assumptions on which such models are based (e.g., retirement ages, life expectancies, income levels, financial resources, replacement income ratios, inflation rates, and rates of return) accompany the models;

3.   To the extent that an asset allocation model identifies any specific investment alternative available under the plan, the model is accompanied by a statement that indicates that other investment alternatives with similar risk and return characteristics may be available under the plan, and that identifies where information on those investment alternatives may be obtained; and

4.   Such asset allocation models are accompanied by a statement that indicates that, in applying particular asset allocation models to their individual situations, participants or beneficiaries should consider their other assets, income, and investments (e.g., home equity, IRAs, savings accounts, and other qualified plan account balances) in addition to their interests in the plan.

The Department of Labor advises, under the regulation, that because the information and materials described above would enable a participant or beneficiary to assess the relevance of

---

1. Labor Reg. §2509.96-1(d)(2).
2. See Labor Reg. §2509.96-1(d)(3).

an asset allocation model to his individual situation, the furnishing of such information would not be considered the rendering of investment advice or the making of recommendations for the purposes of ERISA Section 3(21)(A)(ii).

599. What is the "interactive investment materials" safe harbor under Interpretive Bulletin 96-1?

Interpretive Bulletin 96-1 establishes an "interactive investment materials" safe harbor under which the provision of questionnaires, worksheets, software, and similar materials, which provide a participant or beneficiary the means to estimate future retirement income needs and assess the impact of different asset allocations on retirement income, will not be considered the rendering of investment advice or the making of recommendations, where:

1. Such materials are based on generally accepted investment theories that take into account the historic returns of different asset classes (e.g., equities, bonds, or cash) over defined periods of time;

2. There is an objective correlation between the asset allocations generated by the materials and the information and data supplied by the participant or beneficiary;

3. All material facts and assumptions (e.g., retirement ages, life expectancies, income levels, financial resources, replacement income ratios, inflation rates, and rates of return) that may affect a participant's or beneficiary's assessment of the different asset allocations accompany the materials, or are specified by the participant or beneficiary;

4. To the extent that an asset allocation generated by the material identifies any specific investment alternative available under the plan, the asset allocation is accompanied by a statement indicating that other investment alternatives having similar risk and return characteristics may be available under the plan, and identifying where information on those investment alternatives may be obtained; and

5. The materials either take into account or are accompanied by a statement indicating that, in applying particular asset allocations to their individual situations, participants or beneficiaries should consider their other assets, income, and investments (e.g., home equity, IRAs, savings, and interests in other qualified plans) in addition to their assets under the plan.[1]

The information provided through the use of interactive investment materials enables participants and beneficiaries to independently design and assess multiple asset allocation models, but otherwise these materials do not differ from asset allocation models based on hypothetical assumptions. Accordingly, such information does not constitute the rendering of investment advice or the making of recommendations for purposes of ERISA Section 3(21)(A)(ii).

---

1. Labor Reg. §2509.96-1(d)(4).

600. Are there any other types of information covered by Interpretive Bulletin 96-1?

In Interpretive Bulletin 96-1, the Department of Labor points out that the information and materials described in the four graduated safe harbors detailed within the bulletin (see Q 596 to Q 599) merely represent examples of the type of information and materials that may be furnished to participants and beneficiaries without such information and materials constituting "investment advice" for purposes of ERISA Section 3(21)(A)(ii).

Further, in Interpretive Bulletin 96-1, the DOL states that there may be many other examples of information, materials, and educational services that, if furnished to participants and beneficiaries, would not constitute the provision of investment advice. Accordingly, the DOL advises, no inferences should be drawn from the four graduated safe harbors with respect to whether the furnishing of any information, materials, or educational services not described therein may constitute the provision of investment advice. The DOL cautions that the determination as to whether the provision of any information, materials, or educational services not described within Interpretive Bulletin 96-1 constitutes the rendering of investment advice must be made by reference to the criteria set forth in Labor Regulation Section 2510.3-21(c)(1). That regulation establishes that a person will be deemed to be rendering "investment advice" to an employee benefit plan, within the meaning of ERISA Section 3(21)(A)(ii), only if:

1. Such person renders advice to the plan as to the value of securities or other property, or makes recommendations as to the advisability of investing in, purchasing, or selling securities or other property; and

2. Such person either directly or indirectly has discretionary authority or control, whether or not pursuant to agreement, arrangement, or understanding, with respect to purchasing or selling securities or other property for the plan; or renders any advice described in (1), above, on a regular basis to the plan pursuant to a mutual agreement, arrangement, or understanding, written or otherwise, between such person and the plan or a fiduciary with respect to the plan, that such services will serve as a primary basis for investment decisions with respect to plan assets, and that such person will render individualized investment advice to the plan based on the particular needs of the plan regarding such matters as, among other things, investment policies or strategy, overall portfolio composition, or diversification of plan investments.

601. When will the underlying assets of an insurance company issuing group annuity contracts be considered, or not considered, to be plan assets?

The assets of a plan to which a guaranteed benefit policy is issued by an insurer will be deemed to include that policy, but will not, solely by reason of the issuance of the policy, be deemed to include any assets of the insurer.[1] The term "guaranteed benefit policy" means an

---

1. ERISA Sec. 401(b)(2)(B).

insurance policy or contract to the extent that such policy or contract provides for benefits the amount of which is guaranteed by the insurer. The Court of Appeals for the Second Circuit has ruled that the insurer is a fiduciary with respect to plan assets invested in a policy that are not guaranteed benefits.[1] The court held that the insurer was a plan fiduciary with respect to nonguaranteed benefits even though they are not considered plan assets for purposes of the prohibited transaction provisions of ERISA.

The Department of Labor has stated that if the assets that back a group annuity contract issued to a plan are placed in a separate account that provides for the crediting of income on the group annuity contract based upon the investment performance of the separate account, then the assets of the separate account will be deemed to be plan assets.[2]

In general, under the *Harris Trust* decision, any group annuity contract that provides for variable payments will be deemed "not guaranteed," and that variable portion will be considered plan assets that are subject to ERISA's fiduciary provisions.

The American Council on Life Insurance applied to the DOL for a prohibited transaction class exemption retroactively effective to January 1, 1975, that would provide for exemptive relief from the holdings of the *Harris Trust* case. In response to the application, the DOL issued Prohibited Transaction Class Exemption 95-60, which provides relief, prospectively and retroactively, for certain transactions engaged in by insurance company general accounts containing qualified plan asset investments. The exemption also extends relief to transactions relating to the origination and operation of certain asset pool investment trusts in which insurance company general accounts have an interest as a result of the acquisition of certificates issued by the trust. Further, the exemption extends relief to people who provide services to insurance company general accounts. For a detailed review of the retroactive and prospective relief from the holdings of the *Harris Trust* case provided for under PTE 95-60, see Q 459.

The DOL has issued regulations to clarify the application of ERISA to insurance company general accounts. See Q 589.

602. What are the asset management issues regarding investments in derivatives?

The Department of Labor (DOL) defines "derivatives" as financial instruments whose performance is derived in whole or in part from the performance of an underlying asset (such as a security or index of securities). Examples of these financial instruments include, but are not limited to, futures, options, options on futures, forward contracts, swaps, structured notes, and collateralized mortgage obligations.[3] (See Q 323 for details regarding fiduciary obligations when investing plan assets into derivatives.)

According to the DOL, investments in derivatives are subject to the fiduciary responsibility rules in the same manner as are any other plan investments. In determining whether to invest

---

1. See *Harris Trust & Sav. Bank v. John Hancock Mut. Life Ins. Co.*, 970 F.2d 1138 (2d Cir. 1992).
2. DOL Adv. Op. 83-51A.
3. DOL Information Letter to Comptroller of the Currency (Mar. 21, 1996).

in a particular derivative, plan fiduciaries must engage in the same general procedures and undertake the same type of analysis that is made in any other investment decision. This includes, but is not limited to, considering how the derivative fits within the plan's investment policy, the role the particular derivative plays in the plan's portfolio, and the plan's potential exposure to losses.[1] See also Q 323.

In the view of the DOL, derivatives may be a useful tool for managing a variety of risks and for broadening investment alternatives in a plan's portfolio. However, investments in certain derivatives, such as structured notes and collateralized mortgage obligations, may require a higher degree of sophistication and understanding on the part of plan fiduciaries than other investments would. Characteristics of such derivatives may include extreme price volatility, a high degree of leverage, limited testing by markets, and difficulty in determining the market value of the derivative due to illiquid market conditions. Thus, it is possible the DOL may hold fiduciaries who invest in high-risk derivatives to a higher standard of fiduciary responsibility than that established under the "prudent person" rule.

The DOL also explained that plan fiduciaries who invest in derivatives must secure sufficient information to understand the investment prior to making the investment.[2] For example, plan fiduciaries must secure sufficient information to allow an independent analysis of the credit risk and market risk being undertaken by the plan in making the investment in the particular derivative. The market risks presented by the purchased derivatives must be understood and evaluated in terms of the effects that they will have on the relevant segments of the plan's portfolio as well as the portfolio's overall risk.

Likewise, plan fiduciaries have a duty to determine the appropriate methodology used to evaluate market risk and the information needed to do so. Among other things, this includes stress simulation models showing the projected performance of the derivatives in the plan's portfolio under various market conditions. The DOL believes that stress simulations are particularly important because assumptions that may be valid for normal markets may not be valid in abnormal markets, resulting in significant losses. To the extent that there may be little pricing information available with respect to some derivatives, reliable price comparisons may be necessary. In addition, after purchasing a derivative, a plan fiduciary must obtain timely information from the derivatives dealer regarding the plan's credit exposure and the current market value of its derivatives positions, and, where appropriate, obtain this information from third parties to determine the current market value of the plan's derivatives positions with a frequency that is appropriate to the nature and extent of these positions. If the plan invests in a pooled fund that is managed by a party other than the plan fiduciary, then that plan fiduciary must obtain, among other things, sufficient information to determine the pooled fund's strategy with respect to use of derivatives in its portfolio, the extent of investment by the fund in derivatives, and any other information that is appropriate under the circumstances.[3]

---

1. See DOL Information Letter, above.
2. See DOL Information Letter, above.
3. See DOL Information Letter, above.

In addition, the DOL believes that a fiduciary must analyze the operational risks being undertaken in selecting a derivative as part of its evaluation of the investment. Among other things, the DOL believes that the fiduciary must determine whether it possesses the necessary expertise, knowledge, and information to understand and analyze the nature of the risks and potential returns involved in a particular derivative investment. In particular, the fiduciary must determine whether the plan has adequate information and risk management systems in place given the nature, size, and complexity of the plan's derivatives activity, and whether the plan fiduciary has personnel who are competent to manage these systems. If the investments are made by outside investment managers hired by the plan fiduciary, that fiduciary must consider whether the investment managers have sufficient personnel and controls and whether the plan fiduciary has personnel who are competent to monitor the derivatives activities of the investment managers.[1]

Plan fiduciaries also have a duty to evaluate the legal risk related to the investment. In the DOL's view, this includes ensuring proper documentation of the derivative transaction and, where the transaction is pursuant to a contract, ensuring written documentation of the contract before entering into the contract. Also, as with any other investment, plan fiduciaries must properly monitor their investments in derivatives to determine whether they are still appropriately fulfilling their role in the portfolio. The frequency and degree of the monitoring depends on the nature of the derivatives and their role in the plan's portfolio.[2]

603. Is the cash asset value of a split dollar life insurance policy considered a plan asset?

Split dollar life insurance generally refers to a variety of arrangements between an employer and employees where interests in, and proceeds payable under, a whole life insurance policy are split, and the obligation to pay premiums may be split.

The Department of Labor has advised that the cash value portion of a welfare plan's split dollar life insurance policy that provides life insurance coverage for employees (with premiums paid for by the employees on a voluntary basis through payroll deduction while actively employed, and through direct payment to the carrier after separation from service) and a separate cash value portion providing benefits to the employer and paid for on a discretionary basis by the employer, would not be a plan asset for purposes of Title I of ERISA.[3]

The DOL stated that, the use of a split dollar policy as described above does not, in itself, appear to violate ERISA Section 406(a)(1)(D) (the prohibition against the use of plan assets for the benefit of a party in interest) because the use of the insurance policy to fund the cash value death benefit does not provide any direct or indirect benefit to the employer.

In closing, the DOL stated that a plan fiduciary may, under appropriate facts and circumstances, provide benefits under a death benefit plan through a life insurance policy whose cash value element belongs exclusively to the sponsoring employer, without violating requirements that the

---

1. See DOL Information Letter, above.
2. See DOL Information Letter, above.
3. DOL Adv. Op. 92-22A.

selection and retention of the policy be prudent and made solely in the interests of participants and beneficiaries. However, the DOL continued, if a split dollar life insurance policy were selected to fund a death benefit without due regard to both the cost to the plan of the pure insurance and the financial soundness and claims-paying ability of the insurer, or if such a policy were acquired for the benefit of the employer, this would not meet the fiduciary standards of ERISA Section 404.

604. May plans engage in securities lending arrangements utilizing plan assets?

Yes, but fiduciaries must be cautious that such ventures do not violate the prohibited transaction provisions regarding parties in interest. Securities lending involves the lending of securities to broker-dealers, investment managers, banks, or financial institutions for the purpose of assisting the borrower in covering "short" positions. A "short sale" is an investment practice where the borrower believes the market for a particular stock will go down in the near future. Thus, the borrower sells stock that has been borrowed and holds the proceeds of the sale to purchase an equivalent number of the same shares at the future, lower price. The borrower gets to retain the difference in the sale and purchase price that has been realized due to a drop in the market price of the stock, less any interest that is repaid along with delivery of the borrowed stock.

Securities lending is also a common practice for assistance in covering positions where delivery of promised stock has been delayed, as well as to assist in limited arbitrage situations.

In the absence of an exemption, it would be a prohibited transaction for an ERISA-covered plan to engage in the lending of securities to a financial institution, investment manager, bank, or broker-dealer that is a party in interest to the plan. Fortunately, the Department of Labor has issued Prohibited Transaction Exemption 81-6,[1] which permits the lending of securities by a plan to domestic parties in interest that are:

1. Broker-dealers registered under the Securities Exchange Act of 1934;

2. Dealers in government securities who are exempt from the Securities Exchange Act of 1934; or

3. Banks.

For a detailed review of the lending and collateral requirements of PTE 81-6,[2] see Q 454.

605. May plans engage in repurchase agreements utilizing plan assets?

A repurchase agreement involving a retirement plan is a method utilized by securities dealers to raise cash. These arrangements involve finding a plan to act as a temporary buyer for securities and simultaneously executing a contract with the securities dealer to sell back the securities at a later date at a predetermined price, plus interest (in effect, these are fully collateralized loans).

---

1. As amended and expanded by PTE 2006-16.
2. As amended and expanded by PTE 2006-16.

As with securities lending arrangements, plan fiduciaries must exercise caution when entering into repurchase agreements with parties in interest, as they may be prohibited transactions.

The Department of Labor has issued Prohibited Transaction Exemption 81-8, which provides exemptive relief for repurchase agreements where the securities are sold to the plan by a party in interest under a written agreement to sell them back to the party in interest at a later date for a predetermined price, provided that the requirements spelled out under the exemption are satisfied. Parties in interest who may enter into such repurchase agreements with a plan are:

1.   Broker-dealers registered under the Securities Exchange Act of 1934;

2.   Banks supervised by the United States, or a state thereof; or

3.   Government securities dealers who have complied with specific requirements detailed under the exemption.

For a detailed review of the permissible parties, permissible securities, permissible collateral, and other required elements to be satisfied for such exemptive relief, see PTE 81-8.

Other types of repurchase agreements may be structured as securities lending arrangements (see Q 604 and Q 454), transactions involving bank collective trust funds (see the explanation of PTE 91-38 in Q 448), and those involving insurance company pooled separate accounts (see the explanation of PTE 90-1 in Q 434).

A reverse repurchase agreement involves a dealer agreeing to buy securities from a plan and then selling them back to the plan later at a higher price. Although there is exemptive relief for plans entering into repurchase agreements, there is no class exemption available for plans that enter into reverse repurchase agreements with parties in interest.

606. Under what circumstances may plans enter into "soft dollar" and directed-commission arrangements?

"Soft dollar" and directed-commission arrangements typically involve situations in which an investment manager purchases goods or services with a portion of the brokerage commissions paid by the investor to a broker for executing a securities transaction. Soft-dollar and directed-commission arrangements with ERISA-covered plans involve the payment of a portion of brokerage fees involved in transactions with plan assets to a broker for the provision of goods or services, in addition to the basic execution of the underlying transaction. Soft-dollar arrangements benefit retirement plans by allowing them access to investment research that they may not otherwise be able to afford if they were required to pay for them with "hard" dollars.

In ERISA Technical Release 86-1, the Department of Labor (DOL) set forth its policies regarding soft-dollar and directed-commission arrangements under the limited safe harbor of Section 28(e) of the Securities Exchange Act of 1934 (i.e., "the 1934 Act"). In 1975 Congress added Section 28(e) to the 1934 Act, eliminating the fixed-commission rates on stock exchange transactions. Prior to the elimination of fixed-commission rates, investment managers often purchased with commission dollars additional services beyond simple execution, clearance, and settlement of securities transactions. Section 28(e) of the 1934 Act provides a limited safe harbor from ERISA's fiduciary responsibility rules. It provides that no person who exercises investment discretion with respect to securities transactions will be deemed to have acted unlawfully or to have breached a fiduciary duty solely by reason of paying brokerage commissions for effecting a securities transaction in excess of the amount of the commission another broker-dealer would have charged, if such person determined in good faith that the commission was reasonable in relation to the value of brokerage and research services provided by the broker-dealer. In addition to these requirements, the DOL permits plans to enter into soft-dollar arrangements where the plan has received "best execution" of the transactions.

"Best execution" is defined as execution of a transaction by a money manager in such a manner that the investor's total cost or proceeds in each transaction are the most favorable under the circumstances.[1] This Securities and Exchange Act Release further advises that the investment manager should take into consideration the full range and quality of the broker's services in placing brokerage transactions, including, among other things, the value of the research provided as well as execution capability, commission rate, financial responsibility, and responsiveness to the investment manager. Obviously, "best execution" does not always mean the lowest commission fees; the investment manager must make an evaluation of the relevant facts of each transaction to determine what constitutes "best execution."

In addition to the relief from the general fiduciary provisions, the safe harbor provides relief from the prohibited transaction provisions of: ERISA Section 406(a)(1)(D) (restricting the transfer to, or use by or for the benefit of, a party in interest of any of the assets of the plan); ERISA Section 406(b)(1) (restricting the use of plan assets by a fiduciary in his own interest or for his own account); and ERISA Section 406(b)(3) (prohibiting the receipt by a fiduciary of any consideration for his own account from any party involved in a transaction involving plan assets).

The DOL points out that the Securities and Exchange Commission has ruled that the limited safe harbor provided by Section 28(e) is available only for the provision of brokerage and research services to persons who exercise investment discretion with respect to an account. The investment manager with discretion is still required to act prudently both with respect to a decision to buy or sell securities as well as with respect to the decision as to who will execute the transaction. The named fiduciary to the plan retains the fiduciary obligation for the oversight responsibility of periodically reviewing the investment manager's performance.

607. May plans enter into "soft dollar" and directed-commission arrangements where the plan sponsor has directed brokerage transactions?

Yes, the Department of Labor (DOL) has established in Technical Release 86-1 that plan sponsors may direct brokerage transactions or direct them to specific broker-dealers where the plan trustees have determined that the broker-dealer is able to provide the plan "best execution" (see Q 606) for the brokerage transactions. Trustees are also responsible for the monitoring of services provided by the broker-dealer so as to ensure that the best execution has occurred and that the commissions paid are reasonable in relation to the value of the brokerage and other services received by the plan.

---

1. Securities and Exchange Act Release No. 34-23170 (Apr. 23, 1986).

The DOL has stated that where a plan sponsor or other plan fiduciary directs the investment manager to execute securities trades for the plan through one or more specified broker-dealers, the direction generally requires the investment manager to execute a specified percentage of the plan's trades or a specified amount of the plan's commission business through the particular broker-dealers, consistent with the investment manager's duty to secure best execution for the transactions. The DOL also advises that the plan sponsor's decision to direct brokerage transactions must be made prudently and solely in the interest of the participants and beneficiaries.

However, the DOL advises that the Securities and Exchange Commission has indicated that the limited safe harbor of Section 28(e) is not available for directed-brokerage transactions[1] where plan sponsors who do not have investment discretion with respect to a plan direct the plan's securities trades to one or more broker-dealers in return for research, performance evaluation, other administrative services, or discounted commissions.

608. What types of "soft dollar" and directed-commission arrangements fall outside Technical Release 86-1 and the limited safe harbor?

In ERISA Technical Release 86-1, the Department of Labor (DOL) states that there are several types of "soft dollar" and directed-commission arrangements that do not qualify for the limited safe harbor established under Section 28(e) of the Securities Exchange Act of 1934. The Securities and Exchange Commission has indicated that if a plan fiduciary does not exercise investment discretion with respect to a securities transaction, or uses "soft dollars" to pay for non-research-related services, the transaction falls outside the protection afforded by the limited safe harbor and may be in violation of the securities laws and the fiduciary responsibility provisions of ERISA.

Some examples of improper transactions cited by the DOL include the use of a percentage of brokerage commissions by investment managers or plan sponsors to pay for travel, hotel rooms, and other goods and services that do not qualify as research within the meaning of the limited safe harbor. Such prohibited services would include the provision of bookkeeping services for the benefit of an investment manager from a broker-dealer who has directed plan brokerage transactions through the broker-dealer. Another example would be the provision of tax-exempt securities research services to an investment manager from a broker-dealer in exchange for the execution of plan-related brokerage transactions.

In consideration of such transactions, Technical Release 86-1 states that "soft dollar" and directed-commission arrangements must take the prohibited transaction provisions of ERISA into account. A fiduciary is generally prohibited from causing the plan to engage in a transaction in which she has an interest that may affect her best judgment as a fiduciary.[2] The Release cites as an example that an employer who is the named fiduciary and who does not exercise investment discretion would normally be prohibited from directing the plan's brokerage transactions through a designated broker-dealer who agrees to utilize a portion of the brokerage commissions received from the plan to procure goods or services for the benefit of the plan sponsor.

---

1. As defined under Section VI of Securities Exchange Act Release No. 34-23170 (Apr. 23, 1986).
2. See ERISA Sec. 406(b)(1).

609. How does the limited safe harbor for "soft dollar" arrangements apply to recapture provisions?

A recapture arrangement involves the rebating of commissions from a broker-dealer to one of the parties involved in the brokerage transaction. These arrangements may be permissible under Technical Release 86-1 if the plan is the party receiving the recaptured commissions, and all other fiduciary and prohibited transaction provisions have been satisfied (see Q 606 to Q 608 for details). An improper fiduciary interest in a recapture arrangement that will result in a prohibited transaction is the direction of brokerage transactions through a broker-dealer who, in turn, rebates a portion of the commissions to the employer or trustee to reduce his fees.

610. Are there any proposed changes regarding the rules on "soft dollar" and commission recapture arrangements?

In the Department of Labor's ERISA Advisory Council Working Group on Soft Dollars and Commission Recapture (i.e., "the Advisory Council") is a statutorily mandated aggregation of employee benefit plan professionals, including representatives from private sponsors, governmental plan sponsors, and the financial services industry who issue reports and recommendations to the Department of Labor (DOL).

The Advisory Council reviewed current industry practices on soft-dollar arrangements and applicable ERISA regulations in an effort to determine whether employee benefit plan sponsors and other plan fiduciaries are being provided sufficient disclosure to allow them to adequately protect plan assets. In its report, the Advisory Council reviewed all of the written and oral testimony it had received throughout 1997. That report contains the following recommendations to the Department of Labor, the Securities and Exchange Commission (SEC), and the employee benefits plan industry as a whole:

1. To the DOL, the following recommendations were made:

    a. modify Annual Report Form 5500 so that it requires all plan sponsors to detail all fees greater than $5,000 paid under directed-brokerage arrangements; and

    b. list an additional question in the Annual Report Form 5500 that requires plan sponsors to certify compliance with the requirements of ERISA Technical Release 86-1 regarding directed-brokerage programs.

2. To the SEC, the following recommendations were made:

    a. apply a more stringent definition of the term "research" to Section 28(e) of the Securities Exchange Act of 1934;

    b. establish a detailed list that specifies those brokerage and research services that may be purchased under a soft-dollar or directed-commission arrangement;

    c. require investment managers to disclose to each client the investment manager's soft-dollar policies, all transactions executed for the client in which soft dollars were involved, and details of the benefits received by the investment manager from the soft-dollar arrangement; and

d. establish a requirement that investment managers disclose, on their Form ADV, any external research received.

To the employee benefits plan industry, the Advisory Council recommended further efforts to educate plan sponsors on the legal requirements and industry practices of soft-dollar and directed-brokerage arrangements. Further recommendations include ten guidelines for education efforts on industry practices and appropriate conduct regarding soft-dollar and directed-brokerage arrangements.

The report issued to the Department of Labor by the Advisory Council also included minority positions, which recommended the repeal of Section 28(e) of the Securities Exchange Act of 1934 as it applies to employee benefit plans (which would eliminate the research safe harbor; see Q 606), and the "unbundling" of services by brokerage firms, which would eliminate the use of soft dollars for employee benefit plans. This final minority recommendation would also require investment managers to pay separately for execution and investment research with "hard dollars."

In October 1998, the SEC released the results of its examination of soft-dollar commission practices of the investment advisory and broker-dealer industries. The SEC advised that inadequate disclosure of soft-dollar practices is prevalent. This inadequacy was cited in that the general level of disclosure fails to provide adequate information to enable clients to understand the advisers' soft-dollar practices and policies. The SEC states that advisers and plan sponsors may violate the exclusive purpose provisions of ERISA Sections 403(c)(1) and 404(a)(1) where soft-dollar or directed-brokerage benefits are not received by the benefit plan account whose transactions generated the benefits. The full text of the SEC's report is available on the Internet at http://www.sec.gov/news/studies/softdolr.htm.

611. What are "qualifying employer securities"?

A "qualifying employer security" is defined as an employer security that is (1) stock, (2) a marketable obligation, or (3) an interest in a publicly traded partnership (as described under IRC Section 7704(b)) that is issued by an employer of employees covered by a plan or an affiliate of such employer.[1] After December 17, 1987, a stock or an interest in a publicly traded partnership is a "qualifying employer security" only if, immediately following the acquisition of such stock:

1. No more than 25 percent of the aggregate amount of stock of the same class issued and outstanding at the time of the acquisition is held by the plan; and

2. At least 50 percent of the aggregate amount referred to in item one is held by persons independent of the issuer.[2]

Qualifying employer securities may also include "marketable obligations" that are bonds, debentures, notes or certificates, or other evidence of indebtedness if:

---

1. ERISA Secs. 407(d)(1), 407(d)(5).
2. ERISA Secs. 407(d)(5), 407(f)(1).

1. The obligation is acquired:

   a. on the market, either (i) at the price of the obligation prevailing on a national securities exchange that is registered with the Securities Exchange Commission (SEC), or (ii) if the obligation is not traded on a national securities exchange, at a price not less favorable to the plan than the offering price for the obligation as established by current bid and asked prices quoted by persons independent of the issuer,

   b. from an underwriter, at a price (i) not in excess of the public offering price for the obligation as set forth in a prospectus or offering circular filed with the SEC, and (ii) at which a substantial portion of the same issue is acquired by persons independent of the issuer, or

   c. directly from the issuer, at a price not less favorable to the plan than the price paid currently for a substantial portion of the same issue by persons independent of the issuer; *and*

2. Immediately following the acquisition:

   a. not more than 25 percent of the aggregate amount of obligations issued in such issue and outstanding at the time of acquisition is held by the plan, and

   b. at least 50 percent of the aggregate amount outstanding is held by persons independent of the issuer; *and*

3. Immediately following acquisition of the obligation, not more than 25 percent of the assets of the plan are invested in obligations of the employer or an affiliate of the employer.[1]

Section 901 of PPA 2006 added new ERISA Section 204(j) regarding publicly traded qualifying employer securities. Beginning January 1, 2007, assets attributable to elective deferrals and after-tax employee contributions that are invested in publicly traded employer securities can be diversified at all times. Amounts attributable to employer matching and employer nonelective contributions that are invested in employer securities can be diversified after the participant has completed three years of service. A three-year transition rule applies to amounts invested in employer securities acquired before the first year in which these new rules apply.

Further, plans are required to provide at least three diversified investment options other than employer securities or employer real property. Other investment options offered under the plan must be available, and plans must allow diversification elections at least quarterly, on the same basis as the opportunity to make other investment changes.

Section 507 of PPA 2006 amended ERISA Section 101, effective January 1, 2007, requiring the plan administrator to provide notice at least 30 days before a participant becomes eligible to diversify her investments, setting forth such right and describing the importance of diversifying

---

1. ERISA Sec. 407(e).

investments. Failure to provide this notice can be punished by a civil penalty of up to $100 per day, per participant.[1]

612. What is "qualifying employer real property"?

"Employer real property" is real property (and related personal property) that is leased to an employer of employees covered by a plan, or to an affiliate of such employer.[2] ERISA Section 407(d)(2) "qualifying employer real property" is defined as parcels of employer real property:

1. Where a substantial number of the parcels are dispersed geographically;

2. Where each parcel of real property and the improvements thereon are suitable (or adaptable without excessive cost) for more than one use;

3. Even if all such real property is leased to one lessee (which may be an employer, or an affiliate of an employer); and

4. Where the acquisition and retention of such property comply with the fiduciary provisions of ERISA (except for the diversification and prohibited transaction provisions of ERISA Section 404(a)(1)(C) and ERISA Section 406).

613. What rules apply to the acquisition and holding of employer securities and employer real property?

The general rule is that a plan may not acquire or hold any employer security that is not a "qualifying employer security" (see Q 611) or any employer real property that is not "qualifying employer real property" (see Q 612).[3] Furthermore, a plan may not hold or acquire qualifying employer securities or qualifying employer real property if immediately after such acquisition, the fair market value of employer securities and employer real property held by the plan exceeds 10 percent of the fair market value of the assets of the plan.[4]

"Eligible individual account plans" may invest in qualifying employer securities and qualifying employer real property, provided that the plan explicitly provides for acquisition and holding of qualifying employer securities and qualifying employer real property.[5] Eligible individual account plans include profit sharing, stock bonus, thrift, and savings plans, as well as employee stock ownership plans (see Q 614 through Q 627 for a review of the special rules and restrictions that are applicable to ESOPs). Pre-ERISA money purchase plans, which invested primarily in employer securities prior to the enactment of ERISA, are also included in the definition of eligible individual account plans.[6] Eligible individual account plans are not subject to the 10 percent restriction on the holding of qualifying employer securities or qualifying employer real property.[7] Finally, the 25 percent/50 percent restriction of ERISA Section 407(f)(1)(A) and

---

1. ERISA Sec. 502(c)(7), as amended by PPA 2006, Sec. 507.
2. ERISA Sec. 407(d)(4).
3. ERISA Sec. 407(a).
4. ERISA Sec. 407(a)(2).
5. ERISA Sec. 407(d)(3)(B).
6. ERISA Sec. 407(d)(3)(A).
7. ERISA Sec. 407(b)(1).

ERISA Section 407(f)(1)(B) (see Q 611 for details) does not apply to eligible individual account plans with respect to their investments in qualifying employer securities.

Section 401(k) plans are restricted from mandating that employees place more than 10 percent of their plan funds in company stock or employer real property.[1] (See Q 350 for details of this provision.) Participants in Section 401(k) plans that permit investments into qualifying employer securities or qualifying employer real property may elect, of their own volition, to place more than 10 percent of their plan assets in such qualifying employer investment vehicles.

The Ninth Circuit Court of Appeals has ruled that a rise in stock value alone following a corporate merger, does not dictate that fiduciaries should override a plan's limits regarding the extent to which participants' accounts may be divested of employer securities where the plan calls for a specified minimum percentage of the accounts in such securities.[2]

The DOL, in Advisory Opinion 2012-05A, discussed the ability of a plan sponsor to contribute a single piece of real property to a plan trust without the contribution violating the geographic disbursement requirements of ERISA Section 407(d)(4)(A). "The purpose of requiring that a substantial number of the parcels of employer real property held by a plan be dispersed geographically is to prevent adverse economic conditions peculiar to one area from significantly affecting the economic status of the plan as a whole.... Whether a substantial number of parcels of employer real property are geographically dispersed for this purpose is an inherently factual determination upon which the Department will not opine. However, it is the view of the Department that whether any one parcel of employer real property ... satisfies the requirements of section 407(d)(4)(A) of ERISA is determined by considering the plan's holdings in employer real property immediately after the transaction involving the parcel. Otherwise, a plan could never acquire or sell any single parcel of employer real property even if the other QERP requirements of section 407 of ERISA, besides section 407(d)(4)(A), would be met for the plan's holdings after the acquisition or sale."[3]

614. What is an employee stock ownership plan (ESOP)?

An "employee stock ownership plan" is an individual account plan (Section 401(k), profit sharing, or money purchase) that is a stock bonus plan or a stock bonus plan and money purchase plan, which is qualified under Internal Revenue Code Section 401(a), is designed to invest primarily in qualifying employer securities, and that satisfies the requirements regarding ESOPs provided for under the Internal Revenue Code and regulations thereunder.[4] A provision requiring that more than 50 percent of plan assets be invested in employer stock satisfies the requirement that the plan "be designed to invest primarily in employer securities." ESOPs may require that 100 percent of the assets in the plan be invested in qualifying employer securities.[5]

---

1. ERISA Sec. 407(b)(2)(A).
2. *Wright v. Oregon Metallurgical Corp.*, 32 EBC 1417 (9th Cir. 2004).
3. DOL Advisory Opinion 2012-05A; July 20, 2012.
4. ERISA Sec. 407(d)(6).
5. DOL Adv. Op. 83-6A.

ESOPs are designed to invest primarily in employer stock, and may borrow the funds necessary to purchase such stock from a bank, the plan sponsor, or its shareholders (creating a "leveraged ESOP"; see Q 615, Q 617, and Q 627 for details). Employer stock purchased by the ESOP is held in trust for the participants, and is distributed to them after their employment with the plan sponsor ends and they cease to be active participants in the plan. Employer stock acquired by an ESOP can never revert to the employer.

Because an ESOP is a qualified plan, annual contributions to it by the plan sponsor are generally tax deductible, subject to the 25 percent limitation under IRC Section 404(a)(3)(A). In the case of a leveraged C corporation ESOP, the deductible limit is also 25 percent to the extent of ESOP contributions used to repay principal of a loan incurred to acquire employer securities. Furthermore, contributions applied by the plan to the repayment of interest on a loan used to acquire employer securities may be deducted without limit.[1] The plan sponsor is also permitted to make additional annual contributions of cash or stock to the ESOP. These additional contributions are also tax deductible if they satisfy the limitation requirements imposed by IRC Section 404(a)(3)(A). Finally, limited carry-forward rules permit unused deductions for those years where the employer contributes less than the 25 percent limit to be carried forward into subsequent plan years.

All cash and employer stock contributed to or purchased by an ESOP are allocated on an annual basis to the individual accounts of the participants. Securities purchased by a leveraged ESOP are held in a suspense account and are allocated as the loan is paid off.

Special rules and limitations apply to ESOPs sponsored by S corporations; see Q 616.

615. What is the difference between a stock bonus plan and a leveraged ESOP?

An employee stock ownership plan (ESOP) is a stock bonus plan or a combination of a stock bonus and a money purchase plan qualified under IRC Section 401(a) and designed to invest primarily in qualifying employer securities.[2]

A stock bonus plan is a plan that "is established and maintained by an employer to provide benefits similar to those of a profit sharing plan, except that the contributions by the employer are not necessarily dependent upon profits and the benefits are distributable in stock of the employer company."[3]

A leveraged ESOP is used primarily as a financing vehicle for the plan sponsor. Generally, the plan sponsor will direct the ESOP to borrow money to purchase qualifying employer securities from the plan sponsor or outstanding shareholders.[4] The ESOP then repays the loan using tax-deductible cash contributions made by the plan sponsor. These contributions are traditionally mandated at a fixed rate (similar to the mandatory funding requirements of a money purchase

---

1. IRC Sec. 404(a)(9).
2. ERISA Sec. 407(d)(6); IRC Sec. 4975(e)(7).
3. Treas. Reg. §1.401-1(b)(1)(iii).
4. See IRC Secs. 4975(d)(3), 4975(e)(7).

plan). As the stock loan is paid off, the shares purchased with the proceeds from the loan are released from a suspense account and allocated to the individual participant accounts.

See Q 617 for details on the loan requirements for an ESOP, and Q 627 regarding the fiduciary issues involved in the management of a leveraged ESOP.

616. May an ESOP be maintained by an S corporation?

An employee stock ownership plan (ESOP), a qualified plan trust, may be a shareholder of an S corporation.[1] Furthermore, ESOPs that are established and maintained by S corporations do not need to provide participants the right to demand their distributions in the form of employer securities if the plan permits them the right to receive distributions in cash.[2]

S corporation–sponsored ESOPs are generally exempt (provided certain requirements are met) from the prohibited transaction restriction that forbids the sale of employer securities to an ESOP by certain parties (i.e., a shareholder employee, family member of a shareholder employee, or corporation in which the shareholder employee owns at least 50 percent of the stock).[3]

S corporation–sponsored ESOPs are subject to a series of restrictions designed to limit the application of them to S corporations that will offer them to rank-and-file employees in addition to highly compensated employees. Where there is a "non-allocation year" in an S corporation ESOP (i.e., the plan holds employer securities of an S corporation, and disqualified persons hold at least 50 percent of (a) the number of shares in the S corporation or (b) the aggregate number of outstanding shares of stock, including synthetic equity), three penalty provisions apply:

1. Any amount allocated to a disqualified person in a prohibited allocation (any allocation under the plan to a disqualified person in a non-allocation year) is treated as a distribution in that year to the disqualified person, so the value of such allocation must be included in the disqualified person's income;

2. The S corporation involved in the prohibited allocation will be subject to a 50 percent excise tax on the amount of the prohibited allocation; and

3. The S corporation will also be subject to a 50 percent excise tax on the value of any "synthetic equity" owned by a disqualified person.[4]

"Synthetic equity" means any stock option, warrant, restricted stock, deferred issuance stock right, or similar interest or right that gives the holder the right to acquire or receive stock of the S corporation in the future. Synthetic equity also includes a stock appreciation right, phantom stock unit, or similar right to a future cash payment based on the value of such stock or appreciation in such value.[5]

---

1. IRC Sec. 1361(a).
2. IRC Sec. 409(h)(2)(B).
3. IRC Sec. 4975(f)(6)(B).
4. IRC Sec. 409(p).
5. IRC Sec. 409(p)(6)(C).

These penalty provisions go into effect for plan years beginning after December 31, 2004. However, in the case of an S corporation ESOP established after March 14, 2001, or an ESOP established on or before March 14, 2001, if employer securities held by the plan consist of stock in a corporation for which an "S" election was not in effect on that date, these rules apply to plan years ending after March 14, 2001.[1]

617. What are the requirements of an "exempt loan" used for the purchase of qualifying employer securities by an ESOP?

The prohibited transaction provisions of ERISA Section 406 and the restrictions on the holding of qualifying employer securities found under ERISA Section 407 (see Q 611) do not apply to the acquisition and sale by a plan of qualifying employer securities by an employee stock ownership plan (ESOP) if such acquisition is in exchange for adequate consideration (see below) and no commission is charged for the transaction.[2] An ESOP may use the proceeds of a loan from a party in interest for the acquisition of qualifying employer securities if certain regulatory provisions have been satisfied in the making of the loan.[3]

Adequate Consideration: Adequate consideration is defined under ERISA Section 3(18). If there is a generally recognized market for employer stock, adequate consideration is the price prevailing on a national securities exchange that is registered under Section 6 of the Securities Exchange Act of 1934 (if applicable), or the offering price for the security as established by the current bid and asked prices quoted by persons independent of the issuer and party in interest. In the case of a security for which there is no generally recognized market (e.g., closely held stock), the fair market value of the asset is as determined in good faith by the trustee or named fiduciary pursuant to the terms of the plan, in accordance with generally accepted methods of valuing closely held stock, and in accordance with the regulations provided under ERISA. Where there is no generally recognized market for employer stock, it is very important that a valuation be conducted by an independent appraiser who will apply objective standards of conduct, and who is experienced in the valuation of closely held corporations, in order to establish the adequate consideration to be paid by the ESOP.[4]

Exclusive Benefit Requirement: Exempt loans for the purchase of qualifying employer securities by an ESOP must be for the primary benefit of ESOP participants and their beneficiaries.[5] All surrounding facts and circumstances will be considered in determining whether such a loan satisfies this requirement. At the time the loan is made, the interest rate for the loan and the price of the securities to be acquired should not be such that the plan assets might be drained off.[6]

1. EGTRRA 2001 §656(d).
2. ERISA Sec. 408(e).
3. Labor Reg. §2550.408b-3.
4. Prop. Labor Reg. §2510.3-18.
5. Labor Reg. §2550.408b-3; see also IRC Sec. 4975(d)(3); Treas. Reg. §54.4975-7(b)(3)(i).
6. Treas. Reg. §54.4975-7(b)(3)(ii).

At the time the loan is made, the terms of an exempt loan to an ESOP must be at least as favorable to the ESOP as a comparable loan resulting from arm's-length negotiations between independent parties, whether or not the loan is between independent parties.[1]

Use of Exempt Loan Proceeds: The proceeds of an exempt loan must be used, within a reasonable time after their receipt, only for any, or all, of the following purposes:

1. To acquire qualifying employer securities;

2. To repay such loan; and

3. To repay a prior exempt loan (a new loan, the proceeds of which are so used, must satisfy these requirements).[2]

Reasonable Rate of Interest: The interest rate of an exempt loan must not be in excess of a reasonable rate of interest. All relevant factors will be considered in determining a reasonable rate of interest, including the amount and duration of the loan, the security and guarantee involved (if any), the credit standing of the ESOP and the guarantor (if any), and the interest rate prevailing for comparable loans. When these factors are considered, a variable interest rate may be reasonable.[3]

Collateral Restrictions: An exempt loan must be without recourse against the ESOP. The only assets of the ESOP that may be given as collateral on an exempt loan are qualifying employer securities of two classes:

1. Those acquired with the proceeds of the exempt loan; and

2. Those that were used as collateral on a prior exempt loan repaid with the proceeds of the current exempt loan.[4]

No person entitled to payment under an exempt loan may have any right to assets of the ESOP other than collateral for the loan, contributions made under an ESOP to meet its obligations under the loan, and earnings attributable to such collateral and the investment of such contributions.[5]

Suspense Account Requirement: Employer securities purchased with the proceeds of an exempt loan must be maintained in a suspense account.[6] As the exempt loan is repaid, the shares held in the suspense account are released and allocated to participants in accordance with the Treasury regulations.[7]

The payments made on an exempt loan during a plan year must not exceed an amount equal to the sum of such contributions and earnings received during or prior to the year less

---

1. IRC Sec. 4975(d)(3); Treas. Reg. §54.4975-7(b)(3)(iii); Labor Reg. §2550.408b-3(c)(3).
2. Labor Reg. §2550.408b-3(d).
3. IRC Sec. 4975(d)(3); Labor Reg. §2550.408b-3(g).
4. Labor Reg. §2550.408b-3(e).
5. Labor Reg. §§2550.408b-3(e)(1), 2550.408b-3(e)(2), and 2550.408b-3(e)(3).
6. Treas. Reg. §54.4975-11(c).
7. Treas. Reg. §§54.4975-7(b)(8) and 54.4975-7(b)(15).

such payments in prior years. These earnings and contributions must be accounted for separately in the books of account of the ESOP until the loan is repaid. An exempt loan must provide for the release from encumbrance of plan assets used as collateral. For each plan year during the duration of the loan, the number of securities released must equal the number of encumbered securities held immediately before release for the current plan year multiplied by a fraction. The numerator of the fraction is the amount of principal and interest paid for the year. The denominator of the fraction is the sum of the numerator plus the principal and interest to be paid for all future years (which must be definitely ascertainable without taking into account possible extension or renewal periods).[1]

Practitioner's Pointer: Contributions used by an ESOP to pay the loan are treated as annual additions to participants' accounts and are subject to the IRC Section 415 limits on account contributions. Further, the release of shares from encumbrance in annually varying numbers may reflect a failure on the part of the employer to make substantial and recurring contributions to the ESOP, which may lead to the loss of plan qualification under IRC Section 401(a). The IRS will observe closely the operation of ESOPs that release encumbered securities in varying annual amounts, particularly those that provide for the deferral of loan payments or for balloon payments.[2]

Default: In the event of a default, the value of plan assets transferred in satisfaction of the loan must not exceed the amount of the default.[3] If the lender is a party in interest, a loan must provide for a transfer of plan assets upon default only upon and to the extent of the failure of the plan to meet the payment schedule of the loan.[4]

Scope of the Exemption: The scope of the exemption reaches the prohibited transaction provisions of ERISA Section 406(a) and ERISA Section 406(b)(1) (relating to fiduciaries dealing with assets in their own interest or for their own account) and ERISA Section 406(b)(2) (relating to fiduciaries in their individual or in any other capacity acting in any transaction involving the plan on behalf of a party whose interests are adverse to the interests of its participants or beneficiaries). ERISA Section 408(b)(3) does not provide an exemption from the prohibitions of ERISA Section 406(b)(3) (relating to fiduciaries receiving consideration for their own personal account from any party dealing with a plan in connection with a transaction involving the income or assets of the plan).[5]

Practitioner's Pointer: The exemption under ERISA Section 408(b)(3) includes within its scope certain transactions in which the potential for self-dealing by fiduciaries exists and in which the interests of fiduciaries may conflict with the interests of participants. The Department of Labor advises that to guard against these potential abuses, it will subject these transactions to special scrutiny to ensure that they are primarily for the benefit of participants and their beneficiaries. Although the transactions need not be approved by an independent fiduciary, fiduciaries are cautioned to scrupulously exercise their discretion in approving them.[6]

---

1. Labor Reg. §2550.408b-3(h).
2. Labor Reg. §2550.408b-3; Treas. Reg. §54.4975-7(b)(8)(iii).
3. Treas. Reg. §54.4975-7(b)(6).
4. Treas. Reg. §54.4975-7(b)(6); Labor Reg. §2550.408b-3(f).
5. Labor Reg. §2550.408b-3(b).
6. Labor Reg. §2550.408b-3(b)(2).

Also, the purchase of qualifying employer securities will always be subject to the general fiduciary provisions of ERISA Section 404.

618. Does the use of an independent appraiser by an ESOP fiduciary ensure compliance with ERISA?

Not necessarily. The prohibited transaction provisions of ERISA Section 406 and ERISA Section 407(a) do not apply to the acquisition or sale by a plan of qualifying employer securities, if, among other conditions, the acquisition or sale is for adequate consideration.[1] The definition of the term "adequate consideration" under ERISA is of particular importance to the establishment and maintenance of ESOPs because, under ERISA Section 408(e), an ESOP may acquire employer securities from a party in interest only under certain conditions, including that the plan pay no more than adequate consideration for the securities.

The term "adequate consideration," when used in the case of an ESOP holding securities without a recognized market, means that the fair market value of the securities must be determined in good faith by the trustee or named fiduciary pursuant to the terms of the plan.[2] Regulations addressing the concept of fair market value, as it relates to a determination of "adequate consideration" under this section, state that the good-faith requirement of adequate consideration may be determined using an independent appraisal.[3] In addition, the Internal Revenue Code provides that all valuations of non-publicly traded employer securities with respect to activities carried on by the plan must be conducted by an independent appraiser.[4]

ERISA's requirement that ESOP fiduciaries pay "adequate consideration" for employer stock is interpreted by the courts so as to give effect to the fiduciary requirements of ERISA Section 404, to which ESOP fiduciaries remain subject. In this regard, the adequate consideration test, like the prudent man rule of ERISA Section 404(a)(1)(B), focuses on the conduct of the fiduciaries. Thus, in determining the value of employer securities, an ESOP fiduciary is required to act with the care, skill, and diligence that a prudent person would undertake in acting on behalf of ESOP beneficiaries. In reviewing the acts of ESOP fiduciaries under the objective prudent person standard, courts examine both the process used by the fiduciaries to reach their decision as well as an evaluation of the merits.[5] Thus, whether an ESOP received adequate consideration depends on the thoroughness of the ESOP fiduciaries' investigation.

However, the mere use of an independent appraiser by an ESOP fiduciary does not guarantee thoroughness or compliance with the fiduciary requirements of ERISA. According to the courts, retaining a financial adviser or legal consultant to secure an independent assessment of the value of the ESOP shares is mere evidence of a prudent investigation and not a complete defense to a charge of imprudence.[6] Moreover, "[a]n independent appraisal is not a magic wand that fiduciaries may simply wave over a transaction to ensure that their responsibilities are fulfilled.

---

1. ERISA Sec. 408(e).
2. ERISA Sec. 3(18)(B).
3. Prop. Labor Reg. §2510.3-18(b)(2).
4. IRC Sec. 401(a)(28)(C).
5. *Donovan v. Cunningham*, 716 F.2d 1455 (5th Cir. 1983).
6. *Howard v. Shay*, 100 F.3d 1484 (9th Cir. 1996); *Martin v. Feilen*, 965 F.2d 660 (8th Cir. 1992).

It is a tool and, like all tools, is useful only if used properly."[1] In addition, since securing the advice of an independent third-party appraiser might not insulate a fiduciary from liability per se, a fiduciary also must (according to the court in *Howard v. Shay*): (1) investigate the expert's qualifications; (2) provide the expert with complete and accurate information; and (3) make certain that reliance on the expert's advice is reasonably justified under the circumstances.[2]

An ESOP fiduciary need not become an expert in the valuation of a closely held company; it is entitled to rely on the expertise of others.[3] However, to justifiably rely on an independent appraiser, an ESOP fiduciary must make an honest, objective effort to read the valuation, carefully review and understand it, discuss it with the appraiser, inquire into questionable methods and assumptions, and seek the review of a second firm if uncertainties remain.[4] "The degree to which an [ESOP] fiduciary makes an independent inquiry is crucial."[5] Thus, a fiduciary is responsible to ensure that the methodologies, projections, and assumptions are correct and the appraisal is based on information that is complete and up-to-date.[6] Otherwise, in failing to do so, an ESOP fiduciary breaches its duty of prudence under ERISA Section 404 and likewise cannot establish that it paid adequate consideration.[7]

619. What are the "pass through" voting rights applicable to ESOPs?

The Internal Revenue Code requires that shares of qualifying employer securities that are held in an ESOP and that are readily tradable on an established securities exchange "pass through" full voting rights on all shares allocated to participants so they may direct the voting of their shares on those issues presented to shareholders for consideration and vote.[8] If the shares are not readily tradable on an established securities exchange, participants have the right to vote only on "significant transactions" (e.g., mergers, acquisitions, liquidations, reclassification, sale of substantially all assets, etc.) passed through to them.[9] Where shares are not readily tradable on an established securities exchange, an ESOP may satisfy the limited pass-through voting requirement by allowing each participant in the ESOP one vote with respect to an issue presented to shareholders by the corporate board of directors regardless of the actual number of votes allocated to a participant's account.[10] The plan must provide for this "one vote" rule within the plan documents if the plan fiduciaries decide to allow for it. This "one vote per participant" rule is permitted only where the ESOP trustee votes unallocated shares of the ESOP stock in proportion to the allocated shares voted by the participants.[11]

---

1. *Donovan v. Cunningham*, above.
2. *Howard v. Shay*, above.
3. *Donovan v. Cunningham*, above.
4. *Howard v. Shay*, above.
5. *Eyler v. Commissioner*, 88 F.3d 445 (7th Cir. 1996).
6. *Donovan v. Cunningham*, above.
7. For liberal and conservative views, respectively, of fiduciary breaches involving ESOP security transactions, see *Ershick v. United Missouri Bank of Kansas City*, 705 F. Supp. 1482 (D. Kan. 1990), *aff'd*, 948 F.2d 660 (10th Cir. 1991), and *Reich v. Valley National Bank of Arizona.*, 837 F. Supp. 1259 (S.D.N.Y. 1993).
8. IRC Secs. 409(e)(2), 4975(e)(7).
9. IRC Sec. 409(e)(3).
10. IRC Sec. 409(e)(5).
11. See IRC Sec. 409(e)(5).

Practitioner's Pointer: The voting of shares held in an ESOP is subject to the general fiduciary rules of ERISA; thus, fiduciaries may not use pass-through voting rights to relieve themselves of liability regarding the obligations to oversee the plan in a prudent manner and for the exclusive benefit of participants and beneficiaries.[1] Consequently, fiduciaries are cautioned to carefully review any pertinent issues passed through under the "one vote" rule. The Department of Labor states that the voting of allocated shares is considered a management and control issue over plan assets. If fiduciaries believe that the result of votes presented under the "one vote" rule is not in the best interest of the plan, its participants, and beneficiaries, they should consult competent legal counsel in order to review the possibility of overriding these votes, even if such a move would violate the written provisions of the plan document. In the case of *Danaher Corp. v. Chicago Pneumatic Tool Co.*,[2] the court, in relying on Scott's *Law of Trusts*, stated that "it would be inappropriate (and perhaps a breach of fiduciary obligation) for a trustee to put aside his personal judgment in favor of carrying out the wishes of the [ESOP's] participants." The *Danaher* court instructed that a "neutral trustee" of the ESOP should be appointed, and that this trustee must make an independent evaluation of the tender offer for takeover of the plan sponsor before implementing the participant's instructions.

On the other hand, in *Martin Marietta Corp. v. Bendix Corp.*,[3] the court ordered the pass-through of a tender offer to employees, despite the fact that the plan document did not call for it. A Sixth Circuit Court of Appeals decision held that ESOP fiduciaries who directed ESOP trustees to vote the ESOP stock for themselves in an election of corporate board members, without permitting pass-through of the voting to ESOP participants, did not breach the fiduciary provisions of ERISA. The court ruled that such refusal to pass through the voting on this issue was not a prohibited "self-dealing" issue because the right to vote ESOP stock is not a plan "asset" for prohibited transaction purposes.[4]

620. What special diversification rules apply to ESOPs?

ESOP participants must be provided an opportunity to diversify their individual accounts under the plan as they approach retirement age. For qualifying employer securities purchased by the ESOP after December 31, 1986, the plan must permit an employee who is at least fifty-five years of age and has completed at least ten years of participation in the ESOP an option to diversify 25 percent of his ESOP stock. A participant who qualifies for this treatment must be provided the diversification option annually during a ninety-day election period for six years after the employee attains age fifty-five and ending with the fifth succeeding plan year. At the sixth plan year, the participant must be provided with an option to make a one-time diversification of up to 50 percent of his account balance (less any prior diversified amount).[5]

The ESOP must offer at least three investment options in addition to the employer stock in order to satisfy the diversification requirement.[6] Within ninety days after the diversification election by the eligible participant, the plan must invest that portion of the participant's account covered by the election in accordance with the eligible participant's expressed wishes.[7] As an alternate to providing the three investment options, the ESOP may satisfy the diversification

---

1. *O'Neill v. Davis*, 721 F. Supp. 1013 (N.D. Ill. 1989).
2. 635 F. Supp. 246 (S.D.N.Y. 1986).
3. 697 F.2d 293 (2d Cir. 1982).
4. *Grindstaff v. Green*, 1998 U.S. App. LEXIS 203 (6th Cir. 1998).
5. IRC Sec. 401(a)(28)(B).
6. IRC Sec. 401(a)(28)(B)(ii).
7. See Conference Comm. Rep., TRA '86, Pub. L. No. 99-514.

obligation by making a distribution to the participant of an amount equal to the diversification request. The failure of an eligible participant to make an election to diversify is considered an election under the required diversification option.

For employer stock held in an ESOP that is not readily tradable on a recognized securities exchange, the plan must acquire a valuation of the stock from an independent appraiser, as defined under IRC Section 170(a)(1).[1]

621. With regard to ESOPs, what are the diversification and notice rules regarding publicly traded qualifying employer securities?

The DOL has issued a direct final rule amending the civil penalty regulation under ERISA Section 502(c)(7) to reflect amendments to Section 502(c)(7) under the Pension Protection Act of 2006 (PPA).[2]

PPA Section 901 added ERISA Section 204(j), regarding publicly traded qualifying employer securities. Beginning on January 1, 2007, assets attributable to elective deferrals and after-tax employee contributions that are invested in publicly traded employer securities can be diversified at all times. Amounts attributable to employer matching and employer nonelective contributions that are invested in employer securities can be diversified after the participant has completed three years of service.

PPA Section 507 added ERISA Section 101(m), requiring the plan administrator to provide notice at least thirty days before a participant becomes eligible to diversify her investments, setting forth such right and informing participants of the importance of diversifying investments. Failure to provide this notice can be punishable up to $100 per day, per participant.[3]

Further, plans are required to provide at least three diversified investment options other than employer securities or employer real property. Other investment options offered under the plan must be available and plans must allow diversification elections, at least quarterly, on the same basis as the opportunity to make other investment changes.

The direct final rule makes conforming changes to Labor Regulation Section 2560.502c-7. It does not change the existing penalty assessment procedures of the DOL. Rather; the changes extend the existing procedures for assessing civil penalties to violations under ERISA Section 101(m).

A failure or refusal to provide the notice of diversification rights with respect to any single participant or beneficiary will be treated as a separate violation for purposes of calculating the civil penalty to be assessed.[4] If more than one person is involved in the refusal or failure to provide the notice of diversification in violation of ERISA Section 101(m), joint and several liability for the civil fine will attach.[5]

---

1. IRC Sec. 401(a)(28)(C).
2. 72 Fed. Reg. 44,991 (Aug. 10, 2007).
3. ERISA Sec. 502(C)(7), as amended.
4. Labor Reg. §2560.503c-(b)(2).
5. Labor Reg. §2560.502c-7(j).

The DOL may determine that all or a part of the penalty will be assessed if the plan administrator can show compliance with applicable requirements of ERISA Section 101(m) rules, or demonstrating the existence of mitigating facts and circumstances regarding the degree or willfulness of the noncompliance.[1]

622. What rules apply to the distribution of ESOP benefits?

ESOPs generally must begin to distribute vested benefits to a participant not later than (1) one year after the close of the plan year in which the participant either retires, is disabled, or dies, or (2) the close of the sixth plan year following the participant's separation from service for other reasons.[2] The timing of these ESOP distributions must be specifically outlined in the plan's governing documents; thus, ERISA Section 404(a)(1)(D) (which requires fiduciaries to govern the plan in accordance with its governing documents) mandates that plan fiduciaries adhere to these requirements. Different rules apply in the case of a leveraged ESOP in which the loan used to purchase qualifying employer securities remains outstanding.[3]

The ESOP must also provide that the distribution of the participant's account balance will be in substantially equal periodic payments (not less frequently than annually) over a period of time not to exceed five years.[4] If the participant's account balance exceeds $500,000, there is an extension of the distribution period of one year for every $100,000 by which the participant's account balance exceeds $500,000.[5] These limits are adjusted annually for inflation; for 2013 the indexed amounts are $205,000 and $1,035,000.[6]

Participants may elect to receive their distribution in a different manner than the substantially equal periodic payment method (e.g., a lump sum). Where the employer stock allocated to the participant's account has been purchased in connection with a loan, the distribution of such stock may be restricted until after the loan has been fully repaid. Under this rule, the distribution is not required to be made available to the participant until the close of the plan year following the plan year in which the loan has been fully repaid.[7]

Where the participant has not made an affirmative election regarding his distribution rights, the payment of benefits must begin no later than the sixtieth day after the latest of the close of the plan year in which:

1. The participant attains the earlier of age sixty-five or the normal retirement age established under the plan documents;

2. The tenth anniversary of the participant's participation in the plan occurs; or

3. The participant terminates employment.[8]

---

1. Labor Reg. §2560.502c-7(d).
2. See IRC Sec. 409(o)(1)(A).
3. See IRC Sec. 409(o)(1)(B).
4. IRC Sec. 409(o)(1)(C).
5. IRC Sec. 409(o)(1)(C).
6. IR- 2012-77; IRC Sec. 409(o)(2).
7. IRC Sec. 409(o)(1)(B).
8. IRC Sec. 401(a)(14).

Distributions from ESOPs are traditionally made in the form of employer securities, which the participant may sell on an open market at his discretion, or in cash if the participant does not exercise his option to receive stock. The participant in an ESOP may demand that his benefits be distributed in the form of employer securities.[1]

Put Option: If the employer securities are not readily tradable on an established securities market, the participant has a right to require that the plan sponsor repurchase the employer securities under a fair valuation formula (this is commonly referred to as a "put option").[2] These put options must be exercisable only by a participant, by the participant's donees, or by a person to whom the security passes by reason of the participant's death.[3] The put option must permit a participant to "put" the security to the employer. Under no circumstances may the put option bind the ESOP; however, the put option may grant the ESOP an option to assume the rights and obligations of the employer at the time the put option is exercised. A put option must be exercisable for at least a 15-month period that begins on the date the security subject to the put option is distributed by the ESOP.[4]

Right of First Refusal: The stock may also be subject to a right of first refusal, which permits the plan sponsor or the ESOP to purchase the stock back from the participant before it may be sold to a third party.[5] The plan sponsor exercising a right of first refusal must pay the participant a price no less favorable to the participant than the greater of the value of the security (as determined in accordance with Treasury Regulation Section 54.4975-11(d)(5)) or the purchase price offered by a third party who has made a good-faith offer to purchase the securities. The right of first refusal will lapse no later than fourteen days after the participant provides written notice to the ESOP or the plan sponsor (whichever holds the right of first refusal) that an offer by a third party to purchase the securities has been received.

ESOPs may require the distribution of benefits in the form of cash where the plan sponsor's charter or bylaws mandate that only active employees may own corporate stock and the company is, in fact, "substantially owned" by employees.[6]

623. Does the "put option" apply to bank-sponsored ESOPs?

The Internal Revenue Code provides a special rule for banks, which states that "[i]n the case of a plan established and maintained by a bank (as defined in [IRC] Section 581) that is prohibited by law from redeeming or purchasing its own securities," the put option provision "shall not apply if the plan provides that participants entitled to a distribution from the plan shall have a right to receive a distribution in cash."[7]

---

1. IRC Sec. 409(h)(1)(A).
2. IRC Sec. 409(h)(1)(B).
3. Labor Reg. §2550.408b-3(j).
4. Treas. Reg. §54.4975-7(b)(11).
5. Treas. Reg. §54.4975-7(b)(9).
6. See IRC Sec. 409(h)(2)(B).
7. IRC Sec. 409(h)(3).

624. What are the responsibilities of an ESOP fiduciary where there is a contest for corporate control?

Among the matters that have been addressed by the case law that follows, analyzing fiduciary conduct in the context of a takeover bid, are the effects of: the standard of prudence under ERISA; the exclusive benefit rule; the "business judgment rule" under the state corporate law; the effect of fiduciaries' benefiting from incidental benefits that arise in the management of an ESOP; and the timing of the decision to adopt the ESOP.

The Tenth Circuit Court of Appeals held that an ESOP fiduciary must satisfy ERISA's standard of prudence and the exclusive benefit rule.[1] In *Eaves v. Penn*, the defendant wanted to take control of a corporation using assets of the corporation's profit sharing plan. He had the profit sharing plan converted into an ESOP and had himself appointed as trustee of that newly formed ESOP. Simultaneously, the defendant had himself appointed as treasurer of the corporation and, in that capacity, instructed the corporation to pay a $491,000 contribution to the ESOP. The defendant then used the proceeds of that contribution and the existing profit sharing plan assets to purchase control of 97 percent of the corporation's stock. He then purchased the remaining 3 percent of corporate stock with the proceeds of a $25,000 loan, which he ordered the corporation to extend to him as an individual, and with $5 of his own money. In other words, the defendant took control of the corporation for a total personal expenditure of $5, while the plan spent $1,013,000 for the 97 percent of stock placed into trust as ESOP assets, which had a book value of $76,000 at the time of purchase. The court concluded that the defendant had violated the exclusive benefit rule of ERISA and that he had not acted in a prudent manner in the best interests of the plan, its participants, and beneficiaries.

The responsibilities imposed by ERISA do not preclude fiduciaries from benefiting from incidental benefits that arise in the management of an ESOP, provided that they acted "with an eye single to the interests of participants and beneficiaries" in considering a course of action regarding plan assets involved in a tender offer for control of a corporation. The Second Circuit Court of Appeals has ruled that officers of a corporation who were trustees of an employee benefit plan would not violate their duties as trustees by taking action that, after careful investigation, would best promote the interests of participants even though this action might incidentally benefit the corporation or themselves as corporate officers.[2] However, the court advised that fiduciaries have a duty to avoid placing themselves in a position where their acts as officers and directors would prevent their functioning with complete loyalty to the participants. Where there is such a conflict of interest, the court suggested that trustees either resign for the duration of the takeover attempt or employ independent legal and investment counsel for advice, and conduct an intensive and scrupulous investigation of the facts regarding the takeover attempt.

The adoption of an ESOP in response to a hostile takeover bid (as a defensive maneuver) is protected by the "business judgment rule" under the laws governing corporations (which, in general, protect corporate directors from liability for decisions they have made regarding corporate governance if they have acted on an informed basis, in good faith, and in the honest

---

1. *Eaves v. Penn*, 587 F.2d 453 (10th Cir. 1978).
2. See *Donovan v. Bierworth*, 680 F.2d 263 (2d Cir. 1982).

belief that the action taken by the board was in the best interests of the company).[1] It is important to note, however, that the court in the *NCR* case invalidated the ESOP established by the NCR Board on the grounds that, although they were acting in good faith, they had not been properly informed about the substantive elements of the ESOP. These elements included: potential adverse tax consequences involved in the ESOP; the NCR Human Resources Department's concern that there would be difficulty in getting the employees to enroll in the ESOP; and whether or not the terms of the ESOP were fair to common stockholders of the company. The court also pointed out that NCR always viewed the ESOP as a defensive response to a hostile takeover attempt and that it was used as a tool to entrench the current management.

The court in *NCR* advised that the business judgment rule will be evaluated on the basis of the following factors:

1.   Timing of the formation of the ESOP (e.g., whether it was in response to a hostile takeover attempt);

2.   Consideration of the ESOP's establishment by the board (i.e., by reviewing committee minutes and applicable corporate resolutions);

3.   History of employee participation in the company;

4.   Shareholder neutrality of the ESOP; and

5.   Other legitimate business reasons that may exist for the establishment of an ESOP.

The Delaware Chancery Court upheld the establishment of an ESOP by a plan sponsor who was in the middle of a hostile takeover attempt in *Shamrock Holdings v. Polaroid Corp.*[2] The court in this case determined that the sale of plan sponsor shares to the ESOP was fundamentally fair to the Polaroid shareholders because it involved no increased cost to Polaroid (the ESOP was funded through pay cuts to employees and the elimination of other benefits). In contrast to the NCR rejection of the ESOP attempt, Polaroid Corporation had actually adopted a 5 percent ESOP before it was contacted by Shamrock Holdings regarding their intention to attempt a hostile takeover.

While it may be permissible to establish an ESOP in the midst of a takeover attempt, one federal district court determined that the factors relevant to an evaluation of whether or not the ESOP was created to benefit employees and simply not to entrench management include: the timing of the establishment of the ESOP, the identity of the trustees and voting control of the ESOP shares (in this case they were all insiders), and the financial impact upon the company.[3]

As the foregoing rulings indicate, in the event there has been a takeover attempt, the *timing* of the decision to establish an ESOP is very important in the eyes of the courts in determining whether the establishment of the ESOP will be validated as an effort to act in a prudent manner for the exclusive benefit of plan participants and beneficiaries. Still, timing is not the only matter

---

1. *NCR Corp. v. American Tel. & Tel. Co.*, 761 F. Supp. 475 (S.D. Ohio 1991).
2. 559 A.2d 278 (Del. Ch. 1989).
3. See *Buckhorn, Inc. v. Ropack Corp.*, 656 F. Supp. 209 (S.D. Ohio 1987).

to be considered. There is no hard-and-fast rule regarding the establishment of an ESOP where there has been a tender offer for purposes of obtaining corporate control.

The Department of Labor (DOL) can bring legal action to enjoin any transaction that violates ERISA. Where there has been a filing of a proxy statement with the Securities Exchange Commission (SEC) regarding a buyout that involves an ESOP, the SEC will provide a copy of the filing to the DOL. The DOL will review the transaction to ensure that participants are treated as fairly as all other shareholders. If they are not, the DOL may intervene, seeking different terms or negation of the deal.

625. What are the fiduciary issues regarding the voting of unallocated and nonvoted allocated shares in an ESOP?

As noted in Q 619, the voting of shares held in an ESOP is always subject to the general fiduciary rules of ERISA, including the duty to oversee the plan in a prudent manner and for the exclusive benefit of participants and beneficiaries.[1] Regarding allocated shares, the plan fiduciaries must pass through certain voting rights to participants to whose accounts the shares have been allocated. The general rule regarding voting of these shares requires plan trustees to follow participant instructions. (See Q 619 regarding the voting of allocated shares.)

Plan trustees must take careful consideration with respect to the voting of shares that are unallocated, or the shares that have been allocated but the participants to whom they have been allocated have refused, or failed, to vote. It is a common practice for ESOPs to provide in the governing documents for the "mirror voting" of unallocated and nonvoted allocated shares. "Mirror voting" means that the trustee is instructed to tender unallocated and nonvoted allocated shares held by the plan in the same proportion as it tenders allocated shares. However, mirror voting rules have not always protected trustees from liability for violations of their fiduciary obligations.

In a 1997 ruling, the Eleventh Circuit Court of Appeals provided some much-needed clarification to this issue.[2] There, the court reviewed the voting of unallocated and nonvoted allocated shares in the takeover fight for Polaroid Corporation.[3] The Polaroid ESOP's trustee bank, NationsBank, had received a letter from the Secretary of Labor in the midst of the takeover attempt that outlined the DOL's view of NationsBank's fiduciary responsibilities in light of the competing tender offers.[4] The DOL insisted that an ESOP trustee bears the final responsibility for making tender offer decisions with regard to the plan's unallocated shares and its nonvoted allocated shares.

In following the mirror voting provisions, the trustees tendered the majority of unallocated and nonvoted shares to Polaroid Corporation, leaving the remaining shares to be tendered to Shamrock Holdings, or not tendered (in accordance with participant wishes, including a like percentage withheld under mirror voting rules). Polaroid paid $72,762,200 to the ESOP for the 482,073 shares it accepted that were tendered by NationsBank on behalf of the ESOP.

---

1. *O'Neill v. Davis*, 721 F. Supp. 1013 (N.D. Ill. 1989).
2. See *Herman v. NationsBank Trust Co.*, 126 F.3d 1354 (11th Cir. 1997).
3. This case resulted from the attempted takeover of Polaroid by Shamrock Holdings, Inc.
4. This letter is reprinted at 16 Pens. & Ben. Rep. BNA 390 (1989).

If NationsBank had tendered all of the unallocated shares to Polaroid, the ESOP would have obtained an additional 332,917 shares at a price between $37.41 and $37.67 per share.

The DOL filed suit against NationsBank in 1992, complaining that NationsBank had violated ERISA Section 404(a)(1)(A) and ERISA Section 404(a)(1)(B) by failing to tender all of the unallocated shares and the nonvoted allocated shares to Polaroid. In Count Two of the complaint, the DOL alleged that an indemnification provision in the ESOP created a disincentive for NationsBank to exercise its independent judgment and, therefore, encouraged NationsBank to breach its fiduciary obligations under ERISA. The district court held that NationsBank could not rely on the mirror voting provisions under the ESOP in determining how it would vote unallocated shares.

The Eleventh Circuit was concerned with the issue of whether Polaroid ESOP participants, under the mirror voting provisions of the plan document, could become named fiduciaries who could direct NationsBank's asset management decisions with regard to unallocated and nonvoted shares.

The DOL took the position that ESOP participants may be named fiduciaries *only* with respect to allocated shares for which participants give explicit directions.[1] The DOL also took the position that participants may never be named fiduciaries with regard to unallocated and nonvoted shares and cannot direct a trustee with regard to those shares. The DOL expressed the view that ERISA Section 404(a)(1) must govern the trustee decisions with respect to unallocated and nonvoted shares. As such, the DOL argued that NationsBank's only prudent course of action would have been to tender all unallocated and nonvoted shares to Polaroid.

NationsBank countered that it was acting prudently in following the plan's mirror voting rules and that, consequently, the ESOP participants had the discretion to vote the ESOP's unallocated and nonvoted shares in accordance with their fiduciary obligations in voting the pass-through rights. The DOL responded that Polaroid ESOP participants could not satisfy the definition of fiduciary because whatever control they had regarding the unallocated and nonvoted shares was unknown to them. This left the responsibility for the voting of those shares with NationsBank.

The Eleventh Circuit Court ruled that fiduciaries must know that they can decide an issue and be aware of the choices they have. "Based on the plain language of ERISA, ESOP participants are not fiduciaries when they do not knowingly decide how assets will be managed." Accordingly, (because Polaroid ESOP participants were not aware of their fiduciary responsibility regarding unallocated and nonvoted shares) NationsBank retained exclusive fiduciary authority to manage those shares in accordance with the fiduciary standards of ERISA. The Eleventh Circuit Court further noted that mirror voting language in an ESOP plan document is not per se invalid. However, trustees should not blindly follow mirror voting provisions that lead to an imprudent result[2]—trust documents cannot excuse trustees from their duties under ERISA if following them results in an imprudent result. The Eleventh Circuit Court stated that where plan participants

---

1. Ian D. Lanoff Letter, 22 Pens. & Ben. Rep. BNA 2249 (1995).
2. Citing the holding under *Ershick v. Greb X-Ray Co.*, 705 F. Supp. 1482 (D. Kan. 1989).

are not sufficiently informed to be named fiduciaries, "ERISA dictates that a mirror voting provision that leads to an imprudent result is invalid as applied."

In remanding the case to the district court for final disposition, the Eleventh Circuit Court stated that NationsBank was required to act solely in the interest of participants in voting unallocated shares.

626. May pre-tax salary reduction contributions be used to repay an exempt loan to a leveraged ESOP?

It depends. The Internal Revenue Service issued a national office technical advice memorandum regarding the use of pre-tax salary reduction contributions (i.e., 401(k) elective deferrals) to repay an exempt loan to a leveraged employee stock ownership plan (ESOP) under the exclusive benefit rule of Section 401(a)(2) of the Internal Revenue Code and the regulation that sets forth the permissible assets for repayment of an exempt loan.[1] The IRS concluded that because the applicable regulations designate such contributions as employer contributions, they could be applied to payments under an exempt loan without violating the exclusive benefit rule under the Internal Revenue Code.[2]

In contrast to the IRS's view based on Internal Revenue Code provisions, the Department of Labor (DOL) takes the position that amounts that a participant pays to or has withheld by an employer, whether pursuant to a salary reduction agreement or otherwise, for contribution to an employee benefit plan constitute participant contributions subject to ERISA's general provisions governing the protection of employee benefit rights (Subtitle A of Title I) as well as ERISA's reporting and disclosure provisions (Part 1 of Subtitle B) and fiduciary responsibility provisions (Part 4 of Subtitle B), and for the purposes of the prohibited transaction provisions of IRC Section 4975. Consequently, the DOL believes that the use of pre-tax salary reduction contributions for payments under an exempt loan raises issues with respect to the primary benefit test under ERISA Section 408(b)(3) and the exclusive purpose requirements of ERISA Sections 403 and 404.

Since it is generally understood that an exempt loan to an ESOP is secured primarily by an employer's guarantee of the loan, and its agreement to make annual contributions to the plan sufficient to meet the plan's obligation to repay the principal and interest due under the loan arrangement, the use of participant contributions to satisfy part of the loan obligation serves directly to relieve the employer of its obligation to contribute to the plan. For this reason, the DOL does not believe that a loan that is structured to be repaid with participant contributions will satisfy the general requirements under ERISA Section 408(b)(3) that an exempt loan must be primarily for the benefit of the ESOP's participants and beneficiaries. In addition, when a primary benefit requirement is not met, the DOL takes the position that there is also a violation of the "exclusive purpose" and "solely in the interest" requirements of ERISA Sections 403 and 404.[3]

---

1. See Treas. Reg. §54.4975-7(b)(5).
2. See TAM 9503002; Treas. Reg. §1.401(k)-(a)(4)(ii).
3. DOL Letter to Evelyn Petschek, Internal Revenue Service (Jan. 16, 1996); *see also* TAM 9503002.

627. What are the fiduciary issues regarding ESOP leveraged buyouts?

The most common situation involving an employee stock ownership plan (ESOP) in a leveraged buyout is the coordination of key management personnel in the existing corporation with outside investors in the formation of a new corporation to purchase the outstanding shares of the existing corporation. The investor group will typically furnish a minor initial investment of equity capital (approximately 10 percent) into the new corporation and raise the balance of the necessary funds in a loan from a financial institution or from the issuance of new stock. The new corporation then establishes a leveraged ESOP at the time it is establishing financial arrangements for the takeover of the existing corporation. The newly established ESOP will then borrow funds from a financial institution for the purchase of stock from the new corporation. The new corporation will use the funds received from the purchase of stock by the ESOP, in addition to the equity capital contributed by the investor group and the outside funds borrowed by the new corporation, to complete the purchase of the existing company. In establishing the ESOP, the fiduciaries need to be cognizant of the fact that they are bound by the general fiduciary duties under ERISA.[1]

If the Department of Labor (DOL) has objections (due to perceived violations of ERISA) in an ESOP leveraged buyout, it may intervene in an effort to secure better arrangements for the ESOP, or to stop the completion of the buyout where the terms of the transaction violate ERISA. DOL concerns tend to focus on the valuation of the stock purchased by the ESOP when compared to the price paid by other investors. The DOL also focuses on the adequacy of the consideration (see Q 617 regarding the definition of "adequate consideration") involved in the transaction. In reviewing these two issues, the DOL will ascertain whether the transactions also satisfy the fiduciary duties of general prudence and exclusive purpose, as well as the prohibited transaction provisions (not extended the statutory exemptions) for ESOPs such as conflict of interest, self-dealing, etc.

The acquisition of employer securities must be for adequate consideration.[2] Trustees and other fiduciaries have the obligation to investigate the reasonableness of the appraisal value of employer stock purchased by the ESOP.[3] Furthermore, the DOL will view a valuation as reflecting fair market value where there has been an appropriate demonstration of the level of expertise demonstrated by the parties making the valuation.

Proposed regulations state that the adequacy of consideration paid by an ESOP for privately held employer securities must satisfy a two-part test:[4]

1. The consideration must reflect fair market value; and

2. The valuation must be made in "good faith" (as stated under ERISA Section 3(18)).

The determination of the fair market value of privately held securities must include an assessment of the following factors:

---

1. *Danaher Corp. v. Chicago Pneumatic Tool Co.*, 635 F. Supp. 246 (S.D.N.Y. 1986).
2. ERISA Sec. 408(e).
3. *Donovan v. Cunningham*, 716 F.2d 1455 (5th Cir. 1983).
4. Prop. Labor Reg. §2510.3-18(b)(1)(i).

1.   Nature of the business and the history of the enterprise from its inception;

2.   Economic outlook in general and the condition and the outlook of the specific industry in particular;

3.   Book value of the stock and the financial condition of the business;

4.   Earning capacity of the company;

5.   Dividend-paying capacity of the company;

6.   Whether or not the enterprise has goodwill or other intangible value;

7.   Market price of securities of corporations engaged in the same or a similar line of business, which are traded in a free and open market, either on an exchange or over the counter; and

8.   Sales of the stock and the size of the block of stock to be valued.[1]

Examples of DOL intervention in leveraged buyouts include: objections over ESOP trustees' violating the exclusive benefit rule in paying excessive consideration for ESOP shares after the exercise of options and warrants;[2] the investment of ESOP sale proceeds to be used in a leveraged buyout and restructuring in a highly leveraged firm creating an unreasonable risk of loss;[3] and the payment of a per-share price by the ESOP that was in excess of that paid by other leveraged buyout investors.[4] In the *Valley National Bank* case, the DOL attempted to force recovery of all losses incurred by the ESOP. The DOL has also intervened in a leveraged ESOP situation in which there were conflicting interests by ESOP trustees because they also served as officers in a target or raider corporation. The court ruled that they had a significant personal interest in the outcome of the takeover involving the ESOP, which would have violated the provisions of ERISA Section 406(b)(1). The court ordered the trustees to resign their positions until the control issue was settled.[5]

The DOL is not always successful in its interventions. In a 1990 case, the DOL took the position that the value of the stock involved in an ESOP should be valued on a post-transaction basis in order to establish whether more than adequate consideration was paid by the ESOP. This position received an intense amount of widespread criticism because such hindsight analysis makes it too easy to determine that excessive consideration was paid. In response to this widespread disapproval, the DOL withdrew the complaint on October 4, 1990.[6]

628. What is the Sarbanes-Oxley Act and how does it affect retirement plans?

The Sarbanes-Oxley Act of 2002 ("Sarbanes-Oxley" or the "Act") is aimed at restoring investor trust and confidence in the public markets. Of particular interest to ERISA plans,

---

1. Prop. Labor Reg. §2510.3-18(b)(4)(ii)(H).
2. DOL Letter to Scott & Fetzer ESOP Trustees (July 30, 1985), 12 Pens. & Ben. Rep (BNA) 1182.
3. DOL Letter to C.R. Smith, Blue Bell, Inc. (Nov. 23, 1984), 12 Pens. & Ben. Rep. (BNA) 52.
4. *Reich v. Valley Nat'l Bank of Ariz.*, 837 F. Supp. 1259 (S.D.N.Y. 1993).
5. See *Freund v. Marshall & Ilsley* Bank, 485 F. Supp. 629 (W.D. Wis. 1979).
6. See *Dole v. Farnum, Civ. No.* 900371 (D.R.I. 1990).

Section 306 of the Act contains restrictions on insider trading of publicly traded employer securities within "individual account plans" (see Q 629) during certain "blackout periods" (see Q 629).[1]

Along with the restrictions described above, Section 306 of Sarbanes-Oxley amends Section 101 of ERISA by adding new notice requirements under which plan administrators must provide notice of "blackout periods" (see Q 629) to directors, executive officers, and affected plan participants.[2]

Final labor regulations implement the blackout period notice rules enacted under Sarbanes-Oxley (see Q 629 through Q 636).[3]

The final regulations also provide important clarifications of the effective date. Section 306(c) of the Act provides that the effective date of the blackout period rules[4] is January 26, 2003. Labor Regulation Section 2520.101-3(f) clarifies that for purposes of the notice rules, this means blackout periods that commence *on or after* January 26, 2003. However, for blackout periods that commenced between January 26, 2003, and February 25, 2003 (i.e., where the start of a 30-day advance notice period would have predated the January 26 effective date), plan administrators were required to furnish notice "as soon as reasonably possible" instead of at least 30 days before the blackout period began.[5]

Plan amendments to conform the plan documents with the provisions of the Act, if required, were not necessary until the close of the first plan year beginning on or after January 26, 2003, if the plan was operated in a good-faith effort to comply with the Act and the contents of the anticipated amendment, *and* the amendment was adopted retroactively effective to January 26, 2003.[6]

629. What is a "blackout period" under the Sarbanes-Oxley Act?

Blackout period is described by Section 306(a)(4) of the Act (i.e., for purposes of the insider trading prohibition—see Q 628) as any period of more than three consecutive business days during which the ability of not fewer than 50 percent of the participants or beneficiaries under all "individual account plans" (see below) maintained by the issuer (i.e., employer) to purchase, sell, or otherwise acquire or transfer an interest in any equity of the issuer is temporarily suspended by the issuer or by a fiduciary of the plan. "Individual account plan" has the same meaning as in ERISA Section 3(34), excluding one-participant plans.[7]

Blackout period does *not* include (under regulations to be prescribed by the Securities and Exchange Commission (SEC)):

---

1. Sec. 306(a), Sarbanes-Oxley 2002.
2. ERISA Sec. 101(i)(2), *as added by* Sec. 306(b), Sarbanes-Oxley 2002.
3. Labor Reg. §2520.101-3, 68 Fed. Reg. 3716 (Jan. 24, 2003); Labor Reg. §2560.502(c)(7), 68 Fed. Reg. 3730 (Jan. 24, 2003).
4. Secs. 306(a) and 306(b), Sarbanes-Oxley 2002, above.
5. Labor Reg. §2520.101-3(f).
6. Sec. 306(b), Sarbanes-Oxley 2002.
7. See ERISA Sec. 101(i)(8)(A), *as added by* Sarbanes-Oxley.

1. A regularly scheduled period in which the participants and beneficiaries may not purchase, sell, or otherwise acquire or transfer an interest in any equity of such issuer if such period is:

    a. incorporated into the individual account plan, *and*

    b. timely disclosed to employees before becoming participants under the individual account plan; *or*

2. Any suspension described above that is imposed solely in connection with persons becoming participants or beneficiaries, or ceasing to be participants or beneficiaries, in an individual account plan by reason of a corporate merger, acquisition, divestiture, or similar transaction involving the plan or plan sponsor.[1]

Required Notice of Blackout Periods to Participants. For purposes of the notice rules (see Q 628), the term *blackout period* means, in connection with an "individual account plan" (see above), any period of more than three consecutive business days during which any ability of participants and beneficiaries under the plan (which is otherwise available under the terms of such plan) to do any of the following is temporarily suspended, limited, or restricted:

• Direct or diversify assets credited to their accounts;

• Obtain loans from the plan; or

• Obtain in-service distributions from the plan.[2]

Section 509 of PPA 2006 amended ERISA Section 101(i)(8)(B) by clarifying that blackout notices are not required to be provided to single-participant or partner-only plans, retroactive to the effective date of the Sarbanes-Oxley Act.

630. What is the 30-day notice requirement under Sarbanes-Oxley?

ERISA plan administrators are required to provide individual account plan participants with advance written (or electronic) notice of any "blackout period" (see Q 629) that restricts the availability of trading in publicly available employer securities held in a subject individual account plan, or to receive distributions or loans.[3] Written notices are to be furnished to all participants and beneficiaries under the plan to whom the blackout period applies at least thirty days in advance of the last day on which the participants have the right to give a direction regarding an investment, in-service distribution, or participant loan that will be implemented before the blackout period goes into effect.[4]

---

1. Sec. 306(a)(4)(B), Sarbanes-Oxley 2002.
2. ERISA Sec. 101(i)(7)(A), *as added by* Sarbanes-Oxley 2002.
3. ERISA Secs. 101(i)(1), 101(i)(2)(D), *as added by* Sarbanes-Oxley 2002.
4. ERISA Sec. 101(i)(2)(B), as added by Sarbanes-Oxley 2002.

When a "blackout period" is scheduled or anticipated, and is applicable to a director or executive officer with respect to any equity securities (see Q 629), the issuer of such equity securities shall timely notify such director or officer and the SEC of such blackout period.[1]

The blackout notice may be provided in any manner that is permitted under Labor Regulation Section 2520.104b-1, which includes mailing, private delivery, and electronic delivery.[2] Consequently, if mailed by first-class mail, the notice is treated as given on the date of mailing. If provided through a private delivery service, the notice is treated as given when it is received. If provided by electronic delivery, the notice is treated as given on the date of the electronic transmission.

Although the statute requires notice thirty days before the start of the blackout period, pursuant to the provisions of Labor Regulation Section 2520.101-3(b)(2)(i), this time period may be expanded in two ways:

1. The thirty-day period is clarified to run from the last date on which affected participants and beneficiaries could exercise their affected rights immediately before the commencement of the blackout period. For example, if a blackout period takes effect on May 1, but under the plan the last date before May 1 that participants are allowed to make investment changes is the preceding April 15, the thirty-day period is measured from April 15, not from April 30.

2. A maximum notice period of sixty days is prescribed, so as not to "undermine the importance of the notice to affected participants and beneficiaries."[3]

631. What are the exceptions to the 30-day notice requirement?

In accordance with ERISA Section 101(i)(2)(C) and Labor Regulation Section 2520.101-3(b)(2)(ii), the following *exceptions* to the thirty-day notice requirement may be recognized if:

1. Deferral of the blackout period would violate the exclusive purpose rule under ERISA Section 404(a)(1)(A), or the prudence rule under ERISA Section 404(a)(1)(B); or

2. The inability to provide advance notice of the blackout period is due to events that were unforeseeable or circumstances that were beyond the control of the plan administrator.[4]

In situations (1) and (2), a plan fiduciary must make a written determination that the exception applies, and such determination must be signed and dated by the fiduciary. Furthermore, the blackout notice, when provided, would have to include an explanation as to why thirty-day advance notice was not provided. If either of these situations exists, the plan administrator must give notice "as soon as reasonably possible" under the circumstances.

---

1. Sec. 306(a)(6), Sarbanes-Oxley 2002.
2. Labor Reg. §2520.101-3(b)(3).
3. Preamble, 67 Fed. Reg. 3716, 3718 (Jan. 24, 2003).
4. ERISA Sec. 101(i)(2)(C); Labor Reg. §2520.101-3(b)(2)(ii).

However, if notice in advance of the termination of the blackout period is impracticable, no notice is required.[1]

A third exception provides that in any case in which the blackout period applies only to one or more participants or beneficiaries in connection with a merger, acquisition, divestiture, or similar transaction involving the plan or plan sponsor, *and* occurs solely in connection with becoming or ceasing to be a participant or beneficiary under the plan by reason of a merger, acquisition, divestiture, or similar transaction, the requirement that the notice be provided to all participants and beneficiaries shall be treated as met if the notice required under the Act is provided to such participants or beneficiaries to whom the blackout period applies as soon as reasonably practical.[2]

Exclusions. The term "blackout period"[3] (see Q 629) does *not* include: (1) events that affect only individual participants (e.g., QDROs and beneficiary disputes); and (2) regularly scheduled blackout procedures for upgrades and maintenance so long as they are detailed in the plan's SPD or other required participant communications.[4]

632. What happens if there is a change in the length of the blackout period?

If, following the furnishing of the notice pursuant to these policies and procedures, there is a change in the beginning date or length of the blackout period, the plan administrator must provide affected participants and beneficiaries notice of the change as soon as reasonably practical. In relation to the extended blackout period, the notice must be in writing, except that it may be in electronic or other form to the extent that such form is reasonably accessible to the participant. Furthermore, the notice must specify any material change in the matters required by ERISA Section 101(i)(2)(A) (see Q 633) to be addressed in the notice.[5]

633. What are the content requirements of the thirty-day notice?

Under ERISA Section 101(i)(2)(A) and the applicable regulation, the notice must be written in a manner calculated to be understood by the average plan participant and must include:

1. The reasons for the blackout period;

2. A description of the rights otherwise available to participants and beneficiaries under the plan that will be temporarily suspended, limited, or restricted by the blackout period (e.g., the right to direct or diversify assets in individual accounts, obtain loans from the plan, or obtain distributions from the plan), including identification of any investments subject to the blackout period;

3. The expected beginning date and ending date of the blackout period;

1. ERISA Sec. 101(i)(2)(C); Labor Reg. §2520.101-3(b)(2).
2. ERISA Sec. 101(i)(3).
3. ERISA Sec. 101(i)(7).
4. See ERISA Sec. 101(i)(7)(B); Labor Reg. §2520.101-3(d)(1)(ii).
5. ERISA Sec. 101(i)(4); Labor Reg. §2520.101-3(b)(4).

4. In the case of investments affected, a statement that the participant or beneficiary should evaluate the appropriateness of her current investment decisions in light of her inability to direct or diversify assets in her accounts during the blackout period (a notice that includes the advisory statement contained in Paragraph 4 of the Model Notice (see Appendix A) will satisfy this requirement);

5. In any case in which the required notice is not furnished at least thirty days in advance of the last date on which affected participants and beneficiaries could exercise affected rights immediately before the commencement of the blackout period (except for a notice furnished in the case of the blackout period applying only to one or more participants or beneficiaries solely in connection with their becoming, or ceasing to be, participants or beneficiaries of the plan as a result of a merger, acquisition, divestiture, or similar transaction involving the plan or plan sponsor):

    a. a statement that federal law generally requires that notice be furnished to affected participants and beneficiaries at least thirty days in advance of the last date on which participants and beneficiaries could exercise the affected rights immediately before the commencement of a blackout period (a notice that includes the statement contained in Paragraph 5 of the Model Notice—see Appendix A—will satisfy this requirement), and

    b. an explanation of the reasons why at least thirty days' advance notice could not be furnished; and

6. The name, address, and telephone number of the plan administrator or other person responsible for answering questions about the blackout period.[1]

The final regulation identifies "week" as a calendar week and not as a consecutive seven-day period.[2]

Model Notice. The Model Notice provided by the DOL is intended to assist plan administrators in discharging their notice obligations under ERISA Section 101(i) and Labor Regulation Section 2520.101-3. A copy of the Model Notice can be found in Appendix A.

634. What are the applicable penalties under Sarbanes-Oxley?

The Department of Labor (DOL) is authorized to assess a civil penalty up to $100 per day for noncompliance with the blackout notice requirements.[3] *NOTE*: The plan administrator is the person liable for the civil penalty.[4] Since the liability is a personal liability of the plan administrator, and not a liability of the plan, it is unreasonable to pay the penalty with plan assets (because that would violate the prudence and self-dealing rules under ERISA). Each violation with respect to each participant and each beneficiary is treated as a *separate violation*. For example, if there are

---

1. ERISA Sec. 101(i)(2)(A); Labor Reg. §2520.101-3(b)(1).
2. Labor Reg. §2520.101-3(b)(1)(iii)(B).
3. ERISA Sec. 502(7).
4. Labor Reg. §2560.502c-7.

500 affected participants and beneficiaries, and the failure continues for ten days, the maximum penalty is $100 × 10 (days) × 500 (violations), or $500,000.

The violation is computed from the date of the plan administrator's failure or refusal to provide the notice, up to and including the date that is the final day of the blackout period for which the notice was required.[1] In other words, additional penalties do not accrue after the date that the blackout period ends.

Prior to the enactment of Sarbanes-Oxley, a willful violation of an ERISA requirement regarding a report or a disclosure by an individual carried a maximum criminal penalty of a fine of $5,000, up to one year in prison, or both. The maximum penalty for a willful violation by an entity was previously a fine of up to $100,000. Section 904 of the Sarbanes-Oxley Act amended ERISA Section 501 penalties across the board. The maximum penalty for individuals is now a fine of $100,000, a sentence of up to ten years in prison, or both. Nonindividual entities are now subject to a maximum penalty of $500,000.[2]

From a civil litigation perspective, in order for liability to attach to a service provider involved in assisting a plan sponsor in issuing a blackout notice that resulted in noncompliance with the Sarbanes-Oxley requirements, the plaintiff would need to establish that the service provider, in rendering the assistance that resulted in noncompliance, exercised specified discretion or decision-making authority to the extent that it would render the service provider a fiduciary under ERISA for the matter. Otherwise, the mere transmission of forms and notices is an administrative or ministerial service insufficient to elevate the service provider to the status of a fiduciary under ERISA.[3]

635. What are "prohibited personal loans" to executives under Sarbanes-Oxley?

Section 402(a) of the Sarbanes-Oxley Act of 2002 amends Section 13 of the Securities and Exchange Act of 1934 to prohibit any issuer of publicly traded securities from making an extension of credit in the form of a personal loan to any of its executive officers or directors.[4] This includes assisting in, or arranging for, a personal loan or extension of credit. This prohibition is broadly written, including both indirect as well as direct loans. From an ERISA perspective, the Act, on its face, appears to prohibit the availability of participant loans to officers and executives under individual account plans. Other potential "loan" prohibitions include the cashless exercise of stock options, split-dollar premium payments by the employer, and home purchases under executive relocation programs.

The loan prohibitions became effective immediately upon the signing of the Act, which was July 30, 2002. Arrangements maintained by the issuer on July 30, 2002, were "grandfathered" only if they were not materially modified or renewed after that date.[5]

---

1. See ERISA Sec. 502(7).
2. ERISA Sec. 501.
3. *Milofsky v. American Airlines, Inc.*, 34 EBC 1801 (5th Cir. 2005).
4. 17 CFR 240.13(k)(1).
5. 17 CFR 240.13(k)(1).

636. What Securities Exchange Commission reporting issues under Sarbanes-Oxley affect retirement plans?

ERISA plans generally are not required to report transactions in publicly traded securities to the Securities Exchange Commission. However, individuals and entities that are "insiders" under Section 16(a) of the Securities Exchange Act of 1934 must satisfy reporting obligations. Section 403(a) of the Sarbanes-Oxley Act of 2002 significantly accelerates the timing of the reports required to be filed by insiders under Section 16(a) of the Securities Exchange Act of 1934. Effective August 29, 2002, insider transactions, including certain transactions made within an employee benefit plan, generally must be reported within two business days of the transaction date.[1]

---

1. Sec. 403(b), Sarbanes-Oxley 2002; Sec. 16(a)(2)(C), Securities Exchange Act.

SECTION X

Taft-Hartley Plans

(Multiemployer Plans)

637. What is a "Taft-Hartley" plan?

A "Taft-Hartley" plan, so called after the landmark 1947 collective bargaining legislation, is the same type of plan as a "multiemployer plan," discussed in more detail in Q 638.

638. What is a multiemployer plan?

A multiemployer plan is a plan (1) that is maintained pursuant to a collective bargaining agreement (between one or more employee organizations, see Q 639, and more than one employer) and (2) to which more than one employer is required to contribute.[1]

Note that both elements must be present in order for a plan to be a multiemployer plan. In contrast, for example, a plan subject to a collective bargaining agreement that benefits the employees of two or more members of a controlled group is simply a collectively bargained single-employer plan, while a plan that benefits the employees of two or more unrelated employers, but is not subject to a collective bargaining agreement, is a "multiple employer plan."

ERISA Section 3(37)(A) provides that a multiemployer plan must also satisfy "other requirements as the Secretary [of Labor] prescribes by regulation."[2]

Substantially the same definition of multiemployer plan applies for purposes of the rules relating to the Pension Benefit Guaranty Corporation (PBGC).[3]

Under DOL Advisory Opinion 2004-03A,[4] the DOL has determined that a Taft-Hartley sponsored "Holiday and Vacation" Plan was an employee benefit plan within the meaning of ERISA Section 3(1). The analysis of the DOL's position is found in the text of ERISA Section 3(3) that defines an employee welfare benefit plan as one that, in part, "is maintained for the purpose of providing for its participants or their beneficiaries, through the purchase of insurance or otherwise ... vacation benefits ... [or] any benefit described in section 302(c) of the Labor Management Relations Act, 1947 (other than pensions on retirement or death, and insurance to provide such pensions)." DOL regulations state that because holiday benefits are described in Section 302(c) of the Labor Management Relations Act, the definition of employee welfare benefit plan includes plans that provide holiday benefits.[5]

Conversely, the DOL, through Advisory Opinion 2004-08A,[6] ruled that a "Vacation and Remembrance Fund" funded through a separate trust was not a welfare benefit plan under the

---

1. ERISA Secs. 3(37)(A)(i), 3(37)(A)(ii).
2. See Labor Reg. §2510.3-37.
3. ERISA Sec. 4001(a)(3).
4. DOL Adv. Op. 2004-03A (Apr. 30, 2004).
5. See Labor Reg. §2510.3-1(a)(3).
6. DOL Adv. Op. 2004-08A (July 2, 2004).

provisions of ERISA Section 3(1). In arriving at this decision, the DOL relied upon the ruling of the Massachusetts Supreme Court in *Massachusetts v. Morash*,[1] which held that "the mere presence of a trust or other separate account from which vacation benefits are paid should not automatically result in ERISA coverage in the absence of the trust providing genuine protections to the accrued benefits under the plan or otherwise presenting risks ERISA was intended to address."

639. What is an employee organization?

"Employee organization" means (1) any labor union or any organization of any kind, or any agency or employee representation committee, association, group, or plan, in which employees participate and that exists for the purpose, in whole or in part, of dealing with employers concerning an employee benefit plan, or other matters incidental to employment relationships; or (2) any employees' beneficiary association organized, in whole or in part, for the purpose of establishing such a plan.[2]

640. Who are the fiduciaries in a multiemployer plan?

The general definition of a fiduciary is applicable to multiemployer plans. In general, in order to achieve fiduciary status, an individual or entity must either (1) exercise discretionary authority or control regarding the management of the plan or its assets or (2) exercise discretionary authority or responsibility in the administration of the plan.[3] See Q 215. This would include the power to appoint a plan's trustees.

In order for a participating employer to be considered a fiduciary of a multiemployer plan, it would have to exercise the sort of discretion and authority provided under ERISA Section 3(21)(A). Note that a participating employer in a multiemployer plan would be included in the definition of a party in interest under ERISA Section 3(14)(C). See Q 398.

Because they traditionally have the power, under Labor Management Relations Act Section 302(c)(5), to appoint a portion of a multiemployer plan's trustees, employee organizations (i.e., unions) are considered to be fiduciaries. As is the case with participating employers, an employee organization would be included in the definition of a party in interest under ERISA Section 3(14)(C). See Q 398.

The trustees appointed to operate a multiemployer plan satisfy the statutory definition of fiduciary under ERISA Section 3(21)(A) because they are charged with the power to exercise discretionary authority regarding the control and administration of the plan and its assets. Investment committee members and union-employed plan administrators are usually fiduciaries of a multiemployer plan (unless their duties are limited to ministerial functions) by virtue of performing duties that involve the discretion and authority provided under ERISA Section 3(21)(A).

---

1. 490 U.S. 107 (1989).
2. ERISA Sec. 3(4).
3. ERISA Sec. 3(21)(A).

Other individuals or entities that may be considered to be fiduciaries of a multiemployer plan include service providers who have been granted limited authority regarding the control and administration of the plan or its assets. Such service providers include third-party administrators, investment managers, broker-dealers, and insurance companies.

Fiduciaries of a multiemployer plan are obligated to conduct themselves in accordance with the fiduciary standards of ERISA, which are delineated under ERISA Section 404 (see Section IV for details).

641. May Taft-Hartley plan fiduciaries use plan assets to promote union organizing campaigns or union goals in collective bargaining negotiations?

No. The DOL has issued an Opinion Letter in which it advises that Taft-Hartley plan fiduciaries may not use pension plan assets to promote union organizing campaigns or union goals in collective bargaining negotiations.[1]

642. What is the funding structure of multiemployer plans?

The level of benefits to be funded through a multiemployer plan is traditionally determined by the formula contained within the collective bargaining agreement (CBA) established between the union and the participating employers. Contributions are submitted to plan fiduciaries who either

1.   Administer the type and amount of benefits as they are defined in the CBA, or

2.   Establish the type and amount of benefits provided under the plan.

Multiemployer pension plans are funded through an IRC Section 501(a) tax-exempt trust. Multiemployer welfare plans are traditionally funded through an IRC Section 501(c)(9) tax-exempt trust. Fiduciaries of both types of trusts are charged with investing and managing trust assets in accordance with the general provisions of ERISA (Q 294).[2]

Multiemployer pension plans must satisfy the minimum funding standard, which is satisfied if, as of the end of such plan year, the plan does not have a minimum funding deficiency.[3] Multiemployer welfare plans are not subject to funding limits.[4]

Multiemployer pension plans must establish and maintain a funding standard account. Each year, such account is

1.   Charged with the sum of the normal cost of the plan, the unfunded past service liabilities, net experience losses, net losses resulting from changes in the plan's actuarial assumptions, and the amount necessary to amortize each waived funding deficiency for each prior plan year; and

---

1. ERISA Op. Letter 2008-05A (2008).
2. See PBGC Adv. Op. 94-39A.
3. ERISA Sec. 302(a).
4. IRC Sec. 419A(f)(5).

2.   Credited with the sum of employer contributions, the amount necessary to amortize, in equal annual installments, the net decrease of unfunded past service liabilities, the plan's net experience gains, gains due to changes in the plan's actuarial assumptions, and waived funding deficiencies.[1]

The provisions of ERISA Sections 302(a) and 302(b) are mirrored under IRC Sections 412(a) and 412(b).

IRC Section 413(c)(4) requires pension funding requirements to be applied to multiemployer plans as if all of the participants are employed by a single employer.

643. How can a multiemployer plan be terminated?

There are three ways in which a multiemployer plan can be terminated:

1.   By the adoption of one of two types of amendment:

a.   an amendment that provides that participants will receive no credit under the plan for any period of service for an employer after the date specified by the amendment, or[2]

b.   an amendment that results in the plan's being converted to a defined contribution plan;[3]

2.   By the mass withdrawal of every employer participating in the plan;[4] and

3.   Through proceedings instituted by the PBGC.[5]

Where a multiemployer plan has been terminated through an amendment, the termination is effective on the date when the amendment is adopted or goes into effect, whichever is later.[6] In the case of a termination by mass withdrawal, the termination is effective on the earlier of the date when the last employer has withdrawn from the plan or the first day of the first plan year for which no employer contributions are required under the plan.[7]

In the case of termination by amendment, the plan must file a termination notice with the PBGC. See Q 665.

For details regarding the termination of a plan by the PBGC, see Section XII. Generally, involuntary terminations of single-employer defined benefit plans and multiemployer plans are covered by the same rules as delineated under ERISA Section 4042 (applications specific to each type of plan are spelled out in those rules).

---

1. ERISA Sec. 302(b).
2. ERISA Sec. 4041A(a)(1).
3. ERISA Sec. 4041A(a)(3).
4. ERISA Sec. 4041A(a)(2).
5. ERISA Sec. 4042.
6. ERISA Sec. 4041A(b)(2).
7. ERISA Sec. 4041A(b)(2).

644. What is withdrawal liability? Who is responsible for withdrawal liability?

An employer that withdraws from a multiemployer pension plan is responsible for an allocable share of the multiemployer plan's unfunded vested benefits (sometimes referred to as "UVBs"). ERISA Sections 4201 through 4225 set forth a series of rules that require the withdrawing employer to fund a proportional share of unfunded vested benefits in the plan through a series of annual withdrawal payments to the plan.

For purposes of a multiemployer plan, "employer" means a participating employer, and includes "all trades or businesses (whether or not incorporated) that are under common control within the meaning of section 4001(b)(1)."[1] An individual who owns the entire interest in an unincorporated trade or business is treated as his own employer, and a partnership is treated as the employer of each partner who is an employee within the meaning of IRC Section 401(c)(1).[2]

645. What constitutes a withdrawal for this purpose?

There are two types of withdrawals: a complete withdrawal and a partial withdrawal.

In general, a *complete withdrawal* occurs when an employer

1. Permanently ceases to have an obligation to contribute under the multiemployer plan, or

2. Permanently ceases all covered operations under the plan.[3]

The cessation of an obligation to contribute occurs when the employer is no longer required to make any contributions under the terms of the collective bargaining agreement.[4]

In order for the employer to have permanently ceased all covered operations under the plan, the contributing employer must have completely ceased all operations that are covered by the collective bargaining agreement.[5]

Special rules apply in making the determination of whether a complete withdrawal has occurred for multiemployer pension plans that cover employees in the building and construction industries,[6] the entertainment industry,[7] and the trucking, moving, and warehousing industries.[8]

A *partial withdrawal* occurs when, on the last day of the plan year, there is either (1) a 70 percent contribution decline in or (2) a partial cessation of, the employer's contribution obligation.[9]

---

1. ERISA Sec. 3(37)(B).
2. ERISA Sec. 4001(b)(1).
3. ERISA Sec. 4203(a).
4. *Parmac, Inc. v. I.A.M. Nat'l Pension Fund Benefit Plan*, 872 F.2d 1069 (D.C. Cir. 1989).
5. *Trustees of the Iron Workers Local 473 v. Allied Prods. Corp.*, 872 F.2d 208 (7th Cir. 1989).
6. ERISA Sec. 4203(b).
7. ERISA Sec. 4203(c).
8. ERISA Sec. 4203(d).
9. ERISA Sec. 4205(a).

A *70 percent contribution decline* occurs if the employer's contribution base units do not exceed 30 percent of the employer's contribution base units for the high base year during each plan year in the three-year testing period.[1]

The *three-year testing period* is the period consisting of the current plan year and the immediately preceding two plan years. The number of *contribution base units for the high base year* is the average number of units for the two plan years (within the five plan years immediately preceding the beginning of the three-year testing period) for which the employer's contribution base units were the highest.[2]

Partial cessation of the employer's contribution base units occurs if, during such plan year, the employer permanently ceases to have an obligation to contribute

1.   Under one or more (but fewer than all) collective bargaining agreements under which the employer has been obligated to contribute under the plan, but continues to perform work (of the type for which contributions were previously required) in the jurisdiction of the collective bargaining agreement, or transfers such work to another location; or

2.   With respect to work performed at one or more (but fewer than all) of its facilities, but continues to perform the type of work for which the obligation to contribute ceased at the facility.[3]

An employer that has permanently ceased to perform covered work under one of its collective bargaining agreements but contracts to buy that same service or product from an independent third party has not transferred that work to another location for the purposes of this rule.[4]

A cessation of obligations under a collective bargaining agreement shall not be considered to have occurred solely because, with respect to the same plan, one agreement that requires contributions to the plan has been substituted for another agreement.[5]

According to Section 108(c)(2) of the Multiemployer Pension Plan Amendments Act of 1980,[6] the liability incurred by an employer for a partial withdrawal is a pro rata portion of the liability that the employer would otherwise incur if there had been a complete withdrawal on the same date. See Q 652.

646. Is there withdrawal liability for withdrawal from a multiemployer welfare benefit plan?

This issue remains unsettled, but as of right now, ERISA is silent on the imposition of withdrawal liability against employers that have withdrawn from multiemployer welfare benefit plans. The issue has been subject to litigation.

---

1. ERISA Sec. 4205(b)(1)(A).
2. ERISA Sec. 4205(b)(1)(B).
3. ERISA Sec. 4205(b)(2)(A).
4. PBGC Adv. Op. 86-17.
5. ERISA Sec. 4205(b)(2)(B).
6. Pub. L. No. 96-364.

Courts have held that multiemployer welfare benefit plans have no authority, either under the law of trusts or under ERISA, to unilaterally impose withdrawal liability upon an employer.[1] In *Manchester Knitted Fashions*, the First Circuit Court of Appeals indicated that participating employers in a multiemployer welfare benefit plan may contract for the imposition of withdrawal liability for the funding of post-retirement welfare benefits. But the court cautioned that such a contractual arrangement must be reasonable under the general construction of contracts and must be interpreted in such a way as to "give effect to the expressed intentions of the parties."[2]

647. How is withdrawal liability computed?

The basic method for computing withdrawal liability is the presumptive method. See Q 648. In addition, there are three alternative methods for computing withdrawal liability: the modified presumptive method (see Q 649), the rolling-five method (see Q 650), and the direct attribution method (see Q 651). Note that, in order for any of the alternative methods to be used, the plan must be amended to permit the use of such alternative method.[3]

As a practical matter, the plan's actuary will calculate an employer's withdrawal liability. The withdrawing employer may also wish to engage its own actuary in order to dispute the withdrawal liability determination of the plan's actuary.

648. What is the presumptive method for calculating withdrawal liability?

Under the presumptive method, the amount of unfunded vested benefits (UVBs) allocable to a withdrawing employer (that is, the employer's withdrawal liability) is the sum of

1.   The employer's proportional share of the unamortized amount of the change in the plan's UVBs for plan years ending after September 25, 1980;

2.   The employer's proportional share, if any, of the unamortized amount of the plan's UVBs at the end of the plan year ending before September 26, 1980; and

3.   The employer's proportional share of the unamortized amounts of the reallocated UVBs.[4]

Determining the employer's proportional share of the unamortized amount of the change in the plan's UVBs. This determination is a four-step process. First, the *change in the plan's UVBs* must be determined. For any plan year, this is the amount by which the UVBs at the end of the plan year exceed the sum of

1.   The unamortized amount of the UVBs for the last plan year ending before September 26, 1980; and

---

1. See, e.g., *Manchester Knitted Fashions, Inc. v. Amalgamated Cotton Garment & Allied Indus. Fund*, 967 F.2d 688 (1st Cir. 1992).
2. *Manchester Knitted Fashions, Inc.*, above (citing *Rothenberg v. Lincoln Farm Camp, Inc.*, 755 F.2d 1017 (2d Cir. 1985)).
3. See PBGC Reg. §§4211.1-4211.13.
4. ERISA Sec. 4211.

2.   The sum of

   a.   the unamortized amounts of the change in UVBs for each plan year ending after September 25, 1980, and

   b.   the unamortized amounts of the change in UVBs for the year preceding the plan year for which the change is determined.[1]

Second, the *unamortized amount of the change in the plan's UVBs*, with respect to a plan year, is determined by reducing the change in UVBs for the plan year, as determined in step one, by 5 percent for each succeeding plan year.[2]

Third, the *employer's proportional share of the unamortized amount of the change in a plan's UVBs* is determined by multiplying the amount determined in step two, above, by the following fraction:

   Numerator: the sum of the contributions that the employer must make to the plan for the year in which such change arose, and for the four preceding plan years.

   Denominator: the sum (for the plan year in which such change arose and the four preceding plan years) of all contributions made by all employers that had an obligation to contribute under the plan for the plan year in which such change arose, reduced by the contributions made in such years by employers that had withdrawn from the plan in the year in which the change arose.

Finally, to complete the calculation, add the employer's proportional share amount, determined above, for each plan year. The sum is the employer's proportional share of the unamortized amount of the change in the plan's unfunded benefit obligations for plan years beginning after September 25, 1980.

Determining the employer's proportional share of the unamortized amount of the UVBs for the last plan year ending before September 26, 1980. This is a three-step process. First, establish the *amount of the UVBs* as of the end of that plan year.

Second, determine the *unamortized amount of the UVBs* by reducing the amount of UVBs by 5 percent for each succeeding plan year.[3]

Next, calculate the *employer's proportional share of the unamortized amount of the UVBs* by multiplying the unamortized amount, determined above, by the following fraction:

   Numerator: the sum of all contributions required to be made by the employer under the plan for the most recent five plan years ending before September 26, 1980.

---

1. ERISA Sec. 4211(b)(2)(B).
2. ERISA Sec. 4211(b)(2)(C).
3. ERISA Sec. 4211(b)(2)(B).

Denominator: the sum of all contributions made for the most recent five plan years ending before September 26, 1980, by all employers that had an obligation to contribute under the plan for the first plan year ending on or after such date, and that had not withdrawn from the plan before such date.[1]

Determining the employer's proportional share of the unamortized amounts of the reallocated UVBs. This is a three-step process. First, determine the amount of the *reallocated UVBs.* In general, this is the sum of

1. Amounts that the plan sponsor determines are uncollectible for that year, due to bankruptcy or similar proceedings;

2. Amounts that the plan sponsor determines will not be assessed for that year, due to the operation of the *de minimis* rule of ERISA Section 4209 (see Q 656), the twenty-year limit of ERISA Section 4219(c)(1)(B) (see Q 660), or the limitation on withdrawal liability of ERISA Section 4225 (see Q 676 and Q 677), with respect to employers that have received a notice under ERISA Section 4219 (see Q 658); and

3. Amounts that the plan sponsor determines are uncollectible or unassessable for that plan year, for other reasons that are consistent with applicable regulations.[2]

Second, determine the *unamortized amount of the reallocated UVBs* by reducing the reallocated UVBs, determined above, by 5 percent for each succeeding plan year.[3]

Finally, determine the *employer's proportional share of the unamortized amount of the reallocated UVBs* by multiplying the unamortized amount of the reallocated UVBs by the following fraction:

Numerator: the sum of the contributions that the employer must make to the plan for the year in which such change arose, and for the four preceding plan years.

Denominator: the sum (for the plan year in which such change arose and the four preceding plan years) of all contributions made by all employers that had an obligation to contribute under the plan for the plan year in which such change arose, reduced by the contributions made in such years by employers that had withdrawn from the plan in the year in which the change arose.[4]

649. What is the modified presumptive method for calculating withdrawal liability?

ERISA Section 4211(c) provides for the modified presumptive method. This method, like the presumptive method discussed in Q 648, provides for different calculations for plan years ending before September 26, 1980, and plan years ending after September 25, 1980.

---

1. ERISA Sec. 4211(b)(3).
2. ERISA Sec. 4211(b)(4)(B).
3. ERISA Sec. 4211(b)(4)(C).
4. ERISA Sec. 4211(b)(4)(D).

Under the modified presumptive method, the amount of the unfunded vested benefits (UVBs) allocable to an employer is the sum of (1) and (2), below:

1. The plan's UVBs as of the end of the last plan year ending before September 26, 1980,

    a. reduced, as if those obligations were being fully amortized in level annual installments over fifteen years, beginning with the first plan year ending on or after such date,

    b. multiplied by the following fraction:

    Numerator: the sum of all contributions required to be made by the employer for the last five plan years ending before September 25, 1980.

    Denominator: the sum of all contributions made for the last five plan years ending before September 26, 1980, by all employers that had an obligation to contribute under the plan for the first plan year ending after September 25, 1980, and had not withdrawn from the plan before such date; and

2. The plan's UVBs as of the end of the plan year preceding the plan year in which the employer withdraws, minus the sum of

    a. the value, as of such date, of all outstanding claims for withdrawal liability that can reasonably be expected to be collected, with respect to employers withdrawing before such plan year, and

    b. that portion of the amount to be determined under item 1.a, above, which is allocable to employers that have an obligation to contribute under the plan in the plan year preceding the plan year in which the employer withdraws, and also had an obligation to contribute under the plan for the first plan year ending after September 25, 1980,

    c. multiplied by the following fraction:

    Numerator: the total amount required to be contributed under the plan by all employers for the last five plan years ending before the date on which the employer withdraws.

    Denominator: the total amount contributed under the plan by all employers for the last five plan years ending before the date on which the employer withdraws, increased by the amount of any employer contributions owed with respect to earlier periods, which were collected in those plan years, and decreased by any amount contributed by an employer that withdrew from the plan during those plan years.[1]

---

1. ERISA Sec. 4211(c)(2).

In the case of an employer that did not contribute to the plan for plan years ending prior to September 26, 1980, the amount of the UVBs allocable to the employer is the amount established under item two, above.

650. What is the rolling-5 method for calculating withdrawal liability?

The rolling-5 method for determining withdrawal liability is a statutory alternative to the presumptive method discussed in Q 648. The amount of the unfunded vested benefits (UVBs) allocable to an employer under the rolling-5 method is equal to the product of

1. The UVBs as of the end of the plan year preceding the plan year in which the employer withdraws, less the value, as of the end of such year, of all outstanding claims for withdrawal liability that can reasonably be expected to be collected from employers withdrawing before such year,

2. Multiplied by the following fraction:

    Numerator: the total amount required to be contributed by the employer under the plan for the last five plan years ending before withdrawal.

    Denominator: the total amount contributed under the plan by all employers for the last five years ending before the withdrawal, increased by any employer contributions owed with respect to earlier periods that were collected in those plan years, and decreased by any amount contributed to the plan during those plan years by employers that withdrew from the plan during those plan years.[1]

651. What is the direct attribution method for calculating withdrawal liability?

The direct attribution method for calculating withdrawal liability is a statutory alternative to the presumptive method, discussed in Q 648. The amount of the unfunded vested benefits (UVBs) allocable to an employer under the direct attribution method is equal to the sum of

1. The plan's UVBs that are attributable to participants' service with the employer (determined as of the end of the plan year preceding the plan year in which the employer withdraws), and

2. The employer's proportional share of any UVBs that are not attributable to service with the employer or other employers who are obligated to contribute to the plan in the plan year preceding the plan year in which the employer withdraws (determined as of the end of the plan year preceding the plan year in which the employer withdraws).[2]

---

1. ERISA Sec. 4211(c)(3).
2. ERISA Sec. 4211(c)(4).

652. How is the pro rata determination of partial withdrawal liability calculated?

When there has been a partial withdrawal, the amount of liability for the employer is calculated on a pro rata basis. This pro rata amount of withdrawal liability is determined by multiplying the amount of withdrawal liability that would have been applied in the case of a complete withdrawal by a stipulated fraction.

When there has been a *partial cessation of an employer's obligation* (see Q 645), the withdrawal liability is determined by multiplying the withdrawal liability that would have applied (in the case of a complete withdrawal on the date of the partial withdrawal) by a number, which is one minus the following fraction:

> Numerator: the employer's contribution base units for the plan year following the plan year of the partial withdrawal.

> Denominator: the average of the employer's contribution base units for the five plan years preceding the plan year of partial withdrawal.[1]

When there has been a *70 percent decline in employer contributions*, withdrawal liability is determined as of the last day of the first plan year in the three-year testing period. This amount is multiplied by a number, which is one minus the following fraction:

> Numerator: the employer's contribution base units for the plan year following the plan year of the partial withdrawal.

> Denominator: the average of the employer's contribution base units for the five plan years immediately preceding the three-year testing period.[2]

PBGC Advisory Opinion 93-2 provides that the contribution base units for the plan year following the plan year in which the partial withdrawal occurs are the contribution base units for the plan year following the last plan year in the three-year testing period, and not the plan year that follows the hypothetical withdrawal.

653. What are the plan sponsor's responsibilities when an employer withdraws from a multiemployer plan?

When an employer withdraws from a multiemployer plan, the plan sponsor must

1. Determine the amount of the employer's withdrawal liability (see Q 647),

2. Notify the employer of the amount of the withdrawal liability, and

3. Collect the amount of the withdrawal liability from the employer.[3]

---

1. ERISA Sec. 4206(a)(2).
2. ERISA Sec. 4206(a)(2)(B).
3. ERISA Sec. 4202.

654. Does the sale of the assets or stock of a contributing employer or a merger constitute a plan withdrawal?

Yes and no. In certain situations, a withdrawal has been deemed to have occurred as a result of the sale or merger of the contributing employer. Under other circumstances, no withdrawal has been found to have occurred.

An employer is not deemed to have withdrawn from a multiemployer plan because it ceases to exist by reason of a change in corporate structure through reorganization, liquidation into a parent corporation, merger, consolidation, division, or as a result of a change to an unincorporated form of business enterprise.[1]

Normally, the sale of a contributing employer's assets *does* constitute a withdrawal from a multiemployer pension fund.[2] But a withdrawal will not occur where a seller ceases covered operations or ceases to have an obligation to contribute for such operations as a result of a bona fide, arm's-length sale of assets to an unrelated party, provided that

1. The purchaser has an obligation to contribute to the plan with respect to the operations for substantially the same number of contribution base units for which the seller had an obligation to contribute to the plan;

2. For a period of five plan years (commencing with the first plan year beginning after the sale of assets), the purchaser provides the plan with

    a. a bond issued by a corporate surety company that is listed in IRS Circular 570 as an approved surety provider, or

    b. an amount held in escrow by a bank or similar financial institution satisfactory to the plan, in an amount equal to the greater of (i) the average annual contributions that the seller must make with respect to operations under the plan for the three plan years preceding the plan year in which the sale of assets occurs, or (ii) the annual contribution that the seller must make with respect to the operations under the plan for the last plan year before the plan year in which the sale of employer assets occurs; and

3. The contract for sale provides that, if the purchaser withdraws (in either a complete withdrawal or a partial withdrawal with respect to operations) during the first five plan years following the sale, the seller is secondarily liable for any unpaid liability of the purchaser.[3]

If the purchaser withdraws before the last day of the fifth plan year beginning after the sale and fails to make any withdrawal liability payment when due, then the seller shall pay to the plan an amount equal to the payment that would have been due from the seller but for the sale.[4]

---

1. ERISA Sec. 4218(1).
2. See, e.g., I. *A.M. Nat'l Pension Fund Benefit Plan A v. Cooper Indus., Inc.*, 635 F. Supp. 335 (D.D.Ç. 1986), *rev'd*, 825 F.2d 415 (D.C. Cir. 1987).
3. ERISA Sec. 4204(a)(1).
4. ERISA Sec. 4204(a)(2).

If all, or substantially all, of the seller's assets are distributed, or if the seller is liquidated before the end of the five-plan-year period following the sale, then the seller must provide a bond or escrow an amount equal to the present value of the withdrawal liability that it would have had but for the sale of assets.[1]

Under certain circumstances, an employer may request a "variance" or waiver from the bond or escrow account requirement.[2] But note that a failure to strictly adhere to the requirements of ERISA Section 4204 and the regulations thereunder will result in the asset sale's being treated as a withdrawal from the multiemployer plan.[3]

A second sale of the same business within the five-year period will not result in withdrawal liability, provided that the subsequent sale also meets the requirements of ERISA Section 4204.[4]

655. Does the interruption of business as a result of a labor dispute constitute a withdrawal from a multiemployer pension plan?

No. An employer is not deemed to have withdrawn from a multiemployer pension plan solely because it suspends making contributions to the plan during a labor dispute involving its employees.[5]

656. What are the de minimis and permissive reduction rules of ERISA Section 4209?

The *de minimis reduction rule* provides that the amount of the unfunded vested benefits (UVBs) allocated to an employer that withdraws from a multiemployer pension plan shall be reduced by the lesser of

1.   Three-fourths of 1 percent (.0075) of the plan's unfunded vested obligations (determined as of the end of the plan year preceding the date of withdrawal), or

2. $50,000,

reduced by the amount, if any, by which the employer's portion of UVBs exceeds $100,000.[6]

The *permissive reduction rule* provides that a plan may be amended to provide for reduction of the UVBs allocated to a withdrawing employer by not more than the greater of

1.   The amount established under the *de minimis* rule, above; or

2.   The lesser of

    a.   three-fourths of 1 percent (.0075) of the plan's unfunded vested obligations (determined as of the end of the plan year preceding the date of withdrawal), or

    b. $100,000,

---

1. ERISA Sec. 4204(a)(3).
2. See PBGC Reg. §§4204.11, 4204.12, and 4204.13.
3. See, e.g., *Brentwood Fin. Corp. v. Western Conference of Teamsters Pension Trust Fund*, 902 F.2d 1456 (9th Cir. 1990).
4. PBGC Adv. Op. 90-1.
5. ERISA Sec. 4218(2).
6. ERISA Sec. 4209(a).

reduced by the amount, if any, by which the employer's withdrawal liability amount would otherwise exceed $150,000.[1]

657. What is the "free look" rule of ERISA Section 4210?

Under certain circumstances, discussed subsequently, withdrawal liability may be eliminated for

1.   Employers first obligated to contribute to the plan after September 26, 1980;

2.   Employers obligated to contribute to the plan for no longer than the lesser of

    a.   six consecutive plan years preceding the date of the employer's withdrawal, or

    b.   the number of years required for vesting under the plan;

3.   Employers required to contribute (for each plan year) less than 2 percent of the sum of all employer contributions made to the plan for each year; and

4.   Employers that have never previously avoided withdrawal liability under these provisions.[2]

This "free look" rule applies only to multiemployer plans that

1.   Are amended to provide that the provisions of ERISA Section 4210(a), discussed above, apply;

2.   Provide (or are amended to provide) that the reduction under IRC Section 411(a) (3)(E) applies to the withdrawing employer's employees; and

3.   Have a ratio of plan assets to benefit payments made, during the plan year preceding the first plan year for which the employer was required to contribute to the plan, of at least eight to one.[3]

Note also that, effective for plan withdrawals occurring after 2006, the relief afforded under ERISA Section 4210(a) does apply to multiemployer plans that primarily cover employees in the building and construction industry.[4]

658. What is the notice requirement regarding withdrawal liability?

As soon as practicable after an employer's complete or partial withdrawal, the plan sponsor must notify the employer of the amount of the withdrawal liability and the schedule for liability payments, and demand payment in accordance with the schedule for liability payments.[5]

---

1. ERISA Sec. 4209(b).
2. ERISA Sec. 4210(a).
3. ERISA Sec. 4210(b).
4. ERISA Sec. 4210(b)(1), *repealed by* Pension Protection Act of 2006 Sec. 201.
5. ERISA Sec. 4219(b)(1).

After receiving the notice of withdrawal liability from the plan sponsor, the employer has ninety days in which to

1. Request that the plan sponsor review any specific matter relating to the determination of the employer's liability and the schedule of payments (see Q 659),

2. Identify any inaccuracy in the plan sponsor's determination of the amount of the unfunded vested benefits allocable to the employer, and

3. Furnish any additional relevant information to the plan sponsor.[1]

659. What is the plan sponsor's responsibility after receipt of a request from a contributing employer for a review of the employer's withdrawal liability?

After the receipt of a request from an employer for a review of its withdrawal liability, and reasonable review of any matter raised, the plan sponsor (see Q 658) shall notify the employer of

1. Plan sponsor's decision,

2. Basis for the decision, and

3. Reason for any change in the determination of the employer's liability or the schedule of liability payments.[2]

660. When and how are withdrawal liability payments to be made?

Withdrawal liability payments must begin no later than sixty days after the date on which the plan sponsor demands payment.[3]

The withdrawing employer must pay the withdrawal liability payments over the period of years necessary to amortize the amount in annual level payments, calculated as if the first payment were made on the first day of the plan year following the plan year in which the withdrawal occurs, and as if each subsequent payment were made on the first day of each subsequent plan year. This amortization period may not exceed twenty years.[4]

The Supreme Court ruled that interest begins to accrue on the amortization as of the first day of the plan year after withdrawal, holding that the withdrawing employer's obligation does not begin to accrue until the first day of the year after withdrawal.[5]

Annual withdrawal liability payments must be made in four equal payments, due quarterly, or at other intervals specified in the plan. Interest accrues on late payments from the due date until the date when actually paid.[6]

---

1. ERISA Sec. 4219(b)(2)(A).
2. ERISA Sec. 4219(b)(2)(B).
3. ERISA Sec. 4219(c)(2).
4. ERISA Sec. 4219(c)(1).
5. *Milwaukee Brewery Workers' Pension Plan v. Jos. Schlitz Brewing Co. & Stroh Brewing Co.*, 513 U.S. 414 (1995).
6. ERISA Sec. 4219(c)(3).

There is no prepayment liability if the employer prepays all or a part of the outstanding amount of the unpaid withdrawal liability obligation. If a prepayment has subsequently been determined to be a part of a mass withdrawal (see Q 664), the employer's liability will not be limited to the amount of the prepayment.[1]

The amount of the annual withdrawal liability payment equals

1. The average number of contribution base units for the three consecutive plan years during the ten-year plan period ending before the plan year of withdrawal, in which the number of such units was the highest

   multiplied by

2. The highest contribution rate for required contributions of the employer during the ten-year period ending with the plan year of withdrawal.[2]

661. What happens in the event of a default on withdrawal liability payments?

Default on withdrawal liability payments occurs when the withdrawing employer has failed to make a payment on its withdrawal liability when due, and then fails to make payment within sixty days after receiving written notice from the plan sponsor of such failure.[3] The plan sponsor may also establish rules that include, within the definition of default, other events that indicate a substantial likelihood that an employer would be unlikely to pay its withdrawal liability.[4]

If an employer defaults on the payment of scheduled withdrawal liability, the plan sponsor may require the immediate payment of all or a portion of the outstanding balance of the employer's liability, plus accrued interest from the due date of the first payment in default. Should the plan sponsor accelerate only a portion of the outstanding balance owed, the plan sponsor must establish a new schedule of payments for the remaining amount owed.[5]

662. Does interest accrue on delinquent withdrawal liability payments?

ERISA Section 4219(c)(3) requires that each annual payment that is in default shall accrue interest from the due date until the date on which the payment is made. Such interest rates shall be based on prevailing market rates for comparable obligations, in accordance with PBGC regulations.[6]

Interest on defaulted amounts is charged or credited for each calendar quarter at an annual rate, equal to the average quoted prime rate on short-term commercial loans quoted by large banks (as published by the Federal Reserve Board) on the fiftieth day (or the following business

1. ERISA Sec. 4219(c)(4).
2. ERISA Sec. 4219(c)(1)(C)(i).
3. ERISA Sec. 4219(c)(5)(A); PBGC Reg. §4219.31(b)(1)(i).
4. ERISA Sec. 4219(c)(5)(B); PBGC Reg. §4219.31(b)(1)(ii).
5. ERISA Sec. 4219(c)(5); PBGC Reg. §4219.31(b)(2).
6. ERISA Sec. 4219(c)(6).

day, if the fiftieth day is not a business day) of the month preceding the beginning of the calendar quarter.[1]

Plans may adopt procedures for establishing interest rates that are different from those established under PBGC regulations. But the alternative rates must be consistent with ERISA and reflect "prevailing market rates for comparable obligations."[2]

Any overpayment of withdrawal liability must be refunded with interest at the same rate as that applied to overdue payments. Such overpayments must be refunded in a lump sum, with interest, and may not be applied to future payment obligations.[3]

663. Are payments made by an employer for withdrawal liability deductible?

Yes. IRC Section 404(g)(1) provides that an employer's payments made under Part 1 of Subtitle E of Title VI of ERISA (that is, the withdrawal liability provisions) are treated as deductible employer contributions.

The deduction will be permitted when paid, without regard to the limitation on employer deductions for contributions to tax-qualified plans found elsewhere in IRC Section 404.[4] Withdrawal liability payments will be included in the employer's total plan contributions for purposes of establishing the maximum allowable deduction under the full-funding limitation (see Q 51).[5]

664. What happens when substantially all of the employers withdraw from a plan?

When every employer withdraws from a multiemployer plan, or when substantially all employers withdraw from a multiemployer plan pursuant to an agreement or arrangement, a "mass withdrawal" occurs and there is a plan termination. In the event of a plan termination triggered by such a mass withdrawal, the liability of each withdrawing employer is determined without regard to the twenty-year cap on payments under ERISA Section 4219(c)(1)(B), and the total unfunded vested benefits of the plan will be fully allocated among all of the employers, in a manner "not inconsistent" with PBGC regulations.[6]

Withdrawal from a plan by an employer during a period of three consecutive plan years within which substantially all of the employers withdraw from the plan is presumed to be a withdrawal pursuant to an agreement or arrangement, unless the employer proves otherwise by a preponderance of the evidence.[7]

---

1. PBGC Reg. §4219.32(b).
2. PBGC Reg. §4219.33.
3. PBGC Reg. §4219.31(d).
4. Treas. Reg. §1.404(g)-1(a).
5. Treas. Reg. §1.404(g)-1(c)(3).
6. ERISA Sec. 4219(c)(1)(D).
7. ERISA Sec. 4219(c)(1)(D).

The termination date of a multiemployer plan subject to mass withdrawal is the earlier of (1) the date on which the last employer withdraws; or (2) the first day of the first plan year in which no employer contributions are required under the plan.[1]

When there is a termination of a multiemployer plan as a result of a mass withdrawal of employers (or by a plan amendment),[2] three notice requirements must be satisfied:

1. Notice of termination (see Q 665),

2. Notice of benefit reductions (see Q 666), and

3. Notice of insolvency (see Q 667).

665. What is involved in filing the notice of termination for a multiemployer plan?

When a multiemployer plan has been terminated (whether by mass withdrawal or by a plan amendment), a notice of termination must be filed with the PBGC. In this notice, the plan sponsor is required to certify that all documents and information submitted are true and correct to the best of its knowledge and belief.[3]

If a multiemployer plan is terminated by a mass withdrawal (see Q 664), the notice of termination must contain the following information:

1. Name of the plan;

2. Name, address, and telephone number of the plan sponsor and its duly authorized representative;

3. Name, address, and telephone number of the person who will administer the plan after the date of termination (if other than the plan sponsor);

4. Copy of the plan's most recent annual report (Form 5500) and any schedules attached thereto;

5. Date of plan termination;

6. Copy of the plan document that was in effect five years prior to the termination date and copies of any amendments adopted after that date;

7. Copy of the trust agreement authorizing the plan sponsor to control and manage the operation and administration of the plan;

8. Copy of the most recent actuarial statement and opinion (if any) relating to the plan;

9. A statement of any material change in plan assets or liabilities after the date of either

    a. the most recent actuarial statement, or

    b. the annual report (Form 5500) submitted with the notice;

1. ERISA Sec. 4041A(b)(2).
2. ERISA Sec. 4041A(a)(2).
3. PBGC Reg. §4041A.11(c).

10.   Copies of any IRS determination letters relating to establishment of the plan, disqualification of the plan and any subsequent requalification, and termination of the plan; and

11.   A statement indicating whether the plan assets will cover all benefits in pay status during the twelve-month period following the termination date.[1]

If the plan assets are sufficient to pay all nonforfeitable benefits, the notice is required to contain a brief description of the proposed method of distributing them. Should the plan have insufficient assets to pay all nonforfeitable benefits, the notice must contain the name and address of all employers who have contributed to the plan within three plan years before the termination date.[2]

The notice is required to be filed with the PBGC by the plan sponsor or its duly authorized representative.[3] The notice of termination may be filed with the PBGC by mailing it to the following address:

ATTN: MEPD Insurance Programs Department
PBGC
1200 K Street NW, Suite 930
Washington, DC 20005-4026

In the case of the termination of a multiemployer plan by mass withdrawal, the notice of termination must be filed within thirty days after the earlier of: (1) the date on which the last employer withdrew from the plan, or (2) the first day of the first plan year for which no employer contributions were required under the plan.[4]

For further details on PBGC participation in the termination of a multiemployer plan, including questions on guaranteed limits and benefit payment rules, see Section XII, CIVIL COMPLIANCE AND ENFORCEMENT ISSUES.

666. What is involved in filing the notice of benefit reductions?

When a multiemployer plan is terminated (whether through a mass withdrawal or by amendment), a notice of benefit reductions must be filed with the PBGC and provided to participants and beneficiaries whose benefits are reduced by the termination.[5]

The notice of benefit reductions *to be filed with the PBGC* must contain

1.   Name of the plan;

2.   Name, address, and telephone number of the plan sponsor;

---

1. PBGC Regs. §§4041A.11(a), 4041A.11(b).
2. PBGC Regs. §§4041A.11(b)(7), 4041A.11(b)(8).
3. PBGC Reg. §4041A.11.
4. PBGC Reg. §4041A.11(c)(2).
5. PBGC Reg. §4281.32(a).

3. Employer Identification Number (EIN) and the plan number (PN) assigned to the plan by the plan sponsor;

4. Case number assigned by the PBGC when the plan's notice of termination was filed;

5. A statement that a plan amendment reducing benefits has been adopted, including the adoption and effective dates of the amendment; and

6. A certification, signed by the plan sponsor, that the notice of benefit reductions (containing all of the required information) has been provided to all participants and beneficiaries.[1]

The notice of benefit reductions *to be provided to participants and beneficiaries* must contain

1. Name of the plan;

2. A statement that a plan amendment reducing benefits has been adopted, including the adoption and effective dates of the amendment;

3. A summary of the amendment, including a description of the effect of the amendment on the benefits to which it applies; and

4. Name, address, and telephone number of the plan administrator or other person designated by the plan sponsor to answer inquiries regarding benefits.[2]

The notice of benefit reductions must be filed with the PBGC, and provided to participants and beneficiaries, no later than the earlier of: (1) forty-five days after the amendment is adopted, or (2) the date of the first reduced benefit payment.[3] The notice of benefit reductions must be provided to the PBGC and to participants and beneficiaries who are in pay status (or who are reasonably expected to enter pay status in the plan year after the plan year in which the amendment is adopted) either through regular mail delivery or hand delivery.[4] The plan sponsor may use any method of delivery reasonably calculated to reach participants and beneficiaries not in pay status.

The notice of benefit reductions provided to the PBGC must be mailed or hand delivered to

ATTN: MEPD Insurance Programs Department
PBGC
1200 K Street NW, Suite 930
Washington, DC 20005-4026

---

1. PBGC Reg. §4281.32(d).
2. PBGC Reg. §4281.32(e).
3. PBGC Reg. §4281.32(b).
4. PBGC Reg. §4281.32(c).

667. What is involved in filing the notice of insolvency?

When there has been a plan termination through mass withdrawal, the plan sponsor who has determined that the plan is, or will soon be, insolvent for a plan year must file a notice of insolvency with the PBGC. A notice of insolvency must also be sent to plan participants and beneficiaries.[1]

Thereafter, the plan sponsor must provide annual updates to the PBGC and participants and beneficiaries for each plan year beginning after the plan year for which the notice of insolvency was issued. The plan sponsor need not issue revised annual updates to participants and beneficiaries who have received a notice of insolvency benefit level under PBGC Regulation Section 4281.45 for that plan year.[2] After the plan sponsor has issued annual updates for the plan year, it need not provide revised annual updates if the plan sponsor determines, under PBGC Regulation Section 4041A.25(b), that the plan is, or will be, insolvent for that plan year.[3]

The notice of insolvency *to be filed with the PBGC* must contain

1. Plan sponsor's Employer Identification Number (EIN) and the plan number (PN) assigned to the plan,

2. IRS Key District Office that has jurisdiction over determination letters for the plan,

3. PBGC case number assigned to the filing of the plan's notice of termination,

4. Plan year for which the plan sponsor has determined that the plan is or may be insolvent,

5. Copy of the plan's most recent actuarial valuation,

6. Copy of the plan document currently in effect,

7. Estimated amount of annual benefit payments under the plan for the insolvency year,

8. Estimated amount of the plan's available resources for the insolvency year,

9. Estimated amount of benefits guaranteed by the PBGC for the insolvency year,

10. A statement indicating whether the notice of insolvency is the result of an insolvency determination under the insolvency determination requirements (see Q 676), and

11. A certification signed by the plan sponsor that notices of insolvency have been provided to all participants and beneficiaries containing all required information.[4]

---

1. PBGC Reg. §4281.43(a).
2. PBGC Reg. §4281.43(b).
3. PBGC Reg. §4281.43(b).
4. PBGC Reg. §4281.44(a).

The notice of insolvency *to be provided to participants and beneficiaries* must contain the following

1.   Name of the plan;

2.   Plan year for which the plan sponsor has determined that the plan is or may be insolvent;

3.   A statement that benefits above the amount that can be paid from available resources or the level guaranteed by the PBGC, whichever is greater, will be suspended during the insolvency year, with a brief explanation of which benefits are guaranteed by the PBGC; and

4.   Name, address, and telephone number of the plan administrator or other person designated by the plan sponsor to answer inquiries concerning benefits.[1]

"Available resources" for a plan year are the plan's cash, marketable assets, contributions, and withdrawal liability payments and earnings, less reasonable administrative expenses owed to the PBGC for the plan year under provisions relating to financial assistance repayments.[2]

The plan sponsor must deliver the notices of insolvency no later than thirty days after it determines that the plan is or may be insolvent. The notice to plan participants and beneficiaries in active pay status may be delivered along with the first benefit payment made after the determination of insolvency.[3]

The notice of insolvency must be mailed or hand delivered to the PBGC and to plan participants and beneficiaries in pay status. Participants and beneficiaries who are not in pay status may be provided their notice of insolvency in any manner reasonably calculated to reach them (including posting notices at work sites, placing a notice in union newsletters, or placing a notice in a newspaper of general circulation).[4]

668. What is the penalty for failure to provide any of the required notices under the multiemployer plan provisions of ERISA?

Any person who fails, without reasonable cause, to provide a notice required under the multiemployer plan provisions of ERISA or applicable regulations shall be liable to the PBGC in an amount up to $100 for each day during which such failure continues. The PBGC may bring a civil action against any person who fails to provide a required notice in the U.S. District Court for the District of Columbia, or in any district court of the United States within the jurisdiction in which (1) the plan assets are located, (2) the plan is administered, or (3) a defendant resides or does business. Process may be served in any district where a defendant resides, does business, or may be found.[5]

---

1. PBGC Reg. §4281.44(b).
2. ERISA Secs. 4245(b)(3), 4261(b)(2); PBGC Reg. §4281.2.
3. PBGC Reg. §4281.43(c).
4. PBGC Reg. §§4281.43(e), 4281.43(f).
5. ERISA Sec. 4302.

669. Is the plan sponsor's determination of withdrawal liability presumed to be correct? How can a withdrawing employer challenge the plan sponsor's determination?

Yes. Any determination of withdrawal liability made by a plan sponsor is presumed correct, unless the party contesting the determination shows, by a preponderance of the evidence, that the determination was unreasonable or clearly erroneous.[1]

A dispute between an employer and the plan sponsor of a multiemployer plan regarding the calculation or imposition of withdrawal liability must be resolved through arbitration. See Q 670.

670. What are the rules regarding arbitration of multiemployer plan withdrawal liability disputes?

ERISA Section 4221 mandates that any dispute between an employer and a plan sponsor of a multiemployer plan regarding the calculation or imposition of withdrawal liability be resolved through arbitration. Either party may initiate arbitration within the sixty-day period after the earlier of

1.   The date when the plan sponsor notifies the employer of its decision (see Q 659), following the employer's request for a review of the withdrawal liability determination (see Q 658); or

2.   120 days after the date of the employer's request for review of the withdrawal liability determination (see Q 658).

Both parties may jointly initiate arbitration within the 180-day period after the date of the plan sponsor's initial notice and demand of payment in accordance with the schedule for liability payments.[2] The parties may also waive or extend the statutory time limits at any time by mutual agreement.[3]

Any failure to initiate arbitration within the sixty-day period will result in the employer's waiving the right to contest the assessment of the withdrawal liability,[4] which, consequently, becomes immediately due and payable.[5]

In the absence of an equitable tolling of the deadlines, the employer will be deemed to have waived the right to contest the merits of an assessment if it fails to comply with the statutory time limits.

Where the employer requests arbitration, it must include in its notice of initiation of arbitration a statement that it disputes the plan sponsor's determination of its withdrawal liability, and that it is initiating arbitration. This notice must also contain a copy of the demand

---

1. ERISA Sec. 4221(a)(3).
2. ERISA Sec. 4221(a)(1).
3. PBGC Reg. §4221.3(b).
4. *Philadelphia Marine Trade Ass'n–Int'l Longshoreman's Ass'n Pension Fund v. Rose*, 85 F.3d 612 (3d Cir. 1996).
5. *Robbins v. Admiral Merchs. Motor Freight, Inc.*, 846 F.2d 1054 (7th Cir. 1988).

for payment of withdrawal liability, any request for reconsideration of the withdrawal liability determination, and any response to such request received from the plan sponsor.[1]

Where any other party initiates arbitration, the notice of intent to arbitrate must include a statement that the party is initiating arbitration, along with a brief description of the questions that it seeks to resolve through arbitration.[2]

Where both parties jointly initiate arbitration, the agreement to arbitrate must include a description of the questions that are being submitted to arbitration for resolution.[3]

A party that fails to promptly object to an incomplete or faulty request for arbitration waives its right to object to any filing deficiencies later.[4]

The parties must select an arbitrator within forty-five days after the arbitration is initiated, unless the parties mutually agree upon a different time limit. The parties must provide a notice of appointment to the arbitrator they have selected, which includes (1) a copy of the notice of initiation of arbitration, (2) a statement that the arbitration is to be conducted in accordance with the arbitration rules in the PBGC regulations, and (3) a request for a written acceptance by the arbitrator.[5]

If the arbitrator selected by the parties refuses or fails to accept an appointment within fifteen days after the notice of appointment has been mailed or delivered, the arbitrator is considered to have declined to act. The parties must then select another arbitrator. If the parties fail to select an arbitrator within the statutory time limits, either party may request the appointment of an arbitrator in a United States district court.[6]

An accepting arbitrator is required to disclose to the parties any facts or circumstances that are likely to have an effect upon his impartiality.[7]

If any of the parties to the arbitration believe that the arbitrator should be disqualified because of the information disclosed, that party is required to notify all other parties, as well as the arbitrator, within ten days after the arbitrator makes the disclosure. The arbitrator must withdraw, and the parties must then select another arbitrator.[8]

Any party may also request an arbitrator to withdraw from the proceedings at any time prior to the issuance of a final award on the grounds that the arbitrator is unable to render an impartial award.[9] The request for withdrawal must be provided to all parties and to the arbitrator, either by hand delivery or by certified or registered mail, and must include a statement of the circumstances that have caused the requesting party to question the arbitrator's impartiality, as

---

1. PBGC Reg. §4221.3(d).
2. PBGC Reg. §4221.3(d).
3. PBGC Reg. §4221.3(d).
4. PBGC Reg. §4221.3(e).
5. PBGC Reg. §4221.4(a).
6. PBGC Reg. §4221.4(a).
7. PBGC Reg. §4221.4(b).
8. PBGC Reg. §4221.4(b).
9. PBGC Reg. §4221.4(c).

well as a statement that the requesting party has brought these circumstances to the attention of the arbitrator and the other parties at the earliest practicable point in the proceedings. If, after review, the arbitrator determines that the circumstances raised by the objecting party are likely to affect his impartiality, and that the request was timely presented, the arbitrator must withdraw from the proceedings and notify the parties of the reasons for the withdrawal.[1]

In all cases of an arbitrator vacancy, the parties must select another arbitrator within 20 days after they receive notice of the vacancy.[2]

671. What are an arbitrator's powers and duties?

An arbitrator must conduct an arbitration hearing on withdrawal liability in accordance with arbitration rules found in the PBGC regulations, which provide that an arbitrator has the following powers and duties:

1. An arbitrator must follow applicable law in reaching a decision, including, but not limited to, statutes, regulations, court decisions, and interpretations of those agencies charged with the enforcement of ERISA.

2. An arbitrator may allow any party to conduct pre-hearing discovery, through interrogatories, depositions, requests for documents, and other traditional means, but such attempts at discovery must be shown to be likely to lead to the production of relevant evidence and not to be disproportionately burdensome.

3. An arbitrator may impose sanctions if he determines that a party has failed to respond to good-faith discovery requests or has proceeded with discovery in bad faith, or for the purpose of harassment.

4. An arbitrator may require all parties to provide advance notice of the use of expert witnesses or other witnesses upon which they intend to rely.

5. An arbitrator may determine the admissibility and relevance of evidence presented, but there is no mandate of conformity to the legal rules of evidence.

6. An arbitrator may subpoena witnesses or documents on his own initiative, or upon request of any of the parties.[3]

If an arbitrator should conclude that a pre-hearing conference would expedite the proceedings, he may direct the parties to appear at a pre-hearing conference at any time before the arbitration hearing commences, in order to consider any of the following items:

1. Settlement of the case,

2. Clarification of issues and stipulation of facts not in dispute,

3. Admission of documents to avoid unnecessary proof,

---

1. PBGC Reg. §4221.4(c).
2. PBGC Reg. §4221.4(d).
3. PBGC Reg. §4221.5(a).

4. Limitations on the number of expert or other witnesses, and

5. Any other matters that may hasten the disposition of the proceedings.[1]

An arbitrator is permitted to render an award without conducting a hearing, if all parties so agree and file with the arbitrator all evidence necessary to enable the arbitrator to render an award.[2]

In the absence of a pre-hearing settlement, the arbitrator and the parties must establish a date and a place for the hearing, no later than fifteen days after the arbitrator's written acceptance (see Q 670).[3] The hearing must be scheduled to take place within fifty days after the mailing date of the arbitrator's written acceptance. The arbitrator is then required to provide all parties with written notification of the time and place for the hearing, to be delivered by hand or by certified or registered mail.[4]

At the request of either party, the arbitrator must provide a record of the arbitration hearing, prepared by either stenographic means or by tape recording. The cost of preparing the record, including transcription and copying, is considered part of the cost of arbitration.[5]

No later than thirty days after the proceedings have closed, the arbitrator must render the award regarding the withdrawal liability dispute. The award must

1. State the basis for the award, including findings of fact and conclusions of law;

2. Adjust the amount or schedule of withdrawal liability payments to reflect overpayments or underpayments made before the award was rendered, or require the plan sponsor to refund overpayments; and

3. Provide for an allocation of costs.[6]

A party may seek a modification or reconsideration of the award by filing a written motion with the arbitrator and all opposing parties within twenty days after the award has been issued.[7] Such motion will be granted only if

1. There is a numerical error or mistake in the description of any person, thing, or property referred to in the award;

2. The arbitrator made the award based upon a matter not submitted to the arbitrator, and the matter affects the merit of the decision; or

3. The award is imperfect with respect to a matter of form not affecting the merits of the dispute.[8]

---

1. PBGC Reg. §4221.5(b).
2. PBGC Reg. §4221.5(c).
3. PBGC Reg. §4221.6(a).
4. PBGC Reg. §4221.6(b).
5. PBGC Reg. §4221.6(d).
6. PBGC Reg. §§4221.8(a), 4221.8(b).
7. PBGC Reg. §4221.9(a).
8. PBGC Reg. §4221.9(b).

The arbitrator must render an opinion or denial of the request for a rehearing within twenty days after the request has been filed with him. If an objection to the motion for a rehearing has been filed, the arbitrator must respond in writing within thirty days with a denial of the motion for a rehearing, or render a revised award.[1]

672. How are the awards and costs of arbitration handled?

In general, all costs of the hearing are shared equally by the parties, but each party must bear the costs for their own witnesses, and the cost of tapes or transcripts of the proceedings (see Q 671) is borne by the party requesting them. The parties may agree to a different allocation of costs, provided that they enter into such agreement after the employer has been notified of its withdrawal liability.[2]

But the arbitrator may allocate the costs in an unequal fashion if it deems such an award necessary.[3] For example, the arbitrator may award reasonable attorneys' fees where he has determined that one of the parties has acted in bad faith.[4]

673. May a party to an arbitration bring a post-award court action seeking enforcement, modification, or vacation of the award?

Yes. "Upon completion of the arbitration proceedings in favor of one of the parties, any party thereto may bring an action, no later than thirty days after the issuance of an arbitrator's award, in an appropriate United States district court … to enforce, vacate, or modify the arbitrator's award."[5]

In any post-award court action, there is a rebuttable presumption that the findings of fact made by the arbitrator were correct. Such presumptions are rebuttable only by a preponderance of the evidence.[6]

674. Is a withdrawing employer entitled to a refund for the overpayment of withdrawal liability payments?

Yes. If the plan sponsor or an arbitrator determines that an employer has made an overpayment of its withdrawal liability, the plan sponsor must refund the overpayment and pay the employer interest thereon. The rate of interest to be paid is "based on prevailing market rates for comparable obligations, in accordance with regulations," or the rate applied to overdue payments.[7]

If a withdrawal liability overpayment is refunded to the employer within six months, it will not be considered a prohibited transaction (see Q 403).[8]

---

1. PBGC Reg. §4221.9(c).
2. PBGC Reg. §4221.10.
3. PBGC Reg. §4221.10(b).
4. PBGC Reg. §4221.10(c).
5. ERISA Sec. 4221(b)(2).
6. ERISA Sec. 4221(c).
7. ERISA Sec. 4219(c)(6); PBGC Reg. §4219.31(d).
8. ERISA Sec. 403(c)(3).

675. Must a plan sponsor seek PBGC approval of a plan amendment to utilize a nonstatutory, alternative method for computing withdrawal liability? What information must a request for approval of such an amendment contain?

Yes. An amendment to utilize a nonstatutory, alternative method for computing withdrawal liability under ERISA Section 4211(c)(5)(A) must be approved by the PBGC.[1]

The PBGC will disapprove an amendment to a multiemployer plan "only if the ... [PBGC] determines that the amendment creates an unreasonable risk of loss to plan participants and beneficiaries or to the ... [PBGC]."[2] Likewise, an amendment that provides for an alternative allocation method or modification of allocation will be approved if the PBGC finds that the change will not significantly increase the risk of loss to plan participants and beneficiaries or to the PBGC.[3] Specifically, the amendment will be approved if it meets the following criteria:

1. The method allocates a plan's total unfunded vested benefits (UVBs), on both a current and prospective basis, to the same extent as any of the statutory allocations or permitted modifications.

2. The method calculates the amount allocated to an employer either on the basis of that employer's share of total contributions to the plan over a specified period, or on the basis of UVBs attributable to employers.

3. The method provides a procedure for fully allocating among employers that have not withdrawn from the plan (a) amounts of uncollectible employer liability, and (b) amounts not assessed against withdrawn employers because of the *de minimis* rule, the twenty-year cap, and the insolvent employer provision.[4]

A request for approval of an alternative allocation method, or a modification to an existing method, must contain the following information:

1. Name, address, and telephone number of the plan sponsor and the duly authorized representative of the plan sponsor;

2. Name of the multiemployer plan;

3. Plan sponsor's Employer Identification Number (EIN) and the plan number (PN);

4. Date when the amendment was adopted;

5. Copy of the amendment that sets forth the full text of the alternative allocation method (or modification);

---

1. ERISA Sec. 4220(b).
2. ERISA Sec. 4220(c).
3. PBGC Reg. §4211.23(a).
4. PBGC Reg. §4211.23(b).

6.   Allocation method that the fund currently uses and a copy of the plan amendment that adopted the method; and

7.   A certification that notice of the adoption of the amendment has been given to all employers that have an obligation to contribute under the plan and to all employee organizations that represent covered employees.[1]

A request for approval of an alternative allocation method, or a modification to an existing method, should be sent by first-class mail or courier to:[2]

ATTN: MEPD Insurance Programs Department
PBGC
1200 K Street NW, Suite 930
Washington, DC 20005-4026

The PBGC may request additional information from the plan sponsor that it may need in order to conduct an adequate review of the request for approval of an alternative allocation method or modification of an allocation method.[3]

676. What is the 50 percent insolvency rule?

Special rules apply to a withdrawing employer that is insolvent and going through liquidation or dissolution.[4] In such a case, the employer is minimally liable for the first 50 percent of the normal withdrawal liability, see Q 644 and Q 647. After paying 50 percent of this amount, the employer is liable for that portion of the remaining 50 percent of the allocable unfunded vested benefits not in excess of the liquidation or dissolution value of the employer, as determined at the beginning of the liquidation or dissolution.

An employer is "insolvent" for this purpose if its liabilities (including withdrawal liability) exceed its assets.[5] The liquidation or dissolution value of the employer shall be determined without regard to the withdrawal liability under the plan.[6]

In the case of one or more withdrawals of an employer attributable to the same sale, liquidation, or dissolution, all withdrawals shall be treated as a single withdrawal for the purpose of the 50 percent insolvency rule, and the rule will be applied proportionally to all plans from which the employer has withdrawn.[7]

Reorganization (under Chapter 11 of the Bankruptcy Code) will not qualify a plan for the application of the 50 percent insolvency rule. The employer must be undergoing a process of *liquidation* (under Chapter 7 of the Bankruptcy Code) in order to avail itself of the rule.[8]

---

1. PBGC Reg. §4211.22(d).
2. PBGC Reg. §4211.22(c).
3. PBGC Reg. §4211.22(e).
4. ERISA Sec. 4225(b).
5. ERISA Sec. 4225(d)(1).
6. ERISA Sec. 4225(d)(2).
7. ERISA Sec. 4225(e).
8. *Granada Wines, Inc. v. New England Teamsters & Trucking Indus. Pension Fund*, 748 F.2d 42 (1st Cir. 1984); *Trustees of Amalgamated Cotton Garment & Allied Indus. Fund v. Baltimore Sportswear, Inc.*, 632 F. Supp. 641 (S.D.N.Y. 1986).

677. What rules apply to the sale of assets to an unrelated employer?

In the case of a bona fide sale occurring after 2006 of substantially all assets, in an arm's-length transaction to an unrelated party, for an amount not in excess of $5 million, an employer's withdrawal liability will not be greater than

1.   30 percent of the liquidation or dissolution value of the employer, or

2.   The unfunded vested benefits attributable to the employees of the employer.[1]

Where the sale of assets exceeds $5 million, ERISA Section 4225(a)(2) provides the following sliding scale for determining the withdrawal liability of the employer:

If the liquidation/dissolution value after the sale/exchange is:	The portion is:
$5 million to $10 million	$1,500,000 plus 35% of that amount in excess of $5 million
$10 million to $15 million	$3,250,000 plus 40% of that amount in excess of $10 million
$15 million to $17.5 million	$5,520,000 plus 45% of that amount in excess of $15 million
$17.5 million to $20 million	$6,375,000 plus 50% of that amount in excess of $17.5 million
$20 million to $22.5 million	$7,625,000 plus 60% of that amount in excess of $20 million
$22.5 million to $25 million	$9,125,000 plus 70% of the amount in excess of $22.5 million
More than $25 million	$10,875,000 plus 80% of that amount in excess of $25 million

In cases where withdrawal from two or more plans has occurred, the withdrawal liability is apportioned among all of the plans involved.[2]

678. What are the rules applicable to the merger of multiemployer plans?

A merger is defined as the combining of two or more multiemployer plans into a single multiemployer plan.[3] A plan sponsor may not cause a multiemployer plan to merge with one or more multiemployer plans, or engage in a transfer of assets and liabilities to or from another multiemployer plan, unless the following requirements are satisfied:

1.   One of the plan sponsors notifies the PBGC at least 120 days before the effective date of the merger or transfer.

2.   The accrued benefits of participants and beneficiaries will not be decreased as a result of the merger.

3.   The benefits of participants and beneficiaries are not reasonably expected to be suspended under insolvency provisions.

---

1. ERISA Sec. 4225(a).
2. ERISA Sec. 4225(e).
3. PBGC Reg. §4231.2.

4.   An actuarial valuation of each of the affected plans has been performed during the plan year preceding the effective date of the merger or transfer.[1]

The effective date of the merger or transfer is defined, for this purpose, as the earlier of

1.   The date on which one plan assumes liability for the benefits accrued under another plan involved in the transaction, or

2.   The date on which one plan transfers assets to another plan involved in the transaction.[2]

Where a plan assumes obligations for the payment of benefits to a group of participants as a result of a merger or transfer, that plan must preserve the accrued benefits as determined under the vesting requirements of ERISA Section 411.[3]

679. What occurs if there is a withdrawal following a merger?

In the case of a withdrawal following a merger of multiemployer plans, the withdrawal liability rules of ERISA Section 4211 (see Q 645) will be applied in accordance with PBGC regulations, except that if a withdrawal occurs within the first plan year beginning after a merger of multiemployer plans, withdrawal liability is determined as if each of the multiemployer plans had remained separate.[4]

Withdrawal liability is determined using one of the four methods provided in ERISA Section 4211 (see Q 645), a nonstatutory allocation method that has been adopted by the plan and approved by the PBGC (see Q 675), or one of the allocation methods that have been prescribed by the PBGC specifically for use by merged multiemployer plans (see Q 678).[5]

The four allocation methods provided in ERISA Section 4211 and among which merged plans may choose to determine withdrawal liability are the following:

1.   Presumptive method (see Q 648),

2.   Modified presumptive method (see Q 649),

3.   Rolling-5 method (see Q 650), or

4.   Direct attribution method (see Q 651).[6]

A plan must be amended in order to utilize one of these methods; but PBGC approval of the amendment is not required. See Q 647.

680. How is "transfer of assets or liabilities" defined?

"Transfer of assets or liabilities" is defined, for purposes of the merger rules described in Q 678, as a reduction of assets or liabilities for one plan and the acquisition of those assets or

---

1. ERISA Sec. 4231.
2. PBGC Reg. §4231.8(a).
3. PBGC Reg. §4231.4.
4. ERISA Sec. 4211(f).
5. PBGC Reg. §4211.31.
6. PBGC Reg. §4211.31.

assumption of those liabilities by another plan or plans. The shifting of assets or liabilities under a written reciprocity agreement between two multiemployer plans, in which one plan assumes the liabilities of another plan, is not a transfer of assets or liabilities. Likewise, the transfer of assets among multiple funding media (e.g., trusts) of a single plan does not constitute a transfer of assets or liabilities.[1]

681. Is the transfer of assets or liabilities between plans a prohibited transaction?

Generally speaking, no. The merger or transfer of assets or liabilities between multiemployer plans does not constitute a prohibited transaction under ERISA Section 406(a) or ERISA Section 406(b)(2) if the PBGC determines that the merger or transfer has otherwise satisfied the requirements of ERISA Section 4231 (see Q 678).[2]

682. What are the asset transfer rules for multiemployer plans?

A multiemployer plan must adopt asset transfer rules.[3] The rules adopted must not unreasonably restrict the transfer of plan assets in connection with the transfer of plan liabilities. Such rules are to operate and be uniformly applied with respect to each proposed transfer, except that the rules may provide for reasonable variation taking into account the potential financial impact of a proposed transfer on each affected multiemployer plan. Plan rules authorizing asset transfers under the "in and out" rule between multiemployer and single-employer plans (see Q 683) are deemed to satisfy these requirements.[4]

The transfer of assets provision will only apply where there has been a transfer of assets in connection with a voluntary transfer of liabilities. Under *Vornado, Inc. v. Trustees of the Retail Store Employees Union Local 1262*,[5] a multiemployer association fund could not be compelled, under ERISA, to transfer a share of its assets into a new fund established by employers that had withdrawn from the old association fund. The court found that the transfer of assets provision was inapplicable, because there had been no such transfer of liabilities from the old fund to the new fund.

The PBGC has issued regulations providing that *de minimis* transfers of assets are exempt from the general asset transfer rules of ERISA Section 4234(a). A transfer of assets or liabilities is *de minimis* if

1.   The fair market value of the assets transferred is less than 3 percent of the fair market value of the transferor plan's total assets,

2.   The present value of the accrued benefits transferred (whether or not vested) is less than 3 percent of the fair market value of the transferee plan's total assets, and

---

1. PBGC Reg. §4231.2.
2. ERISA Sec. 4231(c).
3. ERISA Sec. 4234(a).
4. ERISA Sec. 4234.
5. 829 F.2d 416 (3d Cir. 1987).

3. The transferee plan is not a plan that has been terminated pursuant to ERISA Section 4041A(a)(2).[1]

In making the determination of whether a transfer is *de minimis*, assets and accrued benefits transferred in previous *de minimis* transfers within the same plan year must be aggregated. A transfer is not *de minimis*, if, when aggregated

1. The value of the assets *transferred from a plan* equals or exceeds 3 percent of the value of the plan's assets, or

2. The present value of all accrued benefits *transferred to a plan* equals or exceeds 3 percent of the plan's assets.[2]

The asset transfer rules do not apply to a transfer of assets that has occurred in accordance with written reciprocity agreements, except to the extent provided in any regulations that may be prescribed by the PBGC.[3]

683. What rules apply to the transfer of assets between multiemployer and single-employer plans?

Where there is a transfer of assets or liabilities, or a merger, between a multiemployer plan and a single-employer plan, the accrued benefit of any participant or beneficiary may not be less immediately after the transfer or merger than it was immediately before.[4] A multiemployer plan that transfers liabilities to a single-employer plan shall be liable to the PBGC if the single-employer plan terminates within sixty months after the transfer. The amount of such liability is the lesser of

1. The amount of the plan asset insufficiency of the terminated single-employer plan, minus 30 percent of the net worth of the employer maintaining the single-employer plan; or

2. The value of the unfunded benefits, as of the effective date of the transfer, which are transferred to the single-employer plan and are guaranteed by the PBGC.[5]

The PBGC must make a determination as to the multiemployer plan's liability within 180 days after the PBGC has received an application from the multiemployer plan seeking such determination. There will be no liability where the PBGC determines that the interests of participants and beneficiaries are adequately protected, or if the PBGC fails to issue a determination within the 180-day time frame.[6]

---

1. PBGC Reg. §4231.7(c).
2. PBGC Reg. §4231.7(e)(2).
3. ERISA Sec. 4234(c).
4. ERISA Sec. 4232(b).
5. ERISA Sec. 4232(c)(1).
6. ERISA Sec. 4232(c)(2).

Under the "in and out" rule, there is an exception to liability where a multiemployer plan merges with, and later "spins off," a single-employer plan. The "in and out" rule eliminates liability to the multiemployer plan because of the transfer of liabilities to a single-employer plan if

1.   The value of the liabilities transferred to the single-employer plan does not exceed the value of the liabilities for benefits that accrued before the merger, and

2.   The value of the assets transferred to the single-employer plan is substantially equal to the value of the assets that would have been in the single-employer plan if the employer had maintained and funded it as a separate plan under which no benefits accrued after the merger.[1]

The PBGC may make equitable arrangements with a multiemployer plan for the satisfaction of the plan's liability.[2]

684. What special asset transfer rules apply to multiemployer welfare benefit plans?

In distinguishing between cases involving welfare benefits and those involving retirement benefits, one court has ruled that a multiemployer welfare benefit fund must transfer assets to a successor fund if those assets were contributed pursuant to a collective bargaining agreement. The transfer must take place after the affected members are no longer covered by the transferring plan.[3]

685. What rules apply to transfers where there has been a change in collective bargaining representatives?

Where an employer completely or partially withdraws from one multiemployer plan (the "old plan") as a result of a certified change of collective bargaining representatives, and the employer's employees who participated in the old plan will, as a result of that change, participate in another multiemployer plan (the "new plan"), the old plan shall transfer assets and liabilities to the new plan.[4]

The following rules must be satisfied in order to execute an appropriate transfer of assets pursuant to a change in the certified bargaining representatives:

1.   The employer must notify the plan sponsor of the old plan of the change in multiemployer plan participation no later than thirty days after the employer determines that the change will occur.

2.   The plan sponsor of the old plan must notify the employer of the amount of its withdrawal liability, the old plan's intent to transfer the nonforfeitable benefits of employees (no longer in covered service under the old plan because of the change of

---

1. ERISA Sec. 4232(c)(3).
2. ERISA Sec. 4232(c)(4).
3. *Trapani v. Consolidated Edison Emps. Mut. Aid Soc'y, Inc.*, 891 F.2d 48 (2d Cir. 1989).
4. ERISA Sec. 4235(a).

bargaining representatives) to the new plan, and the amount of assets and liabilities that are to be transferred to the new plan.

3. The plan sponsor of the old plan must notify the plan sponsor of the new plan of the benefits, assets, and liabilities that will be transferred to the new plan.[1]

Within sixty days of receiving the notice of the benefits, assets, and liabilities to be transferred, the new plan may file an appeal with the PBGC to prevent the transfer. The transfer will not be made if the PBGC determines that the new plan will suffer substantial financial harm as a result of the transfer.[2]

If (1) the employer fails to object to the transfer within sixty days after receiving notice, or (2) the new plan fails to file an appeal, or (3) the PBGC fails to find, within 180 days after the appeal is filed, that the new plan would suffer substantial financial harm as a result of the transfer, then the plan sponsor of the old plan must transfer the appropriate amount of assets and liabilities to the new plan.[3]

In a transfer of assets pursuant to a change in the certified bargaining representatives, only those assets allocated to active participants shall be transferred.[4]

The plan sponsor shall not transfer any assets to the new plan if the old plan is in reorganization, or if the transfer of assets would cause the old plan to go into reorganization.[5] Where a transfer is so prohibited, the old plan may make a limited transfer to the new plan. If the value of such benefits does not exceed the employer's withdrawal liability, the old plan shall transfer nonforfeitable benefits of all employees who have transferred to the new plan. If, on the other hand, the value of such benefits exceeds the withdrawal liability of the employer, only the portion of such nonforfeitable benefits that is equal to the employer's withdrawal liability is to be transferred.[6]

The plan sponsors of the old plan and the new plan may agree to a transfer of assets and liabilities, so long as their agreement complies with the rules for mergers and transfers between multiemployer plans under ERISA Section 4231 and the asset transfer rules of ERISA Section 4234, and provided that the employer's withdrawal liability under the old plan shall be reduced by the amount by which the value of the unfunded vested benefits allocable to the employer that were transferred to the new plan exceeds the value of the assets transferred.[7]

686. What rules apply where an employer withdraws from a plan after a transfer due to a change in bargaining representatives?

If an employer withdraws from the new plan within 240 months after the effective date of a transfer of assets and liabilities due to a change in certified collective bargaining representatives

---

1. ERISA Secs. 4235(b), 4235(c).
2. ERISA Sec. 4235(b)(3).
3. ERISA Secs. 4235(b)(3)(A), 4235(b)(3)(B).
4. PBGC Adv. Op. 88-6.
5. ERISA Sec. 4234(e)(1).
6. ERISA Sec. 4234(e)(2).
7. ERISA Sec. 4235(f).

(see Q 685), the amount of the employer's withdrawal liability to the new plan shall be the greater of

1. The employer's withdrawal liability, as determined under applicable withdrawal liability provisions, or

2. The amount by which the employer's withdrawal liability to the old plan was reduced by (i) the value of the unfunded vested benefits allocable to the employer (transferred by the plan sponsor of the old plan to the new plan), exceeds (ii) the value of the assets transferred, reduced by 5 percent for each twelve-month period following the effective date of the transfer and ending before the date of the withdrawal from the new plan.[1]

687. Do the rules regarding the transfer of assets and liabilities as a result of a change in collective bargaining representatives apply to a transfer to a defined contribution plan?

No. Where there has been a merger between a defined benefit plan and a defined contribution plan, the rules that govern transfers relating to changes in collective bargaining representatives do not apply to the defined contribution plan, because such plans are not subject to Title IV of ERISA's plan termination rules.[2]

688. When will the PBGC order the partitioning of a multiemployer plan?

A plan sponsor may request that the PBGC order the partition of a multiemployer plan.[3]

In the partitioning of a plan, a portion of the plan's assets and liabilities is segregated and held in a separate trust as the new partitioned plan. The plan created by the partition is the successor plan for the purpose of benefit guarantees under ERISA Section 4022A, and is a plan terminated by mass withdrawal under which only the employer involved in the bankruptcy has withdrawal liability.[4]

Prior to ordering a partition of a plan, the PBGC must find that

1. A substantial reduction in the amount of aggregate contributions under the plan has resulted, or will result, from a bankruptcy proceeding filed by an employer;

2. The plan is likely to become insolvent;

3. Contributions will have to be increased significantly in reorganization to meet the minimum contribution requirement and prevent insolvency; and

4. Partition would significantly reduce the likelihood that the plan will become insolvent.[5]

---

1. ERISA Sec. 4235(f)(2).
2. PBGC Adv. Op. 87-13.
3. ERISA Secs. 4233(a) and 4233(b).
4. ERISA Sec. 4233(e).
5. ERISA Secs. 4233(b)(1) through 4233(b)(4).

The PBGC must provide notice to the plan sponsor and the participants and beneficiaries whose vested benefits will be affected by the ordered partitioning of a plan.[1]

The PBGC's partition order shall provide for a transfer of no more than the nonforfeitable benefits directly attributable to service with the employer that has undergone bankruptcy proceedings and an equitable share of the plan's assets.[2]

The PBGC may seek a court decree partitioning the plan in lieu of ordering the partition. The court must make the findings detailed above in items one through four before it can order the partitioning of the plan. The court order will result in the appointment of a trustee for the terminated portion of the plan.[3]

689. Does ERISA require contributions to a multiemployer plan?

Every employer that is obligated to make contributions to a multiemployer plan under the terms of (1) the plan or (2) a collective bargaining agreement must make such contributions in accordance with the terms and conditions of the plan or agreement.[4]

A fiduciary (see Q 215 through Q 250) may bring suit to compel contributions under ERISA Section 502(g)(2). If the court awards judgment in favor of the plan in such a suit, the court must award the plan the following:

1.   Unpaid contributions;

2.   Interest on the unpaid contributions;

3.   The greater of the unpaid contributions or liquidated damages, as provided in the plan document (but not to exceed 20 percent of the unpaid contributions);

4.   Reasonable attorneys' fees and court costs; and

5.   Such other legal or equitable relief as the court deems appropriate.[5]

Interest on unpaid contributions is determined by using the rate set forth in the plan document, or, if no rate is specified therein, the rate under IRC Section 6621.[6]

Financial hardship is not a legal excuse for failure to make contributions; the employer will be excused from its obligation only if (1) the contributions are illegal or (2) the collective bargaining agreement is void.[7]

In a 2003 Field Assistance Bulletin, the DOL advised that in determining when participant contributions can reasonably be segregated from the assets of a contributing employer in a

---

1. ERISA Sec. 4233(c).
2. ERISA Sec. 4233(d).
3. ERISA Sec. 4233(f).
4. ERISA Sec. 515.
5. ERISA Sec. 502(g)(2).
6. ERISA Sec. 502(g)(2)(E).
7. *Onondaga Cnty. Laborers' Health, Welfare, Pension, Annuity, & Training Funds v. Sal Masonry Contractors, Inc.*, 1992 U.S. Dist. LEXIS 4715 (N.D.N.Y. 1992).

multiemployer defined contribution plan, the time frames established in collective bargaining, employer participation, and similar agreements must be taken into account, provided that the time frames comply with the maximum period mandated under Labor Regulation Section 2510.3-102(b).[1]

690. How are claims for contributions and withdrawal liability handled in bankruptcy?

The Bankruptcy Code gives priority to the expenses and claims for contributions to an employee benefit plan arising from services rendered within 180 days before (1) the date of the filing of the petition or (2) the date of the cessation of the debtor's business, whichever occurs first.[2] But priority is given only to the extent of

1. The number of employees covered by each plan, multiplied by $4,300,

2. Minus

    a. the aggregate amount paid to such employees as pre-petition wages,[3] and

    b. the aggregate amount paid by the bankruptcy estate on behalf of such employees to any other employee benefit plan.[4]

In a case that extended the rules of 11 U.S.C. §507(a)(4) to non-collectively bargained plans, the court held that the insurer was entitled to receive directly the priority payment of employee group life, health, and disability insurance premiums as "unsecured claims for contributions to employee benefit plans." The court observed that it was simpler to grant the priority directly to the insurer, rather than to require employees to seek the premium amount and then pay it over to the insurer, and noted that the employees were protected because 11 U.S.C. §507(a)(4) expressly subordinates the plan contribution priority to the employees' wage priority.[5]

In the case of a reorganization (Chapter 11 bankruptcy), administrative expenses, including the cost of carrying on the debtor's business after the bankruptcy filing, are given the first priority.[6] A claim for withdrawal liability is not an administrative expense, because the debtor's withdrawal liability to a multiemployer plan is deemed to have accrued prior to the filing of the bankruptcy petition, even if the actual withdrawal occurs after the filing. Thus, withdrawal liability has the status of a general unsecured claim.[7]

691. What happens if an employer that has previously withdrawn from a multiemployer plan reenters the plan?

An employer that has completely withdrawn from a multiemployer plan, and subsequently reenters the plan, may have its withdrawal liability "abated" if certain requirements are met.[8]

---

1. Field Assistance Bull. 2003-2 (May 7, 2003).
2. 11 U.S.C. §507(a)(4)(A).
3. Under 11 U.S.C. §507(a)(3).
4. 11 U.S.C. §507(a)(4)(B).
5. *In re Saco Local Dev. Corp.*, 711 F.2d 441 (1st Cir. 1983).
6. 11 U.S.C. §507(a)(1).
7. *Amalgamated Ins. Fund v. William B. Kessler, Inc.*, 55 B.R. 735 (S.D.N.Y. 1985).
8. PBGC Reg. §4207.5(a).

A reentering employer must formally apply for abatement by the due date of the first withdrawal liability payment following the date when the employer resumes covered operations, or, if later, the fiftieth day after the employer resumes covered operations.[1] This application must contain the following information:

1.   Identity of the withdrawing employer;

2.   Date when the employer withdrew;

3.   Identity of the reentering employer (if different from the withdrawing employer), and all entities under common control with the employer, as of both the date of the withdrawal and the date when covered operations resumed;

4.   A list of the operations for which the employer is obligated to make contributions to the plan; and

5.   Date when the employer resumed covered operations.[2]

While the abatement determination is pending, an employer may be relieved from its obligation to make withdrawal liability payments if it (1) posts a bond, or (2) establishes an escrow account, in an amount equal to 70 percent of the withdrawal liability payment that the employer would have otherwise been required to make.[3]

The plan sponsor determines whether a reentering employer has met the following requirements of abatement:

1.   Resumption of covered operations under the plan; and

2.   Assumption of a post-entry level of contribution base units (see Q 645) that exceeds 30 percent of the employer's pre-withdrawal amount.[4]

If the plan sponsor determines that a reentering employer is eligible for abatement, then the employer no longer has an obligation to make payments on its withdrawal liability, and the employer's liability for any subsequent withdrawal will be calculated under modified rules under Labor Regulation Section 4207.7 or 4207.8, as applicable.[5] Under these circumstances, the employer's bond will be canceled, or amounts held in escrow will be returned to the employer.[6] Finally, any withdrawal liability payments that the employer made after reentry will be refunded by the multiemployer plan.[7]

If the plan sponsor determines that a reentering employer is not eligible for abatement, then the plan sponsor must so notify the employer. Within thirty days of the date of the plan sponsor's notice, the bond posted by the employer, or the escrow accounts established by

---

1. PBGC Reg. §4207.5(a).
2. ERISA Sec. 4207; PBGC Reg. §4207.3(a).
3. PBGC Reg. §4207.4.
4. PBGC Reg. §4207.5(a).
5. PBGC Reg. §4207.3(c).
6. PBGC Reg. §4207.3(c)(3).
7. PBGC Reg. §4207.4(c)(4).

the employer, must be paid over to the multiemployer plan, and the employer must also pay the balance of the withdrawal liability that was not satisfied by the bond or escrow account.[1] Thereafter, the employer must resume its schedule for making withdrawal liability payments.[2] The employer will be treated as a new employer for purposes of any future application rules.[3]

692. Who has standing to bring a civil action regarding a multiemployer plan?

A plan fiduciary, employer, plan participant, or beneficiary who is adversely affected by the act or omission of any party under the multiemployer plan provisions of ERISA with respect to a multiemployer plan, or an employee organization that represents such a plan participant or beneficiary for purposes of collective bargaining, has standing to bring a civil action. Such a suit may seek appropriate legal or equitable relief, or both.[4]

ERISA does not authorize any civil actions against the PBGC, the Secretary of Labor, or the Secretary of the Treasury.[5]

693. What is the statute of limitations for civil actions regarding multiemployer plans?

A civil action may not be brought after the later of

1. Six years after the date on which the cause of action arose, or

2. Three years after the earliest date on which the plaintiff acquired, or should have acquired, actual knowledge of the existence of such cause of action, except that, in the case of fraud or concealment, such action may be brought not later than six years after the date of discovery of the existence of such cause of action.[6]

---

1. PBGC Regs. §§4207.3(d)(1), 4207.3(d)(2).
2. PBGC Reg. §4207.3(d)(3).
3. PBGC Reg. §4207.3(d)(4).
4. ERISA Sec. 4301(a)(1).
5. ERISA Sec. 4301(a)(2).
6. ERISA Sec. 4301(f).

SECTION XI

Multiple Employer Benefit Arrangements

694. What are the issues regarding Multiple Employer Welfare Benefit Arrangements (MEWAs)?

Multiple Employer Welfare Benefit Arrangements (MEWAs), also known as multiple employer trusts, have been used for years to market health and welfare benefits to employers for their employees. MEWAs are established by two or more employers for the purpose of pooling resources in a cost-saving manner to provide benefits to their employees. Often, a MEWA is established by a third party, who will then market it to small employers as an attractive low-cost alternative source of health insurance. Typical clients of MEWAs are small employers, who would otherwise have difficulty in obtaining health and welfare benefits coverage for their employees from a traditional insurer. The economies of scale presented by a MEWA allow for the spreading of risk and the resulting decrease in the cost of coverage.

Because MEWAs specifically offer insurance coverage for participants, state insurance regulators have attempted to regulate them, in an effort to eliminate the potential for fraud and abuse that unscrupulous promoters of MEWAs could unleash upon unwitting employers. Many MEWA promoters have represented to employers that MEWAs are employee benefit arrangements subject to the jurisdiction of ERISA and are, therefore, exempt from state insurance regulations under ERISA's preemption provisions. In the past, a number of MEWAs have been unable to pay claims as a result of insufficient funding or inadequate reserves. A few of the more notorious situations of MEWA failures involved individuals who drained the assets out of the MEWA through excessive administration fees and embezzlement.

State regulators who attempted to prevent this type of abuse through administrative and judicial actions were often thwarted by claims that, because the MEWA at issue paid for the type of benefits traditionally covered by an ERISA plan out of a tax-exempt trust (just like an ERISA plan), the MEWA was subject to ERISA preemption. Some plans even filed ERISA-required documents to enhance the appearance of being an ERISA-covered plan. In 1983, Congress amended ERISA, in order to provide relief from the preemption provisions often applied to the regulation of MEWAs for state insurance regulators seeking to establish, apply, and enforce state insurance laws.

In 1998, Sherwin Kaplan, Deputy Associate Solicitor for the DOL's Plan Benefits Security Division, stated that fraudulent MEWAs were one of the top enforcement issues for the DOL. Kaplan spoke at a meeting of a proposed rulemaking committee developed by the DOL for the purpose of developing rules expected to provide guidance in determining when a MEWA had been developed under a collective bargaining agreement. Unscrupulous MEWA operators often attempt to evade state regulation by claiming to have been established under collective bargaining agreements, thereby making them subject to ERISA and exempt from state regulation. Kaplan said that the DOL was conducting 200 to 300 investigations of fraudulent MEWAs.

Unfortunately, there is still a great deal of confusion regarding the enforcement of state and federal laws against MEWAs. The following questions have been designed to help provide a better understanding of MEWAs, how they operate, and how they are subject to the coverage and enforcement provisions of ERISA.

695. What is a Multiple Employer Welfare Arrangement (MEWA)?

The term "multiple employer welfare arrangement" means an employee welfare benefit plan or other arrangement that is established or maintained for the purpose of offering or providing welfare benefit plans to the employees (or their beneficiaries) of two or more employers (including self-employed individuals), except that the term does not include any plan or arrangement that is established or maintained: (1) by one or more collective bargaining agreements; (2) by a rural electric cooperative; or (3) by a rural telephone cooperative association.[1]

The definition of a MEWA includes employee welfare benefit plans and other arrangements that provide coverage for medical, surgical, hospital care, or benefits in the event of sickness, accident, disability, or any other benefit described in ERISA Section 3(1) (see Q 2).

696. When does an arrangement offer or provide benefits to the employees of two or more employers?

If a plan is maintained by a single employer for the exclusive purpose of providing benefits to that employer's employees, former employees (e.g., retirees), or beneficiaries (e.g., spouses, former spouses, dependents) of such employees, the plan will be considered a single-employer plan and not a MEWA within the meaning of ERISA Section 3(40). For purposes of ERISA Section 3(40), certain groups of employers that have common ownership interests are treated as a single employer. In this regard, ERISA Section 3(40)(B)(i) provides that:

> two or more trades or businesses, whether or not incorporated, shall be deemed a single employer if such trades or businesses are within the same control group.

In determining whether trades or businesses are within the "same control group," ERISA Section 3(40)(B)(ii) provides that the term "control group" means a group of trades or businesses under "common control." Pursuant to ERISA Section 3(40)(B)(iii), whether a trade or business is under "common control" is to be determined under regulations issued by the Secretary applying principles similar to those applied in determining whether there is "common control" under ERISA Section 4001(b), except that common control shall not be based on an interest of less than 25 percent. Accordingly, trades or businesses with less than a 25 percent ownership interest will not be considered under "common control" and, therefore, will not be viewed as a single employer for purposes of determining whether their plan provides benefits to the employees of two or more employers under ERISA Section 3(40).

With regard to situations where there is a 25 percent or more ownership interest, it should be noted that the Department of Labor has not adopted regulations under ERISA Section 3(40)(B)(iii). However, regulations issued under ERISA Section 4001(b) and IRC Section 414(c)[2]

---

1. ERISA Sec. 3(40).
2. See Labor Reg. §4001.3 and Treas. Reg. §1.414(c)-2, respectively.

provide that "common control" generally means, in the case of a parent-subsidiary group of trades or businesses, an 80 percent ownership interest, or, in the case of organizations controlled by five or fewer persons, which are the same persons with respect to each organization, at least a 50 percent ownership interest by such persons in each organization.

The DOL has issued guidance in determining what constitutes a "bona fide" employer group or association for adopting a MEWA. Under DOL Advisory Opinion 2003-17A,[1] a group of employers is a "bona fide" group or association if, under the facts and circumstances, the employers meet two tests:

1. They have a commonality of interest; and

2. They exercise control over the plan, both in form and in substance.

The facts underlying Advisory Opinion 2003-17A led the DOL to determine that the employers had a commonality of interest because they were all Department of Energy contractors engaged in interconnecting operations at the same site. This group of contractors had a history of organized cooperation on workplace-related matters. Further, the employers, through the MEWA's board of trustees, exhibited control and directed the MEWA. In form, the participating employers constituted a bona fide group or association for the purpose of adopting a MEWA that was a single ERISA welfare plan.

697. Is a welfare benefit arrangement maintained by a group or association of unrelated employers considered to be provided by two or more employers?

Yes. The term "employer" is defined as "any person acting directly as an employer, or indirectly in the interest of an employer, in relation to an employee benefit plan; and includes a group or association of employers acting for an employer in such capacity."[2]

In order for a group or association to constitute an "employer" within the meaning of ERISA Section 3(5), there must be a bona fide group or association of employers acting in the interest of its employer members to provide benefits for their employees. However, unlike the specified treatment of a controlled group of employers as a single employer, there is no indication in ERISA Section 3(40), or the legislative history accompanying the MEWA provisions, that Congress intended that such groups or associations be treated as "single employers" for purposes of determining the status of arrangements such as MEWAs.

The Department of Labor has said that while a bona fide group or association of employers may constitute an "employer" within the meaning of ERISA Section 3(5), the individuals typically covered by the group- or association-sponsored plan are not employed by the group or association, and, therefore, are not employees of the group or association. The covered participants are actually employees of the employer members of the group or association. Accordingly, to the extent that a plan sponsored by a group or association of employers provides benefits to the

---

1. DOL Adv. Op. 2003-17A (Dec. 12, 2003).
2. ERISA Sec. 3(5).

employees of two or more employer members (which are not a part of a controlled group), the plan would constitute a MEWA within the meaning of ERISA Section 3(40).[1]

Further, clarification on this particular issue is found under DOL Advisory Opinion 2003-17A, which addresses whether ERISA applies at the MEWA level (so that one ERISA plan exists) or at the employer level (so that each separate employer participating in the MEWA is treated as having its own ERISA plan).[2]

The MEWA at issue was established for the benefit of multiple contractors working at a Department of Energy (DOE) site. The contractors had a common labor force. In fact, many of the individuals at the site had been employed by more than one contractor. The DOE contracts with the contractors mandated the provision of similar benefits to employees to be implemented in an integrated fashion. Only contractors working at the site could participate in the MEWA. The participating contractors appointed a board of trustees to oversee and manage the operation of the MEWA. The MEWA requested this advisory opinion to determine whether it was a single-employer welfare benefit plan.

As seen above, ERISA's definition of "employer" includes "a group or association of employers acting for an employer." Under the DOL's analysis, a group of employers is a "bona fide" group or association if, under the facts and circumstances, the employers meet two tests:

1.   They have a commonality of interest; and

2.   They exercise control over the plan, both in form and in substance.

In the advisory opinion, the DOL determined that the employers had a commonality of interest because they were all DOE contractors engaged in interconnecting operations at the same site with a history of organized cooperation on workplace-related matters. In addition, the employers, through the MEWA's board of trustees, appeared to control and direct the MEWA. Consequently, the participating employers constituted a bona fide group or association and the MEWA was a single ERISA welfare plan.

698. Are welfare benefit plans established by employee leasing organizations considered to be provided by "two or more employers"?

Employee leasing organizations often must wrestle with the question of who is the employer of the employees involved in its leasing arrangements. Are the employees considered to be employees of the leasing organization, or of the client employer who is actually receiving the services of these employees? If all of the employees participating in the leasing organization's welfare benefit plan are determined to be employees of the leasing organization, the plan would constitute a "single employer" plan and would not be considered a MEWA. If the employees participating in the welfare benefit plan are considered to be employees of two or more recipient employers, or employees of the leasing organization and at least one recipient employer, the

---

1. DOL Adv. Op. 92-05A.
2. DOL Adv. Op. 2003-17A (Dec. 12, 2003).

welfare benefit arrangement would be considered a MEWA, because it would provide benefits to the employees of two or more organizations.[1]

The term "employee" is defined as "any individual employed by an employer."[2] The Department of Labor takes the position that an individual is employed by an employer when an employee-employer relationship exists. Like a bona fide group or association of employers, an employee leasing organization may be an employer to the extent it is acting directly or indirectly in the interests of an employer. See Q 697. Employer status does not by itself mean that the individuals covered by the leasing organization welfare benefit plan are "employees" of the leasing organization. There must be an employee-employer relationship. In determining the existence of an employee-employer relationship, the payment of wages, the payment of federal, state, and local employment taxes, and the provision of health or pension benefits are not solely determinative of an employee-employer relationship. Rather, the application of established common-law principles, "taking into account the remedial purposes of ERISA," is used to determine the existence of an employee-employer relationship. A contract purporting to create an employee-employer relationship will not be determinative where the facts and circumstances establish that the relationship, in fact, does not exist.[3] For more on the employee-employer relationship, see Q 699.

699. How is employee status determined when considering employers under a Multiple Employer Welfare Arrangement (MEWA)?

The term "employee" is defined to mean "any individual employed by an employer."[4] The Department of Labor takes the position that an individual is employed by an employer when an employee-employer relationship exists. In most instances, the existence of an employee-employer relationship is easy to determine. In general, the existence of an employee-employer relationship is determined on the basis of the facts and circumstances of the particular situation. Common law principles are applied in addition to facts and circumstances, such as the payment of wages, the payment of federal, state, and local employment taxes, and the provision of health or retirement benefits. The common law principles to be applied include, among other things, "whether the person for whom services are being performed has the right to control and direct the individual who performs the services, not only as to the result to be accomplished by the work, but also as to the details and means by which the result is to be accomplished; whether the person for whom services are being performed has the right to discharge the individual performing the services; and whether the individual performing the services is, as a matter of economic reality, dependent upon the business to which he or she renders services...."[5]

In reviewing whether a welfare benefit plan is sponsored by a single employer or two or more employers, the above process for determining employee status must be applied in establishing whether or not the subject plan is sponsored by a person, group, or association that constitutes

---

1. DOL Adv. Op. 92-05A.
2. ERISA Sec. 3(6).
3. DOL Adv. Op. 92-05A.
4. ERISA Sec. 3(6).
5. DOL Adv. Op. 92-05A.

a single employer, or if the plan benefits the employees of two or more employers. If the plan benefits the employees of two or more employers, it is a MEWA.

Certain individuals are not considered "employees" for purposes of ERISA. An individual and his spouse are not "employees" with respect to a trade or business that is wholly owned by the individual or the individual and his spouse. Further, a partner in a partnership and his spouse are not "employees" with respect to the partnership.[1]

700. Is it mandatory that a plan be established by an employer in order for it to be considered a MEWA?

An advisory opinion held that a welfare benefit arrangement that was established by an association to provide health benefits to its members, who were full-time ministers, and other full-time employees of certain schools and churches, was a MEWA, even though there was no employer involvement in the development, adoption, and administration of the plan. The definition of a MEWA refers to an arrangement that offers to provide benefits to the employees of two or more employers; it is not limited to arrangements established or maintained by employers. MEWA status is not affected by the absence of a connection between the plan and the employers of the employees who are covered by the plan.[2]

701. Which welfare benefit arrangements are excluded from the definition of a MEWA?

There are three types of welfare benefit arrangements that are specifically excluded from the definition of a "multiple employer welfare arrangement," even though such arrangements may provide benefits to the employees of two or more employers. The three types of arrangements are plans established and maintained: (1) pursuant to collective bargaining agreements; (2) by rural electric cooperatives; and (3) by rural telephone cooperative associations.[3]

Plans Maintained Pursuant to Collective Bargaining Agreements

Any plan or arrangement that is established and maintained "pursuant to one or more agreements which the Secretary [of Labor] finds to be collective bargaining agreements" is excluded from the definition of a MEWA.[4] This includes those arrangements commonly referred to as "multiemployer plans" (not to be confused with the term "multiple employer welfare arrangement"). See Section X for a discussion of multiemployer plans.

Multiemployer plans are established pursuant to collective bargaining agreements that are negotiated by representatives of unions and employers or an association of employers. Collective bargaining agreements must be negotiated "in good faith" and in accordance with other provisions of the Labor Management Relations Act.[5] Contributions to a plan established by a collective bargaining agreement are held in a trust that is administered jointly by trustees

---

1. Labor Reg. §2510.3-3(c).
2. DOL Adv. Op. 88-5A.
3. ERISA Sec. 3(40)(A).
4. ERISA Sec. 3(40)(A)(i).
5. 29 U.S.C. §§151 et seq.

appointed from both the union (labor trustees) and the participating employers or association of employers (management trustees).

A collective bargaining agreement is a contract that, as mentioned above, is arrived at through the process of good-faith bargaining between bona fide employee representatives (usually selected through a vote of rank-and-file union members) and one or more employers (where the union has been certified as the bona fide representative of the employees by the National Labor Relations Board, or has been elected by a majority of employees of the signatory employers as the exclusive bargaining representative of the employees). In deciding whether or not a collective bargaining agreement was reached through the process of good-faith bargaining, the Department of Labor (DOL) will examine the relevant facts and circumstances (such as the provisions for wages, benefits, working conditions, and grievance resolution), taking into consideration the pertinent provisions of the National Labor Relations Act.

The DOL issued two regulations to assist in the determination of collective bargaining status for welfare benefit plans.[1] Under the first rule, the following criteria must be satisfied in any applicable plan year in order for there to a collective bargaining agreement:

1. The plan satisfies the criteria of an employee welfare benefit plan as required under ERISA Section 3(1);

2. At least 85 percent of the participants in the plan include those who are: (a) actively employed under the collective bargaining agreement, (b) retirees who participated in the plan at least five of the ten years preceding their retirement, or are receiving pension benefits under a plan maintained pursuant to the same bargaining agreement and have at least five years of service under the pension plan, or (c) receiving extended coverage under the plan through COBRA or another applicable statute, or court or administrative agency decision; and

3. The plan is incorporated or referenced in a written agreement between one or more employers and one or more employee organizations, and the agreement: (a) is the product of a bona fide collective bargaining agreement; (b) identifies employers and employee organizations bound by the agreement; (c) identifies the personnel, job classifications, and/or work jurisdiction covered by the agreement; (d) provides terms and conditions of employment in addition to coverage under, or contributions to, the plan; and (e) is not unilaterally terminable or automatically terminated solely for nonpayment of benefits or contributions.[2]

The second rule establishes procedures for hearings for entities seeking individual determinations of collective bargaining status. Where the jurisdiction or law of a state has been asserted against a plan, the plan may petition the Secretary of Labor for a hearing, before an administrative law judge, to determine whether, under ERISA Section 3(40), it is established and/or

---

1. 68 Fed. Reg. 17,472 and 17,484 (Apr. 9, 2003).
2. Labor Reg. §2510.3-40(b).

maintained pursuant to a collective bargaining agreement and thereby exempt from the state law or jurisdiction being applied.[1]

For purposes of a final decision as to collective bargaining status, the plan has the burden of proof in establishing satisfaction of the requisite elements of a collectively bargained plan (see above).[2] However, in the discussion of these rules, the DOL notes that the plan would meet its burden of proof going forward when it makes a prima facie showing that it satisfies the criteria spelled out above.[3]

Rural Electric Cooperatives

Any plan or arrangement established or maintained by a "rural electric cooperative" is excluded from the definition of a MEWA.[4] A rural electric cooperative is (1) an organization exempt from tax under IRC Section 501(a) and engaged primarily in providing electric service on a mutual or cooperative basis; and (2) an organization described in IRC Section 501(c)(4) or IRC Section 501(c)(6), exempt from tax under IRC Section 501(a), and at least 80 percent of the members are organizations described in (1) above.[5]

Rural Telephone Cooperative Associations

Any plan or other arrangement established or maintained by a "rural telephone cooperative association" is excluded from the definition of a MEWA.[6] A rural telephone cooperative association is an organization, described in IRC Section 501(c)(4) or IRC Section 501(c)(6), that is exempt from tax under IRC Section 501(a) and at least 80 percent of the members of which are organizations engaged primarily in providing telephone service to rural areas of the United States on a mutual, cooperative, or other basis.[7]

702. To what extent may states regulate MEWAs covered by ERISA?

States are generally precluded from treating an ERISA-covered plan as an insurance company for purposes of state insurance laws.[8] However, there is an exception to the restriction on treating an ERISA-covered plan as an insurance company with respect to any employee welfare benefit plan that satisfies the statutory definition of a MEWA.[9]

The extent to which state insurance laws may be applied to a MEWA that is an ERISA-covered plan depends upon whether or not the plan is fully insured. An employee welfare benefit plan that is a multiple-employer welfare arrangement and is fully insured (or is a multiple-employer welfare arrangement subject to certain exemptions) may be subject to state laws regulating insurance to the extent that a state law provides (1) standards requiring the maintenance of

---

1. Labor Reg. §2570.151.
2. Labor Reg. §2570.137.
3. 68 Fed. Reg. 17,472 and 17,484 (Apr. 9, 2003).
4. ERISA Sec. 3(40)(A)(ii).
5. ERISA Sec. 3(40)(B)(iv).
6. ERISA Sec. 3(40)(A)(iii).
7. ERISA Sec. 3(40)(B)(v).
8. ERISA Sec. 514(b)(2)(B).
9. ERISA Sec. 514(b)(6)(A).

specified levels of reserves and specified levels of contributions, which any plan, or any trust established under such a plan must meet in order to be considered, under the state law, able to pay benefits in full when due; and (2) provisions to enforce these standards.[1]

The Department of Labor (DOL) has said that nothing in ERISA Section 514(b)(6)(A) limits the application of state insurance laws to only those laws that specifically reference the terms "MEWA" or "multiple employer welfare arrangement."[2]

States may apply and enforce any state insurance law requiring the maintenance of specific reserves or contributions that have been established to ensure that a fully insured MEWA will be able to satisfy its benefit obligations in a timely manner. ERISA Section 514(b)(6)(A)(i) also permits states to subject MEWAs to licensing, registration, certification, financial reporting, examination, audit, and other requirements of state insurance law necessary to ensure compliance with insurance reserve, contribution, and funding requirements. The DOL has stated that "it would be contrary to Congressional intent to conclude that states, while having the authority to apply insurance laws to such plans, do not have the authority to require and enforce ... requirements necessary to establish and monitor compliance with those laws."[3]

State insurance laws may require ERISA-covered MEWAs to meet more stringent standards of conduct, or to provide more protections to plan participants and beneficiaries than required by ERISA.[4]

The DOL has stated that MEWAs rarely qualify as ERISA plans in their own right. When this is the case, the MEWA will be subject to state insurance regulation. This position was clarified under an advisory opinion that concerned the adoption by the state of Washington of a law that would impose premium taxes and high-risk pool assessments on self-funded MEWAs, to the extent that the taxes and assessments would not be preempted by ERISA.[5] The state of Washington asked the DOL to weigh in on whether such premium taxes and high-risk pool assessments were preempted by ERISA.

The DOL opined that the Washington laws, as drafted, regulate insurance under the Supreme Court's two-part test from *Kentucky Ass'n of Health Plans v. Miller*.[6] The proposed Washington laws regulate insurance because self-funded MEWAs engage in the same sort of risk pooling as insurers, consistent with the holding in *Kentucky Ass'n of Health Plans*. The DOL also stated that the state laws were not inconsistent, or in conflict, with ERISA because they did not deny any protection available under ERISA. Finally, the DOL ruled that the imposition of the taxes and assessments would not be inconsistent with ERISA's exclusive purpose requirement. In citing *Atlantic Healthcare Benefits Trust v. Googins*,[7] the DOL ruled that such regulatory fees are legitimate plan administration expenses.[8]

---

1. ERISA Sec. 514(b)(6)(A)(i).
2. DOL Adv. Op. 90-18A.
3. DOL Adv. Op. 90-18A.
4. DOL Adv. Op. 90-18A.
5. DOL Adv. Op. 90-18A.
6. 538 U.S. 329 (2003).
7. F.3d 1, 6 (2d Cir. 1993), cert. denied, 510 U.S. 1043 (1994).
8. OL Adv. Op. 2005-18A (Aug. 1, 2005), http://www.dol.gov/ebsa/regs/aos/ao2005-18a.html.

Conversely, ERISA preempts any applicable state insurance law that would "adversely affect a participant's or beneficiary's rights under Title I of ERISA" to review or receive documents, receive continuation of health coverage, or pursue claims procedures established under ERISA. Further, ERISA preempts any state insurance law that makes compliance a physical impossibility.[1]

Welfare benefit plans that have been established pursuant to a collective bargaining agreement are also exempt from state laws governing MEWAs. In April 2003, the DOL issued two regulations designed to assist the DOL and states in determining whether a welfare benefit arrangement is established or maintained pursuant to a collective bargaining agreement and, therefore, exempt from state regulation. See Q 701 for details on these rules.

The DOL has stated that whether an arrangement is a MEWA under ERISA Section 3(40) is a question of federal law. Therefore, a state statute providing that an employee leasing company shall be deemed to be the employer of its leased employees for the purposes of sponsoring and maintaining any benefit plans, including for the purposes of ERISA, would not govern the determination of whether any particular benefit arrangement sponsored by the employee leasing company is a MEWA for purposes of ERISA.[2]

703. What is a fully insured MEWA?

A multiple employer welfare arrangement is considered fully insured only if the terms of the arrangement provide for benefits and the Department of Labor (DOL) determines that these benefits are guaranteed under a contract or policy of insurance, issued by an insurance company, insurance service, or insurance organization qualified to conduct business in a state.[3]

Under ERISA Section 514(b)(6), it is not mandatory for the DOL to make a determination as to whether a MEWA is fully insured in order for a particular state to treat a MEWA as fully insured and apply its state insurance laws.

The DOL advises that under ERISA Section 514(b)(6)(D), a MEWA is considered fully insured only if the terms of the arrangement provide for benefits guaranteed under a contract, or policy of insurance, issued by an insurance company, insurance service, or insurance organization, qualified to conduct business in a state. This requirement does not refer merely to a financial guaranty running to the plan, but rather requires the insurance company to unconditionally guarantee to pay all benefits due under the plan, and each participant must have a right to those guaranteed benefits that is legally enforceable directly against the insurance company or organization. Where such guaranty does not exist, the MEWA would be subject to state insurance regulation subject to the limitation in ERISA that the state law is "not inconsistent" with Title I of ERISA.[4]

---

1. DOL Adv. Op. 90-18A.
2. ERISA Op Letter 2007-05A (2007).
3. ERISA Sec. 514(b)(6)(D).
4. ERISA Op. Letter 2007-06A (2007).

704. Which state insurance laws may be enforced against a MEWA that is not fully insured?

If a MEWA is not fully insured, the only limitation on the applicability of state insurance laws to the MEWA is that the state law may not conflict with ERISA.[1]

The Department of Labor will consider a state insurance law to be in conflict with ERISA if compliance with the law: (1) would abolish or abridge an affirmative protection or safeguard available to participants and beneficiaries under ERISA (such as a state law that would impede a participant's or beneficiary's right to obtain required disclosure documents under the plan, limit a right to pursue claims procedures described in ERISA, or restrict the right to obtain continuation health coverage under COBRA); or (2) would conflict with any provision of ERISA making compliance with ERISA impossible (such as a state law requiring an ERISA-covered plan to make an imprudent investment).[2]

A state insurance law generally will not be considered in conflict with ERISA if it requires ERISA-covered MEWA plans to meet more stringent standards of conduct or to provide greater protection to plan participants and beneficiaries than required by ERISA. State laws that require a license or certificate of authority to transact insurance business or that subject persons who fail to comply with these requirements to taxation, fines, and other civil penalties are not, when considered by themselves, in conflict with ERISA.[3]

705. Under what circumstances is a state insurance law "inconsistent" with ERISA?

In general, a state law is inconsistent with ERISA if compliance with the state law would abolish or abridge an affirmative protection or a safeguard available to plan participants and beneficiaries under ERISA.[4] A state law is also inconsistent with ERISA if it conflicts with any provision of ERISA, making compliance with ERISA impossible. For example, a state insurance law that adversely affects a participant's or beneficiary's right to request or receive documents described in ERISA, or to pursue claims procedures established in accordance with ERISA Section 503, or to obtain and maintain continuation health coverage in accordance with ERISA would be viewed as inconsistent with ERISA. Similarly, a state insurance law that requires an ERISA-covered plan to make imprudent investments would be inconsistent with ERISA.

On the other hand, a state insurance law generally will not be considered inconsistent with ERISA if it requires MEWAs to meet more stringent standards of conduct, or to provide more or greater protection to plan participants and beneficiaries than required by ERISA.[5] The Labor Department has expressed the view that a state insurance law that sets standards requiring the maintenance of specified levels of reserves and specified levels of contributions

---

1. ERISA Sec. 514(b)(6)(A).
2. DOL Adv. Op. 90-18A.
3. DOL Adv. Op. 90-18A.
4. DOL Adv. Op. 90-18A.
5. DOL Adv. Op. 90-18A.

in order for a MEWA to be considered, under such law, able to pay benefits will generally not be inconsistent with the provisions of ERISA for purposes of ERISA Section 514(b)(6)(A) (ii).[1] The Labor Department has also expressed the view that a state insurance law requiring a license or certificate of authority as a condition precedent or otherwise to transacting insurance business or that subjects persons who fail to comply with such requirements to taxation, fines, and other civil penalties, including injunctive relief, would not in and of itself be inconsistent with ERISA.[2]

706. Has the Department of Labor granted any exemptions from state regulation for MEWAs that are not fully insured?

Pursuant to ERISA Section 514(b)(6)(B), the Department of Labor (DOL) may, under regulations, exempt from ERISA Section 514(b)(6)(A)(ii) MEWAs that are not fully insured. Such exemptions may be granted on an individual or class basis. However, this authority does not extend to the requirements of ERISA Section 514(b)(6)(A)(i) relating to the maintenance of specified levels of reserves and specified levels of contributions under state insurance laws.

The DOL has neither prescribed regulations for such exemptions nor granted any such exemptions since the enactment of the MEWA provisions in 1983.

707. To what extent will the DOL enforce ERISA-governed activities of a MEWA that is not an employee welfare benefit plan?

Persons who exercise discretionary authority or control over the management of ERISA-covered plans or the assets of such plans are considered fiduciaries and are subject to ERISA's fiduciary responsibility provisions.[3] When the sponsor of an ERISA-covered plan purchases health care coverage from a MEWA for its employees and its employee's dependents, the assets of the MEWA are considered to include "plan assets," unless the MEWA is a state-licensed insurance company.[4] In exercising discretionary authority or control over plan assets (e.g., the payment of administration fees or making benefit claim determinations), the individuals operating the MEWA are considered to be conducting fiduciary acts that are subject to ERISA's fiduciary provisions. When a fiduciary breaches a statutorily mandated duty under ERISA (see Q 288 and Q 397), or when an individual knowingly participates in such breach, the Department of Labor (DOL) may investigate and, if such violation is proven, pursue civil sanctions.

The DOL does not have any direct regulatory authority over the insurance business and, as such, ERISA does not cover the typical MEWA as a welfare benefit plan. Because of this, the DOL, through its Pension and Welfare Benefits Administration, focuses its MEWA investigations solely on whether individuals operating MEWAs have breached their fiduciary duties to employee plans that purchase health coverage from a MEWA.

---

1. DOL Adv. Op. 90-18A.
2. DOL Adv. Op. 90-18A.
3. ERISA Sec. 3(21)(A).
4. Labor Regs. §§2510.3-101, 2510.3-102.

Because of the complex nature of MEWAs, investigations of alleged fiduciary breaches typically require a detailed review of financial records and transactions, as well as a detailed review of the documents relating to the establishment and operation of the MEWA and the contracts between the MEWA, service providers, and participating employers and associations. This is a time-consuming and cumbersome process that can result in a determination that the questionable activities of the individuals operating the MEWA have not violated any provisions of ERISA. This is a result of the narrow scope of ERISA's authority over MEWAs. States are usually in a better position to take swift enforcement action against MEWAs, based upon failures to comply with specific statutory requirements such as licensing, reserve, and taxation requirements.

708. What is the scope of ERISA's preemption provisions in regard to MEWA regulation under state insurance laws?

ERISA generally preempts any and all state laws that "relate to any employee benefit plan" subject to ERISA.[1] There are a number of exceptions to the broad preemptive effect of ERISA. They are set forth in ERISA Section 514(b) and are commonly referred to as the "savings clause."

In reviewing the phrase "relate to any employee benefit plan," the Supreme Court held that the phrase should be construed broadly. In the ruling, the Court said that a "law 'relates to' an employee benefit plan, in the normal sense of the phrase, if it has a connection with or reference to such plan."[2]

While a state law may be found to "relate to" an employee benefit plan, that law may be saved from preemption to the extent that the exceptions contained in ERISA Section 514(b) are applicable. ERISA Section 514(b)(2) contains two relevant exceptions to the broad-based preemption found in ERISA. They specifically apply to insurance, banking, and securities regulation at the state level. ERISA provides that nothing in ERISA should be construed to exempt or relieve a person from any law of a state that regulates insurance (the "savings clause"). However, neither an employee benefit plan, nor any trust established under such a plan, is considered an insurance company or other insurer for purposes of a law of a state purporting to regulate insurance companies, or insurance contracts (the "deemer clause").[3]

The "savings clause" of ERISA Section 514(b)(2) reserves to the states the right to regulate the insurance business and persons engaged in that business. On the other hand, the "deemer clause" of ERISA Section 514(b)(2) makes it clear that a state law regulating insurance may not consider an employee benefit plan to be an insurance company in order to establish jurisdiction over such a plan.

Consequently, a state's ability to regulate MEWAs was dependent upon the determination as to whether or not the particular MEWA was an ERISA-covered plan. MEWAs often claimed to be ERISA-covered plans in order to evade state regulation and enforcement activities brought against them under state insurance laws. Congress then added ERISA Section 514(b)(6), which

---

1. ERISA Sec. 514(a).

2. *Shaw v. United Airlines, Inc.*, 463 U.S. 85 (1983).

3. ERISA Sec. 514(b)(2). See *Metropolitan Life Ins. Co. v. Massachusetts*, 471 U.S. 724 (1985), for a discussion of the criteria applied by the Supreme Court to determine if a state law regulates insurance.

allows for a special exception to the broad preemption provisions of ERISA for the application of state insurance laws to ERISA-covered welfare benefit plans that are "multiple employer welfare arrangements." Specifically, ERISA Section 514(b)(6)(A) provides:

Notwithstanding any other provision of this section—

(i)   in the case of an employee welfare benefit plan which is a multiple employer welfare arrangement and is fully insured …, any law of any State which regulates insurance may apply to such arrangement to the extent that such law provides—

(I) standards requiring the maintenance of specified levels of reserves and specified levels of contributions, which any such plan, or any trust established under such a plan, must meet in order to be considered under such law able to pay benefits in full, when due, and

(II) provisions to enforce such standards; and

(ii)   in the case of any other employee welfare benefit plan that is a multiple employer welfare benefit arrangement, in addition to this subchapter, any law of any State which regulates insurance may apply to the extent not inconsistent with the preceding sections of this subchapter.

709. To what extent will ERISA enforcement of MEWAs be taken by the Department of Labor?

Enforcement of the ERISA provisions concerning MEWAs is carried out by the Employee Benefits Security Administration's (EBSA's) Office of Enforcement (national office and fifteen field offices). The national office provides policy direction and technical and management support for the field offices, in addition to conducting investigations in selected sensitive areas. MEWA-related investigations are generally conducted by the field offices under the supervision of an area or district director, with oversight and coordination provided by the national office.

In an effort to facilitate state and federal enforcement efforts in the MEWA area, EBSA's field offices have established, or are in the process of establishing, cooperative arrangements with states in their jurisdictions in which EBSA will share and discuss cases involving MEWAs with the participating states. In addition, field offices will, in accordance with these agreements, make available documents obtained through voluntary production or obtained by a civil subpoena. To ensure proper coordination of MEWA-related initiatives, state officials should direct information or inquiries (other than advisory opinion requests) to the director of the EBSA area office responsible for their particular state.

On December 5, 2011, the DOL issued proposed rules intended to increase DOL oversight and enforcement of MEWAs as well as increase their public reporting requirements.[1] In following up on Section 6606 of the Patient Protection and Affordable Care Act amendment of ERISA

---

1. 76 Fed. Reg. 76,222 (Dec. 5, 2011).

Section 101(g), which grants the DOL authority to require annual reporting by MEWAs that are not ERISA-covered plans and requires them to register with the DOL prior to operating in a state, the DOL has issued rules to provide for these filings.[1] Specifically, MEWAs that are providing medical care benefits and are not ERISA-covered group health plans are covered by these new rules.[2]

The extended disclosure regulations now require existing and new non-ERISA-qualified MEWAs subject to the rule to annually file Form M-1 and any additional statements required pursuant to the instructions to Form M-1 (see Q 711 for full details on the filing requirements of Form M-1).[3] Further, a MEWA is required to register with the DOL by filing a completed Form M-1 and attachments with the DOL thirty days prior to operating in a state.[4] A new registration filing of the Form M-1 is also required in the event of

1.   Operations expanding into a new state;

2.   Merger with another MEWA;

3.   If the number of employees receiving coverage for medical care is at least 50 percent greater than the number of employees receiving coverage for medical care at the close of the last calendar year; or

4.   If there are any material changes (as defined in the Form M-1 instructions).[5]

The DOL is also empowered under the new rules to issue cease and desist orders and summary seizure orders under ERISA Section 521 through amendments to the regulations found under Labor Regulation Sections 2560.521 and 2520.103-1.[6] These powers will be enforced where is apparent that fraud is taking place (i.e., failure to pay claims) or an arrangement is causing immediate danger to the public safety or welfare. The DOL will have the ability to seize assets from a MEWA where there is probable cause that the plan is in a financially hazardous condition (thus preserving the assets before they are dissipated).

The new rules do exclude any MEWA that provides coverage only through group health plans that are not covered by ERISA, including governmental plans, church plans, or plans maintained solely for the purpose of complying with workers' compensation laws.[7]

The DOL has a Web site up and running that allows employers to learn about prospective MEWAs, as well as information on who operates the MEWA and where the funds will be held. This website can be found at: http://askebsa.dol.gov/epds/EPDSUserManual.asp

---

1. Prop. Labor Reg. §2550.101-2(a).
2. Prop. Labor Reg. §2550.101-2(b)(7).
3. Prop. Labor Reg. §2550.101-2(d)(1).
4. Prop. Labor Reg. §2550.101-2(e)(2)(iii).
5. Prop. Labor Reg. §2550.101-2(e)(2)(iv).
6. Prop. Labor Reg. §2550.101-2(g).
7. Prop. Labor Reg. §2550.101-2(c)(1)(D).

710. Does ERISA prohibit the transfer of assets from a terminated MEWA to a tax-exempt foundation?

No. In Advisory Opinion 2008-06A,[1] the DOL advised that ERISA Section 403(d)(2) would not prohibit the transfer of a MEWA trust's surplus assets to an unrelated tax-exempt foundation after the plan was terminated and had satisfied all its liabilities. The DOL also stated that if the trust was properly terminated and all claims were either paid or properly forfeited, the subsequent transfer of the trust's surplus funds would not violate ERISA's prohibited transaction rules.

The facts underlying the request for the advisory opinion show a trade group in the wine and spirits industry that wanted to terminate the MEWA trust due to declining participation. The trust provided insured health and welfare benefits. The association proposed that all remaining assets be transferred to a tax-exempt foundation, previously established by the association to pursue educational and charitable activities on behalf of employers in the industry (such as educating the public about the regulation and safe consumption of alcohol).

The association requested guidance regarding (1) whether it would be permissible under ERISA Section 403(d)(2) to amend the trust to transfer the remaining assets (minus administrative fees) to the foundation; and (2) whether the proposed transfer would violate ERISA's prohibited transaction rules.

Practitioner's Pointer: There is relatively little guidance on the issue of residual assets in a terminating health and welfare plan. While this Advisory Opinion helps detail the DOL's general line of thinking, it is recommended that plan sponsors seek the advice of ERISA counsel before considering a similar transfer of residual assets, as this Opinion still leaves a number of questions related to this topic unanswered.

---

711. What is the Form M-1?

The Form M-1 is a reporting form issued by the Department of Labor (DOL). It is an annual reporting form for MEWAs and certain collectively bargained plans that provide health coverage to the employees of two or more employers.[2]

In 2003, the interim rule issued in 2000, was made final, with some notable modifications (discussed subsequently). The final rule does not significantly modify the reporting requirement established in the interim rule. Instead, several clarifications were added to make clearer the application of the reporting requirement to different types of arrangements.[3]

The DOL has adopted a process pursuant to which a plan or other arrangement may, if subject to an action under state law, seek an individualized finding from a DOL administrative law judge (ALJ).[4] However, because some entities may incorrectly claim the exemption under Labor Regulation Section 2510.3-40, the final rule retains the requirement that entit[ies] claiming exemption (ECEs) file Form M-1 with the Department for three years following

---

1. DOL Adv. Op. 2008-06A (July 10, 2008) (http://www.dol.gov/ebsa/regs/aos/ao2008-06a.html).
2. 65 Fed. Reg. 7152 (Feb. 11, 2000).
3. 68 Fed. Reg. 17,493 (Apr. 9, 2003).
4. See 29 C.F.R. §§2570.150-2570.159.

an "origination" (i.e., the three-year rule—see below). Of course, if an entity does have a determination from an ALJ that it is a collectively bargained plan, that entity does not have to file Form M-1 while the opinion remains in effect unless the circumstances underlying the determination change.

According to the DOL, Form M-1 is designed to assist MEWAs in complying with recent health care–related legislation such as the Women's Health and Cancer Rights Act, the Newborns' and Mothers' Health Protection Act, and HIPAA (see Section II). In effect, the reporting required on Form M-1 will make it more difficult for MEWA operators to manage the plans in an unscrupulous manner by taking premium payments from participants and failing to provide the promised coverage. The information required to be reported on the form will assist the DOL in identifying plans that require closer scrutiny and will assist the DOL in coordinating compliance and enforcement efforts with respect to these plans with state insurance departments.

Under the final rules, administrators of the following plans must file Form M-1:

1.   MEWAs that offer or provide benefits consisting of medical care, regardless of whether the entity is a group health plan; and

2.   Multiemployer collectively bargained group health plans, or entities that claim they are not MEWAs due to collective bargaining status as an ECE.[1]

ECEs are generally not considered MEWAs under ERISA Section 3(40)(A)(i). However, the DOL is requiring ECEs that have been in existence for three or fewer years to file Form M-1.[2] The DOL advises that this requirement is because of a recurring problem with administrators of ECEs attempting to avoid state insurance regulations by mischaracterizing their arrangements as established or maintained pursuant to collective bargaining agreements. Therefore, requiring them to file Form M-1 for the first three years ensures a proper review and analysis of operations by the DOL. The MEWA administrator determination that a particular plan is an ECE does not affect the applicability of state law to the entity during, or after, the initial three-year reporting period.

Under the final rule, as under the interim final rule, the term "origination" continues to be defined as the occurrence of any of the following three events: (1) the MEWA or ECE first begins offering or providing coverage for medical care to the employees of two or more employers (including one or more self-employed individuals); (2) the MEWA or ECE begins offering or providing coverage for medical care to the employees of two or more employers (including one or more self-employed individuals) after a merger with another MEWA or ECE (unless all of the MEWAs or ECEs that participate in the merger previously were last originated at least three years prior to the merger); or (3) the number of employees receiving coverage for medical care under the MEWA or ECE is at least 50 percent greater than the number of such employees on the last day of the previous calendar year (unless the increase is due to a merger

---

1. Labor Reg. §2520.101-2(c).
2. Labor Reg. §2520.101-2(c)(1)(ii).

with another MEWA or ECE under which all MEWAs and ECEs that participate in the merger were last originated at least three years prior to the merger).[1]

The final rule adds a definition of "excepted benefits" and defines the term by reference to Section 733(c) of ERISA and Labor Regulation Section 2590.732(b). This definition was added because of a clarification that MEWAs or ECEs that provide coverage consisting solely of excepted benefits are not required to report under this Labor Regulation section.[2]

The Form M-1 filing requirement does not apply to a MEWA or ECE if it is licensed or authorized to operate as a health insurance issuer in every state in which it offers or provides medical care to employees.[3]

All newly formed MEWAs and ECEs are required to file Form M-1 within ninety days of origination.[4] However, this rule does not apply if the origination date occurs between October 1 and December 1[5] due to the mandatory Form M-1 filing deadline of March 1 for all required Form M-1 filings.[6]

A copy of Form M-1 and instructions for filing electronically are available on the DOL Web site at http://www.dol.gov/ebsa/forms_requests.html.

Finally, the final rule also contains a clarification that reporting is not required if an entity would not constitute a MEWA or ECE but for any of the following three circumstances:

1.   *Common control interest of at least 25 percent.* The final rule clarifies that a filing is not required on behalf of certain plans or other arrangements that provide coverage to the employees of two or more employers that share a common control interest. Specifically, if an entity would not constitute a MEWA or ECE but for the fact that it provides coverage to the employees of two or more trades or businesses that share a common control interest of at least 25 percent at any time during the plan year (applying the principles from Section 414(b) or (c) of the Internal Revenue Code), a Form M-1 filing is not required. However, although use of a 25 percent test may result in a determination of common control for purposes of the Form M-1 filing requirement, common control generally means, under Sections 414 (b) and (c) of the IRC, an 80 percent interest in the case of a parent-subsidiary group of trades or businesses and a more than 50 percent interest in the case of a brother-sister relationship among organizations controlled by five or fewer persons that are the same persons with respect to each organization.

2.   *Temporary MEWAs created by a change in control.* The DOL has modified the final rule to create an exception for arrangements that would not constitute MEWAs but for their creation in connection with a change in control of businesses (such as a merger

---

1. Labor Reg. §2520.101-2(b); 68 Fed. Reg. 17,493 (Apr. 9, 2003).
2. Labor Reg. §2520.101-2(b)(3); 68 Fed. Reg. 17,493 (Apr. 9, 2003).
3. Labor Reg. §2520.101-2(c)(2).
4. Labor Reg. §2520.101-2(e)(2)(iii)(A).
5. Labor Reg. §2520.101-2(e)(2)(iii)(B).
6. Labor Reg. §2520.101-2(e)(2)(i).

or acquisition) and that are temporary in nature (i.e., do not extend beyond the end of the plan year following the plan year in which the change in control occurs). The change in control must occur for a purpose other than avoiding Form M-1 filing.

3. *Very small number of persons who are not employees or former employees.* The final rule provides that any entity is not required to file the Form M-1 if it would not be a MEWA but for the fact that it provides coverage to persons who are not employees nor former employees (including those participants on COBRA continuation coverage) of the sponsor (excluding spouses and dependents) and the number of such persons does not exceed 1 percent of the total number of employees or former employees covered by the arrangement, determined as of the last day of the year to be reported (or, in the case of a ninety-day origination report, determined as of the sixtieth day following the origination date).[1]

---

1. Labor Reg. §§2520.101-2(c)(1)(ii)(A), 2520.101-2(c)(1)(ii)(B), 2520.101-2(c)(1)(ii)(C); 68 Fed. Reg. 17,493 (Apr. 9, 2003).

SECTION XII

Civil Compliance and Enforcement Issues

712. What is involved in the civil compliance and enforcement process?

This section reviews the administration and enforcement of the civil provisions of ERISA, from the individual participant benefits dispute through the investigation and enforcement procedures of the Employee Benefits Security Administration (EBSA) to the administration and enforcement of the plan termination insurance provisions of ERISA and the Pension Benefits Guaranty Corporation (PBGC).

The Department of Labor (DOL), through EBSA, is charged with the enforcement of the reporting, disclosure, and fiduciary provisions of ERISA. The DOL undertakes the majority of its enforcement efforts through the investigative process. This usually results in an administrative settlement of any issues discovered through the course of an investigation. If administrative enforcement efforts fail, the DOL may bring civil actions to compel plan administrators to satisfy their reporting obligations to the DOL and the IRS, as well as their disclosure obligations (i.e., to provide participant statements, summary annual reports, and summary plan descriptions). Likewise, the DOL may bring, or join, civil actions to enforce the fiduciary provisions of ERISA and to recover losses incurred by the plan as a result of fiduciary breaches.

The DOL conducts four major types of investigations: (1) targeting and limited reviews; (2) fiduciary investigations; (3) prohibited person investigations; and (4) criminal investigations. These various actions are reviewed in detail in this section, from the targeting and conduct of the investigations through the negotiation process used to settle any outstanding violations identified in the investigation.

Title IV of ERISA (Plan Termination Insurance) was established to provide for the timely and uninterrupted payment of pension benefits under defined benefit plans that are subject to the jurisdiction of Title IV. The PBGC maintains two pension protection programs that provide termination insurance protection to single-employer defined benefit plans and multiemployer defined benefit plans. The PBGC collects premiums from participating plans that are placed into "revolving funds" that are managed by investment managers selected by the PBGC through a process of competitive bidding. The provisions of Title IV and the termination of defined benefit plans through the plan termination insurance program as well as the PBGC enforcement procedures are reviewed in this section.

This section closes with a brief review of how the DOL and other federal agencies (particularly the IRS) will refer issues identified through their various enforcement efforts to those federal agencies with appropriate jurisdiction. Finally, this section reviews how and when ERISA will and will not preempt state laws.

Employee Benefits Security Administration

713. What is the Employee Benefits Security Administration (EBSA)?

The Employee Benefits Security Administration (EBSA) is an agency within the Department of Labor (DOL) that administers and enforces the provisions of Title I of ERISA (Protection of Employee Benefit Rights). EBSA is directed by an Assistant Secretary, a Presidential appointee, who reports directly to the Secretary of Labor. Though headquartered in Washington, D.C., EBSA's enforcement activities are conducted primarily in its field offices—ten regional offices and five district offices, located in fifteen cities throughout the United States. There are more than 300 investigators and auditors working out of these offices, many of whom are attorneys, certified public accountants, or individuals holding advanced degrees in business and finance. EBSA's Office of Enforcement, located in EBSA's national office, supports the activities of the regional and district offices.[1]

EBSA shares responsibility with the IRS and the Pension Benefit Guaranty Corporation (PBGC) for the administration and enforcement of ERISA. Under ERISA, the Secretary of Labor is responsible for protecting the rights and financial security of employee benefit plan participants and beneficiaries and for ensuring the integrity and effective management of the private pension and welfare benefit system. In carrying out its enforcement responsibilities, EBSA conducts a wide range of activities, including civil and criminal investigations, to determine whether the provisions of ERISA have been violated or whether any crimes have been committed with respect to employee benefit plans. EBSA also issues regulations and interpretations under Title I of ERISA; grants class or individual exemptions regarding the prohibited transactions of ERISA; receives and discloses to the public required annual financial reports filed by employee benefit plans; provides educational, technical, and compliance assistance to the public; and assists plan participants and beneficiaries regarding their plan benefits.[2]

714. What is the mission of the Employee Benefits Security Administration?

The Employee Benefits Security Administration (EBSA) protects the integrity of pensions, health plans, and other employee benefits for more than 150 million people. According to EBSA, its mission is to:

1.   Assist workers in getting the information they need to protect their benefit rights;

2.   Assist plan officials in understanding the requirements of the relevant statutes in order to meet their legal responsibilities;

3.   Develop policies and laws that encourage the growth of employment-based benefits; and

4.   Deter and correct violations of the relevant statutes.[3]

---

1. A list of field offices can be found at: http://www.dol.gov/ebsa/aboutebsa/org_chart.html.
2. *EBSA Enforcement Manual.*
3. See http://www.dol.gov/ebsa/aboutebsa/org_chart.html for contact information and a list of EBSA Officers and Directors.

715. What is the Employee Benefits Security Administration's policy for recruiting and training investigators and auditors?

The Employee Benefits Security Administration (EBSA) prefers to recruit individuals for investigator and auditor positions whose educational and employment background indicates a familiarity with ERISA-related fields of knowledge, such as law, accounting, and finance. The agency's training objectives for newly hired as well as experienced investigators and auditors lie in the areas of (1) basic training, (2) specialized training and skills development, and (3) ongoing continuing education.

Each new investigator or auditor attends a three-week mandatory "Basic Training Course." It consists of an intensive lecture and discussion period, supplemented by practical exercises, to familiarize new employees with the provisions of the federal law that EBSA enforces, as well as presentations and practice sessions to acquaint the investigators and auditors with investigative techniques. This "basic training" course is supplemented by a self-teaching course in the provisions of ERISA, which is mandatory for all new enforcement investigators and auditors.

After basic training, experienced investigators and auditors also attend a seven-day formal classroom presentation in "Financial Institutions." The course provides an understanding of the structure and operation of institutional investment managers, such as banks, registered investment advisers, and insurance companies. Investigators who have no substantial training in accounting also attend a seven-and-a-half-day formal classroom course in "Employee Benefit Plan Accounting." The course concentrates on accounting for employee benefit plans. A formal one-week course in criminal investigation is also presented. In this course, students learn about the applicable criminal statutes and techniques of criminal investigations. These in-house classroom programs are supplemented by additional training. Investigators and auditors may attend these additional training courses, as required in the course of their assignments.

EBSA also provides on-the-job training that is intended primarily for new employees and can range from the use of structured training material to ad hoc discussions between employees and supervisors. It also includes actual casework in the field under the supervision of a supervisor or senior investigator and is primarily designed to address specific needs of individual investigators. EBSA uses continuing education for the purpose of updating the technical knowledge and skills of both new and experienced employees. Legislative changes, regulatory developments, enforcement initiatives, and new investigative techniques are examples of such training.

EBSA also offers investigators and auditors individual development courses that are typically presented at institutions of higher learning or similar establishments. Included are courses of study leading to professional certification, such as Certified Employee Benefit Specialist (CEBS).[1]

---

1. ERISA Enforcement Strategy Implementation Plan, Sept. 1990, at 25-26.

716. What is the Office of Enforcement of the Employee Benefits Security Administration?

The Employee Benefits Security Administration (EBSA) Office of Enforcement promotes the protection of pension and welfare benefits under ERISA by ensuring a strong and effective national and field office enforcement program through:

- Policy formulation;

- Project identification and program planning;

- Guidance development and implementation;

- Field liaison; and

- Field and project evaluation.

The office is headquartered in Washington, D.C. The investigative staff (in EBSA's fifteen regional and district offices) conducts investigations to detect and correct violations of Title I of ERISA and related criminal laws.

EBSA's Office of Enforcement is composed of the Division of Field Operations, which coordinates national civil enforcement policy with EBSA field offices and various governmental agencies; the Division of Enforcement Support, which oversees national targeting efforts and provides technical and administrative assistance to EBSA field offices; and the Criminal Coordinator, who coordinates national criminal enforcement policy with EBSA field offices and with other governmental agencies such as the Department of Justice.[1]

717. What is the Office of the Chief Accountant of the Employee Benefits Security Administration?

The Office of the Chief Accountant (OCA) of the Employee Benefits Security Administration (EBSA) is responsible for enforcing the reporting and disclosure provisions of ERISA and administering a program to audit compliance with the fiduciary requirements of the Federal Employees' Retirement System Act of 1986 (FERSA).

The OCA comprises three divisions: (1) the Division of Accounting Services; (2) the Division of Reporting and Compliance; and (3) the Division of Federal Employees' Retirement System Act of 1986 Compliance.

The Division of Accounting Services actively performs numerous liaison and outreach activities with professional groups that service employee benefit plans and ensures that plan audits are done in accordance with industry standards.

---

1. See http://www.dol.gov/ebsa/aboutebsa/org_chart.html#section5.

The Division of Reporting and Compliance ensures that the ERISA database contains timely, complete, and accurate information about the regulated plan community. This division is also responsible for the administration of the Delinquent Filer Voluntary Compliance Program.

The Division of Federal Employees' Retirement System Act of 1986 (FERSA) Compliance conducts fiduciary compliance audits of thrift savings plans.[1]

In order to leverage its limited resources, OCA implements a multifaceted program to improve compliance with ERISA's reporting and disclosure requirements. One component of this program is a set of traditional enforcement initiatives involving civil penalties imposed against plan administrators for their failure to submit complete and accurate Form 5500 Series Annual Reports with the Department of Labor. OCA reviews Form 5500 Annual Reports to ensure that the information contained therein is complete and accurate. The Non-Filer Enforcement Program is an effort to proactively target employee benefit plans that are required to file annual reports but have not done so.

According to EBSA, non-filers are generally companies and corporations (large and small) that have illegally elected not to file annual reports for various reasons. In EBSA's view, the failure to file annual reports could be a signal that participants' benefits are in jeopardy. The program seeks both retroactive (back to 1988) and prospective compliance. Employee benefit plans targeted through the Non-Filer Enforcement Program, or referred to the program through a Department of Labor investigation or IRS or Pension Benefit Guaranty Corporation (PBGC) referral, are not eligible to participate in other DOL voluntary or reduced-penalty programs.

OCA also has established an ongoing quality review program for employee benefit plan audits to address the concern that independent qualified public accountant (IQPA) audits do not consistently meet professional standards. This program involves a random selection of plan audits for review to ensure that the level and quality of audit work performed supports the opinion rendered by the IQPA on the plan's financial statements, and that such work is adequately documented in the IQPA's work papers as required by established professional standards.[2]

718. What is the Office of Exemption Determinations of the Employee Benefits Security Administration?

The Office of Exemption Determinations of the Employee Benefits Security Administration (EBSA) administers the program for the granting of administrative exemptions from the prohibited transaction provisions of ERISA. The office has two divisions: the Division of Individual Exemptions and the Division of Class Exemptions.

The Division of Individual Exemptions is staffed by a division chief and three teams of analysts, each of which is headed by a supervisor or team leader. The primary responsibilities of

---

1. See http://www.dol.gov/ebsa/aboutebsa/org_chart.html#section9.
2. See http://www.dol.gov/ebsa/aboutebsa/org_chart.html for contact information for the Office of the Chief Accountant.

the Division of Individual Exemptions include analyzing individual exemption applications that involve a wide array of financial transactions, preparing interpretive letters and Federal Register notices, and reviewing petitions for good-faith waivers of ERISA Section 502(*l*) penalties.[1]

The primary responsibilities of the Division of Class Exemptions include analyzing applications for class exemptions and major individual exemptions related thereto, preparing Federal Register notices, reviewing petitions for good-faith waivers of ERISA Section 502(*l*) penalties, drafting advisory opinions and information letters regarding class exemptions, and handling special projects.[2]

The Divisions review applications for such exemptions and determine whether to grant relief. Individual exemptions relate to a particular plan or applicant; class exemptions are applicable to anyone engaging in the described transactions, provided the enumerated conditions are satisfied. See Section V for information on prohibited transaction exemption requests.

719. What is the Office of Regulations and Interpretations of the Employee Benefits Security Administration?

The Office of Regulations and Interpretations of the Employee Benefits Security Administration (EBSA) is primarily responsible for carrying out the agency's regulatory agenda and interpretive activities. The Office also coordinates regulatory and interpretive activities with other federal agencies such as the Department of Treasury, the Internal Revenue Service, and the Pension Benefit Guaranty Corporation (PBGC). The Office also plays a major role in the development, analysis, and implementation of pension and health care policy issues by providing technical assistance and support to the Assistant Secretary, external groups, and other offices within EBSA.

The general interpretive and regulatory responsibilities of the Office are allocated on a subject matter basis between two divisions, the Division of Fiduciary Interpretation and the Division of Coverage, Reporting and Disclosure.

The Division of Fiduciary Interpretations is responsible for interpretive and regulatory matters, including the qualified domestic relations order (QDRO), fiduciary responsibility, preemption, and qualified medical child support order provisions of Parts 2, 4, and 6 of Title I of ERISA, as well as related provisions of the Internal Revenue Code and the Federal Employees' Retirement Security Act (FERSA). The Division of Coverage, Reporting and Disclosure is generally responsible for interpretive and regulatory matters relating to the coverage, reporting, disclosure, suspension of benefits, claims procedure, multiple employer welfare arrangements (MEWA), COBRA, and other provisions of Parts 1, 2, 5, and 6 of Title I of ERISA.[3]

---

1. See http://www.dol.gov/ebsa/aboutebsa/org_chart.html#section4
2. See http://www.dol.gov/ebsa/aboutebsa/org_chart.html#section4.
3. See http://www.dol.gov/ebsa/aboutebsa/org_chart.html#section8.

720. What is the Office of Health Plan Standards and Compliance Assistance of the Employee Benefits Security Administration?

According to the Employee Benefits Security Administration (EBSA):

In response to the significant health care responsibilities given to the Secretary of Labor under the Health Insurance Portability and Accountability Act of 1996, a Task Force was established to develop regulations and other guidance required to implement the new requirements imposed on employer sponsored health plans. These have come to include Part 7 of the Employee Retirement Income Security Act amended by the Health Insurance Portability and Accountability Act of 1996, the Mental Health Parity Act of 1996, and the Newborns' and Mothers' Health Protection Act of 1996. The enactment of these health care laws marks a turning point in how group health plans are regulated at the federal level and significantly changed the nature and scope of the Employee Benefits Security Administration's interpretive and administrative responsibilities. These health care provisions, as well as the provisions of the Women's Health and Cancer Rights Act of 1998, create shared jurisdiction and shared regulatory responsibility for the Departments of Labor, Treasury, and Health and Human Services.[1]

The Office of Health Plan Standards and Compliance Assistance was formed to handle the change in the nature and scope of EBSA's regulatory and interpretive responsibilities as a result of HIPAA. "The Office of Health Plan Standards and Compliance Assistance is the primary source of regulations and interpretive guidance related to health plans and provides education, technical assistance and other types of support to health plans, other government agencies with related responsibilities, policy makers and EBSA program offices on health care matters."[2]

721. What is the Office of Technology and Information Services of the Employee Benefits Security Administration?

DOL guidance states that the Employee Benefits Security Administration's "Office of Technology and Information Services provides computer office automation, information processing, and local wide area, and Internet connectivity for EBSA staff nationwide. The office provides leadership and direction in the use of information technology to support EBSA's management and operations, including the enforcement and public disclosure requirements of the Employee Retirement Income Security Act of 1974 (ERISA)." The Office is also responsible for:

- The automated collection, processing, and dissemination of data and information for EBSA nationwide; and

- The procurement, operation, and maintenance of all computer systems and communication networks for EBSA, including:

   o Network and system security policies and operations;

---

1. See http://www.dol.gov/ebsa/aboutebsa/org_chart.html.
2. See http://www.dol.gov/ebsa/aboutebsa/org_chart.html#section7.

o   Hardware, software, and systems operations support for computer users;

o   Configuration and technical support for the EBSA Web site; and

o   Operation of the EBSA local area network (LAN) for national office communications (e-mail) and the EBSA wide area network (WAN) for nationwide communications with EBSA field offices.[1]

722. What is the Office of Outreach Education and Participant Assistance of the Employee Benefits Security Administration?

According to the DOL, the Office of Outreach Education and Participant Assistance (OOEPA) of the Employee Benefits Security Administration (EBSA) "provides service to EBSA's customers by means of outreach, education [and] technical assistance. OOEPA is responsible for external communications with the public through a variety of vehicles including the media, public outreach, brochures, other educational materials, national educational campaigns, public service announcements, EBSA's web site, and participant and compliance assistance activities. OOEPA coordinates the development of the Agency's strategic plan, establishes policies and operating procedures, and oversees quality reviews and customer satisfaction surveys related to the agency's outreach, education, and assistance program and provides support to the regional offices in carrying out these activities. EBSA's Benefits Advisors respond to approximately 170,000 telephone, written, and electronic inquiries annually from plan participants, employers and plan sponsors, assisting them in understanding their rights and obligations under the law and in obtaining benefits that may have been denied.

"OOEPA's media team coordinates media activities for significant enforcement actions, important litigation actions, and program initiatives. The Office leads the development and publication of a variety of educational materials for consumers and plan officials and the provision of educational information on the agency's web site. The Office is also responsible for the operation of the toll free hotlines for assistance and free publications. The Office is responsible for coordinating two major education campaigns—the Retirement Savings Education Campaign and the Health Benefits Education Campaign, including coordination of three National Summits on Retirement Savings Education in 1998, 2002, and 2005. OOEPA also serves as the Executive Secretary of the ERISA Advisory Council, providing logistical, clerical, and technical support throughout the year. Finally, OOEPA is responsible for the operation of the agency's Public Disclosure Room and responding to Freedom of Information Act requests."[2]

Office of the Solicitor

723. What is the United States Department of Labor's Office of the Solicitor?

The Solicitor of Labor, who is subject to presidential nomination and Senate confirmation, serves as the chief legal officer of the Department of Labor (DOL). The Solicitor's responsibilities include

---

1. See http://www.dol.gov/ebsa/aboutebsa/org_chart.html#section10.
2. See http://www.dol.gov/ebsa/aboutebsa/org_chart.htm/#section11.

enforcing the laws under the DOL's jurisdiction through litigation and providing a full range of legal services to the Secretary of Labor and the numerous agencies and bureaus that make up the DOL.

Within the immediate Office of the Solicitor, there are three Deputy Solicitors, with each one having his own responsibility. The different responsibilities are: (1) National Operations; (2) Regional Operations; and (3) Planning and Coordination.

The attorneys in the Washington, D.C., National Office are divided into eleven divisions, nine of which are program specific.[1] The program-specific divisions are:

- Division of Black Lung and Longshore Legal Services

- Division of Civil Rights and Labor-Management

- Division of Employment and Training Legal Services

- Division of Federal Employees' and Energy Workers' Compensation

- Division of Fair Labor Standards

- Division of Management and Administrative Legal Services

- Division of Mine Safety and Health

- Division of Occupational Safety and Health

- Division of Plan Benefits Security

The two other function-related divisions are: (1) the Division of Special Appellate and Supreme Court Litigation; and (2) the Division of Legislation and Legal Counsel. There are also fifteen regional and branch offices throughout the United States.

724. What is the Plan Benefits Security Division of the Office of the Solicitor?

The Plan Benefits Security Division (PBSD) of the Office of the Solicitor is responsible for the legal work arising out of the Department of Labor's administration and enforcement of ERISA and the Federal Employees' Retirement System Act (FERSA). The Division is headed by an Associate Solicitor and Deputy Associate Solicitor.

PBSD litigates matters that arise under ERISA in federal court. This litigation consists of: (1) federal district court enforcement cases arising out of investigations conducted by EBSA; and (2) an amicus curiae program. This program was designed to clarify and provide consistency to judicial interpretations of ERISA. In addition, the program: (1) expands participant access

---

1. http://www.dol.gov/sol/organizations/divisions/main.htm#.UJK_Y4aoYiY.

under ERISA to the federal courts; (2) ensures that adequate remedies are available to them under ERISA once they secure standing; and (3) interprets the scope of federal preemption of state law in the way intended by the drafters of ERISA.

PBSD is also actively involved in all regulatory and legislative departmental activity involving ERISA and health care reform. PBSD provides technical assistance and support to congressional staffs, to departmental and administration policy makers, and to interested trade and professional groups. Additionally, PBSD is involved in drafting and reviewing legislative proposals, interpretive bulletins, advisory opinions, class exemptions, and other policy initiatives involving ERISA.

ERISA Advisory Council

725. What is the ERISA Advisory Council?

The Advisory Council on Employee Welfare and Pension Benefit Plans is provided for under ERISA Section 512. The Council's members, appointed by the Secretary of Labor, include:

- Three representatives of employee organizations (at least one of whom represents an organization whose members are participants in a multiemployer plan);

- Three representatives of employers (at least one of whom represents employers maintaining or contributing to multiemployer plans);

- One representative from each of the following fields: (1) insurance, (2) corporate trust, (3) actuarial counseling, (4) investment counseling, (5) investment management, and (6) accounting; and

- Three representatives of the general public (one of whom represents those receiving benefits from a pension plan).

The fifteen members of the Council are appointed for three-year terms, with five terms expiring on November 14 of each year. Additionally, no more than eight members of the Council may be from the same political party.

Members of the Council must be qualified to appraise the programs instituted under ERISA. The duties of the Council are to advise the Secretary and submit recommendations regarding the Secretary's functions under ERISA. The Council customarily holds four meetings each year, which are open to the public.[1]

726. How are members of the ERISA Advisory Council appointed?

Each year, vacancies for the Council are announced in the Federal Register. Any person or organization who desires to recommend one or more individuals for appointment to the Council may submit recommendations on or before a specified time and date.

---

1. ERISA Secs. 512(a), 512(b). See http://www.dol.gov/ebsa/aboutebsa/org_chart.html for a list of current ERISA Advisory Council members.

The recommendations may be in the form of letters, resolutions, or petitions signed by the person making the recommendation, or by an authorized representative of the organization if the recommendation is made by an organization. The recommendations should contain the candidate's name, occupation or position, telephone number, and address, as well as a brief description of the candidate's qualifications and the group or field that he or she would represent. The candidate's political party affiliation must be noted because of the requirement that no more than eight Council members may be members of the same political party. Additionally, the recommendation must state whether the candidate is available and would accept appointment to the Council.

The nomination or recommendation letters are evaluated for completeness and qualifications of the candidate. The letters are acknowledged and the nominees are requested to declare their political affiliation. Letters supporting candidates are welcomed and acknowledged. This process continues until the close of business on the termination date previously announced in the Federal Register for receiving nominations.

Upon the completion of the nomination process, the Assistant Secretary of the Employee Benefits Security Administration reviews the nominations and submits his recommendations to the Secretary, who then appoints the five new members. In addition, the Secretary selects the chair and vice chair of the full Council and working groups, based upon the advice and recommendation of the Assistant Secretary.[1]

727. Who is the Executive Secretary of the ERISA Advisory Council?

ERISA Section 512 establishes the position of the Executive Secretary for the ERISA Advisory Council. It is the responsibility of the Executive Secretary to: (1) provide staff support to the Office of the Assistant Secretary of Labor and the Employee Benefits Security Administration regarding Council activities; (2) schedule, coordinate, and provide administrative support to all Council and Working Group meetings; (3) plan and coordinate the selection process for new members of the Council; (4) prepare reports regarding the Council's activities; and (5) establish and maintain the archives of the Council.[2]

728. How does the ERISA Advisory Council work?

After considering and debating various issues that are important to the administration of ERISA, the Council forms a number of working groups to focus on such issues. Additional issues for the Council to examine during the year may be suggested by the Office of the Assistant Secretary of the Employee Benefits Security Administration. The Council usually forms three or four such working groups per year.[3]

The Council receives the working groups' progress reports, discusses the findings, poses questions, and makes recommendations to the working groups during the Council meetings. However, the Council retains the responsibility for all final decisions made in regard to working group reports, and makes its decisions at scheduled meetings open to the general public.

---

1. ERISA Sec. 512(a).
2. ERISA Sec. 512(c).
3. http://www.dol.gov/ebsa/aboutebsa/erisa_advisory_council.html#.UJLE24aoYiY.

The working groups (1) identify and define the various issues; (2) investigate and take testimony from witnesses; and (3) submit final or interim reports of their findings and recommendations to the Council.[1]

Each working group usually uses its first meeting to organize itself. Additionally, during this meeting, a wide variety of witnesses are identified with a view to inviting them to testify before the working group. The working group devises the approach and strategy it will use to study the relevant issue, and reports to the Council for advice and consent.[2] The working groups continue to report their progress to the Council during the course of the Council term, and the Council may offer input and guidance. The Council encourages joint consultation among members of the working groups and their chairs.[3]

A typical working group meeting follows the same general schedule. First, the chair or vice chair calls the meeting to order, welcomes the general public, introduces members of the working group, and states the purpose of the meeting. Next, the chair invites any members who have been given a work assignment to provide a report. Then, any witnesses who have been invited to testify are called forward and requested to speak for a maximum of ten minutes. Also, some witnesses submit written testimony that is distributed to the working group and made part of the official record of the meeting. Members of the working group are invited to pose questions to each witness, and when the working group has no further questions, the chair thanks the witness and excuses him. The process continues with the next witness, until all witnesses scheduled for the meeting have been heard.[4]

Members of the working group are encouraged to discuss the events of the meeting, and to express their views and concerns. After the discussion is completed, the chair invites statements from the general public. When members of the general public have completed their statements and any subsequent discussion has been completed, the chair asks for a motion to adjourn.[5]

During the Council year, the working group studies testimony received and deliberations that took place on various issues. The working group continues to meet and to report to the Council until early November of each year. Near the end of the Council term, members of the working group may be requested to summarize witness testimonies and deliberations of the group in preparation of a final report of findings and recommendations to the Council.[6]

The Council term ends on November 14, at which time the working groups present their final or preliminary findings and recommendations to the full Council. The Council then discusses each working group's report, and either accepts or modifies the report. Finally, the Council Chair transmits the working groups' reports as accepted by the Council to the Secretary of Labor.[7]

---

1. http://www.dol.gov/ebsa/adcoun/acintro.htm.
2. http://www.dol.gov/ebsa/adcoun/acintro.htm.
3. http://www.dol.gov/ebsa/aboutebsa/erisa_advisory_council.html#.UJLE24aoYiY.
4. http://www.dol.gov/ebsa/aboutebsa/erisa_advisory_council.html#.UJLE24aoYiY.
5. http://www.dol.gov/ebsa/adcoun/acintro.htm.
6. http://www.dol.gov/ebsa/aboutebsa/erisa_advisory_council.html#.UJLGHoaoYiY.
7. http://www.dol.gov/ebsa/aboutebsa/erisa_advisory_council.html#.UJLGHoaoYiY.

General Investigative Authority

729. What is the Department of Labor's general investigative authority?

ERISA Section 504(a) grants the Secretary of Labor broad discretion to investigate whether any person has violated or is about to violate any provision of Title I of ERISA (Protection of Employee Benefit Rights), or its attendant regulations. Such investigations may require the submission of reports, books, and records, and the filing of data in support of any information required to be filed with the Department of Labor (DOL).

The DOL may also "enter such places, inspect such books and records and question such persons" as it deems necessary to determine the facts relative to the investigation.[1] This authority extends beyond plans and plan sponsors—it also includes service providers to plans and financial institutions (e.g., banks, savings and loans, insurance companies, and investment management companies) who conduct business with ERISA-covered plans.

The DOL may not require any plan to submit to an investigation more than once in any twelve-month period, unless the DOL has "reasonable cause" to believe that there may be a violation of Title I of ERISA, or its attendant regulations.[2]

The enforcement of Title I of ERISA is handled by the Employee Benefits Security Administration (EBSA). The EBSA has regional and district offices throughout the United States. Under the DOL's 1990 Enforcement Strategy Implementation Plan, the DOL, in an effort to allocate its limited resources in the most effective manner, so as to protect the largest number of plan participants and plan assets, has developed an enforcement strategy designed to:

1. Identify and investigate those areas most prone to abuse;

2. Detect and obtain correction of ERISA violations;

3. Respond to participant complaints, public inquiries, and referrals received from other governmental agencies;

4. Disseminate information and promote voluntary compliance with Title I of ERISA; and

5. Establish a presence in the regulated benefits community.

Under ERISA Section 504(c), the DOL has administrative subpoena authority regarding testimony and the production of books, records, and documents; however, the DOL is required to seek a grant of authority from the Department of Justice to conduct criminal investigations (see Section XIII for details). In criminal investigations, the DOL has no subpoena authority. If the DOL requires a subpoena in the course of a criminal investigation, it must request it through the Department of Justice, specifically, a U.S. Attorney in the district in which the investigation is being conducted.

---

1. ERISA Secs. 504(a)(1), 504(a)(2).
2. ERISA Sec. 504(b).

The DOL has created a new consumer assistance Web page (also available in Spanish) that allows users to submit questions and complaints about plans electronically. The page includes links to various tools and publications with information on benefit plans, as well as answers to questions about "hot topics." Users also have the option to submit a question, file a complaint, or report a problem with their plan. Inquiries and complaints submitted are sent directly to EBSA benefits advisers, who will respond as soon as possible but no later than three business days. Additionally, the system automatically routes the requests to the appropriate EBSA regional office based on users' ZIP codes. The page can be found by going to http://www.dol.gov/ebsa and then selecting "Request Assistance" or "Solicitud de Asistencia" at the top of the page.[1]

730. Does the Department of Labor possess the power to subpoena?

Yes. In accordance with its investigative authority pursuant to ERISA Section 504(c), the Department of Labor (DOL) has the power to subpoena when conducting investigations under Title I of ERISA (Protection of Employee Benefit Rights). This subpoena power is in accordance with the provisions of Sections 9 and 10 of the Federal Trade Commission Act, which relate to the attendance of witnesses and the production of books, records, and documents, and is applicable to the jurisdiction, powers, and duties of the DOL or its designees. Accordingly, these sections provide the DOL with: (1) the authority to administer oaths; (2) the power to compel the attendance of witnesses; and (3) the access to and the right to copy documentary evidence.[2]

The authority of the DOL to execute and issue administrative subpoenas is delegated to the regional directors of the Employee Benefits Security Administration under the guidance and direction of the Director of the Office of Enforcement. Through the use of their subpoena powers, the regional directors issue subpoenas as a method of requiring an individual or entity to produce certain documents and records and to appear for the purpose of providing sworn testimony in connection with an investigation. Prior to its issuance, a subpoena is reviewed by a regional solicitor of the DOL for its legal sufficiency.[3]

The Fourth Circuit Court of Appeals has recognized an ERISA fiduciary exception to the attorney-client privilege in the context of a DOL subpoena.[4] This rule has also been applied in other appellate courts. The case stemmed from a DOL investigation of two multiemployer plans. The DOL sought communications between the defendant funds' fiduciaries and their attorneys in connection with an investigation into the funds' indirect investments in Bernard Madoff's Ponzi scheme, which resulted in a $10.1 million loss in plan assets. The Fourth Circuit Court held that the fiduciary exception to the attorney-client privilege extends to communications between an ERISA trustee and a plan attorney regarding plan administration, as well as when the DOL initiates an investigation or audit under ERISA Section 504.[5] In so holding, the Fourth Circuit Court concluded that applying the fiduciary exception in the context of a DOL

---

1. DOL Consumer Assistance Webpage; DOL News Release 11-1627-NAT (Nov. 10, 2011).
2. ERISA Sec. 504(c).
3. *EBSA Enforcement Manual* ch. 33, at 1-3.
4. *Solis v. Food Emp'rs Labor Relations Ass'n*, 2011 WL 1663597 (4th Cir. 2011).
5. *Solis v. Food Emp'rs Labor Relations Ass'n*, above.

subpoena under ERISA did not require "a showing of good cause; instead, its application turns on the context and content of the individual communications at issue." The court found that the documentation requested related to the funds' administration and was therefore information that ERISA trustees had a fiduciary obligation to disclose, provided that it did not relate to the fiduciary's own legal defense. The court did not reach the issue of whether the work product doctrine is subject to the fiduciary exception because the funds failed to carry their burden to demonstrate applicability of the work product doctrine.[1]

731. What is a subpoena duces tecum?

A subpoena duces tecum is a command to a person or organization to appear at a specified time and place and: (1) to bring certain designated documents in her custody or control; (2) to produce the documents; and (3) to testify as to their authenticity, as well as any other matter concerning the documents to which proper inquiry is made.[2]

732. What is a subpoena ad testificandum?

A subpoena ad testificandum is a command to a named individual or corporation to appear at a specified time and place to give oral testimony under oath. A verbatim transcript is made of this testimony.[3]

733. What is an accommodation subpoena?

An accommodation subpoena is a subpoena issued by the Employee Benefits Security Administration (EBSA) to persons or entities who are willing to testify or to produce the documents requested but are concerned about protecting themselves from any potential adverse consequences of doing so without a legal requirement. These subpoenas are often issued by EBSA as an accommodation to service providers and financial institutions for the foregoing reasons.[4]

734. What methods are used to serve the subpoena?

Subpoenas are generally served by certified or registered mail, with return receipt requested. The Employee Benefits Security Administration's investigators or auditors often arrange service by prior telephone conversation or through the individual's or entity's legal counsel. In all cases, a letter, with references to any earlier telephone discussions, accompanies the subpoena.[5]

In instances where it proves impractical or impossible to serve the subpoena on an individual by mail, EBSA may arrange to have the subpoena served personally, and a copy also may be sent by mail. The DOL instructs its investigators and auditors that personal service is complete when the subpoena is delivered: (1) directly to the individual or entity; (2) to the individual's residence with a person of suitable age and discretion residing there full-time, such as a spouse; or (3) to the person in charge at the office or place of business of the entity.[6]

---

1. *Solis v. Food Emp'rs Labor Relations Ass'n*, above.
2. *EBSA Enforcement Manual* ch. 33, at 1.
3. *EBSA Enforcement Manual* ch. 33, at 1.
4. *EBSA Enforcement Manual* ch. 33, at 1.
5. See *EBSA Enforcement Manual* ch. 33, figs. 1, 2, 3, 4, and 5, for model letters.
6. *EBSA Enforcement Manual* ch. 33 at 3-4.

735. What types of investigations are conducted by the Department of Labor?

The Department of Labor (DOL) conducts investigations of plans, service providers, plan sponsors, and multiemployer organizations. Investigations of these entities are classified by the DOL, depending upon the actual issues being investigated. The classifications are based upon the chapters within the *EBSA Enforcement Manual*. The DOL refers to these investigations as: Program 53, Program 48, Program 52, and Program 47.

Program 53 — Targeting and Limited Reviews

Most investigations are initially opened as Program 53 investigations. The initial on-site investigations for the majority of DOL field audits are conducted as Program 53 investigations (known internally as a "P-53"). (See Q 759 through Q 763 for the details of how the DOL conducts an initial on-site investigation.) The purpose of a P-53 is to investigate the issues upon which the case was targeted and opened (as identified on a Case Opening Form 205), as well as the bonding, reporting, and disclosure obligations applicable to all plans. (See Q 759 for details on how the DOL targets investigations). If a P-53 reveals evidence that a fiduciary violation has occurred, the investigation is converted to a Program 48 ("P-48") investigation. P-53 investigations that fail to uncover any outstanding fiduciary or criminal investigations are quickly closed, and a brief case closing letter is issued.[1]

Program 48 — Fiduciary Investigation

Chapter 48 of the *EBSA Enforcement Manual* details the procedures to be followed in conducting fiduciary investigations. If, in the course of targeting an investigation, the DOL has sufficient evidence to believe that a fiduciary violation has occurred, they will open the investigation as a P-48 and dispense with the formality (and paperwork) involved in a P-53 investigation. P-48 investigations are usually very detailed and involve an in-depth analysis of plan records as well as interviews of, and requests for records from, plan service providers. If the DOL uncovers alleged fiduciary violations of ERISA, the targets of the investigation will likely receive a Voluntary Compliance (VC) letter from the DOL which details: (1) the facts of the alleged violations identified by the DOL; (2) the provisions of ERISA that are alleged to have been violated; and (3) a request that the target of the investigation provide to the DOL, within ten days, a written explanation of the target's plan to reverse the outstanding alleged violations and restore to the plan any alleged losses and lost opportunity costs.

In cases of extreme or egregious violations of ERISA, the target of a P-48 investigation may receive from the Pension Benefits Security Division (PBSD) of the DOL, or from the DOL's Regional Solicitor, a Notice of Intent to Litigate. At this point, the DOL is of the opinion that achieving voluntary compliance from the investigative target is highly unlikely, or that the outstanding violations are of a nature that warrant immediate judicial intervention in order

---

1. *EBSA Enforcement Manual* ch. 53.

to protect plan assets for the benefit of participants and beneficiaries. (See Q 786 regarding information on how investigation subjects should proceed in responding to the DOL voluntary compliance letter).[1]

Program 52 — Criminal Investigation

If a P-53 discovers evidence of criminal activity regarding the subject plan, the evidence will be documented and presented to the United States Attorney's Office for the jurisdiction in which the plan is located.[2] The DOL will present evidence of criminal activity regarding employee benefit plans to the U.S. Attorney along with a request for a Grant of Authority to conduct a criminal investigation. (This is necessary because the DOL does not, by itself, have the authority to issue subpoenas in criminal matters.) All subpoenas issued in the course of a P-52 are issued from the Department of Justice and are carried out by the DOL.

If a P-52 investigation establishes sufficient evidence that criminal activity has occurred in regard to the subject employee benefit plan, and that a certain subject or subjects have committed the violations, the Department of Justice will present the results of the investigation to a federal grand jury for the purpose of securing an indictment against the subject or subjects with respect to whom the investigation has established probable cause to believe that they have committed the crimes for which the indictments were sought.

The most common criminal acts for which indictments are sought under a P-52 investigation are:

1.   Theft or embezzlement from an employee benefit plan;

2.   Making of false statements and concealment of facts in relation to ERISA-required documents;

3.   Acceptance or solicitation of funds to influence the operation of employee benefit plans; and

4.   Mail fraud.

Program 47 — Prohibited Person Investigation

The final type of investigation routinely conducted by the DOL is outlined in Chapter 47 of the *EBSA Enforcement Manual*. That chapter deals with the investigation of certain persons holding certain positions in relation to an employee benefit plan, although they are statutorily barred from serving in such a capacity. This prohibited person investigation is referred to within the DOL as a "P-47" investigation. This chapter is guided by the statutory provisions of ERISA Section 411, which states that "[n]o person who has been convicted of, or has been imprisoned as a result of his conviction for, robbery, bribery, extortion, embezzlement, fraud, grand larceny, burglary, arson, a felony violation of federal or State law" involving controlled substances, "murder, rape,

---

1. *EBSA Enforcement Manual* ch. 48.
2. *EBSA Enforcement Manual* ch. 52.

kidnapping, perjury, assault with intent to kill" or any crime under the Investment Company Act of 1940, may serve or be permitted to serve:

1.   As an administrator, fiduciary, officer, trustee, custodian, counsel, agent, employee, or representative in any capacity of an employee benefit plan;

2.   As a consultant or adviser to an employee benefit plan, including, but not limited to, any entity whose activities are, in whole or substantial part, devoted to providing goods or services to any employee benefit plan; or

3.   In any capacity that involves decision-making authority or custody or control of the monies, funds, assets, or property of any employee benefit plan.

Practitioner's Pointer: This prohibition under ERISA Section 411 is not permanent. It is a restriction that is in place for thirteen years after the conviction, or after the term of incarceration, whichever is later. The thirteen-year restriction can be circumvented if the sentencing judge (in federal court) or a U.S. District Court judge (for a state-level conviction) has determined that the subject's serving in a restricted capacity would not be contrary to ERISA's provision regarding the protection of employee benefit rights.[1] The court reviewing the restoration request must hold a hearing and provide notice by certified mail to the state, county, and federal prosecuting officials in the jurisdiction(s) in which the conviction took place.

If the P-47 investigation establishes that such a prohibited person is serving an employee benefit plan in one of the statutorily defined positions, he may be fined (not more than $10,000) or imprisoned (for not more than five years) or both.

Investigations of Service Providers

736. Does the Employee Benefits Security Administration investigate service providers to employee benefit plans?

Yes. As a result, the DOL investigates service providers, as a national enforcement priority, under the Strategic Enforcement Plan (StEP). The focus on service providers as a national investigative priority under the StEP is not new but rather a continuation of the DOL's long-standing practice under the ERISA Enforcement Strategy Implementation Plan of 1990 (ESIP). Under the ESIP, the Employee Benefits Security Administration (EBSA) devoted 50 percent of EBSA fiduciary investigative time to abusive practices in the areas of welfare plan service providers and financial institutions that provide services to employee benefit plans. By continuing its focus on service providers under the StEP, EBSA is maintaining its position under the ESIP that service provider investigations generally result in larger recoveries for more plans and more participants, and provide a mechanism whereby EBSA can leverage its resources and obtain the maximum impact for the benefit of plan participants and beneficiaries. As under the ESIP, the investigation of service providers generally focuses on the abusive practices committed by the specific service providers rather than on the plans. In contrast to the ESIP, the allocation of appropriate resources under the StEP, however, does not mandate that any specific percentage of fiduciary investigative time be devoted to the targeting and investigation of these issues or entities.

---

1. ERISA Sec. 411(a).

737. What types of issues and service providers are investigated by the Employee Benefits Security Administration?

According to the Employee Benefits Security Administration (EBSA) a number of different types of abuses can be identified that involve service providers. These include, but are not limited to: (1) the payment by plans of large sums of money for the provision of benefits to very few participants; (2) the hiring of individuals as consultants who receive money for no services rendered through an arrangement with plan officials; (3) the purchase of inappropriate, unnecessary, or expensive insurance products for plan participants; (4) the payment of excessive or duplicative administrative fees; (5) the payment of kickbacks to plan fiduciaries by service providers; and (6) the retention of parties in interest to provide services not exempted by ERISA Section 408. The focus of EBSA service provider investigations is on abuses committed by the actual providers of specific services to welfare plans, rather than on the plans themselves.

According to EBSA, a "service provider" is defined as any person or entity who provides a service, directly or indirectly, to an employee benefit plan for compensation. The following are service providers common to employee benefit pension and welfare plans and a brief description of the types of services that they offer to plans:

1. *Contract professional services.* This category includes those individuals, groups of individuals, or firms who enter into a contract with a plan to provide a specific type of professional service (e.g., legal, dental, or vision care) to participants.

2. *Third-party administrators.* Most Taft-Hartley plans (see Section X), as well as other welfare and pension plans, employ third-party administrators to provide a full line of administrative services. Such services include: (a) receiving and depositing contributions; (b) maintaining participant records; (c) processing participant claims; (d) preparing benefit statements; (e) attending trustee meetings; and (f) providing general advice on the day-to-day operation of the plan. Fees are computed in a number of different ways, depending upon the service being provided.

3. *Attorneys.* Employee benefit plans generally have one or more attorneys on retainer, to: (a) prepare plan documents; (b) attend board meetings; (c) review contracts; (d) collect delinquent contributions; (e) provide legal advice in disputes between the plan and its participants or other third parties; and (f) give legal advice in the day-to-day operation of the fund.

4. *Consultants.* Consultants serve a multitude of purposes in the employee benefit plan industry. A consultant might become involved in any of the following matters: (a) analyzing insurance contracts in an insured program; (b) preparing plan documents and benefit booklets; (c) monitoring adherence on the part of an insurance carrier to the contract terms; (d) interpreting the plan documents; and (e) reviewing experience reports in either insured or self-insured programs.

5. *Insurance brokers and agents.* Insurance brokers and agents are often involved in the packaging and selling of insurance coverage and benefits to a plan and may work through a consultant hired by the trustees or a plan administrator responsible for operating the fund.

6. *Computer services.* More and more employee benefit plans are becoming involved with companies set up to provide computer services to plans. Such services can vary significantly, ranging from tracking participant eligibility records and utilization data to monitoring investments.

7. *Accountants.* Accountants, as service providers to plans, generally perform a full line of bookkeeping and accounting activities. They may prepare Form 5500 filings and plan financial statements.

Service provider investigations may have been targeted as a result of evidence discovered in the course of a routine investigation of one of the service providers of ERISA plan clients. Conversely, an investigation of an ERISA service provider that indicates evidence of violations committed by the service provider's client plans may result in the opening of investigations of those client plans by the DOL, or a referral of administrative violations to the IRS for investigation by their Employee Plans Division.[1]

738. What are the goals and objectives of the Employee Benefits Security Administration in the investigation of service providers?

According to the ERISA Enforcement Strategy Implementation Plan of 1990, the objectives of the Employee Benefits Security Administration (EBSA) involving the investigation and audit of service providers are as follows:

- Identifying and conducting investigations of service providers who have the most potential for abuse;

- Establishing a presence in the service provider field nationwide by identifying and conducting investigations of at least one major service provider in each of the fifty states;

- Establishing a presence in areas of high concentration of employee benefit plan service providers by identifying and conducting investigations of at least one major service provider in each of the twenty major population centers in the country;

- Establishing a presence in the entire service provider community by identifying and conducting investigations of service providers based on size (small, medium, and large) and type of service;

---

1. 65 Fed. Reg. 18208 (April 6, 2000).

- Identifying ERISA violations and obtaining corrections of those violations;

- Developing data through investigations of service providers that form a basis for establishing targeting guidelines and for use in pursuing, when violations exist, the correction of those violations; and

- Ensuring the most widespread possible dissemination of knowledge of EBSA's correction of employee abuses through publicity, speeches, etc.

739. What methods are used by the Employee Benefits Security Administration in targeting service providers for investigation?

As a general rule, each regional office of the Employee Benefits Security Administration (EBSA) independently targets service providers for investigation. The service providers selected for audit usually represent a cross-section of the service providers within the jurisdiction, both geographically and by type of provider. The methods used by the regional offices in targeting service providers include the following:

- Access to all Schedule C filings attached to Forms 5500 processed on the EBSA ERISA Access System (or equivalent);

- Computer-generated reports from Form 5500 filings of service providers servicing multiple plans;

- Computer-generated reports from Form 5500 filings analyzing plan administrative expenses;

- Computer-generated reports from Form 5500 filings for various specific health and welfare plans, including: (a) prepaid legal, (b) dental, and (c) vision;

- Office intelligence files, including case filings for various identified potential problem areas with service providers;

- Contacts with other state and federal government agencies to identify potential abusive service providers (e.g., the Federal Bureau of Investigation, Office of Inspector General, Department of Justice, and State Insurance Commissioners);

- Any congressional subcommittee hearing transcripts that may identify potential abusive service providers; and

- Interviews with individuals, companies, and others who might have knowledge of violations in the service provider field.

740. What is the focus of DOL service provider audits?

The Strategic Enforcement Plan and ERISA Enforcement Strategy Implementation Plan of 1990 (ESIP) provide that service provider investigations conducted by the DOL will focus on abusive practices committed by actual providers of specific services to employee benefit plans rather than on the plans themselves. According to the ESIP, each investigation is conducted to determine whether:

1.   A legitimate service is being rendered to the plan or its participants;

2.   The service is necessary to the administration of the plan or the payment of benefits;

3.   The service is being duplicated by other service providers; and

4.   The cost of providing the service is reasonable under the circumstances.

Any entity who provides a service, directly or indirectly, to an employee benefit plan for compensation may be subjected to an investigation by the DOL to determine if a violation of ERISA has been, or is about to be, committed.[1]

Such investigations may have been targeted as a result of evidence discovered in the course of a routine investigation of one of the service providers of ERISA plan clients. Conversely, an investigation of an ERISA service provider that indicates evidence of violations committed by the service provider's client plans may result in the opening of investigations of those client plans by the DOL, or a referral of administrative violations to the IRS for investigation by their Employee Plans Division.[2]

Investigations of Financial Institutions

741. Does the DOL investigate financial institutions that serve employee benefit plans?

Yes. Financial institutions provide services to employee benefit plans in many different capacities. Typically, they provide checking and savings accounts for plans, contribution collection services, and custodial services. With respect to the direct investment of plan assets, financial institutions serve as investment managers and advisers, directed trustees, and co-trustees to plans. In addition, they provide plans with investment vehicles, such as participation loans, pooled or collective investment funds, and deposit administration contracts. Some financial institutions are involved in broker-dealer activities, particularly with discount broker operations.

In accordance with the ERISA Enforcement Strategy Implementation Plan of 1990, the Employee Benefits Security Administration (EBSA) has selected abusive practices by financial institutions for investigation for a variety of reasons. First, ERISA is a very complex law and other regulatory agencies cannot be expected to fully understand the interrelationships among applicable law, ERISA, and the numerous ERISA exemptions and regulations. The absence of any federal regulations in the insurance industry and the unevenness of state regulation

---

1. ERISA Sec. 504(a).
2. *ERISA Enforcement Strategy Implementation Plan*, Sept. 1990.

provide an additional reason for EBSA to protect the interests of employee benefit plans from abusive practices committed by a relatively small number of insurance companies. Finally, and presumably because of resource limitations, federal and state bank regulators have emphasized the commercial operations of banks in their examination activities, as opposed to bank trust department operations where most employee benefit plan assets are held and where most abusive practices relating to employee benefit plans occur.[1]

742. What are the types of issues involving violations of ERISA and financial institutions?

According to the DOL, generally, substantive issues involving violations of ERISA committed by financial institutions acting as fiduciaries to employee benefit plans fall into two categories. The first category involves the financial institution's management of plan assets. Despite the professionalism of many institutions, there exists the possibility of improper and imprudent management and investment of plan assets. The second, and more serious, category of violations concerns conflict-of-interest and self-dealing situations. Examples of these violations include: (1) transfers of bad loans from a bank's commercial department to its trust department; (2) the charging of excessive fees (either directly or through a related entity, such as a stock broker); and (3) the use of plan assets for permanent financing of risky construction projects for which the financial institution has provided interim financing. Also, financial institutions may extend certain "favors" to employee benefit plan fiduciaries in order to retain plan or plan sponsor business. Examples of these "favors" include the making of low-interest or unsecured loans to plan fiduciaries, agreement to plan sponsors' directions of imprudent investments, and the promise of gifts or other gratuities to plan fiduciaries.[2]

743. What types of financial institutions are investigated by the Employee Benefits Security Administration?

The Employee Benefits Security Administration has investigated the following financial institutions:

1. *Banks*. Many employee benefit plans receive services from state or nationally chartered banks. These services range from a bank's providing a simple checking account to a bank's serving as a plan's sole discretionary trustee. Banks are involved in both the short-term and long-term investment of plan assets. Banks provide pooled investments and other collective trusts for plans.

2. *Savings and loan associations*. Similar to banks, savings and loan associations provide a variety of services to employee benefit plans. They manage plan cash in the short-term and provide certificates of deposit for long-term investing. In addition, savings and loan associations provide many investment vehicles for plans such as participation loan packages.

---

1. *ERISA Enforcement Strategy Implementation Plan*, Sept. 1990, at 12 - 13.
2. *ERISA Enforcement Strategy Implementation Plan*, Sept. 1990, at 13.

3. *Trust companies.* Trust companies are primarily involved in managing trust assets and sometimes act as a conduit for plans investing in real estate, mortgages, and other types of investments. Trust companies frequently serve as fiduciaries to employee benefit plans.

4. *Investment management companies.* These entities, although not banks, savings and loan associations, or trust companies, receive large sums of money from employee benefit plans and are responsible for the investment of that money. Often these companies also have money from non-ERISA accounts that they are also responsible for investing. Mutual funds and other investment vehicles are expressly excluded from this category as they do not involve the investment of plan assets.

5. *Insurance companies.* In addition to providing insurance, insurance companies provide a large variety of services and investments to plans, sometimes in a fiduciary capacity, such as deposit administration contracts, annuities, and collective or pooled investment arrangements.[1]

744. What are the goals and objectives of the Employee Benefits Security Administration in investigating financial institutions?

By investigating abuses committed by financial institutions, the Employee Benefits Security Administration (EBSA) attempts to protect participants and beneficiaries of employee benefit plans by ensuring that these institutions are holding, managing, and investing plan assets in accordance with ERISA. The objectives of EBSA in such investigations are as follows:

•   Targeting enforcement efforts on plan assets held by at least two financial institutions located in each state;

•   Concentrating EBSA investigative resources on individuals and entities believed to be involved in the most egregious conflicts of interest and self-dealing violations;

•   Where violations of ERISA are uncovered, seeking to promptly protect and preserve plan assets, recover plan losses, and, if appropriate, remove violators from activities associated with employee benefit plans; and

•   Seeking the assistance and cooperation of federal agencies that regulate financial institutions.[2]

745. What is the focus of DOL financial institution audits?

The Enforcement Strategy Implementation Plan of 1990 (ESIP) required the DOL to allocate 50 percent of its investigative resources to investigations of significant issues. Consequently, in the years following the issuance of the ESIP, the DOL has focused a tremendous amount of

---

1. *ERISA Enforcement Strategy Implementation Plan*, Sept. 1990, at 14.
2. *ERISA Enforcement Strategy Implementation Plan*, Sept. 1990, at 14-15.

time and resources on conducting investigations of financial institutions. Since the Strategic Enforcement Plan (StEP) does not mandate that any specific percentage of fiduciary investigative time be devoted to the targeting and investigation of these issues or entities, it is presumably at the discretion of the Regional Office of the Employee Benefits Security Administration to determine the amount and percentage of its investigative resources that will be allocated to investigations of financial institutions.

Financial institutions that are subject to the DOL's service provider investigations include banks, savings and loans, trust companies, investment management companies, and insurance companies.

The issues and documents reviewed in a financial institution audit by the DOL include the following:

1. *The relationship between the commercial department and the trust department.* This issue involves the review of potentially improper arrangements or relationships between commercial and trust departments of banks or similar departments of other financial institutions.

2. *Prudence and exclusive purpose of the bank as trustee.* This issue involves the failure of financial institutions to act independently or in the sole interest of plans when acting in the capacity of a co-trustee, directed trustee, or fiduciary.

3. *Investment vehicles.* This issue involves the investment of client plan assets in collective investment funds with low earnings and a high concentration of plan asset investments in real estate or other similar investments in a specific geographic or economic area.

4. *Plan equity portfolio management and proxy voting.* This issue involves the failure of financial institutions to manage plan equity portfolios or to vote plan stock in the sole interest of participants and beneficiaries.

5. *Fees charged by the bank.* This issue deals with the appropriateness and reasonableness of fees and other charges of financial institutions to employee benefit plans.

6. *"Soft dollar" arrangements.* This issue involves the propriety of "soft dollar" arrangements involving financial institutions that manage and invest plan assets.[1]

In the conduct of a financial institution audit, the investigation will review a sample of the institution's ERISA plan client files. A rule of thumb for determining how many client files to review is the "twenty-five plus ten" rule. The "twenty-five plus ten" rule requires the investigator to randomly select, from the ERISA plan client list provided by the financial institution, twenty client plans plus 10 percent of the overall number of ERISA client plans serviced by the financial institution. For example, if a financial institution services 200 ERISA covered plans, the "twenty-five plus ten" rule will result in the review of 45 ERISA plan client files. In the review of these files, the investigator will review: (1) the trust agreement and amendments;

---

1. http://www.dol.gov/ebsa/publications/softdolr.htm.

(2) the plan document and amendments; (3) the plan adoption agreement and amendments; (4) the applicable agency agreements; (5) the IRS determination letter; (6) the correspondence file; (7) the trust annual reports (for a minimum of three years); and (8) the Annual Report Forms 5500 (for a minimum of three years).

For a review of specific questions asked by the investigator in reviewing individual ERISA plan client files, see Q 748.

746. How does the Employee Benefits Security Administration select financial institutions as targets of investigation?

The Employee Benefits Security Administration (EBSA) has viewed the selection of financial institutions to be investigated for potential abuse as crucial to the protection of employee benefit plan assets, the efficient use of investigative resources, and the detection of ERISA violations. EBSA selects investigative targets through a detailed review of intelligence data available from a wide variety of sources. These sources include, but are not limited to, the following:

- EBSA case files, and other intelligence files that identify financial institutions providing services to employee benefit plans;

- Data contained in Master Trust and Common Trust Annual Report filings;

- Information contained in Form 5500 Annual Report filings;

- Applications and comments submitted by financial institutions and other interested parties in connection with individual or class exemptions proposed or granted;

- Information on problem institutions obtained from federal and state regulatory agencies, such as state insurance commissioners; and

- Information identified in public sources, such as legislative committee hearings and trade publications.[1]

747. What factors are considered by the Employee Benefits Security Administration in selecting financial institutions for investigation?

The selection of financial institutions for investigation by the Employee Benefits Security Administration (EBSA) takes into consideration the following: (1) the size of the financial institution in terms of plan assets held, managed, or invested; (2) the number and size of employee benefit plan clients; (3) the geographic location of the financial institution; (4) the type and variety of financial services offered to plans; (5) the reputation and standing of the financial institution in

---

1. *ERISA Enforcement Strategy Implementation Plan*, Sept. 1990, at 15.

the community, as determined by industry professionals and government regulators; and (6) the likelihood of finding ERISA violations involving selected areas of significant concern to EBSA.[1]

748. What are the issues covered in a review of individual ERISA plan client files in a financial institution investigation?

Financial institution investigations by the DOL require the investigator to carefully review a specific number of ERISA plan client files. In the review of those files, the investigator is guided by an account examination sheet that details the issues to be examined. The following is a review of the questions detailed in the financial institution account examination checklist:

1. Is the financial institution named as trustee?

2. Does the financial institution have investment responsibility? According to which trust agency/agreement section?

3. Does the plan sponsor direct the financial institution on investment of assets?

   o According to which trust agency/agreement section?

   o Are written investment instructions contained in the file?

4. Does the client plan have an outside investment manager? On all or a part of the assets?

5. What percentage of plan assets are invested in Collective Trust Funds (CTFs) and/or government securities?

6. Is the trustee/custodian/agency fee paid by the plan?

   o Which section of the trust/agency agreement permits the plan to pay this fee?

   o Does the fee appear to be reasonable for the services rendered?

7. Is the plan charged sweep fees?

   o What was the time period for which the fees were incurred?

   o What were the total sweep fees for the last three years?

8. Does the plan hold investments in Bank CTFs? Which trust agreement section permits this?

9. Does the plan hold participant loans?

   o Which section of the plan document permits this?

   o Are all payments current?

---

1. *ERISA Enforcement Strategy Implementation Plan*, Sept. 1990, at 15-16.

- o   Are the loans adequately secured?

- o   Is the rate of interest reasonable?

- o   Is the loan within statutorily defined limits?

10.   Does the plan hold employer securities?

- o   Which section of the trust agreement permits this?

- o   Are the securities qualifying?

- o   Are the holdings within the ERISA Section 407 limits?

11.   Does the plan hold employer real property?

- o   Which section of the trust agreement permits this?

- o   Is the property geographically dispersed?

- o   Is the rent charged adequate and current?

- o   What are the dates of the latest appraisals?

- o   What are the terms of the leases?

- o   Are the lease(s) apparently from an arm's-length transaction?

12.   Does the plan own any interests in limited partnerships?

- o   Which section of the trust agreement permits this?

- o   Is the prospectus in the file?

13.   Does the plan own real estate?

- o   Which section of the trust agreement permits this?

- o   Is it carried on the books at market value?

- o   What was the date of latest appraisal?

- o   Was it appraised free of encumbrance?

- o   Is the real property leased or occupied by a party in interest?

- o   Does the lease appear to be at an arm's-length?

- o   Is the rent adequate and current?

- o   What are the terms of the lease?

14. Does the plan own mortgages?

   o   Which section of the trust agreement permits this?

   o   Is the mortgage adequately secured?

   o   Is the property adequately insured?

   o   Are mortgage payments current?

   o   Are the interest rate and terms of the mortgage reasonable?

   o   How was the mortgage obtained?

15. Does the plan hold promissory notes other than on participant loans?

   o   Which section of the trust agreement permits this?

   o   Does the note represent a loan to a party in interest?

   o   Is the loan adequately secured?

   o   Are payments on the note current?

   o   Are the terms and interest rate on the note reasonable?

16. Does the plan hold precious metals, art, or collectibles?

   o   Which section of the trust agreement permits this?

   o   What percentage of plan assets were represented by the purchase when made?

   o   What percentage of plan assets are currently represented by these holdings?

   o   Are current appraisals of these holdings in the plan file?

   o   What is the appraised value of these holdings?

   o   Where and when were these holdings obtained by the plan?

17. Does the plan invest in commercial paper?

   o   Is the commercial paper issued by a party in interest?

   o   If so, does it satisfy the requirements of PTE 81-8?

18. Does the plan invest in repurchase agreements?

   o   Are the repurchase agreements with a party in interest?

   o   If so, do they satisfy the requirements of PTE 81-8?

19.   Does the plan invest in certificates of deposit?

   o   Are they with a party in interest?

   o   If so, do they satisfy the requirements of PTE 81-8?

This checklist and the general financial institution investigative guidelines are designed to identify improper or imprudent instances of plan asset management, as well as violations involving conflicts of interest and self-dealing between the plan and the financial institution service provider. Such violations include:

1.   Transfers of bad loans from the financial institution's commercial loan department to the trust department;

2.   The charging of excessive fees; and

3.   The use of plan assets for the permanent financing of risky construction projects for which the financial institution has provided interim financing.

The Enforcement Strategy Implementation Plan (ESIP) also cautions that financial institution investigations have discovered situations where the financial institution has extended favors to clients who are ERISA plan fiduciaries in order to retain the plan or the plan sponsor as a client. Such "sweetheart deals" include gifts, gratuities, and unsecured or low-interest loans.[1]

749. What are the issues covered under the DOL's HIPAA service provider enforcement/compliance review?

In mid-1999, the use of HIPAA enforcement/compliance questionnaires originated in one of the DOL's regional offices as an added aspect of their service provider investigations. On June 11, 1999, at the IRS Midwest Benefits Conference in Cincinnati, Ohio, the DOL announced that they would be launching a National Office–directed HIPAA Compliance/Enforcement project in October 1999. The DOL National Office Project was based upon the regional office efforts identified above, and the enforcement checklist is detailed below.

The questionnaire was designed for use in a "desk audit" situation. That is, the target of the inquiry will receive the checklist in the mail or via facsimile, along with a request that a written response and supporting documentation be forwarded to the issuing office within ten business days. The cover letter for the checklist and request for response and documentation also advises that "submission of relevant documents to our office prior to the inception of on-site field investigation can lessen the time subsequently spent with, and the administrative burden placed upon (service provider target) personnel."

---

1. 65 Fed. Reg. 18208 (April 6, 2000).

Compliance with the HIPAA Provisions in
Part 7 of Subtitle B of Title I of ERISA

(Specific Lines of Inquiry Presented by DOL Field Offices
in Conducting Investigations)

If any of the below requested items are voluminous in nature, the DOL advises that the recipient may submit the relevant parts of the requested items that relate to the specific question or following questions.

1.   Provide a copy of the Plan's (a) Summary Plan Description, (b) Plan Document, and (c) Plan Group Policy.

2.   Does the group health plan automatically issue complete certificates of creditable coverage free of charge to individuals who lose coverage under the plan, and to individuals upon request?[1]

3.   Does the group health plan have a written procedure for individuals to request and receive certificates?[2]

4.   If the group health plan imposes a preexisting-condition exclusion period, does the plan or issuer issue a notice informing individuals of such exclusion period, the terms of such exclusion period, and the right of individuals to demonstrate creditable coverage (and any applicable waiting or affiliation periods) to reduce the preexisting-condition exclusion period?[3] [The plan sponsor may be asked to provide copies of the General Notice of Preexisting-Condition Exclusions sent to two different plan participants.]

5.   If the group health plan imposes a preexisting-condition exclusion period, does it issue letters of determination and notification of creditable coverage within a reasonable time after the receipt of individuals' creditable coverage information?[4] [The plan sponsor may be asked to provide a list or log of Individualized Determination of Preexisting-Condition Exclusion letters sent out in the last twelve months.]

6.   Were any of the above individuals *not* provided a certificate of creditable coverage from their prior plan? [If so, the plan sponsor must identify them and explain and provide supporting documentation as to how the matter was resolved. If there have been more than three individuals, the issuing DOL Investigator will select the individuals for which supporting documentation must be applied.]

7.   If the group health plan imposes a preexisting-condition exclusion period, does it comport with HIPAA's limitations on preexisting-condition exclusion periods?[5] [The plan sponsor may be asked to provide a list of all claims that were denied in

---

1. Labor Reg. §§2590.701-5(a)(2)(ii), 2590.701-5(a)(2)(iii).
2. Labor Reg. §2590.701-5(a)(4)(ii).
3. Labor Reg. §2590.701-3(c).
4. Labor Reg. §§2590.701-5(d)(1), 2590.701-5(d)(2).
5. Labor Reg. §§2590.701-2(a), 2590.701-2(b).

the last twelve months due to the imposition of a preexisting-condition exclusion period, as well as records showing the enrollment dates of the individuals involved.]

8. Does the group health plan have written provisions notifying individuals who are ineligible to enroll in the plan of coverage of special enrollment rights, and issue notices of special enrollment rights?[1]

9. Does the group health plan have written procedures that provide special enrollment rights to individuals who lose other coverage and to individuals who acquire a new dependent, if they request enrollment within thirty days of the loss of coverage, marriage, birth, adoption, or placement for adoption?[2]

10. Do the group health plan's rules for eligibility to enroll under the terms of the plan or coverage (including continued eligibility) comply with the nondiscrimination requirements that prohibit discrimination against any individual or a dependent of an individual based on any health status–related factor?[3] [The plan sponsor may be asked to provide a list of any applicants or participants denied eligibility to enroll during the last twelve months.]

11. Does the group health plan comply with the nondiscrimination requirements that prohibit requiring any individual (as a condition of enrollment or continued enrollment) to pay a premium or contribution that is greater than the premium or contribution for a similarly situated individual enrolled in the plan on the basis of any health status–related factor?[4]

12. If the group health plan is a multiemployer plan or a multiple employer welfare arrangement (MEWA), does it comply with Part 7 (guaranteed renewability requirements), which generally prohibits it from denying an employer whose employees are covered under a group health plan continued access to the same or different coverage under the terms of the plan?[5] [The plan sponsor may be asked to provide a list of any employers who have not renewed coverage during the last twelve months.]

General Employee Benefits Security Administration Investigations

750. What is the general framework that governs the enforcement resources of the Employee Benefits Security Administration?

The general framework through which the enforcement resources of the Employee Benefits Security Administration (EBSA) are efficiently and effectively focused to achieve its policy and operational objectives is the Strategic Enforcement Plan (StEP), released on April 6, 2000. The StEP identifies and describes EBSA's enforcement priorities and informs the public of EBSA's current goals, priorities, and methods. The StEP promotes compliance with Title I of ERISA.

---

1. Labor Reg. §2590.701-6(c).
2. Labor Reg. §§2590.701-6(a), 2590.701-6(b).
3. ERISA Sec. 702(a)(1); Labor Reg. §2590.702(a)(1).
4. ERISA Sec. 702(b)(1); Labor Reg. §2590.702(b)(1).
5. ERISA Sec. 703.

EBSA's enforcement strategy is designed to support the Department of Labor's goal of a secure workforce by deterring and correcting violations of ERISA and related statutes.

EBSA's enforcement programs are primarily carried out through civil investigations. The civil investigative program is organized by EBSA using two main approaches: (1) national projects, which are investigative projects that further more broadly established long-range national investigative priorities; and (2) regional projects, which are localized investigative projects undertaken by individual EBSA regional offices. A critical part of EBSA's enforcement program under the Strategic Enforcement Program also includes the prosecution of criminal acts relating to employee benefit plans. Criminal investigations are discussed in detail in Section XIII.

DOL Web Site Containing Form 5500 and Other Enforcement Data

The DOL has introduced a Web site containing searchable enforcement data gathered from several agencies, in addition to EBSA. The data available on the Web site can be searched by agency and up to five states at a time (each search can also be narrowed by ZIP code). The EBSA data includes information on closed Form 5500 cases that resulted in penalties under the agency's programs for deficient, late, or unfiled Form 5500s. The DOL acknowledges that the site is a work in progress and that additional features, functionality, and search criteria will be added over time. The Web site is to be updated quarterly.

The information available on the Web site can be downloaded into a spreadsheet with headings for plan name, plan administrator, state and zip code, plan EIN, plan number and year, case type (deficient, late, or non-filer), closing reason (e.g., closed after correspondence or closed after referral to administrative law judge), closing date, and penalty amount. The Web site containing the enforcement data is available at http://www.ogesdw.dol.gov.

751. What are the Employee Benefits Security Administration's National Investigative Priorities?

The Employee Benefits Security Administration (EBSA) establishes priorities in order to ensure that its enforcement program focuses on the areas that are critical to the well-being of employee benefit plans. Generally, EBSA designates and identifies over several years the various types of plans, benefits, or other broad segments of the regulated employee benefit plan universe that will be emphasized under the enforcement program. Within these national investigative priorities, EBSA annually identifies national investigative projects, to which it dedicates enforcement resources. These national investigative projects are designed to identify and correct the ERISA violations that EBSA believes may be widespread or to focus upon abusive practices that affect many plans. The Strategic Enforcement Plan (StEP) identifies the following three current national investigative priorities: (1) plan service providers; (2) health benefit issues; and (3) defined contribution pension plans.

Plan Service Providers

As discussed in Q 737, the DOL defines a "plan service provider" as any person or entity that provides a direct or indirect service to an employee benefit plan for compensation. The DOL considers third-party administrators, accountants, attorneys, consultants, insurance brokers and agents, computer service providers, and contract service professionals to be plan service providers. The definition also includes financial institutions such as banks, trust companies, investment management companies, and insurance companies, as well as others that manage or administer (directly or indirectly) funds or property owned by employee benefit plans. The DOL believes that the investigation of plan service providers offers the opportunity to address abusive practices that may affect more than one plan. Thus, by focusing investigative resources on plan service providers, the EBSA can address violations involving many plans. The focus on service providers as a national investigative priority under the StEP is not new, but rather a continuation of the DOL's long-standing practice under the ERISA Enforcement Strategy Implementation Plan of 1990 (ESIP). Under the ESIP, EBSA devoted 50 percent of EBSA fiduciary investigative time to abusive practices in the areas of welfare plan service providers and financial institutions that provide services to employee benefit plans. By continuing its focus on service providers under the StEP, EBSA is maintaining its position under the ESIP that service provider investigations generally result in larger recoveries for more plans and more participants, and provide a mechanism whereby EBSA can leverage its resources and obtain the maximum impact for the benefit of plan participants and beneficiaries.

As under the ESIP, the investigation of service providers generally focuses on the abusive practices committed by the specific service providers rather than on the plans. For example, where a third-party administrator has systematically retained an undisclosed fee, the focus of the investigation will be on the third-party administrator rather than the plan that contracted for the services. Although the StEP does not mandate that any specific amount of investigative time be devoted to the investigation of service providers, EBSA is encouraging the field offices to allocate appropriate resources to the targeting and investigation of these issues as a method to leverage its available staffing.

Health Benefit Issues

The DOL estimates that there are a total of 2.6 million ERISA-covered health plans that cover approximately 122 million participants and beneficiaries. In the view of the DOL, several factors have combined in recent years to make the management and administration of ERISA-covered health plans a matter of vital national importance, including: increased health care costs (due in part to improved technology and accessibility); changes in the health care delivery and funding systems; and the evolution of the legal standard under which health plans and their service providers must operate. Additionally, as the cost of health care has increased, the methods for delivering that care have changed. Further, the DOL generally regards the increase in health care costs to be a key factor in the move toward managed care, the stated purpose of which is to control access to health care and its related costs.

Under the StEP, EBSA seeks to ensure that the benefits of participants and beneficiaries under welfare plans are protected. The application of available remedies under ERISA is critical in those cases where federal preemption leaves participants with no other effective statutory or common law cause of action. EBSA seeks to apply the full extent of ERISA's remedies and to promote a legal standard that will increase the availability of appropriate remedies to protect welfare plan participants and beneficiaries.

Because EBSA views health benefits as critically important, in recent years it has applied substantial resources to addressing abusive practices that violate ERISA. For example, EBSA has pursued enforcement actions involving multiple employer welfare arrangements (MEWAs), and insurers and service providers that receive hidden discounts. Moreover, EBSA's role in health care has also expanded as a result of the enactment of new legislation, such as the Health Insurance Portability and Accountability Act of 1996 (HIPAA); the Newborns' and Mothers' Health Protection Act of 1996 (NMHPA); the Mental Health Parity Act of 1996 (MHPA); the Women's Health and Cancer Rights Act of 1998 (WHCRA); the Mental Health Parity and Addiction Equity Act of 2008 (MHPAEA); the Genetic Information Nondiscrimination Act of 2008 (GINA); the Health Information Technology for Economic and Clinical Health Act of 2009 (HITECH Act); and the Children's Health Insurance Program Reauthorization Act of 2009 (CHIPRA). EBSA is charged with implementing new regulatory and enforcement requirements that are found in these laws. In response to its expanding role in the health care area, the StEP provides that EBSA will continue to devote substantial enforcement resources to the targeting and investigation of fiduciary issues relating to health benefit plans. EBSA has also established the Office of Health Plan Standards and Compliance Assistance (see Q 720) to develop regulations, interpretive bulletins, opinions, forms, and rulings relating to health care portability, nondiscrimination requirements, and other related health provisions in furtherance of this role.

Defined Contribution Plans

In the Strategic Enforcement Plan (StEP), EBSA has identified defined contribution plans as a national investigative project. In recent years there has been a tremendous growth in 401(k) defined contribution plans in terms of the number of plans, the number of participants, and the amount of assets in these plans. EBSA has decided that this growth, and the related administrative and investment practices that have developed to accommodate these plans, warrant scrutiny in order to ensure the safety of this large volume of assets. Moreover, because defined contribution plans are not covered by PBGC insurance, plan losses due to a fiduciary breach directly affect plan participants and such losses are irrevocable unless the funds can be recovered through enforcement or other legal actions. Accordingly, EBSA has identified defined contribution plans as a national enforcement priority because the risk of loss in such plans rests entirely on the plan participants.

752. What are the Employee Benefits Security Administration's National Projects?

According to the StEP, national projects are investigative projects that focus on a selected issue or group of related issues of national scope and significance that fall within the established national enforcement priorities. Generally, a field office of the Employee Benefits Security Administration (EBSA) must give priority to conducting investigations and dedicating appropriate resources to the project during the fiscal year. On occasion, however, national projects may address issues that are not necessarily prevalent in all areas of the country, and then only a selected group of EBSA field offices are required to participate in the project. According to EBSA, the issues selected for implementation as national projects are determined in annual planning sessions (or reviewed, since an individual national project may extend over more than one fiscal year), including commentary from EBSA's field offices. National projects may be an expansion of a successful regional project or may arise in connection with field office investigations. Coordination and enforcement policy determinations for national projects are generally directed through the Office of Enforcement (OE), although the field office managers have substantial opportunities to participate and comment. The OE's involvement in national projects includes monitoring and evaluating the project's progression, and, where appropriate, issuing procedural directives and technical guidance.

753. What are some of the national enforcement projects identified by the Employee Benefits Security Administration?

The field offices have been ordered to place particular investigative emphasis upon the following national enforcement projects identified by the Employee Benefits Security Administration (EBSA).

Multiple Employer Welfare Arrangements (MEWAs)

A Multiple Employer Welfare Arrangement (MEWA) is a welfare benefit plan or other arrangement established to benefit the employees of two or more employers. The EBSA has found that small employers may use MEWAs when they are either unable to obtain health care coverage for their employees or cannot afford the cost of such coverage. EBSA investigations continue to reveal instances where MEWAs have failed to pay claims as a result of insufficient funding and inadequate reserves. In the worst situations, MEWAs have been operated by individuals who drained the MEWA's assets through excessive administrative fees or by outright theft. According to the Strategic Enforcement Plan (StEP), EBSA's emphasis is on abusive and fraudulent MEWAs created by unscrupulous promoters, who default on their obligations after promising inexpensive health benefit insurance.

The DOL believes that MEWAs may also be involved in criminal violations.

Administrative Services Only (ASO) Project

The Administrative Services Only (ASO) national project involves investigations of insurance companies that provide administrative services only to self-funded welfare plans. These investigations focus on whether fee reductions or discounts obtained from medical service providers have been passed on to the plans or their participants.

401(k) Fees

Although it does not presently appear to be an investigative-type project, EBSA intends the 401(k) Fees project to educate both plan participants and plan sponsors about the impact of fees on participants' return on investments. (An in-depth discussion of this subject appears in Section IV.) EBSA developed a consumer information brochure on plan investment fees in support of this project, which is designed to educate participants on important ways to monitor investment fees and to remind plan sponsors of their fiduciary obligations to monitor these fees. EBSA reports that this investigative project has increased its knowledge of how 401(k) plans monitor and analyze their investment fees (particularly where the fees are paid from plan assets rather than by the plan sponsor), and how fiduciaries oversee the administration of these types of plans.

Orphan Plans

In response to situations where plans have been abandoned by plan sponsors and fiduciaries, or fiduciaries have completely abdicated their responsibilities to administer plans prudently and in the sole interest of the participants, EBSA began the Orphan Plans project in October 1999. According to EBSA, the objectives of this project are to: (1) locate orphan plans that have been abandoned by fiduciaries as a result of death, neglect, bankruptcy, or incarceration; (2) determine if the fiduciary is available to make fiduciary decisions, such as the termination of the plan and the distribution of plan assets; (3) require fiduciaries to fulfill their duties, file appropriate compliance forms, and ensure that proper actions are undertaken to protect promised benefits; and, where possible, (4) to identify and penalize plan officials that have not fulfilled their responsibilities to plan participants.

Health Benefits Security Project

Established in Fiscal Year 2012, the Health Benefits Security Project (HBSP) is the DOL's comprehensive national health enforcement project, combining DOLs existing health plan enforcement initiatives with the new protections afforded by the Patient Protection and Affordable Care Act of 2010 (PPACA). The HBSP involves a broad range of health care investigations, including examinations for compliance with ERISA Part 7 and PPACA, civil and criminal investigations of Multiple Employer Welfare Arrangements (MEWAs), investigations of insurance companies and claim administrators to ensure that promised benefits are actually provided, and criminal investigations of fraudulent medical providers.

The HBSP investigations examine compliance with applicable provisions of the PPACA, which includes market reforms, patient protections, extension of dependent coverage, internal claims and appeals and external reviews and grandfathered health plans.

The plan document may contain ERISA- and PPACA-compliant language and procedures, but operationally, the promised health benefits are not provided at all or not within the requirements of the law or the plan document. Therefore, the HBSP also focuses on plans' and claims administrators' failure to provide promised health benefits through a lack of disclosure or through the misapplication in substance or in procedure of the plan's terms.

PPACA authorizes the DOL to immediately issue a cease and desist order when fraud is apparent. The DOL may also seize assets from a MEWA when probable cause exists to believe that the plan is in a financially hazardous condition. Final regulations, which became effective on April 1, 2013, establish policies and procedures for implementation of the cease and desist and summary seizure rules.

MEWA Enforcement Project

In December 2011, DOL issued a MEWA Enforcement Fact Sheet (with results through September 2011) reporting that DOL successfully initiated 821 civil investigations and 314 criminal investigations, delivering monetary results of $226 million. These criminal MEWA cases have resulted in jail sentences in excess of 400 years cumulatively and court-ordered restitution against fraudulent MEWA operators. Most of these investigations have been jointly investigated with other agencies, including the Department's Office of Labor Racketeering and Fraud Investigations, the FBI, the U.S. Postal Inspection Service, and the Internal Revenue Service's Criminal Investigative Division.[1]

On December 5, 2011, the DOL issued proposed rules intended to increase DOL oversight and enforcement of MEWAs as well as increase their public reporting requirements.[2] In following up on section 6606 of the Patient Protection and Affordable Care Act amendment of ERISA section 101(g), which grants the DOL authority to require annual reporting by MEWAs that are not ERISA-covered plans and require them to register with the DOL prior to operating in a state, the DOL has issued rules to provide for these filings.[3] Specifically, MEWAs providing medical care benefits which are not ERISA-covered group health plans are covered by these new rules.[4]

The extended disclosure regulations now require existing and new non-ERISA qualified MEWAs subject to the rule to annually file Form M-1 and any additional statements required pursuant to the instructions to Form M-1 (see Question 710 for full details on the filing requirements of Form M-1).[5] Further, a MEWA is required to register with the DOL by filing a completed Form M-1 and attachments with the DOL thirty days prior to operating in a state.[6] A new registration filing of the Form M-1 is also required in the event of

1.   Operations expanding into a new state;

2.   Merging with another MEWA;

3.   If the number of employees receiving coverage for medical care is at least 50 percent greater than the number of employees receiving coverage for medical care at the close of the last calendar year; or

4.   If there are any material changes (as defined in the Form M-1 instructions).[7]

The DOL is also empowered under the new rules to issue cease and desist orders and summary seizure orders under ERISA section 521 through amendments to the regulations found under 2560.521 and 2520.103-1.[8] These powers will be enforced where it is apparent that fraud is taking place (i.e., failure to pay claims) or an arrangement is causing immediate danger to the public safety or welfare. The DOL will have the ability to seize assets from a MEWA where there is probable cause that the plan is in a financially hazardous condition (thus preserving the assets before they are dissipated).

---

1. http://www.dol.gov/ebsa/erisa_enforcement.html; http://www.dol.gov/ebsa/newsroom/fsMEWAenforcement.html.
2. 76 Fed. Reg. 76222 (Dec. 5, 2011).
3. Prop. Reg. Sec. 2550.101-2(a).
4. Prop. Reg. 2550.101-2(b)(7).
5. Prop. Reg. 2550.101-2(d)(1).
6. Prop. Reg. 2550.101-2(e)(iii).
7. Prop. Reg. 2550.101-2(e)(iv).
8. Prop. Reg. 2550.101-2(g).

The new rules do exclude any MEWA that provides coverage only through group health plans that are not covered by ERISA, including governmental plans, church plans, or plans maintained solely for the purpose of complying with workmen's compensation laws.[1]

PPACA added section 521 to ERISA to authorize the Secretary of Labor to issue a cease and desist order, ex parte, when it appears that the alleged conduct of a MEWA is fraudulent, creates an immediate danger to the public safety or welfare, or is causing or can be reasonably expected to cause significant, imminent, and irreparable public injury. The Secretary may also seek a summary seizure order when it appears that a MEWA is in a financially hazardous condition. Systematic failures to pay benefit claims or the diversion of premiums for personal use are common examples of these types of conduct. Before this change, stopping the activities of an abusive arrangement immediately and freezing its assets required a court-issued temporary restraining order and preliminary injunction. With this new authority, the Secretary may take steps to protect plan participants and small employers much earlier in the process, before all of the assets have been exhausted. On March 1, 2013, final rules were published in the Federal Register to facilitate implementation of this new enforcement authority provided to the Secretary.

HIPAA added section 101(g) to ERISA to provide the Secretary with the authority to require, by regulation, annual reporting by MEWAs that are not ERISA-covered plans. The Affordable Care Act amended section 101(g) to require that such MEWAs register with the Department of Labor prior to operating in a state. On March 1, 2013, the Department published final rules in the Federal Register implementing the changes made by the Affordable Care Act.

While reporting requirements for MEWAs have been in place since 1999, the Department often did not find out about insolvent or fraudulent MEWAs until significant harm had occurred to employers and participants. This new registration enhances the existing reporting rules to require all MEWAs as well as certain other entities that offer or provide health benefits to the employees of two or more employers to register with the Department via the Form M-1. These changes also require MEWAs that are ERISA plans which are subject to the Form M-1 filing requirements to file a Form 5500 Annual Report, regardless of plan size. By requiring MEWAs to register with the Department before operating in a State, this rule enhances the State and Federal governments' joint mission to prevent and take enforcement action against fraudulent and abusive MEWAs and limit the losses suffered by American workers, their families, and businesses in instances when abusive MEWAs become insolvent and fail to reimburse medical claims."

DOL Enforcement Activities on Fees

The DOL's web site discussion of National Enforcement Projects states the following: "EBSA's newest National Project will focus on the receipt of improper, undisclosed compensation by pension consultants and other investment advisers. EBSA's investigations will seek to determine whether the receipt of such compensation violates ERISA because the adviser/consultant used

---

1. Prop. Reg. 2550.101-2(c)(1)(D).

its position with a benefit plan to generate additional fees for itself or its affiliates. EBSA may also need to investigate individual plans to address such potential violations as failure to adhere to investment guidelines and improper selection or monitoring of the consultant or adviser. The Consultant/Adviser Project (CAP) will also seek to identify potential criminal violations, such as kickbacks or fraud."

This project is coupled with EBSA's recent Request for Information and Proposed Rule on Fee and Expense Disclosures to Participants in Individual Account Plans.[1]

Both of these items demonstrate that the DOL is stepping up its investigation of plan service providers to identify abusive practices, determine industry trends, and maximize its targeting of plans that may have a high probability of violating the prudence standards of ERISA or plans that could be affected by self-dealing by plan service providers. It is expected that EBSA will continue to increase the number and scope of service provider investigations.

The 401(k) fee standardized disclosure form contains basic information employers may use in calculating and accounting for the total costs of operating a plan. It contains:

1. An overview of the purpose of the form and general description of calculating 401(k) fees;

2. A schedule that summarizes the total plan fees and expenses; and

3. Additional schedules providing information on

    a. investment product fees and estimates,

    b. plan administration expenses,

    c. one-time start-up and conversion expenses, and

    d. service provider termination expenses.

The standardized disclosure form is divided into six parts. It contains a discussion on the four general ways in which service provider fees are calculated (asset based, per person, transaction based, and flat rate), the disclosure schedules, and a glossary of service provider terms defined. The individual schedules require disclosure of the following information, all of which adds up to total plan expenses:

1. Investment product fees

    a. collective investment funds;

    b. insurance/annuity products;

    c. mutual funds;

    d. individually managed accounts;

---

1. EBSA Proposed Rule, "Fee and Expense Disclosures to Participants in Individual Account Plans," 72 Fed. Reg. 20457, April 25, 2007.

      e.   brokerage window; and

      f.   other products (specified).

2.   Plan administration expenses

   a. administration/recordkeeping fees

      i.   daily valuation;

      ii.   payroll processing;

      iii. balance inquiry;

      iv. investment transfer;

      v.   contract administration charge;

      vi. distribution processing;

      vii. QDRO processing;

      viii. participant statements;

      ix. plan sponsor reports;

      x.   VRU/Internet services; and

      xi. other (specified).

   b. participant education/advice

      i.   participant education materials/distribution;

      ii.   education meetings (frequency);

      iii. investment advice programs; and

      iv. other (specified).

   c. trustee custodial services

      i.   certified annual trust statement;

      ii.   safekeeping of plan assets; and

      iii. other (specified).

   d. compliance services

      i.   nondiscrimination testing;

      ii.   signature-ready Form 5500;

          iii.   annual audit; and

          iv.   other (specified).

    e. plan amendment fee

          i.   plan amendment fee;

          ii.   plan document/determination letter fee; and

          iii.   other (specified).

    f. participant loan administration

          i.   loan origination fee;

          ii.   loan processing fee;

          iii.   loan maintenance and repayment tracking fee; and

          iv.   other (specified).

3.   One-time start-up/conversion expenses

        a.   start-up conversion education program;

        b.   start-up/conversion enrollment expense;

        c.   installation fee;

        d.   start-up/conversion plan document fee/filing fee; and

        e.   other (specified).

4.   Service provider termination expenses

    a. investment product expenses

          i.   contract termination charges;

          ii.   back-end load;

          iii.   product termination fee; and

          iv.   other (specified).

    b. plan administration expenses

          i.   service provider termination charge;

          ii.   service contract termination charge; and

          iii.   other (specified).

754. What is the Employee Contributions Project?

Since 1995, the Employee Benefits Security Administration (EBSA) has used the Employee Contributions Project to pursue an aggressive enforcement program that is intended to safeguard employee contributions made to 401(k) plans and health care plans. EBSA investigates situations in which employers delay depositing employee contributions made to these plans. Pursuant to the revised participant contribution regulations, effective February 3, 1997, employee pension benefit plan contributions become plan assets as soon as they can reasonably be segregated from the employer's general assets, but in no event later than fifteen business days after the end of the month in which the contributions are withheld from employees' pay. Employee welfare benefit plan contributions become plan assets as soon as they can reasonably be segregated from the employer's general assets, but in no event later than ninety days after the date when the employer receives them (in the case of amounts that a participant or beneficiary pays to the employer), or the date on which such contributions would otherwise be payable in cash (in the case of amounts withheld by an employer from a participant's wages). EBSA has determined that in some cases, employers do not promptly deposit the contributions in the appropriate funding vehicle, as required by the regulations. In other cases, EBSA has found that the employer simply converts the contributions to other uses, such as business expenses. In EBSA's view, both scenarios may occur when the employer is having fiscal problems and turns to the plan for unlawful financing.

EBSA has amended the plan asset regulations to provide for a safe harbor under which participant contributions to a pension or welfare benefit plan with fewer than one-hundred participants at the beginning of the plan year will be treated as having been made to the plan in accordance with the general rule when contributions are deposited with the plan no later than the seventh business day following the day on which such amount is received by the employer, or the seventh business day on which such amount would otherwise have been payable to the participant in cash.[1] The regulations have been amended to include participant loan repayments under the general provisions and under the safe harbor.[2] These amended regulations will not change the current regulations mandating deposit of the assets by the fiftieth business day of the month following the month in which the assets were withheld from the participants. Rather, it creates a one-week time period in which there is a presumption of compliance for assets deposited to the plan trust by small plans.

755. Are any other enforcement projects aimed at health benefit plans?

In recent years, the Employee Benefits Security Administration (EBSA) has applied substantial enforcement resources to the targeting and investigation of fiduciary violations, as well as criminal violations relating to health benefit plans. EBSA's role with respect to health plans has also expanded as a result of legislation that increased the regulatory and enforcement requirements to be implemented by EBSA. These statutes include the Health Insurance Portability and Accountability Act of 1996 (HIPAA), the Mental Health Parity Act of 1996 (MHPA), the Newborns' and Mothers' Health Protection Act of 1996 (Newborns' Act), the

---

1. Labor Reg. §2510.3-102(a)(2); 75 Fed. Reg. 2068 (Jan. 14, 2010).
2. Labor Reg. §2510.3-102(a)(2); 75 Fed. Reg. 2068 (Jan. 14, 2010).

Women's Health and Cancer Rights Act of 1998 (WHCRA); the Mental Health Parity and Addiction Equity Act of 2008 (MHPAEA); the Genetic Information Nondiscrimination Act of 2008 (GINA); the Health Information Technology for Economic and Clinical Health Act of 2009 (HITECH Act); and the Children's Health Insurance Program Reauthorization Act of 2009 (CHIPRA). EBSA's focus with regard to health plans is primarily to ensure that funded plans are financially sound and that plans are administered prudently and in the participants' sole interest.

756. What are regional projects?

Enforcement initiatives are also conducted as projects by individual regional field offices. Each year, the regional field office managers submit their project proposals to the Office of Enforcement (OE) for review and approval. The subjects selected for regional projects are generally topics that have been identified by a particular region as an enforcement issue that may be unique or particularly problematic within its geographic jurisdiction. Because regional field office staff may be able to identify potential issues through their investigative activities, they have the unique opportunity to observe industry practices firsthand and select issues for development as regional projects that may ultimately be appropriate for adoption as national projects. According to the Employee Benefits Security Administration (EBSA), an issue selected as a regional project will normally be:

- Well-defined both in terms of scope and focus (rather than couched in terms of broad categories, such as "small plan issues");

- Identified in the context of a type of transaction or industry practice; or

- An emerging concern or involving a legal position that is precedential in nature.

In addition, a regional project should have the potential to develop an effective targeting method so that an appropriate number of subjects can be identified for investigation. As noted previously, any number of targeting methods may be used. EBSA considers regional projects that satisfy the criteria listed above to provide a foundation for identifying cutting-edge issues that may ultimately involve matters of national scope and importance. If an issue is subsequently selected as a national project, EBSA believes that the experience and insight gained at the field office level will provide a substantive basis for guiding other field offices in conducting similar investigations. Some regional projects address practices that are more localized in their scope and impact. Because the demographics of each region differ with respect to the concentrations of various types of plans and service providers, the same strategy may not be effective for all regional field offices.

757. What factors are considered by the Employee Benefits Security Administration in targeting cases?

In developing priorities for meeting the objectives for targeting cases, the Employee Benefits Security Administration (EBSA) considers the following factors:

- Preventing dissipation of plan assets;

- Obtaining restitution on behalf of employee benefit plans;

- Removing harmful individuals from contact with plans, through both civil measures and criminal sanctions;

- Establishing legal precedent for the guidance of the public;

- Enlisting the assistance of others, such as plan accountants, in EBSA enforcement efforts;

- Encouraging private initiatives (as contemplated by ERISA Section 502) by fostering greater awareness by plan participants of their rights and increasing their ability to obtain meaningful information about their plans;

- Assisting the public;

- Promoting legislative and public awareness of EBSA enforcement efforts and seeking legislative and regulatory solutions to enforcement problems; and

- Encouraging inter-agency cooperation.[1]

758. What targeting methods are used in selecting plans for investigations?

The Employee Benefits Security Administration (EBSA) uses the following targeting methods in selecting cases for investigation:

- Plan directories for each area office's jurisdiction, based upon its designated geographical territories, participant size, and asset dollar size;

- Specifically designed Form 5500 computer-based targeting reports;

- Comparison of data from the ERISA database to data merged or generated from other databases befitting the criteria under review or investigation (i.e., (1) the Federal Deposit Insurance Corporation (FDIC) database reporting statistical information on financial institutions holding employee benefit trust assets; (2) the Master Trust database maintained by EBSA; (3) the common and collective trusts database; (4) the Office of Labor Management Standards database; and (5) other databases deemed appropriate by EBSA);

- Continued review of significant answers to Form 5500 narrative questions that warrant further inquiry by the appropriate regional office for investigation;

---

1. *ERISA Enforcement Strategy Implementation Plan*, Sept. 1990, at 19-20.

- Targeting techniques to measure whether plan assets are adequately diversified as to decrease the risk of losses to plans using investment strategies;

- Specific "on-line" targeting for special plan characteristics;

- Information from EBSA's Office of Exemption Determinations and Office of Regulations and Interpretations, such as exemption applications and related comments;

- Complaints of abuse in employee benefit plans received from participants, trustees, and interested third parties;

- Information obtained from other federal and state agencies, including the Office of Inspector General, Federal Bureau of Investigation, and state insurance commissioners; and

- Referrals from the Pension Benefit Guaranty Corporation (PBGC) for consideration for investigation by EBSA of those cases relating to areas of potential exposure for PBGC, such as severely underfunded plans, abandoned plans, and special classes of preferred stock by employers to their plans.[1]

759. How does the Employee Benefits Security Administration target a plan for investigation?

The DOL's Employee Benefits Security Administration (EBSA) has approximately 300 auditors and investigators located within its ten regional and five district offices. With the amount of private-sector benefit plans in the United States numbering in the hundreds of thousands, the DOL, with such a relatively small investigative staff, does not randomly target plans for investigation. Consequently, any plan, sponsor, or service provider identified as a target for investigation has been determined to have a high probability of violating ERISA.

There is one exception to this general rule. Plans may be selected for a limited review under the DOL's national computer targeting program, which targets plans based on the information reported on the Annual Report Form 5500. The DOL's national office periodically sends its regional field offices a list of plans within their respective geographic jurisdictions that meet the current targeting criteria for a limited review. At its discretion, the regional office may send an inquiry letter requesting certain information to the plans listed on the targeting report in order to determine whether any violations exist with respect to the issues targeted. A timely response to the regional office, indicating that no violation exists, is likely to result in a closed case.

---

1. *ERISA Enforcement Strategy Implementation Plan*, Sept. 1990, at 20-21.

DOL field offices primarily use the following sources of information to select a plan, sponsor, or service provider for an investigation:

1.   *Complaints.* The DOL may receive information that indicates or alleges that a violation of ERISA has occurred or is about to occur. Complaints may be written or oral and they may be received from individuals, news media, or other governmental agencies. If information in the complaint is indefinite, general, or grounded in rumor or conjecture, an investigation likely will not be conducted. Nevertheless, if a participant complaint indicates and documents ERISA violations that affect a class of participants, the DOL will be interested in investigating. Many of the more egregious civil and criminal violations are brought to the attention of the DOL through participant complaints to the DOL field offices.

2.   *Issues identified through other investigations.* DOL auditors and investigators are trained to identify and investigate evidence of ERISA violations discovered in investigations of plan service providers. If a service provider is being investigated and the provider's actions have left client plans in violation of ERISA, or if violations exist in the plans regardless of the service provider's actions, the DOL may open investigations of the individual plans. Similarly, if a single plan investigation details an ERISA violation that may involve other plans or service providers, further investigations may result.

Practitioner's Pointer: This is why service providers are strongly encouraged to request an accommodation subpoena from the DOL when notified that they are the target of a DOL investigation. An accommodation subpoena is a subpoena issued to persons (or entities) willing to testify or to produce the documents requested, but are concerned about the potential adverse consequences of doing so without a legal requirement. It is not good business to volunteer potentially damaging information to the DOL about one's clients.

Additionally, the attorney-client privilege may protect plan records that have been subpoenaed from plan legal counsel. However, under *Dole v. Milonas*,[1] it has been held that the attorney-client privilege does not permit an attorney to refuse to identify plan participants to the DOL absent a showing that the release of such names would be tantamount to the provision of protected communications protected by the attorney-client privilege. The *Milonas* case also established that the plan (or its service providers) may petition the court to issue a protective order that restricts the use of the subpoenaed information to the agency conducting the investigation and the use of the information solely for the purpose of conducting the ERISA investigation.

---

3.   *Other government agency referrals.* The DOL shares information with the IRS, Office of Inspector General, and other federal agencies about evidence of violations under their respective jurisdictions discovered in the course of investigations.

4.   *Field office computer targeting.* The DOL field offices currently receive digitally scanned images of Annual Report Forms 5500, attached accountants' opinions, and audited financial statements filed with the IRS. The information reported on the Annual Report Form 5500 is entered into a computer database known as

---

1. 889 F.2d 885 (9th Cir. 1989).

"FEDS," and is distributed to the DOL field offices on electronic media, accessible through their computer network. The system does not have the capability to conduct searches or inquiries using targeted criteria. It can only generate a reproduction of the actual Annual Report Forms 5500, attached accountants' opinions, or audited financial statements. Using FEDS, the DOL targets plans for investigation, based upon Annual Report Forms 5500 contained in its database. The targeting criteria are usually determined by the investigators who conduct searches.

5.   *Annual Report Form 5500 review.* Some of the DOL regional offices may periodically send a team of investigators and auditors to an IRS regional storage facility to manually select and review the hard-copy filings of Annual Report Forms 5500, accountants' opinions, and audited financial statements filed by employee benefit plans within their regional jurisdiction. The DOL team then screens, selects, and copies the documents that indicate potential violations of ERISA, according to their experience and judgment. The copied documents are returned to the regional office and used as targeting sources for potential future investigations.

6.   *ESIP targeting programs.* An enforcement strategy implementation plan (ESIP) is periodically undertaken by the DOL, in an effort to allocate limited resources in the most effective manner to achieve and maintain compliance with ERISA. The 1990 ESIP directs the DOL to allocate 50 percent of its investigative resources to investigations of "significant issues": specific areas that have the highest potential for abuse. The objectives of the ESIP are to:

a.   provide protection for the largest number of plan participants and amount of plan assets, given the available resources;

b.   identify and investigate areas with the most potential for abuse;

c.   detect and obtain corrections of ERISA violations;

d.   establish a presence in the regulated community;

e.   disseminate information and promote voluntary compliance; and

f.   respond to participant complaints, public inquiries, and referrals from other government agencies.

In the years immediately following the announcement of the 1990 ESIP, the DOL focused its investigations on financial institutions. Since many of the larger financial institutions across the country have been investigated, the DOL is now focusing its ESIP resources on service providers, such as insurance companies, brokerage houses, third-party administrators, and, most recently, home health care agencies.[1]

---

1. *ERISA Enforcement Strategy Implementation Plan*, Sept. 1990.

Preparing for the Investigation

760. How can an employee benefit plan prepare for a pending Department of Labor investigation?

The target of a pending DOL investigation will be contacted, generally one to three weeks in advance, in order to schedule a convenient date and time for the initial on-site investigation. Unless the situation is urgent, the DOL is usually flexible regarding the scheduling. After the date has been established, the DOL will confirm the appointment with a follow-up letter that includes a list of documents the auditor/investigator will want to review. The auditor/investigator uses this list to prepare for the investigation by identifying the information requested, conducting a pre-investigation analysis of the plan or its operations, and preparing any other necessary documentation and support.

All service providers to the plan should be notified as soon as possible. This allows them time to review their records pertaining to the plan and prepare for any potential inquiries they may receive from the DOL. It also allows the entity and its service providers to obtain a uniform understanding of all of the facts regarding the operation of the plan. It is not uncommon for a DOL investigator/auditor to make unannounced visits to a service provider to follow up on a line of inquiry initiated with the plan sponsor. Preparation may allow these unscheduled visits to confirm, rather than contradict, the information presented by the plan sponsor.

All relevant materials and documents should be organized. Having well-organized documents may result in shorter investigations and minimize follow-up questions that could lead to problems. It may also give the DOL investigator/auditor the impression that the plan is well run and operated in compliance with ERISA. All requested documents may be placed into binders with a labeled dividing tab indicating each document, or if the records are voluminous, using separate, labeled file folders. A copy of the investigator's list of requested records should be placed on the front of the binder or folder with the records it contains highlighted on the list.

The plan sponsor should conduct a thorough pre-investigation internal audit. Depending upon the level of sophistication required to review complex documents, obtaining professional assistance to conduct such an internal audit should be considered. Regardless of who conducts the audit, questionable entries, vague or confusing information, or unanswered questions about plan records should be identified and answers prepared. Many DOL investigations are targeted through an analysis of the information reported on the Annual Report Forms 5500, attached schedules, accountants' opinions, and audited financial statements.

Explanations should be prepared for any unanswered questions or vague or confusing information. DOL investigations are usually based on specific issues that indicate possible ERISA violations. Investigators or auditors must document these possible violations in order to open up an investigation. In that respect, a thorough pre-investigation audit may disclose any possible violations that may be present. If any issues that may support possible violations are identified, responses should be formulated and supporting documentation amassed to deflect or quell the DOL inquiry. Rapid, steadfast, and defensible responses may convince the investigator to disregard the issue. Conversely, hesitant or vacillating responses may indicate that the issue is worth pursuing. See Q 763 through Q 773 for detailed guidance on where to begin a pre-investigation audit.

Any defects identified in the internal audit should be corrected prior to the initial on-site investigation. A targeted entity may minimize its exposure to DOL sanctions and penalties if ERISA violations and defects are corrected before being discovered (or confirmed) during an investigation. In correcting violations, corrections should not be backdated, and documents should never be falsified. This may not only compound civil penalties, it may also be considered a criminal act. If there is a time-related issue, it should be corrected with the current date. Nevertheless, if the violation was also a violation of the Internal Revenue Code, the DOL may notify the IRS under its examination referral program.

Practitioner's Pointer: Although a violation may have existed, penalties may be reduced or eliminated if the underlying violation is corrected. If a breach of a fiduciary responsibility under ERISA is corrected prior to the receipt of a voluntary compliance (VC) letter advising of a violation by the DOL, the 20 percent penalty of ERISA Section 502(*l*) may be inapplicable. That is because, in order for the 20 percent penalty to apply, the applicable recovery amount must be paid pursuant to a settlement agreement with the Secretary of Labor or pursuant to court order in a judicial proceeding instituted by the Secretary of Labor. Note, however, that if a recipient of a VC letter performs the requested action in order to obtain the benefit of the DOL's promise to take no further action, a settlement agreement may be deemed to have occurred, thereby subjecting the recipient to the ERISA Section 502(*l*) penalty. This strategy should be discussed with legal counsel.

It may be necessary to hire outside help. Thorough preparation for the actual investigation may substantially minimize the possibility of surprises later. If the plan sponsor discovers an outstanding violation that it cannot handle alone, retaining outside professional assistance should be considered. Similarly, if the investment, operation, or fiduciary issues are complex or obscure, professional assistance may be warranted to assist in preparing documentation and structuring responses that avoid or minimize the imposition of fines and sanctions. Of course, the plan sponsor should be complete and honest in providing such professionals with all of the information necessary to protect the interests of the plan and fiduciaries because their ability to represent a plan is only as good as the information and cooperation presented to them.

---

761. May the expenses of a compliance audit be charged to a plan?

Maybe. The DOL provided guidance to this question in a July 28, 1998, information letter in which it indicated that the payment of an expense associated with a compliance audit by a multiemployer pension plan may be an appropriate expenditure of plan assets if the plan fiduciaries consider all of the relevant facts and circumstances of a given case. Although this guidance addresses the issue within the context of multiemployer pension plans, the information letter's rationale warrants its extension to single-employer employee benefit pension plans.

Compliance audits examine whether a plan is being operated in accordance with its governing documents, ERISA, and the Internal Revenue Code. Compliance audits include, but are not necessarily limited to, an examination of the administrative aspects of a plan's routine operations, including the plan's collection of contributions, payment of benefits, and investment of assets, as well as its compliance with the qualification provisions of the Internal Revenue Code.

According to the DOL, the fiduciaries must first examine the language of the plan documents in evaluating the payment of compliance audit expenses by a plan. If the expense would be permitted under the terms of the plan documents, then the fiduciaries must determine whether such payment would be consistent with Title I of ERISA. This initial inquiry is consistent with ERISA Section 404(a)(1)(D), which requires plan fiduciaries to discharge their duties in accordance with the documents and instruments governing the plan insofar as such documents and instruments are consistent with the provisions of Title I of ERISA (see Q 352).

Second, the plan's fiduciaries must consider the standards of conduct set forth in Sections 403(c)(1) (see Q 267) and 404(a)(1)(A) of ERISA (see Q 252). With respect to these sections, it is the view of the DOL that, generally, reasonable expenses of administering a plan include direct expenses properly and actually incurred in the performance of a fiduciary's duties to the plan. Consequently, if the trustees of a plan determine that periodic compliance audits are a helpful and prudent means of carrying out their fiduciary duties, including the duty to operate the plan in accordance with its terms, then the use of plan assets to procure compliance audits would not, in and of itself, violate Sections 403 and 404 of ERISA. In support of its conclusion, the DOL referenced the regulatory provision that permits fiduciaries to rely upon information, data, statistics, or analysis furnished by persons performing ministerial functions for the plan, provided that they have exercised prudence in the selection and retention of such persons.[1]

Third, because compliance audits may confer a benefit upon the employer sponsoring plan, the plan fiduciaries have a duty to ensure that the plan's payment of an audit's expenses is reasonable in light of the benefit conferred upon the plan. Moreover, to the extent that the payments are made for the benefit of parties other than the plan's participants or beneficiaries, or involve services for which a plan sponsor or other entity could reasonably be expected to bear the cost in the normal course of such entity's business, the use of plan assets to make such payments would not be a reasonable expense of administering the plan.[2]

Finally, the DOL reiterated, in an information letter, its view that the payment of sanctions or penalties in connection with the settlement of disqualification matters with the IRS may or may not constitute a reasonable administrative expense of the plan under Title I of ERISA. The payment of such penalties will not constitute a reasonable expense of administering the plan for purposes of ERISA Sections 403 and 404 to the extent that the penalties are a personal liability of someone other than the plan (e.g., penalties under IRC Section 6652 imposed on a plan administrator as a personal liability).[3] In contrast, if a plan-disqualifying defect is not caused by a breach of fiduciary duty, the plan can pay for any resulting sanctions or penalties only to the extent that such payment will constitute a reasonable expense of the plan.[4]

---

1. See Labor Reg. §2509.75-8, Q-11.
2. See Letter to David Alter and Mark Hess from Bette Briggs (Sept. 10, 1996); Letter to Kirk F. Maldonado from Elliot I. Daniels (Mar. 2, 1987); see also DOL Adv. Op. 97-03A (Jan. 23, 1997).
3. See Letter to Mark Sokolsky from John J. Canary (Feb. 23, 1996).
4. See DOL Adv. Op. 97-03A (Jan. 23, 1997); Information Letter to Gary E. Henderson from Susan G. Lahne (July 28, 1998).

762. What actions should a plan sponsor take during the course of the initial on-site DOL investigation?

Initial on-site investigations are typically scheduled for no more than three days if the target is a single plan or a single plan sponsor. Service provider investigations are more detailed and usually take one or more weeks, with follow-up on-site visits scheduled as needed.

An official liaison should be ready to meet the DOL investigator/auditor upon his arrival. The liaison should be responsible for working with the investigator/auditor during the on-site investigation. Lower-level employees may assist with the preparation for the investigation, but it is strongly suggested that the plan sponsor should be represented by upper-level management, the key retirement plan administrator, or outside counsel in most dealings with the DOL.

After the initial greeting, the investigator/auditor may make a brief presentation as to how the investigation will proceed. He may have preliminary questions regarding office policies and protocol and may also want to schedule interviews with key personnel in advance. This is an appropriate time for the liaison to ask any general questions regarding the investigation and the DOL. After this initial session, the investigator/auditor may proceed to review the documents that were requested in advance. When the investigator/auditor is escorted to the area prepared for the investigation, he should be assured that the liaison will be available as necessary.

The investigator/auditor may want to make copies of documents relating to the investigation. It is strongly suggested that the target entity make any copies that the investigator/auditor requests, rather than providing unlimited access to a copier. This may prevent the unnecessary copying of documents that do little to prove or disprove an alleged violation of ERISA.

After completing the initial on-site investigation, the investigator/auditor may likely conduct a brief exit interview with the liaison. Responsible parties may attend this meeting so that they may ask any questions or discuss any issues of concern to them.

Practitioner's Pointer: The documents that the investigator requests for copying may likely be used to substantiate an alleged violation of ERISA. Having a clerk make an additional copy of all documents requested may be useful in gaining insight into the potential issues or possible violations of concern to the investigator/auditor.

No one interviewed during the investigation should provide unrequested information. Only those records that the investigator/auditor requests should be made available and individuals should be prepared to cooperate and to respond to requests for records and explanations. However, if the investigator does not request specific information, no information should be volunteered. In many cases, plan sponsor personnel have revealed unsolicited information to the DOL that disclosed violations that were not readily apparent during the investigation.

At the exit meeting, or at any time during the investigation, it may be appropriate to ask the investigator/auditor for his opinion as to the status of the plan with respect to its compliance with ERISA. Quite often the investigator may provide insight as to the potential violations being investigated and whether they have been found to exist. The investigator/auditor may even encourage the plan sponsor to correct the violations in the immediate future before an official notification letter is sent by the DOL.

The motives behind the investigator/auditor's disclosure and encouragement may be purely self-serving. DOL investigators and auditors are formally judged and appraised on their ability to detect violations of ERISA. Informally, but just as important in the performance appraisal process, is the fact that investigators and auditors are judged on the number of cases that were closed, the number of cases in which voluntary compliance was achieved, the number of cases that were referred for litigation, and the dollar amounts that were recovered (although DOL managers and directors would adamantly deny this). In this context, obtaining voluntary compliance relatively early in the investigative process may be seen as reducing the paperwork necessary to bring the case to closure and may further eliminate the paperwork associated with the assessment of an ERISA Section 502(*l*) penalty. Moreover, the investigator is credited with a closed case with voluntary compliance achieved relatively early in the standard investigative time frame.

Investigative Inquiries

763. What are the areas of initial inquiry during a Department of Labor audit?

The initial stages of Department of Labor field audits are intended to inform the auditor/investigator concerning the background of the subject plan. After establishing this foundation of fundamental knowledge, the auditor/investigator may then go forward with the investigation and focus on those areas that had been initially targeted for review. The following is a brief outline of the initial areas of inquiry normally undertaken during the initial on-site investigation of an employee benefit plan. Although it is an informal outline, it is routinely relied upon by field auditors and investigators. (This outline is covered in more detail in Q 764 through Q 773.) In addition to all of the necessary background information, it was designed to identify indicators of potential violations, which would then be reviewed in detail.

The general areas of initial inquiry during a field audit are:

1.   Background of the plan sponsor and key employees;

2.   Background of the plan (type, benefits offered, participants, fiduciaries, etc.);

3.   Related parties to the subject plan;

4.   Reporting and disclosure obligations;

5.   Investment of plan assets;

6.   Plan service providers;

7.   Receipts, expenses, and disbursements;

8.   Non-income-producing assets;

9.   Accounting records and annual review; and

10.   Bonding and insurance.

The areas of initial inquiry are not representative of a complete DOL investigation. It is merely a review of the initial steps taken when a plan has been targeted for an audit. Once all of the above areas have been reviewed by the auditor/investigator, close attention should be paid to the remaining areas of inquiry. More often than not, these are the areas of interest that have been identified for review. All DOL investigative reports are required to review bonding, reporting, and disclosure procedures of a plan. Inquiries into these areas are routine and, most likely, are not the reason the plan has been targeted for an audit.

Practitioner's Pointer: These queries would be an excellent place to begin a due diligence audit or a "pre-audit" prior to the date of an initial on-site visit from a Department of Labor representative. If any "red flags" have been identified through the application of the inquiries (see Q 764 through Q 773), plan counsel should conduct a thorough investigation into problem areas prior to the initial on-site investigation. This would allow for sufficient time to prepare documentation, explanations, and, if necessary, correction of violations or an adequate defense.

If a blatant prohibited transaction is identified for which there is no adequate explanation, plan counsel should consider reversing the transaction prior to the receipt of official notification from the Department of Labor. The Department of Labor will not impose ERISA Section 502(*l*) penalties on a reversed prohibited transaction unless the reversal was the result of a Department of Labor "official notification" of an outstanding violation that the subject plan has been ordered to correct (usually through voluntary compliance).

---

764. What are some of the background areas of initial inquiry during an initial on-site investigation by the Department of Labor?

The first areas of plan information to be reviewed during an initial on-site investigation by a Department of Labor auditor/investigator are likely to be those detailed below:

1. Background information, including:

   a. name or title of the person interviewed;

   b. business address and background of the subject (to establish a foundation of competence); and

   c. name or background of the plan sponsor.

2. Plan information, including:

   a. name and type of plan (i.e., defined benefit, defined contribution, health and welfare);

   b. basic benefits offered under the plan;

   c. number of participants, total assets, and annual contributions;

   d. plan administrator (both currently and over the past five years);

   e. named fiduciaries (both currently and over the past five years);

   f. a list of other plans sponsored;

   g. any functioning committees and the method by which members are selected; and

   h. current investments of the plan.

3.   Information regarding related parties, including:

   a. unions connected with the plan, if any;

   b. names of all stockholders who own a 10 percent or more share of the sponsor;

   c. names of any principal officers or employees who own 10 percent or more of any business with which the plan does business; and

   d. any pending legal proceedings that involve the plan or plan fiduciaries.

This information is intended to provide the auditor/investigator with a detailed overview of the plan, its sponsor, and any related parties who may be involved in the issues under investigation.

765. What are the initial DOL inquiries regarding Summary Plan Descriptions (SPD), Summaries of Material Modifications (SMM), and Summary Annual Reports (SARs)?

When beginning a review of the subject plan's reporting and disclosure obligations under ERISA, the auditor/investigator will review the following questions regarding the plan's Summary Plan Description (SPD), Summary of Material Modifications (SMM), and Summary Annual Reports (SARs):

1.   Is the plan exempt from reporting requirements? If so, why?

2.   Does the SPD meet the style, format, and content requirements of the DOL?[1]

3.   Has the SPD been provided to participants and beneficiaries receiving benefits within 120 days after the plan is subject to ERISA or ninety days after new participants become eligible to participate in the plan?[2]

4.   Is the SPD more than five years old?[3]

5.   If material modifications have occurred, has a summary of material modifications been filed with the DOL and disclosed to participants and beneficiaries within 210 days after the end of the plan year in which the change was made? (Note that for plan years beginning after August 6, 1997, plans are no longer required to provide the Department of Labor with copies of the SMM.)[4]

6.   Has the SAR been disclosed to participants and beneficiaries within nine months after the close of the plan year?[5]

---

1. Labor Reg. §§2520.102-2, 2520.102-3.
2. Labor Reg. §2520.104b-2.
3. Labor Reg. §2520.104b-2.
4. Labor Reg. §2520.104a-7.
5. Labor Reg. §2520.104b-10.

766. What are the initial DOL inquiries regarding Annual Report Forms 5500 and PBGC forms?

When continuing a review of a subject plan's reporting and disclosure obligations under ERISA, the auditor/investigator will review the following items to determine if the plan has satisfied the applicable requirements:

1. Have Annual Report Forms 5500 been filed with the DOL or IRS within 270 days after the close of the plan year?[1]

2. If applicable, have Schedule A (Insurance Information), Schedule B (Actuarial Information), an Opinion of Qualified Public Accountant, an Actuarial Statement, or Financial Statements been included with the Annual Report Forms 5500?[2]

3. If applicable, has Form 5310 (Application for Determination upon Termination; Notice of Merger, Consolidation or Transfer of Plan Assets or Liabilities; Notice of Intent to Terminate) been filed with the IRS or the PBGC?

4. If applicable, has a "Final AR 5500" been filed with the IRS upon complete distribution of assets?

5. If applicable, has the PBGC been notified of a merger, a transfer of assets or liabilities, or the termination of a multiemployer plan covered by the PBGC Insurance Program?

6. For defined benefit plans, has Form PBGC-1 been filed?

767. What are the initial DOL inquiries regarding participant disclosure requirements?

ERISA mandates that plans must disclose certain materials to plan participants under certain circumstances. The following questions were designed to assist field auditors/investigators in determining whether a plan subject to an investigation has satisfied those participant disclosure requirements:

1. Are copies of the plan, summary plan description, latest annual report, and governing documents (under which the plan was established and is operating) made available to plan participants at the principal office of the administrator?[3]

2. For plans that make a charge for documents, is the charge reasonable (generally, up to fifteen cents per page)?[4]

3. Does the plan respond to written disclosure requests within thirty days?[5]

---

1. Labor Reg. §2520.104a-5.
2. Labor Reg. §2520.103-1.
3. Labor Reg. §2520.104b-1.
4. Labor Reg. §2520.104b-30.
5. ERISA Sec. 502(c).

4. For those plans to which vesting standards apply, has a statement concerning the nature, amount, and form of deferred vested benefits been provided to those participants that have terminated employment or had a one-year break in service?[1]

5. For those applicable plans, has a written explanation been provided to participants before the annuity starting date of the terms and conditions of any joint and survivor annuity and the effect of electing against such options?[2]

6. For participants or beneficiaries with claim denials, does the plan provide notice of denial within ninety days?[3]

768. What are the initial DOL inquiries regarding plan investments?

In an initial on-site investigation, the auditor/investigator will review the following questions in order to identify the plan's basic asset investment holdings, procedures, philosophies, and objectives:

1. Does the plan now hold for investment, or has it held for investment in the last six years, any of the following: (a) participant loans; (b) diamonds; (c) gold or other non-income-producing assets; (d) mortgages; (e) loans other than mortgages; (f) limited partnership interests; (g) employer stocks or securities; or (h) stock of a closely held corporation?

2. Who makes the decisions on plan investments, and what criteria are used?

3. What outside advice is obtained to help in investment decisions, and how often is it relied upon?

4. If and when stocks are purchased, who makes the decision and through whom is the transaction executed?

5. What criteria are used in making this decision?

6. Are commissions negotiated, and how?

7. What are the plan's basic investment philosophies and objectives?

769. What are the initial DOL inquiries regarding persons or entities providing services to a subject plan?

In reviewing the background information of a plan under investigation, the auditor/investigator will review the following items to identify the service providers who are involved in the ongoing administration of the plan and the management of the plan's assets. The review will require that the name, functions performed, and contracts of the following service providers be furnished:

•   Accountants;

•   Attorneys;

---

1. ERISA Sec. 105(c).
2. Treas. Reg. §1.401(a)-11(c)(3).
3. Labor Reg. §2560.503-1(e).

- Administrators;

- Actuaries;

- Trustees;

- Insurance agents;

- Investment advisers;

- Broker-dealers;

- Banks; and

- All other service providers not previously identified.

770. What are the initial DOL inquiries regarding plan receipts, expenses, and disbursements?

In an initial on-site investigation, the DOL auditor/investigator will want to ascertain the following information regarding plan receipts, expenses, and disbursements in an effort to establish the protocol utilized by the plan and the persons responsible for these tasks.

1. Regarding receipts, the auditor/investigator will ask:

    a. Who makes the decision regarding the amount of contributions, and when they are made?

    b. What are the plan document's basic funding requirements (within the knowledge of the interviewee)?

    c. How often are contributions received?

    d. If receipts are received by mail, what procedures are used for processing mail receipts?

    e. What is the percentage of receipts received through the mail?

    f. Are contributions received in cash? If so, who handles cash contributions, and how is the accounting for such contributions handled?

    g. What procedures are used to collect delinquent contributions?

    h. Are receipt books used and, if so, are they pre-numbered?

    i. Does the plan maintain a petty cash fund? If so, on what basis is it maintained?

    j. Are all receipts deposited intact? Who makes these deposits?

2.   Regarding expenses and disbursements, the auditor/investigator will ask:

    a. What expenses, other than benefits, are paid by the plan?

    b. What are the basic procedures for making disbursements on service provider invoices?

    c. Are all invoice disbursements made by check? How many signatures are required? Who can sign checks? Are the plan checks ever pre-signed?

    d. What is the basic procedure used to process and approve benefit disbursements?

    e. Are any salaries paid from the plan assets?

    f. If so, who determines salaries, and how is basic payroll accounting set up?

771. What are the initial DOL inquiries regarding non-income-producing assets that may be held by the plan?

During the initial on-site investigation, the DOL auditor/investigator is likely to inquire whether the subject plan holds any of the following non-income-producing assets as plan investments, and what procedures are involved in making such investments. The auditor/investigator may ask the following questions:

1.   What equipment (e.g., cars, office furniture, fixtures, buildings, etc.) is owned by the plan?

2.   What controls are set up to maintain proper safeguards of the assets and to prevent their misuse?

3.   Who approves purchases of any capital item (i.e., purchases over $100 with a useful life in excess of one year); and

4.   Are bids sought on major purchases in order to obtain the best price?

772. What are the initial DOL inquiries regarding the accounting records of a subject plan?

During the initial on-site investigation, the DOL auditor/investigator will want to determine what accounting records are maintained by the subject plan, who maintains them, and who (if anyone) is charged with reviewing them on an annual basis. In order to make this determination, the auditor/investigator may ask the following questions:

1.   Are any of the following accounting records maintained, and who maintains them?

    a. bank accounts,

    b. receipts and disbursements journals,

    c. vouchers, vendors, and invoices,

      d. broker confirmations,

      e. receipt books,

      f. investment acquisition and disposition records, and

      g. Annual Report Forms 5500.

2.   How often and by whom are these records reviewed or audited (internally and externally)?

773. What are the initial DOL inquiries regarding the bonding and insurance coverage of a subject plan?

During the initial on-site investigation, the DOL auditor/investigator will conduct an extensive review of the subject plan's bonding and insurance coverage. This is because the final investigative report that the auditor/investigator will prepare and submit on the case must provide a detailed analysis of these items. Consequently, the auditor/investigator may ask the following questions:

1.   Does a separate trust fund exist?

2.   Are there insurance or annuity contracts?

3.   Are there separate accounts in the books of the employer or do separate funds or other properties exist in the name of the plan? (Note: If the answer to items one or three is "yes," bonding is usually required. It should be determined whether insurance dividends belong to the plan or the plan sponsor. If they belong to the plan, bonding is required. If cash surrender values exist and the plan can obtain those values, bonding is required. See Section VIII for additional bonding rules.)

4.   Are benefits paid from the general assets of the plan sponsor?

5.   Is there any segregation of the plan funds?

6.   Are there separate accounts on the books or are there separate books of account for the plan? (Note: If item four is answered "yes" and items five and six are answered "no," the Plan is unfunded and no bonding is required.)

7.   Do any trustees or plan employees have:

      a. physical possession of plan assets?

      b. power to obtain physical possession of plan assets?

      c. power to transfer assets?

      d. authority to disburse plan funds directly or indirectly?

      e. authority to sign or endorse checks and/or the authority to make investments?

(Note: If any of the items under seven are answered "yes," handling of plan funds is indicated and bonding is required for each individual who has such authority. If a corporate trustee holds the plan assets, but the plan trustees can direct the payment of benefits by the corporate trustee or direct the investments to be made by the corporate trustee, the plan trustees are "handling" funds and bonding is required.)

8. Does the bond provide for payment to the plan in the event of loss? (The plan must be named as an "insured" and the pay-over rider must be attached unless the plan is the sole insured under the bond. The definition of "employee" in the bond must cover all persons who "handle" funds.)

9. How many plans are covered by the bond?

10. How many non-plan entities are covered by the bond?

11. Is the bonding company listed in the Department of the Treasury Circular 570 as an approved surety provider? (The auditor/investigator will require the name of the bonding company and the policy lapse date.)

12. Is the plan named as the insured?

13. If there is more than one plan, or the plan and the plan sponsor are covered, is a pay-over rider attached?

14. If the bond contains a deductible, is an elimination of the deductible rider attached with respect to the plan?

15. Does the bond protect against fraud and dishonesty?

16. Does the bond have a one-year discovery period?

17. Does the bond provide coverage of 10 percent of the funds handled with a maximum amount of $500,000?

18. If the plan or plan sponsor maintains fiduciary liability insurance coverage, what is the name of the insurance company providing coverage and the amount of coverage?

Investigative Findings and Compliance

774. What can a plan sponsor expect after the DOL has completed its investigation?

Once the DOL has completed its investigation of the target plan, it may issue a notice to the fiduciaries, sponsor, or service provider in one of four formats.

1. *No-violation letter.* This is a brief, one-page closing letter advising that the DOL has completed its investigation and no further action is contemplated with regard to the case. This letter is issued in cases in which no violations are detected. The letter closes by thanking the recipient for its cooperation during the investigation.

2.   *Cautionary letter—no action warranted; compliance achieved.* This closing letter is issued when the DOL has discovered violations of ERISA that have been reversed or rectified prior to official notification by the DOL. It is also issued as a caution to fiduciaries, plan sponsors, and service providers for outstanding *de minimis* violations, or if there are no actual or potential monetary damages to the plan (e.g., bonding, reporting, and disclosure issues). This letter cautions the subject of the investigation to exercise prudence in avoiding such violations in the future. Although this letter is used in circumstances that do not appear to justify the commitment of DOL resources, the plan may be notified that the matter will be referred to the IRS for possible imposition of excise taxes.

3.   *Voluntary compliance notice letter.* A voluntary compliance notice (VC) letter notifies plan fiduciaries or others of ERISA violations and requests corrective action. VC letters advise fiduciaries of the DOL's findings and invite the recipient of the letter to discuss with the DOL how the violations may be corrected and any losses restored to the plan. Although the VC letter does not threaten litigation, it informs the recipient that failure to take corrective action may result in referral of the matter to the Office of the Solicitor of Labor for possible legal action. Additionally, the letter advises that if proper corrective action is taken, the DOL will not bring a lawsuit with regard to the issues. However, the assessment of the ERISA Section 502(*l*) penalty is applicable. The recipient is given ten days from the date of the VC letter to advise the DOL, in writing, as to what action it intends to take to correct the violations.

4.   *Demand or litigation notice.* This notice is usually reserved for the most egregious civil violations under ERISA or cases identified as significant under the DOL enforcement strategy. It is mailed from the Plan Benefits Security Division (PBSD) in Washington, D.C., or one of the regional solicitors' offices. This is an official notification to the investigatory target that it has transgressed ERISA to the point that the DOL has deemed that litigation may be warranted. A litigation notice may also be sent in cases of outstanding prohibited transactions that are of sufficient seriousness to warrant judicial action. The DOL may make every attempt to resolve prohibited transactions through the VC letter, but if there is a clear indication that the plan sponsor has no intent to reverse a prohibited transaction and the DOL feels that negotiations would have no success, a case may be referred for litigation. If PBSD or the regional solicitor agrees with the assessment of the field office of the Employee Benefits Security Administration, either may issue a notice demanding corrective action, or litigation may result.

Practitioner's Pointer: Quality legal counsel or other professional assistance competent in ERISA-related matters should be retained upon receipt of a VC, demand, or litigation notice.

775. What techniques does the Employee Benefits Security Administration use to correct ERISA violations?

In accordance with its policy of promoting voluntary compliance with ERISA, in many situations the Employee Benefits Security Administration (EBSA) actively pursues voluntary resolution to correct violations of ERISA. The objective of voluntary correction is to restore the status quo ante. The regional director responsible for the investigation determines whether to pursue corrective action through voluntary compliance in accordance with EBSA national office policy.

If it is decided that correction of the apparent violations should be pursued through voluntary compliance, the EBSA regional office issues a notice letter to plan officials advising them of the results of the investigation. In part, the notice letter describes the ERISA violations and details EBSA's position on acceptable corrective actions. In some cases, violations of a serious nature are corrected through judicial enforcement decrees at the insistence of EBSA. EBSA publicly discloses the results obtained through these situations to inform the employee benefit plan community of the enforcement program and of the issues and legal positions of concern to EBSA. In other cases, some violations, by their nature, may jeopardize plan assets or participants' rights. In these cases, EBSA may bypass voluntary correction efforts and instead pursue immediate court action without discussing the matter with plan officials.[1]

776. Which types of cases involving ERISA violations are appropriate for voluntary compliance?

The regional offices of the Employee Benefits Security Administration (EBSA) actively seek to achieve voluntary resolution of all violations of ERISA because EBSA considers most issues suitable for voluntary compliance. According to EBSA, cases most acceptable for voluntary compliance resolution involve benefit disputes, bonding, reporting, and disclosure issues. EBSA may attempt to resolve these types of issues during the course of an investigation.[2]

777. Which types of cases involving ERISA violations may not be suitable for voluntary compliance?

Although many cases are suitable for resolution through voluntary compliance, the Employee Benefits Security Administration (EBSA) is not bound to seek voluntary compliance in all cases. According to EBSA, voluntary correction of ERISA violations may not be suitable in cases involving issues identified as significant under EBSA enforcement strategy, or cases involving novel or interpretive legal issues, such as (1) when recovery from one who is not a fiduciary can be legally supported, and (2) whether there is a covered plan protected by ERISA.[3]

778. Are any cases involving ERISA violations not suitable for voluntary compliance?

According to the Employee Benefits Security Administration (EBSA), certain types of cases are not considered appropriate for voluntary compliance, either because of the seriousness of the violation or the individual or entities involved. Generally, these cases include:

1. Prudence violations of ERISA Section 404(a) with losses in excess of $500,000 (exclusive of interest on the losses);

---

1. ERISA Sec. 502(a)(2); *ERISA Enforcement Strategy Implementation Plan*, Sept. 1990, at 3, 28.
2. *EBSA Enforcement Manual* ch. 34, at 2.
3. *EBSA Enforcement Manual* ch. 34, at 2.

2.   Prohibited transaction violations of ERISA Section 406 with losses in excess of $500,000;

3.   Cases in which the time for proposed correction of violations will exceed a one-year period;

4.   Violations involving potential fraud or criminal misconduct with respect to dealings with a plan unless a United States Attorney has agreed to a voluntary compliance settlement;

5.   Situations warranting the removal of a fiduciary or a related entity; or

6.   Cases that involve individuals who have previously violated ERISA or other federal statutes.

Thus, EBSA may insist on judicially enforceable decrees in the above situations, or may initiate court action without offering plan officials the opportunity to voluntarily correct the ERISA violations.[1]

779. How are plan fiduciaries or others notified of the opportunity for voluntary compliance?

Although the Employee Benefits Security Administration (EBSA) has adopted the policy of not informing plan officials or others as to the basis or source of its investigation, plan fiduciaries or others are typically notified of the opportunity to voluntarily correct violations of ERISA during the course of an investigation or at its conclusion. During the course of an investigation, investigators/auditors may discuss their personal views of the investigative findings with plan officials. These findings are subject to review by EBSA officials and are generally confirmed in writing by EBSA. The investigator/auditor also may attempt to solicit the position and intentions of the plan officials regarding the actions they might voluntarily take to correct the violations. In addition, the investigator/auditor may attempt to determine the financial condition of the fiduciaries and/or related parties, as well as whether the fiduciaries have fiduciary liability insurance (the latter as a potential source of recovery of monetary loss to the plan).

Officially, the investigator/auditor is generally prohibited from proposing corrective actions or discussing tentative settlement terms without the prior consent of the regional director. If given this consent, the investigator/auditor may discuss proposed corrective actions and the civil penalty process with plan officials at the conclusion of the investigation. The investigator/auditor, however, may not officially discuss specific dollar amounts related to the proposed corrective action or any civil penalty that might be assessed as a result thereof. All discussions with plan officials that relate to findings or proposed corrections may likely be put in writing by the investigator/auditor. In the absence of, or subsequent to, the discussions with plan officials concerning corrective action, plan officials may be notified of the opportunity for voluntary corrective action at the conclusion of an investigation, through the receipt of a voluntary compliance notice letter (see Q 780).[2]

---

1. ERISA Sec. 502(a)(2); *EBSA Enforcement Manual* ch. 34, at 2-3; ERISA *Enforcement Strategy Implementation Plan*, Sept. 1990, at 28.
2. *EBSA Enforcement Manual* ch. 34, at 1-2.

780. What is a voluntary compliance notice letter?

A voluntary compliance (VC) letter is issued by the investigating regional office and advises plan fiduciaries or others of the results of an investigation. A VC letter identifies any violations of ERISA and requests corrective action. The VC letter grants fiduciaries or others an opportunity to comment or discuss with the Employee Benefits Security Administration (EBSA) how to correct the violations and restore any losses to the plan before EBSA determines whether to take action, if any.

Although the VC letter does not threaten litigation, it does state that the matter may be referred to the DOL's Office of the Solicitor for possible legal action should the fiduciaries or others fail to take the prescribed corrective action. In addition, the VC letter advises that EBSA may furnish information to "any person ... actually affected by any matter which is the subject" of an ERISA investigation and that the fiduciaries and others remain subject to suit by other parties, including plan fiduciaries and plan participants or their beneficiaries.[1]

781. How long will the Employee Benefits Security Administration conduct voluntary compliance negotiations?

In an effort to achieve voluntary corrections of ERISA violations, the Employee Benefits Security Administration (EBSA) generally will conduct voluntary compliance negotiations. The period of time devoted to these negotiations varies according to the circumstances of the particular investigation and the parties involved. However, EBSA avoids negotiations with undue delay between the initiation of the voluntary compliance efforts and the conclusion of any negotiations regarding compliance (although the corrective action may occur over a more extended period), especially in instances where the investigation is likely to be referred for litigation should the voluntary compliance process prove unsuccessful.[2]

782. What settlement terms are acceptable under voluntary correction?

Generally, the Employee Benefits Security Administration (EBSA) insists on full recovery to the plan under the terms of a voluntary correction agreement. Recovery includes amounts paid to the plan that represent losses incurred by the plan, disgorged profits, and amounts necessary to achieve correction. Other terms may include, where appropriate, the rescission of prohibited transactions, the removal of fiduciaries, the appointment of a receiver, and the indemnification of the plan against future losses. The amount of the recovery is determined as a part of the "settlement agreement" with the party. Full repayment of losses to the plan must be made over a period of no longer than one year. In instances in which the statute of limitations will toll before the terms of the settlement agreement are completed, EBSA may attempt to obtain a tolling agreement that expires six months after the repayment period terminates. In addition, the settlement agreement should provide that interest on repayments be at appropriate rates, and all notes supporting the payment be adequately secured. Moreover, EBSA will demand proof that payment of the recovery amount is actually made to the plan.[3]

---

1. *EBSA Enforcement Manual* ch. 34, at 3.
2. *EBSA Enforcement Manual* ch. 34, at 7.
3. *EBSA Enforcement Manual* ch. 34, at 4; ch. 48.

783. What actions are taken by the Employee Benefits Security Administration when voluntary compliance attempts are unsuccessful?

In all cases where voluntary compliance attempts prove unsuccessful, in whole or in part, the regional office of the Employee Benefits Security Administration (EBSA) will consider all possible courses of action within its delegated authority for resolving or closing the case, including referral for litigation, referral to the Department of Justice, and referral to the IRS for the imposition of an excise tax under IRC Section 4975. In addition, EBSA may assess the ERISA Section 502(i) civil penalty, if appropriate. In cases where partial compliance is achieved and the ERISA Section 502(l) civil penalty is applicable, EBSA will assess the penalty on the applicable recovery amount. In other situations, where voluntary compliance is not achieved, EBSA may close the case.

In the course of closing a case in which voluntary compliance is not achieved, EBSA may disclose the results of the investigation to affected parties (e.g., by sending them a copy of the closing letter). Disclosure also may be made to a plan participant, beneficiary, or fiduciary in the event the investigation arose as a result of such person's complaint. A disclosure will not be made to these individuals if the information to be disclosed was obtained pursuant to: (1) Rule 6(e) of the Federal Rules of Criminal Procedure; (2) IRC Section 6103; (3) the DOL's agreement with the Federal Financial Institution Regulatory Agencies; or (4) from some other source requiring confidentiality.[1]

784. What is a closing letter?

In instances where it is determined that no further action will be taken, the investigating regional office of the Employee Benefits Security Administration (EBSA) issues a closing letter at the conclusion of an investigation. The closing letter informs plan fiduciaries or others of the results of an investigation, including which sections of ERISA have been violated, if any, and that no further action by the DOL is currently contemplated with respect to the issues described in the letter. In addition, any unresolved reporting issues and their referral to EBSA's Office of the Chief Accountant (OCA) are reflected in the closing letter. (The responsibility for the acceptance or rejection of the Annual Report (Form 5500) or any part thereof is delegated to the OCA.)

A closing letter may be issued in various forms, depending on the situation of the case. For example, a "Pattern Closing Letter" is issued in all cases in which no ERISA violations are detected during the course of the investigation. The letter is typically one page in length and will thank the recipient for its cooperation in the investigation, if appropriate.

In some instances, EBSA issues a closing letter other than the pattern closing letter, even if violations are present. This "No Action Warranted Closing Letter" is issued in instances only if there is no evidence of willful misconduct and (1) the violations are *de minimis* in nature, or (2) there are no actual or potential monetary damages to the plan. For example, EBSA considers it appropriate to use this letter in instances where an investigation disclosed

---

1. *EBSA Enforcement Manual* ch. 34, at 7.

a small prohibited transaction that had been reversed with no harm to the plan, or where a plan failed to submit an accountant's opinion for a particular year, but submitted one for all subsequent years.

A "Compliance Achieved Closing Letter" is issued in instances where corrective action is confirmed and either applicable penalties were paid or the payment period has expired. This letter follows a voluntary compliance notice letter. A modification of this letter is also used in situations where violations were discussed and confirmed with plan officials at the conclusion of an investigation and these violations were or will be corrected by the plan officials pursuant to the discussions with EBSA. The modified compliance achieved closing letter details the violations as well as the specific corrective actions agreed to by the plan officials, including ERISA Section 502(l) and ERISA Section 502(i) matters.

EBSA issues a "Compliance Not Achieved Closing Letter" in instances where a voluntary compliance notice letter has been sent to plan fiduciaries and the fiduciaries: (1) deny the facts disclosed in the investigation; (2) admit to the facts, but deny the facts constitute a violation of ERISA; or (3) otherwise fail to comply with the terms of the VC notice letter. The use of this letter is limited to situations in which no enforcement action is contemplated by EBSA after it has considered all possible courses of action, including referral of the case for possible litigation.

In certain situations where no voluntary compliance was attempted, and when the facts and issues do not appear to justify the commitment of EBSA resources, EBSA may refer the case to the IRS for possible imposition of excise taxes under IRC Section 4975. In these instances, EBSA issues a "Referral to the IRS Closing Letter" to the plan, which notifies it of this action.[1]

785. What action should be taken when fiduciaries agree with the DOL's official findings in an investigation?

If the DOL places a target plan on official notice of outstanding violations of ERISA and plan fiduciaries agree, fiduciaries should follow the instructions for submitting an official response to the DOL office issuing the notice. The plan's response should be tailored to the DOL's notice letter. Each violation should be listed, the fiduciary's agreement stated, and the proposed or completed corrections detailed. The plan sponsor has discretion in the manner of correcting the violations as long as the chosen method does not lead to further violations and plan participants remain unharmed.

In negotiating a settlement with the DOL, the plan sponsor will receive a notice of assessment, issued by the regional office, concerning any penalties assessed under ERISA Section 502(l). The notice will contain a brief description of the violation, the identity of the person being assessed, the amount of the assessment, and the basis for assessing that particular person and that particular penalty amount. If the plan sponsor believes that the 502(l) penalty is unwarranted or extreme, the plan sponsor may, at any time during the sixty-day payment period, petition the Secretary

---

1. *EBSA Enforcement Manual* ch. 34, at 6-7.

of Labor (through the regional director) to waive or reduce the assessed penalty. This petition must be made on the basis that:

1.   Unless such a waiver or reduction is granted, the petitioner will not be able to restore all losses to the plan or any of its participants or beneficiaries without severe financial hardship; and

2.   The petitioner acted in good faith in engaging in the breach or violation.

Additionally, the petitioner is entitled to a conference with the Secretary of Labor regarding a petition for waiver or reduction of the civil penalty. (See Q 786.)

Once the plan sponsor has documented compliance with the DOL order to correct outstanding violations and has reached a settlement with respect to any ERISA Section 502(*l*) penalties, the DOL will issue a case-closing letter confirming its acceptance of the plan's corrective actions. The plan sponsor should retain this case-closing letter in the official plan records file. In the past, the DOL has opened new investigations on previous targets. The case-closing letter serves as protection against the possibility that the DOL will cite the plan again for the same violations.

786. What action should be taken when fiduciaries disagree with the DOL's official findings in an investigation?

If the plan sponsor has received a VC letter from the DOL and plan fiduciaries disagree with some or all of the violations cited, the plan has the right to request a voluntary compliance conference with the DOL. The DOL field office issuing the notice of violations may schedule this conference at its office. Attending the conference on behalf of the DOL may be the investigator/ auditor who conducted the investigation and his direct supervisor. If the case is sufficiently complicated, or involves a substantial amount of money, the regional deputy director (or his equivalent) or the regional director may also be involved. Given the nature of the conference, it is recommended that both the plan and any service provider involved in the contested violation be represented by legal counsel.

The DOL may be reasonable in discussing mitigating facts and circumstances during voluntary compliance conferences. If the plan sponsor's position is reasonable and provides a reasonable alternative to any DOL demands, the DOL may consider it. If plan representatives firmly believe that an action for which the plan has been cited is not a violation of ERISA, this conference is an opportunity to state the plan's case and to convince the DOL to change its position.

In negotiating a settlement, the DOL considers some factors that are unrelated to the facts and circumstances of the violations, such as: (1) the likelihood that the DOL solicitor is willing to litigate the case as originally cited; (2) the seriousness of the violations cited; (3) the case load of the office and the investigator; (4) the working relationship of the regional office with the Pension Benefits Security Division (PBSD) or the regional solicitors; and (5) the likelihood that compliance will not be achieved without a negotiated settlement. For these reasons, voluntary compliance conferences can result in a reduction or elimination of the contested violation.

Alternatively, the plan sponsor may refuse to comply with the DOL's requests for voluntary compliance. This involves a risk, but the risk is much lower if the alleged violation: (1) has a strong defensible position; (2) is not flagrant; (3) has few victims; (4) is technically complex; or (5) involves limited losses to the plan. The DOL field office may respond to the plan sponsor's refusal with a threat of litigation. This may be an intimidation tactic, considering the relatively high rate of rejection of such cases by the PBSD and the regional solicitors.

The regional solicitor offices and the PBSD are most inclined to litigate cases that involve many victims, potentially large recoveries, or unique issues of a timely and newsworthy nature. Although they may be well versed in ERISA, some of these attorneys do not have a strong background in finance, accounting, or investments. With such shortcomings, they may only accept a case for litigation if they understand the underlying technical theories and premises and their relationship to the alleged violations as well as believe it is likely that the case will be won or a favorable settlement reached. These factors should be discussed with plan legal counsel in any decision to refuse the DOL's request for voluntary compliance.

The DOL regional office may even bypass the voluntary compliance step and submit a request for litigation on a case without even offering an opportunity to settle (indeed, the regional office is "credited" when it refers a case for litigation, even if the case is ultimately rejected for litigation by the PBSD or the regional solicitor's office). If the litigation request is rejected, the DOL may attempt voluntary compliance or may close the investigation and leave the target plan "in violation," even though the DOL contemplates no legal action at that time. However, the target plan is still subject to suits by other parties, including plan fiduciaries and plan participants or their beneficiaries. Additionally, the excise tax on disqualified persons under IRC Section 4975 may be applicable. Because of these risks, plan fiduciaries should review any refusal option with the plan's legal counsel.

787. What is the "interagency referral agreement"?

ERISA Section 506 contains the statutory provisions relating to the coordination and responsibility of agencies for enforcing ERISA and related federal laws. ERISA Section 506(a) states that:

[i]n order to avoid unnecessary expense and duplication of functions among Government agencies, the Secretary may make such arrangements or agreements for cooperation or mutual assistance in the performance of his functions under this title and the functions of any such agency as he may find to be practicable and consistent with the law. The Secretary may utilize, on a reimbursable or other basis, the facilities or services of any department, agency, or establishment of the United States or of any State or political subdivision of a State, including the services of any of its employees, with the lawful consent of such department, agency or establishment, and each department, agency, or establishment of the United States is authorized and directed to cooperate with the Secretary and, to the extent permitted by law, to provide such information and facilities as he may request for his assistance in the performance of his functions under this title. The Attorney General or his representative shall receive from the Secretary for appropriate action such

evidence developed in the performance of his functions under this title as may be found to warrant consideration for criminal prosecution under the provisions of this title or other Federal law.

Due to an interagency referral agreement between the IRS and the Employee Benefits Security Administration (EBSA), each field office of the DOL will make arrangements with the field office of the IRS Office of Employee Plans within the appropriate jurisdiction to exchange referrals of evidence and reports indicating potential violations of the other agency's statutory jurisdiction that have been identified in the course of routine investigations. Most DOL field offices have made arrangements to meet with the Office of Employee Plans within its jurisdiction on a monthly basis for the purpose of discussing and exchanging referrals for consideration of investigation.

The DOL and the Securities and Exchange Commission (SEC) have entered into a Memorandum of Understanding (MOU) that has formalized their long-standing practice of sharing information relevant to their regulatory and enforcement responsibilities. The MOU establishes a process for the agency staffs to meet regularly to discuss examination findings and trends, enforcement cases, regulatory requirements affecting the agencies, and other matters of mutual interest. It calls for each agency to designate staff in regional offices who will facilitate information-sharing on enforcement actions and examinations, and it encourages cross-training to increase each agency's understanding of the other's mission and investigative jurisdiction. The MOU gives the DOL standing access to non-public SEC examination information (provided SEC deems that information relevant to the DOL's mission) and creates an access letter procedure intended to facilitate inter-agency sharing of enforcement information. The MOU allows both the DOL and the SEC to reserve their right to transfer information to criminal law enforcement agencies.[1]

These interagency referral agreements are in accordance with the provisions of ERISA Section 506(b), which provides that "[t]he Secretary shall have the responsibility and authority to detect and investigate and refer, where appropriate, civil and criminal violations related to the provisions of this title and other related Federal laws."

DOL Civil Actions

788. What types of civil actions may be brought by the DOL?

ERISA Section 502 permits the DOL to file the following civil actions:

1.   Suits to enforce Title I of ERISA (Protection of Employee Benefit Rights);

2.   Suits to require disclosure of individual benefit statements, in accordance with ERISA Section 105(c);

3.   Suits to enforce the fiduciary provisions of ERISA and to make the plan whole for any losses resulting from a breach of fiduciary duty; and

---

1. Memorandum of Understanding Concerning Cooperation Between the U.S. Securities and Exchange Commission and the U.S. Department of Labor (July 29, 2008). For a copy of the memorandum, go to http://www.dol.gov/opa/media/reports/mou072908.pdf.

4.   Suits to collect civil penalties for:

   a.   failure or refusal to file an Annual Report;

   b.   violation of the prohibited transaction provisions; and

   c.   situations in which a breaching fiduciary or a person who knowingly participates in a fiduciary breach is required to make restitution to the plan.

The Fifth Circuit Court of Appeals has held that the DOL's interest in bringing an ERISA action is to safeguard the integrity of the pension system.[1]

ERISA Section 502(j) provides that in all civil actions brought by the DOL, attorneys appointed by the Secretary of Labor may represent him or her. The exception to this general rule is cases presented to the Supreme Court, which will be subject to the direction and control of the Attorney General.

Actions brought by the DOL are subject to the civil procedure rules regarding: (1) standing to sue; (2) jurisdiction over the claim by the court hearing the proceedings; (3) the proper venue of the suit; and (4) under certain circumstances, the seeking of equitable relief, injunctive relief, and/or attorneys' fees.

The Fourth Circuit Court of Appeals has ruled that there is no personal ERISA action allowed for a fiduciary's failure to carry out participant investment instructions.[2] The participant's claim for damages, equal to the losses that resulted when the plan administrator failed to carry out the instructions, was not actionable under ERISA's breach of fiduciary duty provision or under ERISA's other appropriate equitable relief provision. The court, in relying on *Mertens v. Hewitt*,[3] and *Great-West Life & Annuity Insurance Co. v. Knudsen*,[4] confirmed that ERISA Sections 1132(a)(2) and 1132(a)(3) provide for forms of equitable relief (unjust enrichment, unlawful possession, or self-dealing) that fall outside the relief requested by the plaintiff. As such, a motion for judgment on the pleadings in favor of the defendants was affirmed.

789. Can the DOL intervene in an existing ERISA-related civil action?

A copy of all complaints filed in civil actions brought by a participant, beneficiary, or a fiduciary regarding alleged violations of ERISA must be served upon the Secretary of Labor.

As a result of an Eleventh Circuit decision, the Secretary of Labor may sue a plan fiduciary for money damages even though an identical claim by a class of plan participants against the same fiduciary was the subject of a final judgment or court-approved settlement.[5] See Q 518.

The Secretary of Labor has the right, in his discretion, to intervene in any action, with the exception of suits brought under Title IV (Plan Termination Insurance).[6]

---

1. *Donovan v. Cunningham*, 716 F.2d 1455 (5th Cir. 1983).
2. *LaRue v. DeWolff, Boberg & Assocs., Inc.*, 2006 WL 1668873 (4th Cir. 2006).
3. 508 U.S. 248 (1993).
4. 435 U.S. 204 (2002).
5. *Herman v. South Carolina Nat'l Bank*, 140 F.3d 1413 (11th Cir. 1998), *cert. denied*, 525 U.S. 1140 (1999).
6. ERISA Sec. 502(h).

ERISA Preemption

790. What is the scope of ERISA preemption?

ERISA Section 514(a) says that the provisions of ERISA "shall supersede any and all State laws insofar as they may now or hereafter relate to any employee benefit plan." The objective of this preemption clause is to provide a uniform remedy for the participants and beneficiaries of ERISA-covered employee benefit plans.

An employee benefit plan is one that is established or maintained by an employer or employee organization.[1] This does not include individual retirement accounts.[2]

ERISA Section 514(c)(1) defines a state law as all laws, decisions, rules, regulations, or other state action having effect of law. Any attempt by a state to alter or limit the scope of preemption under ERISA Section 514(a), through legislation, regulatory action, or otherwise, would itself be preempted by ERISA.[3] For these purposes, a "state" includes any political subdivisions, agencies, or instrumentalities of the state.[4]

The United States Supreme Court, as well as United States District Courts and state courts have held in more than 300 cases that state laws and actions have been preempted by ERISA's broad reach.

The United States Supreme Court has held that a state law relates to an employee benefit plan "if it has any connection with or reference to such a plan."[5] In other words, if a claim under state law requires a review of, or reference to the plan, it would be subject to the preemption provisions of ERISA. This is particularly true where a state law has been specifically designed to have an effect upon employee benefit plans, or if the rights or restrictions it creates are based upon the existence of an employee benefit plan.[6] However, the Third Circuit Court of Appeals has ruled that ERISA preemption only applies to claims that an HMO (under the provision of health benefits through an employee welfare benefit plan) failed to provide benefits under the plan through the authorization of medical treatment. It does not prevent a claim under state law regarding the quality of treatment received once it has been authorized by the HMO as a benefit under the employee welfare benefit plan.[7] ERISA preempts state laws invalidating beneficiary designations pursuant to divorce.[8]

ERISA preempts state laws only. It will not preempt other federal laws or regulations. Specifically, ERISA will not be interpreted in such a way as to alter, amend, modify, invalidate, impair, or supersede federal laws and regulations.[9]

---

1. ERISA Secs. 3(1), 3(2).
2. Labor Reg. §2510.3-2(d).
3. DOL Adv. Op. 93-04A.
4. ERISA Sec. 514(c)(2).
5. *Shaw v. Delta Airlines*, 463 U.S. 85 (1983); *Ingersoll-Rand Co. v. McClendon*, 498 U.S. 133 (1990).
6. *United Wire Welfare Fund v. Morristown Mem'l Hosp.*, 995 F.2d 1179 (3d Cir. 1993).
7. *In re U.S. Healthcare, Inc.*, 193 F.3d 151 (3d Cir. 1999).
8. *Egelhoff v. Egelhoff*, 532 U.S. 141 (2001), *rev'g* 989 P.2d 80 (Wash. 1999).
9. ERISA Sec. 514(d).

The City of New York enacted an Equal Benefits Law mandating that no city agency may enter into a contract worth $100,000 or more with any service provider that fails to provide employee benefits to domestic partners of its employees equal to those provided to spouses. The city argued that the law did not mandate the extension of benefits to domestic partners of private industry employees, only that New York City would not conduct business with private entities that do not extend benefits to domestic partners. In rejecting this position, the court ruled that ERISA preempted the Equal Benefits Law because the city was attempting to act as a regulator to achieve public policy goals through dictation of the content of ERISA-covered plans.[1]

The Fourth Circuit Court of Appeals has ruled that Maryland's Fair Share Act is unenforceable due to ERISA preemption. The Fair Share Act was aimed at Wal-Mart and required employers with 10,000 or more Maryland residents on their payroll to spend, at a minimum, a specified level of total Maryland-based wages on health care or insurance. As an alternative, the employer could pay the difference between what is actually spent and the Act minimum to the State Secretary of Labor. In ruling that ERISA preempted the Fair Share Act, the court noted that the Act violated ERISA by mandating a structure of health benefits to meet state minimums. The court also noted that the Fair Share Act, in requiring separate accounting for Maryland residents, interfered with the uniform administration ERISA's plans.[2]

The Sixth Circuit Court of Appeals has ruled that a state law breach of contract claim based on a merger agreement, in which an acquiring employer guaranteed that the participants in an ESOP would receive funds from the employer's general assets if the ESOP's assets were not distributed as described in the merger agreement, was preempted by ERISA.[3] The court saw this case as the plaintiff's seeking damages for the ERISA-regulated actions of an ERISA fiduciary, based on an alleged contract that the fiduciary had entered into before becoming a fiduciary with respect to the plaintiff. The court ruled that ERISA preempted here because the state law contract claim originally filed would have bound fiduciaries to particular choices, thereby functioning as a regulation of the ERISA plan.

As an affirmative defense, ERISA preemption will be waived if not timely asserted.

791. What are the exceptions to the broad reach of ERISA preemption?

State laws that do not directly relate to an employee benefit plan will not be subject to the preemption provisions of ERISA. In addition to state laws that do not directly relate to an employee benefit plan, the following situations are not preempted by ERISA:

1.   Any state law that regulates insurance, banking, or securities;[4]

2.   Any generally applicable criminal law of a state;[5]

---

1. *In the Matter of the Council of the City of New York v. Bloomberg*, 36 EBC 2732 (Feb. 14, 2006).
2. *Retail Industry Leaders Association v. Fielder*, 2007 U.S. App. LEXIS 920 (4th Cir. 2007).
3. *Hutchison v. Fifth Third Bancorp*, 469 F.3d 583 (6th Cir. 2006).
4. ERISA Sec. 514(b)(3)(A).
5. ERISA Sec. 514(b)(3).

3.   The Hawaii Prepaid Health Care Act;[1]

4.   Certain multiple employer welfare arrangements;[2]

5.   Qualified domestic relations orders and qualified medical child support orders;[3] and

6.   Any state cause of action for the recoupment of Medicaid payments.

Further, there have been more than 200 federal and state court cases where the preemption provisions of ERISA have been ruled inapplicable to the state laws at issue. There have also been numerous cases denying ERISA preemption on the grounds that the state law at issue had only a "tenuous" relation to an ERISA-covered plan. Some examples of these cases include the application of state tort laws, fraud laws, breach of contract laws, severance pay laws, prevailing wage laws, malpractice laws, escheat laws, and insurance laws. In addition, the United States Supreme Court has ruled that ERISA does not preempt state garnishment laws.[4]

ERISA does not preempt state workers' compensation laws.[5]

The United States Supreme Court has ruled that state laws that regulate insurance and are directed specifically toward the insurance industry are not preempted by ERISA.[6] Citing the *Dedeaux* case, the Supreme Court has ruled that state level insurance "notice-prejudice" laws (which state that an insurer cannot avoid liability for an untimely claim unless the insurer can show that it suffered actual prejudice from the delay) are not preempted by ERISA.[7]

792. What are EBSA Field Assistance Bulletins?

Field Assistance Bulletins (FABs) are technical guidance provided by the national office of the Employee Benefits Security Administration (EBSA) to its field enforcement staff to ensure that the law is applied consistently across EBSA's various regions. FABs provide insight to the regulated community about EBSA's views on technical applications of ERISA and are available at the Web site of the Department of Labor, Employee Benefits Security Administration, at http://www.dol.gov/ebsa/regs/fabmain.html.

Pension Benefit Guaranty Corporation

793. What is Title IV of ERISA?

Title IV of ERISA established the plan termination insurance program that guarantees the benefits of participants and beneficiaries involved in certain defined benefit plans that, upon plan termination, do not have sufficient assets to cover the actuarially determined benefits that the plan is obligated to pay. In addition, Title IV established the rules applicable to defined benefit plan terminations.

---

1. ERISA Sec. 514(b)(5)(A).
2. ERISA Sec. 514(b)(6)(A).
3. ERISA Sec. 514(b)(7).
4. *Mackey v. Lanier Collection Agency & Serv., Inc.*, 486 U.S. 825 (1988); accord *Retirement Fund Trust of the Plumbing, Heating & Piping Indus. of S. Cal. v. Franchise Tax Bd.*, 909 F.2d 1266 (9th Cir. 1990).
5. ERISA Sec. 4(b)(3).
6. *Pilot Life Ins. Co. v. Dedeaux*, 481 U.S. 41 (1987).
7. *UNUM Life Ins. Co. of Am. v. Ward*, 526 U.S. 358 (1999).

ERISA Section 4002 established the Pension Benefit Guaranty Corporation (PBGC) to administer the plan termination insurance program and to administer and enforce the defined benefit plan termination rules. As a self-financing federal government corporation, the PBGC protects the retirement incomes of approximately 44 million workers and retirees in about 32,500 pension plans. The PBGC is financed through premiums collected from companies that sponsor insured pension plans, investment returns on PBGC assets, and recoveries from employers responsible for underfunded terminated plans. The PBGC's Board of Directors consists of the Secretaries of Labor, Treasury, and Commerce, with the Secretary of Labor serving as Chair. The PBGC is aided by a seven-member Advisory Committee appointed by the President to represent the interests of labor, management, and the general public. The PBGC is headed by an Executive Director.

The plan termination insurance program is a self-funded program in which covered defined benefit plans participating in the program fund it through premium payments based upon the number of plan participants.

Update—Pension Protection Act of 2006: On August 17, 2006, the Pension Protection Act of 2006 was signed into law. This legislation affects many PBGC requirements. The PBGC has provided guidance on how the changes affect practitioners and other persons and is discussed in the following questions.[1]

794. What are the investigative powers and authority of the PBGC and which plans do they cover?

ERISA Section 4003(a) provides that the PBGC "may make such investigations as it deems necessary to enforce any provision of this title (Title IV, Termination Insurance Program) or any rule or regulation thereunder, and may require or permit any person to file with it a statement in writing, under oath or otherwise as the corporation shall determine, as to all the facts and circumstances concerning the matter to be investigated."

ERISA Section 4003(b) permits any member of PBGC's Board of Directors or any officer designated by the Chair to conduct investigations, subpoena witnesses, and require the production of books, papers, correspondence, memoranda, and other records related to an investigation.

ERISA Section 4021(a) provides that the termination insurance program administered by the PBGC applies to any defined benefit plan, which, for a given plan year:

1. Is an employee pension benefit plan established or maintained:

    a. by an employer engaged in commerce or in any industry or activity affecting commerce; or

    b. by any employee organization, or organization representing employees, engaged in commerce or in any industry or activity affecting commerce; or

    c. both (a) and (b); *and*

---

1. Source: http://www.pbgc.gov/practitioners/Whats-New/whatsnew/page15560.html.

2. Has been a qualified pension plan, or has been operated as a qualified pension plan, for the five plan years prior to the year in which the plan terminates.

795. What ERISA-covered plans are exempt from PBGC coverage?

ERISA Section 4021(b) exempts the following plans from PBGC coverage:

1. All individual account (defined contribution) plans;

2. All government plans, including those established pursuant to the Railroad Retirement Act;

3. Any church plan (unless that plan has made an election under IRC Section 410(d), and has notified the PBGC that it wishes to be subject to PBGC coverage);

4. Any plan maintained outside the United States primarily for the benefit of nonresident aliens;

5. Any plan that is unfunded and maintained by an employer primarily for the purpose of providing deferred compensation to a select group of management or highly compensated employees;

6. Any plan that is established and maintained exclusively for substantial owners (sole owner of a trade or business or a greater than 10 percent owner of shares or a greater than 10 percent partner); and

7. Any plan that is established and maintained by a professional service employer that at no time has more than twenty-five active participants.

Further, there are certain nonqualified plans detailed under ERISA Section 4021(b) that are also excluded from PBGC coverage.

796. What is the PBGC premium program?

The primary reason for the establishment of the Pension Benefit Guaranty Corporation (PBGC) is to provide an insurance program that guarantees the provision of pension benefits (within certain limitations) to plan participants and beneficiaries of terminated defined benefit plans. The PBGC program will provide these benefits when a covered plan terminates with insufficient trust assets to cover the actuarially determined vested benefits of participants and beneficiaries.

For 2014, the maximum guarantee for a life annuity with no survivor benefits is $59,318.16 yearly ($4,943.18 monthly) at age sixty-five; $46,861.32 yearly ($3,905.11 monthly) at age sixty-two; and $26,693.16 yearly ($2,224.43 monthly) at age fifty-five [1]

Premium Filings: All plans, regardless of size, must now electronically submit all premium filings for plan years.[2] The PBGC's online application, My Plan Administration Account (My PAA),

---

1. http://www.pbgc.gov/res/factsheets/page/guar-facts.html
2. As of July 1, 2006, large plans (those with 500 or more participants in the prior year) have been required to e-file for plan years beginning on or after January 1, 2006.

is a secure Web-based application available through the Pension Benefit Guaranty Corporation's Web site (http://www.pbgc.gov). This application enables pension plan practitioners to electronically submit their premium filings and payments to the PBGC, in accordance with the PBGC's regulations.

The PBGC's mandatory e-filing requirements apply to estimated and final filings, including both original and amended filings.[1]

ERISA Section 4006(a)(3)(A)[2] establishes premium rates for PBGC-covered single-employer plans at $30 for each plan participant during the plan year. Multiemployer plans are required to submit premium payments at an annual rate of $8 per participant.[3] In the case of underfunded plans, an additional premium is required, which is equal to $9 for each $1,000 of a single-employer plan's unfunded vested benefits divided by the number of participants for whom PBGC coverage premiums were being paid as of the close of the prior plan year.[4] Plan administrators have the option of paying prorated premiums for short plan years instead of paying the premium on a full year and requesting a refund at a later date.[5] After adjustment for inflation, the flat-rate premium for 2012 is $35 for single-employer plans and $9 for multiemployer plans (both unchanged from plan year 2011). By law, the premium rates are adjusted for inflation each year based on changes in the national average wage index. ERISA Section 4006(a)(7) creates a new termination premium of $1,250 per participant to be levied on companies reorganizing under federal bankruptcy laws, payable for the first three years after coming out of bankruptcy.[6]

Participants, for purposes of assessing premium charges, are defined as:

1. Any individual who is currently in employment covered by the plan and who is earning or retaining credited service; this does not include individuals who are earning or retaining credited service if, on the "snapshot" date (see below), they have no accrued benefits (and the plan does not have any other benefit liabilities with respect to them);

2. Any non-vested individual who is not currently in employment covered by the plan, but who is earning or retaining credited service under the plan (excluding any non-vested former employees who (a) have experienced a one-year break in service, (b) are deemed to be cashed out under the terms of the plan, or (c) have died);

3. Any individual who is retired or separated from employment covered by the plan and who is receiving benefits under the plan;

---

1. To access information about My PAA, go to http://www.pbgc.gov/practitioners/premium-filings/content/page13265.html., including "How to Get Started" and online demonstrations.
2. *As amended by Deficit Reduction Act of 2005*, Pub. L. No. 109-171.
3. PBGC Reg. §§4006.3(a)(1), 4006.3(a)(2).
4. PBGC Reg. §4006.3(b).
5. PBGC Reg. §4006.5, as amended, 65 Fed. Reg. 75,160 (Feb. 1, 2000).
6. See *Summary, House–Senate Agreement, The Deficit Reduction Act of 2005*, at 7 (Feb. 1, 2006), at http://www.house.gov/budget/summarys1932.pdf.

4.   Any individual who is retired or separated from service covered by the plan and who is entitled to begin receiving benefits under the plan in the future;

5.   Any deceased individual who has one or more beneficiaries who are receiving or entitled to receive benefits under the plan; and

6.   All other individuals identified as participants under the terms of the plan.[1]

The participant count is made as of the last day of the prior plan year, or for a new defined benefit plan, on the date that it becomes subject to PBGC jurisdiction.

ERISA Section 4007(b) imposes a penalty of up to 100 percent of the amount due as a late-payment charge on unpaid premiums. The late-payment penalty charge is based upon the number of months from the due date to the date when payment is made. For any premium payment year beginning after 1995, the penalty rate is 1 percent per month on any amount of unpaid premium paid on or before the date when the PBGC issues a written notice of the premium delinquency, and 5 percent per month on any amount of unpaid premium paid after that date.[2]

The PBGC has expanded its safe-harbor relief from late-payment penalty charges effective for all PBGC determinations issued on or after December 27, 1999, with respect to premiums for plans years beginning before 1999, as well as PBGC determinations with respect to premiums for 1999 and later plan years. Under the safe harbor, a plan administrator must do two things to qualify and avoid late-payment penalty charges:

1.   By February 28 of the premium payment year, the plan administrator must pay the lesser of: (1) 90 percent of the flat-rate premium due for the premium payment year; or (2) 100 percent of the flat-rate premium that would be due for the premium payment year, if that amount were determined by multiplying the actual participant count for the prior year by the flat-rate premium for the premium payment year; and

2.   By October 15 of the premium payment year, the plan administrator must pay any remaining portion of the flat-rate premium for the premium payment year.[3]

ERISA Section 4011 requires plans that are obligated to pay the variable premium as a result of insufficient funding to provide notice to plan participants and beneficiaries of the plan's funding status and the limit on the PBGC's coverage should the plan terminate while underfunded. If a plan administrator fails to provide a participant with notice of the plan's funding status within the specified time limit or omits material information from such notice, the PBGC may assess a penalty of up to $1,100 a day for each day that the failure continues.[4] The plan administrator must issue the notice no later than two months after the deadline (including extensions) for the filing of the annual report for the previous plan year (i.e., seven months after the close of the plan year).[5]

---

1. PBGC Reg. §4006.2, *as amended*, 65 Fed. Reg. 75,160 (Dec. 1, 2000).
2. PBGC Reg. §4007.8, *as amended*, 64 Fed. Reg. 66,383 (Nov. 26, 1999).
3. PBGC Reg. §4007.8, *as amended*, 64 Fed. Reg. 66,383 (Nov. 26, 1999).
4. PBGC Reg. §4011.3(c).
5. Labor Reg. §2520.104a-5(a)(2).

The PBGC has issued a proposed policy statement on the assessment of penalties for failure to provide participant notices under ERISA Section 4011. The proposed policy would apply to 2004 and later notices, and to certain earlier years' notices that are ineligible for penalty relief under the PBGC's newly established Participant Notice Voluntary Correction Program (VCP).[1]

The proposed guideline penalty amount is equal to the number of plan participants, multiplied by the per-participant penalty rate. There are increases in the penalty for repeat violations and where the corrections occur after the PBGC issues notice of a pending audit. Pre-audit notice corrections would be subject to a $5 per-participant penalty, increased to $20 per participant for a repeat violation. The penalty is increased to $40 per participant and $100 per participant for a repeat violation if the PBGC has issued written notice that it is auditing a plan's compliance with the participant notice requirements. If the corrections have taken place within one year of the notice distribution date, the PBGC will prorate the penalty, based on the number of days before correction. No increases would occur solely because the period exceeds one year.

A repeat violation is a violation occurring after the plan administrator knew, or should have known, that there was a non–*de minimis* failure for an earlier plan year.

If a plan administrator corrects a notice failure on or before the date on which the PBGC issues a written notice that it is auditing the plan's compliance with the notice requirements, the correction would be valid if the PBGC determines, based on the facts and circumstances, that the corrective notice serves the statutory purposes of the notice requirement.

There is a "safe harbor" wherein the PBGC will treat a corrective notice as valid if the notice satisfies both of the following requirements:

1. In addition to the information that must be provided in a participant notice, the corrective notice includes all information that was required in all later notices due on or before the corrective notice is issued.

2. The plan administrator provided the notice to the persons who were entitled to receive the most recent participant notice that was due on or before the date on which the corrective notice was issued.

Defined benefit plans that meet the requirements of IRC Section 412(i) (plans funded exclusively by the purchase of individual insurance contracts) are exempted from the variable-rate premium requirements if the plan fits the description of an IRC Section 412(i) plan on a pre-determined "snap-shot" date in the previous plan year (which in most cases, the PBGC advises, is the last day of the preceding plan year).[2] This is a change from the prior requirement that the elements of IRC Section 412(i) be met on every day of the preceding plan year.

Single-employer plans that are exempt from the variable-premium payment arrangements are required to submit their final premium filing for the year on a simplified Premium

---

1. See Q 805. PBGC News Release 04-44 (May 6, 2004); 69 Fed. Reg. 25,797 (May 7, 2004).
2. PBGC Reg. §4006.5(a)(3), *as amended*, 65 Fed. Reg. 75,160 (Dec. 1, 2000).

Form 1-EZ instead of Form 1 and Schedule A. Nonexempt single-employer plans are still required to file Form 1 and Schedule A. Multiemployer plans are required to file Form 1 only.[1] New and existing Form 1 and schedules may be downloaded from the PBGC Web site at http://www.pbgc.gov.

The PBGC has extended the premium-filing deadline for most plans to nine and one-half months after the beginning of the premium payment year (October 15 for calendar year plans).

The PBGC has issued a proposed rule that would make permanent a procedure that the PBGC has been using on a case-by-case basis to compute liability when employers with underfunded pension plans close down a facility and lay off a significant percentage of their workforce.[2]

797. What are the PBGC proposed regulations that implement PPA changes to variable-rate premiums for single-employer plans?

The PBGC has proposed amendments to its premium payment regulations to implement provisions of the Pension Protection Act of 2006 that changed the variable-rate premium for plan years beginning on or after January 1, 2008.

The PPA enacted changes to the ERISA funding rules on which the variable-rate premium is based, and amended the variable-rate provisions of ERISA Section 4006 to conform with those changes and to eliminate the full-funding limit exemption from the variable-rate premium. The proposed amendments provide much-needed clarity to statutory ambiguity concerning when "unfunded vested benefits" are to be measured. The PBGC proposal establishes dates for variable-rate premium determinations, and revising the premium due date and penalty structure.

A plan's per-participant variable-rate premium is based on the plan's unfunded vested benefits "as of the close of the preceding plan year."[3] Prior to the changes made under PPA, unfunded vested benefits were based on unfunded "current liability." PPA eliminated the "current liability" provisions from the funding rules for single-employer plans. PPA also changed the definition of unfunded vested benefits to reflect the "funding target" for a plan year under ERISA Section 303(d), and amended that provision to establish that the first day of the plan year is the valuation date (with noted exceptions).

Because of PPA's failure to amend ERISA's variable-rate premium rule, there is now ambiguity about the date on which unfunded vested benefits are to be determined.

Due to the burdens imposed in requiring plans to conduct valuations as of the first day of a plan year as well as having to do separate valuations as of the last day for variable-rate premium purposes, the proposed regulations[4] establish a "UVB determination date" that requires that unfunded vested benefits be measured as of the valuation date for the premium payment year.

---

1. PBGC Technical Update 00-6 (Dec. 20, 2000).
2. Prop. PBGC Reg. §4062.8, 70 Fed. Reg. 9258 (Feb. 25, 2005).
3. Section 4006(a)(3)(E).
4. Prop. PBGC Reg. §4006.4.

The proposed regulations[1] also create an "alternative premium funding target" that is intended to be less of a burden.

The proposed regulations allow smaller plans more time to file. They also provide larger plans the ability to make estimated variable-rate premium filings and to correct them without penalty. Under the proposed regulations, PBGC creates a new "mid-size" category of plans and has separate rules for small plans (those with fewer than one-hundred participants), mid-size plans (those with one-hundred or more participants, but fewer than 500), and large plans (those with 500 or more participants).

798. What are the reportable events that must be directed to the attention of the PBGC?

Within thirty days after the plan administrator or the contributing sponsor knows or has reason to know that a reportable event has occurred, she must notify the PBGC.[2] This thirty-day notice is required if any of the following reportable events has occurred:

1. The plan has been disqualified by the IRS, or the DOL has notified the plan that it is not in compliance with the regulatory provisions of ERISA;[3]

2. There has been a plan amendment that would result in a decrease in benefits to any participant payable from employer contributions;[4]

3. Active participation drops below 80 percent of those participating at the beginning of the plan year, or to fewer than 75 percent of those participating at the beginning of the previous plan year;[5]

4. A termination or partial termination has occurred;[6]

5. The plan has been unable to pay vested accrued benefits when they become due;[7]

6. The plan has failed to make the required minimum funding payment;[8]

7. Bankruptcy, liquidation, or dissolution of the plan sponsor, or any member of the plan's controlled group, has occurred;[9]

8. Any distribution has been made to a substantial owner of a contributing sponsor;[10]

9. Plans have been merged or consolidated, or assets or liabilities have been transferred;[11]

---

1. Prop. PBGC Reg. §4006.5.
2. ERISA Sec. 4043(a).
3. PBGC Reg. §4043.21.
4. PBGC Reg. §4043.22.
5. PBGC Reg. §4043.23.
6. As defined under IRC Section 411(d)(3). PBGC Reg. §4043.24.
7. PBGC Reg. §4043.26.
8. PBGC Reg. §4043.25.
9. PBGC Reg. §§4043.35, 4043.30.
10. PBGC Reg. §4043.27.
11. PBGC Reg. §4043.28.

10.   Any transaction has occurred that resulted in a change in the contributing sponsor or in persons' discontinuing membership in the controlled group where the plan had less than $1,000,000 in unfunded benefits or no unfunded vested benefits;[1]

11.   Any declaration of an extraordinary dividend or stock redemption above stated levels has been made by any member of the plan's controlled group;[2]

12.   Any transfer has been made within a twelve-month period (ending on the date of the transfer) of an aggregate of 3 percent or more of the plan's total benefit liabilities to any person or to a plan maintained by a person who is not a member of the contributing sponsor's controlled group;[3]

13.   Any application for a minimum funding waiver has been submitted;[4]

14.   Any default on a loan has occurred with an outstanding balance of $10,000,000 or more by a member of the plan's controlled group;[5] or

15.   Any other event detailed in the regulations has occurred that indicates a need to terminate the plan.[6]

Any failure to make minimum quarterly contributions by small employers (generally, those with fewer than one-hundred plan participants, although, in some cases, as many as 500 participants) need not be reported to the PBGC if the employer makes the payments within thirty days of the due date.[7]

ERISA Section 4010 requires the following information to be included in any thirty-day notice submitted to the PBGC:

1.   Name of the plan;

2.   Name, address, and telephone number of the plan sponsor;

3.   Name, address, and telephone number of the plan administrator;

4.   Plan Sponsor Identification Number (EIN), and the Plan Number (PN);

5.   A brief statement of the facts relating to the reportable event;

6.   Copy of the current plan document;

7.   Copy of the plan's most recent actuarial statement and opinion; and

8.   A statement of any material change in the assets or liabilities of the plan that has occurred after the date of the most recent actuarial statement and opinion relating to the plan.

---

1. PBGC Reg. §4043.29.
2. PBGC Reg. §4043.31.
3. PBGC Reg. §4043.32.
4. PBGC Reg. §4043.33.
5. PBGC Reg. §4043.34.
6. PBGC Reg. §4043.35.
7. PBGC Technical Update 97-4.

The PBGC has established PBGC Form 10 and PBGC Form 10-Advance for use in filing a notice of a reportable event. PBGC Form 10 is to be used by plan sponsors or administrators of single-employer defined benefit plans to notify the PBGC within thirty days of the occurrence of a reportable event (replacing Form 10-SP). PBGC Form 10-Advance is to be filed by single-employer defined benefit plans when they are required to provide the PBGC an advance notice of any reportable event.

The PBGC has made available from their Web site (http://www.pbgc.gov/repevents.htp) the following reportable event forms, which plan sponsors and administrators may fill out and e-mail to the PBGC: Form 10, Form 10-Advance, and Form 200.[1]

Any failure to file a required notice or to include any required information may be subject to a penalty of up to $1,100 per day. This is assessed separately against each individual who is required to provide the PBGC with any notice.[2]

PBGC's Early Warning Program

The PBGC, in July 2000, issued a model participant notice to plans covered by the termination insurance program that provides details on the PBGC "Early Warning Program." The program is designed to assist the PBGC in avoiding the institution of plan termination proceedings under ERISA Section 4042(a)(4) by identifying plan sponsors in need of protection before business decisions or business transactions significantly increase the risk of loss to the corporate sponsored retirement plan covered by the termination insurance program. The PBGC will screen plans covered by the termination insurance program by focusing on two types of companies:

1.   Financially troubled companies; and

2.   Companies with pension plans that are underfunded on a current liability basis.

Financially troubled companies will be identified by a below investment grade bond rating under the most recent ratings published by the major rating agencies (i.e., Moody's and A.M. Best).

Companies with pension plans that have current liability in excess of $25 million and that have an unfunded current liability in excess of $5 million will be identified through data reported to the PBGC on the most recent Form 5500, Schedule B. Such plans, once identified, will be targeted for PBGC intervention under the Early Warning Program.

Those plans identified under the Early Warning Program as being "at risk" will be contacted by the PBGC with a request for further information. This information will assist the PBGC in accurately assessing whether a transaction or financial situation poses a legitimate risk to the underlying pension plan. If, in the estimation of the PBGC, there is a substantial risk to the plan, the PBGC will negotiate with the plan sponsor to obtain protections for the pension insurance program in lieu of terminating the plan.[3] Details on the Early Warning Program, such as a review of those business transactions that are of concern to the PBGC, are available in the text

---

1. PBGC News Release 98-20.

2. ERISA Sec. 4071; PBGC Reg. §4043.3(e).

3. PBGC Technical Update 00-3 (July 24, 2000).

of the model participant notice, which is available on the Internet at http://www.pbgc.gov/legal_info/tech_updates/tech00-3.htm.

On July 23, 2012, the IRS issued a series of questions and answers regarding the issuance of the ERISA Section 101(j) Notice for Funding-Related Benefit Limitations in Single-Employer Defined Benefit Pension Plans. IRS Notice 2012-46, IRB 2012-30 (July 23, 2012). Section 101(j) of ERISA requires the plan administrator of a single-employer defined benefit plan to provide a written notice to plan participants and beneficiaries, generally within thirty days after the plan becomes subject to the benefit limitations of section 206(g)(1) or (3) of ERISA (relating to unpredictable contingent event benefits and prohibited payments). In addition, in the case of a plan that becomes subject to the benefit limitations of section 206(g)(4) of ERISA (relating to the cessation of benefit accruals), the section 101(j) notice must be provided within thirty days after the earlier of the valuation date for the plan year for which the plan's adjusted funding target attainment percentage (AFTAP) is less than 60 percent or the date such percentage is presumed to be less than 60 percent under the rules of section 206(g)(7) of ERISA. Section 502(c)(4) of ERISA provides that the Secretary of Labor may assess a civil penalty of not more than $1,000 a day for each violation by any person of the notice requirement under section 101(j) of ERISA.

Section 101(c)(1)(A)(ii) of the Worker, Retiree, and Employer Recovery Act of 2008, Public Law 110-458 (122 Stat. 5092) (WRERA), amended section 101(j) of ERISA to authorize the Secretary of the Treasury, in consultation with the Secretary of Labor, to prescribe rules applicable to the notice requirements under section 101(j) of ERISA.

Section 206 of ERISA provides benefit limitations that depend on a plan's funding level, which is measured by the plan's Adjusted Funding Target Attainment Percentage (AFTAP), as determined under section 206(g)(9)(B) of ERISA. In general, a plan's AFTAP is based on the plan's Funding Target Attainment Percentage (FTAP) under section 303(d)(2) of ERISA for the plan year. Generally, the plan's FTAP for a plan year is a fraction (expressed as a percentage), the numerator of which is the value of plan assets for the plan year (after subtraction of the plan's funding balances), and the denominator of which is the funding target of the plan for the plan year. The plan's AFTAP for a plan year is determined by adding the aggregate amount of purchases of annuities for employees (other than highly compensated employees, within the meaning of Internal Revenue Code §414(q)) made by the plan during the two preceding plan years to the numerator and the denominator of the fraction used to determine the FTAP.

Under section 206(g)(1) of ERISA, a plan is required to provide that, if a participant is entitled to an unpredictable contingent event benefit payable with respect to any event occurring during a plan year, such benefit may not be paid if the plan's AFTAP for the plan year is less than 60 percent or would be less than 60 percent taking into account the occurrence of the unpredictable contingent event benefit. Section 206(g)(1)(C) of ERISA defines an unpredictable contingent event benefit as any benefit payable solely by reason of a plant shutdown (or similar event, as determined by the Secretary of the Treasury) or an event other than the attainment of any age, performance of any service, receipt or derivation of any compensation, or occurrence of death or disability.

Under section 206(g)(2) of ERISA, a plan amendment increasing the liabilities of the plan by reason of an increase in benefits, establishment of new benefits, changing the rate of benefit accrual, or changing the rate at which a benefit accrual becomes nonforfeitable generally cannot take effect in a plan year if the plan's AFTAP for the plan year is less than 80 percent or would be less than 80 percent taking into account such amendment. The notice requirements of section 101(j) of ERISA do not apply as a result of an amendment that causes the plan to become subject to the benefit limitations in section 206(g)(2).

Section 206(g)(3) of ERISA restricts a plan's ability to make "prohibited payments" if the plan's AFTAP is below 80 percent or the plan sponsor is a debtor in bankruptcy. Section 206(g)(3)(B) of ERISA provides that a "prohibited payment" is generally:

1.   any payment in excess of the monthly amount paid under a single life annuity (plus any social security supplements described in the last sentence of section 204(b)(1)(G) of ERISA to a participant or beneficiary whose annuity starting date occurs during any period that a limitation under section 206(g)(1)(A) or (B) of ERISA is in effect;

2.   any payment for the purchase of an irrevocable commitment from an insurer to pay benefits; and

3.   any other payment specified by the Secretary of the Treasury by regulations.

However, a prohibited payment does not include a payment of a benefit which under section 203(e) of ERISA (relating to benefits with a present value that does not exceed $5,000) may be immediately distributed without the consent of the participant.

Under section 206(g)(3)(A) of ERISA a plan is required to provide that the plan is not permitted to make any prohibited payment for a plan year after the valuation date for the year if the plan's AFTAP for the plan year is less than 60 percent. Under section 206(g)(3)(C) of ERISA, if a plan's AFTAP is at least 60 percent but less than 80 percent, the plan must provide that the plan is not permitted to pay any prohibited payment that is in excess of 50 percent of the amount of the payment that could be made but for the benefit limitation (or, if less, the present value of the maximum guarantee with respect to the participant under section 4022 of ERISA) (partially prohibited payments).

The questions and answers contained in IRS Notice 2012-46 address these complicated issues relating to the issuance of the ERISA 101(j) Notice to affected plan participants.

The PBGC in issuing Technical Update 09-1 has provided temporary guidance on how to apply the advance reporting threshold test and the funding-based waivers and extensions under the reportable events regulations to reflect the PPA 2006 modifications to the way the Variable Rate Premium (VRP) is determined.[1]

PBGC Technical Update 09-3 provided more limited relief for certain small plans with respect to which a reportable event would be triggered, pursuant to PBGC Reg. Section 4043.25, for a failure to timely make a required funding contribution, including a required quarterly

---

1. PBGC Technical Update 13-1 (January 30, 2013). Text available at available http://www.pbgc.gov/res/other-guidance/tu/tu13-.html.

contribution. On November 23, 2009, the PBGC published proposed regulations that will amend the reportable events regulations to accommodate the changes to the VRP rules. The proposed regulations also would eliminate most of the automatic waivers and extensions and would require reporting of a missed quarterly contribution without regard to plan size or the motivation for missing the contribution. Technical Update 13-1 will cover not only 2013 but all subsequent years until superseded. When the revised reportable event regulations become final, they will supersede this interim guidance, except as provided under those regulations.

For post-2012 plan years, if the plan had fewer than twenty-five participants for whom flat-rate premiums were paid for the prior plan year, the reporting requirement under PBGC Reg. section 4043.25 is waived with respect to the failure to make one or more quarterly contributions for the current plan year, but only if financial inability to make the contribution(s) is not the reason for failing to make the contribution. This relief is not conditioned on the plan sponsor's knowing that a quarterly contribution was required.

For post-2012 plan years, if the plan had at least twenty-five participants, but fewer than one-hundred participants for whom flat-rate premiums were paid for the prior plan year, a simplified alternative reporting method is prescribed for the current plan year with respect to missed quarterly contributions, but only if financial inability to make the contribution(s) is not the reason for making the contribution.

Under the simplified reporting method, the plan must file a notice with the PBGC, by the time the first missed-quarterly reportable event report for the current plan year otherwise would be due, which states the following information:

1. the name of the plan and the EIN and Plan Number most recently reported for the plan in a PBGC premium filing;

2. the date the current plan year began;

3. that a quarterly contribution to the plan for the current plan year has not been (or will not be) timely made;

4. that financial inability to make the contribution is not the reason for not making the contribution;

5. the last day for satisfying the minimum funding requirement for the plan for the current plan year (the final payment date);

6. that the filer understands that if the minimum funding requirement for the plan is not satisfied by the final payment date, a reportable event notice must be filed under the reportable events regulation; and

7. the name, telephone number, and e-mail address of a person (who may be the filer) whom PBGC may contact for additional information.[1]

The simplified report must be made either in the manner required for reportable events reports generally or by e-mail to: post-event.report@pbgc.gov. The sample notice language

---

1. PBGC Technical Update 13-1 (January 30, 2013).

provided in Technical Update 09-3 may be used, modified accordingly to reflect missed contributions for the current plan year instead of the 2009 plan year.

799. What are the details of the PBGC streamlined filing and notice requirements to facilitate use of electronic media?

In October 2003, the PBGC finalized rules that simplify and consolidate:

1. The methods that may be used to send a filing to PBGC, or provide an issuance to a third party;

2. The determination of the date on which:

    a. a filing is treated as made, or

    b. an issuance is provided;

3. The computation of time periods (e.g., for filings and issuances); and

4. The rules for maintaining records by electronic means.

The new regulations consolidated the PBGC's filing, notice, and electronic recordkeeping rules into five categories, as follows:

1. Information on how to file with the PBGC (Subpart A of the regulations; see Q 800);

2. How to issue notices to third parties (i.e., persons other than the PBGC) (Subpart B of the regulations; see Q 801);

3. How the PBGC determines the date of a filing or an issuance (Subpart C of the regulations; see Q 802);

4. How to compute time periods (Subpart D of the regulations; see Q 803); and

5. How to comply with recordkeeping requirements under the PBGC regulations using electronic means (Subpart E of the regulations; see Q 804).

These rules apply wherever a particular regulation calls for their application.[1] The PBGC states that these new requirements will facilitate electronic filing and electronic issuances by treating most types of submissions as filed or issued on the date sent rather than on the date received.[2]

The PBGC has issued a final rule mandating that sponsors of insured defined benefit plans submit their premium filings to the PBGC electronically. The requirement became effective for large plans (those with 500 or more participants) with filings for the 2006 plan year that were made on or after July 1, 2006, and for smaller plans starting with filings for plan years that began on or after January 1, 2007. With minor modifications, the final rule adopts the proposed rule that was issued in March 2005.[3]

---

1. PBGC Reg. §4000.1.
2. See PBGC Reg. §§4000 et seq.; 68 Fed. Reg. 61,344 (Oct. 28, 2003).
3. PBGC Reg. 4004.3, 4004.4, and 4004.11.

800. What are the methods of filing provided under the PBGC's streamlined rules?

Regulations finalized in 2003 provide the filing methods for any submission (including a payment) to the PBGC. These methods include submission of paper filings by hand, mail, or commercial delivery. The PBGC has removed the filing addresses for required filings from the regulations and has placed them on its Web site.[1]

In addition, the PBGC provides current information on electronic filings, including permitted methods, fax numbers, and e-mail addresses:

1. On the PBGC's Web site, http://www.pbgc.gov;

2. In printed PBGC forms and instruction packages; and

3. Through the PBGC's Customer Service Center (1200 K Street, NW, Washington, DC 20005-4026, 1-800-400-7242 (for participants), 1-800-736-2444 (for practitioners) (TTY/TDD users may call the federal relay service toll-free at 1-800-877-8339)).[2]

801. What are the methods of issuance under the PBGC's streamlined rules?

The 2003 regulations include rules for the issuance of a notice (or other information) to a person other than the PBGC.[3]

Generally, the method must include measures reasonably calculated to ensure actual receipt of the material by the intended recipient. Posting is not a permissible method of issuance, and payments to third parties are not covered by these rules. Where existing PBGC regulations require compliance with other rules, those other rules must be satisfied (e.g., the sixty-day notice requirement of intent to terminate under PBGC Regulation Section 4041.21; see Q 807).[4]

Safe Harbor Method

The PBGC provides a safe harbor method of providing an issuance by electronic media. This safe harbor generally follows Labor Regulation Section 2520.104b-1 concerning disclosure of employee benefit information through electronic media (see Q 59 for details). Any person using electronic media to satisfy issuance obligations under PBGC regulations may utilize this safe harbor method.[5]

---

1. See PBGC Regs. §§4000.1-4000.10; 68 Fed. Reg. 61,344 (Oct. 28, 2003).
2. See PBGC Reg. §4000.3.
3. See PBGC Reg. §§4000.11-4000.15; 68 Fed. Reg. 61,344 (Dec. 28, 2003).
4. PBGC Regs. §§4000.11 and 4000.13.
5. PBGC Reg. §4000.14.

802. What are the dates of filing or issuance under the PBGC's streamlined rules?

The 2003 regulations provide rules for determining the date a submission is filed with the PBGC, and the date an issuance is provided to someone other than the PBGC (e.g., participants and beneficiaries), for purposes of filings made under applicable PBGC regulations.[1]

Most types of submissions to the PBGC are treated as filed on the date the submission was sent, provided certain requirements are satisfied. If these requirements are not met, the submission, if in a permitted format and sent to the proper address, is treated as filed on the date received.[2]

If a submission is received after 5:00 p.m. on a business day, or any time on a weekend or a federal holiday, the submission is treated as received on the next business day.

The following filings are always treated as filed when the submission is received:

1. Applications for benefits and related submissions (unless the applicable form's instructions provide an earlier date);

2. Advance notices of reportable events;

3. Notices of missed contributions exceeding $1 million; and

4. Requests for approval of a multiemployer plan amendment.

Most types of issuance are treated as provided on the date of issuance, if certain requirements are satisfied. These rules are similar to the rules for the date of filing, except for electronic filings.[3]

The PBGC cautions that these rules do not cover payments to third parties or filings with the PBGC that are not provided for under applicable regulations such as procurement filings, litigations filings, and applications for employment.

Postal Service Delivery. For paper and computer disk submissions or issuances sent by first-class mail (or an equivalent class, such as priority or express) and properly sent by the last scheduled mail collection of the day, the filing or issuance date is the date mailed. If a filing or issuance is properly mailed after the last scheduled mail collection for the day, the filing or issuance date is the date of the next scheduled collection.

If the submission or issuance has a United States Postal Service postmark, the filing or issuance date is presumed to be the date of the postmark, although an earlier date may be proven. The same rule applies if there is a postmark of a private postage meter (but no legible U.S. postmark) and the submission or issuance arrives at the proper address by the time reasonably expected. Postal Service and private postage meter postmarks must be legible.[4]

---

1. See PBGC Regs. §§4000.21-4000.32; 68 Fed. Reg. 61,344 (Oct. 28, 2003).
2. PBGC Reg. §4000.23.
3. PBGC Reg. §4000.23.
4. PBGC Reg. §4000.24.

For submissions and issuances delivered from a foreign postal service, the date of receipt at the proper address will be the applicable filing/issuance date.[1]

Commercial Delivery Service. For a paper or computer disk submission or issuance that is deposited with a commercial delivery service that is a "designated delivery service,"[2] and for which it is reasonable to expect that the submission or issuance will arrive at the proper address by 5 p.m. on the second business day after the date of collection, the filing or issuance date is the date of the deposit if the deposit was made by the last scheduled collection of the day for the type of delivery utilized. If the deposit is made later than the last scheduled collection for the day, or if there is no scheduled collection, the filing or issuance date is the date of the next scheduled collection.[3]

The PBGC Web site provides a detailed listing of the "designated delivery service" providers acceptable under IRC Section 7502(f).

Hand Delivery. The filing or issuance date of a hand-delivered paper or computer disk filing or issuance is the date of receipt at the proper address. A hand-delivered issuance does not have to be delivered while the intended recipient is physically present. Unless the sender has reason to believe that the intended recipient will not receive the notice within a reasonable amount of time, a notice is deemed received when placed in the intended recipient's office mailbox.[4]

Electronic Delivery. The filing date for an electronic submission is the date the submission is transmitted to the PBGC at the proper address, provided the technical requirements for the particular type of submission, as indicated on the PBGC's Web site, are met.

Issuances may be provided electronically and are treated as sent on the date transmitted, provided the PBGC Regulation Section 4000.14 safe harbor rule for issuances made using electronic media (see above) is met.

For either filings or issuances, when sending e-mail with an attachment, the body of the e-mail must contain the name and telephone number of a person for the PBGC to contact if the PBGC is unable to read the attachment.

If the requirements for electronic submission are not met, the PBGC may treat the submission or issuance as invalid. But if the submission or issuance would meet the requirements except that it is sent to the wrong address, the filing or issuance date is the date of receipt at the proper address.[5]

Computer Disk. The regulations include a special requirement for the submission of filings and issuance on computer disk: a paper cover letter or the disk's label must include the name

---

1. See PBGC Reg. §4000.25.
2. Under IRC Sec. 7502(f).
3. PBGC Reg. §4000.26.
4. PBGC Reg. §4000.27.
5. PBGC Reg. §4000.29.

and telephone number of the person to contact if the PBGC or other recipient is unable to read the disk.[1]

Resending. A person sending a filing or issuance can have the benefit of his original filing or issuance date even if he had reason to believe that the PBGC or the intended recipient has not received the issuance (or has received it in a form that is not usable), if the filing or issuance is promptly resent. If the resending is not prompt, or does not include any evidence that the PBGC requires in support of an original filing or issuance date, then the filing or issuance date is the date of the resubmission or reissuance.

If a person is asked to resubmit a filing or an issuance for technical reasons (e.g., inability to open an e-mail attachment), and the resubmission is made by the date that the PBGC specifies for filings or within a reasonable time for issuances, then the original filing or issuance date applies.[2]

De Minimis Issuance Errors. PBGC will not treat an issuance as untimely based on a failure to provide it to a participant or beneficiary in a timely manner if:

1.   The failure resulted from administrative error;

2.   The failure involved only a *de minimis* percentage of intended recipients; and

3.   The issuance is resent to the intended recipient promptly after the error is discovered.[3]

Under previous regulations, this rule applied only to standard and distress termination issuances (under former PBGC Regulation Section 4041.3(c)(3)). The rule under PBGC Regulation Section 4000.31 applies to all issuances under the PBGC's regulations.

803. What are the "computation of time" rules under the PBGC's streamlined requirements?

The "computation of time" rules are set forth at PBGC Regulation Sections 4000.41-4000.43.[4] In computing a time period (whether counting forward or backward) under the final regulations:

1.   The day of the act, event, or default that begins the period is excluded;

2.   The last day of the period is included; and

3.   If the last day is a weekend or federal holiday, the period is extended or shortened (whichever benefits the person making the filing or providing the issuance) to the next regular business day.

The weekend and holiday rule also applies to deadlines for which counting is not required.[5]

---

1. PBGC Reg. §4000.28.
2. PBGC Reg. §4000.30.
3. See PBGC Reg. §4000.31.
4. 68 Fed. Reg. 61,344 (Oct. 28, 2003).
5. See PBGC Reg. §4000.43.

If a time period is measured in months, the period is measured by first identifying the day of the calendar month on which counting is started, and then looking to the corresponding day of the calendar month in which counting is stopped. If counting begins on the last day of a calendar month, the corresponding day of any later (or earlier) calendar month is the last day of that calendar month.

Special February Rule. If counting begins on the twenty-ninth or thirtieth day of a calendar month, the corresponding day of February is the last day of February.[1]

804. What are the electronic means of record retention under the PBGC's streamlined requirements?

The regulations generally follow the rules for retaining records by electronic means set forth in Labor Regulation Section 2520.107-1 (see Q 59 for details). Therefore, electronic media can satisfy the record maintenance and retention requirements if the electronic recordkeeping system has reasonable controls to ensure the accuracy, integrity, authenticity, and reliability of records kept in electronic form, and if the records are maintained in reasonable order and in a safe and accessible place.[2]

The electronic records must also be readily convertible into legible and readable paper copy, and must exhibit a high degree of legibility when displayed on a video display terminal or other method of electronic transmission. There must also be no agreement or restriction that would, directly or indirectly, compromise or limit a person's ability to comply with any reporting and disclosure requirement.

Adequate record management practices (e.g., procedures for labeling electronically maintained or retained records, creating backup electronic copies for storage at an off-site location, etc.) also must be followed.[3]

Original paper records may be disposed of any time after they are transferred to an electronic recordkeeping system that complies with the electronic recordkeeping rules. But original paper records must not be discarded if the electronic record would not be a duplicate or substitute record under the terms of the plan and applicable federal or state law.[4]

The PBGC advises that these recordkeeping requirements are consistent with the goals of the Electronic Signatures in Global and National Commerce Act[5] and are designed to facilitate voluntary use of electronic records, while ensuring continued accuracy, integrity, and accessibility of records required to be kept under PBGC regulations. Furthermore, the PBGC cautions plan sponsors that they remain responsible for following the electronic recordkeeping rules "even if you rely on others for help."[6]

---

1. PBGC Reg. §4000.43(c)(2).
2. See PBGC Regs. §§4000.51-4000.54; 68 Fed. Reg. 61,344 (Oct. 28, 2003).
3. PBGC Reg. §4000.53.
4. PBGC Reg. §4000.54.
5. "E-SIGN," Pub. L. No. 106-229.
6. See Preamble, PBGC Regs §§4000.1 et seq.; 68 Fed. Reg. 61,344 (Oct. 28, 2003).

805. What is the PBGC Participant Notice Voluntary Correction Program?

The PBGC created the Participant Notice Voluntary Correction Program (VCP), through which the plan administrator of an underfunded defined benefit plan may correct a recent failure to provide notice of the plan's underfunded status to participants.[1]

ERISA Section 4011 requires that the administrator of an underfunded defined benefit plan issue notice to the plan participants of the plan's funding status and the limits on the PBGC's guarantee of benefits. The administrator generally must issue the notice for a plan year if the plan is required to pay a variable-rate premium for that year (and in certain other underfunded situations), unless the plan satisfies the two deficit reduction contribution (DRC) exceptions.

Plan administrators are required to certify on their annual PBGC premium filings (Form 1 or Form 1-EZ) that, for the prior plan year, either:

1.   No participant notice was required;

2.   The participant notice was issued as required; or

3.   The participant notice was not issued as required, along with an explanation of why the notice was late or otherwise deficient.

There is a penalty imposed for failure to timely file this required notice. The amount is determined utilizing a formula that takes into account the number of plan participants, multiplied by the per-participant penalty rate.

As a result of the PBGC's expanding its Participant Notice enforcement program, it implemented the VCP to encourage administrators of underfunded pension plans who failed to issue notices on the plan's funding status to correct those failures and to facilitate future compliance with the Participant Notice requirements. The PBGC does not assess penalties for these failures under VCP if the failure was corrected in accordance with the following guidelines:

1.   A corrective notice was issued in accordance with the VCP no later than the 2 years past the participant notice due date; and

2.   The PBGC was notified within 30 days after the participant notice due date that the plan is participating in the VCP.

The notice must include all other information required in a plan year notice (current information on funding waivers, missed contributions, and limitations on the PBGC's guarantee). The VCP corrective notice must provide the funded current liability percentage for the plan year(s), and may include the funded current liability percentage for the plan year, as well. The plan administrator is not required to notify the participants of its failure for. The PBGC advises, however, that a plan administrator may choose to include that information in the VCP corrective notice.

---

1. Internal Revenue Bulletin: 2008-35 (Sep. 2, 2008), Rev. Proc. 2008-50PBGC News Release 04-44 (May 6, 2004); 69 Fed. Reg. 25,791 (May 7, 2004).

The notification filed with the PBGC must include a copy of the VCP corrective notice and the name and telephone number of a person for the PBGC to contact with any questions. Plan administrators may submit this notice electronically through the PBGC Web site at *http://www. pbgc.gov/participantnotice*, by fax at 202-336-4197, or by mail or other delivery at Contracts and Control Review Department, Pension Benefit Guaranty Corporation, 1200 K Street, NW, Suite 580, Washington, DC 20005-4026. PBGC will issue prompt acknowledgment of its receipt of the notification. Plan administrators should keep the acknowledgment as proof of satisfying the PBGC notice requirement under the VCP.

If a plan administrator's only failure for a participant notice was issuing it late, and the administrator corrected the failure, PBGC will treat the plan administrator as having participated in the VCP and will assess no penalty for that failure without requiring that the plan administrator issue a VCP corrective notice or notify the PBGC of the plan's participation in the VCP.

If a plan administrator previously issued an erroneous certification of compliance with the notice requirement as part of a premium filing notifies the PBGC of the plan's participation in the VCP, the PBGC will treat the notification as effectively amending any erroneous certification for a participant notice. The PBGC will take no enforcement action based on the erroneous prior certification if the plan administrator of a plan that meets the requirements for penalty relief under the VCP amends (or effectively amends) the erroneous prior certification.

Plan administrators of all plans that meet the requirements for VCP penalty relief were required to check a box on their PBGC premium filings notifying the PBGC of the plan's participation in the VCP. This requirement supplements the requirement that the administrators notify the PBGC of their participation as a condition of participation in the VCP.

Plan Terminations

806. What is a "standard termination"?

Under a standard termination, the defined benefit plan is voluntarily terminated by the plan sponsor after it has been determined that, as of the effective date of the termination, the plan has sufficient assets to satisfy the actuarially determined benefits it is obligated to pay to plan participants and beneficiaries.

A standard termination of a single-employer defined benefit plan occurs when:

1. The plan administrator provides the sixty-day advance notice of intent to terminate (see Q 807) to affected parties;

2. The plan administrator has completed and issued a notice to the PBGC that contains detailed information and a certification prepared by an enrolled actuary (see Q 808);

3. A notice of benefit commitments to be paid is provided to participants and beneficiaries; and

4. The PBGC has not issued a notice of noncompliance to the plan administrator advising the plan that the PBGC has determined that the plan does not have

sufficient assets for benefit liabilities, and/or that the PBGC determines that there is reason to believe that the requirements of a standard termination have not been met.[1]

ERISA Section 4001(a)(16) provides that benefit liabilities are "the benefits of their (the plan sponsor's) employees and their beneficiaries under the plan" (within the meaning of IRC Section 401(a)(2)).

Practitioner's Pointer: ERISA Section 4041(b)(3)(B) requires that, within thirty days of the final distribution of plan assets, the plan administrator must send notice to the PBGC that the assets of the plan have been distributed in accordance with the standard termination provisions of ERISA. If the actuary has determined that the plan's trust assets are insufficient to satisfy the plan's benefit obligations, the provisions of ERISA Section 4041(b)(3)(B) allow the plan sponsor to execute a standard termination by contributing the plan's shortfall amount prior to the date of final distribution of plan assets.

Update—New Audit Initiative in Standard Terminations. As part of a new enforcement initiative, the PBGC now audits all plans that distribute plan assets in satisfaction of plan benefits before or without filing a standard termination notice (Form 500) in accordance with the PBGC's regulations governing the standard termination process.[2] The PBGC reserves the right to take any other appropriate action in such circumstances.[3]

807. Who must receive notice when a plan sponsor intends to terminate a defined benefit plan? And what information must such individuals receive?

ERISA Section 4041(a)(2) requires that "not less than sixty days before the proposed termination date of a standard termination ... the plan administrator shall provide each affected party a written notice of intent to terminate stating that such termination is intended and the proposed termination date." This is commonly referred to as the "sixty-Day Notice of Intent to Terminate," and it may not be provided more than ninety days before the proposed termination date, although the PBGC may consider the notice to be timely filed if it was early by a *de minimis* number of days and the PBGC finds that the early issuance was the result of an administrative error. If, after the proposed termination date, an individual becomes the beneficiary of a deceased participant or an alternate payee under a QDRO, the notice must also be provided to that individual. The notice must include a statement indicating how the participant or beneficiary can obtain a copy of the plan's summary plan description.[4]

Affected parties are defined as:

1.   Each participant in the plan;

2.   Each beneficiary of a deceased participant;

---

1. ERISA Sec. 4041(b).
2. 29 C.F.R. pt. 4041.
3. http://www.pbgc.gov/practitioners/Whats-New/whatsnew/page15560.html.
4. PBGC Reg. §§4041.3(b)(1), 4041.21(a).

3.   Each alternate payee under an applicable qualified domestic relations order;

4.   Each employee organization that currently represents any group of participants;

5.   The employee organization that last represented a group of currently unrepresented employees within the five-year period preceding the issuance of the notice of intent to terminate; and

6.   The PBGC.

The plan administrator shall issue the sixty-day notice of intent to terminate to the affected parties by hand delivery or first-class mail or courier service to the last known address of the affected parties.[1] The following information must be included in the sixty-day notice:

1.   Name of the plan and the contributing sponsor;

2.   Employer identification number (EIN) and the plan number (PN);

3.   Name, address, and telephone number of the person whom an affected party may contact with questions concerning the plan termination;

4.   A statement that the plan administrator expects to terminate the plan in a standard termination on a proposed termination date that is either a specific date set forth in the notice or a date that is to be determined upon the occurrence of some future event;

5.   The nature of the future event, if the termination date is dependent upon (a) when that event is expected to occur, and (b) when the termination will occur in relation to the event;

6.   A statement that benefit and service accruals will continue until the termination date or, if applicable, that benefit accruals have been frozen as of a specific date in accordance with ERISA Section 204(h);

7.   A statement that, in order to terminate in a standard termination, plan assets must be sufficient to satisfy all benefit liabilities under the plan with respect to each participant and each beneficiary of a deceased participant;

8.   A statement that, after plan assets have been distributed to provide all benefit liabilities with respect to a participant or a beneficiary of a deceased participant, either by the purchase of an irrevocable commitment or commitments from an insurer to provide benefits, or by an alternative form of distribution provided for under the plan, the PBGC's guarantee with respect to that participant's or beneficiary's benefit ends;

9.   If distribution of benefits under the plan may be wholly or partially satisfied by the purchase of irrevocable commitments from an insurer:

      a. name and address of the insurer(s) from whom the plan administrator intends to purchase the irrevocable commitments; or

---

1. PBGC Reg. §4041.21.

      b.   if the plan administrator has not identified an insurer or insurers at the time the notice of intent to terminate is issued, a statement that: (i) irrevocable commitments may be purchased from an insurer to provide some or all of the benefits under the plan; (ii) the insurer(s) have not yet been identified; and (iii) affected parties will be notified at a later date (no later than forty-five days prior to the distribution date) of the name and address of the insurer(s) from whom the plan administrator intends to purchase the irrevocable commitments;

10.   A statement that if the termination does not occur, the plan administrator will notify the affected parties in writing of that fact;

11.   A statement that each affected party, other than the PBGC or any employee organization, will receive a written notification of the benefits that the person will receive; and

12.   For retirees only, a statement that their monthly (or other periodic) benefit amounts will not be affected by the plan's termination.[1]

Any non-vested or partially vested participant who has been cashed out under the provisions of IRC Section 411(a)(7) and Treasury Regulation Section 1.411(a)-7(d) is not a participant who must receive a notice of plan benefits. This includes any 0 percent vested participant who is "deemed" to have been cashed out under the terms of the plan.

808. What other notice requirements are required in a defined benefit plan termination?

The plan administrator must provide a notice to each affected person (as of the proposed termination date) that details the amount of the individual's plan benefits as of the proposed termination date. The notice must include:

1.   Age of the participant or beneficiary;

2.   Length of service to be credited at termination;

3.   Actuarial assumptions used in calculating benefits (including the applicable interest rate);

4.   Wages at the time of termination; and

5.   Any other information that the PBGC may require.

This notice must be provided no later than the date on which the sixty-day notice of intent to terminate has been provided to the PBGC.[2]

In addition, ERISA Section 4041(b)(2)(A) requires the plan administrator to file PBGC Form 500, "Standard Termination Notice Single-Employer Plan Termination," no later than 180 days after the proposed date of termination. Form 500 must be filed with the PBGC. In addition, an

---

1. PBGC Reg. §4041.21(d).
2. ERISA Sec. 4041(b)(2)(A); PBGC Reg. §4041.22.

enrolled actuary must certify: (1) the projected amount of assets of the plan; (2) the actuarial present value of the benefit liabilities; and (3) that the plan is projected to be sufficient (as of the proposed date of final distribution) for such benefit liabilities. The enrolled actuary must submit this information on Schedule EA-S, "Standard Termination Certification of Sufficiency," which is attached to Form 500. The Notice is considered filed with the PBGC as of the date of the mailing, provided that there is evidence of a postmark. If the notice is made through a private delivery service, the date of filing is generally the date of deposit with the delivery service so long as the PBCG receives it within two business days. If the filing is done electronically, the date of filing is generally the date of the electronic transmission to the PBGC. Any information deemed received on a weekend, on a federal holiday, or after 5:00 p.m. on a business day, is considered filed on the next regular business day.[1]

PBGC has issued a final rule for computing liability when employers with underfunded pension plans close down a facility and lay off a significant percentage of their workforce. The final rule adopts the proposed rule without substantive changes, and provides an illustrative example. The regulations are effective for "Section 4062(e) events" occurring on or after July 17, 2006.[2]

809. What is a distress termination?

A distress termination occurs when a defined benefit plan does not have sufficient assets to satisfy the benefit obligations owed to participants and beneficiaries. To voluntarily terminate a defined benefit plan under a distress termination, one of the following conditions must be satisfied:

1. The plan sponsor is in liquidation or bankruptcy proceedings due to insolvency;

2. The plan sponsor is undergoing reorganization in bankruptcy or insolvency proceedings;

3. Termination of the defined benefit plan is required in order to allow the plan sponsor to service the payment of debts while staying in business; or

4. Termination of the defined benefit plan is required in order to allow the plan sponsor to avoid unreasonably burdensome pension costs caused by a declining workforce.[3]

Under a distress termination of a single-employer plan, the plan administrator must provide a 60-day notice of intent to terminate to all affected parties, which includes the proposed termination date.[4] In addition, the plan administrator must provide to the PBGC the following information from a certified enrolled actuary:

1. Amount of the current value of plan assets;

2. Actuarial present value of the benefit liabilities under the plan; and

3. Actuarial present value of benefits under the plan that are guaranteed by the PBGC.[5]

---

1. PBGC Reg. §4041.24.
2. PBGC Reg § 4062.8, 71 Fed. Reg. 34819, (June 16, 2006).
3. ERISA Sec. 4041(c)(2)(B).
4. ERISA Sec. 4041(a)(2).
5. ERISA Sec. 4041(c)(2)(A)(ii).

When the determination has been made that plan assets are not sufficient to satisfy benefit obligations, the PBGC must be provided with:

1.   Name and address of each participant and beneficiary under the plan;

2.   Any additional information required by the PBGC in order for them to make guaranteed payments to participants and beneficiaries; and

3.   Certification by the plan administrator that the information on which the enrolled actuary based his certifications is accurate and complete, and all other information provided to the PBGC is accurate and complete.[1]

810. What are the PBGC proposed regulations on providing information to affected parties in distress or PBGC-initiated plan terminations?

Section 506 of the Pension Protection Act of 2006 (PPA) amended ERISA Sections 4041 and 4042 to add disclosure provisions for distress or PBGC-initiated terminations. These provisions allow an affected party to request information related to a plan termination from the plan administrator in the case of a distress termination under ERISA Section 4041 and from the plan administrator, plan sponsor, and PBGC in the case of a termination under ERISA Section 4042.[2]

"Affected party" is defined in ERISA Section 4001(a)(21) to include each participant in the plan, each beneficiary under the plan, each employee organization representing plan participants, and the PBGC.

These rules require the plan administrator to provide, upon request, to affected parties information it has submitted to PBGC and require that it do so no later than fifteen days after receipt of the request for the information by the affected party.

The new rule also provides a confidentiality provision that allows a court to limit disclosure of confidential information to an authorized representative.

Regarding PBGC-initiated terminations, the rules require that following receipt by the plan administrator of a Notice of Determination, the plan sponsor, plan administrator, and the PBGC must provide information related to the termination to an affected party upon request. The plan sponsor or plan administrator must, not later than fifteen days after receipt of a request, provide copies of any information it provided to the PBGC in connection with the termination. The PBGC must, not later than fifteen days after receipt of a request, provide a copy of the administrative record, including the trusteeship decision record. The confidentiality provision provided for in a distress termination also applies under the new rules to a PBGC-initiated termination.

---

1. ERISA Secs. 4041(c)(2)(A)(iii), 4041(c)(2)(A)(iv).
2. ERISA Secs. 4041(c)(2)(D)(iii), 4042(c)(3)(D).

Information to Be Disclosed in Distress Terminations

In a distress termination, ERISA Section 4041(a)(2) requires a plan administrator to provide to each affected party a notice of intent to terminate containing information as set forth in Section 4041.43 of PBGC's regulation on Termination of Single-Employer Plans.

PBGC regulations also require that a separate notice with additional information be filed with PBGC on PBGC Form 600, Distress Termination, Notice of Intent to Terminate. Additional information must be submitted to the PBGC at a later date in accordance with Section 4041(c)(2) of ERISA and Section 4041.45 of the regulations, if necessary.

"PBGC recognizes that because the statute references only Section 4041(a)(2), which addresses the notice of intent to terminate, it is possible to read Section 4041(c)(2)(D)(i) as requiring that a plan administrator disclose only the Form 600. Such a narrow reading, however, would be at odds with Congress's intent to provide greater disclosure of information submitted to PBGC in connection with a distress termination." Therefore, the PBGC's interpretation, as detailed in the proposed regulations, requires that a request for this information must:

1. Be made in writing to the plan administrator;

2. State the name of the plan and that the request is for information submitted to the PBGC with respect to the application for a distress termination of the plan;

3. State the name of the person making the request, the person's relationship to the plan, and that that relationship meets the definition of "affected party"; and

4. Be signed by the person making the request.[1]

In meeting its disclosure obligations, a plan administrator must, under the proposed regulations, provide the information no later than the fiftieth business day after receipt of the request. However, if the Form 600 has not yet been provided to the PBGC at that time, the administrator has until the fiftieth business day after providing the Form 600 to the PBGC to provide it to the affected party. Similarly, for any additional submission of information to the PBGC a plan administrator has until the fiftieth business day after the submission to provide the information to an affected party that has filed a request.[2]

Information to Be Disclosed in PBGC-Initiated Terminations

Where the PBGC initiates a plan termination and has issued notice of such intent, a plan sponsor or plan administrator of a single-employer plan that has received such notice must provide to an affected party any information provided to the PBGC in connection with the plan termination.[3]

---

1. 29 CFR Sec. 4041 and 4042.
2. PBGC Prop. Reg. §4041.51(b).
3. ERISA Sec. 4042(c)(3)(A)(i).

Pursuant to the PPA amendments to ERISA Section 4042(c)(3) a plan sponsor or plan administrator has fifteen days following a request for this information to provide it to the requesting party. In addition, the PBGC itself must, on request, provide a copy of the administrative record, including the trusteeship decision record, of the terminated plan.

An affected party may file a request for information beginning on the third business day after the PBGC has issued notice that the plan should be terminated.[1]

As with distress terminations, the proposed regulations for PBGC-initiated terminations mandate any disclosure request for information satisfy the four elements detailed above.[2] The proposed regulations allow fifteen business days for providing requested information.[3]

An affected party with respect to the plan covered under the proposed regulations may make a request to PBGC for the administrative record of the PBGC's determination that the plan should be terminated. Requests for information from the PBGC follow the same procedures with respect to when a request may be filed and the contents of the request. In addition, the proposal requires that the request be sent to the PBGC's Disclosure Officer and be prominently identified as an "Administrative Record Request."[4]

Upon receiving the request, the PBGC will promptly notify the plan administrator and plan sponsor that it has received a request for the administrative record and the date by which PBGC will provide it to the affected party.[5]

A plan administrator or plan sponsor that has received notification of a request for the administrative record may seek a court order under which those portions of the administrative record that contain confidential information will be disclosed only to authorized representatives (within the meaning of ERISA Section 4041(c)(2)(D)(iv)) that agree to ensure the confidentiality of such information, and that it will not be disclosed to other affected parties.[6]

In providing that information, the PBGC will use measures, including electronic measures, reasonably calculated to ensure actual receipt of the material by the intended recipient.[7]

811. What must a plan sponsor do if the plan does not satisfy the requirements of a distress termination?

If a plan does not satisfy the statutory requirements for a distress termination and there are insufficient assets to satisfy the plan's benefit obligations, the plan sponsor cannot terminate the plan. In order to terminate an underfunded plan, the plan sponsor must provide sufficient assets that would enable the plan to go forward with a standard termination. Otherwise, the plan sponsor must continue the plan.[8]

---

1. PBGC Prop. Reg. §4042.4(a)(2).
2. PBGC Prop. Reg. §4042.4(a)(2).
3. PBGC Prop. Reg. §4042.4(b).
4. PBGC Prop. Reg. §4042.5(a).
5. PBGC Prop. Reg. §4042.5(b)(1).
6. PBGC Prop. Reg. §§4042.5(b)(2)(ii)(A), 4042.5(b)(2)(ii)(B).
7. PBGC Prop. Reg. §§4042.5(b)(4), 4041.51, 4042.1 et seq.; 72 Fed. Reg. 68,542 (Dec. 5, 2007).
8. PBGC Regs. §§4041.41, 4041.47.

If the plan sponsor must continue the operation of the plan, the plan may be amended to freeze benefit accruals for current participants and to prohibit the addition of new participants. A frozen plan must continue to be maintained in accordance with current law, including any statutorily required amendments.

812. What benefits are guaranteed by the PBGC?

With certain limitations, the PBGC guarantees the payment of all nonforfeitable benefits under a terminated single-employer plan. The limitations restrict the amount of benefits that have been increased through a plan amendment within five years of the termination date.[1]

The guaranteed benefits payable by the PBGC are defined as the amount, as of the date of termination, of a benefit provided under a plan, to the extent that:

1.   The benefit is a nonforfeitable benefit;

2.   The benefit qualifies as a pension benefit; and

3.   The participant is entitled to the benefit.[2]

Qualified preretirement survivor annuities "with respect to a participant under a terminated single-employer plan shall not be treated as forfeitable solely because the participant has not died as of the termination date."[3]

Under ERISA Section 4022(b)(3), the amount of monthly benefits guaranteed by the PBGC cannot have an actuarial value that exceeds the actuarial value of a monthly benefit in the form of a life annuity commencing at age sixty-five. This amount will be adjusted on an annual basis to reflect the cost of living.[4]

The PBGC has issued a regulation that increases the maximum value of benefits payable by the PBGC as a lump-sum distribution from $3,500 to $5,000. This rule has been drafted to reflect the recent amendment of ERISA Section 203(e), which specifies the maximum amount that a plan may pay in a single installment without the participant's consent.[5]

If the guaranteed benefit is payable at an age earlier than age sixty-five, the maximum guaranteed benefit will be actuarially reduced based upon the earlier commencement of benefits.[6]

---

1. ERISA Secs. 4022(a), 4022(b).
2. PBGC Reg. §4022.3.
3. ERISA Sec. 4022(e).
4. PBGC Reg. §4022.23.
5. PBGC Reg. §4022.7(b)(1)(i).
6. PBGC Reg. §4022.23.

The PBGC will recoup an overpayment in a PBGC trusteed plan if, at any time:

1.   The PBGC determines that net benefits paid with respect to any participant in a PBGC trusteed plan exceeded the total amount to which the participant (and any beneficiary) was entitled up to that time; and

2.   The participant (or beneficiary) is, as of the termination date entitled to receive future benefit payments.[1]

For a participant who dies after the termination date, the PBGC will generally not seek recoupment of overpayments from the participant's estate.[2]

The PBGC issues a news release on an annual basis that provides the cost-of-living adjustment.

For 2014, single-employer plans terminated, the maximum guaranteed monthly benefit is $4,943.18 per month ($59,318.16 per year) for workers who begin receiving payments from the PBGC at age sixty-five.[3] If the benefit starts before age sixty-five, or if there are survivor benefits, the maximum guarantee is less. In some instances, a retiree may receive more than the maximum, such as when the plan has sufficient assets to pay non-guaranteed benefits or when portions of funds are recovered from companies on behalf of trusteed plans. Examples of the maximum guarantee for a single life annuity with no survivor benefits are reported on the Internet at *http://www.pbgc.gov/res/laws-and-regulations/code-of-federal-regulations/part-4022— benefits-payable-in-terminated-single-employer-plans.html#93.*

The PBGC provides insurance for more than 1,600 defined benefit multiemployer plans. These multiemployer plans provide retirement benefits to more than 10 million workers and retirees. Under the multiemployer plan program, the PBGC provides financial assistance to plans that become insolvent. A multiemployer plan is considered insolvent if the plan is unable to pay benefits at least equal to the PBGC guaranteed limits when due.[4]

Pension plans pay PBGC yearly insurance premiums. Since 2007, the flat premium rates are adjusted annually. The rates for 2014 are $12 per worker or retiree in multiemployer plans and $49 per worker or retiree in single-employer plans plus $13 for each $1,000 of unfunded vested benefits in single-employer plans. The variable-rate charge for single-employer plans is $400 per participant.[5]

813. Will the PBGC guarantee benefits in a plan that the IRS has disqualified?

ERISA Section 4022(b)(6) states that "no benefits accrued under a plan after the date on which the Secretary of the Treasury (the IRS) issues notice that he has determined that any trust

---

1. PBGC Reg. §4022.81(a).
2. Preamble to PBGC Reg. pt. 4022.
3. Source: http://www.pbgc.gov/res/factsheets/page/guar-facts.html.
4. See http://www.pbgc.gov/res/factsheets/page/pbgc-facts.html.
5. Source: http://www.pbgc.gov/res/factsheets/page/pbgc-facts.html

which is a part of a plan does not meet the requirements of IRC Section 401(a), or that the plan does not meet the requirements of IRC Section 404(a)(2), are guaranteed under this section unless such determination is erroneous."

Benefits accrued under a plan after the date on which the IRS has disqualified a plan, or after the date of the adoption of an amendment that causes the plan to be disqualified, will not be guaranteed by the PBGC.[1]

814. How will a plan amendment affect the PBGC guarantee upon a plan's termination?

ERISA Section 4022(b)(7) provides for a five-year phase-in of benefits that have been increased through a plan amendment within five years of a defined benefit plan's termination. The formula applied to the phase-in rule is spelled out as follows:

Benefits will be guaranteed to the extent of the greater of:

1.   20 percent of the amount guaranteed; or

2. $20 per month;

        multiplied by the number of years (not to exceed five) during which the plan amendment has been in effect.

Benefit increases are defined as "any benefit arising from the adoption of a new plan or an increase in the value of benefits payable arising from an amendment to an existing plan. Such increases include, but are not limited to, a scheduled increase in benefits under a plan or plan amendment, such as a cost of living increase, and any change in plan provisions that advances a participant's or beneficiary's entitlement to a benefit, such as liberalized participation requirements or vesting schedules, reductions in the normal or early retirement age under a plan, and changes in the form of benefit payments."[2]

The definition of year under the phase-in period is each complete twelve-month period prior to the plan's termination date.[3]

Any amendments that benefit a substantial owner will be subject to a thirty-year phase-in rule.[4] A substantial owner is defined as: (1) any individual who owns the entire interest in an unincorporated trade or business; (2) in the case of a partnership, a partner who owns, directly or indirectly, more than 10 percent of either the capital interest or the profits interest in such partnership; or (3) in the case of a corporation, an individual who owns, directly or indirectly, more than 10 percent of either the voting stock or all stock of that corporation.[5]

---

1. PBGC Reg. §4022.27.
2. PBGC Reg. §4022.2.
3. PBGC Reg. §4022.25(c).
4. ERISA Sec. 4022(b)(5)(B); PBGC Reg. §4022.25.
5. ERISA Sec. 4022(b)(5)(A).

815. Who are "affected parties" in a defined benefit plan termination?

"Affected parties" are those individuals who must receive the various notices that must be provided in the defined benefit plan termination process. An affected party is defined as:

1. Each participant in the plan;

2. Each beneficiary under the plan who is the beneficiary of a deceased participant;

3. Each beneficiary who is an alternate payee under a qualified domestic relations order;

4. Each employee organization currently representing participants in the plan;

5. The Pension Benefits Guaranty Corporation (PBGC);

6. The employee organization that last represented such a group of participants within the five-year period preceding the issuance of the notice of intent to terminate; and

7. Any individual identified in writing to receive notice on behalf of an affected party.[1]

816. What is the importance of a defined benefit plan's termination date?

The termination date of a plan is to be determined by the plan sponsor or by the PBGC, depending upon which of the two is terminating the plan.[2] The importance of the plan's termination date is that it is upon that date that certain determinations are made, including:

1. Which rights accrue to which participants;

2. When the plan sponsor's funding obligation ends;[3]

3. The PBGC's obligation for guaranteed benefits; and

4. The plan sponsor's liability for underfunding.

In situations where the plan sponsor has initiated termination proceedings, the notice of intent to terminate must be provided to affected parties at least sixty days before the intended termination date.[4]

817. When will the PBGC initiate a plan termination?

The PBGC may institute proceedings under ERISA Section 4042(a) to terminate a defined benefit plan whenever it has determined that:

1. The plan has not satisfied the minimum funding standards;

2. The plan will be unable to pay benefits when due;

---

1. ERISA Sec. 4001(a)(21); PBGC Reg. §4001.2.
2. ERISA Sec. 4048; H.R. Conf. Rep. No. 93-1280, 93rd Cong. 2nd Sess., 323 (1974) (ERISA Conference Report).
3. *Audio Fidelity Corp. v. PBGC*, 624 F.2d 513 (4th Cir. 1980).
4. ERISA Sec. 4041(a)(2).

3.   A distribution of more than $10,000 was made to a substantial owner in any twenty-four-month period for reasons other than death and, subsequent to such distribution, there remain unfunded vested liabilities; or

4.   A corporation's possible long-run loss with respect to the plan may reasonably be expected to unreasonably increase if the plan is not terminated.

The PBGC will institute termination proceedings in federal court "as soon as practicable" to terminate a single-employer plan whenever the PBGC determines that the plan does not have sufficient assets available to pay benefits that are currently due under the terms of the plan.[1]

The PBGC may reinstitute a plan against which it has begun termination proceedings and return the plan to its pre-termination status if the PBGC determines that circumstances have changed.[2] The *LTV* case prompted the establishment of ERISA Section 4047, which expressly grants the authority of restoration to the PBGC. In the *LTV* case, the plan sponsor terminated three underfunded defined benefit plans covered by the PBGC. After termination proceedings were instituted by the PBGC, the plan sponsor established new defined benefit plans that were to provide the benefits lost as a result of the PBGC's termination of the initial three plans. In effect, the plan sponsor was attempting to provide the entire amount of guaranteed benefits under the first three plans by shifting the burden for the minimum PBGC guaranteed benefits onto the PBGC and picking up the difference through the subsequent plans. The PBGC protested and attempted to reinstitute the initial three plans to their pre-termination status, thereby leaving the full-funding obligation to the plan sponsor. The plan sponsor protested, but the United States Supreme Court sided with the PBGC.

818. What is involved in the final distribution of assets in a defined benefit plan standard termination?

In a standard termination, the PBGC has sixty days within which to issue a notice of noncompliance. The final distribution of assets in a defined benefit plan termination must occur no later than 180 days after the expiration of this sixty-day period (assuming the plan has not received a notice of noncompliance).[3] The PBGC and the plan sponsor may jointly extend the sixty-day noncompliance notice period by a jointly executed written agreement.[4] Such an extension may be necessary in order for the plan to establish, to the satisfaction of the PBGC, that the plan has sufficient assets to meet benefit obligations and has followed the procedural requirements for a standard termination.

The plan is entitled to an automatic extension of the 180-day distribution period if the plan sponsor:

1.   Submits a complete request for a determination letter to the IRS with respect to the plan termination on or before the date when the plan files the standard termination notice (on PBGC Form 500) with the PBGC;

---

1. ERISA Sec. 4002(a).
2. *PBGC v. LTV Corp.*, 496 U.S. 633 (1990).
3. ERISA Sec. 4041(b)(2)(D).
4. ERISA Sec. 4041(b)(2)(C).

2.   Does not receive a determination letter at least sixty days before the expiration of the 180-day period; and

3.   On or before the expiration of the 180-day period, notifies the PBGC in writing that an extension of the distribution deadline is required and certifies that the conditions in items one and two have been met.[1]

The PBGC may grant a discretionary extension of the 180-day period if the plan administrator is unable to complete the distribution of plan assets within that time frame. The PBGC will grant a discretionary extension if it is satisfied that the delay in issuing the final distribution of plan assets is not due to the inaction or action of the plan administrator or the plan sponsor, and that the final distribution can be completed by the date requested.[2]

ERISA Section 4041(b)(3) provides that in the final distribution of assets through a standard termination, the plan administrator will:

1.   Purchase irrevocable commitments from an issuer to satisfy all benefit liabilities under the plan; or

2.   In accordance with the plan provisions and applicable PBGC regulations, otherwise fully satisfy all benefit liabilities under the plan, including the transfer of assets for missing participants to the PBGC (see Q 820).

Within thirty days after the final distribution of all assets, the plan administrator shall send notice to the PBGC certifying that the assets of the plan have been distributed in accordance with the provisions of ERISA Section 4041(b)(3)(A). This notice will be provided on PBGC Form 501, "Post Distribution Certification for Standard Termination."

The PBGC may assess a penalty, payable to the PBGC, for a failure to timely file any required notice or other required material information.[3] The amount of this penalty is not to exceed $1,100 for each day for which such failure continues. This has been reduced regarding Form 501 to $25 per day for the first ninety days of delinquency, and $50 per day for each day beyond that. The PBGC may reduce or eliminate the penalty if the plan sponsor demonstrates reasonable cause for the delay.[4]

Practitioner's Pointer: In issuing the most recent regulations regarding standard termination procedures, the PBGC advises that they intend to conduct post-distribution audits to determine whether these calculations are being made properly. The PBGC says that it is common for them to find errors in their post-distribution audits. The revised forms and packages issued to conform to these new regulations include detailed guidance on calculating lump-sum distributions.[5]

---

1. PBGC Reg. §4041.27(e).
2. PBGC Reg. §4041.27(f).
3. ERISA Sec. 4071.
4. PBGC Statement of Policy, 60 Fed. Reg. 36,837 (July 18, 1995).
5. The revised forms and packages are available on the PBGC's homepage at http://www.pbgc.gov.

819. Does the Pension Benefits Guaranty Corporation (PBGC) retain any responsibility for the provision of benefits after the purchase of annuities by a terminating pension plan?

No. PBGC Opinion Letter 91-1 provides that the purchase of an irrevocable annuity contract for the provision of benefits to participants and beneficiaries in connection with the termination of a pension plan ends the PBGC's obligation to guarantee any of the plan's obligations. Therefore, if the insurance company is unable to provide all of the benefits guaranteed under the annuity contract, the PBGC will not assume the obligation to make up the difference. Furthermore, the PBGC has indicated, in Opinion Letter 91-4, that the plan sponsor is not required to make up such difference if it acted in accordance with the provisions of the plan and in accordance with applicable regulations. They further advise that the plan sponsor has an obligation under the fiduciary provisions of Title I of ERISA to act prudently in the selection of the annuity provider.

820. How are the assets of missing participants handled when a defined benefit plan terminates?

In the termination of a defined benefit plan, the plan sponsor is required to complete a "diligent search" to locate all missing participants.[1] A *diligent search* is one that:

1. Begins not more than six months before notices of intent to terminate are issued and is carried on in such a manner that, if the individual is found, distribution to the individual can reasonably be expected to be made on or before the deemed distribution date (or, in the case of a recently missing participant, on or before the ninetieth day after the deemed distribution date);

2. Includes an inquiry of plan beneficiaries of the missing participant; and

3. Includes the use of a commercial locator service (without charge to the missing participant, or a reduction of their benefit).[2]

If a diligent search yields no result, the plan administrator may request the assistance of the IRS in attempting to locate the missing participants. The IRS will forward a letter to the missing participant's last known address on file with the IRS. The IRS will not levy a charge against the plan if there are fewer than fifty participants in the request for them to forward letters.[3]

Under the PBGC's "Missing Participants Program," for standard terminations, if all attempts to locate a missing participant have failed, the sponsor of the terminating plan is to provide the missing participant's benefits through the purchase of an irrevocable commitment from an insurance company (annuity), or provide a payment of the benefits to the PBGC along with "such information and certifications" as the PBGC specifies.[4] The amount of the

---

1. ERISA Sec. 4050(b)(1).
2. PBGC Reg. §4050.4.
3. Rev. Proc. 94-22, 1994-1 C.B.B 608.
4. ERISA Sec. 4050(a).

designated benefit forwarded to the PBGC shall be determined under the detailed rules of the regulations.[1]

The sponsor of a terminating plan with one or more missing participants is required to file Schedule MP with the Post-Distribution Certification and pay over to the PBGC the value of benefits payable to all missing participants for whom the plan did not purchase irrevocable commitments from an insurance company.

Schedule MP includes the information necessary for the PBGC to attempt to identify and locate missing participants and to compute and pay their benefits. The PBGC will attempt to locate any participant whose benefits have been transferred to the PBGC or for whom the terminating defined benefit plan has purchased an irrevocable annuity.

Schedule MP must be filed at the same time as the Post-Distribution Certification.[2] Relief from this deadline is permitted for "late discovered" or "recently missing participants."

If the PBGC locates the missing participant, the PBGC will inform the participant of the identity of the insurer and the relevant annuity policy number, or the PBGC will pay the benefits in accordance with the actuarial assumptions established by the PBGC at the time when the benefits were transferred from the terminating plan and in accordance with the methods of payment established in the terminated plan.

An additional $300 must be paid to the PBGC "as an adjustment for expenses, for each missing participant whose designated benefit without such adjustment would be greater than $5,000."[3]

821. What help is available from the PBGC for former participants attempting to locate vested benefits in plans of former employers?

The PBGC has issued an online pamphlet entitled "Finding a Lost Pension," which is designed to assist individuals in tracking down information on pension plans of former employers that might still hold vested benefits on their behalf. The booklet is available for viewing on the Internet at http://www.pbgc.gov/lostpendl.htm.

822. Who has authority to enforce certain plan terminations in a civil action?

ERISA Section 4070(a) provides that "any person who is with respect to a single employer plan a fiduciary, contributing sponsor, member of a contributing sponsor's controlled group, participant, or beneficiary, and is adversely affected by an act or practice of any party" (other than the PBGC) in violation of certain provisions of ERISA, may bring an action: (1) to enjoin such act or practice; or (2) to obtain other appropriate equitable relief to redress such

---

1. PBGC Reg. §4050.5.
2. PBGC Reg. §4050.6(a).
3. PBGC Reg. §4050.2.

violation or to enforce such provision. In order to bring such an action, the violation must be a violation of:

1.   Voluntary termination provisions of ERISA Section 4041;

2.   Reporting provisions of ERISA Section 4042;

3.   Distress termination provisions of ERISA Section 4062;

4.   Controlled group withdrawal liability provisions of ERISA Section 4063 and ERISA Section 4064; or

5.   Restriction of transactions to evade liability provisions under ERISA Section 4069.

ERISA Section 4070 does not, however, authorize a civil action against the Secretary of the Treasury (the IRS), the Secretary of Labor, or the PBGC.[1] For civil actions against the PBGC, see Q 825.

A single-employer plan may be sued as an entity under ERISA Section 4070. Service of summons, subpoena, or other legal process of a court upon a trustee or an administrator of a single-employer plan, in his capacity as trustee or administrator, constitutes service upon the plan. If a plan has not designated an agent for the service of process within its summary plan description, service may be made upon any contributing sponsor.[2]

Any money judgment in an ERISA Section 4070 action against a single-employer plan shall be enforceable only against the plan as an entity and not against any other person, unless liability against such person is established in that individual's capacity.[3]

A copy of the complaint or notice of appeal in any action under ERISA Section 4070 shall be served upon the PBGC by certified mail. The PBGC has the right to exercise its discretion to intervene in any action filed under ERISA Section 4070.[4]

Civil Actions under ERISA

823. What is the appropriate jurisdiction and venue to bring a civil action under ERISA Section 4070?

Federal district courts have exclusive jurisdiction over civil actions under ERISA Section 4070. Such actions may be brought in the district court located where the plan is administered, where the violation took place, or where the defendant resides or may be found. Service of process for such civil actions may be served in any district where a defendant resides or may be found. Such jurisdiction resides in the federal district courts without regard to the amount in controversy or the citizenship of the parties.[5]

---

1. ERISA Sec. 4301(a).
2. ERISA Sec. 4070(b).
3. ERISA Sec. 4070(b).
4. ERISA Sec. 4070(d).
5. ERISA Sec. 4070(c).

The federal district court hearing any civil action brought under ERISA Section 4070 may, in its discretion, award all or a portion of the costs and expenses incurred in connection with such action, including reasonable attorneys' fees, to any party who prevails or substantially prevails in such action. There is an exemption that prohibits plans from being required to pay any costs and expenses in any action.[1]

824. What is the statute of limitations for any civil action brought under ERISA Section 4070?

Any civil action under ERISA Section 4070 must be brought within six years after the date on which the cause of action arose, or three years after the earliest date on which the plaintiff acquired, or should have acquired, actual knowledge of the existence of such cause of action.[2]

In the case of a fiduciary plaintiff who brings the action in the exercise of her fiduciary duties, the statute of limitations for bringing an action is the date on which the plaintiff became a fiduciary with respect to the plan if such date is later than six years after the date on which the cause of action arose, or three years after the earliest date on which the plaintiff acquired, or should have acquired, actual knowledge of the existence of such cause of action.[3]

In the case of fraud or concealment, the statute of limitations is six years, instead of three years.[4]

825. Who may bring a civil action against the PBGC?

ERISA Section 4003(f)(1) states that, except with respect to withdrawal liability disputes with multiemployer plans, "any person who is a fiduciary, employer, contributing sponsor, member of a contributing sponsor's controlled group, participant or beneficiary, and is adversely affected by any action of the corporation [PBGC] with respect to a plan in which such person has an interest, or who is an employee organization representing such a participant or beneficiary so adversely affected for purposes of collective bargaining with respect to such plan, may bring an action against the corporation for appropriate equitable relief in the appropriate court."

The court may award all or a portion of the costs and expenses incurred in connection with a civil action brought against the PBGC to any party who prevails or substantially prevails in such action.[5]

826. What is the appropriate jurisdiction and venue in which to bring a civil action against the PBGC?

The provisions of ERISA Section 4003(f)(1) are the exclusive means for bringing civil actions against the PBGC under the plan termination provisions of ERISA, including actions against the PBGC in its capacity as a trustee.[6]

---

1. ERISA Sec. 4070(e).
2. ERISA Sec. 4070(f)(1).
3. ERISA Sec. 4070(f)(2).
4. ERISA Sec. 4070(f)(3).
5. ERISA Sec. 4003(f)(3).
6. ERISA Sec. 4003(f)(4).

The district courts of the United States have exclusive jurisdiction over civil actions brought against the PBGC, without regard to the amount in controversy.[1]

The appropriate court for bringing such actions is the federal district court before which the termination proceedings are being conducted. If no such termination proceedings are being conducted, the appropriate court is the federal district court for the judicial district in which the plan has its principal office, or the federal district court for the District of Columbia.[2]

In any suit, action, or proceeding in which the PBGC is a party or intervenes in any state action, the PBGC may, without bond or security, remove such suit, action, or proceeding from the state court to the federal court for the district or division in which such suit, action, or proceeding is pending.[3]

827. What is the statute of limitations on civil actions brought against the PBGC?

Civil actions may not be brought against the PBGC after the later of:

1.   Six years after the date on which the cause of action arose; or

2.   Three years after the date on which the plaintiff acquired, or should have acquired, actual knowledge of the existence of his cause of action.[4]

In the case of a fiduciary plaintiff who brings the action in the exercise of his fiduciary duties, the three-year statute of limitations begins to run on the date on which the plaintiff became a fiduciary with respect to the plan, if such date is later than the date on which the plaintiff acquired, or should have acquired, actual knowledge of the existence of such cause of action.[5]

In the case of fraud or concealment, the period for the statute of limitations is extended from three years to six years.[6]

828. When may the PBGC bring a civil action?

The PBGC may sue in a federal district court to enforce the termination insurance provisions of ERISA or to seek appropriate equitable or legal relief.[7]

The PBGC may intervene in an action brought for a declaratory judgment that has been instituted by an employee, employer, or plan administrator.[8] The PBGC is also permitted to file a petition for declaratory judgment to appeal an IRS ruling relating to plan qualification, plan amendments, and plan terminations.[9]

---

1. ERISA Sec. 4003(f)(6).
2. ERISA Secs. 4003(f)(2)(A), 4003(f)(2)(B), 4003(f)(2)(C).
3. ERISA Sec. 4003(f)(7).
4. ERISA Secs. 4003(f)(5)(A), 4003(f)(1)(B).
5. ERISA Sec. 4003(f)(5)(B)(ii).
6. ERISA Sec. 4003(f)(6).
7. ERISA Sec. 4003(e)(1).
8. In accordance with IRC Section 7476.
9. ERISA Sec. 3001(c); IRC Sec. 7476.

829. What is the appropriate jurisdiction and venue in which the PBGC may bring civil actions?

The district courts of the United States have exclusive jurisdiction over civil actions brought under the multiemployer plan provisions; however, state courts of competent jurisdiction have concurrent jurisdiction over an action brought by a plan fiduciary to collect withdrawal liability.[1]

ERISA Section 4301(d) establishes jurisdiction in the district court where the plan is administered or where a defendant resides or does business in any civil action under the multiemployer plan provisions. Service of process may be made in any district where a defendant resides, conducts business, or may be found.

The PBGC may remove any state suit, action, or proceeding under the multiemployer plan provisions in which it is a party, or has intervened, to a federal district court.[2]

A copy of the complaint in any civil action under the multiemployer plan provisions must be served upon the PBGC by certified mail. The PBGC may intervene in any such action.[3]

830. What is the statute of limitations for civil actions brought by the PBGC?

The PBGC is held to similar statutes of limitations for civil actions to enforce the termination provisions of ERISA and for other civil actions brought by the PBGC. ERISA Section 4003(e)(6)(A) provides that a civil action brought by the PBGC may not be brought later than:

1. Six years after the date on which the cause of action arose; or

2. Three years after the earliest date on which the PBGC acquired, or should have acquired, actual knowledge of the existence of the cause of action.

If the PBGC brings the action as trustee, the applicable statute of limitations begins to run on the date on which the PBGC became a trustee, if this date is later than the date on which the PBGC acquired, or should have acquired, actual knowledge of the existence of the cause of action.[4]

In the case of fraud or concealment, the statute of limitations on civil actions brought by the PBGC is extended to six years after the earliest date on which the PBGC acquired, or should have acquired, actual knowledge of the existence of the cause of action.[5]

831. Does the PBGC encourage alternative dispute resolution?

In 1999, the PBGC announced the institution of its policy to use alternative dispute resolution for resolving appropriate disputes in a timely and cost-efficient manner. In announcing the new policy, the PBGC stated that "in appropriate circumstances, there may be more effective methods

---

1. ERISA Sec. 4301(c).
2. ERISA Sec. 4003(f)(7).
3. ERISA Sec. 4301(g).
4. ERISA Sec. 4003(e)(6)(B).
5. ERISA Sec. 4003(e)(6)(C).

to resolve issues that would otherwise be resolved through adversarial administrative or judicial processes. Although there is never an entitlement to alternative dispute resolution, the voluntary use of alternative dispute resolution, such as mediation, fact-finding, neutral evaluation, and arbitration, often can provide faster, less expensive, and more effective resolution of disputes that arise with employees, contractors, the regulated community, and others with whom the agency does business."[1]

For further information on the PBGC policy regarding alternative dispute resolution, contact:

PBGC Office of the General Counsel
Pension Benefit Guaranty
Corporation
1200 K St., NW
Washington, DC 20005-4026

832. What are the PBGC notice obligations in light of the events regarding Bernard L. Madoff Investment Securities, LLC?

According to the PBGC in a notice issued on February 6, 2009, concerning single-employer and multiemployer defined benefit pension plans insured by the Pension Benefit Guaranty Corporation (PBGC) that may have experienced significant investment losses resulting from a customer relationship with Bernard L. Madoff Investment Securities LLC, either directly or through an investment adviser, if the losses of a single-employer plan are sufficient to render the plan unable to pay benefits when due, the plan administrator or sponsor is required by ERISA Section 4043 to notify the PBGC of this event within thirty days of knowing or having reason to know that this reportable event has occurred. The plan administrator must notify the PBGC of a reportable event by filing PBGC Form 10, which is available at http://www.pbgc.gov. Questions should be directed to Roger Reiersen of PBGC's Department of Insurance Supervision and Compliance. He may be contacted at 202-326-4000, extension 3704, or reiersen.roger@pbgc.gov.

Multiemployer plans that are covered by Title IV of ERISA do not have an obligation to notify the PBGC when a reportable event under Section 4043 occurs. However, if the trustees believe that benefits cannot be paid when due, *or* all, or substantially all, employers cease contributing to the plan, the trustees have legal responsibilities, which may include reducing benefits, assessing withdrawal liability, and notifying the PBGC. If plan representatives have questions or concerns, they may call the Multiemployer Division at 202-326-4000, ext. 3012, or send an e-mail to Multiemployerprogram@pbgc.gov.

Plan administrators and sponsors of affected single-employer and multiemployer plans should also consult a qualified adviser concerning recovery of funds invested directly or indirectly with Madoff Securities.[2]

---

1. 64 Fed. Reg. 17,696 (Apr. 12, 1999).
2. PBGC No. 09-14.

SECTION XIII

Criminal Enforcement

833. What is the Department of Labor's criminal enforcement program?

The Department of Labor (DOL), through the Employee Benefits Security Administration (EBSA), has statutory authority to conduct investigations.[1] ERISA Section 506(b) expressly confers upon the Secretary of Labor shared responsibility and authority to detect, investigate, and refer, where appropriate, criminal violations of ERISA as well as other related federal laws, including Title 18 of the United States Code.

With the passage of the Comprehensive Crime Control Act,[2] the DOL's statutory authority to investigate criminal matters relating to employee benefit plans is now expressly stated. Accordingly, the DOL is no longer required to obtain delegation on a case-by-case basis; however, EBSA investigators and auditors contact the appropriate United State's Attorney's Office (USAO) after evidence is developed in an investigation that may warrant consideration and interest by the USAO to initiate criminal proceedings under either ERISA or Title 18 of the U.S. Code. The USAO is contacted at the earliest possible stage of the investigation for coordination purposes to determine whether the DOJ is interested in pursuing the matter and, thus, avoid the expenditure of DOL resources on a matter that may not be of interest to the DOJ. When interest in pursuing the investigation is expressed by the DOJ, EBSA continues with the investigation. If the USAO declines pursuing the case, EBSA may either close the investigation, refer it to another agency, or pursue the case with a local or state enforcement agency for prosecution under state criminal laws.

A critical part of EBSA's enforcement program under its Strategic Enforcement Plan is the prosecution of criminal acts relating to employee benefit plans. The criminal enforcement aspects of EBSA's enforcement strategy are integral to EBSA's broader goal of protecting employee benefit plan assets by detecting abuses and deterring future violations. EBSA's policy is to seek the appropriate enforcement remedy under the facts and circumstances as they develop in each investigation. In certain instances, potential improper conduct will be investigated pursuant to a civil investigation and, if appropriate, the case will then be referred to the USAO for criminal prosecution. In some instances, a civil and a criminal investigation will be conducted at the same time using separate investigators and supervisory oversight. In other instances, the investigation may be conducted as a criminal investigation only.[3]

834. How is the Employee Benefits Security Administration's (EBSA) criminal enforcement program operated?

The Employee Benefits Security Administration (EBSA) conducts its criminal enforcement program by decentralizing to the extent possible to its regional offices the decision making and conduct of criminal investigations. Regional office personnel consult with the local

---

1. ERISA Sec. 504.
2. Pub. L. No. 98-473
3. *Strategic Enforcement Plan*, 65 Fed. Reg. 18,208 (Apr. 6, 2000).

U.S. Attorney prior to or at the initiation of any criminal investigation both to obtain a delegation of authority to conduct the investigation and to receive any specific directions as may be necessary. In a number of instances, EBSA conducts joint investigations with other agencies such as the Office of Labor Racketeering, the Office of Labor Management Standards, the Federal Bureau of Investigation, the U.S. Postal Inspectors, the U.S. Department of the Treasury, and other local, state, and federal law enforcement agencies. This team approach brings together the abilities and backgrounds that may be particularly necessary for any individual investigation.[1]

As part of its criminal strategy, EBSA has established a position of Criminal Coordinator within its Office of Enforcement that is held by an individual with extensive criminal investigative experience in the area of complex financial crimes. The Coordinator oversees the implementation of EBSA's criminal enforcement activities and coordinates with other agencies within and outside the Department of Labor, including the Federal Bureau of Investigation, the Department of Justice, and various U.S. Attorneys. The Coordinator also provides guidance to regional office investigators for criminal case referrals, ensures that appropriate criminal investigative training is provided to enforcement staff, and considers whether the criminal enforcement actions are initiated as appropriate based upon the facts obtained in civil investigations.[2]

NOTE: *Major Case Enforcement Priority* – The DOL advises that it will seek to focus its enforcement resources on areas that have the greatest impact on the protection of plan assets and participants' benefits. Beginning in Fiscal Year 2013, the DOL is strategically focusing more investigative resources on professional fiduciaries and service providers with responsibility for large amounts of plan assets and the administration of large amounts of plan benefits. This will be accomplished by a national enforcement priority that directs investigative resources to the conduct of major cases (http://www.dol.gov/ebsa/erisa_enforcement.html.). It is anticipated that additional details will be forthcoming over the 2013/2014 Fiscal Year. This approach has been a non-official position within the DOL field operations for a long time. As noted previously, the DOL has limited numbers of investigators available; therefore, it has always been the best application of manpower to focus on the service provider industry as that is where the ability to review large numbers of plans can best be accomplished through the investigative target's client files. The noted focus on professional fiduciaries is merely a logical extension of the effort to look closer at the service providers. This priority will most likely result in higher levels of activity regarding criminal investigations.

Contributory Plans Criminal Project (CPCP)

In 2010, EBSA initiated the Contributory Plans Criminal Project (CPCP) to combat criminal abuse of contributory benefit plans such as 401(k) retirement programs and participant-paid or partially-paid health care and welfare benefit plan arrangements. EBSA advises that that there are a number of ways in which contributory plans can be vulnerable to criminal abuse. Employers,

---

1. Strategic Enforcement Plan, 65 Fed. Reg. 18,208 (Apr. 6, 2000).
2. Strategic Enforcement Plan, 65 Fed. Reg. 18,208 (Apr. 6, 2000).

or others with authority over plan assets, may convert employee payroll contributions for their own personal use or they may misapply employee contributions to cover business expenses. EBSA has uncovered instances where third parties (usually in the form of contractually obligated service providers) gained access to plan funds and siphoned off the money for their own financial gain. EBSA has uncovered instances where culprits have stolen participants' identity information to gain access to their employee benefit plan accounts (http://www.dol.gov/ebsa/newsroom/fscpcp.html.).

EBSA advises that it works closely with other federal, state, and local agencies to enforce laws safeguarding contributory plan assets under the CPCP. Criminal prosecution of individuals who abuse their authority or control over contributory plans can result in severe criminal penalties, including imprisonment. Those convicted of embezzling or misappropriating moneys intended to fund pension plans or pay health benefits typically are barred from providing services or acting in any capacity for a period of thirteen years.

835. Where does EBSA obtain its leads to pursue a criminal investigation?

The Employee Benefits Security Administration (EBSA) obtains investigative leads for criminal investigations from a variety of sources, including review of a plan's Form 5500, civil investigations, contacts with other law enforcement agencies (including U.S. Attorneys), informants, media, and so forth. EBSA's enforcement strategy involves considering whether there are possible criminal aspects to any of its civil investigations and, if so, to pursue criminal investigative authority from the appropriate U.S. Attorney and seek criminal indictments and convictions where the facts indicate. In this regard, EBSA develops and maintains close contacts and coordination with other law enforcement agencies, and seeks to enhance the ability of its investigators and auditors to conduct criminal investigations.[1]

836. What criminal provisions does EBSA investigate?

The Employee Benefits Security Administration (EBSA) criminal investigations predominately involve Title 18 and Title 29 crimes. The case type, known as Program 52 investigations, is used to conduct investigations of allegations involving potential criminal violations of the following statute sections:

1. ERISA Section 411, "Prohibition Against Certain Persons Holding Certain Positions" (when the issues relate to a reduction of time for a bar against serving in a certain position or an exemption pursuant to ERISA Section 411(a), the investigation is conducted as a Program 47);

2. ERISA Section 501, "Willful Violation of Title I, Part 1";

3. ERISA Section 511, "Coercive Interference";

4. 18 U.S.C. Section 664, "Theft or Embezzlement from Employee Benefit Plan";

---

1. *Strategic Enforcement Plan*, 65 Fed. Reg. 18,208 (Apr. 6, 2000).

5.   18 U.S.C. Section 1027, "False Statements and Concealment of Facts in Relation to Documents Required by the Employee Retirement Income Security Act";

6.   18 U.S.C. Section 1954, "Offer, Acceptance or Solicitation Influence Operations of Employee Benefit Plans"; and

7.   Other criminal statutes that are violated in connection with employee benefit plan operations; such statutes include 18 U.S.C. Section 1341, "Mail Fraud," 18 U.S.C. Section 1343, "Wire Fraud," and 18 U.S.C. Section 371, "Conspiracy."

837. Are EBSA investigators and auditors trained in criminal enforcement matters?

Yes. The Employee Benefits Security Administration (EBSA) has increased its criminal enforcement through increased training for its investigators and auditors on criminal investigative techniques and substantive provisions of applicable criminal laws. EBSA's program for training enforcement investigators includes a segment in its basic training course on criminal investigation and an investigative course devoted solely to criminal investigative techniques and issues. EBSA investigators also may participate in a White-Collar Crime Training Program at the Federal Law Enforcement Training Center located in Glynco, Georgia.

838. Does EBSA disclose the nature and basis of a criminal investigation?

No. It is the policy of the Employee Benefits Security Administration (EBSA) not to inform plan officials or others as to the source of its investigation. However, EBSA will state the purpose of the investigation, by clearly identifying the criminal basis of the investigation and the joint interest in the matter by EBSA and the Department of Justice.[1]

839. Does EBSA utilize administrative subpoenas in the course of a criminal investigation?

No. In light of the fact that the Employee Benefits Security Administration (EBSA) conducts both civil and criminal investigations, it does not use its administrative subpoena power when conducting criminal investigations. This is to avoid potential accusations of improperly using the civil process to obtain information for a criminal case.[2]

840. Does EBSA conduct searches and seizures?

Yes. Employee Benefits Security Administration (EBSA) investigators and auditors conduct and participate in search and seizure actions. Although EBSA investigators and auditors may prepare an affidavit as support for a search and seizure, the application or request for a warrant is likely to be made by the U.S. Attorney's office, or by agents from other law enforcement agencies, who are authorized to apply for a warrant. An EBSA investigator or auditor may serve the warrant; however, on-site search and seizure actions are usually coordinated with the law enforcement agencies applying for the warrant or with the U.S. Marshall's office.[3]

---

1. *EBSA Enforcement Manual* ch. 52.
2. *EBSA Enforcement Manual* ch. 52.
3. *EBSA Enforcement Manual* ch. 52.

ERISA Criminal Code Provisions

841. What are the criminal provisions of ERISA?

The criminal provisions of ERISA address the prohibition against certain persons' holding certain positions with respect to a plan, willful violations of the reporting and disclosure requirements of ERISA, and coercive interference with the rights of participants and beneficiaries.[1] A violation of the prohibition against certain persons' holding certain positions is a felony. Violations of the reporting and disclosure requirements and the prohibition against coercive interference with the rights of participants and beneficiaries are misdemeanors.

842. What is the prohibition against certain persons' holding certain positions under ERISA Section 411?

ERISA bars any person who has been convicted of a broad range of crimes from serving as a fiduciary or service provider of an employee benefit plan. ERISA automatically disqualifies individuals by its terms and subjects those persons to prosecution for violating its provisions. Also, persons who knowingly permit a disqualified person to serve in a prohibited capacity are subject to prosecution. Any person who intentionally violates the statute may be fined up to $10,000, or imprisoned for not more than five years, or both.[2] Section 504 of the Labor Management Reporting and Disclosure Act served as a model for the statute.[3] However, the list of crimes in ERISA Section 411 was expanded by Congress.[4]

The legislative history indicates that Congress considered the prohibitions in the statute necessary because of the large amount of funds involved and the attendant risk of a loss affecting a large number of persons. Without such a provision persons barred from serving as union officers might take positions with employee benefit plans.[5] As a result of amendments made by the Comprehensive Crime Control Act of 1984, a violation of ERISA Section 411 became a felony for convictions occurring after October 12, 1984. That legislation also expanded the class of prohibited persons and lengthened the time in which they are prohibited from serving as a fiduciary or service provider to a plan.[6]

843. What persons are banned from service as fiduciaries?

A person is prohibited from serving as a fiduciary if he has been convicted of, or imprisoned as a result of, the following offenses:

1. Robbery, bribery, extortion, embezzlement, fraud, grand larceny, burglary, arson, murder, rape, kidnapping, perjury, or assault with intent to kill;

---

1. ERISA Secs. 411, 501, 511.
2. ERISA Sec. 411.
3. See 29 U.S.C. §504.
4. *Presser v. Brennan*, 389 F. Supp. 808 (N.D. Ohio 1975).
5. S. Rep. No. 93-127, 93d Cong., 2d Sess., reprinted in 1974 U.S. Code Cong. & Admin. News 4838; *Greenberg v. Brennan*, 1 EBC 2006 (E.D.N.Y. 1975).
6. See S. Rep. No. 98-83, 98th Cong., 1st Sess. (1983), and S. Rep. 98-225, 98th Cong., 1st Sess. (1983), reprinted in 1984 U.S. Code Cong. & Admin. News 3477.

2. A felony violation of a federal or state law involving certain "controlled substances" defined in 21 U.S.C. Section 802(6);[1]

3. Any crime described in 15 U.S.C. Section 80a-9(a)(1);[2]

4. Any crime described in ERISA Section 411, ERISA Section 501, and ERISA Section 511 (see Q 841);

5. A violation of 29 U.S.C. Section 186 (prohibited payments to labor unions, labor union officials, and employee representatives);

6. A violation of 18 U.S.C. Chapter 63;[3]

7. A violation of 18 U.S.C. Section 874, 1027, 1503, 1505, 1506, 1510, 1951, or 1954;

8. A violation of 29 U.S.C. Section 401;[4]

9. Any felony involving abuse or misuse of a person's position or employment in a labor organization or employee benefit plan to seek or obtain an illegal gain at the expense of the members of the labor organization or the beneficiaries of the employee benefit plan;

10. Conspiracy or attempt to commit any crime described above; and

11. Any crime in which any of the crimes described above is an element.

In addition, a person may not knowingly hire, retain, employ, or otherwise place any of the prohibited persons in any of the capacities prohibited by ERISA Section 411. However, a corporation or partnership will not be precluded from acting as an administrator, fiduciary, officer, trustee, custodian, counsel, agent, or employee of an employee benefit plan or as a consultant to an employee benefit plan without a notice, hearing, and determination by a court that the proposed service is inconsistent with the intention of ERISA Section 411.[5]

844. What positions are subject to the prohibition against holding certain positions?

A person convicted of one of the crimes described in Q 843 is banned from serving as a fiduciary in the following positions:

1. As an administrator, fiduciary, officer, trustee, custodian, counsel, agent, employee, or representative in any capacity of an employee benefit plan;

2. As a consultant or adviser to an employee benefit plan, including, but not limited to, any entity whose activities are in whole or substantial part devoted to providing goods or services to an employee benefit plan; or

---

1. Comprehensive Drug Abuse Prevention and Control Act of 1970.
2. Investment Company Act of 1940.
3. 18 U.S.C. §§1341 et seq. (e.g., mail fraud, wire fraud, etc.).
4. Labor-Management Reporting and Disclosure Act of 1959.
5. ERISA Sec. 411(a).

3.   In any capacity that involves decision-making authority or custody or control of the money, funds, assets, or property of an employee benefit plan.[1]

845. How may a prohibited person have the ability to serve as a fiduciary restored?

For convictions after October 12, 1984, the prohibited person may obtain relief from the prohibition under one of the following situations:

1.   By making an application for an exemption from the prohibition against service or employment in a particular prohibited position;

2.   By making an application to a court for a reduction of the length of the prohibition (the length of prohibition may not be less than three years); or

3.   By having fully restored any citizenship rights that were revoked as a result of the disqualifying conviction.[2]

Prior to making any determination under item two, above, the court must hold a hearing and give notice of the proceeding by certified mail to the Secretary of Labor and to state, county, and federal prosecuting officials in the jurisdiction or jurisdictions where the person was convicted. The court's determination in the proceeding is final.[3]

846. What are the penalties for violating ERISA Section 411?

Any person who intentionally violates ERISA Section 411 may be fined up to $10,000, imprisoned for up to five years, or both.[4]

847. When is a person considered to be convicted?

A person is considered convicted and under the disability of a conviction from the date of the judgment of the trial court, regardless of whether the judgment is on appeal.[5]

848. What is a consultant?

The term "consultant" means any person who, for compensation, advises or represents an employee benefit plan, or who provides other assistance to the plan concerning the establishment or operation of the plan.[6]

849. Is a period of parole or supervised release considered part of the period of imprisonment?

No. A period of parole or supervised release is not considered part of a period of imprisonment.[7]

---

1. ERISA Sec. 411(a).
2. ERISA Sec. 411.
3. ERISA Sec. 411(a).
4. ERISA Sec. 411(b).
5. ERISA Sec. 411(c)(1).
6. ERISA Sec. 411(c)(2).
7. ERISA Sec. 411(c)(3).

850. Is there any provision concerning the salary of a person that appeals his conviction?

Yes. A person who is barred from office or other position in an employee benefit plan as a result of a conviction and who has appealed that conviction has any salary that would otherwise be due the person by virtue of the office or position placed in escrow by the individual or organization responsible for payment of the salary. Payment of the salary into escrow must continue for the duration of the appeal or for the period of time during which the salary would be otherwise due, whichever period is shorter. Upon the final reversal of the person's conviction on appeal, the amount in escrow must be paid to the person. Upon the final sustaining of the person's conviction on appeal, the amount in escrow is returned to the individual or organization responsible for payment of that amount. Upon final reversal of a person's conviction, the person is no longer barred from assuming any position from which the person was previously barred.[1]

851. What is the disability period for a disqualified person?

A disqualified person is prohibited from serving employee benefit plans for a period of thirteen years from the entry of judgment of the trial court or the end of imprisonment resulting from the disqualifying conviction, whichever is later. A court may, under appropriate circumstances, reduce the period of prohibition to not less than three years or determine that service in one of the prohibited capacities would not be contrary to the purposes of ERISA.[2]

By the terms of ERISA Section 411, the disability is effective despite any appeal of the disqualifying conviction. For disqualifying convictions on or before October 12, 1984, the period of disability was five years following judgment of conviction, the final sustaining of the judgment on appeal, or end of imprisonment, whichever was later. Congress indicated that the length of the disqualification period is a critical component of the statutory scheme to rid employee benefit plans of corruption.[3]

852. What are the procedures for seeking an application for a certificate of exemption?

ERISA Section 411 establishes the procedures for seeking an exemption from the statutory prohibitions. For a disqualifying crime committed before November 1, 1987, an Application for Exemption must be directed to the United States Board of Parole. The procedures governing the application are found at 28 C.F.R. Part 4. For a disqualifying crime committed on or after November 1, 1987, the Petition for Exemption is directed to the federal sentencing court, or if the conviction is a state offense, the petition is directed to the U.S. District Court for the district where the disqualifying state offense was committed. A Petition for Reduction of the Length of Disability for disqualifying judgments of conviction entered after October 12, 1994, may be made to the state or federal sentencing judge. No such relief was available prior to October 12, 1994.[4]

---

1. ERISA Sec. 411(d).
2. ERISA Sec. 411.
3. See S. Rep. No. 98-225, 98th Cong., 1st. Sess. 227 (1983), *reprinted in* 1984 U.S. Code Cong. & Admin. News 3477.
4. *EBSA Enforcement Manual* ch. 47.

Prior to making a determination on the application, the Department of Labor and the prosecuting officials in the jurisdiction where the person was convicted are notified by the applicable court.[1] The Department of Labor is authorized to conduct investigations when the issues relate to a reduction of the bar or an exemption. The investigation is for the purpose of providing information to the court or Board of Parole, rather than to prove a violation of ERISA.[2]

853. What factors are considered in determining whether a Certificate of Exemption should be granted under ERISA Section 411?

In determining whether a Certificate of Exemption should be granted under ERISA Section 411, the U.S. Board of Parole stated that it was necessary to consider the following factors:

1. Character and gravity of the disqualifying offense;

2. Nature of the position for which the applicant is seeking an exemption; and

3. Extent to which the applicant has been rehabilitated to meet the standards of responsibility required (this is higher than the standard required for release on parole, but the degree of difference depends upon the requirements of the position and any influence the position has on others).[3]

In *Viverito*, the Board of Parole noted that motives and surrounding circumstances may be taken into consideration as mitigating factors under the circumstances. The applicant's motive in *Viverito* appeared to be misplaced loyalty to, and dependence upon, his superior officer, who was a main perpetrator and beneficiary of a scheme to embezzle funds. In addition, the applicant received no personal enrichment from his participation in the scheme. Moreover, the position for which the exemption was sought had little influence on the employing organization or other employees or beneficiaries of the plan, the applicant would have no access to plan funds and no authority or responsibility that could create a substantial risk of loss to the plan, and the record reflected evidence of rehabilitation.

854. What is a Debarment Notice?

A Debarment Notice is a letter sent to a person convicted of one of the enumerated crimes listed in ERISA Section 411. It puts the person on notice that she is prohibited from occupying a position related to employee benefit plan administration, and that the intentional violation of this prohibition is a criminal violation subject to prosecution. A Debarment Notice is generally sent to the convicted person after sentencing, and, if appropriate, a similar letter may be sent to plan officials or service providers.[4]

---

1. ERISA Sec. 411.
2. *EBSA Enforcement Manual* chs. 47, 52.
3. *In re Viverito*, 1 EBC 1102 (U.S. Bd. Parole 1975).
4. *EBSA Enforcement Manual* ch. 47.

855. What is the prohibition against a violation of the reporting and disclosure provisions of ERISA under ERISA Section 501?

ERISA Section 101 through ERISA Section 111 impose elaborate reporting and disclosure requirements on plan administrators. ERISA Section 501 authorizes criminal penalties for willful violations of these reporting and disclosure provisions. By adopting ERISA Section 501, Congress indicated its preference for criminal sanctions, rather than punitive damages, as a deterrent to willful violations of ERISA.[1]

ERISA Section 501 reads as follows:

> Any person who willfully violates any provision of part 1 of this subtitle [Reporting and Disclosure], or any regulation or order issued under any such provision, shall upon conviction be fined not more than $100,000 or imprisoned not more than 10 years, or both; except that in the case of such violation by a person not an individual, the fine imposed upon such person shall be a fine not exceeding $500,000.

856. What is the meaning of the term "willfully" as used in ERISA Section 501?

Anyone who willfully violates the reporting and disclosure requirements of ERISA or a regulation or order issued under those requirements is subject to criminal liability.[2] An act is done "willfully" if it is done with reckless disregard for the requirements of the law. The Eleventh Circuit Court of Appeals upheld a trial court's instruction to a jury that it could find a defendant guilty if he had "knowingly and intentionally committed the acts which [violate Part 1 of Title I of ERISA] and ... [the acts] were not committed accidentally or by some mistake." The court also upheld the trial court's instruction that ERISA Section 501 requires only a general intent and knowledge of one's acts.[3]

857. What are examples of violations of the reporting and disclosure requirements?

Examples of violations of the reporting and disclosure obligations include:

1. Omission or refusal to file an annual financial report (5500 series), terminal, and supplementary report, or to furnish a summary plan description, or modifications and changes to the plan, to a participant or beneficiary as required by ERISA Section 104(a);

2. Omission or refusal to publish a summary plan description and provide annual reports to participants and beneficiaries as required by ERISA Section 104(b);

3. Omission or refusal to furnish certain information concerning benefits to pension plan participants as required by ERISA Section 105; and

4. Failure to maintain records from which reports and other required documents can be verified and checked as required by ERISA Section 107.

---

1. *Whitaker v. Texaco, Inc.*, 566 F. Supp. 745 (N.D. Ga. 1983).
2. ERISA Sec. 501.
3. *United States v. Phillips*, 19 F.3d 1565 (11th Cir. 1994).

858. Is there a good-faith defense to a prosecution for reporting and disclosure violations?

Yes. A statutory defense to an ERISA Section 501 reporting and disclosure violation is codified in ERISA Section 108. Under ERISA Section 108, no person is subject to liability or punishment under ERISA Section 501 on account of a failure to:

1. Comply with the reporting and disclosure requirements, or the bonding requirements of ERISA Section 412, if he pleads and proves that the act or omission complained of was in good faith, in conformity with, and in reliance on any regulation or written ruling of the Department of Labor; or

2. Publish and file any information required by any provision of the reporting and disclosure requirements of ERISA if he pleads and proves that he published and filed the information in good faith, and in conformity with any regulation or written ruling of the Department of Labor issued under those reporting and disclosure requirements regarding the filing of the reports.

If the good-faith (reliance) defense is established, it will prevent a conviction under ERISA Section 501, even if:

1. After the act or omission, the interpretation or opinion is modified or rescinded or is determined by judicial authority to be invalid or of no legal effect; or

2. After publishing or filing annual reports and other required reports, the publication or filing is determined by judicial authority not to be in conformity with the requirements of ERISA.[1]

859. What is the prohibition against coercive interference under ERISA Section 511?

It is a criminal offense to interfere coercively with exercise of the rights of a participant or beneficiary that are protected by ERISA.[2] The essence of the offense is the actual or attempted interference with the exercise of the protected rights of a participant or beneficiary of an employee benefit plan by means of the willful use of actual or threatened force, violence, or fraud.

ERISA Section 511 is one of two provisions in ERISA that prohibit interference with protected rights. The other is ERISA Section 510, which makes it unlawful to interfere with the attainment of any right to which a participant or beneficiary may become entitled. The statute's legislative history reveals that ERISA Section 510 and ERISA Section 511 are companion provisions. As ERISA Section 510 prohibits interference with protected rights; ERISA Section 511 provides criminal penalties where that interference is coercive. The legislative history reveals that the prohibitions were aimed primarily at preventing unscrupulous employers from discharging or harassing their employees in order to keep them from obtaining vested pension rights. These provisions were enacted by Congress in the face of evidence that in some plans a worker's

---

1. ERISA Sec. 108.
2. ERISA Sec. 511.

pension rights or the expectations of those rights were interfered with by the use of economic sanctions or violent reprisals.[1] The intent of Congress was to make ERISA Section 511 coercive interference a subcategory of ERISA Section 510 interference with protected rights.

The interaction of these two sections was expressed by the Sixth Circuit as follows:

> Every employee is to have the right, enforceable by the Secretary of Labor, to be free from interference with his pension benefits. This means that he cannot be discharged, fined, suspended, expelled or otherwise interfered with in order to prevent him from receiving pension benefits or attaining eligibility for pension benefits. There are stiff criminal penalties if this type of interference takes the form of force, fraud or violence or threats of this nature.[2]

The text of ERISA Section 511 reads:

> It shall be unlawful for any person through the use of fraud, force, violence, or threat of the use of force or violence, to restrain, coerce, intimidate, or attempt to restrain, coerce, or intimidate any participant or beneficiary for the purpose of interfering with or preventing the exercise of any right to which he is or may become entitled under the plan, this subchapter, section 1201 of this title, or the Welfare and Pension Plans Disclosure Act (29 U.S.C. 301 et seq.). Any person who willfully violates this section shall be fined $100,000 or imprisoned for not more than ten years, or both.

Section 623 of the Pension Protection Act of 2006,[3] amended ERISA Section 511 by increasing the fine amount from $10,000 to $100,000, and the maximum imprisonment time from one year to ten years, effective for violations occurring on or after August 17, 2006.

Unlike ERISA Section 510, which is a civil prohibition, ERISA Section 511 provides criminal penalties for violators. The component that separates the criminal provision of ERISA Section 511 from the civil provision of ERISA Section 510 is the willful use of actual or threatened force, violence, intimidation, restraint, coercion, or fraud. Under ERISA Section 510, the participant or beneficiary may bring a civil action against any person who interferes with those rights protected under ERISA. By contrast, ERISA Section 511 contains prohibitory language and a criminal penalty provision; it makes no reference to civil enforcement. Thus, ERISA Section 511 punishes coercive forms of conduct that violate ERISA Section 510. As ERISA Section 511 is a criminal provision, its enforcement is the exclusive prerogative of the U.S. Attorney General.

United States Criminal Code Provisions

860. What are the criminal provisions of Title 18 of the United States Code that are applicable to employee benefit plans?

While ERISA provides for a system of administrative penalties, civil actions, and criminal sanctions, the United States Criminal Code (Title 18 of the United States Code) has a number of provisions under which violators can be prosecuted for certain activities involving employee benefit plans. For example, the United States Criminal Code has prohibitions against: (1) theft or embezzlement from employee benefit plans under 18 U.S.C. Section 664; (2) the making

---

1. *West v. Butler*, 621 F.2d 240 (6th Cir. 1980).
2. *West v. Butler*, 621 F.2d 240 (6th Cir. 1980).
3. Pub. L. No. 109-280.

of false statements and concealment of facts in relation to documents required by ERISA under 18 U.S.C. Section 1027; and (3) the offer, acceptance, or solicitation of funds to influence the operation of employee benefit plans under 18 U.S.C. Section 1954.

These three sections of Title 18 were enacted in 1962 as part of the Welfare and Pension Plans Disclosure Act Amendments of 1962 in an effort to strengthen the Welfare and Pension Plans Disclosure Act of 1958.[1] In these enactments Congress intended to provide the "enforcement teeth ... lacking in the existing law."[2]

In addition, prohibitions in other criminal statutes may be violated in connection with employee benefit plan operations. Such statutes include: 18 U.S.C. Section 1341, concerning mail fraud; 18 U.S.C. Section 1343, concerning wire fraud; and 18 U.S.C. Section 371, concerning conspiracy.

861. What is the Criminal Code provision for theft or embezzlement from an employee benefit plan?

Any person who embezzles, steals, or unlawfully and willfully abstracts or converts to his own use or to the use of another, any money, funds, securities, premiums, credits, property, or other assets of an employee welfare benefit plan or employee pension benefit plan, or of any connected fund, may be fined, or imprisoned for up to five years, or both. The term "any employee welfare benefit plan or employee pension benefit plan" means any employee benefit plan subject to any provision of Title I of ERISA.[3]

18 U.S.C. Section 664 was added in 1962 as an amendment to the Welfare and Pension Plans Disclosure Act (former 29 U.S.C. Sections 301 to 309), ERISA's predecessor.[4] Upon the enactment of ERISA in 1974, this section was amended to include the language "ERISA covered plan." It applies to thefts from ERISA- covered plans committed after January 1, 1975.

The legislative history indicates that the purpose of 18 U.S.C. Section 664 is to "preserve the designated funds for those entitled to their benefits."[5] As the court explained in *Andreen*, "[by] enacting [18 U.S.C.] section 664, Congress made it a federal crime to embezzle, steal, and unlawfully convert or abstract assets of an employee benefit plan and to preserve such funds for the protection of those entitled to their benefits." The statute contains no attempt provision, and reimbursement of loss by civil action, insurance, or restitution is no defense.[6] Furthermore, a good-faith intent to return embezzled funds does not negate a showing that the defendant acted with the requisite criminal intent to embezzle the funds in the first instance.[7]

---

1. Pub. L. No. 87-420.
2. H. Rep. No. 87-998, 87th Cong., 2d Sess., *reprinted in* 1962 U.S. Code Cong. & Admin. News 1532, 1537.
3. 18 U.S.C. §664.
4. Pub. L. No. 87-420.
5. *United States v. Andreen*, 628 F.2d 1236 (9th Cir. 1980); H.R. Rep. No. 87-998, 87th Cong., 2d Sess., *reprinted* in 1962 U.S. Code Cong. & Admin. News 1532.
6. *United States v. Daley*, 454 F.2d 505 (1st Cir. 1972).
7. *United States v. Shackleford*, 777 F.2d 1141 (6th Cir. 1985), *cert. denied*, 476 U.S. 1119 (1986).

Cases interpreting 18 U.S.C. Section 664 are few; however, a number of opinions have addressed the meaning of a similar statute that prohibits embezzlement from union funds. 18 U.S.C. Section 664 parallels the language of 29 U.S.C. Section 501(c), which is part of the Labor Management Reporting and Disclosure Act. 29 U.S.C. Section 501(c) provides:

> Any person who embezzles, steals, or unlawfully and willfully abstracts or converts to his own use, or the use of another, any of the moneys, funds, securities, property, or other assets of a labor organization of which he is an officer, or by which he is employed, directly or indirectly, shall be fined not more than $10,000 or imprisoned for not more than five years, or both.

Although in enacting 18 U.S.C. Section 664, Congress provided broader language than 29 U.S.C. Section 501(c), the court in *Andreen* stated that the statutes contain "[p]arallel language" and that "Congress passed the two statutes for a similar purpose: to preserve the designated funds for those entitled to their benefits." The court concluded, "[T]he prohibitory language of both statutes should be given similar interpretation and be applied to similar types of conduct." Further, "our discussion of [29 U.S.C.] Section 501(c) cases ... applies equally to 18 U.S.C. [Section] 664."

862. What is the meaning of the term "embezzlement" under 18 U.S.C. Section 664?

As used in 18 U.S.C. Section 664, the term "embezzlement" is a traditional term that "encompasses the fraudulent appropriation of the property of another by one in lawful possession thereof. The essence of the crime is theft and in the context of union funds or pension funds the offense includes a taking or appropriation that is unauthorized, if accomplished with specific criminal intent."[1] Embezzlement occurs when a person who has lawfully received funds willfully diverts them to his own unauthorized use.[2]

863. Must a person be in a fiduciary relationship to be convicted under 18 U.S.C. Section 664?

No. Criminal culpability under 18 U.S.C. Section 664 does not require that the defendant hold any particular status in relation to an employee benefit plan or fund connected with a plan, or that she act as a fiduciary with respect to an employee welfare benefit plan transaction. In fact, the Seventh Circuit Court of Appeals has held that proof of lawful possession or lawful access to property at the time of appropriation is not required to demonstrate conversion in violation of 18 U.S.C. Section 664.[3] The Eleventh Circuit Court affirmed a conviction pursuant to 18 U.S.C. Section 664 predicated on the disbursement of loan proceeds from a plan, where the loan resulted from the borrower's fraudulent overvaluation of the collateral pledged for the loan.[4]

---

1. *United States v. Andreen*, 628 F.2d 1236 (9th Cir. 1980).
2. *United States v. Marquardt*, 786 F.2d 7710 (7th Cir. 1986).
3. *United States v. Goodstein*, 883 F.2d 1362 (7th Cir. 1989), *cert. denied*, 494 U.S. 1007 (1990).
4. *United States v. Wuagneux*, 683 F.2d 1343 (11th Cir. 1982), *cert. denied*, 464 U.S. 814 (1983).

864. Who can be convicted in an action under 18 U.S.C. Section 664?

18 U.S.C. Section 664, by its terms, applies to "any person." In stating that "[c]riminal culpability under [18 U.S.C.] section 664 does not require that a defendant hold any particular status in relation to an employee benefit plan or fund connected with a plan … Congress intended the statute to be read broadly to include any person who misuses or misappropriates contributions intended for deposit in an employee welfare benefit plan."[1] Thus, "any person" under 18 U.S.C. Section 664 is not limited to an officer, administrator, trustee, or other fiduciary of the plan but may be, for example, a beneficiary, borrower, employer, trustee, or service provider. The language "any person" in 18 U.S.C. Section 664 includes, but is not limited to, the following groups:

1. *Employers who convert plan funds to their own use.* An employer who withheld welfare benefit plan contributions from employees' paychecks and failed to deliver contributions to the plan was convicted under 18 U.S.C. Section 664.[2] The conversion of profit sharing funds by an employer to pay personal and corporate debts of the plan sponsor resulted in a conviction.[3] The same result occurred when an employer converted entrusted monies to its own use.[4]

2. *Borrowers.* The Eleventh Circuit Court of Appeals affirmed a conviction under 18 U.S.C. Section 664 where loan proceeds were disbursed from a plan based on the borrower's fraudulent overvaluation of the collateral (land) pledged for the loan.[5]

3. *Operators of multiple employer welfare arrangements.* An individual was convicted under 18 U.S.C. Section 664 when he operated a fraudulent health insurance scheme where he mismanaged the operation and converted plan assets and, as a result, left many subscribers to the plan with unpaid medical bills.[6]

4. *Union officials and trustees who embezzle funds from local pension and welfare funds.*[7]

865. Is restitution, or lack of personal gain, a defense to a charge under 18 U.S.C. Section 664?

No. The mere fact that the plan recovers the money or property that was unlawfully taken is not a defense under 18 U.S.C. Section 664.[8] Neither is a lack of personal financial gain on the part of the accused.[9] In addition, a good-faith intent to return embezzled funds does not negate a showing that the defendant acted with the requisite criminal intent to embezzle the funds in the first instance.[10]

---

1. *United States v. Goodstein*, 883 F.2d 1362 (7th Cir. 1989), *cert. denied*, 494 U.S. 1007 (1990).
2. *United States v. Grizzle*, 933 F.2d 943 (11th Cir. 1991).
3. *United States v. Goodstein*, 883 F.2d 1362 (7th Cir. 1989), *cert. denied*, 494 U.S. 1007 (1990).
4. *United States v. Panepinto*, 818 F. Supp. 48 (E.D.N.Y. 1993), *aff'd*, 28 F.3d 103 (2d Cir. 1994).
5. *United States v. Wuagneux*, 683 F.2d 1343 (11th Cir. 1982), *cert. denied*, 464 U.S. 814 (1983).
6. *United States v. Rowe*, 999 F.2d 14 (1st Cir. 1993).
7. See *United States v. Busacca*, 863 F.2d 433 (6th Cir. 1988); *United States v. Snyder*, 572 F.2d 894 (2d Cir. 1982).
8. *United States v. Daley*, 454 F.2d 505 (1st Cir. 1972).
9. *United States v. Santiago*, 528 F.2d 1130 (2d Cir.), *cert. denied*, 425 U.S. 972 (1976).
10. *United States v. Shackleford*, 777 F.2d 1141 (6th Cir. 1985), *cert. denied*, 476 U.S. 1119 (1986).

866. What assets are protected by 18 U.S.C. Section 664?

By its terms, 18 U.S.C. Section 664 contains a broad list of assets that are protected. Embezzlement under 18 U.S.C. Section 664 may be accomplished by unlawfully depriving the plan of the beneficial use of money, funds, securities, premiums, credits, property, or other assets. The statute does not define these terms.

In addition, 18 U.S.C. Section 664 is not limited to those who misappropriate assets directly from a plan, but also includes those who divert assets from reaching the plan. "[T]he language of the statute, by its terms, does not limit its reach to protecting only wealth already transferred to a welfare benefit plan or its administrators."[1] The employer in *Panepinto* converted to its own use the required contributions that were held as "credits, property, and other assets" of the plan. Referencing the terms of the collective bargaining agreement, the court in *Panepinto* held that the employer willfully failed to remit funds representing its own contributions to the plan because under the Plan Agreement, the employer surrendered all legal and equitable rights to the contributions due to the plan. Likewise, the term "premiums" include insurance and other premiums. The Fifth Circuit Court of Appeals upheld an 18 U.S.C. Section 664 conviction for the conversion of insurance premiums that were refunded to an employee benefit plan.[2] The plan's employer sponsor retained and used the refunded insurance premiums.

867. What is a connected fund in 18 U.S.C. Section 664?

The language of 18 U.S.C. Section 664 provides for punishment in the case of an embezzlement or theft from "any employee welfare benefit plan or employee pension benefit plan, or of any fund connected therewith." The meaning of the term "fund connected" has not been judicially settled. However, a few cases have applied that term.

One court held that the embezzled proceeds of a first mortgage obtained for the purpose of paying certain plan debts did not constitute property of the pension fund and therefore were not "connected funds" for purposes of the statute. The plan sold its property pursuant to a contract that provided for the purchase price to be payable in notes or bonds, secured by subordinated mortgages on the property. The defendant was to obtain a first mortgage on the property and use the proceeds to discharge the debts previously incurred by the plan in the property's construction and management. Although no provision in the contract gave the plan the right to receive any part of the proceeds, the alleged misappropriation did not constitute property of the plan or "of a fund connected therewith."[3]

More recently, the Eleventh Circuit Court of Appeals addressed the "fund connected with" language and held that it applies only to ERISA plans.[4] In an embezzlement case, the co-defendants administered a welfare and pension fund that provided health and retirement benefits in addition to a fund that provided supplemental income that was distributed at the end of each taxable year. The welfare and pension fund, but not the supplemental income fund, was covered by ERISA.

---

1. *United States v. Panepinto*, 818 F. Supp. 48 (E.D.N.Y. 1993), *aff'd*, 28 F.3d 103 (2d Cir. 1994).
2. *United States v. Moore*, 427 F.2d 38 (5th Cir. 1970).
3. *United States v. Delillo*, 421 F. Supp. 1012 (E.D.N.Y. 1976), *aff'd*, 620 F.2d 939 (2d Cir. 1980).
4. *United States v. Bell*, 22 F.3d 274 (11th Cir. 1994).

Although both plans had common beneficiaries and administrators, the court held that, without more, it would not consider the funds connected for purposes of 18 U.S.C. Section 664.[1]

868. Must the principal taker act willfully to be convicted under 18 U.S.C. Section 664?

Yes. In a prosecution under 18 U.S.C. Section 664, it must be established that the defendant intended to deprive the employee benefit plan of the use of its assets. In such a case, sufficient proof must be gathered to establish that the defendant willfully deprived the plan of its property. Courts have referred to 18 U.S.C. Section 664 as a generic theft statute.[2] As one court stated, "[t]he essence of the crime is theft and in the context of ... pension plans the offense includes a taking or appropriation that is unauthorized, if accomplished with specific criminal intent [to steal]," the essential mental state required for conviction.[3] In order to have specific criminal intent, "the criminal act must have been willful, which means an act done with fraudulent intent or a bad purpose or an evil motive."[4]

A knowing and intentional violation of ERISA's prohibited transaction rules was held to be the basis for the criminal mental state requirement. The defendant, as trustee of a plan, knowingly converted plan funds to his own use and arranged for a loan between the pension fund and a company incorporated by his daughter. The transactions were knowing and intentional violations of the prohibited transaction rules in light of the fact that the defendant received legal admonitions regarding their unlawfulness.[5]

869. What are the rules regarding false statements and concealment of facts in relation to documents required by ERISA?

Whoever, in any document required by ERISA to be published or kept as part of the records of any employee welfare benefit plan or employee pension benefit plan, or certified to the administrator of any such plan, makes any false statement or representation of fact, knowing it to be false, or knowingly conceals, covers up, or fails to disclose any fact the disclosure of which is required by ERISA or is necessary to verify, explain, clarify, or check for accuracy and completeness any report required by ERISA to be published or any information required by ERISA to be certified, may be fined, or imprisoned for up to five years, or both.[6]

18 U.S.C. Section 1027 prohibits any knowingly made false statements or representations of fact, as well as certain knowingly concealed, covered-up, or undisclosed facts. In order to be convicted under the statute, a false statement or representation of fact must be made in a document required by ERISA to be either (1) published by an employee welfare benefit plan or employee pension benefit plan, (2) kept as part of the records of such a plan, or (3) certified to the administrator of such a plan.

---

1. *United States v. Bell*, above.

2. *United States v. Busacca*, 863 F.2d 433 (6th Cir. 1988), *cert. denied*, 490 U.S. 1005 (1989).

3. *United States v. Andreen*, 628 F.2d 1236 (9th Cir. 1980).

4. *Young v. West Coast Indus. Relations Ass'n*, 763 F. Supp. 64 (D. Del. 1991).

5. *United States v. Freel*, 681 F. Supp. 766 (M.D. Fla. 1988), *aff'd without* op., 868 F.2d 1274 (11th Cir. 1989).

6. 18 U.S.C. §1027.

18 U.S.C. Section 1027 also encompasses documents kept as part of the records of an employee welfare benefit plan or employee pension benefit plan. Thus, a concealment, cover-up, or failure to disclose likewise could occur in a similar document, but it also must relate to a fact the disclosure of which is required by ERISA or is necessary to verify, explain, or check for accuracy and completeness any information required by ERISA to be published.[1] No regulations have been promulgated interpreting 18 U.S.C. Section 1027.

870. Is any person subject to conviction under 18 U.S.C. Section 1027?

Yes. 18 U.S.C. Section 1027 provides in broad language, unequivocally and without limitation, that the term "whoever" applies to any person who violates its provisions. For example, "whoever" clearly is sufficiently broad to include criminal prosecutions of fiduciaries, such as a trustee of a union pension fund.[2] The term also included the president of a local chapter of the AFL-CIO, who was also the trustee of the union welfare fund.[3] It also included a defendant who was the salaried supervisor for two employee benefit funds.[4]

"Whoever" also includes employers.[5] Similarly, the term "whoever" was sufficiently broad enough to include medical services providers who filed a false "utilization report."[6] Potential defendants under 18 U.S.C. Section 1027 also may include attorneys or bank trust officers.[7] Plan participants or beneficiaries can also be convicted under 18 U.S.C. Section 1027. An individual who filed a false hospital invoice for medical services and a false coordination of benefits form was convicted under 18 U.S.C. Section 1027.[8]

The Ninth Circuit Court of Appeals, in reviewing 18 U.S.C. Section 1027, held that it is not unconstitutionally vague regarding the criminalization of false statements made on required ERISA forms.[9] The court said that the statute is clear as to what fiduciaries must do—"truthfully fill out the ERISA form according to the instructions." The defendant had accurately reported the value of promissory notes issued on loans made from the plan, but answered "no" to the question of party-in-interest transactions when the promissory notes evidenced extensions of credits from the plan to the fiduciary and certain fiduciary controlled entities.[10]

871. What does the term "knowingly" mean for purposes of 18 U.S.C. Section 1027?

It is a violation of 18 U.S.C. Section 1027 to knowingly make a false statement, representation, or concealment of fact. An act or an omission or failure to act is done knowingly if it is done voluntarily and intentionally, and not because of a mistake or accident or some other innocent

---

1. *United States v. Sarault*, 840 F.2d 1479 (9th Cir. 1988).
2. *United States v. Tolkow*, 532 F.2d 853 (2d Cir. 1976).
3. *United States v. Santiago*, 528 F.2d 1130 (2d Cir.), *cert. denied*, 425 U.S. 972 (1976).
4. *United States v. McCrae*, 344 F. Supp. 942 (E.D. Pa. 1972).
5. *United States v. S & Vee Cartage Co.*, 704 F.2d 914 (6th Cir.), *cert. denied*, 464 U.S. 935 (1983); *Central States, Se. & Sw. Areas Pension Fund v. CRST, Inc.*, 641 F.2d 616 (8th Cir. 1981).
6. *United States v. Martorano*, 596 F. Supp. 621 (E.D. Pa. 1984), *aff'd*, 767 F.2d 63 (3d Cir.), *cert. denied*, 474 U.S. 949 (1985).
7. *United States v. Furst*, 886 F.2d 558 (3d Cir. 1989), *cert. denied*, 493 U.S. 1062 (1990); *United States v. Sarault*, 840 F.2d 1479 (9th Cir. 1988).
8. *United States v. Bartkus*, 816 F.2d 255 (6th Cir. 1987).
9. *United States v. Harris*, 185 F.3d 999 (9th Cir. 1999).
10. *United States v. Harris*, supra.

reason. Proof of specific intent is not required to establish a violation of 18 U.S.C. Section 1027. The term "knowingly" requires "proof of a voluntary conscious failure to disclose without ground for believing that such non-disclosure is lawful, or with reckless disregard for whether or not it is lawful."[1] A conviction was upheld for "knowingly failing to disclose facts" in a required document.[2]

The purpose of adding the word "knowingly" to the statute was to ensure that no one would be convicted of an omission or failure to act due to a mistake, accident, or some other innocent reason. A statement or representation is "false" within the meaning of the statute if it was not true when it was made and the person making it or causing it to be made knew it to be untrue, or if it was made with reckless indifference as to its truth or falsity or with a conscious purpose to avoid learning the truth.[3]

It is not necessary to establish that the defendant was aware of any legal duties imposed upon him by ERISA, or that he was aware of the plan's reporting requirements under ERISA, or that he intended to violate any law.[4] As 18 U.S.C. Section 1027 makes no mention of "fraudulent concealment," it does not require proof of fraud or actual reliance upon any false statement of fact. The statute only requires that the false statement or representation be made knowingly.[5]

872. What documents are covered under the provisions of 18 U.S.C. Section 1027?

A violation of 18 U.S.C. Section 1027 occurs when a false statement or false representation of fact is made in a document required by Title I of ERISA to be (1) published, (2) kept as part of the records of an employee welfare benefit plan, or (3) certified to the administrator of such a plan. The only relevant limitation found in 18 U.S.C. Section 1027 deals with the type of documents containing false statements.

Any concealment, cover-up, or failure to disclose must be of a fact the disclosure of which is required by ERISA, or is necessary to verify, explain, clarify, or check for accuracy and completeness any report required by ERISA to be certified.[6]

873. What documents are "published" for purposes of 18 U.S.C. Section 1027?

The documents required to be published are dependent on the type of plan, number of participants, and the use of service providers. ERISA Section 103 and ERISA Section 104 require that an annual report be published by an employee benefit plan subject to ERISA and filed with the Secretary of Labor. The annual report is submitted on Form 5500 and its attached schedules.[7] Thus, the Form 5500 annual report and its supporting schedules are documents required to

---

1. *United States v. S & Vee Cartage Co.*, 704 F.2d 914 (6th Cir.), *cert. denied*, 464 U.S. 935 (1983).
2. *United States v. Tolkow*, 532 F.2d 853 (2d Cir. 1976).
3. *United States v. S & Vee Cartage Co.*, 704 F.2d 914 (6th Cir.), *cert. denied*, 464 U.S. 935 (1983).
4. *United States v. Tolkow*, 532 F.2d 532 (2d Cir. 1976).
5. *United States v. Martorano*, 596 F. Supp. 621 (E.D. Pa. 1984), *aff'd*, 767 F.2d 63 (3d Cir. 1985).
6. *United States v. Martorano*, 596 F. Supp. 621 (E.D. Pa. 1984), *aff'd*, 767 F.2d 63 (3d Cir.), *cert. denied*, 474 U.S. 949 (1985).
7. Labor Reg. §2520.103-1.

be "published" within the meaning of 18 U.S.C. Section 1027 and any knowingly made false statement of fact or representation of fact on Form 5500 or an attached schedule is proscribed by 18 U.S.C. Section 1027.[1]

The supporting schedules of Form 5500 include:

1. *Schedule A* (Insurance Information). Schedule A is required to be filed by a plan if benefits under the plan are provided by an insurance company, insurance service, or other similar organization; it is certified by the insurer.

2. *Schedule C* (Service Provider and Trustee Information). Schedule C is required to be filed by Form 5500 filers when one or more service providers receive $5,000 or more in compensation for all services rendered to the plan during the plan year, to report trustee information, and to report the termination of certain service providers.

3. *Schedule E* (ESOP Annual Information). Schedule E is required to be filed by every employer sponsoring a pension benefit plan that contains an ESOP benefit; the Schedule E must be filed if required as an attachment to Forms 5500, 5500-C/R, or 5500-EZ.

4. *Schedules MB and SB* (Actuarial Information). Either Schedule MB and SB, depending on whether the plan is a single-employer or multiemployer plan) are required to be filed by defined benefit plans subject to the minimum funding standards; it is certified by an actuary.

5. *Schedule SSA* (Annual Registration Statement Identifying Separated Participants with Deferred Vested Benefits). Schedule SSA is required to be filed by pension plans that have separated participants.

In addition to Form 5500, other documents that are required to be published include:

1. Financial statement for plans with more than 100 participants;

2. Actuarial statement for defined benefit plans; and

3. Stock valuations for ESOPs.

874. What documents are "kept" for purposes of 18 U.S.C. Section 1027?

In addition to documents that are published, 18 U.S.C. Section 1027 also applies to supporting documentation, that is, documents required to be kept as part of plan records. These documents may involve (at least in part) non-financial information that need not be included on Form 5500, but is helpful to verify and check the information that must be included. Examples of these documents include:

1. Plan documents;

2. Trust agreements;

---

1. *United States v. Martorano*, 596 F. Supp. 621 (E.D. Pa. 1984), *aff'd*, 767 F.2d 63 (3d Cir.), *cert. denied*, 474 U.S. 949 (1985).

3.   Checking account statements with canceled checks;

4.   Debit and credit memorandum;

5.   Investment account statements;

6.   Mortgage notes;

7.   Loan agreements with supporting documents;

8.   General ledgers, cash disbursement, and cash receipts journals;

9.   Service provider agreements and reports, including documents containing information from insurance carriers or other similar organizations;[1]

10.   Remittance sheets for collectively bargained plans,[2] where documents misstating the number of eligible employees, the names of employees covered, and the contributions the employer owed were the primary source of that information and necessary to verify ERISA Section 1027 reports;[3]

11.   Claim documents;

12.   Hospital invoices for medical services and Coordination of Benefits forms,[4] the *Bartkus* court holding that a hospital invoice for medical services qualifies as a "receipt" within the meaning of 18 U.S.C. Section 1027, requiring retention of both the Coordination of Insurance Benefits form that verified the eligibility to receive fund payments and the hospital invoice;

13.   Employer payroll records verifying contributions to the plan,[5] the *Combs* court holding that 18 U.S.C. Section 1027 provides a duty to maintain records of hours worked by employees so that trustees can determine the accuracy of an employer's contributions; and

14.   Documents submitted to a plan,[6] where statements made by an attorney representing an assetless insurance company to the trustees of a pension plan who were considering the purchase of fiduciary liability insurance falsely stated the company's assets.

875. What documents are "certified by the plan administrator" for purposes of 18 U.S.C. Section 1027?

These are documents or information that are provided to the plan administrator to complete Form 5500 (Annual Report), filed as an attachment to Form 5500, or maintained

---

1. See *United States v. Martorano*, 596 F. Supp. 621 (E.D. Pa. 1984), *aff'd*, 767 F.2d 63 (3d Cir.), *cert. denied*, 474 U.S. 949 (1985).
2. See *United States v. S & Vee Cartage Co.*, 704 F.2d 914 (6th Cir.), *cert. denied*, 464 U.S. 935 (1983).
3. See also *United States v. Odom*, 736 F.2d 150 (5th Cir. 1984).
4. See *United States v. Bartkus*, 816 F.2d 255 (6th Cir. 1987).
5. See *Combs v. King*, 764 F.2d 818 (11th Cir. 1985).
6. See *United States v. Sarault*, 840 F.2d 1479 (9th Cir. 1988).

as records in support of Form 5500. Certain information provided to a plan administrator is required to be certified as to its accuracy.[1] Examples of certifications include:

1.   *Schedule A* (Insurance Information);

2.   *Schedule MB or SB* (Actuarial Information);

3.   Actuarial Report in support of Schedule MB or SB that is maintained with the plan records;

4.   ESOP valuations (an appraisal of a privately held company that is certified by a valuation company and maintained with the plan records); and

5.   Asset Valuation Reports (stock broker reports, investment manager reports, bank trust reports, etc., that are certified by a broker, manager, or bank and are used to complete Form 5500 and maintained with the records of the plan).

876. What is an offer, acceptance, or solicitation to influence operations of an employee benefit plan?

18 U.S.C. Section 1954 prohibits the receipt, solicitation, giving, offer, or promise to offer of a fee, kickback, commission, gift, loan, money, or thing of value with respect to an employee benefit plan. Violators of the statute may be fined, imprisoned for up to three years, or both.

The text of 18 U.S.C. Section 1954 reads:

Whoever being

(1) an administrator, officer, trustee, custodian, counsel, agent, or employee of any employee welfare benefit plan or employee pension benefit plan; or

(2) an officer, counsel, agent, or employee of an employer or an employer any of whose employees are covered by such plan; or

(3) an officer, counsel, agent, or employee of an employee organization any of whose members are covered by such plan; or

(4) a person who, or an officer, counsel, agent, or employee of an organization which, provides benefit plan services to such plan

receives or agrees to receive or solicits any fee, kickback, commission, gift, loan, money, or thing of value because of or with intent to be influenced with respect to, any of the actions, decisions, or other duties relating to any question or matter concerning such plan or any person who directly or indirectly gives or offers, or promises to give or offer, any fee, kickback, commission, gift, loan, money, or thing of value prohibited by this section, shall be fined under this title or imprisoned not more than three years, or both: Provided, [t]hat this section shall not prohibit the payment to or acceptance by any person of bona fide salary, compensation, or other payments made for goods or facilities actually furnished or for services actually performed in the regular course of his duties as such person, administrator, officer, trustee, custodian, counsel, agent, or employee of such plan, employer, employee organization, or organization providing benefit plan services to such plan.

---

1. ERISA Sec. 103(a)(2).

> As used in this section, the term (a) "any employee welfare benefit plan" or "employee pension benefit plan" means any employee welfare benefit plan or employee pension benefit plan, respectively, subject to any provision of Title I of [ERISA], and (b) "employee organization" and "administrator" as defined respectively in [ERISA Section 3(4) and ERISA Section 3(16)].[1]

18 U.S.C. Section 1954 was enacted as part of the Welfare and Pension Plans Disclosure Amendment Act of 1962. In enacting 18 U.S.C. Section 1954, Congress intended to strictly regulate the administration and operation of employee benefit plans and to provide the "enforcement teeth which [were] lacking in the [Welfare and Pension Plans Disclosure Law of 1958]."[2]

The statute is designed to protect the financial interests of participants in employee benefit plans and their beneficiaries from dishonest or unfaithful fiduciaries, and it is intended to reach a broad class of persons who are connected with the operation of employee benefit plans by encompassing almost every conceivable person who could deal with or administer an employee benefit plan. The statute itself has been construed to reach all persons with the capacity to influence, directly or indirectly, the use of employee benefit plan funds, as well as all fiduciaries who profit as a result of their decisions to invest employee benefit funds.[3]

The statute prohibits the receipt of any fee, kickback, commission, gift, loan, money, or thing of value either "because of" (i.e., a graft provision proscribing the payment or receipt of gratuities), or with "the intent to be influenced" (i.e., a bribery provision proscribing the corrupt payment or receipt of things of value as the primary motivation for the recipient's actions, duties, or decisions with respect to an employee benefit plan matter). Thus, Congress was not only concerned with corrupt transactions as indicated with the "intent to influence" language, it also was concerned with benefit plan fiduciaries' taking advantage of their position in any way. The statute also bans all conflict-of-interest payments by requiring all fiduciaries of benefit plans to be honest and straightforward when handling employee benefit funds. This requires fiduciaries to disclose the financial activities involved in administering plan funds.[4]

877. Who is a recipient for purposes of 18 U.S.C. Section 1954?

In order to demonstrate a violation of 18 U.S.C. Section 1954, the receiver must have served in one of the positions specified in the statute. A person with recipient status must receive, agree to receive, or solicit a thing of value because of, or with the intent to be influenced with respect to any of his actions, decisions, or other duties relating to any question or matter concerning the plan.[5] A receiver may be in one of the following categories.

---

1. 18 U.S.C. §1954.
2. H.R. Rep. No. 87-998, 87th Cong., 2d Sess., *reprinted in* 1962 U.S. Code Cong. & Admin. News 1532, 1532-36.
3. *United States v. Robilotto*, 828 F.2d 940 (2d Cir. 1987); *United States v. Romano*, 684 F.2d 1057 (2d Cir.1982); *United States v. Friedland*, 660 F.2d 919 (3d Cir. 1981).
4. *United States v. Romano*, 684 F.2d 1057 (2d Cir. 1982).
5. *United States v. Palmeri*, 630 F.2d 192 (3d Cir. 1980), *cert. denied*, 450 U.S. 967 (1981).

Category 1—Employee Benefit Plan Personnel

This category includes a plan administrator, officer, trustee, custodian, counsel, agent, or employee of an employee welfare benefit plan or employee pension benefit plan. A trustee of a pension plan was convicted for soliciting and accepting kickbacks, fees, and commissions from borrowers of plan assets in order to influence an employee benefit fund.[1] An administrator of a jointly trusteed pension plan was convicted for receiving television sets as gifts for new depositors from a bank, when the administrator directed the deposit of plan money into savings accounts at the bank.[2] Attorneys who served as general counsel to a pension plan and whom trustees consulted at meetings were convicted for soliciting and receiving payments from a prospective borrower in return for obtaining assistance in obtaining a loan from the plan.[3]

Category 2—Personnel of an Employer

This category includes an officer, counsel, agent, or employee of an employer, or an employer who has employees covered by a plan. For example, an employer's employee and a representative of the employer trustees were convicted for receiving compensation from a service provider seeking a contract with the plan.[4]

Category 3—Personnel of an Employee Organization

This category includes an officer, counsel, agent, or employee of an employee organization any of whose members are covered by the plan. The executive director of a union-sponsored welfare benefit plan was convicted of soliciting and receiving kickbacks (commissions) from a third-party medical laboratory in return for influencing the fund to select the medical laboratory as a service provider.[5] A union president was convicted under 18 U.S.C. Section 1954 for soliciting cash from an employer in exchange for the union president's efforts to not impose a lien on the business of the employer for failing to remit contributions to the plan.[6] Business agents and employees of the employee organization (union) were convicted for accepting personal bank loans in exchange for their efforts in depositing union benefit plan funds into the bank.[7]

Category 4—Personnel of Benefit Service Providers

This category includes a person who provides benefit plan services to the plan. It also includes an officer, counsel, agent, or employee of an organization that provides benefit plan services to the plan. An example is a brokerage firm officer who helped a pension plan manager substantially reduce his personal federal income tax liability by selling to the manager highly

1. *United States v. Pieper*, 854 F.2d 1020 (7th Cir. 1988).
2. *United States v. Romano*, 684 F.2d 1027 (2d Cir.), *cert. denied*, 459 U.S. 1016 (1982).
3. *United States v. Friedland*, 660 F.2d 919 (3d Cir. 1981).
4. *United States v. Fernandez*, 892 F.2d 976 (11th Cir. 1989).
5. *United States v. Wiedyk*, 71 F.3d 602 (6th Cir. 1995).
6. *United States v. Soures*, 736 F.2d 87 (3d Cir. 1984).
7. *United States v. Palmeri*, 630 F.2d 192 (3d Cir. 1980).

illiquid bonds, which the manager sold back to the firm one week later at a loss.[1] The legislative history makes it clear that 18 U.S.C. Section 1954 applies to, among others, an investment broker who provides services to an employee benefit plan.[2]

878. Who is a "giver" under 18 U.S.C. Section 1954?

A "giver" is any person who gives, or offers or promises to give, directly or indirectly, a thing of value because of or with the intent to influence a prohibited recipient's actions, decisions, or other duties relating to any question or matter concerning the plan. Thus, a giver may be any person and, as such, is not required to hold a position affiliated with the plan.[3]

879. Must the "receiver" directly receive a payment to be prosecuted under 18 U.S.C. Section 1954?

No. It is not necessary to prove that a defendant in an action under 18 U.S.C. Section 1954 directly received payment of the fee, kickback, commission, gift, money, or thing of value. If the defendant caused someone other than the plan to receive the fee, kickback, commission, gift, money, or thing of value, then the defendant has also received a thing of value within the meaning of the statute. In other words, being able to control the disposition of the payment is considered a thing of value.[4]

880. Must the defendant receive a kickback both "because of" and "with the intent to be influenced" to be convicted under 18 U.S.C. Section 1954?

No. A defendant may be convicted of receiving a kickback (1) "because of" or (2) "with intent to be influenced with respect to" any actions or decisions relating to the plan involved. The "because of" language of the statute refers to graft and the "with the intent to be influenced" language refers to bribery. Bribery requires that the payment be the motivating factor for the recipient's actions in relation to a plan matter.[5] In contrast, the graft provision does not require that the thing of value paid or received be the primary motivation for the action in connection with a related plan matter.[6] 18 U.S.C. Section 1954 provides for punishment for both graft and bribery because Congress was not only concerned with corrupt transactions as indicated with the "intent to influence" language, it also was concerned with benefit plan fiduciaries' taking advantage of their position in any way. As one court explained, "[i]f only corrupt transactions were intended to be covered, Congress would not have added the 'because of' clause, but would have limited the statute to those possessing the intent to be influenced." Thus, the broad language of the statute reflects the intent of Congress to reach all fiduciaries that profit as a result of their decisions to invest union funds.[7]

1. *United States v. Rosenthal*, 9 F.3d 1016 (2d Cir. 1993).
2. *United States v. Schwimmer*, 700 F. Supp. 104 (E.D.N.Y. 1988); see S. Rep. No. 87-908, 87th Cong., 1st Sess. 11 (1961).
3. 18 U.S.C. §1954.
4. *United States v. Robilotto*, 828 F.2d 940 (2d Cir. 1987); *United States v. Schwartz*, 785 F.2d 673 (9th Cir. 1986); *United States v. Romano*, 684 F.2d 1057 (2d Cir.), *cert. denied*, 459 U.S. 1016 (1982); *United States v. Palmeri*, 630 F.2d 192 (3d Cir. 1980), *cert. denied*, 450 U.S. 967 (1981).
5. 18 U.S.C. §1954.
6. *United States v. Friedland*, 660 F.2d 919 (3d Cir. 1981).
7. *United States v. Romano*, 684 F.2d 1057 (2d Cir. 1982).

881. Must the defendant have the actual ability to control the decisions of a benefit plan to be convicted under 18 U.S.C. Section 1954?

No. Under 18 U.S.C. Section 1954, it is not necessary to prove that a defendant had actual ability to control the decisions of a benefit plan, so long as, because of her status, she had apparent power over decisions regarding the plan. For example, the attorneys who served as the general counsel to a pension plan and whom trustees consulted at meetings and on an ad hoc basis but who had no actual authority over the plan's investments were within the ambit of 18 U.S.C. Section 1954. Thus, it is sufficient that the defendant in a prosecution under 18 U.S.C. Section 1954 was in a position to give evaluation, advice, and recommendation, which though not controlling in the final sense, could have some influence on the operations of a plan.[1]

882. Must the person who paid the kickback know of the recipient's position with respect to a plan in order to be convicted under 18 U.S.C. Section 1954?

No. The state of mind of the person paying the kickback is irrelevant. Rather than focusing on the knowledge of the "giver," it must be established that the defendant received kickbacks "because of" his status, which gave him at least ostensible authority to exercise influence over the decisions of the plan or select the people who did. To accept a contrary position would "create a loophole in the statute by which illegal acts would become decriminalized through delegations and subterfuge."[2] Such a result would fly in the face of Congress's clearly expressed legislative intent "to reach all fiduciaries who profit (other than by regular compensation) as a result of their decisions to invest union pension funds."[3]

883. Is a benefit or lack of injury to the plan a valid defense to a prosecution under 18 U.S.C. Section 1954?

No. It is no defense that a kickback, fee, gift, money, or thing of value was solicited, agreed to be received, or received by a defendant because of actions or decisions that were themselves lawful, beneficial, or not injurious to a plan. The purpose of 18 U.S.C. Section 1954 is to protect the plan from conflict-of-interest payments that may affect the judgment and integrity of persons who exercise direct or indirect control or influence over the operation of the plan.[4] 18 U.S.C. Section 1954 is not limited to actual misuse of pension funds. For example, a defendant could be convicted for soliciting payments in exchange for refraining from reimposing a lien.[5]

---

1. *United States v. Pieper*, 854 F.2d 1020 (7th Cir. 1988); *United States v. Romano*, 684 F.2d 1057 (2d Cir.), *cert. denied*, 459 U.S. 1016 (1982); *United States v. Palmeri*, 630 F.2d 192 (3d Cir. 1980), *cert. denied*, 450 U.S. 967 (1981).
2. *United States v. Pieper*, 854 F.2d 1020 (7th Cir. 1988).
3. *United States v. Romano*, 684 F.2d 1057 (2d Cir. 1982); see S. Rep. No. 87-908, 87th Cong., 1st Sess. 4-5, 11 (1961).
4. *United States v. Pieper*, 854 F.2d 1020 (7th Cir. 1988); *United States v. Soures*, 736 F.2d 87 (3d Cir. 1984); *United States v. Palmeri*, 630 F.2d 192 (3d Cir. 1980), *cert. denied*, 450 U.S. 967 (1981).
5. *United States v. Soures*, 736 F.2d 87 (3d Cir. 1984), *cert. denied*, 469 U.S. 1161 (1985).

884. What is a "thing of value" for purposes of 18 U.S.C. Section 1954?

It is unlawful for a person to directly or indirectly give, offer, or promise to give or offer any fee, kickback, commission, gift, loan, money, or thing of value to an administrator, officer, trustee, custodian, counsel, agent, or employee of an employee pension plan.[1] A "thing of value" is not limited to tangible items with identifiable commercial value, but may include certain intangibles as well, such as providing assistance in arranging for a merger of unions and other services.[2] In addition, the "thing of value" need not be illegal itself for the transaction to violate 18 U.S.C. Section 1954. Television sets given away by a bank in return for opening accounts on behalf of pension funds constituted a prohibited "thing of value."[3] An item is characterized as a "thing of value" if the recipient believed that the item had value, such as when worthless shares of stock nonetheless were considered a "thing of value" because the recipient expected the shares to have substantial worth.[4] The opportunity to purchase stock warrants was also held to be a "thing of value."[5]

885. What payments are not prohibited under 18 U.S.C. Section 1954?

The payment to or acceptance by a person of a bona fide salary, compensation, or other payments made for goods or facilities actually furnished or for services actually performed in the regular course of one's duties is permitted.[6]

886. How is "bona fide" defined for purposes of 18 U.S.C. Section 1954?

18 U.S.C. Section 1954, which prohibits the receipt of fees to influence employee benefit plan operations, contains an exception allowing bona fide salary, compensation, or other payments made for goods or facilities actually furnished or for services actually performed. The term "bona fide" is not restricted to any technical meaning but is used in the statute according to its common and ordinary meaning, which is synonymous with (1) in good faith; (2) without dishonesty, fraud, or deceit; (3) genuine or authentic; and (4) without subterfuge. "Bona fide" is defined as "in good faith, exclusive of fraud or deceit." It contemplates proof of a subjective element that the payment or compensation was given or received in good faith. For example, one who receives a commission from a financial institution for placing employee benefit plan funds, without disclosing to the plan the actual commissions received, is not acting in good faith. Thus, a reasonable construction of bona fide is to require disclosure.[7] In order for beneficiaries to decide whether compensation paid to a fiduciary who handles the investment of union funds is bona fide, the beneficiaries must be told the amount of the compensation. It would be wholly inconsistent with ERISA if a fiduciary could unilaterally decide for herself what is bona fide compensation. This is a decision reserved for the plan beneficiaries.

---

1. 18 U.S.C. §1954.
2. *United States v. Schwartz*, 785 F.2d 673 (9th Cir.), *cert. denied*, 479 U.S. 890 (1986); see also *United States v. Robilotto*, 828 F.2d 940 (2d Cir. 1987), *cert. denied*, 484 U.S. 1011 (1988).
3. *United States v. Romano*, 684 F.2d 1057 (2d Cir.), *cert. denied*, 459 U.S. 1016 (1982).
4. *United States v. Rosenthal*, 9 F.3d 1016 (2d Cir.), *cert. denied*, 464 U.S. 1007 (1993).
5. *United States v. Ostrander*, 999 F.2d 27 (2d Cir. 1993).
6. 18 U.S.C. §1954.
7. *United States v. Schwimmer*, 700 F. Supp. 104 (E.D.N.Y. 1988).

The phrase "bona fide" also contemplates proof of an objective element that the compensation or payments be received for services actually performed (or for goods actually delivered) in the regular course of the recipient's duties. Thus, if a defendant agreed to receive or received salary, compensation, or other payments that he knew were not for services actually performed, or within the regular course of his duties, then the payments are not "bona fide" and do not fall within the exception to the statute. With respect to the term "regular course of duties," the solicitation, agreement to receive, or receipt of compensation, salary, or other payments must comport with the defendant's obligations of his position to the employee benefit plan.[1]

In addition, subject to the limitations of ERISA Section 408(d), ERISA Section 408(b)(2) exempts from the prohibited transaction provisions of ERISA Section 406(a) any contract or reasonable arrangement with a party in interest, including a fiduciary, for office space or legal, accounting, or other services necessary for the establishment or operation of a plan, if no more than reasonable compensation is paid. Regulations clarify the terms "necessary service," "reasonable contract or arrangement," and "reasonable compensation" as used in ERISA Section 408(b)(2).[2] What constitutes a "necessary service" in a particular case, however, can only be resolved by taking into account the relevant facts and circumstances. Thus, the fiduciaries of a plan must review all services provided to determine whether the services are "necessary services" for which payment would be lawful.

887. Do the criminal provisions of ERISA supersede local criminal laws?

No. ERISA does not supersede generally applicable local criminal laws. ERISA exempts generally applicable criminal laws of a state from the scope of ERISA's preemption.[3] With this exception for state criminal laws, it is irrelevant as to whether a plan is an ERISA-covered plan or if the funds misappropriated are "plan assets" under ERISA. Therefore, a criminal proceeding under state theft statutes may apply with respect to misappropriation of employee benefit funds.

---

1. *United States v. Soures*, 736 F.2d 87 (3d Cir. 1984).
2. Labor Reg. §2550.408b-2.
3. ERISA Sec. 514(b)(4).

APPENDIX A

MODEL NOTICES

HIPAA Model Notice

IMPORTANT NOTICE OF YOUR RIGHT TO DOCUMENTATION OF HEALTH COVERAGE

Recent changes in Federal law may affect your health coverage if you are enrolled or become eligible to enroll in health coverage that excludes coverage for preexisting medical conditions.

The Health Insurance Portability and Accountability Act of 1996 (HIPAA) limits the circumstances under which coverage may be excluded for medical conditions present before you enroll. Under the law, a preexisting condition exclusion generally may not be imposed for more than 12 months (18 months for a late enrollee). The 12-month (or 18-month) exclusion period is reduced by your prior health coverage. You are entitled to a certificate that will show evidence of your prior health coverage. If you buy health insurance other than through an employer group health plan, a certificate of prior coverage may help you obtain coverage without a preexisting condition exclusion. Contact your State insurance department for further information.

For employer group health plans, these changes generally take effect at the beginning of the first plan year starting after June 30, 1997. For example, if your employer's plan year begins on January 1, 1998, the plan is not required to give you credit for your prior coverage until January 1, 1998.

You have the right to receive a certificate of prior health coverage since July 1, 1996. You may need to provide other documentation for earlier periods of health care coverage. Check with your new plan administrator to see if your new plan excludes coverage for preexisting conditions and if you need to provide a certificate or other documentation of your previous coverage.

To get a certificate, complete the attached form and return it to:

Entity:

Address:

For additional information contact:

The certificate must be provided to you promptly. Keep a copy of this completed form. You may also request certificates for any of your dependents (including your spouse) who were enrolled under your health coverage.

****

REQUEST FOR CERTIFICATE OF HEALTH COVERAGE

Name of Participant: _____ Date: _____

Address: _____

Telephone Number: _____

Name and relationship of any dependents for whom certificate are requested (and their address if different from above):

_____

_____

917

INFORMATION ON CATEGORIES OF BENEFITS

1. Date of original certificate: _____

2. Name of group health plan providing the coverage: _____

    _____

3. Name of participant: _____

4. Identification number of participant: _____

5. Name of individual(s) to whom this information applies:

    _____

6. The following information applies to the coverage in the certificate
    that was provided to the individual(s) identified above:

    a. MENTAL HEALTH: _____

    b. SUBSTANCE ABUSE TREATMENT: _____

    c. PRESCRIPTION DRUGS: _____

    d. DENTAL CARE: _____

    e. VISION CARE: _____

For each category above, enter "N/A" if the individual had no coverage within the category and either (i) enter both the date that the individual's coverage within the category began and the date that the individual's coverage within the category ended (or indicate if continuing), or (ii) enter "same" on the line if the beginning and ending dates for coverage within the category are the same as the beginning and ending dates for the coverage in the certificate.

HIPAA Model Certificate

CERTIFICATE OF GROUP HEALTH PLAN COVERAGE

1. Date of this certificate: _____

2. Name of group health plan: _____
_____

3. Name of participant: _____

4. Identification number of participant: _____

5. Name of individuals to whom this certificate applies: _____
_____

6. Name, address, and telephone number of plan administrator or issuer responsible for providing this certificate: _____
_____

7. For further information, call: _____

8. If the individual(s) identified in line 5 has (have) at least 18 months of creditable coverage (disregarding periods of coverage before a 63-day break), check here and skip lines 9 and 10:
____

9. Date waiting period or affiliation period (if any) began: _____

10. Date coverage began: _____

11. Date coverage ended (or if coverage has not ended, enter "continuing"): _____

[Note: separate certificates will be furnished if information is not identical for the participant and each beneficiary.]

Statement of HIPAA Portability Rights

IMPORTANT — KEEP THIS CERTIFICATE. This certificate is evidence of your coverage under this plan. Under a federal law known as HIPAA, you may need evidence of your coverage to reduce a preexisting condition exclusion period under another plan, to help you get special enrollment in another plan, or to get certain types of individual health coverage even if you have health problems.

Preexisting condition exclusions. Some group health plans restrict coverage for medical conditions present before an individual's enrollment. These restrictions are known as "preexisting condition exclusions." A preexisting condition exclusion can apply only to conditions for which medical advice, diagnosis, care, or treatment was recommended or received within the 6 months before your "enrollment date." Your enrollment date is your first day of coverage under the plan, or, if there is a waiting period, the first day of your waiting period (typically, your first day of work). In addition, a preexisting condition exclusion cannot last for more than 12 months after your enrollment date (18 months if you are a late enrollee). Finally, a preexisting condition exclusion cannot apply to pregnancy and cannot apply to a child who is enrolled in health coverage within 30 days after birth, adoption, or placement for adoption.

If a plan imposes a preexisting condition exclusion, the length of the exclusion must be reduced by the amount of your prior creditable coverage. Most health coverage is creditable coverage, including group health plan coverage, COBRA continuation coverage, coverage under an individual health policy, Medicare, Medicaid, State Children's Health Insurance Program (SCHIP), and coverage through high-risk pools and the Peace Corps. Not all forms of creditable coverage are required to provide certificates like this one. If you do not receive a certificate for past coverage, talk to your new plan administrator.

You can add up any creditable coverage you have, including the coverage shown on this certificate. However, if at any time you went for 63 days or more without any coverage (called a break in coverage) a plan may not have to count the coverage you had before the break.

Therefore, once your coverage ends, you should try to obtain alternative coverage as soon as possible to avoid a 63-day break. You may use this certificate as evidence of your creditable coverage to reduce the length of any preexisting condition exclusion if you enroll in another plan.

Right to get special enrollment in another plan. Under HIPAA, if you lose your group health plan coverage, you may be able to get into another group health plan for which you are eligible (such as a spouse's plan), even if the plan generally does not accept late enrollees, if you request enrollment within 30 days. (Additional special enrollment rights are triggered by marriage, birth, adoption, and placement for adoption.)

> Therefore, once your coverage ends, if you are eligible for coverage in another plan (such as a spouse's plan), you should request special enrollment as soon as possible.

Prohibition against discrimination based on a health factor. Under HIPAA, a group health plan may not keep you (or your dependents) out of the plan based on anything related to your health. Also, a group health plan may not charge you (or your dependents) more for coverage, based on health, than the amount charged a similarly situated individual.

Right to individual health coverage. Under HIPAA, if you are an "eligible individual," you have a right to buy certain individual health policies (or in some states, to buy coverage through a high-risk pool) without a preexisting condition exclusion. To be an eligible individual, you must meet the following requirements:

- *You have had coverage for at least 18 months without a break in coverage of 63 days or more;*

- *Your most recent coverage was under a group health plan (which can be shown by this certificate);*

- *Your group coverage was not terminated because of fraud or nonpayment of premiums;*

- *You are not eligible for COBRA continuation coverage or you have exhausted your COBRA benefits (or continuation coverage under a similar state provision); and*

- *You are not eligible for another group health plan, Medicare, or Medicaid, and do not have any other health insurance coverage.*

The right to buy individual coverage is the same whether you are laid off, fired, or quit your job.

> Therefore, if you are interested in obtaining individual coverage and you meet the other criteria to be an eligible individual, you should apply for this coverage as soon as possible to avoid losing your eligible individual status due to a 63-day break.

State flexibility. This certificate describes minimum HIPAA protections under federal law. States may require insurers and HMOs to provide additional protections to individuals in that state.

For more information. If you have questions about your HIPAA rights, you may contact your state insurance department or the U.S. Department of Labor, Employee Benefits Security Administration (EBSA) toll-free at 1-866-444-3272 (for free HIPAA publications ask for publications concerning changes in health care laws). You may also contact the CMS publication hotline at 1-800-633-4227 (ask for "Protecting Your Health Insurance Coverage"). These publications and other useful information are also available on the Internet at: http://www.dol.gov/ebsa, the DOL's interactive web pages - Health Elaws, or http://www.cms.hhs.gov/HealthInsReformforConsume.

MODEL DESCRIPTION

If you are declining enrollment for yourself or your dependents (including your spouse) because of other health insurance coverage, you may in the future be able to enroll yourself or your dependents in this plan, provided that you request enrollment within 30 days after your other coverage ends. In addition, if you have a new dependent as a result of marriage, birth, adoption, or placement for adoption, you may be able to enroll yourself and your dependents, provided that you request enrollment within 30 days after the marriage, birth adoption, or placement for adoption.

NATIONAL MEDICAL SUPPORT NOTICE - PART A
NOTICE TO WITHHOLD FOR HEALTH CARE COVERAGE

This Notice is issued under section 466(a)(19) of the Social Security Act, section 609(a)(5)(C) of the Employee Retirement Income Security Act of 1974 (ERISA), and for State and local government and church plans, sections 401(e) and (f) of the Child Support Performance and Incentive Act of 1998. Receipt of this Notice from the Issuing Agency constitutes receipt of a Medical Child Support Order under applicable law. The information on the Custodial Parent and Child(ren) contained on this page is confidential and should not be shared or disclosed with the employee. NOTE: For purposes of this form, the Custodial Parent may also be the employee when the State opts to enforce against the Custodial Parent.

Issuing Agency: _____ Issuing Agency Address: _____ _____ Notice Date: _____ CSE Agency Case Identifier: _____ Telephone Number: _____ FAX Number: _____	Court or Administrative Authority: _____ Order Date: _____ Order Identifier: _____ Document Tracking Identifier: _____ Employer web site: _____ See NMSN Instructions: www.acf.hhs.gov/programs/cse/forms/

_____   RE: _____
Employer/Withholder's Federal EIN Number   Employee's Name (Last, First, MI)

_____   _____
Employer/Withholder's Name   Employee's Social Security Number

_____   _____
_____   _____
Employer / Withholder's Address   Employee's Mailing Address

_____   _____
Custodial Parent's Name (Last, First, MI)   Substituted Official/Agency Name

_____   _____
_____   _____
Custodial Parent's Mailing Address   Substituted Official/Agency Address
                                                 (Required if Custodial Parent's mailing address is left blank)

_____
Child(ren)'s Mailing Address (if different from   _____
Custodial Parent's)   _____
_____
Name and Telephone of a Representative of the   Mailing Address of a Representative of the Child(ren)
Child(ren)

Child(ren)'s Name(s   Gender   DOB   SSN   Child(ren)'s Name(s)   Gender   DOB   SSN
_____ _____ _____ _____   _____ _____ _____ _____
_____ _____ _____ _____   _____ _____ _____ _____
_____ _____ _____ _____   _____ _____ _____ _____

The order requires the child(ren) to be enrolled in ☐ all health coverages available; or only the following coverage(s):
☐ Medical; ☐Dental; ☐Vision; ☐Prescription drug; ☐ Mental health; ☐Other specify):_____

Page 1 of 5

LIMITATIONS ON WITHHOLDING

The total amount withheld for both cash and medical support cannot exceed _____% of the employee's aggregate disposable weekly earnings. The employer may not withhold more under this National Medical Support Notice than the lesser of:

1. The amounts allowed by the Federal Consumer Credit Protection Act (15 U.S.C., section 1673(b));

2. The amounts allowed by the State of the employee's principal place of employment; or

3. The amounts allowed for health insurance premiums by the child support order, as indicated here:_____.

The Federal limit applies to the aggregate disposable weekly earnings (ADWE). ADWE is the net income left after making mandatory deductions such as State, Federal, local taxes; Social Security taxes; and Medicare taxes. As required under section 2.b.2 of the Employer Responsibilities on page 4, complete item 5 of the Employer Response to notify the Issuing Agency that enrollment cannot be completed because of prioritization or limitations on withholding.

PRIORITY OF WITHHOLDING

If withholding is required for employee contributions to one or more plans under this notice and for a support obligation under a separate notice and available funds are insufficient for withholding for both cash and medical support contributions, the employer must withhold amounts for purposes of cash support and medical support contributions in accordance with the law, if any, of the State of the employee's principal place of employment requiring prioritization between cash and medical support, as described here: _____.
As required under section 2.b.2 of the Employer Responsibilities on page 4, complete item 5 of the Employer Response to notify the Issuing Agency that enrollment cannot be completed because of prioritization or limitations on withholdings.

EMPLOYER RESPONSE

If 1, 2, 3, 4 or 5 below applies, check the appropriate box and return this Part A to the Issuing Agency within 20 business days after the date of the Notice, or sooner if reasonable. NO OTHER ACTION IS NECESSARY. If 1 through 5 does not apply, complete item 7 and forward **Part B** to the appropriate Plan Administrator(s) within 20 business days after the date of the Notice, or sooner if reasonable. This includes any organization or labor union that provides group health care benefits to the employee. Check number 5 and return this **Part A** to the **Issuing Agency** if the Plan Administrator informs you that the child(ren) would be enrolled in or qualify(ies) for an option under the plan for which you have determined that the employee contribution exceeds the amount that may be withheld from the employee's income due to State or Federal withholding limitations and/or prioritization. You are required to respond to the Issuing Agency by returning this **Employer Response** regardless of whether you provide group health benefits or the employee named herein is no longer employed by your organization. Information for the Plan Administrator and the Employer Representative at the bottom of this section is required.

☐ 1.   The employee named in this Notice has never been employed by this employer.

☐ 2.   We, the employer, do notoffer our employees the option of purchasing dependent or family health care coverage as a benefit of their employment.

☐ 3.   The employee is among a class of employees (for example, part-time or non-union) that are not eligible for family health coverage under any group health plan maintained by the employer or to which the employer contributes. Do not check this box if the employee is only temporarily ineligible for health care coverage.

☐ 4.   Health care coverage is not available because employee is no longer employed by the employer:

        Date of termination: _____

        Last known telephone number: _____

        Last known address: _____

        New employer (if known): _____

        New employer telephone number: _____

        New employer address: _____

☐ 5   State or Federal withholding limitations and/or prioritization prevent the withholding from the employee's income of the amount required to obtain coverage under the terms of the plan.

☐ 6   The participant is subject to a waiting period that expires _____ (more than 90 days from the date of receipt of this Notice), or has not completed a waiting period, which is determined by some measure other than the passage of time, such as the completion of a certain number of hours worked (describe here: _____). At the completion of the waiting period, the Plan Administrator will process the enrollment.

☐ 7. Employer forwarded Part B to Plan Administrator on _____.
                                   MM/DD/YY

CONTACT FOR QUESTIONS

Plan Administrator Name: _____	FAX Number: _____
Contact Person: _____	Telephone Number: _____
Employer Name: _____	Telephone Number: _____
Employer Representative Name/Title: _____	Federal EIN: _____
	(if not provided on Page 1 of this Notice)
Employee Name: _____	Date: _____

Page 3 of 5

INSTRUCTIONS TO EMPLOYER

This document serves as legal notice that the employee identified on this National Medical Support Notice is obligated by a court or administrative child support order to provide health care coverage for the child(ren) identified on this Notice. This National Medical Support Notice replaces any Medical Support Notice that the Issuing Agency has previously served on you with respect to the employee and the children listed on this Notice.

The document consists of **Part A - Notice to Withhold for Health Care Coverage** for the employer to withhold any employee contributions required by the group health plan(s) in which the child(ren) is/are enrolled; and **Part B - Medical Support Notice to the Plan Administrator**, which **must** be forwarded to the Administrator of each group health plan identified by the employer to enroll the eligible child(ren), or completed by the employer, if the employer serves as the health Plan Administrator.

An employer receiving this legal Notice is required to complete and return **Part A**. If group health coverage is not available to the employee named herein, or the employee was never or is no longer employed, the employer is still required to complete **Part A – Employer Response** and return it to the Issuing Agency with the appropriate response checked. If you, the employer, provide the health care benefits to the employee, forward **Part B – Plan Administrator Response** to the health Plan Administrator of your organization. If the employee's health care benefits are administered through another organization, including a labor union, forward Part B of the Notice to the labor union or other organization acting as the Plan Administrator for completion. If the employee has already enrolled the child(ren) in health care coverage, the employer must forward Part B to the Plan Administrator for completion and submittal to the Issuing Agency.

Keep a copy of **Part A** as it may be used to notify the Issuing Agency if the employee separates from service for any reason including retirement or termination.

EMPLOYER RESPONSIBILITIES

1. If the individual named in this Notice is not your employee, or if the family health care coverage is not available, please complete item 1, 2, 3, 4 or 5 of the Employer Response as appropriate, and return it to the Issuing Agency. NO OTHER ACTION IS NECESSARY.

2. If family health care coverage is available for which the child(ren) identified above may be eligible, you are required to:

   a. Transfer, not later than 20 business days after the date of this Notice, a copy of **Part B - Medical Support Notice to the Plan Administrator** to the Administrator of each appropriate group health plan for which the child(ren) may be eligible, complete item 7, and

   b. Upon notification from the Plan Administrator(s) that the child(ren) is/are enrolled, either

      1) withhold from the employee's income any employee contributions required under each group health plan, in accordance with the applicable law of the employee's principal place of employment and transfer employee contributions to the appropriate plan(s), or

      2) complete item 5 of the Employer Response to notify the Issuing Agency that enrollment cannot be completed because of prioritization or limitations on withholding.

   c. If the Plan Administrator notifies you that the employee is subject to a waiting period that expires more than 90 days from the date of its receipt of **Part B** of this Notice, or whose duration is determined by a measure other than the passage of time (for example, the completion of a certain number of hours worked), complete item 6 of the Employer Response to notify the Issuing Agency of the enrollment timeframe and notify the Plan Administrator when the employee is eligible to enroll in the plan and that this Notice requires the enrollment of the child(ren) named in the Notice in the plan.

Page 4 of 5

DURATION OF WITHHOLDING

The child(ren) shall be treated as dependents under the terms of the plan. Coverage of a child as a dependent will end when conditions for eligibility for coverage under terms of the plan no longer apply. However, the continuation coverage provisions of ERISA may entitle the child to continuation coverage under the plan. The employer must continue to withhold employee contributions and may not disenroll (or eliminate coverage for) the child(ren) unless:

    1.   The employer is provided satisfactory written evidence that:
        a.   The court or administrative child support order referred to in this Notice is no longer in effect; or
        b.   The child(ren) is or will be enrolled in comparable coverage which will take effect no later than the effective date of disenrollment from the plan; or

    2.   The employer eliminates family health coverage for all of its employees.

POSSIBLE SANCTIONS

An employer may be subject to sanctions or penalties imposed under State law and/or ERISA for discharging an employee from employment, refusing to employ, or taking disciplinary action against any employee because of medical child support withholding, or for failing to withhold income, or transmit such withheld amounts to the applicable plan(s) as the Notice directs. Sanctions or penalties may be imposed under State law against an employer for failure to respond and/or for non-compliance with this Notice.

NOTICE OF TERMINATION OF EMPLOYMENT

In any case in which the above employee's employment terminates, the employer must promptly notify the Issuing Agency listed above of such termination. This requirement may be satisfied by sending to the Issuing Agency a copy of Part A with response 4 checked or any notice the employer is required to provide under the continuation coverage provisions of ERISA or the Health Insurance Portability and Accountability Act.

EMPLOYEE LIABILITY FOR CONTRIBUTION TO PLAN

The employee is liable for any employee contributions that are required under the plan(s) for enrollment of the child(ren) and is subject to appropriate enforcement. The employee may contest the withholding under this Notice based on a mistake of fact (such as the identity of the obligor). Should an employee contest the withholding under this Notice, the employer must proceed to comply with the employer responsibilities in this Notice until notified by the Issuing Agency to discontinue withholding. To contest the withholding under this Notice, the employee should contact the Issuing Agency at the address and telephone number listed on the Notice. With respect to plans subject to ERISA, it is the view of the Department of Labor that Federal Courts have jurisdiction if the employee challenges a determination that the Notice constitutes a Qualified Medical Child Support Order.

CONTACT FOR QUESTIONS

If you have any questions regarding this Notice, you may contact the Issuing Agency at the address and telephone number listed on page 1 of this Notice.

NATIONAL MEDICAL SUPPORT NOTICE
PART B
MEDICAL SUPPORT NOTICE TO PLAN ADMINISTRATOR

This Notice is issued under section 466(a)(19) of the Social Security Act, section 609(a)(5)(C) of the Employee Retirement Income Security Act of 1974, and for State and local government and church plans, sections 401(e) and (f) of the Child Support Performance and Incentive Act of 1998. Receipt of this Notice from the Issuing Agency constitutes receipt of a Medical Child Support Order under applicable law. The rights of the parties and the duties of the plan administrator under this Notice are in addition to the existing rights and duties established under such law. The information on the Custodial Parent and Child(ren) contained on this page is confidential and should not be shared or disclosed with the Noncustodial Parent.

Issuing Agency: _____ Issuing Agency Address: _____ _____ Date of Notice: _____ Case Number: _____ Telephone Number: _____ FAX Number: _____ Employer Web Site:_____	Court or Administrative Authority: _____ Date of Support Order: _____ Support Order Number: _____

_____
Employer/Withholder's Federal EIN Number

RE: _____
Employee's Name (Last, First, MI)

_____
Employer/Withholder's Name

_____
Employee's Social Security Number

_____
Employer/Withholder's Address

_____
Employee's Address

_____
Custodial Parent's Name (Last, First, MI)

_____
Custodial Parent's Mailing Address

_____
Substituted Official/Agency Name and Address
(Required if Custodial Parent's mailing address is left blank)

_____
Child(ren)'s Mailing Address (if Different from Custodial Parent's)

_____
_____
_____
Name(s), Mailing Address, and Telephone Number of a Representative of the Child(ren)

Child(ren)'s Name(s)	DOB	SSN	Child(ren)'s Name(s)	DOB	SSN
_____	____	____	_____	____	____
_____	____	____	_____	____	____
_____	____	____	_____	____	____

The order requires the child(ren) to be enrolled in ☐ any health coverages available; or ☐ only the following coverage(s): ☐medical; ☐dental; ☐vision; ☐prescription drug; ☐mental health; ☐other (specify):_____

THE PAPERWORK REDUCTION ACT OF 1995 (P.L. 104-13) public reporting burden for this collection of information is estimated to average 20 minutes per response, including the time reviewing instructions, gathering and maintaining the data needed, and reviewing the collection of information. An agency may not conduct or sponsor, and a person is not required to respond to, a collection of information unless it displays a currently valid OMB control number.

OMB control number: 1210-0113 Expiration Date: 10/31/2012.

PLAN ADMINISTRATOR RESPONSE
(To be completed and returned to the Issuing Agency within 40 business days after the date of the Notice, or sooner if reasonable)

Case #_____ (to be completed by the issuing agency)

This Notice was received by the plan administrator on _____.

1. This Notice was determined to be a "qualified medical child support order," on _____.
Complete **Response 2 or 3, and 4**, if applicable.

2. The participant (employee) and alternate recipient(s) (child(ren)) are to be enrolled in the following family coverage.
　　a. The child(ren) is/are currently enrolled in the plan as a dependent of the participant.
　　b. There is only one type of coverage provided under the plan. The child(ren) is/are included as dependents of the participant under the plan.
　　c. The participant is enrolled in an option that is providing dependent coverage and the child(ren) will be enrolled in the same option.
　　d. The participant is enrolled in an option that permits dependent coverage that has not been elected; dependent coverage will be provided.

Coverage is effective as of __/__/____(includes waiting period of less than 90 days from date of receipt of this Notice). The child(ren) has/have been enrolled in the following option (if plan is insured, identify provider, policy and group numbers): _____. Any necessary withholding should commence if the employer determines that it is permitted under State and Federal withholding and/or prioritization limitations.

3. There is more than one option available under the plan and the participant is not enrolled. The Issuing Agency must select from the available options. Each child is to be included as a dependent under one of the available options that provide family coverage. If the Issuing Agency does not reply within 20 business days of the date this Response is returned, the child(ren), and the participant if necessary, will be enrolled in the plan's default option, if any:
_____.

4. The participant is subject to a waiting period that expires __/__/____ (more than 90 days from the date of receipt of this Notice), or has not completed a waiting period which is determined by some measure other than the passage of time, such as the completion of a certain number of hours worked (describe here: _____). At the completion of the waiting period, the plan administrator will process the enrollment.

5. This Notice does not constitute a "qualified medical child support order" because:

The name of the child(ren) or participant is unavailable.

The mailing address of the child(ren) (or a substituted official) or participant is unavailable.

The following child(ren) is/are at or above the age at which dependents are no longer eligible for coverage under the plan _____ (insert name(s) of child(ren)).

Plan Administrator or Representative:

Name: _____ Telephone Number: _____

Title: _____ Date: _____

Address:_____

INSTRUCTIONS TO PLAN ADMINISTRATOR

This Notice has been forwarded from the employer identified above to you as the plan administrator of a group health plan maintained by the employer (or a group health plan to which the employer contributes) and in which the noncustodial parent/participant identified above is enrolled or is eligible for enrollment.

This Notice serves to inform you that the noncustodial parent/participant is obligated by an order issued by the court or agency identified above to provide health care coverage for the child(ren) under the group health plan(s) as described on **Part B**.

(A) If the participant and child(ren) and their mailing addresses (or that of a Substituted Official or Agency) are identified above, and if coverage for the child(ren) is or will become available, this Notice constitutes a "qualified medical child support order"(QMCSO) under ERISA or CSPIA, as applicable. (If any mailing address is not present, but it is reasonably accessible, this Notice will not fail to be a QMCSO on that basis.) You must, within 40 business days of the date of this Notice, or sooner if reasonable:

(1) Complete Part B - Plan Administrator Response - and send it to the Issuing Agency:

(a) if you checked Response 2:

(i) notify the noncustodial parent/participant named above, each named child, and the custodial parent that coverage of the child(ren) is or will become available (notification of the custodial parent will be deemed notification of the child(ren) if they reside at the same address);

(ii) furnish the custodial parent a description of the coverage available and the effective date of the coverage, including, if not already provided, a summary plan description and any forms, documents, or information necessary to effectuate such coverage, as well as information necessary to submit claims for benefits;

(b) if you checked Response 3:

(i) if you have not already done so, provide to the Issuing Agency copies of applicable summary plan descriptions or other documents that describe available coverage including the additional participant contribution necessary to obtain coverage for the child(ren) under each option and whether there is a limited service area for any option;

(ii) if the plan has a default option, you are to enroll the child(ren) in the default option if you have not received an election from the Issuing Agency within 20 business days of the date you returned the Response. If the plan does not have a default option, you are to enroll the child(ren) in the option selected by the Issuing Agency.

(c) if the participant is subject to a waiting period that expires more than 90 days from the date of receipt of this Notice, or has not completed a waiting period whose duration is determined by a measure other than the passage of time (for example, the completion of a certain number of hours worked), complete Response 4 on the Plan Administrator Response and return to the employer and the Issuing Agency, and notify the participant and the custodial parent; and upon satisfaction of the period or requirement, complete enrollment under Response 2 or 3, and

(d) upon completion of the enrollment, transfer the applicable information on Part B - Plan Administrator Response to the employer for a determination that the necessary employee contributions are available. Inform the employer that the enrollment is pursuant to a National Medical Support Notice.

(B) If within 40 business days of the date of this Notice, or sooner if reasonable, you determine that this Notice does not constitute a QMCSO, you must complete Response 5 of Part B - Plan Administrator Response and send it to the Issuing Agency, and inform the noncustodial parent/participant, custodial parent, and child(ren) of the specific reasons for your determination.

(C) Any required notification of the custodial parent, child(ren) and/or participant may be satisfied by sending the party a copy of the Plan Administrator Response, if appropriate. You may choose to furnish these notifications electronically in accordance with the requirements of the Department of Labor's electronic disclosure regulation codified at 29 C.F.R. 2520.104b-1(c).

UNLAWFUL REFUSAL TO ENROLL

Enrollment of a child may not be denied on the ground that: (1) the child was born out of wedlock; (2) the child is not claimed as a dependent on the participant's Federal income tax return; (3) the child does not reside with the participant or in the plan's service area; or (4) because the child is receiving benefits or is eligible to receive benefits under the State Medicaid plan. If the plan requires that the participant be enrolled in order for the child(ren) to be enrolled, and the participant is not currently enrolled, you must enroll both the participant and the child(ren) regardless of whether the participant has applied for enrollment in the plan. All enrollments are to be made without regard to open season restrictions.

PAYMENT OF CLAIMS

A child covered by a QMCSO, or the child's custodial parent, legal guardian, or the provider of services to the child, or a State agency to the extent assigned the child's rights, may file claims and the plan shall make payment for covered benefits or reimbursement directly to such party.

PERIOD OF COVERAGE

The alternate recipient(s) shall be treated as dependents under the terms of the plan. Coverage of an alternate recipient as a dependent will end when similarly situated dependents are no longer eligible for coverage under the terms of the plan. However, the continuation coverage provisions of ERISA or other applicable law may entitle the alternate recipient to continue coverage under the plan. Once a child is enrolled in the plan as directed above, the alternate recipient may not be disenrolled unless:

(1) The plan administrator is provided satisfactory written evidence that either:
(a) the court or administrative child support order referred to above is no longer in effect, or
(b) the alternate recipient is or will be enrolled in comparable coverage which will take effect no later than the effective date of disenrollment from the plan;

(2) The employer eliminates family health coverage for all of its employees; or

(3) Any available continuation coverage is not elected, or the period of such coverage expires.

CONTACT FOR QUESTIONS

If you have any questions regarding this Notice, you may contact the Issuing Agency at the address and telephone number listed above.

Paperwork Reduction Act Notice

The Issuing Agency asks for the information on this form to carry out the law as specified in the Employee Retirement Income Security Act or the Child Support Performance and Incentive Act, as applicable. You are required to give the Issuing Agency the information. You are not required to respond to this collection of information unless it displays a currently valid OMB control number. The Issuing Agency needs the information to determine whether health care coverage is provided in accordance with the underlying child support order. The average time needed to complete and file the form is estimated below. These times will vary depending on the individual circumstances.

	__Learning about the law or the form__		__Preparing the form__
First Notice	1 hr.__	....	1 hr., 45 min.
Subsequent Notices	-----	....	20 min.

Model Blackout Notice

The model notice provided by the DOL below is intended to assist plan administrators in discharging their notice obligations under ERISA Section 101(i) and Labor Regulation Section 2520.101-3. Use of the model notice is not mandatory. However, a notice that uses the statements provided in Paragraph 4 and Paragraph 5(A) of the Model Notice will be deemed by the DOL to satisfy the notice content requirements of Labor Regulation Sections 2520.101-3(b)(1)(iv) and 2520.101-3(b)(1)(v)(A), respectively. The DOL notes that compliance with the notice content requirements of ERISA Section 101(i) and Labor Regulation Section 2520.101-3 will depend on the facts and circumstances pertaining to the particular blackout period and plan.

The Model Notice is intended to deal solely with the content requirements prescribed in Labor Regulation Section 2520.101-3(b)(1) and not other matters with respect to which disclosure may be required, such as changes in investment options.

Important Notice Concerning Your Rights Under the [Enter Name of Individual Account Plan]

[Enter date of notice]

1. This notice is to inform you that the [enter name of plan] will be [enter reasons for blackout period, as appropriate: changing investment options, changing recordkeepers, etc.].

2. As a result of these changes, you temporarily will be unable to [enter as appropriate: direct or diversify investments in your individual accounts (if only specific investments are subject to the blackout, those investments should be specifically identified), obtain a loan from the plan, or obtain a distribution from the plan]. This period, during which you will be unable to exercise these rights otherwise available under the plan, is called a "blackout period." Whether or not you are planning retirement in the near future, we encourage you to carefully consider how this blackout period may affect your retirement planning, as well as your overall financial plan.

3. The blackout period for the plan will begin on [enter date] and end [enter date]. During these weeks, you can determine whether the **blackout** period has started or ended by [enter instructions for use toll-free number or accessing web site].

4. [In the case of investments affected by the blackout period, enter the following: During the blackout period you will be unable to direct or diversify the assets held in your plan account. For this reason, it is very important that you review and consider the appropriateness of your current investments in light of your inability to direct or diversify those investments during the blackout period. For your long-term retirement security, you should give careful consideration to the importance of a well-balanced and diversified investment portfolio, taking into account all your assets, income and investments. You should be aware that there is a risk to holding substantial portions of your assets in the securities of any one company, as individual securities tend to have wider price swings, up and down, in short periods of time, than investments in diversified funds. Stocks that have wide price swings might have a large loss during the blackout period, and you would not be able to direct the sale of such stocks from your account during the blackout period.]

5. [If timely notice cannot be provided (see paragraph (b)(1)(v) of the Regulation) enter: (A) Federal law generally requires that you be furnished notice of a blackout period at least 30 days in advance of the last date on which you could exercise your affected rights immediately before the commencement of any blackout period in order to provide you with sufficient time to consider the effect of the blackout period on your retirement and financial plans. (B) [Enter explanation of reasons for inability to furnish 30 days advance notice.]]

6. If you have any questions concerning this notice, you should contact [enter name, address and telephone number of the plan administrator or other person responsible for answering questions about the blackout period].

Model COBRA Continuation
Coverage Election Notice[1]
(For use by single-employer group health plans)

[Enter date of notice]

Dear: [Identify the qualified beneficiary(ies), by name or status]

This notice contains important information about your right to continue your health care coverage in the [*enter name of group health plan*] (the Plan), <u>as well as other health coverage alternatives that may be available to you through the Health Insurance Marketplace.</u> Please read the information contained in this notice very carefully.

To elect COBRA continuation coverage, follow the instructions on the next page to complete the enclosed Election Form and submit it to us.

If you do not elect COBRA continuation coverage, your coverage under the Plan will end on [*enter date*] due to [*check appropriate box*]:

❑ End of employment ❑ Reduction in hours of employment

❑ Death of employee ❑ Divorce or legal separation

❑ Entitlement to Medicare ❑ Loss of dependent child status

Each person ("qualified beneficiary") in the category(ies) checked below is entitled to elect COBRA continuation coverage, which will continue group health care coverage under the Plan for up to ____ months [*enter 18 or 36, as appropriate and check appropriate box or boxes; names may be added*]:

❑ Employee or former employee

❑ Spouse or former spouse

❑ Dependent child(ren) covered under the Plan on the day before the event that caused the loss of coverage

❑ Child who is losing coverage under the Plan because he or she is no longer a dependent under the Plan

If elected, COBRA continuation coverage will begin on [*enter date*] and can last until [*enter date*]. [*Add, if appropriate:* You may elect any of the following options for COBRA continuation coverage: [*list available coverage options*].

COBRA continuation coverage will cost: [*enter amount each qualified beneficiary will be required to pay for each option per month of coverage and any other permitted coverage periods.*] You do not have to send any payment with the Election Form. Important additional information about payment for COBRA continuation coverage is included in the pages following the Election Form.

<u>There may be other coverage options for you and your family. When key parts of the health care law take effect, you'll be able to buy coverage through the Health Insurance Marketplace. In the Marketplace, you could be eligible for a new kind of tax credit that lowers your monthly premiums right away, and you can see what your premium, deductibles, and out-of-pocket costs will be before you make a decision to enroll. Being eligible for COBRA does not limit your eligibility for coverage for a tax credit through the Marketplace. Additionally, you may qualify for a special enrollment opportunity for another group health plan for which you are eligible (such as a spouse's plan), even if the plan generally does not accept late enrollees, if you request enrollment within 30 days.</u>

If you have any questions about this notice or your rights to COBRA continuation coverage, you should contact [*enter name of party responsible for COBRA administration for the Plan, with telephone number and address*].

---

1. Revised DOL COBRA election notice with changes tracked. Text insertions are underlined. Text deletions are shown as strikethrough text.

COBRA Continuation Coverage Election Form

Instructions: To elect COBRA continuation coverage, complete this Election Form and return it to us. Under federal law, you must have 60 days after the date of this notice to decide whether you want to elect COBRA continuation coverage under the Plan.

Send completed Election Form to: [*Enter Name and Address*]

This Election Form must be completed and returned by mail [*or describe other means of submission and due date*]. If mailed, it must be post-marked no later than [*enter date*].

If you do not submit a completed Election Form by the due date shown above, you will lose your right to elect COBRA continuation coverage. If you reject COBRA continuation coverage before the due date, you may change your mind as long as you furnish a completed Election Form before the due date. However, if you change your mind after first rejecting COBRA continuation coverage, your COBRA continuation coverage will begin on the date you furnish the completed Election Form.

Read the important information about your rights included in the pages after the Election Form.

I (We) elect COBRA continuation coverage in the [*enter name of plan*] (the Plan) as indicated below:

Name	Date of Birth	Relationship to Employee	SSN (or other identifier)

a. _____

   [*Add if appropriate:* Coverage option elected: _____]

b. _____

   [*Add if appropriate:* Coverage option elected: _____]

c. _____

   [*Add if appropriate:* Coverage option elected: _____]

_____   _____
Signature   Date

_____   _____
Print Name   Relationship to individual(s) listed above

_____
_____   _____
Print Address   Telephone number

Important Information

About Your COBRA Continuation Coverage Rights

What is continuation coverage?

Federal law requires that most group health plans (including this Plan) give employees and their families the opportunity to continue their health care coverage when there is a "qualifying event" that would result in a loss of coverage under an employer's plan. Depending on the type of qualifying event, "qualified beneficiaries" can include the employee (or retired employee) covered under the group health plan, the covered employee's spouse, and the dependent children of the covered employee.

Continuation coverage is the same coverage that the Plan gives to other participants or beneficiaries under the Plan who are not receiving continuation coverage. Each qualified beneficiary who elects continuation coverage will have the same rights under the Plan as other participants or beneficiaries covered under the Plan, including [add if applicable: open enrollment and] special enrollment rights.

How long will continuation coverage last?

In the case of a loss of coverage due to end of employment or reduction in hours of employment, coverage generally may be continued only for up to a total of 18 months. In the case of losses of coverage due to an employee's death, divorce or legal separation, the employee's becoming entitled to Medicare benefits or a dependent child ceasing to be a dependent under the terms of the plan, coverage may be continued for up to a total of 36 months. When the qualifying event is the end of employment or reduction of the employee's hours of employment, and the employee became entitled to Medicare benefits less than 18 months before the qualifying event, COBRA continuation coverage for qualified beneficiaries other than the employee lasts until 36 months after the date of Medicare entitlement. This notice shows the maximum period of continuation coverage available to the qualified beneficiaries.

Continuation coverage will be terminated before the end of the maximum period if:

- any required premium is not paid in full on time,

- a qualified beneficiary becomes covered, after electing continuation coverage, under another group health plan that does not impose any pre-existing condition exclusion for a pre-existing condition of the qualified beneficiary (note: there are limitations on plans' imposing a preexisting condition exclusion and such exclusions will become prohibited beginning in 2014 under the Affordable Care Act),

- a qualified beneficiary becomes entitled to Medicare benefits (under Part A, Part B, or both) after electing continuation coverage, or

- the employer ceases to provide any group health plan for its employees.

Continuation coverage may also be terminated for any reason the Plan would terminate coverage of a participant or beneficiary not receiving continuation coverage (such as fraud).

[If the maximum period shown on page 1 of this notice is less than 36 months, add the following three paragraphs:]

How can you extend the length of COBRA continuation coverage?

If you elect continuation coverage, an extension of the maximum period of coverage may be available if a qualified beneficiary is disabled or a second qualifying event occurs. You must notify [enter name of party responsible for COBRA administration] of a disability or a second qualifying event in order to extend the period of continuation coverage. Failure to provide notice of a disability or second qualifying event may affect the right to extend the period of continuation coverage.

Disability

An 11-month extension of coverage may be available if any of the qualified beneficiaries is determined by the Social Security Administration (SSA) to be disabled. The disability has to have started at some time before the 60th day of COBRA continuation coverage and must last at least until the end of the 18-month period of continuation coverage. [*Describe Plan provisions for requiring notice of disability determination, including time frames and procedures.*] Each qualified beneficiary who has elected continuation coverage will be entitled to the 11-month disability extension if one of them qualifies. If the qualified beneficiary is determined by SSA to no longer be disabled, you must notify the Plan of that fact within 30 days after SSA's determination.

Second Qualifying Event

An 18-month extension of coverage will be available to spouses and dependent children who elect continuation coverage if a second qualifying event occurs during the first 18 months of continuation coverage. The maximum amount of continuation coverage available when a second qualifying event occurs is 36 months. Such second qualifying events may include the death of a covered employee, divorce or separation from the covered employee, the covered employee's becoming entitled to Medicare benefits (under Part A, Part B, or both), or a dependent child's ceasing to be eligible for coverage as a dependent under the Plan. These events can be a second qualifying event only if they would have caused the qualified beneficiary to lose coverage under the Plan if the first qualifying event had not occurred. You must notify the Plan within 60 days after a second qualifying event occurs if you want to extend your continuation coverage.

How can you elect COBRA continuation coverage?

To elect continuation coverage, you must complete the Election Form and furnish it according to the directions on the form. Each qualified beneficiary has a separate right to elect continuation coverage. For example, the employee's spouse may elect continuation coverage even if the employee does not. Continuation coverage may be elected for only one, several, or for all dependent children who are qualified beneficiaries. A parent may elect to continue coverage on behalf of any dependent children. The employee or the employee's spouse can elect continuation coverage on behalf of all of the qualified beneficiaries.

~~In considering whether to elect continuation coverage, you should take into account that a failure to continue your group health coverage will affect your future rights under federal law. First, you can lose the right to avoid having pre-existing condition exclusions applied to you by other group health plans if you have more than a 63-day gap in health coverage, and election of continuation coverage may help you not have such a gap. Second, you will lose the guaranteed right to purchase individual health insurance policies that do not impose such pre-existing condition exclusions if you do not get continuation coverage for the maximum time available to you. Finally~~

In considering whether to elect continuation coverage, you should take into account that you have special enrollment rights under federal law. You have the right to request special enrollment in another group health plan for which you are otherwise eligible (such as a plan sponsored by your spouse's employer) within 30 days after your group health coverage ends because of the qualifying event listed above. You will also have the same special enrollment right at the end of continuation coverage if you get continuation coverage for the maximum time available to you.

How much does COBRA continuation coverage cost?

Generally, each qualified beneficiary may be required to pay the entire cost of continuation coverage. The amount a qualified beneficiary may be required to pay may not exceed 102 percent (or, in the case of an extension of continuation coverage due to a disability, 150 percent) of the cost to the group health plan (including both employer and employee contributions) for coverage of a similarly situated plan participant or beneficiary who is not receiving continuation coverage. The required payment for each continuation coverage period for each option is described in this notice.

~~[If employees might be eligible for trade adjustment assistance, the following information may be added: The Trade Act of 2002 created a new tax credit for certain individuals who become eligible for trade adjustment assistance and~~

~~for certain retired employees who are receiving pension payments from the Pension Benefit Guaranty Corporation (PBGC) (eligible individuals). Under the new tax provisions, eligible individuals can either take a tax credit or get advance payment of 65% of premiums paid for qualified health insurance, including continuation coverage. If you have questions about these new tax provisions, you may call the Health Coverage Tax Credit Customer Contact Center toll-free at 1-866-628-4282. TTD/TTY callers may call toll-free at 1-866-626-4282. More information about the Trade Act is also available at www.doleta.gov/tradeact/2002act_index.cfm.~~

When and how must payment for COBRA continuation coverage be made?

First payment for continuation coverage

If you elect continuation coverage, you do not have to send any payment with the Election Form. However, you must make your first payment for continuation coverage not later than 45 days after the date of your election. (This is the date the Election Notice is post-marked, if mailed.) If you do not make your first payment for continuation coverage in full not later than 45 days after the date of your election, you will lose all continuation coverage rights under the Plan. You are responsible for making sure that the amount of your first payment is correct. You may contact [*enter appropriate contact information, e.g., the Plan Administrator or other party responsible for COBRA administration under the Plan*] to confirm the correct amount of your first payment.

Periodic payments for continuation coverage

After you make your first payment for continuation coverage, you will be required to make periodic payments for each subsequent coverage period. The amount due for each coverage period for each qualified beneficiary is shown in this notice. The periodic payments can be made on a monthly basis. Under the Plan, each of these periodic payments for continuation coverage is due on the [*enter due day for each monthly payment*] for that coverage period. [*If Plan offers other payment schedules, enter with appropriate dates:* You may instead make payments for continuation coverage for the following coverage periods, due on the following dates:]. If you make a periodic payment on or before the first day of the coverage period to which it applies, your coverage under the Plan will continue for that coverage period without any break. The Plan [*select one:* will *or* will not] send periodic notices of payments due for these coverage periods.

Grace periods for periodic payments

Although periodic payments are due on the dates shown above, you will be given a grace period of 30 days after the first day of the coverage period [*or enter longer period permitted by Plan*] to make each periodic payment. Your continuation coverage will be provided for each coverage period as long as payment for that coverage period is made before the end of the grace period for that payment. [*If Plan suspends coverage during grace period for nonpayment, enter and modify as necessary:* However, if you pay a periodic payment later than the first day of the coverage period to which it applies, but before the end of the grace period for the coverage period, your coverage under the Plan will be suspended as of the first day of the coverage period and then retroactively reinstated (going back to the first day of the coverage period) when the periodic payment is received. This means that any claim you submit for benefits while your coverage is suspended may be denied and may have to be resubmitted once your coverage is reinstated.]

If you fail to make a periodic payment before the end of the grace period for that coverage period, you will lose all rights to continuation coverage under the Plan.

Your first payment and all periodic payments for continuation coverage should be sent to:

[*enter appropriate payment address*]

For more information

This notice does not fully describe continuation coverage or other rights under the Plan. More information about continuation coverage and your rights under the Plan is available in your summary plan description or from the Plan Administrator.

If you have any questions concerning the information in this notice, your rights to coverage, or if you want a copy of your summary plan description, you should contact [*enter name of party responsible for COBRA administration for the Plan, with telephone number and address*].

For more information about your rights under ERISA, including COBRA, the Health Insurance Portability and Accountability Act (HIPAA), and other laws affecting group health plans, contact visit the U.S. Department of Labor's Employee Benefits Security Administration (EBSA) website at ~~in your area or visit the EBSA website~~ atwww.dol.gov/ebsa or call their toll-free number at 1-866-444-3272. ~~(Addresses and phone numbers of Regional and District EBSA Offices are available through EBSA's website.)~~ For more information about health insurance options available through a Health Insurance Marketplace, visit www.healthcare.gov.

Keep Your Plan Informed of Address Changes

In order to protect your and your family's rights, you should keep the Plan Administrator informed of any changes in your address and the addresses of family members. You should also keep a copy, for your records, of any notices you send to the Plan Administrator.

Paperwork Reduction Act Statement

According to the Paperwork Reduction Act of 1995 (Pub. L. 104-13) (PRA), no persons are required to respond to a collection of information unless such collection displays a valid Office of Management and Budget (OMB) control number. The Department notes that a Federal agency cannot conduct or sponsor a collection of information unless it is approved by OMB under the PRA, and displays a currently valid OMB control number, and the public is not required to respond to a collection of information unless it displays a currently valid OMB control number. See 44 U.S.C. 3507. Also, notwithstanding any other provisions of law, no person shall be subject to penalty for failing to comply with a collection of information if the collection of information does not display a currently valid OMB control number. See 44 U.S.C. 3512.

The public reporting burden for this collection of information is estimated to average approximately four minutes per respondent. Interested parties are encouraged to send comments regarding the burden estimate or any other aspect of this collection of information, including suggestions for reducing this burden, to the U.S. Department of Labor, Office of the Chief Information Officer, Attention: Departmental Clearance Officer, 200 Constitution Avenue, N.W., Room N-1301, Washington, DC 20210 or email DOL_PRA_PUBLIC@dol.gov and reference the OMB Control Number 1210-0123.

OMB Control Number 1210-0123 (expires 09/30/2013)

Abandoned Plans
Model Notice of Intent to Terminate Plan

A qualified termination administrator may use this notice to inform a plan sponsor of a proposed termination, pursuant to § 2578.1(b)(5).

Appendix A To § 2578.1
Notice of Intent to Terminate Plan

[Date of notice]

[Name of plan sponsor]

[Last known address of plan sponsor]

Re: [Name of plan and account number or other identifying information]

Dear [Name of plan sponsor]:

We are writing to advise you of our concern about the status of the subject plan. Our intention is to terminate the plan and distribute benefits in accordance with federal law if you do not contact us within 30 days of your receipt of this notice. See 29 CFR 2578.1.

Our basis for taking this action is that our records reflect that there have been no contributions to, or distributions from, the plan within the past 12 months. {If the basis for sending this notice is under § 29 CFR 2578.1(b)(1)(i)(B), complete and include the sentence below rather than the sentence above.} Our basis for taking this action is {provide a description of the facts and circumstances indicating plan abandonment}.

We are sending this notice to you because our records show that you are the sponsor of the subject plan. The U.S. Department of Labor requires that you be informed that, as a fiduciary or plan administrator or both, you may be personally liable for all costs, civil penalties, excise taxes, etc. as a result of your acts or omissions with respect to this plan. The termination of this plan by us will not relieve you of your liability for any such costs, penalties, taxes, etc. Federal law also requires us to notify the U.S. Department of Labor, Employee Benefits Security Administration, of the termination of any abandoned plan. For information about the federal law governing the termination of abandoned plans, you may contact the U.S. Department of Labor at 1.866.444.EBSA (3272).

Please contact [name, address, and telephone number of the person, office, or department that the sponsor must contact regarding the plan] within 30 days in order to prevent this action.

Sincerely,

[Name and address of qualified termination administrator or appropriate designee]

Model Notice of Plan Abandonment and Intent to Serve as Qualified Termination Administrator

An entity may use this notice to inform EBSA that it elects to serve as a qualified termination administrator for a particular plan, pursuant to § 2578.1(c)(3).

Appendix B To § 2578.1

Notification of Plan Abandonment and Intent to Serve as Qualified Termination Administrator

[Date of notice]

Abandoned Plan Coordinator, Office of Enforcement
Employee Benefits Security Administration
U.S. Department of Labor
200 Constitution Ave., NW, Suite 600
Washington, DC, 20210

Re:	Plan Identification	Qualified Termination Administrator
	[Plan name and plan number]	[Name]
	[EIN]	[Address]
	[Plan account number]	[E-mail address]
	[Address]	[Telephone number]
	[Telephone number]	[EIN]

Abandoned Plan Coordinator:

Pursuant to 29 CFR 2578.1(b), we have determined that the subject plan is or may become abandoned by its sponsor. We are eligible to serve as a Qualified Termination Administrator for purposes of terminating and winding up the plan in accordance with 29 CFR 2578.1, and hereby elect to do so.

We find that the {check the appropriate box below and provide additional information as necessary}:

❑   There have been no contributions to, or distributions from, the plan for a period of at least 12 consecutive months immediately preceding the date of this letter. Our records indicate that the date of the last contribution or distribution was {enter appropriate date}.

❑   The following facts and circumstances suggest that the plan is or may become abandoned by the plan sponsor {add description below}:

_____

_____

_____

We have also determined that the plan sponsor {check appropriate box below}:

❑   No longer exists

❑   Cannot be located

❑   Is unable to maintain the plan

We have taken the following steps to locate or communicate with the known plan sponsor and have received no objection {provide an explanation below}:

_____

_____

_____

Part I – Plan Information

1. Estimated number of individuals (participants and beneficiaries) with accounts under the plan: [number]

2. Plan assets held by Qualified Termination Administrator:

   A. Estimated value of assets: [value]

   B. Months we have held plan assets, if less than 12:   [number]

   C. Hard to value assets {select "yes" or "no" to identify any assets with no readily ascertainable fair market value, and include for those identified assets the best known estimate of their value}:

		Yes	No	
(a)	Partnership/joint venture interests	❏	❏	[value]
(b)	Employer real property	❏	❏	[value]
(c)	Real estate (other than (b))	❏	❏	[value]
(d)	Employer securities	❏	❏	[value]
(e)	Participant loans	❏	❏	[value]
(f)	Loans (other than (e))	❏	❏	[value]
(g)	Tangible personal property	❏	❏	[value]

3. Name and last known address and telephone number of plan sponsor:

   _____

   _____

4. Other:_____

   _____

   _____

   _____

Part II – Known Service Providers of the Plan

	Name	Address	Telephone
1.			
2.			
3.			

Part III – Services and Related Expenses to be Paid

Services	Service Provider	Estimated Cost

1. _____

2. _____

3. _____

Part IV – Investigation

In the past 24 months {check one box}:

❏   Neither we nor our affiliates are or have been the subject of an investigation, examination, or enforcement action by the Department, Internal Revenue Service, or Securities and Exchange Commission concerning such entity's conduct as a fiduciary or party in interest with respect to any plan covered by the Act.

❏   We or our affiliates are or have been the subject of an investigation, examination, or enforcement action by the Department, Internal Revenue Service, or Securities and Exchange Commission concerning such entity's conduct as a fiduciary or party in interest with respect to any plan covered by the Act.

Part V – Contact Person
{enter information only if different from signatory}:

[Name]

[Address]

[E-mail address]

[Telephone number]

Under penalties of perjury, I declare that I have examined this notice and to the best of my knowledge and belief, it is true, correct and complete.

[Signature]

[Title of person signing on behalf the Qualified Termination Administrator]

[Address, e-mail address, and telephone number]

Model Notice of Plan Termination

A qualified termination administrator may use this notice to inform participants and beneficiaries of the termination, pursuant to § 2578.1(d)(2)(vi).

Appendix C To § 2578.1

Notice of Plan Termination

[Date of notice]

[Name and last known address of plan participant or beneficiary] Re: [Name of plan]

Dear [Name of plan participant or beneficiary]:

We are writing to inform you that the [name of plan] (Plan) has been terminated pursuant to regulations issued by the U.S Department of Labor. The Plan was terminated because it was abandoned by [name of the plan sponsor].

We have determined that you have an interest in the Plan, either as a plan participant or beneficiary. Your account balance on [date] is/was [account balance]. We will be distributing this money as permitted under the terms of the Plan and federal regulations. The actual amount of your distribution may be more or less than the amount stated in this letter depending on investment gains or losses and the administrative cost of terminating the Plan and distributing your benefits.

Your distribution options under the Plan are {add a description of the Plan's distribution options}. It is very important that you elect one of these forms of distribution and inform us of your election. The process for informing us of this election is {enter a description of the election process established by the qualified termination administrator}.

{Select the next paragraph from options 1 through 3, as appropriate.}

{Option 1: If this notice is for a participant or beneficiary, complete and include the following paragraph provided the account balance does not meet the conditions of §2550.404a-3(d)(1)(iii).}

If you do not make an election within 30 days from your receipt of this notice, your account balance will be transferred directly to an individual retirement plan (inherited individual retirement plan in the case of a nonspouse beneficiary) maintained by {insert the name, address, and phone number of the provider if known, other wise insert the following language [a bank or insurance company or other similar financial institution]}. Pursuant to federal law, your money in the individual retirement plan would then be invested in an investment product designed to preserve principal and provide a reasonable rate of return and liquidity. {If fee information is known, include the following sentence: Should your money be transferred into an individual retirement plan, [name of the financial institution] charges the following fees for its services: {add a statement of fees, if any, that will be paid from the participant or beneficiary's individual retirement plan}.}

{Option 2: If this notice is for a participant or beneficiary whose account balance meets the conditions of §2550.404a-3(d)(1)(iii), complete and include the following paragraph.}

If you do not make an election within 30 days from your receipt of this notice, and your account balance is $1,000 or less, federal law permits us to transfer your balance to an interest-bearing federally insured bank account, to the unclaimed property fund of the State of your last known address, or to an individual retirement plan (inherited individual retirement plan in the case of a nonspouse beneficiary). Pursuant to federal law, your money, if transferred to an individual retirement plan would then be invested in an investment product designed to preserve principal and provide a reasonable rate of return and liquidity. {If known, include the name, address, and telephone number of the financial institution or State fund into which the individual's account balance will be transferred or deposited. If the individual's account balance is to be transferred to a financial institution and fee information is known, include the following sentence: Should your money be transferred into a plan or account, [name of the financial institution] charges the following fees for its services: {add a statement of fees, if any, that will be paid from the individual's account}.}

{Option 3: If this notice is for a participant or participant's spouse whose distribution is subject to the survivor annuity requirements in sections 401(a)(11) and 417 of the Internal Revenue Code (or section 205 of ERISA), complete and include the following paragraph.}

If you do not make an election within 30 days from your receipt of this notice, your account balance will be distributed in the form of a qualified joint and survivor annuity or qualified preretirement annuity as required by the Internal Revenue Code. {If the name of the annuity provider is known, include the following sentence: The name of the annuity provider is [name, address and phone number of the provider].}

For more information about the termination, your account balance, or distribution options, please contact [name, address, and telephone number of the qualified termination administrator an4 if different; the name, address, and telephone number of the appropriate contact person].

Sincerely,

[Name of qualified termination administrator or appropriate designee]

As revised effective March 19, 2007 in connection with the amendments to DOL regulation section 2578.1 relating to the termination of abandoned individual account plans, and applicable to distributions made on or after March 19, 2007.

Appendix to § 2550.404a-3

Notice of Plan Termination

[Date of notice]

[Name and last known address of plan participant or beneficiary] Re: [Name of plan]

Dear [Name of plan participant or beneficiary]:

This notice is to inform you that [name of the plan] (the Plan) has been terminated and we are in the process of winding it up.

We have determined that you have an interest in the Plan, either as a plan participant or beneficiary. Your account balance in the Plan on [date] is/was [account balance]. We will be distributing this money as permitted under the terms of the Plan and federal regulations. {If applicable, insert the following sentence: The actual amount of your distribution may be more or less than the amount stated in this notice depending on investment gains or losses and the administrative cost of terminating your plan and distributing your benefits.}

Your distribution options under the Plan are {add a description of the Plan's distribution option). It is very important that you elect one of these forms of distribution and inform us of your election. The process for informing us of this election is {enter a description of the Plan's election process}.

If you do not make an election within 30 days from your receipt of this notice, your account balance will be transferred directly to an individual retirement plan (inherited individual retirement plan in the case of a nonspouse beneficiary). {If the name of the provider of the individual retirement plan is blown, include the following sentence: The name of the provider of the individual retirement plan is [name, address and phone number of the individual retirement plan provider].} Pursuant to federal law, your money in the individual retirement plan would then be invested in an investment product designed to preserve principal and provide a reasonable rate of return and liquidity. {If fee information is known, include the following sentence: Should your money be transferred into an individual retirement plan, [name of the financial institution] charges the following fees for its services: {add a statement of fees, if any, that will be paid from the participant or beneficiary's individual retirement plan}.}

For more information about the termination, your account balance, or distribution options, please contact [name, address, and telephone number of the plan administrator or other appropriate contact person].

Sincerely,

[Name of plan administrator or appropriate designee]

As revised effective March 19, 2007 in connection with the amendments to DOL regulation section 2550.404a-3 relating to the safe harbor for distributions from terminated individual account plans, and applicable to distributions made on or after March 19, 2007.

Model Final Notice

A qualified termination administrator may use this notice to inform EBSA that the termination process has been completed and that all benefits have been distributed, pursuant to § 2578.1(d)(2)(ix).

Appendix D To § 2578.1
Final Notice

[Date of notice]

Abandoned Plan Coordinator, Office of Enforcement
Employee Benefits Security Administration
U.S. Department of Labor
200 Constitution Ave., NW, Suite 600
Washington, DC, 20210

Re:	Plan Identification	Qualified Termination Administrator
	[Plan name and plan number]	[Name]
	[Plan account number]	[Address and e-mail address]
	[EIN]	[Telephone number]
		[EIN]

Abandoned Plan Coordinator:
General Information

The termination and winding-up process of the subject plan has been completed pursuant to 29 CFR 2578.1. Benefits were distributed to participants and beneficiaries on the basis of the best available information pursuant to 29 CFR 2578.1(d)(2)(i). Plan expenses were paid out of plan assets pursuant to 29 CFR 2578.1(d)(2)(v).

{Include and complete the next section, entitled "Contact Person," only if the contact person is different from the signatory of this notice.}

Contact Person

[Name]

[Address and e-mail address]

[Telephone number]

{Include and complete the next section, entitled "Expenses Paid to Qualified Termination Administrator," only if fees and expenses paid to the QTA (or its affiliate) exceeded by 20 percent or more the estimate required by 29 CFR 2578.1(c)(3)(v)(B).}

Expenses Paid to Qualified Termination Administrator

The actual fees and/or expenses we received in connection with winding up the Plan exceeded by {insert either: [20 percent or more] or [enter the actual percentage]} the estimate required by 29 CFR 2578.1(c)(3)(v)(B). The reason or reasons for such additional costs are {provide an explanation of the additional costs}.

Other

Under penalties of perjury, I declare that I have examined this notice and to the best of my knowledge and belief, it is true, correct and complete.

[Signature]
[Title of person signing on behalf the Qualified Termination Administrator]
[Address, e-mail address, and telephone number]
Attachment
Source for the Model Notices: *http://www.dol.gov/ebsa/compliance_assistance.html#section*

Sample Notice – Delinquent Service Provider Disclosure

A qualified termination administrator may use this notice to inform EBSA that the termination process has been completed and that all benefits have been distributed, pursuant to § 2578.1(d)(2)(ix).

[Date of notice]

Delinquent Service Provider Disclosure Coordinator,
Office of Enforcement
Employee Benefits Security Administration
U.S. Department of Labor
200 Constitution Ave., N.W., Suite 600
Washington, DC 20210

Re: [Plan Name]
      [Sponsor EIN/Plan number]
      [Plan sponsor's name;address]

Delinquent Service Provider Disclosure Coordinator:

The employee benefit plan referred to above has entered into a contract or arrangement for the provision of services with the following service provider:

     [Name of covered service provider]
     [Address of covered service provider]
     [EIN of covered service provider, if known]
     [Contact person for covered service provider]
     [Telephone Number of contact person]

This matter relates to the following services provided to the plan by the service provider:

     [Brief description of services provided to plan by covered service provider]

I am the responsible plan fiduciary to whom disclosures must be made pursuant to 29 CFR § 2550.408b-2(c)(1). I have determined that the plan has not received the following information from the service provider as of [INSERT DATE]:

[Brief description of information the covered service provider failed or refused to disclose or furnish]

I requested in writing such missing information from the service provider on [INSERT DATE]. As of the date of this letter, the service provider has not submitted the information pursuant to my request.

I acknowledge that I have 30 days following the earlier of the covered service provider's refusal to furnish the requested information or the date which is 90 days after the date of my written request to the service provider to file this notice with the Department in order to fulfill the requirements of paragraph (c)(1)(v) under the Department's regulations at 29 CFR § 2550.408b-2(c)(1).

The covered service provider [chose one]: continues to provide services under the contract or arrangement or was terminated.

Finally, we have the following additional comments/information relating to this matter:

     [Comments/information]

I declare that I have examined this notice and to the best of my knowledge and belief, it is true, correct and complete.

[Signature]
[Title of person signing on behalf of subject plan = i.e., "responsible plan fiduciary"]
[Address, e-mail address, and telephone number]
[Plan sponsor's name, address and telephone number]

APPENDIX B

VFC PROGRAM CHECKLIST AND SAMPLE VFC PROGRAM NO ACTION LETTER

Revised VFC Program Model Application Form; Revised Checklist; Revised Sample No-Action Letter; and IRC 6621(a)(2) and IRC 6621(c)(1) Underpayment Rates Tables.

On April 19, 2006, the Department of Labor published in the Federal Register a 2006 Update of the Voluntary Fiduciary Correction Program ("VFCP"), which simplified and expanded the original VFCP published in 2002. The VFCP is designed to encourage employers to voluntarily comply with the Employee Retirement Income Security Act ("ERISA"), as amended, by self-correcting certain violations of the law. The 2006 Update of the VFCP describes how to apply, the 19 categories of transactions covered, acceptable methods for correcting violations, and examples of potential violations and corrective actions. The DOL issued the Update in response to public and internal comments on the preliminary revision of the VFCP published in April 2005. The 2006 Update of the VFCP was effective May 19, 2006. The DOL also provides applicants conditional relief from payment of excise taxes for certain VFCP transactions under a class exemption related to the VFCP, which is discussed in more detail in Question 396. The amended class exemption was also effective on May 19, 2006. The VFCP and the class exemption related to the VFCP is available on the DOL's website at www.dol.gov/ebsa.

VFCP Model Application Form

This application form provides a recommended format for your Voluntary Fiduciary Correction Program (VFCP) application. Please make sure you include the required VFCP Checklist and all supporting documents identified on the checklist (for example, proof of payment). Submit your application to the appropriate EBSA field office. For full application procedures, consult www.dol.gov/ebsa.

List separately	
Applicant Name	Address
Applicant Name	Address
Applicant Name	Address

Transactions Corrected

Check which transactions listed in the VFCP you have corrected:

❏ Delinquent Participant Contributions and Participant Loan Repayments to Pension Plans

❏ Delinquent Participant Contributions to Insured Welfare Plans

❏ Delinquent Participant Contributions to Welfare Plan Trusts

❏ Loan at Fair Market Interest Rate to a Party in Interest

❏ Loan at Below-Market Interest Rate to a Party in Interest

❏ Loan at Below-Market Interest Rate to a Non-Party in Interest

❏ Loan at Below-Market Interest Rate Due to Delay in Perfecting Plan's Security Interest

❏ Loans Failing to Comply with Plan Provisions for Amount, Duration or Level Amortization

❏ Default Loans

❏ Purchase of an Asset by a Plan from a Party in Interest

❏ Sale of an Asset by a Plan to a Party in Interest

❏ Sale and Leaseback of Real Property to Employer

❏ Purchase of Asset by a Plan from a Non-Party in Interest at More Than Fair Market Value

❏ Sale of an Asset by a Plan to a Non-Party in Interest at Less Than Fair Market Value

❏ Holding of an Illiquid Asset Previously Purchased by a Plan

❏ Payment of Benefits Without Properly Valuing Plan Assets on Which Payment is Based

❑   Duplicative, Excessive, or Unnecessary Compensation Paid by a Plan

❑   Expenses Improperly Paid by a Plan

❑   Payment of Dual Compensation to a Plan Fiduciary

Correction Amount	
Principal Amount: $	Date Paid
Lost Earnings/Restoration of Profit: $	Date Paid

Narrative And Calculations

1. List all persons materially involved in the Breach and its correction (e.g., fiduciaries, service providers):

2. Explain the Breach, including the date(s) it occurred (attach separate sheets if necessary):

3. Explain how the Breach was corrected, by whom, and when (attach separate sheets if necessary):

4. For correction of Delinquent Remittance of Participant Funds, provide a statement from a Plan Official identifying the earliest date on which participant contributions/loan repayments reasonably could have been segregated from the employer's general assets (attach supporting documentation on which Plan Official relied):

     a. Number of days used to determine the date on which participant contributions/loan repayments withheld from employees' pay could reasonably have been segregated from the employer's general assets:

     b. Description of how this was determined:

5. For correction of Delinquent Remittance of Participant Funds, provide a narrative describing the applicant's contribution and/or repayment remittance practices before and after the period of unpaid or late contributions and/or repayments: (attach separate sheets if necessary)

6. Specific calculations demonstrating how Principal Amount and Lost Earnings or Restoration of Profits was calculated: (if the Online Calculator was used, you only need to indicate this and attach a copy of the "Printable Results" page, attach separate sheets if necessary)

     ❑ Online Calculator ("Printable Results" page attached)   ❑ Manual calculation (see attached calculations)

Supplemental Information		
Plan Sponsor Name:	EIN:	Address:
Plan Name:	Plan Number:	
Plan Administrator Name:	EIN:	Address:
Name of Authorized Representative: (submit written authorization signed by the Plan Official	Address:	Telephone:
Name of Contact Person:	Address:	Telephone
Date of Most Recent Annual Report Form 5500 Filing:	For Plan Year Ending:	

Is Applicant Seeking Relief Under PTE 2002-51?

❏ Yes - Either:

    ❏ Submit a copy of the notice to interested parties within 60 calendar days of this application and indicate date of the notice if not on the notice itself; or

    ❏ If you are relying on the exception to the notice requirement contained in section IV.C. of PTE 2002-51, provide a copy of a completed IRS Form 5330 or other written documentation and proof of payment.

❏ No (3 check boxes)

    ❏ "I will pay any applicable excise tax to the IRS;
    ❏ "I have filed Form 5330 and paid excise tax; or
    ❏ "This transaction is not covered by Section 4975 of the Internal Revenue Code".

Proof of Payment

❏ Signed, dated receipt from the recipient of funds transferred to the plan (such as a financial institution)

❏ Canceled check   ❏ Executed wire transfer

❏ Bank statements for the plan's account   ❏ Other:

Disclosure of a current investigation or examination of the plan by an agency, to comply with Section 3(b)(3)(v):

❑ PBGC

❑ Any state attorney general ❑ State:

❑ Any state insurance commissioner ❑ State:

Contact person for the agency identified:

In order to help us improve our service, please indicate how you learned about the VFCP:

Authorization Of Preparer

I have authorized (name of authorized representative) to represent me concerning this VFCP application.

Name of Plan Official   Signature of Plan Official

Penalty of Perjury Statement - The following statement must be signed and dated by a plan fiduciary with knowledge of the transaction that is the subject of the application and by the authorized representative, if any. Each plan official applying under the VFCP must also sign and date the statement, which must accompany any subsequent additions to the application.

Under penalties of perjury I certify that I am not under investigation (as defined in VFCP Section 3(b)(3)) and that I have reviewed this application, including all supporting documentation, and to the best of my knowledge and belief the contents are true, correct, and complete.

Name and Title	Signature	Date
Name and Title	Signature	Date

This application form provides a recommended format for your Voluntary Fiduciary Correction Program (VFCP) application. Please make sure you include the required VFCP Checklist and all supporting documents identified on the checklist (for example, proof of payment). Submit your application to the appropriate EBSA field office. For full application procedures, consult www.dol.gov/ebsa.

Paperwork Reduction Act Notice

The information identified on this form is required for a valid application for the Voluntary Fiduciary Correction Program of the U.S. Department of Labor's Employee Benefits Security Administration (EBSA). You are not required to use this form; however, you must supply the information identified in order to receive the relief offered under the Program with respect to a breach of fiduciary responsibility under Part 4 of Title I of ERISA. EBSA will use this information to determine whether you have satisfied the requirements of the Program. EBSA estimates that assembling and submitting this information will require an average of 6 to 8 hours. This collection of information is currently approved under OMB Control Number 1210-0118. You are not required to respond to a collection of information unless it displays a currently valid OMB Control Number.

Source: http://www.dol.gov/ebsa/calculator/2006vfcpapplication.html.

Revised Voluntary Fiduciary Correction
Program Checklist (Required)

U.S. Department of Labor
Employee Benefits Security Administration
April 2005

Use this checklist to ensure that you are submitting a complete application. The applicant must sign and date the checklist and include it with the application. Indicate "Yes", "No" or "N/A" next to each item. A "No" answer or the failure to include a completed checklist will delay review of the application until all required items are received.

❑ Yes ❑ No ❑ N/A   1.   Have you reviewed the eligibility, definitions, transaction and correction, and documentation sections of the VFC Program?

❑ Yes ❑ No ❑ N/A   2.   Have you included the name, address and telephone number of a contact person familiar with the contents of the application?

❑ Yes ❑ No ❑ N/A   3.   Have you provided the EIN, Plan Number, and address of the plan sponsor and plan administrator?

❑ Yes ❑ No ❑ N/A   4.   Have you provided the date that the most recent Form 5500 was filed by the plan?

❑ Yes ❑ No ❑ N/A   5.   Have you enclosed a signed and dated certification under penalty of perjury for the plan fiduciary with knowledge of the transactions and for each applicant and the applicant's representative, if any?

❑ Yes ❑ No ❑ N/A   6.   Have you enclosed relevant portions of the plan document and any other pertinent documents (such as the adoption agreement, trust agreement, or insurance contract) with the relevant sections identified?

❑ Yes ❑ No ❑ N/A   7.   "If applicable, have you provided written notification to EBSA of any current investigation or examination of the plan, or of the applicant or plan sponsor in connection with an act or transaction directly related to the plan by the PBGC, any state attorney general, or any state insurance commissioner?

❑ Yes ❑ No ❑ N/A   8.   Where applicable, have you enclosed a copy of an appraiser's report?

❑ Yes ❑ No ❑ N/A   9.   Have you enclosed supporting documentation, including:

        ❑   a.   A detailed narrative of the Breach, including the date it occurred;

        ❑   b.   Documentation that supports the narrative description of the transaction;

        ❑   c.   An explanation of how the Breach was corrected, by whom and when, with supporting documentation;

        ❑   d.   A list of all persons materially involved in the Breach and its correction (e.g., fiduciaries, service providers, borrowers, lenders);

        ❑   e.   Specific calculations demonstrating how Principal Amount and Lost Earnings or Restoration of Profits were computed, and

        ❑   f.   Proof of payment of Principal Amount and Lost Earnings or Restoration of Profits?

        ❑   g.   If application concerns delinquent employee contributions or loan repayments, a statement from a Plan Official identifying the earliest date on which participant contributions/loan repayments reasonably could have been segregated from the employer's general assets and supporting documentation on which the Plan Official relied?

❏ Yes   ❏ No   ❏ N/A   10.   If you are an eligible applicant and wish to avail yourself of excise tax relief under the VFCP Class Exemption:

       a.   Have you made proper arrangements to provide within 60 calendar days after submission of this application a copy of the Class Exemption notice to all interested persons and to the EBSA regional office to which the application is filed; or

       b.   If you are relying on the exception to the notice requirement in section IV.C. of the Class Exemption because the amount of the excise tax otherwise due would be less than or equal to $100.00, have you provided to the appropriate EBSA Regional Office a copy of a completed IRS Form 5330 or other written documentation containing the information required by IRS Form 5330 and proof of payment?

❏ Yes   ❏ No   ❏ N/A   11.   In calculating Lost Earnings, have you elected to use:

❏   a.   The Online Calculator; or

❏   b.   A manual calculation performed in accordance with Section 5(b)?

❏ Yes   ❏ No   ❏ N/A   12.   Where applicable, have you enclosed a description demonstrating proof of payment to participants and beneficiaries whose current location is known to the plan and/or applicant, and for participants who need to be located, have you demonstrated how adequate funds have been segregated to pay missing participants and commenced the process of locating the missing participants using either the IRS and SSA locator services, or other comparable means?

❏ Yes   ❏ No   ❏ N/A   13.   For purposes of the three transactions covered under Section 7.1, has the plan implemented measures to ensure that such transactions do not recur?

Signature of Applicant and Date Signed:_____

Name of Applicant:_____

Title/Relationship to the Plan:_____

Name of Plan, EIN and Plan Number:_____

Paperwork Reduction Act Notice - The information identified on this form is required for a valid application for the Voluntary Fiduciary Correction Program of the U.S. Department of Labor's Employee Benefits Security Administration (EBSA). You must complete this form and submit it as part of the application in order to receive the relief offered under the Program with respect to a breach of fiduciary responsibility under Part 4 of Title I of ERISA. EBSA will use this information to determine that you have satisfied the requirements of the Program. EBSA estimates that completing and submitting this form will require an average of 2 to 4 minutes. This collection of information is currently approved under **OMB Control Number 1210-0118**. You are not required to respond to a collection of information unless it displays a currently valid OMB Control Number.

Source: http://www.dol.gov/ebsa/calculator/vfcpchecklistrevised.html

Revised Voluntary Fiduciary Correction Program
Sample No Action Letter

Applicant (Plan Official)
Address

Dear Applicant (Plan Official):

Re: VFC Program Application No. xx–xxxxxx

The Department of Labor, Employee Benefits Security Administration (EBSA), has responsibility for administration and enforcement of Title I of the Employee Retirement Income Security Act of 1974, as amended (ERISA). EBSA has established a Voluntary Fiduciary Correction (VFC) Program to encourage the correction of breaches of fiduciary responsibility and the restoration of losses to the plan participants and beneficiaries.

In accordance with the requirements of the VFC Program, you have identified the following transactions as breaches, or potential breaches, of Part 4 of Title I of ERISA, and you have submitted documentation to EBSA that demonstrates that you have taken the corrective action indicated.

[Briefly recap the violation and correction. Example: Failure to deposit participant contributions to the XYZ Corp. 401(k) plan within the time frames required by ERISA, from _____ (date) to _____ (date). All participant contributions were deposited by _____ (date) and lost earnings on the delinquent contributions were deposited and allocated to participants' plan accounts on _____ (date).]

Because you have taken the above-described corrective action that is consistent with the requirements of the VFC Program, EBSA will take no civil enforcement action against you with respect to this breach. Specifically, EBSA will not recommend that the Solicitor of Labor initiate legal action against you, and EBSA will not impose the penalties in section 502(l) or section 502(i) of ERISA on the amount you have repaid to the plan.

EBSA's decision to take no further action is conditioned on the completeness and accuracy of the representations made in your application. You should note that this decision will not preclude EBSA from conducting an investigation of any potential violations of criminal law in connection with the transaction identified in the application or investigating the transaction identified in the application with a view toward seeking appropriate relief from any other person.

[If the transaction is a prohibited transaction for which no exemptive relief is available, add the following language: Please also be advised that pursuant to section 3003(c) of ERISA, 29 U.S.C. section 1203(c), the Secretary of Labor is required to transmit to the Secretary of the Treasury information indicating that a prohibited transaction has occurred. Accordingly, this matter will be referred to the Internal Revenue Service.]

In addition, you are cautioned that EBSA's decision to take no further action is binding on EBSA only. Any other governmental agency, and participants and beneficiaries, remain free to take whatever action they deem necessary.

If you have any questions about this letter, you may contact the Regional VFC Program Coordinator at applicable address and telephone number.

Sincerely,

Regional Director (or designated person)

Enclosure

IRC 6621(A)(2) Underpayment Rates Table

Table Of Interest Rates
IRC 6621(a)(2) Underpayment Rates
January 1, 1990 – December 31, 2012

Date	Interest Rate	Date	Interest Rate
Jan 1, 1990 - Mar 31, 1990	11%	Oct 1, 2000 - Dec 31, 2000	9%
Apr 1, 1990 - Jun 30, 1990	11%	Jan 1, 2001 - Mar 31, 2001	9%
Jul 1, 1990 - Sep 30, 1990	11%	Apr 1, 2001 - Jun 30, 2001	8%
Oct 1, 1990 - Dec 31, 1990	11%	Jul 1, 2001 - Sep 30, 2001	7%
Jan 1, 1991 - Mar 31, 1991	11%	Oct 1, 2001 - Dec 31, 2001	7%
Apr 1, 1991 - Jun 30, 1991	10%	Jan 1, 2002 - Mar 31, 2002	6%
Jul 1, 1991 - Sep 30, 1991	10%	Apr 1, 2002 - Jun 30, 2002	6%
Oct 1, 1991 - Dec 31, 1991	10%	Jul 1, 2002 - Sep 30, 2002	6%
Jan 1, 1992 - Mar 31, 1992	9%	Oct 1, 2002 - Dec 31, 2002	6%
Apr 1, 1992 - Jun 30, 1992	8%	Jan 1, 2003 - Mar 31, 2003	5%
Jul 1, 1992 - Sep 30, 1992	8%	Apr 1, 2003 - Jun 30, 2003	5%
Oct 1, 1992 - Dec 31, 1992	7%	Jul 1, 2003 - Sep 30, 2003	5%
Jan 1, 1993 - Mar 31, 1993	7%	Oct 1, 2003 - Dec 31, 2003	4%
Apr 1, 1993 - Jun 30, 1993	7%	Jan 1, 2004 - Mar 31, 2004	4%
Jul 1, 1993 - Sep 30, 1993	7%	Apr 1, 2004 - Jun 30, 2004	5%
Oct 1, 1993 - Dec 31, 1993	7%	Jul 1, 2004 - Sep 30, 2004	4%
Jan 1, 1994 - Mar 31, 1994	7%	Oct 1, 2004 - Dec 31, 2004	5%
Apr 1, 1994 - Jun 30, 1994	7%	Jan 1, 2005 - Mar 31, 2005	5%
Jul 1, 1994 - Sep 30, 1994	8%	Apr 1, 2005 - Jun 30, 2005	6%
Oct 1, 1994 - Dec 31, 1994	9%	Jul 1, 2005 - Sep 30, 2005	6%
Jan 1, 1995 - Mar 31, 1995	9%	Oct 1, 2005 - Dec 31, 2005	7%
Apr 1, 1995 - Jun 30, 1995	10%	Jan 1, 2006 - Mar 31, 2006	7%
Jul 1, 1995 - Sep 30, 1995	9%	Apr 1, 2006 - Jun 30, 2006	7%
Oct 1, 1995 - Dec 31, 1995	9%	Jul 1, 2006 - Sep 30, 2006	8%
Jan 1, 1996 - Mar 31, 1996	9%	Oct 1, 2006 - Dec 31, 2006	8%
Apr 1, 1996 - Jun 30, 1996	8%	Jan 1, 2007 - Mar 31, 2007	8%
Jul 1, 1996 - Sep 30, 1996	9%	Apr 1, 2007-Jun 30, 2007	8%
Oct 1, 1996 - Dec 31, 1996	9%	Jul 1, 2007 - Sep 30, 2007	8%
Jan 1, 1997 - Mar 31, 1997	9%	Oct 1, 2007 - Dec 31, 2007	8%
Apr 1, 1997 - Jun 30, 1997	9%	Jan 1, 2008 - Mar 31, 2008	7%
Jul 1, 1997 - Sep 30, 1997	9%	Apr 1, 2008 - Jun 30, 2008	6%
Oct 1, 1997 - Dec 31, 1997	9%	Jul 1, 2008 - Sep 30, 2008	5%
Jan 1, 1998 - Mar 31, 1998	9%	Oct 1, 2008 - Dec 31, 2008	6%
Apr 1, 1998 - Jun 30, 1998	8%	Jan 1, 2009 - Mar 31, 2009	5%
Jul 1, 1998 - Sep 30, 1998	8%	Apr 1, 2009 - Dec 31, 2010	4%
Oct 1, 1998 - Dec 31, 1998	8%	Jan 1, 2011 - Mar 31, 2011	3%
Jan 1, 1999 - Mar 31, 1999	7%	Apr 1, 2011 - Jun 30, 2011	4%
Apr 1, 1999 - Jun 30, 1999	8%	Jul 1, 2011 - Sep 30, 2011	4%
Jul 1, 1999 - Sep 30, 1999	8%	Oct 1, 2011 - Dec 31, 2011	3%
Oct 1, 1999 - Dec 31, 1999	8%	Jan 1, 2012 - Mar 31, 2012	3%
Jan 1, 2000 - Mar 31, 2000	8%	April 1, 2012 - Jun 30, 2012	3%
Apr 1, 2000 - Jun 30, 2000	9%	Jul 1, 2012 - Sep 30, 2012	3%
Jul 1, 2000 - Sep 30, 2000	9%	Oct 1, 2012 - Dec 31, 2012	3%

Source: http://www.dol.gov/ebsa/calculator/interestratetables.html

IRC 6621(C)(1) Underpayment Rates Table

Table Of Interest Rates
IRC 6621(c)(1) Underpayment Rates
January 1, 1991 – December 31, 2012

Date	Interest Rate	Date	Interest Rate
Jan 1, 1991 - Mar 31, 1991	13%	Apr 1, 2001 - Jun 30, 2001	10%
Apr 1, 1991 - Jun 30, 1991	12%	Jul 1, 2001 - Sep 30, 2001	9%
Jul 1, 1991 - Sep 30, 1991	12%	Oct 1, 2001 - Dec 31, 2001	9%
Oct 1, 1991 - Dec 31, 1991	12%	Jan 1, 2002 - Mar 31, 2002	8%
Jan 1, 1992 - Mar 31, 1992	11%	Apr 1, 2002 - Jun 30, 2002	8%
Apr 1, 1992 - Jun 30, 1992	10%	Jul 1, 2002 - Sep 30, 2002	8%
Jul 1, 1992 - Sep 30, 1992	10%	Oct 1, 2002 - Dec 30, 2002	8%
Oct 1, 1992 - Dec 31, 1992	9%	Jan 1, 2003 - Mar 31, 2003	7%
Jan 1, 1993 - Mar 31, 1993	9%	Apr 1, 2003 - Jun 30, 2003	7%
Apr 1, 1993 - Jun 30, 1993	9%	Jul 1, 2003 - Sep 30, 2003	7%
Jul 1, 1993 - Sep 30, 1993	9%	Oct 1, 2003 - Dec 31, 2003	6%
Oct 1, 1993 - Dec 31, 1993	9%	Jan 1, 2004 - Mar 31, 2004	6%
Jan 1, 1994 - Mar 31, 1994	9%	Apr 1, 2004 - Jun 30, 2004	7%
Apr 1, 1994 - Jun 30, 1994	9%	Jul 1, 2004 - Sep 30, 2004	6%
Jul 1, 1994 - Sep 30, 1994	10%	Oct 1, 2004 - Dec 31, 2004	7%
Oct 1, 1994 - Dec 31, 1994	11%	Jan 1, 2005 - Mar 31, 2005	7%
Jan 1, 1995 - Mar 31, 1995	11%	Apr 1, 2005 - Jun 30, 2005	8%
Apr 1, 1995 - Jun 30, 1995	12%	Jul 1, 2005 - Sep 30, 2005	8%
Jul 1, 1995 - Sep 30, 1995	11%	Oct 1, 2005 - Dec 31, 2005	9%
Oct 1, 1995 - Dec 31, 1995	11%	Jan 1, 2006 - Mar 31, 2006	9%
Jan 1, 1996 - Mar 31, 1996	11%	Apr 1, 2006 - Jun 30, 2006	9%
Apr 1, 1996 - Jun 30, 1996	10%	Jul 1, 2006 - Sep 30, 2006	10%
Jul 1, 1996 - Sep 30, 1996	11%	Oct 1, 2006 - Dec 31, 2006	10%
Oct 1, 1996 - Dec 31, 1996	11%	Jan 1, 2007 - Mar 31, 2007	10%
Jan 1, 1997 - Mar 31, 1997	11%	Apr 1, 2007-Jun 30, 2007	10%
Apr 1, 1997 - Jun 30, 1997	11%	Jul 1, 2007 - Sep 30, 2007	10%
Jul 1, 1997 - Sep 30, 1997	11%	Oct 1, 2007 - Dec 31, 2007	10%
Oct 1, 1997 - Dec 31, 1997	11%	Jan 1, 2008 - Mar 31, 2008	9%
Jan 1, 1998 - Mar 31, 1998	11%	Apr 1, 2008 - Jun 30, 2008	8%
Apr 1, 1998 - Jun 30, 1998	10%	Jul 1, 2008 - Sep 30, 2008	7%
Jul 1, 1998 - Sep 30, 1998	10%	Oct 1, 2008 - Dec 31, 2008	8%
Oct 1, 1998 - Dec 31, 1998	10%	Jan 1, 2009 - Mar 31, 2009	7%
Jan 1, 1999 - Mar 31, 1999	9%	Apr 1 2009 - Dec 31, 2010	6%
Apr 1, 1999 - Jun 30, 1999	10%	Jan 1, 2011 - Mar 31, 2011	5%
Jul 1, 1999 - Sep 30, 1999	10%	Apr 1, 2011 - Jun 30, 2011	6%
Oct 1, 1999 - Dec 31, 1999	10%	Jul 1, 2011 - Sep 30, 2011	6%
Jan 1, 2000 - Mar 31, 2000	10%	Oct 1, 2011 - Dec 31, 2011	5%
Apr 1, 2000 - Jun 30, 2000	11%	Jan 1, 2012 - Mar 31, 2012	5%
Jul 1, 2000 - Sep 30, 2000	11%	Apr 1, 2012 - Jun 30, 2012	5%
Oct 1, 2000 - Dec 31, 2000	11%	Jul 1, 2012 - Sep 30, 2012	5%
Jan 1, 2001 - Mar 31, 2001	11%	Oct 1, 2012 - Dec 31, 2012	5%

Source: http://www.dol.gov/ebsa/calculator/interestratetables.html

APPENDIX C

Sample Automatic Enrollment
and Default Investment Notice

(Relating to Code Sections 401(k)(13) and 414(w)
and ERISA Sections 404(c)(5) and 514(e)(3))

On November 8, 2007, the Internal Revenue Service ("IRS") and the Treasury Department published proposed regulations on new safe-harbor qualified automatic contribution arrangements ("QACAs") under section 401(k)(13) of the Internal Revenue Code of 1986, as amended ("Code"), and on eligible automatic contribution arrangements ("EACAs") under Code section 414(w). 72 FR 63144. A plan sponsor may implement a QACA and may permit withdrawals of certain amounts contributed under an EACA, as early as January 1, 2008 (for calendar year plans). In addition, on October 24, 2007, the Department of Labor ("DOL") issued a final regulation, effective December 24, 2007, on assets invested in a qualified default investment alternative ("QDIA") on behalf of participants and beneficiaries who do not direct the investment of their accounts. DOL Regulation section 2550.404c-5 (72 FR 60452).

Among other things, Code sections 401(k)(13) and 414(w) include notice requirements that plan sponsors must satisfy in order to maintain a QACA or an EACA. The IRS's proposed regulations set forth these notice requirements. Similarly, ERISA sections 404(c)(5) and 514(e)(3) include notice requirements that plan sponsors must satisfy in order to obtain fiduciary relief and preemption of state laws under those sections. The DOL's regulation section 2550.404c-5 sets forth these notice requirements. A plan sponsor's notice must be sufficiently accurate and comprehensive to apprise employees of their rights and obligations under the plan sponsor's particular arrangement and must be written in a manner calculated to be understood by the average employee to whom the arrangement applies. Also, the notice must be provided so that employees have a reasonable period of time after receipt of the notice before automatic elective contributions are made to the plan.

To aid plan sponsors in satisfying the requirements of the IRS's proposed regulations for the 2008 plan year – the first plan year that a plan may include a QACA or EACA – the IRS posted a sample "Automatic Enrollment Notice" on its website that satisfies notice requirements under Code sections 401(k)(13) and 414(w) for a hypothetical QACA that permits EACA withdrawals and has certain other characteristics. Following coordination with the IRS, the DOL indicated that use of this sample notice also satisfies the notice requirements under ERISA sections 404(c)(5) and 514(e)(3) and the DOL's regulation section 2550.404c-5 (i.e., the default investment regulation for a hypothetical plan for which a fiduciary may wish to obtain relief under the regulation). A plan sponsor will need to add to, subtract from, or otherwise change the sample notice to the extent a plan's form and operations differ from the hypothetical QACA described in the sample notice, so that the actual notice accurately reflects the provisions of the plan. For example, a particular plan may satisfy the Code section 401(k)(13) employer contribution requirement through safe-harbor employer nonelective contributions to nonhighly compensated employees, rather than through safe-harbor matching contributions to all eligible

959

participants, or may provide employer nonelective contributions in addition to safe-harbor matching contributions. The plan sponsor will also need to provide details about a plan's QDIA, as directed in italicized notes to plan sponsors in the sample notice, and will need to fill in any blanks in the sample notice.

The hypothetical QACA described in the sample notice includes the following characteristics:

- The QACA is effective January 1, 2008. It is part of a calendar-year defined contribution plan that, before January 1, 2008, provided only for elective contributions under Code section 401(k) (but not for automatic elective contributions).

- The QACA provides for automatic elective contributions at the minimum level permitted under Code section 401(k)(13), and does not restrict employees' ability to elect other elective contribution levels, except to the extent required under other Code provisions (e.g., Code section 402(g)). The plan does not provide for designated Roth contributions described in Code section 402A.

- The QACA provides for matching contributions for all eligible participants at the minimum level permitted under Code section 401(k)(13), and does not provide for additional employer matching or nonelective contributions. The matching contributions are contributed to the plan on a payroll-by-payroll basis (based on the same definition of eligible compensation used to make elective contributions), and are subject to the minimum vesting schedule described in Code section 401(k)(13)(D)(iii)(I) (that is, full vesting upon completion of 2 years of service).

- Employees are eligible to participate in the plan on their date of hire.

- Participants make elective contribution and investment elections under the plan by returning specified election forms to the plan administrator, and may change their elections at any time without restriction.

- Affirmative contribution elections under the plan, whether made before or after the effective date of the QACA, continue in force until changed by the participant.

- The plan permits participants to withdraw automatic elective contributions during a 90- day window period described in Code section 414(w), and treats a withdrawal request as an election to not make further elective contributions to the plan (absent a contrary affirmative election).

- Plan participants may affirmatively choose among various available investment funds. Automatic elective contributions and related employer matching contributions are, absent contrary affirmative election, invested in a QDIA.

- The plan permits distributions and loans to the extent distributions and loans are permitted under Code sections 401(k)(2)(B) and 72(p)(2). Hardship distributions are permitted to the extent the deemed hardship requirements described in Treasury regulation section 1.401(k)-1(d)(3)(iii)(B) and (iv)(E) are satisfied.

- The plan administrator has provided summary plan descriptions to participants that accurately describe eligible compensation, contribution limits, service crediting rules, investment election procedures, the investment funds available under the plan, and hardship withdrawal and loan rules.

Although the sample notice is designed for use in satisfying the QACA and EACA notice requirements, and the notice requirements under ERISA sections 404(c)(5) and 514(e)(3), plan sponsors may also find the sample notice to be helpful in drafting an employee explanation for an automatic contribution arrangement that is neither a QACA nor an EACA.

[Plan Name] Plan (Plan)
Automatic Enrollment Notice

Beginning in 2008, [   ] (Company) is making saving for retirement under our 401(k) Plan even easier. We are offering an automatic enrollment feature, and will make new Company matching contributions.

The new automatic enrollment feature won't change your contribution level if you already turned in a [   ] Form electing the level of your contributions to the Plan or electing not to contribute. Your earlier election will continue to be followed, and matching contributions will be made based on your contribution level. You can change your contribution level by turning in a new [   ] Form at any time. Matching contributions will then be based on your new contribution level.

If you have not turned in a contribution election form, you will be automatically enrolled in the Plan starting with your first paycheck in 2008. This means that amounts will be taken from your pay and contributed to the Plan. For pay during 2008, these automatic contributions will be 3% of your eligible pay each pay period. But, you can choose a different amount. You can choose to contribute more, less, or even nothing.

Keep in mind that the Company will match one dollar for each dollar you contribute, up to 1% of your eligible pay. The Company will also match 50 cents for each dollar you contribute that is between 1% and 6% of your eligible pay. So, to get the most from these matching contributions, you must contribute at least 6% of your eligible pay each pay period. This is more than the 3% automatic contribution rate. It may also be more than your current contribution rate.

This notice gives you important information about some Plan rules, including the Plan's automatic enrollment feature and Company matching contributions. The notice covers these points:

- Whether the Plan's automatic enrollment feature applies to you;

- What amounts will be automatically taken from your pay and contributed to the Plan;

- What other amounts the Company will contribute to your Plan account;

- How your Plan account will be invested;

- When your Plan account will be vested (that is, not lost when you leave your job), and when you can get your Plan account; and

- How you can change your contributions.

You can find out more about the Plan in another document, the Plan's Summary Plan Description (SPD).

1. Does the Plan's automatic enrollment feature apply to me?

The Plan's automatic enrollment feature will not apply to you if you already elected (by turning in a [   ] Form to the Plan Administrator) to make contributions to the Plan or to not 2 contribute. If you made an election, your contribution level will not automatically change. But, you can always change your contribution level by turning in a new contribution form.

If you have not elected a contribution level, you will be enrolled in the Plan starting with your first paycheck in 2008. This means money will be automatically taken from your pay and contributed to your Plan account. If you do not want to be enrolled, you need to turn in the enclosed contribution form to the Plan Administrator by [   ].

2. If I do nothing, how much will be taken from my pay and contributed to the Plan?

If you do not turn in a completed contribution form by [   ], 3% of your eligible pay for each pay period will be taken from your pay and contributed to the Plan. This will start with your first paycheck in 2008 and continue through the end of 2009. After 2009, your contribution level will increase by 1% each year (unless you choose a different level), until it reaches 6% of your eligible pay. To learn more about the Plan's definition of eligible pay, you can review the "[]" section of the Plan's SPD.

Your contributions to the Plan are taken out of your pay and are not subject to federal income tax at that time. Instead, they are contributed to your Plan account and can grow over time with earnings. Your account will be subject to federal income tax only when withdrawn. This helpful tax rule is a reason to save for retirement through Plan contributions.

Contributions will be taken out of your pay if you do nothing. But you are in charge of the amount that you contribute. You may decide to do nothing and become automatically enrolled, or you may choose to contribute an amount that better meets your needs. For example, you may want to get the full amount of the Company's matching contributions by contributing at least 6% of your eligible pay. You can change your contributions by turning in a new contribution form to the Plan Administrator at the address listed at the end of this notice.

If you want to contribute more to your account than would be provided automatically, there are limits on the maximum amount. These limits are described in the "[   ]" section of the Plan's SPD.

3. In addition to the contributions taken out of my pay, what amounts will the Company contribute to my Plan account?

Besides contributing the amounts taken from your pay, the Company will make other contributions to your Plan account. The Company will match, on a dollar-for-dollar basis, the first 1% of eligible pay you contribute each pay period. The Company will also match 50 cents for each dollar you contribute between 1% and 6% of your eligible pay each pay period. These matching contributions will be made if you are automatically enrolled or if you choose your own contribution level.

The Company's matching contributions depend on the amount you contribute out of your pay each pay period.

> *Example:* If you earn $2,000 in eligible pay during a pay period and you elect to contribute 6% of your pay, the Company will deduct $120 from your pay for the pay period (that is, 6% x $2,000). The $120 will be put in your Plan account. The Company will also make matching contributions to your Plan account of $70 for the pay period. In other words, the Company will make a dollar-for-dollar matching contribution on your contributions up to 1% of eligible pay (100% of 1% x $2,000, or $20) plus a 50¢-per-dollar matching contribution on your contributions between 1% and 6% of eligible pay (50% of 5% x $2,000, or $50). Or, if you contribute 3% of your eligible pay for the pay period, the Company will take $60 out of your pay and put it in your Plan account, and will also make $40 in matching contributions for the pay period. Or, if you choose not to contribute to the Plan for a pay period, you will get no matching contributions for the pay period.

Remember, you can always change the amount you contribute to the Plan by turning in a new contribution form.

4. How will my Plan account be invested?

The Plan lets you invest your account in a number of different investment funds. Unless you choose a different investment fund or funds, your Plan account will be invested in the [   ] Fund.

[Note to plan sponsors: In order for the Plan's default investment to satisfy section 404(c)(5) of ERISA, the default investment fund must be a qualified default investment alternative ("QDIA") under DOL Reg. § 2550.404c-5. You must describe the Plan's QDIA, including its investment objectives, risk and return characteristics, and fees and expenses, and must describe other circumstances, if any, under which assets may be invested in the QDIA.]

You can change how your Plan account is invested, among the Plan's offered investment funds, by turning in the enclosed [   ] Form to the Plan Administrator at the address listed at the end of this notice.

[Note to plan sponsors: In order for the Plan's default investment to satisfy section 404(c)(5) of ERISA, you must describe any restrictions, fees, or expenses that apply when participants or beneficiaries transfer assets from the QDIA to other investment funds.]

To learn more about the Plan's investment funds and procedures for changing how your Plan account is invested you can review the "[   ]" section of the Plan's SPD. Also, you can contact the Plan Administrator using the contact information at the end of this notice.

5.   When will my Plan account be vested and available to me?

You will always be fully vested in your contributions to the Plan. You will also be fully vested in matching contributions when you complete two years of service. To be fully vested in Plan contributions means that the contributions (together with any investment gain or loss) will always belong to you, and you will not lose them when you leave your job. For more information about years of service, you can review the "[   ]" section of the Plan's SPD.

Even if you are vested in your Plan account, there are limits on when you may withdraw your funds. These limits may be important to you in deciding how much, if any, to contribute to the 4 Plan. Generally you may only withdraw vested money after you leave your job, reach age 59½, or become disabled. Also, there is generally an extra 10% tax on distributions before age 59½. Your beneficiary can get any vested amount remaining in your account when you die.

You also can borrow certain amounts from your vested Plan account, and may be able to take out certain vested money if you have a hardship. Hardship distributions are limited to the dollar amount of your contributions. They may not be taken from earnings or matching contributions. Hardship distributions must be for a specified reason – for qualifying medical expenses, costs of purchasing your principal residence (or preventing eviction from or foreclosure on your principal residence, or repairing qualifying damages to your principal residence), qualifying post-secondary education expenses, or qualifying burial or funeral expenses. Before you can take a hardship distribution, you must have taken other permitted withdrawals and loans from qualifying Company plans. If you take a hardship distribution, you may not contribute to the Plan or other qualifying Company plans for 6 months.

You can learn more about the Plan's hardship withdrawal and loan rules in the "[   ]" and "[   ]" sections of the Plan's SPD. You can also learn more about the extra 10% tax in IRS Publication 575, Pension and Annuity Income.

6.   Can I change the amount of my contributions?

You can always change the amount you contribute to the Plan. If you know now that you do not want to contribute to the Plan (and you haven't already elected not to contribute), you will want to turn in a contribution form electing zero contributions by [   ]. That way, you avoid any automatic contributions.

But, if you do not turn in the form in time to prevent automatic contributions, you can withdraw the automatic contributions for a short time, despite the general limits on Plan withdrawals. During the 90 days after automatic contributions are first taken from your pay, you can withdraw the prior automatic contributions by turning in a [   ] Form to the Plan Administrator. The amount you withdraw will be adjusted for any gain or loss. If you take out your automatic contributions, you lose Company contributions that matched the automatic contributions. Also, your withdrawal will be subject to federal income tax (but not the extra 10% tax that normally applies to early distributions). If you take out automatic contributions, the Company will treat you as having chosen to make no further contributions. However, you can always choose to continue or restart your contributions by turning in a contribution form.

If you have any questions about how the Plan works or your rights and obligations under the Plan, or if you would like a copy of the Plan's SPD or other Plan documents, please contact the Plan Administrator at:

[Plan administrator name]
[Address]
[Telephone number]
[Email address]

TABLE OF CASES

TABLE OF CASES

TABLE OF CASES

TABLE OF CASES

TABLE OF CASES

TABLE OF ERISA SECTIONS TO USC SECTIONS

ERISA Section	USC Section	ERISA Section	USC Section
2	1001	501	1131
3	1002	502	1132
4	1003	503	1133
101	1021	504	1134
102	1022	505	1135
103	1023	506	1136
104	1024	507	1137
105	1025	508	1138
106	1026	509	1139
107	1027	510	1140
108	1028	511	1141
109	1029	512	1142
110	1030	513	1143
111	1031	514	1144
201	1051	515	1145
202	1052	516	1146
203	1053	517	1147
204	1054	601	1161
205	1055	602	1162
206	1056	603	1163
207	1057	604	1164
208	1058	605	1165
209	1059	606	1166
210	1060	607	1167
211	1061	608	1168
301	1081	609	1169
302	1082	701	1181
303	1083	702	1182
304	1084	703	1183
305	1085	711	1185
306	1085a	712	1185a
307	1085b	713	1185b
308	1086	731	1191
401	1101	732	1191a
402	1102	733	1191b
403	1103	734	1191c
404	1104	3001	1201
405	1105	3002	1202
406	1106	3003	1203
407	1107	3004	1204
408	1108	3021	1221
409	1109	3022	1222
410	1110	3031	1231
411	1111	3032	1232
412	1112	3041	1241
413	1113	3042	1242
414	1114	4001	1301

ERISA Section	USC Section	ERISA Section	USC Section
4002	1302	4204	1384
4003	1303	4205	1385
4004	1304	4206	1386
4005	1305	4207	1387
4006	1306	4208	1388
4007	1307	4209	1389
4008	1308	4210	1390
4009	1309	4211	1391
4010	1310	4212	1392
4011	1311	4213	1393
4021	1321	4214	1394
4022	1322	4215	1395
4022A	1322a	4216	1396
4022B	1322b	4217	1397
4023	1323	4218	1398
4041	1341	4219	1399
4041A	1341a	4220	1400
4042	1342	4221	1401
4043	1343	4222	1402
4044	1344	4223	1403
4045	1345	4224	1404
4046	1346	4225	1405
4047	1347	4231	1411
4048	1348	4232	1412
4049	1349	4233	1413
4050	1350	4234	1414
4061	1361	4235	1415
4062	1362	4241	1421
4063	1363	4242	1422
4064	1364	4243	1423
4065	1365	4244	1424
4066	1366	4244A	1425
4067	1367	4245	1426
4068	1368	4261	1431
4069	1369	4281	1441
4070	1370	4301	1451
4071	1371	4302	1452
4201	1381	4303	1453
4202	1382	4402	1461
4203	1383		

TABLE OF ERISA SECTIONS TO IRC SECTIONS

ERISA Section	IRC Section	ERISA Section	IRC Section
3(3)	4975(e)(1)	204(h)	4980F
3(14)	4975(e)(2)	204(h)(2)	411(d)(6)(B)
3(16)(A)	414(g)	205	401(a)(11)
3(21)	4975(e)(3)	205(b)(2)	401(a)(11)
3(22)	411(a)(9)	205(c)	417(a)
3(23)	411(a)(7)	205(c)(4)	417(a)(4)
3(24)	411(a)(8)	205(d)	417(b)
3(32)	414(d)	205(e)	417(c)
3(33)	414(e)	205(e)(3)	417(c)(3)
3(34)	414(i)	205(g)	417(e)
3(35)	414(j)	205(g)(3)	417(e)(3)
3(37)	414(f)	205(h)(2)	417(f)(2)
3(40)(b)	414(b)-414(c)	205(k)	417(f)(5)
103(a)	6059	206	457(d)
103(a)(4)(C)	7701(a)(35)	206(b)	401(a)(15)
103(d)	6059	206(c)	401(a)(19)
201	401(a)(11), 410(c), 411(e)	206(d)	401(a)(13)
202	401(a)(3), 410(a)	206(d)(3)	414(p)
202(a)(1)	410(a)(1)	206(d)(3)(N)	401(n), 414(p)(12)
202(a)(2)	410(a)(2)	208	401(a)(12)
202(a)(3)	410(a)(3)(C)	210(a)(1)	413(b)(1)
202(a)(4)	410(a)(4)	210(a)(2)	413(b)(4)
202(b)	410(a)(5)	210(a)(3)	413(b)(5)-413(b)(6)
202(b)(4)	410(a)(5)(D)	210(b)	413(c), 414(a)
202(b)(5)	410(a)(5)	210(c)	414(b)
203	401(a)(7)	210(d)	414(c)
203(a)(1)	411(a)(1)	301	412(h)
203(a)(2)	411(a)(2), 413(b)(4)	301(a)(8)	412(h)(1)
203(a)(3)	411(a)(3)	301(b)	412(i)
203(a)(3)(B)	411(a)(3)(B)	301(c)	412(j)
203(a)(3)(C)	411(a)(3)(C)	301(d)	412(k)
203(a)(3)(D)	410(a)(3)(D)	302(a)	412(a)
203(a)(3)(D)(iii)	411(a)(3)(D)	302(a)(3)	412(a)
203(a)(3)(D)(iv)	411(a)(3)(D)	302(b)	412(b)
203(a)(3)(E)	411(a)(3)	302(b)(2)	412(b)(2)(C)
203(a)(3)(F)	411(a)(3)(G)	302(b)(2)(A)	412(b)(2)(A)
203(b)(1)	411(a)(4)	302(b)(3)	412(b)(3)(C)
203(b)(1)(G)	411(a)(4)(G)	302(b)(5)	412(b)(5)
203(b)(2)	411(a)(5)	302(b)(6)	412(b)(6)
203(b)(2)(C)	411(a)(5)(C)	302(b)(7)	412(b)(7)
203(b)(3)(E)	411(a)(6)(E)	302(b)(7)(D)	412(b)(7)(C), 412(b)(7)(D)
203(c)	411(a)(10)	302(c)(1)	412(c)(1)
203(c)(2)	411(d)(2)	302(c)(2)	412(c)(2)
203(e)	411(a)(11)	302(c)(3)	412(c)(3)
203(e)(2)	411(a)(11), 411(a)(11)(B)	302(c)(4)	412(c)(4)
204	411(b)	302(c)(6)	412(c)(6)
204(b)(1)(H)	411(b)(1)(H)	302(c)(7)	412(c)(7)
204(b)(3)(E)	411(a)(6), 411(b)(4)	302(c)(8)	412(c)(8)
204(b)(4)(D)	411(b)(4)	302(c)(9)	412(c)(9)
204(c)(2)	411(c)(2), 411(c)(2)(C)	302(c)(10)	412(c)(10)
204(c)(4)	411(d)(5)	302(c)(11)	412(c)(11)
204(d)	411(a)(7)(B)	302(c)(12)	412(c)(12)
204(g)	411(d)(6)	302(d)(2)	412(l)(2)

ERISA Section	IRC Section	ERISA Section	IRC Section
302(d)(3)	412(l)(3)	408(c)(1)	4975(d)(9)
302(d)(4)	412(l)(4)	408(c)(2)	4975(d)(10)
302(d)(5)	412(l)(5)	408(c)(3)	4975(d)(11)
302(d)(7)	412(l)(7)	408(d)	4975(d)
302(d)(7)(B)	412(l)(7)(B)	408(e)	4975(d)(13)
302(d)(8)(A)	412(l)(8)(A)	408(e)(2)	408(e)
302(d)(8)(B)	412(l)(8)(B)	502(c)(1)(B)	6690
302(d)(10)	412(l)(10)	601	4980B(d)
302(e)	412(m)	602(1)	4980B(f)(2)(A)
302(e)(3)	412(m)(3)	602(2)	4980B(f)(2)(B)
302(e)(5)	412(m)(5)	602(2)(A)	4980B(f)(2), 4980B(f)(2)(B)
302(f)	412(c)(11), 412(n), 412(n)(1)	602(2)(A)(iii)	4980B(f)(2)(B)
302(f)(4)(A)	412(n)(4), 412(n)(4)(A)	602(3)	4980B(f)(2)(C), 4980B(f)(3)
302(f)(6)(B)	412(n)(6)(B)	602(4)	4980B(f)(2)(D)
303	412(d)	602(5)	4980B(f)(2)(E)
303(a)(1)	412(d)(1)	603	4980B(f)(3)
303(c)	412(d)(3)	603(1)	4980B(f)(3)
303(d)(1)	412(d)(4)	603(2)	4980B(f)(3)(B)
303(d)(2)	412(d)(5)	603(3)	4980B(f)(3)(C)
303(e)	412(f)(4)	603(4)	4980B(f)(3)(D)
304	412(e)	603(5)	4980B(g)(1)(A)
304(b)	412(f)	603(6)	4980B(f)(3), 4980B(f)(3)(F)
305	412(g)	604	4980B(f)(4)
306	412(f)(3)	605	4980B(f)(5)
307	401(a)(29)	606	4980B(f)(6)
401	4975(g)	606(a)(2)	4980B(f)(6)(B)
403(a)	401(a)	606(a)(3)	4980B(f)(6)(C)
403(b)(3)	401(f), 408(h)	606(b)	4980B(f)(6)(D)
403(b)(3)(A)	401(f)	606(c)	4980B(f)(6)(D)
403(b)(3)(B)	408(h)	607(1)	5000(b)(1)
403(c)	401(a)(2)	607(2)	4980B(f)(7)
403(c)(2)	401(a)(2)	607(3)	4980B(g)(1)
403(c)(3)	401(a)(2)	607(3)(C)	4980B(g)(1)
404(a)(1)	401(a)(2)	607(5)	4980B(f)(8)
404(d)	4980(d)	609(d)	4980B(f)(1)
404(d)(1)	4980(d)	701	9801
406	4975(e)	702	9802
406(a)(1)	4975(c)(1)	703	9803
406(b)	4975(c)(1)	711	9811
406(c)	4975(f)(3)	712	9812
407(b)(2)(C)	401(m)(4)	2006(b)	401(k)(6)
407(c)(6)	4975(e)(7)	3001	7476
407(d)(1)	409(l), 409(l)(4)	4001(a)(1)	4980B(g)(3)
407(d)(5)	4975(e)(8)	4001(a)(9)	418(b)
408(a)	4975(c)(2)	4001(a)(12)	418(b)(7)(E)
408(b)(1)	4975(d)(1)	4001(a)(14)	4062
408(b)(2)	4975(d)(2)	4044(d)	401(a)(2)
408(b)(3)	4975(d)(3)	4062(e)	411(d)(3)
408(b)(4)	4975(d)(4)	4231	414(l)
408(b)(5)	4975(d)(5)	4232	414(l)
408(b)(6)	4975(d)(6)	4241	418
408(b)(7)	4975(d)(7)	4242	418A
408(b)(8)	4975(d)(8)	4243	418B
408(b)(9)	4975(d)(12)	4244	418C
408(b)(10)	4975(d)(14)	4244(g)	418C(g)
408(b)(11)	4975(d)(15)	4244A	418D
408(b)(12)	4975(d)(13)	4245(f)	418E(f)
408(b)(13)	4975(d)(13)	4303	414(f)(5)

TABLE OF IRC SECTION TO ERISA SECTIONS

IRC Section	ERISA Section	IRC Section	ERISA Section
401(a)	403(a)	411(c)(2)	204(c)(2)
401(a)(2)	403(c), 403(c)(2), 403(c)(3), 404(a)(1), 4044(d)	411(c)(2)(C)	204(c)(2)
401(a)(3)	202	411(d)(2)	203(c)(2)
401(a)(7)	203	411(d)(3)	4062(e)
401(a)(11)	201, 205, 205(b)(2)	411(d)(5)	204(c)(4)
401(a)(13)	206(d)	411(d)(6)	204(g)
401(a)(15)	206(b)	411(d)(6)(B)	204(h)(2)
401(a)(19)	206(c)	411(e)	201
401(a)(29)	307	412(a)	302(a), 302(a)(3)
401(c)	201	412(b)	302(b)
401(f)	403(b)(3), 403(b)(3)(A)	412(b)(2)(A)	302(b)(2)(A)
401(k)(6)	2006(b)	412(b)(2)(C)	302(b)(2)
401(m)(4)	407(b)(2)(C)	412(b)(3)(C)	302(b)(3)
401(n)	206(d)(3)(N)	412(b)(5)	302(b)(5)
408(e)	408(e)(2)	412(b)(6)	302(b)(6)
408(h)	403(b)(3), 403(b)(3)(B)	412(b)(7)	302(b)(7)
409(l)	407(d)(1)	412(b)(7)(C)	302(b)(7)(D)
409(l)(4)	407(d)(1)	412(b)(7)(D)	302(b)(7)(D)
410(a)	202	412(c)(1)	302(c)(1)
410(a)(1)	202(a)(1)	412(c)(2)	302(c)(2)
410(a)(2)	202(a)(2)	412(c)(3)	302(c)(3)
410(a)(3)(C)	202(a)(3)	412(c)(4)	302(c)(4)
410(a)(3)(D)	203(a)(3)(D)	412(c)(6)	302(c)(6)
410(a)(4)	202(a)(4)	412(c)(7)	302(c)(7)
410(a)(5)	202(b), 202(b)(5)	412(c)(8)	302(c)(8)
410(a)(5)(D)	202(b)(4)	412(c)(9)	302(c)(9)
411(a)(1)	203(a)(1)	412(c)(10)	302(c)(10)
411(a)(2)	203(a)(2)	412(c)(11)	302(c)(11), 302(f)
411(a)(3)	203(a)(3), 203(a)(3)(E)	412(c)(12)	302(c)(12)
411(a)(3)(B)	203(a)(3)(B)	412(d)	303
411(a)(3)(C)	203(a)(3)(C)	412(d)(1)	303(a)(1)
411(a)(3)(D)	203(a)(3)(D)(iii), 203(a)(3)(D)(iv)	412(d)(3)	303(c)
411(a)(3)(G)	203(a)(3)(F)	412(d)(4)	303(d)(1)
411(a)(4)	203(b)(1)	412(d)(5)	303(d)(2)
411(a)(4)(G)	203(b)(1)(G)	412(e)	304
411(a)(5)	203(b)(2)(C)	412(f)	304(b)
411(a)(5)(C)	203(b)(2)(C)	412(f)(3)	306
411(a)(6)	204(b)(3)(E)	412(f)(4)	303(e)
411(a)(6)(E)	203(b)(3)(E)	412(g)	305
411(a)(7)	3(23)	412(h)	301
411(a)(7)(B)	204(d), 204(e)	412(h)(1)	301(a)(8)
411(a)(8)	3(24)	412(i)	301(b)
411(a)(9)	3(22)	412(j)	301(c)
411(a)(10)	203(c)	412(k)	301(d)
411(a)(11)	203(e), 203(e)(2)	412(l)(2)	302(d)(2)
411(a)(11)(B)	203(e)(2)	412(l)(3)	302(d)(3)
411(b)	204	412(l)(4)	302(d)(4)
411(b)(1)(H)	204(b)(1)(H)	412(l)(5)	302(d)(5)
411(b)(4)	204(b)(3)(E), 204(b)(4)(D)	412(l)(7)	302(d)(7)

IRC Section	ERISA Section	IRC Section	ERISA Section
412(l)(7)(B)	302(d)(7)(B)	4975(c)(2)	408(a)
412(l)(8)(A)	302(d)(8)(A)	4975(d)	408(d)
412(l)(8)(B)	302(d)(8)(B)	4975(d)(1)	408(b)(1)
412(l)(10)	302(d)(10)	4975(d)(2)	408(b)(2)
412(m)	302(e)	4975(d)(3)	408(b)(3)
412(m)(3)	302(e)(3)	4975(d)(4)	408(b)(4)
412(m)(5)	302(e)(5)	4975(d)(5)	408(b)(5)
412(n)	302(f)	4975(d)(6)	408(b)(6)
412(n)(1)	302(f)	4975(d)(7)	408(b)(7)
412(n)(4)	302(f)(4)(A)	4975(d)(8)	408(b)(8)
412(n)(4)(A)	302(f)(4)(A)	4975(d)(9)	408(c)(1)
412(n)(6)(B)	302(f)(6)(B)	4975(d)(10)	408(c)(2)
413(b)(1)	210(a)(1)	4975(d)(11)	408(c)(3)
413(b)(4)	203(a)(2)	4975(d)(12)	408(b)(9)
413(b)(5)	210(a)(3)	4975(d)(13)	408(b)(12), 408(b)(13), 408(e)
413(b)(6)	210(a)(3)	4975(d)(14)	408(b)(10)
413(c)	210(b)	4975(d)(15)	408(b)(11)
413(b)(4)	210(a)(2)	4975(e)	406
414(a)	210(b)	4975(e)(1)	3(3)
414(b)	3(40)(b), 210(c)	4975(e)(2)	3(14)
414(c)	3(40)(b), 210(d)	4975(e)(3)	3(21)
414(d)	3(32)	4975(e)(7)	407(c)(6)
414(e)	3(33)	4975(e)(8)	407(d)(5)
414(f)	3(37)	4975(f)(3)	406(c)
414(f)(5)	4303	4975(g)	401
414(g)	3(16)(A)	4980(d)	404(d), 404(d)(1)
414(i)	3(34)	4980B(d)	601
414(j)	3(35)	4980B(f)(1)	609(d)
414(l)	208, 4231, 4232	4980B(f)(2)	602(2)(A)
414(p)	206(d)(3)	4980B(f)(2)(A)	602(1)
414(p)(12)	206(d)(3)(N)	4980B(f)(2)(B)	602(2), 602(2)(A), 602(2)(A)(iii)
417(a)	205(c)	4980B(f)(2)(C)	602(3)
417(a)(4)	205(c)(4)	4980B(f)(2)(D)	602(4)
417(b)	205(d)	4980B(f)(2)(E)	602(5)
417(c)	205(e)	4980B(f)(3)	602(3), 603, 603(1), 603(6)
417(c)(3)	205(e)(3)	4980(B)(f)(3)(B)	603(2)
417(e)	205(g)	4980B(f)(3)(C)	603(3)
417(e)(3)	205(g)(3)	4980B(f)(3)(D)	603(4)
417(f)(2)	205(h)(2)	4980B(f)(3)(F)	603(6)
417(f)(5)	205(k)	4980B(f)(4)	604
418	4241	4980B(f)(5)	605
418(b)	4001(a)(9)	4980B(f)(6)	606
418(b)(7)(E)	4001(a)(12)	4980B(f)(6)(B)	606(a)(2)
418A	4242	4980B(f)(6)(C)	606(a)(3)
418B	4243	4980B(f)(6)(D)	606(b), 606(c)
418C	4244	4980B(f)(7)	607(2)
418C(g)	4244(g)	4980B(f)(8)	607(5)
418D	4244A	4980B(g)(1)	607(3), 607(3)(C)
418E(f)	4245(f)	4980B(g)(1)(A)	603(5)
457(d)	206	4980B(g)(3)	4001(a)(1)
4062	4001(a)(14)	4980F	204(h)
4975(c)(1)	406(a)(1), 406(b)	5000(b)(1)	607(1)

TABLE OF IRC SECTION TO ERISA SECTIONS

IRC Section	ERISA Section	IRC Section	ERISA Section
6059	103(a), 103(d)	9802	702
6690	502(c)(1)(B)	9803	703
7476	3001	9811	711
7701(a)(35)	103(a)(4)(C)	9812	712
9801	701		

TABLE OF ERISA SECTIONS CITED

ERISA Section	Q	ERISA Section	Q
3(1)	2, 145, 205, 638, 695, 701, 790	3(40)(B)(v)	701
3(2)	790	4	254
3(3)	254, 638	4(a)	7, 18
3(4)	2, 639, 876	4(b)	8, 62, 255, 396
3(5)	2, 697	4(b)(2)	19
3(6)	698, 699	4(b)(3)	19, 46, 791
3(7)	15	4(b)(4)	19, 46
3(8)	15	5	254
3(9)	216, 224	101	63, 611, 855
3(14)	398, 399, 427, 452, 564	101(b)(4)	63, 72
3(14)(B)	245	101(c)	91
3(14)(C)	640	101(d)	115
3(14)(E)	452	101(f)	114
3(14)(G)	452	101(f)(2)(B)(i)	114
3(14)(H)	412	101(f)(4)(C)	114
3(15)	398, 431	101(g)	709
3(16)	98, 876	101(i)	633
3(16)(A)	232, 233, 389	101(i)(1)	630
3(16)(B)	234, 260	101(i)(2)	628
3(18)	97, 462, 470, 617, 627	101(i)(2)(A)	632, 633
3(18)(B)	618	101(i)(2)(B)	630
3(21)	261, 366, 368, 393, 402	101(i)(2)(C)	631
3(21)(A)	215, 217, 218, 219, 222, 224,	101(i)(2)(D)	630
	225, 226, 227, 229, 235, 239,	101(i)(3)	631
	256, 364, 370, 393, 475, 640, 707	101(i)(4)	632
3(21)(A)(i)	237, 240, 296	101(i)(7)	631
3(21)(A)(ii)	240, 242, 243, 296, 366,	101(i)(7)(A)	629
	381, 393, 595, 596, 598, 599, 600	101(i)(7)(B)	631
3(21)(A)(iii)	219, 233	101(i)(8)(A)	629
3(21)(B)	585, 587	101(i)(8)(B)	629
3(24)	30, 98	101(j)	798
3(26)	67	101(k)	95
3(32)	8, 19, 62, 255	101(m)	621
3(33)	8, 62, 255	102(a)	98, 354, 517
3(34)	260, 629	102(a)(1)	103
3(36)	8, 62, 255	102(b)	174
3(37)(A)	638	103	63, 873
3(37)(A)(i)	638	103(a)(2)	875
3(37)(A)(ii)	638	103(a)(3)(A)	55, 110
3(37)(B)	644	103(a)(4)(A)	368
3(38)	246, 247, 318, 363, 374, 389	103(b)(1)	66
3(38)(A)	374, 389	103(b)(2)	66
3(38)(B)	249	103(b)(3)	66
3(40)	695, 696, 697, 701, 702	103(d)(11)	104
3(40)(A)	701	103(e)	64
3(40)(A)(i)	701, 711	104	873
3(40)(A)(ii)	701	104(a)	857
3(40)(A)(iii)	701	104(a)(6)	88, 89, 90, 96, 98
3(40)(B)(i)	696	104(b)	96, 130, 857
3(40)(B)(ii)	696	104(b)(1)	100, 102, 103
3(40)(B)(iii)	696	104(b)(3)	104
3(40)(B)(iv)	701	104(b)(4)	100, 269

ERISA Section	Q	ERISA Section	Q
502(c)(9)(A)	174	514(d)	40, 790
502(c)(9)(B)	174	514(e)	389
502(g)	540, 543	514(e)(1)	389
502(g)(1)	203, 538, 539, 541	514(e)(2)	389
502(g)(2)	543, 689	514(e)(3)	389
502(g)(2)(B)	543	514(e)(3)(A)	389
502(g)(2)(C)	543	514(e)(3)(B)	389
502(g)(2)(D)	543	515	543, 689
502(g)(2)(E)	689	521	709
502(h)	518, 789	601	189
502(i)	411, 421, 422, 423, 424, 500, 508, 783, 784	602	269
502(I)(6)	96	602(1)	197
502(j)	788	602(2)	199
502(l)	411, 498, 500, 501, 503, 504, 505, 506,	602(2)(A)(i)	199
	507, 508, 509, 510, 519, 718, 760, 762, 763,	602(2)(A)(ii)	199
	774, 783, 784, 785	602(2)(A)(iv)	199
502(l)(2)	501, 503	602(2)(C)	200
502(l)(4)	500	602(3)	200
503	533, 705	602(4)	197
503(1)	42	603	191
503(2)	44	605(1)	193
504	372, 425, 730, 833	606(a)(1)	193
504(a)	411, 729, 740	606(a)(2)	193
504(a)(1)	729	606(a)(3)	193
504(a)(2)	729	606(a)(4)	193
504(b)	729	607(1)	189
504(c)	729, 730	607(2)	191
505	97, 372	609(a)	204
506	372, 787	609(a)(2)	204
506(a)	787	609(a)(5)	204
506(b)	787, 833	609(b)(2)	202
510	511, 512, 513, 514, 515, 524, 536, 859	701(f)(3)(A)(i)	174
511	511, 516, 836, 841, 843, 859	701(f)(3)(A)(ii)	174
512	725, 727	702	209
512(a)	725, 726	702(a)(1)	749
512(b)	725	702(b)(1)	749
512(c)	727	702(b)(3)(A)	206
514	389	702(b)(3)(B)	206
514(a)	276, 389, 708, 790	702(c)	206
514(b)	708	702(c)(1)	206
514(b)(2)	708	702(c)(2)	206
514(b)(2)(B)	702	702(c)(3)(A)	206
514(b)(3)	791	702(c)(4)	207
514(b)(3)(A)	791	702(c)(4)(A)	207
514(b)(4)	887	702(d)(1)	206
514(b)(5)(A)	791	702(d)(3)	206
514(b)(6)	703, 708	702(f)(1)	209
514(b)(6)(A)	702, 704, 708, 791	703	749
514(b)(6)(A)(i)	702, 706	711(d)	103
514(b)(6)(A)(ii)	705, 706	714(a)(1)	214
514(b)(6)(B)	706	714(a)(2)	214
514(b)(6)(D)	703	714(b)(1)(A)	214
514(b)(7)	791	714(b)(2)(A)	214
514(c)(1)	790	714(c)	214
514(c)(2)	790	714(d)	214

ERISA Section	Q	ERISA Section	Q
4204(a)(3)	654	4221(a)(3)	669
4205(a)	645	4221(b)(2)	673
4205(b)(1)(A)	645	4221(c)	673
4205(b)(1)(B)	645	4225	648
4205(b)(2)(A)	645	4225(a)	677
4205(b)(2)(B)	645	4225(a)(2)	677
4206(a)(2)	652	4225(b)	676
4206(a)(2)(B)	652	4225(d)(1)	676
4207	691	4225(d)(2)	676
4209	648, 656	4225(e)	676, 677
4209(a)	656	4231	474, 678, 681, 685
4209(b)	656	4231(c)	681
4210	657	4232(b)	683
4210(a)	657	4232(c)(1)	683
4210(b)	657	4232(c)(2)	683
4210(b)(1)	657	4232(c)(3)	683
4211	648, 679	4232(c)(4)	683
4211(b)(2)(B)	648	4233(a)	688
4211(b)(2)(C)	648	4233(b)(1)	688
4211(b)(3)	648	4233(c)	688
4211(b)(4)(B)	648	4233(d)	688
4211(b)(4)(C)	648	4233(e)	688
4211(b)(4)(D)	648	4233(f)	688
4211(c)	649	4234	682, 685
4211(c)(2)	649	4234(a)	682
4211(c)(3)	650	4234(c)	682
4211(c)(4)	651	4234(e)(1)	685
4211(c)(5)(A)	675	4234(e)(2)	685
4211(f)	679	4235(a)	685
4218(1)	654	4235(b)	685
4218(2)	655	4235(b)(3)	685
4219	648	4235(b)(3)(A)	685
4219(b)(1)	658	4235(b)(3)(B)	685
4219(b)(2)(A)	658	4235(c)	685
4219(b)(2)(B)	659	4235(f)	685
4219(c)(1)	660	4235(f)(2)	686
4219(c)(1)(B)	648, 664	4244A	94
4219(c)(1)(C)(i)	660	4244A(b)(1)(A)	94
4219(c)(1)(D)	664	4245(b)(3)	667
4219(c)(2)	660	4245(e)(1)	94
4219(c)(3)	660, 662	4261(b)(2)	667
4219(c)(4)	660	4301(a)	543, 822
4219(c)(5)	661	4301(a)(1)	692
4219(c)(5)(A)	661	4301(a)(2)	692
4219(c)(5)(B)	661	4301(c)	829
4219(c)(6)	662, 674	4301(d)	829
4220(b)	675	4301(f)	543, 693
4220(c)	675	4301(g)	829
4221	670	4302	668
4221(a)(1)	670		

TABLE OF IRC SECTIONS CITED

IRC Section	Q	IRC Section	Q
4975(b)	409, 416, 417, 418, 419, 482, 483	4980B(f)(7)	191
4975(c)(1)	397	4980B(g)(1)(C)	191
4975(c)(1)(E)	405, 490, 494	4980B(g)(2)	189
4975(c)(1)(F)	405, 425, 490, 494	6033(a)	63
4975(c)(2)	477, 482, 483	6057(b)	63
4975(d)(2)	444, 457, 460	6058(a)	63
4975(d)(3)	615, 617	6103	783
4975(d)(9)	462, 472	6212	416
4975(d)(10)	462, 472	6213(a)	416
4975(e)(2)	398, 426	6501(a)	419
4975(e)(7)	615, 619	6501(e)(3)	419
4975(f)(1)	418	6621	689
4975(f)(2)	416	6621(a)(2)	411, 412
4975(f)(4)	416, 422	6621(c)(1)	411
4975(f)(4)(B)	416	6652	761
4975(f)(5)	417, 482, 483	7422(g)	416
4975(f)(6)(B)	616	7476	828
4975(h)	416	7502(f)	802
4980B	194	7701(a)(37)	261, 278, 444
4980B(b)	203	7704(b)	387, 611
4980B(c)(1)	203	9801(a)	157
4980B(c)(2)	203	9801(a)(1)	158
4980B(c)(3)(B)	203	9801(c)(1)	164
4980B(c)(4)(A)(i)	203	9801(c)(2)(A)	162
4980B(e)(1)(A)	203	9801(d)	160, 173
4980B(f)	189	9801(d)(3)	160
4980B(f)(2)	197, 199	9801(f)(3)(B)(i)(I)	174
4980B(f)(2)(A)	197	9802(a)(1)	172
4980B(f)(2)(B)(i)	177, 199	9802(b)(1)	172
4980B(f)(2)(B)(ii)	199	9813(a)(1)	214
4980B(f)(2)(B)(iii)	200	9813(a)(2)	214
4980B(f)(2)(C)	200	9813(b)(1)(A)	214
4980B(f)(3)	191	9813(b)(2)(A)	214
4980B(f)(4)(C)	200	9813(b)(3)	214
4980B(f)(5)(A)	193	9813(c)	214
4980B(f)(6)(A)	193	9813(d)	214
4980B(f)(6)(B)	193	9813(e)(1)	214
4980B(f)(6)(C)	193	9813(e)(2)	214
4980B(f)(6)(D)	193		

INDEX

A

B

C

G

H

I

M